LAND USE LAW

Fifth Edition

Daniel R. Mandelker
Stamper Professor of Law
Washington University in St. Louis

2003

LexisNexis™
Matthew Bender®

QUESTIONS ABOUT THIS PUBLICATION?

For questions about the **Editorial Content** appearing in these volumes or reprint permission, please call:

Heidi A. Litman, J.D. .... (800) 252-9257 (ext. 2255)
E-mail .... heidi.a.litman@lexisnexis.com
Christopher J. Sollog .... (800) 252-9257 (ext. 2239)
E-mail .... christopher.j.sollog@lexisnexis.com
Outside the United States and Canada please call .... (973) 820-2000

For assistance with replacement pages, shipments, billing or other customer service matters, please call:

Customer Services Department at .... (800) 833-9844
Outside the United States and Canada, please call .... (518) 487-3000
Fax number .... (518) 487-3584

For information on other Matthew Bender publications, please call
Your account manager or .... (800) 223-1940
Outside the United States and Canada, please call .... (518) 487-3000

Library of Congress Card Number: 97-75493
ISBN: 0-327-16269-4

This publication is designed to provide accurate and authoritative information in regard to the subject matter covered. It is sold with the understanding that the publisher is not engaged in rendering legal, accounting, or other professional services. If legal advice or other expert assistance is required, the services of a competent professional should be sought.

LexisNexis, the knowledge burst logo, and Michie are trademarks of Reed Elsevier Properties Inc, used under license. Matthew Bender is a registered trademark of Matthew Bender Properties Inc.

Editorial Offices
744 Broad Street, Newark, NJ 07102 (973) 820-2000
201 Mission St., San Francisco, CA 94105-1831 (415) 908-3200
www.lexis.com

Statement on Fair Use

LexisNexis Matthew Bender recognizes the balance that must be achieved between the operation of the fair use doctrine, whose basis is to avoid the rigid application of the copyright statute, and the protection of the creative rights and economic interests of authors, publishers and other copyright holders.

We are also aware of the countervailing forces that exist between the ever greater technological advances for making both print and electronic copies and the reduction in the value of copyrighted works that must result from a consistent and pervasive reliance on these new copying technologies. It is LexisNexis Matthew Bender's position that if the "progress of science and useful arts" is promoted by granting copyright protection to authors, such progress may well be impeded if copyright protection is diminished in the name of fair use. (See *Nimmer on Copyright* §13.05[E][1].) This holds true whether the parameters of the fair use doctrine are considered in either the print or the electronic environment as it is the integrity of the copyright that is at issue, not the media under which the protected work may become available. Therefore, the fair use guidelines we propose apply equally to our print and electronic information, and apply, within §§107 and 108 of the Copyright Act, regardless of the professional status of the user.

Our draft guidelines would allow for the copying of limited materials, which would include synopses and tables of contents, primary source and government materials that may have a minimal amount of editorial enhancements, individual forms to aid in the drafting of applications and pleadings, and miscellaneous pages from any of our newsletters, treatises and practice guides. This copying would be permitted provided it is performed for internal use and solely for the purpose of facilitating individual research or for creating documents produced in the course of the user's professional practice, and the original from which the copy is made has been purchased or licensed as part of the user's existing in-house collection.

LexisNexis Matthew Bender fully supports educational awareness programs designed to increase the public's recognition of its fair use rights. We also support the operation of collective licensing organizations with regard to our print and electronic information.

(5th Ed.—02/03)

SUMMARY TABLE OF CONTENTS

Table of Contents
Dedication
Acknowledgments
How to Use This Book

Chapter 1 Controlling Land Use: An Overview
Chapter 2 The Constitutional Framework
Chapter 3 The Comprehensive Plan
Chapter 4 The Zoning System
Chapter 5 Zoning For Land Use, Density and Development
Chapter 6 The Zoning Process
Chapter 7 Discriminatory, Exclusionary and Inclusionary Zoning
Chapter 8 Land Use Litigation and Remedies
Chapter 9 Residential Development Controls
Chapter 10 Growth Management and the Control of Public Facilities
Chapter 11 Aesthetics, Sign Regulation and Historic Preservation
Chapter 12 Environmental Land Use Regulation

Table of Cases
Index

(5th Ed.—02/03)

Table of Contents

Dedication
Acknowledgments
How to Use This Book

CHAPTER 1 CONTROLLING LAND USE: AN OVERVIEW

§ 1.01   Providing a Focus.
§ 1.02   Differences in Federal and State Constitutional Law and Litigation.
§ 1.03   The Land Use Control System.
§ 1.04   Zoning for Land Use, Density and Site Development.
§ 1.05   Historic District and Historic Landmark Zoning.
§ 1.06   Environmental Land Use Regulation.
§ 1.07   Sign Regulation and Design Review.
§ 1.08   Growth Management.
§ 1.09   Subdivision Controls and Planned Unit Developments.
§ 1.10   The Exclusion Problem.
§ 1.11   How the Book Is Organized.
§ 1.12   Standards of Judicial Review.
§ 1.13   Rules of Construction.
§ 1.14   Land Use Cases in the Federal Courts.
§ 1.15   Land Use Cases in the State Courts.
§ 1.16   Variations in the States.
§ 1.17   State Appellate Court Structure.
§ 1.18   The Stages of Land Use Law.

CHAPTER 2 THE CONSTITUTIONAL FRAMEWORK

PART A. THE TAKINGS ISSUE.

§ 2.01   The Takings Problem.
§ 2.02   Takings Law.
§ 2.03   Physical Per Se Takings.
§ 2.04   The Noxious Use Cases.
§ 2.05   *Pennsylvania Coal*: Regulatory Takings Recognized.
§ 2.06   *Euclid*: Comprehensive Zoning Upheld.
§ 2.07   *Penn Central*: A Multi-Factor Takings Test.
§ 2.08   The *Agins* Two-Part Takings Test: Herein of Legitimate Governmental Purpose.

Table of Contents

§ 2.09 *Lucas*: A Per Se Test for Regulatory Takings; Nuisance, and other Exceptions.

§ 2.10 Exactions.

§ 2.11 *Nollan*: The Nexus Test.

§ 2.12 *Dolan*: The "Rough Proportionality" Rule.

§ 2.13 *Del Monte Dunes:* Clarifying "Rough Proportionalilty."

§ 2.14 Takings Problems, Principles and Maxims.

§ 2.15 Average Reciprocity of Advantage

§ 2.16 Investment-Backed Expectations.

§ 2.17 The Whole Parcel or Denominator Rule: Herein of Segmentation.

§ 2.18 Conceptual Severance: The Right to Exclude.

§ 2.19 Geographic Segmentation.

§ 2.20 Temporal Severance.

§ 2.21 *Lucas* Applied: When Does a Per Se Regulatory Taking Occur?

§ 2.22 Delay in Decision Making as a Taking.

§ 2.23 Planning and Zoning With Acquisitory Intent.

§ 2.24 Ripeness and Finality.

§ 2.25 Early Supreme Court Cases.

§ 2.26 *Hamilton Bank.*

§ 2.27 *Yolo County.*

§ 2.28 Later Supreme Court Cases.

§ 2.29 Federal Court Cases.

§ 2.30 Final Decision Rule.

§ 2.31 Compensation Requirement.

§ 2.32 Equal Protection and Due Process Claims.

§ 2.33 Returning to Federal Court From State Court.

§ 2.34 *Rooker-Feldman* Doctrine.

§ 2.35 State Court Takings Doctrine.

§ 2.36 "As-Applied" Cases Claiming Total Loss or Diminution in Value.

§ 2.37 Balancing and Multi-Factor Tests.

§ 2.38 State Takings Legislation.

PART B. SUBSTANTIVE DUE PROCESS.

§ 2.39 The Substantive Due Process Problem.

§ 2.40 Barriers to Substantive Due Process Litigation in the Federal Courts.

(5th Ed.—02/03)

Table of Contents

PART C. PROCEDURAL DUE PROCESS.

§ 2.41 The Procedural Due Process Problem.
§ 2.42 In the Federal Courts.
§ 2.43 In the State Courts.

PART D. EQUAL PROTECTION.

§ 2.44 The Equal Protection Problem.
§ 2.45 Judicial Standards for Equal Protection Review.
§ 2.46 Applying the Rational Relationship Standard: The State Courts.
§ 2.47 Applying the Rational Relationship Standard: The Federal Courts.
§ 2.48 *Cleburne*: Rational Relationship "With a Bite."
§ 2.49 Selective Enforcement: The *Olech* Case.

PART E. FREE SPEECH.

§ 2.50 How the Free Speech Clause Applies to Land Use Regulation.
§ 2.51 Retaliatory Governmental Conduct.

PART F. THE CONTRACT CLAUSE.

§ 2.52 General Principles.
§ 2.53 In Land Use Cases.

CHAPTER 3 THE COMPREHENSIVE PLAN

PART A. ROLE OF THE COMPREHENSIVE PLAN.

§ 3.01 Planning and Land Use Regulation.
§ 3.02 The Planning Process and the Plan.
§ 3.03 Criticisms of Planning.
§ 3.04 Planning Today.

PART B. PLANNING LEGISLATION.

§ 3.05 The Standard Planning Act.
§ 3.06 The Planning Commission.
§ 3.07 The Elements of the Plan.
§ 3.08 Plan Adoption.
§ 3.09 State Planning Legislation.
§ 3.10 Required and Optional Planning Elements.
§ 3.11 Planning Policies for Lower-Income Housing.

(5th Ed.—02/03)

Table of Contents

§ 3.12   Mandatory Planning.

PART C. THE COMPREHENSIVE PLAN AND LAND USE CONTROLS.

§ 3.13   Zoning "in Accordance with" a Comprehensive Plan.
§ 3.14   The Majority Judicial View: A Plan Is Not Required.
§ 3.15   The Minority Judicial View: Consistency Is Required.
§ 3.16   Statutory Consistency Requirements.
§ 3.17   Upzoning to Comply With the Plan.
§ 3.18   Land Use Conflicts.
§ 3.19   Plans and the Takings Issue.
§ 3.20   The Plan as a Defense to a Taking.
§ 3.21   The Plan as a Taking of Property.
§ 3.22   Judicial Review of Comprehensive Plans.

CHAPTER 4 THE ZONING SYSTEM

§ 4.01   An Introductory Note.

PART A. JUDICIAL ZONING THROUGH NUISANCE ACTIONS.

§ 4.02   The Private Nuisance Action.
§ 4.03   Anticipatory Nuisances.
§ 4.04   Priority of Occupation.
§ 4.05   Nuisances in Residential Neighborhoods.
§ 4.06   Commercial Uses.
§ 4.07   Funeral Parlors.
§ 4.08   People as Nuisances.
§ 4.09   Aesthetic Nuisances.
§ 4.10   Legalizing Nuisances Through Zoning.
§ 4.11   The Injunction Remedy.
§ 4.12   Balancing the Equities.
§ 4.13   Injunction Not Granted.
§ 4.14   Compensation to Defendant.

PART B. STATUTORY AUTHORITY.

§ 4.15   The Standard Zoning Act.
§ 4.16   Zoning Purposes.
§ 4.17   The District Concept.

Table of Contents

§ 4.18   Adoption and Amendment.

§ 4.19   Board of Adjustment.

§ 4.20   Enforcement.

§ 4.21   Modern Zoning Legislation.

§ 4.22   Extraterritorial Zoning.

§ 4.23   Constitutional Problems.

PART C. HOME RULE.

§ 4.24   Constitutional Home Rule Authority.

§ 4.25   Home Rule Land Use Powers.

PART D. ZONING FOR GOVERNMENT AND GOVERNMENT-REGULATED LAND DEVELOPMENT.

§ 4.26   The Governmental Immunity Problem.

§ 4.27   State Agencies.

§ 4.28   Local Governments Exercising State Functions.

§ 4.29   State-Regulated Facilities and Businesses.

§ 4.30   State Environmental Programs.

§ 4.31   State Permits for Other Private Activities.

§ 4.32   Private Utilities.

§ 4.33   Liquor Licensees.

§ 4.34   Local Governments.

§ 4.35   Governmental-Proprietary Rule.

§ 4.36   Eminent Domain Rule.

§ 4.37   Superior Power Rule.

§ 4.38   Balancing Test.

§ 4.39   Home Rule Problems.

§ 4.40   Legislative Solutions.

PART E. Federal Preemption

§ 4.41   The Federal Preemption Problem.

§ 4.42   Zoning for Cellular Towers.

§ 4.43   Regulation of Airports and Surrounding Areas.

CHAPTER 5 ZONING FOR LAND USE, DENSITY AND DEVELOPMENT

§ 5.01   An Introductory Note.

(5th Ed.—02/03)

Table of Contents

PART A. RESIDENTIAL DISTRICTS.

§ 5.02   *Euclid*: Zoning for Residential Use Held Constitutional.

§ 5.03   Defining the "Family" in Single-Family Residential Districts.

§ 5.04   *Belle Terre* and *Moor*.

§ 5.05   *Belle Terre* in the State Courts.

§ 5.06   Discrimination Against Families With Children Under the Fair Housing Act.

§ 5.07   Group Homes.

§ 5.08   As a Permitted "Family" Use.

§ 5.09   As a Conditional Use.

§ 5.10   State Legislative Regulation.

§ 5.11   Discrimination Against Group Homes for the Handicapped under the Fair Housing Act.

§ 5.12   What the Statute Means.

§ 5.13   Exceptions, Variances and Rezonings.

§ 5.14   Restrictions on Number of Occupants.

§ 5.15   Spacing and Quota Requirements.

§ 5.16   Americans With Disabilities and Rehabilitation Acts.

§ 5.17   Single-Family Use.

§ 5.18   Apartments.

§ 5.19   Accessory Uses.

§ 5.20   Home Occupations.

§ 5.21   Zoning for Mobile (or Manufactured) Homes.

§ 5.22   As a Dwelling.

§ 5.23   Partial Exclusion.

§ 5.24   Total Exclusion.

§ 5.25   As a Conditional Use.

§ 5.26   State and Federal Regulation.

§ 5.27   Private Schools.

PART B. LARGE LOT AND MINIMUM HOUSE SIZE ZONING.

§ 5.28   The Zoning Problem.

§ 5.29   Minimum House Size.

§ 5.30   Large-Lot Zoning.

§ 5.31   Held Valid.

§ 5.32   Held Invalid.

(5th Ed.—02/03)

Table of Contents

PART C. COMMERCIAL AND INDUSTRIAL USES.

§ 5.33   The Zoning Problem.

§ 5.34   Commercial Uses.

§ 5.35   The Mapping Problem.

§ 5.36   Commercial Use Classifications.

§ 5.37   Total Exclusion.

§ 5.38   Ribbon Development.

§ 5.39   Airports and Airport Zoning.

§ 5.40   Industrial Uses.

§ 5.41   Industrial Performance Standards.

§ 5.42   Total Exclusion.

§ 5.43   Noncumulative Zoning: Exclusive Nonresidential Zones.

§ 5.44   Control of Competition.

§ 5.45   As a Zoning Purpose.

§ 5.46   Disapproved.

§ 5.47   Approved.

§ 5.48   Protection of Business Districts.

§ 5.49   Federal Antitrust Law.

§ 5.50   State Action Doctrine.

§ 5.51   *Boulder.*

§ 5.52   *Town of Hallie.*

§ 5.53   *Omni.*

§ 5.54   Land Use Cases after *Omni.*

§ 5.55   *Noerr-Pennington* Doctrine.

§ 5.56   Basis for Liability.

§ 5.57   Local Government Antitrust Act.

§ 5.58   Free Speech Problems in Zoning for Adult Businesses.

§ 5.59   *Mini-Theatres.*

§ 5.60   *Schad.*

§ 5.61   *Renton.*

§ 5.62   *Alameda Books.*

§ 5.63   Zoning Issues in Adult Use Regulation

§ 5.64   Existing Uses.

§ 5.65   Defining Adult Uses

§ 5.66   State Legislation.

(5ᵗʰ Ed.—02/03)

Table of Contents

PART D. RELIGIOUS USES.

§ 5.67 Religious Uses.

§ 5.68 In the State Courts.

§ 5.69 Federal "Free Exercise" and "Establishment" Clauses.

§ 5.70 Federal and State Religious Freedom Acts.

PART E. SITE DEVELOPMENT REQUIREMENTS.

§ 5.71 Yards and Setbacks.

§ 5.72 Frontage Requirements.

§ 5.73 Site Area Ratios.

§ 5.74 Height Limitations.

§ 5.75 Floor Area Ratio.

§ 5.76 Bonuses and Incentives.

§ 5.77 Off-Street Parking.

PART F. NONCONFORMING USES.

§ 5.78 The Zoning Problem.

§ 5.79 Change and Expansion.

§ 5.80 Repair and Reconstruction.

§ 5.81 Abandonment.

§ 5.82 Amortization.

§ 5.83 Highway Beautification Act.

§ 5.84 Constitutional.

§ 5.85 Unconstitutional.

§ 5.86 Reasonableness of Amortization Period.

CHAPTER 6 THE ZONING PROCESS

§ 6.01 An Introductory Note.

PART A. DELEGATION OF POWER.

§ 6.02 The Delegation Problem.

§ 6.03 Zoning Standards.

§ 6.04 Delegation to Neighbors.

§ 6.05 Void for Vagueness.

PART B. MORATORIA AND INTERIM ZONING.

§ 6.06 Purposes and Problems.

Table of Contents

§ 6.07   Statutory Authority and Limitations.

§ 6.08   Constitutionality.

§ 6.09   Revision of Zoning Ordinance or Comprehensive Plan: The *Lake Tahoe* Case.

§ 6.10   Inadequate Public Facilities.

§ 6.11   As Applied.

PART C. ESTOPPEL AND VESTED RIGHTS.

§ 6.12   The Problem.

§ 6.13   The Theory.

§ 6.14   Governmental Act Requirement.

§ 6.15   Building Permit Required.

§ 6.16   Building Permit Not Required.

§ 6.17   Illegal Building Permit.

§ 6.18   Good Faith.

§ 6.19   Detrimental Reliance.

§ 6.20   Substantial Reliance Test.

§ 6.21   What Reliance Is Required.

§ 6.22   Statutory and Ordinance Protection.

§ 6.23   Development Agreements.

PART D. ZONING MAP AMENDMENTS.

§ 6.24   The Zoning Problem.

§ 6.25   Refusals to Rezone.

§ 6.26   The Quasi-Judicial View.

§ 6.27   "Spot" Zoning.

§ 6.28   Definitions.

§ 6.29   The Standard Tests.

§ 6.30   The Public Need and Public Purpose Tests.

§ 6.31   The Change-Mistake Rule.

§ 6.32   Consistency with the Comprehensive Plan.

§ 6.33   Zoning.

§ 6.34   Spot Planning.

§ 6.35   Effect on Adjacent Communities.

§ 6.36   Downzoning.

§ 6.37   The Standard Tests.

§ 6.38   Change-Mistake Rule.

Table of Contents

PART E. VARIANCES, SPECIAL EXCEPTIONS, AND CONDITIONAL USES.

§ 6.39   Role and Function.
§ 6.40   Variances.
§ 6.41   Role and Function.
§ 6.42   Use and Area Variances.
§ 6.43   Use Variances Prohibited.
§ 6.44   Unnecessary Hardship.
§ 6.45   No Reasonable Return.
§ 6.46   Unique to the Owner.
§ 6.47   Impact on the Neighborhood.
§ 6.48   Availability of Area Variances.
§ 6.49   Consistency with the Plan.
§ 6.50   Self-Created Hardship.
§ 6.51   Conditions.
§ 6.52   Findings and Judicial Review.
§ 6.53   Special Exceptions and Conditional Uses.
§ 6.54   Role and Function.
§ 6.55   Delegation to Legislative Body or Plan Commission.
§ 6.56   Judicial Review of Decisions on Exceptions and Conditional Uses.
§ 6.57   Free Speech-Protected and Religious Uses.
§ 6.58   Consistency with the Plan.
§ 6.59   Conditions.

PART F. FLEXIBLE ZONING.

§ 6.60   Role and Function.
§ 6.61   Floating Zones.
§ 6.62   Contract and Conditional Zoning.
§ 6.63   Bilateral.
§ 6.64   Unilateral.
§ 6.65   Proper Purpose View.
§ 6.66   Site Plan Review.

PART G. DECISION-MAKING PROCEDURES.

§ 6.67   The Procedures Problem.
§ 6.68   Legislative vs. Quasi-Judicial.
§ 6.69   Entitlement.
§ 6.70   Procedures Required.

(5th Ed.—02/03)

Table of Contents

§ 6.71   Impartial Decision-Maker.

§ 6.72   Bias and Conflict of Interest.

§ 6.73   Bias.

§ 6.74   Conflicts of Interest.

§ 6.75   Neighborhood Opposition.

§ 6.76   Open Meeting Laws.

PART H. INITIATIVE AND REFERENDUM.

§ 6.77   The Zoning Problem.

§ 6.78   Federal Constitutional Issues.

§ 6.79   Availability in Zoning.

§ 6.80   Referendum.

§ 6.81   Initiative.

CHAPTER 7 DISCRIMINATORY, EXCLUSIONARY AND INCLUSIONARY ZONING

§ 7.01   An Introductory Note.

PART A. THE FEDERAL CONSTITUTION AND FAIR HOUSING ACT.

§ 7.02   Standing to Sue.

§ 7.03   Equal Protection: *Arlington Heights.*

§ 7.04   The Fair Housing Act.

§ 7.05   When Violated.

§ 7.06   Remedies.

PART B. EXCLUSIONARY ZONING IN THE STATES.

§ 7.07   Standing to Sue.

§ 7.08   New Jersey.

§ 7.09   *Mt. Laurel (I).*

§ 7.10   *Weymouth.*

§ 7.11   *Mt. Laurel (II).*

§ 7.12   Fair Housing Act.

§ 7.13   Post *Mt. Laurel (II)* Cases.

§ 7.14   New York.

§ 7.15   *Berenson.*

§ 7.16   *Brookhaven.*

§ 7.17   *Asian Americans for Equality.*

(5th Ed.—02/03)

Table of Contents

§ 7.18   Remedies.

§ 7.19   Pennsylvania.

§ 7.20   *Surrick*: Partial Exclusion.

§ 7.21   *Fernley*: Total Exclusion.

§ 7.22   Remedies.

§ 7.23   Michigan.

§ 7.24   California.

§ 7.25   New Hampshire.

PART C. INCLUSIONARY PLANNING AND ZONING.

§ 7.26   The Planning and Zoning Problem.

§ 7.27   Mandatory Set-Asides and Incentive Zoning.

§ 7.28   Office-Housing Linkage Programs.

§ 7.29   California Inclusionary Legislation.

§ 7.30   Oregon Inclusionary Legislation.

§ 7.31   Affordable Housing Appeals Laws.

CHAPTER 8 LAND USE LITIGATION AND REMEDIES

§ 8.01   An Introductory Note.

PART A. THIRD-PARTY STANDING IN STATE COURTS.

§ 8.02   General Principles.

§ 8.03   Taxpayers and Citizens.

§ 8.04   Resident Landowners.

§ 8.05   Nonresident Landowners.

§ 8.06   Organizations and Associations.

§ 8.07   Municipalities.

PART B. EXHAUSTION OF REMEDIES IN STATE COURTS.

§ 8.08   General Principles: Exhaustion and Ripeness Distinguished.

§ 8.09   The Ripeness Rules in State Courts.

§ 8.10   What Remedies Must Be Exhausted.

§ 8.11   Exceptions.

PART C. JUDICIAL REMEDIES AND RELIEF IN STATE COURTS.

§ 8.12   Judicial Remedies.

Table of Contents

§ 8.13   Appeal and Certiorari.

§ 8.14   Mandamus.

§ 8.15   Injunction.

§ 8.16   Declaratory Judgment.

§ 8.17   Judicial Relief.

§ 8.18   Specific Relief Not Available.

§ 8.19   Specific Relief Available.

§ 8.20   Inverse Condemnation.

§ 8.21   State Cases: Remedy Available.

§ 8.22   State Cases: Remedy Not Available.

§ 8.23   Tort Liability.

PART D. FEDERAL REMEDIES.

§ 8.24   Inverse Condemnation.

§ 8.25   When Available.

§ 8.26   Availability and Measure of Compensation.

§ 8.27   Trial by Jury.

§ 8.28   Section 1983 of the Federal Civil Rights Act.

§ 8.29   Scope of the Statute.

§ 8.30   Land Use Cases Not Actionable Under § 1983.

§ 8.31   Color of Law, Policy, and Custom.

§ 8.32   Fault and Causation.

§ 8.33   Exhaustion and Adequacy of State Remedies.

§ 8.34   Immunities.

§ 8.35   Legislative Bodies.

§ 8.36   Land Use Agencies and Officials.

§ 8.37   Local Governments.

§ 8.38   Damages.

§ 8.39   Implied Constitutional Cause of Action.

§ 8.40   Removal to Federal Court.

§ 8.41   Abstention.

§ 8.42   *Younger* Abstention.

§ 8.43   *Pullman* Abstention.

§ 8.44   *Burford* Abstention.

§ 8.45   *Colorado River* Abstention.

Table of Contents

PART E. SLAPP SUITS.

§ 8.46   SLAPP Suits.
§ 8.47   Anti-SLAPP Statutes.

CHAPTER 9 RESIDENTIAL DEVELOPMENT CONTROLS

§ 9.01   An Introductory Note.

PART A. SUBDIVISION CONTROL.

§ 9.02   History and Purpose.
§ 9.03   Enabling Legislation.
§ 9.04   The Subdivision Control Process.
§ 9.05   Definition of "Subdivision."
§ 9.06   Relationship to Zoning.
§ 9.07   Vested Rights.
§ 9.08   Enforcement.
§ 9.09   Scope of Authority: Discretion to Approve or Reject.
§ 9.10   Variances and Waivers.
§ 9.11   Exactions.
§ 9.12   The Takings Issue.
§ 9.13   *Nollan* and What It Means: Applying the Nexus Test.
§ 9.14   *Dolan* and What It Means.
§ 9.15   On-Site Streets and Improvements.
§ 9.16   Off-Site Streets and Improvements.
§ 9.17   Parks and Schools.
§ 9.18   Statutory Authority.
§ 9.19   The Takings Issue.
§ 9.20   Impact Fees.
§ 9.21   Statutory Authority.
§ 9.22   The Takings Issue.
§ 9.23   Linkage Programs.

PART B. PLANNED UNIT DEVELOPMENT.

§ 9.24   The Land Use Problem.
§ 9.25   The Planned Unit Development Review Process.
§ 9.26   Under the Standard Zoning Act.
§ 9.27   Regulatory Techniques.
§ 9.28   Discretion to Approve or Reject.

Table of Contents

§ 9.29   Amendments to Development Plans.

§ 9.30   Planned Unit Development Legislation.

CHAPTER 10 GROWTH MANAGEMENT AND THE CONTROL OF PUBLIC FACILITIES

§ 10.01   An Introductory Note.

PART A. GROWTH MANAGEMENT PROGRAMS

§ 10.02   What These Programs Do.

§ 10.03   The Legal Problems.

§ 10.04   Timing and Phasing Programs: *Ramapo*.

§ 10.05   Adequate Public Facilities and Concurrency Requirements.

§ 10.06   Development Quotas: *Petaluma*.

§ 10.07   Urban Growth Boundaries and Service Areas.

§ 10.08   Exclusion and The Right to Travel.

§ 10.09   Public Utilities and Service as a Growth Management Control.

§ 10.10   Service Refusals: The Duty to Serve.

§ 10.11   The Takings Issue.

PART B. CORRIDOR PRESERVATION

§ 10.12   The Corridor Preservation Problem.

§ 10.13   Corridor Preservation Legislation.

§ 10.14   The Takings Issue.

CHAPTER 11 AESTHETICS, SIGN REGULATION AND HISTORIC PRESERVATION

§ 11.01   The Aesthetic Regulation Problem.

§ 11.02   Aesthetics as a Regulatory Purpose.

§ 11.03   The Early Period.

§ 11.04   The Minority View: Aesthetics as a Factor in Land Use Regulation.

§ 11.05   The Majority View: Aesthetics Alone as a Regulatory Purpose.

PART A. SIGN CONTROLS.

§ 11.06   Local, State and Federal Regulation.

§ 11.07   Sign Regulation on Highways and Streets: The Takings Issue.

§ 11.08   Billboard Exclusions.

Table of Contents

§ 11.09 Exemption for On-Premise Signs.

§ 11.10 Controls on the Display of Signs.

§ 11.11 Nonconforming Signs.

§ 11.12 Free Speech Issues.

§ 11.13 *Metromedia*.

§ 11.14 *Taxpayers for Vincent*.

§ 11.15 *Ladue*: Residential Signs.

§ 11.16 *Lorillard*: Restrictions on Location.

§ 11.17 What These Cases Decided: Standing, Aesthetics and Content Neutrality.

§ 11.18 Time, Place and Manner Restrictions.

§ 11.19 Prohibition, Classification and Exemption of Off-Premise and On-Premise Signs.

§ 11.20 Portable Signs.

§ 11.21 Content-Based Sign Definitions.

§ 11.22 For Sale Signs.

§ 11.23 Political, Campaign and Temporary Signs.

PART B. ARCHITECTURAL DESIGN REVIEW.

§ 11.24 The Design Review Ordinance.

§ 11.25 Constitutionality.

PART C. HISTORIC PRESERVATION.

§ 11.26 The Historic Preservation Problem.

§ 11.27 Historic Districts.

§ 11.28 Enabling Legislation and Ordinances.

§ 11.29 Constitutionality of Historic Districts.

§ 11.30 Delegation of Power and Vagueness.

§ 11.31 Interim Controls.

§ 11.32 The Takings Issue.

§ 11.33 Historic Landmarks.

§ 11.34 Enabling Legislation and Ordinances.

§ 11.35 The Takings Issue.

§ 11.36 Maintenance and Repair.

§ 11.37 Religious Uses.

§ 11.38 Transfer of Development Rights.

Table of Contents

CHAPTER 12 ENVIRONMENTAL LAND USE REGULATION

PART A. ENVIRONMENTAL LAND USE PROGRAMS

§ 12.01 An Overview.
§ 12.02 Slope and View Protection Ordinances.
§ 12.03 Groundwater Protection.
§ 12.04 Critical Area Controls.

PART B. WETLANDS.

§ 12.05 State and Local Programs.
§ 12.06 Clean Water Act Permit.
§ 12.07 The Takings Issue.

PART C. FLOODPLAINS.

§ 12.08 State and Local Programs.
§ 12.09 The Takings Issue.

PART D. PRESERVATION OF AGRICULTURAL LAND.

§ 12.10 Federal, State and Local Programs.
§ 12.11 Right-to-Farm Laws.
§ 12.12 Agricultural Zoning.
§ 12.13 The Takings Issue.

PART E. COASTAL SETBACK LEGISLATION.

§ 12.14 National and State Programs.
§ 12.15 The Takings Issue.

PART E. TRANSFER OF DEVELOPMENT RIGHTS.

§ 12.16 Transfer of Development Rights.

Table of Cases
Index

(5ᵗʰ Ed.—02/03)

Dedication

This book is dedicated to the late Donald Hagman
scholar, teacher, friend.

(5th Ed.—02/03)

ACKNOWLEDGMENTS

I would like to acknowledge the many people who have contributed to this new edition and must again thank the many colleagues who, over the years, have shaped my ideas and thinking about land use law. The library staff at Washington University School of Law were especially helpful in finding needed research resources, and my faculty assistant, Andrea Powell, provided needed support. I would also like to thank my research assistants for this edition, David R. Gill and Jonathan K. Glassman, who did essential research on issues such as retaliatory government conduct, SLAPP and anti-SLAPP litigation and right-to-farm laws. Dean Joel Seligman of our law school provided welcome financial assistance.

The fifth edition is again dedicated to the late Donald Hagman. His influence on us all is not forgotten.

Daniel R. Mandelker

St. Louis Missouri
November 11, 2002

HOW TO USE THIS BOOK

Land Use Law is a comprehensive review of the law and practice of land use planning and regulation. It has three elements:

- A review of the case law.
- A review of the statutes.
- A review of planning practice.

Discussions of planning practice will usually be found at the beginning of each chapter or section. These briefly review a land use regulation and indicate how it is used in practice, or discuss a legal problem, such as amortization, and indicate how the legal questions it raises can affect practice applications.

There has been a substantial increase in the adoption of legislation in the past few decades, and the publication of the American Planning Associations Legislative Guidebook late in 2001 has provided additional statutory models. Many states had already replaced or modernized the standard planning and zoning acts that provided a statutory model for many years, and the APA Guidebook should provide additional support for statutory change.

The book makes references to the APA model laws throughout and selectively cites typical legislation that provides statutory authority on the practice issue or problem under discussion. Statutes are current as of the date the manuscript was submitted. You can find additional similar legislation by using the "More Like This" search tool in Lexis. Simply highlight the relevant text in a statute you want to find in other states, click on the More Like This tab, and then adjust the library in which you will be searching to cover the jurisdictions you want to search. You can also select mandatory terms that must be included in cases selected by the research program.

Care has been taken in the case law to include selective cases that represent a variety of jurisdictions, yet comprehensively illustrate legal points with typical and influential decisions. Many of the decisions contain a discussion of applicable case law, including conflicting authority, and I sometimes note these decisions with a "citing cases" parenthetical. Because many of the decisions contain comprehensive discussions of the case law, they are excellent starting points for and may also suggest additional research. They may also elaborate points of law that are not discussed in, but are related to issues discussed in, the text. The intention is to provide citations to cases that provide support for textual statements but that also provide a springboard for additional research.

Subsequent history for cases, included certiorari denials in the Supreme Court, is not provided in this edition. Searching for subsequent history in Lexis is quick and simple, and will provide an update on the status of the case at the time of your research. You can also use the "More Like This" feature in Lexis to find additional cases on point with a problem you are researching. You can again highlight critical text in a decision and then click on the More Like This feature as suggested above. For example, in a case discussing the constitutionality of amortization, you might want to highlight text for additional research that says "Amortization of a nonconforming use is constitutional if the amortization period is reasonable." You can again select mandatory terms for inclusion in cases selected by the research program.

(5th Ed.—02/03)

How to Use this Book

I again plan annual supplements to the book that will update the statutory and case law.

Land use law is a fascinating and growing field. Enjoy it!

Chapter 1

CONTROLLING LAND USE: AN OVERVIEW

Synopsis

§ 1.01   Providing a Focus.
§ 1.02   Differences in Federal and State Constitutional Law and Litigation.
§ 1.03   The Land Use Control System.
§ 1.04   Zoning for Land Use, Density and Site Development.
§ 1.05   Historic District and Historic Landmark Zoning.
§ 1.06   Environmental Land Use Regulation
§ 1.07   Sign Regulation and Design Review.
§ 1.08   Growth Management.
§ 1.09   Subdivision Controls and Planned Unit Developments.
§ 1.10   The Exclusion Problem.
§ 1.11   How the Book Is Organized.
§ 1.12   Standards of Judicial Review.
§ 1.13   Rules of Construction.
§ 1.14   Land Use Cases in the Federal Courts.
§ 1.15   Land Use Cases in the State Courts.
§ 1.16   Variations in the States.
§ 1.17   State Appellate Court Structure.
§ 1.18   The Stages of Land Use Law.

§ 1.01 Providing a Focus.

Public control of land use has a long history. The Roman Twelve Tables adopted in the fourth century B.C.E. included building site restrictions. Six centuries of English and American legislation enacted a variety of land use regulations, including restrictions on the growth of London adopted during the reign of Elizabeth I. Early legislation in the United States often dealt with specific regulatory problems such as building and height regulation, but the precedent for more extensive land use control is clear.

Modern land use regulation began with the first comprehensive zoning ordinance, adopted by New York City in 1916. Earlier municipal laws prohibited noxious uses in residential neighborhoods, but New York was the first to adopt a comprehensive zoning ordinance assigning land uses to zoning districts throughout the city. Comprehensive zoning has since spread throughout the country.

All states have legislation authorizing municipal zoning, and all major cities except Houston have zoning ordinances. Practically all states authorize zoning

(5th Ed.—02/03)

by counties. In some states, local governments may adopt and administer zoning and other land use controls under their constitutional home rule powers.

Legislation in all states authorizes local governments to do comprehensive planning and adopt comprehensive plans. Statutes in several states make the adoption of comprehensive plans mandatory. Comprehensive plans include land use policies that guide land use controls. Although the courts did not initially impose this requirement, a number of state statutes also require zoning to be consistent with the comprehensive plan.

State planning and zoning legislation is based on separate Standard Acts for planning and zoning drafted by the U.S. Department of Commerce in the 1920s. Every state adopted the Standard Zoning Act, either as published or with minor variations. The Standard Planning Act was not as widely adopted, but state planning legislation generally follows its format. Many states have now revised their planning and zoning legislation, but the statutory framework provided by these early statutory models still dominates.

This book covers local planning and land use controls. It includes zoning and the regulation of residential development through subdivision controls. It also includes other forms of land use regulation, such as growth management, aesthetic, historic preservation and environmental controls.

Federal and state constitutions impose limitations on land use controls, which local governments adopt under what is known as the "police power." The takings clause is one of the most important. Courts must determine whether a land use regulation "goes so far" that it "takes" property without the just compensation required by the Constitution. If a court holds that a land use regulation violates the takings clause, the U.S. Supreme Court requires compensation for a temporary taking for the period of time the regulation was in effect.

Land use controls must also satisfy the substantive and procedural requirements of due process clauses in the federal and state constitutions. Courts hold a land use regulation satisfies substantive due process if it advances a legitimate governmental purpose. Courts apply procedural due process requirements to land use controls to ensure that the procedures used in land use regulation are fair.

Courts apply equal protection clauses in the federal and state constitutions to the regulatory classifications included in land use controls. They apply a deferential standard of equal protection review when land use controls and their administration affect economic interests in land. Courts apply a more rigorous standard of judicial review when a land use control is suspect or affects a fundamental constitutional right. A racially discriminatory classification is an example of a suspect classification. The right to free speech is an example of a fundamental constitutional right.

This common statutory and constitutional base for land use controls provides a unifying structure for land use law. Extensive state adoption of model legislation provides a common statutory base that makes case law transferable from one state to another. Takings, equal protection, and due process clauses are included in the federal as well as state constitutions and provide a common constitutional base for land use jurisprudence.

§ 1.02 Differences in Federal and State Constitutional Law and Litigation.

State courts for many years decided the vast majority of land use cases, but the federal courts are now more active especially as the Supreme Court continues to decide takings and other land use cases. Similar constitutional provisions provide the basis for litigation in federal and state courts, and plaintiffs may sue on the federal constitution in state courts, but whether a litigant sues in federal or state court can make a difference.

State courts usually apply federal court interpretations of the free speech clause in land use cases, such as sign regulation cases, perhaps because federal courts developed the law of free speech as applied to land use regulation. Supreme Court takings cases also provide at least a minimum of protection to landowners. State courts increasingly apply them, or may decide that state takings doctrine provides equivalent protections.

Due process and equal protection cases are more complicated. The U.S. Supreme Court has held that most land use controls satisfy substantive due process because they advance legitimate governmental purposes, including zoning that separates incompatible uses and historic preservation, open space, and aesthetic controls. State courts agree, but may be more aggressive in applying substantive due process to invalidate exclusionary zoning and other restrictive controls, such as controls on group homes.

Both federal and state courts require procedural due process protections in administrative land use decision making. The Supreme Court has adopted a balancing test to decide procedural due process claims under the federal constitution.. Requirements for fair procedures may not always have a constitutional basis in the state courts, and they differ in how to apply them. In the federal courts, with a few exceptions, plaintiffs must have an entitlement to a land use in order to bring a due process claim, which usually means the municipality must have be required to approve the land use that was denied and that raises a due process claim. In addition, some federal courts will not hear a substantive due process claim if the plaintiff can make a takings claim on the same facts.

Equal protection claims do not face these barriers in federal court but are usually unsuccessful, if there is no claim of racial discrimination, because federal courts apply deferential judicial review when regulations affect only economic interests. Equal protection law under the state constitutions is not always as clear. An equal protection claim is implicit in the ambiguous, but common, state court rule that a zoning restriction is invalid as applied to a tract of land if it is "arbitrary and capricious."

The ripeness rules are another important factor in land use litigation. These rules require plaintiffs to try takings cases arising out of the application of land use regulations in the state courts first. In addition, there must be a final decision at the local level. The lower federal courts are divided on whether to apply the ripeness rules to due process and equal protection claims, and the Supreme Court has not ruled on this question.

§ 1.03   The Land Use Control System.

This section reviews the regulatory goals and purposes of land use controls. It provides illustrations of typical constitutional issues likely to arise under land use control programs and indicates how courts respond to these constitutional claims.

§ 1.04   Zoning for Land Use, Density and Site Development.

Zoning ordinances comprehensively assign compatible land uses to zoning districts throughout the community. The zoning ordinance contains a text and a map. The map designates the location of zoning districts. The text contains use, density, and site development regulations for the land uses permitted in each district. It also contains administrative and enforcement provisions.

Zoning is an elaboration of nuisance doctrines the courts developed in the days before zoning became common. Land use nuisance cases usually arose when a commercial or industrial use planned to locate in a residential neighborhood, where it would be detrimental to residential land uses. Courts recognized the importance of preserving established residential areas by prohibiting the location of these invading uses in residential neighborhoods. The comprehensive zoning ordinance ratifies this land use structure. It divides the municipality into a number of zoning districts that separate residential, commercial, and industrial uses.

Within residential zoning districts, the zoning ordinance makes distinctions among permitted residential uses based on their density. One clear distinction is between single-family and multifamily residential development. The ordinance usually creates a number of single-family and multifamily zoning districts. They permit increasingly higher residential densities as they progress from the most restrictive single-family to the least restrictive multifamily use. Commercial and industrial districts also distinguish between different intensities of land use. For example, the ordinance may contain different commercial districts permitting neighborhood, community, and regional commercial uses. Zoning ordinances were originally cumulative. They permitted "higher" less intensive uses in the "lower" zones that permitted more intensive uses. Most modern zoning ordinances are not cumulative. Each zoning district is exclusive and allows only the uses permitted in that zone.

Much land use litigation arises from the way in which the zoning text and ordinance classify land into zoning districts. This litigation can raise a variety of constitutional questions. A landowner can argue a zoning classification as applied to his land is a taking of property because it does not allow him a reasonable use of his land. Courts determine whether a zoning ordinance is a taking of property "as applied" by comparing the uses allowed by the ordinance on the restricted property with the zoning and land uses in the surrounding area. This method of analysis reflects the nuisance origins of zoning. In the nuisance cases, the courts evaluate the impact of an invading land use on its immediate neighborhood. Adjacent land uses also provide the benchmark for evaluating the impact of a land use regulation on a tract of land under the takings clause. Equal protection problems can also arise. Neighbors may object if the municipality amends the zoning map to allow a commercial use in the middle of a residential neighborhood. They can argue this is "spot" zoning that violates the equal protection clause by unfairly benefitting a single landowner.

§ 1.05 Historic District and Historic Landmark Zoning.

Historic district and landmark zoning enact regulations to preserve the character of historic buildings in historic areas. Municipalities may adopt these regulations in a separate ordinance. Historic district zoning prohibits any development and any change in the exterior of an historic building that is incompatible with the historic buildings in the district. Historic landmark zoning contains similar controls but is applied to individual historic buildings.

Unlike traditional zoning, historic zoning implements aesthetic purposes because it preserves the aesthetic character of historic districts and buildings. This distinction requires qualification because traditional zoning also implements aesthetic purposes. Traditional zoning prohibits nonresidential uses in residential areas, for example, because they can be aesthetically displeasing in a residential environment. Perhaps the aesthetic characterization of historic zoning reflects its novelty. Traditional zoning is based on nuisance law, which historically protected residential areas from incompatible nonresidential uses. The courts did not extend nuisance law to protect the character of historic buildings and historic areas.

The aesthetic purposes of historic zoning raise a substantive due process problem. Courts must decide whether aesthetic land use controls advance a legitimate governmental purpose under the due process clause. A majority of courts now hold that aesthetic purposes alone are a legitimate basis for land use regulation.

Historic zoning also presents a takings problem. The courts have upheld historic district ordinances against taking challenges because they preserve the historic integrity of entire historic areas. Historic landmark regulation presents a more difficult takings problem because landmarks are isolated and the burden of preservation is concentrated on the landmarks owner. However, the Supreme Court upheld a New York City landmark ordinance against a claim the refusal to allow construction of a high-rise office building on Grand Central Station was a taking.

§ 1.06 Environmental Land Use Regulation

Environmental land use controls protect the integrity of vulnerable environmental resources by prohibiting or regulating development within them. Wetland regulations protect the natural habitat of wildlife that uses these areas and help prevent flooding and water pollution by preserving wetlands in their natural state. Floodplain regulation implements public health and safety objectives by preventing development in areas where flooding would cause damage to life and property. Other environmental land use regulations protect groundwater supplies and hillside slopes and may also provide protective controls for areas designated as critical environmental areas. Agricultural zoning allows only agricultural uses or limited residential development in agricultural areas. The courts have held these regulatory objectives serve legitimate governmental purposes.

Environmental land use regulations can raise takings problems. Although these regulations can protect environmental areas by allowing beneficial uses, such as agricultural uses in agricultural land use zones, they may also include restrictions that leave the landowner without an economically beneficial use of the land. Wetland and floodplain zoning are examples. If this occurs, there may be a per se taking because courts cannot consider the purposes of a land use regulation when they decide whether a per se taking has occurred under the Supreme Court's per se takings rule. So far, however, the courts have not usually applied this rule to find a taking when landowners have challenged environmental land use regulations.

§ 1.07 Sign Regulation and Design Review.

Sign regulation, which preceded comprehensive zoning, is an aesthetic regulation. Municipalities initially regulated the size and height of signs, and the courts upheld these regulations. Sign regulations may now be in the zoning ordinance or in a separate ordinance. They regulate the size, height, location and other characteristics of on-premise signs. They may also exclude off-premise signs, usually called billboards, from the entire community or from selected areas, such as residential areas.

Courts have accepted the aesthetic purposes of sign regulation and have upheld the exclusion of billboards from residential areas because they can be a disruptive use in residential surroundings. Most courts also hold a community's interest in its aesthetic appearance justifies a total billboard exclusion.

Sign regulations present more difficult constitutional problems under the free speech clause of the federal constitution. Political and noncommercial messages on signs are protected as noncommercial speech, and courts strictly review ordinances that regulate signs with these messages. Regulations for political and ideological signs are an example. The regulation of commercial messages on signs receives less constitutional protection, but courts apply a heightened standard of judicial review to these regulations as well. However, the Supreme Court has held that traffic safety and aesthetic purposes are valid reasons for regulating signs under the free speech clause.

Design review is another aesthetic control. Many municipalities have architectural design review boards that review the design of signs, residential dwellings and other new developments. The review of major planned developments can also incorporate design review, and some communities have adopted design review ordinances for entire areas, such as downtown areas. The cases have also upheld design review as an appropriate aesthetic control.

§ 1.08 Growth Management.

Growth management has become an important land use regulation program in many areas of the country, and several states have adopted statutes that require growth management programs at the local level. Growth management programs may regulate the timing and phasing of new development, may impose quotas on the amount of new development allowed and may establish urban growth boundaries that determine where new development may occur. Another growth management technique prohibits the approval of new development unless it is served by adequate public facilities. A moratorium on new development may be necessary so that a community can decide whether it wants to adopt growth management regulations.

Growth management programs present a number of constitutional problems. The courts have held these programs serve a legitimate governmental purpose. There may also be a takings problem if a development moratorium, phasing program or similar growth management strategy prohibits development or delays it for a substantial period of time. The Supreme Court has held a temporary delay in development required by a moratorium is not a per se taking, and the courts have also upheld development moratoria when they are reasonably limited in time.

The location of major highways are a major factor in determining where growth will occur. To protect planned highway corridors, a number of states authorize local governments to adopt land use controls to prohibit development on land within a corridor until it is acquired for highway purposes. These ordinances may also apply to parks and other public facilities. There are similar programs in some states to preserve state highway corridors. Corridor preservation can also present a takings problem, though a well-designed program should survive a takings claim.

§ 1.09 Subdivision Controls and Planned Unit Developments.

Controls over residential subdivisions preceded comprehensive zoning. Nineteenth century state legislation authorized the platting of raw land into lots and blocks to facilitate conveyancing. Some states later amended their legislation to add controls over streets. The model planning legislation proposed in the 1920s incorporated an expanded statutory authority for controls over new subdivisions.

Legislation in all states now authorizes local governments to impose a number of requirements on new subdivisions when they are platted and approved. Subdivision control ordinances require the appropriate design of lots and blocks, subdivision access, and such necessary internal improvements as internal streets and drainage, and water and sewer facilities. Developers may also have to provide land without compensation for streets, public schools, or parks, or pay an in-lieu fee the municipality can use for these purposes. Requirements of this type are known as exactions. Some state legislation prohibits subdivisions in floodplain or natural hazard areas.

Courts usually uphold the constitutionality of subdivision control requirements for subdivision design and necessary internal improvements. Other subdivision exactions, such as land dedications for streets and parks, present a more difficult takings problem. Courts uphold these exactions if there is a nexus between the exaction and a need created by the subdivision, but recent U.S. Supreme Court cases, which state courts must follow, have adopted a more demanding nexus test than state courts had previously applied.

An impact fee is another type of exaction on new development. It is usually levied when building permits are issued, not in the subdivision control process. Impact fees are usually used for off-site facilities, such as water and sewage treatment plants. The nexus test also applies to impact fees.

Many local governments have regulations for the approval of planned unit developments, usually as part of the zoning ordinance. These regulations authorize the approval of residential developments as an entity and usually include use, density, circulation, open space and design requirements. They may also authorize mixed-use developments that add nonresidential uses. Though most state legislation does not authorize planned unit regulations, the courts have held that they are authorized by implication and are consistent with the requirements contained in the statutes for zoning ordinances.

§ 1.10 The Exclusion Problem.

If land use controls are too restrictive they will exclude lower income groups from the community. Exclusionary land use controls are primarily a suburban zoning problem. Suburban municipalities may adopt large-lot residential zoning, prohibit multifamily housing or adopt other exclusionary restrictions to exclude lower-income groups and racial minorities.

Exclusionary zoning violates the equal protection clause if it discriminates against racial minorities, though the Supreme Court has made it difficult to prove that racial discrimination has occurred. A few states, such as New Jersey, have restricted the adoption of exclusionary zoning through court decisions

State statutes may contain requirements that deal with the exclusion problem. Several states require a housing element in local comprehensive plans that contains policies for affordable housing. Other programs for affordable housing include statutory provisions for the judicial review of adverse local government decisions, and an affordable housing program as part of the statewide land use program in Oregon. Some communities have inclusionary zoning programs that require developers to provide affordable housing as part of their housing developments or provide incentives for the provision of affordable housing. The economic impact of these programs on developers may create takings problems.

§ 1.11 How the Book Is Organized.

This book is an introduction to the major principles of land use law and concentrates on case law in the federal and state courts. The text is primarily a descriptive summary of land use law concepts and principles. It features a discussion of statutory authority and programs as well as judicial doctrine. and discusses leading and representative cases to illustrate textual principles. The footnotes cite additional selected cases to that provide judicial support for the principles stated in the text.. Selected citations to books and articles are included at the end of each chapter. Periodic supplements will update the statutory, case, and reference material.

The book also discusses the land use practice problems presented by different types of land use regulations and programs. It reviews the Standard Planning and Standard Zoning Acts and how they have been applied in state land use legislation. Statutes cited are current as of the date the text was prepared. References are provided throughout to new model planning and land use regulation proposed by the American Planning Association.

The plan of the book is straightforward. Chapter 2 provides an outline of basic constitutional doctrines. Chapter 3 discusses the comprehensive plan and its role in land use controls. Chapter 4 discusses the nuisance origins of zoning and the basic statutory and governmental structure of the zoning system. Chapter 5 discusses zoning for land use, density, and site development. Chapter 6 discusses the zoning process. The remaining chapters discuss exclusionary zoning, land use litigation and remedies, subdivision control and planned united development, and the newer land use controls such as growth management, historic preservation, sign regulation and design review, and environmental land use controls.

A word on terminology is in order. Land use controls are adopted by a variety of local governments, including cities, villages, and counties. To simplify the textual presentation, these local governments are referred to as "municipalities." This term includes all local governments that have the authority to adopt and administer land use regulations.

§ 1.12 Standards of Judicial Review.

The standard of judicial review courts apply is critical in land use litigation. Land use regulation has historically enjoyed a presumption of constitutionality that courts give to regulation that affects economic interests in property. The presumption has important consequences. It means the party attacking a land use regulation in court has the burden to prove it unconstitutional, and that a court will hold a land use regulation constitutional if the governmental purposes it serves are fairly debatable. A regulation is fairly debatable if reasonable minds disagree about its constitutionality. As the courts sometimes state, they do not sit as super-zoning boards.[1]

Though courts apply the presumption of constitutionality to claims a land use regulation violates equal protection or substantive due process, they will reverse the presumption in equal protection cases when a land use classification is suspect or when a regulation affects a fundamental constitutional interest. The right to free speech is one example of a fundamental constitutional interest.

The courts also reverse the presumption of constitutionality in other types of land use cases, especially when vulnerable land uses are affected. For example, some state courts reverse the presumption of constitutionality when they review exclusionary zoning and ordinances that exclude group homes or unrelated families from single-family zoning districts. The Supreme Court applied a heightened "reasonable basis" standard of review when it held the denial of a permit to a group home for the mentally disabled violated equal protection. Courts have reversed the presumption of constitutionality in so many types of land use cases that it is difficult to claim the presumption usually applies in land use litigation.[2] This shift in judicial attitude is one of the most important recent trends in land use law.[3]

---

[1] See, e.g., Dodd v. Hood River County, 136 F.3d 1219 (9th Cir. 1998); Mayhew v. Town of Sunnyvale, 964 S.W.2d 922 (Tex. 1998).

[2] See Maysom Ltd. Partnership v. Village of Mayfield, 645 N.E.2d 763 (Ohio App. 1994) (refusing to apply presumption when ordinance held unconstitutional twice).

[3] For discussion, see Mandelker & Tarlock, "Shifting the Presumption of Constitutionality in Land Use Law," 24 Urb. Law. 1 (1992).

Judicial review standards in takings cases are less clear. The takings clause includes the equivalent of a substantive due process requirement as one of its takings tests. The Supreme Court has indicated it will apply a more heightened standard of judicial review when applying this test than courts usually apply to land use regulation.[4]

§ 1.13 Rules of Construction.

Another rule that influences land use cases, though it appears out of place in modern legal jurisprudence, is the rule that a court must construe zoning ordinances strictly because they are in derogation of property rights.[1] The rule survives, but its impact is more limited than its statement suggests. Courts usually apply the strict construction rule only when they interpret definitions and restrictions in zoning ordinances. Other courts do not follow the rule.[2]

There is also a strict construction rule, called Dillon's Rule, that courts have historically applied when they interpret the statutory authority delegated to local governments. Courts apply this rule to land use as well as other legislation, but many states have abandoned or modified it in recent years,[3] though it can still be troublesome when courts are asked to imply legislative authority for local land use regulations.[4] However, a number of states have constitutional provisions that confer home rule authority on local governments in addition to statutory authority, and local government may be able to rely on home rule powers to adopt land use regulations.[5]

§ 1.14 Land Use Cases in the Federal Courts.

Land use cases in the federal courts begin at the trial level in the District Courts. A party to a case can take an appeal as of right from these courts to intermediate appellate courts, known as Courts of Appeals. The Supreme Court decides in its discretion whether to take a case from a Court of Appeals, and it can also

---

[4] *See* §§ 2.10–2.13 (exactions).

[1] For typical cases, see Whistler v. Burlington N.R.R., 741 P.2d 422 (Mont. 1987); Knappett v. Locke, 600 P.2d 1257 (Wash. 1979).

[2] Cizek v. Concerned Citizens of Eagle River Valley, Inc., 41 P.3d 140 n.1 (Alaska 2002) (court uses independent judgment if interpretation does not involve agency expertise); City of Portland v. Carriage Inn, 676 P.2d 943 (Or. App. 1984) (casting doubt on rule and stating that primary function of courts is to determine legislative intent); Development Servs. Of America, Inc. v. City of Seattle, 979 P.2d 387 (Wash. 1999) (refusing to follow strict construction rule).

[3] *See* Rotter v. Coconino Cty., 818 P.2d 704 (Ariz. 1991) (strict construction rule not applied to ordinance restricting nonconforming uses because policy favoring their termination should be encouraged).

[4] §§ 9.17, 9.21 (exactions and impact fees).

[5] §§ 4.24, 4.25.

decide to take cases from state courts, but it takes very few cases that are taken to it.

Decisions by the Supreme Court are binding on the lower federal courts, but they often exercise considerable judgment in deciding how to apply Supreme Court land use cases. One reason is that Supreme Court cases often provide only general guidelines for the land use questions they consider. Another is that the Supreme Court may not have decided a question a lower federal courts is asked to decide. Lower federal courts may disagree on how to decide a land use question when the Supreme Court has not considered it or has given incomplete guidance.

It is important to remember that federal courts are courts of limited jurisdiction that can refuse cases they believe more properly belong in state courts. For example, federal courts can abstain from accepting a case if they believe the case presents undecided questions of state law. They can also hold a land use case is not ripe for decision and should be heard in a state court first.

§ 1.15   Land Use Cases in the State Courts.

State courts do not have the same restrictions on jurisdiction as the federal courts, though they will refuse to hear cases that do not present an actual controversy. However, a plaintiff is not entitled to sue a local government in state court unless the suit is authorized by statute, or available under common law judicial writs that may also be codified by statute.[1]

§ 1.16   Variations in the States.

Land use law varies significantly among the states, even though the Standard Zoning and Planning Acts provided a common statutory denominator for land use regulation. This section discusses zoning law, which makes up the vast majority of the decided land use cases. State judicial attitudes on subdivision and other regulations, such as growth management regulations, are more difficult to characterize because the case law is not as developed.

California, New Jersey and New York have decided a substantial number of leading zoning cases, though their highest appellate courts have been deciding fewer zoning cases in recent years. Florida and Texas are populous states whose courts have a growing influence on zoning law. States with smaller populations that have decided important zoning cases include Connecticut, Maryland, Massachusetts, and North Carolina.

The influence of individual state courts on zoning law varies with judicial attitudes toward zoning and the style and content of court decisions. States divide, under one classification, depending on whether they are pro-developer or pro-government. California and Maryland courts have traditionally been pro-government, though changes in these courts may change how they handle land

---

[1] *See* §§ 8.12–8.16.

use cases. Illinois courts may be pro-developer. Other states, such as Texas, Michigan, and Ohio, are either erratic or difficult to characterize. Some states have not produced enough zoning law to be classified. The increasing adoption of statutes on a number of zoning issues also limits judicial discretion and makes it more difficult to characterize state court attitudes. Neither is a court decision that upholds a land use regulation always preferable. Judicial invalidation may be necessary in cases where a land use decision is attacked by neighbors because it is arbitrary, or when a case is brought against an exclusionary land use ordinance. Trying to find neat categories for land use decision may no longer be useful.

The style, content, and even the length of zoning decisions also affects their influence and importance. Some courts, such as the California and New Jersey courts, often consider policy issues in their decisions. Other courts are less policy-oriented. Illinois decisions, especially in the intermediate appellate courts, are often heavily fact-based. Zoning decisions in the Pennsylvania and Florida intermediate courts may also be brief and limited .

Though the statutory framework for land use regulation is similar in all states, statutory differences and differences in judicial doctrine may lead to significant variations across the states in land use law. A statutory example are the state statutes on vested rights, which may modify common law principles. There are also significant variations in judicial doctrine across the board on a number of issues . The treatment of nonconforming uses is an example. Courts tend look to their own precedent to decide cases, especially as land use law within a state matures. Takings and free speech doctrines adopted under the federal constitution are exceptions because the federal constitution applies in state courts.

§ 1.17   State Appellate Court Structure.

A state's appellate court structure has an important influence on the precedential value of its land use decisions. Most states have intermediate appellate, as well as supreme, courts. The supreme court may have a discretionary jurisdiction, and may refuse appeals from intermediate appellate courts in land use cases. In these states intermediate appellate courts decide the vast bulk of land use cases, leaving many issues unresolved if the supreme court takes relatively few land use cases. Some state supreme courts have also indicated they will not consider cases where there is an attack on a land use regulation as applied to a particular property.[1]

The precedential problem is even more complicated when the intermediate appellate court is divided into geographic districts because doctrinal differences can occur among them. California, Illinois, New York and Texas are examples. Pennsylvania has an intermediate Commonwealth Court that hears cases arising

---

[1] Tidewater Oil Co. v. Mayor & Council, 209 A.2d 105 (N.J. 1965), discussed in § 2.46.

in governmental programs, including land use regulation. Trial court decisions are reported in New York in the New York Supplement and in New Jersey in the Atlantic Reporter. Trial court decisions from some states, such as Connecticut, are also available on Lexis.

This book cites and discusses decisions by the highest state courts whenever possible. It includes decisions by intermediate appellate courts only when they establish important doctrine or contain thoughtful discussions of land use law issues.

§ 1.18   The Stages of Land Use Law.

Commentators frequently refer to the different stages through which land use law has moved. This kind of commentary must carefully distinguish between stages of development in the state as compared with the federal courts. A series of distinct stages is more marked in the state courts. The "stages" analysis also applies primarily to zoning, which has produced the vast majority of the decisions.

In the state courts, an early period when they were hostile to zoning ended when the Supreme Court upheld comprehensive zoning in the *Euclid* case.[1] State courts accepted the constitutionality of land use regulation after *Euclid*. Standard judicial attitudes[2] that apply a presumption of constitutionality to land use regulation characterized this stage and still prevail in most states for most land use questions.

The beginning of a new and more judicially assertive stage in land use law, in which courts began to question land use regulations and decisions, is difficult to identify. Though they have accepted the facial constitutionality of land use regulation, state courts have always set aside zoning regulations as applied if they believed they were arbitrary and capricious. Then, beginning in the mid-1960s, state courts became concerned with social issues in zoning and began to hold exclusionary restrictions unconstitutional. *National Land & Inv. Co. v. Kohn*,[3] which struck down large lot zoning, is a major case of this type. This new stage in zoning law reached its peak with the landmark exclusionary zoning decisions in New Jersey.[4] Though judicial concern in the state courts with social zoning issues has subsided, many are still sensitive to zoning that excludes or restricts unwanted land uses, such as group homes.

More recent developments in state courts are cases holding that land use decisions are quasi-judicial rather than legislative, and that zoning must be consistent with an adopted land use plan. Several states have now adopted the consistency requirement by statute.

---

[1] Village of Euclid v. Ambler Realty Co., 272 U.S. 365 (1926), discussed in § 2.06.

[2] § 1.12.

[3] 215 A.2d 597 (Pa. 1965), discussed in § 5.32.

[4] *See* §§ 7.09, 7.11.

At the federal level, an active property rights movement began to challenge land use regulation toward the end of the last century, and the Supreme Court responded with a series of takings clause cases that adopted more rigorous takings doctrine. The Court continues to decide land use takings cases and has placed new limitations on land use regulation, especially as applied to exactions. In addition, the Supreme Court applied the free speech clause to commercial speech in the late 1970s. This decision eventually led the Court to apply the free speech clause to the regulation of signs and adult businesses. These cases effectively reversed the presumption of constitutionality and shifted the burden to municipalities to justify these ordinances. Congress has also adopted legislation that limits zoning for cellular towers, group homes for the disabled and religious land uses. These developments have created a new statutory and judicial environment at the federal level, in which local land use policy is increasingly subject to judicial and statutory scrutiny.

REFERENCES

Books and Monographs

American Planning Association, Growing Smart Legislative Guidebook: Model Statutes for Planning and the Management of Change (S. Meck ed. 2002)

R. Babcock, The Zoning Game (1966).

R. Babcock & C. Siemon, The Zoning Game Revisited (1985).

Trends in Land Use Law from A to Z (American Bar Ass'n, P. Salkin ed., 2001).

Wipeouts and Their Mitigation (J. DiMento ed. 1990).

Articles

Developments in the Law Zoning, 91 Harv. L. Rev. 1427 (1978).

Karkkainen, Zoning: A Reply to the Critics, 10 J. Land Use & Envtl. L. 45 (1994).

Krasnowiecki, The Fallacy of the End-State System of Land Use Control, Land Use L. & Zoning Dig., Vol. 38, No. 4, at 3 (1986).

Libby, The Great Zoning Debate — More Heat Than Light, Land Use L. & Zoning Dig., Vol. 38, No. 11, at 3 (1986).

Rose, New Models for Local Land Use Decision, 79 Nw. L. Rev. 1155 (1985).

Williams, Three Systems of Land Use Control, 25 Rutgers L. Rev. 80 (1970).

Wyckoff, Zoning Critics: Proposed Reforms Over the Past 20 Years, Land Use L. & Zoning Dig., Vol. 38, No. 11, at 5 (1986).

Chapter 2

THE CONSTITUTIONAL FRAMEWORK

Synopsis

A. THE TAKINGS ISSUE.

§ 2.01 The Takings Problem.
§ 2.02 Takings Law.
§ 2.03 Physical Per Se Takings.
§ 2.04 The Noxious Use Cases.
§ 2.05 *Pennsylvania Coal*: Regulatory Takings Recognized.
§ 2.06 *Euclid*: Comprehensive Zoning Upheld.
§ 2.07 *Penn Central*: A Multi-Factor Takings Test.
§ 2.08 The *Agins* Two-Part Takings Test: Herein of Legitimate Governmental Purpose.
§ 2.09 *Lucas*: A Per Se Test for Regulatory Takings, Nuisance and other Exceptions.
§ 2.10 Exactions.
§ 2.11 *Nollan*: The Nexus Test.
§ 2.12 *Dolan*: The "Rough Proportionality" Rule.
§ 2.13 *Del Monte Dunes:* Clarifying "Rough Proportionalilty."
§ 2.14 Takings Problems, Principles and Maxims.
§ 2.15 Average Reciprocity of Advantage
§ 2.16 Investment-Backed Expectations.
§ 2.17 The Whole Parcel or Denominator Rule: Herein of Segmentation.
§ 2.18 Conceptual Severance: The Right to Exclude.
§ 2.19 Geographic Segmentation.
§ 2.20 Temporal Severance.
§ 2.21 *Lucas* Applied: When Does a Per Se Regulatory Taking Occur?
§ 2.22 Delay in Decision Making as a Taking.
§ 2.23 Planning and Zoning With Acquisitory Intent.
§ 2.24 Ripeness and Finality.
§ 2.25 Early Supreme Court Cases.
§ 2.26 *Hamilton Bank*.
§ 2.27 *Yolo County*.
§ 2.28 Later Supreme Court Cases.
§ 2.29 Federal Court Cases.
§ 2.30 Final Decision Rule.
§ 2.31 Compensation Requirement.
§ 2.32 Equal Protection and Due Process Claims.
§ 2.33 Returning to Federal Court From State Court.
§ 2.34 *Rooker-Feldman* Doctrine.
§ 2.35 State Court Takings Doctrine.
§ 2.36 "As-Applied" Cases Claiming Total Loss or Diminution in Value.
§ 2.37 Balancing and Multi-Factor Tests.
§ 2.38 State Takings Legislation.

B. SUBSTANTIVE DUE PROCESS.

§ 2.39 The Substantive Due Process Problem.

(5th Ed.—02/03)

§ 2.40　　Barriers to Substantive Due Process Litigation in the Federal Courts.

C. PROCEDURAL DUE PROCESS.

§ 2.41　　The Procedural Due Process Problem.
§ 2.42　　In the Federal Courts.
§ 2.43　　In the State Courts.

D. EQUAL PROTECTION.

§ 2.44　　The Equal Protection Problem.
§ 2.45　　Judicial Standards for Equal Protection Review.
§ 2.46　　Applying the Rational Relationship Standard: The State Courts.
§ 2.47　　Applying the Rational Relationship Standard: The Federal Courts.
§ 2.48　　*Cleburne*: Rational Relationship "With a Bite."
§ 2.49　　Selective Enforcement: The *Olech* Case.

E. FREE SPEECH.

§ 2.50　　How the Free Speech Clause Applies to Land Use Regulation.
§ 2.51　　Retaliatory Governmental Conduct.

F. THE CONTRACT CLAUSE.

§ 2.52　　General Principles.
§ 2.53　　In Land Use Cases.

A.　THE TAKINGS ISSUE.

§ 2.01　The Takings Problem.

The Fifth Amendment to the U.S. Constitution provides that "private property shall not be taken for public use, without just compensation." Most state constitutions also contain takings clauses, and the Fourteenth Amendment makes the federal takings clause applicable to the states. The takings clause raises the all-important takings issue in land use regulation. Local governments enact land use regulations under their police power, which does not require the payment of compensation. When a land use regulation excessively restricts the use of land without compensation, the restricted landowner can argue a taking of his land without compensation has occurred.

A strict reading of the takings clause suggests it does not apply to land use regulation but only when a government entity takes or physically occupies land for a public use. Judicial doctrine through the latter part of the nineteenth century supported this view. In a leading case, *Mugler v. Kansas*,[1] the Supreme Court held a taking had not occurred when a state prohibition law forced the closing of a brewery without compensation. The Court distinguished the power of eminent domain and the police power. "A prohibition simply upon the use of property" for purposes legislatively declared to be injurious to the health or safety of the community "cannot . . . be deemed a taking . . . of property for the public benefit."

---

[1] 123 U.S. 623 (1887).

This early interpretation of the takings clause gave way to a more expansive view. It holds a restriction on land use through regulation can be a "taking" of property. Under this view, a regulatory restriction on land use is as much a taking as a physical taking of land by a government entity.

Some important distinctions are necessary at this point. The text of a land use regulation may be so restrictive that no application of its requirements can avoid a taking. An example is an open space regulation that does not allow development of any kind. In this type of case the land use regulation may be a "facial" taking, and landowners can bring a facial challenge to its restrictions based on the takings clause. However, the Supreme Court has emphasized more than once that landowners who bring a facial takings claim face an "uphill battle."[2]

Other land use regulations may not be a facial taking but may possibly be a taking "as applied" to a particular property. An example is a zoning ordinance dividing a community into land use districts. The ordinance may not be a taking as applied to some property but may be a taking as applied to other property it covers. This distinction between facial unconstitutionality and unconstitutionality as applied also applies to the equal protection and the due process claims.

If a court holds that a land use regulation is a taking of property it will invalidate the regulation. Compensation is also payable for the temporary period during which the regulation was in effect.

§ 2.02   Takings Law.

Until recently, Supreme Court takings law was not a major factor in land use jurisprudence. The Court did not decide any significant land use takings cases for decades after its landmark *Euclid* decision upholding the constitutionality of comprehensive zoning. Beginning with its 1978 decision in *Penn Central*, however, the Court has decided a number of important land use takings decisions and continues to take these cases for review.

This increase in the number of Supreme Court takings decisions affects the way in which state, as well as federal, courts decide land use cases. Takings rules applied by state courts and the Supreme Court differ in some states, and state courts did not always apply Supreme Court takings law even though the federal constitution is enforceable in state courts. Because the Supreme Court has now decided a number of influential takings cases, state courts are more likely to apply them in their land use decisions. This change has occurred, in part, because some recent Supreme Court decisions provide greater protection to property rights and are more restrictive than takings law the courts had applied in many states.

---

[2] Tahoe-Sierra Preservation Council, Inc. v. Tahoe Regional Planning Agency, 535 U.S. 302 (2002).

The Supreme Court has adopted a number of takings rules that determine the outcome of land use takings cases. One important distinction turns on whether a permanent physical or a regulatory taking has occurred. A physical taking is a categorical taking per se, and occurs when there is a physical condemnation and when a government regulation authorizes permanent physical occupation of land. A regulation that only regulates the use of land, such as a zoning ordinance, may or may not be a taking per se.

A per se regulatory taking, sometimes called a categorical per se taking, occurs under the Supreme Court's *Lucas*[1] decision when the a land use regulation deprives a landowner of all economically beneficial or productive use of her land. If a land use regulation is not a per se taking, it is reviewed under the Supreme Court's *Penn Central* decision that adopted a set of takings factors courts are to balance in their takings decisions. As the Court has indicated, the *Penn Central* balancing test is the "default" rule, and the *Lucas* per se rule applies only in relatively rare cases.[2]

In addition to the per se *Lucas* and *Penn Central* balancing tests, the Court's *Agins*[3] decision adopted a two-part rule that a land use regulation must "substantially advance legitimate state interests" and must not deny "an owner economically viable use of his land." The second prong of this rule became the *Lucas* per se takings rule. The first prong requires courts to examine the purpose of a land use regulation and imports substantive due process requirements into the takings clause. The Court has arguably applied this rule in exaction cases, where the permanent dedication of land has been required as a condition to a development permit. The extent to which the Court will continue to apply a purpose-based rule that is the equivalent of substantive due process is not clear.[4]

There are other examples of takings rules based on the purpose of a regulation. A classic text on the police power proposed a harm-benefit rule at the turn of the century.[5] This rule would uphold a land use regulation that prevents a harm to private landowners and invalidate a regulation that confers a public benefit. For example, a land use regulation prohibiting industrial uses in residential districts prevents a harm because it prevents industrial uses from harming the residential neighborhood. A land use regulation requiring the preservation of historic landmarks confers a public benefit under this theory. It imposes an economic burden on the landmark owner to secure the benefit of landmark

---

[1] § 2.09.

[2] Tahoe-Sierra Preservation Council, Inc. v. Tahoe Regional Planning Agency, 535 U.S. 302 (2002).

[3] § 2.08

[4] *See id.*

[5] E. Freund, The Police Power 546–47 (1904). *See also* Durham, "A Legal and Economic Basis for City Planning." 58 Colum. L. Rev. 650 (1958).

protection for the general public. Though this rule played a role in some state takings tests, the Supreme Court has now rejected it.[6]

§ 2.03 Physical Per Se Takings.

The Court found per se permanent physical takings in two cases where the taking occurred as a result of government regulation. In *Loretto v. Teleprompter Manhattan CATV Corp.,*[1] a New York statute authorized cable TV companies to install equipment on apartment buildings upon payment of reasonable compensation as determined by the state cable regulatory commission. The commission ruled a nominal one dollar payment was sufficient compensation unless a landowner could show that he suffered greater damages.

An apartment owner brought an action claiming a taking occurred when a cable company installed cable lines and boxes containing roof cables on the roof of its building. The Court held a taking occurs when there is "a permanent physical occupation authorized by government . . . without regard to the public interest it may serve," even though the physical interference is minimal. In this case, the government did not take merely a single "strand" from the bundle of property rights but sliced through the bundle and took every "strand." The taking destroyed the property owner's right to exclude, denied her the right to make a nonpossessory use of the property, and emptied the right to sell the property of any value.[2]

The Court held the per se takings rule did not apply to temporary physical invasions, cases where action outside the owner's property caused consequential damage, and to "a regulation that merely restricts the use of property." The Court described the takings test it applies in cases where a physical invasion is not permanent as a "balancing test" or a "multifactor balancing test."

The dissent criticized the majority for having adopted a rigid per se takings rule based on formalistic quibble. The dissent also criticized the takings distinctions made by the majority. It argued, for example, that the statute was not a taking even if it affected the property owner's right to exclude because takings law does not prohibit a legislative redefinition of property rights.

The Supreme Court limited its *Loretto* holding in *Yee v. City of Escondido.*[3] Plaintiffs were mobile home park owners who rented pads of land to owners of mobile homes. Under state law, a park owner may not require the removal of a mobile home when it is sold or disapprove a purchaser who is able to pay rent. A city ordinance rolled back rents to an earlier level and prohibited rent

---

[6] § 2.09.

[1] 458 U.S. 419 (1982).

[2] *See* Ferguson v. City of Mill City, 852 P.2d 205 (Or. App. 1983) (ordinance requiring easement for sewer lines held a taking).

[3] 503 U.S. 519 (1992).

increases without city approval. The Court held a taking by physical occupation had not occurred, and that a regulatory taking claim was not properly before the Court.

The Court rejected an argument that the rent control ordinance authorized a physical taking because, together with the state law's restrictions, it increased the value of a mobile home by giving the owner the right to occupy the pad indefinitely at a sub-market rent. A physical taking occurs only when a law requires an owner to submit to a physical occupation of his land, and here the mobile home park owners voluntarily rented their land to mobile home owners and were not required to do so by either state or local law. These laws merely regulated the landlord-tenant relationship, and a transfer of wealth to mobile home owners does not convert regulation into a physical taking.

These physical takings cases influenced the Court's exaction cases, where landowners were required to dedication an easement in their land as a condition to a development permit. In holding a taking had occurred, the Court compared the easement requirement to a permanent physical taking, which is a taking per se.[4] However, the Court has made it clear that the longstanding distinction between physical and regulatory takings means the rules that apply to physical takings do not apply to regulatory takings.[5]

§ 2.04 The Noxious Use Cases.

In its first set of land use takings cases, the Supreme Court upheld land use regulations applied retroactively to terminate noxious uses in residential neighborhoods. These regulations were not comprehensive zoning ordinances, but were "police power" ordinances that terminated existing noxious uses in neighborhoods where they were out of place. Commentators treated these cases as adopting the rule that courts will uphold a regulation that prevents a harm, but will not uphold a regulation that confers a benefit on the general public.

The present vitality of the noxious use cases is uncertain. Courts today will not uphold a zoning ordinance that terminates an existing nonconforming use. They continue to uphold ordinances that terminate nuisances. The Court referred approvingly to the early noxious use cases in its *Penn Central* decision, and did not characterize them as cases that upheld harm-preventing ordinances. However, the Court's later *Lucas*[1] case cast doubt on these decisions. It characterized them as an "early attempt" to explain the limitations of the takings clause, now replaced with a "contemporary understanding of the broad realm within which government may regulate without compensation."

---

[4] §§ 2.11, 2.12.

[5] Tahoe-Sierra Preservation Council, Inc. v. Tahoe Regional Planning Agency 535 U.S. 302 (2002).

[1] § 2.09.

Hadacheck v. Sebastian[2] is one of the earliest and best known noxious use case. A landowner constructed a brick manufacturing facility on land containing clay worth $800,000 for brick making but only $60,000 for other purposes. The land was isolated at that time and not surrounded by residential development. Residences were built later in the surrounding area, which remained sparsely settled. The city then adopted an ordinance that retroactively prohibited brick works in designated areas of the city, including the area where this brick works was located.

The equities of the case lay strongly with the brick works owner. The residential homeowners had "come to the nuisance" because the brick works was there first. The homeowners might well have lost had they sued to prohibit the brick works as a nuisance. Some courts deny relief in nuisance cases to landowners who come to a nuisance. Los Angeles bypassed this problem by using its regulatory police power to adopt an ordinance requiring the retroactive termination of the brick-making facility. This retroactive application of the ordinance to eliminate a profitable land use raised a takings issue.

The Supreme Court upheld the ordinance in an opinion remarkably unsympathetic to the owner's economic plight. It held the ordinance prohibited only brick making, not clay removal. If he wished, the brick works owner could remove the clay for brick making to another location, though he argued that this alternative was not practicable. The Court did not balance the public gain from the prohibition against the owner's economic loss. It also disregarded the owner's claim that the prohibition was invalid because his use was first in time.

In an enigmatic passage, the Court held that the brick works owner could not assert vested interests against the ordinance because of conditions previously existing in the area:

> To so hold would preclude development and fix a city forever in its primitive conditions. There must be progress, and if in its march private interests are in the way they must yield to the good of the community.[3]

The Court considered a similar ordinance in a later case handed down before it decided its recent string of land use takings cases. In *Goldblatt v. Town of Hempstead,*[4] a confusing opinion, it upheld an ordinance that prohibited additional mining below the water table in a mining pit and the refilling of any

---

[2] 239 U.S. 394 (1915).

[3] *Id.* at 410, *citing* Reinman v. Little Rock, 237 U.S. 171 (1915) (upholding ordinance prohibiting livery stables in designated areas).

[4] 369 U.S. 590 (1962). *Compare* Sucesion Suarez v. Gelabert, 541 F. Supp. 1253 (D.P.R. 1982) (restriction on sand and gravel mining not a taking), *aff'd,* 701 F.2d 231 (1st Cir. 1983), *with* Silva v. Township of Ada, 330 N.W.2d 663 (Mich. 1982) (holding invalid a prohibition on gravel excavation on agriculturally zoned land).

excavation below this level. The ordinance prevented any further use of the property for mining.[5]

§ 2.05 *Pennsylvania Coal*: Regulatory Takings Recognized.

Shortly after the noxious use cases, in *Pennsylvania Coal Co. v. Mahon*,[1] the Supreme Court held the takings clause applies to land use regulations, and that the regulation under review was a taking of property. The brief and opaque opinion by Justice Holmes still provides the starting point for judicial analysis of the takings clause in land use cases, even though a later Supreme Court decision qualified it.

A coal company conveyed the surface rights to a tract of land but reserved the right to remove subsurface coal. The state later adopted a statute that prohibited coal mining that would cause the subsidence of any dwelling unit. The owners of the land brought an action to prohibit the mining of coal that would cause their residence to subside, and the coal company contended that the statute was unconstitutional.

Holmes held the statute accomplished a taking of the coal company's reserved mining rights. He decided the case largely with aphorisms that still remain the most quotable (and conflicting) takings maxims in any court decision:

> Government could hardly go on if to some extent values incident to property could not be diminished without paying for every such change in the general law. . . . But . . . the implied limitation must have its limits . . . . When it reaches a certain magnitude, in most if not all cases there must be an exercise of eminent domain and compensation.[2]

Justice Holmes provided very little additional guidance on when a regulation is a taking because it goes "too far," but some commentators believe he adopted a balancing test to decide this question. At one point in the opinion, Holmes stated that the statute applied to a "single house." He did not consider the widespread incidence of subsidence throughout mining areas in the state. Holmes concluded that damage to a single house was not a public nuisance, that the public interest was limited, and that any personal safety problems caused by coal mining could be handled by a statute requiring notice to property owners. "On the other hand the extent of the taking" was great and the statute abolished an interest in land. It took the right to mine "certain coal.."

Because the statute destroyed a property right reserved to the coal company under this analysis, Holmes could have held the statute unconstitutional because

---

[5] *But see* Nollan v. California Coastal Comm'n, 483 U.S. 825, 836 n.3 (1987) (rejecting assumption in *Goldblatt* that judicial inquiry under takings clause is same as under due process and equal protection clauses). *See* § 2.11.

[1] 260 U.S. 393 (1922).

[2] 260 U.S. at 413.

it transferred an interest in land to a private owner without compensation. The statute effectively destroyed the subsurface mining rights the company reserved and transferred them to residential property owners. A title transfer of this kind requires compensation, as Holmes noted.

Holmes failed to recognize the statute did not expressly prohibit the mining of subsurface coal. It simply prohibited mining that caused subsidence, a consequence the coal company could have avoided by leaving pillars of coal underground. Holmes also failed to indicate how much coal could be extracted had the underground pillars been provided and treated the "certain coal" required to be left in the ground as the property segment for purposes of the takings clause. Brandeis disagreed in his dissent, and argued the Court should have considered the value of the whole property, not just the value of the coal alone.

A later Supreme Court decision, *Keystone Bituminous Coal Ass'n v. DeBenedictis,*[3] upheld a similar statute by holding the act advanced legitimate state interests because it protected the public interest in health, the environment and the fiscal integrity of the area. The Court also held it was reluctant to strike down legislation that restrains a public nuisance. Only two per cent of the coal had to be left in place to prevent subsidence, and the Court refused to treat this coal as a separate segment of property under the takings clause.

§ 2.06 *Euclid*: Comprehensive Zoning Upheld.

Just a few years after *Pennsylvania Coal*, the Supreme Court did an about face on the takings issue and provided the basis for modern zoning in *Village of Euclid v. Ambler Realty Co,*[1] where it upheld the constitutionality of a comprehensive zoning ordinance. The ordinance imposed a fourfold loss on plaintiff's property, which was zoned for residential use, and which it wanted to develop for an industrial use. The complaint relied on this fact to allege that the zoning ordinance confiscated and destroyed a "great part" of the value of its land, but the landowner did not pursue this claim. Its principal complaint was that the zoning ordinance was unconstitutional because it prohibited nonresidential uses in residential zoning districts, but the Court rejected this argument. This claim made *Euclid* a substantive due process and equal protection, rather than a takings case. The Court also noted the case was a claim brought against the "threatened enforcement" of the zoning ordinance, which is a facial constitutional claim. It reserved for another day a decision on the constitutionality of the ordinance as applied to a particular property.

Some commentators claim *Euclid* holds a zoning ordinance is constitutional even though it causes a substantial diminution in the value of the land that is regulated. This interpretation may be correct. The complaint alleged a taking had

---

[3] 480 U.S. 470 (1987).

[1] 272 U.S. 365 (1926). *See also* § 5.02.

occurred, and the Court specifically referred to the drastic reduction in property value caused by the ordinance. However, the Court's treatment of the case as a facial attack on a zoning ordinance rather than an attack on the constitutionality of the ordinance as applied to the landowner's property undercuts this interpretation.

The Court considered an as-applied attack on the constitutionality of a zoning ordinance two years later, in *Nectow v. City of Cambridge*. [2] There it invalidated as applied a zoning ordinance that restricted the property to residential use, apparently as a violation of substantive due process. Although *Nectow* indicated the Court might be willing to review the constitutionality of zoning ordinances when applied to restrict a landowner's property, it has never again decided a similar case.

§ 2.07 *Penn Central*: A Multi-Factor Takings Test.

More than fifty years passed before the Supreme Court again considered a takings issue in a land use case. In *Penn Central Transp. Co. v. New York City*, [1] the Court upheld an historic landmark designation applied to prevent construction of a high-rise office tower over Grand Central Station. Unlike comprehensive zoning, historic landmark designation falls within the public benefit category of land use regulations. The designation imposes a severe restriction on the use of the landmark site to confer the benefits of historic landmark preservation on the general public.

The special circumstances of the *Penn Central* decision weaken, to some extent, its value as a holding on the takings issue. Unlike many historic preservation cases, the *Penn Central* case did not involve a decision that prohibited the demolition of an historic landmark and the use of its site for a more intensive use. *Penn Central* conceded it could earn a reasonable return on the terminal. It argued only that the restriction on its use of the air rights over the terminal required compensation. Curiously, the Court did not address the compensation claim.

The Court's decision vacillated between equal protection, due process, and takings issues and defies generalization. Justice Brennan's opinion for the majority opened with a review of Supreme Court takings doctrine and noted that the Court had never adopted a "set formula" for the takings clause. He adopted a multi-factor balancing test by identifying several factors the Court had considered when it made these "ad hoc, factual inquiries." These factors include the "character of the governmental action." Justice Brennan noted that a taking is more easily found when government physically invades property than when

---

[2] 277 U.S. 183 (1928).

[1] 438 U.S. 104 (1978).

it adjusts "the benefits and burdens of economic life to promote the public good." The second category clearly includes land use regulation.

The takings factors also include the economic impact of the regulation, and particularly whether the regulation interferes with "distinct investment backed expectations." Justice Brennan did not define this phrase, although he noted that Penn Central had not established a taking "simply by showing that they have been denied the ability to exploit a property interest that they heretofore had believed was available for development."[2] He also stated that only a landowner's primary expectation in the use of her property was protected. The Court has referred to this test as a balancing test.[3]

Brennan's discussion of takings doctrine also included a long analysis of the noxious use cases, such as *Hadacheck*. He stated in a footnote that these cases did not rest on the nuisance qualities of the uses prohibited. He explained the Court upheld single-use zoning in the *Hadacheck* line of cases because this zoning implemented a policy intended to produce a widespread public benefit. Historic landmark protection, he believed, accomplishes the same purpose. Justice Brennan also rejected "Penn Central's related contention that a 'taking' must be found to have occurred whenever a land use restriction may be characterized as imposing a 'servitude' on the claimant's property."

Justice Brennan next considered what he termed a "broad" constitutional attack on the landmark program. He noted Penn Central did not claim historic landmark preservation was an inappropriate governmental purpose. He rejected an argument that a taking occurred because the restriction on development deprived the property owner of a valuable property interest in air space. Takings jurisprudence, he observed, "does not divide a single parcel into discrete segments and attempt to determine whether rights in a particular segment have been entirely abrogated." "[T]his Court focuses rather both on the character of the action and on the nature and extent of the interference with rights in the parcel as a whole — here, the city tax block designated as the 'landmark site'." This holding adopted the "whole parcel" rule,[4] which means a court must look at the entire parcel of land owned by a landowner when it applies the takings clause. Brennan added in a footnote that the full use of air rights was not so bound up with investment-backed expectations that a deprivation of their use constitutes a taking, rejecting any implication of such a rule from *Pennsylvania Coal*.

Without recognizing his shift in position, Brennan next considered a number of equal protection problems raised by the ordinance and the landmark designation. He considered an objection that the landmark designation was reverse "spot zoning" because it arbitrarily singled out the terminal for restrictions not imposed

---

[2] *See also* § 2.16

[3] Tahoe-Sierra Preservation Council v. Tahoe Regional Planning Agency, 533 U.S. 302 (2002).

[4] § 2.17.

on its neighbors. Brennan answered that the city's "comprehensive plan" to preserve landmark structures foreclosed this objection. Brennan's reliance on the city's comprehensive plan is questionable. New York may have had a landmark designation ordinance that applied comprehensively throughout the city, but it did not base its ordinance on a true comprehensive plan.

Penn Central also argued the landmark ordinance was "inherently incapable of producing the fair and equitable distribution of benefits and burdens . . . characteristic of zoning." This argument appears to invoke the average reciprocity of advantage rule as a reason for striking down the ordinance. Brennan answered that "more severe" impacts on some landowners do not constitute a taking, again relying on the *Hadacheck* line of cases.

Brennan next turned to Penn Central's argument that it was solely burdened but not benefitted by the landmark designation. He answered that the landmark law "benefits all New York citizens" in economic terms and by improving "the quality of life of the city as a whole." This holding substantially undercut the harm-benefit rule. The rule that a land use restriction is a taking when it confers public benefits loses force if benefits to "all citizen" avoid a taking that could arise from restrictions a single landowner. The Court rejected this rule in a later case.[5] Brennan also held the landmark designation did not fall within the enterprise category of land use regulation because it did not arise "from any entrepreneurial operations of the city."

Brennan easily dismissed arguments that the landmark law was a taking as applied to the terminal. The law neither interfered with the present use of the property nor precluded the possibility of a less intrusive structure in the terminal's airspace. The city's zoning ordinance allowed the transfer of development rights from the terminal to nearby property owned by Penn Central. Brennan held the development rights transfer option could mitigate a takings claim. The Court's holding on the takings issue is also limited by its statement that the terminal owners could reapply for approval of a smaller building. This statement suggests the takings claim was not ripe for decision.

This puzzling mixture of takings and other constitutional doctrines leaves much to be desired. In addition, the three-part multi-factor test adopted by the Court has been limited by later cases. The distinction between physical and regulatory takings is no longer useful because the Court later held a physical taking is a taking per se. The economic impact of the regulation is no longer critical because the Court also held a land use regulation is a taking if it deprives a landowner of all economically beneficial use of her land. These cases make the investment-backed expectations takings factor a prominent element in a takings case when a per se taking has not occurred. It is also possible a taking occurs when a regulation partly but substantially diminishes the value of property. The Court

---

[5] § 2.09.

has now held the *Penn Central* balancing test is the "default" test in takings cases.[6]

§ 2.08 The *Agins* Two-Part Takings Test: Herein of Legitimate Governmental Purpose.

In *Agins v. City of Tiburon*,[1] two years after *Penn Central*, the Court adopted a two-part takings test that differs from the multi-factor test adopted in *Penn Central*. In *Agins* the city placed five acres of undeveloped land in a Residential Planned Development and Open Space Zone to implement an open space element the state law requires in comprehensive plans. The Court dismissed a facial takings attack on the ordinance in which plaintiffs sought compensation for the zoning restriction and stated its two-part takings test as follows:

> The application of a general zoning law to particular property effects a taking if the ordinance does not substantially advance legitimate state interests, . . . or denies an owner economically viable use of his land, . . . [T]he question necessarily requires a weighing of private and public interests.[2]

The Court held the open space zoning ordinance advanced legitimate state goals because it protected the residents of the city from the "ill effects of urbanization." Neither did the ordinance prevent the "best use" of the land nor extinguish a "fundamental attribute of ownership." The landowners would "share with other owners the benefits and burdens of the city's exercise of the police power." The Court confirmed *Agins'* two-part takings test in *Keystone Bituminous Coal Ass'n v. DeBenedictus*,[3] in which it upheld a Pennsylvania statute that prohibited subsidence from coal mining that was very similar to the statute held to be a taking in *Pennsylvania Coal*.

The continuing vitality of the *Agins* takings test is in doubt. In the *Lucas* case, which is discussed next, the Court converted the *Agins* second prong, which requires denial of all economically viable use, into a categorical per se takings test. Doubts also exist about the role of the *Agins* first prong, which requires the governmental interest in a regulation to be legitimate. In the exaction cases[4] the Court arguably applied the first prong to decide whether a dedication required as a condition to a land use permit was a taking.[5] Later, in Lake *Tahoe*,[6] the

---

[6] Tahoe-Sierra Preservation Council, Inc. v. Tahoe Regional Planning Agency 535 U.S. 302 (2002).

[1] 447 U.S. 255 (1980).

[2] *Id.* at 260–61.

[3] 480 U.S. 470 (1987).

[4] *See* §§ 2.10–2.12.

[5] *See also* Tahoe-Sierra Preservation Council, Inc. v. Tahoe Regional Planning Agency 535 U.S. 302 (2002) (issue not raised on appeal).

[6] *Id. See also* § 2.13 (discussing *Del Monte Dunes*).

Court rejected a claim that a restriction on the development of land during a moratorium is a per se taking, and also considered an argument that "fairness and justice" required a contrary result.[7] As part of this inquiry, the Court accepted the district court's conclusion that the moratorium served a legitimate governmental interest, suggesting a legitimacy inquiry is appropriate outside the exaction cases. Critics claim, however, that the *Agins* first prong is an improper application of substantive due process principles in takings law and should be abandoned.[8]

Another difficulty with the *Agins* two-part test is that the Court adopted it in a case where the property owner made a facial takings claim, although the second part of the test would seem to require an as-applied inquiry into the economic impact of a regulation on a property owner. Since *Agins* the Court has applied the two-part takings test to both facial and as-applied takings claims.[9]

§ 2.09   *Lucas*: A Per Se Test for Regulatory Takings, Nuisance and other Exceptions.

Lucas v. South Carolina Coastal Council,[1] a 1992 case, adopted a new per se "categorical" takings rule that holds a taking occurs when a land use regulation deprives a landowner of all economically beneficial use. This per se takings rule adds a bright line test based solely on the economic impact of a land use regulation: regulatory purpose is not a factor. Though the per se takings rule conceivably could threaten many land use regulations, the circumstances in which it might apply are relatively rare.

Lucas bought two lots on a barrier island on which he intended to build homes similar to those on immediately adjacent parcels. At the time of purchase, the lots were not subject to the state's coastal building permit requirement, but a Beachfront Management Act adopted in 1988 prohibited any permanent structures on the property. Lucas brought suit, claiming the prohibition was a taking because the prohibition deprived him of all economically viable use of his property, and the state trial court agreed. The state supreme court reversed, holding a taking does not occur when a regulation restricting the use of property is intended to

---

[7] Quoting the often-cited case, Armstrong v. United States, 364 U.S. 40, 49 (1960), for the view that the takings clause was "designed to bar Government from forcing some people alone to bear burdens which, in all fairness and justice, should be borne by the public as a whole."

[8] Eastern Enterprises v. Apfel, 524 U.S. 498 (1998) (Justice Kennedy would have held pension statute unconstitutional under due process, not takings clause). *See also* South County Sand & Gravel Co.. Inc. v. Town of South Kingston, 160 F .3d 384 (1st Cir. 1998) (governmental purpose analysis similar to substantive due process); Bamber v. United States, 45 Fed. Cl. 162 (1999) (governmental purpose test has not had "fruitful life" and Supreme Court has confined it to exaction cases).

[9] *See* §§ 2.10–2.12 (as-applied takings claim in exaction cases).

[1] 505 U.S. 1003 (1992).

prevent a "serious public harm." The Supreme Court, in an opinion by Justice Scalia, reversed.

After briefing and oral argument in the state court, but before its decision, the beachfront law was amended to authorize the Council to grant a special permit for a dwelling on Lucas' lots. This change raised a ripeness problem because the Court requires landowners to apply for any available land use approval before bringing a takings claim.[2] Scalia decided the ripeness rules did not apply. The state court had decided the case on the merits, not on ripeness grounds. Justice Scalia believed this disposition prevented Lucas from litigating in state court his claim for a temporary taking for the period during which construction on his lots was absolutely prohibited under state law. This claim was ripe.

Justice Scalia next reviewed the Court's takings law, and concluded there were "at least two discrete categories" of regulation that were compensable "without case-specific inquiry into the public interest advanced in support of the restraint." One was a physical invasion of property. The other was a regulation that "denies all economically beneficial or productive use of land." This statement is a slight reformulation of the test adopted in *Agins*, which held a taking would occur if there was a denial of the "economically viable use" of the land. Justice Scalia also quoted this language from *Agins,* as well as its holding that a taking occurs if a land use regulation "does not substantially advance legitimate state interests." He noted that "perhaps" the justification for the rule was that a total deprivation of beneficial use was the equivalent of a physical taking, and that when this occurs there is a risk that private property was being pressed into public service "under the guise of mitigating serious public harm."

Justice Scalia then distinguished early Supreme Court cases holding a regulations was not a taking if it prohibited harmful or noxious uses of property. The reference was to cases thought to establish the rule that government can regulate to prevent a harm, but not to confer a public benefit. These cases, he said, were simply a transition "to our contemporary understanding of the broad realm within which government may regulate without compensation," and a progenitor to the modern rule that land use regulation must advance a legitimate governmental interest. In addition, the distinction between a regulation that prevents a harm and one that confers a public benefit is difficult, if not impossible, to make. Any regulation can be viewed as serving either purpose, and "noxious-use" logic cannot be the basis for distinguishing regulations that are not takings from those that are. The state legislature's recitation, in its legislative findings, "of a noxious-use justification cannot be the basis for departing from our categorical rule that total regulatory takings must be compensated."

Justice Scalia then qualified his "categorical" rule by indicating there are limited circumstances in which a court can uphold a regulation that effects a

---

[2] *See* § 2.26.

total taking. A regulation "so severe" that it prohibits all economically viable use of land must "do no more than duplicate the result that could have been achieved in the courts under the State's law of private nuisance, or by the State under its complementary power to abate nuisances that affect the public generally, or otherwise."

An example he gave was the owner of a lake bed who is denied a permit for land filling that would flood the land of others. However, the nuisance exception has not usually succeeded in land use cases.[3]

The case was remanded to the state court for a new trial under the nuisance exception, but the state court decided a taking occurred and remanded to the trial court to determine compensation.[4] Later, the state bought the property.

In additional language that has become important in takings cases, Justice Scalia adopted another exception to his per se takings rule. He held a regulation so severe that it prohibits all economically viable use of land is not a taking if it "inhere[s] in the title itself, in the restrictions that background principles of the State's law of property and nuisance already place upon land ownership." This reference seemed to include only common law restrictions on title, such as the navigational servitude. Some federal and state courts interpreted this language to mean a taking does not occur when a property owner acquires land after the enactment of a state or local law that restricts the use of his property. However, the Supreme Court has now held[5] the purchase of land after the enactment of a regulation that restricts the use of property is not an absolute bar to a takings claim.

The Court in *Lucas* indicated that total per se takings would be rare, and the Court's later holding, that a per se taking occurs only if a land use regulation permanently obliterates all value, will severely restrict the number of cases in which a *Lucas* takings claim occurs.[6] The Court in its recent takings decisions has also disfavored categorical per se takings rules.[7]

§ 2.10 Exactions.

The Supreme Court has also decided takings cases that deal with exactions. These are requirements that a landowner dedicate land or make a monetary

---

[3] *See* Erb v. Maryland Dep't of the Env't., 676 A.2d 1017 (Md. App. 1996) (applies nuisance exception); State ex rel. R.T.G., Inc. v. State of Ohio, 753 N.E.2d 869 (Ohio App. 2001) (mining operation not a nuisance); Machipongo Land & Coal Co v. Commonwealth of Pennsylvania, (Pa.2002) (mining that pollutes public waterways is public nuisance).

[4] 424 S.E.2d 484 (S.C. 1992).

[5] Palazzolo v. State of Rhode Island, 533 U.S. 606 (2001).

[6] Tahoe-Sierra Preservation Council, Inc. v. Tahoe Regional Planning Agency 535 U.S. 302 (2002) (moratorium not per se facial taking).

[7] *See* § 2.16 (purchase after enactment of regulation not absolute bar to taking).

payment to a municipality as a condition to the approval of development on her land. Local governments usually require exactions as a condition to the approval of a new residential subdivision. However, the exactions that reached the Supreme Court were not imposed in the subdivision review process. They were also dedications of land rather than monetary payments, which affected the Court's consideration of the constitutional issues that exactions present. In these cases the Court applied the first prong of the *Agins* takings test, which requires courts to consider whether a land use regulation serves a legitimate governmental interest. The Court did not consider the economic impact of the dedications, which was not an issue in either case.

§ 2.11 *Nollan*: The Nexus Test.

In *Nollan v. California Coastal Comm'n*,[1] the first exaction case, the Court struck down an exaction required by the California Coastal Commission when the Nollans planned to replace a small bungalow on their beachfront lot with a larger house. A concrete seawall approximately eight feet high separated the beach portion of their property from the rest of their lot. The Commission agreed to grant a permit for the house subject to a condition that they allow the public a lateral easement to cross that part of their property bounded by the high tide line and the seawall. It required the dedication because the new house would contribute to a wall of residential structures that prevented the public from realizing "psychologically" they had a right to enjoy the coastline. The house would also increase private use of the beachfront and, with other development in the area, burden the public's ability to pass along the beach. The Commission had imposed similar access conditions on all but 17 of the 60 development permits it granted in the same tract.

The Court held a taking clearly would have occurred if the Commission had required an easement across the Nollans' property and had not imposed an access requirement as a permit condition. The question was whether requiring access as a condition to a land use permit "alters the outcome." To answer this question, the Court reaffirmed the two-part takings test adopted in *Agins* but elaborated the standard for determining when a regulation "substantially advances" a "legitimate state interest":

> [O]ur opinions do not establish that these standards are the same as those applied to due process or equal-protection claims. To the contrary, our verbal formulations in the takings field have generally been quite different. We have required that the regulation "substantially advance" the "legitimate state interest" sought to be achieved, . . . not that "the State *'could rationally have decided'* the measure adopted might achieve the State's objective."[2]

[1] 483 U.S. 85 (1987).

[2] 483 U.S. at 836 n.3, quoting Agins v. City of Tiburon, 447 U.S. 255, 260 (1980) and Minnesota v. Clover Leaf Creamery Co., 449 U.S. 456, 466 (1981) (emphasis in original).

This holding would modify takings doctrine if it means the Court will apply a heightened standard of judicial review when it considers whether governmental interests are advanced by a land use regulation, but it has had little influence on takings cases.[3]

The Court next reviewed the justifications advanced by the Commission for the permit condition. It held a permit condition is not a taking if it serves the same legitimate governmental purpose that a refusal to issue the permit would serve. As an example, the Court pointed out the Commission could impose a height limitation on a house to preserve the view of the beach if, as the Court only assumed, it could prohibit the construction of the house to preserve the view. This condition would be valid even if it required a "permanent grant of continuous access" so that the public could view the beach from a viewpoint on the property.

A different problem arises, the Court held, if "the condition substituted for the prohibition utterly fails to further the end advanced as the justification for the prohibition." In this case, the "essential nexus is omitted." The Court found none of the reasons given by the Commission for the Nollan access condition provided a "nexus" with the original purpose of the building restriction. The Court noted its holding was consistent with exaction decisions on the nexus requirement in every state except California and cited a long list of these decisions.[4]

The Court next considered a Commission justification for the access condition "unrelated to land use regulation." The Commission found that the condition was part of a comprehensive program to provide continuous access along the beach. Although this was a "good idea," the Commission would have to pay compensation if it wanted the Nollans to provide an access easement across their property.

§ 2.12 *Dolan*: The "Rough Proportionality" Rule.

Dolan v. City of Tigard[1] elaborated the nexus test by adding a rough proportionality requirement. Plaintiffs planned to double the size of their store in the city's central business district, pave a 39-space parking lot, and build an additional structure on the property for a complementary business. The city's comprehensive plan states that flooding had occurred along a creek near plaintiffs' property. The plan suggested a number of improvements to the creek basin, and recommended that the floodplain be kept free of structures and preserved as a greenway to minimize flood damage. A plan for the downtown area proposed a pedestrian/bicycle pathway to encourage alternatives to automobile transportation for short trips in the business district.

---

[3] *See* Builders Service Corp. v. Planning & Zoning Comm'n., 545 A.2d 530, (Conn. 1988) (rejecting footnote). *But see* Mayhew v. Town of Sunnyvale, 964 S.W.2d 922 (Tex. 1998) (1999) (following *Nollan* on standard of review).

[4] 483 U.S. at 838–40, citing a long list of exaction cases.

[1] 512 U.S. 374 (1994).

To implement its plans and land development code, the city conditioned plaintiffs' building permit with a requirement that they dedicate roughly ten percent of their property to the city. The dedication included land within the floodplain for the improvement of a storm drainage system along the creek and a 15-foot adjacent strip for a pedestrian-bicycle pathway. To justify the dedication the city found that the pathway would offset traffic demand and relieve congestion on nearby streets, and the floodplain dedication mitigated the increase in stormwater runoff from plaintiffs' property.

The Court held a "nexus" existed, as required by the *Nollan* case, between a legitimate government purpose and the permit condition on plaintiffs' property. It was "obvious" a nexus existed between preventing flooding along the creek and limiting development in the creek's floodplain. A nexus also existed between the city's attempt to reduce traffic congestion by providing for alternative means of communication and the pedestrian/bicycle pathway requirement. The Court found a taking because "the degree of the exactions demanded by the city's permit conditions [did not] bear the required relationship to the projected impact of [plaintiffs'] proposed development." It reviewed the tests state courts had adopted to decide this question and rejected all of them. It held that the "reasonable relationship" test adopted by a majority of state courts was closest to "the federal constitutional norm," but rejected it because it is "confusingly similar" to the minimal level of scrutiny courts require under the equal protection clause.

Instead, the Court adopted a "rough proportionality" test to determine whether a taking occurred under the federal constitution. "No precise mathematical calculation is required, but the city must make some sort of individualized determination that the required dedication is related both in nature and extent to the impact of the proposed development." In a footnote, the Court added that the city had made an "adjudicative decision" to condition plaintiffs' building permit, and that "in this situation" the burden of proof lies with the city.

Dolan is important because its "rough proportionality" test elevates the level of scrutiny courts must give to exactions. This test suggests that something closer to "strict scrutiny" review is required rather than the more relaxed judicial review most state courts apply under the "reasonable relationship" test. The Court's holding that the burden of proof shifted to the city because the exaction was imposed through adjudication as a condition is also important. An adjudication and a shift in the burden of proof also should occur when a dedication is imposed as a condition to other land use approvals, such as subdivision and planned unit development approvals. However, *Dolan* left open the question whether its rough proportionality rule applies to exactions that are legislatively adopted, and whether it also applies to monetary impact fees as well as dedications of land.

§ 2.13   *Del Monte Dunes:* Clarifying "Rough Proportionalilty."

The Supreme Court clarified the application of the *Dolan* rough proportionality rule for exactions to takings cases in *City of Monterey v. Del Monte Dunes*.[1] In *Del Monte*, the city council rejected a planned unit development proposal for a seafront residential development. The city gave a number of reasons for the rejection, including the impact of the development on an apparently nonexistent endangered butterfly and its impact on traffic congestion. The developer then sued in federal court and introduced evidence tending to show there was no support for any of the city's reasons for rejecting the development. The case went to a jury on general instructions, and the jury awarded compensation on the takings claim. The Supreme Court affirmed a court of appeals decision upholding the verdict.

The Supreme Court's decision is limited because the case came up as an appeal of a jury verdict based on general instructions. One issue raised on appeal was whether the rough proportionality rule the Court applies to exactions also applies to other land use regulations where exactions are not in issue. The Court stated "we have not extended the rough-proportionality test of Dolan beyond the special context of exactions—land-use decisions conditioning approval of development on the dedication of property to public use." This statement apparently means courts can continue to review land use regulations other than exactions under the more relaxed rational basis test,[2] and apparently means that exactions in the form of impact fees are not reviewable under the rough proportionality test either.

However, because the case turned on the legitimacy of the city's reasons for rejecting the development, this is the first time the Court found a taking under the first prong of the *Agins* takings test in a case that did not challenge an exaction. The city challenged the lower court's jury instructions on this prong, but the Court rejected the challenge because the city drafted the instructions, and because it held they were consistent with its earlier decisions.

§ 2.14   Takings Problems, Principles and Maxims.

The takings tests adopted by the Supreme Court include a number of principles and maxims that are important in and often decide takings cases. They include the investment-backed expectations takings factor, the denominator rule, and the rule in *Lucas* that a taking occurs when a land use restriction deprives a landowner of all economically productive and beneficial use of her property. The Court has also adopted an "average reciprocity of advantage" taking maxim for takings cases that it sometimes applies. Other issues in takings cases that receive independent attention are the problems raised by delay in the decision making

---

[1] 526 U.S. 687 (1999).

[2] *See* Bonnie Briar Syndicate, Inc. v. Town of Mamaroneck, 721 N.E.2d 971 (N.Y. 1999).

process and actions by municipalities claimed to have an acquisitory intent. This section discusses these topics.

§ 2.15 Average Reciprocity of Advantage

Justice Holmes proposed this maxim in *Pennsylvania Coal*. Noting an earlier case where the court upheld a law that required mining companies to leave a pillar of coal in place to ensure the safety of miners "secured an average reciprocity of advantage that has been recognized as a justification of certain laws."[1] The Court again relied on the average reciprocity principle in *Penn Central*. Justice Brennan rejected a claim that the historic landmark law "solely burdened and unbenefited" the owners of Grand Central terminal by holding the law "benefitted all New York citizens and all structures."[2] This is a considerable extension of reciprocity of advantage, which is repeated in *Keystone*. There the Court upheld a law that prohibited subsidence from coal mining by holding it restrained uses that are public nuisances. It noted this holding was consistent with the reciprocity of advantage principle: "[E]ach of us is burdened somewhat by such restrictions,[but] we, in turn we greatly benefit from the restrictions that are placed on others. These restrictions are' properly treated as part of the burden of citizenship'."[3]

If membership in society is enough "reciprocity" to defeat a takings claim, the takings clause may be written out of the constitution. Chief Justice Rehnquist's dissent in *Penn Central* would confine this principle to laws, like zoning ordinances, where the benefits and burdens of the regulation are restricted to a geographic area. Within this area, an owner is both burdened and benefitted by the zoning restrictions; they burden him, but they also prevent other landowners from putting their land to uses that could be detrimental to his use. This argument assumes, of course, that the uses restricted by the zoning ordinance are undesirable. The Court did not rely on the average reciprocity principle after *Keystone*, but its *Lake Tahoe* decision referred to it, without discussion, as a basis for its decision upholding a planning moratorium.[4]

§ 2.16 Investment-Backed Expectations.

In *Penn Central*, the Court identified an interference with "distinct" investment-backed expectations as one of the factors courts should consider when applying the three-part balancing test the court adopted in that case. The Court has since indicated that investment-backed expectations must be reasonable, but this difference does not seem to have affected the results in the cases. This takings

---

[1] *Pennsylvania Coal*, 260 U.S. at 415. *See* § 2.05.

[2] *Penn Central*, 433 U.S. at 134. *See* § 2.07.

[3] *Keystone*, 480 U.S. at 491, citing Kimball Laundry Co. v. United States, 338 U.S. 1, 5 (1949).

[4] 535 U.S. 302.

factor has become more important since the other two *Penn Central* takings factors no longer seem critical. Indeed, the Court has indicated that a failure to prove investment-backed expectations can be fatal to a takings claim.[1] The cases do not always acknowledge this rule, but it is clear that proof of investment-backed expectations is an important element in a takings case.

Justice Brennan did not indicate when a landowner can prove she has investment-backed expectations, but he gave several examples of when investment-backed expectations would not exist. For example, he stated that landowners do not have an expectation in the right to develop land, and that only primary expectations are protected. The courts have applied these rules by holding that expectations at the time of purchase are protected.[2] Expectations arising after purchase are not protected.[3] The courts have also recognized an owner's investment-backed expectations when he substantially proceeds in good faith after government approval of his development.[4]

However, the most important development in the application of investment-backed expectations to takings claims was the adoption of a notice rule in *Ruckelshaus v. Monsanto Co.*[5] The Court held a federal statute requiring the disclosure of trade secrets as a condition to a pesticide registration was not a taking; the statute put the company on notice that disclosure was required, and it also knew about this requirement. It also held the "force" of the investment-backed expectations takings factor was so overwhelming that it disposed of the takings claim.

A number of courts applied the notice rule to uphold wetlands, open space and other regulations against takings claims.[6] In some of these cases, the courts held the takings claim was defeated by the purchase of property that was subject to regulation. A footnote in *Nollan* cast doubt on these cases.[7] It held the "right

---

[1] Ruckelshaus v. Monsanto Co., 467 U.S. 986 (1984).

[2] Gil v. Inland Wetlands & Watercourses Agency, 593 A.2d 1368 (Conn. 1991).

[3] *See* MacLeod v. County of Santa Clara, 749 F.2d 541 (9th Cir. 1984) (expectation not primary); Long Beach Equities, Inc. v. Superior Court of Ventura County, 282 Cal. Rptr. 877 (Cal. App. 1991) (right to exploit not protected).

[4] Resolution Trust Corp. v. Town of Highland Beach, 18 F.3d 536 (11th Cir. 1994); County of Kauai v. Pacific Standard Life Ins. Co., 653 P.2d 766 (Haw. 1982). *See* §§ 6.12–6.23 (discussing vested rights). *But see* Bauer v. Waste Management, 662 A.2d 1179 (Conn. 1995) (permit did not create reasonable expectations).

[5] 467 U.S. 986 (1984).

[6] Sucesion Suarez v. Gelabert, 541 F. Supp. 1253 (D.P.R. 1982), *aff'd,* 701 F.2d 231 (1st Cir. 1983); Furey v. City of Sacramento, 592 F. Supp. 463 (E.D. Cal. 1984), *aff'd on other grounds,* 780 F.2d 1448 (9th Cir. 1986); Graham v. Estuary Props., Inc., 399 So. 2d 1374 (Fla.1981); Claridge v. New Hampshire Wetlands Bd., 485 A.2d 287 (N.H. 1984). *But see* Kirby Forest Indus. v. United States, 467 U.S. 1 (1984) (dictum; expectations protected when regulatory burden unforeseeable).

[7] Nollan v. California Coastal Comm'n, 483 U.S. 815, 833 n.2 (1987).

to build on one's own property" is not a unilateral expectation, even though it is subject to government regulation. It also held the purchase of property after a government begins the implementation of a regulatory program does not defeat a takings claim. Despite *Nollan,* some courts continued to hold that landowners did not have investment-backed expectations in the development of their land if they knew[8] or should have known[9] that their land would be restricted by land use regulations. In some of these cases, the landowner had purchased the land after the land use regulation was adopted at the time of purchase.

Additional confusion arose because of the holding in *Lucas,* that a per se taking does not occur if the restriction imposed by a land use regulation inheres in the title or is part of the background principles of state law. Some courts held a land use regulation is a background principle of state law when it is in effect at the time of purchase[10] This interpretation meant that purchase with notice of a land use regulation defeated a *Lucas* per se takings claim, just as it defeated a claim of investment-backed expectations in some courts.

The Supreme Court rejected this interpretation in *Palazzolo.*[11] It held the purchase of land subject to a prior land use restriction does not defeat a per se takings claim. Neither is it an absolute bar to a claim of investment-backed expectations under the *Penn Central* takings factors. The Court held the denial of the development permit was not a per se taking under the *Lucas* case because the landowner could make an economically productive use of his land, and remanded the case so the state court could decide whether a taking had occurred under the *Penn Central* takings factors. Justice O'Connor concurred in the majority opinion. She held that courts should still consider the existence of a

---

[8] National Advertising Co. v. Village of Downers Grove, 561 N.E.2d 1300 (Ill. App. 1990) (sign regulations) (1991); Parranto Bros., Inc. v. City of New Brighton, 425 N.W.2d 585 (Minn. App. 1988) (downzoning); Kelly v. Tahoe Regional Planning Agency, 855 P.2d 1027 (Nev. 1993) (denial of development plans); Gazza v. New York State Dept. of Envtl. Conservation, 679 N.E.2d 1035 (N.Y. 1997) (wetlands); Finch v. City of Durham, 384 S.E.2d 8 (N.C. 1989) (downzoning); Board of Supervisors v. Omni Homes, Inc., 481 S.E.2d 460 (Va. 1997) (risk of acquiring access); Brunelle v. Town of S. Kingston, 700 A.2d 1075 (R.I. 1997); Mayhew v. Town of Sunnyvale, 964 S.W.2d 922 (Tex. 1998).

[9] Good v. United States, 189 F.3d 1355 (Fed. Cir. 1999); Naegele Outdoor Advertising, Inc. v. City of Durham, 803 F. Supp. 1068 (M.D.N.C. 1992) (sign regulation), *aff'd without opinion,* 19 F.3d 11 (4th Cir. 1994), Elias v. Town of Brookhaven, 783 F. Supp. 758 (E.D.N.Y. 1992) (downzoning); McNulty v. Town of Indialantic, 727 F. Supp. 604 (M.D. Fla. 1989) (coastal setback); FIC Homes of Blackstone, Inc. v. Conservation Comm'n, 673 N.E.2d 61 (Mass. App. 1996) (wetlands); Parranto Bros., Inc. v. City of New Brighton, 425 N.W.2d 585 (Minn. App. 1988) (downzoning); White v. City of Brentwood, 799 S.W.2d 890 (Mo. App. 1990) (zoning). *Contra* Carpenter v. Tahoe Regional Planning Agency, 804 F. Supp. 1316 (D. Nev. 1992); Ciampitti v. United States, 22 Cl. Ct. 310 (1991).

[10] Kim v. City of New York, 681 N.E.2d 312 (N.Y. 1997) (denying compensation for fill placed on property and rejecting *Nollan* footnote).

[11] Palazzolo v. State of Rhode Island, 533 U.S. 606 (2001).

prior land use regulation at the time of purchase as a factor in their *Penn Central* analysis. Because the four dissenters concurred with her opinion it was the majority opinion in that case, and a majority of the Court affirmed her opinion in its *Lake Tahoe* decision.

Justice O'Connor's opinion in *Palazzolo* leaves open the possibility that purchase with notice of a regulation may defeat a claim of investment-backed expectations in some cases.[12] Nor did the Court in that case settle the question whether investment-backed expectations and the notice rule are relevant in to a *Lucas* per se takings claim.[13] However, the Court's *Lake Tahoe* decision referred to Justice Kennedy's footnote in *Lucas,* where he said that investment-backed expectations are a factor in *Lucas* cases. Another unsettled issue is whether the Court would apply the notice rule when a landowner purchases land before the adoption of a land use regulation under which the development of his property is prohibited or later denied. Some courts held the notice rule defeats a claim of investment-backed expectations in this situation.[14]

§ 2.17 The Whole Parcel or Denominator Rule: Herein of Segmentation.

An important issue in land use takings cases is the decision on the unit of property, or denominator, to which the takings clause applies. This issue is sometimes called the segmentation issue: should the court segment of portion of the property affected by the regulation and then apply the takings clause only to that segment? Justice Holmes took a narrow view of the denominator issue in *Pennsylvania Coal*, where he held the property to be considered was the coal required to be left in the ground by the statutory prohibition on subsidence. Justice Brandeis dissented, and argued the correct denominator was the "whole property" owned by the coal company. This became the rule adopted by Justice Brennan in *Penn Central*. He held that all the property owned by the railroad was the correct parcel for the application of the takings clause, not just the airspace in which the city rejected an application to build a high-rise office building over Grand Central Station. The Court also adopted the Brandeis position in *Keystone*, where it upheld a statute similar to the statute struck down in *Pennsylvania Coal*.

---

[12] Rith energy, Inc. v. United States, 270 F.3d 1347 (Fed. Cir. 2001) (fact that regulatory regime was in place when landowner purchased property is relevant to takings claim). *See also* pre-*Palazzolo* State Dep't of Envtl. Protection v. Burgess, 772 So.2d 540 (Fla App. 2000) (no investment-backed expectations when landowner bought land as investment and could continue recreational use.

[13] *Compare* Good v. United States, 189 F.3d 1355 (Fed. Cir. 1999) (holding notice rule applies to *Lucas* per se takings cases) *with* Florida Rock Indus. v. United States, 45 Fed. Cl. 21 (1999) (holding contra).

[14] Good v. United States, 189 F.3d 1355 (Fed. Cir. 1999) (denial of permit to develop wetlands under federal Clean Water Act).

The "whole parcel" rule took on more importance after the Supreme Court's decision in *Lucas*. Because the Court held a denial of all economically viable use is a taking, determining the parcel that is the basis for a takings claim is critical.

The denominator, or segmentation, issue arises in a variety of takings cases. In one type of case, known as conceptual segmentation, the issues is whether the denominator is a legal interest in property, such as the right to exclude, that can be segmented for purposes of analysis under the takings clause. In other cases the issue is the geographic extent of the parcel. Temporal segmentation occurs when the question is whether the denial of all economically productive use for a limited period of time is a taking, as when a municipality adopts a moratorium on new development.

§ 2.18　Conceptual Severance: The Right to Exclude.

Justice Brennan rejected conceptual segmentation in *Penn Central*, where he held the plaintiff's property interest in airspace over Grand Central Terminal was not the relevant denominator to which the takings clause applied. Another conceptual severance issue is whether the destruction of one "strand" in a landowner's bundle of property rights is a taking. In *Andrus v. Allard*,[1] for example, the Court applied the whole parcel rule and held that regulations adopted under a federal law that prohibited the sale of Indian artifacts made from certain bird feathers was not a taking. Even though the regulations prohibited the most profitable use of the artifacts, their owners could still possess, transport, donate, or devise them. The destruction of one "strand" in the bundle of property rights was not a taking "because the aggregate must be viewed in its entirety." A loss of future profits, when there is no "physical property restriction, is not a taking.

The Court reached a different conclusion when a government restriction affected a property owner's right to exclude the public from its property. In *Kaiser Aetna v. United States*,[2] a private developer improved a coastal pond and dredged a channel to provide private access to the ocean. The U.S. Army Corps of Engineers sued the developer to prevent it from denying public access to the pond through the channel. The Court held the government's attempt to create a public access was a taking because the property owner's "right to exclude" was a property right "that the Government cannot take without compensation." It also held the improved pond and channel was not navigable water subject to the federal government's navigational servitude. The Court also relied on the Corps' failure to require permits for the improvements to the pond and channel. Though this failure did not estop the government, it created a number of expectancies that are embodied in property the takings clause protects.

---

[1] 444 U.S. 51 (1979). *But see* Hodel v. Irving, 481 U.S. 704 (1987) (invalidating statute providing for automatic escheat of small Indian holdings).

[2] 444 U.S. 164 (1979).

The right to exclude is not absolute. In *PruneYard Shopping Center v. Robins*[3] a shopping center owner brought suit to exclude students who were distributing political literature. The Court held a taking of the "right to exclude" had not occurred. Political solicitation in the shopping center would not "unreasonably impair the value or use" of the property, and the shopping center owner could adopt regulations that would minimize any interference with retailing. The Court distinguished *Kaiser Aetna* because there the developer had a substantial investment in the pond and channel, the navigational servitude did not justify public access, and the federal government did not have the "residual authority" to define property rights. In *PruneYard,* the right to exclude was not "essential to the use or economic value" of the property.

The deprivation of the right to exclude was an important factor in the exaction cases. In these cases the Court held a taking occurred when a landowner was required to convey an easement of public access over his land as a condition to a development permit. The court relied on its cases holding a deprivation of the right to exclude is a taking.[4] It is significant in these cases that the access easement imposed little or no economic loss on the affected properties.

§ 2.19 Geographic Segmentation.

Determining the geographic extent of a parcel for purposes of applying the takings clause is a difficult "whole parcel" problem. The courts have not been consistent in making this determination, but an important factor is whether the property was purchased at one time and is under single ownership. In takings cases of this type that challenge zoning ordinances the courts tend to treat the entire property as the whole parcel, even though different parts of the property are zoned differently.[1]

When more than one parcel is involved, courts tend to take a more flexible approach. Though the factors considered vary, the underlying principle is one of fairness. In one wetlands case, for example, the court held it would consider factors such as the degree of contiguity, dates of acquisition, the extent to which the parcel was treated as a single parcel, and the extent to which the regulated

---

[3] 447 U.S. 74 (1980).

[4] *See* Nollan v. California Coastal Comm'n, 483 U.S. 825, 838 n.1 (1987) (noting that owner in *PruneYard* had opened shopping center to public and that permanent access was not required).

[1] Ramona Convent of the Holy Name v. City of Alhambra, 26 Cal. Rptr. 2d 140 (Cal. App. 1993) (same zoning on entire parcel); Animas Valley Sand & Gravel, Inc. v. Board of County Comm'rs, 38 P.3d 59 (2001); FIC Homes of Blackstone, Inc. v. Conservation Comm'n, 673 N.E.2d 61 (Mass. App. 1996) (wetlands; 38 parcels purchased at one time); Bevan v. Brandon Township, 475 N.W.2d 37 (Mich. 1991) (same); Quirk v. Town of New Boston, 663 A.2d 1328 (N.H. 1995) (part of property zoned as buffer); Zealy v. City of Waukesha, 548 N.W.2d 528 (Wis. 1996) (two zones on property). *Contra* Twain Harte Assocs. v. County of Tuolumne, 265 Cal. Rptr. 737 (Cal. App. 1990) (two zones on property).

lands enhance the value of the remaining lands. The court added that "no doubt many others would enter into the calculus."[2] The court held the individual lots should not be treated as separate parcels when the landowner treated them as a single parcel for purchase and financing purposes. Courts may also apply these factors to single parcels in one ownership. These factors have led courts to broad[3] or narrow[4] definitions of the "whole parcel" affected by the takings claim. Narrowing the parcel, of course, increases the possibility that a takings claim will be successful.

§ 2.20 Temporal Severance.

Temporal severance occurs when a land use regulation prohibits any development of land for a designated period of time. Moratoria are the best examples, but total restrictions on land development for a temporary period of time can also occur under official map and corridor preservation statutes and ordinances.[1] The Supreme Court considered this problem in *Tahoe-Sierra Regional Preservation Council, Inc. v. Tahoe Regional Planning Agency.*[2] The agency imposed two moratoria for a total of 32 months on development within the region while it was preparing a comprehensive plan. The Court rejected a categorical rule that a taking occurs when government deprives a landowner of all economical use of her land for a temporary period, no matter how brief. It reconfirmed the "whole parcel" rule adopted in *Penn Central,* and held a landowner could not "sever a 32-month segment from the remainder of each landowner's fee simple estate, and then ask whether that segment has been taken in its entirety by the moratoria." It noted that "defining the property interest taken in terms of the very regulation

---

[2] Ciampitti v. United States, 22 Cl. Ct. 310 (1991) (lots held not separate when lots treated as single parcel for purpose of purchase and financing).

[3] District Intown Props .Ltd. Partnership v. District of Columbia, 198 F.3d 874 (D.C. Cir. 1999); Forest Props., Inc. v. United States, 177 F.3d 1360 (Fed. Cir. 1999) (parcel treated as whole still had economic value); Tabb Lakes, Ltd. v. United States, 10 F.3d 796 (Fed. Cir. 1993) (wetlands; single parcel); Walcek v. United States (II), 49 Fed. Cl. 248 (2001) (property contiguous and unsubdivided; purchased over a month or two, maintained as single parcel in same ownership with intent to develop as whole), *aff'd,* 393 F.3d 1357 (Fed. Cir. 2002); Broadwater Farms Joint Venture v. United States, 35 Fed. Cl. 232 (1996) (same); Deltona Corp. v. United States, 657 F.2d 1184 (Ct. Cl. 1981) (same); K & K Constr., Inc. v. Department of Natural Resources, 575 N.W.2d 531 (Mich. 1998); Volkema v. Department of Natural Resources, 542 N.W.2d 282 (Mich. App. 1995) (same); Karam v. Department of Envtl. Protection, 723 A.2d 943 (N.J. 1999); Sea Cabins on the Ocean IV Homeowners Ass'n, Inc. v. City of N. Myrtle Beach, 523 S.E.2d 193 (S.C. App. 1999).

[4] Loveladies Harbor, Inc. v. United States, 28 F.3d 1171 (Fed. Cir. 1994) (wetlands permit denial); Florida Rock Indus. v. United States, 18 F.3d 1560 (Fed. Cir. 1994) (same). *See also* American Savings and Loan Association v. County of Marin, 653 F.2d 364 (9th Cir. 1980) (zoning; case remanded); Palm Beach Isles Assocs. v. United States, 208 F.3d 1374 (Fed. Cir. 2000). *See* Clajon Prod. Corp. v. Petera, 70 F.3d 1566 (10th Cir. 1995) (rejecting approach in *Florida Rock*).

[1] *See* §§ 10.12–10.14.

[2] 535 U.S. 302 (2002). *See also* §§ 6.06–6.11.

being challenged is circular," because defining the property in this way would make every moratorium and any delay in obtaining a permit a taking. The Court also noted a fee simple estate does not become valueless because of a temporary prohibition on economic use, because the property recovers its value when the prohibition on use is lifted. The constitutionality of moratoria must be considered under the circumstances of each case.

§ 2.21 *Lucas* Applied: When Does a Per Se Regulatory Taking Occur?

Because a decision on whether a landowner has presented a *Lucas* per se takings claim is the first step in a court's takings analysis, courts must decide how they should apply this test. An initial question is whether a landowner must, in addition, show a land use regulation does not serve a legitimate governmental purpose, the first prong of the *Agins* test. *Lucas* was not clear on this question, and the courts have divided. Some require both, but some require that only one of these tests must be met. [1]

Another important issue is what must be shown to prove a denial of an economically beneficial or productive use of the land. *Lucas* did not answer this question. When courts applied *Lucas* they did not usually find a taking because the land use regulation attacked did not deny the landowner all economically viable use. [2] In *Palazzolo* the Court dismissed a *Lucas* per se takings claim when the uplands portion of the property had a value of $200,000 because a home could be built on it. [3] Only a few cases found a denial of all use sufficient for a per se taking. An example was a case where the municipality denied a landowner the right to build a house on an undersized lot. [4]

An ambiguous opinion by the Federal Circuit in a wetlands permit denial case had suggested there could be a per se taking when there was a partial, though

---

[1] *Compare* City of Pompano Beach v. Yardarm Restaurant, 641 So. 2d 1377 (Fla. App. 1994) (enough to show improper purpose) *and* State ex rel. Shemo v. City of Maryland Heights, 765 N.E.2d 345 (Ohio 2002), *with* Estate & Heirs of Sanchez v. County of Bernalillo, 902 P.2d 550 (N.M. 1995) (contra).

[2] Rith Energy, Inc. v. United States, 271 F.3d 1347 (Fed. Cir. 2001) (91% reduction in value); Cannone v. Noey, 867 P.2d 797 (Alaska 1994) (subdivision denial); Ramona Convent of the Holy Name v. City of Alhambra, 26 Cal. Rptr. 2d 140 (Cal. App. 1993) (no taking where only diminution in value); Tim Thompson, Inc. v. Village of Hinsdale, 617 N.E.2d 1227 (Ill. App. 1993) (same); Iowa Coal Mining Co. v. Monroe City, 494 N.W.2d 664 (Iowa 1993) (zoning change partly blocking proposed land use); McPherson Landfill, Inc. v. Board of County Comm'rs, 49 P.3d 522 (Kan. 2002) (denial of conditional use); Taub v. City of Deer Park, 882 S.W.2d 824 (Tex. 1994) (rezoning denial); Jones v. King County, 874 P.2d 853 (Wash. App. 1994) (downzoning).

[3] *See also* State Dep't of Envtl. Protection v. Burgess, 772 So.2d 540 (Fla. App. 2000) (recreational use of land is economically viable use of land that defeats Lucas per se takings claim).

[4] Moroney v. Mayor & City Council, 633 A.2d 1045 (N.J. App. Div. 1993). *See also* § 12.08 (denial of wetlands permits held a taking).

almost total, deprivation of all economically viable use.[5] Other courts rejected this suggestion.[6] The Supreme Court in *Lake Tahoe* has further qualified *Lucas* by holding a landowner must show a "permanent obliteration" of value rather than a denial of use to prove a *Lucas* taking. This holding is a decisive narrowing of *Lucas*, because most land will continue to have some value, even though all development is prohibited.

§ 2.22　Delay in Decision Making as a Taking.

The Supreme Court held in *First English* that, compensation is payable for the period of time during which a land use regulation was in effect prior to the time a court holds a taking has occurred. The Court in that case also said in dictum that normal delays in decision making are not a taking, and later held in *Lake Tahoe* that a prohibition on development for a temporary period of time during a moratorium is not a per se taking. This later case also reaffirmed an earlier decision, that mere fluctuations in the value of property during the government's decision-making process, absent extraordinary delay, are incidents of ownership and do not give rise to a taking.[1] These decisions leave open the possibility that an extraordinary delay in decision making by a municipality on a land use application may be a taking.

In most of the cases, courts held even prolonged governmental decision making that temporarily deprives a landowner of the use of his property is not an "extraordinary delay" giving rise to a taking of property.[2] The key factor in evaluating the reasonableness of a delay in decision making is whether it is extraordinary.[3] No set standard exists to identify extraordinary delay, and courts evaluate the length of a delay on an ad hoc basis. In *Dufau v. United States*,[4] for example, the court held a sixteen-month delay was not long enough under the circumstances to constitute a temporary taking of the plaintiff's 70 acres of wetlands.

---

[5] Florida Rock Indus. v. United States, 18 F.3d 1560 (Fed. Cir. 1994).

[6] Clajon Prod. Corp. v. Petera, 70 F.3d 1566 (10th Cir. 1995).*See also* Wyer v. Board of Envtl. Protection, 747 A.2d 192 (Me. 2000).

[1] Agins v. City of Tiburon, 477 U.S. 255, 286 n.9 (1980).

[2] Tabb Lakes, Ltd. v. United States, 10 F.3d 796 (Fed. Cir. 1993); Guinanne v. San Francisco, 241 Cal. Rptr. 787 (Cal. App. 1988); McCutchan Estates v. Evansville-Vanderburgh County Airport, 580 N.E.2d 339 (Ind. App. 1991); Lester v. Town of Winthrop, 939 P.2d 1237 (Wash. App. 1997); East Cape May Assocs. v. New Jersey Dep't of Envtl. Protection, 693 A.2d 114 (N.J. App. Div. 1997) (delay must be disproportionate to regulatory scheme).

[3] Lachney v. United States, 22 Env't Rep. Cas. (BNA) 2031 (Fed. Cir. 1985) (two-year delay not extraordinary); 1902 Atlantic Ltd. v. United States, 26 Cl. Ct. 575 (Cl. Ct. 1992) (five-year delay held cost of doing business in regulated society); Philric Assocs. v. South Portland, 595 A.2d 1061 (Me. 1991) (two years deemed adequate to consider subdivision application); Hutchinson v. City of Huntington, 479 S.E.2d 649 (W. Va, 1996) (four months not unreasonable).

[4] Dufau v. United States, 22 Cl. Ct. 156 (Cl. Ct. 1990).

(5th Ed.—02/03)

Courts give extreme deference to the actions of government officials in temporary delay cases.[5] They presume government officials carry out their duties in good faith, and it requires a "well-nigh irrefragable proof" to overcome this presumption.[6] Despite unreasonable, lengthy, and even unlawful delays, courts attribute the actions of zoning administrators to the normal workings of governmental legal processes.[7] Courts also require plaintiffs to show that government delay denied them substantially all economically viable uses of their property during the delay period.[8]

A related problem arises when a court holds a land use regulation is invalid or unconstitutional but does not hold a taking has occurred. Most courts have not applied *First English* in this type of case, and have held a taking has not occurred even though the landowner was unable to make use of her land during the period of time she brought the court action.[9] The hold that *First English* required that compensation must be paid for a temporary denial of all use only when a taking has occurred.

§ 2.23   Planning and Zoning With Acquisitory Intent.

A taking can occur if a municipality improperly uses its condemnation, planning or zoning power in connection with the power to condemn land. These cases are known as cases of acquisitory intent, because the municipality has improperly used its police power as a substitute for the power of eminent domain. The designation of land for acquisition in a comprehensive plan is not enough to make a case of acquisitory intent. It is well-established that mere planning for a public facility, such as the designation of a highway route on a comprehensive plan, is not a taking.[1] However, if a municipality initiates and then delays the condemnation of land the Supreme Court indicated a taking will occur if

---

[5] Wyatt v. United States, 271 F.3d 1090 (Fed. Cir. 2001); Bello v. Walker, 840 F.2d 1124 (3d Cir. 1988) (seven-month delay did not constitute taking); 1902 Atlantic Ltd. v. United States, 26 Cl. Ct. 575 (Cl. Ct. 1992).

[6] Dufau v. United States, 22 Cl. Ct. 156, 164 (Cl. Ct. 1990).

[7] Philric Assocs. v. South Portland, 595 A.2d 1061 (Me. 1991); First Peoples Bank v. Medford, 599 A.2d 1248 (N.J. 1991); Old Tuckaway Assocs. Ltd. Partnership v. City of Greenfield, 509 N.W.2d 323 (Wis. App. 1993).

[8] Tabb Lakes v. United States, 10 F.3d 796 (D.C. Cir. 1993).

[9] Moore v. Costa Mesa, 886 F.2d 260 (9th Cir. 1989); Landgate, Inc. v. California Coastal Comm'n, 953 P.2d 1188 (Cal. 1998); Pheasant Ridge Corp. v. Township of Warren, 777 A.2d 334 (N.J. 2001); Miller & Son Paving, Inc. v. Plumstead Township, 717 A.2d 483 (Pa. 1998); Chioffi v. City of Winooski, 676 A.2d 786 (Vt. 1996). *Contra* Eberle v. Dane County Bd. of Adjustment, 595 N.W.2d 730 (Wis. 1999). *See also* Ali v. City of Los Angeles, 91 Cal. Rptr.2d 458 (Cal. App. 1999).

[1] § 3.21. *See also* § 10.12 (official maps). *Contra* Hager v. Louisville & Jefferson County Planning & Zoning Comm'n, 261 S.W.2d 619 (Ky. 1953).

the delay is extraordinary,[2] even though the municipality does not have "acquisition on its mind."

Courts also find a taking if a municipality prohibits the development of land it or another agency intends to acquire in order to depress its market value prior to condemnation. For example, in *People ex rel. Dep't of Transp. v. Diversified Props. Co. III,*[3] a city cooperated with the state to reject development plans on property the state intended to acquire for a freeway. The court held the delay due to these unreasonable precondemnation activities was a de facto taking. It found the state knew the city's development restrictions made the property virtually unmarketable, that the city's restrictions were imposed because the property was located in a freeway route, and that the state had no intention of condemning the property for many years. Other courts have found that a de facto taking occurred under similar facts.[4] They have not found a taking in these cases when the precondemnation delay was reasonable. In one such case,[5] the city delayed for one year a decision for a building permit on land designated for possible acquisition as a park in its comprehensive plan. The city then decided not to acquire the land and amended its plan to allow development of the land. In a variant of the acquisitory intent case, a municipality adopts a restrictive zoning classification to depress the value of land it intends to acquire but does not announce or begin condemnation. In most of these cases, the municipality adopted a land use classification that was incompatible with surrounding land uses. An example is a restrictive residential zoning classification applied to a tract in an industrial area. Courts hold these zoning restrictions invalid because they do not serve a proper zoning purpose if they were adopted to depress the value of property in advance of acquisition.[6]

[2] Agins v. City of Tiburon, 447 U.S. 255, 263 n.9 (1980). *See also* Martino v. Santa Clara Valley Water Dist., 703 F.2d 1141 (1983); Hotel Coamo Springs, Inc. v. Hernandez Colon, 539 F. Supp. 1008 (D.P.R. 1982). *Compare* Armour & Co., Inc. v. Inver Grove Heights, 2 F.3d 176 (8th Cir. 1993) (lengthy planning and execution of development activity not a taking).

[3] 17 Cal. Rptr. 2d 676 (Cal. App. 1993).

[4] Peacock v. County of Sacramento, 77 Cal. Rptr. 391 (Cal. App. 1969); State ex rel. Senior Estates v. Clarke, 530 S.W.2d 30 (Mo. App. 1975); City of Plainfield v. Borough of Middlesex, 173 A.2d 785 (N.J.L. Div. 1961) (rezoning to park and playground use); San Antonio River Auth. v. Garrett Bros., 528 S.W.2d 266 (Tex. Civ. App. 1977). *See also* Benenson v. United States, 548 F.2d 939 (Ct. Cl. 1977).

[5] Guinnane v. City & County of San Francisco, 241 Cal. Rptr. 787 (Cal. App. 1987). *Accord* Toso v. City of Santa Barbara, 162 Cal. Rptr. 210 (Cal. App.1980); City of Walnut Creek v. Leadership Hous. Sys., Inc., 140 Cal. Rptr. 690 (Cal. App. 1977); Sproul Homes v. State Dep't of Highways, 611 P.2d 620 (Nev. 1980).

[6] Robertson v. City of Salem, 191 F. Supp. 604 (D. Or. 1961); City of Conway v. Housing Auth., 584 S.W.2d 10 (Ark. 1979); Kissinger v. City of Los Angeles, 327 P.2d 10 (1958); Hermanson v. Board of County Comm'rs, 595 P.2d 694 (Colo. App. 1979); Carl M. Freeman Assocs. v. State Roads Comm'n, 250 A.2d 250 (Md. 1969); Riggs v. Township of Long Beach, 538 A.2d 808 (N.J. 1988). *Compare* Mira Dev. Co. v. City of San Diego, 252 Cal. Rptr. 825 (Cal.

§ 2.24 Ripeness and Finality.

A federal court is a court of limited jurisdiction. It may decide to abstain in favor of a state court.[1] A federal court may also not hear a case unless it is ripe for decision. The Supreme Court has adopted a special set of ripeness rules that determine whether federal courts can hear land use cases. The effect of these rules is that litigants must bring as-applied takings cases in state court and may then be precluded from returning to federal court. Many lower federal courts also apply the Supreme Court's ripeness rules to equal protection and due process cases.

A claim a case is not ripe for decision goes to the court's subject matter jurisdiction under the case or controversy requirement of Article III of the federal constitution.[2] The proper way to make this claim is through a motion to dismiss.[3] Ripeness is a question of law subject to de novo judicial review.[4] The ripeness rules do not apply when a federal court has diversity jurisdiction in a land use case.[5] Neither do they apply to a facial takings claim. As the Court pointed out in a rent control case, a facial takings claim does not "depend on the extent to which petitioners are deprived of the economic use of their particular pieces of property or the extent to which these particular petitioners are compensated."[6]

App. 1988) (rezoning denial not done to depress property values); Carl Bolander & Sons v. City of Minneapolis, 378 N.W.2d 826 (Minn. App. 1985) (moratorium on development not adopted to depress property values); Department of Transp. v. Lundberg, 825 P.2d 641 (Or. 1992) (sidewalk dedication requirement did not depress value of property); Howell Plaza, Inc. v. State Hwy. Comm'n, 284 N.W.2d 887 (Wis. 1979) (adopts rule but taking not found).

[1] §§ 8.41–8.45.

[2] E.g., Broughton Lumber Co. v. Columbia River Gorge Comn'n, 975 F.2d 616 (9th Cir. 1992); St. Clair v. City of Chico, 880 F.2d 199 (9th Cir.1989); Unity Ventures v. County of Lake, 841 F.2d 770 (7th Cir.1988). *But see* Buckley v. Valeo, 424 U.S. 1 (1976).

[3] E.g., Taylor Inv., Ltd. v. Upper Darby Township, 983 F.2d 1285 (3d Cir. 1993); St. Clair v. City of' Chico, 880 F.2d 199 (9th Cir. 1989).

[4] East-Bibb Twiggs Neighborhood Ass'n v. Macon Bibb Planning & Zoning Corn., 896 F.2d 1264 (llth Cir. 1989); Herrington v. County of Sonoma, 857 F.2d 567, 568 (9th Cir. 1988).

[5] Vulcan Materials Co. v. City of Tehuacana, 238 F.3d 382 (5th Cir. 2001); SK Finance SA v. La Plata County, Bd. of County Com'rs, 126 F.3d 1272, (10th Cir. 1997); Sinclair Oil Corp. v. County of Santa Barbara. 96 F.3d 401 (9th Cir. 1996). *Contra* Samaad v. City of Dallas. 940 F.2d 925 (5th Cir. 1991).

[6] Yee v. City of Escondido, 503 U.S. 519, 534 (1992). *See also* Lucas v. South Carolina Coastal Council, 503 U.S. 1003, 1014 n.4 (1992) (Blackmun, J., dissenting) ("Facial challenges are ripe when the act is passed; applied challenges require a final decision on the act's application to the property in question."); Loretto v. Teleproinpter Manhattan CATV Corp., 458 U.S. 419 (1982). *See also* Martino v. Santa Clara Water Dist., 703 F.2d 1141 (9th Cir.1983) (final decision rule does not apply to claim of unreasonable condemnation activities).

§ 2.25   Early Supreme Court Cases.

In *Agins v. City of Tiburon,* [1] the city's zoning ordinance permitted one to five single-family residences on plaintiffs' land, and required developers to submit a development plan so the city could determine how many residences it would allow within this range. The Supreme Court remanded the case because the plaintiffs had not submitted the development plan required by the ordinance. The Court did not use the term "ripeness," but the case clearly means an as-applied takings case is not ripe for decision unless the plaintiff has submitted at least one application for development when an ordinance requires one. Other development approval requirements in zoning ordinances, such as site plan review, also trigger the *Agins* rule. [2]

San Diego Gas & Elec. Co. v. City of San Diego [3] applied the final judgment rule. The city adopted an open space zoning ordinance to implement an open space plan. The landowner brought an inverse condemnation action, and the trial court awarded compensation. The California appellate courts dismissed on the authority of *Agins,* and the landowner appealed to the Supreme Court. The Court held the state court judgment was not a final judgment subject to review because the state courts had not finally determined whether a taking had occurred. It remanded to give the landowner an opportunity to resolve disputed facts that would determine whether a taking had occurred.

§ 2.26   *Hamilton Bank.*

The Court extended the ripeness rule in *Williamson County Regional Planning Comm'n v. Hamilton Bank.* [1] The commission gave preliminary subdivision approval for a plat that showed 736 allowable dwelling units but drew lines for only 436 units. After the developer spent 3.5 million dollars on water and sewer facilities and a golf course to serve the entire development, the commission later gave final approval for 212 dwelling units but refused preliminary approval of a revised subdivision plat for the remaining sections of the development. By that time the zoning ordinance had been amended to reduce the number of dwelling units permitted. The commission noted a number of problems with the revised plat, including an excessive number of dwelling units, the placement of dwelling units on slopes where development was prohibited and problems with roads and grading.

---

[1] 447 U.S. 255 (1980). *See* § 2.15. *See also* Penn Cent. Transp. Co. v. New York City, 438 U.S. 104 (1978) (plaintiff did not seek approval for a smaller structure than the high rise building they proposed over Grand Central Terminal).

[2] *See also* Hodel v. Virginia Surface Mining & Reclamation Ass'n, 452 U.S. 264 (1981) (court dismissed takings attack on federal surface mining act because plaintiff had not presented concrete controversy or sought variance or waiver from act's provisions).

[3] 450 U.S. 621 (1981).

[1] 473 U.S. 172 (1985).

The court of appeals affirmed a compensation award to the developer for a temporary taking, but the Supreme Court reversed and remanded. Although the developer submitted a development plan as required by *Agins,* it had not sought variances from the zoning and subdivision ordinances that would have overcome the commission's objections to its plat. The Court could not evaluate the takings claim until the administrative agency arrived at a "final, definitive position" that applied the regulations to the developer's land. It added the developer was not required to file suit for declaratory judgment to review the commission's decision or to appeal the variance decision in a state court, and held an appeal to the board of adjustment was unnecessary because the board did not participate in the commission's decision.

In a holding that has become a substantial barrier to land use takings litigation in federal court, the Court held the case also was not ripe for decision because the developer had not utilized a state statute that authorized compensation awards in inverse condemnation actions in land use takings cases. This is the second prong of the ripeness rule. The Court held that recourse to the state procedure was necessary because the constitution does not prohibit a taking; it only prohibits a taking without compensation. If the state provides an adequate procedure for obtaining just compensation, a property owner cannot claim a taking has occurred until he has used that procedure.

§ 2.27 *Yolo County.*

In the next ripeness case, *McDonald, Sommer & Frates v. Yolo County,*[1] the county board refused to approve a residential subdivision that would help alleviate a severe regional housing shortage. It stated the property could be used only for agricultural purposes, despite its finding that the property was "agriculturally impaired" by insect infestation, the removal of topsoil, and the proximity of residential development. The county's refusal to approve the subdivision was induced by the city, which advised the county the residential use of the subdivision conflicted with the city's designation of the property as an agricultural reserve in its general plan. The city also advised the county it would not annex the property, permit extension of a city street into the subdivision, or provide city services.

In its suit for compensation the plaintiff claimed the county had appropriated the "entire economic use" of its property, and that any application for a zoning change, variance, or other relief was futile. The state trial court sustained a demurrer to the complaint and held that the rejection of plaintiff's development did not preclude "less intensive, but still valuable development," and the state appellate court affirmed.

---

[1] 477 U.S. 340 (1986).

The Supreme Court noted this case was different from its earlier ripeness cases because the plaintiff obtained a ruling on "one" subdivision proposal. However, it had still failed to obtain a final, dispositive position on the application of the regulations to its land because the state court holding left open "the possibility that some development will be permitted." This rule is known as the reapplication rule: a plaintiff whose application for development has been refused must reapply. A claim is not ripe just because the municipality has rejected a developers "grandiose plans". The Court qualified this rule in a footnote where it stated it did not require repeated "futile" development applications.

§ 2.28 Later Supreme Court Cases.

Suitum v. Tahoe Regional Planning Agency[1] considered a ripeness issue that arose in a transfer of development rights program. The agency refused plaintiff permission to build a home on her lot because it was located in an area, classified as a Stream Environment Zone, that carried runoff into the lake's watershed. Plaintiff appealed to the agency's governing board, which affirmed the agency's decision. To ease the impact of its development restrictions on a landowner's property, the agency had adopted a transfer of development rights (TDR) program[2] that granted transferable development rights on property restricted from development that a landowner could sell to other landowners, subject to the agency's approval based on the eligibility of the receiving parcel for development.

Plaintiff sued for a taking without applying for permission to the agency to sell her development rights, but the Court held the plaintiff satisfied the finality requirement of the ripeness rules. The agency had finally determined her land was in a zone in which it did not permit development. Neither was action by the agency allowing the plaintiff to transfer her development rights the type of final action required by the ripeness rules. The parties agreed on the TDRs to which the plaintiff was entitled, and discretionary action by the agency was not necessary for her to obtain them or offer them for sale. *Suitum* has a limited effect on takings claims in land use cases because most land use decisions require an exercise of discretion by government agencies, and in many TDR programs an approval of a TDR transfer is not necessary.

The Supreme Court again considered the ripeness issue in *Palazzolo v. State of Rhode Island*,[3] where it reviewed the denial of a development permit on property that consisted primarily of wetlands. The facts were ambiguous, but the Court held the case ripe because it believed it was clear the agency would not have approved the development he requested, and because it would have approved one house on the uplands portion of the property. The Court allowed

---

[1] 520 U.S. 725 (1997).

[2] *See* §§ 11.38, 12.16.

[3] 533 U.S. 606 (2001).

Palazzolo to base his claim on his application for a 74-unit subdivision, even though it might not have received zoning approval or the necessary septic permits. However, the Court made it clear that landowners could be required to follow normal planning procedures, and could be barred by rules to "control damaged based on hypothetical uses that should have been reviewed in the normal course." A claim of entitlement to value is not enough if the project would not have been allowed under "existing, legitimate land use regulations." Though the Court stretched the facts to find this case ripe, the facts were unique and not likely to be repeated.

The Court decided the compensation remedy and avoided a ripeness problem in *First English* by holding that only the remedial issue, not the takings issue, was before the court.[4] The Court avoided a ripeness problem in *Lucas* by holding the state supreme court precluded the landowner from litigating in state court the temporary taking claim that was at issue in the case.[5]

§ 2.29   Federal Court Cases.[1]

§ 2.30   Final Decision Rule.

Federal court cases have applied the requirement that an as-applied takings case is ripe only when the municipal agency has made a final decision. A case is not ripe unless the plaintiff has made an application for development,[1] and the agency has made a final decision.[2] It is not necessary for an agency to make a formal outright denial of an application. A court can find an agency has made a final decision rejecting an application when an agency's decision is the functional equivalent of a denial.[3] A decision is final when the agency indicates the only development it would allow must be consistent with existing plans and regulations, and the development proposed by the plaintiff does not comply.[4] The courts have also applied the rule in *Yolo County* that a plaintiff must reapply

---

[4] First English Evangelical Lutheran Church v. County of Los Angeles, 482 U.S. 304 (1987). *See* § 8.26.

[5] Lucas v. South Carolina Coastal Council, 505 U.S. 1003 (1992). *See* § 2.09

[1] *See also* § 8.09 (federal ripeness rules applied in state courts).

[1] Kawaoka v. City of Arroyo Grande, 17 F.3d 1227 (9th Cir. 1994) (failure to submit development plan).

[2] Covington Court, Ltd. v. Village of Oak Brook, 77 F.3d 177 (7th Cir. 1996) (no decision made).

[3] A.A. Profiles, Inc. v. City of Ft. Lauderdale, 850 F.2d 1483 (11th Cir. 1988) (city suspended project approval and downzoned property).

[4] Greenbriar, Ltd. v. City of Alabaster, 881 F.2d 1570 (llth Cir. 1989) (city effectively conceded that only alternative plan of development would have been under the existing zoning); Herrington v. County of Sonoma, 857 F.2d 567 (9th Cir. 1988) (county board's decision of inconsistency with plan is final; futile to apply further).

for less intensive development if the municipality rejects her original application.[5]

The Supreme Court in *Palazzolo* provided some guidance on when a decision is final that may make it easier for landowners to claim a takings case is ripe.. The Court held a takings claim is ripe when it is clear the agency lacks discretion to permit any development, "or the permissible uses of the property are known to a reasonable degree of certainty."

Hamilton Bank held a plaintiff must apply for a variance[6] or other administrative relief[7] to make her case ripe, and the courts hold a plaintiff must apply for such relief unless it is not needed or unavailable. The courts are divided on whether an application for a legislative rezoning also is required.[8] Federal courts also have dismissed takings claims because they did not satisfy the holding in *Yolo County*, that a takings claim is not ripe simply because a municipality has rejected a developer's grandiose plans.[9]

The Supreme Court suggested in *Yolo County* that there is a futility exception to the final decision rule.[10] *Kinzli v. City of Santa Cruz*[11] is leading Ninth Circuit case applying this exception. The court held that compliance with the final decision rule is not futile simply because a land use regulation prohibits any beneficial use of the land or inhibits its marketability. This inquiry would require the type of speculation the ripeness rule prohibits. A plaintiff cannot make a futility claim unless he had made at least one "meaningful" application or

---

[5] Southview Assoc., Ltd. v. Bongartz, 980 F.2d 84 (2d Cir. 1992) (might approve another application if it did not affect environmental area); Pace Resources, Inc. v. Shrewsbury Township, 808 F.2d 1023 (3d Cir.) (no showing that alternative uses conclusively barred).

[6] *See* Bateman v. City of West Bountiful, 89 F.3d 704 (10th Cir. 1996); Greenbriar, Ltd. v. City of Alabaster, 881 F.2d 1570 (11th Cir. 1990); Pond Brook Dev. Co. v. Twinsburg Township, 35 F. Supp. 2d 1025 (N.D. Ohio 1999) (must reapply for zoning variance);

[7] *See* Stephans v. Tahoe Regional Planning Agency, 697 F. Supp. 1149 (D. Nev. 1988) (e.g., special development permit or rectification of property); Zilber v. Moraga, 692 F. Supp. 1195 (N.D. Cal. 1988) (status determination).

[8] *Compare* Southern Pacific Transp. Co. v. City of Los Angeles, 922 F.2d 4988 (9th Cir. 1990), *with* Tahoe-Sierra Preservation Council, Inc. v. Tahoe Regional Plan. Agency(II), 938 F.2d 153 (9th Cir. 1991).

[9] Pace Resources, Inc. v. Shrewsbury Twp., 808 F.2d 1023 (3d Cir. 1987). *But see* Del Monte Dunes Ltd. v. City of Monterey, 920 F.2d 1496 (9th Cir. 1990) (final decision rule satisfied when city unfairly protracted application process). *See also* Resolution Trust Corp. v. Town of Highland Beach, 18 F.3d 1536 (11th Cir. 1994) (decision not to extend zoning is final decision).

[10] *See* also Lucas v. South Carolina Coastal Council, 505 U.S. 1003, 1013 n.3 (1992) (submission of plan for development pointless "as the Council stipulated below that no building permit would have been issued under the 1988 Act, application or no application").

[11] 818 F.2d 1449, *amended*, 830 F.2d 968 (9th Cir. 1987),

requested a variance. Ninth Circuit cases since *Kinzli* have not been consistent.[12] Other courts have adopted the *Kinzli* interpretation of the futility rule.[13]

The courts have also considered what kind of showing a plaintiff must make to prove futility.[14] As the First Circuit held in a rent control case, there must be special circumstances indicating a permit application is not a "viable option," or that the "the granting authority has dug in its heels and made it transparently clear" that the permit will not be granted. A "sort of inevitability" is required, and the prospect of refusal must be certain or nearly so.[15]

§ 2.31 Compensation Requirement.

The rule adopted in *Hamilton Bank,* that a plaintiff may not bring an as-applied takings claim in federal court if a state compensation remedy is available,means a plaintiff must bring her as applied takings claim in state court first. The federal courts apply this rule,[1] but do not agree on what kind of a finding a federal court must make on the availability of a state remedy. Some cases find a takings case unripe only if they conclude from an examination of state law that the statute compensation remedy is available.[2] Other cases misapply *Hamilton Bank.* They

---

[12] *See* Hoehne v. County of San Benito, 870 F.2d 529 (9th Cir. 1989) (finding additional applications futile), and Herrington v. County of Sonoma, 857 F.2d 567 (9th Cir. 1988) (need not apply for variance that would not be granted).

[13] Strickland v. Alderman, 74 F.3d 260 (11th Cir. 1996) (futility claim rejected); Landmark Land Co. v. Buchanan, 874 F.2d 717 (10th Cir. 1989); Amwest Investments, Ltd. v. City of Aurora, 701 F. Supp. 1508 (D. Colo. 1988). *But see* A.A. Profiles, Inc. v. City of Ft. Lauderdale, 850 F.2d 1483 (11th Cir. 1988) (case ripe because downzoning not appealable to local board).

[14] Strickland v. Alderman, 74 F.3d 260 (11th Cir. 1996) (obtaining building permit not futile because plaintiff did not make application); Tahoe-Sierra Preservation Council, Inc. v. Tahoe Regional Planning Agency, 911 F.2d 1331, 1338 n. 5 (9th Cir. 1990) (delay); Landmark Land Co. v. Buchanan, 874 F.2d 717 (10th Cir. 1989) (delay); Unity Ventures v. County of Lake, 841 F.2d 770 (7th Cir. 1988) (sewer connection request).

[15] Gilbert v. City of Cambridge, 932 F.2d 51 (1st Cir. 1991). *Compare* Howard W. Heck & Assocs. v. United States, 37 Fed. Cl. 245 (1997) (corps permit; a difficult position is not a futile position); *with* Broadwater Farms Joint Venture v. United States, 35 Fed. Cl. 232 (1996) (Corps objection to permit clear).

[1] *E.g.,* McKenzie v. City of White Hall, 112 F.3d 313 (8th Cir. 1997); Gamble v. Eau Claire County, 5 F.3d 285 (7th Cir. 1993) (unripe; failure to pursue state condemnation claim); Executive 100, Inc. v. Martin Cty., 922 F.2d 1536 (11th Cir. 1991); Bateson v. Geisse, 857 F.2d 1300 (9th Cir. 1988). *Cf.* Samaad v. City of Dallas, 940 F.2d 925 (5th Cir. 1991). *See* Envision Realty, LLC v. Henderson, 182 F. Supp.2d 143 (D. Me. 2002) (pleading state compensation claim in federal lawsuit does not save it from dismissal).

[2] *Compare* Corn v. City of Lauderdale Lakes, 816 F.2d 1514 (11th Cir. 1987) (court concluded state remedy not available) *with* Bickerstaff Clay Prods. Co., Inc. v. Harris County, 89 F.3d 1481 (11th Cir. 1996) (no cases denying remedy); Bateman v. City of West Bountiful, 89 F.3d 704 (10th Cir. 1996) (remedy available); Villager Pond, Inc. v. Town of Darien, 56 F.3d 375 (2d Cir. 1995) (same}; Reahard v. Lee County (II), 30 F.3d 1412 (11th Cir. 1994) (same); Silver v. Franklin Township Board of Zoning Appeals, 966 F.2d 1031 (6th Cir. 1991) (same).

hold a plaintiff must use the state compensation remedy first unless the state court has clearly held it is unavailable.[3] In a few cases the courts held a plaintiff need not use a state remedy if it would be futile.[4]

When the Court decided *Hamilton Bank*, a remedy for compensation in takings cases was not available in federal court. Some courts now hold a compensation remedy is available in state court because *First English* held that compensation is available for a taking under the federal constitution, and a plaintiff can sue for compensation under the federal constitution in state court.[5] A Ninth Circuit panel disagreed, and held correctly that the availability of a compensation claim in state court under the federal constitution does not satisfy the requirement that a state compensation remedy must be available.[6] The court held that to require plaintiffs to sue under the federal constitution for compensation in state court before bringing a federal takings claim would be a draconian result not intended by the Supreme Court's ripeness cases.

§ 2.32 Equal Protection and Due Process Claims.

Hamilton Bank was a takings case, and though the Court has not decided whether its ripeness rules apply to equal protection and due process cases it indicated it might do so in *Yolo County,* where it stated in dictum that "[o]ur cases uniformly reflect an insistence on knowing the nature and extent of permitted development before adjudicating the constitutionality of the regulations that purport to limit it."[1] A number of lower federal courts have relied on this dictum to hold the ripeness rules apply to equal protection due process claims.[2]

---

[3] Deniz v. Municipality of Guaynabo, 285 F.3d 142 (1st Cir. 2002); Southview Assocs., Ltd. v. Bongartz, 980 F.2d 84 (2d Cir. 1992); Estate of Himelstein v. City of Fort Wayne, 898 F.2d 573 (7th Cir. 1990); East-Bibb Twiggs Neighborhood Ass'n v. Macon-Bibb County Planning & Zoning Comm'n, 896 F.2d 1264 (11th Cir. 1989); Austin v. City & County of Honolulu, 840 F.2d 678 (9th Cir. 1988); Littlefield v. City of Afton, 785 F.2d 598 (8th Cir. 1986).

[4] Naegle Outdoor Advertising, Inc. v. City of Durham, 803 F. Supp. 1068 (M.D.N.C. 1992) (futile to require property owner to apply for compensation in state court), *affd mem.,* 19 F.3d 11 (4th Cir. 1994). *Cf.* Schnuck v. City of Santa Monica, 935 F.2d 171 (9th Cir. 1991) (not shown that bringing compensation claim in state court would be futile);

[5] *E.g.,* San Remo Hotel v. City & County of San Francisco, 145 F.3d 1095 (9th Cir. 1998); Tan v. Collier County, 56 F.3d 1533, 1537 n.23 (11th Cir. 1995); Christensen v. Yolo County Bd. of Supervisors, 995 F.2d 161 (9th Cir. 1993)..

[6] Dodd v. Hood River County, 59 F.3d 852 (9th Cir. 1995).

[1] 477 U.S. at 351.

[2] John Corp. v. City of Houston, 214 F.3d 573 (5th Cir. 2000) (procedural due process); Forseth v. Village of Sussex, 199 F.3d 363 (7th Cir. 2000) (substantive due process claim subject to ripeness rules, but not equal protection claim); Sameric Corp. v. City of Philadelphia, 142 F.3d 582 (3d Cir. 1998) (substantive due process); Taylor Inv. Ltd. v. Upper Darby Township, 983 F.2d 1285 (3d Cir. 1993) (equal protection, substantive and procedural due process); Seguin v. City of Sterling Heights, 968 F.2d 584 (6th Cir. 1992) (equal protection); Herrington v. County of Sonoma, 857 F.2d 567 (9th Cir. 1988) (substantive due process and equal protection); Unity Ventures v. County of Lake, 841 F.2d 770 (7th Cir. 1988) (procedural due process).

Other courts hold the ripeness rues do not apply,[3] or hold that only the finality rule applies, not the rule that suit must be brought in state court first for compensation.[4] This latter holding is correct, because equal protection and due process claims do not arise under the takings clause of the federal that requires the payment of just compensation. Some cases have also followed the Supreme Court's lead in the takings cases, and have held the ripeness rules do not apply to facial equal protection and due process claims.[5]

§ 2.33 Returning to Federal Court From State Court.

The ripeness rules require a plaintiff to bring as-applied takings claims in state court first, and a plaintiff may also have to begin an equal protection or due process claim in state court as well. Though the assumption behind this requirement would seem to be that a plaintiff may return to federal court to present her claim after the state suit concludes, there is a split of authority on this question. Cases allowing the refiling of the claim in federal court apply the rule in abstention cases, and allow plaintiffs to return to federal court if they have reserved their federal claim in state court.[1] Cases that do not allow a return to federal court apply res judicata and collateral estoppel rules to bar the federal claim once the state case concludes.[2] They hold it was enough the plaintiff presented, or could have presented, her claim in state court.

§ 2.34 *Rooker-Feldman* Doctrine.

Federal courts may also refuse jurisdiction in land use cases that have been tried in state court under the *Rooker-Feldman* doctrine, named after two United

---

[3] Forseth v. Village of Sussex, 199 F.3d 363 (7th Cir. 2000) (equal protection); Blanche Road Corp. v. Bensalem Township, 57 F.3d 2.53 (3d Cir. 1995) (substantive due process); Pearson v. City of Grand Blanc, 961 F.2d 1211 (6th Cir. 1992) (substantive due process); Harris v. County of Riverside, 904 F.2d 497 (9th Cir. 1990).

[4] McKenzie v. City of White Hall, 112 F.3d 313 (8th Cir. 1997); Strickland v. Alderman, 74 F.3d 260 (11th Cir. 1996); Taylor Inv. v. Upper Darby Township, 983 F.2d 1285 (3d Cir. 19931: Southview Assocs., Ltd. v. Bongartz, 980 F.2d 84 (2d Cir. 1992). *Contra* River Park, Inc. v. City of Highland Park, 23 F.3d 164 (7th Cir. 1994); Sinaloa Lake Owners Assoc. v. Simi Valley, 852 F.2d 1398 (9th Cir. 1989) (property damage case), *See also* Eide v. Sarasota Cty., 895 F.2d 1326 (11th Cir. 1990) (reapplication requirement does not apply to substantive due process claims).

[5] Smithfield Concerned Citizens for Fair Zoning v. Town of Smithfield, 907 F.2d 239 (1st Cir. 1990) (comprehensive rezoning that included extensive downzoning); Beacon Hill Farm Assocs. II, Ltd. Partnership v. Loudoun County Bd. of Supervisors, 875 F.2d 1081 (4th Cir. 1989); Landmark Land Co. v. Buchanan, 874 F.2d 717, 723 n.3 (10th Cir. 1989) (facial racial equal protection claim).

[1] Front Royal & Indus. Park Corp. v. Town of Front Royal, 135 F.3d 275 (4th Cir. 1998); Fields v. Sarasota Manatee Airport Auth., 953 F.2d 1299 (11th Cir. 1992).

[2] Wilkinson v. Pitkin County Bd. of County Comm'rs, 142 F.3d 1319 (11th Cir. 1998); Dodd v. Hood River County, 136 F.3d 1219 (9th Cir. 1998).

States Supreme Court cases.[1] Under this doctrine, federal courts may not reverse or modify a state court judgment or hear issues inextricably involved with a state court decision. *Rooker-Feldman* is based on a federal statute that confers appellate jurisdiction solely in the Supreme Court,[2] and the state court judgment stands unless there is an appeal to that Court. The courts have applied *Rooker-Feldman* to refuse review of state court judgments in land use cases,[3] but the doctrine applies only if the federal issue could have been raised in state court.[4] *Rooker-Feldman* is a basis on which federal courts can refuse jurisdiction in addition to res judicata based on issue and claim preclusion, and in addition to the ripeness and abstention doctrines.

§ 2.35   State Court Takings Doctrine.

State courts developed a substantial body of takings law prior to the time the Supreme Court began a more active role in the decision of takings cases. They have not usually adopted a "set" taking formula, and taking doctrine varies from court to court. As-applied zoning cases are the rule rather than the exception at the state level, although the Supreme Court has not decided an as-applied zoning case since its *Nectow* decision many years ago.

Federal takings law also applies, of course, in the state courts, and they must apply federal takings rules when litigants argue them. Federal takings law thus provides a doctrinal "floor" in takings cases that state courts are bound to follow. Though some state courts still decide takings cases without reference to federal law.[1] State takings law applies only if it has a different doctrinal basis, which is sometimes true.

State courts may also hold their takings law is the equivalent of the federal rules. This tendency is apparent in state court treatment of the Supreme Court's *Lucas* decision, which held a taking occurs when a landowner has been denied all economically beneficial or productive use of her property. Landowners typically make this claim when they argue a zoning restriction prohibits the development of their property. Though state courts have their own rules for this

---

[1] Rooker v. Fidelity Trust Co., 263 U.S. 413 (1923); District of Columbia Court of Appeals v. Feldman, 460 U.S. 4621 (1983).

[2] 28 U.S.C. § 1257.

[3] Anderson v. Charter Township of Ypsilanti, 266 F.3d 487 (6th Cir. 2001) (but suggesting that district court should refrain from dismissal until full scope of state court decision is ascertained); Hill v. Town of Conway, 193 F.3d 33 (1st Cir. 1999); Zealy v. City of Waukesha,153 F. Supp.2d 279 (E.D. Wis. 2001) On whether *Rooke-Feldman* applies when an appeal to a state court is pending see Ahmed v. State of Washington, 262 f.3d 979 (9th Cir 2001).

[4] Parkview Assocs. Partnership v. City of Lebanon, 225 F.3d 321 (3d Cir. 2000) (Fair Housing Act claim); Agripost Inc. v. Miami-Dade County, 195 F.3d 1225 (11th Cir. 1999).

[1] *E.g.,* Homebuilders Ass'n of Dayton v. City of Beavercreek, 729 N.E.2d 359 (Ohio 2000) (upholding impact fee).

kind of case, as the next section illustrates, some state courts hold their takings rules in these cases are the equivalent of the per se rule adopted in the *Lucas* decision.[2]

§ 2.36 "As-Applied" Cases Claiming Total Loss or Diminution in Value.

"As-applied" zoning cases are the major diet of the state courts in land use cases. In these cases a landowner claims a zoning restriction has prevented any economically beneficial or productive use of her land or has caused a diminution in its value. The municipality has zoned the property for a restrictive use, and the landowner wishes to put her land to a more intensive use. She claims the restrictive zoning as applied to her land is a taking. The courts may apply federal or complementary state takings law, but they do not always apply taking theory. If they hold that a land use restriction is unconstitutional as applied, they may sometimes strike it down as "arbitrary and capricious." Because landowners in these cases attack the zoning "line," courts sometimes call them "line-drawing" cases.

Judicial taking analysis in these "as-applied" cases is accompanied by a number of well-established rules that favor the constitutionality of the land use restriction. These rules reflect standard judicial attitudes, described earlier,[1] which most state courts usually apply. One of these rules places the burden on the property owner to prove that the zoning restriction is unconstitutional.[2] The zoning restriction is not a taking just because the property owner wishes to put her property to a more profitable use, and a court will uphold it if it is reasonably debatable. *Robinson v. City of Bloomfield Hills*[3] is a leading case that illustrates the standard adopting a highly deferential of judicial review these line-drawing cases:

> But many of the cases coming to us involve merely the legislative judgment. They are the peripheral problems (should the line be drawn here, or there?) and the allegations of more advantageous use, with its corollary of "confiscation" (the property is worth more if devoted to some other use). Save in the most extreme instances, involving clearly whimsical action, we will not disturb the legislative judgment.[4]

---

[2] Bauer v. Waste Management, 662 A.2d 1179 (Conn. 1995); Security Mgt. Corp. v. Baltimore County, 655 A.2d 1326 (Md. App. 1995); Zealy v. City of Waukesha, 548 N.W.2d 528 (Wis. 1996).

[1] § 1.15. *See* City of McDonough v. Tusk Partners, 492 S.E.2d 206 (Ga. 1997) (trial court ruling will be affirmed unless clearly erroneous); Tilles v. Town of Huntington, 547 N.E.2d 90 (N.Y. 1989) (landowner attacking residential zoning failed to rebut presumption of constitutionality).

[2] City of Phoenix v. Beall, 524 P.2d 1314 (Ariz. App. 1974); Northern Westchester Professional Park Assocs. v. Town of Bedford, 458 N.E.2d 809 (N.Y. 1983); Lakewood Dev. Co. v. Oklahoma City, 534 P.2d 23 (Okla. App. 1975); Tillo v. City of Sioux Falls, 147 N.W.2d 128 (S.D. 1966).

[3] 86 N.W.2d 166 (Mich. 1957).

[4] *Id.* at 172.

The economic impact of a land use restriction is another factor in these cases. Though a substantial diminution in value is a factor the courts may consider,[5] a majority of state courts find a taking only if the landowner cannot make any economically viable use of her land under the zoning restriction.[6] State courts usually decide whether an economically viable use of the land is possible by determining whether the use allowed by the zoning ordinance is reasonable in the area in which it is located. A court may characterize the zoning restriction as "confiscatory" if it holds an economically viable use of the land is impossible. The U.S. Supreme Court will find a per se taking in this situation.[7]

Stevens v. Town of Huntington[8] illustrates the state court approach. The municipality downzoned to residential use a tract of land in an area of mixed uses. The tract was surrounded on three sides by extensive commercial development, including a shopping center, and on one side by a residentially zoned area. This area contained only one residential dwelling. The rest of this area was to be used for storing electronic equipment, a permitted use in the residential zone. As the court put it, the restricted tract was "immersed in a well-traveled, highly commercial shopping area."

The municipality defended the downzoning as necessary to maintain the character of the adjacent residentially zoned area and to avoid traffic congestion, but the court held the downzoning. unconstitutional. "These aims, admirable as they may be, have the effect of depriving a property owner of making any reasonable use of his property."[9] The presence of adjacent commercial uses made the land unsuitable for residential development.

The dissent saw the matter differently:

Although the court is acting upon words having heavy implications of invalidity, such as "confiscatory," . . . the issue in actuality amounts to a routine controversy turning on a difference of opinion between local zoning

---

[5] Galt v. Cook County, 91 N.E.2d 395 (Ill. 1950); Alsensas v. Brecksville, 281 N.E.2d 21 (Ohio App. 1972).

[6] Maider v. Town of Dover, 306 N.E.2d 274 (Mass. App. 1974); Krause v. City of Royal Oak, 160 N.W.2d 769 (Mich. App. 1968); Megin Realty Corp. v. Baron, 387 N.E.2d 618 (N.Y. 1979). As-applied attack on zoning restriction rejected: Terminals Equip. Co. v. City & Cty. of San Francisco, 270 Cal. Rptr. 329 (Cal. App. 1990); Gerchen v. City of Ladue, 784 S.W.2d 232 (Mo. App. 1989); Buskey v. Town of Hanover, 577 A.2d 406 (N.H. 1990); Columbia Oldsmobile, Inc. v. City of Montgomery, 564 N.E.2d 455 (Ohio 1990). *But see* Reuschenberg v. Town of Huntington, 532 N.Y.S.2d 148 (App. Div. 1988) (need not show deprivation of all use if restriction invalid as discriminatory); MC Props., Inc. v. City of Chatanooga, 994 S.W.2d 132 (Tenn. App. 1999).

[7] § 2.09.

[8] 229 N.E.2d 591 (N.Y. 1967).

[9] *Id.* at 593.

officials and property owners on zoning classifications. The merits are arguable either way, but it takes more than that to invalidate a zoning restriction.[10]

Stevens illustrates a typical "line-drawing" case in which the area surrounding the restrictively zoned property is mixed. Courts in these cases must determine the dominant character of the surrounding area in order to decide whether the ordinance is a taking as applied to the restricted land. As the opinions in *Stevens* indicate, this determination is not always easy. The majority viewed the residentially restricted property as a "zoning island" and struck down the ordinance. The dissent believed the case raised a debatable line-drawing issue and would have applied the presumption of validity to uphold the zoning restriction.

§ 2.37 Balancing and Multi-Factor Tests.

At the federal level, the *Penn Central* multi-factor takings test applies when a court holds a per se taking has not occurred.[1] The Supreme Court has referred to this test as a balancing test.[2] Some state courts apply their own balancing test in this type of case in which they weigh the diminution in value of the property against the benefit of the zoning restriction to the community.[3] Balancing often is implicit rather than explicit. The court explicitly applied a balancing test in *State v. Pacesetter Constr. Co.*[4] and rejected taking objections to a state statute restricting the height of buildings in coastal areas to prevent a loss of view. The court applied a balancing test even though it acknowledged that the test only considers legislative purpose and disregards the economic impact of the regulation. Other state courts have applied a balancing test to uphold environmentally protective land use regulation.[5]

The Illinois Supreme Court adopted a multi-factor test for as-applied land use cases in *LaSalle Nat'l Bank v. County of Cook.*[6] The six *LaSalle* factors are: (1) the existing uses and zoning of nearby property; (2) the extent to which property values are diminished by the particular zoning restriction; (3) the extent to which the destruction of property value promotes health, safety, morals, or

10 *Id.* at 595. *See* Grimpel Assocs. v. Cohalan, 361 N.E.2d 1022 (N.Y. 1977) (zoning island case). *Compare* McGowan v. Cohalan, 361 N.E.2d 1025 (N.Y. 1977).

1 *See* R & Y, Inc. v. Municipality of Anchorage, 34 P.3d 289 (Alaska 2001) (applying similar test under state law).

2 Tahoe-Sierra Preservation Council v. Tahoe Regional Planning Agency, 533 U.S. 302 (2002).

3 *See* White v. City of Brentwood, 799 S.W.2d 890 (Mo. App. 1990)plying balancing test).

4 571 P.2d 196 (Wash. 1977). *See* Orion Corp. v. State (II), 747 P.2d 1062 (Wash. 1987).

5 Pope v. City of Atlanta, 249 S.E.2d 16 (Ga. 1978); Krahl v. Nine Mile Creek Watershed Dist., 283 N.W.2d 538 (Minn. 1979). *But see* Northern Westchester Professional Park Assocs. v. Town of Bedford, 458 N.E.2d 809 (N.Y. 1983).

6 145 N.E.2d 65 (Ill. 1957). *See, e.g.,* Northern Trust Bank/Lake Forest v. County of Lake, 723 N.E.2d 1269 (Ill. App. 2000) (proposed development not consistent with surrounding area).

general welfare purposes; (4) the relative gain to the public as compared to the hardship of the individual property owner; (5) the suitability of the property for the zoned use; and (6) the length of time the property has been vacant as zoned. Note the mixture of diminution in value, substantive due process, and balancing criteria. The *LaSalle* factors are a call for active judicial intervention. The Illinois courts often find for landowners when they attack zoning restrictions as an as-applied taking. A few other states have adopted the *LaSalle* factors.[7]

§ 2.38   State Takings Legislation.

A number of states have considered or adopted takings legislation, and at least 20 states have adopted takings legislation so far. This legislation is usually an attempt to codify a takings rule this more favorable to landowners. Some of this legislation is based on a takings Executive Order issued by President Reagan in 1988 that requires a "takings impact analysis" by federal agencies on actions that might generate a takings claim.[1] Most of these laws apply only to state agencies and require a takings assessment, or in some states an impact statement, on agency rules and regulations.[2] The agency carries out the assessment in most states, but the attorney general conducts the review in a few states. Some statutes contain a list of factors to be included in a checklist, which becomes the basis for the takings assessment. A few laws require takings assessments by local governments, but the state guidelines are only advisory. Most of the statutes do not specify any legal consequences if a takings assessment is not done.

A few state takings acts go beyond takings impact analysis and require compensation for takings. Florida legislation requires compensation when a regulation places an "inordinate burden" on property. An inordinate burden exists if a property owner is unable to attain the reasonable investment-backed expectations to an existing or vested use of the property or, in the alternative, if the owner must permanently bear "a disproportionate share of a burden imposed for the good of the public, which in fairness should be borne by the public at large."[3]

---

[7] Guhl v. Holcomb Bridge Road Corp., 232 S.E.2d 830 (Ga. 1977); Landau v. City Council, 767 P.2d 1290 (Kan. 1989) (court adopts deferential review standards and holds Golden factors only suggestive); Par Mar v. City of Parkersburg, 398 S.E.2d 532 (W.Va. 1990) (applies La Salle factors to as-applied taking attack).

[1] Executive Order 12630, 53 Fed. Reg. 8859 (1988).

[2] *E.g.,* Idaho Code §§ 67-8001 to 67-8004; Ind. Code Ann. § 4-22-32; Mont. Code Ann. §§ 2-20-104, 2-10-105; Tenn. Code Ann. §§ 12-1-203 to 12-1-206; Utah Code Ann. §§ 63-90-1 to 63-90-4; W. Va. Code §§ 22-1A-1 to 22-1A-6.

[3] Fla. Stat. Ann. § 70.001. *See also* Tex. Gov't Code § 2007.001 et seq. (compensation for 25% reduction in value).

B. SUBSTANTIVE DUE PROCESS.

§ 2.39   The Substantive Due Process Problem.

Land use controls must satisfy the substantive limitations imposed on land use regulation by the due process clause.[1] Courts interpret this clause to mean that land use controls must advance legitimate governmental interests that serve the public health, safety, morals, and general welfare. State zoning legislation restates these purposes as the guiding objectives in land use regulation, though the general welfare predominates in this litany of police power nouns. Whether land use regulation serves the general welfare is the major substantive due process question.

Substantive due process overlaps other constitutional limitations on land use regulations. In takings cases, for example, the U.S. Supreme Court requires a similar showing that a land use regulation must advance a legitimate governmental interest. Equal protection doctrine demands that a legitimate governmental purpose must justify zoning and other land use classifications. The overlap with substantive due process is clear.

Judicial review in substantive due process cases is deferential, and substantive due process objections to the purposes of land use regulations do not usually succeed. The Supreme Court has approved the governmental purposes advanced by most land use regulations, including landmark preservation. In the federal courts, and open space and residential zoning.[2] The Seventh Circuit has especially been reluctant to apply substantive due process to strike down land use cases.[3] State courts have also been receptive. A majority approve aesthetic zoning, for example, which once presented serious substantive due process problems.[4]

Though federal courts apply the traditional rational relationship standard, it is phrased differently in different circuits. Some require a stronger showing, such as whether the municipality's conduct "shocked the conscience" of the court, before they will hold a land use restriction unconstitutional.[5] Different rules may

---

[1] *But see* § 8.30.

[2] Nollan v. California Coastal Comm'n, 483 U.S. 825, 834 (1987).

[3] *E.g.,* Coniston Corp. v. Village of Hoffman Estates, 844 F.2d 461 (7th Cir. 1988).

[4] § 11.02.

[5] *E.g.,* Natale v. Town of Ridgefield, 170 F.3d 258 (2d Cir. 1999) ("outrageously arbitrary so as to constitute a gross abuse of governmental authority"); Richardson v. City & County of Honolulu, 124 F.3d 1150 (9th Cir. 1997) (arbitrary and irrational); DeBlasio v. Zoning Bd. of Adjustment, 53 F.3d 592 (3d Cir. 1995); Chesterfield Dev. Corp. v. City of Chesterfield, 963 F.2d 1102 (8th Cir. 1992) (something more than arbitrary and capricious); Pearson v. City of Grand Blanc, 961 F.2d 1211 (6th Cir. 1992) (reviewing standards applied in the federal circuits);Spence v. Zimmennan, 873 F.2d 256 (llth Cir. 1989) (pretextual, arbitrary and capricious, and without rational basis). Shelton v. City of College Station, 780 F.2d 475, 477 (5th Cir. 1986) (no conceivable rational basis).

apply when a plaintiff claims a denial of a permit or some other land use approval violated substantive due process. Although some circuits apply the relaxed standard of substantive due process review in these cases,[6] other federal courts find substantive due process violations when municipalities arbitrarily withheld a building permit or other approval or refused approval for political or other improper reasons.[7] The Supreme Court has now held that the arbitrary and irrational test applies to the review of legislative action, but that the "shocks the conscience" test applies to the review of executive action.[8]

§ 2.40 Barriers to Substantive Due Process Litigation in the Federal Courts.

Substantive due process litigation presents additional problems in federal courts. They rely on Supreme Court doctrine adopted in non-land use cases to create substantial barriers to substantive due process litigation. For example, the Supreme Court has held a substantive due process claim cannot be made if another, more specific, constitutional claim is available, such as the Fourth Amendment.[1] In land use cases, this rule will usually eliminate substantive due process claims because a takings claim will also be available. Since as-applied takings claims must be brought in state court first, this rule will also keep zoning cases out of federal courts unless an equal protection claim is possible. Some circuits have rejected this rule in land use cases,[2] but others have accepted it.[3]

[6] Anderson v. Douglas County, 4 F.3d 574 (8th Cir. 1993) (conditional use permit); Corn v. City of Lauderdale Lakes, 997 F.2d 1369 (11th Cir. 1993) (denial of shopping center development); Neston Colon Medina & Sucesores, Inc. v. Custodio, 964 F.2d 32 (1st Cir. 1992) (landfill and tourist complex).

[7] Woodwind Estates, Ltd. v. Gretkowski, 205 F.3d 118 (3d Cir.2000); Phillips v. Borough of Keyport, 107 F.3d 164 (3d Cir. 1997) (denial based on dislike of adult use); Resolution Trust Corp. v. Town of Highland Beach, 18 F.3d 1536 (11th Cir. 1994) (denial of vested right to develop); Marks v. City of Chesapeake, 883 F.2d 308 (4th Cir. 1989) (neighborhood opposition); Bateson v. Geisse, 857 F.2d 1300 (9th Cir. 1988) (municipality refused to issue building permit when all requirements met); Brady v. Town of Colchester, 863 F.2d 205 (2d Cir. 1988) (refusal to issue site plan or certificate of occupancy). See Doherty v. City of Chicago, 75 F.3d 318 (7th Cir. 1996) (rejecting claim and discussing conflicting cases on whether substantive due process applies).

[8] County of Sacramento v. Lewis, 523 U.S. 833 (1998).

[1] Graham v. Connor, 490 U.S. 386 (1990) (Fourth Amendment claim). See also Collins v. City of Harker Heights, 503 U.S. 115 (1992) (suggesting substantive due process clause has limited application in constitutional adjudication).

[2] Tri County Indus., Inc. v. District of Columbia, 104 F.3d 455 (D.C. Cir. 1997); Pearson v. City of Grand Blanc, 961 F.2d 1211 (6th Cir. 1992). See also John Corp. v. City of Houston, 214 F.3d 573 (5th Cir. 2000).

[3] Sinclair Oil Corp. v. County of Santa Barbara, 96 F.3d 401 (9th Cir. 1996). See also Bickerstaff Clay Prods. Co. v. Harris County, 89 F.3d 1481 (11th Cir. 1996) (substantive due process police power limitation subsumed within takings clause). Accord Miller v. Campbell County, 945 F.2d 348 (10th Cir. 1991) (non-zoning case); South County Sand & Gravel Co. v. Town of South Kingstown, 160 F.3d 834 (1st Cir. 1998); Macri v. King County, 126 F.3d 1125 (9th Cir. 1997); Villas of Lake Jackson v. Leon County, 121 F.3d 610 (11th Cir. 1997).

In addition, the Eleventh Circuit does not apply substantive due process to claims to executive denials of a state-created property right, such as the denial of a license for a legal nonconforming use.[4]

Another important barrier to substantive due process litigation is the requirement, in all but one circuit, that a plaintiff must have an entitlement in order to sue on a substantive due process claim. The due process clause protects "property," and the entitlement rule means a litigant must be entitled to the land use approval for his property. Ownership of property is not enough. As in procedural due process cases,[5] a plaintiff must show it is entitled to a land use or land use approval because the land use agency does not have the discretion to deny the use. If an agency has the discretion to refuse a land use approval, such as a subdivision or site plan approval, the cases find an entitlement does not exist.[6] The Third Circuit does not require an entitlement,[7] and in a few cases the courts either assumed an entitlement existed or did not discuss the issue.[8] The Supreme Court has not decided whether an entitlement rule applies in substantive due process claims in land use cases, and no such rule applies in takings cases, where the ownership of land enough for a takings claim against discretionary refusals to approve a land development project.

C. PROCEDURAL DUE PROCESS.

§ 2.41 The Procedural Due Process Problem.

Administrative decision making in the land use control process must meet procedural due process requirements.[1] These requirements are constitutional and statutory. The due process clause of the federal constitution includes a procedural

---

[4] DeKalb Stone, Inc. v. County of DeKalb, 106 F.3d 956 (11th Cir. 1997).

[5] § 2.42.

[6] Carpenter Outdoor Advertising Co. v. City of Fenton, 251 F.3d 686 (8th Cir. 2001) Hyde Park Co. v. Santa Fe City Council, 226 F.3d1207 (10th Cir. 2000); Woodwind Estates, Ltd. v. Gretkowski, 205 F.3d 118 (3d Cir. 2000); DLC Mgmt. Corp. v. Town of Hyde Park, 163 F.3d 124 (2d Cir. 1998); Bituminous Materials v. Rice County, 126 F.3d 1068 (8th Cir. 1997); Triomphe Investors v. City of Northwood, 49 F.3d 198 (6th Cir. 1995) (city had discretion to deny special use permit); Sylvia Dev. Co. v. Calvert County, 48 F.3d 810 (4th Cir. 1995) (approval of transfer zone); Gardner v. City of Baltimore, 969 F.2d 63 (4th Cir. 1992); MacKenzie v. City of Rockledge, 920 F.2d 1554 (11th Cir. 1991); Spence v. Zimmerman, 873 F.2d 256 (11th Cir. 1989); R.R.I. Realty Corp. v. Village of Southampton, 870 F.2d 911 (2d Cir. 1989).

[7] De Blasio v. Board of Zoning Adjustment, 53 F.2d 592 (3d Cir. 1995); Coniston Corp. v. Village of Hoffman Homes, 844 F.2d 461 (7th Cir. 1988).

[8] Jacobs, Visconsi & Jacobs v. City of Lawrence, 927 F.2d 1111 (10th Cir. 1991) (rezoning); G.M. Eng'rs & Assocs., Inc. v. West Bloomfield Township, 922 F.2d 328 (6th Cir. 1990) (lot split); Scott v. Greenville County, 716 F.2d 1409 (4th Cir. 1983) (vested right).

[1] But see § 8.30.

as well as a substantive element and requires constitutionally acceptable procedures in administrative decision making. State zoning legislation requires only minimum procedures, such as a notice and hearing. State courts impose additional procedural requirements, such as findings of fact on variance decisions, but they do not usually base these requirements on the state constitution.

§ 2.42 In the Federal Courts.

Procedural due process protections apply if a land use decision is administrative or quasi-judicial rather than legislative.[1] The federal courts treat zonings and rezonings as legislative. In *Rogin v. Bensalem Township*,[2] the court held a downzoning was legislative and said:

> The act of legislating necessarily entails political trading, compromise, and ad hoc decision making which, in the aggregate, produce policies that at least approximate a fair and equitable distribution of social resources and obligations.[3]

The court indicated it would hold a land use decision administrative only if it "inherently treats a particular class of persons inequitably." However, actions by a governing body affecting a single landowner, such as the review of a site plan, may be held legislative.[4] Though a general plan amendment is usually held legislative,[5] the Ninth Circuit held a plan amendment adjudicative because it reclassified a single parcel of land to a more restrictive use and was directed solely to that landowner.[6]

Even if a land use decision is administrative, procedural due process requirements apply in the federal courts only if a landowner has an entitlement to a property interest protected by state law rather than a mere expectancy. This problem arises when a landowner claims a procedural due process violation occurred when a land use agency or official denied his application for a land use permit or approval. Whether a landowner has an expectancy rather than an entitlement depends on whether the decision on his application requires an

---

[1] But see § 8.33 (procedural due process claim not available in federal court if postdeprivation state remedy available).

[2] 616 F.2d 580 (3d Cir. 1980). *Accord* Pro-Eco, Inc. v. Board of Comm'rs, 57 F.3d 305 (7th Cir. 1995); Jackson Court Condominiums, Inc. v. City of New Orleans, 874 F.2d 1070 (5th Cir. 1989).

[3] 616 F.2d at 693. *But see* Bogan v. Scott-Harris, 523 U.S. 44 (1998) (in immunity case, action held legislative if it is formally legislative).

[4] Conniston Corp. v. Village of Hoffman Estates, 844 F.2d 461 (7th Cir. 1988).

[5] Holbrook, Inc. v. Clark County, 49 P.3d 142 (Wash. App. 2002).

[6] Harris v. County of Riverside, 904 F.2d 497 (9th Cir. 1990). *Accord,* Naierowski Bros. Inv. Co. v. City of Sterling Heights, 949 F.2d 890 (6th Cir. 1992).

exercise of discretion by the agency or official. The courts have held that subdivision and other similar approval procedures are discretionary.[7]

The Supreme Court has adopted a three-part test to determine which procedural due process limitations apply when a landowner has an entitlement.[8] Bias is a clear case of a procedural due process violation.[9] The courts usually hold that decision making procedures violate procedural due process, but there are exceptions when procedures are clearly inadequate.[10]

§ 2.43   In the State Courts.

Procedural due process requirements in the state courts apply to administrative zoning decisions, such as decisions on variances.[1] They do not apply to zoning map amendments by local governing bodies in most states because the courts hold these decisions are legislative. This characterization can lead to abuses in the zoning process. Members of governing bodies can make ex parte contacts outside the hearing, and participants in the hearing cannot challenge the information obtained through these contacts or cross-examine witnesses. The governing body can also inhibit judicial review by making generalized findings of fact or by failing to make any findings at all.

---

[7] Weinberg v. Whatcom County, 241 F.3d 746 (9th Cir. 2001) (short plats and permits); Hyde Park Co. v. Santa Fe City Council, 226 F.3d 1207 (10th Cir. 2000) (subdivision plat); Sylvia Dev. Co. v. Calvert County, 48 F.3d 810 (4th Cir. 1995) (rezoning); Jacobs, Visconsi & Jacobs v. City of Lawrence, 927 F.2d 1111 (10th Cir. 1991) (rezoning; federal court not bound by state determination of what is legislative); Walker v. City of Kansas City, 911 F.2d 80 (8th Cir. 1990) (rezoning); Bateson v. Geisse, 857 F.2d 1300 (9th Cir. 1988) (approval of plat); Yale Auto Parts, Inc. v. Jackson, 758 F.2d 54 (2d Cir. 1985) (junkyard permit). *See also* Fusco v. State of Connecticut, 815 F.2d 201 (2d Cir. 1987) (neighboring property owner does not have property interest in statutory right to appeal land use approval).

[8] Mathews v. Eldridge, 424 U.S. 319, 335 (1976) (private interest affected; risk of erroneous deprivation of such interest and probable value of additional procedural safeguards; and government's interest, including fiscal and administrative burdens of additional safeguards).

[9] Smith-Birch v. Baltimore County, 68 F. Supp.2d 602 (D. Md. 1999 (bias not found); Leverett v. Town of Limon, 567 F. Supp. 471 (D. Colo. 1983) (bias found). *See* Withrow v. Larkin, 421 U.S. 35 (1976) (bias found in licensing procedures).

[10] Violation not found: Pro-Eco, Inc. v. Board of Comm'rs, 57 F.3d 505 (7th Cir. 1995 (hearing); Bender v. City of St. Ann, 36 F.3d 57 (8th Cir. 1994) (notice and hearing); Licari v. Ferruzzi, 22 F.3d 344 (1st Cir. 1994 (same); First Assembly of God v. Collier County, 20 F.3d 419 (11th Cir. 1994) (deficiencies in notice of hearing); Anderson v. Douglas County, 4 F.3d 574 (8th Cir. 1993) (plaintiff failed to take advantage of available procedures); Landmark Land Co. v. Buchanan, 874 F.2d 717 (10th Cir. 1989) (ex parte contacts); Chongris v. Board of Appeals, 811 F.2d 36 (1st Cir. 1987) (notice and opportunity to be heard; no right of cross-examination).

Violation found: Resolution Trust Corp. v. Town of Highland Beach, 18 F.3d 1536 (11th Cir. 1994) (notice inadequate); Harris v. County of Riverside, 904 F.2d 497 (9th Cir. 1990) (same); Herrington v. County of Sonoma, 857 F.2d 567 (9th Cir. 1988) (notice and hearing inadequate).

[1] §§ 6.67–6.76 (discussing decision-making procedures).

Decision-making procedures at the local level are rudimentary in many states because the Standard Zoning Act and state legislation that follows it provide only minimal notice and hearing requirements. State courts supplement the statutory requirements, though bias and conflict of interest problems often receive the most attention. The American Planning Association's model legislation contains a comprehensive code for the administrative and judicial review of land use decisions that remedies this lack of procedure in state zoning legislation.[2]

D.   EQUAL PROTECTION.

§ 2.44   The Equal Protection Problem.

The equal protection clause requires fair treatment in governmental regulation. Zoning and other land use controls raise an equal protection problem because they classify land uses and because municipalities can administer them in an unfair manner.. Landowners can make two types of equal protection objections to zoning ordinances. They can object to classifications among land uses in the zoning ordinance text. They can also accept the textual classifications but object to how a municipality applies the ordinance., either through land use classifications in the zoning map, or in its administration. The entitlement requirement does not apply to equal protection cases because the equal protection clause protects persons, not property.[1]

An equal protection claim can be either a facial attack or an as-applied attack on an ordinance. In a typical as-applied case, a landowner agrees the zoning ordinance properly distinguishes between residential and commercial uses, but claims these classifications as applied by the zoning map violate equal protection. He may argue, for example, that the zoning map has improperly placed his land in a residential district because commercial zoning for his land is more appropriate. This is a typical "line-drawing" zoning case, discussed earlier as a takings problem. Often a court does not indicate whether it is considering a takings or an equal protection claim in cases of this kind. In another kind of as-applied case, a landowner can argue she has been unfairly treated in the administrative or adjudicative process. For example, she can argue she has been denied approval of her site plan for development though the municipality has approved other site plans comparable to hers.

Equal protection, as noted earlier, overlaps with substantive due process. The equal protection standard applied to land use regulation also requires a rational

---

[2] American Planning Association, Growing Smart Legislative Guidebook: Model Statutes for Planning and the Management of Change Ch. 10 (S. Meck ed. 2002)

[1] On whether equal protection claims are preempted by the takings clause *compare* Bateman v. City of W. Bountiful 89 F.3d 704 (equal protection claim preempted), with Armendirez v. Penman, 76 F.3d 1311 (9th Cir. 1996) (recognizing equal protection claim while dismissing substantive due process claim as preempted). *See* § 2.42.

relationship between an ordinance or land use decision and the legitimate governmental purpose it is intended to serve. Courts apply a similar standard when landowners challenge land use regulation under the due process clause.

§ 2.45 Judicial Standards for Equal Protection Review.

The judicial review standard courts apply to equal protection claims differs depending on the interest affected by the legislative classification. The majority and dissenting opinions in *Village of Belle Terre v. Boraas*,[1] illustrate the different standards courts use. The Court upheld a zoning ordinance that defined a family in a single-family zoning district as no more than two unrelated persons and applied the relaxed rational relationship standard. Under this standard, a court will uphold a legislative classification if it finds any rational basis for its justification.

The Supreme Court's *Euclid*[2] decision illustrates the application of the rational relationship standard to uphold the usual zoning district classifications in zoning ordinances. The Court upheld the exclusion of industrial and multifamily uses from single family residential districts. It held that any legislation needs "inclusion of a reasonable margin to insure effective enforcement," and that, in some fields, "the bad fades into the good by . . . insensible degrees." The Court added that the exclusion of nonresidential uses from residential districts "bears a rational relation to the health and safety of the community."

The Supreme Court also applies a strict scrutiny standard in equal protection cases. To apply this standard, a court must find that the classification is suspect, or that it burdens a fundamental interest. Racially discriminatory classifications are an example of suspect classifications subject to strict scrutiny review. In *Village of Arlington Heights v. Metropolitan Hous. Dev. Corp.*,[3] the Court held a suburban municipality's refusal to rezone to allow construction of a federally subsidized multifamily housing project was not racially discriminatory. It also held, however, that the burden shifts to the municipality to justify its zoning action if a plaintiff can show it was racially motivated, even in part. The Court required proof of discriminatory intent rather than discriminatory effect as the basis for an equal protection zoning violation based on racial discrimination. The Court's discriminatory intent requirement makes it very difficult to find racial discrimination in zoning except in extreme cases. Justice Marshall's dissenting opinion in *Belle Terre* illustrates the application of the more rigorous strict scrutiny standard when fundamental interests are affected. Justice Marshall believed the exclusion of unrelated families with more than two members burdened a fundamental interest in privacy and association.

---

[1] 416 U.S. 1 (1974).

[2] Ambler Realty Co. v. Village of Euclid, 272 U.S. 365 (1926). *See* § 2.06.

[3] 429 U.S. 252 (1977). *See* § 7.03.

Free speech is another fundamental interest. Land use regulations that burden free speech, such as ordinances that regulate signs or adult uses can affect the exercise of free speech and do not enjoy the usual protection afforded by the rational relationship standard of judicial review.

The strict scrutiny standard requires a compelling governmental interest to justify the classification, but the courts hardly ever find a governmental interest compelling. In *Belle Terre,* for example, Justice Marshall did not find a compelling governmental interest for the restriction on unrelated families. It did not achieve its goal of protecting residential neighborhoods because it did not prohibit large related families from living together. It prohibited large unrelated families from living together even though they did not impair residential quiet.

Justice Marshall's attempt to find fundamental interests in the zoning process has not borne fruit in the Supreme Court apart from the free speech cases. Although the Court under Justice Warren created a number of fundamental interests entitled to strict scrutiny review, such as the right to vote, it has not extended these categories since. The Court might have laid a foundation for strict scrutiny review in zoning cases had it found that the right to housing is a fundamental right. This holding would have applied strict scrutiny review to any zoning ordinance that restricted the right to housing opportunity, but the Supreme Court dashed any hope that it might adopt this position in *Lindsey v. Normet.*[4] A state landlord-tenant law did not allow tenants to defend an eviction action by showing that their dwelling was uninhabitable, and a tenant claimed this law violated equal protection because defenses in other civil actions were not subject to this restriction. The Court held the federal constitution did not guarantee a right to housing and rejected this claim under the rational relationship standard.

The Supreme Court has also adopted a middle-tier judicial review standard in equal protection cases when classifications are quasi-suspect. The middle-tier standard requires a legislative classification to bear a substantial rather than a necessary relationship to an important rather than a compelling governmental interest. The Court refused to apply this standard in a group home zoning case,[5] but one state court held that it applies to the judicial review of all zoning ordinances.[6] State courts can also be more aggressive than the Federal Courts in applying the equal protection clause to land use regulation.

§ 2.46 Applying the Rational Relationship Standard: The State Courts.

Since *Euclid,* the traditional zoning classifications have usually been safe from an equal protection attack in the state courts because the rational relationship

---

[4] 405 U.S. 56 (1972).

[5] § 2.48

[6] Town of Chesterfield v. Brooks, 489 A.2d 600 (N.H. 1985).

standard applies when the only question how a land use regulation applies to an economic interest in land.[1] State courts occasionally strike down underinclusive commercial zoning,[2] and several have invalidated exclusions of lower income housing, mobile homes, unrelated families, and group homes from residential districts.[3]

Restrictive land use classifications adopted by zoning maps raise equal protection problems similar to the line-drawing problems considered in as-applied takings cases.[4] As in the takings cases, a court may apply the rational relationship standard and the presumption of constitutionality and approve a zoning classification. A court can also take a more aggressive view and invalidate the zoning classification adopted by the zoning map even though the presumption applies.

A court's reaction to a zoning map classification may depend on whether the municipality adopted the classification as part of a comprehensive zoning ordinance. For example, assume a municipality wants to distinguish between "heavy" and "light" commercial uses. It creates "limited" and "general" commercial use districts as part of a comprehensive rezoning. Automobile service stations are allowed in the general but not in the limited district. At a street intersection where the two districts meet, a service station is located on the southeast corner in a general commercial district. The southwest corner across the street is in the limited commercial district. Can the owner of the southwest corner, who wants to construct a service station, claim the ordinance violates equal protection? In *State ex rel. American Oil Co. v. Bessent*,[5] the court sustained a mapped zoning classification of this type. Though it was troubled by the distinction between the two districts, it was influenced by the adoption and mapping of the districts in a comprehensive zoning ordinance, which "rests upon the interdependency of adjoining parcels of land in a community."

Equal protection problems also arise in a municipality's administration of a zoning ordinance. Assume a municipality grants a number of multifamily rezonings on street corners adjacent to commercial development. A landowner then applies for a similar rezoning and is refused. May she claim an equal protection violation? Most courts do not find an equal protection violation in

---

[1] *E.g.*, Mayhew v. Town of Sunnyvale, 964 S.W.2d 922 (Tex. 1998).

[2] § 5.36.

[3] *See* Chapter 5.

[4] § 2.36.

[5] 135 N.W.2d 317 (Wis. 1965). *See also* Westbrook v. Board of Adjustment, 262 S.E.2d 785 (Ga. 1980); Perron v. Village of New Brighton, 145 N.W.2d 425 (Minn. 1966) (upholding street centerline as dividing line between multifamily and single family residential area); City of Miami Beach v. Wiesen, 86 So.2d 442 (Fla. 1956); Carlson v. City of Bellevue, 435 P.2d 957 (Wash. 1968);

this type of case. They hold that each zoning case depends on its own facts and refuse to bind the municipality by its earlier rezoning decisions.[6]

A few cases hold as-applied attacks on zoning classifications are not appealable to the state's supreme court as-of-right as matters arising under the state constitution, even though the appeal is based on the equal protection clause. These cases treat the zoning classification problem as statutory rather than constitutional. As one case noted,[7] zoning legislation contains a clause that requires uniform regulations within zoning districts, and that an arbitrary classification in a zoning map violates this statutory requirement. It then held that "[w]hile these statutory prerequisites have loose constitutional connotations, the fundamental question here resolves itself into a matter of application of statutory standards to a particular fact situation under long established principles."

§ 2.47 Applying the Rational Relationship Standard: The Federal Courts.

The federal courts hold that land use regulations and decisions to not violate equal protection when the rational relationship standard of judicial review applies. In one group of cases, for example, the courts do not find an equal protection violation when a landowner is denied a zoning, site plan, subdivision or similar land use approval.[1] They rejected arguments that there was no rational basis for the denial, or that the denial was arbitrary because similar applications were approved. The federal courts have also rejected equal protection claims when a municipality prohibited a land use or restricted the area where a land use could be located,[2] and when claims were made that a land use ordinance implemented

---

[6] See Houston v. Board of City Comm'rs, 543 P.2d 1010 (Kan. 1975); Krause v. City of Royal Oak, 160 N.W.2d 769 (Mich. App. 1968); Ranken v. Lavine, 363 N.E.2d 343 (N.Y. 1977); State ex rel. Miller v. Cain, 242 P.2d 505 (Wash. 1952). Compare Aspen Hill Venture v. Montgomery County Council, 289 A.2d 303 (Md. App. 1972); Wilson v. Borough of Mountainside, 201 A.2d 540 (N.J. 1964). But see City of Birmingham v. Morris, 396 So. 2d 53 (Ala. 1981).

[7] Tidewater Oil Co. v. Mayor and Council of Carteret, 209 A.2d 105, 108 (N.J. 1965). Accord, First Nat'l Bank & Trust Co. v. City of Evanston, 197 N.E.2d 705 (Ill. 1964).

[1] Sylvia Dev. Co. v. Calvert, 48 F.3d 819 (4th Cir. 1995) (rezoning denial); Anderson v. Douglas County, 4 F.3d 574 (8th Cir. 1993) (conditional use permit); Jacobs, Visconsi & Jacobs Co. v. City of Lawrence, 927 F.2d 1111 (10th Cir. 1991) (rezoning for suburban shopping center); Conti v. City of Fremont, 919 F.2d 1385 (9th Cir. 1990) (refusal to amend zoning permit); New Burnham Prairie Homes, Inc. v. Village of Burnham, 910 F.2d 2474 (7th Cir. 1990) (building permit); Studen v. Beebe, 588 F.2d 560 (6th Cir. 1978) (extension of nonconforming use); Sylvia Dev. Co. v. Calvert County, 48 F.3d 810 (4th Cir. 1995) (rezoning denial); Anderson v. Douglas County, 4 F.3d 574 (8th Cir. 1993) (denial of conditional use permit); Nelson v. City of Selma, 881 F.2d 836 (9th Cir. 1989) (zoning denial); Scudder v. Town of Greendale, 704 F.2d 999 (7th Cir. 1983) (building permit).

[2] Crider v. Board of County Comm'rs, 246 F.3d 1285 (10th Cir. 2001) (rural Reservation); Vulcan Materials Co. v. City of Tehucacana, 238 F.3d 382 (5th Cir. 2001) (ban on heavy equipment for quarrying); Bannum, Inc. v. City of Fort Lauderdale, 157 F.3d 819 (11th Cir. 1998) (special

or enforced in an arbitrary manner.[3] However, some cases have upheld selective enforcement claims,[4] and selective enforcement claims may now be easier to prove under a recent Supreme Court decision.[5]

§ 2.48 *Cleburne*: **Rational Relationship "With a Bite."**

City of Cleburne v. Cleburne Living Center[1] indicated the Supreme Court might have adopted a more stringent rational relationship standard for land use cases. The Court struck down the denial of a special use permit for a group home for the mentally retarded. The group home planned to locate in an "apartment house" district, where the zoning ordinance required a special use permit for homes for the "insane or feeble-minded" and for alcoholics and drug addicts. It did not require a special use permit in this district for hospitals, sanitariums, nursing homes, or homes for convalescents or the aged.

The group home argued that middle tier equal protection review applied to the permit denial, but the Court disagreed. It held there were legitimate reasons to distinguish the mentally retarded from other groups that were entitled to middle-tier review. They could not claim they should all be treated alike because the mentally retarded, as a class, were very different from each other. Neither was there a principled basis for distinguishing the mentally retarded from other groups, such as the aged and mentally ill, who could also claim they were a quasi-suspect class because they were subject to public prejudice. The Court also noted that federal and state legislation protected the mentally retarded, and that this legislation indicated they were not politically powerless. It pointed out that

---

permit requirement); Mount Elliott Cemetery Ass'n v. City of Troy, 171 F.3d 398 (6th Cir. 1999); Hayes v. City of Miami, 52 F.3d 918 (11th Cir. 1995); Howard v. City of Garland, 917 F.2d 898 (5th Cir. 1990); Greene v. Town of Blooming Grove, 879 F.2d 1061 (2d Cir. 1989); Grant v. County of Seminole, 817 F.2d 731 (11th Cir. 1987) (mobile home); City of Highland Park v. Train, 519 F.2d 861 (7th Cir. 1977).

[3] Martin v. City of Brentwood, 200 F.3d 1205 (8th Cir. 2000) (liquor license); Brandt v. Davis, 191 F.3d 887 (8th Cir. 1999) (zoning enforcement); LaTrieste Restaurant v. Village of Port Chester, 188 F.3d 65 (2d Cir. 1999) (ordinance violations); Mount Elliott Cemetery Ass'n v. City of Troy, 171 F.3d 398 (6th Cir. 1999) (denial of zoning request for cemetery); Poppell v. City of San Diego, 149 F.3d 951 (9th Cir. 1998); Crowley v. Courville, 76 F.3d 47 (2d Cir. 1996); Strickland v. Alderman, 74 F.3d 260 (11th Cir. 1996); Zahra v. Town of Southold, 48 F.3d 674 (2d Cir. 1995) (arbitrary enforcement); Muckway v. Craft, 789 F.2d 517 (7th Cir. 1986); Kuzinich v. County of Santa Clara, 689 F.2d 1345 (9th Cir. 1982); Cook v. City of Price, 566 F.2d 699 (10th Cir. 1977).

[4] Lisa's Party City, Inc. v. Town of Henrietta, 185 F.3d 12 (2d Cir. 1999) (sign ordinance); Rubinovitz v. Rogato, 60 F.3d 906 (1st Cir. 1995) (building code); Thomas v. City of West Haven, 734 A.2d 535 (Conn. 1999) (site plan); Thorp v. Town of Lebanon, 612 N.W.2d 59 (Wis. 2000) (failure to rezone).

[5] § 2.49.

[1] 473 U.S. 432 (1985).

legislatures might not adopt protective legislation for the mentally retarded if courts subjected this legislation to stringent judicial review.

Although the Court did not invalidate the special permit requirement for the group home, it held the permit denial unconstitutional under the rational relationship standard. It pointed out the zoning ordinance did not require a permit for similar uses in the district, but that the differences between these uses and a home for the mentally retarded were largely irrelevant to the city's legitimate zoning interests. Neither were the reasons for denying the permit acceptable. The city denied the permit because of neighborhood fears, but "mere negative attitudes" were not a sufficient reason for the denial. Neither were fears that nearby junior high school students might harass the group home residents. Objections that the group home would be overcrowded and located in a floodplain were not acceptable because the same objections applied to similar group homes the ordinance allowed without a permit.

Cleburne suggested a higher standard of judicial review was appropriate when municipalities discriminated against group homes and other vulnerable uses in their zoning ordinances — rational relationship "with a bite." Some courts followed *Cleburne* and struck down zoning restrictions in such cases.[2] Other courts did not follow *Cleburne* and took a contrary position.[3] The Supreme Court has now indicated that *Cleburne* did not make a major change in equal protection law.[4] It held *Cleburne* does not mean that decision making based on negative attitudes or fear is enough, standing alone, for an equal protection violation. *Cleburne* stood only for the "unremarkable and widely acknowledge" rule that governmental action is not invalid under rational basis scrutiny when it rationally furthers a governmental purpose.

§ 2.49   Selective Enforcement: The *Olech* Case.

In *Village of Wildwood v. Olech*,[1] the Supreme Court may have breathed new life into equal protection cases based on the selective enforcement of land use

---

[2] Bannum, Inc. v. City of Louisville, 958 F.2d 1354 (6th Cir. 1992) (conditional use permit for group homes); Cornerstone Bible Church v. City of Hastings, 948 F.2d 464 (8th Cir. 1991) (remanding claim that exclusion of church from central business district violated equal protection); Burstyn v. City of Miami Beach, 663 F. Supp. 528 (S.D. Fla. 1987) (zoning restrictions on housing for elderly); Kirsch v. Prince George's County, 626 A.2d 372 (Md. 1993) (occupancy restrictions on student housing). *Contra*

[3] Bannum, Inc. v. City of Fort Lauderdale, 157 F.3d 819 (11th Cir. 1998) (group home); Texas Manufactured Housing Ass'n v. City of Nederland, 101 F.3d 1095 (5th Cir. 1996) (restriction on mobile homes); Howard v. City of Garland, 917 F.2d 898 (5th Cir. 1990) (zoning ordinance prohibiting operation of day care center); Bannum, Inc. v. City of St. Charles, 2 F.3d 267 (8th Cir. 1993) (halfway house for convicted criminals); Freedom Ranch, Inc. v. Board of Adjustment, 878 P.2d 380 (Okla. App. 1994).

[4] Board of Trustees v. Garrett, 531 U.S. 356 (2001).

[1] 528 U.S. 562 (2000) (per curiam).

ordinances. The village refused to supply water to the plaintiffs unless they granted he village an additional street easement it had not required from other property owners. It was alleged the village did so to retaliate for the plaintiffs having brought (and won) an earlier, unrelated law suit against the village.

The district court dismissed the complaint, the court of appeals reversed, and the Supreme Court affirmed. The Court confirmed it had recognized successful equal protection claims "brought by a "class of one," where the plaintiff alleges she has been intentionally treated differently from others similarly situated, and there is no rational basis for the difference in treatment." Unlike the court of appeals, it did not require proof of vindictive action, illegitimate animus or will against the plaintiff as a required element in a selective enforcement case. Justice Breyer concurred in the result and held the decision would transform "run-of-the-mill zoning cases into cases of constitutional right" unless the additional factors relied on by the court of appeals were included.

The Supreme Court's decision leaves many questions unanswered. The intent requirement is consistent with an early Supreme Court decision that was not cited,[2] and most lower federal courts had dismissed selective enforcement claims based on equal protection under tests similar to those adopted in *Olech*.[3] The decisions since *Olech* have taken conflicting views on what that case means for selective enforcement equal protection claims.[4] Other cases since *Olech* have decided selective enforcement equal protection claims without discussing that decision.[5]

---

[2] Snowden v. Hughes, 321 U.S. 1 (1944).

[3] *E.g.*, Mount Elliott Cemetery Ass'n v. City of Troy, 171 F.3d 398 (6th Cir. 1999); Poppell v. City of San Diego, 149 F.3d 951 (9th Cir. 1998); Crowley v. Courville, 76 F.3d 47 (2d Cir. 1996).

[4] Nevel v. Village of Schaumburg, 297 F.3d 673 (7th Cir. 2002) (village had legitimate reason to enforce ordinance and similarly situated property owners did not receive more favorable treatment); Cruz v. Town of Cicero, 275 F.3d 579 (7th Cir. 2001) (upholding verdict for plaintiff based on showing of deliberate animus); Harlen Assocs. v. Incorporated Village of Mineola, 273 F.3d 494 (2d Cir. 2001) (not deciding whether animus required but rejecting claim assuming it is not); Bryan v. City of Madison, 213 F.3d 267 (5th Cir. 2000) (dismissing selective enforcement claim and interpreting *Olech* to require improper motive); Purze v. Village of Winthrop Harbor, 236 F.3d 452 (7th Cir. 2002) (dismissing selective enforcement claim because unequal treatment not found); Hilton v. City of Wheeling, 209 F.3d 1005 (7th Cir. 2000) (police case, restating animus test); McDonald's Corp. v. City of Norton Shores, 102 F. Supp. 2d 432 (W.D. Mich. 2000) (upholding rejection of site plan under *Olech* test).

[5] Polk v. Town of Lubec, 756 A.2d 510 (Me. 2000) (claim of discriminatory enforcement rejected); Pope v. Little Bear's Head Dist., 764 A.2d 932 (N.H. 2000) (conscious and intentional discrimination required); 421 Corp. v. Metropolitan Gov't of Nashville & Davidson County, 36 S.W.3d 469 (Tenn. App. 2001) (dismissing claim that county selectively enforced zoning ordinance against adult business).

E. FREE SPEECH.

§ 2.50 How the Free Speech Clause Applies to Land Use Regulation.

The free speech clause has always applied to land use regulations that affect noncommercial speech. An example is a sign ordinance that regulates signs with political or noncommercial messages. The Supreme Court extended the application of the free speech clause to commercial speech in the mid-1970s, and this decision means the free speech clause also applies to land use regulation that affects commercial speech.[1] A zoning ordinance that regulates adult book stores and movie theaters is an example of a land use ordinance that affects commercial speech. Another example is a sign ordinance that regulates signs with commercial messages. This section outlines the doctrines the Supreme Court applies to laws, such as land use regulations, that affect free speech. Later sections discuss the application of the free speech clause to adult uses and signs.[2]

Most land use ordinances that implicate the free speech clause regulate commercial speech. The Supreme Court reviews the constitutionality of laws that affect commercial speech under a multi-part test it adopted in *Central Hudson Gas & Elec. Co. v. Public Serv. Comm'n*.[3] Under this test, if the speech is protected, the Court will uphold a land use regulation against free speech objections if (1) the governmental interest is substantial; (2) the regulation directly advances that governmental interest; and (3) The regulation is not more extensive than necessary to serve that interest. This test resembles the tests the courts impose under the substantive due process clause but are more rigorous. The *Central Hudson* tests effectively reverse the presumption of constitutionality the courts usually apply to land use regulations.[4]

Time, place and manner regulations are a type of regulation that has a special place in free speech law. A time, place and manner regulation protects governmental interests other than the content of speech. The Supreme Court has adopted tests for time, place, and manner regulations that are similar to the tests it adopted for commercial speech in *Central Hudson*.[5] Land use regulations affecting commercial speech are often in this category, although they are usually hybrids.

---

[1] Virginia State Bd. of Pharmacy v. Virginia Citizens Consumer Council, 425 U.S. 748 (1976); Bigelow v. Virginia, 421 U.S. 809 (1975).

[2] §§ 5.59–5.66 (adult uses); § 6.57 (conditional uses); §§ 11.12–11.23 (signs).

[3] 447 U.S. 557 (1980). *See* Lorillard Tobacco Co. v. Reilly, 533 U.S. 525 (affirming *Central Hudson* tests).

[4] *But see* Board of Trustees v. Fox, 492 U.S. 469 (1989) (*Central Hudson* rules do not include "less restrictive alternative" test; Court requires only "reasonable fit" between legislative ends and means).

[5] United States v. O'Brien, 391 U.S. 367 (1968).

An example is a zoning ordinance that requires the spacing of adult movie theaters. The ordinance is a time, place, and manner regulation because it prevents the neighborhood deterioration that would result from the overconcentration of adult businesses in one neighborhood. The ordinance also regulates the content of speech because the content of the movies shown determines whether a movie theater is adult. The Supreme Court has upheld carefully tailored land use regulations that affect commercial speech by treating them as time, place, and manner regulations, despite their hybrid character.

Another important distinction the Supreme Court makes under the free speech clause is the distinction between a law affecting speech that is content-neutral and a law affecting speech that is viewpoint-neutral. A regulation is not viewpoint-neutral if it prohibits a point of view. An example is a sign ordinance prohibiting messages on signs that oppose nuclear power. A regulation is not content-neutral if it regulates the content of speech. An example is a sign ordinance that prohibits signs with any messages on nuclear power, no matter what point of view they take.[6]

The tests the Supreme Court applies to laws that are not content-neutral are more rigorous than the *Central Hudson* tests and more rigorous than the tests it applies to laws that are not viewpoint-neutral. If a law is not content-neutral, the Court requires government to justify its effect on free speech by a "compelling" rather than a "substantial" governmental interest.[7]

§ 2.51 Retaliatory Governmental Conduct.

Free speech problems arise in another type of case in which a municipality engages in retaliatory conduct against a landowner because she has exercised her free speech rights. It is well-established that state actors may not retaliate against a person's exercise of his free speech rights, and the courts have begun to apply this rule to land use cases. In a typical case, a landowner has spoken out against a mayor or councilman who was up for reelection, and who subsequently won. The landowner then applies to the municipality for a site plan approval. The landowner claims similar site plans were approved for other landowners,[1] and argues she was denied approval because of her political speech and that her constitutional right to free speech has been violated. This case raises

---

[6] Ward v. Rock Against Racism, 491 U.S. 781, 791 (1989) (principal inquiry in determining content neutrality in speech and time, place, or manner cases is whether government has adopted regulation of speech because of disagreement with message it conveys; government's purpose is the controlling consideration).

[7] City of Ladue v. Gilleo, 114 S. Ct. 2038 (1994) (invalidating sign regulation; concurring opinion of O'Connor, J.).

[1] *But see* Welch v. Paicos, 66 F.Supp.2d 138 (D. Mass. 1999) (plaintiff need not show that others similarly situated were treated differently; proof of necessary motive enough).

an equal protection problem, but the free speech issue is an alternate ground for recovery.

These are mixed motive cases. The municipality may have had a legitimate reason to deny approval of the site plan in the example above, but may also have denied approval in retaliation of the landowner's exercise of her free speech rights. Similar problems arise when a landowner claims a municipality's land use decision is racially discriminatory.[2] In these cases the courts have usually applied a rule from a Supreme Court free speech case,[3] also applied by the Court in its racial discrimination zoning case, where the plaintiff carries the burden to show her conduct was protected by the free speech clause,[4] and that this conduct was a "motivating factor" in the agency's decision. If that burden is met, the municipality must show by a "preponderance of the evidence" that it would have reached the same decision "even in the absence of the protected conduct."[5]

For example, in *Gagliardi v. Village of Pawling*,[6] the court held the plaintiffs had stated a cause of action that the village had failed to enforce its zoning ordinance against a neighbor in retaliation for plaintiffs' beginning legal proceedings and attending public hearings and meetings to express concern about the lack of enforcement. The court also held the plaintiffs had proved the requisite "nexus" between the plaintiff's conduct and the subsequent retaliatory conduct by the municipal defendants. This issue was ultimately one of motive, and it was sufficient under the federal rules to allege facts from which a retaliatory intent "reasonably may be inferred."[7] Problems arise, however, in holding multi-member bodies liable for constitutional violations based on motivation. A plaintiff may sue members in their individual capacities,[8] but a court may be unwilling to hold an entire legislative body liable for merely concurring with another member who had a political motive for his vote.[9]

---

[2] § 7.03

[3] Mt. Healthy School Dist. Bd Of Educ. V. Doyle, 429 U.S. 274 (1977). *See* Allen v. Iranon, 283 F.3d 1070 (9th Cir. 2002) (*Mt. Healthy* is correct test in free speech retaliation cases, not *McDonnell Douglas* test); Nestor Colon Successores, Inc. v. Custodio, 964 F.2d 32 (1st Cir. 1992) (applying four-part *McDonnell Douglas* test used in cases of employment discrimination under Title VII); Arrington v. Dickerson, 915 F.Supp 1516 (M.D. Ala 1996) (*McDonnell Douglas* test not essentially different).

[4] Brady v. Town of Colchester, 863 F.2d 205 (2d Cir. 1988) (lease of property for commercial reasons not protected by free speech clause).

[5] Mt. Healthy, 429 U.S. at 287.

[6] 18 F.3d 188 (2d. Cir. 1994). *See also* Dougherty v. Town of North Hempstead Bd. Of Zoning, 282 F.3d 83 (2d. Cir 2002) (retaliation claim ripe for decision and not subject to dismissal); Baker v. Coxe, 230 F.3d 470 (1st Cir. 2001) (defendants had legitimate reason to reject permit, and holding plaintiff must show she was entitled to permit); Rolf v. City of San Antonio, 77 F.3d 823 (5th Cir. 1996) (only plaintiffs' property was targeted for condemnation).

[7] Federal Rules of Civil Procedure 9(b).

[8] Welch v. Paicos, 66 F.Supp.2d 138 (D. Mass. 1999).

[9] Arroyo Vista Partners v. County of Santa Barbara, 732 F. Supp. 1046 (C.D. Cal. 1990).

F. THE CONTRACT CLAUSE.

§ 2.52 General Principles.

The Constitution provides: "No State shall pass any . . . Law impairing the Obligation of Contracts. . . ."[1] Although the contract clause is not often a factor in land use cases, a claim under the clause can sometimes be made. One example is the case of a developer who obtains an option on a property on which he plans a development that is permitted by the zoning ordinance. A contract clause claim may arise if the municipality downzones the property to impose a more restrictive classification.

The contract clause remained dormant for many years, but in *United States Trust Co. v. New Jersey,*[2] the Supreme Court held invalid a legislative repeal of a statutory covenant that prohibited the use of port authority revenues for mass transit subsidies. The contract clause is not an absolute bar to a land use regulation that impairs a contract. A court must first find that an impairment of a contract has occurred, but even an impairment is valid if it is justified by a legitimate governmental purpose. Judicial scrutiny of contract impairment under the contract clause is heightened when the state or local government is party to a contract.[3]

§ 2.53 In Land Use Cases.

The Supreme Court considered a contract clause objection in a land use case, *Keystone Bituminous Coal Ass'n v. Benedictus,*[1] that also decided important takings issues. Property owners in land conveyances from mining companies had contractually waived any liability for surface damage from mining. The companies claimed a state statute prohibiting subsidence from mining violated the contract clause by not allowing the company to hold the property owners to the waivers.

The Court held the statute was a substantial impairment of a contractual relationship, and the critical inquiry was whether the impairment was justified.[2] The Court held the state had a "strong public interest" in preventing harm from

---

[1] U.S. Const. art. I, § 10.

[2] 431 U.S. 1 (1977).

[3] *See generally* Energy Reserves Group, Inc. v. Kansas Power & Light Co., 459 U.S. 400 (1983); Allied Structural Steel Co. v. Spannaus, 438 U.S. 234 (1978). *See* Board of Cty. Comm'rs v. East Prince Frederick Corp., 559 A.2d 822 (Md. App. 1989) (no contract clause violation when county imposed two-year limit on use of sewer and water service allocation unless developer paid user fee; impairment not severe and justified by need to allocate limited capacity).

[1] 480 U.S. 470 (1987).

[2] *Compare* Northwestern Nat'l Life Ins. Co. v. Tahoe Reg'l Planning Agency, 632 F.2d 104 (9th Cir. 1980) (adoption of restrictive zoning ordinance not a contract impairment solely because it made collection of assessment for payment of improvement bonds more difficult).

subsidence, and the environmental effect of the harm transcended any private contractual agreements. The Court then noted that a significant and legitimate public purpose is not enough to justify a contract impairment. The legislative adjustment of contractual rights must also be based on reasonable conditions and must be appropriate to the public purpose that justified the legislation.

The Court then held it must defer to the legislative judgment on this issue unless the state was a contracting party, and concluded that the environmental purposes of the subsidence act "clearly survived" its standards for evaluating contract impairment. The few additional land use cases that have considered contract clause claims have also dismissed them.[3]

---

[3] Pitts v. Pilkerton, 714 F. Supp. 285 (M.D. Tenn. 1989) (ordinance prohibiting display of portable signs that affected existing leases for the display of these signs); Beasley v. Potter, 493 F. Supp. 1059 (W.D. Mich. 1980) (denial of special use permit that caused loan default). *But see* JSS Realty Co., LLC v. Town of Kittery, 177 F. Supp.2d 64 (D. Me. 2001) (cause of action stated based on repeal of transferable development rights that were under contract)

REFERENCES

Books and Monographs

Takings: Land-Development Conditions and Regulatory Takings After *Lucas* and *Dollan* (D. Callies ed. 1996).

F. Bosselman, D. Callies, & J. Banta, The Takings Issue (1973).

S. Eagle, Regulatory Takings (2nd ed. 2001).

Land Use and The Constitution: Principles for Planning Practice (B. Blaesser & A. Weinstein eds., 1989).

R. Meltz, D. Merriam & R. Frank, the Takings Issue (1999).

Articles

Allee, Drawing the Line in Regulatory Takings Law: How a Benefits Fraction Supports the Fee Simple Approach to the Denominator Problem, 70 Fordham L. Rev. 1957 (2002).

Berger, Supreme Bait & Switch: The Ripeness Ruse in Regulatory Takings, 3 Wash. U. J.L. & Pol'y 137 (2000).

Blaesser, Closing the Federal Courthouse Door on Property Owners: The Ripeness and Abstention Doctrines in Section 1983 Land Use Cases, 2 Hofstra Prop. L.J. 73 (1989).

Blaesser, Substantive Due Process Protection at the Outer Margins of Municipal Behavior, 3 Wash. U. J.L. & Pol'y 583 (2000).

Blais, Takings, Statutes, and the Common Law: Considering Inherent Limitations on Title, 70 S. Cal. L. Rev. 1 (1996).

Bley & Axelrad, The Search for Constitutionally Protected "Property" in Land-Use Law, 29 Urb. Law. 251 (1997).

Brauneis, "The Foundation of our 'Regulatory Takings' Jurisprudence": The Myth and Meaning of Justice Holmes' Opinion in *Pennsylvania Coal Co. v. Mahon*, 106 Yale L.J. 613 (1996).

Brownstein, Illicit Legislative Motive in the Municipal Land Use Regulation Process, 57 U. Cin. L. Rev. 1 (1988).

Buchsbaum, Did *Palazzolo* Answer the Tough Takings Questions?, Land Use L. & Zoning Dig. vol. 53, no. 11, at 8 (2001).

Burling, The Latest Take on Background Principles and the States' Law of Property After *Lucas* and *Palazzolo*, 24 U. Hawaii L. Rev. 497 (2002).

Burton, Predatory Municipal Zoning Practices: Changing the Presumption of Constitutionality in the Wake of the Takings Trilogy, 44 Ark. L. Rev. 65 (1991).

Callies, & Breemer, The Right to Exclude Others From Private Property: A Fundamental Constitutional Right, 3 Wash. U. J.L. & Pol'y 39 (2000).

Chesney, Old Wine or New? The Shocks-the-Conscience Standard and the Distinction Between Legislative and Executive Action, 50 Syracuse L. Rev. 981 (2000).

Cobb, Land Use Law: Marred by Public Agency Abuse, 3 Wash. U.J.L. & Pol'y 195 (2000).

Cordes, Leapfrogging the Constitution: The Rise of State Takings Legislation, 24 Ecology L.Q. 187 (1997).

Cordes, Property Rights and Land Use Controls: Balancing Private and Public Interests, 19 N. Ill. U. L. Rev. 629 (1999).

Coursen, Property Rights Legislation: A Survey of Federal and State Assessment and Compensation Measures, 29 Envtl. L. Rptr. 10239 (1996).

Delaney & Desiderio, Who Will Clean Up the "Ripeness Mess"? A Call for Reform so Takings Plaintiffs Can Enter the Federal Courthouse, 31 Urb. Law. 195 (1999).

DiMento, Mining the Archives of *Pennsylvania Coal*: Heaps of Constitutional Mischief, 11 J. Legal Hist. 349 (1990).

Eagle, Just Compensation for Permanent Takings of Temporal Interests, 10 Fed. Circuit B.J. 485 (2001).

Eagle, The 1997 Regulatory Takings Quartet: Retreating From the "Rule of Law," 42 N.Y.L. Sch. L. Rev. 345 (1998).

Eagle, Substantive Due Process and Regulatory Takings: A Reappraisal, 51 Ala. L. Rev. 977 (2000).

Eagle, The Rise and Rise of "Investment-Backed Expectations," 32 Urb. Law. 437 (2000).

Echeverria, A Turning of the Tide: The *Tahoe-Sierra* Regulatory Takings Decision, 32 Envtl. L. Rep. 11235 (2002).

Echeverria, Does a Regulation that Fails to Advance a Legitimate Governmental Interest Result in a Regulatory Takings?, 29 Envtl. L. 853 (1999).

Echeverria, Is the *Penn Central* Three-Factor Test Ready for History's Dustbin?, Land Use L. & Zoning Dig., Vol. 52, No. 1, at 3 (2000).

Echeverria, Takings and Errors, 51 Ala. L. Rev. 1047 (2000).

Ellis, Neighborhood Opposition and the Permissible Purposes of Zoning, 7 Land Use & Envt'l L. Rev. 275 (1992).

Frieden, Towards a Political Economy of Takings, 3 Wash. U. J.L. & Pol'y 137 (2000).

Freyfogle, Regulatory Takings, Methodically, 31 Envt. L. Rep. 10251 (2001).

Glicksman, Making a Nuisance of Takings Law, 3 Wash. U.J.L. & Pol'y 149 (2000).

Guy & Holloway, The Direction of Regulatory Takings Analysis in the Post-Lochner Era, 102 Dick. L. Rev. 327 (1998).

Halper, Why the Nuisance Knot Can't Undo the Takings Muddle, 28 Ind. L. Rev. 329 (1995).

Haar & Wolf, *Euclid* Lives: The Survival of Progressive Jurisprudence, 115 Harv. L. Rev. 2158 (2002).

Jacobs, The Impact of State Property Rights Laws: Those Laws and My Land, Land Use L. & Zoning Dig., Vol. 50, No. 3, at 3 (1998).

Kanner, Hunting the Snark, Not the Quark: Has the U.S. Supreme Court Been Competent in Its Effort to Formulate Coherent Regulatory Takings Law?, 30 Urb. Law. 307 (1998).

Kmiec, The "Substantially Advance" Quandary: How Closely Should Courts Examine the Regulatory Means and Ends of Legislative Applications?, 22 Zoning & Plan. L. Rep. 97 (1999).

Lisker, Regulatory Takings and the Denominator Problem, 27 Rutgers L.J. 663 (1996).

Lyman, Finality Ripeness in Federal Land Use Cases From *Hamilton Bank* to *Lucas*, 9 J. Land Use & Envtl. L. 101 (1994).

Mandelker, Entitlement to Substantive Due Process: Old Versus New Property in Land Use Regulation, 3 Wash. U. J.L. & Pol'y 61 (2000).

Mandelker, Investment-Backed Expectations in Takings Law, 27 Urb. Law. 215 (1995).

Mandelker & Tarlock, Shifting the Presumption of Constitutionality in Land Use Law, 24 Urb. Law. 1 (1992).

Martinez, Statutes Enacting Takings Law: Flying in the Face of Uncertainty, 26 Urb. Law. 327 (1994).

Martinez & Martinez, A Prudential Theory for Providing a Forum for Federal Takings Claims, 36 Real Prop., Prob. & Trust J. 445 (2001).

McGuiness, Equal Protection for Non-Suspect Class Victims of Governmental Misconduct: Theory and Proof of Disparate Treatment and Arbitrariness Claims, 18 Campbell L. Rev. 333 (1996).

Overstreet, The Ripeness Doctrine of the Takings Clause: A Survey of Decisions Showing Just How Far Federal Courts Will Go to Avoid Adjudicating Land Use Cases, 10 J. Land Use & Envtl. L. 91 (1994).

Roberts, Facial Takings Claims Under *Agins-Nectow*: A Procedural Loose End, 24 U. Hawaii L.J. 623 (2002).

Roberts, Mining With Justice Holmes, 39 Vand. L. Rev. 287 (1986).

Roberts, Procedural Implications of Williamson/First English in Regulatory Takings Legislation: Reservations, Removal, Diversity, Supplemental Jurisdiction, *Rooker-Feldman*, and Res Judicata, 31 Envt. L. Rep. 10350 (2001).

Saxer, Zoning Away First Amendment Rights, 53 W.U.J. Urb. & Contemp. L. 1 (1998).

Sherry, Judicial Federalism in the Trenches: The *Rooker-Feldman* Doctrine in Action, 74 Notre Dame L. Rev. 1085 (1999).

Stein, Who Gets the Takings Claim? Changes in Land Use Law, Pre-Enactment Owners, and Post-Enactment Buyers, 61 Ohio St. L.J. 89 (2000).

Sullivan, Emperors and Clothes: The Genealogy and Operation of the Agins' Tests, 33 Urb. Law 343 (2001).

Sullivan, Return of the Platonic Guardians: *Nollan* and *Dolan* and the First Prong of *Agins*, 34 Urb. Law. 39 (2002).

Thomas, The Illusory Restraints and Empty Promises of New Property Protection Laws, 28 Urb. Law. 223 (1996).

Wade, *Penn Central's* Economic Failings Confounded Takings Jurisprudence, 31 Urb. Law. 277 (1999).

Washburn, "Reasonable Investment-Backed Expectations" As a Factor in Defining Property Interest, 49 J. Urb. & Contemp. L. 63 (1996).

White, State Property Rights Laws: Recent Impacts and Future Implications, Land Use L. & Zoning Dig., Vol. 52, No. 7, at 3 (2000).

Wilson, Nasty Motives: A Consideration of Recent Federal Damages Claims in Land-Use Cases, 31 Urb. Law. 937 (1999).

Wright & Laughner, Shaken, Not Sirred: Has *Tahoe-Sierra* Settled or Muddied the Regulatory Takings Waters?, 32 Envtl. L. Rep. 11177 (2002).

Student Work

Note, Conceptual Severance and Takings in the Federal Circuit, 85 Cornell L. Rev. 586 (2000).

Note, The Demise of Three-Tier Review: Has the United States Supreme Court Adopted a "Sliding Scale"' Approach Toward Equal Protection Jurisprudence? 23 J. Contemp. L. 475–514 (1997).

Note, Florida's Takings Law: A Bark Worse Than Its Bite, 16 Va. Envtl. L.J. 313 (1997).

Note, From Lucas to Palazzolo: A Case Study of Title Limitations. 16 J. Land Use & Envtl. L. 225 (2001).

Note, Have They Gone "Too Far"? An Evaluation and Comparison of 1995 State Takings Legislation, 30 Ga. L. Rev. 1061 (1996).

Note, Is the Court One Step Closer to Unraveling the Takings and Due Process Clauses?, 77 N.C. L. Rev. 1525 (1999).

Note, The Origins and Original Significance of the Just Compensation Clause of the Fifth Amendment, 94 Yale L.J. 694 (1985).

Note, A Standard for "Class of One" Claims Under the Equal Protection Clause of the Fourteenth Amendment: Protecting Victims of Non-Class Based Discrimination From Vindictive State Action, 35 Val. U.L. Rev. 197 (2000).

Note, Trying to Halt the Procedural Merry-Go-Round: The Ripeness of Regulatory Takings Claims After *Palazzolo v. Rhode Island*,46 St. Louis U.L.J. 833 (2002).

Note, Ultra Vires Takings, 97 Mich. L. Rev. 245 (1998).

Comment, Freedom of Expression and Adult Entertainment: The Naked Truth. 37 Duq. L. Rev. 103 (1998).

Comment, Texas Private Real Property Rights Preservation Act: A Political Solution to the Regulatory Takings Problem, 27 St. Mary's L.J. 557 (1996).

Comment, Unearthing the Denominator in Regulatory Takings Cases, 61 U. Chi. L. Rev. 1535 (1994).

Student article. Protecting the "Class of One" (Village of Willowbrook v. Olech, 2001 Real Prop.Prob. & Tr. J. 331–363 (2001).

SELECTION OF ARTICLES ON THE SUPREME COURT'S 1987 Takings TRILOGY

Berger, Happy Birthday, Constitution: The Supreme Court Establishes New Ground Rules for Land-Use Planning, 20 Urb. Law. 735 (1988).

Berger, The Year of the Takings Issue, 1 B.Y.U.J. Pub. L. 262 (1987).

Callies, Property Rights: Are There Any Left?, 20 Urb. Law. 597 (1988).

Epstein, Takings: Descent and Resurrection, 1987 Sup. Ct. Rev. 1 (1987).

Freilich & Morgan, Municipal Strategies for Imposing Valid Development Exactions: Responding to *Nollan*, 10 Zoning & Plan. L. Rep. 169 (1987).

Large, The Supreme Court and the Takings Clause: The Search for a Better Rule, 18 Envtl. L. 3 (1987).

Lawrence, Means, Motives, and Takings: the Nexus Test of Nollan v. California Coastal Commission, 12 Harv. Envtl. L.J. 231 (1988).

Lawrence, Regulatory Takings: Beyond the Balancing Test, 20 Urb. Law. 389 (1988).

Mandelker, Waiving the Taking Clause: Mixed Signals from the Supreme Court, Land Use L. & Zoning Dig., Vol. 40, No. 11, at 3 (1988).

Martinez, A Critical Analysis of the 1987 Takings Trilogy: The *Keystone, Nollan and First English* Cases, 1 Hofstra Prop. L.J. 39 (1988).

Myers, Some Observations on the Analysis of Regulatory Takings in the Rehnquist Court, 23 Val. U.L. Rev. 527 (1989).

Peterson, The Takings Clause: In Search of Underlying Principles Part I — A Critique of Current Takings Clause Doctrine, 77 Calif. L. Rev. 1299 (1989).

Peterson, The Takings Clause: In Search of Underlying Principles Part II — Takings as Intentional Deprivations of Property Without Moral Justification, 78 Calif. L. Rev. 53 (1990).

Salsich, *Keystone Bituminous Coal, First English* and *Nollan*: A Framework for Accommodation?, 34 Wash. U.J. Urb. & Contemp. L. 173 (1988).

Sax, Property Rights in the U.S. Supreme Court: A Status Report, 7 UCLA J. Envtl. L. & Pol'y 139 (1988).

Siemon, Who Owns Cross Creek? 5 J. Land Use & Envtl. L. 323 (1990).

Siemon & Larson, The Takings Issue Trilogy: The Beginning of the End, 33 Wash. U.J. Urb. & Contemp. L. 169 (1988).

Williams & Ernst, And Now We Are Here on a Darkling Plain, 13 Vt. L. Rev. 635 (1989).

SELECTED ARTICLES ON THE SUPREME COURT'S *LUCAS* DECISION

Berlin, Just Compensation Doctrine and the Workings of Government: The Threat From the Supreme Court and Possible Responses, 17 Harv. Envtl. L. Rev. 97 (1993).

Brown, Takings: Who Says it Needs to be So Confusing?, 22 Stetson L. Rev. 379 (1993).

Delaney, Advancing Private Property Rights: The Lessons of *Lucas*, 22 Stetson L. Rev. 395 (1993).

Hartman, *Lucas v. South Carolina Coastal Council*: The Takings Test Turns a Corner, 23 Envt'l L. Rep. 10003 (1993).

Humbach, Evolving Threshold of Nuisance and the Takings Clause, 18 Colum. J. Envtl. L. 1 (1993).

Lazarus, Putting the Correct "Spin" on *Lucas*, 45 Stan. L. Rev. 1411 (1993).

Lucas v. South Carolina Coastal Council, Colloquium, 10 Pace Envt'l L. Rev. 1 (1992).

Mandelker, Of Mice and Missiles: A True Account of *Lucas v. South Carolina Coastal Council*, 8 J. Land Use & Envt'l L. 285 (1993).

Morgan, Takings Law: Strategies for Dealing with *Lucas*, Land Use L. & Zoning Dig., Vol. 45, No. 1, at 3 (1993).

Pershkow & Houseman, In the Wake of *Lucas v. South Carolina Coastal Council*: A Critical Look at Six Questions Practitioners Should be Asking, 23 Envt'l. L. Rep. 10008 (1993).

Sax, Property Rights and the Economy of Nature: Understanding *Lucas v. South Carolina Coastal Council*, 45 Stan. L. Rev. 1433 (1993).

Washburn, Land Use Control, the Individual, and Society: *Lucas v. South Carolina Coastal Council*, 52 Md. L. Rev. 162 (1993).

Chapter 3

THE COMPREHENSIVE PLAN

Synopsis

A. ROLE OF THE COMPREHENSIVE PLAN.

§ 3.01   Planning and Land Use Regulation.
§ 3.02   The Planning Process and the Plan.
§ 3.03   Criticisms of Planning.
§ 3.04   Planning Today.

B. PLANNING LEGISLATION.

§ 3.05   The Standard Planning Act.
§ 3.06   The Planning Commission.
§ 3.07   The Elements of the Plan.
§ 3.08   Plan Adoption.
§ 3.09   State Planning Legislation.
§ 3.10   Required and Optional Planning Elements.
§ 3.11   Planning Policies for Lower-Income Housing.
§ 3.12   Mandatory Planning.

C. THE COMPREHENSIVE PLAN AND LAND USE CONTROLS.

§ 3.13   Zoning "in Accordance with" a Comprehensive Plan.
§ 3.14   The Majority Judicial View: A Plan Is Not Required.
§ 3.15   The Minority Judicial View: Consistency Is Required.
§ 3.16   Statutory Consistency Requirements.
§ 3.17   Upzoning to Comply With the Plan.
§ 3.18   Land Use Conflicts.
§ 3.19   Plans and the Takings Issue.
§ 3.20   The Plan as a Defense to a Taking.
§ 3.21   The Plan as a Taking of Property.
§ 3.22   Judicial Review of Comprehensive Plans.

A.   ROLE OF THE COMPREHENSIVE PLAN.

§ 3.01 Planning and Land Use Regulation.

As any planner can tell you, comprehensive plans come first. Municipalities adopt and administer land use controls, such as zoning, in order to implement comprehensive plans. As any land use lawyer can tell you, the courts were slow to recognize this relationship. For the first fifty years or so of zoning, the courts did not require a comprehensive plan as the basis for the adoption and administration of zoning ordinances. Several state legislatures rejected this rule by mandating the adoption of local comprehensive plans and consistency between plans and zoning. A few courts have also required consistency between zoning and plans. This chapter reviews the role of planning in the land use regulation process.

Comprehensive plans, sometimes known as "general" or "master" plans, have a number of standard characteristics. They plan for the physical development of the community. They are future-oriented and project the development of a community to a future point in time or a future point in the community's growth. Comprehensive plans are geographically and functionally comprehensive. They cover all of the geographic area of the community and include all of the physical elements that determine future community development. Land use, public facilities, and transportation elements are common to all plans. The zoning ordinance is based on and implements the development policies contained in the land use element of the comprehensive plan.

Comprehensive plans usually contain both textual policies and maps. For the land use element the text states the land use policies adopted by the plan. The land use map indicates where development proposed by land use policies should occur. Some comprehensive plans contain highly generalized maps or may dispense with maps altogether and rely on the text to state the community's planning policies. The zoning ordinance implements the land use policies in the comprehensive plan through textual zoning regulations that create land use districts and specify the land uses permitted in these districts. A zoning map classifies all land within the community into one of these zoning districts.

§ 3.02   The Planning Process and the Plan.

Planners prepare comprehensive plans for community adoption in a "rational" planning process. The rational planning process is well-established in planning practice. It requires a series of steps leading up to the preparation and adoption of the comprehensive plan.

The rational planning process begins with a survey and analysis of the data that provide the basis for the plan's policies. Projections are then made for the future development of the community. These projections cover population, the economy, public services and facilities, and private land use. The planning staff then develops a set of goals for the future growth of the community that take these projections into account. Planning goals are highly generalized. They provide the rationale for more detailed planning policies for land development and the other elements in the comprehensive plan. Some plans have three levels of textual statement, although the names given to these levels may vary. In one type of textual hierarchy, planning objectives provide the basis for planning goals, which in turn provide the basis for the more detailed planning policies.

Multifamily housing illustrates how a plan with two levels of textual statement is organized. The plan's housing goal may state that a balanced housing supply is one of the goals the plan seeks to implement. This goal contemplates multifamily development. A detailed planning policy on multifamily housing would then indicate the conditions under which this kind of development can occur. The policy may state, for example, that multifamily housing should occur at highway interchanges near nonresidential development to minimize journeys to work.

Problems can arise in translating the land use map into mapped zoning districts when a comprehensive plan contains a land use map. Land use categories in the plan's land use map are usually more generalized than the land use districts in the zoning ordinance. The zoning map must translate these generalized land use categories into more detailed land use districts in a manner that implements the policies of the comprehensive plan.

Planners usually develop more than one set of planning goals and policies for the comprehensive plan. They test these goals and policies for feasibility and acceptability, usually through public hearings and other forms of public participation. The goals and policies selected form the basis for the preparation of the final comprehensive plan.

§ 3.03 Criticisms of Planning.

Critics raise several objections to rational planning. They claim the political process is unable to specify planning goals and policies with sufficient precision. They claim that land use policies for future development are subject to error because the planner cannot control all of the factors that influence new development. He cannot control changes in economic conditions, for example, which may depress housing construction or require industrial developers to modify development plans.

Critics also claim planning ignores the nonphysical consequences of community development. One criticism is that planners ignore the social impact of their plans, which is difficult to measure and quantify. Until recently, comprehensive plans also paid little or no attention to the environmental impact of new development. These omissions lead to what some call "partial planning" — the inability to integrate all of the necessary variables affected by community development in a comprehensive plan.

A final criticism of comprehensive planning concentrates on the limitations of a process that assembles complex data to make conditional predictions. Professor Lindblom articulated these criticisms in a leading article.[1] He argued that limited intellectual capacity and resources, the interdependence between fact and value judgments, inadequate analytic systems, and the diversity of forms in which problems actually arise prevent successful comprehensive planning.

---

[1] "The Science of Muddling Through," 19 Pub. Admin. Rev. 79 (1959). *See also* Lindblom, "Still Muddling, Not Yet Through," 39 Pub. Admin. Rev. 517 (1979).

Lindblom suggested an alternative planning process known as "incremental" planning.

Problems are not "solved" through incremental planning but are marginally and repeatedly attacked. Ends and means are chosen simultaneously and are continually explored. Policy analysis and policy making are incomplete at any one point. They are remedial because they move away from perceived problems rather than toward fixed objectives. The political process ensures that issues ignored at one stage in the planning process receive attention at a later stage. Incrementalists claim that incremental planning can avoid the errors that may occur in a comprehensive planning process.

§ 3.04 Planning Today.

Planning practice today has overcome many of these criticisms. The criticism that planning is not sufficiently comprehensive or politically connected is blunted by new consensus-building approaches through citizen participation. Although citizen participation is not without its critics, it can provide a source of information and innovative approaches, secure feedback for planners, and help define the public interest in the planning process more accurately. Statutes have also made plans more comprehensive by including additional elements, such as housing and environmental elements, that were lacking historically.

A related change in comprehensive planning ties the planning process more closely with the political process. As originally conceived, planning was policy-neutral. Planners served an independent and politically removed planning commission and did not always seek political input into the planning process. Most planning directors are now appointed by the chief executive and work directly with the executive branch. Planners produce alternative goals and policies for political decision makers to consider and adopt in the political process. This view of planning sees the political decision maker as responsible for the adoption of planning policy. Planners assist by presenting and clarifying policy alternatives.

Planners can avoid the difficulties of plans that project long-range development policies in favor of plans that cover a shorter time frame. This approach helps avoid planning errors arising from inaccurate projections. These so-called "middle-range" plans are now common, and some statutes require them. Planning error is also avoidable through periodic revision of the plan, often at yearly intervals. As an alternative, the community can adopt short-range periodic plans to implement the policies of the long-range comprehensive plan.

Communities can also achieve more flexibility in planning by adopting a geographic hierarchy of land use plans. They supplement a comprehensive plan for the entire community with more detailed plans for subareas and even local neighborhoods. This planning technique allows planners to implement the plan in sequence and over time as development trends become clearer and projections are revised.

New computer-based systems have moderated criticisms that planning cannot assemble complex data to make conditional predictions. These systems include electronic spreadsheets and geographic information systems that make it much easier to test out development scenarios and impacts and react to proposed changes quickly.

Land use plans today fall into four prototypes, although many communities combine them into hybrids.[1] The traditional land use design plan proposes a future and long-range urban form that consists of designated land uses and a circulation system. The land use classification plan is a more proactive general map of growth policy areas that indicates where growth will occur. The policy plan uses verbal policy statements to project land use futures and de-emphasizes mapping. The development management plan proposes specific policy actions to guide development, such as a public investment program, and assumes the public sector will influence growth management.

B. PLANNING LEGISLATION.

§ 3.05 The Standard Planning Act.

Model acts proposed by the U.S. Department of Commerce in the 1920s still dominate state legislation for planning and zoning. One model act provided legislative authority for planning and the other authorized zoning. The model planning legislation also authorized controls over subdivisions. Although the planning act should have come first, the strong political demand for legislation authorizing zoning led to the publication of the zoning act first. This inverted publication sequence contributed to the early failure to integrate zoning with the planning process. The model planning act was entitled A Standard City Planning Enabling Act and will be called the Standard Planning Act or Standard Act. Much modern planning legislation still shows the influence of the Standard Act, even though this Act was not as popular as its sister zoning act and did not adopt it.

Several policy decisions made in the Standard Planning Act continue to influence land use planning today. In one of its most important decisions, the Act made planning optional rather than mandatory and most states followed this model. This decision had important consequences for land use regulation, because the Standard Planning Act did not prevent a municipality from zoning without having adopted a comprehensive plan. Language in the zoning act might have compelled a different result, but the courts did not initially read that statute this

---

[1] This paragraph is based on Kaiser & Godschalk, Twentieth Century Land Use Planning: A Stalwart Family Tree, 61 J. Am. Plan. Ass'n 365 (1995).

way. The absence of planning in some communities may have led courts to hold that the adoption and implementation of zoning ordinances did not depend on the adoption of a comprehensive plan.

The Standard Planning Act was process-oriented. It provided the authority for planning and specified the role local agencies were to play in that process. It also specified the issues and elements that local comprehensive plans were required to address. The Standard Act did not include substantive planning policies but left the development of these policies to the local planning process. This decision was probably wise, because the variety of settings in which planning occurs may make the inclusion of substantive planning policies in state planning legislation undesirable. There are some exceptions, such as planning policies for lower-income housing. Some critics also claim the process-oriented requirements in the Standard Planning Act led to an elevation of process over substance. They argue that the Act's process orientation allows communities to adopt regressive social policies. Exclusionary land use policies are an example. The American Planning Association has proposed model legislation intended to replace the Standard Planning and Zoning Acts.[1] Unlike the Standard Acts, the APA model legislation is the product of a lengthy collaborative process that included an advisory committee representing the important interest groups. The APA legislation also contains alternate legislative proposals rather than a single model for legislative adoption.

§ 3.06   The Planning Commission.

The Standard Planning Act delegated the development of planning policy to a planning commission appointed by the local chief executive. This choice was deliberate. Reformist local government theory at the time held that independent local commissions responsible for policy development should be independent of local politics. In the case of planning, this independence was considered a strength. Many communities reinforce this political independence by making planning staff responsible to the planning commission.

The Standard Act contemplated a lay planning commission. In an important footnote to the Act, its drafters pointedly stated that the Act provided no professional qualifications for commission members. "Capacity for leadership in city planning . . . constitutes the best qualification." The planning commission was expected to promote the advantages of city planning to the community and to the political decision makers. Many modern-day reformers criticize the political isolation of the planning process and even propose abolition of the planning commission.

---

[1] American Planning Association, Growing Smart Legislative Guidebook: Model Statutes for Planning and Management of Change (S. Meck ed. 2002). The legislation is available at www.planning.org.

The independent planning commission is partly responsible for the fragmented decision making that is typical in planning and land use regulation. It usually reviews and approves the zoning ordinance and any amendments to it, and may also approve subdivisions, site plans, planned unit developments and conditional uses. Early reformers may have considered fragmentation desirable, but it dilutes political responsibility in a decision-making process in which political responsibility for policy decisions is essential. The APA Model legislation does not require the creation of a planning commission and authorizes the preparation of the comprehensive plan by the planning staff as an alternative.[1]

§ 3.07   The Elements of the Plan.

The Standard Planning Act provided a "shopping list" of public capital facilities and private and public utility facilities for which the plan was required to provide policies. The Standard Act did not detail the contents of plan elements, establish planning priorities, require the integration of planning policies, or demand internal consistency. Modern state planning legislation follows the Standard Act model but groups the facilities for which policies are required into several planning "elements," including a capital facilities and a transportation element. The Standard Planning Act did not require the municipality to follow the plan when making capital facility decisions. Section 9 provided that the "location, character and extent thereof of any public capital improvement covered by an adopted plan, as well as any private utility improvement, must be submitted to the planning commission for approval. If the planning commission disapproved, the legislative body could override it but only by a two-thirds vote. Much modern planning legislation retains this provision.

The Standard Act did not require a land use element. It did require a zoning plan to control the "height, area, bulk, location, and use of buildings and premises." The zoning plan element created much confusion, and the drafters did not provide a satisfactory explanation for its inclusion. A comprehensive plan is future-oriented and general, while the zoning "plan" contemplated standards regulating the detailed use of property. Modern planning legislation does not usually require a zoning plan but does require a land use element.

§ 3.08   Plan Adoption.

Section 6 of the Standard Planning Act authorized both the preparation and the adoption of the plan by the planning commission rather than the council. The drafters made this decision intentionally. They pointed out in a footnote that the plan covered a period of years longer than the term of any one council, that the council dealt only with "pressing and immediate" needs, and that a hostile council could reject a plan adopted by an earlier council. The decision to require

---

[1] APA Guidebook at §§ 7-102, 7-103.

adoption of the plan by the planning commission reflected the related decision to insulate the planning process from local politics.[1]

Some critics would require adoption of the plan by the legislative body so that the plan will be politically endorsed. The APA model legislation authorizes this alternative.[2]

§ 3.09   State Planning Legislation.

State legislation that authorizes comprehensive planning shows the influence of the Standard Planning Act in many states. Statutory authority for the comprehensive plan may still track the language of the Standard Act and provide a comparable shopping list of elements the plan must contain.[1] A number of states have modernized their planning legislation by revising and adding to the required and optional planning elements, by providing substantive planning policies for lower-income housing, and by mandating planning.

§ 3.10   Required and Optional Planning Elements.

Most modern planning legislation does not adopt the Standard Act's shopping list. Instead, it contains a set of mandatory and optional planning elements that define what the comprehensive plan should contain.[1] Like the Standard Act, most state statutes do not specify the content of plan elements in detail. All states have transportation elements, practically all have land use elements, about two-third have environmental elements and half have housing elements. Pennsylvania is typical.[2] The plan is to include maps, charts and textual matter and is to include "a statement of objectives of the municipality concerning its future development." Elements in the plan are to address issues such as land use, housing needs, the "movement of people and goods," and community facilities. The plan also must include "a discussion of short-and long-range plan implementation strategies."

Florida legislation contains detailed guidelines for the land use element of the comprehensive plan and also specifies more detailed guidance for the comprehensive plan through administrative regulations.[3] It is to show the "proposed future distribution, location, and extent" of land uses, and must have "standards" for the control and distribution of population and building densities. In addition, "the

---

[1] *See* Alameda County Land Use Ass'n v. City of Hayward, 45 Cal. Rptr. 2d 752 (Cal. App. 1995) (giving other jurisdictions veto on plan is improper delegation of legislative authority)

[2] APA Guidebook at § 7-201.

[1] Ohio Rev. Code § 713.02.

[1] Colo. Rev. Stat. § 30-28-106; .Del. Code Ann. tit. 9, § 2656; Fla. Stat. Ann. § 163.3177; Md. Ann. Code art. 66B, § 3.05; N.H. Rev. Stat. Ann. § 674:2; S.C. Code Ann. § 6-29-510; Tex. Local Gov't Code § 219.002; Va. Code § 15.2-2223; Wis. Stat. § 66.1001.

[2] Pa. Stat. Ann. tit. 53, § 10301.

[3] Fla. Stat. Ann. § 163.3177(6)(a).

proposed distribution, location, and extent of the various categories of land use shall be shown" on a land use map. This degree of detail provides necessary guidance in determining whether zoning is consistent with a plan, which Florida requires. The Florida statute also encourages innovative planning and development strategies to accommodate growth in an environmentally acceptable manner, such as clustering, urban villages, and mixed-use development.[4]

Planning statutes may also authorize additional required and optional planning elements.[5] Optional elements may include environmental,[6] recreational, housing and community design elements, though in some states some or all of these elements may be mandatory. Statutes may also require growth management elements in comprehensive plans, including the designation of urban growth boundaries.[7] An urban growth boundary marks the dividing line between areas where growth can and cannot occur. The APA model legislation contains a list of required and optional elements for comprehensive plans.[8] Land use and other traditional plan elements, such as a transportation element are required.

One of the problems with the Standard Act was that it did not require integration and internal consistency among plan elements. Some states have remedied this problem. For example, California provides in its statement of legislative intent that the comprehensive plan and its elements must be "an integrated internally consistent and compatible statement."[9]

§ 3.11 Planning Policies for Lower-Income Housing.

A significant number of states require a housing element in their planning legislation, and the statute usually requires the adoption of policies for lower-income housing.[1] The California legislation is a good example. It states:

> The housing element shall consist of an identification and analysis of existing and projected housing needs and a statement of goals, policies, quantified objectives, financial resources, and scheduled programs for the preservation,

---

[4] Fla. Stat. Ann. § 161.3177(11)(b).

[5] *E.g.*, Cal. Gov't Code § 65303; Fla. Stat. Ann. § 163.3177; Utah Code Ann. § 17-27-301 (wildlife habitat and economic stability); Wash. Rev. Code Ann. §§ 36.70.340–350.

[6] *E.g.*, Md. Ann. Code art. 66B, § 3.05(1)(viii); N.Y. Town Law § 272-a(d).

[7] E.g., Ariz. Rev. Stat. §§ 9-461.05 (D0(2), 11-826; Maine Ann. Art.30A, § 4326.3A; Oregon Dep't of Land Conserv. & Dev., Statewide Goals & Guidelines, Goal 14; Tenn. Code Ann. § 6-58-104; Wash. Rev. Code §§ 36.70A.106, 36.70A.040. *See also* APA Guidebook at (authorizing designation of urban growth boundaries by regional agency).

[8] APA Guidebook at § 7-702. *See also* § 12-101 (authorizing environmental analysis in comprehensive plan).

[9] Cal. Gov't Code § 65300.5, *applied in* Hernandez v City of Encinitas, 33 Cal Rptr. 2d 875 (Cal. App. 1994). *See also* Wash. Rev. Code Ann. § 36.70A.070.

[1] *E.g.*, Ariz. Rev. Stat. Ann. § 9-461.05(D)(6) (municipalities); Conn. Gen. Stat. § 8-23; N.Y. Town Law § 277-a(3)(h); R.I. Gen. Laws § 45-22.2-6(C); Vt. Stat. Ann. tit. 24, § 4302(C)(11).

improvement, and development of housing. The housing element shall identify adequate sites for housing, including rental housing, factory-built housing, and mobile homes, and shall make adequate provision for the existing and projected needs of all economic segments of the community.[2]

The legislation requires an inventory and analysis of housing needs and a five-year schedule of actions to be implemented, in part, through "the administration of land use and development controls."

Florida has similar legislation that requires "a housing element consisting of standards, plans, and principles to be followed in" meeting housing needs including "the provision of housing for all current and anticipated future residents of the jurisdiction."[3] The housing element must also designate "adequate sites" for needed housing. Oregon legislation includes a comparable lower-income housing policy for its state land use planning program.[4] Local plans and land use regulations must comply with this policy. The Oregon legislation also states that "any approval standards, special conditions and the procedures for approval adopted by a local government shall be clear and objective and shall not have the effect, either in themselves or cumulatively, of discouraging needed housing through unreasonable cost or delay."[5]

§ 3.12 Mandatory Planning.

Legislation in a number of states makes planning mandatory for all or some units of local government.[1] These states require the adoption of comprehensive plans, but they may or may not require consistency between land use controls and the plan.[2] About half the states make planning conditionally mandatory by requiring the adoption of a plan, at least by the planning commission, if a municipality decides to create one.

---

[2] Cal. Gov't Code § 65583. *See also* § 65584. For additional discussion of the California legislation, see § 7.28.

[3] Fla. Stat. Ann. § 163.3177(6)(f)1.

[4] Or. Rev. Stat. §§ 197.303, 197.307.

[5] Or. Rev. Stat. § 107.307(6).

[1] *E.g.,* Cal. Gov't Code § 65103; Fla. Stat. Ann. § 163.3167; Ky. Rev. Stat. § 100.183; Nev. Rev. Stat. § 278.150; Or. Rev. Stat. § 197.175(2)(a); R.I. Gen. Laws § 45-22.2-5; Wash. Rev. Code Ann. § 36.70A.040.

[2] § 3.16.

C. THE COMPREHENSIVE PLAN AND LAND USE CONTROLS.

§ 3.13 Zoning "in Accordance with" a Comprehensive Plan.

Whether or not a comprehensive plan is mandatory, the courts must determine whether zoning must be consistent with the comprehensive plan.[1] The Standard Zoning Enabling Act states in § 3 that zoning must be "in accordance with a comprehensive plan." A majority of states include this language in their zoning legislation. At first glance, this language means what it says and supports a judicial interpretation that zoning must be "in accordance" with a comprehensive plan if one exists.

Commentary to the Standard Zoning Act suggests a different view and indicates the draftsmen meant only that zoning be done comprehensively and not in a piecemeal manner.[2] This interpretation indicates that courts can find the "comprehensive plan" contemplated by the Act in the provisions of the zoning ordinance and that a comprehensive plan as a separate document is not necessary.[3] This interpretation, which a majority of the courts have adopted, is discussed in the next section.

§ 3.14 The Majority Judicial View: A Plan Is Not Required.

Most courts that have considered the question hold that the "in accordance" requirement does not mandate the adoption of a comprehensive plan as a condition to the exercise of the zoning power.[1] The leading case is *Kozesnik v. Township of Montgomery*.[2] New Jersey had incorporated the "in accordance" language in its zoning legislation. The plaintiff argued that a zoning amendment was ultra vires because the municipality violated the statutory requirement by

---

[1] *See also* holding that a comprehensive plan is not a zoning ordinance that regulates land use, Theobald v. Board of County Comm'rs, 644 P.2d 942 (Colo. 1982); Ash Grove Cement Co. v. Jefferson County, 943 P.2d 85 (Mont. 1997).

[2] The Standard Zoning Act § 3, n. 22.

[3] Ford v. Board of County Commr's, 924 P.2d 91 (Wyo. 1996), explains the difference between a comprehensive plan and a zoning ordinance.

[1] Theobald v. Board of County Comm'rs, 644 P.2d 942 (Colo. 1982); Furtney v. Simsbury Zoning Comm'n, 271 A.2d 319 (Conn. 1970); Dawson Enters., Inc. v. Blaine County, 567 P.2d 1257 (Idaho 1977); Iowa Coal Mining Co. Inc. v. Monroe County, 494 N.W.2d 664 (Iowa 1993); Nottingham Village, Inc. v. Baltimore County, 292 A.2d 680 (Md. 1972); State ex rel. Chiavola v. Village of Oakwood, 886 S.W.2d 74 (Mo. App. 1994); Udell v. Haas, 235 N.E.2d 897 (N.Y. 1968); Cleaver v. Board of Adjustment, 200 A.2d 408 (Pa. 1964); Hadley v. Harold Realty Co., 198 A.2d 149 (R.I. 1964); West Hall Citizens for Controlled Dev. Density v. King County Council, 627 P.2d 1002 (Wash. App. 1981); Bell v. City of Elkhorn, 364 N.W.2d 144 (Wis. 1985) (quoting this treatise). *See also* Colo. Rev. Stat. §§ 30-28-106(3)(F), 31-23-206(3) (master plan advisory).

[2] 131 A.2d 1 (N.J. 1957).

not adopting a comprehensive plan. The court disagreed, and relied on the history of the state's planning and zoning legislation to hold that it did not require an independently adopted comprehensive plan. The court noted that New Jersey, following the model act sequence, adopted its zoning legislation before its planning legislation.

Although it held the "in accordance" requirement did not require a comprehensive plan, the court held that this requirement imposed a fairness and reasonableness test on zoning. It relied on early zoning cases to hold that the intent of the "in accordance" requirement was to prevent a "capricious exercise" of the zoning power. Although it did not supply a definition of "in accordance," the court held that the term plan "connotes an integrated product of a rational process and 'comprehensive' requires something beyond a piecemeal approach, both to be revealed by the ordinance considered in relation to the physical facts and the [statutory] purposes." Later New Jersey legislation modified this holding.[3]

Other courts have adopted a weak limitation on zoning, which is based on the "in accordance" requirement. As the Rhode Island court put it, this requirement means only that "the zoning regulation reflect the necessary relation between . . . the zoning power and the grounds upon which the police power of the state may properly be exercised."[4] This decision means that the "in accordance" requirement only restates substantive due process limitations, which require zoning to implement the health, safety, morals, and general welfare.

New York follows the majority view but also imposes a reasonableness requirement as an interpretation of the "in accordance" language. In *Udell v. Haas*,[5] in response to local pressure, the municipality quickly downzoned a property from commercial to residential in an area that the community's zoning policy had long identified as appropriate for commercial development. These circumstances led the court to hold that the downzoning was not "in accordance" with the comprehensive plan. More than "mock" obedience to this statutory requirement is necessary. Communities must show that a zoning change does not conflict with its basic land use policies. In states where a statute or judicial decision requires consistency with an adopted land use plan, courts apply a plan "consistency" requirement to reach similar results.[6]

§ 3.15   The Minority Judicial View: Consistency Is Required.

Fasano v. Board of County Comm'rs,[1] an Oregon case, adopted a consistency requirement in the absence of legislation imposing one. The court invalidated

---

[3] *See* § 3.16, n. 42.

[4] Hadley v. Harold Realty Co., 198 A.2d 149, 153 (R.I. 1964).

[5] 235 N.E.2d 897 (N.Y. 1968).

[6] § 3.15.

[1] 507 P.2d 23 (Or. 1973). *But see* Green v. County Council, 508 A.2d 882 (Del. Ch. 1986) (interpreting statute to require plan as basis for zoning).

a zoning map amendment because it was not consistent with the local plan. *Fasano* was not an interpretation of the "in accordance" requirement, and Oregon legislation now mandates the adoption of comprehensive plans and requires local land use actions to be consistent with them.

Fasano placed a limitation on the consistency requirement. It held the proponent of a zoning change must also prove the public need for the change and show that no other alternative available property serves that need better. A later case, *Neuberger v. City of Portland*,[2] dropped this limitation because the statute now required local comprehensive plans to comply with state planning goals.

Fasano applied only to a rezoning. A later decision, *Baker v. City of Milwaukee*,[3] required the land use restrictions in a zoning ordinance to be consistent with a comprehensive plan. Neighbors challenged a zoning ordinance allowing a residential density more intensive than a subsequently adopted comprehensive plan permitted. The court required a revision of the zoning ordinance to comply with the plan. "Upon passage of a comprehensive plan a city assumes a responsibility to effectuate that plan and conform prior conflicting zoning ordinances to it."[4] *Baker* implied the converse of its holding also is true: A local government must amend its zoning ordinance to allow a more intensive use as designated in the comprehensive plan. However, a later Oregon intermediate court of appeals case rejected this interpretation and limited *Baker* to its facts.[5]

Although no other court has adopted the *Fasano* and *Baker* consistency requirements, an Illinois appellate court adopted a weak variant.[6] The court held it would not give zoning the usual presumption of constitutionality if a municipality does not have a comprehensive plan. The court shifted the burden to the municipality to justify its land use regulations in this situation.[7] A Pennsylvania Supreme Court decision, which appeared to require the adoption of a comprehensive plan as the basis for land use regulation, is no longer good law in that state.[8] However, if a municipality has adopted a comprehensive plan a court will treat

---

[2] 603 P.2d 771 (Or. 1979).

[3] 533 P.2d 772 (Or. 1975).

[4] *Id.* at 779.

[5] Marracci v. City of Scappoose, 552 P.2d 552 (Or. App. 1976). *Accord,* Board of County Comm'rs. V. Snyder, 627 So. 2d 469 (Fla. 1993); Bone v. City of Lewiston, 693 P.2d 1046 (Idaho 1984). *See also* Boyds Civic Ass'n v. Montgomery County Council, 526 A.2d 598 (Md. 1987).

[6] Forestview Homeowners' Ass'n v. County of Cook, 309 N.E.2d 763 (Ill. App. 1974).

[7] *Accord,* Raabe v. City of Walker, 174 N.W.2d 789 (Mich. 1970); Board of County Comm'rs v. City of Las Vegas, 622 P.2d 695 (N.M. 1980). *Contra,* First Nat'l Bank of Highland Park v. Village of Vernon Hills, 371 N.E.2d 659 (Ill. App. 1977).

[8] Eves v. Zoning Bd. of Adjustment, 164 A.2d 7 (Pa. 1960). *See* Russell v. Penn Twp. Planning Comm'n, 348 A.2d 499 (Pa. Commw. 1975).

the plan as a guide and give it some weight when it reviews a zoning ordinance or land use decision..[9]

§ 3.16 Statutory Consistency Requirements.

Legislation in several states requires zoning to be consistent with a comprehensive plan,[1] but most of this legislation does not define consistency. The California legislation provides a definition. Its mandatory planning legislation provides that consistency requires:

> The various land uses authorized by the [zoning] ordinance are [to be] compatible with the objectives, policies, general land uses, and programs specified in . . . [the] plan.[2]

The Florida legislation provides a more comprehensive definition:

> A development approved or undertaken by a local government shall be consistent with the comprehensive plan if the land uses, densities, or intensities, capacity or size, timing, and other aspects of the development are compatible with and further the objectives, policies, land uses, and densities or intensities in the comprehensive plan and if it meets all other criteria enumerated by the local government.[3]

> A municipality may define, in its charter or by ordinance, the relationship between a comprehensive plan and development regulations and may provide standards for determining the consistency required between a plan and development regulations.[4]

---

[9] Palatine Nat'l Bank v. Village of Barrington, 532 N.E.2d 955 (Ill. App. 1988) (plan to be given weight in zoning decisions); Nova Horizon, Inc. v. City Council, 769 P.2d 721 (Nev. 1989) (plan commands deference and presumption of validity in zoning decisions); West Bluff Neighborhood Ass'n v. City of Albuquerque, 50 P.3d 182 (N.M. App. 2002); Mayhew v. Town of Sunnyvale, 774 S.W.2d 284 (Tex. App. 1989).

[1] E.g., Ariz. Rev. Stat. Ann. § 9-462.01(F) (municipalities); Cal. Gov't Code § 65860; Del. Code Ann. tit. 22, § 702(d). Fla. Stat. Ann. § 163.3194; Ky. Rev. Stat. § 100.213 (unless findings made on whether zoning appropriate or changes have occurred); N.J. Stat. Ann. § 40:55D-62 (governing body may waive); Or. Rev. Stat. § 197.010(3). See also N.J. Rev. Stat. § 40:55D-89.1 (land use regulations lose presumption if plan not updated regularly). See Olson v. City of Deadwood, 480 N.W.2d 170 (S.D. 1992) (ordinance that allows use-on-review procedure is consistent with mandatory planning statute). See Town of Jonesville v. Powell Valley Village Ltd. Partnership, 487 S.E.2d 207 (Va. 1997) (allowing zoning ordinance to substitute for plan would undermine statutory requirement that zoning ordinances must be drawn with "reasonable consideration" of comprehensive plan).

[2] Cal. Gov't Code § 65860(a)(ii).

[3] Fla. Stat. Ann. § 163.3194(3)(b). See also id, § 163.3194(3)(a) (similar provision for development orders and land development regulation); id. § 163.3194(4)(a) (court in reviewing local government action on land development regulations to consider reasonableness of plan and relationship of plan to action).

[4] 235 N.E.2d 897 (N.Y. 1968).

When the statute does not define consistency the courts have developed their own rules to determine when zoning is consistent with a comprehensive plan.[5]

The Texas statute allows municipalities to define consistency:

A municipality may define, in its charter or ordinance, the relationship between a comprehensive plan an development regulations and may provide standards for determining the consistency required between a plan and development regulations.[6]

§ 3.17 Upzoning to Comply With the Plan.

A landowner may apply for an amendment to a zoning ordinance to rezone her property to a more intensive use in order to comply with the land use policies in a comprehensive plan. If the municipality refuses to approve the rezoning, the landowner may argue the consistency requirement mandates the municipality to grant the rezoning so the zoning ordinance will be consistent with the plan. The courts have rejected this argument, holding the consistency requirement does not deprive a municipality of the discretion to decide when an amendment to the zoning ordinance is appropriate.[1] Courts take the same position when the plan states that development at the more intensive use can occur at a later time.[2] However, the Idaho court has also held that failure to upzone to comply with a comprehensive plan is evidence that the refusal to rezone was arbitrary .[3]

§ 3.18 Land Use Conflicts.

Courts apply a "rule of reason" to decide whether land use classifications in a zoning ordinance conflict with land use designations in the comprehensive plan.[1] [2] This problem arises because land uses permitted by the zoning ordinance

---

[5] Little v. Board of County Comm'rs, 631 P.2d 1282 (Mont. 1981) (statutes require substantial compliance with comprehensive plan in zoning); Manalapan Realty v. Tp. Committee, 658 A.2d 1230 (N.J. 1995) ("the concept of 'substantially consistent' permits some inconsistency, provided it does not substantially or materially undermine or distort the basic provisions and objectives of the Master Plan").

[6] Tex. Local Gov't Code § 213.002(c).

[1] Board of County Comm'rs. V. Snyder, 627 So. 2d 469 (Fla. 1993); Bone v. City of Lewiston, 693 P.2d 1046 (Idaho 1984); Marracci v. City of Scappoose, 552 P.2d 552 (Or. App. 1976).

[2] Phillipi v. City of Sublimity. 662 P.2d 325 (Or.1983). *See also* Building Indus. Ass'n. V. City of Oceanside, 33 Cal. Rptr. 2d 137 (Cal. App. 1994) (numerical growth control initiative inconsistent with plan); Dade County v. Inversiones Rafamar, S.A., 360 So. 2d 1130 (Fla. App. 1978); City of Jacksonville Beach v. Grubbs, 461 So. 2d 160 (Fla. App. 1984); Clinkscales v. City of Lake Oswego, 615 P.2d 1164 (Or. App. 1980) *But see* Board of Suplers v. Hillman. 211 S.E.2d 48 (Va. 1975) (contra, when county allowed similar development nearby).

[3] Bone v. City of Lewiston, 693 P.2d 1046 (Idaho 1984).

[1] Flavell v. City of Albany, 25 Cal. Rptr. 2d 21 (Cal. App. 1993) (no nexus between zoning ordinance increasing residential parking spaces and housing element of plan); Victor Rechhia

may be different from the land uses designated by the plan. The court must then decide whether the zoning ordinance is consistent with the plan.

This question arose in an Oregon case, *Gillis v. City of Springfield*.[3] A comprehensive plan and a more detailed community plan designated an area of the municipality for medium density residential use. To implement the plan, the city adopted a zoning district that allowed office and certain service uses as of right but required a conditional use permit for residential uses.

Noting that the comprehensive plan stated only "broad" criteria for use, the court held that it did not prohibit nonresidential uses. But the court held that the plan's residential designation "requires at least that the area be zoned so that residential uses predominate." The court held the city's zoning district lacked "this essential feature." Although the intensity of use in the zoning district was comparable to intensity of use in a residential district, this did not transform this predominantly commercial district into one possessing a residential character. The case indicates that type of use, rather than intensity, is the key factor in determining consistency with a plan.

In another Oregon case, *Alluis v. Marion County*,[4] the county rejected a partition of land into lots of less than 1.5 acres. The ordinance authorized a one-acre minimum, but the county decided it conflicted with the comprehensive plan because the plan required a 1.5-acre minimum. The court disagreed. It read a reference in the plan to a 1.5-acre minimum as establishing only a "general" maximum density, an "optimum lot size," and an "overall" density minimum. *Allius* indicates how ambiguous plans give the courts an opportunity to establish planning policy through interpretation when they apply the consistency requirement.

Residential Constr., Inc. v. Zoning Bd. Of Adjustment, 768 A.2d 803 (N.J. App. 2001) (refusal to allow residential development held consistent with plan); Manalapan Realty, L.P. v. Township Comm., 658 A.2d 1230 (N.J. 1995) (zoning exclusion of unenclosed uses from shopping centers consistent with shopping center element of plan). *See also* Lesher Communications, Inc. v. City of Walnut Creek, 802 P.2d 317 (Cal. 1990) (initiative measure enacting zoning ordinance that conflicts with comprehensive plan is invalid). *See* §§ 6.32–6.34 for a discussion of when rezoning and refusals to zone are consistent with comprehensive plans.

[2] 668 P.2d 1242 (Or. App. 1983).

[3] 611 P.2d 355 (Or. App. 1980).

[4] Miller v. Council of City of Grants Pass, 592 P.2d 1088 (Or. App. 1979) (county incorrect in interpreting plan to require maximum density); Board of Supvrs. v. Jackson, 269 S.E.2d 381 (Va. 1980) (upheld county's interpretation of ambiguous residential infill policy in comprehensive plan). *See also* City of Jacksonville Beach v. Prom, 656 So.2d 581 (Fla. App. 1995) (landowner entitled to zoning approval for less intensive use than comprehensive plan contemplates if there are no present plans for the more intensive use.

§ 3.19 Plans and the Takings Issue.

§ 3.20 The Plan as a Defense to a Taking.

Although a comprehensive plan does not provide an absolute defense to a taking claim, some courts give weight to comprehensive plans when they consider taking problems. They are impressed by the municipality's efforts in the plan and planning process to comprehensively balance land use opportunities throughout the community.

Norbeck Village Joint Venture v. Montgomery County Council[1] is a leading case. The county comprehensively downzoned twenty square miles to low-density residential use. The downzoning implemented an area plan adopted by the county to provide a greenbelt around a suburban community designated as a growth center. The area plan implemented a county general plan, which in turn implemented a regional growth management plan for the Washington, D.C., metropolitan area.

The court held the downzoning constitutional and relied heavily on the policies of the county plans. It noted that the plaintiffs disputed the validity of the concept underlying the plan and its legality but "did not suggest that it was not conceived and adopted in the utmost good faith." They did not overcome the strong presumption that the plan was valid legislative action.

Another leading case relying on a comprehensive plan to reject a taking claim is *Golden v. Planning Bd. of Town of Ramapo.*[2] The Town of Ramapo adopted a growth management program deferring development in the community for as much as eighteen years. It implemented the program through a residential development permit system under which it allowed new development only if adequate public services and facilities were available. The plaintiff objected that the plan as implemented through the permit system was a taking because development could be deferred in some areas for the eighteen-year growth management period. The court rejected this claim and partly based this holding on the community's adoption of the comprehensive plan as the basis for the growth management program. "The restrictions [in the growth management program] conform to the community's considered land use policies as expressed in its comprehensive plan and represent a bona fide effort to maximize population density consistent with orderly growth."[3]

§ 3.21 The Plan as a Taking of Property.

A comprehensive plan indicates proposals for future land use, and these proposals inevitably affect property values. A California court forcefully made

---

[1] 254 A.2d 700 (Md. 1969).

[2] 285 N.E.2d 291 (N.Y. 1972).

[3] *Id.* at 302. *See also* § 10.04.

this point.[1] Nevertheless, the prevailing rule is that the designation of a land use in a comprehensive plan is not a taking of property. The rule applies if a municipality designates property on a plan for future acquisition to a public facility, such as a highway.[2] *Selby Realty Co. v. City of San Buenaventura*[3] is a leading case. A joint city and county area plan showed an extension of a public street over plaintiff's property. The city refused to issue a necessary building permit when the plaintiff refused to dedicate the land required for the street extension. The court rejected a taking claim because the only action taken by the county that affected plaintiff's property was the adoption of the plan. It held that "[t]he plan is by its very nature merely tentative and subject to change," and that whether any part of plaintiff's property would be taken "depends on unpredictable future events." Plaintiff could seek relief if the plan was implemented at some future time in a manner that affected the "free use" of its property.

A court may reach a different result in states with mandatory planning statutes. Oregon cases have held the designation of a public facility in a plan can be a taking if it precludes all economically feasible use prior to acquisition, or if the designation results in a governmental intrusion that does irreversible damage.[4]

Only a few cases have considered whether the designation of a private land use in a plan is a taking. An early New Jersey case held a residential property owner had not suffered a taking when a plan designated adjacent land for an expansion of a parking area for a commercial building.[5] The court noted the plan at that time was simply a declaration of policy and did not have to be implemented by ordinance. It also noted there was no injury to plaintiff's property because a buffer zone would separate it from the parking lot, and held the plaintiff could not claim a taking until his property was actually destroyed or damaged. In Florida, where planning is mandatory, a court held a facial taking did not occur when a village amended its plan to change the land use designation on a landowner's property from commercial to conservation and open space.[6] The court noted the plan was not a "complete ban" development, and that the residual uses did not deprive the property owner of all economically viable use.

---

[1] O'Loane v. O'Rourke, 42 Cal. Rptr. 283 (Cal. App. 1965) (plan held subject to referendum).

[2] Santini v. Connecticut Hazardous Waste Mgt. Serv., 739 A.2d 680 (Conn. 1999); Lone Star Indus., Inc. v. Department of Transp., 671 P.2d 511 (Kan. 1983); Arnold v. Prince George's County, 311 A.2d 223 (Md. 1973); Marvin E. Neiberg Real Estate Co. v. St. Louis County, 488 S.W.2d 626 (Mo. 1973); 37 A.L.R.3d 127 (1971).

[3] 514 P.2d 111 (Cal. 1973).

[4] Suess Bldrs. Co. v. City of Beaverton, 656 P.2d 306 (Or. 1982) (plan designating property for public acquisition could be taking if landowner induced to abandon all development), *on remand*, 714 P.2d 229 (Or. App. 1986) (upholding directed verdict for city); Fifth Ave. Corp. v. Washington County, 581 P.2d 50 (Or. 1978).

[5] Cochran v. Planning Bd., 210 A.2d 99 (N.J.L. Div. 1965).

[6] Taylor v. Village of North Palm Beach, 659 So. 2d 1167 (Fla. App. 1995).

§ 3.22   Judicial Review of Comprehensive Plans.

Courts have reviewed the content of comprehensive plans to decide whether they satisfy statutory requirements.[1] The California courts have decided many of these cases. The California statute authorizes judicial review of comprehensive plans and authorizes the court to suspend local authority to grant building permits and zoning changes until the local government adopts a plan that complies with the statute.[2] The statutes provide that the adoption and amendment of a comprehensive plan is a legislative act,[3] and courts elsewhere have also held that plan amendments are legislative acts.[4]

The California courts require "actual compliance" with the statute but hold a plan inadequate only if the local government has acted arbitrarily, capriciously, or without evidentiary basis.[5] They have invalidated comprehensive plans when plan elements required by the statute were missing[6] and when the plan was so grossly inadequate that it did not comply with the statute.[7] They have upheld plan amendments that were consistent with the plan.[8]

The California courts have reviewed comprehensive plans to determine whether they comply with the statutory requirements for plan elements and with its internal consistency requirement. In *Twain Harte Homeowners Ass'n v. County of Tuolumne*,[9] the court held that the residential density limitations in a plan

---

[1] Sprenger, Grubb & Assocs. v. City of Hailey, 986 P.2d 343 (Idaho 1999) (plan must contain all statutory elements unless it states why they are not needed); Diehl v. Mason County, 972 P.2d 543 (Wash. App. 1999) (plan did not satisfy requirements of Growth Management Act).

[2] Cal. Gov't Code §§ 65754, 65755 (residential development excepted in certain cases).

[3] § 65301.5.

[4] Martin County v. Yusem, 690 So.2d 1288 (Fla. 1997); Westside Hilltop Survival Comm. v. King County, 634 P.2d 862 (1981). *See also* Kindred Homes, Inc. v. Dean, 605 S.W.2d 15 (Ky. App. 1979); Coastal Dev. of North Florida, Inc. v. City of Jacksonville, 788 So. 2d 204 (small scale amendment to comprehensive plan held legislative).

[5] Buena Vista Gardens Apt. Ass'n v. City of San Diego Planning Dep't, 220 Cal. Rptr. 732 (Cal. App. 1985). *See also* Napa Citizens for Honest Gov't. V. Napa County Bd. Of Supervisors, 100 Cal. Rptr. 2d 579 (Cal. App. 2001) (specific plan inconsistent with comprehensive plan).

Plans held adequate: Garat v. City of Riverside, 3 Cal. Rptr. 2d 504 (Cal. App. 1991); Kings Cty. Farm Bur. v. City of Hanford, 270 Cal. Rptr. 650 (Cal. App. 1990). *See also* Environmental Coalition of Florida, Inc. v. Broward Cty., 586 So. 2d 1212 (Fla. App. 1991) (plan map); Treisman v. Town of Bedford, 563 A.2d 786 (N.H. 1989).

[6] Save El Toro Ass'n v. Days, 141 Cal. Rptr. 282 (Cal. App. 1977).

[7] Camp v. Mendocino County Bd. of Supvrs., 176 Cal. Rptr. 620 (Cal. App. 1981).

[8] Hernandez v. City of Encinitas, 33 Cal. Rptr. 2d 875 (Cal. App. 1994) (housing element); Environmental Council of Sacramento v. Board of Supvrs., 185 Cal. Rptr. 363 (Cal. App. 1982) (land designation changed from agricultural to agricultural-residential when plan called for agricultural preservation).

[9] 188 Cal. Rptr. 233 (Cal. App. 1982) (housing element and implementation measures held adequate). *See* § 3.10. *See also* Concerned Citizens of Calaveras County v. Calaveras County Bd. of Supvrs., 212 Cal. Rptr. 273 (Cal. App. 1985) (plan held internally inconsistent).

were not properly stated and that the transportation element was not sufficiently correlated with the land use element. The courts have been especially strict in requiring compliance with the detailed requirements for the housing element.[10]

A court may decide to review the policies of a comprehensive plan to determine whether they are adequate. In *Holmes v. Planning Bd. of Town of New Castle*,[11] a detailed plan for a neighborhood commercial area attempted to relieve traffic congestion by requiring the dedication of common access driveways to interior parking lots. A landowner challenged a condition attached to a site plan that implemented the neighborhood plan by requiring the dedication of an easement for a common driveway. The court set aside the condition, partly because it found the plan so vague and amorphous in its impact on individual properties that it could raise taking problems. The court held that the board must prepare an "implementation strategy" that would "identify potential conflicts and assemble strategies that will achieve results."

---

[10] Hoffmaster v. City of San Diego, 64 Cal. Rptr. 2d 684 (Cal. App. 1997) (housing element does not identify sites as required by statute); Black Prop. Owners Ass'n v. City of Berkeley, 28 Cal. Rptr. 2d 305 (Cal. App. 1994) (housing element held adequate); Buena Vista Gardens Apt. Ass'n v. City of San Diego Planning Dep't, 220 Cal. Rptr. 732 (Cal. App. 1985). *See* § 7.26.

[11] 433 N.Y.S.2d 587 (App. Div. 1980). *See also* Christine Bldg. Co. v. City of Troy, 116 N.W.2d 816 (Mich. 1962) (court struck down large-lot zoning partly because it did not accept the plan's population limitation).

REFERENCES

Books and Monographs

R. Burby & P. May, Making Governments Plan: State Experiments in Managing Land Use (1997).

J. DiMento, The Consistency Doctrine and the Limits of Planning (1980).

R. Fishman ed., Housing for All Under Law ch. 5 (1978).

E. Kelly & B. Becker, Community Planning: An Introduction to the Comprehensive Plan (2000).

E. Netter & J. Vranicar, Linking Plans and Regulations: Local Responses to Consistency Laws in California and Florida (American Planning Ass'n, Planning Advisory Serv. Rep. No. 363, 1981).

J. DeNeufville ed., The Land Use Policy Debate in the United States (1981).

F. So & J. Getzels, The Practice of Local Government Planning (2d ed. 1988).

Articles

Brooks, Law of Plan Implementation in the United States, 16 Urb. L. Ann. 225 (1979).

Cobb, Mandatory Planning: An Overview, American Planning Ass'n, PAS Memo, Feb. 1994.

Cobb, Toward Modern Statutes: A Survey of State Laws on Local Land Use Planning, in Modernizing State Planning Legislation: The Growing Smart Papers, Vol. 2, at 21, American Planning Ass'n, Planning Advisory Serv. Rep. Nos. 462–463 (1998).

Cox, Recent Progress in Planning Legislation, Land Use L. & Zoning Dig., Vol. 51, No. 10, at 3 (1999).

Day, Citizen Participation in the Planning Process: An Essentially Contested Concept?, 11 J. Plan. Lit. 421 (1997).

DeGrove & Stroud, New Developments and Future Trends in Local Government Comprehensive Planning, 17 Stetson L. Rev. 573 (1988).

Glenn & Apgar, Concurrency and Growth Management: A Lawyer's Primer, 7 Fla. St. Land Use & Envtl. L. Rev. 1 (1991).

Haar, In Accordance with a Comprehensive Plan, 68 Harv. L. Rev. 1154 (1955).

Haar, The Master Plan: An Impermanent Constitution, 20 Law & Contemp. Probs. 353 (1955).

Knaap, Toward Model Statutes for the Land-Use Element: An Assessment of Current Requirements on Practice in Modernizing State Planning

Legislation: The Growing Smart Papers, Vol. 2, at 39, American Planning Ass'n, Planning Advisory Serv. Rep. Nos. 462–463 (1998).

Mandelker, The Role of the Local Comprehensive Plan in Land Use Regulation, 74 Mich. L. Rev. 899 (1976).

Meck, The Legislative Requirement That Zoning and Land Use Controls be Consistent With an Independently Adopted Local Comprehensive Plan: A Model Statute, 3 Wash. U. J.L. & Pol'y 295 (2000).

Meck, Model Planning and Zoning Enabling Legislation: A Short History in Modernizing State Planning Legislation: The Growing Smart Papers, Vol. 1, at 1, American Planning Ass'n, Planning Advisory Serv. Rep. Nos. 462–463 (1996).

Stach, Zoning — To Plan or to Protect?, 2 J. Plan. Literature 472 (1987).

Sullivan, The Evolving Role of the Comprehensive Plan, 32 Urb. Law. 813 (2000).

Sullivan, The Rise of Reason in Planning Law: Daniel R. Mandelker and the Relationship of the Comprehensive Plan in Land Use Regulation, 3 Wash. U. J.L. & Pol'y 323 (2000).

Tarlock, Consistency with Adopted Land Use Plans as a Standard of Judicial Review: The Case Against, 9 Urb. L. Ann. 69 (1975).

Weitz, Toward a Model Statutory Plan Element: Transportation, Land Use L. & Zoning Dig., Vol.49, No. 2, at 3 (1997).

Chapter 4

THE ZONING SYSTEM

Synopsis

§ 4.01   An Introductory Note.

A. JUDICIAL ZONING THROUGH NUISANCE ACTIONS.

§ 4.02   The Private Nuisance Action.
§ 4.03   Anticipatory Nuisances.
§ 4.04   Priority of Occupation.
§ 4.05   Nuisances in Residential Neighborhoods.
§ 4.06   Commercial Uses.
§ 4.07   Funeral Parlors.
§ 4.08   People as Nuisances.
§ 4.09   Aesthetic Nuisances.
§ 4.10   Legalizing Nuisances Through Zoning.
§ 4.11   The Injunction Remedy.
§ 4.12   Balancing the Equities.
§ 4.13   Injunction Not Granted.
§ 4.14   Compensation to Defendant.

B. STATUTORY AUTHORITY.

§ 4.15   The Standard Zoning Act.
§ 4.16   Zoning Purposes.
§ 4.17   The District Concept.
§ 4.18   Adoption and Amendment.
§ 4.19   Board of Adjustment.
§ 4.20   Enforcement.
§ 4.21   Modern Zoning Legislation.
§ 4.22   Extraterritorial Zoning.
§ 4.23   Constitutional Problems.

C. HOME RULE.

§ 4.24   Constitutional Home Rule Authority.
§ 4.25   Home Rule Land Use Powers.

D. ZONING FOR GOVERNMENT AND GOVERNMENT-REGULATED LAND DEVELOPMENT.

§ 4.26   The Governmental Immunity Problem.
§ 4.27   State Agencies.
§ 4.28   Local Governments Exercising State Functions.
§ 4.29   State-Regulated Facilities and Businesses.
§ 4.30   State Environmental Programs.
§ 4.31   State Permits for Other Private Activities.
§ 4.32   Private Utilities.
§ 4.33   Liquor Licensees.
§ 4.34   Local Governments.

§ 4.35   Governmental-Proprietary Rule.
§ 4.36   Eminent Domain Rule.
§ 4.37   Superior Power Rule.
§ 4.38   Balancing Test.
§ 4.39   Home Rule Problems.
§ 4.40   Legislative Solutions.

E. Federal Preemption

§ 4.41   The Federal Preemption Problem.
§ 4.42   Zoning for Cellular Towers.
§ 4.43   Regulation of Airports and Surrounding Areas.

§ 4.01   An Introductory Note.

This chapter examines the zoning system. It opens with a review of cases in which the courts applied nuisance law to resolve conflicts between land uses. The courts in the nuisance cases established a judicial basis for resolving land use conflicts that provided a model for zoning legislation and the zoning ordinance. Next, the chapter reviews statutory and constitutional authority for the enactment of zoning ordinances. It examines the Standard Zoning Enabling Act, which provided the model for all state zoning legislation, and the adoption of land use controls under constitutional home rule powers. It then considers legislation that confers extraterritorial zoning powers on local governments. It concludes with a discussion of zoning for government and government-regulated land development.

A. JUDICIAL ZONING THROUGH NUISANCE ACTIONS.

§ 4.02   The Private Nuisance Action.

Anglo-American courts have recognized the action for nuisance ever since the Elizabethan English decision in Aldred's Case.[1] Nuisance actions are an extension of the private tort of trespass to land. In the trespass action, the landowner sues for a physical invasion of her property by another. No physical invasion occurs in nuisance cases. The plaintiff landowner complains that the use of adjacent land unreasonably affects her land, and that a court can enjoin this use and award damages for any injury suffered.[2] This chapter considers only private nuisances. It does not consider public nuisances, which are usually defined as a criminal violation that interferes with the rights of the community at large.[3] Some states have codified the judicial law of nuisance.[4]

---

[1] [1611] 9 Coke R.D.F. 57b.

[2] Pestey v. Cushman, 788 A.2d 496 (2002) (upholding jury instruction).

[3] W. Prosser & W. Keeton, The Law of Torts 618 (5th ed. 1984).

[4] *E.g.*, Ky. Rev. Stat. §§ 411.500–411.570.

The Supreme Court's taking decision in *Lucas v. South Carolina Coastal Council*[5] gives nuisance rules a role to play in land use law. The Court held a land use regulation that denies a landowner all economically beneficial use of his land is a taking per se unless the use is a nuisance under state nuisance law.

The tort origins of nuisance law make its conceptual underpinnings unclear to this day. Whether success in a nuisance action requires proof of negligence on the part of the offending user, for example, continues to be a problem for some courts.[6] These conceptual difficulties tend to disappear in the land use nuisance cases. They reflect the Latin maxim that a landowner may make any use of his land if he does not unreasonably interfere with the use of land by others.

Courts determine the reasonableness of a use claimed to be a nuisance by determining whether it is compatible with land uses in the surrounding area. This decision requires a judicial "line-drawing" that is the same as the "line-drawing" municipalities make when they adopt zoning maps. The difference is that the courts make line-drawing decisions in land use nuisance cases. These cases are called judicial zoning for this reason. The Supreme Court's *Euclid* case[7] relied on this element in nuisance law to construct a constitutional justification for zoning. Courts award either damages or an injunction in land use nuisance cases.

Although nuisance law does not require a physical invasion, courts more easily find a nuisance when a defendant's land use has a physical impact on plaintiff's land. The polluting industry in a residential neighborhood is the clearest example. Proof of physical impact is not always necessary in nuisance law because some courts enjoin aesthetic nuisances in residential areas, such as funeral homes.

A helpful way to look at nuisance law in land use cases is to construct an invader-defender model of nuisance litigation. The defendant who proposes a land use in an area is the invader. The plaintiff who resists the defendant's use is the defender. The land use claimed to be a nuisance is usually adjacent or close to the plaintiff's property.

Land use nuisances are either a nuisance *per se* or a nuisance *per accidens*. A nuisance *per se* is a nuisance wherever it locates. A nuisance *per accidens* is a nuisance only in areas in which its location is detrimental to surrounding uses. Hardly any land uses are in the *per se* category. In the usual land use nuisance case, the plaintiff claims a land use is a nuisance *per accidens*.[8] The courts have adopted an implicit land use hierarchy they apply in the *per accidens*

---

[5] 505 U.S. 1003 (1992). *See* § 2.18.

[6] Copart Indus. v. Consolidated Edison Co., 362 N.E.2d 968 (N.Y. 1977).

[7] Village of Euclid v. Ambler Realty Co., 272 U.S. 365 (1926). *See* 5.02

[8] State v. Feezell, 400 S.W.2d 716 (Tenn. 1966).

cases. Residential land uses are at the top of the hierarchy, and courts hold that nonresidential uses that seek to enter residential neighborhoods are nuisances *per accidens.*

Nuisance actions have declined in importance as a method for resolving land use conflicts because most municipalities have adopted zoning ordinances. A nuisance action may still have advantages that enforcement of the zoning ordinances does not have. If a plaintiff is successful in securing an injunction, a court can order the removal of the nuisance without compensation. A plaintiff can also secure damages in a nuisance action.

§ 4.03 Anticipatory Nuisances.

Because most land use nuisances are in the *per accidens* category, it is not surprising that courts refuse to grant injunctions against anticipatory nuisances, which are nuisances that have not yet been established. The courts hold they will not enjoin an anticipatory nuisance unless it is a nuisance *per se.*[1] Other cases, while not expressly holding that an anticipatory nuisance must be a nuisance per se, hold the threat of substantial future injury must be inherent,[2] or that it must appear with reasonable certainty that irreparable harm and damage may occur.[3]

Judicial reluctance to enjoin anticipatory nuisances reflects the requirement that the vast majority of land uses are not nuisances *per se*, and are held to be nuisances *per accidens* only if incompatible with the area in which they plan to locate. Courts are reluctant to make this determination in many cases when the nuisance has not yet been established. They find the potential harm to a plaintiff too speculative to justify an injunction.

The judicial reluctance to enjoin anticipatory nuisances has important consequences for new residents in an undeveloped area. New arrivals who build residences there will find themselves in the position of "coming to the nuisance"

---

[1] Brammer v. Housing Auth., 195 So. 256 (Ala. 1940) (housing project); Miniat v. McGinnis, 762 S.W.2d 390 (Ark. 1988) (long-term care facility); Davis v. Miller, 96 S.E.2d 498 (Ga. 1957) (harm from automobile service station too speculative); Olsen v. City of Baton Rouge, 247 So. 2d 889 (La. App. 1971) (garbage transfer facility); Leatherbury v. Gaylord Fuel Corp., 347 A.2d 826 (Md. 1975) (quarry); Marshall v. Consumers' Power Co., 237 N.W.2d 266 (Mich. 1975) (nuclear power plant); Wallace v. Andersonville Docks, Inc., 489 S.W.2d 532 (Tenn. App. 1972) (motorcycle course). *But see* Dill v. Brinkley, 1988 Tenn. App. LEXIS 118 (Tenn. App. 1988) (granting injunction against construction of mud race track in residential neighborhood).

[2] Connecticut Bank & Trust Co. v. Mularcik, 174 A.2d 128 (Conn. 1961) (rock crusher and stone screener).

[3] Camp v. Warrington, 182 S.E.2d 419 (Ga. 1971) (injunction granted; airport). *See also* Green v. Castle Concrete Co., 509 P.2d 588 (Colo. 1973) (quarry); Conner v. Smith, 433 S.W.2d 911 (Tex. Civ. App. 1968) (hide plant); Freedman v. Lewis, 776 S.W.2d 212 (Tex. App. 1989) (parking lot); 55 A.L.R. 880 (1928).

if a land use they consider to be a nuisance is established later. If they then sue to enjoin the new land use as a nuisance, some courts will not grant an injunction because the nuisance enjoys priority in occupation.

One court noted the relationship between anticipatory nuisance actions and the failure to enact comprehensive zoning. In *Henn v. Universal Atlas Cement Co.*,[4] plaintiffs sued to enjoin the operation of a quarry as an anticipatory nuisance after a referendum on a zoning ordinance lost at the polls. A second referendum was pending. The court noted the granting of an injunction would determine future land use in the area and would lend the weight of the court to one of the factions in the "zoning battle." It held that "[t]he benefits of zoning must be won at the polls, not in the courtroom."

§ 4.04 Priority of Occupation.

Priority of occupation is a factor some courts consider in nuisance cases. If the defendant's use is in existence when a plaintiff establishes his use, a court may apply the priority of occupation rule and deny relief to the plaintiff because he "came" to the nuisance. The priority of occupation rule derives from principles of equity that require plaintiffs to come into court with "clean hands." Because the plaintiff came into the area knowing the nuisance existed, he does not have "clean hands." Courts do not consider priority of occupation an absolute defense for a defendant whose use came first. They treat priority of occupation as one factor and weigh it in the balance when they decide whether to grant relief to a plaintiff. The courts are less likely to grant an injunction when the plaintiff seeking the injunction "came" to the nuisance.[1]

Courts may especially be willing to deny relief to a plaintiff who "comes to a nuisance" by building a residence in an industrial area if the area is clearly incompatible with residential uses.[2] A court may also deny relief when a plaintiff builds a home in an area that later becomes industrial if the area was likely to be developed for industrial purposes when the plaintiff built her home. In *Bove v. Donner-Hanna Coke Corp.*,[3] a plaintiff sued to enjoin coke works constructed after she had built her home. The court held for the coke works because the plaintiff "should have known" that the area would eventually be developed industrially because "in a growing community, changes are inevitable."

---

[4] 144 N.E.2d 917 (Ohio C.P. 1957). *See also* Menger v. Pass, 80 A.2d 702 (Pa. 1951).

[1] Kriener v. Turkey Valley Community School Dist., 212 N.W.2d 526 (Iowa 1973); Schlotfelt v. Vinton Farmers' Supply Co., 109 N.W.2d 695 (Iowa 1961); Williams v. Oeder, 659 N.E.2d 379 (Ohio App. 1995); Weida v. Ferry, 493 A.2d 824 (R.I. 1985); Kellogg v. Village of Viola, 227 N.W.2d 55 (Wis. 1975); Abdella v. Smith, 149 N.W.2d 537 (Wis.1967); 42 A.L.R.3d 344 (1972). *But see* Jerry Harmon Motors, Inc. v. Farmers Union Grain Term. Ass'n, 337 N.W.2d 427 (N.D. 1983) (plaintiff coming to nuisance has "heavy burden to establish liability").

[2] Powell v. Superior Portland Cement, 129 P.2d 536 (Wash. 1942).

[3] 258 N.Y.S. 229 (App. Div. 1932).

The rule denying relief to a plaintiff who "comes" to the nuisance is questionable. If a court applies this rule to deny relief against a nuisance, an accidental priority in time will determine the future development of the area. The nuisance that is "first in time" will impose a "negative servitude" on the surrounding area that allows it to remain even though it is incompatible with how the area develops. Cases like *Bove* reject the "negative servitude" doctrine implicit in the priority of occupation rule.

§ 4.05 Nuisances in Residential Neighborhoods.

Courts recognize the land use hierarchy implicit in nuisance cases by granting relief to plaintiffs who sue to prohibit noxious nonresidential uses in residential neighborhoods. Nuisance suits against industrial uses seldom present difficulties. In *Schlotfelt v. Vinton Farmers' Supply Co.*,[1] for example, the court enjoined a feed grinding and mixing business in a residential neighborhood. No case was found in which a plaintiff attempted to prohibit a different type of residential dwelling, such as multifamily apartments, in residential neighborhoods.[2]

§ 4.06 Commercial Uses.

The physical basis for nuisance actions leads to mixed results when plaintiffs attempt to prohibit commercial uses in residential neighborhoods. A commercial use is not usually physically noxious. Homeowners in residential neighborhoods must rely on some other physically intrusive aspect of commercial uses if they seek to prohibit them as nuisances.[1]

A pair of Pennsylvania cases indicates the mixed judicial view toward commercial uses in residential areas. In *Essick v. Shillam*,[2] residential homeowners asked for an injunction to prohibit the construction of a supermarket in a residential area. They claimed a nuisance would be created by the traffic congestion caused by the store's parking lot and patrons who would shop in the store. They also claimed that bright lights that would illuminate the store would

---

[1] 109 N.W.2d 695 (Iowa 1961). *See also* Wilson v. Interlake Steel Co., 649 P.2d 922 (Cal. 1982); Padillo v. Lawrence, 685 P.2d 964 (N.M. App. 1984). *Compare* Rose v. Chaiken, 453 A.2d 1378 (N.J. Ch. Div. 1982) (noise from windmill held a nuisance in a residential neighborhood); Perkins v. Madison County Livestock & Fair Ass'n, 613 N.W.2d 264 (Iowa 2000) (racetrack held nuisance as to one landowner); A to Z Paper Co., Inc., 775 So.2d 42 (La. 2000) (concrete batching plant held not a nuisance in industrial neighborhood); Citizens for a Safe Grant v. Lone Oak Sportsmen's Club, Inc. 624 N.W.2d 796 (Minn. App. 2001) (Shooting range held nuisance).

[2] *But cf.* Scoville v. Ronalter, 291 A.2d 222 (Conn. 1971) (suggesting that apartments are not nuisances in single-family neighborhoods).

[1] GTI Mobilnet v. Pascouet, 61 S.W.2d 599 (Tex. App. 2001) (cellular tower and building held nuisance).

[2] 32 A.2d 416 (Pa. 1943). *See also* Hannum v. Oak Lane Shopping Center, Inc., 119 A.2d 213 (Pa. 1956) (supermarket in residential neighborhood not nuisance per se).

be a nuisance. The court denied an injunction, noting in part that the expected disturbance from the store was anticipatory.[3]

In *Reid v. Brodsky,*[4] the court held the establishment of a taproom-restaurant in a quite residential neighborhood was a nuisance. It was clear the patrons of the restaurant would come from other areas, and that their conduct would be offensive to residents of the neighborhood.[5] Judicial holdings on filling stations as nuisances in residential areas are also mixed.[6]

§ 4.07 Funeral Parlors.

Funeral parlors are usually located in well-kept residences or buildings, do not attract substantial amounts of traffic on a regular basis, are pleasant and attractive in appearance, and certainly do not create noise or disturbances. Despite these characteristics, the majority of courts enjoin a funeral parlor in residential areas as an anticipatory nuisance.

The funeral parlor cases usually point out that funeral parlors are different from similar commercial uses as nuisances, such as stores and restaurants that are not drive-ins. They invade the integrity of residential neighborhoods and disturb the seclusion to which residents of these neighborhoods are entitled. Reminders of death, and the coming and going of caskets and mourners, are depressing. When the neighborhood is clearly residential, the majority of courts enjoin the establishment of funeral parlors for these reasons.[1]

§ 4.08 People as Nuisances.

In a few cases, the courts considered actions to prohibit as nuisances the establishment of half-way houses and other group homes in residential areas. Like funeral parlors, these uses are located in residential dwellings and do not have the physically noxious characteristics that lead courts to enjoin a use as a nuisance.

Nicholson v. Connecticut Half-Way House, Inc.[1] is a leading case refusing to enjoin the establishment of a home for prison parolees in a dwelling in a

---

[3] *Accord* Winget v. Winn-Dixie Stores, Inc., 130 S.E.2d 363 (S.C. 1963); 146 A.L.R. 1407 (1943).

[4] 156 A.2d 334 (Pa. 1959). *See also* Diehl v. Lockard, 385 A.2d 550 (Pa. Super. 1978) (granting injunction against construction of drive-in restaurant in residential neighborhood).

[5] *Accord* Wade v. Fuller, 365 P.2d 802 (Utah 1961). *See* Reid v. Brodsky, 156 A.2d 334 (Pa. 1959); 91 A.L.R.2d 572 (1963).

[6] Bortz v. Troth, 59 A.2d 93 (Pa. 1948); 124 A.L.R. 383 (1940).

[1] Potter v. Bryan Funeral Home, 817 S.W.2d 882 (Ark. 1991) (not enjoinable; area not residential); Powell v. Taylor, 263 S.W.2d 906 (Ark. 1954); Dawson v. Laufersweiler, 43 N.W.2d 726 (Iowa 1950); Travis v. Moore, 377 So. 2d 609 (Miss. 1979); 8 A.L.R.4th 324 (1981).

[1] 218 A.2d 383 (Conn. 1966). *Accord* Deep East Texas Regional Mental Health & Mental Retardation Servs. v. Kinnear, 877 S.W.2d 550 (Tex. App. 1994).

residential neighborhood. The court's opinion is consistent with other cases refusing injunctions against anticipatory nuisances. It held it would not grant an injunction based solely on the fears and apprehensions of neighborhood residents. The court left for another day the question whether it would grant an injunction if problems arose in the operation of the home.

Other courts granted injunctions against similar group homes after they began operation and after disturbing incidents occurred,[2] although some "incidents," such as a conversation with a resident who acted "silly," hardly justified an injunction. One case that granted an injunction was based on the fears and apprehensions rejected in the *Nicholson* opinion.[3]

§ 4.09   Aesthetic Nuisances.

The decisions on aesthetic nuisances are also divided. The automobile junkyard cases illustrate the aesthetic nuisance problem. Junkyards are visually offensive but physically passive. In *Parkersburg Bldrs. Material Co. v. Barrack*,[1] an early and leading junkyard case, the court reversed a trial judge who refused an injunction and explicitly addressed the aesthetics issue. It noted that "a thing visually offensive may seriously affect the residents of a community in the reasonable enjoyment of their homes, and may produce a decided reduction in property values." It added that a court should act "only when there is presented a situation which is offensive to the view of the average persons in the community." Other cases have agreed[2] or disagreed[3] with this decision in junkyard as well as other cases brought against uses as diverse as a used-car lot and the raising of livestock. The cases rejecting *Parkersburg* are questionable, as most courts now recognize aesthetic purposes in zoning. Two recent cases have also held that the deprivation of light and air is a nuisance, a rejection of the majority view on this question.[4] Some of the land uses that raise aesthetic

---

[2] Smith v. Gill, 310 So. 2d 214 (Ala. 1975). *Compare* Everett v. Paschall, 111 P. 879 (Wash. 1910) (injunction granted against tuberculosis sanitarium).

[3] Arkansas Release Guidance Found. v. Needler, 477 S.W.2d 821 (Ark. 1972) (home for parolees). *See also* Armory Park Neighborhood Ass'n v. Episcopal Community Serv., 712 P.2d 914 (Ariz. 1985) (indigent food distribution center held a public nuisance).

[1] 191 S.E. 368, 192 S.E. 291 (W. Va. 1937).

[2] Allison v. Smith, 695 P.2d 791 (Colo. App. 1984); Robie v. Lillie, 299 A.2d 155 (N.H. 1972) (unaesthetic quality of an activity important consideration in balancing process); Hay v. Stevens, 530 P.2d 37 (Or. 1975). Cf. Foley v. Harris, 286 S.E.2d 186 (Va. 1982).

[3] Oliver v. AT&T Wireless Servs., 90 Cal. Rptr.2d 491 (Cal. App. 1999) (shape of structure permitted by law is not nuisance per se); Green v. Castle Concrete Co., 509 P.2d 588 (Colo. 1973); Noakes v. Gaiser, 315 P.2d 183 (Colo. 1957); B & W Mgt., Inc. v. Tasea Inv. Co., 451 A.2d 879 (D.C. App. 1982); Ness v. Albert, 665 S.W.2d 1 (Mo. App. 1983); Robie v. Lillis, 299 A.2d 155 (N.H. 1972); Crabtree v. City Auto Salvage Co., 340 S.W.2d 940 (Tenn. App. 1960). *Cf.* Carroll v. Hurst, 431 N.E.2d 1344 (Ill. App. 1982).

[4] Tenn v. 889 Assocs., 500 A.2d 366 (N.H. 1985); Prah v. Moretti, 321 N.W.2d 182 (Wis. 1982).

nuisance problems are now regulated under statutory programs. All states, for example, regulate junkyards under requirements imposed by the federal Highway Beautification Act.[5]

§ 4.10   Legalizing Nuisances Through Zoning.

A zoning ordinance that authorizes a use claimed to be a nuisance creates a problem in nuisance law. Courts enjoin nuisances because they are unreasonable uses in the areas in which they want to locate, but the zoning ordinance is a legislative declaration that the use is compatible with the surrounding area. Some courts give the zoning ordinance at least some weight when they decide whether to enjoin a nuisance.[1] However, the majority view is that a zoning ordinance allowing a use is not an absolute bar to an injunction against a nuisance,[2] but a minority of courts adopt the contrary view.[3] Cases following the majority rule are short on analysis but usually hold that a municipality may not legalize a use that could be a nuisance in the area in which it is located.

This conclusion requires some qualification. The decisions are best explained by the effect the court gives to the zoning ordinance. They indicate that the enactment of a zoning ordinance authorizing a use only precludes a holding that the use is a nuisance *per se*.[4] A zoning ordinance cannot preclude a court from holding the use a nuisance *per accidens*.[5] This distinction may explain what courts mean when they hold that a zoning ordinance may not legalize the creation of a nuisance. Some statutes cover the zoning question.[6]

---

[5] 23 U.S.C. § 136.

[1] Harrison v. Indiana Auto Shredders Co., 528 F.2d 1107 (7th Cir. 1976); Weltshe v. Graf, 82 N.E.2d 795 (Mass. 1948); Rockenbach v. Apostle, 47 N.W.2d 636 (Mich. 1951).

[2] Armory Park Neighborhood Ass'n v. Episcopal Community Serv., 712 P.2d 914 (Ariz. 1985); Sierra Screw Prods. v. Azusa Greens, Inc., 151 Cal. Rptr. 799 (Cal. App. 1979); Allison v. Smith, 695 P.2d 791 (Colo. App. 1984); Ferreira v. D'Asaro, 152 So. 2d 736 (Fla. App. 1963); Valley Poultry Farms, Inc. v. Preece, 406 S.W.2d 413 (Ky. 1966); Weltshe v. Graf, 82 N.E.2d 795 (Mass. 1948); Rockenbach v. Apostle, 47 N.W.2d 636 (Mich. 1951); Kozesnsik v. Township of Montgomery, 131 A.2d 1 (N.J. 1957); Dunaway v. City of Austin, 290 S.W.2d 703 (Tex. App. 1956).

[3] Kirk v. Mabis, 246 N.W. 759 (Iowa 1933); Winget v. Winn-Dixie Stores, Inc., 130 S.E.2d 363 (S.C. 1963).

[4] Weaver v. Bishop, 52 P.2d 853 (Okla. 1935).

[5] *Cf.* City of St. Louis v. Golden Gate Corp., 421 S.W.2d 4 (Mo. 1967) (city ordinance may not confer jurisdiction on court).

[6] Cal. Civ. Proc. Code § 731(a) (manufacturing, commercial, or airport uses authorized by zoning enjoinable if employ unnecessary and injurious methods of operation, and nuisance can be eliminated at reasonable cost). *See* Sierra Screw Prods. v. Azusa Greens, Inc., 151 Cal. Rptr. 799 (Cal. App. 1979); Venuto v. Owens-Corning Fiberglas Corp., 99 Cal. Rptr. 350 (Cal. App. 1971).

§ 4.11   The Injunction Remedy.

§ 4.12   Balancing the Equities.

A plaintiff must be able to enjoin the continuation of a nuisance to obtain an effective remedy in a nuisance case. However, the availability of an injunction in a nuisance case is not certain.[1] Under standard equity principles, a court will not grant an injunction as a matter of right. It balances the equities to determine whether an injunction is appropriate. In many nuisance cases, the balancing test works to the disadvantage of the plaintiff. He may be a single homeowner who seeks to prohibit a use, such as a manufacturing plant, that provides substantial economic benefit to the community.

In most states the courts will balance the equities in nuisance cases when they decide whether an injunction will issue. Courts consider a number of factors when applying the balancing test in land use cases. As in equity cases generally, the availability of damages as an adequate legal remedy is one factor.[2] The economic impact on the defendant and the economic importance of the defendant's use are other factors courts consider.[3] A court may conclude the benefits to the plaintiff when balanced against the costs to the defendant do not warrant an injunction under the facts of the case.

The balancing test takes on a somewhat different coloration in land use nuisance cases. Because the appropriateness of a use at its location is so decisive in these cases, the nature of the area in which the nuisance use is located may help decide the injunction issue. If the court characterizes the area as mixed residential and industrial, for example, it may decide that the equities do not require an injunction.[4] The decision on whether the offending use is a nuisance merges with the decision on the remedy.

A court is in a quandary if it believes the offending use is a nuisance, but that it cannot modify its operations to avoid damage to adjacent homeowners. A decision in this kind of case to grant an injunction may impose substantial costs on the defendant because it may be forced to move. Damages may be an adequate legal remedy in this situation but do not give the plaintiff the relief he seeks from continuing disturbance by the nuisance. A damages remedy also leaves the residential neighborhood permanently impaired.

---

[1] Helmkamp v. Clark Ready Mix Co., 214 N.W.2d 126 (Iowa 1974); Storey v. Central Hide & Rendering Co., 226 S.W.2d 615 (Tex. 1950); 40 A.L.R.2d 601 (1971).

[2] Daigle v. Continental Oil Co., 277 F. Supp. 875 (1967); McCarty v. Macy & Co., 334 P.2d 156 (Cal. App. 1959); Haack v. Lindsay Light & Chem. Co., 66 N.E.2d 391 (Ill. 1946).

[3] Riter v. Keokuk Electro-Metals Co., 82 N.W.2d 151 (Iowa 1957); York v. Stallings, 341 P.2d 529 (Or. 1959).

[4] McCarty v. Macy & Co., 334 P.2d 156 (Cal. App. 1959); Roy v. Chevrolet Motor Car Co., 247 N.W. 774 (Mich. 1933); York v. Stallings, 341 P.2d 529 (Or. 1959).

Some courts resolve this quandary by favoring the plaintiff, even though the economic loss to the defendant is substantial. In *Schlotfelt v. Vinton Farmers' Supply Co.*,[5] for example, the court held a feed grinding, feed mixing, and fertilizer sales business was a nuisance in a residential neighborhood. The disturbance to the plaintiff was partly physical, consisting of vibrations from defendant's machinery, as well as dust and noxious odors from the grinding and mixing.

Although the trial court decree would have allowed the defendant to continue its operations if it could remedy the physical disturbances to the plaintiff, the defendant claimed it could not meet this requirement. Closing the business was the only alternative. The court weighed the equities and granted an injunction even though the plant might have to close, partly because priority of occupation favored the plaintiff. The plaintiff had found its "clean and quiet" residential neighborhood invaded by this noxious use. Other courts reached similar results.[6]

§ 4.13 Injunction Not Granted.

In a leading case, *Boomer v. Atlantic Cement Co.*,[1] the plaintiff sought an injunction against a cement plant because of vibrations and air pollution caused by the plant's operation. The court rejected the previously accepted rule in New York, that courts will grant an injunction in a nuisance case if the damage to the plaintiff is substantial. It held that payment of compensation to the plaintiff for permanent injury was the proper remedy.

The facts of the case clearly influenced the court. It noted the disparity between the damage suffered by the plaintiff and the loss to the community should the defendant's plant close. It observed that the defendant could abate the nuisance by making technological improvements in its operations, but that its ability to achieve the technological advances necessary for these improvements was uncertain. Nor should the defendant be burdened with the research necessary to develop a new technology, a need common to the entire industry. The court held that damages would adequately redress the harm to the plaintiff and spur the research necessary to produce the required technological improvements. The dissent viewed the majority opinion as a judicially mandated private inverse condemnation not supported by judicial precedent. *Boomer* could apply to many land use nuisance cases in which physical disturbance by the defendant is an

---

[5] 109 N.W.2d 695 (Iowa 1961).

[6] Pendoley v. Ferreira, 187 N.E.2d 142 (Mass. 1963); Mahoney v. Walter, 205 S.E.2d 692 (W. Va. 1974). *But see* Hartford Penn-Cann Serv. v. Zymblosky, 549 A.2d 554 (Pa. Super. 1988) (court should have ordered alternative to remedy dust problem rather than issuing order that closed business).

[1] 257 N.E.2d 870 (N.Y. 1970).

issue, but may not apply when a nuisance is incompatible with the surrounding area and technological modification is not an issue.[2]

§ 4.14   Compensation to Defendant.

A modification of the injunction remedy can avoid the imposition of excessive costs on a defendant. This alternative, which some scholars recommend, allows the court to grant an injunction if the plaintiff pays damages to the defendant to meet its relocation costs. Advocates of this remedy claim it is more efficient. Plaintiffs will not provide compensation for relocation unless the benefits of the defendant's relocation exceed the relocation costs they must pay. Only one case approved this remedy. In *Spur Indus. v. Del E. Webb Dev. Co.*,[1] a plaintiff that developed a new residential community in an agricultural area sued to enjoin the operation of an adjacent feedlot. The developer had "come" to the feedlot by expanding its development. The court recognized that this fact justified a denial of an injunction only if the plaintiff had alleged a private nuisance. Plaintiff also alleged a public nuisance based on an injury to all homeowners in the surrounding area, and the court granted an injunction because the defendant's nuisance was public as well as private. It required the plaintiff to compensate the defendant for its relocation costs as a condition to injunctive relief because the defendant enjoyed priority of occupation.

Whether this remedy is practicable in many situations is problematic. In *Spur,* the plaintiff was a developer of a large residential community and could afford the compensation costs. It also was the only landowner in the area. A court would not likely place all of the costs of relocation on an individual plaintiff who sues for an injunction. Overcoming the "freeloader" problem by requiring other adjacent homeowners to participate in the compensation burden may stretch judicial competence.

B.   STATUTORY AUTHORITY.

§ 4.15   The Standard Zoning Act.

All state zoning legislation is based on a Standard Zoning Enabling Act proposed by the U.S. Department of Commerce in the mid-1920s that preceded by a few years the publication of a Standard Planning Act.[1] Although many states have modified the Standard Zoning Act, some substantially, these changes do not modify the basic statutory framework of this legislative model. The Standard Zoning Act provides a common statutory basis for zoning that makes court decisions on zoning applicable nationwide.

---

[2] *Compare* Little Joseph Realty, Inc. v. Town of Babylon, 363 N.E.2d 1163 (N.Y. 1977) (asphalt plant enjoined as violation of zoning ordinance).

[1] 494 P.2d 700 (Ariz. 1972).

[1] § 3.05.

The drafters of the Standard Zoning Act built carefully on the nuisance concept as applied in land use cases. They noted that courts draw lines to determine the established residential districts that are protected from invading offensive uses. The Zoning Act adopted this concept as the basis for the zoning ordinance. The Act authorized municipalities to designate zoning districts in which only compatible uses are allowed and incompatible uses are excluded. As implemented at the local level, the zoning ordinance establishes a land use hierarchy with residential districts at the top of the land use pyramid.

Careful inspection of the Standard Zoning Act also indicates that the drafters contemplated a static zoning system in which the zoning districts authorize land uses permitted "as of right" throughout the community. This legislative intent is apparent from the limited opportunities the Standard Act provided for administrative relief. The Act created a board of adjustment with limited powers to grant hardship variances authorized by the statute and special exceptions authorized by the zoning ordinance. The drafters borrowed the variance idea from the local building code, and indicated that the variance was an experiment subject to statutory modification as localities gained experience with zoning. The zoning variance has become standard practice, but major modification has not occurred.

Although the drafters contemplated a zoning system in which uses are permitted as of right and modifications few, everyone knows that municipalities do not manage the zoning process in this manner. In urban areas with little land available for development, the zoning ordinance is comparatively stable. Incremental modifications through variances and exceptions are the rule. In suburban areas, localities usually adopt low-density residential zones that do not permit intensive land development. This practice allows localities to adopt a "wait and see" zoning system in which developers must obtain a major zoning change before they can develop their land. Because almost all development requires a zoning change, the "wait and see" approach allows local zoning agencies to exercise considerable control over the land development process.

The Standard Act also contains an anachronism no longer common in zoning practice. It authorized a "zoning commission" with the authority to recommend the adoption of zoning districts and regulations. The Act stated that "[w]here a city plan commission already exists, it may be appointed as the zoning commission." The drafters authorized a zoning commission because the Standard Zoning Act preceded the Standard Planning Act. Although state legislation may authorize a zoning commission, the planning commission carries out the functions of the zoning commission in almost all communities.

§ 4.16 Zoning Purposes.

Section 1 of the Standard Zoning Act provides the basic "Grant of Power." It authorizes the local legislative body to regulate and restrict the height, number of stories, and size of buildings and other structures, the percentage of lot that may be occupied, the size of yards, courts, and other open spaces, the density of population, the location and use of buildings, structures, and land for trade, industry, residence, or other purposes. [1]

This section provides the statutory authority for density, site development, bulk, and use restrictions. Note that the Act contemplates regulation of the "use" of land for the three major land use categories. The reference to "land for trade" is intended to cover commercial development.

Section 3, which states the "purposes" of local zoning regulations, further elaborates the scope of zoning:

Sec. 3. Purposes in View. Such regulations shall be made in accordance with a comprehensive plan and designed to lessen congestion in the streets; to secure safety from fire, panic, and other dangers; to promote health and the general welfare; to provide adequate light and air; to prevent the overcrowding of land; to avoid undue concentration of population; to facilitate the adequate provision of transportation, water, sewerage, schools, parks, and other public requirements. Such regulations shall be made with reasonable consideration, among other things, to the character of the district and its peculiar suitability for particular uses, and with a view to conserving the value of buildings and encouraging the most appropriate use of land throughout such municipality. [2]

This section is critical. Its quaint language indicates the origins of zoning in New York City and a concern with zoning problems specific to Manhattan. The concern over "safety from fire" and "adequate light and air" reflects the drafters' concern with the height and siting of the tall skyscrapers that, even then, were common to that city.

Sections 1 and 3 provide the statutory authority for zoning ordinances. They have not proved especially troublesome for courts asked to consider the statutory basis for a zoning regulation, although some modern forms of land use regulation are not included. Aesthetic regulation is one example. Nor have all of the statutory authorizations received extensive judicial consideration. The statutory direction to conserve "the value of buildings" is an example. Some courts rely on this delegation of authority to uphold architectural design review ordinances that protect the aesthetic integrity of residential areas. [3]

---

[1] *See* Bittinger v. Corporation of Bolivar, 395 S.E.2d 554 (W.Va. 1990) (explaining distinction between planning and zoning).

[2] *See* Board of Township Trustees v. Funtime, Inc., 563 N.E.2d 717 (Ohio 1990) (act does not authorize control of hours of operation).

[3] § 11.03.

§ 4.17 The District Concept.

Section 2 of the Standard Zoning Act provides the necessary authority to divide the community

> into districts of such number, shape, and area as may be deemed best suited to carry out the purposes of this act; and within such districts . . . [to] regulate and restrict the erection, construction, reconstruction, alteration, repair, or use of buildings, structures, or land.

The Act appears to provide authority to regulate building construction as well as land use, but that was not the intent. The Act was intended to authorize land use regulations in zoning ordinances that municipalities apply when buildings are erected, constructed, reconstructed, altered, or repaired. A final sentence in this section requires uniformity of regulations within districts but allows regulations in the various zoning districts to differ from each other.

§ 4.18 Adoption and Amendment.

Sections 4 and 5 of the Standard Act authorize the local legislative body to adopt and amend zoning "regulations and restrictions and . . . [district] boundaries."[1] The Act does not provide statutory standards to guide the adoption and amendment process, which the drafters apparently treated as a legislative function. The Act also requires notice by publication and a hearing for all zoning ordinance adoptions and amendments. A three-fourths vote by the legislative body is required to adopt a zoning amendment if twenty percent of the affected property owners or twenty percent of adjacent or opposite property owners protest its adoption. The cases indicate that this provision does not apply to a comprehensive revision of a zoning ordinance.[2]

§ 4.19 Board of Adjustment.

The Standard Act confers the administrative powers to be exercised under the zoning ordinance on a board of adjustment, which is called a board of zoning adjustment in some state legislation and some zoning ordinances. The board has three powers. It may hear appeals from interpretations of the zoning ordinance. It may "hear and decide special exceptions to the terms of the ordinance upon which such board is required to pass under such ordinance." It may also authorize variances from the zoning ordinance not "contrary to the public interest, where, owing to special conditions, a literal enforcement of the provisions of the ordinance will result in unnecessary hardship, and so that the spirit of the ordinance shall be observed and substantial justice done."

---

[1] Red Dog Saloon v. Sedgwick County Bd. of Comm'rs, 33 P.3d 869 (Kan. App. 2001) (settlement agreement cannot bind county to amendment or repeal of ordinance).

[2] Wanamaker v. City Council, 19 Cal. Rptr. 554 (Cal. App. 1962); Benesh v. Township of Frenchtown, 228 N.W.2d 459 (Mich. App. 1975).

In practice, and in the court decisions, the distinction between special exceptions and variances is confused. The conventional understanding is that a special exception is a use in a zoning district that is authorized by the zoning ordinance and requires permission from the board. Zoning ordinances may use the term "conditional use" as an alternative. Unlike a variance, conditional uses (or special exceptions) do not require proof of unnecessary hardship.

§ 4.20   Enforcement.

Section 8 of the Standard Act provides that any violation of the Act or a zoning ordinance is a misdemeanor, punishable by fine, imprisonment, or civil penalties. The municipality may also bring "appropriate" proceedings against any violation of the Act or a zoning ordinance.

§ 4.21   Modern Zoning Legislation.

A number of states have adopted comprehensive revisions of their zoning enabling legislation in recent years.[1] The innovations adopted in these states do not usually change the basic structure of the Standard Act. They retain the zoning district concept and do not usually modify the role of the legislative body or the board of adjustment.

California zoning legislation illustrates changes in the Standard Act that expand its regulatory authority and change the distribution of administrative responsibilities. This legislation specifically authorizes regulations for site development, such as off-street parking, setbacks and land use intensity; signs and billboards and sexually-oriented businesses.[2] It strengthens the role of the planning commission by making the commission's recommendation against a zoning map change final unless "otherwise provided by ordinance" or unless an "interested party" requests a hearing before the legislative body.[3]

California authorizes the creation of a board of zoning adjustment, the office of zoning administrator, or both.[4] The zoning administrator may grant variances and the zoning ordnance may also authorize him to grant conditional uses or other permits.[5] A local government may establish a board of appeals to hear appeals from the board of zoning adjustment or the zoning administrator.[6] A municipality may also authorize the planning commission to exercise the functions of the board of adjustment or zoning administrator.[7]

---

[1] *E.g.,* R.I. Gen. Laws § 45-22.2-1 et seq.; Utah Code Ann. § 10-9-101 et seq., § 17-27-101 et seq.

[2] Cal. Gov't Code § 65850.

[3] *Id.* § 65856.

[4] *Id* . § 65900.

[5] *Id.* § 65901.

[6] *Id.* § 65903.

[7] *Id.* § 65902.

In addition, states have authorized new zoning techniques, such as historic preservation exactions, and the transfer of development rights, may not be authorized by the Standard Zoning Act. An example is legislation that authorizes regulations for traditional neighborhood development (TND).[8]

The American Planning Association's model legislation retains the traditional format of the zoning ordinance but authorizes the adoption of zoning techniques not included in the Standard Act.[9] It also authorizes a zoning board of review that has, with some modifications, the same authority as the board of adjustment.[10]

§ 4.22 Extraterritorial Zoning.

Land development beyond municipal borders presents a difficult regulatory problem. Areas adjacent to a municipality may develop without the benefit of planning or zoning, or may develop under county zoning regulations that are inconsistent with the municipality's planning and zoning policies.

Municipalities can acquire some control over adjacent areas by prezoning adjacent land. This technique requires statutory authority.[1] California legislation, for example, authorizes the municipalities to prezone adjacent areas to predetermine the zoning that will take effect upon annexation.[2]

State courts have upheld extraterritorial zoning as a reasonable exercise of the police power. However, State legislation authorizing extraterritorial zoning usually limits this power. Illinois legislation states that municipal extraterritorial zoning "shall be reasonable with respect to the area outside the corporate limits so that future development will not be hindered or impaired."[3] Nor may a municipality exercise extraterritorial zoning powers if a county has adopted a zoning ordinance. North Carolina has a similar prohibition and, municipalities must define their extraterritorial zoning area by ordinance, "based upon existing or projected urban development and areas of critical concern to the city."[4] Florida requires an agreement between the city and the county on the boundaries of the extraterritorial zoning area, and on joint procedures in the preparation and

---

[8] *See* Conn. Gen. Stat. § 8-2j(b) (authorizing regulations for village districts); Pa. Stat. Ann. tit. 53 § 10-702A et seq.

[9] American Planning Association, Growing Smart Legislative Guidebook: Model Statutes for Planning and Management of Change § 8-201 (S. Meck ed. 2002).

[10] *Id.*, §§ 10-401 to 10-405.

[1] *Cf.* City of Carlsbad v. Caviness, 346 P.2d 310 (N.M. 1959). *See also* Smeltzer v. Messer, 225 S.W.2d 96 (Ky. 1949) (extraterritorial zoning statute did not authorize zoning in another county).

[2] Cal. Gov't Code § 65859.

[3] § 65 Ill. Comp. Stat. Ann. 5/11-13-1.

[4] N.C. Gen. Stat. § 160A-360.

adoption of comprehensive plans and the administration of land development regulations.[5]

§ 4.23   Constitutional Problems.

State courts have upheld extraterritorial zoning as a reasonable exercise of the police power.[1] However, state legislation that authorizes municipalities to adopt extraterritorial zoning does not give residents in the extraterritorial area the right to vote on the zoning ordinance, and may also raise problems under the U.S. Supreme Court's right-to-vote cases. *Holt Civic Club v. City of Tuscaloosa*[2] upheld a similar statute that extended the city's licensing, police, sanitary, and criminal court jurisdiction to a three-mile extraterritorial area against right-to-vote objections.

The Court held a right-to-vote problem arises only when a city denies the vote to individuals physically resident within its limits. Any other rule, it held, would be difficult to apply. Nonresidents could argue that many municipal actions taken within municipal limits require voting by nonresidents because they affect their interests. The Court also held a state legislature has a legitimate interest in the exercise of necessary governmental powers in developed but unincorporated areas adjacent to cities. Extraterritorial legislation reasonably advances this interest.

Holt may not apply to extraterritorial zoning because the Court pointed out in a footnote that the statute upheld did not include the power to zone, levy property taxes, and use eminent domain, which it characterized as "vital and traditional authorities." However, state courts have applied *Holt* to uphold extraterritorial zoning against right-to-vote objections.[3]

C.   HOME RULE.

§ 4.24   Constitutional Home Rule Authority.

A majority of state constitutions authorize municipal home rule, and some state constitutions authorize home rule for counties. Local governments in home rule states may be able to exercise land use control powers under their constitutional home rule authority.[1] The exercise of land use controls under constitutional home

---

[5] Fla. Stat. Ann. § 163.3171(1).

[1] Board of County Comm'rs v. Kokomo City Planning Comm'n, 310 N.E.2d 877 (Ind. App. 1974), *rev'd on other grounds*, 330 N.E.2d 92 (Ind. 1975); City of Raleigh v. Morand, 100 S.E.2d 870 (N.C. 1957); Walworth v. City of Elkhorn, 133 N.W.2d 257 (Wis. 1965).

[2] 439 U.S. 60 (1978).

[3] Town of Northville v. Village of Sheridan, 655 N.E.2d 22 (Ill. App. 1995); Schlientz v. City of North Platte, 110 N.W.2d 58 (Neb. 1961); Schmidt v. City of Kenosha, 571 N.W.2d 892 (Wis. App. 1997).

[1] *See also* N.J. Const. art. IV, § 6, ¶ 2 (authorizes state legislature to adopt zoning legislation); Ga. Const. art. 9, § 2, ¶ 4 (counties and municipalities may exercise zoning power subject to general laws establishing procedures).

rule provisions has several advantages. Local governments may be able to modify the administrative structure provided by the Standard Act for the zoning process, reassigning zoning responsibilities and even substituting alternate agencies for the agencies specified in the Act. One possibility is the substitution of an administrative hearings officer for the board of adjustment. Local governments could also exercise substantive land use control powers under their constitutional home rule authority that the Standard Zoning Act does not expressly confer. Aesthetic controls are an example.[2]

Whether land use controls are authorized by constitutional home rule depends to some extent on the type of home rule provision the constitution contains.[3] Under the traditional form of home rule the constitution specifies an area of concern in which local governments can legislate without statutory authority.[4] A traditional home rule provision may authorize local governments to legislate concerning their "municipal" or "corporate" affairs. Traditional home rule provisions do not usually elaborate the powers that are of local concern, a function the courts have assumed.

Courts usually classify areas of regulatory concern under traditional home rule as belonging exclusively to the state, exclusively local, or of concern both to the state and its local governments. If the area of concern is both state and local, the local government may regulate but state legislation may preempt. If the area of concern is exclusively local, a local government has the authority to regulate and state legislation may not preempt. If the area of concern belongs to the state, a local government may not regulate in that area at all. Home rule cases considering land use powers in states adopting the traditional form of home rule appear to treat land use powers as falling in the shared state-local category.

A number of states have adopted a newer form of constitutional home rule, which is called legislative home rule.[5] Under this type of home rule, local governments may exercise all powers the state legislature is capable of delegating to them even though the legislature has not delegated the power.[6] Legislative home rule clearly confers land use control powers.[7] It also allows the state

---

[2] Adams Outdoor Advertising v. City of Holland, 600 N.W.2d 339 (Mich. App. 1999) (upholding sign regulation.

[3] D. Mandelker, D. Netsch, P. Salsich & J. Wegner, State and Local Government in a Federal System (5th ed. 2002).

[4] Goodell v. Humboldt County, 575 N.W.2d 486 (Iowa 1998) (state regulation of animal feeding operations preempts local ordinance); Munroe v. Town of East Greenwich, 733 A.2d 703 (R.I. 1999) (state land development act preempts home rule charter provision on assignment of subdivision review function).

[5] See, e.g., National Municipal League Alternative Home Rule Model § 8.02.

[6] E.g., City of Miami Beach v. Fleetwood Hotel, Inc., 261 So.2d 801 (1972) (rent control).

[7] E.g., State ex rel. City of Beford v. Board of Elections, 577 N.E.2d 645 (Ohio 1991) (advisory referendum).

legislature to deny a home rule power a local government might otherwise exercise, and some state courts allow legislative denial by implication. These courts could construe state zoning legislation as an implied denial of local zoning powers.

Local governments usually implement their constitutional home rule powers by adopting a charter that specifies their home rule authority. Most state courts hold that local governments have only those home rule powers granted by their charters. A few state courts hold that local charters only limit home rule powers granted by the constitution.

§ 4.25   Home Rule Land Use Powers.

Although a few courts hold that zoning is not included in a home rule grant under traditional home rule,[1] most courts hold to the contrary. In some of these states, zoning is a matter of shared state and local concern, and the exercise of zoning powers by home rule municipalities is subject to controlling provisions in the state zoning enabling act.[2]

Other states hold that zoning is a matter only of local concern, and that state statutes do not control. In *Service Oil Co. v. Rhodus*,[3] a city adopted a zoning ordinance requiring the termination of an abandoned nonconforming use. The state zoning statute did not authorize this provision. The court held that zoning was a matter of purely local concern and that the legislature could not limit the local zoning power. Some courts also hold that the procedures used in zoning and other land use controls are a matter of local concern, and are governed by local charters or ordinances despite conflicting statutory provisions.[4]

---

[1] City of Livonia v. Department of Social Servs., 378 N.W.2d 402 (Mich. 1985); Asian Americans for Equality v. Koch, 514 N.Y.S.2d 939 (App. Div. 1987). *See also* City of Moore v. Atchison, Topeka & Santa Fe Ry. Co., 699 F.2d 507 (10th Cir. 1983) (zoning based on statute if not authorized by charter).

[2] Gumprecht v. City of Coeur D'Alene, 661 P.2d 1214 (Idaho 1983); Scadron v. City of Des Plaines, 606 N.E.2d 1154 (Ill. 1992) (signs); Adams Outdoor Advertising v. East Lansing, 483 N.W.2d 38 (Mich. 1992) (sign ordinance authorized by home rule act); A.C.E. Equip. Co. v. Erickson, 152 N.W.2d 739 (Minn. 1967); Rispo Realty & Dev. Co. v. City of Parma, 564 N.E.2d 425 (Ohio 1990) (procedures in zoning ordinance conflicted with state law); State ex rel. Ekern v. City of Milwaukee, 209 N.W. 860 (Wis. 1926). *Compare* Nelson v. City of Seattle, 395 P.2d 82 (Wash. 1965) (city may reject statutory authority and zone under home rule powers).

[3] 500 P.2d 807 (Colo. 1972). *See also* Board of County Comm'rs v. City of Thornton, 629 P.2d 605 (Colo. 1981) (home rule city has standing to object to zoning in adjacent county); Moore v. City of Boulder, 484 P.2d 134 (Colo. App. 1971) (zoning for low-income housing a local concern).

[4] Thompson v. Cook County Zoning Bd. of Appeals, 421 N.E.2d 285 (Ill. 1981); Vito v. City of Garfield Heights, 200 N.E.2d 501 (Ohio App. 1962); Bartle v. Zoning Bd. of Adjustment, 137 A.2d 239 (Pa. 1958).

A municipality in some traditional home rule states may exercise home rule powers, including land use powers, unless a statutory or other limitation prohibits the exercise of the power. In *Ayres v. City Council*,[5] the court held a city could require land dedications from a residential developer even though the state subdivision control legislation, the city's charter, and the city's subdivision ordinance did not authorize these dedications. California is a "limitation" home rule state. The court found no limitation on the dedication requirement in the statute, the charter, or the ordinance.[6]

White v. City of Dallas[7] is a similar case. A home rule zoning ordinance gave the board of adjustment an original jurisdiction to hear and decide cases on the continuance of nonconforming uses. The court upheld the ordinance against a contention that it was inconsistent with the state zoning statute, which gave the board the authority only to hear and decide appeals.

Land use controls are clearly a delegated home rule power in the legislative home rule states because the constitution delegates all powers the legislature could exercise.[8] The issue in these states is whether a statute has denied a home rule municipality the power to adopt a land use ordinance. The answer to this question turns on the legislative intent.[9]

---

[5] 207 P.2d 1 (Cal. 1949). *Compare* City of Los Angeles v. State, 187 Cal. Rptr. 893 (Cal. App. 1982) (home rule cities subject to requirement that zoning be consistent with plan).

[6] *See also* Brougher v. Board of Pub. Works, 271 P. 487 (Cal. 1928) (statutory procedures for adoption of zoning ordinance do not apply to home rule city); Boulder Bldrs. Group v. City of Boulder, 759 P.2d 752 (Colo. 1988) (growth control ordinance limiting development held authorized under home rule powers); Adams Outdoor Advertising v. City of Holland, 600 N.W. 2d 339 (Mich. App. 1997) (sign regulation); School Dist. of Philadelphia v. Zoning Bd. of Adjustment, 207 A.2d 864 (Pa. 1965). *See also* Sherman v. Frazier, 446 N.Y.S.2d 372 (App. Div. 1982) (zoning authority of towns).

[7] 517 S.W.2d 344 (Tex. Civ. App. 1974). *See also* City of College Station v. Turtle Rock Corp., 680 S.W.2d 802 (Tex. 1984); Hollingsworth v. City of Dallas, 931 S.W.2d 699 (Tex. App. 1996).

[8] Hollywood, Inc. v. Broward County, 431 So. 2d 606 (Fla. App. 1983) (subdivision exactions). *See* City of Boca Raton v. State, 595 So. 2d 25 (Fla. 1992) (home rule city may levy special assessment; reviews development of home rule powers).

[9] Schillerstrom Homes, Inc. v. City of Naperville, 762 N.E.2d 494 (2001) (ordinance and statute held complementary); Tisei v. Town of Ogunquit, 491 A.2d 564 (Me. 1985) (sewage usage ordinance held not in conflict with state law); Board of Appeals of Hanover v. Housing Appeals Comm., 294 N.E.2d 393 (Mass. 1973) (local zoning subject to state "snob zoning" law); City of Springfield v. Goff, 918 S.W.2d 786 (Mo. 1996) (city may not modify zoning protest provision in state statute).

D. ZONING FOR GOVERNMENT AND GOVERNMENT-REGULATED LAND DEVELOPMENT.

§ 4.26 The Governmental Immunity Problem.

The Standard Zoning Act does not limit the application of zoning ordinances to private land uses. Nothing in the Act prevents a local government from applying its zoning ordinance to governmental facilities. The courts take a different view. They have adopted a number of rules to determine when zoning applies to the capital facilities of public agencies. Earlier cases found an absolute immunity based on sovereign immunity principles. The leading case adopting the sovereign immunity rule for state facilities is *Kentucky Institute for Educ. of the Blind v. City of Louisville.*[1] Although some courts still confer an absolute immunity on state agencies, some of the more recent cases have adopted a more flexible "balancing test" that views sovereign immunity as only one factor to consider in intergovernmental immunity cases.

A variant of the intergovernmental immunity problem arises when a municipality applies its zoning ordinance to a public or private facility licensed or approved by a state agency. Examples are a local waste disposal facility licensed under a state environmental protection law, a private utility power transmission line approved by a state public utility commission, and a group home for mentally retarded children licensed by a state welfare agency.

In the intergovernmental land immunity cases considered here, the zoning ordinance prohibits the facility claiming immunity. A different question arises if the zoning ordinance only applies to off-street parking or similar restrictions on site development.[2] In this situation a court may not confer immunity. Nor may a court confer immunity for a use accessory to a public facility even if the local zoning ordinance is prohibitory.[3]

Although a few states have legislation expressly addressing the intergovernmental immunity problem,[4] in most states the planning and zoning legislation does not explicitly address this issue. The Standard Planning Act requires a three-fourths approval of the local governing body to override a planning commission determination that a proposed capital facility is not consistent with the local comprehensive plan. This provision does not address the zoning problem. Section 9 of the Standard Zoning Act also provides that "higher standards" contained in the zoning ordinance prevail over standards imposed under other legislation. This provision does not explicitly address the intergovernmental conflict problem,

---

[1] 97 S.W. 402 (Ky. 1906). *See also* Montgomery v. Town of Sherburne, 514 A.2d 702 (Vt. 1986) (federal immunity); 53 A.L.R.5th 1 (1997).

[2] School Dist. of Philadelphia v. Zoning Bd. of Adjustment, 207 A.2d 864 (Pa. 1965).

[3] Shell Oil Co. v. Board of Adjustment, 185 A.2d 201 (N.J. 1962).

[4] § 4.40.

although a few courts have relied on it to accord priority to a zoning regulation that applies to a public facility.

The absence of explicit legislative direction on the intergovernmental immunity problem sometimes leads courts to consider legislative intent when resolving intergovernmental conflicts in land use cases. Courts rely on legislative intent even though the absence of published legislative histories in most states makes it difficult to make this determination. The rule applied by some courts, that priority goes to the agency exercising the superior governmental power, is an application of the legislative intent rule. The courts determine whether the legislature intended the local zoning power or the public agency's power to undertake capital facility projects to be the superior power. This view gives the courts considerable discretion. A court will usually observe that both powers come from the state legislature and that both are presumptively entitled to equal stature. The court then applies its own analysis of legislative intent to determine which power is superior.

Although a court may apply the same rule, such as the legislative interpretation rule, to a variety of intergovernmental conflict problems, the cases tend to divide depending on the status of the government seeking zoning immunity. Cases in which a state agency claims immunity, for example, may take a different view than cases in which one local government claims immunity from the zoning ordinance of another local government. The sections that follow divide the cases along these lines.

§ 4.27 State Agencies.

The primary sovereign status of the state initially led courts to give the capital projects of state agencies an absolute immunity from local zoning ordinances. Many of these cases simply follow *Kentucky Institute* and hold that the sovereign status of the state confers an absolute immunity on state agencies from local zoning.[1] Some of these cases limit state immunity to governmental as distinguished from proprietary functions. A judicial rule conferring absolute immunity

---

[1] Board of Regents v. City of Tempe, 356 P.2d 399 (Ariz. 1960); Regents of Univ. of Cal. V. City of Santa Monica, 143 Cal Rptr. 276 (Cal. App. 1978); City of New Orleans v. State, 364 So. 2d 1020 (La. 1978); Morse v. Vermont Div. Of State Bldgs., 388 A.2d 371 (Vt. 1978). *But see* Varnado v. Southern Univ. at New Orleans, 621 So. 2d 176 (La. App. 1993) (university not agent of state when its parking lots violated zoning ordinance); Town of Bourne v. Plante, 708 N.E. 2d 103 (Mass. 1999) (parking facility); Senders v. Town of Columbia Falls, 647 A.2d 93 (Me. 1994) (lessee from state agency immune from zoning); City of Detroit v. Volunteers of America, 426 N.W.2d 743 (Mich. App. 1988) (independent contractor operating group home does not have state immunity); Town of Bourne v. Plante, 708 N.E.2d 103 (Mass. 1999) (steamship authority); 84 A.L.R.3d 1187 (1978). *See also* City of Joliet v. Snyder, 741 N.E.2d 1051 (Ill. App. 2000) (state facility of sexually violent persons not subject to conditional use requirement because housing of such persons does not pertain to "government affairs" of city as home rule unit).

on state agencies is questionable. It exalts sovereignty over substance, disregarding the impact a state facility can have on local zoning policies.[2]

A few courts have adopted a balancing test for state agency immunity that takes local zoning policies into account. The leading case is *Rutgers v. Piluso*.[3] The university was unable to build a dormitory for married students because it violated a local zoning ordinance limiting the number of dormitories for married, but not unmarried, students. The court held the university was immune from the ordinance, and that the "true test" of immunity in these cases was to determine the legislative intent by considering a number of "obvious and common" factors, including

> the nature and scope of the instrumentality seeking immunity, the kind of function or land use involved, the extent of the public interest to be served thereby, the effect local land use regulation would have upon the enterprise concerned and the impact of legitimate local interests.[4]

The court indicated this list of factors was not all-inclusive.

The court emphasized that state agency immunity was not unbridled, and that a state agency must not assert immunity in an unreasonable and arbitrary manner. It held that the local zoning restriction did not serve a legitimate interest in this case. The municipality's interest in avoiding the cost of educating children living in university housing was not a legitimate zoning concern. Other courts have adopted the *Rutgers* balancing test and have applied it to some or all state agencies.[5]

In *Commonwealth, Dep't of Gen. Servs. v. Ogontz Area Neighbors Ass'n*,[6] the municipality refused to issue permits for a state workshop and development center for mentally handicapped persons that did not comply with the zoning ordinance. The court overruled an earlier case adopting the balancing test and held that courts should resolve state and local land use conflicts by determining the legislative intent. Because legislative intent was difficult to determine from

---

[2] *But see* Snohomish County v. State, 648 P.2d 430 (Wash. 1982) (legislature expressly provided exemption for state prison).

[3] 286 A.2d 697 (N.J. 1972). *See* Township of West Orange v. Whitman, 8 F. Supp.2d 408 (D.N.J. 1998) (*Rutgers* rule does not apply to group homes for disabled protected by federal Fair Housing Act); Mayor & Council v. Clark, 516 A.2d 1126 (N.J. App. Div. 1986) (citing cases applying *Rutgers*); §§ 5.12–5.16.

[4] 286 A.2d at 702.

[5] Hayward v. Gaston, 542 A.2d 760 (Del. 1988); City of Newark v. University of Del., 304 A.2d 347 (Del. Ch. 1973); Kunimoto v. Kawakami, 545 P.2d 684 (Haw. 1976); Herrmann v. Board of Cty. Comm'rs, 785 P.2d 1003 (Kan. 1990); Brown v. Kansas Forestry, Fish & Game Comm'n, 576 P.2d 230 (Kan. App. 1978); Brownfield v. State, 407 N.E.2d 1365 (Ohio 1980).

[6] 483 A.2d 448 (Pa. 1984). *See also* Olon v. Commonwealth, 626 A.2d 533 (Pa. 1993) (finding legislative intent to override local zoning ordinance); Kee v. Pennsylvania Turnpike Comm'n, 722 A.2d 1123 (Pa. Commw. 1998) (Commission subject to local zoning).

the applicable statutes, the court applied the rule of construction that determines legislative intent by considering the consequences of a particular interpretation. The court concluded that giving priority to the zoning ordinance would give effect to the legislative mandates of both government entities. Allowing the state agency to override local zoning would frustrate local zoning powers, and a state agency prohibited from using one location could always find another.

Although *Ogontz* rejected the balancing test, its legislative intent rule is similar to the multifactor "balancing" rule adopted in *Rutgers* that also emphasizes legislative intent. These decisions illustrate a growing line of cases that refuse to give absolute immunity to state agencies under a superior sovereignty theory.[7]

§ 4.28   Local Governments Exercising State Functions.

State-transferred immunity can bar local zoning in a category of cases in which local governments exercise state functions. Counties and school districts are in this category. Courts view these local government units as state "agencies" in the loose sense that they carry out state-delegated functions at the local level. County authority for the administration of justice is an example. Courts classify these governmental units as "quasi-local governments" to distinguish them from local governments exercising comprehensive local government powers.

A number of cases transfer the absolute immunity of the state to quasi-local governments exercising state functions.[1] These cases rely on the role of these governmental units in carrying out responsibilities for the state, such as the administration of justice, within their territorial areas. These cases are a strained interpretation of the state immunity rule. All local governments exercise powers delegated by the state. To separate so-called "quasi-local government" entities, such as counties and school districts, from general-function municipalities is improper. Decisions granting them immunity from local zoning are another example of exalting sovereignty over substance.

School districts present a special problem. Most courts exempt school districts from local zoning because the state retains extensive control over the education function. They may also rely on the statutory authority delegated to school districts to determine locations for school facilities.[2] These cases conclude that

---

[7] *See also* Dearden v. City of Detroit, 245 N.W.2d 700 (Mich. App. 1976); City of Hattiesburg v. Region XII Comm'n on Mental Health & Retardation, 654 So. 2d 516 (Miss. 1995) (regional mental health facility subject to local zoning).

[1] Vagim v. Board of Supvrs., 40 Cal. Rptr. 760 (Cal. App. 1964); County of Los Angeles v. City of Los Angeles, 28 Cal. Rptr. 32 (Cal. App. 1963); Lake Charles Harbor & Term. Dist. v. Calcasieu Parish Police Jury, 613 So. 2d 1031 (La. App. 1993); Glascock v. Baltimore Cty., 581 A.2d 822 (Md. 1990); County Comm'rs v. Conservation Comm'n of Dartmouth, 405 N.E.2d 637 (Mass. 1980).

[2] Town of Atherton v. Superior Court, 324 P.2d 328 (Cal. App. 1958); Normandy School Dist.

the grant of statutory authority to determine "location" overrides the authority of a local government to make the same decision under its zoning ordinance. Off-street parking requirements are an exception,[3] but they do not force school districts to select another site for a school.

Many states have constitutional provisions requiring the establishment of a system of public education. Some courts view state enabling legislation for school districts as a statutory implementation of this constitutional requirement. This constitutional authority for establishing a system of public education is another reason courts give for exempting school districts from local zoning.

The school cases stand apart. Provision of an adequate educational system requires the location of schools close to or within the neighborhoods they serve. Municipalities may attempt to exclude schools from these locations because residential neighbors consider schools an intrusive land use. The courts believe that educational necessity overrides local zoning powers often used to exclude schools at locations the school district considers appropriate.

§ 4.29 State-Regulated Facilities and Businesses.

State legislation commonly provides for the licensing and regulation of a number of public and private facilities and private businesses. This legislation may authorize a state agency to permit the operation of a business or the construction of a facility at a designated location if the regulatory standards in the legislation are satisfied. An example is a permit for the operation of a private airport issued by the state aeronautics agency. Conflicts arise when a zoning ordinance prohibits the facility or business at the location the state agency designates. The state legislation may indicate whether the state agency can override the local zoning ordinance. If the legislation does not resolve the state-local conflict, the courts must determine whether the state agency can override local zoning.

The cases that have considered conflicts between state regulation and licensing and local zoning do not usually turn on the superior sovereignty of the state.

---

v. City of Pasadena Hills, 70 S.W.3d 488 (Mo. App. 2002); Board of Coop. Educ. Serv. v. Gaynor, 303 N.Y.S.2d 183 (Sup. Ct. 1969); Appeal of Radnor Twp. School Auth., 252 A.2d 597 (Pa. 1969); Hazleton Area School Dist. v. Zoning Hearing Bd., 720 A.2d 220 (Pa. Commw. 1998) (statute does not preempt zoning authority over non-school related activities). Austin Indep. School Dist. v. City of Sunset Valley, 502 S.W.2d 670 (Tex. 1973); 71 A.L.R.3d 136 (1976). *See also* § 5.28 (zoning for private schools). *But see* Council Rock School Dist. v. Wrightstown Township Zoning Hearing Bd., 709 A.2d 453 (Pa. Commw. 1998) (holding *Ogontz* decision, discussed *supra* § 4.27, modifies earlier decisions).

[3] Robinson v. Indianola Mun. Separate School Dist., 467 So. 2d 911 (Miss. 1985); School Dist. of Philadelphia v. Zoning Bd. of Adjustment, 207 A.2d 864 (Pa. 1965). *See also* Hazleton Area School Dist. v. Zoning Hearing Bd., 778 A.2d 1205 (Pa. 2001) (no immunity for lease of athletic field).

Most courts examine the legislative intent to determine whether the state legislation preempts the local zoning ordinance, either expressly or by implication. To decide this question courts look at a number of factors, including the purpose of the statute, whether the subject matter requires a uniform system of state regulation, and whether the local regulation conflicts with or frustrates the purposes and objectives of the state law.

§ 4.30 State Environmental Programs.

Many states, prodded by federal environmental legislation, have adopted statutes that require permits for environmental facilities. Legislation requiring permits for hazardous waste disposal facilities is an important example. A statute may make an environmental permit subject to local zoning regulations.[1] It may also provide that a local government may not require permits for state-permitted hazardous waste facilities.[2] In the absence of an express provision covering local zoning, the courts must decide whether the legislature intended, by implication, that the state legislation overrides local zoning powers.

Courts are split on the issue of implied preemption. Although some courts hold to the contrary,[3] other courts hold a state statute preempts local zoning even without an express preemption provision.[4] Often when a court decides a state law does not preempt local zoning the reason is that the state law has a different purpose,[5] that the legislature did not intend to cover the entire regulatory field[6] or that the state statute included only minimum standards, which the local ordinance could exceed.[7] The home rule status of the zoning municipality may affect the resolution of this question.[8]

Welsh v. City of Orono[9] illustrates the cases finding preemption. The Minnesota Supreme Court held a municipality did not have the authority to require

[1] Conn. Gen. Stat. § 22a-124; § 415 Ill. Comp. Stat. Ann. 5/39(c); La Stat. Ann. § 30:2180(C); Minn. Stat. Ann. § 115.28.

[2] N.C. Gen. Stat. § 130A-293; Pa. Stat. Ann. tit. 52, § 681.20c.

[3] Water Dist. No. 1 of Johnson County v. City Council of Kansas City, 871 P.2d 1256 (Kan. 1994) (state monofill law does not preempt); IT Corp. v. Solano County Bd. of Supvrs., 820 P.2d 1023 (Cal. 1991) (same; hazardous waste disposal); Council of Middletown Twp. v. Benhjam, 523 A.2d 311 (Pa. 1987) (same); Resource Conservation Mgt., Inc. v. Board of Supvrs., 380 S.E.2d 879 (Va. 1989) (same; landfills).

[4] Holmes v. Maryland Reclamation Assocs., 600 A.2d 864 (Md. 1992) (solid waste management law); Applied Chem. Tech., Inc. v. Town of Merrimack, 490 A.2d 1348 (N.H. 1985) (hazardous waste); Little Falls Twp. v. Bardin, 414 A.2d 559 (N.J. 1979) (landfills).

[5] Palermo Land Co. v. Planning Comm'n, 561 So. 2d 482 (La. 1990).

[6] Resource Conservation Mgt., Inc. v. Board of Supvrs., 380 S.E.2d 879 (Va. 1989). *See also* Town of Beacon Falls v. Posick, 549 A.2d 656 (Conn. App. 1988) (statute interpreted to deny immunity).

[7] IT Corp. v. Solano County Bd. of Supvrs., 820 P.2d 1023 (Cal. 1991).

[8] *See* § 4.39.

[9] 355 N.W.2d 117 (Minn. 1984).

a conditional use permit for dredging and filling. The court held the legislature had clearly delegated water resource conservation, particularly jurisdiction over dredging and filling, to the state resources agency.[10] *Ad + Soil, Inc. v. County Commissioners*[11] held the state sewage management legislation did not preempt local zoning. The court found the state legislation intended to foster local control under state supervision, and that its purpose was to coordinate and supplement local zoning through the enactment of a statewide regulatory program. A statute may cover the preemption problem by specifying what local regulations are allowed.[12]

§ 4.31 State Permits for Other Private Activities.

State legislation often requires a location permit for a number of private activities that can also be regulated by zoning ordinances. Examples are motor vehicle storage,[1] airports or heliports,[2] agricultural and forestry activities,[3] oil and gas well drilling and petroleum storage,[4] and gambling.[5] Courts again will

---

[10] *See also* Arthur Whitcomb, Inc. v. Town of Carroll, 686 A.2d 743 (N.H. 1996) (comprehensive state legislation on commercial excavation preempts local zoning); River Springs Ltd. Liability Co. v. Board of County Comm'rs, 899 P.2d 1329 (Wyo. 1995) (state agency has pervasive control over mining);67 A.L.R.4th 822 (1988).

[11] 513 A.2d 893 (Md. 1986). *See also* Fafard v. Conservation Comm'n of Barnstable, 733 N.E.2d 66 (Mass. 2000) (state pier regulations do not address impact of pier construction on zoning regulations, public safety, creation of nuisances, or other spheres traditionally within municipal authority); Town of Parishville v. Contore Co., 667 N.Y.S.2d 453 (App. Div. 1998) (mined reclamation law does not preempt local zoning). *But see* Soaring Vista Props. v. Board of County Comm'rs, 741 A.2d 1110 (Md. 1999) (statute authorizing sewage sludge permit held to preempt local zoning).

[12] *E.g.* Va. Code §§ 10.1-1126.1 (indicating local regulations that can apply to forestry practices). See Dull v. York County, 528 S.E.2d 447 (Va. 2000) (holding local buffer zone requirement and clearcutting prohibition consistent with state law). *See also* Sawyer Env't Recovery Facilities, Inc. v. Town of Hampden, 760 A.2d 257 (Me. 2000) (ban on expansion of solid waste facility inconsistent with state law).

[1] Board of County Comm'rs v. Martin, 856 P.2d 62 (Colo. App. 1993) (zoning preempted); Joe Horisk's Salvage Pool Systems of Ohio v. City of Strongsville, 631 N.E.2d 1097 (Ohio App. 1993) (contra).

[2] Helicopter Assocs. v. City of Stamford, 519 A.2d 49 (Conn. 1986) (zoning not preempted); Garden State Farms, Inc. v. Bay, II, 390 A.2d 1177 (N.J. 1978) (same); County of DuPage v. Harris, 231 N.E.2d 195 (Ill. App. 1967) (same).

[3] Big Creek Lumber Co. v. County of San Mateo, 37 Cal. Rptr. 2d 159 (Cal. App. 1995) (timber harvesting; zoning ordinance not preempted).

[4] Newbury Twp. Bd. of Twp. Trustees v. Lomak Petroleum (Ohio), Inc. 583 N.E.2d 302 (Ohio 1992) (oil and gas well drilling; zoning preempted); Northeastern Gas Co. v. Foster Twp. Zoning Hearing Bd., 613 A.2d 606 (Pa. 1992) (gasoline storage; zoning not preempted).

[5] St. Charles Gaming Co. v. Riverboat Gaming Comm'n, 648 So. 2d 1310 (La. 1995) (zoning not preempted).

look at the usual factors they apply in preemption cases to determine whether the local zoning ordinance is preempted. For example, in *Big Creek Lumber Co. v. County of San Mateo*,[6] the county zoning ordinance prohibited timber harvesting in designated rural areas within 1,000 feet of any dwelling. The court held the state Forest Practice Act did not preempt the county zoning ordinance. The Act regulated how timber operations should be conducted, while the county zoning ordinance regulated where they can take place.[7]

§ 4.32 Private Utilities.

State utility regulation authorizes comprehensive regulations of an entire industry by the state utility agency. As part of its regulatory authority the state agency must approve the location of utility facilities, such as transmission lines and power stations. Municipalities may object to these facilities and exclude them through zoning or impose financially burdensome requirements, such as requiring the undergrounding of utility lines.

Exclusion of a utility's facility from a municipality may compel it to select a more expensive location. Rerouting of a power transmission line, for example, may be more expensive because the new route may be less direct. Most utilities also serve an area wider than the municipality that excludes or burdens its operations. State agency resolution of conflicts with local governments may be necessary to take the needs of the wider service area into account.

Many of the utility cases do not present a zoning problem. The overhead power line cases are an example. A municipality may simply adopt a "police power" ordinance that requires the utility to place power lines underground. Most courts hold that the state utility commission's approval of the overhead line under state legislation comprehensively regulating the utility industry confers immunity from this ordinance.[1]

Most courts reach the same result in the zoning cases for the same reason and grant immunity from zoning ordinances prohibiting a utility company facility.[2]

---

[6] 37 Cal. Rptr. 2d 159 (Cal. App. 1995).

[7] *See also* Barnhill v. City of North Myrtle Beach, 511 S.E.2d 361 (S.C. 1999) (state regulation of watercraft does not preempt local regulation of activity on beach); Willow Creek Ranch, LLC v. Town of Shelby, 611 N.W.2d 693 (Wis. 2000) (town may apply zoning ordinance to game bird farm licensed by state).

[1] Union Elec. Co. v. City of Crestwood, 499 S.W.2d 480 (Mo. 1973); Cohen v. Ford, 339 A.2d 175 (Pa. Commw. 1975).

[2] For zoning cases, see Harbor Carriers, Inc. v. City of Sausalito, 121 Cal. Rptr. 577 (Cal. App. 1975); Commonwealth Edison Co. v. City of Warrenville, 680 N.E.2d 465 (Ill. App. 1997); Graham Farms, Inc. v. Indianapolis Power & Light Co., 233 N.E.2d 656 (Ind. 1968); Howard Cty. v. Potomac Elec. Power Co., 573 A.2d 821 (Md. 1990); Consolidated Edison Co. of N.Y. v. Village of Briarcliff Manor, 144 N.Y.S.2d 379 (Sup. Ct. 1955); Duquesne Light Co. v. Upper St. Clair Twp., 105 A.2d 287 (Pa. 1954); Commonwealth v. Delaware & Hudson Ry. Co., 339 A.2d 155 (Pa. Commw. 1975); Potomac Edison Co. v. Jefferson County Planning & Zoning Comm'n, 512 S.E.2d 576 (W.Va. 1998).

The few zoning cases reaching a contrary result have not always considered the effect of comprehensive utility regulation on local zoning.[3] The cases that give priority to the state utility agency's decision effectively decide the land use controversy these cases present. The state utility agency is primarily concerned with the economic health and efficiency of the utility industry and is not likely to uphold a prohibitory local zoning ordinance. Some state legislation expressly authorizes the state utility agency to preempt local zoning.[4] The court decisions tend to uphold the state utility agency under this legislation when it sets aside a local zoning decision.[5] Legislation in other states requires utilities that receive state permits to comply with local zoning.[6]

Some states have adopted legislation dealing expressly with the siting of electric power stations and transmission lines. This legislation authorizes the governor or a specially created state siting agency to make the siting decision. Like the utility agency legislation, this legislation may expressly preempt local zoning.[7] Court decisions under these laws have upheld decisions by state agencies authorizing utility facilities not permitted by local zoning even though the state legislation does not authorize preemption. They rely on the legislative intent to provide a comprehensive state-wide solution to the siting problem that considers land use as well as industry problems.[8]

§ 4.33   Liquor Licensees.

State liquor control legislation raises a zoning preemption problem. In addition to determining the fitness of the applicant for a liquor license, the state liquor control agency also grants a license for the sale of liquor at a designated location. The question that arises is whether the state liquor control law preempts a zoning restriction that prohibits the sale of liquor at the location designated in a state license.

[3] Wolf v. Village of Mt. Prospect, 40 N.E.2d 778 (Ill. App. 1942); Porter v. Southwestern Pub. Serv. Co., 489 S.W.2d 361 (Tex. 1972); City of Richmond v. Southern Ry., 123 S.E.2d 641 (Va. 1962).

[4] *E.g.,* Md. Nat. Res. Code Ann. § 3-306.1; Mass. Gen. L. ch. 40A, § 3; N.Y. Pub. Serv. Law § 126 (state agency may refuse to apply restrictive local law). *See also* Ohio Rev. Code Ann. § 4905.65(B) (limits local authority).

[5] New England LNG Co. v. City of Fall River, 331 N.E.2d 536 (Mass. 1975); Public Serv. Co. v. Town of Hampton, 411 A.2d 164 (N.H. 1980); In re Monmouth Consol. Water Co. v. Board of Pub. Util. Comm'rs, 220 A.2d 189 (N.J. 1966).

[6] *E.g.,* Ky. Rev. Stat. Ann. § 278.040(2); Nev. Rev. Stat. § 704.890(2).

[7] *Compare* Conn. Gen. Stat. § 16-50x(d) (preserves local zoning power) *with* Or. Rev. Stat. § 469.401(3) (contra) *and* Wash. Rev. Code Ann. § 80.50.110(2) (same).

[8] Detroit Edison Co. v. Township of Richmond, 388 N.W.2d 296 (Mich. App. 1986); Vermont Elec. Power Co. v. Bandel, 375 A.2d 975 (Vt. 1977); Petition of Vermont Elec. Power Co., 306 A.2d 687 (Vt. 1973).

Some state liquor licensing statutes expressly provide that a liquor licensee must comply with local zoning.[1] The courts divide on whether the state liquor control law preempts local zoning in the absence of such a provision, though recent cases have not found preemption..[2] Courts that find preemption usually base their holding on the comprehensive scope of the state liquor control law. Even when this legislation is not comprehensive, a court may conclude that local zoning is preempted by holding that the zoning ordinance attempted to "veto" or set aside the state license. Courts that hold to the contrary find that the state liquor control legislation does not provide the authority to resolve land use conflicts. They hold that this authority is conferred on the municipality under state zoning legislation.

§ 4.34 Local Governments.

Intergovernmental land use conflicts arise when a local government plans to build a facility that a zoning ordinance prohibits. The courts apply a variety of rules to determine whether a local government not enjoying state immunity is subject to the zoning ordinance of another municipality. The sections that follow discuss these rules. Local governments must comply with their own zoning ordinance unless exempted by the ordinance or protected by one of these judicially adopted immunity rules.[1]

§ 4.35 Governmental-Proprietary Rule.

Most courts originally applied a governmental-proprietary rule to local government land use conflicts. This rule exempts a local government facility from the zoning ordinance of another municipality if the facility is to be used to carry

---

[1] *E.g.,* Cal. Bus. & Prof. Code § 23790; Conn. Gen. Stat. § 30-44; Tex. Alco. Bev. Code Ann. § 109.32 (authorizing regulation of sale of beer).

[2] Preempted: Application of Melkonian, 355 S.E.2d 503 (N.C. App. 1987); 7-Eleven, Inc. v. McClain, 422 P.2d 455 (Okla. 1967); Wetlake v. Mascot Petroleum Co., 573 N.E.2d 1068 (Ohio 1991); Salt Lake County v. Liquor Control Comm'n, 357 P.2d 488 (Utah 1960). Not preempted: Korean American Legal Advocacy Found. v. City of Los Angeles, 28 Cal. Rptr. 2d 530 (Cal. App. 1994); O'Banion v. State ex rel. Shively, 253 N.E.2d 739 (Ind. App. 1969); Town Pump, Inc. v. Board of Adjustment, 971 P.2d 349 (Mont. 1998); DJL Restaurant Corp. v. City of New York, 749 N.E.2d 186 (N.Y. 2001) (adult use); Tex-1, Inc. v. City of Dayton Bd. of Zoning Appeals, 758 N.E.2d 768 (Ohio App. 2001) (brewery manufacturing); Town of Hilton Head Island v. Fine Liquors, Ltd., 397 S.E.2d 662 (S.C. 1990); City of Clute v. Linscomb, 446 S.W.2d 377 (Tex. Civ. App. 1969); County of Chesterfield v. Windy Hill, Ltd., 559 S.E.2d 627 (Va. 2002); Longwell v. Hodge, 297 S.E.2d 820 (W. Va. 1982) (reviewing cases). *See* 9 A.L.R.2d 877 (1950).

[1] Clark v. Town of Estes Park, 686 P.2d 777 (Colo. 1984) (rejecting governmental-proprietary rule); Sinn v. Board of Selectmen of Acton, 259 N.E.2d 557 (Mass. 1970); Hagfeldt v. City of Bozeman, 757 P.2d 753 (Mont. 1988) (applies legislative intent test); Scotch Plains Twp. v. Town of Westfield, 199 A.2d 673 (N.J.L. Div. 1964); Davidson County v. City of High Point, 354 S.E.2d 280 (N.C. App. 1987) (legislative intent rule); Nunes v. Town of Bristol, 232 A.2d 775 (R.I. 1967). *Compare* City of Lubbock v. Austin, 628 S.W.2d 49 (Tex. 1982).

out a governmental as distinguished from a proprietary function.[1] Courts borrowed the governmental-proprietary rule from local government tort law. Local governments historically were immune from tort liability when exercising governmental functions but were liable for torts committed in the exercise of proprietary functions.

Almost all courts have abandoned the governmental-proprietary rule in local government tort liability cases. They concluded that the rule is irrelevant to the solution of local government tort liability problems. Many critics also argue that this rule is irrelevant to the solution of intergovernmental land use conflicts, and some courts have rejected this rule as a test for resolving these conflicts.

§ 4.36   Eminent Domain Rule.

The eminent domain rule is another well-established rule courts use to resolve local government land use conflicts. Under this rule, courts exempt the local government that plans to construct a public facility from compliance with the zoning ordinance of another municipality if it has the authority to exercise the power of eminent domain.[1] These courts believe that the eminent domain power is superior to the zoning power. They reason that the exercise of the power of eminent domain is an attribute of state sovereignty limited only by the constitution.

The eminent domain rule also is questionable. It is irrelevant to the land use conflict problem and favors the local government that plans to build the facility because this government usually has the power of eminent domain.

§ 4.37   Superior Power Rule.

Some courts decide intergovernmental land use conflicts by determining which local government has the superior power. The court must choose between the zoning power and the power under which a local government plans to construct a public facility. The superior power rule may require the courts to examine the legislative intent to determine which power is superior.

---

[1] Lauderdale County Bd. of Educ. v. Alexander, 110 So. 2d 911 (Ala. 1959); City of Scottsdale v. Municipal Court of Tempe, 368 P.2d 637 (Ariz. 1962); AIA Mobile Home Park v. Brevard County, 246 So. 2d 126 (Fla. App. 1971); Macon-Bibb County Hospital Auth. v. Madison, 420 S.E.2d 586 (Ga. App. 1992); Baltis v. Village of Westchester, 121 N.E.2d 495 (Ill. 1954); Taber v. City of Benton Harbor, 274 N.W. 324 (Mich. 1937); City of Vinita Park v. Girls Sheltercare, Inc., 664 S.W.2d 256 (Mo. App. 1984) (court also applied superior power rule).

[1] Mayor of Savannah v. Collins, 84 S.E.2d 454 (Ga. 1954); City of Des Plaines v. Metropolitan San. Dist., 268 N.E.2d 428 (Ill. 1971); City of Washington v. Warren County, 899 S.W.2d 863 (Mo. 1995); Seward County Bd. of Comm'rs v. City of Seward, 242 N.W.2d 849 (Neb. 1976); State ex rel. Helsel v. Board of County Comm'rs, 78 N.E.2d 694 (Ohio App. 1948); South Hill Sewer Dist. v. Pierce County, 591 P.2d 877 (Wash. App. 1979); 53 A.L.R.5th 1 (1997).

Wilkinsburg-Penn Joint Water Auth. v. Borough of Churchill[1] illustrates the superior power rule. A water authority planned to construct an elevated water tower at a site where a zoning ordinance did not permit it. The court held that the authority was subject to the zoning ordinance. It noted that the state zoning act, like the Standard Act, required zoning to be in accordance with a comprehensive plan and to implement a number of statutory objectives, including the adequate provision of water. These provisions indicated "that the objectives of zoning regulation are more comprehensive than and, in fact, include the objectives of the water authority." Some courts take the contrary position. They hold that the legislation authorizing the construction of a public facility is superior to the zoning legislation.[2]

Courts may accord a special status to historic preservation. In *Mayor of Annapolis v. Anne Arundel County*[3] the court upheld a decision by the city's Historic District Commission that prohibited the demolition of a church owned by the county in an historic district. The court held that historic preservation ordinances were entitled to more judicial protection than conventional zoning because they regulate the preservation of building exteriors rather than land use. Historic preservation also imposes more rigorous procedural requirements. Governmental noncompliance would frustrate the goals of historic zoning because "a valuable building is just as much lost by destruction by a public body as it would by a private owner."

§ 4.38 Balancing Test.

A number of courts have adopted a balancing test to resolve land use conflicts between local governments. These cases reject the traditional tests, such as the governmental-proprietary rule, because they believe they are not appropriate for resolving local government land use conflicts. As some courts note, the traditional tests are acceptable when a local government seeks exemption from its own zoning ordinance. They should not apply when a local government seeks exemption from another local government's zoning ordinance.[1] New Jersey adopted a balancing test for state-local land use conflicts in *Rutgers v. Piluso*.[2]

[1] 207 A.2d 905 (Pa. 1965). *Accord* Jefferson County v. City of Birmingham, 55 So. 2d 196 (Ala. 1951); Wilmette Park Dist. v. Village of Wilmette, 490 N.E.2d 1282 (Ill. 1986) (but holding that zoning decision is judicially reviewable); County of Venango v. Borough of Sugarcreek Zoning Hearing Bd., 626 A.2d 489 (Pa. 1993) (county's zoning power superior under court's legislative intent rule; see § 4.28); City of Richmond v. Board of Supvrs., 101 S.E.2d 641 (Va. 1958).

[2] Village of Swansea v. County of St. Clair, 359 N.E.2d 866 (Ill. App. 1977). *Cf.* City of Kirkwood v. City of Sunset Hills, 589 S.W.2d 31 (Mo. App. 1979).

[3] 316 A.2d 807 (Md. 1974). *Accord* City of Ithaca v. County of Tompkins, 355 N.Y.S.2d 275 (Sup. Ct. 1974). *Contra* State v. City of Seattle, 615 P.2d 461 (Wash. 1980).

[1] Orange County v. City of Apopka, 299 So. 2d 652 (Fla. App. 1974).

[2] 286 A.2d 697 (N.J. 1972), discussed in § 4.27.

Under this test, the court considers a number of factors to determine the legislative intent in allocating power between different local government entities. The New Jersey courts have applied the *Rutgers* balancing test to local government land use conflicts, and other courts have adopted it for land use conflicts between local governments.[3]

Some courts adopted a different version of the balancing test. *In City of Temple Terrace v. Hillsborough Ass'n for Retarded Citizens*,[4] a home for the mentally retarded, which operated under a contract with a state agency, planned to locate in an area where a local zoning ordinance did not allow it. Although the case was not a land use dispute between two local governments, the court held that it would apply a balancing test to local government land use conflicts.

Unlike *Rutgers, Temple Terrace* did not investigate legislative intent to resolve the land use conflict. It held that legislation granting an exemption from a zoning restriction must be explicit and added that:

> When the state legislature is silent on the subject, the governmental unit seeking to use land contrary to local zoning regulations should have the burden of proving that the public interests favoring the proposed use outweigh those mitigating against a use not sanctioned by the zoning regulations of the local government.[5]

The court also held that, "under normal circumstances," a local government should attempt to secure the approvals required by a zoning ordinance before raising the exemption issue.

Temple Terrace favors the local zoning ordinance over the public facility. Its holding that a local government carries the burden to justify a violation of a zoning ordinance is contrary to *Rutgers,* which appears to put the burden on the opposing municipality to justify its zoning.

Lincoln County v. Johnson[6] also adopted a different version of the balancing test. A city planned to locate a waste disposal facility outside its limits, but within the county, at a site where the county zoning ordinance did not permit it. The city made no attempt to obtain a zoning change. The state agency issued a permit for the facility but declined to decide the zoning issue.

---

[3] City of Crown Point v. Lake County, 510 N.E.2d 684 (Ind. 1992); Pittsfield Charter Township v. Washtenaw County, 633 N.W.2d 10 (Mich. App. 2001) (zoning power preferred based on legislative intent); City of Bridgeton v. City of St. Louis, 18 S.W.2d 107 (Mo. App. 2000); City of St. Louis v. City of Bridgeton, 705 S.W.2d 524 (Mo. App. 1985); Hagfeldt v. City of Bozeman, 757 P.2d 753 (Mont. 1988); Matter of Cty. of Monroe, 530 N.E.2d 202 (N.Y. 1988) (overruling case adopting governmental-proprietary test); Independent School Dist. No. 89 v. City of Oklahoma City, 722 P.2d 1212 (Okla. 1986); Smithfield v. Fanning, 602 A.2d 939 (R.I. 1992).

[4] 322 So. 2d 571 (Fla. App. 1975), *aff'd,* 332 So. 2d 610 (Fla. 1976).

[5] *Id.* at 579.

[6] 257 N.W.2d 453 (S.D. 1977) (also adopting burden of proof rule of *Temple Terrace*).

This case also favored the zoning power. It held that a local government should apply for a zoning change when it plans to build a facility on a site where the zoning ordinance does not allow it. If it is not satisfied with the zoning decision, the local government can appeal to a trial court. The court should then consider the "zoning factors," the local government's legislative authority, the public need for the facility, and alternative locations and methods for carrying out the project. Other courts have adopted modified versions of the balancing test for local government land use conflicts.[7]

Proponents of the balancing test favor it because the traditional tests often give priority to the local government facility and do not allow courts to consider local zoning policies. Balancing test proponents view the traditional tests as bad land use law. This argument overlooks the difficulties the balancing test presents. It allows courts to displace local zoning policies with their own policy for resolving local government land use conflicts, a form of judicial zoning that may be unwise. The case-by-case adjudication required by the balancing test also makes the application of zoning restrictions to the public facilities of other local governments dependent on the uncertainties of judicial review. Some courts have rejected the balancing test for some or all of these reasons.[8]

As an alternative to the balancing test, a court could hold that the local zoning power is superior because zoning, especially if it implements a comprehensive plan, can comprehensively resolve local government land use conflicts. A court should set aside the zoning ordinance only if it improperly excludes a needed governmental facility that cannot find a feasible alternative location. This test contemplates judicial policy-making, but the court's role is more limited and better focused.

Courts should also be sensitive to the status of the public agency whose facility violates the local zoning ordinance. The superior state sovereignty view has merit when a state agency administers a state program that requires a comprehensive resolution of intergovernmental land use conflicts. State waste disposal programs are an example. Local governments and private entities that have state agency approval in these programs are entitled to immunity from zoning restrictions. Status counts least when one local government invades the territory of another. Judicial resolution of these intergovernmental land use disputes is necessary and probably inevitable.

---

[7] City of Ames v. Story County, 392 N.W.2d 145 (Iowa 1986); City of Fargo v. Harwood Twp., 256 N.W.2d 694 (N.D. 1977).

[8] City of New Orleans v. State, 364 So. 2d 1020 (La. 1978); Dearden v. City of Detroit, 269 N.W.2d 139 (Mich. 1978); Everett v. Snohomish Cty., 772 P.2d 992 (Wash. 1989) (adopting legislative intent test). See also Commonwealth, Dep't of Gen. Servs. v. Ogontz Area Neighbors Ass'n, 483 A.2d 448 (Pa. 1984) (rejecting balancing test for state agencies; see § 4.27).

§ 4.39 Home Rule Problems.

Under the traditional grant of constitutional home rule powers to local governments, the legislature can preempt local home rule authority, including zoning authority, through general legislation. A court could find a home rule zoning ordinance preempted under this rule by a statute that authorizes the construction of a public facility to implement a state legislative policy. A school built by a school district is an example.[1]

Constitutional home rule powers can favor the zoning ordinance in the resolution of intergovernmental land use conflicts. If a municipality adopts its zoning ordinance under its home rule powers, a court may rely on the constitutional grant of home rule authority to give priority to the zoning ordinance.[2] *Temple Terrace*[3] took a different view. In a case in which a state-supervised group home violated a local zoning ordinance, the court held that home rule authority for the zoning ordinance "weakened" the immunity of the state-regulated agency.

Home rule status may sometimes protect an invading local government. In one case, a city exercising home rule powers to construct a campsite outside its limits was exempted from compliance with a county zoning ordinance.[4]

§ 4.40 Legislative Solutions.

The usual failure of state legislation to provide more guidance on intergovernmental land use conflicts is surprising in view of the conflicting court decisions. A few statutes resolve this problem for specific facilities,[1] and an occasional statute enacts a more general rule. An Oregon statute,[2] provides that local zoning ordinances are applicable to publicly owned property.

---

[1] Board of Educ. v. Houghton, 233 N.W. 834 (Minn. 1930). *See also* Town of Atherton v. Superior Court, 324 P.2d 328 (Cal. App. 1958).

[2] City of Plano v. City of Allen, 395 S.W.2d 927 (Tex. App. 1965).

[3] 322 So. 2d 571 (Fla. App. 1975), *aff'd*, 332 So. 2d 610 (Fla. 1976). *See* § 4.39. *See also* City of New Orleans v. Board of Comm'rs, 640 So. 2d 237 (La. 1994) (home rule authority is basis for applying zoning ordinance to state agency).

[4] McDonald v. City of Columbus, 231 N.E.2d 319 (Ohio App. 1967).

[1] Bielunski v. Tousignant, 149 N.E.2d 801 (Ill. App. 1958); Zubli v. Community Mainstreaming Assocs., 423 N.Y.S.2d 982 (1979); Town of Westborough v. Department of Pub. Utils., 267 N.E.2d 110 (Mass. 1971); Vermont Div. of State Bldgs. v. Town of Castleton Bd. of Adjustment, 415 A.2d 188 (Vt. 1980).

[2] Or. Rev. Stat. § 227.286. *See also* Cal. Gov't Code §§ 53,090, 53091; City of Lafayette v. East Bay Mun. Utility Dist., 20 Cal. Rptr. 2d 658 (Cal. App. 1993); Lawler v. City of Redding, 9 Cal. Rptr. 2d 392 (Cal. App. 1992).

E. Federal Preemption

§ 4.41 The Federal Preemption Problem.

Several federal statutes have a preemptive effect on local zoning.[1] These statutes provide preemptive requirements in several ways. They may provide regulations for facilities, such as airports, which have a preemptive effect on local zoning. They may also may require local zoning ordinances and decisions to comply with criteria contained in the federal law. The next two sections discuss federal statutes that have a preemptive effect on zoning for cellular towers and for airports and surrounding areas.

§ 4.42 Zoning for Cellular Towers.

The Telecommunications Act of 1996[1] contains a number of requirements that apply to local zoning for cellular towers. The Act contains substantive and procedural limitations on local zoning and zoning decisions, and it preempts statutes and local ordinances that violate the Act.[2] Local authorities have the first opportunity to decide how to regulate wireless communication facilities, but the Act provides a cause of action for "any person adversely affects by an final action" of a local government that is inconsistent with the act. A court may grant relief to a wireless provider if it finds a local authority's actions violate the Act, including injunctive relief.[3] Finally, local governments cannot regulate cellular towers on the basis of the environmental effects of radio frequency emissions that comply with FCC regulations. The cases are divided on whether a moratorium on the approval of cellular towers violates the act.[4]

---

[1] *E.g.,* 47 C.F.R. § 25.104 (satellite earth stations, receiving dishes and antennas); Ensco v. Dumas, 807 F.2d 743 (8th Cir. 1986) (Resource Recovery and Conservation Act; invalidating prohibitory ordinance); Leisure Time Cruise Corp. v. Town of Barnstable, 62 F. Supp.2d 202 (D. Mass 1999); (Gambling Act; upholding order removing gambling boat from its berth); In re Vermont Railway, 769 A.2d 648 (Vt. 2000) (condition on permit not preempted by Railroad Safety Act). *See also* §§ 5.12–5.16 (group homes under Fair Housing Act); § 5.70 (Land Use and Institutionalized Persons Act); § 11.16 (sign regulation).

[1] 47 U.S.C. § 337 (amending Communications Act of 1934). *See* Nextel West Corp. v. Unity Township, 282 F.3d 257 (3d Cir. 2002) (amendment to ordinance did not moot claim under statute and claim ripe for decision); Sprint Spectrum, L.P. v. Borough of Upper Saddle River Zoning Bd. of Adjustment, 801 A.2d 336 (N.J. App. Div. 2002) (discussing Act and federal court decisions).

[2] Town of Amherst v, Omnipoint Communications Enters., Inc., 173 F.3d 9 (1st Cir. 1999).

[3] New Par v. City of Saginaw, 301 F.3d 390 (6th Cir. 2002) (discussing cases); National Tower, L.L.C. v. Plainville Zoning Bd. of Appeals, 297 F.3d 14 (1st Cir. 2002).

[4] National Telecommunications Advisors v. Board of Selectman, 27 F. Supp.2d 184 (D. Mass. 1998) (discussing division in cases on validity of moratoria under the Act).

One provision in the Act is that local governments must "not unreasonably discriminate among providers of functionally equivalent services."[5] Decisions that selectively favor a provider must be reasonable.[6]

The Act also states that local government actions may not prohibit or have the effect of prohibiting the placement, construction, or modification of personal wireless services. One case held an express prohibition is not necessary, but that a prohibition could be implied from one rejection if further reasonable efforts would be fruitless.[7] Another view is there is prohibition when a local government does not allow service providers to fill gaps in the ability of wireless telephones to have access to landlines, though this must be done by the least intrusive means.[8] At the other extreme, one court ruled the statute is not violated by an individual zoning decision, but only if there is a blanket prohibition and a general ban or policy.[9]

The Act requires decisions[10] on requests for personal wireless service facilities to be made within a reasonable time, and any decision to deny a request for a facility must be "in writing and supported by substantial evidence contained in a written record."[11] The courts are divided on whether the "in writing" provision requires formal findings and explanation of the agency's decision.[12] They have reversed denials when a local government did not rely on factors acceptable under the statute or denied permission for a cellular tower to restrict market entry.[13]

[5] Nextel W. Corp. v. Unity Township, 282 F.3d 257 (3d Cir. 2002) (remanding case); Aegerter v. City of Delafield, 174 F.3d 886 (7th Cir. 1999) (services not functionally equivalent).

[6] Sprint Spectrum, L.P. v. Willoth, 176 F.3d 630 (2d Cir. 1999); AT & T Wireless PCS, Inc. v. City Council, 155 F.3d 423 (4th Cir. 1998).

[7] Town of Amherst v. Omnipoint Communications Enters., 173 F.3d 9 (1st Cir. 1999).

[8] Sprint Spectrum, L.P. v. Willoth, 176 F.3d 630 (2d Cir. 1999); Cellular Telephone Co. v. Zoning Bd. of Adjustment, 197 F.3d 64 (3d Cir. 1999).

[9] AT & T Wireless PCS, Inc. v. City Council, 155 F.3d 423 (4th Cir. 1998). *But see* 360 Degree Communications Co. v. Board of Supervisors, 211 F.3d 79 (4th Cir. 2000) (suggesting that individual denial may be enough if preclusive).

[10] *See* Southwestern Bell Mobile Systems v. Todd, 244 F.3d 51 (1st Cir. 2001) (formal findings not required; notes cases contra); Petersburg Cellular Partnership v. Board of Supervisors, 29 F. Supp.2d 701 (E.D. Va. 1998) (discussing disagreement in cases on how much formality is required).

[11] Omnipoint Corp. v. Zoning Hearing Bd., 181 F. 3d 403 (3d Cir. 1999) (defining phrase). *See* Cellular Telephone Co. v. Town of Oyster Bay, 166 F.3d 490 (2d Cir. 1999) (noting division in cases on weight to be given to aesthetic concerns).

[12] New Par v. City of Saginaw, 301 F.3d 390 (6th Cir. 2002) (separate statement describing reasons for denial and explanation of reasons); Southwestern Bell Mobile Systems, Inc. v. Todd, 244 F.3d 51 (1st Cir. 2001) ("sufficient explanation"); AT & T Wireless PCS, Inc. v. City Council, 155 F.3d 423 (4th Cir. 1998) (stamping of "denial" on zoning application satisfies requirement).

[13] New Par v. City of Saginaw, 301 F.3d 390 (6th Cir. 2002) (variance; generalized concern about aesthetics not enough); Preferred Sites, LLC v. Troup County, 296 F.3d 1210 (11ty Cir. 2002) (same); Omnipoint Corp. v. Zoning Hearing Bd., 181 F.3d 403 (3d Cir. 1999) (same); Cellular

They upheld denials when there were reasons for differential treatment of different providers, when existing facilities were adequate, or when the proposed tower would create aesthetic, risk or compatibility problems.[14] There are conflicting decisions on whether the Act changes the burden of proof in zoning litigation.[15]

§ 4.43   Regulation of Airports and Surrounding Areas.

The Federal Aviation Act of 1958[1] may preempt municipal regulation of airports and surrounding areas. The statute does not expressly preempt local land use regulations, but in *City of Burbank v. Lockheed Air Terminal*,[2] the court held a city regulations that limited the noise created by its airport by placing a night curfew on jet flights was preempted by the federal law. It found the regulation preempted federal airspace management by increasing congesting and intruding on the comprehensive federal scheme for noise regulation.[3]

However, despite arguments that they affect the preempted area of navigable space by affecting flight approaches, height restrictions on building or other structures near runways have been upheld as valid local regulations.[4] *City of Cleveland v. City of Brook Park*[5] upheld an ordinance requiring a special permit

---

Telephone Co. v. Town of Oyster Bay, 166 F.3d 490 (2d Cir. 1999) (same); Smart SMR of N.Y., Inc. v. Zoning Comm'n, 995 F. Supp. 52 (D. Conn. 1998) (special permit); Sprint Spectrum L.P. v. Town of Easton, 982 F. Supp. 47 (D. Mass. 1997).

[14] American Tower LP v. City of Huntsville, 295 F.3d 1203 (11th Cir. 2002); Southwestern Bell Mobile Systems, Inc. v. Todd, 244 F.3d 51 (1st Cir. 2001); Aegerter v. City of Delafield, 174 F.3d 886 (7th Cir. 1999); AT & T Wireless PCS, Inc. v. City Council, 155 F.3d 423 (4th Cir. 1998); Iowa Wireless Servs. v. City of Moline, 29 F. Supp.2d 915 (C.D. Ill. 1998); National Telecommunications Advisors v. Board of Selectman, 27 F. Supp.2d 184 (D. Mass. 1998).

[15] *See* Cellular Telephone Co. v. Town of Oyster Bay, 166 F.3d 490 (2d Cir. 1999); AT & T Wireless PCS, Inc. v. City Council, 155 F.3d 423 (4th Cir. 1998).

[1] 49 U.S.C. § 40101.

[2] 411 U.S. 624 (2973). *See also* Griggs v. Allegheny County, 369 U.S. 84 (1961) (airport proprietors may limit liability for noise damage).

[3] *Accord* County Aviation, Inc. v. Tinicum Township, 9 F.3d 1539 (3rd Cir. 1993) (noise control ordinance); Pirolo v. City of Clearwater, 711 F.2d 1006 (11th Cir. 1983) (regulations prohibiting night operations and prescribing air traffic patterns); American Airlines v. Town of Hempstead, 398 F.2d 369 (2d Cir. 1969) (noise ordinance). For cases upholding airport regulations under the municipal proprietorship exception *see* Alaska Airlines, Inc. v. City of Long Beach, 951 F.2d 977 (9th Cir. 1991) (flight and noise limitations); Western Air Lines, Inc. v. Port Auth., 817 F.2d 222 (2d Cir. 1987) (rule prohibiting takeoff or landing of flights from certain distance).

[4] LaSalle Nat'l Bank v. County of Cook, 340 N.E.2d 79 (Ill. App. 1975).

[5] 893 F. Supp. 742 (N.D. Ohio 1995). *Accord* City of Burbank v. Burbank-Glendale-Pasadena Airport Auth., 85 Cal. Rptr.2d 28 (Cal. App. 1999); In re Commercial Airfield, 752 A.2d 13 (Vt. 2000). *But see* Burbank-Glendale-Pasadena Airport Auth. v. City of Los Angeles, 979 F.2d 1338 (9th Cir. 1992). *See also* Condor Corp. v. City of St. Paul, 912 F.2d 215 (8th Cir. 1990) (upholding denial of conditional use to operate heliport in industrial area located within 1100 feet of residential

for airport use that applied to an airport expansion. It relied on congressional intent and federal regulatory policy that indicated there was no intent to preempt local zoning powers.

---

area); Guillot v. Brooks, 651 So.2d 345 (La. App. 1995) (upholding special permit for ultralight landing strip); Riggs v. Burson, 941 S.W.2d 44 (Tenn. 1997) (upholding statute prohibiting heliport within nine miles of national park).

REFERENCES

Books

M. Brough, A Unified Development Ordinance (1987).

J. Hand & J. Smith, Neighboring Property Owners (1988).

W. Prosser & W. Keeton, The Law of Torts (5th ed. 1984).

B. Siegan, Land Use Without Zoning (1972).

R. Wakeford, American Development Control (1990).

Articles

Baldwin, The Telecommunications Act of 1996: Developing Caselaw of Towering Propositions, 31 Urb. Law. 555 (1999).

Beuscher & Morrison, Judicial Zoning Through Recent Nuisance Cases, 1955 Wis. L. Rev. 440.

Carrel & Foster, Twin Towers: The Developing Split in Interpretation of Facility Siting Law Under the Telecommunications Act of 1996, 32 Urb. Law. 839 (2000).

Chapman, Land Use Regulatory Jurisdiction of Local Governments Over State Agencies and Other Local Governments, 25 Gonz. L. Rev. 65 (1989-90).

Ellickson, Alternatives to Zoning: Covenants, Nuisance Rules, and Fines as Land Use Controls, 40 U. Chi. L. Rev. 681 (1973).

Halper, Untangling the Nuisance Knot, 26 B.C. Envtl. Aff. L. Rev. 89 (1998).

Kosman, Toward an Exclusionary Jurisprudence: A Reconceptualization of Zoning, 54 Cath. U. L. Rev. 59 (1993)

Knack, Meck & Stollman, The Real Story Behind the Standard Planning and Zoning Acts of the 1920s, Land Use L. & Zoning Dig., Vol. 48, No. 2, at 3 (1996).

Levi, Gehring & Groethe, Application of Municipal Ordinances to Special Purpose Districts and Regulated Industries: A Home Rule Approach, 12 Urb. L. Ann. 77 (1976).

Lewin, Comparative Nuisance, 50 U. Pitt. L. Rev. 1009 (1989).

Madigan, State Liquor Control Boards v. Local Government: Who Should Control the Location of Liquor Establishments?, 26 Duq. L. Rev. 851 (1988).

Meck, Present at the Creation: A Personal Account of the APA Growing Smart Project, Land Use L. & Zoning Dig. vol. 54, no. 3, at 3 (2002).

Rabin, Nuisance Law: Rethinking Fundamental Assumptions, 63 Va. L. Rev. 1299 (1977).

Rasso, Exempting Government From Zoning: Court Tests, Land Use L. & Zoning Dig., Vol. 38, No. 10, at 3 (1986).

Riseberg, Exhuming the Funeral Home Cases: Proposing a Private Nuisance Action Based on the Mental Anguish Caused by Pollution, 21 B.C. Envtl. L. Rev. 557 (1994).

Reynolds, The Judicial Role in Intergovernmental Land Use Disputes: The Case Against Balancing, 71 Minn. L. Rev. 611 (1987).

Reynolds, Of Time and Feedlots: The Effect of *Spur Industries* on Nuisance Law, 40 Wash. U.J. Urb. & Contemp. L. 75 (1992).

Smith & Fernandez, The Price of Beauty: An Economic Approach to Aesthetic Nuisance, 15 Harv. Envtl. L. Rev. 53 (1991).

Sterk, Neighbors in American Land Law, 87 Colum. L. Rev. 55 (1987).

Travalio, Pay Up or Shut Down: Some Cautionary Remarks on the Use of Conditional Entitlements in Private Nuisance Cases, 38 U. Fla. L. Rev. 209 (1986).

Van Gorder, Alternative Solutions to the Judicial Doctrine of Strict Compliance With Statutory Procedures for the Adoption of Local Land Use Regulations, 29 Wash. U.J. Urb. & Contemp. L. 133 (1985).

Ziegler, Governmental Immunity From Zoning: Balancing of Interests and Legislative Intent, 14 Zoning & Plan. L. Rep. 105 (1991).

Ziegler, Zoning Regulation Based On Identity of Land User, or Form of Ownership, 11 Zoning & Plan. L. Rep. 73 (1988).

Student Work

Note, Allocating the Aesthetic Costs of Cellular Tower Expansion: A Workable Regulatory Regime, 19 Stan. Envtl. L.J. 373 (2000).

Note, Governmental Immunity From Zoning, 22 B.C.L. Rev. 783 (1981).

Note, Transmission Line Siting: Local Concerns Versus State Energy Interests, 19 Urb. L. Ann. 183 (1980).

Note, Wireless Facilities are a Towering Problem: How Can Local Zoning Boards Make the Call Without Violating Section 704 of the Telecommunications Act of 1996? 40 Wm. & Mary L. Rev. 975 (1999).

Comment, Applying the Basic Principles of Cognitive Science to the Standard State Enabling Act, 27 B.C. Envtl. Aff. L. Rev. 519–566 (2000).

Comment, Limited Local Zoning Regulation of Electric Utilities: A Balanced Approach in the Public Interest, 23 U. Balt. L. Rev. 563 (1994).

Comment, An Ounce of Prevention: Rehabilitating the Anticipatory Nuisance Doctrine, 15 B.C. Envtl. Aff. L. Rev. 627 (1988).

Chapter 5

ZONING FOR LAND USE, DENSITY AND DEVELOPMENT

Synopsis

§ 5.01   An Introductory Note.

A. RESIDENTIAL DISTRICTS.

§ 5.02   *Euclid*: Zoning for Residential Use Held Constitutional.
§ 5.03   Defining the "Family" in Single-Family Residential Districts.
§ 5.04   *Belle Terre* and *Moor*.
§ 5.05   *Belle Terre* in the State Courts.
§ 5.06   Discrimination Against Families With Children Under the Fair Housing Act.
§ 5.07   Group Homes.
§ 5.08   As a Permitted "Family" Use.
§ 5.09   As a Conditional Use.
§ 5.10   State Legislative Regulation.
§ 5.11   Discrimination Against Group Homes for the Handicapped under the Fair Housing Act.
§ 5.12   What the Statute Means.
§ 5.13   Exceptions, Variances and Rezonings.
§ 5.14   Restrictions on Number of Occupants.
§ 5.15   Spacing and Quota Requirements.
§ 5.16   Americans With Disabilities and Rehabilitation Acts.
§ 5.17   Single-Family Use.
§ 5.18   Apartments.
§ 5.19   Accessory Uses.
§ 5.20   Home Occupations.
§ 5.21   Zoning for Mobile (or Manufactured) Homes.
§ 5.22   As a Dwelling.
§ 5.23   Partial Exclusion.
§ 5.24   Total Exclusion.
§ 5.25   As a Conditional Use.
§ 5.26   State and Federal Regulation.
§ 5.27   Private Schools.

B. LARGE LOT AND MINIMUM HOUSE SIZE ZONING.

§ 5.28   The Zoning Problem.
§ 5.29   Minimum House Size.
§ 5.30   Large-Lot Zoning.
§ 5.31   Held Valid.
§ 5.32   Held Invalid.

C. COMMERCIAL AND INDUSTRIAL USES.

§ 5.33   The Zoning Problem.
§ 5.34   Commercial Uses.
§ 5.35   The Mapping Problem.
§ 5.36   Commercial Use Classifications.

(5th Ed.—02/03)

§ 5.37   Total Exclusion.
§ 5.38   Ribbon Development.
§ 5.39   Airports and Airport Zoning.
§ 5.40   Industrial Uses.
§ 5.41   Industrial Performance Standards.
§ 5.42   Total Exclusion.
§ 5.43   Noncumulative Zoning: Exclusive Nonresidential Zones.
§ 5.44   Control of Competition.
§ 5.45   As a Zoning Purpose.
§ 5.46   Disapproved.
§ 5.47   Approved.
§ 5.48   Protection of Business Districts.
§ 5.49   Federal Antitrust Law.
§ 5.50   State Action Doctrine.
§ 5.51   *Boulder.*
§ 5.52   *Town of Hallie.*
§ 5.53   *Omni.*
§ 5.54   Land Use Cases after *Omni.*
§ 5.55   *Noerr-Pennington* Doctrine.
§ 5.56   Basis for Liability.
§ 5.57   Local Government Antitrust Act.
§ 5.58   Free Speech Problems in Zoning for Adult Businesses.
§ 5.59   *Mini-Theatres.*
§ 5.60   *Schad.*
§ 5.61   *Renton.*
§ 5.62   *Alameda Books.*
§ 5.63   Zoning Issues in Adult Use Regulation
§ 5.64   Existing Uses.
§ 5.65   Defining Adult Uses
§ 5.66   State Legislation.

D. RELIGIOUS USES.

§ 5.67   Religious Uses.
§ 5.68   In the State Courts.
§ 5.69   Federal "Free Exercise" and "Establishment" Clauses.
§ 5.70   Federal and State Religious Freedom Acts.

E. SITE DEVELOPMENT REQUIREMENTS.

§ 5.71   Yards and Setbacks.
§ 5.72   Frontage Requirements.
§ 5.73   Site Area Ratios.
§ 5.74   Height Limitations.
§ 5.75   Floor Area Ratio.
§ 5.76   Bonuses and Incentives.
§ 5.77   Off-Street Parking.

F. NONCONFORMING USES.

§ 5.78   The Zoning Problem.
§ 5.79   Change and Expansion.
§ 5.80   Repair and Reconstruction.
§ 5.81   Abandonment.

§ 5.82   Amortization.
§ 5.83   Highway Beautification Act.
§ 5.84   Constitutional.
§ 5.85   Unconstitutional.
§ 5.86   Reasonableness of Amortization Period.

§ 5.01   An Introductory Note.

Land use, density, and site development regulations are the heart of the zoning ordinance. The standard zoning format contains the three basic residential, commercial, and industrial use categories and subdivides each category into a number of zoning districts. The textual regulations for each zoning district specify permitted use and density limitations. The ordinance usually regulates densities through minimum lot size requirements and by limiting the number of dwelling units that are allowed on an acre of land.

Zoning ordinances also contain site development regulations for each zoning district that include minimum front, rear, and side yard requirements and a limit on the height of buildings. They may also include a minimum street frontage requirement and a limit on the percentage of a lot a building can occupy. Height, setback, and other site development requirements control density indirectly. The table that follows illustrates a simplified standard zoning format for a typical zoning ordinance.

A Standard, Simplified Zoning Format

SF-1, Single-Family Large Lot	One-Acre Lots
SF-2, Single-Family Medium	Half-Acre Lots
SF-3, Single-Family Standard	6,000 Sq. Ft. Lot Minimum
MF-1, Multifamily Low Density	18–26 Units/Acre
MF-2, Multifamily Medium Density	27–36 Units/Acre
MF-3, Multifamily High Density	37–44 Units/Acre
GO, General Office	Offices and Limited Uses Serving Community and City-Wide Needs
NC, Neighborhood Commercial	Neighborhood Retail and Office Facilities
CC, Community Commercial	Shopping Centers Providing Sub-Regional and Regional Retail and Office Facilities
SC, Service Commercial	Commercial Service Facilities Incompatible with Retail and Office Development
CBD, Central Business District	Office and Commercial Facilities in Central Business Area

LI, Limited Industrial   Light Manufacturing
HI, Heavy Industrial   Heavy Manufacturing

The constitutionality of comprehensive zoning is well-established since the Supreme Court's *Euclid* decision. Problems arise when courts must decide whether a zoning restriction is constitutional as applied to a particular property, or whether a zoning ordinance advances suspect governmental purposes or affects a fundamental constitutional right. Examples are restrictions on group homes, mobile homes, and adult or religious uses.

A.   RESIDENTIAL DISTRICTS.

§ 5.02   *Euclid*: Zoning for Residential Use Held Constitutional.

The key to comprehensive zoning is the division of the municipality into districts. Most modern zoning ordinances are noncumulative. Each district is exclusive, and only uses permitted in the district are allowed. For example, only residential uses are allowed in residential districts. Moreover, as the zoning format illustrate, each district is further divided into subcategories. For example, residential districts are subdivided into single-family and multifamily districts, and the ordinance excludes multifamily as well as other nonresidential uses from the single-family district.

The Supreme Court upheld a residential district in a comprehensive zoning ordinance that excluded nonresidential and multifamily uses in *Village of Euclid v. Ambler Realty Co.*.[1] a landmark case decided in 1926. These exclusions raised equal protection and substantive due process problems.

Euclid upheld these exclusions by looking to nuisance law as "a fairly helpful clew" in zoning cases. It applied the rule from nuisance cases that the acceptability of a land use designation depends on "the circumstances and the locality." "A nuisance may be merely a right thing in the wrong place — like a pig in the parlor instead of the barnyard."[2] The Court held that the exclusion of nonresidential uses presented "no difficulty" because it increased the safety and security of home life and reduced street accidents. The apartment exclusion was more difficult, probably because the nuisance cases had not considered the exclusion of apartment houses from residential districts. To justify the apartment house exclusion, the Court adopted a "parasite" theory to describe the effect of apartment houses on residential areas. Apartment houses, the court held, destroyed areas devoted to single-family use, interfered with light and air, and attracted large numbers of automobiles that block public streets.

---

[1] 272 U.S. 365 (1926).

[2] *Id.* at 388.

The Supreme Court clearly had a model of apartment development in mind when it wrote these words. Apartments in that day were built on single lots, towered over adjacent homes and did not provide off-street parking. Modern apartment developments in the typical "garden apartment" complex avoid all of these problems. Some courts accept,[3] but some reject, the *Euclid* characterization of apartment development.[4]

Although the Court's decision upholding the exclusion of multifamily dwellings is clear, the basis on which municipalities can make this exclusion is not clear. *Euclid* relied primarily on density, height, and parking problems presented by multifamily dwellings to uphold their exclusion from residential districts. This analysis suggests the differences between apartments and other residential dwellings is a density and bulk problem, but the state courts treat this separation as a problem in use classification. This characterization is questionable, now that apartment development no longer fits the *Euclid* model. The exclusion of multifamily dwellings from residential districts remains an important and troublesome land use issue.

§ 5.03 Defining the "Family" in Single-Family Residential Districts.

A threshold problem in residential zoning how to define the "family" entitled to reside in single-family dwellings, and the critical issue is whether to place numerical limits on family members. Zoning ordinances do not limit the number of related family members who can live together but often limit the number of unrelated persons who can live together as a family. The numerical limitation on unrelated families may have been an attempt to prohibit boardinghouse living in single-family neighborhoods.[1]

§ 5.04 *Belle Terre* and *Moor*.

The Supreme Court upheld a zoning ordinance that limited the number of unrelated persons who could live together as a family in *Village of Belle Terre v. Boraas*.[1] A zoning ordinance in a small suburban residential community near New York City defined a "family" as no more than two unrelated individuals. Plaintiffs, who rented their home to six unrelated college students, challenged

---

[3] Krause v. City of Royal Oak, 160 N.W.2d 769 (Mich. App. 1968).

[4] Allred v. City of Raleigh, 173 S.E.2d 533 (N.C. App. 1970), *rev'd on other grounds*, 178 S.E.2d 432 (N.C. 1971).

[1] *Compare* Borough of Glassboro v. Vallorisi, 568 A.2d 888 (N.J. 1990) (group of college students living together held to be family) *and* Appeal of Miller, 515 A.2d 904 (Pa. 1986) (boarders held to be housekeeping unit) *with* Appeal of Summers, 551 A.2d 1134 (Pa. Commw. 1988) (temporary care of mentally retarded held not a family) *and* Commonwealth v. Jaffe, 494 N.E.2d 1342 (Mass. 1986) (boarders held to be unrelated tenants).

[1] 416 U.S. 1 (1974).

this definition on several constitutional grounds, some of which suggested a substantive due process violation. They claimed, for example, that the definition was unconstitutional because "social homogeneity is not a legitimate interest of government."

The Court upheld the ordinance in an opinion by Justice Douglas. He did not separate the due process and equal protection problems, but he clearly held the definition did not violate substantive due process:

> The regimes of boarding houses, fraternity houses and the like present urban problems. More people occupy a given space; more cars continuously pass by; more cars are parked; noise travels with crowds. A quiet place where yards are wide, people few, and motor vehicles restricted are legitimate guidelines in a land use project addressed to family needs.

> This goal is a permissible one within *Berman v. Parker.* . . . The police power . . . is ample to lay out zones where family values, youth values, and the blessings of quiet seclusion, and clean air make the area a sanctuary for people.[2]

Berman v. Parker[3] was an urban renewal decision also written by Justice Douglas. It contains a much-quoted dictum that defines the "public welfare" to include spiritual and aesthetic as well as physical values.

Belle Terre does not provide a satisfactory link between the limitation in the zoning ordinance on the number of unrelated individuals who can live together and the broad social objectives Justice Douglas endorsed. One interpretation of the decision is that the due process clause justifies zoning ordinances that distinguish between different types of families, a holding some state courts reject.[4]

The Supreme Court qualified *Belle Terre* in *Moore v. City of East Cleveland.*[5] *Moore* struck down a local housing code that restricted the number of related individuals who could live together, but the decision also applies to zoning ordinances. The Court distinguished *Belle Terre* but could not produce a majority opinion. The plurality opinion made the point that the restriction in *Belle Terre* applied only to unrelated rather than related individuals.

The Court clearly viewed *Moore* as a substantive due process case, but the opinions were troubled by this latter-day attempt to invoke the substantive due process clause. Not for some time had the Supreme Court struck down a police power regulation as a violation of substantive due process. The plurality noted, quite properly, that the restriction on related individuals living together did little

---

[2] *Id.* at 9.

[3] 348 U.S. 26 (1954).

[4] § 5.06.

[5] 431 U.S. 494 (1977).

to meet legitimate community objectives, such as the prevention of overcrowding and traffic congestion. Yet it viewed substantive due process as a "treacherous field," and struck down the ordinance because it interfered with the sanctity of the family. For this reason, *Moore* does not affect the holding in the *Belle Terre* decision.

§ 5.05   *Belle Terre* in the State Courts.

A number of states followed *Belle Terre* and upheld zoning ordinances limiting the size of unrelated families.[1] Several states have also held them invalid,[2] though these cases may allow municipalities to limit the use of single-family dwellings to "functional" families.[3]

City of Santa Barbara v. Adamson[4] is a leading case that invalidated a restriction on the size of unrelated families on state constitutional grounds. A zoning ordinance allowed no more than five unrelated persons to live together as a family unit. The court relied on a right of privacy guaranteed by the state constitution's declaration of rights to strike down this "rule of five." Applying an "ends and means" analysis similar to strict scrutiny equal protection review, the court demanded a "compelling public need" to justify the restriction. It found none. The restriction did not enhance the maintenance of a residential environment because the "rule of five" was irrelevant to noise, parking, or other conditions that might affect residential areas. Neither was the ordinance justified by a belief that unrelated families create an immoral environment for families with children. The court applied the "least restrictive alternative" rule and held that other regulations, such as population density and parking restrictions, could accomplish the purposes the "rule of five" attempted to serve. Zoning ordinances,

---

[1] 4. Zavala v. City & Cty. of Denver, 759 P.2d 664 (Colo. 1988); Dinan v. Board of Zoning Appeals, 595 A.2d 864 (Conn. 1991); State v. Champoux, 566 N.W.2d 763 (Neb.1997); Town of Durham v. White Enters., Inc., 348 A.2d 706 (N.H. 1975); Farley v. Zoning Hearing Bd., 636 A.2d 1232 (Pa. Commw. 1994) (student housing); City of Brookings v. Winker, 554 N.W.2d 827 (S.D. 1996).

[2] Dvorak v. City of Bloomington, 768 N.E.2d 490 (Ind. App. 2002); Kirsch v. Prince George's County, 626 A.2d 372 (Md. 1993) (occupancy limitation on student housing violates equal protection); Charter Twp. of Delta v. Dinolfo, 351 N.W.2d 831 (Mich. 1984); Borough of Glassboro v. Vallorisi, 529 A.2d 1028 (N.J. Ch. Div. 1987); Ocean Cty. Bd. of Realtors v. Township of Long Beach, 599 A.2d 1309 (N.J.L. 1991); State v. Baker, 405 A.2d 368 (N.J. 1979); Baer v. Town of Brookhaven, 537 N.E.2d 619 (N.Y. 1989); McMinn v. Town of Oyster Bay, 488 N.E.2d 1240 (N.Y. 1985). *See also* City of Chula Vista v. Pagard, 171 Cal. Rptr. 738 (Cal. App. 1981). *See* 71 A.L.R.3d 693 (1976); 12 A.L.R.4th 238 (1982). *See also* Dvorak v. City of Bloomington, 702 N.E.2d 1121 (Ind. App. 1998) (remanded for further proceedings).

[3] Stegeman v. City of Ann Arbor, 540 N.W.2d 724 (Mich. App. 1995).

[4] 610 P.2d 436 (Cal. 1980). *See also* College Area Renters & Landlord Ass'n v. City of San Diego, 50 Cal. Rptr. 2d 515 (Cal. App. 1996) (occupancy requirements cannot distinguish between tenant-occupied and owner-occupied dwellings).

the court noted, are much less suspect when they focus on uses rather than the users.

Strict scrutiny judicial review was a key factor in many of the cases invalidating limitations on the size of unrelated families. It was based either on an equal protection clause or a state constitutional provision that recognized a fundamental interest, such as the right of privacy. Cases that apply strict scrutiny judicial review reverse the presumption of constitutionality and require a compelling governmental interest to justify the restriction, which they find lacking. Some state courts have also held that restrictions on the size of unrelated families are unauthorized by the zoning legislation.[5]

§ 5.06　Discrimination Against Families With Children Under the Fair Housing Act.

In 1988, Congress added discrimination against "familial status" as another type of discrimination covered by the Fair Housing Act.[1] Congress adopted this amendment to prohibit discrimination against families with children in the sale and rental of housing, but the amendment may invalidate zoning that restricts residences in single family zoning districts to older persons. The effect of this zoning is to prohibit families with children from occupying residences in these districts. The amendment may also invalidate zoning ordinances that prohibit occupancy by families in group homes.[2]

The Act exempts "housing for older persons" from the prohibition against familial status discrimination.[3] This exemption was clearly intended to apply to private owners of such housing, not age-restricted zoning.[4] However, this provision may invalidate zoning ordinances limiting the number of persons who can live together because the it protects individuals who have custody of minor children.[5]

The Act also exempts governmentally-imposed occupancy restrictions from the prohibition against familial discrimination.[6] *City of Edmonds v. Oxford*

---

[5] City of Des Plaines v. Trottner, 216 N.E.2d 116 (Ill. 1966), *rev'd by* § 65 Ill. Comp. Ann. Stat. 5/11-13-1(9).

[1] 42 U.S.C. § 3602(k).

[2] Doe v. City of Butler, 892 F.2d 315 (3d Cir. 1989) (remanding claim that Act violated by limitation on occupancy in group home for abused women because limitation would prevent abused mothers from bringing children into home).

[3] 42 U.S.C. § 3607(b)(1).

[4] H.R. Rep. No. 711, 100th Cong., 2d Sess. 31–32 (1988). *See* Gibson v. County of Riverside, 181 F. Supp.2d 1057 (C.D. Cal. 2002) (age-restricted zoning did not qualify for exemption); 24 C.F.R. § 100.304.

[5] Keys Youth Servs. v. City of Olathe, 52 F. Supp.2d 1284 (D. Kan. 1999) (invalidating ordinance limiting to eight the persons who can live together in the custody of a guardian).

[6] 42 U.S.C. § 3607(b)(1). *See* H.R. Rep. No. 711, 100th Cong., 2d Sess. 31 (1988) (though exemption in text applies to all types of discrimination prohibited by the Act).

House,[7] held the exemption did not include a zoning provision that limited to five the number of unrelated people who could live together. The Court held that congressional intent was to distinguish between land use and maximum occupancy restrictions, which are intended to protect health and safety by limiting the overcrowding of buildings. Only the latter are exempt.[8]

§ 5.07   Group Homes.

§ 5.08   As a Permitted "Family" Use.

The definition of "family" contained in zoning ordinances also comes under attack if it is applied to exclude group homes from residential districts. State legislation that regulates group homes may exempt them from zoning restrictions.[1] The courts have also held that the group that plans to live in a group home is a "family" as defined by the zoning ordinance or that the application of a "family" definition to exclude a group home is unconstitutional.[2]

Belle Terre upheld an ordinance limiting the number of unrelated people who can live together, and some courts hold the application of a family definition to exclude a group home from a residential district is constitutional.[3] The U.S. Supreme Court approved one of these cases as a correct interpretation of the *Belle Terre* decision.[4] In *Doe v. City of Butler,*[5] the Third Circuit relied on *Belle Terre* to uphold, as applied to a medium density residential district, a zoning ordinance that allowed group homes as conditional uses in all residential districts. The ordinance limited to six and a supervisor the number of persons who could live in these homes. The court remanded for trial the question whether the numerical limitation was valid in higher-density residential districts, where apartments and other high-density uses were permitted.

---

[7] 514 U.S. 725 (1995) (quoting this treatise).

[8] Fair Housing Advocates Ass'n v. City of Richmond Heights, 209 F.3d 626 (6th Cir. 2000) (occupancy restrictions based on number of square feet in unit exempt).

[1] § 5.26. *See* My Brother's Keeper v. Scott County, 621 N.W.2d 1121 (Ind. App. 1998) (remanded for further proceedings).

[2] Cherry Hill Township v. Oxford House, Inc., 621 A.2d 952 (N.J. App. Div. 1993).

[3] Behavioral Health Agency of Cent. Ariz. (BHACA) v. City of Casa Grande, 708 P.2d 1317 (Ariz. App. 1985); Hayward v. Gaston, 542 A.2d 760 (Del. 1988); Penobscot Area Hous. Dev. Corp. v. City of Brewer, 434 A.2d 14 (Me. 1981). *See also* Browndale Int'l, Ltd. v. Board of Adjustment, 208 N.W.2d 121 (Wis. 1973) (can allow foster homes but exclude therapeutic home).

[4] City of Cleburne v. Cleburne Living Center, 473 U.S. 432 (1985), approving Macon Ass'n for Retarded Citizens v. Macon-Bibb County Planning & Zoning Comm'n, 314 S.E.2d 218 (Ga.), *appeal dismissed,* 469 U.S. 802 (1984). *See* Frazier v. City of Grand Lodge, 135 F. Supp. 2d 845 (W.D. Mich. 2001) (zoning ordinance excluding foster care home did not violate equal protection); § 2.48.

[5] 892 F.2d 315 (3d Cir. 1989).

A number of cases avoided constitutional issues by interpreting a definition of family or a definition of accessory use in a zoning ordinance to include group homes.[6] Some of these cases contain constitutional overtones, and suggest that constitutional problems would arise if the ordinance excluded group homes. They may stress, for example, that the zoning ordinance may regulate only uses, not the users, implying that a regulation based on users would violate substantive due process.[7] Some of these cases require the group home to be the functional equivalent of a family,[8] but other cases do not adopt this requirement.[9]

City of White Plains v. Ferraioli[10] is a leading case that adopted the functional equivalency rule. The court held a foster home headed by a married couple and including two of their own natural children was a family as defined by the zoning ordinance. The court distinguished *Belle Terre,* and noted the foster home in this case was a "relatively normal, stable, and permanent family unit." Because the group home "bears the generic character of a family unit" and was not a place for transients, it was consistent with the purposes of single-family zoning.

Several cases held the functional equivalency rule was not satisfied, or interpreted the family definition to hold that the zoning ordinance excluded group homes.[11] These cases usually relied on *Belle Terre,* and sometimes emphasized that the group home was supervised by resident staff rather than a resident married couple.[12]

---

[6] White v. Board of Zoning Appeals, 451 N.E.2d 756 (Ohio 1983) (held accessory use); Saunders v. Clark County Zoning Dep't, 421 N.E.2d 152 (Ohio 1981) (delinquent boys); Collins v. City of El Campo, 684 S.W.2d 756 (Tex. App. 1984); Citizens for a Safe Neighborhood v. City of Seattle, 836 P.2d 235 (Wash. App. 1992).

[7] Linn County v. City of Hiawatha, 311 N.W.2d 95 (Iowa 1981); City of West Monroe v. Ouachita Ass'n for Retarded Children, Inc., 402 So. 2d 259 (La. App. 1981); Hopkins v. Zoning Hearing Bd., 423 A.2d 1082 (Pa. Commw. 1980); State ex rel. Catholic Family & Children's Servs. v. City of Bellingham, 605 P.2d 788 (Wash. App. 1979).

[8] City of Vinita Park v. Girls Sheltercare, Inc., 664 S.W.2d 256 (Mo. App. 1984); Unification Theological Seminary v. City of Poughkeepsie, 607 N.Y.S.2d 383 (App. Div. 1994) (upholds ordinance limiting number of unrelated people unless functional equivalent of a family); Eichlin v. Zoning Hearing Bd., 671 A.2d 1173 (Pa. Commw. 1996) (group home met functional family requirements of ordinance). Act I, Inc. v. Zoning Hearing Bd., 704 A.2d 732 (Pa. Commw. 1997).

[9] Hessling v. City of Broomfield, 563 P.2d 12 (Colo. 1977); Oliver v. Zoning Comm'n, 326 A.2d 841 (Conn. C.P. 1974); Y.W.C.A. v. Board of Adjustment, 341 A.2d 356 (N.J. 1975).

[10] 313 N.E.2d 756 (N.Y. 1974). *See also* Group House of Port Wash., Inc. v. Board of Zoning & Appeals, 380 N.E.2d 207 (N.Y. 1978).

[11] Civitans Care, Inc. v. Board of Adjustment, 437 So. 2d 540 (Ala. 1983); Behavioral Health Agency of Cent. Ariz. (BHACA) v. City of Casa Grande, 708 P.2d 1317 (Ariz. App. 1985); Planning & Zoning Comm'n v. Synanon Found., Inc., 216 A.2d 442 (Conn. 1966); City of Kenner v. Normal Life of La., Inc., 483 So. 2d 903 (La. 1986); Metropolitan Dev. Comm'n v. Villages, Inc., 464 N.E.2d 367 (Ind. App. 1984); Northern Maine Gen. Hosp. v. Ricker, 572 A.2d 479 (Me. 1990); Open Door Alcoholism Program, Inc. v. Board of Adjustment, 491 A.2d 17 (N.J. App. Div. 1985).

[12] Wengert v. Zoning Hearing Bd., 414 A.2d 148 (Pa. Commw. 1980); Culp v. City of Seattle, 590 P.2d 1288 (Wash. App. 1979); 100 A.L.R.3d 876 (1980).

§ 5.09   As a Conditional Use.

A zoning ordinance may authorize the approval of a group home as a conditional use. The state cases apply the usual rules governing conditional uses[1] when they decide whether to uphold or reverse a denial of a conditional use for a group home.[2] In *City of Cleburne v. Cleburne Living Center*,[3] the U.S. Supreme Court invalidated the denial of a conditional use permit for a group home for the mentally retarded under the rational relationship standard of equal protection review. The Court held that fears of neighbors were not a sufficient reason for denying the permit, and that the city could not reject the group home for reasons that applied to group homes the ordinance allowed without a permit. The cases since *Cleburne* have divided on whether a municipality can constitutionally require a conditional use permit for a group home.[4]

§ 5.10   State Legislative Regulation.

Group homes operate under state supervision and must obtain state approval. State approval includes the authority to operate the home at a designated location but does not consider its land use impacts. State funding may also be available. Even though there is no express exemption in these statutes, most courts exempt group homes operating under state approval from zoning restrictions.[1] They hold the state legislation authorizing group homes implies that local zoning restrictions may not frustrate the treatment policy of the state law by restricting their location.

---

[1] §§ 6.56–6.58.

[2] Bannum, Inc. v. City of Fort Lauderdale, 157 F.3d 819 (11th Cir. 1998) (upholding denial); Gaslight Villa, Inc. v. Governing Body, City of Lansing, 518 P.2d 410 (Kan. 1974) (same); Normal Life of La., Inc. v. Jefferson Parish Dep't of Inspection & Code Enforcement, 483 So. 2d 1123 (La. App. 1986) (same); City Planning Comm'n of Greensburg v. Threshold, Inc., 315 A.2d 311 (Pa. Commw. 1974) (reversing denial); Bannum, Inc. v. City of Columbia, 516 S.E.2d 439 (S.C. 1999) (same).

[3] 473 U.S. 432 (1985). *See* § 2.48.

[4] *Compare* Bannum, Inc. v. City of Fort Lauderdale, 157 F.3d 819 (11th Cir. 1998) (upholding ordinance); Bannum, Inc. v. City of Louisville, 958 F.2d 1354 (6th Cir. 1992) (invalidating requirement), *with* Bannum, Inc. v. City of St. Charles, 2 F.3d 267 (8th Cir. 1993) (contra); Freedom Ranch, Inc. v. Board of Adjustment, 878 P.2d 380 (Okla. App. 1994) (same); Avalon v. Residential Care Homes v. City of Dallas, 130 F. Supp. 2d 833 (N.D. Tex. 2000) (upholding denial).

[1] City of Temple Terrace v. Hillsborough Ass'n for Retarded Citizens, 322 So. 2d 571 (Fla. App. 1975), *aff'd,* 332 So. 2d 610 (Fla. 1976); Berger v. State, 364 A.2d 993 (N.J. 1976); Town of Southern Pines v. Mohr, 226 S.E.2d 865 (N.C. 1976); Region 10 Client Mgt., Inc. v. Town of Hampstead, 424 A.2d 207 (N.H. 1980); Abbott House v. Tarrytown, 312 N.Y.S.2d 841 (App. Div. 1970) (neglected children). *Contra* Macon Ass'n for Retarded Citizens v. Macon-Bibb County Planning & Zoning Comm'n, *314 S.E.2d 218 (Ga.), appeal dismissed,* 469 U.S. 802 (1984); Board of Child Care v. Harker, 561 A.2d 219 (Md. 1989); Village of Nyack v. Daytop Village, Inc., 583 N.E.2d 928 (N.Y. 1991) (drug treatment facility). *See also* §§ 5.12–5.16 (discrimination against group homes under the federal Fair Housing Act).

Legislation in a number of states specifically considers the group home zoning problem, though some statutes apply only to one type of group home, such as a group home for the mentally disabled.[2] Some statutes require municipalities to allow small group homes as a permitted use in residential districts. Other statutes allow municipalities to approve group homes as a conditional use in residential districts. The statute usually requires state licensing and may require the dispersal of group homes throughout residential areas to avoid excessive concentration through spacing or other requirements. Model legislation proposed by the American Bar Association's Commission on the Mentally Disabled includes similar protective provisions but does not authorize conditional use permits.[3]

Most courts have upheld statutes that regulate zoning for group homes. They find that these statutes bear a substantial relation to a legitimate governmental purpose and reject arguments that they infringe on land use controls adopted under home rule charters.[4] Zoning ordinances requiring a minimum spacing between group homes have been upheld as not in violation of these laws.[5]

§ 5.11   Discrimination Against Group Homes for the Handicapped under the Fair Housing Act.

§ 5.12   What the Statute Means.

Amendments to the Fair Housing Act in 1988 apply it to discrimination against handicapped persons.[1] The definition of "handicap" incorporates the definition

---

[2] *E.g.,* Ariz. Rev. Stat. Ann. §§ 36-581, 36-582; Cal. Welf. & Inst. Code §§ 5115–5116; Kan. Stat. Ann. § 12-736; Me. Rev. Stat. tit. 30-A, § 4357-A; N.J. Stat. Ann. §§ 40:55D-66.1, 30:4C-26(d). *See* Campbell v. City Council, 616 N.E.2d 445 (Mass. 1993) (group home protected by state educational use law); Trible v. Bland, 458 S.E.2d 297 (Va. 1995) (statute allows municipality to be more permissive in definition of group home).

[3] *See* Hopperton, "A State Legislative Strategy for Ending Exclusionary Zoning of Community Homes," 19 Urb. L. Ann. 47, 77 (1980).

[4] Los Angeles v. State Dep't of Health, 133 Cal. Rptr. 771 (Cal. App. 1976); Glennon Heights, Inc. v. Central Bank & Trust, 658 P.2d 872 (Colo. 1983); Hayward v. Gaston, 542 A.2d 760 (Del. 1988) (statutory zoning exemption may distinguish between different types of group homes); City of Livonia v. Department of Social Servs., 333 N.W.2d 151 (Mich. App. 1983); Zubli v. Community Mainstreaming Assocs., 423 N.Y.S.2d 982 (Sup. Ct. 1979); Nichols v. Tullahoma Open Door, Inc., 640 S.W.2d 13 (Tenn. App. 1982). *Contra* Garcia v. Siffrin Residential Ass'n, 407 N.E.2d 1369 (Ohio 1980) (held to violate local home rule powers). *See also* City of Torrance v. Transitional Living Centers for Los Angeles, Inc., 638 P.2d 1304 (Cal. 1982) (interpreting state statute); Northwest Residence, Inc. v. City of Brooklyn Center, 352 N.W.2d 764 (Minn. App. 1984) (group home law generally preemptive of local zoning).

[5] Verland C.L.A., Inc. v. Zoning Hearing Bd., 556 A.2d 4 (Pa. Commw. 1989) (one mile); Shannon & Riordan v. Board of Zoning Appeals, 451 N.W.2d 479 (Wis. App. 1989) (2500 feet).

[1] 42 U.S.C. § 8604(f). *See* Gromme Resources Ltd., L.L.C. v. Parish of Jefferson, 234 F.3d 192 (5th Cir. 2000) (held constitutional).

used in section 504 of the Rehabilitation Act of 1973.[2] This definition is broad. It includes, for example, persons with AIDS.[3] Although the amendments do not expressly apply to zoning, the legislative history makes it clear that the Act applies to zoning practices, such as restrictions on group homes, that discriminate against housing for handicapped persons.[4] The legislative history also indicates that the courts are to apply a discriminatory effect test to discrimination against the handicapped in zoning ordinances, and that the statute incorporates a prima facie case rule that shifts to the defendant municipality the burden to show that a zoning restriction is justified by a legitimate reason not related to discrimination against the handicapped.[5] A municipality also violates the Act if it is guilty of a discriminatory intent.[6]

The statute defines as discrimination as

a refusal to make reasonable accommodation in rules, policies, [or] practices . . . when such accommodations may be necessary to afford such person equal opportunity to use and enjoy a dwelling.[7]

This provision applies only to cases of discrimination against handicapped persons. Note that it requires proof that a reasonable accommodation is both necessary and reasonable. Courts divide on which party has the burden of proof on these issues.[8] Courts usually apply the reasonable accommodation requirement when decide the extent of municipal responsibility to comply with the Act.

Some courts have held that the Americans with Disabilities Act[9] and the Rehabilitation Act[10] apply to zoning ordinances. They have held that discriminatory actions by municipalities against facilities for persons covered by these acts are a violation of these acts.[11]

---

[2] 29 U.S.C. § 794. *See* 54 Fed. Reg. 3232, 3245 (1989).

[3] Bragdon v. Scott, 524 U.S. 624 (1998). *See also* Suttton v. United States Airlines, 527 U.S. 471 (1999) (not disabled if correctable by medication or other measures); Sullivan v. City of Pittsburgh, 815 F.2d 171 (3rd Cir. 1987) (alcoholics).

[4] H.R. Rep. No. 711, 100th Cong., 2d Sess. 24 (1988).

[5] *See* Children's Alliance v. City of Bellevue, 950 F. Supp. 1491 (W.D. Wash. 1997) (also reviewing cases discussing applicable standard of judicial review).

[6] Tsombandis v. City of West Haven, 180 F. Supp.2d 262 (D. Conn. 2001).

[7] 42 U.S.C. § 3604(f)(3)(B). *See* Advocacy Center for Persons With Disabilities, Inc. v. Woodlands Estates Ass'n, Inc. 192 F. Supp.2d 1344 (M.D. Fla. 2002) (reviewing cases interpreting reasonable accommodation requirement).

[8] Lapid Laurel, L.L.C. v. Zoning Bd. of Adjustment, 284 F.3d 442 (3d Cir. 2002) (different for different issues); Grover v. Golden Gate Gardens Apartments, 250 F.3d 1039 (6th Cir. 2001) (plaintiff); Bryant Woods Inn, Inc. v. Howard County, 124 F.3d 597 (4th Cir. 1997) (same).

[9] *See* 42 U.S.C. § 12132.

[10] *See* 29 U.S.C. § 794(a).

[11] Mx Group, Inc. v. City of Covington, 293 F.3d 326 (6th Cir. 2002) (ban prohibiting center from locating anywhere in city); Bay Area Addiction Research & Treatment Inc. v. City of Antioch,

§ 5.13 Exceptions, Variances and Rezonings.

Many municipalities treat group homes for the handicapped as special exceptions and conditional uses, and group home owners may also apply for zoning variances. The courts will invalidate a denial of a special use permit or a variance for a group homes for the handicapped if they find the denial had a discriminatory impact, was based on a discriminatory intent, or was required as a reasonable accommodation.[1] Legitimate zoning reasons may support a denial of a special use.[2] However, a court of appeals held the reasonable accommodation requirement did not exempt a group home from applying for and receiving a special use permit.[3] The court held that any burdens that residents of the group home might suffer from going through the special use procedure did not outweigh the municipality's interest in applying this requirement to all applicants for special use approval.

The courts have also considered whether the Act requires a zoning amendment as a reasonable accommodation ford a group home. The Sixth Circuit held a city must make reasonable accommodation through its zoning ordinance for a group home, but held the district court did not have the power to compel an amendment to the ordinance to enforce this requirement.[4] However, the court upheld a district court decision that an amendment was required, and which rejected arguments

179 F.3d 725 (9th Cir. 1999) (ordinance prohibited location near residential area; case remanded); Forest Daly Housing, Inc. v. Town of North Hempstead, 173 F.3d 144 (2d Cir. 1999) (home not entitled to exception when traditional homes would also be denied exception); Innovative Health Systems, Inc. v. City of White Plains, 117 F.3d 37 (2d Cir. 1997) (refusal to give building permit to group home).

[1] Special use: Regional Economic Community Action Program, Inc. v. City of Middletown, 294 F.3d 35 (2d Cir. 2002) (reversing summary judgment for city on disparate treatment claim); Lapid-Laurel, L.L.C. v. Zoning Bd. of Adjustment, 284 F.3d 442 (3rd Cir. 2002) (required); Association of Relatives & Friends of AIDS Pations v. Regulations and Permits Admin., 740 F. Supp. 95 (D.P.R. 1990) (required); Baxter v. City of Belleville, 720 F. Supp. 720 (S.D. Ill. 1989) (same).

Variance: Howard v. City of Beavercreek, 276 F.3d 802 (6th Cir. 2002) (upholding denial of variance for privacy fence because handicapped person not required to move from neighborhoo); Hovson's, Inc. v. Township of Brick, 89 F.3d 1096 (3d Cir. 1996) (required).

[2] Hemisphere Bldg. Co., Inc. v. Village of Richton Park, 171 F.3d 437 (7th Cir. 1999) (presence of housing at higher densities in surrounding area does not require density increase for proposed group home); Erdman v. City of Fort Atkinson, 84 F.3d 960 (7th Cir. 1996); Gamble v. City of Escondido, 104 F.3d 300 (9th Cir. 1997). See also Elderhaven, Inc. v. City of Lubbock, 98 F.3d 175 (5th Cir. 1996).

[3] United States v. Village of Palatine, 37 F.3d 1230 (7th Cir. 1994).

[4] Smith & Lee Assocs. v. City of Taylor (II), 102 F.3d 781 (6th Cir. 1996). See also "K" Care, Inc. v. Town of Lac du Flambeau, 510 N.W.2d 697 (Wis. App. 1993) (invalidating refusal to rezone).

that the amendment would fundamentally alter the city's zoning policies. Other courts have held the facts did not require a rezoning.[5]

§ 5.14   Restrictions on Number of Occupants.

Courts have held a definition of "family" in zoning ordinances that excludes group homes for the handicapped from single family residential districts violates the Act.[1] Whether occupancy restrictions violate the Act is less clear. The statute contains an exemption for "reasonable . . . restriction[s] regarding the maximum number of occupants permitted to occupy a dwelling."[2] In *City of Edmonds v. Oxford House, Inc.,*[3] The Supreme Court limited the exemption to claims of discrimination based on familial status. The Court left open the question of whether a limitation on the number of persons who can live together is valid under the federal act. Some courts have held a limit on the number of unrelated persons who can live together does not violate the federal Act, even though the effect of the restriction is to prohibit the location of the group home at its intended location.[4]

§ 5.15   Spacing and Quota Requirements.

Provisions regulating the density of group homes for the handicapped by regulating the spacing between them are common in zoning ordinances and in statutes providing zoning protection for these homes. Although the Eighth Circuit held that a spacing requirement in a zoning ordinance did not violate the Act,[1] this decision is clearly wrong. The Sixth Circuit invalidated a similar requirement in a state statute.[2] The court rejected arguments that the spacing requirement

---

[5] Forest City Daly Housing, Inc. v. Town of North Hempstead, 175 F.3d 144 (2d Cir. 1999) (does not require rezoning from business use when existing zoning prohibited non-disabled persons from residing in the district); Hemisphere Bldg. Co. v. Village of Richton Park, 171 F.3d 437 (7th Cir. 1999) (rezoning to higher density held not a reasonable accommodation).

[1] Support Ministries for Persons With AIDS, Inc. v. Village of Waterford, 808 F. Supp. 120 (N.D.N.Y. 1992); Oxford House v. Township of Cherry Hill, 799 F. Supp. 450 (D.N.J. 1992). *See also* Easter Seal Soc'y of New Jersey, Inc. v. Township of North Bergen, 798 F. Supp. 228 (D.N.J. 1992) (classifying group home as non-family use held discriminatory).

[2] 42 U.S.C. § 3607(b)(1).

[3] 514 U.S. 725 (1995) (quoting this treatise). *See* § 5.06.

[4] Oxford House-C v. City of St. Louis, 77 F.3d 249 (8th Cir. 1996); City of St. Joseph v. Preferred Family Healthcare, Inc., 859 S.W.2d 723 (Mo. App. 1993).

[1] Familystyle of St. Paul, Inc. v. City of St. Paul, 923 F.2d 91 (8th Cir. 1991). *Accord* Plymouth Charter Twp. v. Department of Soc. Servs., 501 N.W.2d 186 (Mich. App. 1993).

[2] Larkin v. State of Michigan Dep't of Soc. Servs., 89 F.3d 295 (6th Cir. 1996). *Accord* Oconomowoc Residential Programs, Inc. v. City of Greenfield, 23 F. Supp.2d 941 (E.D. Wis. 1998); Horizon House Develpmt'l Servs., Inc. v. Township of Upper Southampton, 804 F. Supp. 683 (E.D. Pa. 1992), *aff'd without opinion,* 995 F.2d 217 (3d Cir. 1993).

was valid because it integrated the disabled into the community and prevented "ghettoization." Integration is not a justification for maintaining quotas, the court held, and any clustering that occurs is caused by the free choice of the disabled.

§ 5.16   Americans With Disabilities and Rehabilitation Acts.

These statutes provide that a disabled person may not be subject to discrimination.[1] The Rehabilitation Act (RA) applies only to municipalities receiving federal assistance, but the Americans With Disabilities Act (ADA) applies to anyone "denied the benefits of the services, programs or activities of a "private entity." These acts provide wider coverage than the Fair Housing Act because they are not limited to discrimination against handicapped persons.

A Second Circuit case held that both acts applied to zoning discrimination against group homes, and that the municipality had violated them.[2] The court held the city's refusal to give a building permit for a group home for drug-dependent individuals was discriminatory conduct covered by both statutes and granted the plaintiffs a preliminary injunction. Though the city could consider legitimate zoning considerations in its decisions on group homes, it could not consider perceived harm based on stereotypes and perceived fears; the denial was tainted with discriminatory intent.[3]

§ 5.17   Single-Family Use.

Ever since the U.S. Supreme Court's landmark *Euclid* decision, the separation of residential uses by building type has been a well-established practice in zoning. Most zoning ordinances contain a set of single-family zoning districts in which single-family dwellings are the exclusive use. The ordinance permits multifamily residential uses in a separate set of residential districts.

Judicial acceptance of single-family zoning leads many municipalities to rely on it as the key element in a "wait and see" development timing strategy. They effectively preclude development by zoning more land for single-family use than the market requires, often at low densities. No development is likely to occur until the municipality adopts a zoning change to authorize either nonresidential development or residential development at a higher density. Courts have allowed municipalities to maintain the character of single-family residential districts by

---

[1] 42 U.S.C. § 12132 (ADA); 29 U.S.C. § 794(a) (RA).

[2] Innovative Health Systems, Inc. v. City of White Plains, 177 F.3d 37 (2d Cir. 1997). *See also* Bay Area Addiction & Research, Inc. v. City of Antioch, 179 F.3d 715 (9th Cir. 1999) (remanding case attacking distance requirement); Wisconsin Correctional Serv. v. City of Milwaukee, 173 F. Supp.2d 842 (E.D. Wis. 2001) (statute requires board of zoning appeals to reconsider standard criteria for special use permits).

[3] *See also* Forest City Daly Housing, Inc. v. Town of North Hempstead, 175 F.3d 144 (2d Cir. 1999) (group home not entitled to special exception in business zone when traditional homes would also have been denied a special exception).

prohibiting transient rentals,[1] denying the construction of an accessory unit,[2] prohibiting more than one kitchen in a dwelling unit,[3] and zoning a townhouse buffer between a residential area and commercial development.[4]

Arverne Bay Constr. Co. v. Thatcher,[5] a leading early New York case, indicates a municipality may not use single-family zoning as a holding zone when it is not appropriate for the site to which it applies. The court struck down an exclusive single-family zone on a major boulevard in Brooklyn because it was premature. The plaintiff wanted to construct an automobile service station. The court noted that the area was undeveloped, that single-family development probably would not occur for some time, and that conditions near the site, including an incinerator and garbage disposal plant and a dumping ground, made the area unsuitable for single-family use.[6] An implication from *Arverne Bay*, that municipalities may not use single-family zoning to hold undeveloped areas for future residential development is qualified by a later New York decision.[7]

A suburban municipality may attempt to preserve the quality of its residential environment by zoning its entire area for single-family use. This type of zoning raises obvious exclusionary problems. A few decisions upheld single-family zoning for an entire community against objections by developers who planned to build either commercial or industrial facilities. They emphasized the availability of adequate facilities of this type in adjacent communities but did not consider the exclusionary zoning problem.[8]

§ 5.18   Apartments.

Although *Euclid* held that the exclusion of apartments from residential districts does not violate due process or equal protection, it did not tell municipalities how they should map zoning districts that separate apartments from other residential uses. This problem frequently arises when a landowner attacks the constitutionality of a single-family zoning restriction on property he would like

---

[1] Cope v. City of Cannon Beach, 855 P.2d 1083 (Or. 1993).

[2] Desmond v. City of Contra Costa, 25 Cal. Rptr. 2d 842 (Cal. App. 1993).

[3] Zarrinnia v. Zoning Hearing Bd., 639 A.2d 1276 (Pa. Commw. 1994).

[4] Central Motors Corp. v. City of Pepper Pike, 653 N.E.2d 639 (Ohio 1995).

[5] 15 N.E.2d 587 (N.Y. 1938).

[6] *See also* Petersen v. City of Decorah, 259 N.W.2d 553 (Iowa App. 1977) (may not use agricultural use district to reserve land for future industrial development). *Compare* Rodo Land, Inc. v. Board of County Comm'rs, 517 P.2d 873 (Colo. App. 1974) (upholding single-family zoning in rural area).

[7] § 10.04.

[8] Valley View Village, Inc. v. Proffett, 221 F.2d 412 (6th Cir. 1955); Barolomeo v. Town of Paradise Valley, 631 P.2d 564 (Ariz. App. 1981); Cadoux v. Planning & Zoning Comm'n, 294 A.2d 582 (Conn. (1972); Blank v. Town of Lake Clarke Shores, 161 So. 2d 683 (Fla. 1964). *See also* Folsom Rd. Civic Ass'n v. Parish of St. Tammany, 407 So. 2d 1219 (La. 1981).

to develop for apartment use. The state courts have decided practically all of these cases. Although they clearly raise an as-applied taking problem, state courts may not consider the takings issue but simply hold a zoning restriction is "arbitrary and capricious" if they invalidate it.[1]

Courts usually examine the zoning and existing development in the area surrounding land restricted to single-family use to determine whether the restriction is a taking or is arbitrary and capricious. If the surrounding area is zoned and developed for single-family use, a court will uphold the single-family restriction because single-family development is a reasonable use of the restricted property.

More difficult problems arise when the area surrounding property restricted to single-family use contains a mixture of single-family and multifamily development. *Krause v. City of Royal Oak*[2] is a typical case. Plaintiff owned a 3.5-acre tract that formed an imperfect right triangle at an intersection of two roads. A railroad ran along the hypotenuse of the triangle. Northeast of the railroad the land was zoned and partially developed for single-family use. The area south of the triangle was developed with apartments. A golf course was located across the road to the west. A row of single-family dwellings was located on the western fringe of plaintiff's property, across from the golf course. The governing body refused to rezone plaintiff's tract for multifamily use.

The plaintiff, who wished to build apartments on his property, claimed that the single-family zoning was a taking. The court disagreed. It held that the neighborhood affected by the plaintiff's proposed apartments was the single-family area lying to the northeast. The court quoted *Euclid* for the proposition that apartments are "parasites" in single-family neighborhoods and held that noise and congestion from the plaintiff's apartment development would detrimentally affect this single-family area. It then held that the disparity between the value of plaintiff's property for multi-as compared with single-family use was not enough to "subvert the interests of the public" in the single-family zoning of plaintiff's land.

In an interesting holding on the use of apartments to buffer single-family residences from more intensive uses, the court dismissed the presence of the railroad tracks as a significant factor. As the court noted, more people live in apartments than in single-family housing. To place apartments next to the railroad tracks would subject even more people to the noise and inconvenience of railroad traffic. The court also believed that the plaintiff's case was weakened because he did not challenge a previous downzoning of his property but asked instead

---

[1] § 2.36. *See* Ewing v. City of Carmel-by-the-Sea, 286 Cal. Rptr. 382 (Cal. App. 1991) (ordinance prohibiting temporary occupancy held not a taking).

[2] 160 N.W.2d 769 (Mich. App. 1968).

for an upzoning to allow a more profitable use of his property. This point of view is unusual in as-applied taking cases.

The dissenting opinion would have held the single-family zoning "confiscatory" because it prevented any reasonable use of plaintiff's property, whether or not it had some "exchange value" under the single-family zoning. In the dissent's view, the railroad tracks made the plaintiff's property unsuitable for residential development. This holding would have made the restriction a per se taking under the Supreme Court's *Lucas* decision.[3]

Although unusual in its treatment of the upzoning and buffer issues, the *Krause* majority illustrates a typical as-applied taking opinion on single-family zoning. The disagreement between the majority and dissenting opinions indicates how courts can go either way in cases where a mixed-use area surrounds the property whose owner brings a taking challenge. Most courts review the facts in as-applied taking attacks on single-family zoning without so clearly specifying the criteria that govern their decision.[4]

A total exclusion of apartments is another matter. A few early cases invalidated zoning ordinances that totally excluded apartments from suburban communities but did not provide a comprehensive review of exclusionary zoning problems. *Appeal of Girsh*[5] is the leading case. The court held that a suburban zoning ordinance that excluded apartments was an improper limitation on suburban growth. It refused to accept the community's justification that apartment development would fiscally burden municipal services. "[I]f . . . [this suburb] is a logical place for development to take place, it should not be heard to say that it will not bear its rightful part of the burden."[6] Later cases have elaborated the tests the Pennsylvania court applies to exclusionary zoning.[7]

The supply of rental housing is also reduced by the conversion of rental apartments to condominium ownership. Some municipalities attempt to regulate condominium conversions through the zoning ordinance by requiring a conditional use permit or by limiting conversions to certain areas of the community. The courts have invalidated these restrictions by holding that condominium

---

[3] *See* § 2.09.

[4] Davis v. Sails, 318 So. 2d 214 (Fla. App. 1975); Wheeler v. City of Berkeley, 485 S.W.2d 707 (Mo. App. 1972).

[5] 263 A.2d 395 (Pa. 1970).

[6] *Id.* at 398–99. *See also* Dowsey v. Village of Kensington, 177 N.E. 427 (N.Y. App. 1937) (accord); Zelvin v. Zoning Bd. of Appeals, 306 A.2d 151 (Conn. C.P. 1973) (contra); Countrywalk Condominiums, Inc. v. City of Orchard Lake Village, 561 N.W.2d 405 (Mich. App. 1997) (upholding exclusion of apartments).

[7] §§ 7.19–7.22.

conversions are a change in ownership, not a change in use the zoning ordinance can regulate. [8]

§ 5.19 Accessory Uses.

Accessory uses are secondary activities that are necessary and convenient to the principal use of the property. Zoning ordinances usually allow accessory uses that are related, subordinate, and customarily incidental to the principal use. They also require the location of accessory uses on the same lot as the principal use and may prohibit them if they alter the character of the surrounding area. [1] The cases apply these criteria to determine whether a particular use is allowable as an accessory use under the ordinance. [2]

Zoning ordinances often allow accessory uses or buildings that are "customarily incidental" to a residential use, and courts impose a similar requirement if the ordinance does not contain one. The test is whether the accessory use is normally incidental to a residential use. [3] It is not necessary to show that a majority or even a substantial number of homes in a neighborhood have a particular accessory use, such as a tennis court. [4]

A zoning ordinance may permit homeowners to rent rooms in single-family dwellings and will often limit the number of rooms the homeowner can rent and

---

[8] Griffin Dev. Co. v. City of Oxnard, 199 Cal. Rptr. 739 (Cal. App. 1984); McHenry State Bank v. City of McHenry, 46 N.E.2d 521 (Ill. App. 1983) (may not restrict conversion to condominium zones); Graham Court Assocs. v. Town Council, 281 S.E.2d 418 (N.C. App. 1981); Backer v. Town of Sullivan's Island, 310 S.E.2d 433 (S.C. 1983). *See* San Remo Hotel v. City & County of San Francisco, 41 P.3d 87 (Cal. 2002) (holding ordinance requiring replacement of residential hotel units lost by conversion not a taking).

[1] Redfearn v. Creppel, 455 So. 2d 1356 (La. 1984).

[2] Perron v. City of Concord, 150 A.2d 403 (N.H. 1959) (use of large part of house by roofing contractor held not incidental); Charlie Brown of Chatham, Inc. v. Board of Adjustment, 495 A.2d 119 (N.J. App. Div. 1985) (sleeping accommodation in restaurant held not accessory); Presnell v. Leslie, 144 N.E.2d 381 (N.Y. 1959) (tall amateur radio transmitting tower not appropriate in small compact neighborhood); Boreth v. Philadelphia Zoning Bd. of Adjustment, 151 A.2d 474 (Pa. 1959) (home beauty shop not incidental); Pearson v. Evans, 320 P.2d 300 (Wash. 1958) (boathouse held incidental to house one-quarter its size); 60 A.L.R.4th 901 (1988); 54 A.L.R.4th 1034 (1987).

[3] Dupont Circle Citizens Ass'n v. District of Columbia Bd. of Zoning Adjustment, 749 A.2d 1258 (D.C. App. 2000) (bed and breakfast held accessory); Pratt v. Building Inspector, 113 N.E.2d 816 (Mass. 1953); Maselbas v. Zoning Bd. of Appeals, 694 N.E.2d 1314 (Mass. App. 1998) (garage and swimming pool held accessory); KSC Realty Trust v. Town of Freedom, 772 A.2d 321 (N.H. 2001) (transport and sale of water held accessory to permitted use of water storage facility); Colt's Run Civic Ass'n v. Colts Neck Township Zoning Bd., 717 A.2d 456 (N.J. 1998) (domestic animal shelter allowed); Dettmar v. County Bd. of Zoning Appeals, 273 N.E.2d 921 (Ohio Misc. 1971); Allegheny West Civic Council v. Zoning Bd. of Adjustment, 716 A.2d 600 (Pa. 1998) (engineering consulting business not accessory);Town of Alta v. Ben Hame Corp., 836 P.2d 797 (Utah 1992) (overnight rental as lodging facility not customarily incidental).

[4] Klien v. Township of Lower Macungie, 395 A.2d 609 (Pa. 1978).

their total floor area. Some courts hold that this practice is an impermissible business activity if the zoning ordinance does not permit it,[5] but other courts approve the occasional renting of a small number of rooms.[6] The ordinance may prohibit separate residential apartments located in accessory structures or within the primary dwelling.[7] The courts have allowed accessory apartments for friends, relatives, or domestic servants if the ordinance does not prohibit them.[8] A California court has held unconstitutional an ordinance that restricted the occupancy of accessory housing to property owner, his or her dependent, or caregiver for the property owner or dependent.[9] The court held the ordinance violated the right of privacy under the California constitution and the equal protection clause.

An accessory structure is a building located on the same lot as the principal building that either houses or serves as an accessory use. Accessory structures must comply with special height, size, and location requirements that keep them away from lot lines and prevent inappropriate placement. Placement in the front yard is usually prohibited. The courts hold that additions to principal buildings are not accessory structures.[10]

The courts have usually held that the parking of commercial or recreational vehicles is neither accessory nor incidental to residential uses.[11] They hold that commercial vehicles create excessive noise and that their overnight parking or permanent storage adversely affects the character of residential neighborhoods.[12]

---

[5] Kewseling v. City of Baltimore, 151 A.2d 726 (Md. 1959); Township of Berlin v. Christiansen, 215 A.2d 593 (N.J.L. Div. 1965).

[6] Brady v. Superior Court, 19 Cal. Rptr. 242 (Cal. App. 1962); Baddour v. City of Long Beach, 18 N.E.2d 18 (N.Y. 1938).

[7] Sanders v. Board of Adjustment, 445 So. 2d 909 (Ala. App. 1983) (accessory structure); City of Peru v. Nienaber, 424 N.E.2d 85 (Ill. App. 1981) (within dwelling).

[8] Trent v. City of Pittsburg, 619 P.2d 1171 (Kan. 1980); Township of Randolph v. Lamprecht, 542 A.2d 36 (N.J. App. Div. 1988) (separate dwelling unit for servant held accessory use); Farr v. Board of Adjustment, 326 S.E.2d 382 (N.C. App. 1985).

[9] Coalition Advocating Legal Housing Options v. City of Santa Monica, 105 Cal. Rptr. 2d 802 (Cal. App. 2001).

[10] Olson v. Zoning Bd. of Appeal, 84 N.E.2d 544 (Mass. 1949) (garage and connecting breezeway); City of Cleveland v. Young, 111 So. 2d 29 (Miss. 1959) (carport).

[11] Sechrist v. Municipal Court, 134 Cal. Rptr. 733 (Cal. App. 1976) (motor vehicles and junk); Becker v. Town of Hampton Falls, 374 A.2d 653 (N.H. 1977) (road grader); Galliford v. Commonwealth, 430 A.2d 1222 (Pa. Commw. 1981) (large truck). See Whaley v. Dorchester County Zoning Bd. of Appeals, 524 S.E.2d 404 (S.C. 1999) (ordinance prohibiting parking of commercial vehicle held constitutional).

[12] People v. Tolman, 168 Cal. Rptr. 328 (Cal. App. 1980); Recreational Vehicle United Citizens Ass'n v. City of Sterling Heights, 418 N.W.2d 702 (Mich. App. 1987) (setback restrictions on motor vehicle parking upheld); Township of Livingston v. Marchev, 205 A.2d 65 (N.J. App. Div. 1964).

§ 5.20 Home Occupations.

Home occupations are income-producing activities that take place within dwellings or accessory structures in residential districts. Most zoning ordinances define home occupations in general terms, but some list home occupations that are prohibited or permitted. They may also limit the amount of floor space home occupations can use, prohibit equipment not normally used for domestic purposes, and prohibit or limit the number of nonresident employees. Zoning ordinances may also confine home occupations to indoor activity, regulate exterior signage, and prohibit structural alterations.[1] The courts have rejected substantive due process and equal protection objections to these restrictions.[2]

Courts approve home occupations that are incidental and subordinate to the principal use if the ordinance does not list permitted home occupations. Some courts compare the scale of the home occupation with the scale of the principal use.[3] They usually approve professional offices for the practice of law, medicine, dentistry, and architecture and the use of the home to give music and dance lessons.[4] The cases divide on whether the sale of real estate is an acceptable home occupation.[5] They usually allow minor commercial services in large apartment buildings.[6]

---

[1] State v. Baudier, 334 So. 2d 197 (La. 1976) (limited floor space to 15% of dwelling unit); Holsheimer v. Columbia County, 890 P.2d 447 (Or. App. 1995) (commercial business requiring daily movement of vehicles and equipment not allowed under statute); City of Aberdeen v. Herrmann, 301 N.W.2d 674 (S.D. 1981) (limiting nonresident employees).

[2] Farrell v. City of Miami, 587 F. Supp. 413 (S.D. Fla. 1984); Levinson v. Montgomery County, 620 A.2d 961 (Md. App. 1993); City of Manassas v. Rosson, 294 S.E.2d 799 (Va.), *appeal dismissed,* 459 U.S. 1166 (1982); City of Florence v. Turbeville, 121 S.E.2d 437 (S.C. 1961).

[3] Metropolitan Dev. Comm'n v. Mullin, 399 N.E.2d 751 (Ind. App. 1979); Adams v. DelMonte, 707 A.2d 1061 (N.J. App. Div. 1998) (septic tank cleaning business held not home occupation); Franchi v. Zoning Hearing Bd., 543 A.2d 239 (Pa. Commw. 1988).

[4] Eisner v. Farrington, 209 N.Y.S.2d 673 (App. Div. 1961) (veterinarian's office); Osborne v. Planning Bd., 536 N.Y.S.2d 244 (Sup. Ct. 1989) (social worker); Stewart v. Humpheries, 132 N.E.2d 758 (Ohio 1955) (dance studio); Parks v. Board of Adjustment, 566 S.W.2d 365 (Tex. Civ. App. 1978) (music school with 110 students). *But see* County of Butte v. Bach, 218 Cal. Rptr. 613 (Cal. App. 1985) (law office not permitted when lawyer did not reside in residence); Schweitzer v. Board of Zoning Appeals, 167 N.Y.S.2d 767 (Misc. 1957) (ceramics class not permitted). *But see* Frederick v. Zoning Hearing Bd., 713 A.2d 139 (Pa. Commw. 1998) (cannot park trucks used in business on adjacent street); Appeal of Herrick, 742 A.2d 752 (Vt. 1999) (interpreting statutes to allow day care center).

[5] *Compare* People v. Cully Realty, Inc., 442 N.Y.S.2d 847 (Misc. 1981) (not permitted) *with* Vislisel v. Board of Adjustment, 372 N.W.2d 316 (Iowa App. 1985) (contra). *See also* Board of Adjustment v. Levinson, 244 S.W.2d 281 (Tex. Civ. App. 1951) (beauty shop not a home occupation).

[6] City of Newark v. Daley, 214 A.2d 410 (N.J. 1965) (vending machine); 140 Riverside Drive v. Murdock, 95 N.Y.S.2d 860 (App. Div. 1950) (newsstand).

§ 5.21   Zoning for Mobile (or Manufactured) Homes.

Mobile homes are a residential building type that zoning ordinances often exclude from the community or restrict to undesirable areas or mobile home parks. A mobile home is a dwelling that is manufactured off-site and shipped fully assembled to a building site. It is then placed on a foundation or on supports and is seldom moved again. Some legislation now refers to this type of housing as "manufactured" housing. This term also applies to housing that is assembled on site from manufactured modular components.

Municipalities object to mobile homes for a number of reasons, such as their transient use, their unpleasant appearance, their unsafe construction, and the inadequate tax revenues that are produced by their taxation as personal rather than real property. Many of these objections are no longer valid. New developments in mobile home construction can make them comparable to conventional construction. Legislation can remedy taxation problems, and federal, state and local legislation now imposes safety requirements. Mobile home residents are no longer transient rather than permanent occupants.

The discussion that follows reviews a number of common zoning restrictions on mobile homes, including total or partial exclusion and zoning that limits mobile homes to mobile home parks. A municipality may also place other burdensome restrictions on mobile homes, such as a conditional use requirement, appearance requirement, or a limitation on the number of mobile homes permitted in the municipality.[1] Judicial reaction to these prohibitions is mixed. The courts have upheld appearance codes for manufactured housing that contained exterior finish, roof construction and pitch requirements.[2] The courts are also divided on whether a municipality can distinguish between different types of manufactured housing, such as an ordinance allowing modular housing but not allowing mobile homes shipped from the factory as a unit.[3]

---

[1] *Compare* Riverview Park, Inc. v. Town of Hinsdale, 313 A.2d 733 (N.H. 1973) (upholds numerical limit) *with* Begin v. Inhabitants of Town of Sabattus, 409 A.2d 1269 (Me. 1979) (contra), *and* Town of Glocester v. Olivo's Mobile Home Court, Inc., 300 A.2d 465 (R.I. 1973) (same); 42 A.L.R.3d 598 (1972).

[2] Georgia Manufactured Hous. v. Spalding County, 148 F.3d 1304 (11th Cir. 1998); CMH Mfg. v. Catawba County, 994 F. Supp. 697 (W.D.N.C. 1998). *But see* Campbell v. Monroe County, 426 So. 2d 1158 (Fla. App. 1983) (ordinance requiring masonry construction held to violate state statute prohibiting differential treatment of mobile homes). *See* 2002 Ky. S.B. 197 (authorizing municipalities to adopt compatibility standards for manufactured homes).

[3] Bourgeois v. Parish of St. Tammany, 628 F. Supp. 159 (E.D. La. 1986) (invalidating ordinance excluding mobile homes but not modular homes from residential district); Geiger v. Zoning Hearing Bd., 507 A.2d 361 (Pa. 1986) (invalidating ordinance allowing two-section but prohibiting one-section homes delivered to the site). *Contra* Warren v. Municipal Officers, 431 A.2d 624 (Me. 1981); Bibco Corp. v. City of Sumter, 504 S.E.2d 112 (S.C. 1998).

§ 5.22   As a Dwelling.

Single-family zoning restricts single-family uses to residential "dwellings," a building type classification. A mobile home owner may claim that her mobile home is permitted as a "dwelling" in a single-family district. The court must then decide whether the mobile home qualifies under the definition of a dwelling in the zoning ordinance. *Town of Manchester v. Phillips,*[1] an early leading case, held that the exclusion of mobile homes from a definition of a "dwelling" in a zoning ordinance applied to a mobile home placed on a foundation. The court was hostile to mobile homes and held that the town could limit them to areas where they would not injure the investment in conventional houses, "hurt taxable values, and impede town development."

Other cases, perhaps easier because the ordinance did not expressly exclude mobile homes, held that the definition of a "dwelling" included mobile homes.[2] These cases usually turned on an analysis of legislative intent. Their refusal to distinguish mobile homes from conventional dwelling units implies a rejection of the older mobile home image.

§ 5.23   Partial Exclusion.

A zoning ordinance may exclude mobile homes from designated zoning districts. Some courts uphold their exclusion from residential districts,[1] and some even uphold their exclusion from industrial and commercial districts and from rural and agricultural areas.[2] A partial exclusion problem also arises when a municipality allows mobile homes only in mobile home parks and excludes them from its residential districts. Most of the cases have upheld ordinances that contained these restrictions.[3] They relied on the usual presumption of

---

[1] 180 N.E.2d 333 (Mass. 1962).

[2] Fedorich v. Zoning Bd. of Appeals, 424 A.2d 289 (Conn. 1979); Village of Moscow v. Skeene, 585 N.E.2d 493 (Ohio App. 1989) (after mobile home placed on foundation); In re Willey, 140 A.2d 11 (Vt. 1958); State v. Work, 449 P.2d 806 (Wash. 1969).

[1] Jensen's, Inc. v. Town of Plainville, 150 A.2d 297 (Conn. 1959); City of Lewiston v. Knieriem, 685 P.2d 821 (Idaho 1984) (excluded from farm zone but allowed in residential districts); Mack T. Anderson Ins. Agency, Inc. v. City of Belgrade, 803 P.2d 648 (Mont. 1990) (although modular homes allowed); Village Bd. of Trustees v. Zoning Bd. of Appeals, 562 N.Y.S.2d 973 (App. Div. 1990); Duggins v. Town of Walnut Grove, 306 S.E.2d 186 (N.C. App. 1981); Corning v. Town of Ontario, 121 N.Y.S.2d 288 (Sup. Ct. 1953); Duckworth v. City of Bonney Lake, 586 P.2d 860 (Wash. 1978).

[2] Camboni's, Inc. v. County of Du Page, 187 N.E.2d 212 (Ill. 1962) (upholds exclusion from industrial zone); Lakeland Bluff v. County of Will, 252 N.E.2d 765 (Ill. App. 1969) (contra, rural area); 42 A.L.R.3d 598 (1972). *But see* Town of Chesterfield v. Brooks, 489 A.2d 600 (N.H. 1985) (may not confine to areas with unpaved roads).

[3] Colorado Housing Ass'n v. City of Salida, 977 F. Supp. 1080 (D. Colo. 1997); Cooper v. Sinclair, 66 So. 2d 702 (Fla. 1953); People of Village of Cahokia v. Wright, 311 N.E.2d 153 (Ill.

constitutionality or found that placement in mobile home parks made supervision easier or was necessary to protect property values. These reasons reflect traditional perceptions that mobile homes have negative effects on residential areas.

A landmark Michigan case, *Robinson Twp. v. Knoll,*[4] held a *per se* prohibition on the location of mobile homes outside mobile home parks unconstitutional. The court reviewed the usual objections to mobile homes but noted that changes in mobile home construction made them as attractive as conventional single-family dwellings. Aesthetic objections to mobile homes were no longer justified, and the investment required for a modern mobile home precluded any objections based on transient occupancy. More appropriate regulations, such as local plumbing codes and a regulation requiring attachment to a solid foundation, could handle health and safety problems. A municipality could also prohibit the exposure of the wheels and chassis.

Though limited to a mobile home park restriction, *Robinson Township* has broader implications for mobile home zoning. The court rejected a *per se* restriction on the location of mobile homes and adopted the less restrictive alternative test to demand the regulation of mobile home problems outside the zoning ordinance. The case suggests that any restrictive zoning of mobile homes is suspect.

§ 5.24   Total Exclusion.

In *Barre Mobile Home Park v. Town of Petersham,*[1] a federal district court upheld the exclusion of mobile home parks from a Massachusetts town. The court held a mobile home park would increase the population density of the town, alter its rural character of the town and affect the town's ability to provide adequate social and other municipal services, including sewage and waste disposal services. as well as other municipal services. The prohibition was also designed to preserve property values and keep commercial enterprises out of residential areas.

1974); McCollum v. City of Berea, 53 S.W.3d 106 (Ky. 2001); City of Saco v. Tweedie, 314 A.2d 135 (Me. 1974); Town of Granby v. Landry, 170 N.E.2d 364 (Mass. 1960); State v. Larson, 195 N.W.2d 180 (Minn. 1972); Mobile Home Owners Protective Assoc. v. Town of Chatham, 305 N.Y.S.2d 334 (App. Div. 1969); Town of Scranton v. Willoughby, 412 S.E.2d 424 (S.C. 1991); Mobile Home City of Chattanooga v. Hamilton County, 552 S.W.2d 86 (Tenn. App. 1976); City of Brookside Village v. Comeau, 633 S.W.2d 790 (Tex..(1982); Town of Stonewood v. Bell, 270 S.E.2d 787 (W. Va. 1980); 17 A.L.R.4th 106 (1982).

[4] 302 N.W.2d 146 (Mich. 1981). *See also* Cannon v. Coweta Cty., 389 S.E.2d 329 (Ga. 1990) (exclusion held unconstitutional); Carpenter v. City of Petal, 699 So.2d 928 (Miss. 1997) (invalidating exclusion); Luczynski v. Temple, 497 A.2d 211 (N.J. Ch. Div. 1985) (following *Robinson*). *See also* Gackler Land Co. v. Yankee Springs Twp., 359 N.W.2d 226 (Mich. App. 1984) (upholding restrictions promoting compatibility and relative uniformity of site-built and mobile home housing).

[1] 592 F. Supp. 633 (D. Mass. 1984), *aff'd without opinion,* 767 F.2d 904 (1st Cir. 1985).

However, the New Jersey Supreme Court invalidated a prohibition on mobile homes in its second *Mt. Laurel* exclusionary zoning decision,[2] and other courts have invalidated total exclusions that were not part of an exclusionary ordinance.[3]

§ 5.25 As a Conditional Use.

Municipalities often authorize mobile homes as a special exception in designated zoning districts.[1] Although a municipality may provide reasonable opportunities for mobile homes through special exceptions, it may also draft or administer a special exception provision so that it is exclusionary. Some courts are sensitive to these possibilities and strike down vaguely drafted special exception provisions, such as a provision requiring proof of "necessity" as the basis for allowing a mobile home use.[2]

§ 5.26 State and Federal Regulation.

The courts do not imply a preemption of local zoning from legislation that merely authorizes the state licensing of mobile homes.[1] Some states have legislation that explicitly prohibits the discriminatory treatment of mobile homes in zoning ordinances.[2] The language enacting this type of prohibition varies, though courts have invalidated a number of local restrictions held to violate the state law.[3] A number of states have also adopted legislation authorizing the state

---

[2] Southern Burlington County NAACP v. Township of Mt. Laurel, 456 A.2d 390 (N.J. 1983). *See* § 7.09.

[3] Oak Forest Mobile Home Park v. City of Oak Forest, 326 N.E.2d 473 (Ill. App. 1975) (holding mobile home is legitimate use and noting need for affordable housing). *See* also Town of Pompey v. Parker, 377 N.E.2d 741 (N.Y. 1978) (validity of mobile home exclusion reserved).

[1] Jensen's, Inc. v. City of Dover, 547 A.2d 277 (N.H. 1988) (upholding conditional use requirement because of density increase).

[2] Pioneer Trust & Sav. Bank v. County of McHenry, 241 N.E.2d 454 (Ill. 1968) (necessity requirement invalidated); Lakewood Estates, Inc. v. Deerfield Twp. Zoning Bd. of Appeals, 194 N.W.2d 511 (Mich. App. 1977) (vague standards); Walworth Leasing Corp. v. Sterni, 316 N.Y.S.2d 851 (Sup. Ct. 1970) (denial as special use reversed); 42 A.L.R.3d 598 (1972).

[1] Adams v. Cowart, 160 S.E.2d 805 (Ga. 1968); County of Winnebago v. Hartman, 242 N.E.2d 916 (Ill. App. 1968).

[2] Cal. Gov't Code § 65852.3 (if certified under federal law); Fla. Stat. Ann. §§ 553.36, 553.38; Idaho Code § 67-6509B; N.H. Rev. Stat. § 674:32; Or. Rev. Stat. § 197.314. Vt. Stat. Ann. tit. 24, § 4406(4)(A). *See* Marion County v. Department of Community Affairs, 817 So.2d 1062 (Fla. App. 2002) (statute held constitutional and invalidating moratorium); Pope v. Town of Hinsdale, 624 A.2d 1360 (N.H. 1993) (existing nonconforming manufactured housing park not covered by statute). *See also* Idaho Code § 67-6509A (imposes minimum size and design requirements); Neb. Rev. Stat. § 14-402(2)(a) (same).

[3] Bangs v. Town of Wells, 760 A.2d 632 (Me. 2000) (ordinance prohibiting expansion of mobile home park conflicts with state statute requiring municipalities to give "reasonable consideration'" to expansion); Paladac v. City of Rockland, 558 A.2d 372 (Me. 1989) (invalidating setback requirement; statute required municipalities to find locations for mobile homes); Ettinger v. City

certification of mobile homes that meet state construction standards. This legislation preempts local regulation of mobile homes under building codes, and some of these laws preempt local zoning.[4]

Federal legislation requires mobile home manufacturers to comply with federal construction and safety standards.[5] This legislation does not preempt local zoning,[6] but some states have adopted legislation that prohibits municipalities from adopting restrictive zoning for manufactured housing certified under the federal law.[7] The Eleventh Circuit invalidated an ordinance that allowed mobile homes certified under federal law in residential areas only if they met additional safety requirements.[8] The court held the city could not do land use planning through a safety provision that is preempted by federal law.

§ 5.27   Private Schools.

Private nonsectarian schools present special regulatory problems in residential districts. Public schools are often not subject to zoning regulations because they are state-supervised.[1] Attempts are still made to prohibit private schools from residential zones, or to require a conditional use permit for them. Although arguments can be made that private schools present special zoning problems, the majority rule is that attempts to prohibit private nonsectarian schools while allowing other schools in residential zones are invalid.[2] The courts have upheld

---

of Lansing, 546 N.W.2d 652 (Mich. App. 1996) (ordinance allowing mobile home parks in residential districts on special permit did not "generally" exclude them); Jensen's, Inc. v. City of Dover, 547 A.2d 277 (N.H. 1988) (statute requiring reasonable opportunities for mobile homes did not invalidate ordinance limiting mobile homes to rural zones); Northfield Dev. Co., Inc. v. City of Burlington, 523 S.E.2d 743 (N.C. App) (statute prohibiting exclusion of manufactured homes from entire jurisdiction does not require "substantial presence'" in the jurisdiction), aff'd, 535 S.E.2d 532 (N.C. 2000); In re Lunde, 688 A.2d 1312 (Vt. 1997) (ordinance restricting mobile homes to mobile home parks violates statute).

[4] Warren v. Municipal Officers, 431 A.2d 624 (Me. 1981).

[5] 42 U.S.C. § 5415.

[6] CMH Mfg., Inc. v. Catawba County, 994 F. Supp. 697 (W.D.N.C. 1998); Gackler Land Co. v. Yankee Springs Twp., 398 N.W.2d 393 (Mich. 1986);Bibco Corp. v. City of Sumter, 504 S.E.2d 112 (S.C. 1998); City of Brookside Village v. Comeau, 633 S.W.2d 790 (Tex.1982); Washington Manufactured Housing Ass'n v. Public Util. Dist. No. 3, 878 P.2d 1213 (Wash. 1994) (federal law does not preempt public utility district's new facility charge for connecting electricity).

[7] Iowa Code Ann. § 414.28; Me. Rev. Stat. Ann. tit. 30(A), § 4358(2).

[8] Scurlock v. City of Lynn Haven, 858 F.2d 1521 (11th Cir. 1988) (provision also held invalid under state law).

[1] See § 4.28.

[2] Roman Catholic Welfare Corporation of San Francisco v. City of Piedmont, 289 P.2d 438 (Cal. 1955) (invalidating ordinance permitting public schools but not private or parochial schools); Catholic Bishop of Chicago v. Kingery, 20 N.E.2d 583 (Ill. 1939) (same; ordinance permitting public schools but not parochial schools); City of Miami Beach v. State ex rel. Lear, 175 So. 537 (Fla. 1937) (same; public schools allowed but private schools prohibited in multifamily zone); State

special use permit requirements for private schools because they are less onerous than total prohibition.[3] Religious schools receive different judicial treatment because of the protection accorded religious uses under federal and state constitutions.[4] Statutes may also protect private schools.[5]

B. LARGE LOT AND MINIMUM HOUSE SIZE ZONING.

§ 5.28   The Zoning Problem.

Municipalities often control residential densities and amenities through large-lot zoning and minimum house size restrictions. These restrictions are exclusionary if they are excessive, and minimum house size requirements are especially suspect. Large lot zoning may also be exclusionary, but courts uphold it if it serves a legitimate zoning purpose, such as ensuring a low density environment to minimize environmental pollution. A trend toward building oversized home in existing residential neighborhoods of smaller homes has also prompted the adoption of restrictions on house size to maintain the residential character of a neighborhood.

§ 5.29   Minimum House Size.

Proponents of minimum house size restrictions advance a number of justifications. They claim they serve an aesthetic purpose, but why the size of a house is related to its aesthetic qualities is not clear. They also claim that minimum house size restrictions advance the health objective of zoning by preventing overcrowding. Housing codes provide a less restrictive alternative that can accomplish the same objective. These codes commonly require a minimum floor area for each habitable room.[1] Proponents of minimum house size restrictions also argue that they implement the statutory purposes of zoning by conserving property values.

---

v. Northwestern Preparatory School, 37 N.W.2d 370 (Minn. 1949) (same public and religious schools permitted but private schools prohibited); Trustees of Union College v. Members of Schenectady City Council, 690 N.E.2d 862 (N.Y. 1998) (cannot exclude educational institutions from historic district). *Contra* Wisconsin Lutheran High School Conference v. Sinar, 65 N.W.2d 43 (Wis. 1954). *Compare* Yanow v. Seven Oaks Park, 94 A.2d 482 (N.J. 1953) (upholding ordinance that allowed public and parochial schools but disallowed schools of higher learning and specialty schools).

[3] Creative Country Day School, Inc. v. Montgomery County Board of Appeals, 219 A.2d 789 (Md. 1966).

[4] *See* §§ 5.69–5.70 (zoning for religious uses); § 6.57 (conditional use permits).

[5] Trustees of Tufts College v. City of Medford, 616 N.E.2d 433 (Mass. 1993) (statute prohibiting zoning of educational institutions except for reasonable regulations.)

[1] Nolden v. East Cleveland City Comm'n, 232 N.E.2d 421 (Ohio C.P. 1966).

Early decisions that considered substantive due process attacks on minimum house size restrictions were divided.[2] They usually turned on the willingness of the court to recognize aesthetic objectives and the conservation of property values as a legitimate zoning purpose. A pair of New Jersey cases indicates how judicial views have changed since these early decisions. An early, leading, and much-debated decision, *Lionshead Lake, Inc. v. Wayne Twp.*,[3] upheld a minimum house size restriction adopted by a suburban community that was not substantially developed. The court viewed the restriction as far-sighted planning intended to protect the quality of the community's environment, its health and its property values.

The New Jersey Supreme Court overruled *Lionshead* in *Home Bldrs. League of S. Jersey, Inc. v. Township of Berlin.*[4] It held the minimum house size restriction raised overlapping constitutional and statutory "general welfare" issues, but noted that minimum house size restrictions may serve the general welfare but may be exclusionary because they are clearly cost-related. It held a minimum house size provision unrelated to any other factor would be presumed enacted for improper purposes. The municipality then has the burden to establish a valid basis for the provision, and the court must then weigh and balance its "exclusionary and salutary effects." The court specifically noted its decision in *Mt. Laurel* that had invalidated exclusionary zoning.[5]

The court held the municipality had not justified the minimum house size restriction. Its impact on health and safety was indirect, and housing code occupancy requirements could better serve this purpose. The court noted that minimum house size restrictions varied by zoning district, even though minimum health and safety needs were "unquestionably the same" throughout the municipality.[6] The court also rejected a property conservation justification, and noted that the minimum house size requirement would not maintain the aesthetic quality of the municipality's residential environment because beauty is not related to size.

This case may suggest that restrictions on maximum house size are also invalid, though they serve the very different purpose of limiting rather than increasing

---

[2] Valid: Flower Hill Bldg. Corp. v. Village of Flower Hill, 100 N.Y.S.2d 903 (Sup. Ct. 1950); Thompson v. City of Carrollton, 211 S.W.2d 970 (Tex. App. 1948). Invalid: Northwood Props. Co. v. Perkins, 39 N.W.2d 25 (Mich. 1949); Elizabeth Lake Estates v. Waterford Twp., 26 N.W.2d 788 (Mich. 1947); Senefsky v. Lawler, 12 N.W.2d 387 (Mich. 1943). *See* 87 A.L.R.4th 294 (1991).

[3] 89 A.2d 693 (N.J. 1952).

[4] 405 A.2d 381 (N.J. 1979). *But see* Country Club Estates v. Town of Loma Linda, 281 F.3d 723 (8ith Cir. 2002) (applying deferential standard of review to uphold minimum house size requirement).

[5] § 7.09.

[6] *See also* Appeal of Medinger, 104 A.2d 118 (Pa. 1954) (invalidating variable minimum house size requirements).

price. The New Jersey Appellate Division distinguished *Berlin* and held an ordinance placing a maximum cap on house size was authorized by the zoning statute.[7] It served the purpose of ensuring that residences would be proportionate to the size of other homes in the area, and provided appropriately priced housing in a municipality limited in area and available housing stock.

§ 5.30 Large-Lot Zoning.

Suburban municipalities often adopt zoning ordinances that require large lots of one acre or more for single family residential development. Large-lot zoning can serve a number of zoning purposes. A common purpose is to maintain the character of a low density residential neighborhood. Another is to ensure the provision of low density housing so that the impact on environmentally sensitive areas will be limited. A municipality may also overzone for low density housing by providing more land for large lots than the market can absorb. This strategy may be intended to keep land off the market as a permanent open space or "green belt" preserve. It may also be intended as a temporary holding zone with the expectation that the municipality will rezone for higher residential densities or nonresidential use when developers apply for a zoning change. The large-lot holding zone is a "wait and see" zoning policy.

Large-lot zoning is exclusionary if it increases the cost of land for housing, but a price increase is not inevitable. A builder can build only one dwelling on a lot, no matter what its size, so that increasing the size of the lot does not necessarily increase its price. The price of land per square foot may decrease sufficiently to offset the increased size of the lot. Whether this price effect occurs is not clear. Some of the more convincing studies indicate that increasing the size of a lot increases its price.[1]

If a large-lot requirement increases the price of a lot it will increase the cost of housing because builders usually maintain a constant ratio between the price of a lot and the price of the dwelling that is built on it. Assume the constant ratio between lot price and house price is 1:4. If this ratio applies, the price of a house will increase by $4.00 for each $1.00 increase in the price of a lot. The ratio amplifies the exclusionary effect of large-lot zoning if this zoning increases lot prices.

The courts have usually upheld large lot zoning despite its potential for exclusion. However, a few cases struck down large lot zoning when it was excessive or exclusionary.[2]

---

[7] Rumson Estates, Inc. v. Mayor & Council, 795 A.2d 290 (N.J. App. Div. 2002).

[1] W. McEachern, "Large-Lot Zoning in Connecticut: Incentives and Effects," U. Conn. Center for Real Est. & Urb. Econ. Studies (1979); Nat'l Comm'n on Urban Problems, Building the American City 213–15 (1968).

[2] *But see* § 7.09 (invalid as exclusionary zoning in New Jersey). *See also* 2 A.L.R.5th 553 (1992); 1 A.L.R.5th 622 (1992).

§ 5.31   Held Valid.

An early Massachusetts case, *Simon v. Needham*[1] , illustrates the cases that uphold large-lot zoning as a method of providing a low density residential environment..A comparatively small and primarily residential suburb, twelve miles from the center of Boston, placed nearly all of its southern area in a one-acre residential zone. The court held that language in the state zoning act that authorized the regulation of "the size and width of lots" authorized large-lot zoning. The Standard Zoning Act contains different but equally sufficient language that authorizes the municipality to regulate "the size of yards . . . and other open spaces."

The court held the one-acre zoning implemented legitimate zoning purposes that included the establishment of residential neighborhoods of high quality that "would tend to improve and beautify the town and would harmonize with the natural characteristics of the locality." One-acre lots would also provide more residential amenities. They ensured more freedom from noise, less danger from fire, and a better opportunity for rest and relaxation. The court held the benefits of large-lot zoning made its constitutionality fairly debatable, and held the ordinance did not violate substantive due process. Though these justifications for the large lot requirement seem dubious, the case represents the tendency to uphold large lot zoning by applying the reasonably debatable rule associated with the presumption of constitutionality. The court reserved decision on whether it would uphold larger minimum lot sizes.

The court dismissed a taking objection because the ordinance only diminished the value of the developer's land. Most of the decisions apply this rule to reject taking objections to large-lot zoning. It does not prohibit residential development but only makes it less profitable by limiting the number of dwellings allowed.

Simon also rejected an exclusionary zoning claim. Assuming, but not deciding, that municipalities could not use zoning for fiscal purposes, the court stated that it would not tolerate an ordinance that was used to exclude. The court also decided that large-lot zoning served the public interest because nearby communities also had large-lot zoning. Later, more sophisticated, exclusionary zoning cases recognize that large-lot zoning can have exclusionary effects if applied extensively in metropolitan areas.

The argument that large-lot zoning will provide a high-quality, low-density, residential environment is more acceptable. Large lot zoning reinforces existing low residential densities in partly developed communities, and if the community is undeveloped it "plans" for a low-density residential environment by requiring development at low-density levels. This use of large-lot zoning is an application of the compatibility rationale in the nuisance cases. Exclusionary problems aside,

---

[1] 42 N.E.2d 516 (Mass. 1942).

it ensures that residential development will take place on compatible, low-density residential lots. Many of the favorable cases upheld large lot zoning as a measure that would ensure the character and appearance of suburban and developing communities.[2] A related purpose is the use of large lot zoning to implement a comprehensive plan by creating predominantly open "green belts" between communities to preserve community identity.[3]

Courts often rely on environmental justifications to uphold large lot zoning. Preservation of sites for low density development which are not easily buildable for higher density development because of their topography is one example.[4] Another is the provision of large enough building sites to assure a safe water supply and safe sewage disposal in areas without a public water supply, public sanitary sewers, or both.[5] Though these cases were decided before *Lucas*, a Maryland court upheld large lot zoning intended to limit development in a watershed. It rejected an argument that the zoning denied the landowner all economically viable use of the property under the *Lucas* per se takings test.[6]

Courts may exercise some caution in approving large lot zoning in these cases. For example, the Massachusetts Supreme Judicial Court[7] upheld three-acre zoning on Martha's Vineyard, but carefully noted that neither the provision of open space nor the protection of plant and animal life would "singly" support large lot zoning. Neither did the court decide whether the zoning was justified

[2] Rodo Land, Inc. v. Board of County Comm'rs, 517 P.2d 873 (Colo. App. 1974); Senior v. Zoning Comm'n of New Canaan, 153 A.2d 415 (Conn. 1959); Honeck v. County of Cook, 146 N.E.2d 35 (Ill. 1957); Flora Realty & Inv. Co. v. City of Ladue, 246 S.W.2d 771 (Mo.); Levitt v. Incorporated Village of Sands Point, 160 N.E.2d 501 (N.Y. 1959; Mayhew v. Town of Sunnyvale, 964 S.W.2d 922 (Tex. 1998) (upholding rejection of planned unit development that did not comply with one-acre zoning requirement because of impact development would have on community). For cases approving large-lot zoning in rural areas, see Steel Hill Dev., Inc. v. Town of Sanbornton, 469 F.2d 956 (1st Cir. 1972); County Comm'rs of Queen Anne's County v. Miles, 228 A.2d 450 (Md. 1967) (preservation of historic site and building).

[3] Norbeck Village Joint Venture v. Montgomery County Council, 254 A.2d 700 (Md. 1969) (two acres). See also Morse v. County of San Luis Obispo, 55 Cal. Rptr. 710 (Cal. App. 1967); Fisher v. Viola, 789 A.2d 782 (Pa. Commw. 2001).

[4] Larsen v. Zoning Comm'n, 217 A.2d 715 (Conn. 1966) (one acre); Metropolitan Homes, Inc. v. Town Planning & Zoning Comm'n, 202 A.2d 241 (Conn. 1964) (30,000 sq. ft.); Bogert v. Washington Twp., 135 A.2d 1 (N.J. 1957) (one acre) (preservation of natural capacity of soil to absorb rainfall to provide protection against flooding and soil erosion after heavy rains); Honeck v. County of Cook, 146 N.E.2d 35 (Ill. 1957) (five acres).

[5] Zygmont v. Planning & Zoning Comm'n, 210 A.2d 172 (Conn. 1965) (four acres); De Mars v. Zoning Comm'n, 115 A.2d 653 (Conn. 1955) (one acre); Salamar Bldrs. Corp. v. Tuttle, 275 N.E.2d 585 (N.Y. 1971) (two acres); Carruthers v. Board of Adjustment, 290 S.W.2d 340 (Tex. Civ. App. 1956) (one acre); *See also* Albano v. Mayor & Twp. Comm., 476 A.2d 852 (N.J. App. Div. 1984) (three acres; to prevent pollution of lake).

[6] Security Mgt. Corp. v. Baltimore County, 655 A.2d 1326 (Md. App. 1995.

[7] Johnson v. Town of Edgartown, 680 N.E.2d 37 (Mass. 1997).

by the need to provide a safe source of drinking water on-site for a lot with its own septic system. The court accepted evidence that the three-acre zoning was necessary to limit the amount of damaging nutrient pollution flowing into a nearby pond, and to protect the amenities and character of a rural resort in order to assist its economic stability, including the shellfish industry and tourism.

§ 5.32   Held Invalid.

Though courts often accept the facial validity of large lot zoning, they may hold it unconstitutional as applied. The courts have held large-lot zoning invalid when it would make residential development economically infeasible,[1] or that the large lot zoning did not implement the purposes for which it was adopted.[2] In some of these as-applied cases the courts held the large-lot zoning was inconsistent with residential densities in the surrounding area.[3] In *Aronson v. Town of Sharon*,[4] the Massachusetts court held a large-lot zoning ordinance improperly substituted the police power for the use of eminent domain. A suburban community twenty-one miles southwest of Boston zoned one-third of its area for two-and-one-half-acre lots to implement a comprehensive plan that included a land acquisition program for conservation purposes. The court seized on this point to hold that the municipality improperly used the large-lot ordinance as a substitute for eminent domain. It distinguished *Simon*, which upheld one-acre zoning. A "law of diminishing returns" sets in, the court held, and a two-acre lot did not improve on the environmental amenities provided by one-acre lots.

Other courts have held that large-lot zoning is exclusionary.[5] The most important cases invalidating large-lot zoning come from Pennsylvania. In the first case, *National Land & Inv. Co. v. Kohn*,[6] a small suburban municipality in the path of development in the Philadelphia area adopted a four-acre lot size minimum that applied to thirty percent of its area. The court noted the land zoned for four acres had no "readily available market." It applied a balancing test,

---

[1] Zeltig Land Dev. Corp. v. Bainbridge Township Bd. of Trustees, 599 N.E.2d 383 (Ohio App. 1991) (bedrock made public sewers necessary but development then not economically feasible at required five-acre lot size).

[2] Scott Ventures v. Hayes Township, 537 N.W.2d 610 (Mich. App. 1995) (real motivations behind facade of "public health and welfare" was aesthetics, retention of "rural character," and desire to exclude new homeowners from township); Pheasant Ridge Corp. v. Township of Warren, 777 A.2d 334 (N.J. 2001) (no environmental justification for six-acre zoning).

[3] Hamer v. Town of Ross, 382 P.2d 375 (Cal. 1963); LaSalle Nat'l Bank v. City of Highland Park, 189 N.E.2d 302 (Ill. 1963); Du Page County v. Halkier, 115 N.E.2d 635 (Ill. 1953); Guy v. Brandon Twp., 450 N.W.2d 279 (Mich. App. 1989) (2½ acres; taking found).

[4] 195 N.E.2d 341 (Mass. 1965).

[5] Board of County Supvrs. v. Carper, 107 S.E.2d 390 (Va. 1959) (invalidating two-acre zoning the covered two-third of county near Washington, D.C.).

[6] 215 A.2d 597 (Pa. 1965).

weighed the purposes of the four-acre zoning against the loss in value suffered by the landowner, and held the four-acre zoning unconstitutional. It found testimony on drainage and sewage problems unconvincing, held the municipality could adopt sanitary regulations to handle these problems, and concluded that four-acre zoning was neither "a necessary nor a reasonable method" to protect the community from pollution. The municipality argued that fire and road services were inadequate, but the court held that zoning "may not be used . . . to avoid the increased responsibilities and economic burdens which time and natural growth inevitably bring."

The court also rejected an argument the four-acre zoning was constitutional because it created a green belt that was necessary to preserve the "character" of the community. A greenbelt would be created if four-acre lots were unmarketable, but then the zoning would be confiscatory. Alternative measures were available to achieve open space preservation, including condemnation and cluster zoning, which reduces lot sizes in return for common open space. In the second case, *Concord Twp. Appeal (Kit-Mar)*,[7] the court struck down two-and three-acre zoning adopted by a suburban municipality and required "extraordinary justification" for lots of this size. The court also held that the size of a lot was irrelevant to sewage disposal.

The Pennsylvania court decided these cases before it adopted its more comprehensive rules for exclusionary zoning.[8] In recent cases since then it has continued to apply a balancing test to decide whether large lot zoning ordinances are constitutional.[9]

C. COMMERCIAL AND INDUSTRIAL USES.

§ 5.33 The Zoning Problem.

Commercial and industrial uses present a number of zoning problems. Municipalities must decide how to classify and map these uses in zoning districts. They may face constitutional objections if they exclude these uses entirely or place them in noncumulative zoning districts. Restrictive commercial zoning may also violate the rule that control of competition is not a proper zoning purpose and raises a problem under federal antitrust laws. Free speech problems arise

---

[7] 268 A.2d 765 (Pa. 1970).

[8] §§ 7.19–7.21.

[9] Fisher v. Viola, 789 A.2d 782 (Pa. Commw. 2001) (invalidating 1.5 and 1.25 acre zoning); Kirk v. Zoning Hearing Bd., 713 A.2d 1225 (Pa. Commw. 1998) (upholding 1.5 and 1.0 acre zoning adopted to preserve agricultural land); Hock v. Board of Supvrs., 622 A.2d 431 (Pa. Commw. 1993) (rejecting agricultural justification); Berman v. Board of Comm'rs, 608 A.2d 585 (Pa. Commw. 1992) (invalidating 2+ acre zoning that prevented subdividing);; Martin v. Township of Millcreek, 413 A.2d 764 (Pa. Commw. 1980 (invalidating 10-acre requirement).

if a municipality adopts zoning restrictions on the location of adult businesses, such as adult movie theaters.

§ 5.34   Commercial Uses.

§ 5.35   The Mapping Problem.

The mapping of commercial use districts also creates as-applied problems in the application of the zoning ordnance. One common mapping problem arises when a municipality maps small, scattered zoning districts for neighborhood retail uses. Courts usually hold that the need to provide convenience neighborhood shopping overcomes objections that this type of mapping is discriminatory.[1]

Mapping problems also arise when a property owner wants to make a commercial use of a site the zoning ordinance has zoned for residential use. In this situation, the property owner may bring an as-applied attack on the residential land use restriction. The issue in most state courts is whether classification is arbitrary and capricious, but the landowner may also claim a taking has occurred. A typical case is brought by an owner of a residentially zoned lot that is located on a street or highway. The owner argues she could make a more profitable use of the land if it were zoned commercial. As usual, courts decide these cases by examining the zoning and land use in the surrounding area. They uphold the residential classification if the residential development of the land is reasonable in the area in which it is located. Location on a busy thoroughfare, and a claim the land is more valuable for commercial use, are not enough to overturn the residential zoning under the standard presumption of constitutionality and the fairly debatable rule.[2] Courts have also upheld restrictive commercial zoning that prohibits another commercial use the ordinance does not permit.[3]

The landowner will probably succeed if the residentially restricted property is an "island" surrounded by commercial uses. The court will not apply the presumption of constitutionality in this type of case and will hold that the residential land use classification is not fairly debatable. The court must determine which use is dominant if the surrounding area is mixed. Although municipalities are not bound by their prior zoning actions, a court may hold a residential zoning

---

[1] See Marshall v. Salt Lake City, 141 P.2d 704 (Utah 1943).

[2] For typical cases, see Wood Marine Serv., Inc. v. City of Harahan, 858 F.2d 1061 (5th Cir. 1988); Kelber v. City of St. Louis Park,, 185 N.W.2d 526 (Minn. 1971); Tealin Co. v. City of Ladue, 541 S.W.2d 544 (Mo. 1976); Englin v. Board of County Comm'rs, 48 P.3d 39 (Mont. 2002); Central Motors Corp. v. City of Pepper Pike, 653 N.E.2d 639 (Ohio 1995); Leslie v. City of Toledo, 423 N.E.2d 123 (Ohio 1981); Lakewood Dev. Co. v. Oklahoma City, 534 P.2d 23 (Okla. App. 1975); Harmon City, Inc. v. Draper City, 997 P.2d 321 (Utah App. 2001).

[3] Restigouche, Inc. v. Town of Jupiter, 59 F.3d 1208 (11th Cir. 1995).

restriction is invalid as applied if the municipality changed the character of the area by approving a large number of commercial uses.[4]

§ 5.36 Commercial Use Classifications.

Zoning ordinances classify commercial uses into a number of commercial zoning districts. Incompatible commercial uses are excluded from each district. The exclusion of filling stations from retail commercial districts is a common example. Courts uphold these use classifications if they are reasonable.[1] As in residential districts,[2] zoning ordinances for commercial districts usually allow accessory uses that are customary and incidental to the principal use.[3]

Municipalities may also impose site development standards on commercial development. For example, the Georgia Supreme Court held a requirement for minimum barrier curbs and landscaping areas equal to at least ten percent of a lot was not a physical taking.[4] Big box retail is another growing commercial use problem. Municipalities may try to deal with it by limiting the size of stores in commercial districts. A federal district court refused to dismiss claims that a zoning ordinance limiting the size of retail stores was unconstitutional,[5] but an Ohio court held a similar ordinance constitutional.[6]

A New Jersey court held the owner of property zoned for commercial use can sell or use the property for uses permitted by the zoning ordinance, even if the uses differ from the present use of the property by its owner.[7] It pointed out a planning board cannot dictate "in perpetuity" who can use, buy, own or rent property.

---

[4] City of Birmingham v. Morris, 396 So. 2d 53 (Ala. 1981) (affirmative governmental action permitting nonconforming uses frustrated development of residential area).;

[1] Caldwell v. Pima County, 837 P.2d 154 (Ariz. 1992) (requirement that business be conducted within enclosed buildings); Manalapan Realty, L.P. v. Township Comm., 658 A.2d 1230 (N.J. 1995) (ordinance excluding unenclosed uses from shopping center); Mahony v. Township of Hampton, 651 A.2d 525 (Pa. 1994) (ordinance prohibiting private operation of gas wells but allowing public operation); State ex rel. American Oil Co. v. Bessent, 135 N.W.2d 317 (Wis. 1965).

[2] § 5.19.

[3] Eastern Serv. Ctrs., Inc. v. Cloverland Farms Dairy, Inc., 744 A.2d 63 (Md. App. 2000) (gasoline service station upheld as accessory use to convenience store); Borough of Fleetwood v. Zoning Hearing Bd., 649 A.2d 651 (Pa. 1994) (gas pump is accessory use to convenience store).

[4] Parking Ass'n of Ga. v. City of Atlanta, 450 S.E.2d 200 (Ga. 1994) (with dissent from denial of certiorari claiming recent Supreme Court cases should apply).

[5] Great Atlantic & Pacific Tea Co. v. Town of East Hampton, 997 F. Supp. 340 (E.D.N.Y. 1998).

[6] Loreto Dev. Co., Inc. v. Village of Chardon, 695 N.E.2d 1151 (Ohio App. 1996) See also Home Depot U.S.A., Inc. v. City of Portland, 10 P.3d 316 (Or. App. 2000) (restrictive treatment of big box retail uses does not violate state economic development planning goal).

[7] Mt. Plainsboro Limited Partnership v. Township of Plainsboro, 719 A.2d 1285 (N.J. App. Div. 1998).

A court may strike down a commercial use exclusion if it finds no basis for the classification. In *Board of Supvrs. v. Rowe,*[8] the court struck down a number of exclusions from a commercial use district. The commercial district included hotels but excluded banks and included restaurants but excluded drive-in restaurants. The court found equal protection and substantive due process violations. It noted that the district excluded a large number of "legitimate retail uses" from a retail business district, even though the excluded uses were no more detrimental than the uses included.

Rowe applies the compatibility principle that underlies zoning. It suggests that this principle requires commercial zoning categories that allow an adequate range of commercial uses.[9] Most zoning ordinances take this approach, often by including long lists of permitted uses within each commercial district. This practice creates problems when a landowner requests a commercial rezoning. His neighbors may not find his proposed development objectionable, but they may oppose the rezoning if it allows other commercial uses that they consider undesirable.[10] This concern has prompted the use of "conditional" zoning, under which the landowner voluntarily restricts his property to the intended use through a contract or a recorded covenant. Flexible zoning techniques, such as conditional uses and the floating zone, are another answer to this problem. These techniques allow the municipality to restrict its approval to the use the landowner proposes.

Neighborhood Conservation or urban design districts are another alternative. They can include graphic and textual use and urban design criteria that can provide the basis for attractive and mutually compatible residential, commercial and office development. Downtown and other mixed use areas are good examples of areas where this technique can be successful. The courts have upheld the establishment and implementation of this kind of district.[11]

§ 5.37 Total Exclusion.

A total commercial exclusion problem arises when small residential suburban communities zone their entire area for residential use. A few cases upheld this

---

[8] 216 S.E.2d 199 (Va. 1975).

[9] *Compare* Reedy v. City of Wheaton, 430 N.E.2d 273 (Ill. App. 1981) (upholding exclusion of gasoline filling stations from local business district) *with* Gas 'N Shop, Inc. v. City of Kearney, 539 N.W.2d 423 (Neb. 1995) (cannot require off-premises liquor retailer to sell liquor from separate premises), *and* Layne v. Zoning Bd. of Adjustment, 460 A.2d 1088 (Pa. Commw. 1983) (boarding houses cannot be excluded from residential districts where rooming houses are permitted).

[10] *See* Pierson Trapp Co. v. Peak, 340 S.W.2d 456 (Ky. 1960) (invalidating a rezoning to a single commercial use).

[11] BP America, Inc. v. Avon City Council, 753 N.E.2d 947 (Ohio App. 2001) (upholding denial of gas station rezoning in downtown preservation district); Franchise Devs., Inc. v. City of Cincinnati, 505 N.E.2d 966 (Ohio 1987) (upholding environmental quality overlay district); Bell v. City of Waco, 835 S.W.2d 211 (Tex. App. 1992) (upholding neighborhood conservation district).

type of zoning, usually because adequate commercial facilities were available nearby in the surrounding area.[1]

Courts review the total exclusion of one type of commercial use from a community on a case-by-case basis to decide whether the exclusion advances legitimate zoning purposes.[2] *Town of Los Altos Hills v. Adobe Creek Props., Inc.*[3] illustrates these cases. The court upheld an ordinance that excluded almost all commercial uses from a suburban community. It noted the town had a rural-residential character, that it had a small population, and that it was in close proximity to urban areas.

Pennsylvania has long taken the singular position that a zoning ordinance that totally excludes a land use type is unconstitutional and has applied this rule to apartments as well as nonresidential uses.[4] The court invalidated a total exclusion of gasoline filling stations in *Beaver Gasoline Co. v. Zoning Hearing Bd.*[5] The court held that the usual presumption of constitutionality does not apply when a municipality excludes "an otherwise legitimate business activity," and that the burden shifts to the municipality to justify the exclusion. The exclusion of a "particularly objectionable" business would be prima facie reasonable. Other states have not followed *Beaver,* and Florida has explicitly rejected it.[6]

In a variant of the exclusion case, a landowner who plans a commercial development may attack a residential zoning restriction on her site because her development will serve commercial needs in the area outside the community. In *Wrigley Props., Inc. v. City of Ladue,*[7] a suburb in a metropolitan area zoned a tract of land on a highway intersection at its city limits for residential use. The court held that the need to provide land for commercial development to satisfy regional shopping demand did not make the residential zoning unconstitutional. It added that commercial development on the site would have a negative impact on an adjacent residential neighborhood. The court also noted that land across the highway in another municipality was zoned for commercial use.

---

[1] § 5.17.

[2] Town of Beacon Falls v. Posick, 563 A.2d 285 (Conn. 1989) (upholding exclusion of landfill); Ottowa County Farms, Inc. v. Township of Polkton, 345 N.W.2d 672 (Mich. App. 1983) (invalidating exclusion of landfill); McNeil v. Township of Plumstead, 522 A.2d 469 (N.J. App. Div. 1987) (remanding for determination whether prohibition on soil removal was reasonable).

[3] 108 Cal. Rptr. 271 (Cal. App. 1973). *See also* City of Alameda v. Van Horn, 219 Cal. Rptr. 764 (Cal. App. 1985) (massage parlor).

[4] § 5.14.

[5] 285 A.2d 501 (Pa. 1971). *See* Montgomery Crossing Assocs. v. Township of Lower Gwynedd, 758 A.2d 285 (Pa. Commw. 2000) (ordinance held not to exclude shopping centers).

[6] Lambros, Inc. v. Town of Ocean Ridge, 392 So. 2d 993 (Fla. 1981). *Compare* Suburban Ready Mix Corp. v. Village of Wheeling, 185 N.E.2d 665 (Ill. 1962) (cannot exclude ready-mix concrete plant).

[7] 369 S.W.2d 397 (Mo. 1963).

§ 5.38 Ribbon Development.

Ribbon commercial development along major streets and highways is a major zoning problem. Once a community allows some commercial development along these thoroughfares, the pressure to zone additional frontage for commercial use is overwhelming. The unattractive commercial ribbon development typical of American cities indicates that these pressures are difficult to resist. Some communities attempt to halt the spread of commercial ribbon development by inserting a buffer zone covering one or two lots between residential and commercial segments on a street or highway. The community may limit the buffer zone to a nonintensive commercial use, such as a small office building, to provide a transition between residential and commercial development. This strategy is not always successful. A commercial developer can successfully attack a buffer zone if he can convince the court that commercial uses dominate the surrounding area or that land uses in the area are irreversibly mixed.[1]

A community can also prevent ribbon development by limiting intensive commercial uses to intersections and by zoning thoroughfares between intersections for residential use. The Arizona court upheld this practice in *City of Phoenix v. Fehlner*.[2] The zoning ordinance applied the least restrictive residential zone, which allowed some of the less intensive commercial uses, to land adjacent to thoroughfares. An owner of land that was included in this residential zone challenged its constitutionality. The land was an "island" in the middle of a commercially zoned strip 6,400 feet in length. The court did not consider the "island" problem but upheld the ordinance under the fairly debatable rule.[3]

§ 5.39 Airports and Airport Zoning.

Safety standards adopted by the Federal Aviation Commission require height limitations in the approach zone adjacent to airports that is used for takeoffs and landings, and an adjacent transition zone that provides an additional margin of safety if circumstances such as engine failure require a deviation from the normal flight path.[1] State legislation commonly authorizes airport zoning,[2] and

---

[1] Spaid v. Board of County Comm'rs, 269 A.2d 797 (Md. 1970); City of Tulsa v. Swanson, 366 P.2d 629 (Okla. 1961). *See also* Jefferson County v. O'Rorke, 394 So. 2d 937 (Ala. 1981). *But see* State v. Gallop Bldg., 247 A.2d 350 (N.J. App. Div. 1968) (upholding landscaped buffer requirement).

[2] 363 P.2d 607 (Ariz. 1961).

[3] *See also* City of Tempe v. Rasor, 536 P.2d 239 (Ariz. App. 1975); Primerica v. Planning & Zoning Comm'n, 558 A.2d 646 (Conn. 1989) (upholding ordinance limiting office building occupancy to one occupant as valid method of controlling traffic and not confiscatory).

[1] 14 C.F.R. § 77.1, *et seq.*

[2] *E.g.*, Ariz. Rev. Stat. § 28-8467; Fla. Stat. Ann. § 333.03; Tex. Local Gov't Code § 241.014. *See* § 4.43 (discussing federal preemption of airport zoning).

municipalities comply with these regulations by adopting zoning restrictions with height and use limitations because this is necessary in order to secure federal funding.

Height and use restrictions adopted under airport zoning present a takings problem because they may prohibit or severely limit development in the airport zone. The Supreme Court rejected a per se "conceptual severance" rule that would hold that airspace in which development is prohibited is a severable property interest that has been taken by an airport zoning restriction.[3] The possibility remains that courts can find a taking when the height restriction imposes a severe restriction on development that deprives a landowner of all economically beneficial and productive use of her land under *Lucas* per se takings test.[4]

Fitzgerrald v. City of Iowa City[5] is a post-*Lucas* case holding that height and land use restrictions on property used as a mobile home within the approach zone of an airport. The court looked at the whole parcel that was affected by the restrictions, and held they only imposed a diminution in the value of the land. A number of cases pre-*Lucas* held airport zoning restrictions constitutional.[6] In some of these cases the court rejected a facial attack on the zoning restrictions.[7]

In other cases the courts held airport zoning unconstitutional.[8] These cases were all decided before the Supreme Court adopted the whole parcel rule and several relied on the theory a taking had occurred because the landowner's

[3] Tahoe-Sierra Preservation Council v. Tahoe Regional Planning Agency, 535 U.S. 302 (2002).

[4] § 2.09.

[5] 492 N.W.2d 659 (Iowa 1992).

[6] Land Assocs. v. Metropolitan Airport Auth., 547 F. Supp. 1128 (M.D. Tenn. 1982) (refusal to upzone), *aff'd per curiam,* 712 F.2d 248 (6th Cir. 1983); Harrell's Candy Kitchen, Inc. v. Sarasota-Manatee Airport Auth., 111 So.2d 439 (Fla. 1959) (height restriction did not deprive landowner of beneficial use of land); LaSalle Nat'l Bank v. County of Cook, 340 N.E.2d 79 (Ill. 1975); Kimberlin v. City of Topeka, 710 P.2d 682 (Kan. 1985); Greenberg v. State, 502 A.2d 522 (Md. App. 1986); Davis v. City of Princeton, 401 N.W.2d 391 (Minn. App. 1987) (no measurable diminution in market value); Patzau v. New Jersey Dep't of Transp., 638 A.2d 866 (N.J. App. Div. 1994) (state airport zoning act held not facial taking).Eck v. City of Bismarck (II), 302 N.W.2d 739 (N.D. 1981) (holding ordinance was comprehensive attempt to zone for city and permitted agricultural uses were reasonable); Rogers v. City of Cheyenne, 747 P.2d 1137 (Wyo. 1987).

[7] *E.g.,* Harris v. City of Wichita, 862 F. Supp. 287 (D. Kan. 1994); Baggett v. City of Montgomery, 160 So. 2d 6 (Ala. 1963);

[8] Sneed v. County of Riverside, 32 Cal. Rptr. 318 (Cal. App. 1962); Roark v. City of Caldwell, 394 P.2d 641 (Idaho 1964);Roark v. City of Caldwell, 394 P.2d 641 (Idaho 1964) (recognizing property right of owner in airspace); Indiana Toll Rd. Comm'n v. Jankovich, 193 N.E.2d 237 (Ind. 1963) (same); McShane v. City of Faribault, 292 N.W.2d 253 (Minn. 1980) (relying on enterprise theory of takings law and requiring substantial and measurable decline in market value); Yara Eng'r Corp. v. City of Newark, 40 A.2d 559 (N.J. 1945); State v. City of Columbus, 209 N.E.2d 405 (Ohio 1965); Ackerman v. Port of Seattle, 348 P.2d 64 (Wash. 1960) (recognizing property right of owner in airspace).

property right in airspace had been taken. They relied for this conclusion on an early Supreme Court case, *United States v. Causby*,[9] which had awarded damages to a landowner when airplane overflights severely interfered with the existing surface use of land.

§ 5.40　Industrial Uses.

The courts uphold industrial zoning classifications if they are reasonable[1] and not a taking of property.[2] An interesting New York case upheld density restrictions adopted in an industrial zoning ordinance. In *Marcus v. Town of Huntington*,[3] the zoning ordinance limited each building or "premises" to no more than three industrial uses. It also required each industrial use to occupy no less than 20,000 square feet of a building's gross floor area. The court rejected a substantive due process objection and noted that density regulation was a legitimate purpose in industrial as well as residential zoning. It upheld the town's density regulation because it was intended to preserve the industrial character of the community. Existing industrial development met the density requirements.

§ 5.41　Industrial Performance Standards.

Industrial performance standards are a zoning technique that attempts to control industrial use incompatibilities more effectively than traditional zoning. Industrial use classifications in zoning ordinances cannot control industrial use incompatibilities effectively because uses allowed in the same district may have different impacts on the surrounding area. Performance standards attempt to remedy this problem by imposing specific requirements for noise, vibrations, smoke, odors, and the emission of air pollutants. Many of the problems covered by industrial performance standards are also covered by federal and state environmental legislation, but there are gaps in this legislation that need to be addressed by local standards.

Although theoretically an excellent technique for regulating the nuisance qualities of industrial uses, industrial performance standards have significant limitations. Administration is expensive and difficult, and most communities are unlikely to impose drastic remedies on noncomplying industries. Performance standards are also imprecise, and may not effectively protect neighbors against adverse effects from industrial uses.

Because they deal with health and nuisance problems, the courts have had no difficulty upholding industrial performance standards against constitutional

---

[9] 328 U.S. 256 (1945). *See also* Griggs v. County of Allegheny, 369 U.S. 84 (1962).

[1] Tidewater Oil Co. v. Mayor & Council, 209 A.2d 105 (N.J. 1965).

[2] Bernardsville Quarry v. Borough of Bernardsville, 608 A.2d 1377 (N.J. 1992) (holding ordinance limiting depth below which property could not be quarried not a taking).

[3] 382 N.E.2d 1323 (N.Y. 1978).

attacks. For example, in *DeCoals, Inc. v. Board of Zoning Appeals*[1] an industrial use was denied a building permit because it was unable to comply with industrial dust, noise, and sound performance standards. The dust standard was absolute and prohibited dust "of any kind." The court held that industrial performance standards were clearly an appropriate exercise of the police power. It would not interfere with the legislative judgment that a "no-dust" standard was appropriate. Citing air pollution control cases, the court held that "[a]lleged technical infeasibility or economic hardship need not be considered" and noted that the courts had upheld "technology-forcing" air pollution regulations. The court added that a different question might arise if a no-dust standard precluded "development of any industry in an industrial zone." The courts have also considered claims that industrial performance standards are unconstitutional because they are too vague, with mixed results.[2]

§ 5.42   Total Exclusion.

The leading case upholding a zoning ordinance that excluded all industrial uses is *Duffcon Concrete Prods., Inc. v. Borough of Cresskill.*[1] The court took a regional view of municipal zoning obligations and upheld the exclusion because sites for industrial development were available in the surrounding area.[2] The Pennsylvania cases have also struck down total exclusions of industrial uses in an application of their rule that a zoning ordinance is invalid if it totally excludes a particular use.[3]

§ 5.43   Noncumulative Zoning: Exclusive Nonresidential Zones.

Early zoning ordinances were cumulative. They allowed "higher" uses in the "lower" zoning districts. Under this system a residential use can locate in a commercial or industrial zone, and commercial uses can locate in industrial zones. Cumulative zoning is undesirable. It prevents municipalities from adopting

---

[1] 284 S.E.2d 856 (W. Va. 1981). *See also* City of Rochester v. Superior Plastics, Inc., 480 N.W.2d 620 (Mich. App. 1992) (standard requiring control of noise held authorized by zoning law); Terino v. Town of Hartford Zoning Bd. of Adj., 538 A.2d 160 (Vt. 1987) (town properly applied performance standard to deny industrial use; consideration of offsite problems held authorized by statute).

[2] *See also* State v. Zack, 674 P.2d 329 (Ariz. App. 1983) (performance standard prohibiting "offensive vibration" held not vague); Stephen Renedy Mem. Fund v. Town of Old Saybrook, 492 A.2d 533 (Conn. App. 1985) (same; lighting standard). *But see* Lithonia Asphalt Co. v. Hall Cty. Planning Comm'n, 364 S.E.2d 860 (Ga. 1988) (performance zoning standard held vague). *See also* § 6.05.

[1] 64 A.2d 347 (N.J. 1949).

[2] *See* Oregon City v. Hartke, 400 P.2d 255 (Or. 1965) (upholding junkyard exclusion on aesthetic grounds).

[3] Exton Quarries, Inc. v. Zoning Bd. of Adjustment, 228 A.2d 169 (Pa. 1967); General Battery Corporation v. The Zoning Hearing Board of Alsace Township, 371 A.2d 1030 (Pa. Commw. 1977).

industrial and commercial zones in which only industrial and commercial development is permitted. Cumulative zoning also creates development expectations the community may not have intended. A landowner in an industrial zone can use his land for residential and commercial uses. This development expectation may increase land values and make local attempts to zone away these expectations politically difficult.

Modern zoning ordinances are noncumulative. The land use permitted in each district is the exclusive and only use allowed. The Supreme Court upheld exclusive residential zoning in *Euclid* because it protected residential uses from incompatible nonresidential development. This could imply that exclusive nonresidential zoning is unconstitutional because "lower" commercial and industrial uses do not require protection from "higher" residential uses.

The courts have not accepted this line of reasoning. In *People ex rel. Skokie Town House Bldrs., Inc. v. Village of Morton Grove*,[1] a builder who planned to build townhouses in an exclusive industrial district attacked the exclusive industrial zoning. He claimed that "such an ordinance conflicts sharply with the generally acknowledged principle that zoning is intended to preserve rather than to restrict dwellings."

The court disagreed, and held that the compatibility principle cuts both ways. A legislative body could assume that the exclusion of residences from industrial and commercial areas "would tend in the long run to insure a better and more economical use of municipal services." It noted that industrial or commercial development would be impossible or prohibitively expensive if a few lots were sold for residential use "at important points in a district."[2]

Exclusive industrial zoning can raise a taking problem if the demand for industrial development is not sufficient to absorb exclusively zoned industrial land in a reasonable period of time. Exclusive commercial zoning raises the same problem. The *Skokie* case indicated that excessive mapping for exclusive industrial use might be unconstitutional. Another case held an exclusive industrial zoning ordinance unconstitutional partly for this reason.[3] Excessive mapping of exclusive nonresidential districts can also be exclusionary. In the *Mt. Laurel* exclusionary zoning case, the New Jersey Supreme Court held that zoning for exclusive industrial use far in excess of expected demand was a major element

---

[1] 157 N.E.2d 33 (Ill. 1959).

[2] *Id.* at 36. *Accord* Roney v. Board of Supvrs., 292 P.2d 529 (Cal. App. 1956); Lamb v. City of Monroe, 99 N.W.2d 566 (Mich. 1959); Kozesnik v. Township of Montgomery, 131 A.2d 1 (N.J. 1957). *Compare* Grubel v. MacLaughlin, 286 F. Supp. 24 (D.C.V.I. 1968) (upholding exclusive commercial district); Katobimar Realty Co. v. Webster, 118 A.2d 824 (N.J. 1955) (invalidating exclusion of retail business from light industrial district).

[3] Corthouts v. Town of Newington, 99 A.2d 112 (Conn. 1953).

in the community's exclusionary residential zoning strategy and effectively excluded lower-income housing.[4]

The use of exclusive industrial zoning for fiscal purposes is constitutional if it does not exclude lower-income housing. "[A] zoning scheme seeking balanced land use to obtain a sound municipal economy by encouraging industry on which taxes may be levied to help meet the deficit in the cost of municipal services to home owners is a proper exercise of the zoning power, subject always to the reasonableness of the classification and regulations. . . ."[5]

§ 5.44 Control of Competition.

The use of zoning to control market demand creates a special set of commercial zoning problems. A hypothetical case illustrates the problem. Assume a municipality does a market study showing that market demand will support only two regional shopping centers in the community. It then designates two sites in its comprehensive plan for regional shopping centers. A developer applies for a rezoning for a regional shopping center at a site not designated on the comprehensive plan and the municipality denies it. The shopping center developer then brings suit claiming that the municipality has improperly used the zoning power to control competition. This problem also arises when a municipality rezones land for a shopping center. If the owner of another shopping center brings an action to challenge the rezoning, the municipality may ask the court to dismiss the suit because its purpose is to protect the plaintiff's competitive position.

A court may decide for the developer who was denied a rezoning in the problem by applying the well-established maxim that zoning may not be used to control competition. The maxim is not absolute. Some courts recognize that zoning always affects competitive opportunities in the use of land. They uphold zoning that affect competition if control of competition is not its primary purpose and if it implements other legitimate zoning objectives.

§ 5.45 As a Zoning Purpose.

§ 5.46 Disapproved.

A large number of cases hold, apparently without qualification, that the control of competition is not a proper purpose in zoning.[1] A close examination of these

---

[4] § 7.09.

[5] Newark Milk & Cream Co. v. Parsippany-Troy Hills Twp., 135 A.2d 682, 695 (N.J.L. 1957). *Accord* Gruber v. Raritan Twp., 186 A.2d 489 (N.J. 1962).

[1] Benson v. Zoning Bd. of Appeals, 27 A.2d 389 (Conn. 1942); Chicago Title & Trust Co. v. Village of Lombard, 166 N.E.2d 41 (Ill. 1960); Pearce v. Village of Edina, 118 N.W.2d 659 (Minn. 1962); Herman Glick Realty Co. v. St. Louis County, 545 S.W.2d 320 (Mo. App. 1977); Schneiderman v. Shenkenberg, 281 N.Y.S.2d 459 (Sup. Ct. 1967); State v. City of East Cleveland, 153 N.E.2d 177 (Ohio App. 1958), *aff'd*, 160 N.E.2d 1 (Ohio 1959).

cases indicates that they do not support so broad a rule. In some of them, a competitor opposed or attempted to prevent commercial rezoning in order to maintain a competitive advantage. Courts adopt the rule that control of competition is not a proper purpose in zoning when a competitor attempts to use zoning solely to shield its competitive position.

Circle Lounge & Grill, Inc. v. Board of Appeal[2] illustrates these decisions. Circle Lounge, which was in a commercial zone, brought an action challenging a zoning variance the board granted for a restaurant in a residential zone across the street. The court held that the threat of competition did not give Circle Lounge standing to challenge the variance. Nor was the action brought by the Lounge based on a proper zoning interest. Zoning, the court held, ensures the compatibility of land uses. Homeowners in a residential district could object to a variance for a commercial use in their district. The Lounge was in a commercial district and could not object to a variance in a neighboring residential district for a commercial use that was consistent with its own commercial use.[3]

Some courts invoke the rule that zoning may not be used to control competition to strike down ordinances that require a minimum distance between commercial uses, such as filling stations.[4] They may also invalidate the denial of a special exception for a commercial use if the denial is based on a finding that other businesses adequately serve the same commercial need.[5] These zoning problems are discussed more fully in the next section, which indicates that some courts take a different view.

§ 5.47 Approved.

Control of competition problems arise when a zoning ordinance authorizes the approval of a commercial use as a special exception only if there is a "need"

---

[2] 86 N.E.2d 920 (Mass. 1949).

[3] *Accord* Earth Movers of Fairbanks, Inc. v. Fairbanks North Star Borough, 865 P.2d 741 (Alaska 1993); Westwood Meat Mkt., Inc. v. McLucas, 361 P.2d 776 (Colo. 1961); Nautilus of Exeter, Inc. v. Town of Exeter, 656 A.2d 407 (N.H. 1995); Sun-Brite Car Wash, Inc. v. Board of Zoning & Appeals, 508 N.E.2d 130 (N.Y. 1987); Cord Meyer Dev. Co. v. Bell Ray Drugs, Inc., 229 N.E.2d 44 (N.Y. 1967). *See also* Swain v. County of Winnebago, 250 N.E.2d 439 (Ill. App. 1969). *But see* Westgate Shopping Village v. City of Toledo, 639 N.E.2d 126 (Ohio App. 1994) (rival mall has standing to challenge rezoning for mall competitor when there is property injury from increased traffic).

[4] Mobil Oil Corp. v. Board of Adjustment, 283 A.2d 837 (Del. Super. 1971); Costco Wholesale Corp. v. Orange County, 780 So.2d 198 (Fla. App. 2001) (invalidating ordinance prohibiting liquor package stores within 5,000 feet of each other;.Chicago Title & Trust Co. v. Village of Lombard, 166 N.E.2d 41 (Ill. 1960); Exxon Co., U.S.A. v. Township of Livingston, 489 A.2d 1218 (N.J. App. Div. 1985); Caudill v. Village of Milford, 225 N.E.2d 302 (Ohio C.P. 1967). *See also* Fogg v. City of South Miami, 183 So. 2d 219 (Fla. App. 1966) (drive-in businesses prohibited in commercial zoning district).

[5] Metro 500, Inc. v. City of Brooklyn Park, 211 N.W.2d 358 (Minn. 1973); Cardinal Props. v. Borough of Westwood, 547 A.2d 316 (N.J. App. Div. 1988).

for the use. A zoning board can find that a commercial use is not needed if existing commercial uses satisfy the market demand for that use in the community. Some courts approve zoning ordinances that authorize the approval of a conditional use only if need is shown and hold that they do not violate the control of competition rule.[1] *Van Sicklen v. Browne*[2] illustrates these cases. A planning commission refused to approve a special permit for a filling station. It partly based its decision on a showing that there was no demonstrated need for an additional station in the neighborhood. Although it accepted the maxim that zoning cannot be used to control competition, the court noted that planning and zoning also serve a number of legitimate public purposes. They include the maintenance of property values and neighborhood economic and social stability. The court added:

> Whether these be classified as "planning considerations" or "economic considerations," we hold that so long as the primary purpose of the zoning ordinance is not to regulate competition, but to subserve a valid objective pursuant to a city's police powers, such ordinance is not invalid even though it might have an indirect impact on economic competition.[3]

Cases like *Van Sicklen* illustrate the rule some courts adopt that control of competition may be a factor in zoning if it is not its primary purpose.[4] The gasoline filling station cases also illustrate this rule. In the typical case, a zoning board refuses to approve a filling station as a special exception because there is no community need for additional filling stations. The board may also rely on more traditional zoning reasons for the refusal, such as the traffic congestion the filling station would create. Some cases uphold the board in this type of case and avoid the control of competition issue by relying on the traditional zoning reasons for the denial.[5] Cases that uphold minimum distance requirements between filling stations and other uses also rely on noncompetitive justifications for the restriction, such as the avoidance of fire and other hazards.[6]

Ensign Bickford Realty Corp. v. City Council[7] indicates that commercial zoning may not be invalid as an improper control of competition if it is based

---

[1] Technical & Professional Serv. v. Board of Zoning Adjustment, 558 S.W.2d 798 (Mo. App. 1977).

[2] 92 Cal. Rptr. 786 (Cal. App. 1971).

[3] *Id.* at 790.

[4] Appeal of Lieb, 116 A.2d 860 (Pa. 1955).

[5] American Oil Co. v. Board of Appeals, 310 A.2d 796 (Md. 1973); Peterson v. Mayor & Council, 21 A.2d 777 (N.J. 1941); Application of Max Kirsch, Inc., 202 N.Y.S.2d 547 (Sup. Ct. 1960).

[6] Stone v. City of Maitland, 446 F.2d 83 (5th Cir. 1971); Consolidated Gov't of Columbus v. Barwick, 549 S.E.2d 73 (Ga. 2001) (power to license liquor business); Chicago Title & Trust Co. v. Village of Lombard, 166 N.E.2d 41 (Ill. App. 1961).

[7] 137 Cal. Rptr. 304 (Cal. App. 1977). *Accord* Lucky Stores, Inc. v. Board of Montgomery County, 312 A.2d 758 (Md. 1973). *Compare* Fallon v. Baker, 455 S.W.2d 572 (Ky. 1970) (invalidating shopping center rezoning inconsistent with plan).

on a comprehensive plan. The city's comprehensive plan designated a site for a shopping center in one of its neighborhoods. The court upheld the city when it turned down an application for another shopping center in the same neighborhood. It noted that the zoning decision was based on the city's comprehensive plan and added that "a zoning ordinance may be expected to depress the value of some land while it operates, in its total effect, to achieve an end which would benefit the whole community."

§ 5.48 Protection of Business Districts.

Rezonings for shopping malls in outlying areas threatens the existence of established downtown and main street business districts. Downtown or main street merchants may bring suit to challenge a shopping mall rezoning because it is a threat to their commercial future. Their lawsuit raises a standing problem.

In *Swain v. County of Winnebago*,[1] the court refused to grant standing to downtown city merchants who challenged a rezoning in the county for a regional shopping center located "a substantial distance" from the central business district. They claimed that the rezoning would adversely affect the value of their property as well as the use and development of public facilities. They did not claim that the rezoning would increase general tax burdens in the city. The court held that distance alone did not preclude a showing of the special damage necessary to confer standing but added that a distant plaintiff who claims standing has a more onerous pleading and proof burden.

Some municipalities have adopted zoning ordinances that protect the downtown business core by limiting retail uses outside the core to neighborhood shopping facilities. *Forte v. Borough of Tenafly*[2] is a leading case upholding a zoning ordinance of this type against a control of competition objection. The borough acted on a planning consultant's recommendation and adopted a zoning ordinance which stated that one of its purposes was to protect the economic health of the central business core. About ninety-three percent of the borough's retail businesses were located in the central core area. To implement this purpose, the ordinance established a retail use district for the area outside the central core, which was limited to neighborhood convenience retail stores. This district did not allow general retail businesses of the type located in the central core.

The plaintiffs planned to build a supermarket in the limited retail use district, where it was a prohibited use. They argued that the district was unconstitutional

---

[1] 250 N.E.2d 439 (Ill. App. 1969).

[2] 255 A.2d 804 (N.J. App. Div. 1969). *Accord* Carty v. City of Ojai, 143 Cal. Rptr. 506 (Cal. App. 1978); Sprenger, Grubb & Assocs., Inc. v. City of Hailey, 903 P.2d 741 (Idaho 1995); E & G Enters. v. City of Mount Vernon, 373 N.W.2d 693 (Iowa App. 1985); Chevron Oil Co. v. Beaver County, 449 P.2d 989 (Utah 1969). *But cf.* Cape Ann Dev. Corp. v. City Council, 373 N.E.2d 218 (Mass. 1978); State ex rel. Diehl v. City of Helena, 593 P.2d 458 (Mont. 1979).

as an improper control of competition because the municipality adopted it "for the sole benefit of the merchants in the central business core." The court rejected this argument and held that the use of zoning to maintain and revitalize central business districts is valid, even though "the ordinance may give the central area a virtual monopoly over retail business." It held that the limited retail district was reasonable even though there were a number of nonconforming retail uses in the vicinity of plaintiffs' property that were similar to its proposed use. The court noted that "plaintiffs may use their property for the many purposes allowed by the ordinance."

§ 5.49   Federal Antitrust Law.

Anticompetitive commercial zoning may violate the federal antitrust law. Section 1 of the Sherman Act prohibits contracts, combinations, or conspiracies that restrain trade in interstate commerce. This section could apply to a zoning ordinance or decision that restricted competition. An example is a denial of a shopping center rezoning to protect a rezoning for a shopping center for another developer. However, although the Supreme Court has withdrawn the absolute immunity of local governments from liability under the antitrust law, it has also indicated that anticompetitive zoning is unlikely to violate the Sherman Act.

§ 5.50   State Action Doctrine.

Anticompetitive zoning had not been an issue under the federal antitrust law because municipalities were from liability under a state action doctrine adopted by the Supreme Court in *Parker v. Brown*[1] as a matter of federal comity. The state action doctrine holds that states are absolutely immune from antitrust liability, and this doctrine extended to municipalities. However, in *City of Lafayette v. Louisiana Power & Light Co.*,[2] the Court for the first time held that the state action doctrine did not absolutely protect municipalities from federal antitrust liability. A plurality of the Court held that municipalities are immune under this doctrine only if the state legislation under which the municipality acted clearly articulates and affirmatively expresses a policy to displace competition. In *California Retail Liquor Dealers Ass'n v. Midcal Aluminum Co.*,[3] an antitrust action against a state agency, the Court added as a requirement for antitrust immunity that the state must supervise the practices claimed to restrain competition.

---

[1] 317 U.S. 341 (1943).

[2] 435 U.S. 389 (1978).

[3] 445 U.S. 97 (1980).

§ 5.51   *Boulder.*

In *Community Communications Co. v. City of Boulder.*[1] the Court held that a city's home rule status did not afford it immunity under the state action doctrine. The city granted a twenty-year nonexclusive license to a cable television company but later adopted a three-month moratorium on additional expansion of the company's business so it could consider granting licenses to potential competitors. The company brought an action under Section 1 of the Sherman Act to enjoin enforcement of the moratorium. The Court held that the city was not immune from the antitrust law.

A majority of the Court confirmed the rule adopted in *Lafayette* that municipal immunity from the antitrust law requires clearly and affirmatively expressed state policy to displace competition. The Court held that the constitutional home rule authority under which the city adopted the moratorium did not confer immunity under this test. The test is not satisfied when the state's position concerning the municipal action challenged as anticompetitive is neutral. A state does not contemplate anticompetitive action by allowing a municipality to do as it pleases under a home rule delegation of authority. Municipalities may exercise land use control authority under home rule powers in some states.[2] The Court left open the question whether local government immunity requires active state supervision.

§ 5.52   *Town of Hallie.*

Town of Hallie v. City of Eau Claire[1] eased the application of the federal antitrust law to municipalities acting under statutory authority. Four adjacent unincorporated townships brought an antitrust action against the city. They claimed they were potential competitors and that the city used its monopoly power over sewage treatment to gain an unlawful monopoly in the provision of sewage collection and transportation services. The Court upheld the trial court's dismissal of the complaint.

Wisconsin statutes gave cities the authority to construct sewage systems and determine the area they wish to serve. The Court held these statutes evidenced a clearly articulated and affirmatively expressed state policy to displace competition in the municipal provision of sewage service. It is enough if the suppression of competition is the "foreseeable result" of the statutory authority. The Court also held that municipalities are entitled to state action immunity even though the state has not "compelled" the city to act. The legislature need not state explicitly that it expected the city to engage in anticompetitive conduct.

---

[1] 455 U.S. 405 (1982).

[2] § 4.25.

[1] 471 U.S. 34 (1985).

Anticompetitive effects would logically result from the broad, delegated statutory authority to provide sewage services and determine the area to be served.

The Court also held the active state supervision requirement does not apply to municipalities because there is little or no danger that a municipality will engage in private price-fixing. The only real danger is that a municipality will advance parochial public interests instead of compelling state goals, but the requirement that a municipality must act under a clearly articulated state policy minimizes this possibility.[2]

§ 5.53 Omni.

In *City of Columbia v. Omni Outdoor Adv., Inc.*,[1] the Supreme Court held that state action immunity protected a municipality from antitrust liability claimed to arise from a billboard regulation and rejected a conspiracy exception. Because the basis for antitrust liability in *Omni* was especially strong, and because the city acted under the Standard Zoning Enabling Act,[2] the decision substantially protects municipalities from antitrust liability that can arise from land use regulation.

Columbia Outdoor Advertising controlled 95% of the local market in billboards. When Omni began erecting billboards in the city, Columbia worked with city officials, with whom it had close relationships, to adopt billboard regulations that would block Omni. A six-month moratorium on new billboards was held unconstitutional by a state court because it conferred too much discretion on the city council to authorize exceptions. The city then adopted, after comprehensive study, an ordinance restricting the size, location, and spacing of billboards. These restrictions, especially those on spacing, benefitted Columbia because they already had billboards in place and severely hindered Omni.

Omni brought an antitrust action against the city and the billboard company in which it claimed the city's billboard ordinances were the result of an anticompetitive conspiracy that stripped the city of antitrust immunity. Omni was awarded damages after a jury trial, but the Supreme Court held that the city was entitled to state action immunity.

The Court held that state action immunity was conferred by the city's "unquestioned zoning power over the size, location, and spacing of billboards" that was authorized by the state zoning act. The Court rejected an argument that

---

[2] *See also* Fisher v. City of Berkeley, 475 U.S. 260 (1986) (Court applied preemption doctrine to hold that federal antitrust law did not preempt city rent control ordinance adopted by popular initiative).

[1] 499 U.S. 365 (1991). *See* The Supreme Court, 1990 Term: Leading Cases, 105 Harv. L. Rev. 177, 361 (1991). *See also* Fisichelli v. Town of Methuen, 956 F.2d 12 (1st Cir. 1992) (refusal to issue development bonds for development protected by immunity, applying *Omni*).

[2] §§ 4.15–4.21.

state action immunity does not apply if a municipality acts beyond its delegated authority because its regulation is substantively or procedurally defective. This defense would undermine "the very interests of federalism" the state action doctrine was designed to protect. This holding means immunity is available even if a state court holds a zoning regulation invalid under the well-established state doctrine that the control of competition is not a proper purpose in zoning.[3]

The Court next held the "clear articulation" rule was "amply met here" because "[t]he very purpose of zoning regulation is to displace unfettered business freedom in a manner that regularly has the effect of preventing normal acts of competition, particularly on the part of new entrants." An ordinance restricting the size, location, and spacing of billboards, which the Court characterized as "a common form of zoning," necessarily protects existing billboards from new competition. The Court's discussion of the foreseeability requirement indicates that any "common" form of zoning that limits market entry is entitled to state action immunity.

The Court in *Omni* did not overrule or even discuss its holding in *Boulder* that the delegation of constitutional home rule power to municipalities does not confer state action immunity under the antitrust act. The home rule exception may be of limited application. Home rule municipalities can also exercise land use and other powers under statutory authority, and there do not seem to be serious limitations under state law that prohibit municipalities from making this election.[4] Several states have also adopted legislation conferring state action immunity on local governments from federal antitrust laws.[5]

Early antitrust cases suggested a conspiracy exception to the state action immunity; the court of appeals in *Omni* adopted it, but the Supreme Court held that "[t]here is no such conspiracy exception." Language in *Parker v. Brown* suggesting a conspiracy exception meant only that state action immunity "does not necessarily obtain where the State acts not in a regulatory capacity but as a commercial participant in a given market." Alternatively, the Court held that application of the co-conspirator exception would be impracticable and would "swallow up" the *Parker* rule. "Since it is both inevitable and desirable that public officials often agree" with their constituency, such a definition would make "all anticompetitive regulation . . . vulnerable to a 'conspiracy' charge."

The Court also held that bribery and misconduct would not make state action immunity unavailable. The Antitrust Act condemned trade restraints, not political

---

[3] § 5.46.

[4] *E.g.,* Nelson v. City of Seattle, 395 P.2d 82 (Wash. 1964) (reliance on zoning legislation held to be optional with home rule city). *See* Note, Land-Use Control, Externalities, and the Municipal Affairs Doctrine, 8 Loy. L.A.L. Rev. 432 (1975).

[5] *E.g.,* Ga Code Ann. § 36-65-1 (local governments exercising powers specifically granted are acting pursuant to state policy); Iowa Code Ann. § 553.6(5); N.D. Cent. Code § 40-01-22 (exempting local governments from federal antitrust liability); Utah Code Ann. § 76-10-915(1)(f).

activity, and the Court held that this type of problem should be dealt with by statutes created specifically for this purpose.

Notably, the Court also did not distinguish for purposes of immunity between the city and the private company, implicitly overruling earlier precedent that private parties are immune under the act only if there is active state supervision.[6] A later case indicates, however, that private immunity is distinguishable and requires comprehensive state supervision over regulatory detail.[7]

§ 5.54 Land Use Cases after *Omni.*

Federal court cases decided after *Boulder* but before *Town of Hallie* held that anticompetitive zoning decisions violated the federal antitrust law.[1] Some of these cases were decided on the conspiracy theory now rejected by *Omni.*[2] Cases decided after *Hallie* held local government zoning actions immune under the state action doctrine for antitrust liability.[3] In *Racetrac Petroleum, Inc. v. Prince George's County,*[4] for example, the county denied Racetrac a special exception for a gasoline filling station because a needs analysis found there were thirty-one filling stations within a two-mile radius of the Racetrac site. The court held the state planning and zoning legislation contained a clearly articulated and affirmatively expressed policy to displace competition among owners and users of land with "local regulation by planning and zoning." This policy authorized the county to consider public need for a land use in special exception cases. *Omni* confirms

---

[6] Southern Motor Carriers Rate Conference, Inc. v. United States, 471 U.S. 48 (1985).

[7] FTC v. Ticor Title Ins. Co., 504 U.S. 621 (1992).

[1] Parks v. Watson, 716 F.2d 646 (9th Cir. 1983) (city refused to vacate platted streets unless plaintiff dedicated land); Mason City Center Assocs. v. City of Mason City, 468 F. Supp. 737 (N.D. Iowa) (city denied commercial rezoning after entering into agreement with developers of a competing downtown shopping facility), *aff'd on immunity holding,* 671 F.2d 1146 (8th Cir. 1982).

[2] Westborough Mall, Inc. v. City of Cape Girardeau, 693 F.2d 733 (8th Cir.1983), *remanded for new trial,* 794 F.2d 330 (8th Cir.), *reh'g denied,* 804 F.2d 108 (8th Cir. 1986).

[3] Jacobs, Visconsi & Jacobs Co. v. City of Lawrence, 927 F.2d 1111 (10th Cir. 1991) (suburban shopping center zoning denied to implement plan designating downtown as primary retail area); Traweek v. City & Cty. of San Francisco, 920 F.2d 989 (9th Cir. 1990) (prohibition of condominium conversion); LaSalle Nat'l Bank v. County of DuPage, 777 F.2d 377 (7th Cir. 1985) (denial of sewage service and special use permit); Russell v. Kansas City (I), 690 F. Supp. 947 (D. Kan. 1988) (city denied office rezoning to protect renewal area development for office use; court found zoning action implemented renewal law); Pinehurst Enters. v. Town of Southern Pines, 690 F. Supp. 444 (M.D.N.C. 1988) (rezoning on condition that developer hook up to town sewage system), *aff'd without opinion,* 887 F.2d 1088 (4th Cir. 1989); Pendleton Constr. Co. v. Rockbridge County, 652 F. Supp. 312 (W.D. Va. 1987) (refusal to renew conditional use permit); Plaza Mobile & Modular Homes, Inc. v. Town of Colchester, 639 F. Supp. 140 (D. Conn. 1986) (mobile home moratorium), *aff'd mem.,* 810 F.2d 1160 (2d Cir. 1986).

[4] 601 F. Supp. 892 (D. Md. 1985), *aff'd per curiam post-Hallie,* 786 F.2d 202 (4th Cir. 986).

the *Racetrac* holding. Cases since *Omni* have extended antitrust immunity to zoning actions claimed to violate the antitrust act.[5]

§ 5.55 *Noerr-Pennington* Doctrine.

The *Noerr-Pennington* doctrine provides a first amendment antitrust defense for competitors who petition to influence governmental action. This doctrine protects private parties who participate in anticompetitive zoning actions. The doctrine is named after two U.S. Supreme Court decisions that exempted anticompetitive lobbying from the antitrust laws.[1] The courts have extended the *Noerr-Pennington* doctrine to administrative and judicial proceedings brought to challenge competitive commercial activity. An example in the zoning context is a lawsuit challenging a zoning amendment that allows a competitive use. Local governments are protected under *Noerr-Pennington* by legislative process immunity. This immunity covers a governmental entity that listens to "anticompetitive pleas" if "the public body acts within its legal discretion and in what it considers the public interest."[2]

Noerr-Pennington immunity does not protect "sham" proceedings brought by an antitrust defendant to prevent a competitor from gaining access to the courts and public agencies.[3] The Court has adopted a two-part test for the sham exception. A lawsuit must be objectively baseless, and it "must conceal an attempt to interfere directly with the business relationship of a competitor."[4]

Racetrac[5] indicates how the sham exception applies in land use cases. The court held the sham exception does not apply if a defendant attempts to influence a government decision that would harm a competitor. The exception applies if a defendant attempts to bar a competitor from the decision-making process, or if the defendant's motive was to corrupt the decision-making process through

---

[5] Jacobs, Visconsi & Jacobs v. City of Lawrence, 927 F.2d 111 (10th Cir. 1991); Superior-FCR Landfill, Inc. v. County of Wright, 59 F. Supp.2d 929 (D. Minn. 1999) (exclusion of landfill); James Emory, Inc. v. Twiggs County, 883 F. Supp. 1546 (M.D. Ga. 1995) (zoning exclusion of landfill); Pate v. City Council, 622 So.2d 405 (Ala. Civ. App. 1993) (billboard prohibition); Phillips v. Town of Brookhaven, 628 N.Y.S.2d 723 (App. Div. 1995) (rezoning to protect established businesses by limiting competition from shopping centers). *But see* Pine Ridge Recycling, Inc. v. Butts County, 855 F. Supp. 1264 (M.D. Ga. 1994) (county's attempt to exclude private landfill would violate commerce clause so not protected by state immunity).

[1] United Mine Workers v. Pennington, 381 U.S. 657 (1965); Eastern R.R. Presidents' Conference v. Noerr Motor Freight Co., 365 U.S. 127 (1961).

[2] Duke & Co. v. Foerster, 521 F.2d 1277 (3d Cir. 1975). *But see* Racetrac Petroleum, Inc. v. Prince George's County, 601 F. Supp. 892 (D. Md. 1985), (*Noerr-Pennington* does not apply to local governments), *aff'd per curiam* post-*Hallie,* 786 F.2d 202 (4th Cir. 1986).

[3] California Motor Transp., Inc. v. Trucking Unlimited, 404 U.S. 508 (1972).

[4] Professional Real Estate Investors, Inc. v. Columbia Pictures Indus., Inc., 508 U.S. 49, 60–61 (1993)

[5] § 5.54.

bribery or misrepresentation. The court held the trade association's conduct was not disqualifying under either of these tests. Though it influenced the county to deny a competitor a special exception, the competitor initiated the conditional use proceedings and it did not show that the trade association corrupted the decision-making process.[6] The Supreme Court has now held that the sham exception defense is based on an objective, not a subjective, evaluation of a competitor's conduct.[7]

Although some courts applied a conspiracy exception to the *Noerr-Pennington* doctrine, the Supreme Court rejected this exception in *Omni*. The Court held that "*Parker* and *Noerr* are complementary expressions of the principle that the antitrust laws regulate business, not politics." The elimination of the conspiracy exception greatly expands the scope of *Noerr-Pennington* immunity. *Noerr-Pennington* immunity is not limited to antitrust actions but extends to other actions claiming a violation of constitutional rights.[8]

§ 5.56   Basis for Liability.

The Supreme Court applies two different rules to determine whether there is a restraint on competition that violates the antitrust act. It applies a *per se* invalidity rule to conduct that is inherently anticompetitive. It evaluates conduct not inherently anticompetitive by considering the facts peculiar to the business, the history of the restraint, and the reasons why it was imposed.[1] This test is called a "rule of reason."

Chief Justice Rehnquist's dissent in *Boulder*[2] argued that courts should not apply traditional antitrust liability standards to municipalities. The *per se* standard would force municipalities to obtain legislation authorizing for anticompetitive

---

[6] Sham not found: Baltimore Scrap Corp. v. David J. Joseph Co., 81 F. Supp.2d 602 (D. Md. 2000); Miracle Mile Assocs. v. City of Rochester, 617 F.2d 18 (2d Cir. 1980); Vim, Inc. v. Somerset Hotel Ass'n, 19 F. Supp. 2d 422 (W.D. Pa. 1998), *aff'd without opinion*, 187 F.3d 627 (3d Cir. 1999); Pendleton Constr. Co. v. Rockbridge County, 652 F. Supp. 312 (W.D. Va. 1987); Interstate Props., Inc. v. Pyramid Co., 586 F. Supp. 1160 (S.D.N.Y. 1984); Zeller v. Consolini, 758 A.2d 376 (Conn. App. 2000); Alfred Weissman Real Estate, Inc. v. Big V Supermarkets, Inc., 707 N.Y.S.2d 647 (App. Div. 2000).

Ernest W. Hahn, Inc. v. Codding, 615 F.2d 830 (9th Cir. 1980); Ross v. Bremer, 1982-2 Trade Cas. (CCH) Par. 64747 (W.D. Wash. 1982) (denying exemption for bringing zoning suit even though suit successful); Sham found: Hi-Top Steel Corp. v. Lehrer, 29 Cal. Rptr.2d 646 (Cal. App. 1994).

[7] Professional Real Estate Investors, Inc. v. Columbia Pictures Industries, Inc., 508 U.S. 49 (1993).

[8] White v. Lee, 227 F.3d 1214 (9th Cir. 2000) (extending immunity to First Amendment retaliation cases and holding that immunity applied); Pellegrino Food Prods. Co. v. City of Warren, 136 F. Supp. 2d 391 (W.D. Pa. 2000) (immunity applied to some defendants).

[1] National Soc'y of Professional Eng'rs v. United States, 435 U.S. 679 (1980).

[2] § 5.49.

activities, and the rule of reason would subject municipal activities to wide-ranging judicial review. Later Supreme Court decisions have not endorsed Chief Justice Rehnquist's concerns, but the Court indicated in *Town of Hallie*[3] that it might apply a more liberal antitrust liability standard to local governments. Although the Court has rejected a conspiracy exception to state action immunity, municipalities remain liable for conspiracies in restraint of trade if state action immunity does not apply. Corporations are liable for intra-enterprise conspiracies between parent corporations and partially owned subsidiaries.[4] At the municipal level, an intra-enterprise conspiracy is a unilateral governmental action, as the adoption of a zoning ordinance that restricts competitive opportunity. The Supreme Court has held that the intra-enterprise conspiracy doctrine does not apply to the unilateral adoption of a regulatory ordinance by a city council.[5]

§ 5.57 Local Government Antitrust Act.

Prior to 1984, local governments faced the possibility of substantial monetary liability under the antitrust act because it authorizes the recovery of treble damages and attorney's fees. The Local Government Antitrust Act of 1984 eliminated the recovery of monetary damages against local governments in cases in which a court holds that a local government is not immune from liability under the state action doctrine.[1] Plaintiffs may still obtain injunctions against local governments in antitrust cases, and may attorney's fees only if they are successful in an injunction case.

Statutory immunity from damages applies "in any claim against a person based on any official action directed by a local government, or official or employee thereof acting in an official capacity."[2] Legislative history indicates the statute applies to any action or inaction of a local government that could "reasonably" be construed to be within its authority.[3] This interpretation is broad enough to include home rule as well as statutory authority. Legislative history also indicates that immunity attaches only if local government officials act in good faith, which means a reasonable belief that the conduct was within a local government's authority.[4]

---

[3] § 5.50.

[4] Copperweld Corp. v. Independence Tube Corp., 467 U.S. 752 (1984).

[5] Fisher v. City of Berkeley, 475 U.S. 260 (1986) (rent control ordinance). *See* Russell v. Kansas City (II), 1988 U.S. Dist. Lexis 12170 (D. Kan. 1988) (intra-enterprise conspiracy doctrine does not apply to city and its official implicated in zoning actions).

[1] 15 U.S.C. §§ 34–36.

[2] 15 U.S.C. § 36.

[3] H.R. Rep. No. 965, 98th Cong., 2d Sess. 20 (1984). *See* Montauk-Caribbean Airways, Inc. v. Hope, 784 F.2d 91 (2d Cir. 1986) (Congress intended broad meaning; affirmative authority not required).

[4] *Id.*

The relief from damages provided by the Act also applies to claims against private defendants "based on any official action directed by a local government" or an official or employee acting in an official capacity.[5] Legislative history indicates that the private activity must be "expressly required." It cited a "zoning permit" requiring the building of a hotel with certain specifications on rezoned land as an example that "probably" meets this test.[6]

§ 5.58   Free Speech Problems in Zoning for Adult Businesses.

Zoning for adult businesses raises a special set of legal problems because adult uses, such as move theaters and book stores, are a form of commercial speech protected by the free speech clause of the federal constitution.[1] Zoning ordinances for adult uses raise free speech issues because they may exclude them from the community or may restrict their location. Municipalities usually restrict location through dispersal requirements that prohibit adult uses from locating within a certain distance of each other, and which may also prohibit their location within a certain distance of residential areas and sensitive uses such as hospitals, schools and religious uses. Another alternative, less frequently used, is to concentrate adult uses in specified areas of the community. Municipalities also license adult businesses, and may require them to obtain a special permit or conditional use under the zoning ordinance.[2]

The exclusion of adult uses from a community or their restriction to designated area raises suppresses commercial speech because it limits the number of locations in a community where adult uses are allowed. The following sections first discuss Supreme Court decisions that have decided how the free speech clause affects zoning ordinances that regulate adult uses. It then discusses federal and state court cases that have applied these decisions to zoning problems raised by adult use zoning regulations. The case law on adult uses is reasonably settled, but the decisions of some Supreme Court cases by plurality opinions leave some issues open.

§ 5.59   Mini-Theatres.

Young v. American Mini Theatres, Inc.[1] was the first Supreme Court decision that considered an adult use regulation. In a plurality opinion, the Court upheld a deconcentration zoning strategy for adult businesses adopted by the City of

---

[5] 15 U.S.C. § 36(a).

[6] H.R. Rep. No. 965, 98th Cong., 2d Sess. 21, 22 (1984).

[1] § 2.50. *See* 10 A.L.R.5th 538 (1993). *See also* Deerfield Med. Center v. City of Deerfield Beach, 661 F.2d 328 (5th Cir. 1981) (invalidating prohibition on abortion clinics as interference with constitutional right of privacy).

[2] § 6.57.

[1] 427 U.S. 50 (1976).

Detroit. The zoning ordinance required a distance of 1,000 feet between adult businesses, and this requirement applied to a number of other businesses, such as hotels and bars. The ordinance also prohibited any of these businesses from locating within 500 feet of a residential area. Operators of two adult movie theaters brought an action challenging the constitutionality of both requirements as a free speech violation. Justice Stevens wrote a plurality opinion upholding the ordinance, in which Justice Powell concurred.

Justice Stevens noted that the free speech clause did not absolutely prohibit the deconcentration ordinance. The ordinance did not regulate free speech because of its viewpoint, and he would not give adult sexual expression the same protection under the free speech clause that he would give to political debate. He upheld the city's adoption of a spacing requirement for adult theaters because it did not suppress speech and was adopted to avoid its "secondary effects." Justice Stevens found a factual basis for concluding that the zoning ordinance would have its desired effect of preserving the character of city neighborhoods. He held that "the city's interest in attempting to preserve the quality of urban life is one that must be accorded high respect." He emphasized the case would raise a different question if the ordinance "had the effect of suppressing, or greatly restricting access to, lawful speech."

§ 5.60   Schad.

Schad v. Borough of Mount Ephraim[1] was the next Supreme Court case. A suburban municipality adopted a zoning ordinance that excluded all live entertainment, including nude dancing. An adult bookstore owner installed glass booths in which customers could observe nude dancers. He brought an action challenging the ordinance as a violation of free speech. The Court wrote five opinions, including a plurality opinion signed by three Justices, three concurring opinions that adopted different views of the case, and a dissenting opinion. The actual holding in the case was quite narrow. The seven Justices whose different opinions made up a majority agreed only that the ordinance was facially overbroad and that the borough had not justified it.

The plurality opinion rejected a borough claim that the ordinance was constitutional because it authorized only businesses that met the "immediate needs" of its residents. The plurality could not accept this claim because the ordinance permitted businesses such as motels and lumber yards that met more than local needs. The plurality also rejected a borough argument that it could exclude live entertainment businesses because they presented parking, trash, police, and medical protection problems. The borough did not present evidence on these problems, and it was "immediately apparent as a matter of experience"

---

[1] 452 U.S. 61 (1981).

that live entertainment businesses did not present any more problems than businesses the ordinance permitted.

The plurality rejected a borough argument that the ordinance did not violate the free speech clause because it was a reasonable time, place, and manner regulation.[2] Under this exception, a regulation of a land use protected by the free speech clause is constitutional if it advances a governmental interest other than the suppression of free speech. The borough did not offer evidence that justified a prohibition on live entertainment under this exception because it did not show that live entertainment was "basically incompatible" with uses normally permitted in a commercial district. The ordinance also closed adequate channels of communication for live entertainment uses. The plurality added that *Young* "did not purport to approve the total exclusion from the city of theaters showing adult, but nonobscene, materials."

§ 5.61 *Renton.*

The Court wrote a majority opinion that clarified many of the uncertainties left open by its earlier adult business zoning cases in *City of Renton v. Playtime Theatres, Inc.,*[1] Renton is a small city in the Seattle metropolitan area that did not have any adult uses at the time the ordinance was passed. Its zoning ordinance prohibited adult theaters within 1,000 feet of any residential zone, single-family or multifamily dwelling, church, park, or school. The plaintiffs, who planned to exhibit adult movies in two theaters, challenged the constitutionality of the ordinance.

The Court held its decision was "largely dictated" by *Mini Theatres,* and held the Renton ordinance was a content-neutral time, place, and manner regulation because its purpose was unrelated to the suppression of speech and it did not regulate a point of view. The Court will uphold a content-neutral time, place, and manner regulation if it serves a substantial governmental interest and allows for reasonable alternative avenues of communication. The Renton ordinance passed this test. It was entitled to "high respect" because it served the governmental interest of preserving the quality of urban life. Renton had not made independent studies of the adult business problem, but the free speech clause did not require new studies independent of studies done elsewhere. Renton relied on a state supreme court decision reviewing studies in nearby Seattle, and this was enough.

Although the ordinance dispersed rather than concentrated adult businesses, the Court held that either strategy was acceptable and that cities should be allowed to experiment with different zoning techniques. The ordinance was not overbroad,

---

[2] § 2.50.

[1] 475 U.S. 41 (1986). *See also* Boos v. Barry, 485 U.S. 312 (1988) (explaining *Renton* as upholding ordinance aimed at manner of expression and not content of speech).

like the ordinance in *Schad,* because it was narrowly tailored to cover only theaters that would create the problem the city was trying to eliminate.

The Court held that adequate alternative channels of communication were available even though the ordinance limited adult theaters to 520 acres, which was about five percent of the city's land area. The trial court found that this area contained "ample, accessible real estate" in all stages of development and was "criss-crossed" by highways and roads. The Court dismissed an argument that much of this land was occupied, and that "practically none" was for sale or lease. It held the free speech clause is not violated just because adult businesses "must fend for themselves in the real estate market on an equal footing with other prospective purchasers and lessees." Renton need only provide a "reasonable opportunity" for adult theaters to open and operate.

§ 5.62   *Alameda Books.*

The Court's next adult use case raised questions concerning proof of the links between adult uses and their secondary effects. In *City of Los Angeles v. Alameda Books, Inc.,*[1] the city had adopted a typical distance requirement in 1977 after conducting a study concluding that adult businesses were associated with higher rates of prostitution, robbery, assaults and thefts in surrounding communities. Later, to close a loophole in the ordinance, the city amended it to prohibit "the establishment or maintenance of more than one adult entertainment business in the same building, structure or portion thereof." Suit was brought challenging the amendment by two adult use establishments that did not violate the distance requirement but operated in the same building. The effect of the ordinance was to make one of these businesses close or relocate. The district court granted the plaintiff's motion for summary judgment, but the Court reversed and remanded for trial.

The Court upheld the ordinance. Justice O'Connor, joined by three other Justices, wrote a plurality opinion. The plurality accepted the city's theory, that reducing the concentration of adult uses in a neighborhood would reduce crime whether the uses were in separate establishments or one large establishment. It held the city did not have to provide evidence that ruled out every theory about the link between adult uses and secondary effects, but the city "bears the burden of providing evidence that supports a link between concentrations of adult operations and asserted secondary effects."

The Court t repeated its holding in *Renton* that the city could rely on studies "reasonably believed to be relevant," but cautioned a city could not get away with "shoddy data or reasoning." If a plaintiff casts doubt on a municipality's rationale, then "the burden shifts back to the municipality to supplement the record with evidence renewing support for a theory that justifies its ordinance."

---

[1] 535 U.S. 425 (2002).

The Court held it was adhering to its rule of intermediate scrutiny of adult use ordinances it had adopted in *Renton*.

Justice Kennedy concurred, though he believed calling adult use zoning content-neutral was a fiction, and took a different view of the city's burden of proof. He believed the amended ordinance could be justified only if one of the two businesses required to split would move rather than close, thus reducing their secondary effects while not diminishing their speech. If this were so, he was willing to accept the city's conclusion that two businesses in one building had the same effect as two businesses in adjacent buildings, and that dispersing one of these businesses would reduce their secondary effects by proportionately decreasing the number of customers at each site. Justice Kennedy's support of the plurality opinion is critical and suggests the Court has not yet reached agreement on what municipalities must do to justify adult use zoning.

§ 5.63   Zoning Issues in Adult Use Regulation

Federal and state courts have considered a number of issues in adult use zoning that were left unresolved by the Supreme Court or that require an application of the principles adopted in the Supreme Court case.[1] After *Renton*, the courts relaxed the requirement that municipalities must make independent studies of the adult use problem as the basis for adopting adult use ordinances,[2] but they may have to revisit this issue after *Alameda Books*.[3] The courts have usually upheld distance and spacing requirements if they did not effectively preclude adult uses from a community.[4] They also uphold ordinances that limit adult

---

[1] City of Crystal v. Fantasy House, Inc., 569 N.W.2d 225 (Minn. App. 1997) (upholding moratorium to consider adoption of adult use ordinance).

[2] Jakes, Ltd., Inc. v. City of Coates, 284 F.3d 884 (8th Cir. 2002); Ward v. County of Orange, 217 F.3d 1350 (11th Cir. 2000); ILQ Investments, Inc. v. City of Rochester, 25 F.3d 1413 (8th Cir. 1994); Alexander v. City of Minneapolis, 928 F.2d 278 (8th Cir. 1991); Thames Enterprises v. City of St. Louis, 851 F.2d 199 (8th Cir. 1988); Town of Islip v. Caviglia, 540 N.E.2d 215 (N.Y. 1989). *But see* World Wide Video, Inc. v. City of Tukwila, 816 P.2d 18 (Wash. 1991) (en banc). *But see* Ranch House, Inc. v. Amerson, 238 F.3d 1273 (11th Cir. 2001) (remanding because no evidence of secondary effects).

[3] Encore Videos, Inc. v. City of San Antonio, 310 F.3d 812 (5th Cir. 2002); (studies did not meet *Alameda*-based test); Baby Dolls Topless Saloons, Inc. v. City of Dallas, 295 F.3d 471 (5th Cir. 2002) (applying *Alameda* and holding study adequate).

[4] LLEH, Inc. v. City of Wichita Falls, 289 F.3d 359 (5th Cir. 2002); Z.J. Gifts D-2, L.L.C. v. City of Aurora, 136 F.3d 683 (10th Cir. 1998); Ambassador Books & Video, Inc. v. City of Little Rock, 20 F.3d 858 (8th Cir. 1994); Lakeland Lounge of Jackson, Inc. v. City of Jackson, 973 F.2d 1255 (5th Cir. 1992); International Eateries of America, Inc. v. Broward County, 941 F.2d 1157 (11th Cir. 1991); Hart Bookstores, Inc. v. Edmisten, 612 F.2d 821 (4th Cir. 1979); City of National City v. Wiener, 838 P.2d 223 (Cal. 1992); Stringfellow's of New York v. City of New York, 91 N.E.2d 382 (N.Y. 1998). *See also* DiMas Corp. v. Town of Hallie, 185 F.3d 823 (7th Cir. 1999) (upholding ordinance regulating hours of business).

businesses to certain districts, such as commercial districts, or exclude them from other districts, such as residential districts, if they do not raise an effective preclusion problem.[5]

An effective preclusion claim arises from the *Renton* holding, that "reasonable alternative channels of communication" must be available for adult uses. In effective preclusion cases the claim is that areas zoned for adult uses, though reasonably plentifully, are not truly available, or that they are too undesirable, too few or too small to be meaningful.[6] Some courts have rejected effective preclusion claims.[7] Other courts found effective preclusion post-*Renton*,[8] but differed in defining the circumstances in which an effective preclusion claim would be justified.[9]

Municipalities need only identify general areas, not exact sites.[10] Nor is there a free speech violation even if the cost of relocating puts the adult use out of business.[11] Courts have looked at a variety of factors to determine whether there

---

[5] Z.J. Gifts D-2, L.L.C. v. City of Aurora, 136 F.3d 683 (10th Cir. 1998) (limited to industrial areas); Holmberg v. City of Ramsey, 12 F.3d 140 (8th Cir. 1994); Lakeland Lounge of Jackson, Inc. v. City of Jackson, 973 F.2d 1255 (5th Cir. 1992); U.S. Partners Financial Corp. v. Kansas City, 707 F. Supp. 1090 (W.D. Mo. 1989); Jeffrey Lauren Land Co. v. City of Livonia, 326 N.W.2d 604 (Mich. 1982); Northend Cinema, Inc. v. City of Seattle, 585 P.2d 1153 (Wash. 1978). *But see* CLR Corp. v. Henline, 702 F.2d 637 (6th Cir. 1983).

[6] *See* Isbell v. City of San Diego, 258 F.3d1108 (9th Cir. 2001).

[7] SDJ, Inc. v. City of Houston, 636 F. Supp. 1359 (S.D. Tex. 1986), *aff'd*, 837 F.2d 1268 (5th Cir. 1988); County of Cook v. Renaissance Arcade & Bookstore, 522 N.E.2d 73 (Ill. 1993); North Avenue Novelties, Inc. v. City of Chicago, 88 F.3d 441 (7th Cir. 1996); Stringfellow's of New York v. City of New York, 91 N.E.2d 382 (N.Y. 1998).

[8] Walnut Properties, Inc. v. City of Whittier (II), 861 F.2d 1102 (9th Cir. 1988) (would force only adult theater in district to close); People Tags, Inc. v. Jackson County Legislature, 636 F. Supp. 1345 (W.D. Mo. 1986) (ordinance intended to close one business invalidated); City of Stanton v. Cox, 255 Cal. Rptr. 682 (Cal. App. 1989) (locations zoned for adult businesses severely limited); A.F.M., Ltd. v. City of Medford, 704 N.E.2d 184 (Mass. 1999) (0.11% of city not enough).

[9] Lim v. City of Long Beach, 217 F.3d 1050 (9th Cir. 2000) (holding sites must have genuine possibility of coming available for commercial use); Woodall v. City of El Paso, 959 F.2d 1305 (5th Cir. 1992) (may consider physical or legal but not economic unsuitability of land), *followed in* Woodall v. City of El Paso, 49 F.3d 1120 (5th Cir. 1995); Topanga Press, Inc. v. City of Los Angeles, 989 F.2d 1524 (9th Cir. 1993) (disagreeing with *Woodall* and holding property not potentially available when it is unreasonable to believe it would ever become available to any commercial enterprise);*See also* Young v. City of Simi Valley, 216 F.3d 807 (9th Cir. 2000) (invalidating ordinance allowing affected "sensitive" uses to veto adult use). Gammoh v. City of Anaheim, 86 Cal. Rptr.2d 194 (Cal. App. 1999) (invalidating rezoning that prevented adult use of vacant lot located next to freeway).

[10] Hickerson v. City of New York, 146 F.3d 99 (2d Cir. 1998). *See also* Vincent v. Broward County, 200 F.3d 1325 (11th Cir. 2000) (summarizing the cases and holding a site is not unavailable even though some development is required, and that lot need not be ideal).

[11] Holmberg v. City of Ramsey, 12 F.3d 149 (8th Cir. 1993).

are a sufficient number of available sites. One approach is to consider "the percentage of land within the city available to adult businesses, or the number of sites compared with the number of adult businesses currently in existence or seeking to open."[12] There is no requirement that a specific proportion of a municipality be available for adult businesses.[13] Florida cases have relied on the ratio of sites to population,[14] while other courts have compared the availability of sites to market demand.[15] Though the Supreme Court in *Schad* suggested that courts could consider the availability of sites outside a municipality, this question has not yet been decided in the lower federal courts.[16]

§ 5.64 Existing Uses.

The Supreme Court in *Mini-Theatres* observed in a footnote that the adult business ordinance it upheld did not apply to existing uses but did not say that a grandfather clause was essential. Most courts have not required them, and have upheld provisions in zoning ordinances that require the amortization of a nonconforming adult use after a period of time.[1] A court may strike down an ordinance prohibiting advertising by adult businesses if it finds the ordinance restricts speech and is not supported by other governmental purposes, such as preventing loss of property values.[2] The courts have upheld ordinances and

---

[12] Diamond v. City of Taft, 215 F.3d 1057 (9th Cir. 2000). *See also* Boss Capital, Inc. v. City of Casselberry, 187 F.3d 1251 (11th Cir. 1999).; Young v. City of Simi Valley, 216 F.3d 807 (9th Cir. 2000) (holding number of sites adequate and refusing to apply "supply and demand" analysis).

[13] D.H.L. Assocs., Inc. v. O'Gorman, 199 F.3d 50 (1st Cir. 1999).

[14] *See* Centerfold Club v. City of St. Petersburg, 969 F. Supp. 1288 (M.D. Fla. 1997) (striking down one site per 12,516 residents, and noting that Florida cases have upheld ratios of about 1/6000).

[15] North Avenue Novelties, Inc. v. City of Chicago, 88 F.3d 441 (7th Cir. 1996) (number of sites adequate because demand limited and a number of adult businesses operated in the city); Lakeland Lounge of Jackson, Inc. v. City of Jackson, 973 F.2d 1255 (5th Cir. 1992).

[16] Boss Capital, Inc. v. City of Casselberry, 187 F.3d 1251 (11th Cir. 1999).

[1] Ambassador Books & Video, Inc. v. City of Little Rock, 20 F.3d 585 (8th Cir. 1994); Hart Bookstores, Inc. v. Edminsten, 612 F.2d 821 (4th Cir. 1979); County of Cook v. Renaissance Arcade & Bookstore, 522 N.E.2d 73 (Ill. 1988); Town of Islip v. Caviglia, 540 N.E.2d 215 (N.Y. 1989); Northend Cinema, Inc. v. City of Seattle, 585 P.2d 1153 (Wash. 1978). *Contra* Ebel v. City of Corona, 767 F.2d 635 (9th Cir. 1985) (invalidating 60-to 120-day period when user had five-year lease and had made substantial investment); 751 Orange Ave, Inc. v. City of W. Haven, 761 F.2d 105 (2d Cir. 1985). *See also* E. Brooks Books v. City of Memphis, 48 F.3d 220 (6th Cir. 1995) (contra when state law requires continuation of nonconforming uses); Foreman v. Union Township Zoning Hearing Bd., 787 A.2d 1099 (Pa. Commw. 2001) (increased frequency of adult entertainment did not change status as nonconforming use).

[2] MD II Entertainment, Inc. v. City of Dallas, 28 F.3d 492 (5th Cir. 1994). *But see* Hamilton Amusement Center, Inc. v. Poritz, 689 A.2d 201 (N.J. App. Div. 1997) (upholding state statute limiting size, number and content of signs).

statutes limiting the display of signs by adult businesses.[3]

§ 5.65 Defining Adult Uses

Defining adult uses presents problems because establishments may conduct non-adult as well as adult activities, and because the terms used in definitions may be unconstitutionally vague.[1] In *Mini-Theatres*,[2] a majority of the Supreme Court upheld a definition of an adult motion picture theater defined as an enclosed building used to present "material distinguished or characterized by their emphasis" on sexual matter. The Court rejected an argument the definition was vague because the plaintiff "regularly" offered adult fare and so fell within the definition.[3] The courts have also upheld ordinances against vagueness charges that define and adult book store as an establishment that carries a "substantial or significant portion" of adult material.[4] Though municipalities may prefer a definition that makes an establishment adult if a certain percentage of its business is in adult material, courts have struck down definitions of this kind if they are too restrictive.[5]

---

[3] Pleasureland Museum, Inc. v. Beutter, 288 F.3d 988 (7th Cir. 2002) (but invalidating provision limiting sign to name of business); Excaliber Group, Inc. v. City of Minneapolis, 116 F.3d 1216 (8th Cir. 1997); SDJ, Inc. v. City of Houston, 837 F.2d 1268 (5th Cir. 1988); Hamilton Amusement Center, Inc. v. Poritz, 716 A.2d 1137 (N.J. 1998).

[1] § 6.05.

[2] § 5.59. *See also accord* Baby Dolls Topless Saloons, Inc. v. City of Dallas, 295 F.3d 471 (5th Cir. 2002) (similar definition); Pleasureland Museum, Inc. v. Beutter, 288 F.3d 988 (7th Cir. 2002); Blue Canary Corp. v. City of Milwaukee (II), 270 F.3d 1156 (7th Cir. 2001) (upholding ordinance prohibiting use "similar" to listed adult uses); Chez Sez VIII, Inc. v. Poritz, 688 A.2d 119 (N.J. App. Div. 1997) (upholding statute that prohibited the provision by commercial establishments of booths that facilitated sexual activity). *But see* Central Ave. Enters., Inc. v. City of Las Cruces, 845 F. Supp. 1499 (D.N.M. 1994) (invalidating statute that failed to define terms).

[3] See FW/PBS v. City of Dallas, 493 U.S. 215, 260 (1990) ("regularly features" means "a continuous presentation of the sexual material as one of the very objectives of the commercial enterprise," Justice Scalia concurring). Compare Tollis v. San Bernardino County, 827 F.2d 1329 (9th Cir. 1987) (invalidating ordinance construed to apply when only one adult feature shown).

[4] Excaliber Group, Inc. v. City of Minneapolis, 116 F.3d 1216 (8th Cir. 1997); ILQ Invs., Inc. v. City of Rochester, 25 F.3d 1413 (8th Cir. 1994); Town of Islip v. Caviglia, 540 N.E.2d 215 (N.Y. 1989). *See accord* Stansberry v. Holmes, 613 F.2d 1285 (5th Cir. 1980) ("major business").

[5] Christy v. City of Ann Arbor, 824 F.2d 489 (6th Cir. 1987) (20 per cent); Golden Triangle News, Inc. v. Corbett, 689 A.2d 974 (Pa. Commw. 1997) (sales percentage test would be arbitrary); Worldwide Video v. Tukwila, 816 P.2d 18 (Wash. 1991) (10 per cent). *Contra* Alexander v. City of Minneapolis, 928 F.2d 278 (8th Cir. 1991) (30 per cent); Maloy v. City of Lewisville, 848 S.W.2d 380 (Tex. App. 1993) (20 per cent). *See* City of New York v. Hommes, 724 N.E.2d 368 (N.Y. 1999) (avoiding regulation by maintaining sufficient non-adult stock).

§ 5.66   State Legislation.

A few states have statutes that either put restrictions on adult businesses or authorize local regulation of adult businesses.[1] California law, for example, authorizes counties and cities to adopt ordinances regulating adult businesses that advance a substantial governmental interest and that do not unreasonably restrict avenues of communication.[2] Kansas authorizes reasonable regulations for the elimination of nonconforming adult businesses.[3] Statutes have also prohibited the location of adult businesses within a certain distance of specified designated uses.[4]

D. RELIGIOUS USES.

§ 5.67   Religious Uses.

§ 5.68   In the State Courts.

Religious uses present a controversial zoning problem. Their status in the zoning ordinance classification system is unclear. Though arguably a non-intrusive use in residential neighborhoods, they can also be activity centers that can be incompatible with residential neighborhoods.

The cases are divided on whether a zoning ordinance may exclude religious uses, such as churches, from residential areas. Several courts hold that the ordinance may exclude religious uses from residential areas if they create traffic problems or have an adverse effect on property values or municipal services.[1]

---

[1] N.C. Gen. Stat. §§ 160A-181.1 (same); Nev. Rev. Stat. § 278.0222 (same); N.J. Stat. Ann. § 2C:34-7 (distance requirements and limitations on signs); N.C. Gen. Stat. § 160A-181.1 (authorizing regulation); Tenn. Code Ann. §§ 7-51-1401 to 7-51-1406 (hours of operation and design of premises); Tex. Local Gov't Code §§ 243.001–243.011 (authorizes local regulation). *See* Township of Saddle Brook v. A.B. Family Center, Inc., 722 A.2d 530 (N.J. 1999) (interpreting statute to allow consideration of sites in other municipalities); Onslow County v. Moore, 499 S.E.2d 780 (N.C. App. 1998) (statute prohibiting more than one adult use in building preempts municipal spacing requirements).

[2] Cal. Gov't Code 65850.4.

[3] Kan. Stat. Ann.. § 12-770.

[4] Ala. Code §§ 13A-12-200.5(4).

[1] Seward Chapel, Inc. v. City of Seward, 655 P.2d 1293 (Alaska 1982) (exclusion of parochial school); Corporation of Presiding Bishop of Church of Jesus Christ of Latter-Day Saints v. City of Porterville, 203 P.2d 823 (Cal.), *appeal dismissed,* 338 U.S. 805 (1949); West Hartford Methodist Church v. Zoning Bd. of Appeals, 121 A.2d 640 (Conn. 1956); Lutheran High School Ass'n v. City of Farmington Hills, 381 N.W.2d 417 (Mich. App. 1986); Cornell Univ. v. Bagnardi, 503 N.E.2d 509 (N.Y. 1986); Milwaukie Company of Jehovah's Witnesses v. Mullen, 330 P.2d 5 (Or. 1958). *But see* Jehovah's Witness Assembly Halls of New Jersey, Inc. v. City of Jersey City, 597 F. Supp. 972 (D.N.J. 1984) (may not exclude from commercial area).

When the impact on residential areas is less extreme, the cases suggest that allowing religious uses as a conditional use is a more "balanced" alternative.[2]

A number of cases treat religious uses as a preferred use and hold a zoning ordinance may not exclude them from residential neighborhoods. Some of these cases rely on state constitutions that protect the free exercise of religion, and some reverse the presumption of constitutionality the courts usually apply to zoning ordinances.[3] Religious uses must comply with reasonable site development regulations, such as parking requirements.[4] A wide variety of uses that accompany the operation of a religious institution have been held to be appropriate accessory uses.[5]

§ 5.69 Federal "Free Exercise" and "Establishment" Clauses.

Whether zoning ordinances and actions violate the free exercise clause is governed by the Supreme Court's holding in *Employment Division v. Smith (II)*[1] that valid, neutral laws generally applied and free of a "system of individual exemptions" do not violate that clause if there is a rational basis for their application. The courts have upheld zoning restrictions on religious uses when

---

[2] Cornell Univ. v. Bagnardi, 503 N.E.2d 509 (N.Y. 1986). *Contra* Love Church v. City of Evanston, 671 F. Supp. 508, 515 (N.D. Ill. 1987). *See* § 6.56.

[3] Ellsworth v. Gercke, 156 P.2d 242 (Ariz. 1945); City of Colorado Springs v. Blanche, 761 P.2d 212 (Colo. 1988) (qualifying earlier case adopting rule); Village Lutheran Church v. City of Ladue, 935 S.W.2d 720 (Mo. App. 1997) (municipalities only have power to adopt safety regulations); Jehovah's Witnesses Assembly Hall v. Wollrich Twp., 532 A.2d 276 (N.J.L. Div. 1987) (citing cases); State ex rel. Synod of Ohio v. Joseph, 39 N.E.2d 515 (Ohio 1942); Simms v. City of Sherman, 181 S.W.2d 100 (Tex. Civ. App.), *aff'd*, 183 S.W.2d 415 (Tex. 1944); Lake Shore Drive Baptist Church v. Village of Bayside Bd. of Trustees, 108 N.W.2d 288 (Wis. 1961). *See* State v. Cameron, 498 A.2d 1217 (N.J. 1985) (ordinance excluding church held vague).

[4] East Side Baptist Church v. Klein, 487 P.2d 549 (Colo. 1971); Board of Zoning Appeals v. Decatur, Ind. Congregation of Jehovah's Witnesses, 117 N.E.2d 115 (Ind. 1954); Wellspring Zendo, Inc. v. Trippe, 625 N.Y.S.2d 334 (App. Div. 1995) (screening buffer). *See also* Lucas Valley Homeowners Ass'n v. County of Marin, 284 Cal. Rptr. 427 (Cal. App. 1991) (permit conditions). *See* Colo. Rev. Stat. §§ 29-1-1201 to 29-1-1203 (prohibiting regulation of private residences for religious services).

[5] Keeling v. Board of Zoning Appeals, 69 N.E.2d 613 (Ind. App. 1946) (parking lot for members); City of Richmond Heights v. Richmond Heights Presbyterian Church, 764 S.W.2d 647 (Mo. 1989) (day care center); Application of Faith for Today, Inc., 204 N.Y.S.2d 751 (App. Div. 1960) (correspondence school and television studio), *aff'd*, 174 N.E.2d 743 (N.Y. 1961); Slevin v. Long Island Jewish Medical Center, 319 N.Y.S.2d 937 (Misc. 1971) (center for counseling drug users); Henley v. City of Youngstown Bd. of Zoning Appeals, 735 N.E.2d 433 (Ohio 2000) (residential accommodations in church buildings); Solid Rock Ministries Int'l v. Board of Zoning Appeals, 740 N.E.2d 320 (Ohio App. 2000) (conditional use permit for church construed to allow home for pregnant unwed teenage girls). *See* Or. Rev. Stat. §§ 227.500, 214.441 (county shall allow reasonable use of property for activities customarily associated with practices of the religious activity).

[1] 419 U.S. 872 (1990).

they satisfy this requirement.[2] For example, in *First Assembly of God v. Collier County,*[3] the court upheld a zoning ordinance that applied to all homeless shelters and that prohibited a church from operating a shelter on its premises. The ordinance also defined areas in which a shelter could be operated. However, a municipality must have a compelling interest for its regulation if a court finds it substantially burdens a religious belief.[4]

The Court in *Smith (II)*, however, left undisturbed the rule that the strict scrutiny rule applies to cases where laws contain "a system of individualized exceptions", that "create[] a mechanism for individualized exemptions" or that lend themselves to "individualized governmental assessment" of the conduct governed.[5] Government decisions in this instance must be justified by a compelling interest. This requirement can apply to actions taken under zoning ordinances. The courts have applied the individualized assessment exception to invalidate zoning actions that require the exercise of discretion.[6]

---

[2] Mount Elliot Cemetery Ass'n v. City of Troy, 171 F.3d 398 (6th Cir. 1999) (zoning ordinance that prohibited cemeteries); Daytona Rescue Mission, Inc. v. City of Daytona Beach, 885 F. Supp. 1554 (M.D. Fla. 1995) (fire standards);First Baptist Church v. Miami-Dade County, 768 So.2d 1114 (Fla. App. 2000) (upholding ordinance under which church was denied permission for expansion); Korean Buddhist Dae Won Sa Temple v. Zoning Bd. of Appeals, 953 P.2d 1315 (Hawaii 1998) (denial of height variance); Village Lutheran Church v. Village of Ladue, 997 S.W.2d 506 (Mo. App. 1999) (exercising some control over religious institutions not a per se violation of constitutional rights). *See also* Church of the Lukumi Babalu Aye v. City of Hialeah, 508 U.S. 520 (1993) (invalidating local zoning and other laws targeting use of animal sacrifice for religious purposes); Bethel Evangelical Lutheran Ch. v. Village of Morton, 559 N.E.2d 533 (Ill. App. 1990) (upholding enrollment cap on church school). *See* 11 A.L.R.4th 1084 (1982).

Pre-*Smith* cases *accord*: Messiah Baptist Ch. v. County of Jefferson, 859 F.2d 820 (10th Cir. 1988) (upholding denial of building permit for house of worship); Grosz v. City of Miami Beach, 721 F.2d 729 (11th Cir. 1983) (conduct of religious services in home); Lakewood, Ohio Congregation of Jehovah's Witnesses, Inc. v. City of Lakewood, 699 F.2d 303 (6th Cir. 1983) (prohibition on church in residential district); Congregation Beth Yitzchok of Rockland, Inc. v. Town of Ramapo, 593 F. Supp. 655 (S.D.N.Y. 1984) (fire and safety regulations).

[3] 20 F.3d 419 (11th Cir. 1994).

[4] Fifth Ave. Presbyterian Church v. City of New York, 293 F.3d 570 (2d Cir. 2002) (cannot prohibit homeless shelter);Cornerstone Bible Ch. v. City of Hastings, 948 F.2d 464 (8th Cir. 1991) (church excluded from central business district); Western Presbyterian Church v. Board of Zoning Adjustment, 849 F. Supp. 77 (D.D.C. 1994) (food for homeless program). Pre-*Smith*: Islamic Center of Miss., Inc. v. City of Starkville, 840 F.2d 293 (5th Cir. 1988) (invalidating prohibition on church building). *See also* Society of Jesus v. Boston Landmarks Comm'n, 564 N.E.2d 571 (Mass. 1990) (designation of church interior as landmark violates state free exercise clause when adopted to prevent renovation).

[5] Sherbert v. Verner, 374 U.S. 398 (1963), confirmed in Church of the Lukumi Babalu Aye, Inc. v. City of Hialeah, 508 U.S. 520 (1993).

[6] Cottonwood Christian Center v. Cypress Redev. Agency, 218 F. Supp.2d 1203 (C.D. Cal. 2002) (denial of conditional use permit and condemnation of property); Keeler v. Mayor & Council, 949 F. Supp. 879 (D. Md. 1999) (certificate of appropriateness in historic preservation ordinance); Cam

In *Larkin v. Grendel's Den, Inc.*,[7] the Supreme Court invalidated a Massachusetts statute providing that a city could not issue a liquor license if a church or school located within 500 feet of the premises vetoed it. The Court held that the statutory veto violated the "establishment of religion" clause of the federal constitution. The statute could advance or inhibit religion because it did not contain standards for the exercise of the veto, which churches could use for religious purposes. The veto also "enmeshes churches in the process of government" and could create political fragmentation on religious issues. *Grendel's Den* casts doubt on the cases that give churches a preferred use status under zoning ordinances. However, the courts have upheld zoning ordinances that exempt religious institutions from special exception and special use permit procedures, holding that the exemption served the secular purpose of avoiding governmental interference in religious affairs.[8]

§ 5.70 Federal and State Religious Freedom Acts.

Congress passed a Religious Freedom Restoration Act[1] in 1993 to restore the "compelling" governmental interest test the Supreme Court previously required to justify governmental action affecting the free exercise of religion. The Act applied to state and local governments. It did not mention zoning, but it was clear from the legislative history that Congress intended the Act to apply to zoning actions,[2] and courts applied it in zoning cases. However, the Supreme Court held the Act unconstitutional as an unauthorized exercise of congressional power because it redefined the meaning of the free exercise clause.[3]

Congress enacted a new Religious Land Use and Institutionalized Persons Act of 2000 that reinstates the compelling interest test. It prohibits a government from imposing or implementing a land use regulation that imposes a "substantial burden"[4] on religious exercise, unless that burden is in furtherance of a

---

v. Marion County, 987 F. Supp. 854 (D. Or. 1997) (cannot deny permission to worship in pre-existing barn); First Covenant Ch. v. City of Seattle, 840 P.2d 174 (Wash. 1992) (historic landmarking of church).

[7] 459 U.S. 116 (1982).

[8] Ehlers-Renzi v. Connelly School of the Holy Child, 224 F.3d 283 (4th Cir. 2000) (and that exemption was not government activity or influence that advanced religion); Cohen v. City of Des Plaines, 8 F.3d 484 (7th Cir. 1993). *See also* Boyajian v. Gatzunis, 212 F.3d 1 (1st Cir. 2000) (upholding statute and ordinances that prohibit municipalities from excluding residential uses from any zoning district).

[1] Formerly 42 U.S.C. §§ 2000b to 2000b-4.

[2] *See, e.g.,* H.R. Rep. No. 103-88, 103d Cong., 1st Sess. 6, n. 14 (1993) (disapproving, *e.g.,* *Saint Bartholomew's Church* decision, discussed in § 11.37).

[3] City of Boerne v. Flores, 521 U.S. 507 (1997).

[4] Murphy v. Zoning Comm'n, 148 F. Supp.2d 173 (D. Conn. 2001) (finding substantial burden and invalidating prohibition on prayer meeting in home)

"compelling governmental interest" and is the "least restrictive means'" of furthering that interest. A "substantial burden" includes cases where "government makes, or has in place formal or informal procedures or practices that permit [it] to make, individualized assessments of the proposed uses for the property involved," which codifies this exception to *Smith (II)*. The Act also prohibits a government from imposing or implementing a land use regulation that treats a land use assembly or institution in "less than equal terms," and from imposing or implementing a land use regulation that "discriminates against any assembly or institution on the basis of religion or religious denomination."[5] The definition of "religious exercise" protected by the act is broad and may include typical accessory uses.[6] Finally, the act codifies the "individualized assessment" exception to Smith. A constitutional challenge to the statute is expected.

Several states have adopted religious freedom acts modeled on the federal act the Supreme Court held unconstitutional,[7] but the state acts do not, of course, face constitutional challenges similar to those made under the federal constitution. Like the federal act, the state acts apply to land use regulations that affect religious uses.[8]

E.   SITE DEVELOPMENT REQUIREMENTS.

§ 5.71   Yards and Setbacks.

The constitutionality of yard and setback requirements has been secure since a post-*Euclid* Supreme Court case, *Gorieb v. Fox*.[1] The Court relied on *Euclid* to uphold a street setback requirement in a residential area because it separated residences from the noise of the street, improved the attractiveness of residential environments, and ensured the availability of light and air. The courts have upheld the constitutionality of setback and yard requirements since *Gorieb*.[2]

---

[5] 42 U.S.C. §§ 2000cc, *et seq.*

[6] *See* Prater v. City of Burnside, 289 F.3d 417 (6th Cir. 2002) (city decision to develop rather than close street not covered by act).

[7] *E.g.,* Ariz. Rev. Stat. § 41-1493.01; Cal. Gov't Code §§ 25373(d), 37361(c); Mass. Gen. Laws Ch. 40A, § 3; Fla. Stat. Ann. § 761.03; § 775 Ill. Comp. Stat. Ann. 35/15 to 35/25; R.I. Gen. Laws §§ 42-80.1-1 to 42-80.1-4; S.C. Code §§ 1-32-10 to 1-32-60; Tex. Civ. Practice & Remedies Code §§ 110.001–110.012.

[8] *See also* Martin v. Corporation of Presiding Bishop, 747 N.E.2d 131 (Mass. 2001) (upholding zoning variance for church steeple under state law prohibiting restrictions on land used for religious purposes).

[1] 274 U.S. 603 (1927).

[2] City of Leadville v. Rood, 600 P.2d 62 (Colo. 1979); Quirk v. Town of New Boston, 663 A.2d 1328 (N.H. 1995) (buffer zone); Miller & Son Paving, Inc. v. Wrightstown Twp., 451 A.2d 1002 (Pa. 1982); In re Letourneau, 726 A.2d 31 (Vt. 1998).93 A.L.R.2d 1223 (1964); 94 A.L.R.2d 398 (1964).

Cases occasionally invalidate setback requirements when they do not serve the zoning purposes approved in *Gorieb*. The Pennsylvania Supreme Court held that the zoning purposes that support the constitutionality of setbacks in urban areas do not apply in rural areas.[3] A court may also hold setback and yard requirements invalid as a taking of property if they excessively restrict the area available for building. In *Board of Supvrs. v. Rowe*,[4] the court invalidated front setback and perimeter open space requirements that eliminated twenty-nine percent of the buildable area of a lot.

§ 5.72   Frontage Requirements.

Courts uphold minimum street frontage requirements for the same reasons that the Supreme Court upheld street setbacks in *Gorieb*. Minimum street frontage requirements control density and the open space required around dwellings because they effectively determine the size of the lot.[1] Large-lot zoning provisions often contain frontage requirements, although the large-lot zoning cases do not usually consider the frontage requirement separately.

Frontage requirements can be exclusionary if they require excessive additional expense for streets, curbs, and sewer and water lines, as this can substantially . increase housing costs. The comprehensive exclusionary zoning cases have not yet considered frontage requirements, although the zoning ordinance held exclusionary in the *Mt. Laurel* case included excessive frontage requirements as well as other exclusionary zoning measures.[2]

Doubts about the zoning purposes served by frontage requirements occasionally produce an unfavorable decision. In *Metzger v. Town of Brentwood (II)*,[3] the zoning ordinance required a 200-foot frontage for single-family dwellings, but the property owner had only a 123-foot frontage on part of a road that was open to the public. The court noted that "frontage requirements can be justified on the basis that they are a method of determining lot size to prevent overcrowding" but pointed out that the size of the property owner's lot far exceeded the frontage requirement. Nor did the shorter frontage restrict access by fire trucks and other public vehicles.

---

[3] Schmalz v. Buckingham Twp. Zoning Bd. of Adjustment, 132 A.2d 233 (Pa. 1957).

[4] 216 S.E.2d 199 (Va. 1975). *See also* Dallen v. City of Kansas City, 822 S.W.2d 429 (Mo. App. 1991) (setback requirement held unreasonable); Giambrone v. City of Aurora, 621 N.E.2d 475 (Ohio App. 1993).

[1] Di Salle v. Giggal, 261 P.2d 499 (Colo. 1953). *See* Emond v. Board of Appeals, 541 N.E.2d 380 (Mass. App. 1989) (upholding special permit provision that authorized frontage limitation based on neighborhood average); 96 A.L.R.2d 1367 (1964).

[2] § 7.09.

[3] 374 A.2d 954 (N.H. 1977). *Contra* McNeil v. Town of Avon, 435 N.E.2d 1043 (Mass. 1982). *See also* Damurjian v. Board of Adjustment, 890 A.2d 655 (N.J. App. Div. 1997) (method of calculation vague).

§ 5.73   Site Area Ratios.

Site ratios regulate building bulk by specifying the maximum percentage of a lot a building may occupy. When applied along with height limitations in multifamily and office districts, the site area ratio controls density by limiting the square footage allowed in apartment and office buildings. Developers can vary density somewhat by varying the size of apartment and office units, but the allowable square footage imposes an important density control.

Although obviously quite important as a zoning control, site area ratio requirements have received little judicial attention. A much-cited leading case, *La Salle Nat'l Bank v. City of Chicago*,[1] upheld a site area ratio requirement that applied to multifamily dwellings. The evidence in the case did not indicate that the site area ratio was unreasonable, and the court upheld it under the usual presumption of constitutionality.

§ 5.74   Height Limitations.

Zoning district regulations usually contain height limitations as part of the site development controls package. Height limitations are an important density control because they limit the building bulk permitted by other site development requirements, such as the site ratio. The height limitation also ensures access to light and air.

In Welch v. Swasey,[1] the U.S. Supreme Court upheld a Massachusetts statute that adopted two height districts for the city of Boston. A landowner challenged the lower height requirement in the residential district. The Court upheld the statute in a traditional substantive due process decision and relied especially on the "aesthetic" considerations underlying the height limitation. The Court also upheld the differential height requirements in the two districts. The landowner did not make a taking objection.

Although there are few recent decisions, the courts have upheld height limitations contained in comprehensive zoning ordinances.[2] A few cases considered the usual mapping problems and upheld or struck down a height limitation depending on whether it was consistent with building heights in the surrounding area.[3]

---

[1] 125 N.E.2d 609 (Ill. 1955).

[1] 214 U.S. 91 (1909).

[2] Landmark Land Co. v. City & County of Denver, 728 P.2d 1281 (Colo. 1986) (to protect views); Loyola Fed. Sav. & Loan Ass'n v. Buschman, 176 A.2d 355 (Md. 1961); Alexander v. Hampstead, 525 A.2d 276 (N.H. 1987); 8 A.L.R.2d 963 (1949).

[3] *Compare* LaSalle Nat'l Bank v. City of Chicago, 125 N.E.2d 609 (Ill. 1955) (invalid), and Anderson v. City of Seattle, 390 P.2d 994 (Wash. 1964) (same), *with* LaSalle Nat'l Bank v. City of Evanston, 312 N.E.2d 625 (Ill. 1974) (contra).

The U.S. Supreme Court's *Penn Central* decision[4] held the property interest in airspace is not absolutely protected from regulation under the taking clause. Height limitations may be vulnerable to "as-applied" taking claims despite this holding. In *William C. Haas & Co. v. City & County of San Francisco*,[5] the city adopted a building height limitation as part of an urban design plan. A property owner on Russian Hill challenged the limitation and claimed it imposed a $1.9 million dollar loss on a $2 million dollar land investment. The court rejected the taking claim because the ordinance merely diminished the value of the property. It also held that the height limitation was not "reverse" spot-zoning because it was part of a comprehensive plan and all property owners in the area were equally affected.[6] *Haas* is an extreme case and is suspect post-*Lucas*.[7]

§ 5.75   Floor Area Ratio.

Site development regulations can create design problems when they are applied to multifamily and office development. Conventional setback, yard, site ratio, and height requirements can produce a uniform building design that is monotonous and unattractive. The floor area ratio is a zoning technique that attempts to avoid these design problems. It specifies a ratio between the square footage allowable in a building and the square footage of the lot. A floor area ratio of 1:1, for example, allows one square foot of building for each square foot of the lot. A developer can use the square footage allowed by the floor area ratio in any building shape he prefers if it complies with any applicable perimeter open space and height requirements. If the floor area ratio is 1:1, a two-story building would occupy one-half of the lot. A three-story building would occupy one-third of the lot. Floor area ratios in the more intensive multifamily and office districts are usually higher and allow even more variation in building design.

Though no court has considered the constitutionality of floor area ratios, they do not present constitutional questions different from those raised by other site development regulations. An important California case reviewing a floor area ratio variance stressed the importance of the floor area ratio as a zoning control.[1]

---

[4] § 2.07.

[5] 605 F.2d 1117 (9th Cir. 1979).

[6] *See also* City of St. Paul v. Chicago, St. Paul, Minneapolis & Omaha Ry., 413 F.2d 762 (8th Cir. 1969) (limitation applied to single-property owner); State v. Pacesetter Constr. Co., 571 P.2d 196 (Wash. 1977) (residential height limitation in shoreline management act).

[7] *See also* § 5.39 (discussing height limitations near airports as taking of property).

[1] Broadway, Laguna, Vallejo Ass'n v. Board of Permit Appeals, 427 P.2d 810 (Cal. 1967). *See* Raritan Dev. Corp. v. Silva, 689 N.E.2d 1373 (N.Y. 1997) (FAR calculation does not include cellar space).

§ 5.76   Bonuses and Incentives.

A number of cities have adopted an innovative zoning technique that authorizes density bonuses to office and commercial developers in return for on-site and other facilities available to the public. The city usually increases densities by increasing the floor area ratio. A street-level plaza or open space is an example of an on-site facility, although cities utilize density bonuses to secure other facilities, such as pedestrian skyways linking commercial uses in downtown areas. New York City used its density bonus program to secure the provision of commercial theaters in new office buildings.[1]

The zoning ordinance can make a density bonus available as a matter of right by specifying the density increases permitted for designated facilities. This type of density bonus, like conventional site development regulations, can produce monotonous designs. A city can avoid this problem by awarding density bonuses on a discretionary, case-by-case basis. This approach requires an even-handed administration of the density bonus option, which may be difficult to achieve. Under another alternative, the city can prepare a detailed plan for a commercial area that specifies the density bonuses available on each lot. New York City has used this approach.

The density bonus is intended to avoid the taking problem that would arise if a municipality required developers to provide a facility for public use without a density increase that offsets its cost. A different taking problem may arise if the density bonus is optional. In an optional program, a city must make the density bonus so attractive that developers will want to participate in the bonus program. A city can improve developer participation by adopting restrictive densities that make development economically unattractive. Developers will then seek the higher densities available in the bonus program.

In *Montgomery County v. Woodward & Lothrop, Inc.*,[2] the county adopted a density bonus program for a suburban business district. A developer claimed a taking occurred because the density and other requirements established as-of-right in the business district were "superficial." Landowners would not be able to develop their land under these requirements and would have to apply for a density bonus. The court dismissed the taking challenge. It held that nothing in the record showed that the developer had to obtain a density bonus in order to make a reasonable use of its land.

§ 5.77   Off-Street Parking.

Zoning ordinances usually contain off-street parking requirements for uses permitted in zoning districts. In multifamily districts the ordinance usually

---

[1] *See* N.Y. Town Law § 261-6; Village Law § 7-703 (authorizing incentive zoning and bonuses).
[2] 376 A.2d 483 (Md. 1977).

requires a specified number of parking spaces, usually two or more, for each dwelling unit. In commercial districts the parking requirement depends on the type of use and the amount of traffic it will generate. Variations in off-street parking requirements by district are constitutional if they have a reasonable basis.[1]

Off-street parking requirements serve purposes similar to those served by other site development regulations. The courts have easily upheld them, although there are not many cases. In *Zilinsky v. Zoning Bd. of Adjustment*,[2] the court upheld a zoning ordinance that required every one-family dwelling to have at least two off-street parking spaces, one of which had to be in a garage. The lower courts held the ordinance unconstitutional because it did not penalize property owners who did not park a car in the garage. The state supreme court reversed. It applied the presumption of constitutionality and held that "[e]ven without mandating use, off-street parking is a rational means of advancing the legitimate municipal interest in decreasing traffic congestion."

F. NONCONFORMING USES.

§ 5.78   The Zoning Problem.

The nonconforming use is a difficult problem in zoning administration. The mixed land use pattern that exists in built-up cities means that some uses will not conform to newly adopted or amended zoning ordinances. A zoning ordinance cannot achieve its goal of separating incompatible uses in this situation unless it requires the elimination of nonconforming uses. Municipalities have long struggled with a variety of techniques to accomplish this objective, but they have usually been unsuccessful. Nonconforming uses have remained and have often become more entrenched. They are an especially serious problem in sign control programs, which must secure the removal of nonconforming signs to achieve the visual environment they seek to create. Registration can help considerably in regulating nonconforming uses because it provides a record of the nonconforming uses that exist in a community.[1] Municipalities can also regulate a nonconforming use so long as they do not abrogate them altogether.[2]

---

[1] Montgomery County v. Woodward & Lothrop, Inc., 376 A.2d 483 (Md. 1977); 71 A.L.R.4th 529 (1989).

[2] 521 A.2d 841 (N.J. 1987). *Accord* Stroud v. City of Aspen, 532 P.2d 720 (Colo. 1975); Parking Ass'n of Georgia v. City of Atlanta, 450 S.E.2d 200 (Ga. 1994) (upholding barrier curb and landscaping requirements); Yates v. Mayor & Comm'rs, 244 So. 2d 724 (Miss. 1971); Grace Baptist Church v. City of Oxford, 358 S.E.2d 372 (N.C. 1987) (paved off-street parking).

[1] *See* Board of Zoning Appeals v. Leinz, 702 N.E.2d 1026 (Ind. 1998) (ordinance requiring registration advances legitimate governmental purpose and is not a taking when it merely reduces the number of rental units in a dwelling); Uncle v. New Jersey Pinelands Comm'n, 645 A.2d 788 (N.J. App. Div. 1994) (upholding registration provision).

[2] Suzuki v. City of Los Angeles, 51 Cal. Rptr.2d 880 (Cal. App. 1996) (nuisance abatement);

Nonconforming "use" may not be an accurate term for zoning nonconformities. A true nonconforming use is a use of land or a building that does not conform with the use restrictions of the zoning ordinance. A zoning nonconformity also occurs when an undeveloped tract of land or a building does not conform with the site development regulations of the zoning ordinance, such as lot size and frontage requirements.

The U.S. Supreme Court held in early decisions that municipalities could adopt land use ordinances that applied retroactively to eliminate an existing use.[3] These cases suggested that municipalities could apply comprehensive zoning ordinances to eliminate nonconforming uses retroactively. The early zoning ordinances did not take advantage of this opportunity. They protected nonconforming uses from immediate termination, apparently to avoid political problems. The courts now hold that a municipality may not zone retroactively to terminate a nonconforming use.[4] Some state zoning statutes impose this limitation.[5]

Some critics believe the need to eliminate nonconforming uses is overemphasized. They argue that nonconforming uses occur in mixed areas of the city where their removal is not necessary. They would limit measures for the elimination of nonconforming uses to well-established homogenous areas where a nonconforming use is a true anomaly.[6]

Two competing philosophies influence the court decisions that consider the constitutionality of ordinances providing for the elimination of nonconforming use. One philosophy favors the gradual elimination of nonconforming uses to accomplish the zoning objective of compatible and homogenous land use environments. This philosophy has its roots in an expansive view of the police power and supports zoning requirements that eliminate nonconforming uses. A

Petruzzi v. Zoning Board of Appeals, 176 Conn. 479, 483–84, 408 A.2d 243 (1979); Taylor v. Zoning Bd. of Appeals, 783 A.2d 526 (Conn. App. 2001) (special permit); Mayor & City Council v. Dembo, 719 A.2d 1007 (Md. App. 2001) (licensing); Rhod-A-Zalea & 35th, Inc. v. Snohomish County, 959 P.2d 1024 (Wash. App. 1998) (grading permit).

[3] § 2.04*See* City of Dublin v. Finkes, 615 N.E.2d 690 (Ohio App. 1993) (regulations based on protection of public health or safety can be applied retroactively to nonconforming uses).

[4] Jones v. City of Los Angeles, 295 P. 14 (Cal. 1930) (leading case); *See* Town of Lyons v. Bashor, 867 P.2d 159 (Colo. App. 1993) (nonconforming use runs with the land); Missouri Rock, Inc. v. Winholtz, 614 S.W.2d 734 (Mo. App. 1981). *But see* City Council v. Lindsey Trusts, 520 S.E.2d 181 (Va. 1999) (charter held to confer power to regulate nonconforming uses); Rhod-A-Zalea & 35th, Inc. v. Snohomish County, 959 P.2d 1024 (Wash. 1998) (nonconforming use subject to grading permit requirement).

[5] Ky. Rev. Stat. § 100.253; Mass. Ann. Laws ch. 40A, § 6; Ohio Rev. Code Ann. § 713.15; R.I. Gen. Laws § 45-24-39; Utah Code Ann. § 10-9-408. *But see* Village of Valatie v. Smith, 632 N.E.2d 1264 (N.Y. 1994) (ordinance terminating nonconforming use when in ownership changes is facially constitutional).

[6] The American Law Institute's Model Land Development Code adopts this recommendation. Model Land Dev. Code § 5-102.

competing philosophy stems from the cases that invalidate the retroactive elimination of nonconforming uses and is based on the takings clause. This philosophy places primary emphasis on protecting the "vested" rights of property owners in nonconforming uses.[7] Courts adopting this philosophy tend to strike down zoning requirements that eliminate nonconforming uses.

Neither of these competing philosophies has triumphed in the cases. The judicial view of nonconforming use controls varies, often illogically, with the zoning technique used. Nor do the courts always address the constitutional issues implicit in the vested rights philosophy. For example, zoning provisions that prohibit the resumption of abandoned nonconforming uses raise a constitutional problem because they terminate a "vested" property right. Courts seldom address this constitutional issue but concentrate instead on how they should interpret the abandonment provision.

The courts explicitly consider the constitutional problems only in the amortization cases. Although most courts still uphold amortization, some recent decisions have struck down amortization requirements.

§ 5.79   Change and Expansion.

A nonconforming use may lose its protected status if it changes or expands. Most zoning ordinances contain provisions covering this problem. One common provision states that a nonconforming use "shall not change except to a use permitted in the district in which it is located."An ordinance prohibiting a change in a nonconforming use is not a taking of property.[1] A zoning ordinance may also specify the type of changes allowed in nonconforming uses or may require a permit from the board of adjustment for nonconforming use changes.[2] A few zoning statutes regulate changes in nonconforming uses[3] and a zoning ordinance may also require an approval of any change.

The cases usually determine whether a change or expansion of a nonconforming use is permitted by considering the degree of change from the existing use and the effect of the change on the neighborhood. Many cases turn on an

---

[7] *See* Taylor v. Zoning Bd. of Appeals, 783 A.2d 526 (Conn. App. 2001).

[1] Ragucci v. Metropolitan Dev. Comm'n, 702 N.E.2d 677 (Ind. 1998); City of Sugar Creek v. Reese, 969 S.W.2d 888 (Mo. App. 1998).

[2] Ragucci v. Metropolitan Dev. Comm'n, 702 N.E.2d 677 (Ind. 1998) (holding that terms of ordinance determine whether change allowed); Kopietz v. Zoning Bd. of Appeals, 535 N.W.2d 910 (Mich. App. 1995); McLaughlin v. City of Brockton, 587 N.E.2d 251 (Mass. App. 1992).

[3] Ky. Rev. Stat. § 100.253; Neb. Rev. Stat. § 19-904.01; N.H. Rev.. Stat.§ 674:19. Va. Code Ann. § 15.1-2307; W. Va. Code § 8-24-50. *See also* Town of Seabrook v. Vachon Mgt., Inc., 745 A.2d 1155 (N.H. 2000) (statute does not apply to site plan approval); City of Chesapeake v. Gardner Enters., Inc., 482 S.E.2d 812 (Va. 1997) (statute authorizing regulation of nonconforming uses authorizes regulation of new structures).

interpretation of the zoning ordinance. A court's view on the need to eliminate nonconforming uses may also influence its decision.

In one common case, a nonconforming use claims that an expansion in its business is protected by its nonconforming use status. Permissible expansions include an increase in business volume if there are no structural alterations that increase the size of a building.[4] Courts have held that alterations in signs necessary to change sign messages do not trigger a loss of nonconforming use status.[5] Courts also usually allow a change from one conforming use to another conforming use within a nonconforming structure.[6] A nonconforming use may expand to occupy an entire tract or building if the character of the use and the nature of the property indicates that use of the entire tract or building was contemplated at the time the nonconforming use was established.[7] Relocation to another site or within the site may terminate the nonconforming use status, however.[8]

A change in a nonconforming business may also result in a loss of nonconforming use status.[9] For example, *Belleville v. Parrillo's, Inc.*[10] held that a change

---

[4] Change approved: State v. Szymanski, 189 A.2d 514 (Conn. Cir. Ct. App. Div. 1967) (increase in number of cars parked); Board of Adjustments v. Brown, 969 S.W.2d 214 (Ky. App. 1998) (modifications and enlargement of auction house); Redfearn v. Creppel, 455 So.2d 1356 (La. 1984) (expansion of restaurant); Feldstein v. La Vale Zoning Bd., 227 A.2d 731 (Md. 1967) (increase in quality and height of stored junk); Powers v. Building Inspector, 296 N.E.2d 491 (Mass. 1973) (increase in business); Racine County v. Cape, 639 N.W.2d 782 (Wis. App. 2001) (addition of portable concrete crusher).

Change not approved: Blake v. City of Phoenix, 754 P.2d 1368 (Ariz. 1988) (plant nursery drastically expanded retail sales); SLS Partnership v. City of Apple Valley, 496 N.W.2d 429 (Minn. App. 1993) (increase in size of mobile home); Grey Rocks Land Trust v. Town of Hebron, 614 A.2d 1048 (N.H. 1992) (construction of new building); 61 A.L.R.4th 806, 902 (1988); 87 A.L.R.2d 4 (1963).

[5] Rogers v. Zoning Board of Adjustment, 707 A.2d 1090 (N.J. App. Div. 1998); Ray's Stateline Market v. Town of Pelham, 605 A.2d 1068 (N.H. 1995). *See* Motel 6 Operating Ltd. Partnership v. City of Flagstaff, 991 P.2d 272 (Ariz. App. 1999).

[6] Appeal of Miserocchi, 749 A.2d 607 (Vt. 2000).

[7] Ollinger v. Collins, 470 So. 2d 1183 (Ala. 1985) (intent to use entire property not enough); Hansen Bros. Enters. v. Board of Supervisors, 907 P.2d 1324 (Cal. 1995) (mining); Fred McDowell, Inc. v. Board of Adjustment, 757 A.2d 822 (N.J. App. Div. 2000) (subjective intent to use additional area for quarrying not enough); Syracuse Aggregate Corp. v. Weise, 414 N.E.2d 651 (N.Y. 1980) (quarrying exception); Town of West Greenwich v. A. Cardi Realty Assocs., 786 A.2d 354 (R.I. 2001); (earth removal and gravel business); City of University Place v. McGuire, 30 P.3d 453 (Wash. 2001) (mining; discussing cases); Keller v. City of Bellingham, 600 P.2d 1276 (Wash. 1979) (manufacturing plant); 56 A.L.R.4th 769 (1987).

[8] Jones v. County of Coconino, 35 P.3d 422 (Ariz. App. 2001) (within site); Stuckman v. Kosciusko County Bd. of Zoning Appeals, 506 N.E.2d 1079 (Ind. 1987) (moving automobile salvage yard to adjacent lots not allowed); Hurley v. Town of Hollis, 729 A.2d 998 (N.H. 1999) (relocation to new building with expanded parking lot not natural expansion).

[9] Change in use approved: DiBlasi v. Zoning Bd. of Appeals, 624 A.2d 372 (Conn. 1993) (use

in the use of a nonconforming business from a restaurant to a renovated discotheque was impermissible. The court held that the "entire character" of the business had been altered and the effect of the change on the general welfare of the surrounding neighborhood was "demonstrably" adverse.

Baxter v. City of Preston[11] provides an extensive review of the case law on the change and expansion of nonconforming uses. The court adopted a flexible approach that focuses on the character of the expansion and enlargement on a case-by-case basis. It held that the nonconforming use of land for grazing livestock could not be converted to a year-round use as a feed lot.

§ 5.80   Repair and Reconstruction.

Zoning ordinances usually contain a number of provisions that are intended to achieve the gradual elimination of nonconforming uses. One common provision permits the repair, but not the alteration or construction, of a nonconforming use. Some zoning statutes contain similar provisions.[1] The courts have upheld these restrictions against constitutional attacks,[2] but most of the cases have considered how these statutory and ordinance provisions have been applied.

---

change to probation office); Ray's Stateline Market, Inc. v. Town of Pelham, 665 A.2d 1068 (N.H. 1995) (minor change in business); Institute for Evaluation & Planning, Inc. v. Board of Adjustment, 637 A.2d 235 (N.J.L. Div. 1993) (from residential to group home); Limley v. Zoning Hearing Bd., 625 A.2d 54 (Pa. 1993) (from nonprofit private club to public restaurant and bar).

Change in use not approved: Anderson v. Board of Adjustment for Zoning Appeals, 931 P.2d 517 (Colo. App. 1996) (addition of automatic car wash to filling station); Boivin v. Town of Sanford, 588 A.2d 1197 (Me. 1991) (change from auction barn to antique business); Comforti v. City of Manchester, 677 A.2d 147 (N.H. 1996) (change from movies to live entertainment); Aboud v. Wallace, 463 N.Y.S.2d 572 (App. Div. 1983) (change from doctor's office to professional lobbying office); Knowlton v. Browning-Ferris Indus. of Va., 260 S.E.2d 232 (Va. 1979) (change from small trucking business to large trash collection business).

[10] 416 A.2d 388 (N.J. 1980).

[11] 768 P.2d 1340 (Idaho 1989) (citing treatise). *See also* Township of Chartiers v. William H. Martin, Inc., 542 A.2d 985 (Pa. 1988) (reviewing Pennsylvania law); 61 A.L.R.4th 912 (1988); 61 A.L.R.4th 806 (1988); 61 A.L.R.4th 724 (1988); 56 A.L.R.4th 769 (1987); 10 A.L.R.4th 1122 (1981).

[1] Cal. Gov't Code § 65852.25; Mich. Comp. Laws § 125.126; N.J. Stat. Ann. § 40:55D-68; Or.. Rev. Stat. 215.130; Utah Code Ann. § 10-9-408. *See* City of Tempe v. Outdoor Systems, Inc., 32 P.3d 31 (Ariz. App. 2001) (statute prevails over conflicting ordinance); Gannett Outdoor Co. v. City of Mesa, 768 P.2d 191 (Ariz. App. 1989) (replacement of multi-pole with monopole billboard not allowed); Avalon Home & Land Owners Ass'n v. Borough of Avalon, 543 A.2d 950 (N.J. 1988) (ordinance allowing demolition and total reconstruction not authorized).

[2] O'Mara v. Council of City of Newark, 48 Cal. Rptr. 208 (Cal. App. 1965); Palazzola v. City of Gulfport, 52 So. 2d 611 (Miss. 1951); Williams v. Town of Spencer, 500 S.E.2d 473 (N.C. App. 1998); State ex rel. Miller v. Cain, 242 P.2d 505 (Wash. 1952).

Granger v. Board of Adjustment[3] is a typical case. A nonconforming manufacturer of burial vaults replaced the brick and frame walls of his building with concrete and steel. The court held that this work was a reasonable repair rather than a prohibited structural alteration, which it defined as an alteration that converts an existing building into a different one.[4] Similar problems arise when changes are made in nonconforming signs. Most courts hold a sign loses its nonconforming status when it is relocated,[5] and when there have is major reconstruction, such as the removal or replacement of support poles, or a change in the size or dimension of a sign.[6] Minor changes do not change nonconforming use status.[7] The zoning ordinance, or state agency regulations for the state outdoor advertising program, may deal with this problem by defining what a "substantial change" in a nonconforming use is.[8]

A municipality may require the demolition of a nonconforming building under a building or housing code if it is seriously deteriorated. The question that then arises is whether the owner of the nonconforming building may reconstruct it. In *Application of O'Neal*,[9] a city ordered the demolition of a nonconforming nursing home under a state building code. The zoning ordinance did not prohibit structural alterations of nonconforming uses. The court held the owners of the home could reconstruct a building of the same size. It pointed out the reconstruction of the home was not a voluntary act but was necessary to meet state building code requirements. The courts have held that reconstruction is not permitted when

---

[3] 44 N.W.2d 399 (Iowa 1950); *contra* Moore v. Pettus, 71 So. 2d 814 (Ala. 1954). *See* 63 A.L.R.4th 275 (1988). *See also* Mossman v. City of Columbus, 449 N.W.2d 214 (Neb. 1989) (nonconforming mobile home may not be replaced).

[4] *But see* Marris v. City of Cedarburg, 498 N.W.2d 842 (Wis. 1993) (structural repair is work that affects structural quality or contributes to longevity or permanence).

[5] City of Tuscon v. Whiteco Metrocom, Inc., 983 P.2d 759 (Ariz. App. 1999). *See also* Kasha v. Department of Transp. 782 A.2d 15 (Pa. Commw. 2001) (nonconforming status lost when on-premise sign changed to advertise off-premise business.

[6] U.S. Outdoor Advertising v. Indiana Dep't of Transp., 714 N.E.2d 1244 (Ind. App. 1999) (new sign face and support posts, changed dimensions); Meredith Outdoor Advertising, Inc. v. Iowa Dep't of Transp., 648 N.W.2d 109 (Iowa 2002) (dimensions, size, and number of signs increased); Royal Foods Systems, Inc. v. Missouri Hwy. & Transp. Comm'n, 876 S.W.2d 38 (Mo. App. 1994) (change in advertising message); Appalachian Poster Advertising, Inc. v. Zoning Bd. of Adjustment, 278 S.E.2d 321 (N.C. App. 1981) (replacement with larger pole, new lighting for larger sign); Keystone Outdoor Advertising v. Commonwealth, 687 A.2d 47 (Pa. Commw. 1996) (owner changed dimensions, added posts, and used more durable materials). *See* 80 A.L.R.3d 6230 (1977).

[7] State v. World Diversified, Inc., 576 N.E.2d 198 (Neb 1998) (change to electronic messages did not constitute an erection of a new sign); Rothrock v. Zoning Hearing Bd. 319 A.2d 432 (1974) (sign put in new concrete base, text changed, extra support pole added).

[8] *E.g.,* Meredith Outdoor Advertising, Inc. v. Iowa Dep't of Transp., 648 N.W.2d 109 (Iowa 2002).

[9] 92 S.E.2d 189 (N.C. 1956). *Accord* Money v. Zoning Hearing Bd., 755 A.2d 732 (Pa. Commw. 2000).

the zoning ordinance prohibits structural alterations, and when reconstruction is not required under a building or housing code.[10]

Many zoning ordinances limit the expenditure an owner is allowed to make on the restoration of a nonconforming building. These provisions apply to deteriorated buildings as well as buildings destroyed by fire or other calamity. The ordinance usually states that the owner of a nonconforming building may not restore it if the cost of restoration exceeds a maximum percentage of its value or its cost of reproduction. The maximum specified is usually at least fifty percent. The courts uphold fifty and sixty-five percent cost ratios and will uphold a municipality that applies them to prohibit restoration if the cost of restoration is substantial.[11] Some of the cases that upheld cost ratios noted that the land could be put to a conforming use once the nonconforming building was removed. Courts strike down a prohibition on restoration as confiscatory if the cost of restoration is not a substantial portion of the nonconforming building's value.

§ 5.81   Abandonment.

Zoning ordinances attempt to achieve the gradual elimination of nonconforming uses by terminating them when they are abandoned. Most zoning ordinances have nonconforming use abandonment provisions, and a few zoning statutes authorize them.[1] Abandonment provisions present interpretive problems that have constitutional implications. A municipality could apply an abandonment provision to prevent the resumption of a nonconforming use if its owner discontinued it. A court could then hold the termination of the nonconforming use was unconstitutional because its abandonment by its owner was involuntary.[2]

Most courts avoid this constitutional problem by holding the abandonment of a nonconforming use must be voluntary, and that discontinuance is not enough.

---

[10] Bixler v. Pierson, 188 So. 2d 681 (Fla. App. 1966); Selligman v. Von Allmen Bros., Inc., 179 S.W.2d 207 (Ky. 1944); Hanna v. Board of Adjustment, 183 A.2d 539 (Pa. 1962); State ex rel. Miller v. Cain, 242 P.2d 505 (Wash. 1952); 87 A.L.R.2d 4 (1963).

[11] Palazzola v. City of Gulfport, 52 So. 2d 611 (Miss. 1951); Adcock v. King, 520 S.W.2d 418 (Tex. Civ. App. 1975); State v. Burt, 127 N.W.2d 270 (Wis. 1964); State v. Steinke, 96 N.W.2d 356 (Wis. 1959); 57 A.L.R.3d 419 (1974). *See* Manhattan Sepulveda, Ltd. v. City of Manhattan Beach, 27 Cal. Rptr. 2d 565 (Cal. App. 1994) (value defined as fair market value at time of fire). *See* Buss v. Johnson, 624 N.W.2d 781 (Minn. App. 2001) (ordinance that allows reconstruction of nonconforming use notwithstanding percentage of destruction conflicts with statute prohibiting reconstruction if destruction exceeds more than 50% of market value).

[1] Neb. Rev. Stat. § 19-904.01 (if discontinued for 12 months); Ohio Rev. Code Ann. § 713.15 (voluntary discontinuance); Or. Rev. Stat. § 215.30(7); R.I. Gen. Laws § 45-24-39 (requires overt act); Vt. Stat. Ann. tit. 24, § 4408(b). *See* Camara v. Board of Adj., 570 A.2d 1012 (N.J. App. Div. 1990). *See also* Conn. Gen. Stat. § 8-2 (prohibits ordinance terminating nonconforming use "as a result of nonuse for a specified period of time without regard to the intent of the property owner"); 57 A.L.R.3d 279 (1974); 56 A.L.R.3d 138 (1974); 56 A.L.R.3d 14 (1974).

[2] *See* The Ansley House, Inc. v. City of Atlanta, 397 S.E.2d 419 (Ga. 1990).

An abandonment is voluntary if a municipality can prove an intent to abandon and an overt act of abandonment.[3] Some courts adopt this rule even when the zoning ordinance requires only a "discontinuance" rather than an "abandonment" of a nonconforming use. They interpret "discontinuance" to mean "abandonment" and apply the intent to abandon and overt act rule.

A municipality may attempt to avoid this rule by providing in the zoning ordinance that discontinuance is proof of abandonment whatever the intent of the owner of the nonconforming use.[4] An even more stringent provision states a nonconforming use is abandoned if it is discontinued for a stated period of time. The time period usually is very short and may range from six months to two years.

Some courts hold that ordinances of this type create a presumption the nonconforming use has been abandoned.[5] Other courts go further and interpret these ordinances to mean that proof of intent to abandon is not required when a zoning ordinance provides a nonconforming use may not resume if it is discontinued for the required time period, if one is required.[6] In some of these cases, the ordinance provided that proof of intent to abandon was not necessary.[7]

---

[3] Magnano v. Zoning Bd. of Appeals, 449 A.2d 148 (Conn. 1982); Lewis v. City of Atlantic Beach, 467 So. 2d 751 (Fla. App. 1985); Ernst v. Johnson County, 522 N.W.2d 599 (Iowa 1994) (circumstances beyond control of parties not enough); Union Quarries, Inc. v. Board of County Comm'rs, 478 P.2d 181 (Kan. 1970); Dusdal v. City of Warren, 196 N.W.2d 778 (Mich. 1972); Forsyth County v. Shelton, 329 S.E.2d 730 (N.C. App. 1985); Town of West Greenwich v. A. Cardi Realty Associates, 786 A.2d 354, (R.I. 2001); City of Myrtle Beach v. Jual P. Corp., 543 S.E.2d 538 (S.C. 2001); Boles v. City of Chattanooga, 892 S.W.2d 416 (Tenn. App. 1994); Badger v. Town of Frerrisburgh, 712 A.2d 911 (Vt. 1998); City of University Place v. McGuire, 30 P.3d 453 (Wash. 2001); 40 A.L.R.4th 1012 (1985); 57 A.L.R.3d 279 (1974); 56 A.L.R.3d 138 (1974); 56 A.L.R.3d 14 (1974). *See also* Villari v. Zoning Bd. of Adjustment, 649 A.2d 98 (N.J. App. Div. 1994) (abandonment sustainable under either intent or objective abandonment test).

[4] *See also* Toys "R" Us v. Silva, 676 N.E.2d 862 (N.Y. 1996) (New York City ordinance prohibited continuation of nonconforming use if, during a two-year period, "the active operation of substantially all the non-conforming uses . . . is discontinued").

[5] The Ansley House, Inc. v. City of Atlanta, 397 S.E.2d 419 (Ga. 1990); Miller v. City of Bainbridge Island, 43 P.3d 1250 (Wash. App. 2002); Snake River Brewing Co. v. Town of Jackson, 39 P.3d 397 (Wyo. 2002). *See* Latrobe Speedway, Inc. v. Zoning Hearing Bd., 720 A.2d 127 (Pa. 1998) (discontinuance evidence of intent to abandon and burden is then with person challenging claim of abandonment).

[6] Essex Leasing, Inc. v. Zoning Bd. of Appeals, 539 A.2d 101 (Conn. 1988).

[7] Anderson v. City of Paragould, 695 S.W.2d 851 (Ark. App. 1985);Hartley v. City of Colorado Springs, 764 P.2d 1216 (Colo. 1988) (held constitutional); Essex Leasing Co. v. Zoning Bd. of Appeals, 539 A.2d 101 (Conn. 1988) (contains extensive discussion of issue); Smith v. Board of Adj., 460 N.W.2d 854 (Iowa 1990); Ka-Hur Enters., Inc. v. Zoning Bd. of Appeals, 676 N.E.2d 838 (Mass. 1997); Fuller v. City of New Orleans, 311 So. 2d 466 (La. App. 1975); Canada's Tavern, Inc. v. Town of Glen Echo, 271 A.2d 664 (Md. 1970); Estate of Cuomo v. Rush, 708 N.Y.S.2d 695 (App. Div. 2000) (opening night club for one night out of year does not prevent abandonment); Latrobe Speedway, Inc. v. Zoning Hearing Bd., 720 A.2d 127 (Pa. 1998) (presumption of intent

This interpretation has been held constitutional.[8] Though some courts do not require an intent to abandon, they do require that the abandonment must be permanent and caused by conduct within the control of and attributable to the owner.[9] This conduct may consist of negligence, inadvertence, criminal or civil misconduct that leads to the closure of the nonconforming use.[10] Discontinuance because of problems beyond the control of the owner, such as financial problems, does not result in abandonment,[11] nor is there usually an abandonment if a nonconforming use is discontinued because it is offered for sale or lease.[12]

Most courts hold the transfer of ownership of a nonconforming use does not terminate nonconforming use status.[13] Similar problems arise when there is a nonconforming sign on a property and the business changes,[14] or when a sign is unused for a period of time.[15] A court may also hold the failure to apply for

to abandon); Marchese v. Norristown Borough Zoning Bd. of Adjustment, 277 A.2d 176 (Pa. Commw. 1971); Badger v. Town of Ferrisburgh, 712 A.2d 911 (Vt. 1998); 57 A.L.R.3d 279 (1974); *See* Toys R Us v. Silva, 676 N.E.2d 862 (N.Y. 1996) (ordinance interpreted to require substantial, not complete, abandonment).

[8] Franmor Realty Co. v. Le Boeuf, 104 N.Y.S.2d 247 (Sup. Ct. 1951), *aff'd,* 109 N.Y.S.2d 525 (App. Div. 1952); Copechal v. Township of Bristol, 668 A.2d 1222 (Pa. Commw. 1995); *See* Prudco Realty Corp. v. Palermo, 455 N.E.2d 483 (N.Y. 1983). *Cf.* Lytle Co. v. Clark, 491 F.2d 834 (10th Cir. 1974); Service Oil Co. v. Rhodus, 500 P.2d 807 (Colo. 1972). *But see* A.T. & G., Inc. v. Zoning Bd. of Review, 322 A.2d 294 (R.I. 1974).

[9] Cizek v. Concerned Citizens of Eagle River Valley, 41 P.3d 140 (Alaska 2002) (sporadic use of airport not enough); Church v. St. Charles Parish, 767 So.2d 913 (La. App. 2000) (closure of lounge); Estate of Cuomo v. Rush, 708 N.Y.S.2d 695 (App. Div. 2000) (sporadic use of nightclub not enough); Forsyth County v. Shelton, 329 S.E.2d 730 (N.C. App. 1985) (abandonment because of claimed ill health not involuntary). *But see* Caster v. West Valley City, 29 P.3d 22 (Utah App. 2001) (storage of vehicles enough).

[10] City of Glendale v. Aldabbagh, 939 P.2d 418 (Ariz. 1997); Smith v Board of Adjustment, 460 N.W.2d 854 (Iowa 1990); Sapakoff v. Town of Hague Zoning Bd. of Appeals, 621 N.Y.S.2d 215 (App. Div. 1995) (criminal forfeiture).

[11] Southern Equipment Co. v. Winstead, 342 S.E.2d 524 (N.C. App. 1986).

[12] Magnano v. Zoning Bd. of Appeals, 449 A.2d 148 (Conn. 1982); Kinnard v. Carrier, 175 So.2d 920 (La. App. 1965); Latrobe Speedway v. Zoning Hearing Bd., 720 A.2d 1197 (Pa. 1998).

[13] Budget Inn of Daphne, Inc. v. City of Daphne, 789 So.2d 154 (Ala. 2000) (citing cases); Town of Lyons v. Bashor, 867 P.2d 159 (Colo. App. 1993); O'Connor v. City of Moscow, 202 P.2d 401 (Idaho 1941); Poole v. Berkeley County Planning Comm'n, 488 S.E.2d 349 (W. Va. 1997). *Contra* City of Lakewood v. Olson, 2001 Wash. App. Lexis 2475) (unpublished),

[14] Camara v. Board of Adjustment, 570 A.2d 1012 (N.J. App. Div. 1990) (nonconforming use status lost). *Contra* Rodgers v. Zoning Bd. of Adjustment, 707 A.2d 1090 (N.J. App. Div. 1998). *See also* § 5.80.

[15] National Advertising Co. v. Department of Transp., 932 P.2d 871 (Colo. App. 1997) (nonconforming use abandoned when signs left blank or displayed obsolete advertising material for required discontinuance period); City of Myrtle Beach v. Juel P. Corp., 543 S.E.2d 538 (S.C. 2001) (no intent to abandon when sign removed because of storm).

a license for a nonconforming use does not terminate it because the power to license is distinct from the power to zone..[16]

§ 5.82 Amortization.

Amortization is the most effective zoning technique for eliminating nonconforming uses. Most amortization provisions require the removal of a nonconforming use after a stated period of time. Other amortization provisions do not contain a fixed time period but specify the factors a municipality must apply on a case-by-case basis when it amortizes a nonconforming use, such as the original investment in the property and the extent to which it has depreciated.

The constitutional theory that supports amortization is that the amortization period allows the nonconforming user a reasonable period of time to continue his nonconforming use before it is terminated. At that point, the municipality can terminate the nonconforming use without compensation under the police power. The courts do not always require an amortization period that fully amortizes the value of the nonconforming use. Some only require an amortization period that strikes a reasonable balance between the owner's property interest in the nonconforming use and the interest of the municipality in the integrity of its zoning ordinance. Courts that hold amortization unconstitutional view it as an unconstitutional termination of property rights.

The success of amortization programs and the time period required for amortization vary with the nonconforming use that is amortized. Substantial nonconforming buildings, such as factories, require substantial amortization periods, and amortization programs applied to them are not always successful. Municipalities can amortize less substantial structures, such as signs, in a relatively short two-to five-year period. A study of amortization programs indicated that they were most successful when applied to billboards and land-intensive uses, such as junkyards.[1]

Some zoning statutes address the amortization problem. A few authorize the continuation of nonconforming uses and by implication preclude their amortization.[2] Some states explicitly authorize amortization.[3] In the absence of express

---

[16] Dempsey v. Newport Bd. of Adjustments, 941 S.W.2d 483 (Ky. App. 1997); Mayor & City Council v. Dembo, Inc., 719 A.2d 1007 (Md. App. 1998); Board of Selectmen v. Monson, 247 N.E.2d 364 (Mass. 1969); City of Franklin v. Gerovac, 197 N.W.2d 772 (Wis. 1972). *Contra*: Town of Scituate v. O'Rourke, 239 A.2d 176 (R.I. 1968); *In re* Chamberlin, 360 A.2d 100, (Vt. 1976).

[1] R. Scott, The Effect of Nonconforming Land-Use Amortization (American Planning Ass'n, Planning Advisory Serv. Rep. No. 280, 1972).

[2] De Mull v. City of Lowell, 118 N.W.2d 232 (Mich. 1962). *See also* Scottsdale v. Scottsdale Assoc. Merchants, 583 P.2d 891 (Ariz. 1978).

[3] Colo. Rev. Stat. § 30-28-120; 65 Ill. Comp. Stat. 5/11-13-1; Okla. Stat. § 11-44-107.1; Utah Code Ann. § 10-9-408(2)(b).

statutory authority, some courts hold the statutory authority to zone does not confer the power to amortize nonconforming uses.[4] A statutory delegation of general welfare powers or a constitutional home rule provision may authorize the use of amortization.[5] A statute may prohibit amortization.[6]

§ 5.83   Highway Beautification Act.

Political pressure prevented the use of amortization in the state outdoor advertising control programs authorized by the federal Highway Beautification Act. The act requires the payment of compensation by states and municipalities for the removal of nonconforming signs along federal interstate and primary highways. The compensation requirement prohibits amortization by municipalities. A state could lose ten percent of its federal highway funds if a municipality attempted to remove a nonconforming sign located on one of these highways under an amortization provision.[1] A number of states have adopted legislation that prohibits municipalities from amortizing nonconforming signs on highways covered by the federal act.[2]

§ 5.84   Constitutional.

Early U.S. Supreme Court decisions upholding retroactive single-use zoning suggested that eliminating nonconforming uses retroactively in comprehensive zoning also was constitutional. Early decisions in Louisiana also upheld short amortization periods in comprehensive zoning ordinances.[1] Despite these precedents, the courts adopted the rule that a zoning ordinance cannot apply retroactively to eliminate a nonconforming use.[2] Owners of nonconforming uses argued that amortization is unconstitutional under this rule because a nonconforming use is a vested property right that a municipality can eliminate only by paying compensation.

---

[4] State v. Bates, 305 N.W.2d 426 (Iowa 1981).

[5] Service Oil Co. v. Rhodus, 500 P.2d 807 (Colo. 1972) (home rule); Naegele Outdoor Adv. Co. v. Village of Minnetonka, 162 N.W.2d 206 (Minn. 1968) (general welfare clause).

[6] Minn. Stat. Ann. § 394.21.

[1] 23 U.S.C. § 131(g). *But see* National Adv. Co. v. City of Ashland, 678 F.2d 106 (9th Cir. 1982) (federal act does not preempt amortization by municipalities).

[2] City of Ft. Collins v. Root Outdoor Adv., Inc., 788 P.2d 149 (Colo. 1990); Battagliani v. Town of Red River, 669 P.2d 1082 (N.M. 1983). *See also* N.Y. Gen. Mun. Law § 74-c (compensation required for removal of nonconforming signs in industrial and commercial districts; amortization schedule imposed for nonconforming signs outside these districts).

[1] State ex rel. Dema Realty Co. v. McDonald, 121 So. 613 (La.), *appeal dismissed,* 280 U.S. 656 (1929).

[2] § 5.78.

An early California case rejected this argument in a comprehensive opinion that fully discussed the constitutional issues. *City of Los Angeles v. Gage*[3] upheld a five-year amortization provision the city applied to remove a plumbing supply business conducted in a residential dwelling. The court held that the gradual elimination of nonconforming uses was "a logical and reasonable method" for securing the integrity of residential areas. It pointed out that every zoning ordinance "effects some impairment of property rights . . . [either prospectively or retroactively] because it affects property already owned by individuals at the time of its enactment." The court believed there was no distinction between amortization and other methods for eliminating nonconforming uses, such as abandonment provisions or provisions limiting the right of restoration:

> The distinction between an ordinance restricting future uses and one requiring the termination of present uses within a reasonable period of time is merely one of degree, and constitutionality depends on the relative importance to be given to the public gain and the private loss. . . . Use of a reasonable amortization scheme provides an equitable means of reconciliation of the conflicting interests in satisfaction of due process requirements.[4]

The court also noted that the loss suffered by the nonconforming user was spread over a number of years, and that the nonconforming use enjoyed a monopoly position during the amortization period. The Maryland court applied similar reasoning to uphold a five-year amortization period for a nonconforming sign in a case decided soon after *Gage*.[5]

A majority of courts upheld the constitutionality of zoning ordinances that amortized nonconforming uses prior to the Supreme Court's 1987 taking trilogy.[6]

---

[3] 274 P.2d 34 (Cal. App. 1954). *See also* Tahoe Reg'l Planning Agency v. King, 285 Cal. Rptr. 335 (Cal. App. 1991) (*First English* and *Nollan* do not require change in rule that amortization is constitutional). *See* 8 A.L.R.5th 391 (1992).

[4] *Id.* at 44.

[5] Grant v. Mayor & City Council, 129 A.2d 363 (Md. 1957).

[6] Art Neon Co. v. City & County of Denver, 488 F.2d 118 (10th Cir. 1973); Donrey Communications Co. v. City of Fayetteville, 660 S.W.2d 900 (Ark. 1983); Metromedia, Inc. v. City of San Diego, 610 P.2d 407 (Cal. 1980), *rev'd on other grounds,* 453 U.S. 490 (1981); Mayor & Council v. Rollings Outdoor Adv., Inc., 475 A.2d 355 (Del. 1984); Lamar Adv. Assocs. of E. Fla. v. City of Daytona Beach, 450 So. 2d 1145 (Fla. App. 1984); Village of Glenview v. Velasquez, 463 N.E.2d 873 (Ill. App. 1984) (balancing test); Spurgeon v. Board of Comm'rs, 317 P.2d 798 (Kan. 1957); Naegele Outdoor Adv. Co. v. Village of Minnetonka, 162 N.W.2d 206 (Minn. 1968); University City v. Dively Auto Body Co., 417 S.W.2d 107 (Mo. 1967) (signs); Temple Baptist Church, Inc. v. City of Albuquerque, 646 P.2d 565 (N.M. 1982); Modjeska Sign Studios, Inc. v. Berle, 373 N.E.2d 255 (N.Y. 1977), *appeal dismissed,* 439 U.S. 809 (1978); Goodman Toyota, Inc. v. City of Raleigh, 306 S.E.2d 192 (N.C. App. 1983); Sullivan v. Zoning Bd. of Adjustment, 478 A.2d 912 (Pa. Commw. 1984); Collins v. City of Spartanburg, 314 S.E.2d 322 (S.C. 1984); Rives v. City of Clarksville, 618 S.W.2d 502 (Tenn. App. 1981); Lubbock Poster Co. v. City of Lubbock, 569 S.W.2d 935 (Tex. Civ. App. 1978); City of Seattle v. Martin, 342 P.2d 602 (Wash. 1959); 22 A.L.R.3d 1134 (1968).

These courts did not always accept the reasoning in *Gage* that the distinction between prospective zoning and amortization is a matter of degree.

Post-trilogy cases have rejected claims that amortization was a taking under either the per se taking or traditional balancing tests.[7] The courts have also upheld other techniques for removing nonconforming uses, such as a requirement that a nonconforming sign must be removed when a lot is developed.[8] Decisions in the Fourth Circuit since the taking trilogy made it more difficult to uphold the constitutionality of amortization provisions in sign ordinances. *Georgia Outdoor Adv. Co. v. City of Waynesville (II)*[9] attempts to reconcile these decisions. The court held that an amortization provision does not automatically validate or invalidate a sign ordinance but is only one fact to consider in deciding the taking issue. Summary judgment upholding the constitutionality of an amortization provision is proper only in those few cases where there are no facts to try. The court remanded for a new trial.

§ 5.85 Unconstitutional.

Some courts have held amortization unconstitutional if not used to eliminate nuisances. The Indiana Supreme Court held that amortization could not eliminate a nonconforming junkyard that was "continuing and lawful" when a municipality adopted a zoning ordinance.[1] It noted there was no claim that the junkyard was a nuisance. New Hampshire held the amortization of signs unconstitutional if based on aesthetic reasons, but indicated an ordinance that amortized nonconforming signs that are nuisances would be constitutional.[2] The Missouri Supreme Court held that amortization was unconstitutional as applied to open storage uses but held later that the amortization of billboards was constitutional.[3]

---

[7] Outdoor Graphics, Inc. v. City of Burlington, 103 F.2d 690 (8th Cir. 1996) (no per se taking because plaintiff purchased nonconforming billboard); Lone v. Montgomery County, 584 A.2d 142 (Md. App. 1991) (multifamily dwellings).

[8] Outdoor Systems, Inc. v. City of Mesa, 997 F.2d 604 (9th Cir. 1993) (held not a per se taking under *Lucas*); Circle K Corp. v. Mesa, 803 P.2d 457 (Ariz. App. 1990); Adams Outdoor Advertising v. City of East Lansing, 614 N.W.2d 634 (Mich. 2000); Red Roof Inns, Inc. v. City of Ridgeland, 797 So.2d 898 (Miss. 2001).

[9] 900 F.2d 783 (4th Cir. 1990).

[1] Ailes v. Decatur County Area Planning Comm'n, 448 N.E.2d 1057 (Ind. 1983). *But see* Board of Zoning Appeals v. Leinz, 702 N.E.2d 1026 (Ind. 1998) (overruling *Ailes* insofar as it applied the federal constitution, and reserving judgment under the Indiana constitution).

[2] Loundsbury v. City of Keene, 453 A.2d 1278 (N.H. 1982). *See also* Stoner McCray Sys. v. City of Des Moines, 78 N.W.2d 783 (Iowa 1956) (indicating it would uphold amortization if period of amortization reasonable and nonconforming use endangered health, safety and welfare); Northern Ohio Sign Contractors Ass'n v. City of Lakewood, 513 N.E.2d 324 (Ohio 1987) (amortization constitutional if applied to remove public nuisance).

[3] Hoffman v. Kinealy, 389 S.W.2d 745 (Mo. 1965). *See* § 5.80,

The Georgia[4] and Pennsylvania[5] courts held amortization unconstitutional. The Pennsylvania case held that its state constitution mandates the payment of compensation to owners of nonconforming uses that are required to be discontinued. Amortization is not a substitute, and any requirement that a nonconforming use be terminated without compensation is per se unconstitutional.

§ 5.86   Reasonableness of Amortization Period.

Even though the constitutionality of amortization is well established in principle, constitutional problems can arise when a court is asked to determine whether amortization is constitutional as applied to remove a nonconforming use. Some amortization provisions specify amortization factors the municipality must consider when it determines the length of an amortization period. *Metromedia, Inc. v. City of San Diego*[1] upheld an amortization provision that required amortization in one to four years depending on the "adjusted market value" of a nonconforming sign. The ordinance defined this term as the sign's original cost less ten percent of the original cost for each year the sign was standing prior to the effective date of the ordinance.

Many amortization provisions do not specify amortization factors but require the removal of a nonconforming use after a designated period of years. The courts have upheld the removal of nonconforming signs under amortization periods ranging from three to seven years.[2] When a municipality removes a nonconforming use after the amortization period has expired, a court must decide whether the amortization period is constitutional as applied. In *Metromedia,* for example, the court held that the constitutionality of amortization as applied depends in part on facts peculiar to the nonconforming structure:

> Such facts include the cost of the billboard, its depreciated value, remaining useful life, the length and remaining term of the lease under which it is

---

[4] Lamar Adv. of South Ga., Inc. v. City of Albany, 389 S.E.2d 216 (Ga. 1990).

[5] Pennsylvania Nw. Distribs., Inc. v. Zoning Hearing Bd., 584 A.2d 1372 (Pa. 1990).

[1] 610 P.2d 407 (Cal. 1980), *rev'd on other grounds,* 453 U.S. 490 (1981); County of Cook v. Renaissance Arcade & Bookstore, 522 N.E.2d 73 (Ill.) (adult business; one year upheld), *appeal dismissed,* 488 U.S. 882 (1988); Lone v. Montgomery Cty., 584 A.2d 142 (Md. App. 1991) (upholding ten years for multifamily use of dwellings). *See also* Art Neon Co. v. City & County of Denver, 488 F.2d 118 (10th Cir. 1973) (invalidating ordinance basing length of amortization on replacement cost); La Mesa v. Tweed & Gambrell Planning Mill, 304 P.2d 803 (Cal. App. 1957) (implying amortization must be based on physical life of nonconforming building); Murmur Corp. v. Board of Adjustment, 718 S.W.2d 790 (Tex. App. 1986) (ordinance required amortization based on investment cost of structures).

[2] Major Media of the Southeast, Inc. v. City of Raleigh, 621 F. Supp. 1446 (E.D.N.C. 1985) (five and one-half years), *aff'd,* 792 F.2d 1269 (4th Cir. 1986); Hatfield v. City of Fayetteville, 647 S.W.2d 450 (1983) (seven years); County of Cumberland v. Eastern Fed. Corp., 269 S.E.2d 672 (N.C. App. 1980) (three years).

maintained, and the harm to the public if the structure remains standing beyond the prescribed amortization period.[3]

The highest New York court approved similar amortization factors. In *Modjeska Sign Studios, Inc. v. Berle,*[4] the court held that the critical amortization factors were the length of the amortization period in relation to the investment in the nonconforming use and whether the public gain from amortization outweighed the loss suffered by the owner of the nonconforming use. The court held that the owner of the nonconforming use did not have to recover his entire investment but added that he must not suffer a substantial loss. The court held that consideration of the following factors would determine whether the loss was substantial: the owner's initial capital investment, the extent to which that investment had been realized and its life expectancy, the existence or nonexistence of lease obligations, and whether there was a contingency clause allowing the termination of a lease. Other courts approved amortization factors similar to those approved by the California and New York courts.[5]

Some courts have also considered the extent to which a nonconforming use has been depreciated for tax purposes.[6] A more controversial issue is whether municipalities must consider the remaining useful economic or expected life of the nonconforming use in determining the amortization period. Some courts have rejected this factor.[7]

---

[3] 610 P.2d at 428. *See* note 281, *supra. See also* National Adv. Co. v. County of Monterey, 464 P.2d 33 (Cal. 1970) (upholding amortization of nonconforming signs which were fully amortized under federal income tax law).

[4] 373 N.E.2d 255 (N.Y. 1977), *appeal dismissed,* 439 U.S. 809 (1978); *See also* Suffolk Outdoor Adv. Co. v. Town of Southampton, 449 N.Y.S.2d 766 (App. Div. 1982), *aff'd,* 455 N.E.2d 1245 (N.Y. 1983).

[5] Fisher Buick, Inc. v. City of Fayetteville, 689 S.W.2d 350 (Ark. 1985); Lamar Adv. Assocs. of E. Fla. v. City of Daytona Beach, 450 So. 2d 1145 (Fla. App. 1984); AVR, Inc. v. City of St. Louis Park, 585 N.W.2d 411 (Minn. App. 1998) (upholding two-year amortization period for ready-mix concrete plant; determination of individual amortization period not quasi-judicial); Board of Adjustment v. Winkles, 832 S.W.2d 803 (Tex. App. 1992); Lubbock Poster Co. v. City of Lubbock, 569 S.W.2d 935 (Tex. Civ. App. 1978). *Compare* Naegele Outdoor Adv. Co. v. Village of Minnetonka, 162 N.W.2d 206 (Minn. 1968) (need not consider right to renew lease) *with* Art Neon Co. v. City & County of Denver, 488 F.2d 118 (10th Cir. 1973) (contra).

[6] Art Neon Co. v. City & County of Denver, 488 F.2d 118, (10th Cir. 1973); National Advertising Co. v. County of Monterey, 464 P.2d 33 (Cal. 1970); Village of Skokie v. Walton on Dempster, Inc., 456 N.E.2d 293 (Ill. App. 1983); Philanz Oldsmobile, Inc. v. Keating, 381 N.Y.S.2d 916 (App. Div. 1976).

[7] AVR, Inc. v. City of St. Louis Park, 585 N.W.2d 411 (Minn. App. 1998) (substantial return on investment and depreciation for tax purposes justified amortization period). *Compare* City of La Mesa v. Tweed & Gambrell Planing Mill, 304 P.2d 803 (Cal. App. 1956). *See also* Murmur Corp. v. Board of Adjustment, 718 S.W.2d 790 (Tex. App. 1986) (rejecting market value and replacement cost standards).

REFERENCES

Books and Monographs

R. Babcock & W. Larsen, Special Districts: The Ultimate in Neighborhood Zoning (1990).

Bergthold, Effective Zoning of Sexually Oriented Businesses in Protecting Free Speech and Expression: The First Amendment and Land Use Law (American Bar Ass'n, D. Mandelker & R. Rubin eds. 2001).

J. Butler & J. Getzels, Home Occupation Ordinances, American Planning Ass'n, Planning Advisory Serv. Rep. No. 391 (1985).

A. Cibulskis & M. Ritzdorf, Zoning for Child Care, American Planning Ass'n, Planning Advisory Serv. Rep. No. 422 (1992).

R. Cook, Zoning for Downtown Urban Design (1980).

M. Gellen, Accessory Apartments in Single-Family Housing (1985).

Gerard, Adult Uses, The First Amendment and the Supreme Court in Trends in Land Use Law from A to Z Ch. 4 (P. Salkin ed. 2001).

J. Gerard, Local Regulation of Adult Businesses (2001).

J. Getzels & M. Jaffe, Zoning Bonuses in Central Cities, American Planning Ass'n, Planning Advisory Serv. Rep. No. 410 (1988).

P. Hare, Accessory Apartments, American Planning Ass'n, Planning Advisory Serv. Rep. No. 365 (1981).

M. Jaffe, Regulating Videogames, American Planning Ass'n, Planning Advisory Serv. Rep. No. 370 (1982).

M. Jaffe & T. Smith, Siting Group Homes for Developmentally Disabled Persons, American Planning Ass'n, Planning Advisory Serv. Rep. No. 397 (1986).

E. Kelly & C. Cooper, "Everything you always wanted to know about regulating sex business xxx", American Planning Ass'n, Planning Advisory Serv. Rep. No. 495/496 (2000).

L. Kendig, New Standards for Nonresidential Uses, American Planning Ass'n, Planning Advisory Serv. Rep. No. 405 (1987).

D. Mandelker & W. Ewald, Street Graphics and the Law (1988).

W. Sanders, Manufactured Housing: Regulation, Design Innovations, with Development Options, American Planning Ass'n, Planning Advisory Serv. Rep. No. 478 (1998).

W. Sanders, Regulating Manufactured Housing, American Planning Ass'n, Planning Advisory Serv. Rep. No. 398 (1986).

W. Sanders, J. Getzels, E. Mosena & J. Butler, Affordable Single-Family Housing, American Planning Ass'n, Planning Advisory Serv. Rep. No. 385 (1984).

J. Schwab, Industrial Performance Standards for a New Century, American Planning Ass'n, Planning Advisory Serv. Rep. No. 444 (1993).

T. Smith, Flexible Parking Requirements, American Planning Ass'n, Planning Advisory Serv. Rep. No. 377 (1983).

C. Weaver & R. Babcock, City Zoning: The Once and Future Frontier (1980).

C. Wunder, Regulating Home-Based Businesses in the Twenty-First Century, American Planning Ass'n, Planning Advisory Serv. Rep. No. 499 (2000).

Articles

Baers, Zoning Code Revisions to Permit Mixed Use Development, 7 Zoning & Plan. L. Rep. 81 (1984).

Bergthold, How to Avoid the Top Ten Pitfalls of Adult Business Regulation, Land Use L. & Zoning Dig., Vol. 54, No.5, at 3; No. 6, at 3 (2002)..

Brownstein, Illicit Legislative Motive in the Municipal Land Use Regulation Process, 57 U. Cin. L. Rev. 1 (1988).

Cobb, Amortizing Nonconforming Uses, Land Use L. & Zoning Dig., Vol. 37, No. 1, at 3 (1985).

Collins, Methods of Determining Amortization Periods for Non-conforming Uses, 3 Wash. U. J.L. & Pol'y 215 (2000).

Connor, How the Federal Fair Housing Act Protects Persons with Handicaps in Group Homes, Land Use L. & Zoning Dig., Vol. 50, No. 1, at 3 (1998).

Davis & Gaus, Protecting Group Homes for the Non-Handicapped: Zoning in the Post-Edmonds Era, 6 U. Kan. L. Rev. 777–817 (1998).

Dennison, Changing or Expanding Nonconforming Uses, Zoning News, Mar. 1997, at 1.

Dennison, Home Occupations as Accessory Uses, Zoning News, Jan. 1996, at 1.

Duerksen, Modern Industrial Performance Standards: Key Implementation and Legal Issues, 18 Zoning & Plan. L. Rep. 33 (1995).

Edmonds & Merriam, Zoning and the Elderly: Issues for the 21st Century, Land Use L. & Zoning Dig., Vol. 47, No. 3, at 3 (1995).

Elliott, The Fair Housing Act's 'Reasonable Accommodation' Requirement, Land Use L. & Zoning Dig., Vol. 52, No. 4, at 3 (2000).

Fahringer, Zoning Out Free Expression: An Analysis of New York City's Adult Zoning Resolution, 46 Buff. L. Rev. 403 (1998).

Fox, Smut, Smokes and Spirits: The First Amendment Re-Examined, 32 Urb. Law. 449 (2000).

Fredericks, Adult Use Zoning: New York City's Journey on the Well-Traveled Road from Suppression to Regulation of Sexually Oriented Expression, 46 Buff. L. Rev. 433 (1998).

Garnett, On Castles and Commerce: Zoning Laws and the Home-Based Business Dilemma, 42 Wm. & Mary L. Rev. 1191 (2001).

Gerard, New Developments in the Effective Preclusion of Adult Businesses by Zoning Ordinances, 17 Zoning & Plan. L. Rep. 26 (1994).

Gerencser, Removal of Billboards: Some Alternatives for Local Governments, 31 Stetson L. Rev. 899 (1992).

Jaffe, Performance Zoning: A Reassessment, Land Use L. & Zoning Dig., Vol. 45, No. 9, at 3 (1993).

Jaffe, Redesigning Industrial Performance Standards, Land Use L. & Zoning Dig., Vol. 47, No. 11, at 3 (1995).

Jaffe, Quantum Zoning, Land Use L. & Zoning Dig., Vol. 43, No. 10, at 3 (1991).

Jaffe & Netter, Zoning for Child Day Care Facilities, Land Use L. & Zoning Dig., Vol. 37, No. 2, at 5 (1985).

Kayden, Statutory Preference for Religious Land Use: Divining What is Religious and What is Reasonable, Land Use L. & Zoning Dig. vol. 53, no. 9, at 3 (2001).

Kayden, Using and Misusing Zoning Law to Design Cities: An Empirical Study of New York City's Privately Owned Public Spaces, Land Use L. & Zoning Dig., Vol. 53, No. 2, at 3, id. No. 3 at 3 (2001).

Kayden, Zoning for Dollars: New Rules For an Old Game? Comments on the Municipal Art Society and Nollan Cases, 39 Wash. U.J. Urb. & Contemp. L. 3 (1991).

Kelly, Local Regulation of Lawful Sex Businesses, Land Use L. & Zoning Dig., Vol. 51, No. 9, at 3 (1999).

Kolosky & Merriam, Group Homes for Recovering Alcoholics and Substance Abusers, 24 Zoning & Plan. L. Rep. 33 (2001).

Leitel & Somppi, Perspectives on Group Homes, 4 J. Plan. Literature 357 (1989).

Marwedel, Opting for Performance: An Alternative to Conventional Zoning for Land Use Regulation, 13 J. Plan. Lit. 220 (1998).

Meck, Religious Land Use and Institutionalized Persons Act, Zoning News, Jan. 2001, at 1.

Mullin & Kotval, The Industrial Zoning Crisis, Zoning News, Nov. 2000, at 1.

O'Neil, Religious Freedom and Nondiscrimination: State RFRA Laws Versus Civil Rights, 32 U.C. Davis L. Rev. 785 (1999).

Osborne, Zoning Private and Parochial Schools — Could Local Governments Restrict Socrates and Aquinas, 24 Urb. Law. 305 (1992).

Peterson & McCarthy, Amortization of Legal Land Use Nonconformities as Regulatory Takings: An Uncertain Future, 35 Wash. U.J. Urb. & Contemp. L. 37 (1989).

Pollak, Zoning Matters in a Kinder, Gentler Nation: Balancing Needs, Rights and Political Realities for Shared Residences for the Elderly, 10 St. Louis U. Pub. L. Rev. 501 (1991).

Power & Bowyer, Diversification of Housing Supply to Accommodate Smaller Households: Can Single and Multiple Households Coexist in Suburban Settings?, 23 Zoning & Plan. L. Rep. 81 (2000).

Reynolds, The Reasonableness of Amortization Periods for Nonconforming Uses — Balancing the Private Interest and the Public Welfare, 34 Wash. U.J. Urb. & Contemp. L. 99 (1988).

Roberts, The Regulation of Home Occupations Under Zoning Ordinances: Some Constitutional Considerations, 56 Temp. L. Rev. 49 (1983).

Saphire, Equal Protection, Rational Basis Review, and the Impact of Cleburne Living Center, Inc., 88 Ky. L.J. 591 (1999-2000).

Saxer, Local Autonomy or Regionalism?: Sharing the Benefits and Burdens of Suburban Commercial Development, 30 Ind. L. Rev. 659 (1997).

Saxer, When Religion Becomes a Nuisance: Balancing Land Use and Religious Freedom When Activities of Religious Institutions Bring Outsiders into the Neighborhood, 84 Ky. L.J. 507 (1995-1996).

Schonfeld, "Reasonable Accommodation"' Under the Federal Fair Housing Amendments Act, 25 Fordham Urb. L.J. 413 (1998).

Sellman, Equal Treatment of Housing: A Proposed Model State Code for Manufactured Housing, 20 Urb. Law. 73 (1988).

Storzer & Picarello, The Religious Land Use and Institutionalized Persons Act of 2000: A Constitutional Response to Unconstitutional Zoning Practices, 9 Geo. Mason L. Rev.929 (2001).

Strauss & Giese, Elimination of Nonconformities: The Case of Voluntary Discontinuance, 25 Urb. Law. 159 (1993).

Sullivan, Antitrust Regulation of Land Use: Federalism's Triumph Over Competition, The Last Fifty Years, 3 Wash. U.J.L. & Social Policy 473 (2000).

Sullivan, The Religious Land Use and Institutionalized Persons Act of 2000: An Update, 25 Zoning & Plan. L. Rep., 25 (2002).

The Supreme Court, 1985 Term, 100 Harv. L. Rev. 1, 195 (1986) (*Renton* decision).

Weaver & Duerksen, Central Business District Planning and the Control of Outlying Shopping Centers, 14 Urb. L. Ann. 57 (1977).

Weinstein, Courts Take Close Look at Adult Use Ergs, Land Use L. & Zoning Dig., Vol. 46, No. 5, at 3 (1994).

Weinstein, The *Renton* Decision: A New Standard for Adult Business Regulation, 32 Wash. U.J. Urb. & Contemp. L. 91 (1987).

White, State and Federal Planning Legislation and Manufactured Housing: New Opportunities for Affordable, Single-Family Shelter, 28 Urb. Law. 163 (1996).

Ziegler, Shaping Megalopolis: The Transformation of Euclidean Zoning by Special Zoning Districts and Site-Specific Development Review Techniques, 15 Zoning & Plan. L. Rep. 57 (1992).

Student Work

Note, Adult Uses and the First Amendment: The Stringfellow Decision and Its Impact on Municipal Control of Adult Businesses, 15 Toro L. Rev. 241 (1998).

Note, Behind the Smokescreen: Exclusionary Zoning of Mobile Homes, 25 Wash. U.J. Urb. & Contemp. L. 235 (1983).

Note, *Belle Terre* and Single-Family Home Ordinances: Judicial Perceptions of Local Government and the Presumption of Validity, 74 N.Y.U. L. Rev. 447 (1999).

Note, Broadway's Newest Hit: Incentive Zoning for Preserving Legitimate Theatres, 3 Cardozo Arts & Ent. L.J. 377 (1984).

Note, The Devil is in the Details: Neutral, Generally Applicable Laws and Exceptions from *Smith*, 75 N.Y.U.L. Rev. 1045 (2000).

Note, The Fair Housing Act Amendments of 1988: New Zoning Rules for Group Homes for the Handicapped, 37 St. Louis U. L.J. 1033 (1993).

Note, Fair Housing Laws and Fear of Adult Family Homes, 18 Seattle U.L. Rev. 425 (1995).

Note, Judicial Acquiescence in Large Lot Zoning: Is It Time to Rethink the Trend? 16 Colum. J. Envtl. L. 183 (1991).

Note, Municipal Antitrust Immunity After *City of Columbia v. Omni Outdoor Advertising, Inc.,* 67 Wash. L. Rev. 479 (1992).

Note, Not In My Backyard: The Disabled's Quest For Rights in Local Zoning Disputes Under the Fair Housing, the Rehabilitation, and the Americans with Disabilities Acts, 33 Val. U. L. Rev. 581 (1999).

Note, Put a Rein on That Unruly Horse: Balancing the Freedom of Commercial Speech and the Protection of Children in Restricting Cigarette Billboard Advertising, 52 Wash. U. J. Urb. & Contemp. L. 307 (1997).

Note, The Qualitative vs. Quantitative Approach to Nonconforming Uses Under Section 52-61 of the New York City Zoning Resolution: The Toys case, 62 Alb. L. Rev. 323 (1998) (abandonment of nonconforming use).

Note, Religion, Zoning, and the Free Exercise Clause: The Impact of *Employment Division v. Smith,* 7 B.Y.U. J. Pub. L. 395 (1993).

Note, Rescuing Manufactured Housing from the Perils of Municipal Zoning Laws, 37 Wash. U.J. Urb. & Contemp. L. 189 (1991).

Note, The Tension Between Local Zoning and the Development of Elderly Housing: Analyzing the Use of the Fair Housing Act and the Americans with Disabilities Act to Override Zoning Decisions, 33 Suffolk U. L. Rev. 317 (2000).

Note, Zoning Away the Evils of Alcohol, 61 S. Cal. L. Rev. 1373 (1988).

Comment, Challenging Restrictive Family Definitions in Zoning Ordinances: *City of Santa Barbara v. Adamson,* 23 Wash. U.J. Urb. & Contemp. L. 235 (1983).

Comment, Looking Back: The Full-Time Baseline in Regulatory Takings Analysis, 24 B.C. Envtl. Aff. L. Rev. 199 (1996) (discusses amortization).

Comment, A Matter of Arithmetic: Using Supply and Demand to Determine the Constitutionality of Adult Entertainment Ordinances, 51 Emory L.J. 319 (2002).

Comment, Overlay Zoning, Performance Standards, and Environmental Protection After *Nollan,* 16 B.C. Envtl. Aff. L. Rev. 615 (1989).

Comment, Playing the Numbers: Local Government Authority to Apply Use Quotas in Neighborhood Commercial Districts, 14 Ecology L.Q. 325 (1987).

Comment, Zoning Adult Entertainment: A Reassessment of *Renton,* 79 Calif. L. Rev. 119 (1991).

Case Comment, *City of Edmonds v. Oxford House, Inc.:* A Comment on the Continuing Validity of Single-Family Zoning Restrictions, 71 Notre Dame L. Rev. 829 (1996).

Recent Development, Exclusionary Zoning of Abortion Facilities, 32 Wash. U.J. Urb. & Contemp. L. 361 (1987).

Recent Development, The Manoa Valley Special District Ordinance: Commu-
nity-Based Planning in the Post-Lucas Era, 19 U. Hawaii L. Rev. 449
(1997).

Chapter 6

THE ZONING PROCESS

Synopsis

§ 6.01   An Introductory Note.

A. DELEGATION OF POWER.

§ 6.02   The Delegation Problem.
§ 6.03   Zoning Standards.
§ 6.04   Delegation to Neighbors.
§ 6.05   Void for Vagueness.

B. MORATORIA AND INTERIM ZONING.

§ 6.06   Purposes and Problems.
§ 6.07   Statutory Authority and Limitations.
§ 6.08   Constitutionality.
§ 6.09   Revision of Zoning Ordinance or Comprehensive Plan: The *Lake Tahoe* Case.
§ 6.10   Inadequate Public Facilities.
§ 6.11   As Applied.

C. ESTOPPEL AND VESTED RIGHTS.

§ 6.12   The Problem.
§ 6.13   The Theory.
§ 6.14   Governmental Act Requirement.
§ 6.15   Building Permit Required.
§ 6.16   Building Permit Not Required.
§ 6.17   Illegal Building Permit.
§ 6.18   Good Faith.
§ 6.19   Detrimental Reliance.
§ 6.20   Substantial Reliance Test.
§ 6.21   What Reliance Is Required.
§ 6.22   Statutory and Ordinance Protection.
§ 6.23   Development Agreements.

D. ZONING MAP AMENDMENTS.

§ 6.24   The Zoning Problem.
§ 6.25   Refusals to Rezone.
§ 6.26   The Quasi-Judicial View.
§ 6.27   "Spot" Zoning.
§ 6.28   Definitions.
§ 6.29   The Standard Tests.
§ 6.30   The Public Need and Public Purpose Tests.
§ 6.31   The Change-Mistake Rule.
§ 6.32   Consistency with the Comprehensive Plan.
§ 6.33   Zoning.
§ 6.34   Spot Planning.
§ 6.35   Effect on Adjacent Communities.

(5th Ed.—02/03)

§ 6.36   Downzoning.
§ 6.37   The Standard Tests.
§ 6.38   Change-Mistake Rule.

E. VARIANCES, SPECIAL EXCEPTIONS, AND CONDITIONAL USES.

§ 6.39   Role and Function.
§ 6.40   Variances.
§ 6.41   Role and Function.
§ 6.42   Use and Area Variances.
§ 6.43   Use Variances Prohibited.
§ 6.44   Unnecessary Hardship.
§ 6.45   No Reasonable Return.
§ 6.46   Unique to the Owner.
§ 6.47   Impact on the Neighborhood.
§ 6.48   Availability of Area Variances.
§ 6.49   Consistency with the Plan.
§ 6.50   Self-Created Hardship.
§ 6.51   Conditions.
§ 6.52   Findings and Judicial Review.
§ 6.53   Special Exceptions and Conditional Uses.
§ 6.54   Role and Function.
§ 6.55   Delegation to Legislative Body or Plan Commission.
§ 6.56   Judicial Review of Decisions on Exceptions and Conditional Uses.
§ 6.57   Free Speech-Protected and Religious Uses.
§ 6.58   Consistency with the Plan.
§ 6.59   Conditions.

F. FLEXIBLE ZONING.

§ 6.60   Role and Function.
§ 6.61   Floating Zones.
§ 6.62   Contract and Conditional Zoning.
§ 6.63   Bilateral.
§ 6.64   Unilateral.
§ 6.65   Proper Purpose View.
§ 6.66   Site Plan Review.

G. DECISION-MAKING PROCEDURES.

§ 6.67   The Procedures Problem.
§ 6.68   Legislative vs. Quasi-Judicial.
§ 6.69   Entitlement.
§ 6.70   Procedures Required.
§ 6.71   Impartial Decision-Maker.
§ 6.72   Bias and Conflict of Interest.
§ 6.73   Bias.
§ 6.74   Conflicts of Interest.
§ 6.75   Neighborhood Opposition.
§ 6.76   Open Meeting Laws.

H. INITIATIVE AND REFERENDUM.

§ 6.77   The Zoning Problem.
§ 6.78   Federal Constitutional Issues.

§ 6.79 Availability in Zoning.
§ 6.80 Referendum.
§ 6.81 Initiative.

§ 6.01 An Introductory Note.

The Standard Zoning Act clearly contemplated a limited use of an administrative decision making process to review allowable land uses under the zoning ordinance. The Act authorized municipalities to adopt a zoning text and map designating the land uses permitted in zoning districts "as of right." The only administrative relief it authorized was the authority of the board of adjustment to grant relief from zoning restrictions through variances and special exceptions. Although the Act authorized the local governing body to amend the zoning text and map, it is doubtful that the drafters intended the zoning map amendment to play a major role in the day-to-day administration of the zoning ordinance.

Zoning does not conform to this model. Development usually occurs only when it is authorized through one of the zoning change techniques that are available in the zoning process. Governing bodies frequently adopt zoning map amendments to allow development on single lots. Many boards of adjustment grant zoning variances frequently. Zoning ordinances often contain long lists of special exceptions the board can authorize in the zoning districts where they are allowed. Municipalities have also adopted flexible zoning techniques to manage zoning change the Standard Zoning Act did not authorize. They include floating zones and contract zoning.

This chapter reviews the standard and newer zoning techniques that are commonly used in the zoning process, including interim zoning and moratoria. The chapter also considers related doctrines, such as delegation of power, estoppel and vested rights that determine how the zoning process functions. A final section discusses procedural issues in the land use regulation. Planned unit development controls, a zoning process in which municipalities approve large-scale residential developments, are discussed in Chapter 9.

A. DELEGATION OF POWER.

§ 6.02 The Delegation Problem.

Although the U.S. Supreme Court has not held a statute or ordinance unconstitutional as a delegation of legislative power since the 1930s, the delegation doctrine is alive and well in the states. In the zoning cases, most state courts continue to resolve delegation problems by determining whether the standards provided in the zoning ordinance are adequate. A few courts have adopted an alternative doctrine that upholds a delegation of power if the statute or ordinance provides adequate procedural safeguards. They hold a zoning ordinance has not improperly delegated legislative power if it imposes fact-finding or hearing requirements, or if administrative, legislative, or judicial review of a zoning decision is available.[1]

A municipality may attempt to avoid delegation of power problems by delegating the authority to grant special exceptions or other administrative permits to the legislative body. This alternative is available because the doctrine of separation of powers does not apply at the local level. A local legislative body may exercise administrative functions.

Some courts hold a legislative body acts legislatively even when it exercises administrative functions and do not require standards for the exercise of these functions.[2] The absence of standards does not mean administrative determinations by the legislative body are unreviewable. Courts can always review arbitrary and unreasonable decisions and impose standards similar to those they consider appropriate for inclusion in zoning ordinances.[3] The contrary view holds the character of the function the legislative body exercises is determinative and requires standards for the exercise of administrative functions.[4] Some courts also hold the legislative body acts quasi-judicially when it considers amendments to the zoning map for individual parcels of land.[5]

A number of communities have experimented with an administrative innovation under which discretionary zoning decisions, such as amendments, variances, and special exceptions, are heard by an appointed hearing examiner. His decision is usually appealable to the legislative body or zoning board. One case held that the use of a hearing examiner was not a delegation of power because the governing body made the "ultimate decision."[6] Statutes in a few states expressly authorize the use of hearing examiners.[7]

---

[1] Economy Whsle. Co. v. Rodgers, 340 S.W.2d 583 (Ark. 1960); Ward v. Scott, 93 A.2d 385 (N.J. 1952); Katzin v. McShain, 89 A.2d 519 (Pa. 1952).

[2] Kotrich v. County of DuPage, 166 N.E.2d 601 (Ill.(1960); Green Point Sav. Bank v. Board of Zoning Appeals, 24 N.E.2d 319 (N.Y. 1939); Olp v. Town of Brighton, 19 N.Y.S.2d 546 (Sup. Ct. 1940), aff'd, 29 N.Y.S.2d 956 (App. Div. 1941).

[3] Larkin Co. v. Schwab, 151 N.E. 637 (N.Y. 1926).

[4] Wheeler v. Gregg, 203 P.2d 37 (Cal. App. 1949); Osius v. City of St. Clair Shores, 75 N.W.2d 25 (Mich. 1956); State v. Guffey, 306 S.W.2d 552 (Mo. 1957); In re Clements' Appeal, 207 N.E.2d 573 (Ohio App. 1965).

[5] § 6.26.

[6] West Slope Community Council v. City of Tacoma, 569 P.2d 1183 (Wash. App. 1977).

[7] Or. Rev. Stat. § 227.165; Wash. Rev. Code Ann. § 36.70.970.

§ 6.03 Zoning Standards.

The Standard Zoning Act authorized the board of adjustment to grant zoning variances and special exceptions, and state zoning legislation usually includes this grant of authority. State zoning acts follow the Standard Act by authorizing the board to grant variances for "unnecessary hardship," and the courts have held that this statutory standard is adequate.[1]

The special exception, now usually called a special or conditional use, is a use of land authorized in designated zoning districts when approved by the board of adjustment. State zoning acts usually follow the Standard Act by authorizing the board to grant special exceptions "in harmony with . . . [the] general purpose and intent" of the zoning ordinance. The Standard Act contemplated the adoption of standards for special exceptions in the zoning ordinance, and courts find an unconstitutional delegation of power if the ordinance does not provide them.[2]

Special exception uses are presumptively compatible with the zoning district in which they are authorized, but the board must review them so it can determine whether they are appropriate in the area in which they plan to locate. Zoning ordinances commonly implement this requirement by authorizing special exceptions when they are compatible with adjacent uses. A negative form of this standard authorizes a denial if the special exception would be a nuisance to its neighbors. A municipality can elaborate a compatibility standard by requiring consideration of the intensity of the use, its impact on traffic congestion and public facilities, and similar factors. Courts usually uphold these standards because they implement the land use compatibility principles on which zoning is based.[3]

---

[1] Devaney v. Board of Zoning Appeals, 45 A.2d 828 (Conn. 1946); Clarke v. Morgan, 327 So. 2d 769 (Fla. 1976); Gardner v. Harahan, 504 So. 2d 1107 (La. App. 1987); Application of Arlington Village Dev. Corp., 124 N.Y.S.2d 172 (Sup. Ct. 1953), aff'd, 128 N.Y.S.2d 596 (App. Div. 1954); Consolidated Mgt., Inc. v. City of Cleveland, 452 N.E.2d 1287 (Ohio 1983); City of Madison v. Clarke, 288 N.W.2d 312 (S.D. 1980); 58 A.L.R.2d 1083 (1958).

[2] City of St. Petersburg v. Schweitzer, 297 So. 2d 74 (Fla. App. 1974); State v. Waddill, 318 S.W.2d 281 (Mo. 1958); Rogue Valley Ass'n of Realtors v. City of Ashland, 970 P.2d 685 (Or. 1999) (ordinance lacked clear and objective standards as required by statute); Dooling's Windy Hill v. Zoning Bd. of Adjustment, 89 A.2d 505 (Pa. 1952).

[3] C & M Sand & Gravel v. Board of County Comm'rs, 673 P.2d 1013 (Colo. App. 1983); Alachua County v. Eagle's Nest Farms, Inc., 473 So. 2d 257 (Fla. App. 1985); Cyclone Sand & Gravel Co. v. Zoning Bd. of Adjustment, 351 N.W.2d 778 (Iowa 1984); Gorham v. Town of Cape Elizabeth, 625 A.2d 898 (Me. 1993) ("adverse effect" criterion); Certain-Teed Prods. Corp. v. Paris Twp., 88 N.W.2d 705 (Mich. 1958); Ours Properties v. Ley, 96 S.E.2d 754 (Va. 1957). See also Suddeth v. Forsyth Cty., 373 S.E.2d 746 (Ga. 1988) (ordinance required balancing of costs and benefits as basis for approving airports as special use); Button Gwinnett Landfill, Inc. v. Gwinnett Cty., 353 S.E.2d 328 (Ga. 1987) (delegation of conditional use authority to board of adjustment); Kopietz v. Zoning Bd. of Appeals, 535 N.W.2d 910 (Mich. App. 1995) (upholding standard authorizing change in nonconforming use if "more appropriate to the district"); Save the Pine Bush,

Municipalities sometimes adopt generalized standards that authorize special exceptions when they are in the "public interest," when they serve the "general welfare," or when they are consistent with the "purpose or intent" of the zoning ordinance. Municipalities defend vague standards of this kind by arguing that more specific standards are difficult to draft and that zoning agencies are entitled to exercise discretion when they administer the zoning ordinance. The decisions on the constitutionality of these general standards are divided.[4] Cases that invalidate these standards emphasize the unlimited discretion they confer on zoning agencies. Cases that uphold these standards emphasize the need for flexibility in zoning administration and the difficulty of drafting more precise criteria.

§ 6.04   Delegation to Neighbors.

The Standard Zoning Act required a three-fourths vote by the legislative body to adopt a zoning amendment if it was protested by twenty percent of the owners of the affected or adjacent area.[1] Many state zoning acts and local zoning ordinances contain similar requirements. Most courts hold that this requirement is not an unconstitutional delegation of power. They note that the local legislative body retains the authority to approve or disapprove the amendment, and that amendments require closer scrutiny when landowners who are most affected indicate their objection.[2]

A related delegation to neighbors provision, which is less frequently found in zoning statutes and ordinances, is more troublesome. This provision requires

---

Inc. v. City of Albany, 512 N.E.2d 526 (N.Y. 1987) (site plan review standards).*See also* Hardin County v. Jost, 897 S.W.2d 592 (Ky. App. 1995) (holding invalid ordinance that required development approval under point system); Kosalka v. Town of Georgetown, 752 A.2d 183 (Me. 2000) (invalidating "natural beauty" standard); Chandler v. Town of Pittsfield, 496 A.2d 1058 (Me. 1985) (ordinance authorizing board to "consider" or "evaluate" factors held invalid).

[4] Valid: Burrell v. Lake County Plan Comm'n, 624 N.E.2d 526 (Ind. App. 1993); Schultz v. Board of Adjustment, 139 N.W.2d 448 (Iowa 1966); Mobil Oil Corp. v. City of Clawson, 193 N.W.2d 346 (Mich. App. 1971); Ward v. Scott, 93 A.2d 385 (N.J. 1952); Peachtree Dev. Co. v. Paul, 423 N.E.2d 1087 (Ohio 1981); Town of Richmond v. Murdock, 235 N.W.2d 497 (Wis. 1975). Invalid: Redwood City Company of Jehovah's Witnesses, Inc. v. City of Menlo Park, 335 P.2d 195 (Cal. App. 1959); Clark v. Board of Appeals, 204 N.E.2d 434 (Mass. 1965); Fitanides v. Crowley, 467 A.2d 168 (Me. 1983); Osius v. City of St. Clair Shores, 75 N.W.2d 25 (Mich. 1956); Flynn v. Zoning Bd. of Review, 73 A.2d 808 (R.I. 1950).

[1] Standard Act, § 5.

[2] Hope v. City of Gainesville, 355 So. 2d 1172 (Fla. 1978); Bredberg v. City of Wheaton, 182 N.E.2d 742 (Ill. 1962); Northwood Props. Co. v. Perkins, 39 N.W.2d 25 (Mich. 1949). *See also* City of Springfield v. Goff, 918 S.W.2d 786 (Mo. 1996) (home rule city may not modify state statute); Levin v. Township of Parsippany-Troy Hills, 411 A.2d 704 (N.J.1980); Board of Adjustment v. Patel, 887 S.W.2d 90 (Tex. App. 1994) (citizen right to initiate termination of nonconforming use held constitutional); Strucker v. Summit County, 870 P.2d 283 (Utah App. 1994).*See also* Schwarz v. City of Glendale, 950 P.2d 167 (Ariz. App. 1997) (buffer area created by property owner does not prevent statutory trigger);

the consent of neighbors for a zoning amendment, variance, or special exception. The cases on the constitutionality of zoning consent provisions are mixed. A trio of early U.S. Supreme Court cases appeared to hold that consent provisions are valid if they waive a previously applicable zoning restriction, but are invalid if they impose a new zoning restriction.[3]

The distinction between waiver and imposition is not clear, but the state courts that have considered consent provisions have generally followed the U.S. Supreme Court holdings.[4] The state cases sometimes turn on the offensiveness of the use that is subject to the provision. A leading case, *Concordia College Inst. v. Miller*,[5] held that a consent provision is invalid when a landowner proposes an inoffensive use such as an educational building.[6]

§ 6.05   Void for Vagueness.

Legislation that contains vague or ambiguous language violates due process if a court holds it is void for vagueness.[1] The Supreme Court has adopted tests to determine when a law affecting only economic interests is facially challenged as void for vagueness.[2] The law must be vague in all its applications. A plaintiff cannot complain that a law is vague as applied to others, but only as it is applied to it.

Courts hold a land use law void for vagueness when persons of common intelligence must guess at what it requires or forbids,[3] and when a law lacks

---

[3] Washington ex rel. Seattle Title Trust Co. v. Roberge, 278 U.S. 116 (1928); Thomas Cusack Co. v. City of Chicago, 242 U.S. 526 (1917); Eubank v. City of Richmond, 226 U.S. 137 (1912). *See* Schulz v. Milne, 849 F. Supp. 708 (N.D. Cal. 1994) (claim of de facto delegation of power to neighbors stated a cause of action).

[4] Howard Twp. Bd. of Trustees v. Waldo, 425 N.W.2d 180 (Mich. App. 1988) (approving consent requirement but disapproving ordinance because consent of 100 percent of neighbors required); Shannon v. City of Forsyth, 666 P.2d 750 (Mont. 1982); Cary v. City of Rapid City, 559 N.W.2d 891 (S.D. 1997) (invalidating statute giving veto power to landowners); Davis v. Blount County Beer Bd., 621 S.W.2d 149 (Tenn. 1981); Williams v. Whitten, 451 S.W.2d 535 (Tex. App. 1970); County of Fairfax v. Fleet Indus. Park Ltd. Pt'ship, 410 S.E.2d 669 (Va. 1991) (invalidating statute giving veto power to landowners); Town of Westford v. Kilburn, 300 A.2d 523 (Vt. 1973); 21 A.L.R.2d 551 (1952). *See also* Rispo Inv. Co. v. City of Seven Hills, 629 N.E.2d 3 (Ohio App. 1993) (relying on right-to-vote cases to uphold city charters requiring approval of zoning change by voters in ward in which property located).

[5] 93 N.E.2d 632 (N.Y. 1950).

[6] *See also* Valkanet v. City of Chicago, 148 N.E.2d 767 (Ill. 1958) (home for aged); O'Brien v. City of Saint Paul, 173 N.W.2d 462 (Minn. 1969) (apartments); 21 A.L.R.2d 551 (1952).

[1] *See also* § 5.65 (adult use ordinances).

[2] Village of Hoffman Estates v. Flipside, Hoffman Estates, 455 U.S. 489 (1982).

[3] Arizona v. Zack, 674 P.2d 329 (Ariz. App. 1983); Trice v. City of Pine Bluff, 649 S.W.2d 179 (Ark. 1983); Price v. City of Lakewood, 818 P.2d 763 (Colo. 1991); Gouge v. City of Snellville, 287 S.E.2d 539 (Ga. 1982); City of Council Bluffs v. Cain, 342 N.W.2d 810 (Iowa 1983).

standards clear enough to prevent arbitrary or discriminatory enforcement,[4] but are generally deferential when reviewing land use laws challenged as vague.[5] They will attempt curative constructions by relying on common meanings or dictionary definitions.[6] If standards are claimed to be imprecise, courts may try to derive precision from their narrow applicability,[7] from related[8] or in pari materia provisions,[9] or from factors enumerated to guide authorities charged with its enforcement.[10] Courts have upheld ordinances regulating signs,[11] home occupations,[12] accessory[13] and nonconforming uses;[14] defining historical significance in historical preservation districts;[15] and establishing front-yard set-back requirements.[16]

[4] City of Mobile v. Weinacker, 720 So.2d 953 (Ala. Civ. App. 1998) (design guidelines for signs); Fisher v. City of Berkeley, 693 P.2d 261 (Cal. 1976); Miller v. Maloney Concrete Co., 491 A.2d 1218 (Md. App. 1985); Commonwealth v. Jaffe, 494 N.E.2d 1342 (Mass. 1986); West Bloomfield Charter Twp. v. Karchon, 530 N.W.2d 99 (Mich. App. 1995); Alexander v. Town of Hampstead, 525 A.2d 276 (N.H. 1987); State v. Cameron, 498 A.2d 1217 (N.J. 1985); People v. New York Trap Rock Corp., 442 N.E.2d 1222 (N.Y. 1982).

[5] Franchise Developers, Inc. v. City of Cincinnati, 505 N.E.2d 966 (Ohio 1987 (zoning ordinance puts property owner on notice that property is subject to regulation).

[6] Rolling Pines Ltd. Partnership v. City of Little Rock, 40 S.W.3d 828 (Ark. App. 2001) (compatibility standard); Sellon v. Manitou Springs, 745 P.2d 229 (Colo. 1987) (definition of plat); Life Concepts, Inc. v. Harden, 562 So. 2d 726 (Fla. App. 1990) (compatibility standard); Town of Freeport v. Brickyard Cove Assocs., 594 A.2d 556 (Me. 1991) ("timber harvesting"); Burke v. Denison, 630 N.Y.S.2d 421 (App. Div. 1995) (definition of "take-out" restaurant).

[7] Lentine v. Town of St. George, 599 A.2d 76 (Me. 1991).

[8] Town of Warren v. Hazardous Waste Facility Site Safety Council, 466 N.E.2d 102 (Mass. 1984); Matter of Save the Pine Bush, Inc. v. City of Albany, 512 N.E.2d 526 (N.Y. 1987).

[9] Miami Dolphins, Ltd. v. Metropolitan Dade Cty., 394 So. 2d 981 (Fla. 1981).

[10] Ackman v. Board of Adjustment, 596 N.W.2d 96 (Iowa 1999); Charter Township of Canton v. Department of Soc. Servs., 340 N.W.2d 306 (Mich. App. 1983) (group home licensing statute).

[11] Asselin v. Town of Conway, 628 A.2d 247 (N.H. 1993) (sign illumination ordinance); State v. Schad, 733 A.2d 1159 (N.J. 1999); J.B. Advertising Co. v. Sign Bd. of Appeals, 883 S.W.2d 443 (Tex. App. 1994) (term "premises" in sign code).

[12] City of Los Altos v. Barnes, 5 Cal. Rptr.2d 77 (Cal. App. 1992).

[13] State v. Trachtman, 947 P.2d 905 (Ariz. App. 1997); City of Parma Heights v. Jaros, 591 N.E.2d 726 (Ohio App. 1990).

[14] Smith v. Town of Normal, 605 N.E.2d 727 (Ill. App. 1992); City of Las Vegas v. 1017 S. Main Corp., 885 P.2d 552 (Nev. 1994) (ordinance prohibiting alteration of nonconforming use).

[15] South of Second Assocs. v. Georgetown, 580 P.2d 807 (Colo. 1978) ("historical and architectural significance"); Faulkner v. Town of Chestertown, 428 A.2d 879 (Md. 1981) (visible changes to structure); In re Vermont Nat'l Bank, 597 A.2d 317 (Vt. 1991) (local "heritage").

[16] Weiner v. City of Los Angeles, 441 P.2d 293 (Cal. 1968); Adams v. Brian, 212 So. 2d 128 (La. App. 1968). *See also* Echevarrieta v. City of Rancho Palos Verdes, 103 Cal. Rptr. 2d 165 (Cal. App. 2001) (authorizing reasonable conditions on view restoration permit); Briggs v. City of Rolling Hills Estates, 47 Cal. Rptr. 2d 29 (Cal. App. 1995) (privacy factor in neighborhood compatibility ordinance); Mann v. Mack, 202 Cal. Rptr. 296 (Cal. App. 1984) (noise ordinance);

Courts engage in heightened scrutiny when a challenged law burdens a substantial amount of constitutionally protected activity [17] or imposes a prohibitory or stigmatizing civil penalty. [18] They most commonly apply heightened scrutiny when the violation of a challenged land use law is a misdemeanor. [19] For example, although courts usually uphold zoning ordinances that permit accessory uses "incidental to the use of a premises," [20] they have struck down such provisions when their violation constitutes a misdemeanor. [21]

A land use regulation may be found unconstitutionally vague even if it does not impose civil penalties. Examples are an ordinance so ambiguous that property owners subject to it could reasonably interpret it three different ways, [22] and design review ordinances. [23]

The vagueness challenge is not available when a party applies for a variance or special exception and fails to secure it. [24] Having made use of the provisions of the zoning ordinance, a party can no longer claim not to know what it prohibits or requires.

B. MORATORIA AND INTERIM ZONING.

§ 6.06 Purposes and Problems.

Moratoria and interim development control ordinances are an important part of the zoning process. Local governments often adopt these ordinances when

Barbarino Realty & Dev. Co. v. Planning & Zoning Comm'n, 610 A.2d 1205 (Conn. 1992) (adequate facilities criteria in subdivision control ordinance);Wolff v. Mooresville Planning Comm'n, 754 N.E.2d 589 (Ind. App. 2001) (criteria for subdivision review); Farley v. Zoning Hearing Bd., 636 A.2d 1232 (Pa. Commw. 1994) (definition of "student" in occupancy ordinance).

[17] State v. Jones, 865 P.2d 138 (Ariz. App. 1993); State v. Cameron, 498 A.2d 1217 (N.J. 1985).

[18] Village of Hoffman Estates v. Flipside, Hoffman Estates, 455 U.S. 489 (1982). *See also* ABN 51st Street Partners v. City of New York, 724 F. Supp. 1142 (S.D.N.Y. 1989).

[19] *But see* West Chester Township Zoning v. Fromm, 762 N.E.2d 400 (Ohio App. 2001) (zoning ordinance not criminal).

[20] Goode v. City of Dallas, 554 S.W.2d 753 (Tex. Ct. App. 1977).

[21] Arizona v. Owens, 562 P.2d 738 (Ariz. App. 1977), following Wiley v. County of Hanover, 163 S.E.2d 160 (Va. 1968). *Accord* Miller v. Maloney Concrete Co., 491 A.2d 1218 (Md. App. 1985) (public nuisance prohibition); City of Independence v. Richards, 666 S.W.2d 1 (Mo. App. 1983) ("unsightly" or "annoying" accumulation of rubbish); People v. New York Trap Rock Corp., 442 N.E.2d 1222 (N.Y. 1982) (noise ordinance).

[22] Lionshead Woods Corp. v. Kaplan Bros., 595 A.2d 568 (N.J.L. Div. 1991).

[23] Waterfront Estates Dev., Inc., v. City of Palos Hills, 597 N.E.2d 641 (Ill. App. 1992); Anderson v. City of Issaquah, 851 P.2d 754 (Wash. App. 1993). *See also* Potomac Greens Assocs. Pt'ship v. City Council of Alexandria, 761 F. Supp. 416 (E.D. Va. 1991) (traffic management plans); U-Haul Co. v. City of St. Louis, 855 S.W.2d 424 (Mo. App. 1993) (historic preservation).

[24] Spero v. Zoning Bd. of Appeals, 586 A.2d 590 (Conn. 1991); Bonnell, Inc. v. Board of Adj., 791 P.2d 107 (Okla. Ct. App. 1989).

they undertake a comprehensive revision of their zoning ordinance or comprehensive plan. An interim ordinance can allow only new development that is consistent with existing zoning regulations, it can prohibit all development or certain types of intensive development, such as apartments or nonresidential uses, or it can prohibit any development unless it is approved by a local zoning agency.

A municipality may also impose a development moratorium so it can correct inadequate public facilities. The moratorium usually imposes a total or partial ban on new development until adequate facilities are provided. This kind of moratorium is common in growth management programs. Communities also impose moratoria to prevent development in transportation corridors where transportation facilities are planned for construction.[1] Statutory authority for adopting moratoria and the takings issue are two important problems in their use.

§ 6.07 Statutory Authority and Limitations.

The recent cases have usually implied the authority to adopt interim zoning if the statute does not authorize it.[1] In most of the decisions that did not find an implied power to adopt interim zoning the municipality did not comply with statutory procedural requirements, such as the notice and hearing requirement for the adoption of zoning ordinances.[2] Courts in some of the strong home rule states allow municipalities to adopt interim zoning ordinances under their home rule powers.[3] A growing number of statutes authorize moratoria.[4] These statutes

---

[1] See also § 10.12.

[1] Arnold Bernhard & Co. v. Planning & Zoning Comm'n, 479 A.2d 801 (Conn. 1984) (reviewing cases); Collura v. Town of Arlington, 329 N.E.2d 733 (Mass. 1975); Almquist v. Town of Marshan, 245 N.W.2d 819 (Minn. 1976); Brazos Land, Inc. v. Board of County Comm'rs, 848 P.2d 1095 (N.M. App. 1993); State ex rel. SCA Chem. Waste Serv. v. Konigsberg, 636 S.W.2d 430 (Tenn. 1982). Contra, Naylor v. Township of Hellam, 773 A.2d 770 (Pa. 2001). Compare Board of Supvrs. v. Horne, 215 S.E.2d 453 (Va. 1975) (subdivision statute did not authorize moratoria), with Matthews v. Board of Zoning Appeals, 237 S.E.2d 128 (Va. 1977) (zoning statute; contra).

[2] Deighton v. City Council, 902 P.2d 426 (Colo. App. 1995); City of Sanibel v. Buntrock, 409 So. 2d 1072 (Fla. App. 1981); Kline v. City of Harrisburg, 68 A.2d 182 (Pa. 1949); 30 A.L.R.2d 1196 (1970). But see Schrader v. Guilford Planning & Zoning Comm'n, 418 A.2d 93 (Conn. Super. 1980).

[3] Fletcher v. Porter, 21 Cal. Rptr. 452 (Cal. App. 1962). See § 4.28.

[4] Ariz. Rev. Stat. § 9-463.06 (to prevent shortage of essential public facilities in urban and urbanizable areas); Cal. Evid. Code § 669.5; Cal. Gov't Code § 65858; Minn. Stat. Ann. § 394.34 (one year for revision in comprehensive plan or ordinance); N.J. Stat. Ann. § 40:55D-90(b) (for six months when clear and imminent danger to health); S.D. Codified Laws § 11-2-10.1 (authorizes injunction against temporary zoning ordinance that does not serve public health, safety and general welfare); Wash. Rev. Code Ann. § 36.70.790 (no time limit); 36.70.795 (time limit). See Bank of the Orient v. Town of Tiburon, 269 Cal. Rptr. 690 (Cal. App. 1990) (statute applies to moratorium adopted by initiative); Minster v. Town of Gray, 584 A.2d 646 (Me. 1990) (authority to adopt under statute allowing moratoria); Davis v. City of Bandon, 805 P.2d 709 (Or. App. 1991)

may limit the purposes for which a moratorium may be adopted and place time limits on how long a moratorium can last.[5]

§ 6.08 Constitutionality.

§ 6.09 Revision of Zoning Ordinance or Comprehensive Plan: The *Lake Tahoe* Case.

The courts have upheld interim zoning ordinances and development moratoria when they were necessary to provide time to comprehensively revise a local plan or zoning ordinance.[1] In most of these cases the municipality adopted interim land use controls for the interim period, but some cases upheld a partial prohibition on new development while the municipality was revising a zoning ordinance.[2] The courts viewed the interim control as a necessary measure to protect the municipality from development that might be inconsistent with the revised plan or ordinance.

Moratoria raised potential takings problems after the Supreme Court's *Lucas* and *First English* cases[3] because an absolute prohibition on development for a

(approving moratorium adopted under statutory authority). *See* Building Industry Legal Defense Foundation v. Superior Court, 85 Cal. Rptr.2d 828 (Cal. App. 1999) (moratorium did not comply with statute); Home Builders Ass'n of Maine, Inc. v. Town of Eliot, 750 A.2d 566 (Me. 2000) (ordinance placing quota on annual building permits held not to be a moratorium under the statute); Toll Bros., Inc. v. West Windsor Township, 712 A.2d 266 (N.J. App. 1998) (timed growth plan held moratorium under statute to extent it deferred right to develop). For model legislation see American Planning Association, Growing Smart Legislative Guidebook: Model Statutes for Planning and Management of Change § 8-604 (S. Meck ed. 2002).

[5] *See* Or. Rev. Stat. §§ 197.505–197.540 (limited to facility shortage and must accommodate housing needs); R.I. Gen. Laws § 45-22.2-13 (may limit building permits for period of time in case of emergency).

[1] Metro Realty v. County of El Dorado, 35 Cal. Rptr. 480 (Cal. App. 1963); TPW, Inc. v. City of New Hope, 388 N.W.2d 390 (Minn. App. 1986); Compana v. Clark Twp., 197 A.2d 711 (N.J. 1964); Meadowland Regional Dev. Agency v. Hackensack Meadowlands Dev. Comm'n, 293 A.2d 192 (N.J. App. Div. 1972); Walworth Co. v. City of Elkhorn, 133 N.W.2d 257 (Wis. 1965).

[2] Schafer v. City of New Orleans, 743 F.2d 1086 (5th Cir. 1984) (rejecting substantive due process and equal protection objections to moratorium on building permits for fast food restaurants in city neighborhood); Arnold Bernhard & Co. v. Planning & Zoning Comm'n, 479 A.2d 801 (Conn. 1984) (nine-month moratorium on business development in business district); Fischer v. Kellenberger, 392 N.E.2d 733 (Ill. App. 1979) (apartments); Collura v. Town of Arlington, 329 N.E.2d 733 (Mass. 1975) (same); Naylor v. Township of Hellam, 717 A.2d 629 (Pa. Commw. 1998) (ordinance reasonable in time and did not discriminate because it only prohibited residential development)..

[3] §§ 2.09, 8.25. *But see* Williams v. City of Central, 907 P.2d 701 (Colo. App. 1995), following Woodbury Place Partners, Inc. v. City of Woodbury, 492 N.W.2d 258 (Minn. App. 1992) (moratorium for corridor preservation held not a taking; development prohibited only for limited period of time).

limited period time appeared to be an absolute per se taking. However, the Court, in *Tahoe-Sierra Preservation Council v. Tahoe Regional Planning Agency*,[4] held that the time during which a moratorium is in effect is not the unit of property denominator to which the takings clause applies, so that the restriction on development during the moratorium period at issue in that case was not a per se taking.[5]

The Court went on to consider whether "fairness and justice," which are benchmarks for the application of the takings clause to land use regulation, required it to consider seven other theories that would have held the moratorium a taking. It rejected four of these theories, noting the district court found the moratorium was adopted for a public purpose and was adopted in good faith. The Court also rejected any categorical rule that would hold moratoria unconstitutional, noting that moratoria were widely used as a planning strategy, and that any such rule would cause agencies to rush through the planning process or abandon it altogether. Ill-conceived growth could then occur, as developers would have an incentive to develop quickly before comprehensive plans were adopted. In addition, moratoria have a reciprocity of advantage because they protect the interests of all developers against immediate development.

Though *Lake Tahoe* rejected a per se takings rule that would hold moratoria unconstitutional, the Court left open the possibility that a moratorium could be unconstitutional as applied in a particular case. It noted, for example, that any moratorium over one year could possibly be viewed with "special skepticism." It refused to apply a per se one-year rule based on the length of the moratorium, however, because the district court had held the 32-month moratorium at issue in the case to be reasonable. The Court concluded that the duration of a moratorium was an "important" factor to consider.

§ 6.10   Inadequate Public Facilities.

Prior to *Lake Tahoe*, the courts approved development moratoria that municipalities adopted when sewer and other public facilities were inadequate because they prohibited development that could cause environmental damage.[1] *Cappture Realty Corp. v. Board of Adjustment*[2] is a leading case. To provide time to construct flood control facilities, an ordinance prohibited all development in a flood-prone area unless allowed by a special exception permit. An industrial

---

[4] 535 U.S. 302 (2002).

[5] The Court quoted Agins v. City of Tiburon, 447 U.S. 266 (1980) (mere fluctuations in value during government decision making, absent extraordinary delay, are not a taking).

[1] Tisei v. Town of Ogunquit, 491 A.2d 564 (Me. 1985); SCA Chem. Waste Serv., Inc. v. Konigsberg, 636 S.W.2d 430 (Tenn. 1982) (hazardous waste); Sun Ridge Dev., Inc. v. City of Cheyenne, 787 P.2d 583 (Wyo. 1990) (drainage).

[2] 313 A.2d 624 (N.J.L. Div. 1973), *aff'd,* 336 A.2d 30 (N.J. App. Div. 1975).

developer who was denied a permit challenged the interim ordinance as unconstitutional. The court held that the ordinance was reasonable in time and that a taking had not occurred.[3]

The courts upheld sewer service moratoria that were in effect for a reasonable period of time to provide an opportunity to remedy inadequate facilities.[4] Environmental moratoria can raise exclusionary zoning problems. In *Associated Home Bldrs. of Greater Eastbay, Inc. v. City of Livermore*,[5] city voters adopted a ban on additional residential building permits unless adequate educational, sewage, and water supply facilities were available. The court held the rational relationship rather than the strict scrutiny standard of judicial review applied. It remanded the case to determine whether the moratorium unreasonably excluded new growth and development.[6]

§ 6.11 As Applied.

The courts have considered whether moratoria served legitimate purposes when landowners brought as-applied attacks.[1] They held moratoria arbitrary when they did not find a necessity for them.[2] Some of these cases relied on the equities of the landowner's case to hold that the interim control did not apply.[3] Courts were especially inclined to invalidate an interim control as applied if the

---

[3] *Compare* Westwood Forest Estates, Inc. v. Village of South Nyack, 244 N.E.2d 700 (N.Y. 1969) (invalidating ban on apartments when sewage problem not related to apartment development), *with* Belle Harbor Realty Corp. v. Kerr, 323 N.E.2d 697 (N.Y. 1974) (upholding revocation of building permit because sewers at project site inadequate).

[4] Kaplan v. Clear Lake City Water Auth., 794 F.2d 1059 (5th Cir. 1986); Ocean Acres, Ltd. Partnership v. Dare County Bd. of Health, 707 F.2d 103 (4th Cir. 1983); Unity Ventures v. County of Lake, 631 F. Supp. 181 (N.D. Ill. 1986), *aff'd on other grounds,* 841 F.2d 770 (7th Cir 1988); Smoke Rise, Inc. v. Washington Sub. San. Comm'n, 400 F. Supp. 1369 (D. Md. 1975); Kopetzke v. County of San Mateo Bd. of Supvrs., 396 F. Supp. 1004 (N.D. Cal. 1975); Ungar v. State, 492 A.2d 1336 (Md. 1985). *But see* Lockary v. Kayfetz, 917 F.2d 1150 (9th Cir. 1990) (remanding taking and other constitutional claims). *Cf.* Wincamp Partnership v. Anne Arundel County, 458 F. Supp. 1009 (D. Md. 1978).

[5] 557 P.2d 473 (Cal. 1976).

[6] *See also* Smoke Rise, Inc. v. Washington Sub. San. Comm'n, 400 F. Supp. 1369 (D. Md. 1975) (rejecting exclusionary objection to the development moratorium).

[1] Home Depot U.S.A., Inc. v. Village of Rockville Centre, 743 N.Y.S.2d 541 (App. Div. 2002) (moratorium held to be legitimate response to uncertainty created by challenge to application of zoning ordinance amendments to pending building permit applications).

[2] Q.C. Constr. Co. v. Gallo, 549 F. Supp. 1331 (D.R.I. 1986), *aff'd mem.* 836 F.2d 1340 (1st Cir. 1987); Pritchett v. Nathan Rodgers Constr. & Realty Corp., 379 So. 2d 545 (Ala. 1979) (case-by-case ban arbitrary); DeKalb County v. Townsend Assocs., 252 S.E.2d 498 (Ga. 1979) (no necessity for moratorium).

[3] *Compare* Almquist v. Town of Marshan, 245 N.W.2d 819 (Minn. 1976) (valid) *with* Alexander v. City of Minneapolis, 125 N.W.2d 583 (Minn. 1963) (invalid). *See also* Medical Servs., Inc. v. City of Savage, 487 N.W.2d 263 (Minn. App. 1992) (held invalid after 1987 trilogy).

municipality downzoned the property to prohibit development it permitted before it adopted an interim control ordinance.[4]

Most of the pre-*Lucas* cases that rejected takings objections to moratoria held the moratorium was adopted to prevent a harm, or that the landowner was not denied all reasonable use of her land.[5] Though the harm prevention defense is no longer available in a per se takings case, a holding that some use remains on land subject to a moratorium prevents the application of the *Lucas* per se takings rule. Cases holding a taking had not occurred after the 1987 takings trilogy held either that the moratorium had not denied all reasonable use of the land, or relied on Supreme Court statements that reasonable delays in government decision making are not a taking.[6]

C. ESTOPPEL AND VESTED RIGHTS.

§ 6.12 The Problem.

Changes in zoning regulations often affect development in progress when the zoning changes are made. A developer may argue that she is entitled to proceed with her development because she has acquired a vested right in the prior zoning or because the municipality is estopped from making the zoning change. Vested rights and estoppel problems have become more serious because residential and other development projects are larger and require more time to complete.

The law of vested rights and estoppel must strike a fine balance between the competing interests of the developer and the municipality. A developer needs some protection from changes in land use requirements that prevent him from completing his project or that make completion more expensive. Municipalities need the freedom to revise their land use requirements to meet new land use problems or to implement new land use policies.[1] The courts have developed an amorphous body of vested rights and estoppel law that determines when developers are protected from changes in land use regulations. A few states and

[4] Ogo Assocs. v. City of Torrance, 112 Cal. Rptr. 761 (Cal. App. 1974).

[5] Jackson Ct. Condominiums, Inc. v. City of New Orleans, 874 F.2d 1070 (5th Cir. 1989); Smoke Rise, Inc. v. Washington Sub. San. Comm'n, 400 F. Supp. 1369 (1975); Ungar v. State, 492 A.2d 1336 (Md. 1985); Capture Realty Corp. v. Board of Adjustment, 313 A.2d 624 (N.J.L. Div. 1973), *aff'd*, 336 A.2d 30 (N.J. App. Div. 1975). *See also* Golden v. Planning Bd. of Town of Ramapo, 285 N.E.2d 291 (N.Y.1972).

[6] Moore v. City of Costa Mesa, 886 F.2d 260 (9th Cir. 1989) (delay in development approval did not deny all use of land); Zilber v. Town of Moraga, 692 F. Supp. 1195 (N.D. Cal. 1988) (rejecting facial taking claim because development not totally prohibited); S.E.W. Friel v. Triangle Oil Co., 543 A.2d 863 (Md. App. 1988); Guinanne v. City & County of San Francisco, 241 Cal. Rptr. 787 (1987) . *But see* Lockary v. Kayfetz, 917 F.2d 1150 (9th Cir. 1990).

[1] Carty v. City of Ojai, 143 Cal. Rptr. 506 (Cal. App. 1978); Petrosky v. Zoning Hearing Bd., 402 A.2d 1385 (Pa. 1979).

some municipalities have also adopted statutes and ordinances that provide vested rights protection for developers. If a landowner does not have a vested right, and if a municipality changes its land use regulation after the owner files an application to approve a change in use, most courts hold that the amended regulation applies unless the municipality acted in bad faith.[2]

§ 6.13 The Theory.

Estoppel and vested rights doctrines provide two distinct theories for protecting landowners from changes in zoning regulations.[1] The estoppel doctrine is based in equity. The majority rule requires substantial expenditures by a landowner in good faith reliance on some act of the government agency. Vested rights doctrine has a constitutional base. It confers constitutional protection on property rights a landowner has acquired in the use of his land. The factual basis for showing a vested right is the same as the factual basis for proving an estoppel, and courts may apply both theories with identical results.[2] This discussion makes no distinction between these two theories and uses the two terms interchangeably.

§ 6.14 Governmental Act Requirement.

A landowner may not rely on the protection provided by existing zoning and may not complain when the municipality changes this zoning to his disadvantage. He is protected under the vested rights and estoppel rule only if he relies on an affirmative governmental act by the municipality. This rule arises from the implicit right of government to change its regulatory policy.[1] Some courts relax this rule in the vested rights and estoppel cases or may invalidate a downzoning that affects a landowner's development even if he cannot make an estoppel or vested rights claim.[2]

§ 6.15 Building Permit Required.

Most courts hold that a building permit is necessary to provide a basis for a zoning estoppel.[1] *Avco Community Devs., Inc. v. South Coast Regional*

---

[2] United States Cellular Corp. v. Board of Adjustment, 589 N.W.2d 712 (Iowa 1999) (reviewing cases).

[1] Kohn v. City of Boulder, 919 P.2d 822 (Colo. App. 1996) (estoppel claim not a tort claim); City of Key West v. R.L.J.S. Corp., 537 So. 2d 641 (Fla. App. 1989) (vested rights doctrine does not apply to tax increase or impact fees).

[2] Allen v. City & County of Honolulu, 571 P.2d 328 (Haw. 1977). *But see* Sycamore Realty Co., Inc. v. People's Counsel, 684 A.2d 1331 (Md. 1996) (applying vested rights and rejecting estoppel doctrine).

[1] Golden Gate Corp. v. Town of Narragansett, 359 A.2d 321 (R.I. 1976).

[2] §§ 6.36–6.38.

[1] Bass River Assocs. v. Mayor of Bass River Twp., 573 F. Supp. 205 (D.N.J. 1983), *aff'd,* 743

Comm'n[2] is a leading case. The court noted that giving estoppel protection to a developer who had not been issued a building permit would impair the right of government to "control land use policy." A few jurisdictions provide absolute protection to the property owner once a building permit is issued.[3] As the *Avco* decision also held, preliminary development approvals preceding a building permit are not enough to provide a basis for a vested rights claim.[4]

§ 6.16   Building Permit Not Required.

Some courts do not require a building permit as the basis for a vested rights claim. They extend vested rights protection to a landowner who was entitled to a building permit when he applied but who was denied a permit because the municipality changed the zoning ordinance after he submitted his application. Some decisions protect the property owner who was entitled to a permit at the time of application, even though he did not substantially rely on his right to a permit by making substantial expenditures.[1] Other courts require substantial reliance.[2] Some decisions do not apply the zoning ordinance retroactively unless it was pending at the time the landowner submitted his application.[3] This rule

F.2d 159 (3d Cir. 1984); Consaul v. City of San Diego, 8 Cal. Rptr. 2d 762 (Cal. App. 1993); City of Aspen v. Marshall, 912 P.2d 56 (Colo. 1996); Palermo Land Co. v. Planning Comm'n of Calcasieu Parish, 561 So. 2d 482 (La. 1990); County Council v. District Land Corp., 337 A.2d 712 (Md. 1975); Town of Seabrook v. Yachon Mgt., Inc., 745 A.2d 1155 (N.H. 2000) (license not enough); Morris v. Postma, 196 A.2d 792 (N.J. 1964); Twin Rocks Watseco Defense Comm. v. Sheets, 516 P.2d 472 (Or. App. 1973); Town of Stephens City v. Russell, 399 S.E.2d 814 (Va. 1991); State ex rel. Humble Oil & Refining Co. v. Wahner, 130 N.W.2d 304 (Wis. 1964); 26 A.L.R.5th 736 (1994). *See* County of Kauai v. Pacific Stds. Life Ins. Co., 653 P.2d 766 (Haw. 1982) (no estoppel; referendum repeal before final discretionary approval given).

[2] 553 P.2d 546 (Cal. 1976).

[3] Clark v. International Horizons, Inc., 252 S.E.2d 488 (Ga. 1979).

[4] *Accord* Zoning Comm'n v. Lescynski, 453 A.2d 1144 (Conn. 1982) (preliminary permits; unauthorized unofficial acts; certificate of occupancy); Denning v. County of Maui, 485 P.2d 1048 (Haw. 1971); Kaloo v. Zoning Bd. of Appeals, 654 N.E.2d 493 (Ill. App. 1995) (oral assurance); Sterling Homes Corp. v. Anne Arundel County, 695 A.2d 1238 (Md. App. 1997) (grading permit not enough; must be demonstrated, inextricable connection between permit and ultimate construction); Gosselin v. City of Nashua, 321 A.2d 593 (N.H. 1974); Aragon & McCoy v. Albuquerque Nat'l Bank, 659 P.2d 306 (N.M. 1983) (site development plan approval).

[1] Folsom Enters. v. City of Scottsdale, 620 F. Supp. 1372 (D. Ariz. 1985); WMM Props., Inc. v. Cobb County, 339 S.E.2d 252 (Ga. 1986); Pokoik v. Silsdorf, 358 N.E.2d 874 (N.Y. 1976) (municipality may not delay action on permit application); Smith v. Winhall Planning Comm'n, 436 A.2d 760 (Vt. 1981).

[2] American Nat'l Bank & Trust Co. v. City of Chicago, 311 N.E.2d 325 (Ill. App. 1974) (reviewing Illinois cases); Pure Oil Div. v. City of Columbia, 173 S.E.2d 140 (S.C. 1970).

[3] Smith v. City of Clearwater, 383 So. 2d 681 (Fla. App. 1980); Casey v. Zoning Hearing Bd., 328 A.2d 464 (Pa. 1974). *See also* Ben Lomond, Inc. v. City of Idaho Falls, 448 P.2d 209 (Idaho 1968); 50 A.L.R.3d 596 (1973). *But see* Gulf Oil Corp. v. Township Bd. of Supvrs., 266 A.2d 84 (Pa. 1970) (good faith required).

reflects the equities of zoning estoppel and is sometimes adopted to promote stability in zoning.

Several cases found an estoppel when a municipality changed its zoning solely to frustrate a landowner who was entitled to a permit under existing regulations when he applied for one.[4] The courts find an estoppel in these cases to discipline municipalities that arbitrarily rezone to frustrate a landowner's development plans.

Another group of cases holds that an act by the municipality other than the issuance of a building permit can provide the basis for an estoppel. Some courts estop a municipality when it rezones property at the request of a landowner who relies substantially on the rezoning. A subsequent zoning change is held ineffective.[5] Other cases recognize the realities of zoning administration by holding that a municipality is estopped by informal acts on which a developer substantially relied.[6] In the typical case, the developer makes an inquiry at the zoning office and is told that his development complies with the zoning ordinance. He then relies substantially on this information. Site plan and special exception approvals may also provide the basis for an estoppel.[7] These approvals are similar to the construction approval which is provided by a building permit. However, the Virginia court holds, if a building permit is not issued, that there must be "an official response to a detailed request for a use of a particular property that would not be allowed under the law."[8] A letter of support to a state agency,

[4] Sunset View Cem. Ass'n v. Kraintz, 16 Cal. Rptr. 317 (Cal. App. 1961); Marmah, Inc. v. Town of Greenwich, 405 A.2d 63 (Conn. 1978); Rockville Fuel & Feed Co. v. City of Gaithersburg, 291 A.2d 672 (Md. 1972); Interstate Power Co., Inc. v. Nobles County Bd. of Comm'rs, 617 N.W.2d 566 (Minn. 2000) (refusing to apply revised ordinance when revision occurred after remand from court decision); Whitehead Oil Co. v. City of Lincoln (II), 515 N.E.2d 390 (Neb. 1994) (downzoning arbitrary and capricious); Bankoff v. Board of Adjustment, 875 P.2d 1138 (Okla. 1994); Commercial Props., Inc. v. Peternel, 211 A.2d 514 (Pa. 1965); Lake Bluff Housing Partners v. City of South Milwaukee, 525 N.W.2d 59 (Wis. App. 1994).

[5] Franklin County v. Leisure Props., Ltd., 430 So. 2d 475 (Fla. App. 1983); Town of Largo v. Imperial Homes Corp., 309 So. 2d 571 (Fla. App. 1975); Benson v. City of DeSoto, 510 P.2d 1281 (Kan. 1973). *See also* Disabatino v. New Castle County, 781 A.2d 687 (Del. 2001) (subdivision approval).

[6] Nemmers v. City of Dubuque (I), 716 F.2d 1194 (8th Cir. 1983) (road improvement and receptiveness to development); Project Home, Inc. v. Town of Astatula, 373 So. 2d 710 (Fla. App. 1979); Abbeville Arms v. City of Abbeville, 257 S.E.2d 716 (S.C. 1979); 6 A.L.R.2d 960 (1949). *Contra* Colonial Inv. Co. v. City of Leawood, 646 P.2d 1149 (Kan. App. 1982) (advice from planning staff); Howard Township Bd. of Trustees v. Waldo, 425 N.W.2d 180 (Mich. App. 1988) (casual advice from township officials). *See* Healey v. Town of New Durham Zoning Bd. of Adjustment, 665 A.2d 360 (N.H. (1995).

[7] Pingitore v. Town of Cave Creek, 981 P.2d 129 (Ariz. App 1999) (variety of permits, variances and zoning clearance); Board of Supvrs. v. Medical Structures, Inc., 192 S.E.2d 799 (Va. 1972).

[8] Board of Zoning Appeals v. CasLin Systems, Inc., 501 S.E.2d 397 (Va. 1998). *See also* Town of Rocky Mount v. Southside Investors, Inc., 487 S.E.2d 855 (Va. 1997).

a variance, a rezoning or the partial processing of a subdivision or site plan application are not sufficient under this test.

The judicial view that recognizes the right of a developer to vested rights protection prior to the issuance of a building permit is captured in *Western Land Equities, Inc. v. City of Logan.*[9] The court first noted the competing interests that estoppel and vested rights doctrine must reconcile. Although governments should not impose economic waste on developers by halting projects without a compelling justification, "important public interests . . . may legitimately require interference with planned private development." The court then held

> that an applicant is entitled to a building permit if his proposed development meets the zoning requirements in existence at the time of his application and if he proceeds with reasonable diligence, absent a compelling, countervailing public interest.[10]

The court added that a landowner is not entitled to rely on the original zoning if he applies for a building permit after the municipality has initiated proceedings to amend the zoning ordinance.

Courts may have adopted the building permit rule because it provides a convenient and identifiable governmental act as the basis for a vested rights claim. Decisions relaxing this rule may believe that it tips the scales too heavily against the developer. A municipality can block a development simply by withholding a building permit until it has revised its zoning ordinance. The *Western Land* rule provides more equitable criteria for balancing public and private interests.

§ 6.17 Illegal Building Permit.

A different problem arises when a municipality issues a building permit that is illegal because it was issued in violation of the zoning ordinance. The equities are with the developer if she did not know that the permit was illegal, but estopping the municipality makes it responsible for the illegal acts of its official.

Most courts allow a municipality to revoke an illegally issued building permit, but their reasons differ.[1] Some allow revocation because they hold that the

---

[9] 617 P.2d 388 (Utah 1980).

[10] *Id.* at 396.

[1] Smith v. County of Santa Barbara, 9 Cal. Rptr. 2d 120 (Cal. App. 1992); Miller v. Board of Adjustment, 521 A.2d 642 (Del. Super. 1986); Town of Lauderdale-by-the-Sea v. Meretsky, 773 So.2d 1245 (Fla. App. 2000); Corey Outdoor Adv., Inc. v. Board of Zoning Adjustments, 327 S.E.2d 178 (Ga. 1985); Harris Used Car Co. v. Anne Arundel County, 263 A.2d 520 (Md. 1970); Parkview Assocs. v. City of New York, 519 N.E.2d 1372 (N.Y. 1988); Stratford Arms, Inc. v. Zoning Bd. of Adjustment, 239 A.2d 325 (Pa. 1968); Highland Park Community Club v. Zoning Bd. of Adjustment, 475 A.2d 925 (Pa. Commw. 1984); Almeida v. Zoning Bd. of Review, 606 A.2d 1318 (R.I. 1992); Grant v. City of Folly Beach, 551 S.E.2d 229 (S.C. 2001); City of Hutchins v. Prasifka, 450 S.W.2d 829 (Tex. 1970).

landowner should have known about the zoning restrictions even though the municipality issued a permit. Other courts allow revocation because they hold that a municipality may not waive its right to enforce the zoning ordinance. Some courts protect the developer if she did not know the permit was illegally issued and made expenditures in reliance on it.[2]

§ 6.18 Good Faith.

Landowners who want to claim an estoppel or a vested right must also show that they acted in good faith. The courts usually find that a property owner acted in good faith if he proceeded in reliance on his permit at a normal pace in the absence of any indication that a zoning change might occur.[1] The courts hold a landowner acted in bad faith if he rushed to begin or complete his project with knowledge of a possible zoning change.[2]

Although the good faith rule would seem to require a subjective evaluation of a landowner's conduct, some courts have adopted an objective test of good faith. Under this test, the court asks whether a landowner's conduct was consistent with how a reasonable property owner would have acted in the same circumstances.[3]

A key issue in the bad faith cases is whether a court may infer bad faith from knowledge by the landowner that a revision of the zoning ordinance was pending. The courts are divided on this point, although the "objective" good faith courts are more likely to hold that a landowner acted in good faith in this situation.[4] The courts require some positive indication that a revision of the zoning ordinance was contemplated before they will hold that knowledge of a pending revision is bad faith. Mere knowledge of pending studies, or a landowner's expectation

---

[2] Town of West Hartford v. Rechel, 459 A.2d 1015 (Conn. 1983); Saah v. District of Columbia Bd. of Zoning Adjustment, 433 A.2d 1114 (D.C. App. 1981); City of Peru v. Querciagrossa, 392 N.E.2d 778 (Ill. App. 1979); City of Berea v. Wren, 818 S.W.2d 274 (Ky. 1991); Petrosky v. Zoning Hearing Bd., 402 A.2d 1385 (Pa. 1979); Abbeville Arms v. City of Abbeville, 257 S.E.2d 716 (S.C. 1979). See also § 8.22.

[1] Aries Dev. Co. v. California Coastal Zone Conservation Comm'n, 122 Cal. Rptr. 315 (Cal. App. 1975); Deshotel v. Calcasieu Parish Police Jury, 323 So. 2d 155 (La. App.), aff'd, 326 So. 2d 371 (La. 1976); Price v. Smith, 207 A.2d 887 (Pa. 1965); 49 A.L.R.3d 13 (1973).

[2] Stowe v. Burke, 122 S.E.2d 374 (N.C. 1961); A.J. Aberman, Inc. v. City of New Kensington, 105 A.2d 586 (Pa. 1954).

[3] Pingitore v. Town of Cave Creek, 981 P.2d 129 (Ariz. App 1999); Carty v. City of Ojai, 143 Cal. Rptr. 506 (Cal. App. 1978); Graham Corp. v. Board of Zoning Appeals, 97 A.2d 564 (Conn. 1953); Bosse v. City of Portsmouth, 226 A.2d 99 (N.H. 1967). Contra Miller v. Dassler, 155 N.Y.S.2d 975 (Sup. Ct. 1956).

[4] Bad faith not found: Kasparek v. Johnson County Bd. of Health, 288 N.W.2d 511 (Iowa 1980); Yocum v. Power, 157 A.2d 368 (Pa. 1960). Bad faith found: Smith v. City of Clearwater, 383 So. 2d 681 (Fla. App. 1980); Morris v. Postma, 196 A.2d 792 (N.J. 1964); Clackamas County v. Holmes, 508 P.2d 190 (Or. 1973); Boron Oil Co. v. L.C. Kimple, 284 A.2d 744 (Pa. 1971).

that political change might bring a revision of the ordinance, may not be enough.[5] A court may also require the municipality to act on a pending revision without unreasonable delay.[6]

The courts are also divided on the effect of an appeal by the landowner on his estoppel or vested rights claim.[7] The cases that hold against the landowner in this situation emphasize that the right to appeal would be meaningless if a landowner could assert a vested right based on activity undertaken during the appeal period.[8]

§ 6.19   Detrimental Reliance.

Detrimental reliance is the final element necessary for proof of an estoppel claim. Most courts require substantial reliance by the developer, usually through substantial expenditures on actual construction. This is a judicial rule of convenience that requires some visible and substantial act as the basis for an estoppel. The rule has no other justification. Some courts have adopted a more flexible balancing test that does not require actual construction but turns on the equities of the developer's commitment to his project.

§ 6.20   Substantial Reliance Test.

The cases have adopted three versions of the substantial reliance test. A majority hold the landowner must have devoted a "set quantum" of expenditures to the project.[1] The courts never indicate precisely how much expenditure is necessary to meet the "set quantum" test, and some courts avoid this dilemma by adopting a "ratio" test. This test requires that the expenditures devoted to the project must represent a substantial percentage of the total project cost.[2] A few cases reject both tests. They adopt a "balancing" test under which the expenditures made on a project are only one factor to consider. The court adopted a balancing test in a leading New Jersey case, in which it found an estoppel when

---

[5] Sakolsky v. City of Coral Gables, 151 So. 2d 433 (Fla. 1963); Application of Campsites Unlimited, Inc., 215 S.E.2d 73 (N.C. 1975).

[6] Boron Oil Co. v. L.C. Kimple, 284 A.2d 744 (Pa. 1971). *See* Hill v. Zoning Hearing Bd., 626 A.2d 510 (Pa. 1993) (municipality, not neighbors, must decide whether pending ordinance applies).

[7] *Compare* Grandview Baptist Church v. Zoning Bd. of Adjustment, 301 N.W.2d 704 (Iowa 1981) (landowners barred) *with* Petty v. Barrentine, 594 S.W.2d 903 (Ky. App. 1980) (contra on facts).

[8] Ebzery v. City of Sheridan, 982 P.2d 1251 (Wyo. 1999) (good faith lacking when variance granted to plaintiff could be appealed by objectors, and expenditures made during appeal period).

[1] Gackler Land Co. v. Yankee Springs Twp., 398 N.W.2d 393 (Mich. 1986); Town of Orangetown v. Magee, 665 N.E.2d 1061 (N.Y. 1996) (serious loss); 38 A.L.R.5th 737 (1996).

[2] City of Rochester v. Barcomb, 169 A.2d 281 (N.H. 1961); Waterman v. Kaufman, 221 N.Y.S.2d 526 (Sup. Ct. 1961). *Contra* Clackamas County v. Holmes, 508 P.2d 190 (Or. 1973).

a municipality revoked a building permit and changed the zoning ordinance to stop the plaintiff's development:

> The ultimate objective is fairness to both the public and the individual property owner. We think there is no profit in attempting to fix some precise concept of the nature and *quantum* of reliance which will suffice. Rather a balance must be struck between the interests of the permittee and the right and duty of the municipality . . . [to implement planning and zoning for the general welfare].[3]

Attempts at precise formulations like the set quantum and ratio rules consider only the amount of expenditure made by the developer and do not consider the impact of the zoning change on his development. A zoning change that imposes a marginal additional cost, such as an increase in a setback, may not substantially affect the developer's return even though he has made a substantial expenditure on the project. Conversely, a developer who has made a minimal expenditure may face severe costs if the zoning change is substantial. Courts that concentrate on the amount of expenditure ignore this problem. The balancing test is preferable because it allows a court to consider the before-and-after impact of a zoning change.[4]

§ 6.21 What Reliance Is Required.

Most courts require actual physical construction before they will find an estoppel,[1] but how much progress must be made in actual construction is not clear. Completion of a building is usually sufficient,[2] but the courts divide on whether excavation of the site is enough.[3] Developers have even less luck with

---

[3] Whitehead Oil Co. v. City of Lincoln, 451 N.W.2d 702 (Neb. 1990); Tremarco Corp. v. Garzio, 161 A.2d 241, 245 (N.J. 1960) (emphasis in original). *See also* Nott v. Wolf, 163 N.E.2d 809 (Ill. 1960); Clackamas County v. Holmes, 508 P.2d 190 (Or. 1973).

[4] *See* Even v. City of Parker, 597 N.W.2d 670 (S.D. 1999) (court will consider financial position of landowner when deciding whether expenditure is substantial).

[1] Phoenix City Council v. Canyon Ford, Inc., 473 P.2d 797 (Ariz. App. 1970); County Council v. District Land Corp., 337 A.2d 712 (Md. 1975); Gruber v. Mayor & Twp. Comm., 186 A.2d 489 (N.J. 1962); Beeshos Restaurant, Inc. v. State Liquor Auth., 281 N.Y.S.2d 720 (Sup. Ct. 1967). *Contra* Town of Paradise Valley v. Gulf Leisure Corp., 557 P.2d 532 (Ariz. App. 1976) (citing cases); Town of Hillsborough v. Smith, 170 S.E.2d 904 (N.C. 1969).

[2] Township of Pittsfield v. Malcolm, 134 N.W.2d 166 (Mich. 1965); Price v. Smith, 207 A.2d 887 (Pa. 1965). *See* Village of Palatine v. LaSalle Nat'l Bank, 445 N.E.2d 1277 (Ill. App. 1983) (completion of first phase of multi-phase project entitled developer to building permits for completion of project).

[3] Sufficient: Boise City v. Blaser, 572 P.2d 892 (Idaho 1977); Prince George's County v. Blumberg, 407 A.2d 1151 (Md. 1979); Pemberton v. Montgomery County, 340 A.2d 240 (Md. 1975). Not sufficient: Verner v. Redman, 271 P.2d 468 (Ariz. 1954); Prince George's County v. Sunrise Dev. Ltd. Partnership, 623 A.2d 1296 (Md. 1993); Gackler Land Co. v. Yankee Springs Twp., 398 N.W.2d 393 (Mich. 1986); Kiges v. City of St. Paul, 62 N.W.2d 363 (Minn. 1953).

less substantial commitments to their projects. The courts are likely to find that site preparation short of excavation is not sufficient.[4] They may find preliminary contractual and financial obligations sufficient but hold that other preliminary expenditures are not enough.[5] Most courts do not usually find an estoppel when the only expenditure is the cost of purchasing the land.[6]

This summary is a fair reading of the case law, but generalization is difficult. The developer usually relies on more than one category of expenditure, the court does not always indicate how much expenditure is sufficient, and the equitable basis for an estoppel claim makes an evaluation of the decisions difficult. The judicial requirement of some tangible commitment to the project is clear. The application of this rule may be unfair when the developer makes substantial commitments sufficient to show a change in position but falls short of actual construction. An example is the developer who makes substantial expenditures on preliminary approvals, site plans, and other preliminary stages, only to find the rules of the game changed when the municipality revokes his permit and revises the zoning regulations.

§ 6.22 Statutory and Ordinance Protection.

The unsatisfactory state of estoppel and vested rights law has led some municipalities and states to adopt vested rights provisions in their zoning ordinances and statutes.[1] These statutes vary, and the critical issue is to balance the need for the property owner from protection against arbitrary change against

[4] Not sufficient: Weiner v. City of Los Angeles, 441 P.2d 293 (Cal. 1968); Sterling Homes Corp. v. Anne Arundel County, 695 A.2d 1238 (Md. App. 1997) (grading, bulkheading and revetment construction); Heath Twp. v. Sall, 502 N.W.2d 627 (Mich. 1993); County Council v. District Land Corp., 337 A.2d 712 (Md. 1975); County of Saunders v. Moore, 155 N.W.2d 317 (Neb. 1967); Sufficient: Griffin v. County of Marin, 321 P.2d 148 (Cal. App. 1958); Pure Oil Div. v. City of Columbia, 173 S.E.2d 140 (S.C. 1970); H.R.D.E., Inc. v. Zoning Officer, 430 S.E.2d 341 (W. Va. 1993).

[5] Carson v. Miller, 370 So. 2d 10 (Fla. 1979); Mattson v. City of Chicago, 411 N.E.2d 1002 (Ill. App. 1980); Stone v. City of Wilton, 331 N.W.2d 398 (Iowa 1983); Brackett v. City of Des Moines, 67 N.W.2d 542 (Iowa 1954); Robert L. Rieke Bldg. Co. v. City of Olathe, 697 P.2d 72 (Kan. App. 1985); Thomas v. Zoning Bd. of Appeals, 381 A.2d 643 (Me. 1978); Murrell v. Wolff, 408 S.W.2d 842 (Mo. 1966).

[6] Anderson v. City Council, 40 Cal. Rptr. 41 (Cal. App. 1964); North Georgia Mountain Cross Network, Inc. v. City of Blue Ridge, 546 S.E.2d 850 (Ga. App. 2001); Sgro v. Howarth, 203 N.E.2d 173 (Ill. App. 1964); Union Oil Co. v. Board of County Comm'rs, 724 P.2d 341 (Or. App. 1986); Daniels v. City of Goose Creek, 431 S.E.2d 256 (S.C. App. 1993). *But see* Tremarco Corp. v. Garzio, 161 A.2d 241 (N.J. 1960) (premium paid); Gulf Oil Corp. v. Township Bd. of Supvrs., 266 A.2d 84 (Pa. 1970). *See also* Raum v. Board of Supvrs., 370 A.2d 777 (Pa. Commw. 1977) (carrying costs).

[1] *See* American Planning Association, Growing Smart Legislative Guidebook: Model Statutes for Planning and Management of Change § 8-501 (S. Meck ed. 2002) (model vested rights legislation).

the municipality's need to revise its zoning ordinance when required by new or unforeseen problem.

A Washington statute provides ones solution to this problem by granting vested rights to a landowner on the date he files a valid and fully complete building application for a structure permitted under the zoning or other land use control ordinances. The statute codifies existing vested rights law.[2] Other states have adopted similar provisions.[3]

A New Jersey statute protects an applicant who receives preliminary subdivision or site plan approval from any change in use requirements, and generally from any requirements applicable to layout or design, for three years.[4] Health and safety regulations are excepted. A Colorado law protects developers for three years after local approval of a site-specific plan.[5]

A Massachusetts law protects the holder of a building or special permit from a zoning change if the permit was granted before notice was given of the zoning change, if construction began within six months after the permit was issued and proceeded as continuously and expeditiously as possible.[6] Some zoning ordinances contain similar vested rights provisions.[7]

---

[2] Wash. Rev. Code Ann. § 19.27.095; Erickson & Assoc. v. McLerban, 872 P.2d 1090 (Wash. 1994); Valley View Indus. Park v. City of Richmond, 733 P.2d 182 (Wash. 1987). *See* Noble Manor Co. v. Pierce County, 943 P.2d 1378 (Wash. 1997) (law applies to short subdivisions). *See also* FM Props. Operating Co. v. City of Austin, 93 F.3d 167 (5th Cir. 1996) (no due process violation in retroactive application of ordinance); City of Portland v. Fisherman's Wharf Assocs. (II), 541 A.2d 160 (Me. 1988))(statute prevented application of ordinance to pending application).

[3] Conn. Gen. Stat. § 8-2h(a) (application in compliance with zoning regulations at time of filing not to be denied because of change in regulations); Or. Rev. Stat. § 227.178(3) (when complete application submitted); Tex. Gov't Code § 481.143(a) (permit approval to be based on regulations in effect on date of application). *See also* Vt. Stat. Ann. tit. 24, § 4443(d) (municipality to review new applications filed after notice of first public hearing on zoning amendment; application to be reviewed under existing regulations if amendment rejected or not adopted within 150 days).

[4] N.J. Stat. Ann. § 40:55D-49. *See* Board of Comm'rs v. Toll Bros., 607 A.2d 824 (Pa. Commw. 1992) (developer protected under similar statute from increase in water and sewer connection fees). *See also* Ariz. Rev. Stat. §§ 9-1202, 11-1202 (protects rights established in protected development right plan); N.C. Gen. Stat. §§ 153A-344.1, 160A.385.1 (approved site-specific development plan protected for two years); Va. Code Ann. § 15.2-2307 (good faith reliance on affirmative governmental act). *See* Weinman Assocs. General Partnership v. Town of Huntersville, 555 S.E.2d 342 (N.C. App. 2001) (statutory requirements met).

[5] Colo. Rev. Stat. §§ 24-68-101 to 24-68-106 (municipality must reimburse developer for expenses incurred in development if change in law makes development impossible). *See* Villa at Greely, Inc. v. Hopper, 917 P.2d 350 (Colo. App. 1996) (interpreting exception to vested rights claim).

[6] Mass. Gen. Laws ch. 40A, § 6 (also protects approved subdivision for eight years). *See also* Va. Code § 15.2-2307 (requires good faith reliance on significant governmental act).

[7] *Compare* West Main Assocs. v. City of Bellevue, 720 P.2d 782 (Wash. 1986) (holding local vested rights provision unconstitutional) *with* Comparo v. Woodbridge Twp., 222 A.2d 28 (N.J. App. Div. 1966) (contra).

Commencement of construction and similar requirements in vested rights provisions create interpretive problems similar to those that arise under judicial vested rights doctrine, although the language of the protective provision influences the court's decision. With this qualification, the cases are again divided on whether commencement of construction or preliminary work such as excavation is sufficient to secure vested rights protection.[8] The courts require good faith diligence in the completion of construction when reasonable diligence is required by the vested rights provision or when it imposes a time period for completion.[9]

Under an alternative method of vested rights protection, the municipality provides an administrative procedure for granting exemptions when the zoning ordinance is changed. The ordinance can utilize an existing zoning technique, such as the special exception, or can create a new procedure. The ordinance should provide criteria for the vested rights determination. Possibilities include an "extraordinary hardship" or "reasonableness" standard that balances the need for landowner protection against the need to protect the integrity of newly adopted zoning requirements.

§ 6.23 Development Agreements.

A number of states protect developers from zoning change by authorizing the execution of development agreements between a developer and a municipality.[1] The California law is illustrative.[2] It authorizes agreements that specify permitted uses and densities and the maximum height and size of buildings. The agreement must also include provisions for the reservation or dedication of land for public purposes. The Florida law requires agreement between the parties on the responsibility for and timing of public facilities.[3]

Under the California law, the development of the property must comply with use, density, design, improvement, and construction standards applicable at the

---

[8] Must commence construction: First Nat'l Bank & Trust v. City of Rockford, 361 N.E.2d 832 (Ill. App. 1977); Murphy v. Crosby, 298 N.E.2d 885 (Mass. App. 1973); Prince George's County v. Equitable Trust Co., 408 A.2d 737 (Md. 1970). Preliminary work enough: O'Neill v. Burns, 198 So. 2d 1 (Fla. 1967); Williams v. Wofford, 140 S.E.2d 190 (Ga. 1965). *See also* Temkin v. Karagheuzoff, 313 N.E.2d 770 (N.Y. 1974); 49 A.L.R.3d 1150 (1973).

[9] League to Save Lake Tahoe v. Crystal Enters., 490 F. Supp. 995 (D. Nev. 1980); Papalia v. Inspector of Bldgs., 217 N.E.2d 911 (Mass. 1966); City of Monett v. Buchanan, 411 S.W.2d 108 (Mo. 1967).

[1] 110 Fla. Stat. Ann. §§ 163.3220–163.3243; Hawaii Rev. Stat. §§ 46-121 to 46-132; Nev. Rev. Stat. §§ 278.0201–278.0207; S.C. Code Ann. §§ 6-31-10 to 6-31-160.; Wash. Rev. Code §§ 36.70B.170.–36.170.210 *See* 216 Sutter Bay Assocs. v. Sutter County, 68 Cal. Rptr.2d 492 (Cal. App. 1997) (upholding county's recission of development agreement). City of N. Las Vegas v. Parde Constr. Co., 21 P.3d 8 (Nev. 2001) (agreement construed to allow only pass-through of cost-based fees to developer).

[2] Cal. Gov't Code §§ 65864–65869.5.

[3] Fla. Stat. Ann. § 163.3227(1)(d).

time the agreement is executed unless it provides otherwise. The agreement may authorize subsequent discretionary action by the municipality if it does not prevent development that complies with the agreed uses, densities or intensities. It may also provide that the developer must commence or complete construction within a specified period of time. The municipality must review the agreement every twelve months. It may terminate or modify the agreement if it finds that the developer has not complied with it in good faith.

Development agreements raise a number of constitutional questions. The courts have upheld agreements in which a landowner agrees to annex to a municipality in return for a municipality's promise to provide public services, especially when the agreement is authorized by a statute.[4] These cases support the constitutionality of similar provisions in development agreements. The constitutionality of development agreements that freeze existing land use restrictions is more doubtful. A court could hold that a freeze on land use restrictions is an unconstitutional bargaining away of the police power.[5]

However, in *Santa Margarita Residents Together v. San Luis Obispo County*,[6] a California court held a development agreement can establish the scope of the project and precise parameters for future construction and a procedure to process project approvals. The statute is not limited to approval of agreements to complete construction of a project according to specific plans. A five year zoning freeze in the agreement was not a surrender of governmental function because the agreement required development in accordance with the county's general plan and county approval of detailed building plans.

---

[4] Morrison Homes Corp. v. City of Pleasanton, 130 Cal. Rptr. 196 (Cal. App. 1976); Carruth v. City of Medera, 43 Cal. Rptr. 855 (Cal. App. 1965).

[5] Delucchi v. County of Santa Cruz, 225 Cal. Rptr. 43 (Cal. App. 1086) (zoning freeze in agricultural land preservation agreement would be invalid); City of Louisville v. Fiscal Court, 621 S.W.2d 219 (Ky. 1981) (annexation agreement in which city agreed to "assist and cooperate fully" in rezoning held invalid); City of New York v. 17 Vista Assocs., 642 N.E.2d 606 (N.Y. 1994) (agreement to expedite decision on development in return for payment of money to low income housing trust held invalid). *But see* Union Nat'l Bank v. Village of Glenwood, 348 N.E.2d 226 (Ill. App. 1976) (annexation agreement authorized by statute may limit land to existing zoning); Mayor & City Council v. Crane, 352 A.2d 786 (Md. 1976) (city bound by agreement providing for density increase in exchange for donation of land to city executed by developer). *See also* §§ 6.62–6.65 (contract and conditional zoning). *See* County Mobilehome Positive Action Comm., Inc. v. County of San Diego, 73 Cal. Rptr. 2d 409 (Cal. App. 1998) (invalidating accord between county and mobilehome park owners' association containing standard lease and rent stabilization measures in return for county's promise not to adopt rent control for 15 years).

[6] 116 100 Cal. Rptr.2d 740 (Cal. App. 2000). *See also* Stephens v. City of Vista, 994 F.2d 650 (9th Cir. 1993) (city can guarantee density and retain review of design features of development without surrendering control of its land use power); Save Elkhart Lake, Inc. v. Village of Elkhart Lake, 512 N.W.2d 202 (Wis. App. 1993) (village agreed to cooperate and extend good faith in attempting to make agreement successful). *But see* Morgran Co., Inc. v. Orange County, 818 So.2d 640 (Fla. App. 2002) (agreement containing promise to rezone invalid as contract zoning).

The court also rejected an argument that a development agreement may be approved only after a project has been approved for actual construction. It noted the statute recognized the importance of planning and early public and private participation in the planning process, and held the statute allowed development agreements when significant financial and personnel commitments to a project were required from the municipality and the developer.

D. ZONING MAP AMENDMENTS.

§ 6.24   The Zoning Problem.

The Standard Zoning Enabling Act authorized the local governing body to amend the zoning ordinance.[1] State zoning acts contain comparable provisions, and the typical zoning ordinance authorizes the local governing body to make zoning text and map amendments. This section discusses the zoning map amendment. A map amendment changes the zoning regulations for a tract of land by reclassifying it to a different zoning classification.

Legal remedies to challenge a refusal to rezone and a zoning map amendment are quite different. The map amendment process is legislative in most states, so a refusal to rezone cannot be appealed. An action for declaratory judgment or injunction can be brought by a landowner whose application for a map amendment is refused.[2] Neighboring landowners can bring a similar suit to challenge a rezoning map amendment.

§ 6.25   Refusals to Rezone.

When a zoning ordinance does not allow a land use a landowner wants to make of her land, one option is to apply for a rezoning. that will change the zoning district that applies to the land to one that will allow the landowner's proposed use.[1] If the council refuses to grant a rezoning, the landowner can then bring a collateral attack on the refusal by way of an injunction. In state court, this action is not a direct appeal of the refusal to zone but is a collateral attack on the refusal that challenges the legality of the zoning restriction that applies to the land.[2]

One approach in state court is to claim a refusal to rezone is arbitrary and capricious. Courts apply a presumption of constitutionality in these cases when the zoning function is legislative, and will uphold a refusal to rezone if the

---

[1] Standard Zoning Enabling Act §§ 4, 5.

[2] §§ 8.15, 8.16.

[1] See § 4.18 (Standard Act conferred power to amend zoning ordinance).

[2] F.S. Plummer Co. v. Town of Cape Elizabeth, 612 A.2d 856 (Me. 1992); Copple v. City of Lincoln, 315 N.W.2d 628 (Neb. 1982); East Lampeter Township v. County of Lancaster, 744 A.2d 359 (Pa. Commw. 1999) (refusal to rezone not directly appealable).

decision is reasonably debatable.[3] They will invalidate a refusal to rezone they consider arbitrary.[4] Another option is an as-applied attack that claims the existing restrictive zoning is a taking of property. State courts in these cases utilize the rules that usually apply to as-applied taking cases.[5] They usually require a showing the existing zoning has left the landowner without an economically viable use of his property,[6] but some state courts apply a balancing test in as-applied taking cases.[7] Landowners who succeed in these cases usually cannot obtain a decree rezoning their land for the more intensive use they proposed.[8]

Landowners must usually sue in state court on a claim a refusal to rezone is an as-applied taking under the federal constitution.[9] When courts have considered these claims they have usually refused to find a taking under the *Penn Central*[10] balancing test because the zoning ordinance has left the landowner with some use of her land.[11] A landowner can also argue a refusal to rezone is a per se taking under the *Lucas* case,[12] but these cases will not usually succeed if the zoning ordinance allows some beneficial or productive use of the property. Landowners can bring a substantive due process challenge in federal court if they can overcome the obstacles to litigation in federal courts, but the federal courts usually apply the presumption of constitutionality to uphold refusals to rezone.[13]

---

[3] City of Atlanta v. Tap Assocs., 544 S.E.2d 433 (Ga. 2001) (upholding refusal to rezone area near transit station from residential to mixed-use development under detriment-benefit test); Englin v. Board of County Comm'rs, 48 P.3d 39 (Mont. 2002); Harmon City, Inc. v. Draper City, 997 P.2d 321 (Utah App. 2000); MC Props., Inc. v. City of Chattanooga, 994 S.W.2d 132 (Tenn. App. 1999). *See* Arthur Land Co., LLC v. Ostego County, 645 N.W.2d 50 (Mich. App. 2002) (court not limited to record in appeal of legislative refusal to rezone and plaintiff entitled to hearing de novo).

[4] Henry County v. The Jones Props., 539 S.E.2d 167 (Ga. 2000) (refusal to rezone to higher residential density); Lenette Realty & Inv. Co. v. City of Chesterfield, 35 S.W.3d 399 (Mo. App. 2001) (refusal to rezone to retail use).

[5] § 2.36.

[6] *Cf.* Iowa Coal Mining Co. Inc. v. Monroe County, 494 N.W.2d 664 (Iowa 1993); Eternalist Foundation, Inc. v. City of Platteville, 593 N.W.2d 84 (Wis. App. 1999).

[7] D'Addario v. Planning & Zoning Comm'n, 593 A.2d 511 (Conn. App. 1991); § 2.37.

[8] § 8.18.

[9] § 2.31.

[10] § 2.07.

[11] Baytree of Inverarry Realty Partner v. City of Lauderhill, 873 F.2d 1407 (11th Cir. 1989) (refusal to rezone for low income housing).

[12] § 2.09.

[13] Pearson v. City of Grand Blanc, 961 F.2d 1211 (6th Cir. 1992); Jacobs, Visconsi & Jacobs Co. v. City of Lawrence, 927 F.2d 1111 (10th Cir. 1991); South Gwinnett Venture v. Pruitt, 491 F.2d 5 (5th Cir.1974).

§ 6.26 The Quasi-Judicial View.

The adoption and rejection of amendments to the zoning map is held to be a legislative act in the majority of states. This characterization means governing bodies do not have to make findings of fact and give reasons for their zoning decisions, and it also means courts will give zoning map amendment decisions the usual deference accorded to legislative acts. A break in these standard rules occurred in *Fasano v. Board of County Comm'rs*,[1] a case holding a mobile home rezoning was quasi-judicial. The court held that ordinances laying down legislative policies were entitled to the usual constitutional presumptions. Ordinances applying these policies to individual properties were "an exercise of judicial authority" and subject to different tests. The mobile home rezoning fell in the second category.

The courts review zoning map amendments more rigorously if they hold that a rezoning is a quasi-judicial, rather than a legislative, act. The presumption of constitutionality accorded legislative actions disappears, and the municipality has the burden of proof to justify the zoning change. The legislative body must also adopt adjudicative procedures for zoning changes and make adequate findings of fact.

The reception of *Fasano* in other states has been mixed. Several states have also held the zoning amendment process is quasi-judicial, and they apply this characterization to rezoning denials as well as approvals.[2] The most important recent case holding the zoning process quasi-judicial is *Snyder v. Board of County Comm'rs*.[3] The court held a denial of a rezoning quasi-judicial. The court held that "comprehensive rezonings affecting a large portion of the public are legislative." It concluded that rezonings are quasi-judicial when they affect a limited number of persons or property owners and identifiable parties and interests, when the decision is based on facts arrived at from distinct alternatives presented at a hearing, and when the decision can be functionally viewed as policy application.

The reasons for holding that the zoning amendment process is quasi-judicial vary. The Oregon court believed this rule would limit destructive piecemeal

---

[1] 507 P.2d 23 (Or. 1973). *See* Cherry Hills Resort Dev. Co. v. Cherry Hills Village, 757 P.2d 622 (Colo. 1988) (explaining nature of quasi-judicial actions in zoning and holding approval of PUD quasi-judicial).

[2] New Castle Cty. Council v. BC Dev. Assocs., 567 A.2d 1271 (Del. 1989); Golden v. City of Overland Park, 584 P.2d 130 (Kan. 1978); City of Louisville v. McDonald, 470 S.W.2d 173 (Ky. 1971); Woodland Hills Conservation Ass'n v. City of Jackson, 443 So. 2d 1173 (Miss. 1983) (change-mistake and public need test make rezoning quasi-judicial); West Old Town Neighborhood Ass'n v. City of Albuquerque, 927 P.2d 529 (N.M. App. 1996); Fleming v. City of Tacoma, 502 P.2d 327 (Wash. 1972). *See also* Devaney v. City of Burlington, 545 S.E.2d 763 (N.C. App. 2001) (approval of application for overlay district held quasi-judicial).

[3] 627 So. 2d 469 (Fla. 1996).

zoning changes adopted in response to pressures from developers. The Idaho Supreme Court adopted a somewhat different rationale:

> The great deference given true legislative action stems from its high visibility and widely felt impact, on the theory that appropriate remedy can be had at the polls. . . . This rationale is inapposite when applied to a local zoning body's decision as to the fate of an individual's application [to] rezone. Most voters are unaware or unconcerned that fair dealing and consistent treatment may have been sacrificed in the procedural informality which accompanies action deemed legislative.[4]

A respectable number of courts have rejected the *Fasano* rule and continue to follow the majority rule that a zoning map amendment is legislative.[5] *Arnel Dev. Co. v. City of Costa Mesa*[6] is a leading California case that rejected the *Fasano* rule, although the court did not discuss it. The voters adopted a downzoning of a fifty-acre single-family and multifamily development by initiative. Because the initiative process is available only for legislative acts, the court had to determine whether downzoning a mixed-use development of this size was legislative or quasi-judicial.

The court reaffirmed the "generic" classifications it had previously adopted, which classify zoning actions depending on the nature of the zoning process. This approach classifies zoning amendments as legislative and variances and special permits as adjudicative. The court noted that any other classification, such as a classification based on the size of the parcel or the number of landowners affected, would create uncertainty because courts would have to apply it on a case-by-case basis. The court believed that the public interest in "rational and orderly land-use planning" was adequately protected by the statutory plan coexistence requirement and by a regional general welfare requirement for zoning it had previously adopted.

Courts hold a zoning action is quasi-judicial when it affects specific individuals and requires the application of previously-adopted policy to the fact situation presented to a governmental body.[7] Difficulties arise in applying this test. In

---

[4] Cooper v. Board of County Comm'rs, 614 P.2d 947 (Idaho 1980).

[5] South Gwinnett Venture v. Pruitt, 491 F.2d 5 (5th Cir 1974)l Carana v. Kenai Peninsula Borough, 21 P.3d 833 (Alaska 2001); Wait v. City of Scottsdale, 618 P.2d 601 (Ariz. 1980); Hall Paving Co. v. Hall County, 226 S.E.2d 728 (Ga. 1976); Montgomery Cty. v. Woodward & Lothrop, 376 A.2d 483 (Md. 1977); State v. City of Rochester, 268 N.W.2d 885 (Minn. 1978); Quinlan v. City of Dover, 614 A.2d 1057 (N.H. 1992); Hampton v. Richland County, 357 S.E.2d 463 (S.C. 1987); Bell v. City of Elkhorn, 364 N.W.2d 144 (Wis. 1985).

[6] 620 P.2d 565 (Cal. 1980).

[7] Cherry Hills Resort Dev. Co. v. City of Cherry Hills Village, 757 P.2d 622 (Colo. 1988); Raynes v. Leavenworth, 821 P.2d 1204 (Wash. 1992). *See* Wash. Rev. Code Ann. § 42.36.010.

Neuberger v. City of Portland[8] the city rezoned a 601-acre parcel of land to a more intensive single-family residential density. The court held the rezoning quasi-judicial, but not without difficulty. It noted that a land use decision is quasi-judicial "when a particular action by a local government is directed at a relatively small number of identifiable persons, and when that action also involves the application of existing policy to a specific factual setting."[9]

A zoning determination also is quasi-judicial if "the process is bound to result in a decision." The court held that the zoning ordinance in this case satisfied this test because it required quasi-judicial procedures. It then considered whether the rezoning was legislative because it was a "free choice among competing policies" or quasi-judicial because it was the "application of existing policy." The court concluded that both kinds of decision making were present. The rezoning required major policy determinations because it was large and would have a substantial impact on municipal services. It was quasi-judicial because it required the application of the statutory zoning criteria as well as state-wide planning goals adopted by a state agency.

Arnel and *Neuberger* indicate the trade-offs courts must make when they must decide how they should characterize the zoning process. A holding that the process is legislative allows the voters to adopt zoning amendments by initiative and but makes judicial review more difficult. A holding that the process is quasi-judicial allows more rigorous judicial review but makes the initiative and referendum process unavailable.[10] The court in *Arnel* held that rezoning is legislative because it believed that initiatives and referenda on individual rezoning actions were unlikely.

§ 6.27 "Spot" Zoning.

§ 6.28 Definitions.

Probably no term in zoning jurisprudence is used more frequently by the courts and is less understood than "spot" zoning. Zoning statutes and ordinances authorize amendments to the zoning map without differentiating between "spot" and other types of rezonings. A "spot zoning" is a zoning map amendment that rezones a tract of land from a less intensive to a more intensive use district. Spot zoning comes under attack because objectors believe it confers a zoning "favor" on a single landowner without justification.

---

[8] 603 P.2d 771 (Or. 1979). *See also* Stuart v. Board of County Comm'rs, 699 P.2d 978 (Colo. App. 1985) (comprehensive plan amendment held not quasi-judicial when development and its impact not known).

[9] 603 P.2d at 775.

[10] *But see* Margolis v. District Court, 638 P.2d 297 (Colo. 1981) (rezoning subject to referendum though held quasi-judicial when judicially reviewed).

The courts have adopted a definition of spot zoning that they use to decide spot zoning cases. Although the definitions vary, the definition adopted by a Texas Court of Appeals is typical. It held that the term spot zoning is descriptive of the process of singling out a small parcel of land for a use classification different and inconsistent with the surrounding area, for the benefit of the owner of such property and to the detriment of the rights of other property owners.[1] The Texas Supreme Court adopted a similar definition and added that spot zoning "is piecemeal zoning, the antithesis of planned zoning."[2]

§ 6.29   The Standard Tests.

These definitions highlight the equal protection objection to spot zoning. They also modify the presumption of constitutionality that courts usually apply to zoning map amendments. The courts apply the presumption of constitutionality to uphold a zoning map amendment that comprehensively covers all or a substantial part of a municipality.[1] Courts are suspicious of spot zonings because of their potential for abuse and will aggressively review a spot-zoning amendment to determine whether it meets constitutional and statutory requirements. A court may review a rezoning under a reasonableness test if it holds that rezoning for individual tracts is quasi-judicial.[2]

The basis for a constitutional attack on spot zoning is unclear. Because a spot zoning is an upzoning to a more intensive use, the landowner usually is satisfied and will not bring a taking claim. An action challenging the spot zoning is usually brought by neighbors. They cannot claim a taking based on a more intensive use of neighboring property. Their objection is that the spot zoning violates equal protection because it arbitrarily favors a single landowner.[3] Courts examine the public purposes for a spot zoning to determine whether they overcome the claim of arbitrary action. Objecting neighbors can also claim that a spot zoning violates the statutory requirement that zoning must be "in accordance" with a comprehensive plan because it is arbitrary.[4]

Spot zoning definitions contain spatial and non-spatial zoning criteria that courts apply to determine whether a spot zoning is invalid. These definitions indicate that a spot zoning is invalid if it covers a small parcel of land and is

---

[1] Burkett v. City of Texarkana, 500 S.W.2d 242, 244 (Tex. Civ. App. 1973). *See also* Griswold v. City of Homer, 925 P.2d 1015 (Alaska 1996).

[2] City of Pharr v. Tippitt, 616 S.W.2d 173 (Tex. 1981); 73 A.L.R.5th 223 (1999).

[1] Mraz v. County Comm'rs, 433 A.2d 771 (Md. 1981); Fasano v. Board of County Comm'rs, 507 P.2d 23 (Or. 1973).

[2] Board of County Comm'rs v. City of Olathe, 952 P.2d 1302 (Kan. 1998).

[3] *See also* Clawson v. Harborcreek Twp. Zoning Hearing Bd., 304 A.2d 184 (Pa. Commw. 1973) (due process).

[4] §§ 3.13–3.18.

inconsistent with the surrounding area. This criterion is spatial. They also indicate that a spot zoning is invalid because it confers a private benefit and injures other property owners.[5] This criterion is non-spatial. The American Planning Association's model planning legislation authorizes the establishment of a Land-Use Review Board, which has the authority to grant area (but not use) variances and conditional authorizes similar to authority conferred by the Standard Zoning Act. The model legislation also contains authority for Mediated Agreements that allow an applicant for a development and the municipality to negotiate changes in land development regulations.[6]

Many courts elaborate these criteria by adopting a balancing test under which they weigh the benefits of a spot zoning to the public against its detriments to other landowners.[7] A court can uphold a spot zoning under the balancing test if it finds that its benefits outweigh its detriments.[8] A court may add that a spot zoning must be "in accordance" with the comprehensive plan, as required by many zoning statutes.[9] The "in accordance" requirement means that a court must find an acceptable planning or zoning purpose for a spot zoning that overcomes the objection that it is arbitrary. This requirement does not necessarily mean that the spot zoning must be consistent with the planning policies in a comprehensive plan.

The criteria that apply to spot zoning are flexible and provide guidelines rather than rigid rules. Not all rezonings for small parcels are necessarily invalid, and not all rezonings for large parcels are necessarily valid.[10] The courts usually require consistency with surrounding land uses and zoning, but inconsistency

---

[5] Lee v. District of Columbia Zoning Comm'n, 411 A.2d 635 (D.C. App. 1980); Greater Yellowstone Coalition, Inc. v. Board of County Comm'rs, 25 P.3d 168 (Mont. 2001); Goodrich v. Town of Southampton, 355 N.E.2d 297 (N.Y. 1976); Cannon v. Murphy, 600 N.Y.S.2d 965 (App. Div. 1993); City of Rusk v. Cox, 665 S.W.2d 233 (Tex. App. 1984); Anderson v. Island County, 501 P.2d 594 (Wash. 1972); 51 A.L.R.2d 263 (1957).

[6] American Planning Association, Growing Smart Legislative Guidebook: Model Statutes for Planning and Management of Change §§ 10-401 to 10-507 (S. Meck ed. 2002)

[7] Some courts apply this test when they review refusals to rezone.

[8] Woodland Estates, Inc. v. Building Inspector of Methuen, 358 N.E.2d 468 (Mass. App. 1976); Rando v. Town of North Attleboro, 692 N.E.2d 544 (Mass. App. 1998) (rezoning to commercial); Boland v. City of Great Falls, 910 P.2d 890 (Mont. 1996); Randolph v. Town of Brookhaven, 337 N.E.2d 763 (N.Y. 1975); Godfrey v. Union County Board of Comm'rs, 300 S.E.2d 273 (N.C. App. 1983); Galanes v. Town of Brattleboro, 388 A.2d 406 (Vt. 1978). Compare Covington v. Town of Apex, 423 S.E.2d 537 (N.C. App. 1992) (held invalid).

[9] Luery v. Zoning Bd. of City of Stamford, 187 A.2d 247 (Conn. 1962); Bosse v. City of Portsmouth, 226 A.2d 99 (N.H. 1967); Palisades Props., Inc. v. Brunetti, 207 A.2d 523 (N.J. 1965).

[10] Griswold v. City of Homer, 925 P.2d 1015 (Alaska 1996) (7.29 acres; held valid); Fifteen Fifty N. State Bldg. Corp. v. City of Chicago, 155 N.E.2d 97 (Ill. 1959) (single tract; held invalid); McWhorter v. City of Winnsboro, 525 S.W.2d 701 (Tex. Civ. App. 1975) (5.29 acres; held valid); Chrobuck v. Snohomish County, 480 P.2d 489 (Wash. 1971) (635 acres; held invalid).

is not necessarily fatal.[11] Recent cases have emphasized that spot zoning rules are flexible, and that "spot zoning" is merely a descriptive term. The ultimate test is the reasonableness of the zoning as determined by a number of factors such as compatibility with surrounding uses and consistency with the comprehensive plan.[12]

§ 6.30   The Public Need and Public Purpose Tests.

Courts often rely on a public need for a land use allowed by a spot zoning to reject a claim that it arbitrarily confers a benefit on a landowner. A court can find the basis for a public need in a comprehensive plan but must base this determination on its own *ad hoc* judgment if a comprehensive plan does not exist. This judicial attitude distinguishes the spot zoning from the "as-applied" taking cases, where the public need to be served by a landowner's proposed use is not a factor in the taking decision.

The courts have upheld spot zonings in which the municipality rezoned land to a more intensive multifamily use because of a need for multifamily development in the community as indicated by a housing shortage.[1] As one court pointed

---

[11] Fox v. Polk County Bd. of Supervisors, 569 N.W.2d 503 (Iowa 1997) (upholding rezoning for softball field); Little v. Winborn, 518 N.W.2d 384 (Iowa 1994) (rezoning small parcel in agricultural zone to nonagricultural uses held spot zoning); Tennison v. Shomette, 379 A.2d 187 (Md. App. 1978) (suggesting inconsistency not always required); Sharp v. Zoning Hearing Bd., 628 A.2d 1223 (Pa. Commw. 1993) (rezoning extended preexisting institutional use in accordance with plan); Bell v. City of Elkhorn, 364 N.W.2d 144 (Wis. 1985) (upholding spot zoning consistent with adjacent uses and zoning).

[12] Bossman v. Village of Riverton, 684 N.E.2d 427 (Ill. App. 1997) (commercial rezoning invalidated; reviews cases); Fabiano v. City of Boston, 730 N.E.2d 311 (Mass. App. 2000) (upholding residential rezoning to protect surrounding residential character of surrounding area); Watson v. Town Council, 805 P.2d 641 (N.M. App. 1991); Yellow Lantern Kampground v. Town of Cortlandville, 716 N.Y.S.2d 786 (App. Div. 2000) (invalidating rezoning for asphalt plant; must also consider availability of alternate sites and recommendations of planning staff); Save Our Forest Action Coalition Inc. v. City of Kingston, 675 N.Y.S.2d 451 (App. Div. 1998) (upholding rezoning to retain large industrial employer); Good Neighbors of South Davidson v. Town of Denton, 559 S.E.2d 768 (N.C. 2002) (invalidating rezoning of 50 acres surrounded by residential and agricultural use to industrial); Chrismon v. Guilford Cty., 370 S.E.2d 579 (N.C. 1988) (citing this treatise); Bigwood v. City of Wahpeton, 565 N.W.2d 498 (N.D. 1997) (upholding rezoning for lower income housing); Baker v. Chartiers Tp. Zoning Hearing Bd., 677 A.2d 1274 (Pa. Commw. 1996); Granger v. Town of Woodford, 708 A.2d 1345 (Vt. 1998) (commercial rezoning); Smith v. Town of St. Johnsbury, 554 A.2d 233 (Vt. 1988).

[1] Malafronte v. Planning & Zoning Bd., 230 A.2d 606 (Conn. 1967); Miles v. Dade County Bd. of County Comm'rs, 260 So. 2d 553 (Fla. App. 1972); Decuir v. Town of Marksville, 426 So. 2d 766 (La. App. 1983) (housing shortage); State v. City of Rochester, 268 N.W.2d 885 (Minn. 1978); Fallin v. Knox County Bd. of Comm'rs, 656 S.W.2d 338 (Tenn. 1983). *See also* Ballenger v. Door County, 388 N.W.2d 624 (Wis. App. 1986) (upholding text amendment allowing ferry terminals in resort commercial district). *But see* Coughlin v. City of Topeka, 480 P.2d 91 (Kan. 1971).

out in a decision upholding a rezoning from single-family detached to single-family row house dwellings:

> [Z]oning decisions which allow the erection of apartments in districts previously classified for construction of detached residential dwellings only are not disturbed by appellate courts when a need for housing exists and injury to the land is minimal.[2]

Courts adopt a similar analysis in spot zoning cases in which a municipality rezones land from residential to commercial use in order to provide for commercial facilities. A court may consider the need for such facilities as a factor that supports the commercial rezoning.[3] It may also consider a need to broaden an area's employment base as a factor supporting the rezoning.[4]

Incompatibility with surrounding land uses may defeat a spot zoning, even if it serves a public need. A need for employment opportunities, for example, may not justify a spot zoning for an industrial use in a residential neighborhood.[5] A court may uphold a spot zoning that serves a public need if the parcel is large enough that the developer can avoid compatibility problems through a buffer and landscaping. A rezoning for a large regional shopping center is an example,[6] especially if it extends an existing commercial zone.[7]

§ 6.31 The Change-Mistake Rule.

A change-mistake rule for zoning map amendments, first adopted in Maryland and later exported to a few other states, provides more control on spot zoning than the traditional spot zoning rules. A court will uphold a zoning map amendment under the change-mistake rule only if it is based on a change in conditions in the surrounding neighborhood or a mistake in the original zoning. This rule stabilizes existing zoning by making it more difficult to secure piecemeal changes. Although the change-mistake rule does not mean that existing zoning classifications are immutable, it clearly gives objecting neighbors much greater leverage when they object to piecemeal amendments to a zoning ordinance.

---

[2] Lee v. District of Columbia Zoning Comm'n, 411 A.2d 635, 642 (D.C. App. 1980).

[3] *Compare* Griswold v. City of Homer, 925 P.2d 1015 (Alaska 1996) (held valid), *and* Bartram v. Zoning Comm'n of City of Bridgeport, 68 A.2d 308 (Conn. 1949) (same) *with* Kuehne v. Town Council, 72 A.2d 474 (Conn. 1950) (contra); 51 A.L.R.2d 263 (1957); 76 A.L.R.2d 172 (1961). *See also* Protect Hamden/North Haven From Excessive Traffic & Pollution, Inc. v. Planning & Zoning Comm'n, 600 A.2d 757 (Conn. 1991) (upholding text amendment for shopping centers).

[4] Save Our Rural Env't v. Snohomish County, 662 P.2d 816 (Wash. 1983). *See also* Save a Neighborhood Env't v. City of Seattle, 676 P.2d 1006 (Wash. 1984) (subsidized housing).

[5] Fritts v. City of Ashland, 348 S.W.2d 712 (Ky. 1961) (industrial rezoning). *See also* §§ 5.44–5.48 (control of competition problem).

[6] Willott v. Village of Beachwood, 197 N.E.2d 201 (Ohio 1964).

[7] McNaughton v. Boeing, 414 P.2d 778 (Wash. 1966).

In addition to Maryland,[1] a few other states have adopted the change-mistake rule.[2] Other courts rely on evidence of changed conditions when they consider a zoning amendment even though they have not adopted this rule.[3] Some courts have rejected the change-mistake rule.[4]

Unless there is a mistake in the zoning ordinance, the change-mistake rule limits zoning map amendments to cases where some change in the area surrounding the rezoned parcel has occurred. The change is usually an intensification in land use. The change-mistake rule requires the court to make a planning judgment to determine whether the changed conditions justify the rezoning. In apartment zoning cases, for example, the Maryland court has had to determine whether apartments provide an appropriate buffer zone, whether highways can properly divide different land uses, and whether improved public facilities justify the rezoning.[5]

In Maryland, a municipality may not defend a zoning map amendment by arguing that it is justified by a change in municipal land use policy. In *Chapman v. Montgomery County Council*,[6] the county rezoned a 5.8-acre parcel for a neighborhood convenience shopping center to avoid the expansion of a nearby shopping center, which the comprehensive plan did not favor. The court disapproved the amendment, even though the population in the area had grown substantially. Population growth, the court held, would justify a rezoning to higher residential densities but would not support a shopping center rezoning.

---

[1] The leading case is Wakefield v. Kraft, 96 A.2d 27 (Md. 1953). *See also* MacDonald v. Board of County Comm'rs, 210 A.2d 325 (Md. 1965). *See* Md. Ann. Code art. 66B, § 4.05(a) (codifies rule).

[2] Zoning Comm'n v. New Canaan Bldg. Co., 148 A.2d 330 (Conn. 1959); Harvey v. Town of Marion, 756 So.2d 835 (Miss. App. 2000) (upholding rezoning from residential to commercial along highway); Lewis v. City of Jackson, 184 So. 2d 384 (Miss. 1966); Miller v. City of Albuquerque, 554 P.2d 665 (N.M. 1976); Hayden v. City of Port Townsend, 613 P.2d 1164 (Wash. 1980); Tugwell v. Kittitas County, 951 P.2d 272 (Wash. App. 1998) (change of circumstances found; rule does not apply if zoning is consistent with plan). *See also* Ky. Rev. Stat. § 100.213(1) (must show substantial change in area involved if rezoning not consistent with plan); City of Beechwood Village v. Council of & City of St. Matthews, 574 S.W.2d 322 (Ky. 1978).

[3] King's Mill Homeowners Ass'n v. City of Westminster, 557 P.2d 1186 (Colo. 1976); Lanner v. Board of Appeal, 202 N.E.2d 777 (Mass. 1964).

[4] Dye v. City of Phoenix, 542 P.2d 31 (Ariz. App. 1975); Conner v. Shellburne, Inc., 281 A.2d 608 (Del. 1971); Oka v. Cole, 145 So. 2d 233 (Fla. 1962); Levitt v. Incorporated Village of Sands Point, 174 N.Y.S.2d 283 (Sup. Ct. 1958).

[5] Palermo Land Co. v. Planning Comm'n of Calcasieu Parish, 561 So. 2d 482 (La. 1990) (citing cases rejecting rule); Brown v. Wimpress, 242 A.2d 157 (Md. 1968); Park Constr. Corp. v. Board of County Comm'rs, 227 A.2d 15 (Md. 1967). *See* D. Mandelker, The Zoning Dilemma 87-105 (1971).

[6] 271 A.2d 156 (Md. 1970). *But see* Bjarnson v. Kitsap County, 899 P.2d 1290 (Wash. App. 1995) (change-mistake rule does not apply when rezoning implements comprehensive plan).

States that apply the change-mistake rule may also shift the burden of proof to the proponent of an amendment.[7]

§ 6.32   Consistency with the Comprehensive Plan.

Much of the judicial concern with spot zoning arises from a belief that piecemeal rezoning undercuts the community's comprehensive planning and zoning policies. The change-mistake rule and the quasi-judicial view of zoning amendments are judicial attempts to avoid this problem by securing more judicial control over the rezoning process. A number of states take a direct approach to this problem by requiring zoning to be consistent with the comprehensive plan.[1] A court may require consistency with a comprehensive plan if the municipality has adopted one, even in states that do not have a consistency requirement.[2]

§ 6.33   Zoning.

The courts apply the consistency requirement by upholding refusals to rezone[1] and rezonings[2] that are consistent with a comprehensive plan and by invalidating

---

[7] Pattey v. Board of County Comm'rs, 317 A.2d 142 (Md. 1974); Hughes v. Mayor & Comm'rs of City of Jackson, 296 So. 2d 689 (Miss. 1974); Parkridge v. City of Seattle 573 P.2d 359 (Wash. 1978). *Compare* West Ridge, Inc. v. McNamara, 160 A.2d 907 (Md. 1960) (contra). *See* Buckel v. Board of Cty. Comm'rs, 562 A.2d 1297 (Md. App. 1989) (reconciling change-mistake and fairly debatable rules).

[1] §§ 3.16–3.18.

[2] Webb v. Giltner, 468 N.W.2d 838 (Iowa App. 1991) (compliance required); Watson v. Town Council, 805 P.2d 641 (N.M. App. 1991); Daniels v. Van Voris, 660 N.Y.S.2d 758 (App. Div. 1997).

[1] Fritz v. Lexington-Fayette Urban County Gov't, 986 S.W.2d 456 (Ky. App. 1998); F.S. Plummer Co. v. Town of Cape Elizabeth, 612 A.2d 856 (Me. 1992); City of Mounds View v. Johnson, 377 N.W.2d 476 (Minn. App. 1985) (refusal to rezone consistent with plan); Witt v. Borough of Maywood, 746 A.2d 73 (N.J.L. Div. 1998), *aff'd*, 746 A.2d 25 (N.J. App. Div. 1999) (consistency with plan subject to reasonable debate);Neighbors for Livability v. City of Beaverton, 35 P.3d 1122 (Or. App. 2001); Petersen v. Dane County, 402 N.W.2d 376 (Wis. App. 1987). *See also* Board of Supvrs. v. Jackson, 269 S.E.2d 381 (Va. 1980) (refusal to rezone held consistent with plan);

[2] Griswold v. City of Homer, 925 P.2d 1015 (Alaska 1996); Spenger, Grubb & Assocs. v. City of Hailey, 903 P.2d 741, (Idaho 1995); City of Old Town v. Dimoulas, 803 A.2d 1018 (Me. 2002) (failure in plan to mention commercial use nonfatal to change to that use); Adelman v. Town of Baldwin, 750 A.2d 577 (Me. 2000); Holmgren v. City of Lincoln, 256 N.W.2d 686 (Neb. 1977); Watson v. Town Council, 805 P.2d 641 (N.M. App. 1991); Cleaver v. Board of Adjustment, 200 A.2d 408 (Pa. 1964); Bjarnson v. County of Kitsap, 899 P.2d 1290 (Wash. App. 1995) (need not be changed circumstances when rezoning consistent with plan). *See also* Greenebaum v. City of Los Angeles, 200 Cal. Rptr. 237 (Cal. App. 1984) (approval of tract map); Pinecrest Lakes, Inc. v. Shidel, 795 So.2d 191 (Fla. App. 2001) (can enjoin construction of building approved inconsistent with plan); Vella v. Town of Camden, 677 A.2d 1051 (Me. 1996) (text amendment expanding commercial uses). *But see* Hugham v. Lexington-Fayette Urban County Gov't, 29 S.W.3d 370 (Ky. 2000) (statute does not mandate approval of rezoning consistent with plan and refusal to approve upheld).

rezonings and upholding refusals to rezone that are inconsistent with a comprehensive plan.[3] Judicial review to determine consistency with the plan requires judicial interpretation of planning policy, which may be inconsistent or ambiguous. Although courts often defer to a municipality's interpretation, they will review the policies in the plan and disagree with its interpretation if they decide it was incorrect.[4] There is a trend toward treating a rezoning subject to a consistency requirement as a quasi-judicial act that requires more stringent judicial review.[5]

In *Green v. Hayward*,[6] a county adopted a rezoning to allow a lumber mill to expand its operations. The court upheld the rezoning even though the county plan designated the area for agricultural uses to implement an urban containment policy. The court held that the plan indicated the "broad allocation" of land uses but did not "put a limit on the permissible uses of each and every tract within" the area. One or a few statements in a plan should not be used "in isolation as justification for a rezoning decision."

The court next considered a set of "minimum location standards" for industrial development in areas not shown for industrial development in the plan. It upheld

---

[3] Families Unafraid to Uphold Rural El Dorado County v. Board of Supervisors, 74 Cal. Rptr. 2d 1 (Cal. App. 1998) (zoning inconsistent with land use element of plan); Mira Dev. Co. v. City of San Diego, 252 Cal. Rptr. 825 (Cal. App. 1988) (rezoning held consistent with land use plan but violated adequate public facilities policy); Green v. County Council, 508 A.2d 882 (Del. Ch.) (rezoning held contrary to plan), *aff'd per curiam,* 516 A.2d 480 (Del. 1986); Dixon v. City of Jacksonville, 774 So.2d 763 (Fla. App. 2000) (refusal to rezone for hotel); Windward Marina, L.L.C. v. City of Destin, 743 So.2d 635 (Fla. App. 1999) (refusal to issue development order was consistent with plan); Gillis v. City of Springfield, 611 P.2d 355 (Or. App. 1980) (rezoning held contrary to plan); City of Bellevue v. East Bellevue Community Council, 983 P.2d 602 (Wash. 1999) (can reject rezoning when range of densities allowable under the plan); Schofield v. Spokane County, 980 P.2d 277 (Wash. App. 1999) (refusal to rezone consistent with plan). *See also* deBottari v. Norco City Council, 217 Cal. Rptr. 790 (Cal. App. 1985) (cannot hold referendum on zoning ordinance that would be inconsistent with plan); Amcon Corp. v. City of Eagan, 348 N.W.2d 66 (Minn. 1984) (refusal to give rationale for not following plan when denying rezoning held "evidence of arbitrary action"). *See also* 21st Century Dev. Co. v. Watts, 958 S.W.2d 25 (Ky. App. 1997) (remanding so more adequate consideration could be given to comprehensive plan).

[4] Alluis v. Marion County, 668 P.2d 1242 (Or. App. 1983); Miller v. Council of City of Grants Pass, 592 P.2d 1088 (Or. App. 1979). *See also* Bridger Canyon Property Owners' Ass'n v. Planning & Zoning Comm'n, 890 P.2d 1268 (Mont. 1995) (plan must be internally consistent); *In re* Kisiel, 772 A.2d 135 (Vt. 2001) (steep slope and road improvement planning policies).

[5] Dixon v. City of Jacksonville, 774 So.2d 763 (Fla. App. 2000) (defining and applying strict scrutiny review); Snyder v. Board of County Comm'rs, 627 So. 2d 469 (Fla. 1993); Love v. Board of City Comm'rs, 671 P.2d 471 (Idaho 1983) (council must make specific findings on consistency); Nattress v. Land Use Regulation Comm'n, 600 A.2d 391 (Me. 1991); Smith v. Town of St. Johnsbury, 554 A.2d 233 (Vt. 1988).

[6] 552 P.2d 815 (Or. 1976). For similar holdings see Haines v. City of Phoenix, 727 P.2d 339 (Ariz. App. 1986); Las Virgnenes Homeowners Fed'n, Inc. v. County of Los Angeles, 223 Cal. Rptr. 18 (Cal. App. 1986); LaBonta v. City of Waterville, 528 A.2d 1262 (Me. 1987).

the rezoning even though it was not convinced that findings by the county board showed compliance with these standards. The court noted that the plant expansion would be compatible with adjacent uses and would not disrupt neighborhood continuity because it was an expansion of an existing use.

These cases indicate that requiring zoning to be consistent with a comprehensive plan may give the courts rather than municipalities the final authority to interpret planning policy. The courts may also refuse to give effect to a plan if it is outdated,[7] and may uphold a rezoning that is inconsistent with a plan if the previous restriction was arbitrary.[8]

When a plan proposes a use for a tract of land that is different from the use permitted by the zoning ordinance, a question arises whether its owner may compel a rezoning that complies with the use proposed by the plan. In *Baker v. City of Milwaukie*,[9] the comprehensive plan showed a density for a tract of land that was lower than the density permitted by the zoning ordinance. The Oregon court ordered the city to downzone the property to the density specified in the plan. Later Oregon cases refused to order upzonings to comply with a land use designation in a plan. They held that the municipality has the discretion to determine when it will approve an upzoning, at least when the plan does not contain guidelines indicating when more intensive uses in compliance with the plan should occur.[10]

§ 6.34   Spot Planning.

A municipality can evade the consistency requirement by changing the land use designation in a plan for a tract of land so that it is consistent with a zoning map amendment it would like to adopt, a practice known as spot planning. Some courts condone "spot planning" by upholding an amendment to a comprehensive plan made at the same time as a zoning amendment.[1] Other courts review a plan

---

[7] Security Nat'l Bank v. City of Olathe, 589 P.2d 589 (Kan. 1979); Town of Bedford v. Village of Mount Kisco, 306 N.E.2d 155 (N.Y. 1973).

[8] Ferguson v. Board of County Comm'rs, 718 P.2d 1223 (Idaho 1986). *See also* Holmes v. Planning Bd. of Town of New Castle, 433 N.Y.S.2d 587 (Sup. Ct. 1980) (requiring plan to include implementation program to implement complex planning policies).

[9] 533 P.2d 772 (Or. 1975).

[10] Clinkscales v. City of Lake Oswego, 615 P.2d 1164 (Or. App. 1980); Marracci v. City of Scappoose, 552 P.2d 552 (Or. App. 1976). *Accord* Mira Dev. Co. v. City of San Diego, 252 Cal. Rptr. 825 (Cal. App. 1988) (California consistency statute does not affect city's discretionary zoning decisions); Bone v. City of Lewiston, 693 P.2d 1046 (Idaho 1984). *But see* Nova Horizon, Inc. v. City Council, 769 P.2d 721 (Nev. 1989) (council decision refusing to rezone in accordance with plan held improper); Citizens for Mount Vernon v. City of Mount Vernon, 947 P.2d 1208 (Wash. 1997). *But see* County of Clark v. Doumani, 952 P.2d 13 (Nev. 1998) (refusal to consider master plan held improper).

[1] Weigel v. Planning & Zoning Comm'n, 278 A.2d 766 (Conn. 1971); Donahue v. Zoning Bd. of Adjustment, 194 A.2d 610 (Pa. 1963). *But see* Price v. Fayette County Bd. of County Comm'rs, 958 P.2d 583 (Idaho 1998) (statute prohibits this procedure).

amendment to determine whether it is consistent with other elements in the plan.[2] In some of these states, the courts hold that the amendment of a plan is a quasi-judicial act.

The Hawaii Supreme Court adopted substantive limitations on plan amendments in *Dalton v. City & County of Honolulu*.[3] The council amended its plan and zoning ordinance on the same day to allow a medium-density residential development. The court invalidated the amendments because the council did not refer them to the planning commission and planning director for advice, as its charter required.[4] The court also held the plan amendments required new studies that showed a need for additional housing and that the site selected was the "best site" available.

Some states and municipalities attempt to control spot planning by limiting the number of times a plan can be amended each year.[5] This limitation requires a municipality to consider the cumulative effect of a group of plan amendments at one time and avoid piecemeal changes that may undercut the plan. Some zoning ordinances impose similar requirements. They allow the governing body to consider zoning amendments only at stated times during the year or require frequent comprehensive rezonings on a cyclical schedule.[6]

§ 6.35 Effect on Adjacent Communities.

In some cases, a rezoned tract is located on the border of the municipality that rezones it. In this situation, some courts invalidated commercial rezonings that were inconsistent with land uses in the adjacent community. They upheld commercial rezonings that were consistent with uses in the adjacent community, even though the uses surrounding the rezoned site in the community that adopted the rezoning were residential.[1]

---

[2] Karlson v. City of Camarillo, 161 Cal. Rptr. 260 (Cal. App. 1980); South of Sunnyside Neighborhood League v. Board of Comm'rs, 569 P.2d 1063 (Or. 1977); Marggi v. Ruecker, 533 P.2d 1372 (Or. App. 1975). *Compare* Wolff v. Dade County, 370 So. 2d 839 (Fla. App. 1979). *Cf.* City of St. Charles v. DeVault Mgt. Co., 959 S.W.2d 815 (Mo. App. 1998) (redevelopment plan inconsistent with comprehensive plan).

[3] 462 P.2d 199 (Haw. 1969).

[4] *See also* Colorado Leisure Prods., Inc. v. Johnson, 532 P.2d 742 (Colo. 1975); Houser v. Board of Comm'rs, 247 N.E.2d 670 (Ind. 1969); Save Our Rural Env't v. Snohomish County, 662 P.2d 816 (Wash. 1983).

[5] Cal. Gov't Code § 65358(b).

[6] Coppolino v. County Bd. of Appeals, 328 A.2d 55 (Md. 1974).

[1] Liberty Nat'l Bank of Chicago v. City of Chicago, 139 N.E.2d 235 (Ill. 1957); Huttig v. City of Richmond Heights, 372 S.W.2d 833 (Mo. 1963); Borough of Cresskill v. Borough of Dumont, 104 A.2d 441 (N.J. 1954).

The Washington Supreme Court adopted a "regional general welfare" test for commercial rezonings in *Save a Valuable Env't (SAVE) v. City of Bothell.*[2] An environmental organization challenged a rezoning for a major regional shopping center in an outlying agricultural and low-density residential area of the city. The court struck down the rezoning and noted that the shopping center would have "serious detrimental effects" on areas outside the city's jurisdiction. It held the municipality must consider the "welfare of the entire affected community" if a rezoning may have serious environmental effects outside its jurisdiction. The court found the shopping center would have adverse impacts on surrounding agricultural and low-density development, create a demand for new public facilities, and cause flooding.

§ 6.36 Downzoning.

A downzoning is the reserve of an upzoning and downzones and to a less restrictive use. Downzoning has become more frequent as municipalities tighten zoning regulations in comprehensive zoning revisions or growth management programs that limit growth in a community. For example, a municipality may downzone an area zoned for commercial use to residential use to reduce an oversupply of commercially-zoned land. Downzonings may also be discriminatory. A municipality may downzone land zoned for multifamily housing to residential use to block a development it disapproves. Because the landowner will not have obtained a permit in this type of case, she will not have vested rights protection. Her only recourse is to attack the legality of the downzoning.

Attempts to attack downzoning in the federal courts are seldom successful. They apply deferential federal takings[1] and substantive due process[2] rules to uphold downzoning actions. The sections that follow discuss the rules applied to downzonings in the state courts.

---

[2] 576 P.2d 401 (Wash. 1978). *See also* Committee for Sensible Land Use v. Garfield Twp., 335 N.W.2d 216 (Mich. App. 1983) (township adequately considered regional effects of shopping center rezoning).

[1] Buckles v. King County, 191 F.3d 1127 (9th Cir. 1999) (downzoning part of comprehensive plan); Pace Resources, Inc. v Shrewsbury Township, 808 F.2d 1023 (3d Cir. 1987); Park Ave. Tower Assocs. v. City of New York, 746 F.2d 135 (2d Cir. 1984); Rogin v. Bensalem Township, 616 F.2d 680 (3d Cir. 1980); William C. Haas & Co. v. City & County of San Francisco, 605 F.2d 1117 (9th Cir. 1979). *But see* A.A. Profiles, Inc. v. City of Ft. Lauderdale, 850 F.2d 1483 (11th Cir. 1988) (downzoning following revocation of building permit held invalid); JSS Realty Co. v. Town of Kittery, 177 F. Supp.2d 64 (D. Me. 2001) (refusing to dismiss substantive due process claim).

[2] New Port Largo, Inc. v. Monroe County, 95 F.3d 1084 (11th Cir. 1996); Smithfield Concerned Citizens for Fair Zoning v. Town of Smithfield, 907 F.2d 239 (1st Cir. 1990) (comprehensive rezoning); Couf v. De Blaker, 652 F.2d 585 (5th Cir. 1981); Rogin v. Bensalem Township, 616 F.2d 680 (3d Cir. 1980);

§ 6.37 The Standard Tests.

An important issue in the downzoning cases is whether the municipality carried out the downzoning as part of a comprehensive zoning revision, or whether it applied the downzoning to only one or a few properties. Comprehensive downzonings usually receive deferential and favorable judicial review.[1] Downzonings adopted for single tracts of land receive more rigorous judicial scrutiny. A downzoning of this type is known as a reverse "spot zoning." Some courts apply their spot zoning rules to this type of downzoning, although there are important differences.

Because a downzoning changes the land use classification to a less intensive use, a landowner can argue that the downzoning is a taking of property.[2] Courts also use the estoppel and vested rights doctrines to protect a landowner from a downzoning,[3] and will invalidate a downzoning that is adopted to depress the value of property prior to its acquisition.[4]

Although courts may apply the usual presumption of validity and fairly debatable rules to a downzoning and place the burden of proof on the landowner who challenges a downzoning,[5] they are sensitive to possibilities for abuse in the downzoning process. They may invalidate a downzoning if they believe it was adopted to benefit adjoining landowners who preferred a less intensive use of the downzoned land,[6] just as they may invalidate an upzoning if they believe a municipality adopted it to benefit a landowner.

Compatibility with adjacent uses is an important factor in the downzoning as well as the "spot" zoning cases. Courts usually uphold a downzoning to uses that are compatible with uses in the surrounding area, even though the downzoning substantially reduces the value of the downzoned property.[7] Incompatibility

---

[1] Norbeck Village Joint Venture v. Montgomery County Council, 254 A.2d 700 (Md. 1969); Sullivan v. Town of Acton, 645 N.E.2d 700 (Mass. App. 1995) (downzoning to control traffic along highway).

[2] Jafay v. Board of County Comm'rs, 848 P.2d 892 (Colo. 1993); Sprenger, Grubb & Assocs., Inc. v. City of Hailey, 903 P.2d 741 (Idaho 1995) (no taking); Tim Thompson, Inc. v. Village of Hinsdale, 617 N.E.2d 1227 (Ill. App. 1993) (same); Smith Inv. Co. v. Sandy City, 958 P.2d 245 (Utah App. 1998) (rejecting facial takings claim because property not deprived of all economically viable use).

[3] Kempf v. City of Iowa City, 402 N.W.2d 393 (Iowa 1987) (held invalid).

[4] § 2.23.

[5] Bird v. City of Colorado Springs, 489 P.2d 324 (Colo. 1971).

[6] Four States Realty Co. v. City of Baton Rouge, 309 So. 2d 659 (La. 1975); Trust Co. of Chicago v. City of Chicago, 96 N.E.2d 499 (Ill. 1951); Pace Resources, Inc. v. Shrewsbury Twp. Planning Comm'n, 492 A.2d 818 (Pa. Commw. 1985); 51 A.L.R.2d 263 (1957). *But see* Parranto Bros. v. City of New Brighton, 425 N.W.2d 585 (Minn. App. 1988).

[7] Ex parte City of Jacksonville, 693 So.2d 465 (Ala. 1996); Lum Yip Kee, Ltd. v. City & Cty.

with uses in the surrounding area can lead to an invalidation that may be based on a holding that a taking has occurred. The courts apply this rule to residential downzonings to a more restrictive residential zoning classification[8] and to downzonings from a nonresidential to a residential use.[9]

In *McGowan v. Cohalan*,[10] for example, the court invalidated a downzoning from business to residential use of a parcel surrounded by business uses and major thoroughfares. It noted that the downzoning reduced the value of the property by ninety-two percent. This proof, though not dispositive, "tends to establish that the property is not reasonably suited for the uses prescribed."

As in the upzoning cases, a court will uphold a downzoning if it implements a comprehensive plan[11] and will invalidate a downzoning that is inconsistent with a plan.[12] In the absence of a comprehensive plan, a court must find an acceptable zoning purpose that justifies the downzoning. In *Mountcrest Estates, Inc. v. Mayor & Twp. Comm.*,[13] the township adopted a downzoning that increased lot sizes in one of its residential districts. The court applied the presumption of validity and upheld the ordinance even though the downzoning

---

of Honolulu, 767 P.2d 815 (Hawaii 1989) (citing treatise); Palermo Land Co. v. Planning Comm'n of Calcasieu Parish, 561 So. 2d 482 (La. 1990); Coppolino v. County Bd. of Appeals, 328 A.2d 55 (Md. 1974); Hyland v. Mayor & Twp. Comm., 327 A.2d 675 (N.J. App. Div. 1974); Grimpel Assocs. v. Cohalan, 361 N.E.2d 1022 (N.Y. 1977); Kelly v. Zoning Bd. of Adjustment, 276 A.2d 569 (Pa. Commw. 1971). *See* Gregory v. County of Harnett, 493 S.E.2d 786 (N.C. App. 1997) (invalidating downzoning for failure to consider these factors).

[8] City of Cherry Hills Village v. Trans-Robles Corp., 509 P.2d 797 (Colo. 1973); Aronovitz v. Metropolitan Dade County, 290 So. 2d 536 (Fla. App. 1974); Neuzil v. Iowa City, 451 N.W.2d 159 (Iowa 1990); Odabash v. Mayor & Council of Borough of Dumont, 319 A.2d 712 (N.J. 1974).

[9] Carty v. City of Ojai, 143 Cal. Rptr. 506 (Cal. App. 1978); Washington Sub. San. Comm'n v. TKU Assocs., 376 A.2d 505 (Md. 1977); National Amusements, Inc. v. City of Boston, 560 N.E.2d 138 (Mass. App. 1990); Finch v. City of Durham, 384 S.E.2d 9 (N.C. 1989) (extensive discussion of taking doctrine); Superior Uptown, Inc. v. City of Cleveland, 313 N.E.2d 820 (Ohio 1974).

[10] 361 N.E.2d 1025 (N.Y. 1977). *Accord* D'Addario v. Planning & Zoning Comm'n, 593 A.2d 511 (Conn. App. 1991).

[11] Carty v. City of Ojai, 143 Cal. Rptr. 506 (Cal. App. 1978); Lum Yip Kee, Ltd. v. City & Cty. of Honolulu, 767 P.2d 815 (Hawaii 1989) (citing treatise); Sprenger, Grubb & Assocs., Inc. v. City of Hailey, 903 P.2d 741 (Idaho 1995); Hibernia Nat'l Bank v. City of New Orleans, 455 So. 2d 1239 (La. App. 1984) (even though downzoning adopted because of neighbor objections); Riggs v. Township of Long Beach, 514 A.2d 45 (N.J. App. Div. 1986); Horizon Adirondack Corp. v. State of New York, 388 N.Y.S.2d 235 (Ct. Cl. 1976).

[12] Pace Resources, Inc. v. Shrewsbury Twp. Planning Comm'n, 492 A.2d 818 (Pa. Commw. 1985). *See also* Udell v. Haas, 235 N.E.2d 897 (N.Y. 1968).

[13] 232 A.2d 674 (N.J. App. Div. 1967); Miller v. Town of Tilton, 655 A.2d 409 (N.H. 1995) (extending agricultural buffer area); Smith Inv. Co. v. Sandy City, 958 P.2d 245 (Utah App. 1998) (rejecting facial substantive due process challenge because downzoning to residential justified to reduce commercial area, support adjacent neighborhood and avoid traffic problems).

was inconsistent with development in much of the surrounding area. "The municipality's problems with respect to congestion, overcrowding and inability to provide public facilities due to the population explosion [will be lessened by the downzoning]."[14] Courts have also upheld downzonings to protect water supplies and environment areas and avoid health problems, even when the downzoning severely restricted the use of the downzoned land.[15]

Some courts invalidated downzonings because they found that they were exclusionary. In *Kavanewsky v. Zoning Bd. of Appeals,*[16] the court invalidated a downzoning that reduced residential densities in one of the town's zoning districts. It noted that the downzoning "'was made in demand of the people to keep Warren a rural community with open spaces and keep undesirable businesses out.'" The Iowa court upheld a downzoning from multifamily to single-family use that a municipality adopted to block a federally-subsidized multifamily housing project. The court accepted the city's claim that the multifamily zoning was inconsistent with the expected growth of the area and would create traffic and pedestrian flow problems and that public services were inadequate for multifamily development.[17]

§ 6.38   Change-Mistake Rule.

When a court holds the rezoning process is quasi-judicial it may also require a change in circumstances to justify a downzoning. In *Parkridge v. City of Seattle,*[1] for example, the court held there is no presumption of validity favoring the action of rezoning, that the proponents of the rezone have the burden of proof in demonstrating that conditions have substantially changed since the original zoning, and that the rezone must bear a substantial relationship to the public health, safety, morals or welfare.

The Virginia Supreme Court adopted a similar rule in *Board of Supvrs. v. Snell Constr. Corp.*[2] Once a landowner introduces evidence showing that a piecemeal

---

[14] 232 A.2d at 677.

[15] Chucta v. Planning & Zoning Comm'n, 225 A.2d 822 (Conn. 1967); Lee Cty. v. Morales, 557 So. 2d 652 (Fla. App. 1990) (barrier island); Moviematic Indus. v. Board of County Comm'rs, 349 So. 2d 667 (Fla. App. 1977); Parranto Bros. v. City of New Brighton, 425 N.W.2d 585 (Minn. App. 1988) (and because market for previously zoned use saturated); Pacific Blvd. Assocs. v. City of Long Beach, 368 N.Y.S.2d 867 (Sup. Ct. 1975). *Compare* Steel Hill Dev., Inc. v. Town of Sanbornton, 469 F.2d 956 (1st Cir. 1972).

[16] 279 A.2d 567 (Conn. 1971).

[17] Stone v. City of Wilton, 331 N.W.2d 398 (Iowa 1983). *But see* Ogo Assocs. v. City of Torrance, 112 Cal. Rptr. 761 (Cal. App. 1974).

[1] 573 P.2d 359 (Wash. 1978), *applied in* Englund v. King County, 839 P.2d 339 (Wash. App (1992). *Accord,* Board of Supervisors v. Snell Constr. Corp., 202 S.E.2d 889 (Va. 1974), *applied in* City of Virginia Beach v. Virginia Land Inv. Ass'n No. 1, 389 S.E.2d 312 (Va. 1990). *See also* Davis v. City of Albuquerque, 648 P.2d 777 (N.M. 1982).

[2] 202 S.E.2d 889 (Va. 1974).

downzoning is not justified by changed circumstances, the municipality must introduce evidence of mistake, fraud, or changed circumstances sufficient to make the downzoning a reasonably debatable issue. The usual presumption of validity is weakened. Nor is a political change in the governing body a sufficient change in circumstances to justify a downzoning.

E. VARIANCES, SPECIAL EXCEPTIONS, AND CONDITIONAL USES.

§ 6.39 Role and Function.

The drafters of the Standard Zoning Act clearly contemplated a zoning process in which the uses designated by the zoning ordinance were permitted "as of right," but they also provided for an administrative zoning function. The Standard Act delegated this function to the board of adjustment. It authorized the board to grant variances from the zoning ordinance in cases of hardship, as defined in the Act, and to grant special exceptions authorized by provisions in the zoning ordinance. Many zoning ordinances use the term "special" or "conditional" use rather than "special exception." Notice that the authority for variances is based on criteria contained in the Act, but that the governing body has the authority to determine when the board may grant special exceptions.

Courts often confuse the variance with the special exception, but the distinction should be clear. The highest New York court has provided the following distinction:

> A variance is an authority to a property owner to use property in a manner forbidden by the ordinance while a special exception allows the property owner to put his property to a use expressly permitted by the ordinance.[1]

The court added that a variance is harder to obtain than a special exception, and that the applicant in a variance case bears a higher burden of proof. This definition is reflected in the frequently quoted judicial maxim that variances should be granted "sparingly."[2] Courts often adopt a contrary presumption for special exceptions.[3]

---

[1] North Shore Steak House, Inc. v. Board of Appeals, 282 N.E.2d 606, 609 (N.Y. 1972). For similar definitions, see Vogelaar v. Polk County Zoning Bd. of Adjustment, 188 N.W.2d 860 (Iowa 1971); Luger v. City of Brunsville, 295 N.W.2d 609 (Minn. 1980); Verona, Inc. v. Mayor & Council of West Caldwell, 229 A.2d 651 (N.J. 1967); Nucholls v. Board of Adjustment, 560 P.2d 556 (Okla. 1977).

[2] Dolan v. Zoning Bd. of Appeals, 242 A.2d 713 (Conn. 1968); Broderick v. Board of Appeal, 280 N.E.2d 670 (Mass. 1972); Cook v. Zoning Hearing Bd., 408 A.2d 1157 (Pa. Commw. 1979).

[3] § 6.56.

§ 6.40   Variances.

§ 6.41   Role and Function.

The authority to grant variances[1] is found in § 7 of the Standard Zoning Act, which most states adopted and which authorizes the board of adjustment:

> To authorize upon appeal in specific cases such variance from the terms of the ordinance as will not be contrary to the public interest, where, owing to special conditions, a literal enforcement of the provisions of the ordinance will result in unnecessary hardship, and so that the spirit of the ordinance shall be observed and substantial justice done.

This provision authorizes a hardship variance. A number of states also authorize a variance because of "practical difficulties," a standard applied principally to area variances. Some statutes and ordinances contain an additional provision that requires the board to consider the impact of the variance on the surrounding area. The language of the Standard Act that requires that the "spirit" of the ordinance be observed and "substantial justice" done does not often receive attention in the cases.[2] Statutes and ordinances may also contain a requirement, contained in the Standard Zoning Act, that a zoning variance must not be contrary to the public interest.[3] A few states have adopted standards for variances that are more detailed than the Standard Act,[4] and New Jersey has a unique hybrid provision that authorizes a variance for "special reasons."[5] A variance runs with the land and is not personal to the landowner who receives it.[6]

The zoning act provides the standards zoning boards must apply when they grant variances. Municipalities in home rule states may be able to modify the statutory standards,[7] but if a municipality's zoning power is based on the zoning statute it may not adopt standards that conflict with the statute,[8] though a

---

[1] *See* Cromwell v. Ward, 651 A.2d 424 (Md. App. 1995) (discusses role of variances).

[2] *But see* Belanger v. City of Nashua, 430 A.2d 166 (N.H. 1981); Fobe Assocs. v. Mayor & Council, 379 A.2d 31 (N.J. 1977).

[3] Larsen v. Zoning Bd. of Adjustment, 672 A.2d 286 (Pa. 1996); State v. Winnebago County, 540 N.W.2d 6 (Wis. App. 1995).

[4] Pa. Stat. Ann. tit. 53, § 10910.2; Va. Code Ann. § 15.1-495(2).

[5] N.J. Stat. Ann. § 40:55D-70(d). *See* Sica v. Board of Adj., 603 A.2d 30 (N.J. 1992); Medici v. BPR Co., 526 A.2d 109 (N.J. 1987).

[6] Stop & Shop Supermarket Co. v. Board of Adjustment, 744 A.2d 1169 (N.J. 2000) (citing cases).

[7] § 4.25.

[8] Nelson v. Donaldson, 50 So. 2d 244 (Ala. 1951); Celentano, Inc. v. Board of Zoning Appeals, 184 A.2d 49 (Conn. 1962); Dsuban v. Union Township Zoning Bd. of Appeals, 748 N.E.2d 597 (Ohio App. 2000) (statute did not authorize practical difficulties standard); Sorg v. North Hero Zoning Bd. of Adjustment, 378 A.2d 98 (Vt. 1977).

municipal ordinance can supplement the statutory standards.[9] A court may reverse a zoning board if its decision is not based on the statutory standards. An example is a zoning board decision that denies a variance because of neighborhood opposition.[10] A board may grant a variance to modify a definition in a zoning ordinance.[11] A zoning board may not decline jurisdiction of a variance application because it believes it should be treated as a rezoning.[12]

The discussion that follows considers each of the standards separately but requires qualification because a court may consider all of the statutory standards together and may not indicate which standard it finds controlling. The "unnecessary hardship" standard probably receives more judicial attention than any of the others.[13]

§ 6.42 Use and Area Variances.

Although the zoning statutes do not usually make this distinction, the courts have always distinguished use from area variances. The following judicial distinction is typical:

> A use variance is one which permits a use other than that prescribed by the zoning ordinance. . . . An area variance . . . is primarily a grant to erect, alter, or use a structure for a permitted use in a manner other than that prescribed by . . . the zoning ordinance.[1]

---

[9] Gould v. Santa Fe County, 37 P.3d 122 (N.M. App. 2001).

[10] Arkules v. Board of Adjustment, 728 P.2d 657 (Ariz. App. 1986); Silverco, Inc. v. Zoning Bd. of Adjustment, 109 A.2d 147 (Pa. 1954); Appeal of Lindquist, 73 A.2d 378 (Pa. 1950); Kent v. Zoning Bd. of Review, 58 A.2d 623 (R.I. 1948). *See also* Knipple v. Geistown Borough Zoning Hearing Bd., 624 A.2d 766 (Pa. Commw. 1993) (finding conscious discrimination in denial of variance).

[11] Cricklewood Hill Realty Assocs. v. Zoning Bd. of Adj., 558 A.2d 178 (Pa. Commw. 1989) (definition of family).

[12] TWC Realty Partnership v. Zoning Bd. of Adjustment, 717 A.2d 439 (N.J.L. Div. 1998), *aff'd*, 728 A.2d 338 (N.J. App. Div. 1999).

[13] *See also* Klein v. Hamilton County Bd. of Zoning Appeals, 716 N.E.2d 268 (Ohio App. 1999) (need not grant variance for commercial use in residential zone when it is less discreet than other uses allowed in that zone).

[1] Jenney v. Durham, 707 A.2d 752 (Del. Super. 1997) (variance from steep slope ordinance is use variance to which unnecessary hardship test applies), *aff'd*, 696 A.2d 396 (Del. 1997); Alumni Control Bd. v. City of Lincoln, 137 N.W.2d 800, 802 (Neb. 1965). *See also* Anderson v. Board of Appeals of Chesapeake Beach, 322 A.2d 220 (Md. App. 1974); Consolidated Edison Co. of N.Y. v. Hoffman, 374 N.E.2d 105 (N.Y. 1978). *See* Bella Vista Apartment Co. v. Bennett, 678 N.E.2d 198 (N.Y. 1997) (cannot sell portion of lot that received use variance to adjoining owner to avoid need to seek area variance); Hertzberg v. Zoning Bd. of Adjustment, 721 A.2d 53 (Pa. 1998) (conversion of vacant building to homeless shelter is dimensional variance); Segal v. Zoning Hearing Bd., 771 A.2d 90 (Pa. Commw. 2001) (relief from prohibition against filling of wetlands not an area variance).

An area variance modifies site development requirements for permitted uses, such as lot size, yard, setback, and frontage restrictions. A variance that would change a prohibited use is not an area variance.[2] A landowner may also request an area variance for an increase in densities. An example is an area variance that substantially increases multifamily densities. The courts are divided on whether an increase in density requires a use or an area variance. Some courts hold that only an area variance is required.[3] Other courts are not as lenient. In *O'Neill v. Zoning Bd. of Adjustment*,[4] the landowner obtained a variance that increased the floor space permitted in a multifamily building by two and one-half times. The court held that this change had to be made by the governing body.[5]

§ 6.43 Use Variances Prohibited.

Although most cases hold that zoning statutes based on the Standard Act authorize a use variance,[1] a substantial number hold that use variances are prohibited.[2] The decisions that prohibit a use variance hold that a change in use requires an amendment to the zoning ordinance and that a use variance would usurp the amendment power. A few zoning statutes prohibit use variances.[3] Field studies that found substantial abuses in the granting of use variances lend support to decisions and statutes that prohibit them.

Some courts that do not absolutely prohibit use variances take an intermediate view and disapprove a particular use variance if they believe it constitutes an improper amendment of the zoning ordinance. The size of the parcel affected by the variance was a controlling factor in most of these cases.[4] *Township of*

---

[2] Society Created to Reduce Urban Blight (SCRUB) v. Zoning Bd. of Adjustment, 787 A.2d 1123 (Pa. Commw. 2001) (prohibition on billboard).

[3] Wilcox v. Zoning Bd. of Appeals, 217 N.E.2d 633 (N.Y. 1966).

[4] 254 A.2d 12 (Pa. 1969).

[5] *See also* Broadway, Laguna, Vallejo Ass'n v. Board of Permit Appeals, 427 P.2d 810 (Cal. 1967); Taylor v. District of Columbia Bd. of Zoning Adjustment, 308 A.2d 230 (D.C. App. 1973); Mavrantonis v. Board of Adjustment, 258 A.2d 908 (Del. 1969); Board of Adjustment v. Willie, 511 S.W.2d 591 (Tex. Civ. App. 1974).

[1] Clarke v. Morgan, 327 So. 2d 769 (Fla. 1976); Strange v. Board of Zoning Appeals, 428 N.E.2d 1328 (Ind. App. 1981); Appeal of Kennedy, 374 N.W.2d 271 (Minn. 1985); Matthew v. Smith, 707 S.W.2d 411 (Mo. 1986) (quoting treatise); Nucholls v. Board of Adjustment, 560 P.2d 556 (Okla. 1977).

[2] Bradley v. Zoning Bd. of Appeals, 334 A.2d 914 (Conn. 1973); Stice v. Gribben-Allen Motors, Inc., 534 P.2d 1267 (Kan. 1975); Standard Oil Co. v. City of Warrensville Heights, 355 N.E.2d 495 (Ohio App. 1976); Banks v. City of Bethany, 541 P.2d 178 (Okla. 1975); Swain v. Board of Adjustment, 433 S.W.2d 727 (Tex. App. 1968). *Compare* Swann v. Board of Adjustment, 459 So. 2d 896 (Ala. Civ. App. 1984) (ordinance cannot prohibit use variance), *with* Zoning Bd. of Appeals v. Planning & Zoning Comm'n, 605 A.2d 885 (Conn. App. 1992) (contra).

[3] Cal. Gov't Code § 65906.

[4] Sinclair Pipe Line Co. v. Village of Richton Park, 167 N.E.2d 406 (Ill. 1960); Staller v. Cranston Zoning Bd. of Review, 215 A.2d 418 (R.I. 1965). *Compare* Cavanaugh v. DiFlumera, 401 N.E.2d 867 (Mass. 1980); DeSimone v. Greater Englewood Hous. Corp. No. 1, 267 A.2d 31 (N.J. 1970).

Dover v. Board of Adjustment[5] considered parcel size along with other related factors to determine whether the board of adjustment had engaged in "proscribed legislation" when it granted a use variance. It held that "[t]he basic inquiry in each such case must be whether the impact of the requested variance will be to substantially alter the character of the district as that character has been prescribed by the zoning ordinance."[6] The court suggested a number of factors to consider in making this determination, including the size of the parcel, its size and character in relation to the size and character of the zoning district and the municipality, and the "degree and extent of the variation from district regulations."

Dover also suggested an inverse relationship between a use variance and a rezoning. It suggested that a property that was too small for a rezoning might be eligible for a use variance. A large tract that is ineligible for a variance might be eligible for a rezoning.

§ 6.44   Unnecessary Hardship.

The classic statement of the unnecessary hardship test appears in a New York case, *Otto v. Steinhilber*:[1]

> Before the Board may . . . grant a variance upon the ground of unnecessary hardship, the record must show that (1) the land in question cannot yield a reasonable return if used only for a purpose allowed in that zone; (2) that the plight of the owner is due to unique circumstances and not to the general conditions of the neighborhood which may reflect the unreasonableness of the zoning ordinance itself; and (3) that the use to be authorized by the variance will not alter the essential character of the locality.[2]

A number of courts have adopted these criteria for unnecessary hardship, which reflect the restrictive judicial view toward variances.[3] Not all of these criteria apply to the unnecessary hardship determination. The second criterion reflects the limitation on variances noted earlier, that a board may not grant a variance when an amendment of the zoning ordinance is indicated.[4] For example, a court

---

[5] 386 A.2d 421 (N.J. App. Div. 1978).

[6] *Id.* at 427.

[1] 24 N.E.2d 851 (N.Y. 1939).

[2] *Id.* at 853.

[3] Deardorf v. Board of Adjustment, 118 N.W.2d 78 (Iowa 1962); Lovely v. Zoning Bd. of Appeals, 259 A.2d 666 (Me. 1969); Puritan-Greenfield Imp. Ass'n v. Leo, 153 N.W.2d 162 (Mich. App. 1967); Matthew v. Smith, 707 S.W.2d 411 (Mo. 1986). *Compare* Larsen v. Zoning Bd. of Adjustment, 672 A.2d 286 (Pa. 1996) (may not base hardship on need for additional space in dwelling); Joseph B. Simon & Co. v. Zoning Bd. of Adjustment, 168 A.2d 317 (Pa. 1961). *See* 168 A.L.R. 13 (1957).

[4] In re Dunnett, 776 A.2d 406 (Vt. 2001).

may not grant a variance based on a hardship that does not distinguish it from other uses in the area, such as the historic character of a building. Neither may a board grant a variance because a zoning enforcement officer acted arbitrarily in applying an ordinance, or because the language of an ordinance is uncertain.[5] New York has codified its judicially-adopted variance test, and the statutes also require proof that the applicant has been deprived of "all economic use or benefit from the property."[6] New Hampshire has liberalized its tests for unnecessary hardship.[7]

§ 6.45 No Reasonable Return.

The requirement adopted in *Otto*,[1] that the board may grant a variance only if it finds that the landowner cannot make a reasonable return on her property, is a standard requirement in variance law.[2] This rule is similar to the rule that a landowner must show an inability to make a reasonable use of her land in order to prove an as-applied taking.[3] The "no reasonable return" rule means that the use variance is an administrative alternative to litigation that claims the zoning restriction on the land is an as-applied taking. A variance can avoid the damage that can occur to a zoning ordinance as a result of successful as-applied taking litigation.[4] Whether changes in taking doctrine adopted by the U.S. Supreme Court will result in changes in the proof of economic impairment required for a variance is not yet clear. The Maryland court has held the "reasonable return" or "reasonable use" test is less restrictive than the tests for a taking of property because otherwise the variance standard would be "superfluous" to the constitutional takings standard.[5]

---

[5] Wnuk v. Zoning Bd. of Appeals, 626 A.2d 698 (Conn. 1993). *See* Moroney v. Mayor & Council, 633 A.2d 1045 (N.J. App. 1993) (court may award compensation for variance denial).

[6] N.Y. Gen. City Law § 81-b; N.Y. Town Law § 267-b(2)(b); N.Y. Village Law § 7-712-b.

[7] Simplex Technologies, Inc. v. Town of Newington, 766 A.2d 713 (N.H. 2001) (zoning restriction as applied interferes with reasonable use considering unique setting in environment; no fair and substantial relationship between general purposes of zoning ordinance and specific restriction; variance would not injure public or private rights of others).

[1] § 6.44.

[2] Baker v. Connell, 488 A.2d 1303 (Del. 1985); Jenney v. Durham, 707 A.2d 752 (Del. Super. 1997) (rejecting steep slope variance), *aff'd*, 606 A.2d 396 (Del. 1997); Joy Street Condominium Ass'n v. Board of Appeal, 688 N.E.2d 1363 (Mass. 1998) (invalidating variance allowing conversion of residential unit to beauty salon); Grey Rocks Land Trust v. Town of Hebron, 614 A.2d 1048 (N.H. 1992); Soho Alliance v. New York City Bd. of Standards & Appeals, 741 N.E.2d 106 (N.Y. 2000) (proof shown). *But see* Allegheny West Civic Council, Inc. v. Zoning Bd. of Adjustment, 689 A.2d 225 (Pa. 1997) (need not show that property has no value).

[3] *See* Belvoir Farms Homeowners Ass'n, Inc. v. North, 734 A.2d 227 (Md. 1999) (citing cases to show that majority of courts adopt the "reasonable use" standard); Village Bd. v. Jarrold, 423 N.E.2d 385 (N.Y. 1981) (two rules are "much the same").

[4] *See* Puritan-Greenfield Imp. Ass'n v. Leo, 153 N.W.2d 162 (Mich. App. 1967).

[5] Belvoir Farms Homeowners Ass'n, Inc. v. North, 734 A.2d 227 (Md. 1999).

The "no reasonable return" rule means that a landowner does not make a case for a variance simply by showing that his property could be used for a more profitable use if the board granted the variance. The typical judicial point of view in this type of case is illustrated by *Carbonneau v. Town of Exeter*.[6] An applicant for a variance had been using the bottom floor of his home as a funeral business, which was an established nonconforming use. He applied for a variance to operate a beauty parlor on the bottom floor of a barn located on his property. The court held that a desire to make a more profitable use of the property did not justify a variance.[7]

The New York court expanded the *Otto* tests by holding, in *Forrest v. Evershed*,[8] that the applicant must show that he made diligent efforts to sell his property without success. Although not always applied in New York, this requirement has some following elsewhere in cases that either require efforts to sell or that accept such efforts as evidence of hardship.[9] Other courts reject or are critical of the requirement that the applicant must show actual efforts to sell. They allow evidence of inability to sell to show that a reasonable return is not possible under the existing zoning restriction.[10]

This rule is preferable. The ability to sell a property may depend on factors other than the zoning ordinance, such as the state of the property market. A rule that requires diligent efforts to sell contradicts the assumption underlying the "no reasonable return" rule that variances are based on an inability to use the property under the zoning ordinance, not on circumstances personal to the user.

§ 6.46 Unique to the Owner.

The requirement adopted in *Otto*[1] that the applicant for a use variance must show a unique hardship to his property restates the rule that a variance is not proper when other forms of relief from the zoning ordinance are available. As the New York court stated in *Otto*:

---

[6] 401 A.2d 675 (N.H. 1979).

[7] *Accord* Graziano v. Board of Adjustment, 323 N.W.2d 233 (Iowa 1982); State ex rel. Pitts v. Board of Zoning Adjustments, 327 So. 2d 140 (La. App. 1976); City Council of Waltham v. Vinciullo, 307 N.E.2d 316 (Mass. 1974); Lovely v. Zoning Bd. of Appeals, 259 A.2d 666 (Me. 1969); Olszak v. Town of New Hampton, 661 A.2d 768 (N.H. 1995); Enterprise Citizens Action Comm. v. Clark County Bd. of Comm'rs, 918 P.2d 305 (Nev. 1996); MacLean v. Zoning Bd. of Adjustment, 185 A.2d 533 (Pa. 1962); State v. Winnebago County, 540 N.W.2d 6 (Wis. App. 1995).

[8] 164 N.E.2d 841 (N.Y. 1959).

[9] Puritan-Greenfield Imp. Ass'n v. Leo, 153 N.W.2d 162 (Mich. App. 1967); Chirichello v. Zoning Bd. of Adjustment, 397 A.2d 646 (N.J. 1979).

[10] Culinary Inst. of Am. v. Board of Zoning Appeals, 121 A.2d 637 (Conn. 1956); Valley View Civic Ass'n v. Zoning Bd. of Adjustment, 462 A.2d 637 (Pa. 1983); Guenther v. Zoning Bd. of Review, 125 A.2d 214 (R.I. 1956).

[1] § 6.44.

[T]he fault may lie in the fact that the particular zoning restriction is unreasonable in its application to a certain locality. . . . In . . . [this] situation, the relief is by way of direct attack upon the terms of the ordinance.[2]

Other courts allow a landowner to apply for an amendment of the zoning ordinance in this situation. Some states have codified the uniqueness requirement.[3]

The courts generally hold that a board may not grant a variance because of conditions general to the neighborhood.[4] This rule is an application of the uniqueness requirement. If strictly applied, it would substantially limit the power of zoning boards to grant use variances, which are often requested because of changes in the character of a neighborhood. In a typical case of this type, an owner of a single-family dwelling on the edge of a business district applies for a variance to allow a commercial use of the dwelling. He claims that the adjacent commercial uses and an increase in motor vehicle traffic in the neighborhood make a residential use of the dwelling unreasonable. A court that applies the rule that a variance cannot be based on conditions general to a neighborhood will not approve a variance in this case.

Courts will not accept policy reasons as the basis for a variance, such as a claim that a housing shortage justifies a variance for apartments in a single-family residential area.[5] Although this type of claim may indicate that the variance serves the public interest, it does not establish conditions unique to the property. Policy reasons of this kind may justify a rezoning.

---

[2] 24 N.E.2d at 852. *Accord* State v. Winnebago County, 540 N.W.2d 6 (Wis. App. 1995). *See also* North v. St. Mary's County, 638 A.2d 1175 (Md. App. 1994) (discussing uniqueness requirement); Douglaston Civic Ass'n v. Klein, 416 N.E.2d 1040 (N.Y. 1980).

[3] Cal. Gov't Code § 64906.

[4] Smith v. Zoning Bd. of Appeals, 387 A.2d 542 (Conn. 1978); Kelly v. Zoning Bd. of Appeals, 575 A.2d 249 (Conn. App. 1990); Town of Indialantic v. Nance, 419 So. 2d 1041 (Fla. 1982); Puritan-Greenfield Imp. Ass'n v. Leo, 153 N.W.2d 162 (Mich. App. 1967); Moore v. City of Rochester, 427 A.2d 10 (N.H. 1981); Vidal v. Lisanti Foods, 679 A.2d 206 (N.J. App. 1996). *Contra,* Sherwood v. Grant County, 699 P.2d 243 (Wash. App. 1985). *Compare* Wolfman v. Board of Appeals, 444 N.E.2d 942 (Mass. App. 1983) (soil conditions justified variance to avoid height increase), *with* Governor's Island Club, Inc. v. Town of Gilford, 467 A.2d 246 (N.H. 1983) (substandard lot size not a unique problem), *and* City of Burley v. McCaslin Lumber Co., 693 P.2d 1108 (Idaho App. 1984) (increasing density to make investment economically feasible not condition unique to property).

[5] Zaruta v. Zoning Hearing Bd., 543 A.2d 1282 (Pa. Commw. 1988) (structure for homeless); Cass v. Board of Appeal, 317 N.E.2d 77 (Mass. 1974); Farah v. Sachs, 157 N.W.2d 9 (Mich. App. 1968); Downtown Neighborhood Ass'n v. City of Albuquerque, 783 P.2d 962 (N.M. App. 1989) (historic structure); Xanthos v. Board of Adjustment, 685 P.2d 1032 (Utah 1984) (retention of low-cost housing units). *But see* Kessler-Allisonville Civic League, Inc. v. Marion County Bd. of Zoning Appeals, 209 N.E.2d 43 (Ind. App. 1965).

§ 6.47 Impact on the Neighborhood.

The *Otto* case[1] also adopted this requirement. It noted that "the use to be authorized by the variance . . . [should] not alter the essential character of the locality."[2] Zoning statutes and ordinances may include this requirement, which courts may refer to as the "negative" criterion. A related provision that appears in some statutes requires that "relief can be granted without substantial detriment to the public good."[3]

Commons v. Westwood Zoning Bd. of Adjustment[4] illustrates a judicial application of the negative criterion. A landowner requested a variance to build a house on an undersized lot. The court noted that "if the size and layout of the proposed house would have adversely affected the character of the neighborhood . . . a board may justly conclude that a variance should not be granted." Other courts apply the negative criterion by balancing the hardship to the property owner against detrimental impacts on the surrounding area.[5]

§ 6.48 Availability of Area Variances.

The Standard Zoning Act did not make a distinction between area and use variances and provided a single "unnecessary hardship" test for both. A number of zoning statutes and ordinances modify the Standard Act by authorizing a variance for "practical difficulties" as well as for unnecessary hardship.[1] Many cases hold this type of statute does not create a dual standard and apply the unnecessary hardship test and other tests for use variances to area variances.[2]

---

[1] § 6.44.

[2] *See* Jackson v. City of San Mateo, 307 P.2d 451 (Cal. App. 1957); Culinary Inst. of Am. v. Board of Zoning Appeals, 121 A.2d 637 (Conn. 1956); Janssen v. Holland Charter Bd. of Zoning Appeals, 651 N.W.2d 464 (Mich. App. 2002) (court took note of changing character of surrounding agricultural area); Gullickson v. Stark County Bd. of County Comm'rs, 474 N.W.2d 890 (N.D. 1991).

[3] N.J. Stat. Ann. § 40:55D-70(d). *See* Smart SMR of N.Y., Inc. v. Borough of Fair Lawn Bd. of Adjustment, 704 A.2d 1271 (N.J. 1998) (reversing denial of use variance for cellular tower).

[4] 410 A.2d 1138 (N.J. 1980).

[5] Amberley Swim & Country Club v. Zoning Bd. of Appeals, 191 N.E.2d 364 (Ohio App. 1963).

[1] *See also* American Planning Association, Growing Smart Legislative Guidebook: Model Statutes for Planning and Management of Change § 10-503 (S. Meck ed. 2002) (authorizing area variances).

[2] Abel v. Zoning Bd. of Appeals, 374 A.2d 227 (Conn. 1977); Graziano v. Board of Adjustment, 323 N.W.2d 233 (Iowa 1982); City of Merriam v. Board of Zoning Appeals, 748 P.2d 883 (Kan. 1988); Marchi v. Town of Scarborough, 511 A.2d 1071 (Me. 1986); Matthew v. Smith, 707 S.W.2d 411 (Mo. 1986) (citing this treatise); Alumni Control Bd. v. City of Lincoln, 137 N.W.2d 800 (Neb. 1965); Ouimette v. City of Somersworth, 402 A.2d 159 (N. H.1979); Chirichello v. Zoning Bd. of Adjustment, 397 A.2d 646 (N.J. 1979); Brown v. Fraser, 467 P.2d 464 (Okla. 1970); Kelley v. Clackamas County, 973 P.2d 916 (Or. App. 1999) difficulties standard); Cummings v. City of Seattle, 935 P.2d 663 (Wash. App. 1997) (citing this treatise); Snyder v. Waukesha County Zoning

City & Borough of Juneau v. Thibodeau[3] is a leading decision. The court pointed out that, in the cases holding that the statute adopted a separate practical difficulties test for area variances, the statute or zoning ordinance stated the two variance tests disjunctively. The court refused to adopt a separate practical difficulties test for area variances because the Juneau zoning ordinance stated the two tests conjunctively.

Thibodeau illustrates the application of the unnecessary hardship rule to deny an area variance. A landowner was granted a rezoning to expand a store and then applied for and received an area variance to reduce the required number of parking spaces. The court reversed. It noted that a variance must be based on "physical conditions of the land itself which distinguished it from other land in the general area." It added that if the property has substantially the same value for the permitted uses as other property within the same zoning classification, the "assertion that the ordinance merely deprives the landowner of a more profitable operation" is not sufficient.[4]

Courts have adopted a variety of tests for area variances when they do not apply the unnecessary hardship test. They have made it clear that the difference between the tests for use and area variances is a matter of degree, but have also emphasized that the test for area variances is less stringent. Courts that apply the practical difficulties test have also adopted a set of factors that determine when this test justifies an area variance. These usually include the significance of the economic injury, the magnitude of the variance sought, whether the difficulty was self-created, and whether other feasible alternatives could avoid the difficulty.[5] The effect of the variance on the surrounding neighborhood is also considered.[6]

Bd. of Adjustment, 247 N.W.2d 98 (Wis. 1976). *See also* Bennett v. Sullivan's Island Bd. of Adjustment, 438 S.E.2d 273 (S.C. App. 1993) ("peculiarity" requirement interpreted not to mean "unique"). *See* Me. Rev. Stat. Ann. tit. 30-A, § 4353(4) (adopting practical difficulties test).

[3] 595 P.2d 626 (Alaska 1979).

[4] *Accord* Margate Motel, Inc. v. Town of Gilford, 534 A.2d 717 (N.H. 1987). *But see* City of Olathe v. Board of Zoning Appeals, 696 P.2d 409 (Kan. App. 1986) (applying use variance criteria to approve variance for name change on sign); Marchi v. Town of Scarborough, 511 A.2d 1071 (Me. 1986) (same; setback variance); State *ex rel.* Klawuhn v. Board of Zoning Adjustment, 952 S.W.2d 725 (Mo. App. 1997) (cannot base variance on conditions personal to owner); State v. Kenosha County Bd. of Adjustment, 577 N.W.2d 813 (Wis. 1998) (reversing setback variance on lake so landowner could build deck).

[5] Doyle v. Amster, 594 N.E.2d 911 (N.Y. 1992); Human Dev. Serv. of Porth Chester v. Zoning Bd. of Appeals, 493 N.Y.S.2d 481 (App. Div. 1985) (now modified by statute), *aff'd mem.*, 480 N.E.2d 927 (N.Y. 1986); Burkholder v. Twinsburg Township Bd. of Zoning Appeals, 701 N.E.2d 766 (Ohio App. 1997). *See also* Metropolitan Bd. of Zoning Appeals v. McDonald's Corp., 481 N.E.2d 141 (Ind. App. 1985) (statutory test); McLean v. Soley, 270 Md. 208 (Md. 1973); National Boatland, Inc. v. Farmington Hills Zoning Bd. of Appeals, 380 N.W.2d 472 (Mich. App. 1985); Duncan v. Village of Midfield, 491 N.E.2d 692 (Ohio 1986).

[6] Four M Constr. Corp. v. Fritts, 543 N.Y.S.2d 213 (App. Div. 1989); Cardamone v. Whitpain Township Zoning Hearing Bd., 771 A.2d 103 (Pa. Commw. 2001)

Not all courts apply these criteria, and statutes or ordinances may contain different standards.[7] For example, local ordinances or judicial decisions may modify this test by requiring "extraordinary" or "exceptional" difficulties,[8] while other courts seem to soften this test by requiring only "adverse impact" that is more than mere inconvenience.[9] Courts, or statutes and ordinances, may also impose a uniqueness requirement under the practical difficulties test.[10] New York statutes require a balancing of the benefit to the applicant against the detriment to the neighborhood or community through consideration of five statutory factors.[11] These factors are similar to factors adopted by other courts to apply the practical difficulties test.[12] In a case in which the owner of a vacant building planned to convert it to a homeless shelter, the Pennsylvania Supreme Court held a court may consider factors that include economic detriment if the variance denied, financial hardship created by work necessary to bring a building into strict zoning compliance, and the character of the surrounding neighborhood. Any other standard, it held, would inhibit neighborhood rehabilitation by prohibiting a variance that would allow the rehabilitation of a dilapidated building.[13]

---

[7] 257 Md. Code Ann. art. 66B, § 4.05(d) (authorizing administrative adjustments); N.J. Stat. Ann. § 40:55D-70(c)(1); R.I. Gen. Laws §§ 45-24-41(c)(2) (amounts to more than a mere inconvenience, which means that there is no other reasonable alternative to enjoy a legally permitted beneficial use of one's property). *See* Miami-Dade County v. New Life Apostolic Church, 750 So.2d 738 (Fla. App. 2000) (ordinance standards: basic intent and purpose of zoning; stability and appearance of community; compatible with surrounding land uses and not detrimental to community).

[8] Ivancovich v. City of Tucson, 529 P.2d 242 (Ariz. App. 1975); Board of Adjustment v. Kwik-Check Realty, Inc., 389 A.2d 1289 (Del. 1978); Palmer v. Board of Zoning Adjustment, 287 A.2d 535 (D.C. App. 1972). *See also* Ebzery v. City of Sheridan, 982 P.2d 1251 (Wyo. 1999) (fence variance not minimum variance possible as required by statute).

[9] Cellco Partnership v. Bellows, 692 N.Y.S.2d 203 (App. Div. 1999) (applying statute to upheld denial of area variance for communications tower); Gara Realty, Inc. v. Zoning Bd. of Review, 523 A.2d 855 (R.I. 1987).

[10] Cromwell v. Ward, 651 A.2d 424 (Md. App. 1995) (thorough review of the cases); Lang v. Zoning Bd. of Adjustment, 733 A.2d 464 (N.J. 1999) (reviewing basis for variances). *See also* Orinda Ass'n v. Board of Supervisors, 227 Cal. Rptr. 688 (Cal. App. 1986).

[11] N.Y. Town Law § 267-b(3); N.Y. Village Law § 7-712-b(3). The factors are: whether there will be an undesirable change to the neighborhood or detriment to nearby properties; whether there is a feasible alternative; whether the requested variance is substantial; whether there will be an adverse physical or environmental effect on the neighborhood; and whether the variance was self-created. *Id. See also In re* Baker, 670 N.Y.S.2d 216 (App. Div. 1998) (reversing variance for concrete patio); Kaufmann v. Planning Bd., 542 A.2d 457 (N.J. 1988) (interpreting similar statute); Cellco Partnership v. Bellows, 692 N.Y.S.2d 203 (App. Div. 1999) (applying statute to upheld denial of area variance for communications tower).

[12] *But see* Sasso v. Osgood, 657 N.E.2d 254 (N.Y. 1995) (statute repeals tests previously applied to area variances).

[13] Hertzberg v. Zoning Bd. of Adjustment, 721 A.2d 53 (Pa. 1998) (remanded for additional evidence). *See* Yeager v. Zoning Hearing Bd., 779 A.2d 595 (Pa. Commw. 2001) (cannot grant

Because the tests for area variances vary so widely it is difficult to generalize the situations in which an area variance will be granted. Area variances based on the physical condition of a property are usually upheld.[14] Courts may also hold that conditions inherent in a building justify an area variance.[15]

The courts almost always approve area variances under either the unnecessary hardship or practical difficulties test for landowners who wish to build a dwelling on a substandard lot.[16] The owner of the substandard lot must show that he cannot build on the lot under the applicable zoning restrictions.[17]

§ 6.49 Consistency with the Plan.

Most of the cases that considered the question did not require variances to be consistent with a comprehensive plan.[1] Consistency is desirable when the

---

variance because of personal needs of car dealer); Society Created to Reduce Urban Blight v. Zoning Bd. of Adjustment, 771 A.2d 874 (Pa. Commw. 2001) (rejecting variance to make sign more visible); Cardamone v. Whitpain Township Zoning Hearing Bd., 771 A.2d 103 (Pa. Commw. 2001) (rejecting variance to build additional house on lot). *Compare* City of Burley v. McCaslin Lumber Co., 693 P.2d 1108 (Idaho 1984) (reversing variance for increase in density needed to make remodeling economically feasible).

[14] Bressman v. Gash, 621 A.2d 476 (N.J. 1993) (setback for garage); Lang v. Zoning Bd. of Adjustment, 733 A.2d 464 (N.J. 1999) (setback for pool). *But see* Board of Zoning Adjustment v. Summers, 814 So.2d 851 (Ala. 2001) (topography did not justify area variance); Stickelman v. Harrison Township Bd. of Zoning Appeals, 772 N.E.2d 683 (Ohio App. 2002) (upholding denial of variance from lot size requirement).

[15] Wolf v. District of Columbia Bd. of Zoning Adjustment, 397 A.2d 936 (D.C. App. 1979) (reduction in lot size to allow conversion of large home to four, rather than two, dwelling units); Rowell v. Board of Adj., 446 N.W.2d 917 (Minn. App. 1989) (upholding substantial setback variance for extension of nonconforming building to conform to function and aesthetics of building); Husnander v. Town of Barnstead, 660 A.2d 477 (N.H. 1995) (zoning restrictions created unreasonable design for dwelling). *But see* Gilmartin v. District of Columbia Bd. of Adj., 579 A.2d 1164 (D.C. App. 1990) (remanding on-premise parking variance because parking inside building might be possible); Korean Buddhist Dae Won Sa Temple v. Zoning Bd. of Appeals, 953 P.2d 1315 (Hawaii 1998) (rejecting height variance for church).

[16] Russell v. District of Columbia Bd. of Adjustment, 402 A.2d 1231 (D.C. App. 1979); Chater v. Board of Appeals, 202 N.E.2d 805 (Mass. 1964); Tall Trees Constr. Corp. v. Zoning Bd. of Appeals, 761 N.E.2d 565 (N.Y. 2001); Filangeri v. Foster, 684 N.Y.S.2d 50 (App. Div. 1999); Neilson v. Zoning Hearing Bd., 786 A.2d 1050 (Pa. Commw. 2001) (landlocked lot); Lincoln v. Zoning Bd. of Review, 201 A.2d 482 (R.I. 1964). *But see* Miriam Homes, Inc. v. Board of Adjustment, 384 A.2d 147 (App. Div. 1976), *aff'd mem.*, 384 A.2d 143 (N.J. 1978) (upholding denial of variance).

[17] Khan v. Zoning Bd. of Appeals, 662 N.E.2d 783 (N.Y. 1996) (rejecting absolute exemption from lot size requirement); Ron Rose Group, Inc. v. Baum, 712 N.Y.S.2d 174 (App. Div. 2000) (petitioner was aware before it purchased the property of the substandard size of the two lots, and that previous owner's variance application was denied).

[1] Belanger v. City of Nashua, 430 A.2d 166 (N.H. 1981); C. Miller Chevrolet, Inc. v. City of Willoughby Hills, 313 N.E.2d 400 (Ohio 1974).

variance allows a major change in use, and courts could impose this requirement under consistency statutes. The New Jersey Supreme Court has interpreted its consistency statute to require variances to be consistent with the comprehensive plan.[2] A few statutes expressly apply the consistency requirement to variances.[3]

§ 6.50 Self-Created Hardship.

Courts usually hold that a board may not grant a variance when the hardship claimed by the applicant is self-created.[1] In a typical case, the landowner creates a substandard lot by conveying part of it and then seeks a variance from the lot size restrictions of the zoning ordinance,[2] or by other acts such as constructing a building without a building permit.[3] This rule is correct. The purpose of a variance is to provide relief from over restrictive zoning enacted by the municipality, not from over restrictive zoning created by the voluntary acts of landowners.

A more complicated problem is presented when self-created hardship is claimed because the landowner purchased a lot with knowledge of the zoning restrictions. The rule that hardship is self-created in this situation stems from early New York cases[4] and is followed in some states.[5] A number of other courts either reject this rule[6] or hold that purchase with knowledge of the zoning

[2] Medici v. BPR Co., 526 A.2d 109 (N.J. 1987).

[3] Suess v. Vogelgesang, 281 N.E.2d 536 (Ind. App. 1972).

[1] Chapman v. Board of Adjustment, 485 So. 2d 1161 (Ala. 1986); Farrington v. Zoning Bd. of Appeals, 413 A.2d 817 (Conn. 1979); Foxhall Community Citizens Ass'n v. District of Columbia Bd. of Zoning Adjustment, 524 A.2d 759 (D.C. App. 1987); Clarke v. Morgan, 327 So. 2d 769 (Fla. 1976); In re Schrader, 660 P.2d 135 (Okla. 1983).

[2] Baker v. Connell, 488 A.2d 1303 (Del. 1985); Johnson v. Township of Robinson, 359 N.W.2d 526 (Mich. 1984); In re Volpe's Appeal, 121 A.2d 97 (Pa. 1956); Sciacca v. Caruso, 769 A.2d 578 (R.I. 2001) (created hardship by recreating substandard lots).

[3] Ad + Soil, Inc. v. County Comm'rs, 513 A.2d 893 (Md.1986); Frank v. Russell, 70 N.W.2d 306 (Neb. 1995).

[4] Clarke v. Board of Zoning Appeals, 92 N.E.2d 903 (N.Y. 1950). See Overhill Bldg. Co. v. Delany, 271 N.E.2d 537 (N.Y. 1971). See Doyle v. Amster, 594 N.E.2d 911 (N.Y. 1992) (considered as factor in rejecting area variance). See also § 6.48 (discussing recent statute codifying rules for area variances in New York and making self-created hardship relevant but not determinative).

[5] Kalimian v. Board of Zoning Appeals, 783 A.2d 506 (Conn. App. 2001); Association for Preservation of 1700 Block of N St., N.W., & Vicinity v. District of Columbia Bd. of Zoning Adjustment, 384 A.2d 674 (D.C. App. 1978) (use variances); Josephson v. Autrey, 96 So. 2d 784 (Fla. 1957); Sanchez v. Board of Zoning Adjustments, 488 So. 2d 1277 (La. App. 1986); Marino v. City of Baltimore, 137 A.2d 198 (Md. 1957); Beaudoin v. Rye Beach Village Dist., 369 A.2d 618 (N.J. 1976).

[6] Landmark Universal, Inc. v. Pitkin County Bd. of Adjustment, 579 P.2d 1184 (Colo. App. 1978); Adolphson v. Zoning Bd. of Appeals, 535 A.2d 799 (Conn. 1988); Hehir v. Bowers, 407 N.E.2d 149 (Ill. App. 1980); Reinking v. Metropolitan Bd. of Zoning Appeals, 671 N.E.2d 137 (Ind. App. 1996); Twigg v. Town of Kennebunk, 662 A.2d 914 (1995); Richard Roesser

restriction is only one factor to consider.[7] Pennsylvania adopted a more limited form of the rule. It holds that self-created hardship exists when the landowner pays a premium for a property that makes it unprofitable to put it to its permitted use.[8]

The cases that reject the rule that purchase with knowledge of existing zoning in self-created hardship are correct. The rule is fair in cases where a prior owner created a hardship through some action relating to the land. Purchase should not relieve a subsequent owner of this infirmity. To hold that mere purchase with knowledge of existing zoning is self-created hardship improperly makes the purchase of land a basis for denying a variance. The cases are on better ground when they deny a variance where the purchaser pays a premium for the land and uses the premium payment as the basis for claiming financial hardship. This rule is also consistent with the Supreme Court's holding in *Palazzolo*,[9] that purchase of property subject to a land use restriction is not an absolute bar to a landowner's claim that his investment-backed expectations in his property were frustrated.

§ 6.51 Conditions.

Although the Standard Zoning Act and most state zoning acts do not expressly authorize the board of adjustment to attach conditions to variances, the power to do so is recognized everywhere as inherent in the statutory power to grant variances. As the court pointed out in *Town of Burlington v. Jencik*,[1] "[s]ince variances allow uses forbidden by the regulations, the attachment of conditions to the granting of a variance alleviates the harm which might otherwise result."[2] A few zoning statutes confer the authority to impose conditions on variances.[3]

Professional Bldr., Inc. v. Anne Arundel County, 793 A.2d 545 (Md. 2002) (quoting this treatise); Myron v. City of Plymouth, 562 N.W.2d 21 (Minn. App. 1997); Board of Adjustment v. Shanbour, 435 P.2d 569 (Okla. 1968); Spence v. Board of Zoning Appeals, 496 S.E.2d 61 (Va. 1998); Hoberg v. City of Bellevue, 884 P.2d 1339 (Wash. App. 1994); Schalow v. Waupaca County, 407 N.W.2d 316 (Wis. App. 1987).

[7] Arant v. Board of Adjustment, 126 So. 2d 100 (Ala. 1961); Twigg v. Town of Kennebunk, 662 A.2d 914 (Me. 1995); Hill v. Town of Chester, 771 A.2d 559 (N.H. 2001) (hardship self-inflicted because knew or constructively knew lot was inadequate under zoning ordinance); Chirichello v. Zoning Bd. of Adjustment, 397 A.2d 646 (N.J. 1979); In re Zoning Variance Application, 449 A.2d 910 (Vt. 1982) (hardship self-created when landowner purchased part of lot that violated zoning ordinance).

[8] Appeal of Gro, 269 A.2d 876 (Pa. 1970). *See also* POA Co. v. Findlay Township Zoning Hearing Bd., 679 A.2d 1342 (Pa. Commw. 1996) (self-inflicted because applicant limited access to property).

[9] Palazzolo v. State of Rhode Island, 533 U.S. 606 (2001).

[1] 362 A.2d 1338 (Conn. 1975).

[2] *Accord* Everson v. Zoning Bd. of Adjustment, 149 A.2d 63 (Pa. 1959); Town of Warren v. Frost, 301 A.2d 572 (R.I. 1973).

[3] Cal. Gov't Code § 65906.

The accepted limitation on variance conditions is that they must relate to the use of the land, not the user. Conditions that affect the development of the site, such as landscaping, paving and access conditions, are clearly acceptable.[4] Some courts void conditions that limit hours of operation[5] or that limit the variance to a period of time[6] or to the applicant[7] because they do not properly relate to the use of the land.[8]

When a use permitted by a variance will increase traffic congestion, boards of adjustment sometimes attach a condition requiring the dedication of land for a street widening. A few cases hold that the zoning board has the implied power to attach such conditions.[9] To avoid a takings problem, the dedication should be based on traffic problems generated by the use permitted by the variance. A California statute codifies this requirement.[10]

§ 6.52   Findings and Judicial Review.

Although a few zoning statutes require boards of adjustment to make findings of fact in variance cases,[1] the Standard Zoning Act and most state zoning acts do not impose this requirement. A number of courts require findings of fact in

---

[4] Wright v. Zoning Bd. of Appeals, 391 A.2d 146 (Conn. 1978); Town of Burlington v. Jencik, 362 A.2d 1338 (Conn. 1975); St. Onge v. Donovan, 522 N.E.2d 1019 (N.Y. 1988) (disapproving condition terminating variance person using property changes); Gomez v. Zoning Bd. of Appeals, 740 N.Y.S.2d 139 (App. Div. 2002) (disapproving condition limiting height of house to single story); Nicholson v. Zoning Bd. of Adjustment, 140 A.2d 604 (Pa. 1958).

[5] Bora v. Zoning Bd. of Appeals, 288 A.2d 89 (Conn. 1972); 99 A.L.R.2d 227 (1965).

[6] Huntington v. Zoning Bd. of Appeals, 428 N.E.2d 826 (Mass. App. 1981); Vlahos Realty Co. v. Little Boar's Head Dist., 146 A.2d 257 (N.H. 1958); DeFelice v. Zoning Bd. of Adjustment, 523 A.2d 1086 (N.J. App. Div. 1987) (requiring demolition of building on sale of land). *Compare* Wentworth Hotel v. Town of New Castle, 287 A.2d 615 (N.H. 1972).

[7] National Black Child Dev. Inst. v. District of Columbia Bd. of Adjustment, 483 A.2d 687 (D.C. App. 1984).

[8] 763 A.2d 1011 (Conn. 2001) (continued maintenance of no rental condition violates strong public policy against restrictions on free alienability of property); Gay v. Zoning Bd. of Appeals, 757 A.2d 61 (Conn. App. 2000) (invalidating condition that lot never be used as a building lot); Brous v. Planning Bd., 594 N.Y.S.2d 816 (App. Div. 1993) (condition on area variance prohibiting expansion of beach house not related to public welfare). *But see* Gangemi v. Zoning Bd. of Appeals Berninger v. Board of Adj., 603 A.2d 954 (N.J. App. Div. 1991) (upholds original variance although illegal condition invalidated).

[9] Bringle v. Board of Supvrs., 351 P.2d 765 (Cal. 1960); Alperin v. Mayor & Twp. Comm., 219 A.2d 628 (N.J. 1966). *See also* Black v. City of Waukesha, 371 N.W.2d 389 (Wis. 1985) (building permit). *But cf.* City of Corpus Christi v. Unitarian Church, 436 S.W.2d 923 (Tex. Civ. App. 1968).

[10] Cal. Gov't Code § 65909. *See also* §§ 9.11–9.15.

[1] 65 Ill. Comp. Stat. Ann. 5/11-13-11. *See also* Warren v. Board of Appeals, 416 N.E.2d 1382 (Mass. 1981) (statute requires); LaVallee v. Britt, 383 A.2d 709 (N.H. 1978) (ordinance may require).

variance cases even though they are not required by the zoning statute. Courts require findings of fact to facilitate judicial review because findings link the statutory standards to the variance decision. The reason for requiring findings was best stated in a leading California case, *Topanga Ass'n for a Scenic Community v. County of Los Angeles*:[2]

> [A] findings requirement serves to conduce the administrative body to draw legally relevant subconclusions supportive of its ultimate decision; the intended effect is to facilitate orderly analysis and minimize the likelihood that the agency will randomly leap from evidence to conclusions. . . . [F]indings enable the reviewing court to trace and examine the agency's mode of analysis.[3]

Some courts do not require findings of fact in variance cases.[4]

The Standard Zoning Act, which most states adopted, authorizes the use of the writ of certiorari to review board of adjustment decisions, including variance decisions. Although the Standard Act does not provide a judicial review standard, the courts apply the judicial review standard they usually apply to administrative proceedings they review on a record. Judicial review is deferential, and a court must uphold a board's decision if there is substantial evidence to support it in the record. The court may reverse only if the board's decision was arbitrary or capricious.[5] Statutes also govern judicial review of trial court decisions reviewing grant or denial of variances.[6]

This judicial review standard overstates the deference the courts give to board of adjustment variance decisions. Despite this standard, courts retain sufficient control over board of adjustment variance decisions to implement the judicial policy that variances should be granted "sparingly." They may review board of adjustment findings of fact critically, and may always reverse the grant of a

---

[2] 522 P.2d 12 (Cal. 1974).

[3] *Id.* at 18. *Accord* Zieky v. Town Plan & Zoning Comm., 196 A.2d 758 (Conn. 1963); Board of Adjustment v. Henderson Union Ass'n, 374 A.2d 3 (Del. 1977); Harrington Glen, Inc. v. Municipal Bd. of Adjustment, 243 A.2d 233 (N.J. 1968); Village Bd. v. Jarrold, 423 N.E.2d 385 (N.Y. 1981); Potter v. Hartford Zoning Bd. of Adjustment, 407 A.2d 170 (Vt. 1979).

[4] Deardorf v. Board of Adjustment, 118 N.W.2d 78 (Iowa 1962); South Maple St. Ass'n v. Board of Adjustment, 230 N.W.2d 471 (Neb. 1975).

[5] Farrington v. Zoning Bd. of Appeals, 413 A.2d 817 (Conn. 1979); Wolf v. District of Columbia Bd. of Zoning Adjustment, 397 A.2d 936 (D.C. App. 1979); Town of Indialantic v. Nance, 400 So. 2d 37 (Fla. App. 1981); Evesham Twp. Zoning Bd. of Adjustment v. Evesham Twp. Council, 404 A.2d 1274 (N.J. 1979); Cowan v. Kern, 363 N.E.2d 305 (N.Y. 1977); Cole v. Board of Adjustment, 616 N.W.2d 483 (S.D. 2000) (trial court improperly considered case de novo on the merits).

[6] Sciacca v. Caruso, 769 A.2d 578 (R.I. 2001) (in review of trial court decision supreme court shall not reverse unless trial justice misapplied law, misconceived, or overlooked material evidence, or made findings that were clearly wrong).

variance for errors of law, such as a decision that based a variance on self-created hardship.

Although the Standard Zoning Act appeared to contemplate judicial review of zoning variances on the record before the board in the certiorari appeal, it also authorized the trial court to take additional evidence.[7] Many states adopted this provision. Some courts interpret this provision to authorize a de novo trial in the trial court, with judicial review based on the trial court record rather than the board proceedings.[8]

§ 6.53 Special Exceptions and Conditional Uses.

The Standard Zoning Act and state zoning acts authorize the board of adjustment to grant "special exceptions" under standards provided by the zoning ordinance. Some zoning statutes also contain criteria for special exceptions.[1] The term "special exception" is vague and unclear[2] and was an unfortunate choice. The term "conditional" or "special" use or permit is more frequently used in zoning ordinances, and the courts often use both terms interchangeably.

The zoning ordinance usually contains a provision that details the standards for all conditional uses and also indicates the conditional uses allowable in the different zoning districts. The standards provided for conditional uses are usually quite general and typically authorize the approval of a conditional use if it is compatible with the surrounding area. A zoning ordinance may include even vaguer standards authorizing conditional uses that are in the "public interest," serve the "public welfare," or are consistent with the "spirit and intent" of the zoning ordinance. Some courts hold that this type of standard is an unconstitutional delegation of legislative power.[3]

Some land uses almost always require approval as a conditional use. One example is a land use that may be appropriate in a zoning district but which requires review to determine whether it will have an adverse impact on the surrounding area. Gasoline filling stations in commercial districts and apartments in single-family residential districts are in this category. A second example is a use that may have an adverse impact on the surrounding area but that deserves

---

[7] Standard Zoning Act § 7. *See also* American Planning Association, Growing Smart Legislative Guidebook: Model Statutes for Planning and Management of Change § 10-502 (S. Meck ed. 2002) (provision similar to Standard Act and requiring consistency with comprehensive plan).

[8] Whitcomb v. City of Woodward, 616 P.2d 455 (Okla. App. 1980); Overstreet v. Zoning Hearing Bd., 412 A.2d 169 (Pa. Commw. 1980); Chioffi v. Winooski Zoning Bd., 556 A.2d 103 (Vt. 1989) (upholding statute allowing de novo review). *But see* Bentley v. Chastain, 249 S.E.2d 38 (Ga. 1978) (de novo trial unconstitutional).

[1] 55 Ill. Comp. Stat. Ann. 5/5-12009.5.

[2] BCT Partnership v. City of Portland, 881 P.2d 176 (Or. App. 1994) (ordinance must contain provisions that can reasonably be interpreted and explained as embodying standards and criteria).

[3] § 6.03.

consideration as a conditional use because it serves community needs. A community facility, such as a hospital, is in this category.

§ 6.54   Role and Function.

Because conditional uses are expressly authorized by the zoning ordinance and are not granted to avoid unnecessary hardship, courts view them as uses that can be appropriate in the zoning districts established by the zoning ordinance. This distinction was captured in what is still the classic judicial statement of the role of the conditional use:

> [C]ertain uses, considered by the local legislative body to be essential or desirable for the welfare of the community . . ., are entirely appropriate and not essentially incompatible with the basic uses in any zone . . ., but not at every or any location . . . or without conditions being imposed by reason of special problems the use . . . presents from a zoning standpoint . . . .[1]

Proof of hardship is not required for a conditional use.[2]

A threshold question is whether the zoning ordinance has properly classified a use as one that requires conditional use approval. In *Board of Supvrs. v. Southland Corp.*,[3] the ordinance classified quick-service food stores as a conditional use in a commercial district. It permitted grocery stores with more than 5,000 square feet in area in this district as-of-right. The court held the governing body's decision to treat a land use as a conditional use was entitled to a presumption of constitutionality and that the decision to classify quick-food stores as a conditional use was fairly debatable. The governing body found that peak traffic at quick-service stores came at peak traffic times, that peak traffic at the larger grocery stores permitted as-of-right did not come at peak times, and that quick-service stores were located on smaller parcels and had less flexibility in locating entrances.

The courts approved the classification of other uses as conditional uses when they found a reasonable distinction between these uses and uses permitted

---

[1] Tullo v. Millburn Twp., 149 A.2d 620, 624, 625 (N.J. App. Div. 1959). *See also* Kotrich v. County of DuPage, 166 N.E.2d 601 (Ill. 1960); Eberhart v. Indiana Waste Sys., 452 N.E.2d 455 (Ind. App. 1983); M.S.W., Inc. v. Board of Zoning Appeals, 24 P.3d 175 (Kan. App. 2001) (granting of conditional use at time of initial zoning regulation did not violate due process rights of landowner though it avoided creation of nonconforming use); Hofmeister v. Frank Realty Co., 373 A.2d 273 (Md. App. 1977); Anderson v. Peden, 587 P.2d 59 (Or. 1978). *But see* Delta Biological Resources, Inc. v. Board of Zoning Appeals, 467 N.W.2d 164 (Wis. App. 1991) (no presumption in favor of special exceptions). Special use defined: N.Y. Town Law § 274-b, Village Law 7-725-b.

[2] In re Gage's Appeal, 167 A.2d 292 (Pa. 1961).

[3] 297 S.E.2d 718 (Va. 1982). *See also* Walters City of Greenville, 751 So.2d 1206 (Miss. App. 1999) (transfer of business from permitted to conditional use upheld to avoid transfer to irresponsible owners when neighborhood was having crime and nuisance problems).

as-of-right in the same district.[4] One court struck down an ordinance that required a special exception for all uses in a commercial district as "a roving and virtually unlimited power to discriminate . . . between landowners similarly situated."[5] Modifications in site development standards, such as setbacks, require a variance and may not be approved as a conditional use.[6]

Problems also arise in distinguishing an exception from a variance. In theory, the special exception provision of the Standard Zoning Act delegates to the governing body the decision on how to define an exception, but an argument can be made that it may not improperly characterize an action as an exception when it should properly be classified as a variance. One basis for making this distinction is that an exception is a use permitted by the ordinance, while a variance is a use or other change prohibited by the ordinance.[7] A Wisconsin case held a municipality could authorize a departure from a floor area ratio as an exception because the ordinance permitted the use, but a departure from a dimensional standard of this kind would seem to require a variance.[8]

§ 6.55 Delegation to Legislative Body or Plan Commission.

Although the Standard Act and most zoning acts delegate the authority to grant conditional uses to the zoning board, many zoning ordinances do not follow this practice. The ordinance may delegate the authority to grant conditional uses to the planning commission, to the commission with a further appeal to the legislative body, or to the legislative body. This practice reflects a belief that the review of conditional uses should be carried out by the planning staff, which advises the commission and council but which does not usually advise the zoning board. A zoning statute may allow this option. California allows a delegation to a zoning administrator, the legislative body, the planning commission, or the zoning board.[1]

Several cases invalidated a delegated of power to the planning commission[2]

---

[4] Bierman v. Township of Taymouth, 383 N.W.2d 235 (Mich. App. 1985) (can classify junkyards but not landfills as special exception in agricultural district); LaRue v. Township of East Brunswick, 172 A.2d 691 (N.J. App. Div. 1961) (apartments in single-family district). See High Meadows Park v. City of Aurora, 250 N.E.2d 517 (Ill. App. 1969) (requiring special exception for mobile homes). Cf. People v. Perez, 29 Cal. Rptr. 781 (Cal. App. 1963).

[5] SCIT, Inc. v. Planning Bd., 472 N.E.2d 269 (Mass. App. 1984). See also Jachimek v. Superior Ct., 819 P.2d 487 (Ariz. 1991) (cannot limit special use for pawn shops to overlay zone for commercial district).

[6] One Hundred Two Glenstone, Inc. v. Board of Adjustment, 572 S.W.2d 891 (Mo. App. 1978).

[7] City of Chicago Heights v. Living Word Outreach Full Gospel Church & Ministries, Inc., 749 N.E.2d 916 (Ill. 2001)

[8] Fabyan v. Waukesha County Bd. of Adjustment, 632 N.W.2d 116 (Wis. App. 2001). See § 6.48.

[1] Cal. Gov't Code §§ 65901–65904.

[2] Langer v. Planning & Zoning Comm'n, 313 A.2d 44 (Conn. 1972); Franklin County v. Webster, 400 S.W.2d 693 (Ky. 1966); Swimming River Golf & Country Club v. Borough of New Shrewsbury, 152 A.2d 135 (N.J. 1959).

or the legislative body[3] to grant special exceptions. In these states the zoning statute followed the Standard Act and delegated the authority to grant special exceptions to the board of adjustment. This interpretation is too restrictive. The Standard Act provides that the legislative body "may" authorize the board of adjustment to grant special exceptions. The legislative body could decide not to grant this power to the board and to retain the special exception function. Courts have upheld a delegation to the legislative body in states where the authority to delegate to the board is omitted or where the statute leaves the delegation question open.[4]

Courts are divided on whether a legislative body acts legislatively or quasi-judicially when it is authorized to grant an exception or conditional use,[5] and so they also divide on whether the zoning ordinance must provide standards when the legislative body has this authority.[6] They hold the legislative body must act reasonably, even when standards are not required. They review the legislative body's decision under the same criteria they apply to the board of adjustment when it has the power to grant a special exception.[7]

§ 6.56 Judicial Review of Decisions on Exceptions and Conditional Uses.

Judicial review of decisions on conditional uses differs from judicial review of decisions on variances because a conditional use is permitted by the ordinance if it meets the standards contained in the ordinance. Most courts hold an applicant has the initial burden to show that his conditional use satisfies the criteria contained in the ordinance, but that the burden then shifts to objectors to show that the use does not satisfy the criteria and is adverse to the public interest.[1]

---

[3] City of Des Moines v. Lohner, 168 N.W.2d 779 (Iowa 1969); Goerke v. Township of Middletown, 205 A.2d 338 (N.J. 1964); Salt Lake County Cottonwood Sanitary Dist. v. Sandy City, 879 P.2d 1379 (Utah App. 1994); American Tower Corp. v. Common Council, 557 S.E.2d 752 (W. Va. 2001) (council may not review decisions by zoning board); State ex rel. Skelly Oil Co. v. Common Council, 207 N.W.2d 585 (Wis. 1973). *Compare* State ex rel. Ludlow v. Guffey, 306 S.W.2d 552 (Mo. 1957).

[4] Kotrich v. County of DuPage, 166 N.E.2d 601 (Ill. 1960); Corporation Way Realty Trust v. Building Comm'r of Medford, 205 N.E.2d 718 (Mass. 1965); Detroit Osteopathic Hosp. Corp. v. City of Southfield, 139 N.W.2d 728 (Mich. 1966); Green Point Sav. Bank v. Board of Zoning Appeals, 24 N.E.2d 319 (N.Y. 1939).

[5] City of Chicago Heights v. Living Word Outreach Full Gospel Church & Ministries, Inc., 749 N.E.2d 916 (Ill. 2001).

[6] § 6.02.

[7] Zylka v. City of Crystal, 167 N.W.2d 45 (Minn. 1969); Golden v. City of St. Louis Park, 122 N.W.2d 570 (Minn. 1963); Lemir Realty Corp. v. Larkin, 181 N.E.2d 407 (N.Y. 1962).

[1] Irvine v. Duval County Planning Comm'n, 495 So. 2d 167 (Fla. 1986); Commonwealth of Pa., Bureau of Cors. v. City of Pittsburgh City Council, 532 A.2d 12 (Pa. 1987); In re: Brickstone Realty Corp., 789 A.2d 333 (Pa. Commw. 2001) (protestors evidence not credible). *See* Damascus

Courts may again reinforce judicial control of conditional use decisions by requiring findings of fact,[2] and some statutes impose this requirement.[3] Courts will reverse a denial or approval of a conditional use permit if the denial or approval was arbitrary and capricious or not supported by substantial evidence on the record,[4] which some courts view as the equivalent of the usual administrative law rule that a decisions will be upheld if it is fairly debatable.[5]

There is a tendency in the cases to treat the special exception or conditional use as presumptively entitled to approval. *Archdiocese of Portland v. County of Washington*[6] states the rationale for this result. The court distinguished the conditional use from the zoning amendment and added the following comments on the role of conditional uses in zoning:

> Because . . . [conditional] uses are generally compatible with the design of the zone the possibility that a permitted use will not comport with the comprehensive plan is not as great as it is when a variance or amendment is sought.
>
> . . .
>
> [T]he ordinance itself reveals the legislative plan . . . . The suspicion which is cast upon the approval of a change involving an incompatible use . . . is not warranted where the change has been anticipated by the governing body.[7]

Courts will therefore reverse a denial of a conditional use when the applicant has complied with the standards provided in the ordinance.[8] For example, a board

---

Community Church v. Clackamas County Bd. of Comm'rs, 573 P.2d 726 (Or. App. 1978) (ordinance may place burden on applicant); Delta Biological Resources, Inc. v. Board of Zoning Appeals, 467 N.W.2d 164 (Wis. App. 1991).

[2] Cormier v. Town of Danville Zoning Bd. of Adjustment, 710 A.2d 401 (N.H. 1998); Melucci v. Zoning Bd. of Review, 226 A.2d 416 (R.I. 1967); Ames v. Town of Painter, 389 S.E.2d 702 (Va. 1990); Harding v. Board of Zoning Appeals, 219 S.E.2d 324 (W. Va. 1975); Heiss v. City of Casper Planning & Zoning Comm'n, 941 P.2d 27 (Wyo. 1997). *See also* Heiney v. Sylvania Township Bd. of Zoning Appeals, 710 N.E.2d 725 (Ohio App. 1998) (no evidence to support denial of conditional use).

[3] 65 Ill. Comp. Stat. Ann. 5/5-12009.5(d).

[4] 314 Quality Sand & Gravel, Inc. v. Planning & Zoning Comm'n, 738 A.2d 1157 (Conn. App. 1999) (substantial evidence did not support denial); Ackman v. Board of Adjustment, 596 N.W.2d 96 (Iowa 1999); Jenkins v. St. Tammany Parish Police Jury, 736 So.2d 1287 (La. 1999) (reversing denial when conditional use had been granted for three other similar uses); Coyote Flats, L.L.C. v. Sanborn County Comm'n, 596 N.W.2d 347 (S.D. 1999) (upholding denial).

[5] Alviani v. Dixon, 775 A.2d 1234 (Md. 2001); Board of Supervisors v. Stickley, 556 S.E.2d 748 (Va. 2002).

[6] 458 P.2d 682 (Or. 1969).

[7] *Id.* at 685, 686.

[8] Raczkowski v. Zoning Comm'n, 733 A.2d 862 (Conn. App. 1999); Jesus Fellowship, Inc. v. Miami-Dade County, 752 So.2d 708 (Fla. App. 2000); (church expansion, private school and day

may disapprove an unwanted use, such as a group home or a landfill, if there is substantial public opposition. Courts reverse disapprovals in these cases if the use complies with the criteria for approval contained in the ordinance,[9] but they will uphold a denial of a conditional use when the evidence shows that it does not meet approval requirements, as when it would have an adverse effect on the surrounding area.[10]

However, judicial review of conditional use decisions is complicated by the vague standards zoning ordinances often include, such as a standard that authorizes the approval of a conditional use if it serves the "general welfare." The courts limit the discretion of zoning agencies under provisions of this type by holding the ordinance authorizes only the consideration of appropriate criteria, such as the impact of a conditional use on the surrounding area.[11] Nor is community pressure an acceptable reason for denying a conditional use.[12]

care center); Lazarus v. Village of Northbrook, 199 N.E.2d 797 (Ill. 1964); Town of Merrillville Bd. of Zoning Appeals v. Public Storage, Inc., 568 N.E.2d 1092 (Ind. App. 1991); Picha v. County of McLeod, 634 N.W.2d 739 (Minn. App. 2001) (cemetery); Amoco Oil Co. v. City of Minneapolis, 395 N.W.2d 115 (Minn. App. 1986); State ex rel. Presbyterian Church of Washington County v. City of Washington, 911 S.W.2d 697 (Mo. App. 1995); Verona, Inc. v. Mayor & Council of West Caldwell, 229 A.2d 651 (N.J. 1967); North Shore Steak House, Inc. v. Board of Appeals, 282 N.E.2d 606 (N.Y. 1972); Retail Property Trust v. Board of Zoning Appeals, 722 N.Y.S.2d 244 (App. Div. 2001) (mall expansion); C.B.H. Props., Inc. v. Rose, 613 N.Y.S.2d 913 (App. Div. 1994); Sun Suites Holdings, LLC v. Board of Aldermen, 535 S.E.2d 525 (N.C. App. 2000) (extended stay facility); Clark v. City of Asheboro, 524 S.E.2d 46 (N.C. App. 1999) (mobile home park); Hydraulic Press Brick Co. v. Council of City of Independence, 475 N.E.2d 144 (Ohio App. 1984); Bankoff v. Board of Adjustment, 875 P.2d 1138 (Okla. 1994); Mehring v. Zoning Bd., 762 A.2d 1137 (Pa. Commw. 2000) (day care home).

[9] Pollard v. Palm Beach Cty., 560 So. 2d 1358 (Fla. App. 1990) (group home); Fulton Cty. v. Bartenfeld, 363 S.E.2d 555 (Ga. 1988) (landfill, when opponents based testimony on fear; applicant had obtained state permit); Framike Realty Corp. v. Hinck, 632 N.Y.S.2d 177 (App. Div. 1995);Ralph L. Wadsworth Constr., Inc. v. West Jordan City, 999 P.2d 1240 (Utah App. 2000); Davis Cty. v. Clearfield City, 756 P.2d 704 (Utah App. 1988) (group home).

[10] Rolling Pines Ltd. Partnership v. City of Little Rock, 40 S.W.3d 828 (Ark. App. 2001) (manufactured home); White Bear Docking & Storage, Inc. v. City of White Bear Lake, 324 N.W.2d 174 (Minn. 1982); Mann Media, Inc. v. Randolph County Planning Bd., 565 S.E.2d 9 (N.C. 2002) (broadcast tower; safety problems);Vulcan Materials Co. v. Guilford County, 444 S.E.2d 639 (N.C. App. 1994) (stone quarry); Visionquest Nat'l, Ltd. v. Board of Supvrs., 569 A.2d 915 (Pa. 1990) (correctional camp for juveniles); Atlantic Richfield Co. v. City of Franklin Zoning Hearing Bd., 465 A.2d 98 (Pa. Commw. 1983).

[11] Tandem Holding Corp. v. Board of Zoning Appeals, 373 N.E.2d 282 (N.Y. 1977); Piney Mt. Neighborhood Ass'n v. Town of Chapel Hill, 304 S.E.2d 251 (N.C. App. 1983) (may not consider racial status of subsidized housing occupants); Harts Book Stores v. City of Raleigh, 281 S.E.2d 761 (N.C. App. 1981). See also Schultz v. Pritts, 432 A.2d 1319 (Md. 1981); Atlantic Richfield Co. v. City of Franklin Zoning Hearing Bd., 465 A.2d 98 (Pa. Commw. 1983).

[12] Conetta v. City of Sarasota, 400 So. 2d 1051 (Fla. App. 1981); City of Barnum v. County of Carlton, 386 N.W.2d 770 (Minn. App. 1986); Robert Lee Realty Co. v. Village of Spring Valley, 462 N.E.2d 1193 (N.Y. 1984). See also Chernik v. McGowan, 656 N.Y.S.2d 392 (App. Div. 1997)

Moreover, the courts will uphold a conditional use denial only if it is based on criteria included in the ordinance.[13] *C.R. Invs., Inc. v. Village of Shoreview*[14] illustrates this rule. A developer applied for a conditional use to construct nineteen "quad" apartments adjacent to single-family homes located across a county road. As one of the reasons for denying the conditional use, the council found that there was an "insufficient buffer from existing single-family homes." It apparently based this finding on the applicant's failure to plan for single-family homes on its site in the area nearest to the adjacent single-family homes. The court held this reason for denial was inappropriate in the absence of evidence that the development would adversely affect the welfare of the area or the "value of surrounding property." The zoning ordinance did not require a buffer, and the city planner stated that the buffer provided by the road was sufficient.

Other cases found that statutes and ordinances granting the authority to approve conditional uses conferred a broad discretion to deny a conditional use application[15] or that the board had the discretion to decide whether an applicant for a special exception has met the standards contained in the ordinance.[16] In these cases the zoning ordinance or statute either contained generalized approval standards or stated that the zoning board "may" grant conditional uses.

For example, in *Crooked Creek Conserv. & Gun Club, Inc. v. Hamilton County N. Bd. of Zoning Appeals*,[17] the ordinance provided that the board must find

---

(cannot base denial on objections and concerns of neighbors); Washington State Dep't of Corrections v. City of Kennewick, 937 P.2d 1119 (Wash. App. 1997) (same).

[13] Harris v. City of Costa Mesa, 31 Cal. Rptr. 2d 1 (Cal. App. 1994) (accessory apartment); Inland Constr. Co. v. City of Bloomington, 195 N.W.2d 558 (Minn. 1972); Value Oil Co. v. Town of Irvington, 377 A.2d 1225 (N.J.L. 1977); Brentwood Borough v. Cooper, 431 A.2d 1177 (Pa. Commw. 1981).

[14] 304 N.W.2d 320 (Minn. 1981)..*Accord* Trisko v. City of Waite Park, 566 N.W.2d 349 (Minn. App. 1997). *See also* Barbaro v. Wroblewski, 689 N.E.2d 1369 (Mass. App. 1998) (approving limited remand to board to correct minor error); Nevada Contrs. v. Washoe Cty., 792 P.2d 31 (Nev. 1990) (decision discretionary and denial must be sustained if supported by substantial evidence).

[15] Mobil Oil Corp. v. Zoning Bd. of Appeals, 644 A.2d 401 (Conn. App. 1994); Connecticut Health Facilities, Inc. v. Zoning Bd. of Appeals, 613 A.2d 1358 (Conn. App. 1992);Gulf Oil Corp. v. Board of Appeals, 244 N.E.2d 311 (Mass. 1969); Davis v. Zoning Bd., 754 N.E.2d 101 (Mass. App. 2001); Molnar v. County of Carver Bd. of Comm'rs, 568 N.W.2d 177 (Minn. App. 1997) (and inconsistent with comprehensive plan); Lindteigen v. City of Bismarck, 565 N.W.2d 47 (N.D. 1997); Anderson v. Peden, 587 P.2d 59 (Or. 1978); Kleck v. Zoning Bd. of Adjustment, 319 S.W.2d 406 (Tex. App. 1958). *See also* Health Mgt., Inc. v. Union Township Bd. of Zoning Appeals, 692 N.E.2d 667 (Ohio App. 1997) (health and safety problems justified denial). *See* Board of Supervisors v. McDonald's Corp., 544 So.2d 334 (Va. 2001) (denial held not discriminatory).

[16] Native Village of Eklutna v. Board of Adjustment, 995 P.2d 641 (Alaska 2000) (remanding because board did not consider effect on cultural resources as required by plan); Irwin v. Planning & Zoning Comm'n, 711 A.2d 675 (Conn. 1998).

[17] 677 N.E.2d 544 (Ind. App. 1997).

that the specially excepted use "will not be injurious to the public health, safety, morals, or general welfare of the community" and that the use "will not affect the use and value of other property in the immediate area in a substantially adverse manner." The court held "that these criteria, having no absolute objective standards against which they can be measured, involve discretionary decision making on the part of the board." A court can also rely on a municipality's broad discretion in reviewing conditional uses to uphold a decision approving a conditional use.[18]

§ 6.57 Free Speech-Protected and Religious Uses.

Different rules apply to conditional uses protected by the first amendment to the federal constitution, such as adult uses, signs and religious uses. A requirement that one of these uses must be approved as a conditional use before the use can be established is a prior restraint on first amendment rights.[1] A conditional use requirement for these uses is unconstitutional as a prior restraint on speech unless the ordinance contains precise standards. Some courts have invalidated standards they approve for other uses, such as a standard requiring compatibility with adjacent uses, when compliance with these standards was required for uses protected by the free speech clause.[2] A court may invalidate even a seemingly innocuous standard, such as a requirement that the use "Will be sufficiently accessible to permit entry onto the property by fire, police, rescue and other services."[3]

---

[18] City of Reno v. Harris, 895 P.2d 663 (Nev. 1995); Mayor & Alderman v. Hudson, 774 So.2d 448 (Miss. App. 2000) (church expansion).

[1] §§ 5.5–5.71 (adult businesses), 11.12–11.23 (signs). *See also* §§ 5.07–5.10 (group homes), 5.21.–5.26 (mobile homes); Marty's Adult World of Enfield, Inc. v. Town of Enfield, 20 F.3d 512 (2d Cir. 1994) (upholds special permit requirement for parking when no permit needed to operate viewing booths); Fisher v. Pilcher, 341 A.2d 713 (Del. Super. 1975) (day care center).

[2] Lady J Lingerie, Inc. v. City of Jacksonville, 176 F.3d 1358 (11th Cir. 1999) ("cases show that virtually any amount of discretion beyond the merely ministerial is suspect. Standards must be precise and objective;" emphasis in original); TJ's South, Inc. v. Town of Lowell, 895 F. Supp. 1124 (N.D. Ind. 1995); Diamond v. City of Taft, 29 F. Supp. 2d 633 (E.D. Cal. 1998) (reviewing cases); Dease v. City of Anaheim, 826 F. Supp. 336 (C.D. Cal. 1993); Smith v. County of Los Angeles, 29 Cal. Rptr. 2d 680 (Cal. App. 1994); City of Indio v. Arryo, 191 Cal. Rptr. 565 (Cal. App. 1983) (sign); City of Imperial Beach v. Palm Ave. Books, 171 Cal. Rptr. 197 (Cal. App. 1981) (adult business); Zebulon Enters. v. County of DuPage, 496 N.E.2d 1256 (Ill. App. 1986) (adult business); Landover Books, Inc. v. Prince George's Cty., 566 A.2d 792 (Md. App. 1989) (same); Barbulean v. City of Newburgh, 640 N.Y.S.2d 935 (Sup. Ct. 1996) (same); White Adv. Metro v. Zoning Hearing Bd., 453 A.2d 29 (Pa. Commw. 1982) (sign). *But see* Rodriguez v. Solis, 2 Cal. Rptr.2d 50 (Cal. App. 1991) (sign permit denial not content-based; standards upheld). *See also* Outdoor Systems, Inc. v. City of Merriam, 67 F. Supp.2d 1258 (D. Kan. 1999) (authority to remove "unattractive" signs).

[3] Lady J Lingerie, Inc. v. City of Jacksonville, 176 F.3d 1358 (11th Cir. 1999)

However, other courts have upheld conditional use standards that contained detailed approval criteria, and some of these ordinances appeared to authorize as much discretion as ordinances the courts have disapproved.. [4] Comparisons are difficult because the ordinances reviewed were similar but not identical. The Supreme Court held an ordinance that provided the agency "may"approve a park permit if it met criteria contained in the ordinance did not confer too much discretion. [5] In cases in which the courts approved the standards contained in an ordinance they also usually approved a denial of a conditional use.

Prior restraint doctrine also imposes procedural requirements on decision making that affects free speech-protected uses. These requirements come from a Supreme Court case, *Freedman v. State of Maryland*[6] a movie censorship case. The Court held that any restraint prior to judicial review could be imposed only for a brief period, that prompt judicial review of decisions had to be available, and that government had the burden of going to court to suppress the speech and had the burden of proof once in court. However, the Court relaxed these procedural requirements for a licensing scheme for adult uses in *FW/PBS v. City of Dallas, Inc.*[7] A three-Justice plurality held that the licensing scheme was not presumptively invalid, like the censorship statute in *Freedman*, because it did not require a review of speech content. For this reason, the municipality in this type of program did not have to carry the burden of proof in court, and only the other two procedural requirements applied. Courts since *FW/PBS* have

---

[4] Blue Canary Corp. v. City of Milwaukee, 251 F.3d 1121 (7th Cir. 2001) (liquor license; compatibility with neighborhood test, and noting that strict prior restraint doctrine does not apply to nonexpressive activity); Steakhouse, Inc. v. City of Raleigh, 166 F.3d 634 (4th Cir. 1999) (adversely affect public services); People v. Nadeau, 227 Cal. Rptr. 644 (Cal. App. 1986) (six specific criteria, including that it be "sufficiently buffered" so that it does not "adversely affect" residential areas); Pulaski Hwy., Inc. v. Town of Perryville, 519 A.2d 206 (Md. App. 1987) (upholding 13 criteria such as noise, availability of services and contribution to deterioration in neighborhood); Lamar Corp. v. City of Twin Falls, 981 P.2d 1146 (Idaho 1999) (six criteria related to detailed aesthetic impacts); Area Plan Comm'n v. Wilson, 701 N.E.2d 856 (Ind. App. 1998) (six criteria including adverse effect on surrounding area and availability of facilities). *See also* Jakes, Ltd., Inc. v. City of Coates, 284 F.3d 884 (8th Cir. 2002) (upholding license suspension if licensee "a menace to the health, safety, or general welfare of the community");Outdoor Sys., Inc. v. City of Mesa, 997 F.2d 604 (9th Cir. 1993) (discretion to distinguish between commercial and noncommercial signs upheld); Jeffrey Lauren Land Co. v. City of Livonia, 326 N.W.2d 604 (Mich. App. 1982) (conditional use requirement for general audience movie theater justified by traffic and parking concerns); Media Art Co. v. City of Gates, 974 P.2d 249 (Or. App. 1999) (upholding requirement that sign be "incidental, appropriate and subordinate" use).

[5] Thomas v. Chicago Park Dist., 534 U.S. 316 (2002) (also approving ordinance standards for permits).

[6] 380 U.S. 51 (1965).

[7] 493 U.S. 215 (1990).

invalidated licensing and conditional use requirements for adult and religious uses,[8] but some courts held licensing procedures were adequate.[9]

The Court addressed additional questions raised by licensing and permit procedures in *Thomas v. Chicago Park District*,[10] where it upheld a permit requirement for activities in public parks. Because the permit requirement was a content-neutral time, place and manner requirement, the Court held the District did not have to initiate litigation every time it denied a permit, and that the ordinance did not have to specify a deadline for judicial review of a challenge to a permit denial. Though the Court emphasized the permit requirement applied to activities in a public forum, the decision would seem to apply to other content-neutral decision making procedures, such as procedures for the review of uses protected by the free speech clause that occur outside a public forum.

The Court in *Thomas* left open the question whether the *Freedman* rules require a municipality to provide in its ordinance for prompt judicial review of permit denials, or whether the availability of judicial review through statutory or other means is enough.[11] The cases are divided on this point,[12] and the Court's specific reference to this problem suggests it is willing to take a case to decide it.

Though courts have upheld a conditional use permit requirement for religious uses,[13] a state court's treatment of a conditional use denial depends on whether

---

[8] Nightclubs, Inc. v. City of Paducah, 202 F.3d 884 (6th Cir. 2000) (licensing; decision period too long and no provision for prompt judicial review); Baby Tam & Co. v. City of Las Vegas II, 199 F.3d 111 (9th Cir. 2000) (decision period not circumscribed); Baby Tam & Co. v. City of Las Vegas, 154 F.3d 1097 (9th Cir. 1998) (prompt judicial review not available);1126 Baltimore Blvd., Inc. v. Prince George's County, 58 F.3d 988 (4th Cir. 1995) (zoning; decision and judicial review period too long); Redner v. Dean, 29 F.3d 1495 (11th Cir. 1994) (licensing; risk that expressive activity repressed for indefinite time periods, judicial review not timely); Alpine Christian Fellowship v. County Comm'rs, 870 F. Supp. 991 (D. Colo. 1994) (church school); JJR, Inc. v. City of Seattle, 891 P.2d 720 (Wash. 1997) (stay not provided).

[9] Steakhouse, Inc. v. City of Raleigh, 166 F.3d 634 (4th Cir. 1999).

[10] 534 U.S. 316 (2002).

[11] *See* City News & Novelty, Inc. v. City of Waukesha, 531 U.S. 278 (2001) (question raised but case held moot).

[12] Rejecting ordinance requirement: Boss Capital, Inc. v. City of Casselberry, 187 F.3d 1251 (11th Cir. 1999) (reviewing the cases); TK's Video, Inc. v. Denton County, 24 F.3d 705 (5th Cir. 1994); Graff v. City of Chicago, 9 F.3d 1309 (7th Cir. 1993) (en banc). Contra: Nightclubs, Inc. v. City of Paducah, 202 F.3d 84 (6th Cir. 2000); Baby Tam & Co. v. City of Las Vegas, 154 F.3d 1097 (9th Cir. 1998); 11126 Baltimore Blvd., Inc. v. Prince George's County, 58 F.3d 998 (4th Cir. 1995) (en banc). *See* Nev. Rev. Stat. § 34.185 (providing for prompt judicial review in first amendment cases).

[13] Christian Gospel Ch. v. City & Cty. of San Francisco, 896 F.2d 1221 (9th Cir. 1990); Grace Community Church v. Planning & Zoning Comm'n, 622 A.2d 591 (Conn. App. 1993); Area Plan Comm'n v. Wilson, 701 N.E.2d 856 (Ind. App. 1998); City of Las Cruces v. Huerta, 692 P.2d 1331 (N.M. App. 1984); Tran v. Gwinn, 554 S.E.2d 63 (Va. 2001); Open Door Baptist Church v. Clark County, 995 P.2d 33 (Wash. 2000). *See* §§ 5.68–5.70. *See also* Cohen v. City of Des

it gives religious uses a preferred use status. States that give religious uses a preferred status rely on their constitutionally-protected status or a showing that a church would not substantially increase traffic congestion to reverse conditional use denials.[14] States that do not apply the preferred status rule have upheld conditional use denials for religious uses that would create traffic congestion.[15] A federal court of appeals reversed the denial of a special use permit for a Moslem center.[16] It held the denial was based only on community opposition and that different standards were applied than had been applied to other churches. A court will apply the arbitrary and capricious standard of judicial review to a board decision approving a conditional use.[17]

§ 6.58   Consistency with the Plan.

State statutes that require zoning to be consistent with the comprehensive plan do not always indicate whether the consistency requirement applies to conditional uses,[1] and a court may not require consistency.[2] A California statute requires

Plaines, 8 F.3d 484 (7th Cir. 1993) (special permit requirement exemption for churches did not violate Establishment Clause).

[14] Aluminum Co. of Am. v. Lipke, 320 S.W.2d 751 (Ark. 1959); City of Englewood v. Apostolic Christian Church, 362 P.2d 172 (Colo. 1961); Columbus Park Congregation of Jehovah's Witnesses, Inc. v. Board of Appeals, 182 N.E.2d 722 (Ill. 1962); Our Saviour's Evangelical Lutheran Ch. v. City of Naperville, 541 N.E.2d 1150 (Ill. App. 1989) (parking lot variance); Lubavitch Chabad House of Ill., Inc. v. City of Evanston, 445 N.E.2d 343 (Ill. App. 1982) (in mixed use area); Kali Bari Temple v. Board of Adjustment, 638 A.2d 839 (N.J. App. Div. 1994) (home in residential area; adverse effects reduced by conditions); Harrison Orthodox Minyan, Inc. v. Town Bd., 552 N.Y.S.2d 434 (App. Div. 1990) (must treat religious uses flexibly; denial improper). *See also* Mooney v. Village of Orchard Lake, 53 N.W.2d 308 (Mich. 1952).

[15] West Hartford Methodist Church v. Zoning Bd. of Appeals, 121 A.2d 640 (Conn. 1956); First Baptist Church v. Miami-Dade County, 768 So.2d 1114 (Fla. App. 2000) (traffic study flawed); Milwaukie Company of Jehovah's Witnesses v. Mullen, 330 P.2d 5 (Or. 1958). *See also* First Assembly of God v. City of Alexandra, 739 F.2d 942 (4th Cir. 1984) (landscaping and enrollment conditions); Abram v. City of Fayetteville, 661 S.W.2d 371 (Ark. 1983) (church exceptions does not authorize school); Allendale Congregation of Jehovah's Witnesses v. Grosman, 152 A.2d 569 (N.J. 1959), (upholding denial of conditional use for church); Macedonian Orthodox Church v. Planning Bd., 636 A.2d 96 (N.J. App. Div. 1994) (denial of expansion and relocation of previously approved community hall); City of Pasco v. Rhine, 753 P.2d 993 (Wash. App. 1988) (upholding condition prohibiting external display of posters for X-rated films).

[16] Islamic Center of Miss., Inc. v. City of Starkville, 840 F.2d 293 (5th Cir. 1988).

[17] Mayor & Board of Aldermen v. Hudson, 774 So.2d 448 (Miss. 2000) (upholding conditional use approval).

[1] *But see* Fla. Stat. Ann. § 163.3194(consistency required). *See* Baker v. Metropolitan Dade County, 774 So.2d 14 (Fla. App. 2000) (held inconsistent with plan); *See also* Adelman v. Town of Baldwin, 750 A.2d 577 (Me. 2000) (applying zoning consistency requirement to conditional use and finding consistency).

[2] City of Chicago Heights v. Living Word Outreach Full Gospel Church & Ministries, Inc., 749 N.E.2d 916 (Ill. 2001) (plan cannot override zoning ordinance designation of exception as appropriate for zone). .

land uses "authorized" by the zoning ordinance to be consistent with the plan. *Neighborhood Action Group v. County of Calaveras*[3] held that this statute requires a conditional use to be consistent with a comprehensive plan. The court held the consistency requirement is "implied from the hierarchical relationship of the land use laws." A conditional use "is struck from the mold of the zoning law," and the zoning law must comply with the comprehensive plan. The court also held that a conditional use approval is invalid if plan elements required by the statute are inadequate.

Some cases based their review of a conditional use decision on the policies of a comprehensive plan even though the statute did not require consistency with the plan.[4] In Oregon, the consistency requirement does not apply to conditional uses because they are a presumptively permitted use under the zoning ordinance.[5]

§ 6.59   Conditions.

The Standard Zoning Act[1] and the state zoning acts that follow it authorize the board of adjustment to impose conditions on special exceptions. The case law on conditions attached to special exceptions is the same as the case law on conditions attached to variances.[2] The decisions approve conditions that relate to the use of the land, such as conditions that require access and parking.[3] They

---

[3] 203 Cal. Rptr. 401 (Cal. App. 1984). *Contra,* Hawkins v. County of Marin, 126 Cal. Rptr. 754 (Cal. App. 1976). *See* Elysian Heights Residents Ass'n v. City of Los Angeles, 227 Cal. Rptr. 226 (Cal. App. 1986) (building permit need not be consistent).

[4] Cadiz Land Co. v. Rail Cycle, L.P., 99 Cal. Rptr.2d 378 (Cal. App. 2000) (conditional use consistent with plan); Gatri v. Blane, 962 P.2d 367 (Hawaii 1998) (upholding denial); International Villages, Inc. of Am. v. Board of County Comm'rs, 585 P.2d 999 (Kan. 1978); Richmarr Holy Hills, Inc. v. American PCS, L.P., 701 A.2d 879 (Md. App. 1997) (upholding grant of special exception); Hubbard Broadcasting, Inc. v. City of Afton, 323 N.W.2d 757 (Minn. 1982); SuperAmerican Group, Inc. v. City of Little Canada, 539 N.W.2d 264 (Minn. App. 1995) (upholding denial); City of Reno v. Harris, 895 P.2d 663 (Nev. 1995); Piney Mt. Neighborhood Ass'n v. Town of Chapel Hill, 304 S.E.2d 251 (N.C. App. 1983); 40 A.L.R.2d 372 (1955).

[5] Kristensen v. City of Eugene Planning Comm'n, 544 P.2d 591 (Or. App. 1976). *But see* Trademark Constr., Inc. v. Marion County Bd. of Comm'rs, 962 P.2d 772 (Or. 1998).

[1] Standard Zoning Act § 7. *See, e.g.,* N.Y. Town Law §§ 274-a(4), 274-b(4).

[2] § 6.51.

[3] Exxon, Inc. v. City of Frederick, 375 A.2d 34 (Md. 1977) (denial of access to street); Rockford Blacktop Constr. Co. v. County of Boone, 635 N.E.2d 1077 (Ill. App. 1994) (five-year limitation on special use for quarry upheld); Water Dist. No. 1 v. City Council, 871 P.2d 1256 (Kan. 1994) (conditions on operation of sludge lagoon valid); Titman v. Zoning Hearing Bd., 408 A.2d 167 (Pa. Commw. 1979) (parking area); Hemontolor v. Wilson County Bd. of Zoning Appeals, 883 S.W.2d 613 (Tenn. App. 1994). *See* Cal. Gov't Code § 65909 (condition must be reasonably related to use of property).

disapprove conditions that do not relate to the use of the land, such as a condition
that terminates the conditional use when there is a change in ownership.[4]

F. FLEXIBLE ZONING.

§ 6.60 Role and Function.

Many zoning ordinances include flexible zoning techniques that are not
authorized by the Standard Zoning Act. These techniques give the municipality
more control over the details of land development than zoning regulations usually
allow. Contract or conditional zoning, under which detailed conditions are
imposed concurrently with a zoning amendment, is one example. The floating
zone, which defers the mapping of a zoning district until the developer makes
an application for development, is another.

Zoning statutes doe not usually authorize flexible zoning techniques,[1] but
elsewhere the courts must decide whether they should imply the authority to use
a flexible zoning technique from a zoning statute that does not expressly authorize
it. Though some courts were initially hostile to the use of flexible zoning
techniques, the trend is now the other way.

§ 6.61 Floating Zones.

"Floating zone" is the term used for a zoning technique under which the
municipality adopts a zoning district in the text of its zoning ordinance but does
not map it immediately. The municipality reserves the mapping decision until

---

[4] Anza Parking Corp. v. City of Burlingame, 241 Cal. Rptr. 175 (Cal. App. 1987) (making use
nontransferable); Board of Zoning Adjustment v. Murphy, 438 S.E.2d 134 (Ga. App. 1994)
(requiring parking attendant at off-site location); Middlesex & Boston St. Ry. v. Board of Aldermen,
359 N.E.2d 1279 (Mass. 1977) (requiring lease to public housing authority at reduced rents); Solar
v. Zoning Bd. of Appeals, 600 N.E.2d 187 (Mass. App. 1992) (making use nontransferable);
Sandbothe v. City of Olivette, 647 S.W.2d 198 (Mo. App. 1983) (restricting hours of operation
and prohibiting drive-through facility for fast food restaurant); Mechem v. City of Santa Fe, 634
P.2d 690 (N.M. 1981) (terminating use if change in ownership); Plandome Doughnuts v. Mammima,
692 N.Y.S2d 111 (App. Div. 1999) (requirement that parking area be open to retail and restaurant
customers between designated hours); Geiben v. Town of Pomfret Zoning Bd. of Appeals, 688
N.Y.S.2d 303 (App. Div. 1999) (relocation of dwelling); Old Country Burgers v. Town Bd. of
Oyster Bay, 553 N.Y.S.2d 843 (App. Div. 1990) (prohibiting drive-in business for fast-food
restaurant during mealtimes); Woodinville Water Dist. v. King County, 21 P.3d 209 (Wash. App.
2001) (can limit number of employees business can have without applying for new permit). *See
also* Halfway House v. City of Waukegan, 641 N.E.2d 1005 (Ill. App. 1994) (condition prohibiting
group home from accepting sexual offenders held vague); Elkhart County Bd. of Zoning Appeals
v. Earthmovers, Inc., 631 N.E.2d 927 (Ind. App. 1994) (conditions may sometimes regulate who
uses land). *But see* Hopengarten v. Board of Appeals, 459 N.E.2d 1271 (Mass. App. 1984)
(upholding conditions terminating use if title alienated and requiring renewal every three years).

[1] Ariz. Rev. Stat. §§ 9-462.01(D); 11-821(E) (authorizing overlay zoning that modifies zoning
regulations in another district with which the overlay district is combined).

a developer makes an application to have the floating zone applied to his property. The ordinance includes standards for the approval of the floating zone, such as density and site development standards. Floating zones are usually limited to major nonresidential uses, such as multifamily, industrial, and commercial development. Floating zones are sometimes called "overlay zones."

Because the Standard Zoning Act does not authorize the floating zone, it does not specify the zoning agency that must approve them. The municipality may delegate the authority to approve a floating zone to the legislative body, the board of adjustment, or the planning commission. It may also require concurrent approval by one or more of these bodies.

The floating zone may provide more control over development than the special exception. As one court noted,[1] the municipality can impose more limitations on development through the floating zone technique, which is not limited by the traditional special exception standards. The zoning agency may also have more discretion to reject a floating zone, especially if a court characterizes the floating zone review process as legislative. The usual rules governing conditional uses, which require approval when all standards in the ordinance have been met, may not apply.

The floating zone raised a number of legal problems when it first became popular. Objectors argued that floating zones were unauthorized because zoning legislation required the mapping of a zoning district concurrently with its textual adoption. They also argued that floating zones were improper spot zoning and an improper delegation of legislative power.

The courts approved the floating zone in the limited number of cases in which it was considered. The first and leading case, *Rodgers v. Village of Tarrytown*,[2] illustrates the typical judicial view. The village adopted a new zoning district for garden apartments that contained detailed site and density standards and required a minimum tract of ten acres. The boundaries of the zone were to be determined later "by amendment" to the zoning map as applications were made. The planning board was authorized to approve amendments, with a further appeal to the governing body if the planning board denied an application.

After the board and governing body approved a floating zone for garden apartments, a neighboring landowner challenged the map amendment and the textual adoption of the floating zone district. The court approved the map amendment "in the light of the area involved" and because the amendment met the housing needs of the community. It also approved the floating zone procedure. It held that the village could decide on "the choice of methods" to amend the

---

[1] Sheridan v. Planning Bd., 266 A.2d 396 (Conn. 1969).

[2] 96 N.E.2d 731 (N.Y. 1951). *See* Beyer v. Burns, 567 N.Y.S.2d 599 (Sup. Ct. 1991) (upholding floating zone including reverter provision if construction not commenced within two years of rezoning).

ordinance and could adopt a procedure that authorized map amendments on application by a landowner. The minimum acreage requirement was valid because garden apartments "would blend more attractively and harmoniously . . . if placed upon larger tracts of land."

The court rejected a number of other objections to the floating zone. It held it was not spot zoning because it applied to the entire village and was not designed for the benefit of a single landowner. Nor did the floating zone divest the village of the "power to regulate future zoning." The decision to map a floating zone remained within the discretion of the planning board and governing body. The floating zone was not a "device" for granting a variance but was enacted "to permit the development of the property for the general welfare of the entire community." The village did not need to set boundaries for the floating zone at the time it was adopted textually because the ordinance "prescribed specifications for a new use district." *Tarrytown* reviewed the major problems raised by floating zones, and other court decisions have accepted its reasoning.[3]

A few cases invalidated an extreme use of discretionary zoning.[4] In these cases a suburban zoning ordinance zoned an entire municipality for residential use and required the discretionary approval of all nonresidential uses. The courts held the zoning statute required the municipality to regulate land use by dividing the community into appropriate zoning districts. These cases are a hostile judicial reaction to the conversion of zoning into a process that is entirely discretionary.

Courts have approved floating zones when they were not consistent with a comprehensive plan in states in which the plan is advisory.[5] The consistency problem has not yet arisen in states that have a consistency requirement. Consistency with the plan is preferable when the floating zone authorizes intensive uses that may impair the policies of a comprehensive plan.

---

[3] Sheridan v. Planning Bd., 266 A.2d 396 (Conn. 1969); Pleasant Valley Neighborhood Ass'n v. Planning & Zoning Comm'n, 543 A.2d 296 (Conn. App. 1988); Bellemeade Co. v. Priddle, 503 S.W.2d 734 (Ky. 1974); Huff v. Board of Zoning Appeals, 133 A.2d 83 (Md. 1957); Treme v. St. Louis County, 609 S.W.2d 706 (Mo. App. 1980); 80 A.L.R.3d 95 (1977). *But see* Lutz v. City of Longview, 520 P.2d 1374 (Wash. 1974). *See also* Carron v. Board of County Comm'rs, 976 P.2d 359 (Colo. App. 1998) (approving "delineation" procedure); Montgomery County v. Colesville Citizens Ass'n, 521 A.2d 770 (Md. App. 1987) (basis for approving floating zone). *Compare* Homart Dev. Co. v. Planning & Zoning Comm'n, 600 A.2d 13 (Conn. App. 1991) (commission has discretion to deny or approve floating zone; denial upheld).

[4] Rockhill v. Chesterfield Twp., 128 A.2d 473 (N.J. 1957); Town of Hobart v. Collier, 87 N.W.2d 868 (Wis. 1958). *Compare* Eves v. Zoning Bd. of Adjustment, 164 A.2d 7 (Pa. 1960), *with* Klem v. Zoning Hearing Bd., 387 A.2d 667 (Pa. Commw. 1978).

[5] Loh v. Town Plan & Zoning Comm'n, 282 A.2d 894 (Conn. 1971). *See* McQuail v. Shell Oil Co., 183 A.2d 572 (Del. 1962); Floyd v. County Council, 461 A.2d 76 (Md. App. 1983).

§ 6.62   Contract and Conditional Zoning.

Contract or conditional zoning is another zoning technique that provides more flexibility in the administration of the zoning ordinance. Contract zoning is used because of problems created by the zoning district system. In the typical zoning ordinance, each zoning district allows a wide range of permitted uses. An example is a neighborhood commercial zone, which may allow a wide variety of neighborhood commercial uses.

Adjacent property owners may object to a rezoning because the landowner may use his land for any of the uses permitted in the new zone, not just the use he contemplates. In contract zoning, the landowner agrees to restrict the use of his land to the use for which he seeks the zoning amendment. The landowner may agree to other protective conditions, such as a landscaped buffer adjacent to the residential dwellings. Municipalities may also use contract zoning to secure street widening or other contributions from the landowner.

Contract zoning can take several forms. One frequently used classification distinguishes between unilateral and bilateral contract zoning. In unilateral contract zoning, the landowner unilaterally agrees to impose restrictions on his land in a written document, which he records. The municipal governing body or planning commission indicates the restrictions it wants the landowner to adopt but does not formally agree to a rezoning if the landowner complies. In bilateral contract zoning, a landowner and the municipality execute a bilateral contract in which the municipality promises to rezone in return for the landowner's promise to record a document that contains the restrictions the municipality requires. A landowner can also execute a bilateral contract with adjacent landowners.

Some courts refer to the case in which a landowner imposes restrictions on his land unilaterally as conditional zoning. They apply the term "contract zoning" only to a true bilateral contract between a landowner and a municipality. This text uses all of these terms interchangeably.

Contract zoning advocates defend it as an appropriate zoning technique that tailors land development to its environment and assures its compatibility with adjacent land uses. The objections to contract zoning are similar to those raised against floating zones. Contract zoning is claimed to be invalid because it is unauthorized by the zoning statute, because it is arbitrary spot zoning and an illegal bargaining away of the zoning power, and because it violates the statutory provision that requires uniform land use regulations within zoning districts. Several states now authorize contract zoning.[1]

---

[1] Ariz. Rev. Stat. Ann. § 11-832; Idaho Code § 67-6511A; Md. Code Ann. art. 66B, § 4.01(c)(1); R.I. Gen. Laws. § 45-24-53(h); Va. Code Ann. §§ 15.2-2303, 15.2-2297. *See* Sweetman v. Town of Cumberland, 364 A.2d 1277 (R.I. 1977) (statute held constitutional).

The case law on contract and conditional zoning is mixed, although most of the more recent decisions approve this technique. Whether the conditions on development are imposed bilaterally or unilaterally makes a difference. The courts usually disapprove bilateral contract zoning but approve conditions on development that are imposed unilaterally.

Despite growing judicial approval of conditional zoning, its use by municipalities is unwise. Individually negotiated zoning agreements undercut the uniformity of the land use regulations imposed by the zoning ordinance. The proliferation of a large number of zoning agreements throughout a municipality complicates zoning enforcement. Although a municipality may be able to amend the zoning ordinance to impose restrictions that conflict with a rezoning agreement, this problem is also troublesome.[2] Detailed control over land development is possible under acceptable zoning techniques that impose development standards subject to approval by the zoning agency. Floating zones and site plan review are two examples.

The terminology used by the courts in the "contract" zoning cases is not clear, and it is difficult to find accepted terms that describe the results in the cases. The discussion that follows divides the cases into the "bilateral" and "unilateral" categories, but the text indicates that the courts have different views of these terms. One court has adopted the term "concomitant agreement zoning" for this zoning device.[3]

The Nebraska court upheld a rezoning for a mixed use development that included four agreements executed by the city and the developer incorporating the development plan.[4] The court held that the distinction between contract and conditional zoning was irrelevant and that the critical question was whether the conditions on the rezoning advanced the public health, safety and general welfare. The court held that the city was entitled to make agreements with developers requiring them to follow their plans, because otherwise these plans are difficult to enforce.

§ 6.63   Bilateral.

A number of cases have held bilateral contract zoning invalid.[1] In these cases the municipality and the developer executed a bilateral contract, or the ordinance

---

[2] Delucchi v. County of Santa Cruz, 225 Cal. Rptr. 43 (Cal. App. 1986); Nicholson v. Tourtellotte, 293 A.2d 909 (R.I. 1972).

[3] State ex rel. Myhre v. City of Spokane, 422 P.2d 790 (Wash. 1967).

[4] Giger v. City of Omaha, 442 N.W.2d 182 (Neb. 1989) (court also found no bargaining away of police power). *See also* Bradley v. City of Trussville, 527 So. 2d 1303 (Ala. Civ. App. 1988) (no delegation of legislative power).

[1] Hale v. Osborn Coal Enters., Inc., 729 So.2d 853 (Ala. Civ. App. 1997); Hartman v. Buckson, 467 A.2d 694 (Del. Ch. 1983); Hartnett v. Austin, 93 So. 2d 86 (Fla. 1956); Cederberg v. City

that adopted the rezoning included the terms of a bilateral agreement. *Houston Petroleum Co. v. Automotive Prods. Credit Ass'n* [2] best expresses the reasoning these cases adopt. The court held invalid an agreement in which the developer agreed to impose site development restrictions and stated:

> Contracts thus have no place in a zoning plan and a contract between a municipality and a property owner should not enter into the enactment or enforcement of zoning regulations. [3]

The purpose of a rezoning agreement may make it invalid. Municipalities sometimes insist on "reverter" agreements under which the land reverts to its initial zoning classification if the landowner does not begin development in a reasonable period of time. The cases hold these agreements invalid because they accomplish a rezoning without recourse to the usual notice and hearing requirements that apply to zoning amendments. [4]

A court may uphold a bilateral agreement when it is made with third parties, such as neighbors. In *State ex rel. Zupancic v. Schimenz*, [5] an applicant for a zoning change executed an agreement with neighbors that restricted the site to a specified use and imposed site development restrictions. The agreement was executed and recorded after the neighbors expressed concern about the rezoning at a plan commission meeting.

The court upheld the rezoning and noted that there was no agreement with the city and no agreement to rezone. A rezoning is not invalid contract zoning when "a zoning authority . . . is motivated to zone by agreements as to use of the land made by others." Private agreements that "underlie" zoning provide the "flexibility and control" that allow "a municipality to meet the ever-increasing demands for rezoning in a rapidly changing area." [6] The court also held that the rezoning must be "otherwise valid" and suggested that the imposition of

---

of Rockford, 291 N.E.2d 249 (Ill. App. 1972); Baylis v. City of Baltimore, 148 A.2d 429 (Md. 1959); Rodriguez v. Prince George's Cty., 558 A.2d 742 (Md. App. 1989); Carlino v. Whitpain Invs., 453 A.2d 1385 (Pa. 1982). *See also* Chung v. Sarasota County, 686 So.2d 1358 (Fla. App. 1996) (settlement agreement). But see Broward County v. Griffey, 366 So. 2d 869 (Fla. App. 1979). *See generally* 70 A.L.R.3d 125 (1976).

[2] 87 A.2d 319 (N.J. 1952).

[3] *Id.* at 322.

[4] Scrutton v. County of Sacramento, 79 Cal. Rptr. 872 (Cal. App. 1969); Hausmann & Johnson, Inc. v. Berea Bd. of Bldg. Code Appeals, 320 N.E.2d 685 (Ohio App. 1974). *But see* Goffinet v. County of Christian, 357 N.E.2d 442 (Ill. 1976); Colwell v. Howard County, 354 A.2d 210 (Md. App. 1976). *See also* Dexter v. Town Bd., 324 N.E.2d 870 (N.Y. 1975). *Contra,* Beyer v. Burns, 567 N.Y.S.2d 599 (Sup. Ct. 1991) (in floating zone ordinance).

[5] 174 N.W.2d 533 (Wis. 1970).

[6] *See also* City of Greenbelt v. Bresler, 236 A.2d 1 (Md. 1967); Pressman v. City of Baltimore, 160 A.2d 379 (Md. 1960).

conditions on land development "might better be done by uniform ordinances providing for special uses, special exceptions and overlaid districts."

§ 6.64 Unilateral.

A growing number of cases uphold contract zoning when the restrictions on the rezoned property are imposed unilaterally by the landowner.[1] Courts sometimes refer to this type of zoning as conditional zoning. In these cases there was no evidence of a bilateral contract between the landowner and the municipality, although the rezoning ordinance may have contained the restrictions the landowner imposed on the land.[2] The cases emphasized the protective function of restrictions unilaterally imposed on the land that avoided or mitigated the adverse impacts of the development on adjacent property owners. In other cases the municipality executed a contract with the developer, concurrent with the rezoning, in which he agreed to dedicate land or make a contribution to street widenings and other improvements. Some cases upheld these agreements, emphasizing that the municipality did not agree to rezone and that the improvements to which the owner contributed were reasonably required by the development.[3]

The favorable judicial view of conditional zoning was expressed in extensive dictum in *Collard v. Incorporated Village of Flower Hill*.[4] The court indicated conditional zoning is not objectionable as a form of spot zoning. It held that, if a zoning change is proper, it is not automatically invalid simply because conditions are imposed. The court pointed out that "imposing limiting conditions while benefitting surrounding properties, normally adversely affects the premises on which the conditions are imposed."

The court held that conditional zoning is not an improper bargaining away of the police power "absent proof of a contract purporting to bind the local legislature in advance." It held the zoning act did not prohibit conditional zoning,

---

[1] Haas v. City of Mobile, 265 So.2d 564 (Ala. 1972); J-Marion Co. v. County of Sacramento, 142 Cal. Rptr. 723 (Cal. App. 1977); Martin v. Hatfield, 308 S.E.2d 833 (Ga. 1983); Ogden v. Premier Props., USA, Inc., 755 N.E.2d 661 (Ind. App. 2001); Sylvania Elec. Prods., Inc. v. City of Newton, 183 N.E.2d 118 (Mass. 1962); Rando v. Town of North Attleboro, 692 N.E.2d 544 (Mass. App. 1998); Bucholz v. City of Omaha, 120 N.W.2d 270 (Neb. 1963); Church v. Town of Islip, 168 N.E.2d 680 (N.Y. 1960); Chrismon v. Guilford Cty., 370 S.E.2d 579 (N.C. 1988) (citing this treatise); Hall v. City of Durham, 372 S.E.2d 564 (N.C. 1988) (same).

[2] King's Mill Homeowners Ass'n v. City of Westminster, 557 P.2d 1186 (Colo. 1976).

[3] Scrutton v. County of Sacramento, 79 Cal. Rptr. 872 (Cal. App. 1969); Gladwyne Colony, Inc. v. Township of Lower Merion, 187 A.2d 549 (Pa. 1963); State ex rel. Myhre v. City of Spokane, 422 P.2d 790 (Wash. 1967). *But see* Transamerica Title Ins. Co. v. City of Tucson, 533 P.2d 693 (Ariz. App. 1975). *See also* §§ 9.11–9.15.

[4] 421 N.E.2d 818 (N.Y. 1981). *Accord* DePaolo v. Town of Ithaca, 694 N.Y.S.2d 235 (App. Div. 1999). *See also* Chrismon v. Guilford Cty., 370 S.E.2d 579 (N.C. 1988) (reviewing benefits of conditional zoning; citing this treatise);

which was "within the spirit" of the enabling legislation as a means of harmonizing "the landowner's need for rezoning with the public interest." It added that preventing the legislative body from imposing conditions that protect adjacent property would not be "in the best interests of the public."

Some courts do not approve unilateral conditional zoning. In *Bartsch v. Planning & Zoning Comm'n,*[5] a municipality conditioned a rezoning on the filing of a restrictive covenant that limited the use of the land to a medical office building. The court held the covenant was a "blatant violation" of the "strict" statutory provision that requires uniform regulations within zoning districts.

§ 6.65 Proper Purpose View.

Collard[1] represents a judicial view which holds that unilateral conditions do not necessarily invalidate a rezoning if they serve proper zoning purposes and if the rezoning is valid under the usual zoning map amendment tests. This point of view is illustrated by *Cross v. Hall County,*[2] which held that neighbors cannot attack conditions imposed for their "benefit and protection . . . to ameliorate the effects of the zoning change." *Goffinet v. County of Christian*[3] is a similar case. The county imposed site development conditions on a rezoning for a synthetic gas production facility. The court held that the conditions "are not of such a nature as to constitute an abrupt departure from the comprehensive zoning plan . . ., which emphasizes substantial industrial development for the future." The court reviewed and upheld the rezoning under its traditional zoning tests and rejected a spot zoning objection to the zoning amendment.

These cases treat zoning conditions as a neutral factor in their review of zoning map amendments. They take the reasonable view that neighbors should not be allowed to complain of zoning conditions imposed for their benefit. Some courts still show concern over possible abuses of the conditional zoning process.[4]

§ 6.66 Site Plan Review.

Site plan review is a zoning technique that allows municipalities to exercise control over the site details of a development. In the typical site plan review procedure, the applicant for an amendment, conditional use, variance, or building permit submits a detailed site plan to the plan commission, zoning board, or

---

[5] 506 A.2d 1093 (Conn. App. 1986). *Accord* Board of County Comm'rs v. H. Manny Holtz, Inc., 501 A.2d 489 (Md. App. 1985); Dacy v. Village of Ruidoso, 845 P.2d 793 (N.M. 1992) (municipality promised to rezone).

[1] § 6.64.

[2] 235 S.E.2d 379 (Ga. 1977).

[3] 357 N.E.2d 442 (Ill. 1976). *See* Thornber v. Village of N. Barrington, 747 N.E.2d 513 (Ill. App. 2001) (contract zoning not found).

[4] Nolan v. City of Taylorville, 420 N.E.2d 1037 (Ill. App. 1981).

administrative staff. Approval of the site plan is required before development may proceed. Site plan review usually applies to nonresidential and multifamily development on individual lots. It is a useful supplement to subdivision controls, which do not usually apply to this type of development because it does not require the subdivision of land.

Some courts have assumed that the authority to use site plan review exists even in the absence of express statutory authority.[1] Other courts implied the power to require site plan review as a step in the approval of special exceptions and zoning amendments.[2] A few zoning statutes authorize site plan review and specify the site development requirements the municipality can impose in the site plan review process.[3]

The role of site plan review as compared with the variance and special exception is not always clear. The limitations on the site plan review procedure authorized by the New Jersey legislation were explored in *Lionel's Appliance Center, Inc. v. Citta.*[4] A local planning board approved a site plan for an office building and two restaurants. Neighbors objected that the board should have disapproved the site plan because the development would cause off-site traffic problems.

The court disagreed and distinguished site plan review from similar zoning controls, such as variances and conditional uses. It concluded that traffic problems were an appropriate concern in the administration of these controls, but that the statutory provision authorizing site plan review did not authorize the denial of a site plan because of off-site traffic congestion. "[T]he planning board may deny

---

[1] McCrann v. Town Plan. & Zoning Comm'n, 282 A.2d 900 (Conn. 1971); Charter Twp. of Harrison v. Calisi, 329 N.W.2d 488 (Mich. App. 1982); Sun Oil Co. v. Zoning Bd. of Adjustment, 169 A.2d 294 (Pa. 1961) (ordinance also held constitutional).

[2] Colwell v. Howard County, 354 A.2d 210 (Md. App. 1976) (amendment); Y.D. Dugout, Inc. v. Board of Appeals, 255 N.E.2d 732 (Mass. 1970) (special exception); Southwick, Inc. v. City of Lacey, 795 P.2d 712 (Wash. App. 1990) (council may delegate site plan review to administrative agency after zoning approved). *See also* Kozesnik v. Township of Montgomery, 131 A.2d 1 (N.J. 1957) (under statute authorizing governing body to refer "any action" to planning commission); KCI Mgt., Inc. v. Board of Appeal, 764 N.E.2d 377 (Mass. App. 2002); Town of Grand Chute v. U.S. Paper Converters, Inc., 600 N.W.2d 33 (Wis. App. 1999) (site plan review ordinance authorized by statute granting general welfare powers).

[3] N.J. Stat. Ann. §§ 40:55D-37 to 42; N.Y. Town Law § 274-a; N.Y. Village Law § 7-725-a. *See* Bragdon v. Town of Vassalboro, 780 A.2d 299 (Me. 2001) (site plan review not subject to statutory comprehensive plan requirement); Moriarty v. Planning Bd., 506 N.Y.S.2d 184 (App. Div. 1986) (site plan denial because of distance from fire hydrants exceeded authority; citing treatise). *See also* American Planning Association, Growing Smart Legislative Guidebook: Model Statutes for Planning and Management of Change § 9-302 (S. Meck ed. 2002).

[4] 383 A.2d 773 (N.J.L. Div. 1978). *Accord* TLC Dev. Co. v. Planning & Zoning Comm'n, 577 A.2d 288 (Conn. 1990); New England Brickmaster, Inc. v. Town of Salem, 582 A.2d 601 (N.H. 1990); Dunkin' Donuts of N.J., Inc. v. Township of North Brunswick Plan. Bd. 475 A.2d 71 (N.J. App. Div. 1984).

a site plan application only if the ingress and egress proposed by the plan creates an unsafe and inefficient vehicular circulation."[5] The court held that, if a site plan affected off-site conditions such as traffic, the site plan review ordinance could require a contribution from the developer for a street widening that would remedy the traffic congestion.[6]

This decision is consistent with decisions elsewhere. They hold that site plan review is limited to conditions relating to the site.[7] Some courts also hold that the site plan review ordinance may not require developer contributions for off-site improvements.[8]

If a site plan complies with site plan review requirements and if the proposed use is authorized by the zoning ordinance, the reviewing agency may not disapprove the site plan because it finds the proposed use objectionable. In *Kosinski v. Lawlor*,[9] a site plan proposed a retail complex that met all of the requirements in the zoning ordinance for site plans, but the planning and zoning commission rejected the plan because it was a "poor use for the site." The court held that site plan review "may be used . . . only in conjunction with and not as an alternative" to zoning standards.[10] Courts review decisions approving or

---

[5] 383 A.2d at 779.

[6] *See* N.J. Stat. Ann. § 40:55D-42 (municipality may, by ordinance, require applicant to pay pro-rata share of off-site improvements necessitated by site plan).

[7] Coscan Washington, Inc. v. Maryland-National Capital Park & Planning Comm'n, 590 A.2d 1080 (Md. App. 1991) (can impose condition designating building materials and condition upheld); Southland Corp. v. Mayor & City Council, 541 A.2d 653 (Md. App. 1988) (can deny site plan because of traffic hazards); Holmes v. Planning Bd. of Town of New Castle, 433 N.Y.S.2d 587 (Sup. Ct. 1980) (may impose access conditions).

[8] *Compare* Robbins Auto Parts, Inc. v. City of Laconia, 371 A.2d 1167 (N.H. 1977) (authorized) *with* Riegert Apts. Corp. v. Planning Bd., 441 N.E.2d 1067 (N.Y. 1982) (contra).

[9] 418 A.2d 66 (Conn. 1979).

[10] Accord Sherman v. City of Colorado Springs Planning Comm'n, 680 P.2d 1302 (Colo. App. 1983), *aff'd on appeal from remand,* 729 P.2d 1014 (Colo. App. 1986); Allen Plywood, Inc. v. Planning & Zoning Comm'n, 480 A.2d 584 (Conn. App. 1984); East Lake Partners v. City of Dover Planning Comm'n, 655 A.2d 821 (Del. Super. 1995); S.E.W. Friel v. Triangle Oil Co., 543 A.2d 863 (Md. App. 1988); Prudential Ins. Co. v. Board of Appeals, 502 N.E.2d 137 (Mass. App. 1986); PRB Enters. v. South Brunswick Planning Bd., 518 A.2d 1099 (N.J. 1987); Bongiorno v. Planning Bd., 533 N.Y.S.2d 631 (App. Div. 1988) (reversing disapproval of site plan for permitted use when denial based on opposition); Brooks v. Fisher, 705 S.W.2d 135 (Tenn. App. 1985). *See also* Saddle River Country Day School v. Borough of Saddle River, 144 A.2d 425 (N.J. App. Div. 1958) (may not interfere with board of adjustment variance and special exception powers), *aff'd,* 150 A.2d 34 (N.J. 1959). *Compare* Wesley Inv. Co. v. County of Alameda, 198 Cal. Rptr. 872 (Cal. App. 1984) (ordinance allowed site plan denial of permitted use); City of Colorado Springs v. Securecare Self Storage, Inc., 10 P.3d 1244 (Colo. 2000) (ordinance provided authority to reject site plan for permitted uses); Hansel v. City of Keene, 634 A.2d 1351 (N.H. 1993) (cannot impose condition on site plan approval less stringent than zoning ordinance requires).

denying site plans under the rules they usually apply to the review of administrative zoning decisions.[11]

G. DECISION-MAKING PROCEDURES.

§ 6.67 The Procedures Problem.

Zoning legislation provides only the most basic procedural protections in the decision-making process, such as notice and hearing requirements. Section 7 of the Standard Zoning Act, and statutes based on that Act, require notice of hearings before the board of adjustment and the administration of oaths, compelling the attendance of witnesses, and the taking of minutes.[1] Courts may require additional procedural protections under the due process clause of federal and state constitutions. They may also require adequate procedures to ensure fairness in the decision making process, and some procedural safeguards, such as open meeting requirements, are mandated by statute. Chapter 2 discusses procedural protections available under the federal constitution.[2] This part discusses procedural protections required by the state courts.

Another major problem with providing procedural protections in the zoning process is that the decision making process is fragmented. A land use change or development may require several approvals, including a rezoning, a variance and a site plan approval. Only some of these approval procedures require a quasi-judicial decision making process; zonings and rezonings are legislative in the clear majority of states. Model legislation proposed by the American Planning Association unifies these procedures by requiring a development permit that includes most required quasi-judicial land use approvals, and that can include

---

[11] Lindborg/Dahl Invs., Inc. v. City of Garden Grove, 225 Cal. Rptr. 154 (Cal. App. 1986) (upholding site plan denial); Crann v. Town Plan & Zoning Comm'n, 282 A.2d 900 (Conn. 1971) (can reverse approval only if arbitrary or abuse of discretion); Kurlanski v. Portland Yacht Club, 782 A.2d 783 (Me. 2001) (findings inadequate); Star Vector Corp. v. Town of Windham, 776 A.2d 138 (N.H. 2001) (upholding denial of site plan for shooting range); W.L. Goodfellows & Co. v. Washington Township Planning Bd., 783 A.2d 750 (N.J. App. Div. 2001) (approval required); Black v. Summers, 542 N.Y.S.2d 837 (App. Div. 1989) (invalidating condition prohibiting development); Heidrich v. City of Lee's Summit, 26 S.W.3d 179 (Mo. App. 2000) (upholding site plan approval); Hudson Canyon Constr., Inc. v. Town of Cortlandt, 692 N.Y.S.2d 158 (App. Div. 1999) (reversing site plan denial based in part on public opposition). *See* City of Boynton Beach v. V.S.H. Realty, Inc., 443 So. 2d 452 (Fla. App. 1984) (site plan review held discretionary). *See also* Village of Key Biscayne v. Tesaurus Holdings, Inc., 761 So.2d 397 (Fla. App. 2000) (not denial of due process to require compliance with master plan as required by state law); Bowen v. Board of Appeals, 632 N.E.2d 858 (Mass. App. 1994) (ordinance does not require detailed findings); Leda Lanes Realty, Inc. v. City of Nashua, 293 A.2d 320 (N.H. 1972); Palatine I v. Planning Bd., 628 A.2d 321 (N.J. 1993) (interpreting statutory protection of preliminary site plan approval).

[1] 397 U.S. Dep't of Commerce, Standard State Zoning Enabling Act (1926). *See* § 4.18.

[2] § 2.42.

zoning map amendments at local option. The model act includes a detailed procedural process for decisions on development permits that can include consolidated permit procedures and the use of hearings examiners.[3] Some state legislation also provides detailed procedural safeguards for administrative and quasi-judicial decision making.[4]

§ 6.68 Legislative vs. Quasi-Judicial.

In state as in federal courts, the threshold question is whether a land use decision is legislative or quasi-judicial, for only quasi-judicial decisions implicate procedural due process. Comprehensive rezoning is legislative, as is a zoning map amendment for a single parcel in a majority of states.[1] Administrative actions, such as subdivision approvals,[2] variances, conditional use permits and building permits, are held quasi-judicial.[3]

§ 6.69 Entitlement.

Assuming a land use decision is adjudicatory, another questions is whether a party challenging it as a violation of procedural due process must also show it deprived her of a protectible property interest or "entitlement." In the federal courts, an entitlement does not include an expectancy interest.[1] A landowner has an expectancy rather than an entitlement under federal law if a decision on her application for a land use approval requires an exercise of discretion by the land use agency or official. Some state courts follow the federal rules on entitlement,[2] but a minority provide procedural due process protection even if the landowner

---

[3] American Planning Association, Growing Smart Legislative Guidebook: Model Statutes for Planning and Management of Change ch. 10 (S. Meck ed. 2002).

[4] *E.g.,* Ga. Code Ann. § 36-66-1 et seq.; N.J. Stat. Ann. § 40:55D-10; Or. Rev. Stat. § 197.763.

[1] §§ 2.43, 6.26.

[2] Horn v. County of Ventura, 596 P.2d 1134, 1138 (Cal. 1979); Shaw v. Planning Comm'n, 500 A.2d 1338 (Conn. App. 1985); Mutton Hill Estates, Inc. v. Town of Oakland, 468 A.2d 989 (Me. 1983).

[3] Building permits: Sclavenitis v. Cherry Hills Bd. of Adj., 751 P.2d 661 (Colo. App. 1988); Thomson v. State, Dep't of Envtl. Reg., 493 So. 2d 1032 (Fla. App. 1986). *See also* County of Lancaster v. Mecklenburg County, 434 S.E.2d 604 (N.C. 1993) (landfill permit).

Conditional use permits: Scott v. City of Indian Wells, 492 P.2d 1137 (Cal. 1972); Barton Contr'g Co. v. City of Afton, 268 N.W.2d 712 (Minn. 1978).

Variances: Speedway Bd. of Zoning Appeals v. Popcheff, 385 N.E.2d 1179 (Ind. App. 1979); White v. Town of Hollis, 589 A.2d 46 (Me. 1991); Horn v. Township of Hilltown, 337 A.2d 858 (Pa. 1975); Schalow v. Waupaca Cty., 407 N.W.2d 316 (Wis. App. 1987); Cook v. Zoning Bd. of Adj., 776 P.2d 181 (Wyo. 1989).

[1] § 2.42.

[2] Red Maple Properties v. Zoning Comm'n, 610 A.2d 1238 (Conn. 1992); Sandy Beach Defense Fund v. City Council, 773 P.2d 250 (Hawaii 1989).

has only an expectancy interest.[3] Some state courts also provide procedural due process protections to adjacent landowners affected by a zoning approval.[4]

§ 6.70 Procedures Required.

Once a court has determined that a land use decision is adjudicatory and that an entitlement was affected, it must determine what process is due. The Supreme Court employs a three-part balancing test to decide this question,[1] and some state courts also apply this test.[2]

Some state courts refuse to impose the full range of trial-type procedures on adjudicatory decision-making by zoning authorities.[3] Other courts virtually judicialize adjudicatory decision-making by local land use authorities.[4] They may require adequate notice,[5] hearings by a neutral arbiter, the right to present

---

[3] Goldberg v. City of Rehoboth Beach, 565 A.2d 936, 942 (Del. Super. Ct.) (partitioning request), aff'd, 567 A.2d 421 (Del. 1989); Fairbairn v. Planning Bd., 360 N.E.2d 668 (Mass. App. 1977) (subdivision approval).

[4] Scott v. City of Indian Wells, 492 P.2d 1137 (Cal. 1972); Roosevelt v. Beau Monde Co., 384 P.2d 96 (Colo. 1963); Rodine v. Zoning Bd. of Adj., 434 N.W.2d 124 (Iowa App. 1988); Koppel v. City of Fairway, 371 P.2d 113 (Kan. 1962). *But see* Sandy Beach Defense Fund v. City Council, 773 P.2d 250 (Hawaii 1989) (only abutting owners protected); Wells v. Village of Libertyville, 505 N.E.2d 740 (Ill. App. 1987) (notice by publication enough); *Compare* Lawrence Preservation Alliance, Inc. v. Allen Realty, Inc., 819 P.2d 138 (Kan. App. 1991) (historical preservation groups have protectible interests at stake in requests for demolition permits).

[1] Mathews v. Eldridge, 424 U.S. 319 (1976).

[2] Goldberg v. City of Rehoboth Beach, 565 A.2d 936 (Del. Super. Ct.) (partitioning request), aff'd, 567 A.2d 421 (Del. 1989); Horn v. County of Ventura, 596 P.2d 1134 (Cal. 1979). *See also* Waste Management of Illinois, Inc. v. Pollution Control Bd., 530 N.E.2d 682 (Ill. App. 1988) (similar balancing test adopted as state requirement).

[3] Petersen v. Chicago Plan Comm'n, 707 N.E.2d 150 (Ill. App. 1998) (cross examination not required); Kletschka v. LeSueur Cty. Bd. of Comm'rs, 277 N.W.2d 404 (Minn. 1979) (no cross-examination required in administrative appeal from denial of conditional use permit).

[4] Cardillo v. Council of South Bethany, 1991 Del. Super. Lexis 224 (Super. Ct. 1991) (subdivision application); Coral Reef Nurseries, Inc. v. Babcock Co., 410 So. 2d 648, 652 (Fla. App. 1982) (right to present evidence and cross-examine and be informed of factual basis for decision); Cooper v. Board of Cty. Comm'rs, 614 P.2d 947 (Idaho 1980) (notice; transcribable verbatim record of proceedings; specific findings of fact and conclusions); Kaelin v. City of Louisville, 643 S.W.2d 590, 591 (Ky. 1983); Fairbairn v. Planning Bd., 360 N.E.2d 668 (Mass. App. 1977) (same); Neuberger v. City of Portland, 607 P.2d 722, 725 (Or. 1980) (ex parte contacts); Board of Cty. Comm'rs v. Teton Cty. Youth Servs., 652 P.2d 400 (Wyo. 1982) (hearing, taking of evidence, findings of fact, orders based on substantial evidence, judicial review). *See also* American Planning Association, Growing Smart Legislative Guidebook: Model Statutes for Planning and Management of Change §§ 10-201 to 10-211(S. Meck ed. 2002) (completeness determination on application, record hearing after notice, time limits on decisions); § 6.48.

[5] Grimes v. Conservation Comm'n, 703 A.2d 101 (Conn. 1997) (published notice of site visit held adequate); Nazarko v. Conservation Comm'n, 717 A.2d 853 (Conn. App. 1998) (notice inadequate); Comer v. County of Twin Falls, 942 P.2d 557 (Idaho 1997) (failure to provide notice

evidence,[6] the right to cross-examine witnesses, the right to respond to written submissions, the right to counsel, and a decision on the record with stated reasons.[7] Procedural due process rights may vary with the administrative posture of the case. For example, when a final decision-maker must engage in de novo fact-finding, a planning board need not submit its findings of fact in writing.[8]

Claims of procedural due process violations may be difficult to sustain. State courts may require plaintiffs that complain of unfair hearings to defeat the presumption that local authorities performed their duties properly,[9] prove that they were prejudiced (*e.g.*, that they had been denied variances although they had not shown undue hardship),[10] and preserve their rights of appeal to the courts by objecting to procedural due process violations at the hearing level.[11] Substantial compliance with procedural requirements may be enough.[12]

Nevertheless, there have been successful challenges to hearings and fact-finding by local agencies. For example, procedural due process was denied when a board of adjustment told the plaintiff's attorney the hearings were over, and

---

of site visit violated due process rights); Gallo v. Mayor & Township Council, 744 A.2d 1219 (N.J. App. Div. 2000) (published notice sufficient for revision of land use ordinance pursuant to review of plan); Perlmart of Lacey, Inc. v. Lacey Township Planning Bd., 684 A.2d 1005 (N.J. App. Div. 1996) (notice inadequate); Gernatt v. Town of Sardinia, 664 N.E.2d 1226 (N.Y. 1996) (notice adequate); Prekeges v. King County, 990 P.2d 405 (Wash. App. 1999) (lack of notice does not excuse untimely filing of appeal when appellant had actual notice). *But see* Quality Refrigerated Servs. v. City of Spencer, 586 N.W.2d 202 (Iowa 1998) (comprehensive zoning amendment does not require personal notice).

[6] Howard v. City of Kinston, 558 S.E.2d 221 (N.C. App. 2002) (may limit testimony and rely on unsworn testimony).

[7] People *ex rel*. Klaeren v. Village of Lisle, 737 N.E.2d 1099 (Ill. App. 2000) (cross-examination required), noted, Land Use L. & Zoning Dig., Vol. 53, No.7, at 3 (2001); Crispin v. Town of Scarborough, 736 A.2d 241 (Me. 1999) (applicants had adequate opportunity to be heard).

[8] Jago-Ford v. Planning & Zoning Comm'n, 642 A.2d 14 (Conn. App. 1994) (member absent from some hearings sufficiently acquainted with case); Riverside Groups, Inc. v. Smith, 497 So. 2d 988 (Fla. App. 1986); Petersen v. City of Clemson, 439 S.E.2d 317 (S.C. App. 1993) (extensive minutes by Planning Board given to council with oral report satisfied written report requirement). *See also* Restivo v. Lynch, 707 A.2d 663 (R.I. 1998) (personal knowledge of decision maker is legally competent evidence if disclosed in record).

[9] Messer v. Snohomish Cty. Bd. of Adj., 578 P.2d 50 (Wash. App. 1978).

[10] Speedway Bd. of Zoning Appeals v. Popcheff, 385 N.E.2d 1179 (Ind. App. 1979); White v. Town of Hollis, 589 A.2d 46 (Me. 1991). *See also* Danville-Boyle County Planning & Zoning Comm'n v. Prall, 840 S.W.2d 205 (Ky. 1992); Barton Contr'g Co. v. City of Afton, 268 N.W.2d 712 (Minn. 1978); Pease Hill Community Group v. County of Spokane, 816 P.2d 37 (Wash. App. 1991).

[11] Speedway Bd. of Zoning Appeals v. Popcheff, 385 N.E.2d 1179 (Ind. App. 1979); Jorgensen v. Board of Adj., 336 N.W.2d 423 (Iowa 1983).

[12] Bennett v. City Council, 973 P.2d 871 (N.M. App. 1999) (notice).

then, in the attorney's absence, reopened the hearings to take adverse testimony.[13] Other courts found procedural due process violations when local agency fact-finding was not supported by the record.[14]

§ 6.71   Impartial Decision-Maker.

Procedural due process guarantees the parties an impartial decision-maker. That means a decision-maker free of bias and conflict of interest.[1] An impartial decision-maker must also be a decision-maker untainted by ex parte contacts,[2] though state courts are careful to point out that ex parte contacts do not render a decision void per se.[3] Some courts hold that ex parte contacts are not actionable at all if discoverable in time to be rebutted.[4] Other courts hold that ex parte contacts are actionable if prejudicial, and they may adopt a rebuttable presumption of prejudice.[5] A court may also require plaintiffs to show prejudice — at least when the alleged contacts are open contacts with public entities[6] rather than concealed contacts with individual decision-makers.[7] Moreover, ex parte contacts are not prejudicial if they are disclosed.[8] 16 Although a decision-maker may not rely on extrinsic evidence in making a decision, it is well-established she

---

[13] Sclavenitis v. Cherry Hills Bd. of Adj., 751 P.2d 661 (Colo. App. 1988). *Accord* Clark v. City of Hermosa Beach, 56 Cal. Rptr. 2d 223 (Cal. App. 1996). *Compare* Board of County Comm'rs v. Webber, 658 So. 2d 1069 (Fla. App. 1995) (reconsideration held proper).

[14] Bryan v. Salmon Corp., 554 S.W.2d 912 (Ky. App. 1977); In re Rocky Point Plaza Corp., 621 N.E.2d 566 (Ohio App. 1993); Schalow v. Waupaca Cty., 407 N.W.2d 316 (Wis. App. 1987) (county made no record and took no evidence). *See also* McKinstry v. Wells, 548 S.W.2d 169 (Ky. App. 1977) (cannot rely on legislative fact-finding by planning commission).

[1] §§ 6.72–6.74.

[2] American Planning Association, Growing Smart Legislative Guidebook: Model Statutes for Planning and Management of Change § 10-207(7) (S. Meck ed. 2002) (proposing two alternatives for handling parte contacts), based on Or. Rev. Stat. §§ 215.422, 227.180 and Wash. Rev. Code § 42.36.060. *See also* Fla. Stat. Ann. 268.0115.

[3] Blaker v. Planning & Zoning Comm'n, 562 A.2d 1093 (Conn. 1989); Hougham v. Lexington-Fayette Urban County Gov't, 29 S.W.3d 370 (Ky. 2000) (contact with neighborhood groups, letters from constituents, information gathered from staff, does not, by itself, constitute improper ex parte contact); Neuberger v. City of Portland, 607 P.2d 722, 725 (Or. 1980).

[4] Jennings v. Dade Cty., 1991 Fla. App. Lexis 12672 (Fla. App. 1991).

[5] *Id.*; Waste Management v. Pollution Control Bd., 530 N.E.2d 682 (Ill. App. 1986).

[6] Neuberger v. City of Portland, 607 P.2d 722 (Or. 1980). *See* Or. Rev. Stat. § 227.180(3); Opp v. City of Portland, 16 P.3d 520 (Or. App. 2000) (LUBA order that respondent conduct a hearing that afforded interested parties an opportunity to present evidentiary and rhetorical responses to the ex parte communication cured ex parte contact); Horizon Constr. Co. v. City of Newberg, 834 P.2d 523 (Or. App. 1992) (ex parte contact not cured);

[7] Smith v. Fair Haven Zoning Bd. of Adjustment, 761 A.2d 111 (N.J. App. 2000) (no prejudice; contacts did not go beyond arguments at hearing); 1000 Friends of Oregon v. Wasco Cty. Ct., 723 P.2d 1034 (Or. App. 1986) (incorporation).

[8] Idaho Historic Preservation Council, Inc. v. City Council, 8 P.3d 646 (Idaho 2000).

may rely on competent personal knowledge.[9] Finally, several courts have held that the right to an impartial decision-maker is impaired when attorneys for a party before a zoning board also serve on it,[10] or when a single attorney or a single law firm provides both advocacy and adjudicatory counsel in a single proceeding.[11]

§ 6.72 Bias and Conflict of Interest.

The traditional rule that judicial and administrative decision makers must not be tainted with prejudice when passing on claims that come before them applies to the zoning process. Courts examine administrative and quasi-judicial decision making in zoning to determine whether bias or a conflict of interest was present. Bias and conflict-of-interest claims are less successful when brought against legislative decision makers because of the rule, applied to zoning as well as other legislative actions, that courts will not investigate the motives of legislative bodies.[1] Fraud in the legislative process is an exception to this rule.[2] Bias and conflict of interest claims may also be made against members of legislative bodies when they act in a quasi-judicial capacity, or when they are covered by a statute that makes them subject to such claims.[3]

The bias and conflict-of-interest disqualification applies to members of the governing body in states where the courts hold that rezoning and other actions by the governing body are quasi-judicial. A minority of courts disqualify a member of a governing body because of bias and conflict of interest even though they hold that the governing body acts in a quasi-legislative manner in the zoning process.[4]

---

[9] Adelman v. Town of Baldwin, 750 A.2d 577 (Me. 2000); Smith v. Fair Haven Zoning Bd. of Adjustment, 761 A.2d 111 (N.J. App. 2000).

[10] Washington Cty. Cease, Inc. v. Persico, 473 N.Y.S.2d 610 (App. Div. 1984), aff'd, 477 N.E.2d 1084 (N.Y. 1985).

[11] Horn v. Township of Hilltown, 337 A.2d 858 (Pa. 1975) (proof of prejudice not required).

[1] Brown v. Town of Davidson, 439 S.E.2d 206 (N.C. App. 1994); Fiser v. City of Knoxville, 584 S.W.2d 659 (Tenn. App. 1979).

[2] Schauer v. City of Miami Beach, 112 So. 2d 838 (Fla. 1959); Lindsey Creek Area Civic Ass'n v. Consolidated Gov't of Columbus, 292 S.E.2d 61 (Ga. 1982); Athey v. City of Peru, 317 N.E.2d 294 (Ill. App. 1974). *Cf.* Woodland Hills Residents Ass'n v. City Council, 609 P.2d 1029 (Cal. 1980) (campaign contributions do not create appearance of unfairness). *See* 63 A.L.R.2d 1072 (1975) (effect of abstention on voting majority requirement).

[3] Breakzone Billiards v. City of Torrance, 97 Cal. Rptr. 2d 467 (Cal. App. 2000) (statute applied; campaign contributions not disqualifying). *See* Ind. Code Ann. § 36-7-4-223(b).

[4] Olley Valley Estates, Inc. v. Fussell, 208 S.E.2d 801 (Ga. 1974); Netluch v. Mayor & Council, 325 A.2d 517 (N.J. 1974). *But see* Sugarloaf Citizens Ass'n v. Gudis, 573 A.2d 1325 (Md. 1990) (ordinance authorizing court to void zoning ordinance because of conflict of interest violates separation of powers).

Washington has adopted a unique "appearance of fairness" rule that applies to legislative and administrative proceedings in which a hearing is required.[5] This rule incorporates a two-part fairness test. A reasonable person attending a hearing must be able to conclude that everyone entitled to a hearing obtained one. The agency holding the hearing must also give due weight to the matters presented.

Several states have statutory provisions covering bias and conflict-of-interest problems. These statutes usually apply to planning commission and board of adjustment members and prohibit any direct or indirect personal or financial interest.[6] The statutory prohibition sometimes extends to members of legislative bodies.[7] New York has enacted a full disclosure requirement for amendments, variances, and other land use decisions.[8]

§ 6.73 Bias.

The courts have found bias when a member of a local zoning agency makes outspoken public statements on a zoning matter she subsequently heard.[1] In a typical case, a board member made it openly clear that she would oppose an application for a variance or similar approval no matter what evidence an applicant introduced. The court disqualified the board member from sitting when the board heard the variance application. Participation by members of a decision body in a project for which they later grant a zoning approval may not constitute bias.[2]

---

[5] Fleming v. City of Tacoma, 502 P.2d 327 (Wash. 1972), *overruled in part by statute,* Raynes v. City of Leavenworth, 821 P.2d 1204 (Wash. 1992). *See* Wash. Rev. Code Ann. § 42.36.010. *See also* Golden Gate Corp. v. Town of Narragansett, 359 A.2d 321 (R.I. 1976); 71 A.L.R.2d 568 (1960).

[6] Cal. Gov't Code § 87100; Colo. Rev. Stat. § 24-18-105; Conn. Gen. Stat. §§ 8-11, 8-21; Fla. Stat. Ann. § 112.3143 (duty to disclose); N.J. Stat. Ann. § 40:55D-69; Or. Rev. Stat. § 244.120; Pa. Stat. Ann. tit. 65, § 401 et seq.;Va. Code Ann. § 15.2-852. *See also* American Planning Association, Growing Smart Legislative Guidebook: Model Statutes for Planning and Management of Change § 10-207(8) (S. Meck ed. 2002).

[7] Ga. Code Ann. §§ 36-67A-1 to 36-67A-4 (applies only to rezoning); Idaho Code § 67-6506.

[8] N.Y. Gen. Mun. Law § 809.

[1] Lage v. Zoning Bd. of Appeals, 172 A.2d 911 (Conn. 1961); Acierno v. Folsom, 337 A.2d 309 (Del. 1975); Barbara Realty Co. v. Zoning Bd. of Review, 128 A.2d 342 (R.I. 1957); Chrobuck v. Snohomish County, 480 P.2d 489 (Wash. 1971); Marris v. City of Cedarburg, 498 N.W.2d 842 (Wis. 1993). *See also* Marmah, Inc. v. Town of Greenwich, 405 A.2d 63 (Conn. 1978). *But see* McPherson Landfill, Inc. v. Board of County Comm'rs, 49 P.3d 522 (Kan. 2002) (board members kept open mind and considered all evidence).

[2] In re Application of City of Raleigh, 421 S.E.2d 179 (N.C. App. 1992) (contrary holding would destroy community's orderly planning process). *But see* South Brunswick Assocs. v. Township Council, 667 A.2d 1 (N.J.L. Div. 1995) (council president may not represent opposition to project before zoning board and then participate in council review of board decision). *See also* Wyzkowski v. Rizas, 626 A.2d 406 (N.J. 1993) (discussing whether mayor may make application to planning board).

The cases have not disqualified a public official because of campaign statements when he later voted in accordance with his campaign promises.[3] As one court pointed out:

> Campaign promises made in political races do not disqualify . . . . Under our theory of government the voters desire and even demand to be informed as to how candidates stand on the issues of the campaign.[4]

Neither may campaign contributions be disqualifying.[5]

§ 6.74 Conflicts of Interest.

Conflicts of interest usually arise when a member of a zoning agency has a pecuniary interest in a zoning decision or a personal relationship with the applicant for a zoning change.[1] A pecuniary interest based on the ownership of property affected by the zoning change is a typical example. A court may find an improper pecuniary interest even though a zoning action is extensive and the board member's property is not the only property affected. In *Kovalik v. Planning & Zoning Comm'n*,[2] the chairman of the commission owned eight percent of the land that the commission upgraded to two-acre residential zoning. The court found a disqualifying conflict of interest.[3]

A pecuniary benefit from property ownership may not create a conflict of interest if the benefit is indirect. In *Dana-Robin Corp. v. Common Council*,[4] the

---

[3] City of Fairfield v. Superior Court of Solano County, 537 P.2d 375 (Cal. 1975); Turf Valley Assocs. v. Zoning Bd., 278 A.2d 574 (Md. 1971); Kramer v. Board of Adjustment, 212 A.2d 153 (N.J. 1965); Wollen v. Borough of Fort Lee, 142 A.2d 881 (N.J. 1958); Webster Assocs. v. Town of Webster, 451 N.E.2d 189 (N.Y. 1983). *See also* Izaak Walton League of Am. v. Monroe County, 448 So. 2d 1170 (Fla. App. 1984) (applying rule to statements made during term of office).

[4] City of Farmers Branch v. Hawnco, Inc., 435 S.W.2d 288, 292 (Tex. Civ. App. 1968).

[5] Woodland Hills Residents Ass'n v. City Council, 609 P.2d 1029 (Cal. 1980); Breakzone Billiards v. City of Torrance, 97 Cal. Rptr.2d 467 (Cal. App. 2000).

[1] State v. Schenkolewski, 693 A.2d 1173 (N.J. App. Div. 1997) (indictment for bribery upheld).

[2] 234 A.2d 838 (Conn. 1967).

[3] *See also* Griswold v. City of Homer, 925 P.2d 1015 (Alaska 1996) (zoning change would benefit council member's property); Brunswick v. Inland Wetlands Comm'n, 617 A.2d 466 (Conn. App. 1992) (board member voted for subdivision for which he might build roads); O'Ko'olau v. Pacarro, 666 P.2d 177 (Haw. App. 1983) (project would benefit board member's property); Manookian v. Blaine County, 735 P.2d 1008 (Idaho 1987) (commission members voted to route power line away from their property); McNamara v. Borough of Saddle River, 166 A.2d 391 (N.J. 1960); Gunthner v. Planning Bd., 762 A.2d 710 (N.J.L. Div. 2000) (members of yacht club had disqualifying interest in adjacent development but court disregarded because disqualification would prevent a quorum); Segalla v. Planning Bd., 611 N.Y.S.2d 287 (App. Div. 1994) (mere ownership of property not enough); Town of North Hempstead v. Village of North Hills, 342 N.E.2d 566 (N.Y. 1975); Segalla v. Planning Bd., 611 N.Y.S.2d 287 (App. Div. 1995) (ownership of property in town not enough); Amerikohl Mining Co. v. Zoning Hearing Bd., 597 A.2d 219 (Pa. Commw. 1991) (having residence near proposed use that was denied not enough); 10 A.L.R.3d 694 (1966).

[4] 348 A.2d 560 (Conn. 1974).

court did not find a conflict of interest when the council disapproved an application for a multifamily development, even though members of the council owned competing multifamily developments in the city.[5]

A court may refuse to find a pecuniary conflict of interest when the pecuniary benefit is contingent or remote. In *Copple v. City of Lincoln*,[6] a council member voted for a comprehensive plan that designated property he owned for commercial use. He later abstained from voting on the commercial rezoning of his property. The court did not find a conflict of interest. It held that the designation on the comprehensive plan was "speculative" because it depended on future action by the city, including "the future staging of development and zoning."

Members of local zoning boards and commissions often belong to unions and other organizations that benefit indirectly from zoning decisions. An example is a conditional use a zoning board grants for a development project that will employ workers who belong to a board member's union. A court will not find a conflict of interest if the member of the organization does not receive a direct pecuniary benefit.[7] Courts do not want to prohibit service on a zoning agency by an individual whose organization gains indirectly from the zoning process.[8]

Courts find an improper conflict of interest when close personal or business relationships exist between a member of a zoning board and an applicant for a zoning change. A board member was disqualified when his wife was the applicant for a zoning amendment.[9] Board members who sold property to an

---

[5] *Compare* Perry-Worth Concerned Citizens v. Board of Comm'rs, 723 N.E.2d 457 (Ind. App. 2000) (ownership by spouse in adjacent property not enough); S & L Assocs. v. Township of Washington, 160 A.2d 635 (N.J. 1960) (disqualifying board member who voted to exclude competing land from industrial area).

[6] 274 N.W.2d 520 (Neb. 1979). *See also* White v. Board of Comm'rs, 555 S.E.2d 45 (Ga. App. 2001) (financial interest remote and speculative); Bluffs Dev. Co. v. Board of Adjustment, 499 N.W.2d 12 (Iowa 1993) (family and business relationships with opponents of zoning proposal held remote); Lincoln Heights Ass'n v. Township of Cranford Planning Bd., 714 A.2d 995 (N.J.L. Div. 1998) (benefit to parents speculative), *aff'd*, 720 A.2d 50 (N.J. App. Div. 1999).

[7] Tangen v. State Ethics Comm'n, 550 P.2d 1275 (Haw. 1976); Rowell v. Board of Adj., 446 N.W.2d 917 (Minn. App. 1989) (church member may vote on variance for church). *Compare* Narrowsview Preservation Ass'n v. City of Tacoma, 526 P.2d 897 (Wash. 1974).

[8] For other pecuniary interest cases, *see* Hochberg v. Borough of Freehold, 123 A.2d 46 (N.J. 1956); Save a Valuable Env't v. City of Bothell, 576 P.2d 401 (Wash. 1978).

[9] Low v. Town of Madison, 60 A.2d 774 (Conn. 1948); Care of Tenafly, Inc. v. Tenafly Zoning Bd. of Adjustment, 704 A.2d 1032 (N.J. App. Div. 1998) (mother of board member owned competing commercial business within 500 feet of commercial use approved by board). *See also* Barrett v. Union Twp. Comm., 553 A.2d 62 (N.J. App. Div. 1989) (board member disqualified to vote on zoning amendment for nursing home where his wife was patient); Sokolinski v. Municipal Council, 469 A.2d 96 (N.J. App. Div. 1983) (board members or their wives employed by school district granted a variance); Zagoreos v. Conklin, 491 N.Y.S.2d 358 (App. Div. 1985) (employees of applicant disqualified). *But see* Petrick v. Planning Bd., 671 A.2d 140 (N.J. App. Div. 1996) (occasional employment of board member by successful applicant for site plan approval not enough).

individual who subsequently made an application for a zoning change on the property also were disqualified.[10] A board member was disqualified when his nephew was a member of the law firm that represented the applicant.[11] Indirect business relationships, such as writing insurance for an applicant for a zoning amendment, are not disqualifying.[12] Personal interests are also disqualifying,[13] but a mayor's personal interest in an amendment he proposed to a zoning ordinance did not disqualify.[14] A statute may require the full disclosure of conflicts of interest and disqualify an official from voting on an action in which he has a conflict.[15]

§ 6.75 Neighborhood Opposition.

Zoning boards often react to neighborhood opposition, either in approving or rejecting a land use application. Courts may set aside a zoning decision if they believe that a favorable response to neighborhood opposition tainted the zoning action with an improper motive or purpose. *Chanhassen Estates Residents Ass'n v. City of Chanhassen*[1] states the typical judicial concern that denial of a zoning approval must based "on something more than neighborhood opposition and expressions of concern for public safety and welfare." These decisions are often based on substantive due process concerns.[2]

---

[10] Daly v. Town Plan & Zoning Comm'n, 191 A.2d 250 (Conn. 1963); Piggott v. Borough of Hopewell, 91 A.2d 667 (N.J. 1952). *See also* Aldom v. Borough of Roseland, 127 A.2d 190 (N.J. 1956); Zell v. Borough of Roseland, 125 A.2d 890 (N.J. 1956).

[11] Kremer v. City of Plainfield, 244 A.2d 335 (N.J. 1968). *Accord,* Dick v. Williams, 452 S.E.2d 172 (Ga. App. 1994) (conflict of interest to vote on matter represented by son's law partner); Carroll County Ethics Comm'n v. Lennon, 703 A.2d 1338 (Md. App. 1998) (commission member represented private clients on matters regulated by commission and participated in approval of client proposals by commission); Paruszewski v. Township of Elsinboro, 711 A.2d 273 (N.J. 1998) (appearance of township attorney before zoning board not conflict of interest); Trust Co. of New Jersey v. Planning Bd., 582 A.2d 1295 (N.J. App. Div. 1990). *Compare* Strandberg v. Kansas City, 415 S.W.2d 737 (Mo. 1967).

[12] Moody v. City of Univ. Park, 278 S.W.2d 912 (Tex. Civ. App. 1955). *See* Ahearn v. Zoning Bd. of Appeals, 551 N.Y.S.2d 392 (App. Div. 1990) (generalized claims of conflict not enough); West Slope Community Council v. City of Tacoma, 569 P.2d 1183 (Wash. App. 1977). *But see* Parker v. Town of Gardiner, 585 N.Y.S.2d 571 (App. Div. 1992) (financial interest de minimis).

[13] Clark v. City of Hermosa Beach, 56 Cal. Rptr.2d 223 (Cal. App. 1996) (council member's enjoyment of home); Jock v. Shire Realty, Inc., 684 A.2d 921 (N.J. App. Div. 1996) (member of board testified in favor of variance for property in which he had interest).

[14] Ghent v. Zoning Comm'n, 600 A.2d 1010 (Conn. 1991).

[15] 446 Ga. Code Ann. § 36-67A-2 (financial and property interests must be disclosed). *See* Little v. City of Lawrenceville, 528 S.E.2d 515 (Ga. 2000) (action in support of rezoning application, including supplementation, responding to inquiries from zoning authorities, or altering the property at issue or business conducted not covered by disqualification requirement).

[1] 342 N.W.2d 335 (Minn. 1984).

[2] *See also* City of Cleburne v. Cleburne Living Center, 473 U.S. 432 (1985) (denial of special use permit for group home based partly on neighborhood opposition held to violate equal protection). *See* § 2.48.

A number of cases have invalidated zoning approvals found to have been improperly influenced by neighborhood opposition.[3] Courts will uphold a zoning decision, despite neighborhood opposition, if they believe the decision was based on legitimate zoning purposes. In *Nelson v. City of Selma*,[4] the court upheld a refusal to rezone, despite neighborhood opposition, because it served the legitimate purpose of preventing heavy traffic and preserving the residential character of the neighborhood.

§ 6.76 Open Meeting Laws.

All states have open meeting laws, popularly known as "sunshine laws." Statutes may require all state and local governing bodies, including municipalities and counties, to hold open meetings.[1] Statutes more commonly require governmental bodies that receive or disburse public funds or act under authority delegated by the state constitution, statute, charter, or ordinance to hold open meetings.[2] This includes municipal governing bodies. It also includes planning commissions and boards of adjustment[3] that are required by statute to hold public hearings.[4] Statutes and courts frequently exempt deliberations by judicial and quasi-judicial bodies from the reach of open meeting laws, such as a zoning board meeting in closed session to weigh evidence previously presented at an open meeting on a special use permit application.[5] A public hearing may be required but deliberation may be allowed in private.[6] Other statutes[7] and courts[8] require

---

[3] Marks v. City of Chesapeake, 883 F.2d 308 (4th Cir. 1989); National Amusements, Inc. v. City of Boston, 560 N.E.2d 138 (Mass. App. 1990); Huntington Health Care Partnership v. Zoning Bd. of Appeals, 516 N.Y.S.2d 99 (App. Div. 1987); Davis County v. Clearfield City, 756 P.2d 704 (Utah App. 1988); Washington State Dept. of Corrections v. City of Kennewick, 937 P.2d 1119 (Wash. App. 1997).

[4] 881 F.2d 836 (9th Cir. 1989). *Accord* Fleckinger v. Jefferson Parish Council, 510 So. 2d 429 (La. App. 1987).

[1] Ariz. Rev. Stat. Ann. § 38-431(5); Utah Code Ann. §§ 52-4-2 to 54-2-10.

[2] N.J. Stat. Ann. § 10:4-6 *et seq. See also* § 5 Ill. Comp. Stat. Ann. 120/1–120/5.

[3] Town of Palm Beach v. Gradison, 296 So. 2d 473 (Fla. App. 1974); Hudspeth v. Board of County Comm'rs of Routt, 667 P.2d 775 (Colo. App. 1983). *But see* Goodson Todman Ent. v. Town Bd. of Milan, 542 N.Y.S.2d 373 (App. Div. 1989) (zoning revision committee created to recommend changes in zoning ordinance held not subject to open meeting because function merely advisory).

[4] *E.g.,* Wash. Rev. Code Ann. § 36.70.840; Wis. Stat. Ann. § 62.23(7)(d).

[5] Concerned Citizens v. Town of Guilderland, 458 N.Y.S.2d 13 (App. Div. 1982). *But see* Ridenour v. Jessamini County Fiscal Court, 842 S.W.2d 532 (Ky. App. 1992) (fiscal court not exempt); Kennedy v. Upper Milford Township Zoning Hearing Bd., 779 A.2d 1257 (Pa. Commw. 2001) (deliberative official action not exempt); Hays County v. Hays County Water Planning Partnership, 69 S.W.3d 253 (Tex. App. 2002) (no legislative immunity).

[6] Sullivan v. Northwest Garage & Storage Company, 165 A.2d 881 (Md. 1960); State ex rel. Cities Service Oil Co. v. Board of Appeals, 124 N.W.2d 809 (Wis. 1963). *See* State ex rel. Long v. Village of Cardington, 748 N.E.2d 58 (Ohio 2001) (minutes must contain full and accurate record

all phases of the decision-making process of quasi-judicial bodies to be open to the public.

"Meetings" required to be held open to the public are defined as a gathering of a quorum of the members of the public body in order to transact public business.[9] Public business which must be conducted at an open meeting normally includes formal action of the governmental body as well as informal discussion on public issues.[10] A meeting also may occur even where a quorum is gathered for the purpose of attending the meeting of another governmental agency.[11] Most state statutes exclude social and chance gatherings from the definition of meeting.[12]

Violations of the open meeting statute occur when public bodies required to hold open meetings, conduct meetings that are closed to the public. Courts usually interpret the "open to the public" requirement as mandating that the meeting be reasonably open to the public.[13] Most courts require that all aspects of the decision-making process be open to the public.[14] Open meeting laws almost always contain provisions requiring notice of public meetings.

Almost all open meeting laws contain specific, enumerated exemptions to the public meeting requirements. Typical exemptions include meetings to discuss

of meeting and contain sufficient facts and information to allow public to understand rationale behind decision).

[7] Ariz. Rev. Stat. Ann. § 38-431 (exempts only judicial deliberations in court of law); Ky. Rev. Stat. Ann. § 61.810 (excludes zoning boards and commissions). See Wesley Chapel Bluemount Ass'n v. Baltimore County, 699 A.2d 434 (Md. 1997) (law applies to review of development plans).

[8] Remington v. City of Boonville, 701 S.W.2d 804 (Mo. App. 1985) (includes administrative bodies, such as boards of adjustment, unless exempted).

[9] Cal. Gov't Code § 54952.6; N.Y. Pub. Off. Law § 102. See Bryant v. Cleveland Township, 608 N.W.2d 101 (Mich. App. 2000) (township supervisor's comments to planning commission not a deliberation amounting to an open meeting); Sovereign v. Dunn, 498 N.W.2d 62 (Minn. App. 1993) (mediation sessions not a meeting); Harper v. Summit County, 26 P.3d 193 (Utah 2001) (issuance of certificate of compliance and building permit not included).

[10] Brookwood Area Homeowners Ass'n v. Anchorage, 702 P.2d 1317 (Alaska 1985); Orange County Publications v. Council of City of Newburgh, 401 N.Y.S.2d 84 (App. Div. 1978); Danis Montco Landfill Co. v. Jefferson Twp. Zoning Comm'n, 620 N.E.2d 140 (Ohio App. 1993) (no decision made at meeting); Moore v. Township of Raccoon, 625 A.2d 737 (Pa. Commw. 1993) (plan commission recommendations on junkyard ordinance). But see Board of County Comm'rs v. Webber, 658 So. 2d 1069 (Fla. App. 1995) (ex parte discussions not substantive).

[11] State ex rel. Badke v. Village Bd., 494 N.W.2d 408 (Wis. 1993) (quorum of members of village board attended meetings of planning commission).

[12] Ind. Code Ann. § 5-14-1.5-2(c)(1); Iowa Code Ann. § 21.2(2).

[13] State ex rel. Badke v. Village Bd., 494 N.W.2d 408 (Wis. 1993).

[14] Beck v. Crisp County Bd. of Zoning Appeals, 472 S.E.2d 558 (Ga. App. 1996) (meeting closed to public after evidentiary hearing); Yaro v. Board of Appeals of Newburyport, 410 N.E.2d 725 (Mass. App. 1980).

pending or potential litigation, meetings to discuss real estate transactions, meetings to discuss personnel matters, and emergency meetings. Courts in some states have narrowed the scope of the exception, holding that only discussions of strategy and position on pending or actual litigation may be closed.[15] Many statutes require a majority vote for a closed meeting, a statement of the exemption that covers the closed meeting, and a posting of the meeting agenda.

Open meeting laws typically provide that actions or deliberations that violate the open meeting law are void or voidable by the court. Such statutes typically give the court discretion in voiding decisions and actions taken in violation of an open meeting law.[16] In addition, statutes may provide for costs and attorney fees to be paid by the losing party and for criminal or civil sanctions against those who violate open meeting laws.

Although open meeting laws void actions taken in violation of open meeting requirements, many courts allow violations to be "cured" by subsequent meetings conforming to the open meeting law.[17] Courts also overlook violations when there has been "substantial compliance" with the act.[18]

H. INITIATIVE AND REFERENDUM.

§ 6.77 The Zoning Problem.

Many states authorize the use of the initiative and referendum at the municipal level, and the use of these direct electoral techniques to secure zoning change has become increasingly popular. An initiative is a procedure that allows the voters to propose a municipal ordinance, such as a text amendment to a zoning ordinance. The ordinance takes effect if it is approved by the voters. A referendum is a vote on an action by a local legislative body, such as a rezoning that amends

---

[15] *Compare* Schoen v. Cherokee County, 530 S.E.2d 226 (Ga. App. 2000) (closed meeting to discuss pending litigation fell within statutory exception allowing closed meeting to consult and meet with legal counsel concerning pending litigation and settlement); Manning v. City of East Tawas, 593 N.W.2d 649 (Mich. App. 1999) (any attorney who helps a municipality prepare for litigation is covered by this exemption); Caldwell v. Lambrou, 391 A.2d 590 (N.J. App. Div. 1978) (violation; attorney met with board of adjustment in closed session to discuss board's power to modify site plan), *with* Whispering Woods v. Township of Middleton Planning Bd., 531 A.2d 770 (N.J. App. Div. 1987) (no violation; discussion of revised plan for litigation), *and* State ex rel. Hodge v. Town of Turtle Lake, 508 N.W.2d 603 (Wis. 1993) (hearing on junkyard permit not a "case" on which town board can later hold closed meeting).

[16] Oshry v. Zoning Bd. of Appeals, 713 N.Y.S.2d 564 (App. Div. 2000) (trial court properly exercised discretion in voiding variance when violation of open meetings law was accompanied by other concerns regarding the procedures followed in granting variances).

[17] Brookwood Area Homeowners Ass'n v. Anchorage, 702 P.2d 1317 (Alaska 1985) (violation not cured); Moore v. Township of Raccoon, 625 A.2d 737 (Pa. Commw. 1993).

[18] State v. City of Hailey, 633 P.2d 576 (Idaho 1981) (annexation and rezoning).

the zoning map. The voters decide whether to accept or reject the legislative action.

Referenda are usually permissive and are called only after a specified number of voters have filed a petition. Some municipalities require mandatory referenda on zoning amendments. The initiative is also usually permissive, and an initiative election is called only after the required number of voters have filed the necessary petition.

A zoning referendum is usually called to secure voter review of a zoning change, such as an amendment to a zoning ordinance upzoning a property to a more intensive use or to provide for lower-income housing. An initiative is usually called to propose a major change in the zoning ordinance, such as a growth moratorium. The initiative may also be used as a substitute for a referendum in most states.[1] If a municipality adopts an amendment to the zoning ordinance that upzones land to a more intensive use, the voters may petition for an initiative in the form of a repeal of the zoning amendment.

Referenda and initiatives are available only on legislative as distinguished from administrative or quasi-judicial actions. An ordinance that amends the zoning map is a legislative action in most states. Special exceptions and conditional uses are administrative actions and are not subject to an initiative or referendum. Referenda and initiatives are not available if a statute confers authority to act solely on the municipal governing body. For example, the Washington Supreme Court held a referendum unavailable on a county-wide planning policy required by a Growth Management Act because a statute delegated the authority to adopt that policy solely to the county council.[2]

§ 6.78   Federal Constitutional Issues.

The U.S. Supreme Court has held that referenda may violate the equal protection clause if they are racially discriminatory. In *Hunter v. Erickson,*[1] the Court struck down an amendment to a city charter that required a referendum on fair housing ordinances. It held the amendment was "an explicitly racial classification treating racial housing matters differently from other racial and housing matters."

James v. Valtierra[2] qualified *Hunter.* The Court upheld a California constitutional provision that required a mandatory referendum on federally-subsidized

---

[1] *Contra* Christensen v. Carson, 533 N.W.2d 712 (S.D. 1995).

[2] Snohomish County v. Anderson, 868 P.2d 116 (Wash. 1994). *Accord* Whatcom County v. Brisane, 884 P.2d 1326 (Wash. 1994) (zoning ordinance adopted to implement plan); Save Our State Park v. Board of Clallam County Comm'rs, 875 P.2d 673 (Wash. App. 1994) (initiative).

[1] 393 U.S. 385 (1969).

[2] 402 U.S. 137 (1971) (also rejecting wealth discrimination claim).

public housing projects. It distinguished *Hunter* because the California constitutional provision "requires referendum approval for any low-rent public housing project, not only for projects which will be occupied by a racial minority." The Court found no support for "any claim that a law seemingly neutral on its face is in fact aimed at a racial minority." A later Supreme Court case resurrected *Hunter*. It invalidated as racially discriminatory a constitutional provision adopted by referendum that prohibited the busing of school children to achieve racial integration.[3]

Claims that zoning referenda are racially discriminatory have been difficult to prove under the equal protection clause because the Supreme Court requires proof of a racially discriminatory intent.[4] The Court may clarify this issue.[5] The federal courts rejected claims that referenda repealing zoning amendments that allowed lower-income housing projects were racially discriminatory.[6] They were unwilling to investigate voter motivation to determine whether the voters had a racially discriminatory intent.

City of Eastlake v. Forest City Enters.[7] rejected due process objections to zoning referenda. A city charter required the approval of any land use change in a referendum receiving fifty-five percent of the vote. The Court held that the referendum provision did not improperly delegate legislative power and noted that a referendum "is a means for direct political participation." Neither did the Court find it objectionable that the referendum provision provided no standards. "[W]e deal with a power reserved by the people to themselves." As the Court noted, if "the referendum result . . . [is] unreasonable, the zoning restriction is open to challenge in state court." The Court pointed out that voter rejection of the referendum would leave in place the zoning restriction that the rejected amendment changed. The landowner could then challenge the zoning restriction in state court or apply for a variance.

The Court rejected a claim that the referendum requirement was unconstitutional under Supreme Court decisions that invalidated neighbor consent provisions in zoning ordinances.[8] The Court held that "the standardless delegation

---

[3] § 2.52. *Compare* Washington v. Seattle School Dist. No. 1, 458 U.S. 457 (1982) (busing referendum held racially discriminatory). *But see* Crawford v. Board of Educ., 458 U.S. 527 (1982) (*contra*).

[4] Washington v. Davis, 426 U.S. 229 (1976).

[5] Buckeye Community Hope Foundation v. City of Cuyahoga Falls, 263 F.3d 627 (6th Cir. 2001), *cert. granted*, 2002 U.S. LEXIS 4691 (June 24, 2002).

[6] Southern Alameda Spanish Speaking Org. v. City of Union City, 424 F.2d 291 (9th Cir. 1970); Ranjel v. City of Lansing, 417 F.2d 321 (6th Cir. 1969); 15 A.L.R. Fed. 613 (1973).

[7] 426 U.S. 668 (1976). *Accord* Taylor Props., Inc. v. Union County, 583 N.W.2d 638 (S.D. 1998); Moore Bldg. Co. v. Committee for the Repeal of Ordinance R(C)-88-13, 391 S.E.2d 587 (Va. 1990).

[8] § 6.04.

of power to a limited group of property owners . . . is not to be equated with decisionmaking by the people through the referendum process." Justices Powell and Stevens wrote separate dissents in which they argued that the referendum denied property owners the fair procedures to which they were entitled in the zoning process.

Although *Eastlake* rejected a federal constitutional challenge to a zoning referendum, it does not mean that zoning is always subject to referendum procedures. Some state courts have found state statutory and constitutional barriers to the use of the initiative and referendum in the zoning process.

§ 6.79　Availability in Zoning.

§ 6.80　Referendum.

Although the referendum is potentially available on all local legislative zoning actions, some state courts refuse to allow zoning referenda because they conflict with required statutory procedures for the enactment of zoning ordinances, such as notice and hearing requirements. The courts may also hold that the referendum improperly adds to the zoning procedures provided by the zoning legislation.

Township of Sparta v. Spillane[1] held that a referendum was not available on a zoning ordinance amendment for these reasons. The court noted that the statutory comprehensive plan requirement and the goal that zoning reflect "the social, economic and physical characteristics of the community . . . might well be jeopardized by piecemeal attacks on the zoning ordinances if referenda were permissible for review of any amendment." The New Jersey zoning statute now exempts zoning ordinances and amendments from the initiative and referendum.[2]

Whether a state court will hold that the zoning referendum is inconsistent with the statutory zoning process may depend on how the referendum is authorized. When the referendum is authorized by statute, as in *Spillane,* the court may treat the availability of the referendum as a question of statutory conflict. A court can hold the referendum unavailable if it finds that the statutory authority for a referendum conflicts with the statutory procedural requirements for zoning enactments. The statute in *Spillane* provided general authority for referenda and did not expressly make referenda available in the zoning process.

---

[1] 312 A.2d 154 (N.J. App. 1973). *Accord* Elliott v. City of Clawson, 175 N.W.2d 821 (Mich. App. 1970); Nordmarken v. City of Richfield, 641 N.W.2d 343 (Minn. App. 2002); Westgate Families v. County Clerk, 667 P.2d 453 (N.M. 1983); San Pedro N., Ltd. v. City of San Antonio, 562 S.W.2d 260 (Tex. Civ. App. 1978); I'On, L.L.C. v. Town of Mt. Pleasant, 526 S.E.2d 716 (S.C. 2000); State ex rel. Foster v. City of Morgantown, 432 S.E.2d 195 (W. Va. 1993). *See* State ex rel. MacQueen v. City of Dunbar, 278 S.E.2d 636 (W. Va. 1981); 72 A.L.R.3d 1030 (1976). *See also* Great Atlantic & Pacific Tea Co. v. Borough of Point Pleasant, 644 A.2d 598 (N.J. 1994) (statutory prohibition of referendum does not prohibit nonbinding referendum).

[2] N.J. Stat. Ann. § 40:55D-62(b).

Courts may reach a different result when, as in many states, the state constitution authorizes the use of the referendum. These courts liberally construe the constitutional referendum provision and hold it superior to zoning legislation as a "fundamental right" guaranteed to the people. They stress that the zoning statute is not violated because the referendum is held after notice and hearing procedures have been observed in the zoning process. They may also hold that zoning procedures are not violated because the referendum simply restores the zoning regulations to what they were before they were changed.[3] This holding ignores the point that restoration of the original zoning is an amendment to the zoning ordinance, which also requires a statutory notice and hearing.

City of Fort Collins v. Dooney[4] held that the evasion of notice and hearing procedures through a referendum does not violate procedural due process. "The fact that due process requirements may be met in one manner when the change is by council action does not preclude other procedures from meeting due process requirements under the referendum."[5] The court noted that the election campaign and debate is an alternative to the public hearing the statute requires before the adoption of a zoning ordinance.

The referendum is available on a comprehensive plan or comprehensive zoning amendment if a court characterizes these actions as legislative.[6] It is not available on a limited zoning map amendment if a court characterizes it as quasi-judicial rather than legislative.[7] Administrative zoning decisions, such as special

---

[3] Queen Creek Land & Cattle Corp. v. Yavapai County Bd. of Supvrs., 501 P.2d 391 (Ariz. 1972); City of Fort Collins v. Dooney, 496 P.2d 316 (Colo. 1972); Florida Land Co. v. City of Winter Springs, 427 So. 2d 170 (Fla. 1983) (relying on constitutional provision for referendum); Cook-Johnson Realty Co. v. Bertolini, 239 N.E.2d 80 (Ohio 1968); Taylor Props., Inc. v. Union County, 583 N.W.2d 638 (S.D. 1998); R.G. Moore Bldg. Co. v. Committee for the Repeal of Ordinance R(C)-88-13, 391 S.E.2d 587 (Va. 1990) (referendum authorized by ordinance).

[4] 496 P.2d 316 (Colo. 1972).

[5] *Id.* at 319. *Accord* City of Coral Gables v. Carmichael, 256 So. 2d 404 (Fla. App. 1972).

[6] O'Loane v. O'Rourke, 42 Cal. Rptr. 283 (Cal. App. 1965) (plan); State ex rel. Wahlmann v. Reim, 445 S.W.2d 336 (Mo. 1969). *See also* Allison v. Washington County, 548 P.2d 188 (Or. App. 1976).

[7] Fritz v. City of Kingman, 957 P.2d 337 (Ariz. 1998) (rezoning held legislative); Margolis v. District Court, 638 P.2d 297 (Colo. 1981); Kelley v. John, 75 N.W.2d 713 (Neb. 1956); Leonard v. City of Bothell, 557 P.2d 1306 (Wash. 1976). Amendment held legislative: Pioneer Trust Co. v. Pima Cty., 811 P.2d 22 (Ariz. 1991) (conditional rezoning); Johnston v. City of Claremont, 323 P.2d 71 (Cal. 1958); Albright v. City of Portage, 470 N.W.2d 657 (Mich. App. 1991); Denney v. City of Duluth, 202 N.W.2d 892 (Minn. 1973); Greens at Fort Missoula, LLC v. City of Missoula, 897 P.2d 1078 (Mont. 1995); Wilson v. Manning, 657 P.2d 251 (Utah 1982). *See also* Citizens for Quality Growth Petitioners' Comm. v. City of Steamboat Springs, 807 P.2d 1197 (Colo. App. 1991) (council approval of specific use held legislative); Forman v. Eagle Thrifty Drugs & Mkts., Inc., 516 P.2d 1234 (Nev. 1974); Citizen's Awareness Now v. Marakis, 873 P.2d 1117 (Utah 1994) (adopting criteria for zoning change is administrative).

exceptions and variances, are not subject to referendum because the courts usually hold that they are administrative actions.[8] Judicial review of a referendum is limited to whether it is arbitrary and capricious. For example, one court held that voters may disapprove a plan amendment for a development even though it is consistent with a comprehensive plan.[9]

§ 6.81   Initiative.

Most courts hold the initiative is not available to amend or adopt a zoning ordinance because it bypasses the required statutory notice and hearing.[1] These courts hold the lack of a notice and hearing violates the statutory requirement or is unconstitutional as a violation of procedural due process. The cases that disallow the use of the initiative in zoning do not distinguish the use of the initiative as a referendum substitute.[2]

California takes a different view. In *Associated Home Bldrs. of Greater Eastbay, Inc. v. City of Livermore*,[3] a zoning ordinance enacted by initiative prohibited the issuance of building permits until adequate educational, sewerage, and water facilities were available. The constitution authorizes the initiative and referendum in California. The court noted that the constitutional amendment that authorizes the initiative and referendum was an "outstanding" achievement and held that the initiative did not conflict with the zoning statutes because the constitutional provision was supreme. "[T]he notice and hearing provisions of the state zoning law, if interpreted to bar initiative land use ordinances, would be of doubtful constitutionality."[4] The California court has also upheld the use

---

[8] Southwest Diversified, Inc. v. City of Brisbane, 280 Cal. Rptr. 869 (Cal. App. 1991) (revision in boundaries of area covered by development plan), noted, 29 San Diego L. Rev. 561 (1993); State ex rel. Srovnal v. Linton, 346 N.E.2d 764 (Ohio 1976). *See also* W.W. Dean & Assocs. v. City of South San Francisco, 236 Cal. Rptr. 11 (Cal. App. 1987); Fishman v. City of Palo Alto, 150 Cal. Rptr. 326 (Cal. App. 1974).

[9] Chandis Securities Co. v. City of Dana Point, 60 Cal. Rptr.2d 481 (Cal. App. 1996).

[1] Transamerica Title Ins. Co. Trust v. City of Tucson, 757 P.2d 1055 (Ariz. 1988); City of Scottsdale v. Superior Court, 439 P.2d 290 (Ariz. 1968); Andover Dev. Corp. v. City of New Smyrna Beach, 328 So. 2d 231 (Fla. App. 1972); Kaiser Hawaii Kai Dev. Co. v. City & Cty. of Honolulu, 777 P.2d 244 (Hawaii 1989); Gumprecht v. City of Coeur D'Alene, 661 P.2d 1214 (Idaho 1983); State ex rel. Childress v. Anderson, 865 S.W.2d 384 (Mo. App. 1993) (charter city); Smith v. Township of Livingston, 256 A.2d 85 (N.J. Ch.), *aff'd*, 257 A.2d 698 (N.J. 1969); L.A. Ray Realty v. Town Council, 603 A.2d 311 (R.I. 1992); I'On, L.L.C. v. Town of Mt. Pleasant, 526 S.E.2d 716 (S.C. 2000); Hancock v. Rouse, 437 S.W.2d 1 (Tex. Civ. App. 1969); Lince v. City of Bremerton, 607 P.2d 329 (Wash. App. 1980); 72 A.L.R.3d 991 (1976).

[2] *But see* Storegard v. Board of Election, 255 N.E.2d 880 (Ohio 1969) (may use initiative to repeal zoning ordinance).

[3] 557 P.2d 473 (Cal. 1976). *See* Devita v. County of Napa, 889 P.2d 1019 (Cal. 1995) (plan amendment initiative to require voter approval of land use changes for 30 years). *Accord* State ex rel. Hickman v. City Council, 690 S.W.2d 799 (Mo. App. 1985).

[4] 557 P.2d at 480.

of the initiative to enact zoning amendments, which are legislative in that state.[5] Like the referendum, an initiative may not be had on administrative zoning actions.[6]

A court may invalidate an initiative under the same tests they apply to zoning ordinances adopted by a municipality. In *Arnel Dev. Co. v. City of Costa Mesa*,[7] for example, a California court invalidated an initiative that repealed a zoning amendment for moderate-income housing. It did not find a change in conditions or circumstances that justified the initiative repealer and held it was adopted for the "sole and specific purpose of defeating" the housing development and did not sufficiently accommodate the regional interest in the provision of moderate-income housing.[8]

---

[5] Arnel Dev. Co. v. City of Costa Mesa, 620 P.2d 565 (Cal. 1980). *But see* L.I.F.E. Comm. v. City of Lodi, 262 Cal. Rptr. 166 (Cal. App. 1989) (initiative requiring plan amendment before annexation conflicted with annexation statute). *See also* San Diego Bldg. Contractors Ass'n v. City Council, 529 P.2d 570 (Cal. 1974) (building height limit), *appeal dismissed*, 427 U.S. 901 (1976); Lesher Communications, Inc. v. City of Walnut Creek, 262 Cal. Rptr. 337 (Cal. App. 1989) (upholding initiative as amendment to general plan).

[6] Camden Community Dev. Corp. v. Sutton, 5 S.W.3d 439 (Ark. 1999) (recommendation of planning commission on rezoning held administrative).

[7] 178 Cal. Rptr. 723 (Cal. App. 1981).

[8] *See also* Northwood Homes, Inc. v. Town of Moraga, 265 Cal. Rptr. 363 (Cal. App. 1989) (repeal of plan amendment for residential development had *de minimis* impact on regional housing need); Patterson v. County of Tehama, 235 Cal. Rptr. 867 (Cal. App. 1987) (initiative ordinance prohibiting zoning to implement comprehensive plan held invalid); Wiltshire v. Superior Court, 218 Cal. Rptr. 199 (Cal. App. 1985) (initiative ordinance transferring approval of waste-to-energy plant to voters invalid as displacement of council adjudicatory powers).

REFERENCES

Books and Monographs

B. Blaesser, Discretionary Land Use Controls (1997).

City Deal Making (T. Lassar ed. 1990).

E. Kelly, Enforcing Zoning and Land-Use Codes, American Planning Ass'n, Planning Advisory Serv. Rep. No. 409 (1988).

M. Morris, Incentive Zoning: Meeting Urban Design and Affordable Housing Objectives, American Planning Ass'n, Planning Advisory Serv. Rep. No. 494 (2000).

C. Siemon & W. Larson, Vested Rights (1982).

Articles

Alperin & King, Ballot Box Planning: Land Use Planning Through the Initiative Process in California, 21 Sw. L. Rev. 1 (1992).

Baker, Ethical Limits on Attorney Contact with Represented and Unrepresented Officials: The Example of Municipal Zoning Boards Making Site-Specific Land Use Decisions, 31 Suffolk U. L. Rev. 349 (1997).

Blaesser, Negotiating Entitlements, Urb. Land, Vol. 50, No. 12, at 30 (1991).

Blaesser, Special Use Permits: The "Wait-and-See" Weapon of Local Communities, 21 Zoning & Plan. L. Rep. 69 (1998).

Callies, Neuffer & Calibaoso, Ballot Box Zoning: Initiative, Referendum and the Law, 39 Wash. U.J. Urb. & Contemp. L. 53 (1991).

Callies & Tappendorf, Unconstitutional Land Development Conditions and the Development Agreement Solution: Bargaining for Public Facilities After *Nollan* and *Dolan*, 52 Case Wes. Res. L. Rev. 663 (2001).

Campanella, Elliott & Merriam, New Vested Property Rights Legislation: States Seek to Steady a Shaky Judicial Doctrine, 11 Zoning & Plan. L. Rep. 81 (1988).

Cordes, Policing Bias and Conflicts of Interest in Zoning Decisionmaking, 65 N.D.L. Rev. 161 (1989).

Crew, Development Agreements After *Nollan v. California Coastal Commission*, 22 Urb. Law. 23 (1990).

Curtin, Protecting Developer's Permits to Build: Development Agreement Practice in California and Other States, 18 Zoning & Plan. Rep. 85 (1995).

Curtin, Effectively Using Development Agreements to Protect Land Use Entitlements: Lessons From California, 25 Zoning & Plan. Rep. 85 (2002).

Delaney, Development Agreements: The Road from Prohibition to "Let's Make a Deal!", 25 Urb. Law. 49 (1993).

Delaney, Vesting Verities and the Development Chronology: A Gaping Disconnect? 3 Wash. U. J.L. & Pol'y 603 (2000).

Delaney & Vaias, Recognizing Vested Development Rights as Protected Property in Fifth Amendment Due Process and Taking Claims, 49 J. Urb. & Contemp. L. 27 (1996).

Delogu, Land Use and Vested Rights: Mixed Law and Policy Issues, Land Use L. & Zoning Dig., Vol. 41, No. 1, at 3 (1989).

Dennison, Estoppel as a Defense to Enforcement of Zoning Ordinance, 19 Zon. & Plan. Rep. 69 (1996).

Dukeminier & Stapleton, The Zoning Board of Adjustment: A Case Study in Misrule, 50 Ky. L.J. 273 (1962).

Dyas, Conflicts of Interest in Planning and Zoning Cases, 17 J. Legal Prof. 219 (1993).

Ellis, Neighborhood Opposition and the Permissible Purposes of Zoning, 7 J. Land Use & Envtl. L. 275 (1992).

Freilich & Guemmer, Removing Artificial Barriers to Public Participation in Land-Use Policy: Effective Zoning by Initiative and Referenda, 21 Urb. Law. 511 (1989).

Goetz, Direct Democracy in Land Use Planning: The State Response to *Eastlake*: 19 Pac. L.J. 793 (1988).

Goldwich, Development Agreements: A Critical Introduction, 4 J. Land Use & Envtl. L. 249 (1989).

Haar, Sawyer & Cummings, Computer Power and Legal Reasoning: A Case Study of Judicial Decision Prediction in Zoning Amendment Cases, 1977 Am. B. Found. Res. J. 651.

Hammes, Development Agreements: The Intervention of Real Estate Finance and Land Use Controls, 23 U. Balt. L. Rev. 119 (1993).

Hanes & Minchew, On Vested Rights to Land Use and Development, 46 Wash. & Lee L. Rev. 373 (1989).

Heeter, Zoning Estoppel: Application of the Principles of Equitable Estoppel and Vested Rights to Zoning Disputes, 1971 Urb. L. Ann. 63.

Johannessen, Zoning Variances: Unnecessarily an Evil, Land Use L. & Zoning Dig., Vol. 41, No. 7, at 3 (1989).

Kessler, The Development Agreement and Its Use in Resolving Large Scale, Multi-Party Development Problems: A Look at the Tools and Suggestions for Its Application, 1 Fla. St. U.J. Land Use & Envtl. L. 451 (1985).

Larson, A Model Ethical Code for Appointed Municipal Officials, 9 Hamline J. Pub. L. & Pol'y 395 (1989).

Larsen & Larsen, Moratoria as Taking Under *Lucas*, Land Use L. & Zoning Dig., Vol. 46, No. 6, at 3 (1994).

Liebmann, Devolution of Power to Community and Block Associations, 25 Urb. Law. 385 (1993).

Mandelker, Delegation of Power and Function in Zoning Administration, 1963 Wash. U.L.Q. 60.

Mandelker, The Role of the Local Comprehensive Plan in Land Use Regulation, 74 Mich. L. Rev. 899 (1976).

McClendon, Reforming the Rezoning Process, Land Use L. & Zoning Dig., Vol. 36, No. 4, at 5 (1984).

McClendon, Standards and Criteria for Zoning Administration, 8 Zoning & Plan. L. Rep. 129 (1985).

Morgan, Vested Rights Legislation, 34 Urb. Law. 131 (2002).

Nadel, This Land is Your Land . . . Or Is It? Making Sense of Vested Rights in California, 22 Loyola L.A.L. Rev. 791 (1989).

Novak & Blaesser, Invitations to Abuse of Discretion: Aesthetic and Automatic Reviews, Land Use L. & Zoning Dig., Vol. 42, No. 11, at 3 (1990).

Reynolds, Self-Induced Hardship in Zoning Variances: Does a Purchaser Have No One But Himself to Blame?, 20 Urb. Law. 1 (1988).

Reynolds, "Spot Zoning" — A Spot That Could Be Removed From the Law, 48 Wash. U. J. Urb. & Contemp. L. 117 (1995).

Reynolds, The "Unique Circumstances" Rule in Zoning Variances—An Aid in Achieving Greater Prudence and Less Leniency, 31 Urb. Law. 127 (1999).

Rosenburg, Referendum Zoning: Legal Doctrine and Practice, 53 Cinn. L. Rev. 381 (1984).

Rosenzeig, From Euclid to Eastlake Toward a More Responsive Approach to Procedural Protection, 82 Dick. L. Rev. 59 (1977).

Sager, Insular Majorities Unabated: Warth v. Seldin and City of Eastlake v. Forest City Enterprises, Inc., 91 Harv. L. Rev. 1373 (1978).

Salkin, Legal Ethics and Land-Use Planning, 30 Urb. Law. 383 (1998).

Schultz, Vested Property Rights in Colorado: The Legislature Rushes in Where. . . ., 66 Den. U.L. Rev. 31 (1988).

Shortlidge, The "*Fasano* Doctrine": Land Use Decisions as Quasi-Judicial Acts, in Proceedings of the Institute on Planning, Zoning, and Eminent Domain, ch. 3 (1985).

Steele, Participation and Rules: The Functions of Zoning, 1986 Am. B. Found. Res. J. 709.

Tarlock, Challenging Biased Zoning Board Decisions, 10 Zoning & Plan. L. Rep. 97 (1987).

Tarlock, Not in Accordance with a Comprehensive Plan: A Case Study of Regional Shopping Center Location Conflicts in Lexington, Kentucky, 1970 Urb. L. Ann. 133.

Taub, Development Agreements, Land Use L. & Zoning Dig., Vol. 42, No. 10, at 3 (1990).

Valletta, Unnecessary Hardship: The Financial Standard for Zoning Variances in New York City, 1 Hofstra Prop. L.J. 1 (1988).

VanderVelde, Legal Pluralism and Equal Treatment in the Context of Zoning Variances, 33 J. L. Pluralism & Unofficial Law 91 (1993).

Van Gorder, Alternative Solutions to the Judicial Doctrine of Strict Compliance with Statutory Procedures for the Adoption of Local Land Use Regulations, 29 Wash. U.J. Urb. & Contemp. L. 133 (1985).

Vietzen, Controlling Conflicts of Interest in Land Use Decisions, Land Use L. & Zoning Dig., Vol. 38, No. 1, at 3 (1986).

Wegner, Moving Toward the Bargaining Table: Contract Zoning, Development Agreements, and the Theoretical Foundations of Government Land Use Deals, 65 N.C.L. Rev. 957 (1987).

Williamson, Constitutional and Judicial Limitations on the Community's Power to Downzone, 12 Urb. Law. 157 (1980).

Student Work

Note, The Ad Hominem Element in the Treatment of Zoning Problems, 109 U. Pa. L. Rev. 992 (1961).

Note, Adjudication by Labels, Referendum Rezoning and Due Process, 55 N.C.L. Rev. 517 (1977).

Note, Administrative Discretion in Zoning, 82 Harv. L. Rev. 668 (1969).

Note, The Changing Weather Forecast: Government in the Sunshine in the 1990s — An Analysis of State Sunshine Laws, 71 Wash. U. L.Q. 1165 (1993).

Note, Concomitant Agreement Zoning: An Economic Analysis, 1985 U. Ill. L. Rev. 89.

Note, Instant Planning — Land Use Regulation by Initiative in California, 61 S. Cal. L. Rev. 497 (1988).

Note, Kaiser Hawaii Kai Development Company v. City and County of Honolulu: Zoning by Initiative in Hawaii, 12 Hawaii L. Rev. 181 (1990).

Note, The Prior Restraints Doctrine and the *Freedman* Protections: Navigating a Gigantic Labyrinth, 52 Fla. L. Rev. 809 (2000).

Note, The Proper Use of Referenda in Rezoning, 29 Stan. L. Rev. 819 (1977).

Note, Zoning: Looking Beyond Municipal Borders, 1965 Wash. U.L.Q. 107.

Note, Zoning and the Referendum: Converging Powers, Conflicting Processes, 6 N.Y.U. Rev. L. & Soc. Change 97 (1977).

Note, Zoning Variances, 74 Harv. L. Rev. 1396 (1961).

Comment, A Constitutional Safety Valve: The Variance in Zoning and Land-Use Based Environmental Controls, 22 B.C. Envtl. Aff. L. Rev. 307 (1995).

Comment, Delegation of Land Use Decisions to Neighborhood Groups, 57 UMKC L. Rev. 101 (1988).

Comment, Ex Parte Communications in Local Land Use Decisions, 15 B.C. Envtl. Aff. L. Rev. 181 (1987).

Comment, The Initiative and Referendum's Use in Zoning, 64 Calif. L. Rev. 74 (1976).

Comment, Land Use By, For, and of the People: Problems With the Application of Initiatives and Referenda to the Zoning Process, 19 Pepp. L. Rev. 99 (1991).

Comment, Land-Use Applications Not Acted upon Shall Be Deemed Approved: A Weighing of Interests, 57 UMKC L. Rev. 607 (1989).

Comment, Shattered Plans: Amending a General Plan Through the Initiative Process, 26 U.C. Davis L. Rev. 1055 (1993).

Comment, When Real Property Rights Vest in California: What Happens When a Plaintiff Has Not Secured Required Governmental Approvals?, 28 Santa Clara L. Rev. 417 (1988).

Contemporary Studies Project, Rural Land Use in Iowa: An Empirical Analysis of County Board of Adjustment Practices, 68 Iowa L. Rev. 1083 (1983).

Recent Development, Developer's Vested Rights, 23 Wash. U.J. Urb. & Contemp. L. 487 (1983).

Chapter 7

DISCRIMINATORY, EXCLUSIONARY AND
INCLUSIONARY ZONING

Synopsis

§ 7.01   An Introductory Note.

A. THE FEDERAL CONSTITUTION AND FAIR HOUSING ACT.

§ 7.02   Standing to Sue.
§ 7.03   Equal Protection: *Arlington Heights*.
§ 7.04   The Fair Housing Act.
§ 7.05   When Violated.
§ 7.06   Remedies.

B. EXCLUSIONARY ZONING IN THE STATES.

§ 7.07   Standing to Sue.
§ 7.08   New Jersey.
§ 7.09   *Mt. Laurel (I)*.
§ 7.10   *Weymouth*.
§ 7.11   *Mt. Laurel (II)*.
§ 7.12   Fair Housing Act.
§ 7.13   Post *Mt. Laurel (II)* Cases.
§ 7.14   New York.
§ 7.15   *Berenson*.
§ 7.16   *Brookhaven*.
§ 7.17   *Asian Americans for Equality*.
§ 7.18   Remedies.
§ 7.19   Pennsylvania.
§ 7.20   *Surrick*: Partial Exclusion.
§ 7.21   *Fernley*: Total Exclusion.
§ 7.22   Remedies.
§ 7.23   Michigan.
§ 7.24   California.
§ 7.25   New Hampshire.

C. INCLUSIONARY PLANNING AND ZONING.

§ 7.26   The Planning and Zoning Problem.
§ 7.27   Mandatory Set-Asides and Incentive Zoning.
§ 7.28   Office-Housing Linkage Programs.
§ 7.29   California Inclusionary Legislation.
§ 7.30   Oregon Inclusionary Legislation.
§ 7.31   Affordable Housing Appeals Laws.

(5th Ed.—02/03)

§ 7.01   An Introductory Note.

Many zoning regulations, such as large lot zoning and the exclusion of multifamily development, can exclude lower-income and racial minorities. This chapter reviews the problem of exclusionary zoning, and how it has been treated as a problem of racial discrimination under the fourteenth amendment to the federal constitution and the federal Fair Housing Act. It also considers court decisions and legislation in several states that have attempted to remedy exclusionary zoning problems, as well as inclusionary zoning programs that have provided opportunities for affordable housing.

A. THE FEDERAL CONSTITUTION AND FAIR HOUSING ACT.

§ 7.02   Standing to Sue.

Federal litigation, whether under the constitution or the Fair Housing Act, is based on discrimination. Racial discrimination is a common claim. Standing to sue to challenge racially discriminatory zoning is a major problem for plaintiffs if the plaintiff is not the person directly suffered the discrimination. They must meet the requirements of federal standing law, which is based on the case and controversy requirement of the federal constitution and on prudential limitations on standing adopted by the Supreme Court. Two of these constitutional requirements are critical in litigation claiming that zoning was racially discriminatory. A plaintiff must show that she suffered an "injury in fact," and there must be a causal link between the injury asserted and the judicial relief demanded.

Both requirements proved fatal to the plaintiffs in *Warth v. Seldin*,[1] a Supreme Court case. A number of nonresident plaintiffs challenged a restrictive zoning ordinance adopted by Penfield, a suburb of Rochester, New York, that zoned practically all of the community for single-family development. The plaintiffs included a nonprofit organization dedicated to expanding housing opportunities, a homebuilders' organization, Rochester taxpayers, and several low-and moderate-income residents in the Rochester area who were members of minority racial and ethnic groups. Plaintiffs claimed that the ordinance had the purpose and effect of excluding low-and moderate-income groups but did not make a racial discrimination claim.

The Court denied standing to all of the plaintiffs. It noted that none of the nonresident individual plaintiffs had an interest in any property in Penfield. These plaintiffs claimed they had been unable to locate affordable housing in Penfield

---

[1] 422 U.S. 490 (1975). *Accord* Hope, Inc. v. County of DuPage, 738 F.2d 797 (7th Cir. 1984).

and that the Penfield zoning ordinance precluded the construction of housing they could afford. The Court held that these claims did not confer standing. Although two efforts to build affordable housing in Penfield had failed,

> the record is devoid of any indication that these projects, or other like projects, would have satisfied . . . [plaintiffs'] needs at prices they could afford, or that, were the court to remove the obstructions attributable to . . . [the zoning ordinance], such relief would benefit . . . plaintiffs]. Indeed, . . . their inability to reside in Penfield is the consequence of the economics of the area housing market, rather than . . . [the zoning ordinance].[2]

The Court held that there must be "specific, concrete facts demonstrating" harm to the plaintiff and that "he personally would benefit from the court's intervention." An important footnote added that "usually the initial focus should be on a particular project." Plaintiffs had not demonstrated a "substantial probability" of a "causal relationship" between the exclusionary zoning ordinance and their injuries, nor had they shown that the requested relief would probably remedy their harm.

The Court denied standing to the Rochester taxpayers and the nonprofit housing organization partly because they asserted the constitutional rights of third parties excluded by the Penfield ordinance. The Court denied standing to the home-builders' organization because no member of the organization claimed it had been excluded by the Penfield zoning ordinance or had applied "for a building permit or a variance with respect to any particular project."

The Court granted standing to a developer and an individual seeking lower-income housing in a later case, *Village of Arlington Heights v. Metropolitan Housing Dev. Corp.*[3] A virtually all-white Chicago suburb refused to rezone from single-family to multifamily so that a developer could build a federally subsidized multifamily housing project. The plaintiffs claimed that the refusal to rezone was racially discriminatory. The Court granted standing to the developer even though the invalidation of the ordinance would not necessarily guarantee construction of the project. It noted that "all housing developments are subject to some extent to similar uncertainties." The developer suffered economic injury in its predevelopment expenditures for the project, but economic injury was not necessary to support standing. The developer had "an interest in making suitable low-cost housing available in areas where such housing is scarce."[4]

The Court did not consider the developer's right to assert the standing of third parties because an individual plaintiff in the lawsuit, a black, claimed that the

---

[2] *Id.* at 506.

[3] 429 U.S. 252 (1977).

[4] *Accord* Baytree of Inverrary Realty Ptn. v. City of Lauderhill, 873 F.2d 1407 (11th Cir. 1989); Keith v. Volpe, 858 F.2d 467 (9th Cir. 1988); Cutting v. Mazzey, 724 F.2d 259 (1st Cir. 1984); Scott v. Greenville County, 716 F.2d 1409 (4th Cir. 1983).

zoning refusal frustrated his search for housing near his place of employment. The Court distinguished *Warth* and granted standing to this plaintiff. It held there was a "substantial probability" the developer would build the project, which would meet the plaintiff's needs, if it held the refusal to rezone unconstitutional. The black plaintiff's claim "focuses on a particular project and is not dependent on speculation about the possible actions of third parties not before the court." The Court did not consider the possibility that the black plaintiff would have to compete with others for a dwelling unit in the project and might not obtain one.

§ 7.03 Equal Protection: *Arlington Heights*.

Exclusionary zoning raises an equal protection problem, but an equal protection attack on exclusionary zoning is likely to succeed in federal court only if the plaintiff claims discrimination against minorities, such as racial discrimination. A claim of minority discrimination triggers strict scrutiny equal protection review, which requires a compelling governmental interest to avoid an equal protection violation.

The Supreme Court held that a refusal to rezone was not racially discriminatory in *Arlington Heights*.[1] A developer applied for a multifamily rezoning on a vacant tract located in a single-family area so that it could build a federally subsidized multifamily housing project. The comprehensive plan for some time had included a "buffer" policy that allowed multifamily zoning only on sites lying between single-family and other more intensive development. The village had applied this policy in a reasonably consistent manner. It denied the plaintiff's rezoning under the buffer policy because its site was surrounded by single-family development. The village also claimed the denial was necessary to protect the property values of adjacent single-family development from the adverse impacts of the plaintiff's multifamily project.

The Court upheld the refusal to rezone. It held that proof of racial discrimination under the equal protection clause requires proof of a racially discriminatory intent as a motivating factor[2] but added that proof of a racially "disproportionate impact" is relevant as evidence of a racially discriminatory intent. One example is the case in which "a clear pattern unexplainable on grounds other than race, emerges from the effect of state action even when the governing legislation appears neutral on its face." The Court did not explain why the virtually all-white character of Arlington Heights failed to raise an inference that the refusal to rezone implemented a "clear pattern" of racial exclusion. Departures from an established policy are also relevant to a finding of discriminatory intent. To

---

[1] § 7.02.

[2] Applying Washington v. Davis, 426 U.S. 229 (1976). *See also* Personnel Adm'r of Mass. v. Feeney, 442 U.S. 256 (1979).

illustrate this point, the Court cited a lower federal court case in which the city's zoning actions blocked a lower-income housing project only after plans to build the project became known.[3] Departures from normal procedural sequence are also evidence of improper purpose.

The Court held that "[s]ubstantive departures too may be relevant, particularly if the factors usually considered important by the decisionmaker strongly favor a decision contrary to the one reached." The village, the Court emphasized, had relied on "zoning factors" that were "not novel criteria in the Village's rezoning decision." Neighboring property owners had also relied on the maintenance of the single-family zoning on the plaintiff's site.

The Court cited *Dailey v. City of Lawton*[4] to illustrate the "zoning factors" principle. In *Dailey* the court found a racially discriminatory intent in a refusal to rezone to allow a lower-income multifamily project when the surrounding area was zoned multifamily. Two city officials testified that the rezoning would have been proper from a "zoning standpoint." A municipality can apparently zone its entire area for single-family development and defend a refusal to rezone for multifamily development as consistent with its "zoning factors."

The Supreme Court has substantially limited attacks on exclusionary zoning based on claims of minority discrimination under the equal protection clause. Wholesale attacks on exclusionary zoning brought by nonresidents are foreclosed by *Warth v. Seldin. Arlington Heights* indicates the Court will uphold site-specific discrimination claims only in blatant cases.[5] Claims of racially discriminatory zoning have survived a motion to dismiss or for summary judgment when they were adequately pleaded.[6]

---

[3] Kennedy Park Homes Ass'n v. City of Lackawanna, 436 F.2d 108 (2d Cir. 1970).

[4] 425 F.2d 1037 (10th Cir. 1970).

[5] Racial discrimination not found: Macone v. Town of Wakefield, 277 F.3d 1 (1st Cir. 2002) (recission of approval for housing project); Kawaoka v. City of Arroyo Grande, 73 F.3d 1227 (9th Cir. 1994) (density restrictions; specific plan requirement; moratorium); Orange Lake Assocs. v. Kirkpatrick, 21 F.3d 1214 (2d Cir. 1994); Henry v. Jefferson County Planning Comm'n, 148 F. Supp.2d 698 (N.D. W. Va. 2001); Jackson v. City of Auburn, 41 F. Supp.2d 1300 (M.D. Ala. 1999); Brian B. Brown Constr. Co. c. St. Tammany Parish, 17 F.. Supp.2d 786 (E.D. La. 1998); Litton Int'l Dev. Co. v. City of Simi Valley, 616 F. Supp. 275 (C.D. Cal. 1985); In re Malone, 592 F. Supp. 1135 (E.D. Mo. 1984), *aff'd mem.,* 794 F.2d 680 (8th Cir. 1986); Beasley v. Potter, 493 F. Supp. 1059 (W.D. Mich. 1980); Cowart v. City of Ocala, 478 F. Supp. 744 (M.D. Fla. 1979); Stone v. City of Wilton, 331 N.W.2d 398 (Iowa 1983). *But see* In re Township of Warren, 622 A.2d 1257 (N.J. 1993) (suggesting preference for municipal residents and employees in affordable housing violated federal Act).

[6] Scott v. Greenville County, 716 F.2d 1409 (4th Cir. 1985) (refusal to issue building permit); Housing Investors, Inc. v. City of Clanton, 68 F. Supp.2d 1287 (M.D. Ala. 1999) (rejection of housing project); Barnes Foundation v. Township of Lower Merion, 982 F. Supp. 970 (E.D. Pa. 1997) (some of plaintiff's trustees were African-American).

§ 7.04   The Fair Housing Act.

Plaintiffs have been more successful in challenging exclusionary zoning as racially discriminatory under Title VIII of the Civil Rights Act of 1968, the federal fair housing act. Most federal courts hold that this act requires only proof of a racially discriminatory effect.[1] Although the fair housing act is directed primarily at racial discrimination in the sale or rental of housing, the act also makes it "unlawful . . . [t]o make unavailable or deny . . . a dwelling to a person because of race."[2] The federal courts have applied this provision to strike down racially discriminatory exclusionary zoning.[3] They have also granted standing to nonresidents and developers who challenged racially discriminatory zoning.[4]

§ 7.05   When Violated.

The Supreme Court remanded *Arlington Heights*[1] so the court of appeals could determine whether a violation of the fair housing act had occurred. The court of appeals held that proof of discriminatory effect was sufficient to show a violation of the act and that courts should review claims of racial discrimination under the act under a four-factor test.[2] The factors are: (1) the strength of the discriminatory effect; (2) the presence of "partial evidence" of discriminatory intent, which is evidence insufficient to satisfy the constitutional equal protection standard; (3) whether the municipality acted within the scope of its authority; and (4) whether the relief requested was affirmative or remedial. The court remanded the case to the district court, but the parties settled.[3] Other courts

---

[1] *But see* Ward's Cove Packing Co. v. Atonio, 490 U.S. 642 (1989) (shifting burden of proof to plaintiffs in Title VII fair employment cases, *applied in* United States v. Incorporated Village of Island Park, 888 F. Supp. 419 (E.D.N.Y. 1995) (claiming discrimination in federal housing subsidy program). Congress overruled *Ward's Cove* in part as applied to employment discrimination claims. *See* 42 U.S.C. § 2000e-2(k)1); Mojica v. Gannett Co., 7 F.3d 552 (7th Cir. 1993).

[2] 42 U.S.C. § 3604(a).

[3] *See also* 42 U.S.C. § 3610(g)(2)(c) (if Secretary of Housing and Urban Development determines in a proceeding that a "matter involves the legality of any State or local zoning or other land use law or ordinance," he is to immediately refer the matter to attorney general for appropriate action).

[4] Baytree of Invarerray Realty Partners v. City of Lauderhill, 873 F.2d 1407 (11th Cir. 1989); Park View Heights Corp. v. City of Black Jack, 467 F.2d 1208 (8th Cir. 1972) (nonresidents); In re Malone, 592 F. Supp. 1135 (E.D. Mo. 1984), *aff'd mem.,* 794 F.2d 680 (8th Cir. 1986) (developer) *Contra* Nasser v. City of Homewood, 671 F.2d 432 (11th Cir. 1982) (developer).

[1] § 7.03.

[2] Metropolitan Hous. Dev. Corp. v. Village of Arlington Heights, 558 F.2d 1283 (7th Cir. 1977). *See also* In re Malone, 592 F. Supp. 1135 (E.D. Mo. 1984) (finding no violation of act under similar facts; *Arlington Heights* factors not applied), *aff'd mem.,* 794 F.2d 680 (8th Cir. 1986).

[3] Metropolitan Hous. Dev. Corp. v. Village of Arlington Heights, 616 F.2d 1006 (7th Cir. 1980).

adopted the four-factor test and applied it to racial discrimination claims under the fair housing act in zoning and similar cases.[4]

Huntington Branch, NAACP v. Town of Huntington[5] modified *Arlington Heights*. It held the act was violated by a zoning ordinance restricting private multifamily housing to a largely minority urban renewal area and a refusal to rezone land in a white neighborhood for federally subsidized multifamily housing. The court held it would apply the disparate impact test adopted under the federal equal employment opportunity act to determine when a facially neutral government policy, such as a zoning law, violated the fair housing act.

A plaintiff need not prove a discriminatory intent under this test. He can establish a prima facie case, the court held, by showing that the defendant's policy or practice has a discriminatory effect. Plaintiffs made a strong prima facie case under this standard by showing that the zoning restriction and refusal to rezone had a discriminatory effect in two ways. They perpetuated segregation in the town and had a greater proportionate effect on blacks because a larger percentage of blacks needed affordable housing.

Once a prima facie case is established, the court held that a court must weigh the adverse discriminatory effect against the justification offered by the defendant. This inquiry has two components. The court must first determine whether a less discriminatory alternative is feasible. This concern is "plan-specific" and requires less discriminatory design modifications in the project. The court must then consider whether the reasons for the decision are bona fide and legitimate. The inquiry is whether the justification is a "substantial concern" that would justify a decision by a "reasonable official." The court held that the town's reasons for refusing the rezoning were weak and that it could encourage the rehabilitation of the renewal area through less discriminatory means, such as tax incentives. However, not all courts have found zoning to be racially discriminatory in violation of the act.[6]

---

[4] No violation: Arthur v. City of Toledo, 782 F.2d 565 (6th Cir. 1986) (refusal to extend services to public housing project; three of four factors adopted). Violation: Resident Advisory Bd. v. Rizzo, 564 F.2d 126 (3d Cir. 1977) (public housing site selection).

[5] 844 F.2d 926 (2d Cir. 1988), *aff'd*, 488 U.S. 15 (1988) (Court reviewed holding on zoning ordinance only; was satisfied with court of appeals findings without endorsing court's "precise analysis"). *See generally* United States v. Black Jack, 508 F.2d 1179 (8th Cir. 1974). *Accord* Keith v. Volpe, 858 F.2d 467 (9th Cir. 1988).

[6] Violation not found: Macone v. Town of Wakefield, 277 F.3d 1 (1st Cir. 2002) (no proof of discrimination though town not racially integrated); Orange Lake Assocs. v. Kirkpatrick, 21 F.3d 1214 (2d Cir. 1994) (racial discrimination not found); New Burnham Prairie Homes, Inc. v. Burnham, 910 F.2d 1474 (7th Cir. 1990) (affirming jury verdict for municipality); Suffolk Interreligious Coalition on Housing v. Town of Brookhaven, 575 N.Y.S.2d 548 (App. Div. 1991) (denial of individual zoning requests held not exclusionary).

Violation found: Dews v. Town of Sunnyvale, 109 F. Supp. 2d 526 (N.D. Tex. 2000) (one-acre zoning and ban on apartments by suburban community held to violate Act).

§ 7.06   Remedies.

In *Huntington*, the court provided site-specific relief to the plaintiff to remedy the statutory violation. In another case, the developer and prospective residents of a federally-subsidized housing project brought an action seeking damages and equitable relief.[1] The court had invalidated a downzoning to block the project under the act, but the project was not built. The city agreed to pay damages to the plaintiffs under a consent judgment, but the judgment did not prohibit further declaratory or equitable relief. The plaintiffs then sought an injunction ordering the city to undertake measures to make 108 dwelling units available within a reasonable time for multi-racial, moderate-income occupancy. This was the number of dwelling units the project would have provided. The plaintiffs suggested a number of inclusionary zoning measures, such as density bonuses and a waiver of building and zoning requirements, that could satisfy this obligation. The district court refused to grant an injunction, but the court of appeals reversed.

The court held the invalidation of the zoning ordinance would not provide effective relief. The enactment of the restrictive zoning "predictably" delayed the project, with the "inevitable and foreseeable" result that a rise in construction costs during the delay period made the project economically infeasible. On remand, the court of appeals ordered the district court to consider the City's duty to seek out and make land sites available for purchase by the plaintiff class. These sites must be properly zoned and so located with reference to public facilities and services as to meet established criteria for low and moderate income family housing.[2]

B.   EXCLUSIONARY ZONING IN THE STATES.

§ 7.07   Standing to Sue.

Third party standing to sue in state courts presents fewer problems because state constitutions, unlike the federal constitution, do not usually limit litigation to "cases and controversies." Standing is a prudential matter within the discretion of the state court.

Although the Supreme Court severely limited standing for nonresidents,[1] some state courts have taken a more generous view and have recognized nonresident standing. *Stocks v. City of Irvine*[2] is a strong statement on this issue. The plaintiffs

---

[1] Park View Heights Corp. v. City of Black Jack, 605 F.2d 1033 (8th Cir. 1979).

[2] *Id.* at 1040. *See also* United States v. City of Parma, 494 F. Supp. 1049 (N.D. Ohio 1980), *aff'd*, 661 F.2d 562 (6th Cir. 1981).

[1] § 7.02.

[2] 170 Cal. Rptr. 724 (Cal. App. 1981).

were nonresidents of the city who claimed they wished to live in Irvine but that the city's zoning prevented the construction of housing they could afford. Plaintiffs also claimed the city's zoning affected the housing market in the surrounding region and increased the cost of housing where they presently lived. The court granted standing. It noted that the more restrictive a city's zoning becomes, the less likely a developer will propose housing for lower-income families. Without a developer to challenge the exclusionary zoning ordinance, the *Warth* test could not be satisfied. The court rejected the *Warth* "substantial probability" test for standing and held it would not deny access to the courts simply because "granting relief . . . will not remove all obstacles . . . to complete redress." The plaintiffs were only required to show a "causal relationship" between the city's zoning and their alleged harm.

The New Jersey Supreme Court granted standing to nonresidents to challenge exclusionary zoning in *Home Bldrs. League of S. Jersey, Inc. v. Township of Berlin*.[3] The court partly relied on a provision in the zoning statute that defined an "interested party" as "any person, whether residing within or without the municipality."[4]

Some state courts are more restrictive. A Pennsylvania court dismissed an exclusionary zoning suit by nonresidents that challenged the zoning ordinances of all fifty-four municipalities in the county.[5] The court characterized the suit as hypothetical, far-ranging, and unparticularized. *Bucks* suggests that exclusionary zoning litigation joining several municipalities which is not based on specific development proposals may fail on justiciability grounds. New Hampshire held a landowner whose land is restricted by a zoning ordinance may not challenge the restriction claiming it limits opportunities to build affordable housing if he is not a developer and has no plans to build affordable housing. His generalized interest in a diverse community is not enough to confer standing to make this claim.[6]

§ 7.08   New Jersey.

§ 7.09   *Mt. Laurel (I)*.

In *Southern Burlington County NAACP v. Township of Mt. Laurel (Mt. Laurel I)*,[1] the New Jersey Supreme Court adopted a regional general welfare doctrine

---

[3] 405 A.2d 381 (N.J. 1979).

[4] N.J. Stat. Ann. § 40:55D-4. *Accord* Suffolk Hous. Serv. v. Town of Brookhaven, 397 N.Y.S.2d 302 (Sup. Ct. 1978), *aff'd as modified,* 405 N.Y.S.2d 302 (App. Div. 1978).

[5] Commonwealth v. County of Bucks, 302 A.2d 897 (Pa. Commw. 1973). *See also* Fair Hous. Dev. Fund v. Burke, 55 F.R.D. 414 (E.D.N.Y. 1972).

[6] Caspersen v. Town of Lyme, 661 A.2d 759 (N.H. 1995).

[1] 336 A.2d 713 (N.J.), *appeal dismissed and cert. denied,* 423 U.S. 808 (1975).

to test the constitutionality of exclusionary zoning. *Mount Laurel (I)* was brought by a number of plaintiffs, including residents, nonresidents, and the NAACP. They challenged the zoning ordinance of a New Jersey suburb in the Philadelphia and Camden commuting area. Although a substantial part of Mt. Laurel was undeveloped, its zoning ordinance contained a number of exclusionary restrictions, including excessive exclusive zoning for industrial use, that effectively prevented residential development and extensive low-density residential zoning. Plaintiffs did not have an interest in any land in Mt. Laurel that was subject to the exclusionary zoning restrictions, but the court held they had standing to bring the case.

The court invalidated the Mt. Laurel ordinance under equal protection and substantive due process principles it found embedded in the state constitution. It held that Mt. Laurel had excluded lower-and moderate-income groups and that proof of a discriminatory intent to accomplish this purpose was not necessary. The heart of the decision was the court's conclusion that municipalities in New Jersey must meet their "fair share of the present and prospective regional need" for low-and moderate-income housing.

The court adopted a prima facie case rule to implement this holding. A municipality carries a heavy burden to establish a valid basis for its actions once a plaintiff makes a prima facie case that it has not met its fair share obligations. The court held a municipality cannot refuse to meet its fair share obligation because it does not want to provide necessary public services, a clear rejection of fiscal exclusionary zoning. The court recognized that imposing a fair share obligation on every municipality in the state might be arbitrary but noted the state legislation conferred zoning authority on all municipalities. The court concluded that all municipalities must responsibly exercise their zoning authority by meeting their fair share housing obligations. The court indicated the fair share doctrine applied only to "developing" municipalities, a limitation it later rejected.

The court provided only limited guidance on how courts should determine a municipality's fair share obligation. It did not elaborate criteria for determining the region in which the fair share rule should apply and indicated that planning "expertise" at the local, county, and state level could determine the municipality's fair share. The court invalidated the objectionable features in the ordinance, gave the municipality three months to correct these deficiencies, and suggested that anyone disappointed with the revision could challenge it in court.

§ 7.10   *Weymouth.*

In its next exclusionary zoning case, *Taxpayers Ass'n of Weymouth Twp. v. Weymouth Twp.*,[1] the New Jersey Supreme Court upheld a zoning ordinance that established a zoning district limited to the elderly. It held the zoning ordinance met the special needs of the elderly and was not invalid as a regulation of users rather than use, and noted the legislature had authorized zoning for the elderly in the state zoning act. The court applied the rational relationship test to reject equal protection and due process objections. Zoning for the elderly was not presumptively exclusionary and "must be assessed against the background of general land use regulation by the municipality." Although these plaintiffs had not proved a prima facie case of exclusion, extensive zoning for the elderly within a community could be exclusionary because it could exclude families with children.[2]

§ 7.11   *Mt. Laurel (II).*

On remand, Mt. Laurel revised its zoning ordinance to limit substantial areas of the community to low-density residential use and to restrict apartment projects to small dwelling units. *Oakwood at Madison, Inc. v. Township of Madison*[1] invalidated the ordinance in a decision that somewhat restricted the *Mt. Laurel (I)* decision.

A trial court then upheld the rezoning even though the municipality rezoned only twenty acres out of a total of 22.4 square miles for higher density housing.[2] Plaintiffs appealed and the New Jersey Supreme Court consolidated this appeal with appeals in five other cases raising questions concerning the fair share rule. In *Mt. Laurel (II)*,[3] the court reversed and remanded these cases.

The court confirmed and expanded the fair share doctrine adopted in *Mt. Laurel (I)*, including the prima facie case rule. It held that the fair share obligation was not limited to "developing" municipalities but extended to all municipalities designated in a 1980 State Development Guide Plan as growth areas. A municipality could rebut a growth area designation if it showed it was arbitrary or capricious or no longer appropriate. The court indicated that the plan was only presumptively valid and that it must be periodically revised. The legislature has

---

[1] 364 A.2d 1016 (N.J. 1976). *See also* Shepard v. Woodland Twp. Comm. & Planning Bd., 364 A.2d 1005 (N.J. 1976). *Accord* Maldini v. Ambro, 330 N.E.2d 403 (N.Y.), *appeal dismissed*, 423 U.S. 993 (1975). *Contra* Hinman v. Planning & Zoning Comm'n, 214 A.2d 131 (Conn. C.P. 1965). *See also* § 5.06 (federal Fair Housing Act).

[2] *See also* Home Bldrs. League of S. Jersey, Inc. v. Township of Berlin, 405 A.2d 381 (N.J. 1979) (minimum house size ordinance held unconstitutional). *See* § 5.29.

[1] 371 A.2d 1192 (N.J. 1977).

[2] 391 A.2d 935 (N.J.L. Div. 1978).

[3] 456 A.2d 390 (N.J. 1983).

since adopted legislation authorizing the preparation and adoption of a State Development and Redevelopment Plan.[4] The growth designations in the plan will indicate the municipalities that are subject to the fair share obligation.

The court also held the *Mt. Laurel* obligation requires quantitative proof of a municipality's fair share of low-and moderate-income housing. It recognized the complexities inherent in calculating fair shares but did not propose substantive criteria for making this calculation. Instead, the court mandated the appointment of three special judges authorized to make fair share determinations on a case-by-case basis.

To strengthen the *Mt. Laurel* obligation the court then ruled the fair share obligation requires more than the elimination of "unnecessary cost-producing requirements," although it also held that municipalities must at least eliminate these requirements. The court approved and required affirmative governmental actions to meet the fair share obligation, including density bonuses and mandatory set-aside requirements for lower-income housing in residential developments. Municipalities could choose to adopt additional affirmative measures, including measures to facilitate the use of housing subsidies and tax abatements for subsidized housing. Providing least-cost housing would satisfy the fair share obligation only if a municipality could not satisfy it in any other manner, and only after a municipality considered all alternatives and affirmative actions. The court rejected holdings in *Oakwood* that courts need only consider the "substance" of exclusionary zoning ordinances and that municipalities need only make "bona fide" efforts to provide for low-and moderate-income housing. The court also qualified an earlier decision upholding a zoning ordinance that excluded mobile homes.[5] It held a municipality must zone land for mobile homes if this is necessary to comply with the fair share obligation.

The court held the *Mt. Laurel* doctrine did not affect "the clear obligation to preserve open space and prime agricultural land." A municipality that meets its fair share obligation may plan for its development consistent with sound land use planning, environmental considerations, and community preferences. Once a municipality has satisfied its fair share obligation, any restrictive zoning regulations it adopts will not be held invalid *per se* under the fair share doctrine.[6]

To provide a method to enforce *Mt. Laurel* obligations the court held that builder's remedies should be afforded to *Mt. Laurel* plaintiffs on a case-by-case basis when a developer is successful in *Mount Laurel* litigation and proposes a project with a substantial amount of lower income housing. Courts can refuse a builder's remedy if it is clearly contrary to sound land use planning because

---

[4] N.J. Stat. Ann. §§ 52:18A-196 to 52:18A-207.

[5] *See* §§ 5.21–5.26.

[6] *See also* Samaritan Center, Inc. v. Borough of Englishtown, 683 A.2d 611 (N.J.L. Div. 1996) (adjacent municipality must provide water and sewer service for *Mount Laurel* housing).

of environmental or other substantial planning concerns, but a court should not refuse a builder's remedy just because the municipality prefers another location.

The court added that care should be taken that so that the builder's remedy is not used as an unintended bargaining chip in negotiations with municipalities. It suggested the timing of the remedy could be adjusted to cushion its impact, and that the municipal planning board should be involved in its formulation. Neither should the builder's remedy should not be used as a license for unnecessary litigation when a variance can be obtained, and courts should condition the remedy so that the developer will construct a substantial amount of lower-income housing.

§ 7.12   Fair Housing Act.

The supreme court in *Mt. Laurel (II)* asked for legislative action on the fair share obligation, and the legislature responded by adopting a Fair Housing Act in 1985.[1] The Act creates a state Council on Affordable Housing to implement the *Mt. Laurel* doctrine. The Council is to determine the housing regions of the state and adopt criteria and guidelines for municipal fair share determinations. It also provides state funding to help municipalities meet their fair share obligations. The supreme court held the Act constitutional in *Hills Dev. Co. v. Township of Bernards.*[2]

The Act requires a housing element in local plans and authorizes municipalities to submit their housing elements to the Council for certification.[3] The housing element must include an analysis of present and future housing needs and employment characteristics, a present and future fair share calculation, and an analysis of land suitable to meet the fair share housing obligation.[4]

In preparing its housing element, a municipality must consider a number of techniques for providing low-and moderate-income housing. They include tax abatements, a plan for infrastructure expansion and rehabilitation, if necessary, and a "[d]etermination of the total residential zoning necessary to assure that the municipality's fair share is achieved."[5] A municipality may transfer up to twenty percent of its fair share obligation to another municipality in its region under a voluntary contractual agreement approved by the Council.

---

[1] N.J. Stat. Ann. §§ 52:27D-301 to 52:27D-329.

[2] 510 A.2d 621 (N.J. 1986).

[3] N.J. Stat. Ann. § 52:27D-310.

[4] *See also* N.J. Stat. Ann. § 52-27D-311.2 (Council cannot require counties to consider sites improved with sound residential structures as available for affordable housing).

[5] § 52:27D-311(a)(2).

A municipality may petition the Council for a "substantive certification" of its housing element.[6] Once a housing element is substantively certified, any person who brings an exclusionary zoning suit against a municipality must first exhaust mediation and review procedures before the Council. A suit may be filed once these procedures are exhausted, but the plaintiff must overcome a substantial presumption in favor of the certified housing element.[7] Objectors may still make conventional zoning objections to zoning adopted to comply with *Mt. Laurel* requirements.[8] Municipalities sued in *Mt. Laurel* litigation may demand a "phase-in schedule" from the court for meeting its fair share obligations, including a separate schedule for inclusionary zoning.

The courts have upheld most of COAH's regulations applying the act.[9] However, the Supreme Court disapproved a Council on Affordable Housing rule authorizing municipalities to provide preferences in affordable housing for local residents and employees.[10] The court held the rule was inconsistent with a municipality's *Mt. Laurel* obligation to provide for regional as well as local needs.

§ 7.13 Post *Mt. Laurel (II)* Cases.

The New Jersey courts have applied the *Mt. Laurel* doctrines in recent cases and have considered whether inclusionary zoning plans and proposals meet the *Mt. Laurel (II)* criteria.[1] In one case, the Appellate Division rejected a builder's

---

[6] *In re* Petition for Substantive Certification, Township of Southampton, 768 A.2d 233 (N.J. App. Div. 2001) (rejecting substantive certification because of problem with affordable housing site).

[7] § 52:27D-317(a). Dynasty Bldg. Corp. v. Borough of Upper Saddle River, 632 A.2d 544 (N.J. App. Div. 1993) (intervention allowed by court to interested borough held too limited).

[8] Alexander's Department Stores v. Borough of Paramus, 592 A.2d 1168 (N.J. 1991) (trial court can hear conventional zoning challenge against municipality whose affordable housing plan was substantively certified by Council); Sartoga v. Borough of West Paterson, 788 A.2d 841 (N.J. App. Div. 2002). *See also* East/West Venture v. Borough of Fort Lee, 669 A.2d 260 (N.J. App. Div. 1996) (approving settlement agreement for *Mount Laurel* litigation).

[9] *In re* Adoption of Amendments to N.J.A.C., 772 A.2d 9 (N.J. App. Div. 2001) (approving regulation allowing COAH to certify fair share housing plan for sites that did not have in place plans for sewer infrastructure that has been approved by department of environmental protection); Non-Profit Affordable Housing Network of N.J. v. New Jersey Council on Affordable Housing, 627 A.2d 1153 (N.J. App. Div. 1993) (approving regulation authorizing housing credit without affordability requirement but remanding constitutional challenge); Calton Homes, Inc. v. Council on Affordable Housing, 582 A.2d 1024 (N.J. App. Div. 1990) (disapproving 1,000-unit cap rule and approving accessory apartment rule and rental unit bonus rule); Township of Bernards v. State Dep't of Community Affairs, 558 A.2d 1 (N.J. App. Div. 1989) (rule requiring consideration of per capita income in determining municipal need for affordable housing approved); Bi-County Dev. Corp. v. Mayor & Council, 540 A.2d 927 (N.J.L. Div. 1988) (approving most regulations including minimum density requirement).

[10] In re Township of Warren, 622 A.2d 1257 (N.J. 1993).

[1] Shire Inn v. Borough of Avon-By-The-Sea & Planning Bd. of Avon-By-The-Sea, 729 A.2d

remedy because of laches and held a downzoning to five acres as compatible with the surrounding area and consistent with the state plan.[2]

In an important Supreme Court case, *Toll Bros., Inc. v. Township of West Windsdor*,[3] the court held the township had engaged in an unconstitutional pattern of exclusionary zoning in violation of the *Mount Laurel* doctrine and the Fair Housing Act. Prior litigation had established the township's required affordable housing units. COAH had modified that number, and the township submitted a housing plan and zoned 11 affordable housing sites. However, by 1994 only two of the sites had been developed, which the developer claimed was due to the township's failure to include conventional single-family housing in its zoning for inclusionary sites, which were limited primarily to multifamily housing. The plaintiff filed suit asking for a builder's remedy that would allow single-family conventional housing on its 293-acre site. By the time of the suit the township's period of protection under the Fair Housing Act had expired.

The supreme court held that existing affordable housing sites in the township did not meets its affordable housing obligations, and that market demand is an appropriate factor in meeting *Mt. Laurel* obligations. It rejected the township's claim that considering the volatility of market demand would prevent it from planning for affordable housing with certainty, adding that planners should be able to anticipate "some level of volatility" in developing land use plans. The supreme court also affirmed the grant of a builder's remedy. It found the plaintiff's lawsuit had been the catalyst for change in the township's affordable housing program, and that the plaintiff's development proposal was not a good candidate for a variance because of its size and its importance in the township's compliance plan.

The supreme court had previously held that municipalities could levy develop- ment fees to provide for affordable housing,[4] but in a companion case it held a municipality could not levy a development fee as an alternative to including a tract of land in its affordable housing inventory.[5] An earlier trial court decision held an adjacent municipality was required to provide access to its sewer system to an affordable housing development in an adjacent municipality, when access to the system was essential for the project to go forward.[6] This is an exception

---

473 (N.J. App. Div. 1999) (builder's remedy not available for nonconforming use); Livingston Builders, Inc. v. Township of Livingston, 707 A.2d 186 (N.J. App. Div.1998) (settlement not invalid because site could have contained more housing); Rosenschein Assocs. v. Borough of Paradise Park, 701 A.2d 448 (N.J. App. Div. 1997) (financial position of plaintiff not a factor).

[2] Mount Olive Complex v. Township of Mount Olive, 774 A.2d 704 (N.J. App. Div. 2001).

[3] 803 A.2d 53 (N.J. 2002).

[4] 7.26.

[5] Fair Share Housing Center, Inc. v. Township of Cherry Hill, 802 A.2d 512 (N.J. 2002).

[6] Samaritan Center, Inc. v. Borough of Englishtown, 683 A.2d 611 (N.J.L. Div. 1996).

to the usual rule. In a second companion case, the supreme court refused to extend this exception to a developer that paid a development fee as an alternative to the construction of affordable housing. The developer was not actually building affordable housing, and the success of the development did not depend on sewer access.[7]

§ 7.14   New York.

§ 7.15   *Berenson.*

The court of appeals, which is New York's highest court, adopted a two-tiered test for exclusionary zoning in *Berenson v. Town of New Castle.*[1] New Castle is in Westchester County, which is adjacent to New York City. Its zoning ordinance required low residential densities and excluded multifamily development. Suit was brought by a developer who planned to build a multifamily condominium development on a fifty-acre site in a one-acre zone and who failed to obtain municipal approval for the necessary zoning change. The development was not intended for low-or moderate-income occupants.

The court relied on the statutory requirement that zoning must serve the general welfare as the basis for a two-tier test it adopted for exclusionary zoning. It held first that the "primary goal of a zoning ordinance must be to provide for the development of a balanced, cohesive community which will make efficient use of the town's available land." This requirement did not necessarily call for "a certain relative proportion between various types of development," nor did it necessarily prohibit the creation of specialized land use zones. An apartment exclusion "may" be acceptable in a community that already has apartment development but unacceptable in a community where no apartments presently exist.

The second part of the test examines the effect of a municipality's zoning on neighboring communities. A municipality that excludes multifamily housing must consider "the needs of the region" as well as its own need for such housing. The court added that a municipality need not permit a use "solely for the sake of the people of the region" if regional housing needs are met in an adequate manner. It indicated a municipality is excused from meeting regional housing needs only if they are met "by other accessible areas in the community at large."

In *Blitz v. Town of New Castle,*[2] an intermediate appellate court upheld a zoning revision adopted by the town to comply with the *Berenson* decision. The

---

[7] Bi-County Dev. of Clinton, Inc. v. Borough of High Bridge, 805 A.2d 433 (N.J. 2002).

[1] 341 N.E.2d 236 (N.Y. 1975). *See* Gernatt Asphalt Prods., Inc. v. Town of Sardinia, 664 N.E.2d 1226 (N.Y. 1996) (*Berenson* rule does not apply to exclusion of industrial uses); Robert E. Kurzius, Inc. v. Incorporated Village of Upper Bronxville, 414 N.E.2d 680 (N.Y. 1980) (five-acre zoning held not to violate *Berenson* tests).

[2] 463 N.Y.S.2d 832 (App. Div. 1983).

ordinance contained extensive provisions for multifamily development, either as a permitted use or when approved as a floating zone or by special permit. The court accepted the county housing policy's estimate of housing need and held the town's multifamily zoning made adequate provision for meeting its share of that need.

Although noting that *Berenson* did not adopt the New Jersey fair share doctrine, the court found the revised zoning allowed a significantly greater number of new housing units than its share of the county's population, land area, housing units, and vacant land required. The court held it would test compliance with the regional housing need requirement by considering what the zoning ordinance allowed, not the housing units that probably would be built. The court noted that market forces determine what will be built in the absence of government subsidies. It need determine only whether the zoning ordinance "on its face" allowed a sufficient number of housing units to meet regional need, assuming this housing was physically and economically feasible. The court held the revised ordinance met this test.

§ 7.16 *Brookhaven.*

The court of appeals again adopted a restrictive reading of *Berenson* in *Suffolk Hous. Serv. v. Town of Brookhaven.*[1] Plaintiffs brought an action claiming the town's administration of its zoning ordinance prevented the development of lower-income housing. They claimed the town's failure to pre-map sufficient land for multifamily housing inflated the cost of housing because the town required developers to engage in a lengthy and expensive special permit process to have land approved for multifamily development, and that the town usually did not grant approval.

The court held the plaintiffs had not stated a cause of action. It noted the lower courts had found the town had granted numerous developer applications for multifamily housing and that the inadequate development of low-cost, multi-family housing was due to factors such as rising construction and financing costs and economic stagnation. The court found no need to apply *Berenson* because in that case the plaintiff challenged the facial validity of the ordinance, while here the plaintiffs challenged its implementation. The court also held the plaintiffs had asked for improper radical judicial rezoning of the town to accommodate multifamily development, even though they did not challenge the denial of a specific special permit.[2]

---

[1] 511 N.E.2d 67 (N.Y. 1987).

[2] *See also* Suffolk Interreligious Coalition on Housing v. Town of Brookhaven, 575 N.Y.S.2d 548 (App. Div. 1991) (denial of individual zoning requests held not exclusionary); North Shore Unitarian Universalist Soc'y v. Town of Upper Brookville, 493 N.Y.S.2d 564 (App. Div. 1985) (court rejected suit brought by developer denied rezoning for multifamily housing to be occupied by the elderly).

§ 7.17   *Asian Americans for Equality.*

In *Asian Americans for Equality v. Koch,*[1] the court of appeals rejected a claim that a special New York City zoning district adopted for Chinatown was exclusionary. The district included a density bonus incentive partly intended to promote lower-income housing. Plaintiffs claimed the bonuses favored higher-income housing developments and requested relief requiring the city to adopt additional programs to provide lower-income housing in the district. The court held the special district was a well-considered plan that advanced legitimate governmental goals. It refused to apply the *Mt. Laurel* doctrine to areas within cities, noting that both *Mt. Laurel* and *Berenson* dealt with suburban zoning exclusion. The court held the entire city was the appropriate community for making exclusionary zoning determinations. There was no evidence the city had excluded lower-income persons from Chinatown, and it had made substantial efforts to improve lower-income housing throughout the city. Nor had the plaintiffs shown the incentive plan for lower-income housing in the Chinatown district was inadequate.

§ 7.18   Remedies.

The trial court ordered an extensive judicial remedy on remand in the *Berenson* case,[1] but the appellate division substantially modified the trial court's order.[2] The trial court determined the municipality's fair share of regional low-and moderate-income housing need, but the appellate division rejected this determination. It believed the court of appeals did not intend lower courts to "remedy the [zoning] deficiency by judicial fiat." The record showed an unmet regional need for multifamily housing, and a remedy directing "developing" municipalities to meet this need would be appropriate. The appellate division remanded the case to give the municipality six months to remedy this zoning deficiency.

The trial court also ordered the municipality to rezone plaintiff's land for multifamily use. The appellate division upheld this order, but held the trial court erred by mandating a specific "allowable density of development" and by ordering the issuance of a building permit when the developer complied with the amended zoning ordinance. Density was a matter for the town to consider when it revised its ordinance. A building permit could issue only if the developer also complied with the state's Freshwater Wetlands Act, which applied to the development. The case was subsequently settled.

---

[1] 527 N.E.2d 265 (N.Y. 1988).

[1] § 7.15.

[2] 415 N.Y.S.2d 669 (App. Div. 1979).

§ 7.19 Pennsylvania.

Pennsylvania took preliminary steps toward a comprehensive exclusionary zoning doctrine in cases striking down large-lot zoning and the exclusion of multifamily housing.[1] In later cases the supreme court adopted a *per se* invalidity rule for zoning ordinances that are totally exclusionary and a fair share multi-factor test for partial exclusions. The Pennsylvania statutes also require zoning ordinances to provide "for residential housing of various dwelling types encompassing all basic forms of housing," but an ordinance need not provide a specific dwelling type.[2]

§ 7.20 *Surrick*: Partial Exclusion.

In *Surrick v. Zoning Hearing Bd.*,[1] a suburban Philadelphia municipality denied a developer a rezoning for multifamily development. The court invalidated the ordinance, which it characterized as a partial exclusion of multifamily dwellings because it zoned only 1.14% of the municipality's area for multifamily development. The court noted it had adopted the New Jersey fair share doctrine in an earlier exclusionary zoning case,[2] but held this doctrine merely stated a "general precept" for zoning. It applied substantive due process analysis to hold its scope of review would be limited

> to determining whether the zoning formulas fashioned by these [governmental] entities reflect a balanced and weighted consideration of the many factors which bear upon local and regional housing needs and development.[3]

A court that carries out this review should first determine whether the municipality was a logical place for development as indicated by the proximity of a metropolis and projected metropolitan growth. It should next examine the present level of community development as indicated by population density, available undeveloped land, and land available for multifamily development. If the court found the community was a logical place for development and was not highly developed, it should apply an exclusionary impact test to determine whether the zoning ordinance was exclusionary. Proof of an exclusionary motive or intent "is not of critical importance." The court invalidated the ordinance

---

[1] §§ 5.14, 5.32.

[2] Pa. Stat. Ann. tit. 53, § 10604(4).*See also id.* § 10604(5) ("to accommodate reasonable overall community growth, including population and employment growth, and opportunities for development of a variety of residential dwelling types and nonresidential uses").

[1] 382 A.2d 105 (Pa. 1977).

[2] Township of Willistown v. Chesterdale Farms, Inc., 341 A.2d 466 (Pa. 1975), noted, 13 Urb. L. Ann. 277 (1977).

[3] 382 A.2d at 109–10.

because it did not provide for the municipality's fair share of land for multifamily housing.[4]

The supreme court applied *Surrick* in *BAC, Inc. v. Board of Supervisors of Millcreek Township.*[5] Plaintiff claimed the township's ordinance was exclusionary because it excluded mobile homes. The court noted the ordinance was entitled to a presumption of constitutionality, and that plaintiff had not overcome this presumption. Plaintiff did not introduce evidence showing the township had excluded mobile homes, only evidence the township had not made adequate allowance for housing for low-and moderate-income families. The court held this evidence insufficient because it showed the exclusion of certain classes of people, not a restriction on the use of property.

§ 7.21 *Fernley*: Total Exclusion.

In *Fernley v. Board of Supvrs.*,[1] the court held the *Surrick* tests did not apply to a zoning ordinance that totally excluded multifamily uses:

> Where the challenger proves a total prohibition of a legitimate use, the burden shifts to the municipality to establish that the prohibition promotes public health, safety, morals and general welfare.[2]

The court held the *Surrick* fair share tests apply only to a zoning ordinance that enacts a *de facto* exclusion of a particular use as distinguished from an ordinance that enacts a total or *de jure* exclusion. The considerations underlying the *Surrick* tests were irrelevant to a total exclusion of a basic form of housing, such as apartments.

The court in *Fernley* rejected the municipality's claim the ordinance was not exclusionary because projections indicated only minimal growth. The growth projection was irrelevant because the ordinance possibly excluded families who wanted to live in the municipality but could not move there because apartments

---

[4] *See, e.g.,* Heritage Bldg. Group, Inc. v. Bedminster Township Bd. of Supervisors, 742 A.2d 708 (Pa. Commw. 1999) (township not in path of growth); Farley v. Zoning Hearing Bd., 636 A.2d 1232 (Pa. Commw. 1994) (exclusion of student housing not shown); Stahl v. Upper Southampton Twp. Zoning Hearing Bd., 606 A.2d 960 (Pa. Commw. 1992) (restrictive density requirement for mobile home parks held exclusionary); Cambridge Land Co. v. Township of Marshall, 560 A.2d 253 (Pa. Commw. 1989) (zoning for apartments and commercial uses satisfies fair-share criteria); Weiner v. Board of Supvrs., 547 A.2d 833 (Pa. Commw. 1988) (same, commercial zoning; special permit requirement does not violate fair-share rule).

[5] 633 A.2d 144 (Pa. 1993). *See also* Precision Equities, Inc. v. Franklin Park Borough Zoning Hearing Bd., 646 A.2d 756 (Pa. Commw. 1994) (small lot single-family housing not a protected housing type).

[1] 502 A.2d 585 (Pa. 1985). The court ignored In re M.A. Kravitz Co., 460 A.2d 1075 (Pa. 1983), an earlier case that did not adopt this interpretation.

[2] 502 A.2d at 587.

were unavailable. The court invalidated the ordinance because the municipality had not shown the apartment exclusion served a legitimate public purpose.[3]

§ 7.22 Remedies.

Pennsylvania statutes and court decisions provide effective site-specific relief for developers who challenge exclusionary zoning. A developer may submit a challenge to a zoning ordinance to the local governing body with a request for a curative amendment.[1] He must accompany the request with "plans and other materials describing the [proposed] use or development."[2] If the court finds the zoning ordinance "unlawfully prevents or restricts a development or use" that is described in the plans and materials, it may order the described use approved. The court may also approve the described use in part and refer unapproved elements back to the governing body for further consideration, including the adoption of alternative restrictions.[3] The statute also requires a municipality to declare its zoning ordinance invalid and propose its own curative amendment.[4]

The statute codified court decisions that awarded site-specific relief.[5] It contains criteria for site-specific relief based primarily on the suitability of the site for the proposed use and its impact on "regional housing needs" and public facilities.[6] The *Fernley* case noted that "approval of the developer's plan is not automatic but, instead, must be predicated on the suitability of the proposed site and various health and safety considerations."

§ 7.23 Michigan.

The Michigan intermediate Courts of Appeals at one time adopted a rule that required municipalities to justify zoning ordinances that excluded preferred uses. Mobile homes and apartments were in the preferred use category.[1] The Michigan

---

[3] *See also* Upper Salford Township v. Collins, 669 A.2d 335 (Pa. 1995) (ordinance did not exclude mobile homes); Appeal of Shore, 573 A.2d 1011 (Pa. 1990) (invalid prohibition of mobile home parks); Township Bd. of Supvrs. v. Golla, 452 A.2d 1337 (Pa. 1982) (upholding statute limiting basis for judicial review of exclusionary zoning); H & H Bldrs., Inc. v. Borough Council, 555 A.2d 948 (Pa. Commw. 1989) (exclusion of townhouses held de jure exclusionary).

[1] Pa. Stat. Ann. tit. 53, § 10609.1.

[2] § 10916.1(c).

[3] § 11006-A(c).

[4] § 10609.2.

[5] Casey v. Zoning Hearing Bd., 328 A.2d 464 (Pa. 1974); Ellick v. Board of Supvrs., 333 A.2d 239 (Pa. Commw. 1975).

[6] § 10609.1(c). *See* H.R. Miller Co. v. Board of Supvrs. of Lancaster Twp., 605 A.2d 321 (Pa. 1992) (site-specific relief not required when ordinance not exclusionary); H & H Bldrs., Inc. v. Borough Council, 555 A.2d 948 (Pa. Commw. 1989) (criteria do not apply to total exclusion).

[1] *See* Bristow v. City of Woodhaven, 192 N.W.2d 322 (Mich. App. 1971) (mobile home park).

Supreme Court overruled the preferred use rule in *Kropf v. City of Sterling Heights*[2] but held it would take a different view of a total exclusion:

> On its face, an ordinance which *totally* excludes from a municipality a use recognized by the Constitution or other laws of this state as legitimate also carries with it a strong taint of unlawful discrimination and a denial of equal protection of the law as to the excluded use.[3]

Kropf also held that "the purely arbitrary, capricious, and unfounded exclusion of other types of legitimate land use from the area in question" would raise a substantive due process question. The supreme court later invalidated a zoning ordinance limiting mobile homes to mobile home parks.[4] The state zoning statutes also provide that counties and municipalities may not totally exclude a land use for which there is a "demonstrated need" within the township or the surrounding area unless there is no appropriate location for the use or it is unlawful.[5]

§ 7.24 California.

The California Supreme Court provided extensive dicta on exclusionary zoning in *Associated Home Bldrs. of Greater Eastbay, Inc. v. City of Livermore*,[1] in which it upheld a local growth moratorium. The court rejected the *Mt. Laurel* fair share doctrine[2] but suggested criteria that apply when a zoning ordinance influences "the supply and distribution of housing for an entire metropolitan region."

The first step is to forecast "the probable effect and duration of the restriction." The second is to identify the competing interests the restriction affects. These interests include the conflict between environmental protectionists and egalitarian humanists. They also include the conflict between suburban residents who wish to restrict immigration to their community and outsiders seeking a place to live in the face of a growing housing shortage.

The final step is "to determine whether the ordinance, in light of its probable impact, represents a reasonable accommodation of the competing interests." The

---

[2] 215 N.W.2d 179 (Mich. 1974).

[3] *Id.* at 185 (emphasis in original).

[4] § 5.24.

[5] Mich. Comp. Laws §§ 125.227a, 125.297a, 125.592. *See* Mt. Elliott Cemetery Ass'n v. City of Troy, 171 F.3d 398 (6th Cir. 1999) (applying state law);English v. Augusta Twp., 514 N.W.2d 172 (Mich. App. 1994) (denial of rezoning for mobile home park violates statute); Fremont Twp. v. Greenfield, 347 N.W.2d 204 (Mich. App. 1984).

[1] 557 P.2d 473 (Cal. 1976). *See* City of Del Mar v. City of San Diego, 183 Cal. Rptr. 898 (Cal. App. 1983) (applying *Livermore* doctrine to uphold approval of new community). *But see* Town of Los Altos Hills v. Adobe Creek Props., Inc., 108 Cal. Rptr. 271 (Cal. App. 1973) (refusing to apply exclusionary zoning doctrine to commercial exclusions).

[2] § 7.09.

burden rests on the party challenging the ordinance to provide the necessary evidence and documentation for this constitutional analysis. California has also enacted extensive legislation mandating local adoption of fair share housing plans and restricting other forms of exclusionary zoning.[3]

§ 7.25 New Hampshire.

The New Hampshire Supreme Court adopted the "regional general welfare" rule to hold exclusionary a zoning ordinance that prohibited multifamily housing in *Britton v. Town of Chester.*[1] The town was a bedroom community located near Manchester, a major city, and was projected to have one of the highest growth rates in New Hampshire over the next two decades. Although the town permitted multifamily housing in planned residential districts, the court held this did not save the ordinance, because only a limited amount of land was available for these districts. The ordinance was also a "substantial disincentive" to the development of these districts, because it allowed the town to control their approval without reference to any objective criteria.

Relying on New Hampshire cases addressing the responsibility of municipalities in adopting growth management ordinances, the court held the ordinance invalid as applied to the facts of the case because it did not address regional needs for affordable housing. The governing body of the town was given a "reasonable time period" to bring its ordinance into compliance with the regional housing-need requirement. The court also held that a builder's remedy was available and affirmed the trial court's grant of a builder's remedy to the developer. It did not follow the New Jersey rule on builder's remedies, however. It adopted the rule applied in Illinois and other states[2] to hold that the remedy is available only if the development will provide a reasonable opportunity for affordable housing consistent with "sound zoning concepts and environmental concerns."

C. INCLUSIONARY PLANNING AND ZONING.

§ 7.26 The Planning and Zoning Problem.

This section discusses inclusionary zoning techniques and state inclusionary legislation that can assist in the provision of affordable housing. Providing zoning opportunities for affordable housing requires extensive revisions in zoning and land use programs. These revisions include increasing housing densities, streamlining the development approval process, and making provision for housing in which development costs are reduced through techniques such as cluster zoning.

---

[3] § 7.29.

[1] 595 A.2d 492 (N.H. 1991).

[2] § 8.19.

Municipalities can also use flexible zoning techniques, such as the floating zone, to provide for affordable housing.[1] Revisions in excessive zoning and development standards, such as curb and gutter and street width requirements, must also be considered. Some states have adopted legislation authorizing zoning for affordable housing.[2] A number of states, in response to the availability of federal assistance,[3] have also enacted laws to remove regulatory barriers to affordable housing, which include land use restrictions.[4]

Comprehensive plans should require municipalities to plan for affordable housing, to make zoning revisions necessary to provide for affordable housing and to designate sites in their comprehensive plans they will zone for affordable housing. Several states, such as California, require municipalities to include affordable housing elements in their comprehensive plans. These statutes can require municipalities to designate sites for affordable housing in their housing elements.[5] The American Planning Association's model legislation contains provisions for housing elements in state, regional and local plans that can include a state or regional fair share allocation plan.[6]

§ 7.27   Mandatory Set-Asides and Incentive Zoning.

Mandatory set-aside ordinances are another inclusionary zoning technique that can provide affordable housing. These ordinances require residential developments over a minimum size to include a minimum percentage of units for sale or rental to low-or moderate-income households. Under some ordinances, the set-aside requirement applies only if federal or state housing subsidies are available for the lower-income units or if the local public housing authority will acquire or lease them. When the provision of lower-income housing is not linked to housing subsidies, zoning incentives may be necessary to absorb losses incurred by the developer on the lower-income units. Density bonuses are a possibility, and the ordinance can also relax site development requirements. Under California legislation, for example, developers who provide a specified percentage of housing for households with low or very low incomes are entitled

---

[1] Moore v. City of Boulder, 484 P.2d 134 (Colo. App. 1971) (approving rezone). *See also* Cameron v. Zoning Agent of Bellingham, 260 N.E.2d 143 (Mass. 1970) (upholding ordinance exempting public housing from site development restrictions and allowing it as permitted use in any zoning district).

[2] Conn. Gen. Stat. § 8-2.

[3] 42 U.S.C. § 12705c.

[4] *E.g.*, Wash. Rev. Code Ann. § 43.185B.030(1)(d) (Affordable Housing Advisory Board to analyze proposals to remove "state and local regulatory barriers" to affordable housing "where appropriate and not detrimental to the public health and safety or environment").

[5] §§ 3.11, 7.29. *See, e.g.,* Conn. Gen. Stat. § 8-23; Fla. Stat. Ann. 163.3177.

[6] American Planning Association, Growing Smart Legislative Guidebook: Model Statutes for Planning and Management of Change §§ 4-208, 6-203, 7-207 (S. Meck ed. 2002).

to a density bonus or other cost reduction incentives.[1] Some states have also have statutes authorizing zoning incentives that can be used to help provide affordable housing.[2]

Although inclusionary ordinances usually require the provision of affordable dwelling units on-site, they can also provide alternatives for meeting the affordable housing requirement. These alternatives include the off-site provision of affordable units; the dedication of land for affordable housing, either on-site or off-site; and in-lieu cash payments to a fund to be used for affordable housing. The municipality can use the fund to construct affordable housing or to assist such housing through write-downs on the cost of land, loans or grants to lower-income households, and similar measures.

Inclusionary ordinances often contain controls that maintain the availability of affordable housing for lower-income households once this housing is built. The ordinance may regulate the price and rents of the lower-income housing, including the resale price, and may give the municipality or its housing authority an option to purchase when lower-income units are offered for sale.

Mandatory inclusionary ordinances present a number of legal problems. Developers may make a taking objection if they suffer a loss on the sale or rental of the lower-income dwellings. They may also claim the mandatory ordinance violates equal protection and substantive due process and is not authorized by the state zoning legislation.[3] The statutory authority and substantive due process objections are interrelated. Developers can argue that mandatory inclusionary ordinances violate due process and are unauthorized by the zoning act because they do not serve a legitimate zoning purpose.

The Virginia court invalidated a mandatory inclusionary zoning ordinance invalid because it "exceeds the authority granted by the [zoning] enabling act . . . [and] because it is socio-economic zoning and attempts to control the compensation for the use of land and the improvements thereon."[4] The court also found a taking because the ordinance required the developer to sell or rent

---

[1] Cal. Gov't Code § 65915. *See* Building Indus. Ass'n v. City of Oceanside, 33 Cal. Rptr. 2d 137 (Cal. App. 1994) (growth control initiative conflicts with state laws protecting and encouraging lower income housing). See also American Planning Association, Growing Smart Legislative Guidebook: Model Statutes for Planning and Management of Change § 9-501 (S. Meck ed. 2002).

[2] Conn. Gen. Stat. § 8-2g; Md. Ann. Code Art. 66B, § 12.01; N.H. Rev. Stat. § 674:21; N.Y. Town Law § 261-b; N.Y. Village Law § 7-703; R.I. Gen. Laws § 45-24-33; Va. Code Ann. § 15.2-2286(10).

[3] *See* N.Y. Gen. City Law § 81-d (authorizing incentive zoning).

[4] Town of Telluride v. Lot Thirty-Four Venture, L.L.C., 3 P.2d 30 (Colo. 2000) (rental rate requirement in set-aside program violates state law prohibiting rent control); Board of Supvrs. v. DeGroff Enters., 198 S.E.2d 600 (Va. 1973). *See also* Middlesex & Boston St. Ry. v. Board of Aldermen, 359 N.E.2d 1279 (Mass. 1977) (condition on special exception requiring lease of apartments to city housing authority held invalid). *See* 62 A.L.R.3d 880 (1975).

dwelling units to lower-income households "at rental or sales prices not fixed by a free market."

This case was wrongly decided. The loss that a mandatory lower-income housing requirement is likely to impose on a developer is not substantial enough for a taking. The developer should be able to make a reasonable return on his development. Density bonuses can partially or totally offset any loss the developer may suffer.

The New Jersey Supreme Court rejected the Virginia decision and approved inclusionary zoning measures, including mandatory set-asides, in *Mt. Laurel (II)*:[5]

It is nonsense to single out inclusionary zoning (providing a realistic opportunity for the construction of lower income housing) and label it "socio-economic" if that is meant to imply that other aspects of zoning are not. . . . It would be ironic if inclusionary zoning to encourage the construction of lower income housing were ruled beyond the power of a municipality because it is "socio-economic" when its need has arisen from the socio-economic zoning of the past that excluded it.[6]

The New Jersey Supreme Court has also held that mandatory development fees for affordable housing imposed on commercial and non-inclusionary residential development are authorized by the Fair Housing Act and the zoning act.[7] The court rejected the nexus test as the basis for upholding the fee requirement and based their validity on the relationship between nonresidential development and the need for affordable housing.

§ 7.28 Office-Housing Linkage Programs.

Several cities have adopted programs that require office developers either to construct affordable housing or to pay an in-lieu fee into a fund for the construction of such housing. The programs assume that the new workers who are hired to fill new office space inflate housing prices by creating pressures on the housing market. Most of these programs are limited to downtown areas and some include retail developers. The construction or in-lieu payment requirement is usually based on a calculation that estimates the housing need created by each square foot of new office or commercial space.

---

[5] 456 A.2d 390 (N.J. 1983), discussed in § 7.11. *See also* Home Builders Ass'n of N. California v. City of Napa, 108 Cal. Rptr. 2d 60 (Cal. App. 2001) (rejecting facial attack on set-aside ordinance and holding heightened judicial review of Supreme Court exaction cases does not apply). In re Egg Harbor Assocs. (Bayshore Center), 464 A.2d 1115 (N.J. 1983) (holding mandatory set-aside imposed as condition to coastal development permit was impliedly authorized).*But see* N.J. Stat. Ann. § 13:19-11.1 (prohibiting coastal zone permit conditions that require lower-income housing in residential developments).

[6] 456 A.2d at 449.

[7] Holmdel Bldrs. Ass'n v. Township of Holmdel, 583 A.2d 277 (N.J. 1990).

Office-housing linkage programs raise a number of legal questions. One is whether municipalities have the implied authority to adopt them.[1] Another is whether these programs meet the nexus test for developer exactions. This issue is discussed in a later chapter.[2]

§ 7.29   California Inclusionary Legislation.

California has adopted extensive legislation to implement inclusionary housing objectives, including the authorization of density bonuses for affordable housing.[1] Zoning discrimination against low-and moderate-income housing is prohibited.[2]

The planning legislation requires a housing element in comprehensive plans.[3] This element must contain an "assessment of housing needs and an inventory of resources and constraints relevant to the meeting of these needs." The analysis of existing and projected housing need must identify each locality's "share of the regional housing need." The statute specifies criteria for the distribution of regional housing need, which include market demand for housing, employment opportunities, and the availability of suitable sites and public facilities.[4] The distribution is to be made by regional councils of government or by the state housing and community development department in areas where councils of government do not exist. The housing element must analyze "potential and actual governmental constraints" on the "development of housing for all income levels, including land use controls." Additional requirements include an analysis of "the availability of financing, the price of land, and the cost of construction."

The housing element must include a five-year housing program. Among other requirements, the housing program must

[i]dentify adequate sites which will be made available through appropriate zoning and development standards and with public services and facilities needed to facilitate and encourage the development of a variety of types of housing for all income levels . . . [and] [a]ddress and, where appropriate and

---

[1] Blagden Alley Ass'n v. District of Columbia Zoning Comm'n, 590 A.2d 139 (D.C. App. 1991) (implying authority to require linkage for planned unit developments); 1956 Mass. Acts ch. 665, §§ 15–20, added by 1987 Mass. Acts ch. 371, § 3 (authorizing Boston program). *But see* San Telmo Assocs. v. City of Seattle, 735 P.2d 673 (Wash. 1987) (invalidating ordinance that required owners who demolished low-income housing and replaced it with nonresidential use to provide other suitable housing or contribute to low-income housing replacement fund).

[2] § 9.23.

[1] § 7.27.

[2] Cal. Govt. Code § 65008.

[3] Cal. Gov't Code §§ 65580–65589.3. *See also id.* § 65590 (requiring replacement of lower income dwellings converted or demolished in coastal zone). *See also id.* § 65683 (prohibiting density reductions).

[4] Gov't Code § 65584.

legally possible, remove governmental constraints to the . . . development of housing.[5]

Local governments must "zone sufficient vacant land for residential use with appropriate standards . . . to meet housing needs as identified in the general plan."[6] They may not impose subdivision control requirements "for the purpose of rendering infeasible the development of housing for all economic segments of the community."[7] The California legislation codifies the *Mt. Laurel* fair share doctrine as a planning and plan implementation requirement.

§ 7.30 Oregon Inclusionary Legislation.

Oregon has adopted state legislation that requires local governments to adopt comprehensive plans and land use regulations that comply with state planning goals. The state Land Conservation and Development Commission reviews local plans and land use regulations to determine whether they comply with the state goals. One of the major state goals is an urbanization goal that requires local governments to adopt urban growth boundaries that contain land sufficient to meet projected urban growth.

A state housing goal requires local plans to encourage the availability of adequate housing at prices and rents affordable by Oregon households. The Commission held that this goal incorporated the *Mt. Laurel* fair share doctrine[1] and later extended this interpretation in an unofficial Commission policy. The legislature codified this policy:

When a need has been shown for housing within an urban growth boundary at particular price ranges and rent levels, needed housing . . . shall be permitted in one or more zoning districts . . . of sufficient buildable land to satisfy that need.[2]

Amendments to urban growth boundaries must also include sufficient buildable land to accommodate estimated housing needs for the next twenty years for all types of housing.[3]

The statute requires local governments to permit needed housing "in a zone or zones with sufficient buildable land to satisfy that need." They may adopt approval standards and procedures for housing and impose special conditions

---

[5] Gov't Code § 65583(c)(1) & (3). *See* § 3.22.

[6] Gov't Code § 65913.1 (and with "appropriate standards" that "contribute significantly" to the production of lower income housing).

[7] Gov't Code § 65913.2.

[1] Seaman v. City of Durham, LCDC No. 77-025 (1978).

[2] Or. Rev. Stat. § 197.307(3). *See* City of Happy Valley v. Land Conservation & Dev. Comm'n, 677 P.2d 43 (Or. App. 1984) (statute codifies housing goal).

[3] Or. Rev. Stat. § 197.296.

on approvals. Approval standards and procedures and special conditions must be "clear and objective" and must not have the effect, either singly or cumulatively, "of discouraging the needed housing types through unreasonable cost or delay."[4]

§ 7.31   Affordable Housing Appeals Laws.

A few states have adopted legislation authorizing appeals to a court or state agency if a local government denies or restrictively conditions an application for affordable housing. Connecticut legislation authorizes a court appeal if affordable housing is denied or approved with restrictions that have a substantial adverse impact on its viability or affordability.[1] The municipality has the burden to justify its decision with substantial public interests in health, safety and other legal matters that outweigh the affordable-housing's need, and must show that changes in the housing cannot protect these interests. Affordable housing is assisted housing, or developments in which at least 35 percent of the housing is deed-restricted to lower-income persons.

In its first decision the supreme court reversed a denial of an affordable housing development application and held the law applies to legislative zoning changes. The court also held the trial court had properly applied traditional judicial review standards, and that the statute authorized an order for a requested zone change and the approval of a special development district.[2] Later decisions held a court can approve an affordable housing application even though it does not comply with local zoning,[3] and that traffic and environmental problems did not justify denial of an affordable housing application.[4]

However, the Supreme Court later held a zoning commission meets its burden under the statute when there is sufficient evidence to reasonably conclude the public interest clearly outweighs the need for affordable housing, and that this interest could not be protected by reasonable change in the development. The court also held the need for affordable housing could be addressed on a local, rather than a regional, basis. The town could reject the affordable housing to

---

[4] Or. Rev. Stat. § 197.307(6). *See* Rogue Valley Ass'n of Realtors v. City of Ashland, 970 P.2d 685 (Or. App. 1999) (interpreting statute).

[1] Conn. Gen. Stat. § 8-30g; Ensign-Bickford Realty Corp. v. Zoning Comm'n, 715 A.2d 701 (Conn. 1998) (statute does not afford direct appeal to appellate court).

[2] West Hartford Interfaith Coalition, Inc. v. Town Council, 636 A.2d 1342 (Conn. 1994).

[3] Wisniowski v. Planning Comm'n, 655 A.2d 1146 (Conn. 1995). *See also* Town Close Assocs. v. Planning & Zoning Comm'n, 679 A.2d 378 (Conn. App. 1996) (public interest test applies though land zoned for affordable housing).

[4] Kaufman v. Zoning Comm'n, 653 A.2d 798 (Conn. 1995). *See also* National Associated Props. v. Planning & Zoning Comm'n, 658 A.2d 114 (Conn. App. 1995) (reversing denial of affordable housing application).

preserve the parcel for open space.[5] The legislative amended the statute to require courts to conduct their own review of the record to determine whether a denial of affordable housing was justified under the statute. The supreme court has decided the amendment was intended to clarify the scope of judicial review.[6]

Massachusetts has similar legislation, limited to federal-or state-subsidized low-or moderate-income housing projects.[7] If a local board of zoning appeals denies or restrictively conditions a "comprehensive permit" for a project, a state Housing Appeals Committee reviews the denial to determine whether it was "reasonable and consistent with local needs." This test requires a balancing of the regional need for low-and moderate-income housing, "considered with the number of low income persons" in the municipality, with the municipality's need for health, safety, design, and open space regulations.[8] Local requirements or regulations must be applied "as equally as possible" to both subsidized and unsubsidized housing. Local requirements or regulations must be applied "as equally as possible" to both subsidized and unsubsidized housing.

If the Committee reverses a denial, "it shall direct the [local] board to issue a comprehensive permit or approval to the applicant." The Committee may also order the removal or modification of any "condition or requirement" that makes the project uneconomic.[9] Rhode Island has comparable legislation.[10]

---

[5] Christian Activities Council, Congregational v. Town Council, 735 A.2d 231 (Conn. 1999).

[6] Quarry Knoll II Corp. v. Planning & Zoning Comm'n, 780 A.2d 1 (Conn. 2001) (and applying statute retroactively). *See also* JPI Partners v. Planning & Zoning Bd., 791 A.2d 552 (Conn. 2002) (board to make a collective statement of its reasons on the record when it denies an affordable housing land use application).

[7] Mass. Ann. Laws ch. 40B, §§ 20–23.

[8] *See also* § 20 (standard met when existing lower-income housing exceeds 10% of land area or application will provide housing on sites comprising more than .3% of land area or ten acres).

[9] *See* Zoning Bd. of Appeals v. Ardemore Apartments, 767 N.E.2d 584 (Mass. 2002) (rents must be maintained as affordable as long as project not in compliance with local zoning); Pheasant Ridge Assocs. v. Town of Burlington, 506 N.E.2d 1152 (Mass. 1987) (invalidating taking that blocked lower income housing project); Board of Appeals v. Housing Appeals Comm., 357 N.E.2d 936 (Mass. App. 1976) (Committee may not authorize noncompliance with state building code); Wilson v. Town of Sherborn, 326 N.E.2d 922 (Mass. App. 1975) (court relied on availability of law to uphold two-acre lot requirement).

[10] R.I. Gen. Laws § 45-53-1 et seq. *See* Curran v. Church Community Hous. Corp., 672 A.2d 453 (R.I. 1996) (upholding approval of affordable housing under the statute). See also R.I. Gen. Laws § 34-39.1-1 et seq. (making restrictions that preserve affordable housing legally enforceable).

REFERENCES

Books and Monographs

M. Danielson, The Politics of Exclusion (1976).

A. Downs, Opening Up the Suburbs, An Urban Strategy for America (1973).

A. Mallach, Inclusionary Housing Programs: Policies and Practices (1984).

M. Morris, Incentive Zoning: Meeting Urban Design and Affordable Housing Objectives, American Planning Ass'n, Planning Advisory Serv. Rep. No. 494 (2000).

S. White, Affordable Housing: Proactive & Reactive Planning Strategies, American Planning Ass'n, Planning Advisory Serv. Rep. No. 441 (1992).

Articles

Berger, Inclusionary Zoning Devices as Takings: The Legacy of the Mount Laurel Cases, 70 Neb. L. Rev. 183 (1991).

Brownstein, Illicit Legislative Motive in the Municipal Land Use Regulation Process, 57 U. Cin. L. Rev. 1 (1988).

Calavita, Grimes & Mallach, Inclusionary Zoning in California and New Jersey: A Comparative Analysis, 8 Hous. Pol'y Debate 109 (1997).

Connerly & Smith, Developing a Fair Share Housing Plan for Florida, 12 J. Land Use & Envtl. L. 63 (1996).

Cummins, Recasting Fair Share: Toward Effective Housing Law and Principled Social Policy, 14 Law & Ineq. 339 (1996).

Daye, Whither Fair Housing? Meditations on Wrong Paradigms, Ambivalent Answers, and a Legislative Proposal, 3 Wash. U. J.L. & Pol'y 241 (2000).

Dietderich, An Egalitarian's Market: The Economics of Inclusionary Zoning Reclaimed, 24 Fordham Urb. L.J. 23 (1996).

Fox, The Selling Out of Mount Laurel: Regional Contribution Agreements in New Jersey's Fair Housing Act, 16 Fordham Urb. L.J. 535 (1987-88).

Franzese, Mount Laurel III: The New Jersey Supreme Court's Judicial Retreat, 18 Seton Hall L. Rev. 30 (1988).

Galowitz, Interstate Metro-Regional Responses to Exclusionary Zoning, 27 Real Prop. Prob. & Tr. J. 49 (1992).

Inman & Rubinfeld, The Judicial Pursuit of Local Fiscal Equity, 92 Harv. L. Rev. 1662 (1979).

Jaffe, Government Code § 65008: New Strategies to Combat Exclusionary Zoning, 24 Colum. Hum. Rts. L. Rev. 165 (1992-93).

Johnston, Schwartz, Wandesorde-Smith & Caplan, Selling Zoning: Do Density Bonus Incentives for Moderate-Cost Housing Work?, 36 J. Urb. & Contemp. L. 45 (1989).

Kleven, Inclusionary Ordinances — Policy and Legal Issues in Requiring Private Developers to Build Low Cost Housing, 21 U.C.L.A. L. Rev. 1432 (1974).

Kmiec, Exclusionary Zoning and Purposeful Racial Discrimination: Two Wrongs Deserving Separate Remedies, 18 Urb. Law. 393 (1986).

Lamar, Mallach & Payne, *Mount Laurel* at Work: Affordable Housing in New Jersey, 41 Rutgers L. Rev. 1197 (1989).

Mandelker, Racial Discrimination and Exclusionary Zoning: A Perspective on Arlington Heights, 55 Tex. L. Rev. 1217 (1977).

McGuire, The Judiciary's Role in Implementing the *Mt. Laurel* Doctrine: Deference or Activism?, 23 Seton Hall L. Rev. 1006 (1993).

McDougall, From Litigation to Legislation in Exclusionary Zoning Law, 22 Harv. C.R.-C.L. L. Rev. 623 (1987).

McDougall, Regional Contribution Agreements: Compensation for Exclusionary Zoning, 60 Temp. L.Q. 665 (1987).

Monaghan & Penkethman, The Fair Housing Act: Meeting the Mount Laurel Obligation with a Statewide Plan, 9 Seton Hall Legis. J. 581 (1986).

Mount Laurel Housing Symposium, 27 Seton Hall. L. Rev. 1268 (1997).

Mount Laurel II Symposium, 14 Seton Hall L. Rev. 829 (1984).

Netter, The Massachusetts Approach to Affordable Housing, Urb. Land, Vol. 49, No. 6, at 32 (1990).

Patrick, Gilbert & Wheeler, Trading the Poor, Intermunicipal Housing Negotiation in New Jersey, 2 Harv. Negotiation L. Rev. 1 (1997).

Padilla, Reflections on Inclusionary Zoning and a Renewed Look at its Viability, 23 Hofstra L. Rev. 539 (1995).

Payne, Fairly Sharing Affordable Housing Obligations: The Mount Laurel Matrix, 22 W. New Eng. L. Rev. 365 (2001).

Payne, Norman Williams, Exclusionary Zoning, and the Mount Laurel Doctrine: Making the Theory Fit the Facts, 20 Vt. L. Rev. 665 (1996).

Payne, Reconstructing the Constitutional Theory of Mount Laurel II, 3 Wash. U. J.L. & Pol'y 555 (2000).

Payne, Remedies for Affordable Housing: From Fair Share to Growth Share, Land Use L. & Zoning Dig., Vol. 49, No. 6, at 3 (1997).

Payne, Rethinking Fair Share: The Judicial Enforcement of Affordable Housing Policies, 16 Real Estate L.J. 20 (1987).

Roisman & Tegeler, Improving and Expanding Housing Opportunities for Poor People of Color: Recent Developments in Federal and State Courts, 24 Clearinghouse Rev. 312 (1990).

Sager, Insular Majorities Unabated: Warth v. Seldin and City of Eastlake v. Forest City Enterprises, Inc., 91 Harv. L. Rev. 1373 (1978).

Schill, The Federal Role in Reducing Regulatory Barriers to Affordable Housing in the Suburbs, 8 J.L. & Politics 703 (1992).

Schukoske, Housing Linkage: Regulating Development Impact on Housing Costs, 76 Iowa L. Rev. 1011 (1991).

Schuman, From Washington to Arlington Heights and Beyond: Discriminatory Purpose in Equal Protection Litigation, 1977 U. Ill. L.J. 961.

Schwartz, The Disparate Impact Theory of Discrimination in Employment and Housing: The Limits of Analogy, 59 UMKC L. Rev. 815 (1991).

Smith, Delaney & Liou, Inclusionary Housing Programs: Issues and Outcomes, 25 Real Estate L.J. 155 (1996).

Solinski, Affordable Housing Law in New York, New Jersey, and Connecticut: Lessons for Other States,, 8 J. Affordable Hous. & Community Dev. L. 36 (1998).

Span, How the Courts Should Fight Exclusionary Zoning, 32 Seton Hall L. Rev. 1 (2001).

Symposium — Mount Laurel II and Developments in New Jersey, 15 Rutgers L.J. 513 (1984).

Symposium [on Housing], 22 W. New Eng. L. Rev. 323 (2001) (articles discussing New England zoning appeals systems).

Wheeler, Negotiating NIMBYs: Learning From the Failure of the Massachusetts Siting Law, 11 Yale J. on Reg. 241 (1994).

White, Using Fees and Taxes to Promote Affordable Housing, Land Use L. & Zoning Dig., Vol. 43, No. 9, at 3 (1991).

Williams, The Background and Significance of Mount Laurel II, 26 W.U.J. Urb. & Contemp. L. 3 (1984).

Williams, The Need for Affordable Housing: The Constitutional Viability of Inclusionary Zoning, 26 J. Marshall L. Rev. 75 (1992).

Student Work

Note, Alternatives to Warth v. Seldin: The Potential Resident Challenger of an Exclusionary Zoning Scheme, 11 Urb. L. Ann. 223 (1976).

Note, Anti-Snob Zoning in Massachusetts: Assessing One Attempt at Opening the Suburbs to Affordable Housing, 78 Va. L. Rev. 535 (1992).

Note, Breaking the Exclusionary Land Use Regulation Barrier: Policies to Promote Affordable Housing in the Suburbs, 82 Geo. L.J. 2039 (1994).

Note, Connecticut Retrenches: A Proposal to Save the Affordable Housing Appeals Procedure, 110 Yale L. J. 1247 (2001).

Note, Expanding the Effectiveness of the Massachusetts Comprehensive Permit Law by Eliminating its Subsidy Requirement, 28 B.C. Envtl. Aff. L. Rev. 651 (2001).

Note, Racial Diversity in Residential Communities: Societal Housing Patterns and a Proposal for a "Racial Inclusionary Ordinance," 63 S. Cal. L. Rev. 1151 (1990).

Note, Standing to Challenge Exclusionary Land Use Devices in Federal Courts After Warth v. Seldin, 29 Stan. L. Rev. 323 (1977).

Note, State-Sponsored Growth Management as a Remedy for Exclusionary Zoning, 108 Harv. L. Rev. 1127 (1995).

Comment, Building Housing From the Ground Up: Strengthening California Law to Ensure Adequate Locations for Affordable Housing, 39 Santa Clara L. Rev. 503 (1999).

Comment, Fundamental Issues in Housing Discrimination Litigation, 14 N.C. Cent. L.J. 555 (1984).

Comment, In Defense of Inclusionary Zoning: Successfully Creating Affordable Housing, 36 U.S.F.L. Rev. 971 (2002).

Comment, Judicial Deference and the Perpetuation of Exclusionary Zoning: A Case Study, Theoretical Overview, and a Proposal for Change, 37 Buff. L. Rev. 863 (1988-89).

Comment, Zoning for All: Using Inclusionary Zoning Techniques to Promote Affordable Housing, 44 Emory L.J. 359 (1995).

Recent Decision, Land Use — Lack of Judicial Guidance in Exclusionary Zoning, 64 Temp. L. Rev. 339 (1991).

Chapter 8

LAND USE LITIGATION AND REMEDIES

Synopsis

§ 8.01   An Introductory Note.

A. THIRD-PARTY STANDING IN STATE COURTS.

§ 8.02   General Principles.
§ 8.03   Taxpayers and Citizens.
§ 8.04   Resident Landowners.
§ 8.05   Nonresident Landowners.
§ 8.06   Organizations and Associations.
§ 8.07   Municipalities.

B. EXHAUSTION OF REMEDIES IN STATE COURTS.

§ 8.08   General Principles: Exhaustion and Ripeness Distinguished.
§ 8.09   The Ripeness Rules in State Courts.
§ 8.10   What Remedies Must Be Exhausted.
§ 8.11   Exceptions.

C. JUDICIAL REMEDIES AND RELIEF IN STATE COURTS.

§ 8.12   Judicial Remedies.
§ 8.13   Appeal and Certiorari.
§ 8.14   Mandamus.
§ 8.15   Injunction.
§ 8.16   Declaratory Judgment.
§ 8.17   Judicial Relief.
§ 8.18   Specific Relief Not Available.
§ 8.19   Specific Relief Available.
§ 8.20   Inverse Condemnation.
§ 8.21   State Cases: Remedy Available.
§ 8.22   State Cases: Remedy Not Available.
§ 8.23   Tort Liability.

D. FEDERAL REMEDIES.

§ 8.24   Inverse Condemnation.
§ 8.25   When Available.
§ 8.26   Availability and Measure of Compensation.
§ 8.27   Trial by Jury.
§ 8.28   Section 1983 of the Federal Civil Rights Act.
§ 8.29   Scope of the Statute.
§ 8.30   Land Use Cases Not Actionable Under § 1983.
§ 8.31   Color of Law, Policy, and Custom.
§ 8.32   Fault and Causation.
§ 8.33   Exhaustion and Adequacy of State Remedies.
§ 8.34   Immunities.
§ 8.35   Legislative Bodies.

§ 8.36   Land Use Agencies and Officials.
§ 8.37   Local Governments.
§ 8.38   Damages.
§ 8.39   Implied Constitutional Cause of Action.
§ 8.40   Removal to Federal Court.
§ 8.41   Abstention.
§ 8.42   *Younger* Abstention.
§ 8.43   *Pullman* Abstention.
§ 8.44   *Burford* Abstention.
§ 8.45   *Colorado River* Abstention.

E. SLAPP SUITS.

§ 8.46   SLAPP Suits.
§ 8.47   Anti-SLAPP Statutes.

§ 8.01   An Introductory Note.

Land use litigation presents complex problems. Plaintiffs in state courts must have standing to sue, must exhaust administrative remedies, and must select an appropriate judicial remedy. Courts may be reluctant to provide affirmative relief that requires a municipality to rezone its land to allow the development the landowner has proposed.

Land use plaintiffs may also sue in federal court, where remedies are available for damages and equitable relief under § 1983 of the federal Civil Rights Act, and in an action for inverse condemnation to secure compensation in takings cases. Ripeness rules in takings and perhaps in other cases brought under the federal constitution may keep land use cases out of federal court.

The chapter discusses land use litigation issues in state and federal courts. The ripeness barrier to federal court land use actions is discussed in Chapter 2.[1] Though the chapter concentrates on zoning litigation, the law that applies to zoning cases also applies to other land use regulations as well.

A.   THIRD-PARTY STANDING IN STATE COURTS.

§ 8.02   General Principles.

A party must have standing to sue in order to be able to sue in state court. Landowners who challenge land use regulations in court have a property interest sufficient to confer standing.[1] More difficult standing problems arise when third

---

[1] §§ 2.24–2.32.

[1] Frank Hardie Adv., Inc. v. City of Dubuque Zoning Bd. of Adjustment, 501 N.W.2d 521 (Iowa 1993) (citing cases holding that lessee of property has standing).

parties, such as neighboring property owners or nonresidents, challenge land use regulations. Standing to sue is more difficult to obtain in these cases because third parties do not own property that is directly affected by a zoning restriction. This section reviews the law of third-party standing in state court zoning litigation. It does not discuss third-party standing in exclusionary zoning litigation, which is reviewed in Chapter Seven.[2]

Standing law in state courts differs from standing law in federal courts, which is governed by constitutional "case and controversy" and prudential standing principles.[3] State constitutions do not have "case and controversy" limitations on state court jurisdiction. State courts impose a "prudential" standing limitation by limiting their jurisdiction to justiciable controversies.[4]

Third-party standing in zoning litigation also is controlled by the Standard Zoning Enabling Act. The Act authorized appeals from decisions of the board of adjustment by "persons . . . aggrieved" and "any taxpayer."[5] Almost all state statutes contain the "person aggrieved" provision, but only a minority extend standing to taxpayers. An occasional statute makes zoning decisions reviewable under the state's administrative procedure act.[6] The courts usually assume that the statutory aggrievement requirement for standing to appeal zoning board decisions also governs nonstatutory judicial remedies, such as injunction and declaratory judgment actions.[7]

Most statutes allow a plaintiff to appeal an administrative decision even though he did not participate in the administrative proceedings in which the decision was made.[8] Some courts do not follow this rule if the statute does not enact it. They require participation in the administrative proceedings by the party who brings an appeal.[9] These courts require participation even if the interests represented by the party bringing the appeal were not adequately represented in the administrative proceedings.

---

[2] See also § 7.07.

[3] § 7.02.

[4] Bremner v. City & County of Honolulu, 28 P.2d 350 (Hawaii App. 2001); Pence v. State, 652 N.E.2d 486 (Ind. 1995).

[5] Standard Zoning Enabling Act § 7. See also American Planning Association, Growing Smart Legislative Guidebook: Model Statutes for Planning and Management of Change § 10-101(S. Meck ed. 2002) (defining aggrievement for standing).

[6] 65 Ill. Comp. Stat. Ann. 5/11-13-13.

[7] Palmer v. St. Louis County, 591 S.W.2d 39 (Mo. App. 1980). See Society Created to Reduce Urban Blight (SCRUB) v. Zoning Bd. of Adjustment, 729 A.2d 117 (Pa. Commw. 1999) (city has power to define standing).

[8] See Mass. Gen. L. ch. 40A, § 17.

[9] Bryniarski v. Montgomery County Bd. of Appeals, 230 A.2d 289 (Md. 1967); Abrams v. Gearhart, 184 N.E.2d 411 (Ohio App. 1961); Frank v. Mobil Oil Corp., 296 A.2d 300 (Pa. Commw. 1973). Contra State ex rel. Brookside Poultry Farms, Inc. v. Jefferson County Bd. of Adjustment, 388 N.W.2d 593 (Wis. 1986).

Under the usual formulation of the rule, third-party standing requires "special" damage to an interest or property right that is different from the damage the general public suffers from a zoning restriction.[10] Competitive injury, for example, is not enough.[11] This rule reflects the nuisance basis of zoning, which protects property owners only from damage caused by adjacent incompatible uses. Although the special damage rule is well-entrenched in zoning law, a few courts have modified it. New Jersey has adopted a liberal third-party standing rule which requires only a showing of "a sufficient stake and real adverseness."[12]

§ 8.03 Taxpayers and Citizens.

If the statute does not grant standing, most courts deny standing to citizens and taxpayers who do not own property affected by a zoning restriction they wish to challenge.[1] This rule is less liberal than the rule that grants standing to taxpayers to challenge illegal municipal expenditures. A few state courts grant standing to taxpayers and citizens to challenge zoning restrictions.[2]

§ 8.04 Resident Landowners.

Landowners who reside in a municipality and are adjacent or close to land on which a zoning agency has allowed a more intensive use are usually held to have suffered special damage which is sufficient to confer standing.[1] Some

[10] Hall v. Planning Comm'n, 435 A.2d 975 (Conn. 1981); Renard v. Dade County, 261 So. 2d 832 (Fla. 1972); Harvard Square Defense Fund v. Planning Bd., 540 N.E.2d 182 (Mass. App. 1989); Bryniarski v. Montgomery County Bd. of Appeals, 230 A.2d 289 (Md. 1967); Palmer v. St. Louis County, 591 S.W.2d 39 (Mo. App. 1980); Develo-Cepts, Inc. v. City of Galveston, 668 S.W.2d 790 (Tex. App. 1984).

[11] Multiplex Corp. v. Hartz Mountain Indus., 564 A.2d 146 (N.J. App. Div. 1989); Nernberg v. City of Pittsburgh, 620 A.2d 692 (Pa. Commw. 1993). See also § 5.41.

[12] Home Bldrs. League of S. Jersey, Inc. v. Township of Berlin, 405 A.2d 381 (N.J. 1979).

[1] Wine v. Council of City of Los Angeles, 2 Cal. Rptr. 94 (Cal. App. 1960); Bell v. Planning & Zoning Comm'n, 391 A.2d 154 (Conn. 1978); Lewis v. Swan, 716 A.2d 127 (Conn. App. 1998) (developer does not have standing to challenge lack of enforcement that put him at competitive disadvantage); Citizens Growth Mgt. Coalition of W. Palm Beach, Inc. v. City of West Palm Beach, Inc., 450 So. 2d 204 (Fla. 1984) (consistency of zoning with comprehensive plan); Bremner v. City & County of Honolulu, 28 P.2d 350 (Hawaii App. 2001) (plan and zoning for Waikiki);; Tate v. Stephens, 265 S.E.2d 811 (Ga. 1980); Garner v. County of Du Page, 133 N.E.2d 303 (Ill. 1956); Amherst Growth Study Comm'n, Inc. v. Board of Appeals, 296 N.E.2d 717 (Mass. App. 1973); Blumberg v. Hill, 119 N.Y.S.2d 855 (Sup. Ct. 1953). See Committee for Responsible Dev. on 25th Street v. Mayor & City Council, 767 A.2d 906 (Md. App. 2001) (statute allows appeal by taxpayer if aggrieved); Munch v. City of Mott, 311 N.W.2d 17 (N.D. 1981) (ordinance may confer standing).

[2] Towle v. Nashua, 212 A.2d 204 (N.H. 1965); Booth v. Board of Adjustment, 234 A.2d 681 (N.J. 1967); Roeder v. Borough Council, 266 A.2d 691 (Pa. 1970). See also Renard v. Dade County, 261 So. 2d 832 (Fla. 1972) (challenge to validity in enactment).

[1] Steadham v. Board of Zoning Adjustment, 629 So. 2d 647 (Ala. 1993); Mings v. City of Ft.

cases hold that adjacent landowners have standing prima facie.[2] Other cases hold that proximity alone is not enough, even when a statute confers standing on neighboring landowners. These courts insist on specific proof of special damage.[3] Fear of harmful adverse effects, such as a fear of apartment development, increased traffic, or the aesthetic "blight" created by an adjacent parking lot, may not be enough.[4] Courts have granted standing to owners of land affected by amendments to zoning or subdivision regulations.[5]

The courts do not usually confer standing on property owners who wish to challenge a favorable zoning action on a site that is some distance away.[6] These

Smith, 701 S.W.2d 705 (Ark. 1986); Buckelew v. Town of Parker, 937 P.2d 368 (Ariz. App. 1997); Butters v. Hauser, 960 P.2d 181 (Idaho 1998); Reynolds v. Dittmer, 312 N.W.2d 75 (Iowa App. 1981); Christy's Realty Ltd. Partnership v. Town of Kittery, 663 A.2d 59 (Me. 1995); Ramirez v. City of Santa Fe, 852 P.2d 690 (N.M. App. 1993) (applying liberal Supreme Court rules); Roach v. Town of Milton Zoning Bd. of Appeals, 530 N.Y.S.2d 321 (App. Div. 1988); Anderson v. Island County, 501 P.2d 594 (Wash. 1972); Hoke v. Moyer, 865 P.2d 624 (Wyo. 1994); 37 A.L.R.2d 1137 (1954). *But see* Sherrill House, Inc. v. Board of Appeal, 473 N.E.2d 716 (Mass. App. 1986).

[2] Concerned Citizens of Murphys v. Jackson, 140 Cal. Rptr. 531 (Cal. App. 1977); Snyder v. City Council, 531 P.2d 643 (Colo. App. 1975); Hobbs v. Markey, 398 S.W.2d 54 (Ky. 1966); Marashlian v. Zoning Bd. of Appeals, 660 N.E.2d 369 (Mass. 1996) (rebuttable presumption of standing); Massiello v. Town Board, 684 N.Y.S.2d 330 (App. Div. 1999); Sun-Brite Car Wash, Inc. v. Board of Zoning & Appeals, 508 N.E.2d 130 (N.Y. 1987).

[3] Foran v. Zoning Bd. of Appeals, 260 A.2d 609 (Conn. 1969), applying Conn. Gen. Stat. § 8-8; Florida Rock Props. v. Keyser, 709 So.2d 175 (Fla. App. 1998) (standing denied to adjacent property owner); Davis v. City of Archdale, 344 S.E.2d 369 (N.C. App. 1986); Midwest Fireworks Mfg. Co. v. Deerfield Township Board of Zoning Appeals, 743 N.E.2d 894 (Ohio 2001) (owner of property across highway had standing to challenge substantial enlargement of fireworks factory). *See* Hendel's Investor Co. v. Zoning Bd. of Appeals, 771 A.2d 182 (Conn. App. 2001) (statute requires showing of effect on public safety as basis for appealing decision authorizing gasoline station).

[4] Gulf House Ass'n v. Town of Gulf Shores, 484 So. 2d 1061 (Ala. 1985); Walls v. Planning & Zoning Comm'n, 408 A.2d 252 (Conn. 1979); Columbus v. Diaz-Verson, 373 S.E.2d 208 (Ga. 1988) (flooding threat); AT&T Wireless PCS, Inc. v. Leafmore Forest Condominium Ass'n of Owners, 509 S.E.2d 374 (Ga. App. 1998) (same); Dunaway v. City of Marietta, 308 S.E.2d 823 (Ga. 1983); Bagnall v. Town of Beverly Shores, 726 N.E.2d 782 (Ind. 2000); 222 E. Chestnut St. Corp. v. Board of Appeals, 152 N.E.2d 465 (Ill. 1958); Wilkinson v. Atkinson, 218 A.2d 503 (Md. 1966); Marashlian v. Zoning Bd. of Appeals, 660 N.E.2d 369 (Mass. 1996); Sanitary & Imp. Dist. No. 347 v. City of Omaha, 589 N.W.2d 160 (Neb. App. 1999) (increase in traffic); Tata v. Town of Babylon, 276 N.Y.S.2d 426 (Sup. Ct. 1967). *But see* Dalton v. City & County of Honolulu, 462 P.2d 199 (Haw. 1969).

[5] Harris v. Zoning Comm'n, 788 A.2d 1239 (Conn. 2002).

[6] Victoria Corp. v. Atlanta Merchandise Mart, Inc., 112 S.E.2d 793 (Ga. App. 1960); Garner v. County of Du Page, 133 N.E.2d 303 (Ill. 1956); Pattison v. Corby, 172 A.2d 490 (Md. 1961); Nickerson v. Zoning Bd. of Appeals, 761 N.E.2d 544 (Mass. App. 2002) (plaintiff one mile away); Palmer v. St. Louis County, 591 S.W.2d 39 (Mo. App. 1980). *But see* Exchange Invs., Inc. v. Alachua County, 481 So. 2d 1223 (Fla. App. 1985); Jenkins v. City of Gallipolis, 715 N.E.2d 196 (Ohio App. 1998) (granting standing to property owner one-half mile from site because decrease in property values will occur).

cases reflect the assumption in nuisance law that special damage from an incompatible land use occurs only to property that is close enough to be affected.

§ 8.05   Nonresident Landowners.

Although a few courts hold to the contrary,[1] the recent decisions hold that nonresident landowners have standing to challenge another municipality's zoning if they own property contiguous or near to the rezoned land.[2] *Scott v. City of Indian Wells*[3] is a leading case. The court held:

> To hold, under these circumstances, that defendant city may zone the land within its borders without any concern for adjacent landowners would indeed "make a fetish out of invisible boundary lines and mockery of the principles of zoning."[4]

The court also held that individual property interests are "often affected by local land use controls," and that municipalities owe nonresidents as well as residents a "duty" to hear and consider their views before acting on a rezoning. Some of the cases that granted standing to nonresident landowners relied on decisions holding that land uses in an adjacent municipality are relevant to the constitutionality of a municipality's zoning.

§ 8.06   Organizations and Associations.

Although some courts hold that neighborhood and other organizations are not entitled to standing as aggrieved persons,[1] the trend is toward granting standing to these organizations in a representational capacity.[2] Many of these cases follow

---

[1] Clark v. City of Colorado Springs, 428 P.2d 359 (Colo. 1967); Cablevision — Div. of Sammons Communications, Inc. v. Zoning Hearing Bd., 320 A.2d 388 (Pa. Commw. 1974).

[2] Brandywine Park Condo. Council v. Members of City of Wilmington Zoning Bd. of Adjustment, 534 A.2d 286 (Del. Super. 1987); Whittingham v. Village of Woodridge, 249 N.E.2d 332 (Ill. App. 1969); Stokes v. City of Mishawaka, 441 N.E.2d 24 (Ind. App. 1982); Koppel v. City of Fairway, 371 P.2d 113 (Kan. 1962); Allen v. Coffel, 488 S.W.2d 671 (Mo. App. 1972); 69 A.L.R.3d 805 (1976).

[3] 492 P.2d 1137 (Cal. 1972).

[4] *Id.* at 1141.

[1] Lindsey Creek Area Civic Ass'n v. Consolidated Gov't of Columbus, 292 S.E.2d 61 (Ga. 1982); Westwood Forum, Inc. v. City of Springfield, 634 N.E.2d 1154 (Ill. App. 1994); Amherst Growth Study Comm'n, Inc. v. Board of Appeals, 296 N.E.2d 717 (Mass. App. 1973); Stocksdale v. Barnard, 212 A.2d 282 (Md. 1965); Acorn Corp. v. Zoning Hearing Bd., 523 A.2d 436 (Pa. Commw. 1987) (denying right to intervene); Beaufort Realty Co., Inc. v. Beaufort County, 551 S.E.2d 588 (S.C. App. 2001) (injury not shown; Supreme Court cases followed);Virginia Beach Beautification Comm'n v. Board of Zoning Appeals, 344 S.E.2d 899 (Va. 1986). *See* Mo. Rev. Stat. § 89.100 (neighborhood organizations may take appeals to board of adjustment).

[2] Colorado Manufactured Housing Ass'n v. Pueblo County, 857 P.2d 507 (Colo. App. 1993); Timber Trails Corp. v. Planning & Zoning Comm'n, 610 A.2d 620 (Conn. 1992); Dupont Circle Citizens Ass'n v. Barry, 455 A.2d 417 (D.C. App. 1983); Life of the Land v. Land Use Comm'n,

the lead of *Hunt v. Washington State Apple Advertising Comm'n*,[3] a U.S. Supreme Court case. It held an organization can sue on behalf of its members if its members would have standing to sue in their own right, if it seeks to protect interests germane to the organization's purpose, and if neither the claim nor the relief requested requires the participation of its individual members in the suit. Many of the state cases have also ignored *Warth v. Seldin*,[4] which denied standing to a housing organization to challenge an exclusionary suburban zoning ordinance.

Residents of Beverly Glen, Inc. v. City of Los Angeles[5] illustrates the cases that grant standing to organizations. A neighborhood organization brought suit claiming a planned unit development was inconsistent with density policies contained in a comprehensive plan. The court noted that "environmental concerns underlie this action . . . [and] are the proper subject of judicial consideration." It held that "there is no insuperable obstacle to the maintenance of an action by a group whose members find themselves directly and adversely affected by the governmental action involved."

Douglaston Civic Ass'n v. Galvin[6] is a leading case that granted standing to a neighborhood organization. The court found an "economic disparity" in zoning litigation that justified organizational standing. A landowner who stands to gain from the relaxation of zoning restrictions is not reluctant to engage in litigation to achieve this result. Individual landowners in the neighborhood may not realize the impact of the change on their property or may not have the finances to effectively oppose the zoning change. "By granting the neighborhood and civic associations standing in such situations, the expense can be spread out over a number of property owners putting them on an economic parity with the developer."[7]

---

594 P.2d 1079 (Haw. 1979); Glengary-Gamlin Protective Ass'n v. Bonner County Bd. of Comm'rs, 675 P.2d 344 (Idaho App. 1983); Bellhaven Imp. Ass'n v. City of Jackson, 507 So. 2d 41 (Miss. 1987); 1000 Friends of Or. v. Land Conservation & Dev. Comm'n, 593 P.2d 1171 (Or. App. 1979); Save a Valuable Env't v. City of Bothell, 576 P.2d 401 (Wash. 1978). *Cf.* Montana Wildlife Fed'n v. Sager, 620 P.2d 1189 (Mont. 1980) (statute conferred standing). *See also* Citizens Coordinating Comm. on Friendship Heights, Inc. v. TKU Assocs., 351 A.2d 133 (Md. 1976) (intervention). *See* Fla. Stat. Ann. § 163.3215 ("alleged adverse interest may be shared in common with other members of the community at large, but shall exceed in degree the general interest in community good shared by all persons'"), applied in Putnam County Envtl. Council, Inc. v. Board of County Comm'rs, 757 So.2d 590 (Fla. App. 2000) (construction of middle school complex would cause specific injuries to organization).

[3] 432 U.S. 333 (1977), as restated in United Food & Commercial Workers Union Local 751 v. Brown Group, Inc., 116 S. Ct.2 1529 (1996). *See also* Sierra Club v. Morton, 405 U.S. 727 (1972).

[4] 422 U.S. 490 (1974), discussed in § 7.02.

[5] 109 Cal. Rptr. 724 (Cal. App. 1973).

[6] 324 N.E.2d 317 (N.Y. 1974).

[7] *Id.* at 320.

The court held that "an appropriate representative association" should have standing to assert the rights of members affected by a zoning change. The court listed a number of factors courts should consider in determining whether the association was sufficiently representative. They include the capacity of the association to assume an adversary position and a requirement that the association be "fairly representative of the community or interests which it seeks to protect."[8]

§ 8.07 Municipalities.

The courts recognize the standing of municipalities to challenge actions by their zoning boards and planning commissions. They may deny standing if no harm is shown, unless they construe a statutory provision authorizing judicial actions by municipalities and municipal officials as a waiver of the harm requirement.[1]

More difficult problems are presented when a municipality challenges the zoning of an adjacent municipality. Harm is difficult to show unless the municipality owns property in the area affected by the adjacent municipality's zoning. A municipality may also claim harm based on more generalized injuries, such as increased traffic from a land use in an adjacent municipality that increases traffic control costs. Some courts refuse to recognize this kind of harm as sufficient to confer standing.[2]

In *Village of Barrington Hills v. Village of Hoffman Estates*,[3] the court took a contrary view in a case in which two municipalities challenged the approval of an open-air theater in an adjacent municipality. The court noted that the municipalities would suffer "special damages in their corporate capacities," such as a decline in property values, increased traffic control costs, and air quality

---

[8] *See also* American Law Inst., Model Land Dev. Code § 2-307 (similar requirements for organizational standing).

[1] City of Irvine v. Irvine Citizens Against Overdevelopment, 30 Cal. Rptr. 2d 797 (Cal. App. 1994); City of Burley v. McCaslin Lumber Co., 693 P.2d 1108 (Idaho App. 1984); County of Cook v. Priester, 342 N.E.2d 41 (Ill. 1976); City of Plattsburgh v. Mannix, 432 N.Y.S.2d 910 (Sup. Ct. 1980); City of East Providence v. Shell Oil Co., 290 A.2d 915 (R.I. 1972); 13 A.L.R.4th 1130 (1982). *Compare* Township of Dover v. Board of Adjustment, 386 A.2d 421 (N.J. App. Div. 1978). *See also* Town of Northville v. Village of Sheridan, 655 N.E.2d 22 (Ill. App. 1995) (applying usual rule that municipality may not challenge legislation as unconstitutional). *See* State *ex rel.* Smith v. Grant, 943 S.W.2d 319 (Mo. App. 1997) (statute does not confer standing on aldermen to appeal grant of variance).

[2] City of New Haven v. Allen County Bd. of Zoning Appeals, 694 N.E.2d 306 (Ind. App. 1998) (personal and pecuniary interest claims insufficient); City of Greenbelt v. Jaeger, 206 A.2d 694 (Md. 1965); Town of Huntington v. Town Bd. of Oyster Bay, 293 N.Y.S.2d 558 (Sup. Ct. 1968). *See* Town of North Hempstead v. Village of North Hills, 342 N.E.2d 566 (N.Y. 1975) (statute).

[3] 410 N.E.2d 37 (Ill. 1980). *Accord* Town of Mesilla v. Town of Las Cruces, 898 P.2d 121 (N.M. App. 1995) (aesthetic, environmental and economic harm).

degradation caused by motor vehicle exhaust. Other decisions allowed a municipality to sue an adjacent municipality in a representative capacity without showing proof of harm.[4]

B. EXHAUSTION OF REMEDIES IN STATE COURTS.

§ 8.08 General Principles: Exhaustion and Ripeness Distinguished.

A plaintiff cannot challenge a zoning ordinance or restriction in state court unless he has exhausted his administrative remedies. The courts adopted the exhaustion doctrine to maintain an appropriate separation of governmental powers. They require exhaustion of administrative remedies because they want to give an administrative agency the opportunity to grant administrative relief that can avoid a court challenge. The exhaustion doctrine in zoning also reflects a judicial belief that zoning agencies, not the courts, are the proper forum in which to resolve questions concerning the applicability of zoning ordinances.

A failure to exhaust administrative remedies is jurisdictional in many states, and municipalities can raise it as an affirmative defense.[1] The exhaustion requirement is different from the rule that bars plaintiffs from using a particular judicial remedy, such as mandamus, if another judicial remedy is available.[2]

The exhaustion doctrine must be distinguished from the ripeness doctrine that is a barrier to bringing land use cases in federal court.[3] The ripeness doctrine, which is similar to but theoretically different from the exhaustion of remedies doctrine, does not allow a plaintiff to bring suit until the administrative agency has made a final, definitive decision applying its regulation. A number of state courts apply the federal ripeness doctrine to taking claims in land use cases, but it is not always clear whether the usual exhaustion rules also apply. The issue in the state cases is whether there is a final decision, because the availability of a state compensation remedy only affects federal jurisdiction. Applying the federal ripeness rules in state courts is incorrect because the U.S. Supreme Court adopted these rules to determine federal jurisdiction to hear questions arising

---

[4] Board of County Comm'rs v. City of Thornton, 629 P.2d 605 (Colo. 1981) (home rule city); Borough of Roselle Park v. Township of Union, 272 A.2d 762 (N.J. 1970); 49 A.L.R.3d 1126 (1973). *See also* Maryland-Nat'l Capital Park & Planning Comm'n v. City of Rockville, 305 A.2d 122 (Md. 1973) (regional commission).

[1] Poe v. City of Baltimore, 216 A.2d 707 (Md. 1966); Nodell Inv. Corp. v. City of Glendale, 254 N.W.2d 310 (Wis. 1977). *Contra* Boomhower v. Cerro Gordo County Bd. of Supvrs., 173 N.W.2d 95 (Iowa 1969); Deal Gardens, Inc. v. Board of Trustees, 226 A.2d 607 (N.J. 1967). *See* Palmieri v. Zoning Bd. of Appeals, 349 A.2d 731 (Conn. Super. 1975) (can compel administrative agency to act).

[2] G.S.T. v. City of Avon Lake, 357 N.E.2d 38 (Ohio 1976).

[3] §§ 2.24–2.32

under state law. Nevertheless, the tendency of state courts to apply the federal ripeness rules seems entrenched and is likely to continue. The American Planning Association's model legislation contains provisions on exhaustion of remedies and ripeness.[4]

§ 8.09   The Ripeness Rules in State Courts.

State courts considering ripeness claims in takings cases have followed ripeness doctrines adopted by the federal courts. Like the federal courts, they require a meaningful application[1] and a final decision by the local government.[2] State courts also require a reapplication following an initial denial.[3] A case is not ripe unless the plaintiff has applied for a variance,[4] but the cases divide on whether an appeal is necessary.[5]

The state cases apply a futility rule adopted by some federal circuits that does not require an application for approval or administrative relief if it would be futile. In most of the cases, the courts held a futility claim had not been proved.[6]

---

[4] American Planning Association, Growing Smart Legislative Guidebook: Model Statutes for Planning and Management of Change §§ 10-603 (ripeness), 10-604 (exhaustion), § 10-605 (reserving federal claims in state court) (S. Meck ed. 2002).

[1] Metropolitan Baptist Church v. District of Columbia Dep't of Consumer & Reg. Aff.. 718 A.2d 119 (D.C. 1998); City of Riviera Beach v. Shillingburg, 659 So.2d 1174 (Fla. App. 1995); Messer v. Town of Chapel Hill, 479 S.E.2d 221 (N.C. App.), *vacated as moot*, 485 S.E.2d 269 (N.C. 1997). *See also* Long Beach Equities, Inc. v. County of Ventura, 282 Cal. Rptr. 877 (Cal. App. 1991) (no application for annexation, specific plan, zoning change or other favored uses). *See* MC Assocs. v. Town of Cape Elizabeth, 773 A.2d 439 (Me. 2001) (federal and state takings claims need not be tried separately in state court).

[2] Reale Inv., Inc. v. City of Colorado Springs, 856 P.2d 91 (Colo. 1993); Canal/Norcrest/Columbus Action Comm. v. City of Boise, 39 P.3d 606 (Idaho 2001) (conditional use approval final); Bothwell v. City of Eagle, 938 P.2d 1212 (Idaho 1997) (preliminary plat approval not final); Galbraith v. Planning Dep't, 627 N.E.2d 850 (Ind. App. 1994); MFH Holding Co. v. New Jersey Dep't of Envtl. Protection, 713 A.2d 1096 (N.J.L. Div. 1997).

[3] Toigo v. Town of Ross, 82 Cal.Rptr. 2d 649 (Cal. App. 1998); Port Clinton Assocs. v. Board of Selectmen, 587 A.2d 126 (Conn. 1991); Daddario v. Cape Cod Comm'n, 681 N.E.2d 833 (Mass. 1997); Joyce v. Multnomah County, 835 P.2d 127 (Or. App. 1992); Killington, Ltd. v. State, 668 A.2d 1278 (Vt. 1995).

[4] Drovers Bank of Chicago v. Village of Hinsdale, 566 N.E. 2d 899 (Ill. App. 1991); Paragon Props. Co. v. City of Novi, 550 N.W.2d 772 (Mich. 1996) (extensive dissent); Bonge v. County of Madison, 573 N.W.2d 448 (Neb. 1998); April v. City of Broken Arrow, 775 P.2d 1347 (Okla. 1989). *But see* Cumberland Farms, Inc. v. Town of Groton, 719 A.2d 465 (Conn. 1998) (one denial of variance enough when board decision could not change).

[5] *Compare* Ben Lomond, Inc. v. Municipality of Anchorage, 761 P.2d 119 (Alaska 1988) (not ripe where plaintiff failed to appeal revocation of permit), *with* Cumberland Farms, Inc. v. Town of Groton, 719 A.2d 465 (Conn. 1998) (not required to bring administrative appeal to court when monetary relief could not be provided for taking claim).

[6] Futility not found: Toigo v. Town of Ross, 82 Cal. Rptr. 2d 649 (Cal. App. 1998) (possibility

Although it would seem to be a requirement only for federal jurisdiction, a few state courts held a plaintiff must use available state remedies to seek compensation in state court to make a state takings claim ripe.[7] State courts have also applied the final decision rule to equal protection, substantive and procedural due process claims.[8]

§ 8.10   What Remedies Must Be Exhausted.

The exhaustion of remedies requirement means plaintiffs must pursue all available administrative remedies, including exceptions, variances, site plan review,[1] and appeals to the board of adjustment for administrative interpretations of the zoning ordinance.[2] A plaintiff must also pursue any additional remedies that are available under the zoning ordinance.[3]

The exhaustion doctrine in most states does not require landowners to seek legislative relief through a zoning amendment,[4] but a few courts hold to the

---

of administrative reprieve existed for well-designed, less-dense proposal); Paragon Props. Co. v. City of Novi, 550 N.W.2d 772 (Mich. 1996) (must seek variance though board grants variances sparingly); Bonge v. County of Madison, 573 N.W.2d 448 (Neb. 1998) (regulation clearly allowed for variances); Messer v. Town of Chapel Hill, 479 S.E.2d 221 (N.C. App.) (no allegations on futility), *vacated as moot*, 485 S.E.2d 269 (N.C. 1997); Joyce v. Multnomah County, 835 P.2d 127 (Or. App. 1992) (outcome not precluded); Killington, Ltd. v. State, 668 A.2d 1278 (Vt. 1995) (board indicated reasonable mitigation measures and comprehensive plan would allow rezoning); Estate of Friedman v. Pierce County, 768 P.2d 462 (Wash. 1989) (futility not shown).

Futility found: Taylor v. City of Riviera Beach, 801 So.2d 259 (Fla. App. 2001) (plan amendment futile); Whitehead Oil Co. v. City of Lincoln (III), 515 N.W.2d 401 (Neb. 1994) (futility established by city's past actions); Mayhew v. Town of Sunnyvale, 964 S.W.2d 922 (Tex. 1998) (futile because plaintiff's alleged anything but their only application would be a regulatory taking).

[7] Beverly Bank v. Illinois Department of Transportation, 579 N.E.2d 815 (Ill. 1991); Bakken v. City of Council Bluffs, 470 N.W.2d 34 (Iowa 1991). *Contra See* Cox v. City of Lynnwood, 863 P.2d 578 (Wash. App. 1993) (noting rule that exhaustion of remedies not required for § 1983 substantive due process claims).

[8] Drovers Bank of Chicago v. Village of Hinsdale, 506 N.E.2d 899 (Ill. App. 1991); Messer v. Town of Chapel Hill, 479 S.E.2d 221 (N.C. App.), *vacated as moot*, 485 S.E.2d 269 (N.C. 1997). *See* Cox v. City of Lynnwood, 863 P.2d 578 (Wash. App. 1993) (noting rule that exhaustion of remedies not required for § 1983 substantive due process claims).

[1] Exception: Holt-Lock, Inc. v. Zoning & Planning Comm'n, 286 A.2d 299 (Conn. 1971). Variance: Pan Pac. Props. v. County of Santa Cruz, 146 Cal. Rptr. 428 (Cal. App. 1978); Lange v. Town of Woodway, 483 P.2d 116 (Wash. 1971). Site Plan Review: Bruni v. City of Farmington Hills, 293 N.W.2d 609 (Mich. App. 1980). *See also* Park Area Neighbors v. Town of Fairfax, 35 Cal. Rptr. 2d 334 (Cal. App. 1994) (not excused from exhaustion because no legal representation and agency misadvice); Howland Realty Co. v. Wolcott, 457 N.E.2d 883 (Ohio App. 1982) (petition for referendum not required).

[2] Minor v. Cochise County, 608 P.2d 309 (Ariz. 1980); Cunningham v. Kittery Planning Bd., 400 A.2d 1070 (Me. 1979); Westside Enters. v. City of Dexter, 559 S.W.2d 638 (Mo. App. 1977).

[3] County of Platte v. Chipman, 512 S.W.2d 199 (Mo. App. 1974).

[4] G.S.T. v. City of Avon Lake, 357 N.E.2d 38 (Ohio 1976).

contrary.[5] A zoning amendment is an administrative remedy a plaintiff must exhaust in states that characterize the zoning amendment process as quasi-judicial.[6]

§ 8.11 Exceptions.

The exhaustion doctrine is discretionary, and the courts have adopted a number of exceptions. Under one important exception, exhaustion is not required when administrative remedies are inadequate.[1] Remedies are inadequate when the board of adjustment cannot grant a use variance that can avoid an attack on the constitutionality of a zoning regulation, or when a variance or exception is unavailable.[2] Exhaustion is not required when a landowner claims a vested right, because a vested right confers absolute protection from a change in the zoning ordinance and does not require an administrative determination.[3] Exhaustion of an appeal procedure is not required when the person who was to exercise that right did not have notice there was a decision to appeal.[4]

Another commonly applied exception does not require exhaustion when a plaintiff claims a zoning ordinance is unconstitutional in its entirety or is facially illegal.[5] This exception arises from the rationale of the exhaustion rule, which requires an administrative interpretation only when a plaintiff claims the ordinance is unconstitutional as applied to her property. The courts require exhaustion in as-applied cases because the administrative agency may foreclose constitutional attack by giving the landowner administrative relief. Administrative

---

[5] Village Centers, Inc. v. DeKalb County, 281 S.E.2d 522 (Ga. 1981); Bright v. City of Evanston, 139 N.E.2d 270 (Ill. 1957).

[6] Fifth Ave. Corp. v. Washington County, 581 P.2d 50 (Or. 1978).

[1] Shors v. Johnson, 581 N.W.2d 648 (Iowa 1998) (remedy adequate); In re Fairchild, 616 A.2d 228 (Vt. 1992) (statutory appeal not adequate remedy); Town of Jonesville v. Powell Valley Village Ltd. Partnership, 487 S.E.2d 207 (Va. 1997) (board did not have authority to rule on validity of zoning ordinance); Smoke v. City of Seattle, 937 P.2d 186 (Wash. 1997) (interpretation of ordinance not available as remedy). *But see* Riley v. Boxa, 542 N.W.2d 519 (Iowa 1996) (remedy adequate though board cannot award damages and charges fee); Holiday Point Marina Partners v. Anne Arundel County, 707 A.2d 829 (Md. 1998) (no constitutional or validity exception when administrative remedy exclusive).

[2] City of Rome v. Pilgrim, 271 S.E.2d 189 (Ga. 1980); Sinclair Pipe Line Co. v. Village of Richton Park, 167 N.E.2d 406 (Ill. 1960); Montgomery County v. Citizens Bldg. & Loan Ass'n, 316 A.2d 322 (Md. 1974). *But see* Pa. Stat. Ann. tit. 53, § 11004 (landowners must submit constitutional challenge to board of adjustment or governing body).

[3] O'Mara v. Council of City of Newark, 48 Cal. Rptr. 208 (Cal. App. 1966); Town of Hillsborough v. Smith, 167 S.E.2d 51 (N.C. App. 1969). *Compare* State ex rel. Foreman v. City Council, 205 N.E.2d 398 (Ohio 1965) (nonconforming use).

[4] Loulis v. Parrott, 695 A.2d 1040 (Conn. 1997).

[5] Gingell v. Board of County Comm'rs, 239 A.2d 903 (Md. 1968); Deal Gardens, Inc. v. Board of Trustees, 226 A.2d 607 (N.J. 1967); Golden Gate Corp. v. Town of Narragansett, 359 A.2d 321 (R.I. 1976).

review cannot remedy a constitutional attack that does not depend on an application of the zoning ordinance to the landowner's property.[6] In the clearest case, the plaintiff claims a zoning ordinance is invalid because of some underlying illegality, such as a lack of adequate notice or statutory authority.[7] Nor is exhaustion required when the plaintiff claims that the zoning ordinance contains facially arbitrary classifications or is confiscatory in its entirety.[8] Exhaustion is not required when a third party brings an action to enforce a zoning ordinance because nothing is gained by administrative consideration of this type of claim.[9]

The rule that a landowner who attacks a zoning ordinance as facially illegal need not exhaust administrative remedies stems from the *Euclid* case.[10] The U.S. Supreme Court did not require exhaustion in *Euclid* because the landowner attacked as unconstitutional the textual provisions in a zoning ordinance that excluded multifamily dwellings from residential zones. *Golden v. Planning Bd. of Town of Ramapo*[11] is a leading growth management case in which the court did not require exhaustion. The plaintiffs attacked a growth management ordinance in its entirety. The court did not require exhaustion because a holding that the ordinance was unconstitutional would make it unnecessary to apply for the development permit required by the ordinance.[12]

A court may not require exhaustion even when a zoning restriction is attacked as applied to a plaintiff's property. In *Grimpel Assocs. v. Cohalan*,[13] the plaintiff attacked as applied a downzoning to residential use of a tract of land on which it planned to construct a shopping center. The court did not require exhaustion. It held that the plaintiff's use was "absolutely prohibited by the zoning classification," and that the plaintiff had attacked the "validity of the zoning ordinance itself as confiscatory."

In *Environmental Law Fund, Inc. v. Town of Corte Madera*,[14] a California court created an exception to the exhaustion doctrine for third parties asserting

---

[6] *See* Mountain View Chamber of Commerce v. City of Mountain View, 143 Cal. Rptr. 441 (Cal. App. 1978); Poe v. City of Baltimore, 216 A.2d 707 (Md. 1966).

[7] Horn v. County of Ventura, 596 P.2d 1134 (Cal. 1979); Morland Dev. Co. v. City of Tulsa, 596 P.2d 1255 (Okla. 1979); Kingsley v. Miller, 388 A.2d 357 (R.I. 1978); Sparks v. Bolton, 335 S.W.2d 780 (Tex. Civ. App. 1960).

[8] Baum v. City & County of Denver, 363 P.2d 688 (Colo. 1961); Board of Supvrs. v. Rowe, 216 S.E.2d 199 (Va. 1975).

[9] Simko v. Ervin, 661 A.2d 1018 (Conn. 1995); Frye Constr., Inc. v. City of Monongahela, 584 A.2d 946 (Pa. 1991); Culbertson v. Board of County Comm'rs, 41 P.3d 642 (Utah 2002). *See* § 8.15

[10] Village of Euclid v. Ambler Realty Co., 272 U.S. 365 (1926), discussed in § 5.02.

[11] 285 N.E.2d 291 (N.Y.1972).

[12] *But see* Northwestern Univ. v. City of Evanston, 383 N.E.2d 964 (Ill. 1978) (attack not facial when it requires assessment of uses authorized by ordinance).

[13] 361 N.E.2d 1022 (N.Y. 1977).

[14] 122 Cal. Rptr. 282 (Cal. App. 1975). *But see* Sage & Audubon Soc'y, Inc. v. Planning Comm'n,

public rather than private rights in opposition to developments that receive local approval. The court emphasized that the plaintiff organization did not participate in and did not receive notice of the administrative proceedings in which the development was approved, and that the development would affect a substantial area of the community. Similarly, a court may restrict the exhaustion requirement to permit applicants who are directly affected by a public official's decision.[15]

Courts will not require exhaustion if an attempt to secure administrative relief would be futile. In the typical futility case, the municipality's opposition to the proposed development is clear and a denial of the project is inevitable.[16] *Ogo Assocs. v. City of Torrance*[17] is an extreme example of this situation. The court held that exhaustion would be futile when the plaintiff attacked the constitutionality of an ordinance that purposely downzoned its property to frustrate a subsidized housing project it planned to build. The cases also find futility when a development was previously disapproved, and no change in circumstances indicated that a different decision would be forthcoming if the landowner made a new application.[18]

A court may apply the futility rule when a landowner asserts a defense in an enforcement action brought by a municipality.[19] The courts hold that the

668 P.2d 664 (Cal. 1983). (not ruling on validity of case but holding contra, when plaintiffs did have notice of administrative proceedings and actively participated at every stage of hearing process).

[15] Bixler v. LaGrange County Bldg. Dep't, 730 N.E.2d 818 (Ind. App. 2000) (plaintiff not required to exhaust remedies before challenging building permit issued for adjacent property); Frye Constr., Inc. v. City of Monongahela, 584 A.2d 946 (Pa. 1991) (neighbor can bring action in equity to enforce ordinance). *But see* Bennion v. Sundance Dev. Corp., 897 P.2d 1232 (Utah App. 1997).

[16] O & G Indus. v. Planning & Zoning Comm'n, 655 A.2d 1121 (Conn. 1995) (rejecting futility claim based on claimed bias); Halifax Area Council v. City of Daytona Beach, 385 So. 2d 184 (Fla. App. 1980); Van Laten v. City of Chicago, 190 N.E.2d 717 (Ill. 1963); Town Council of New Harmony v. Parker, 726 N.E.2d 1217 (Ind. 2000) (rejecting futility claim); Amcon Corp. v. City of Eagan, 348 N.W.2d 66 (Minn. 1984); Napierkowski v. Township of Gloucester, 150 A.2d 481 (N.J. 1959); Karches v. City of Cincinnati, 526 N.E.2d 1350 (Ohio 1988); League of Women Voters of Appleton, Inc. v. Outagamie County, 334 N.W.2d 887 (Wis. 1983). *But see* Sea & Sage Audubon Soc'y, Inc. v. Planning Comm'n, 668 P.2d 664 (Cal. 1983); Corsino v. Grover, 170 A.2d 267 (Conn. 1961); Northwestern Univ. v. City of Evanston, 383 N.E.2d 964 (Ill. 1978); City of Iowa City v. Hagen Electronics, Inc. 545 N.W.2d 530 (Iowa 1996); Presbytery of Seattle v. King County, 787 P.2d 907 (Wash.1990); Estate of Friedman v. Pierce Cty., 752 P.2d 936 (Wash. App. 1988).

[17] 112 Cal. Rptr. 761 (Cal. App. 1974). *But see* Mountain View Chamber of Commerce v. City of Mountain View, 143 Cal. Rptr. 441 (Cal. App. 1978).

[18] *Compare* Town of Paradise Valley v. Gulf Leisure Corp., 557 P.2d 532 (Ariz. App. 1976) *with* National Brick Co. v. City of Chicago, 235 N.E.2d 301 (Ill. App. 1968).

[19] Board of County Comm'rs v. Goldenrod Corp., 601 P.2d 360 (Colo. App. 1979); Johnson's Island v. Board of Twp. Trustees, 431 N.E.2d 672 (Ohio 1982). *Contra* Metropolitan Dev. Comm'n v. Ching, Inc., 460 N.E.2d 1236 (Ind. App. 1984). *See also* City of St. Ann v. Elam, 661 S.W.2d 632 (Mo. App. 1983).

municipality admits a zoning regulation is valid if it brings an action to enforce it. Any attempt by the landowner to seek administrative relief would be futile.

C. JUDICIAL REMEDIES AND RELIEF IN STATE COURTS.

§ 8.12 Judicial Remedies.

The Standard Zoning Act contained little in the way of judicial remedies. Section 7 of the Act provided for the review of board of adjustment decisions by writ of certiorari, and most state zoning acts contain this provision. The Standard Act and most state zoning acts do not provide for the judicial review of decisions by the planning commission or governing body. The statutory appeal provided by state administrative procedure acts often is unavailable to review decisions by these bodies because courts hold that the act does not apply to local zoning agencies.[1] Plaintiffs who challenge zoning decisions by these bodies must use one of the so-called extraordinary remedies that are available to challenge local government actions.

The injunction and declaratory judgment are the remedies most used by plaintiffs in zoning cases in which the appeal provided by the zoning statute is not available. In the typical case, a landowner claims a zoning restriction as applied to his land is a taking of property. He usually asks for an injunction to prohibit the municipality from enforcing the zoning restriction against him and a declaratory judgment that the zoning restriction is unconstitutional. The disadvantage of the injunction and declaratory judgment is that most courts will only invalidate a zoning restriction if it holds it is a taking. They do not usually give affirmative relief that orders a rezoning or the issuance of a building permit that authorizes the landowner's proposed use. Mandamus is an alternative remedy that allows a landowner to compel the issuance of a building permit or a zoning approval, but it is available only in those infrequent cases in which the zoning ordinance imposes a mandatory duty.

Some states now provide more comprehensive judicial review procedures for zoning decisions. The American Planning Association model legislation contains a comprehensive judicial review procedure for quasi-judicial decisions taken on development permits.[2] The statute is modeled on the Washington state Land Use Petition Act.[3]

---

[1] Schlega v. Detroit Bd. of Zoning Appeals, 382 N.W.2d 737 (Mich. App. 1985); Davis Cty. v. Clearfield City, 756 P.2d 704 (Utah App. 1988).

[2] American Planning Association, Growing Smart Legislative Guidebook: Model Statutes for Planning and Management of Change §§ 10-601 to 10-618 (S. Meck ed. 2002)

[3] Wash. Rev. Code Ann. § 36.70C.005 et seq.

§ 8.13   Appeal and Certiorari.

Section 7 of the Standard Zoning Act, which most state zoning acts include, authorized a petition to a "court of record" stating that a board of adjustment decision is "illegal." The court may then "allow a writ of certiorari directed to the board of adjustment to review such decision."[1] Certiorari is an extraordinary remedy available in the court's discretion to review the decisions of courts and administrative agencies for jurisdictional defects or illegality in the exercise of jurisdiction. A court will not grant a writ of certiorari when a statutory appeal is available.[2]

Legislation in some states provides for a statutory appeal of zoning decisions and regulations to the courts, and some of this legislation applies to governing bodies as well as zoning boards and planning commissions.[3] However, an appeal is not available if the governing body acts in a legislative capacity.[4] A state statute or charter provision may also provide for certiorari review of zoning amendments or actions by the planning commission or governing body.[5]

Certiorari is the standard judicial review procedure available in administrative law to review quasi-judicial and administrative decisions including zoning decisions,[6] such as the denial of a special use permit.[7] These decisions are usually made by a board of adjustment or similar zoning agency, although the planning

---

[1] *See also* Jackson v. Spaulding County, 462 S.E.2d 361 (Ga. 1995) (ordinance may specify certiorari to review denial of variance by board).

[2] Ledbetter v. Roberts, 98 S.E.2d 654 (Ga. App. 1957); Massachusetts Feather Co. v. Aldermen of Chelsea, 120 N.E.2d 766 (Mass. 1954); Rhodes v. Town of Woodstock, 318 A.2d 170 (Vt. 1974).

[3] Alaska Stat. § 29.40.060 (local governing body may provide for appeal); Ark. Stat. § 14-363-208; Conn. Gen. Stat. § 8-8 (boards and commissions); Mass. Gen. Laws Ch. 40A, § 17 (board of appeals); Minn. Stat. Ann. § 462.361 (board of appeals); N.H. Rev. Stat. Ann. § 677:4 (governing body and board of appeals).

[4] Sun Communities v. Leroy Township, 617 N.W.2d 42 (Mich. App. 2000); Copple v. City of Lincoln, 315 N.W.2d 628 (Neb. 1979).

[5] Dade County v. Metro Imp. Corp., 190 So. 2d 202 (Fla. App. 1966); City Plan Comm'n v. Pielet, 338 N.E.2d 648 (Ind. App. 1975); County Council v. Carl M. Freeman Assocs., 376 A.2d 860 (Md. 1977). *See also* McCallen v. City of Memphis, 786 S.W.2d 633 (Tenn. 1990) (council PUD approval held administrative).

[6] Broward County v. G.B.V. Internat'l, Inc., 787 So.2d 838 (Fla. 2001) (describing writ); Handicraft Block Ltd. Partnership v. City of Minneapolis, 611 N.W.2d 16 (Minn. 2000) (designation of historic building is quasi-judicial); Allen v. Coffel, 488 S.W.2d 671 (Mo. App. 1972); Currey v. Kimple, 577 S.W.2d 508 (Tex. Civ. App. 1979); Leavitt v. Jefferson County, 875 P.2d 681 (Wash. App. 1994); Bridle Trails Community Club v. City of Bellevue, 724 P.2d 1110 (Wash. App. 1986).

[7] Hirt v. Polk Cty. Bd. of Comm'rs, 578 So. 2d 415 (Fla. App. 1991) (approval of planned unit development); City Council v. Trebor Constr. Corp., 254 So. 2d 51 (Fla. App. 1971); Florka v. City of Detroit, 120 N.W.2d 797 (Mich. 1963).

commission and the governing body can also act in a quasi-judicial or administrative manner. An injunction against the enforcement of an ordinance is the usual remedy for challenging legislative actions by the governing body, such as rezonings in most states.[8] Certiorari is available to review rezonings by the governing body in states where the courts hold that rezoning is quasi-judicial.[9] Direct review through certiorari or a statutory appeal is also available when the legislative body makes an administrative decision, such as the approval or denial of a variance,[10] or if it reviews a decision of a zoning board.[11] Decisions by planning commissions are directly reviewable if they are quasi-judicial.[12] Advisory decisions are not reviewable.[13]

Review by certiorari is usually on the record made before the zoning agency. The courts are divided on whether a reviewing court may take additional evidence.[14] They also divide on whether they will consider the constitutionality of a zoning ordinance in an appeal from a variance.[15] Courts usually apply a substantial evidence test when reviewing decisions by zoning agencies in a certiorari review.[16]

§ 8.14   Mandamus.

Mandamus is an extraordinary remedy that is useful in zoning litigation because it can provide affirmative relief, such as the issuance of a building permit. The writ lies to compel ministerial as distinguished from discretionary acts.[1]

---

[8] Sherman v. City of Colorado Springs Planning Comm'n, 763 P.2d 292 (Colo. 1988); Copple v. City of Lincoln, 315 N.W.2d 628 (Neb. 1982); Bama Invs., Inc. v. Metropolitan Dade County, 349 So. 2d 207 (Fla. App. 1977). *See also* Walton Cty. v. Scenic Hills Estates, 401 S.E.2d 513 (Ga. 1991) (municipality may not create right of appeal).

[9] Snyder v. City of Lakewood, 542 P.2d 371 (Colo. 1975).

[10] Talbut v. City of Perryburg, 594 N.E.2d 1046 (Ohio App. 1991); Frederico v. Moore, 395 N.Y.S.2d 535 (App. Div. 1977). *See* Lowell v. M & N Mobile Home Park, 916 S.W.2d 95 (Ark. 1996) (applying usual arbitrary and capricious standard of judicial review).

[11] Bieger v. Village of Moreland Hills, 209 N.E.2d 218 (Ohio App. 1965); Sun Ray Homes, Inc. v. County of Dade, 166 So. 2d 827 (Fla. App. 1964).

[12] Maher v. Town Planning & Zoning Comm'n, 226 A.2d 397 (Conn. 1967).

[13] Downing v. Board of Zoning Appeals, 274 N.E.2d 542 (Ind. App. 1971).

[14] § 6.52.

[15] City of Cherokee v. Tatro, 636 P.2d 337 (Okla. 1981).

[16] Florida Power & Light Co. v. City of Dania, 761 So.2d 1089 (Fla. 2000) (discussing test and holding test incorrectly applied by lower court).

[1] Held ministerial: City of Coachella v. Riverside County Airport Land Use Comm'n, 258 Cal. Rptr. 795 (Cal. App. 1989((plan did not meet statutory requirements); 350 Lake Shore Assocs. v. Hill, 761 N.E.2d 760 (Ill. App. 2001) (approval letter); State ex rel. Burger King Corp. v. Oakwood, 594 N.E.2d 116 (Ohio App. 1991) (appeal to zoning board); Lindy Homes, Inc. v. Sabatini, 453 A.2d 972 (Pa. 1982) (to reinstate building permit); In re Fairchild, 616 A.2d 228 (Vt. 1992) (ministerial duties of executive officer); Town of Jonesville v. Powell Valley Ltd. Partnership, 487 S.E.2d 207 (Va. 1997) (building permit).

As one court stated in a zoning case:

The prerequisites for a writ of mandamus are (1) that the defendant be obliged by law to perform a duty in which there is no permitted discretion, (2) that the plaintiff have a clear legal right to have the duty performed, and (3) that the plaintiff have no other sufficient remedy.[2]

This decision illustrates the type of case in which a writ of mandamus will issue. The court held that the municipality did not have the statutory authority to adopt a nine-month development moratorium. It granted a writ of mandamus directing the commission to accept an application the moratorium barred.

Note that the court only ordered the commission to accept the application. A court can also grant a writ of mandamus that orders a zoning agency to exercise a discretionary responsibility, even though the court cannot order the agency to act in a particular manner.[3] A court will also grant a writ of mandamus to review the exercise of a discretionary function, and it will set aside the agency's decision if it was arbitrary or capricious.[4] Mandamus will issue to compel a government agency to act if a plaintiff has shown a clear legal right to have a duty performed because she has satisfied all of the requirements necessary for the exercise of a ministerial duty. An example is a case in which an applicant complies with all of the requirements for the issuance of a building permit, but the building official refuses to issue it.[5]

Held discretionary: Brant v. Custom Design Constructors Corp., 677 N.E.2d 92 (Ind. App. 1997) (subdivision approval and variance); Rodrock Enters., L.P. v. City of Olathe, 21 P.3d 598 (Kan. App. 2001) (review of subdivision application); Tranner v. Helmer, 878 P.2d 787 (Idaho 1994) (same); Allen v. St. Tammany Parish Police Jury, 690 So.2d 150 (La. App. 1997 (same); Hart v. City of Albuquerque, 975 P.2d 366 (N.M. App. 1999) (mandamus not available to compel rezoning); Jordan Partners v. Goehringer, 611 N.Y.S.2d 626 (App. Div. 1994) (stop work order).

[2] Schrader v. Guilford Planning & Zoning Comm'n, 418 A.2d 93, 94 (Conn. Super. 1980). Stratos v. Town of Ravenel, 376 S.E.2d 783 (S.C. App. 1989). For the distinction in California between an administrative and ordinary mandamus see Agins v. City of Tiburon, 598 P.2d 25 (Cal. 1979); Toso v. City of Santa Barbara, 162 Cal. Rptr. 210 (Cal. App.1980).

[3] Griffin Homes, Inc. v. Superior Ct., 274 Cal. Rptr. 456 (Cal. App. 1990) (to compel hearing on denial of building approval); Ratliff v. Phillips, 746 S.W.2d 405 (Ky. 1988) (to compel hearing); Portland Sand & Gravel v. Town of Gray, 663 A.2d 41 (Me. 1995) (to compel review of application); Weed v. King County, 677 P.2d 179 (Wash. App. 1984) (cannot compel rezoning). Compare Fontana Unified School Dist. v. City of Rialto, 219 Cal. Rptr. 254 (Cal. App. 1985); Dougherty County v. Webb, 350 S.E.2d 457 (Ga. 1986).

[4] Fulton County v. Bartenfeld, 363 S.E.2d 555 (Ga. 1988); Steinlage v. City of New Hampton, 567 N.W.2d 438 (Iowa App. 1997); Curtis Oil v. City of North Branch, 364 N.W.2d 880 (Minn. App. 1985); Nova Horizon, Inc. v. City Council, 769 P.2d 721 (Nev. 1989); Davis Cty. v. Clearfield City, 756 P.2d 704 (Utah App. 1988). But see Gwinnett County v. Ehler Enters., Inc. 512 S.E.2d 239 (1999) (denial of special permit not arbitrary).

[5] Par Developers v. Planning & Zoning Comm'n, 655 A.2d 1164 (Conn. App. 1995); DeKalb County v. Publix Super Markets, 452 S.E.2d 471 (Ga. 1994) (no clear right to subdivision approval); Clark v. City of Shreveport, 655 So. 2d 617 (La. App. 1995) (granting of variance when all

Conditional use and site plan review illustrate the application of these rules. Conditional use provisions typically authorize the approval of a conditional use if it is "compatible" with other uses in the surrounding area. A court will not compel the approval of a conditional use under a provision of this type if it holds that approval requires an exercise of discretion by the zoning agency.[6] The criteria for site plan review also will usually require the exercise of discretion.[7] A court may issue a writ of mandamus to compel the approval of a conditional use or site plan if an applicant exhausts a zoning agency's discretion by satisfying the approval criteria in a zoning ordinance.[8]

A court will not grant a writ of mandamus if a statutory appeal or other remedy is available. An example is the statutory appeal that is available from actions by the board of zoning adjustment.[9] Mandamus may issue to compel a decision by a zoning board if the statute does not provide an alternative remedy.[10]

Mandamus is available to compel the enforcement of a zoning ordinance. Although the enforcement function is discretionary, mandamus will lie when the violation of the zoning ordinance is clear.[11] An example is a mandamus action to compel a municipality to take action against a landowner who illegally uses land in a residential area for off-street business parking. Courts also grant mandamus to compel municipal officials to take action against landowners who are issued illegal permits.[12] Other courts hold that mandamus is unavailable to compel the enforcement of a zoning ordinance if the duty to enforce is not clear or if an alternative remedy is available.[13]

---

requirements met); State v. Ludewig, 187 N.E.2d 170 (Ohio App. 1962); Bell Atlantic Mobile Systems, Inc. v. Borough of Clifton Heights, 661 A.2d 909 (Pa. Commw. 1995) (no clear right to permit); Lake Bluff Housing Partners v. City of S. Milwaukee, 540 N.W.2d 189 (Wis. 1995) (no vested right).

[6] City of Miami Beach v. Mr. Samuel's, Inc., 351 So. 2d 719 (Fla. 1977).

[7] § 6.66

[8] Kosinski v. Lawlor, 418 A.2d 66 (Conn. 1979).

[9] Big Train Constr. Co. v. Parish of St. Tammany, 446 So. 2d 889 (La. App. 1984); The Chapel v. City of Solon, 530 N.E.2d 1321 (Ohio 1988).

[10] City of Atlanta v. Wansley Moving & Storage Co., 267 S.E.2d 234 (Ga. 1980). *See also* State Bd. of Health v. Atnip Design & Supply Center, Inc., 385 So. 2d 1307 (Ala. 1980).

[11] Tustin Heights Ass'n v. Board of Supvrs., 339 P.2d 914 (Cal. App. 1959); Rebholz v. Floyd, 327 So. 2d 806 (Fla. App. 1976); Stratford v. Crossman, 655 S.W.2d 500 (Ky. App. 1983); Brady v. Board of Appeals, 204 N.E.2d 513 (Mass. 1965); Green v. Board of App., 529 N.E.2d 159 (Mass. App. 1988); Garrow v. Teaneck Tryon Co., 94 A.2d 332 (N.J. 1953); Petition of Fairchild, 616 A.2d 228 (Vt. 1992). *See also* State ex rel. Long v. Council of Cardington, 748 N.E.2d 58 (Ohio 2001)(enforcement of open meeting law).

[12] Parks v. Board of County Comm'rs, 501 P.2d 85 (Or. App. 1972); 68 A.L.R.3d 166 (1976).

[13] Board of Educ. v. Idle Motors, Inc., 90 N.E.2d 121 (Ill. App. 1950); Fried v. Fox, 373 N.Y.S.2d 197 (Sup. Ct. 1975).

§ 8.15 Injunction.

The injunction is an equitable remedy that lies to restrain illegal action.[1] Like mandamus, it is not available to compel a discretionary decision. Neither is it available if there is an alternative legal remedy. A plaintiff in an injunction action may be able to obtain temporary relief through a temporary restraining order or preliminary injunction. Most states require a plaintiff to post a bond as a condition to obtaining temporary or permanent injunctive relief. The bond protects the developer from damage caused by the litigation delay if she should ultimately prevail. Injunction bonds may be substantial and may create an effective financial barrier to injunctive relief.

An injunction is the proper remedy to challenge zoning actions by the governing body in states holding that the zoning process is legislative. An injunction lies because an alternative legal remedy is not available. Appeal and certiorari are not available to review zoning actions by the governing body if these actions are legislative. In the typical case, the governing body adopts a restrictive zoning classification that applies to a landowner's land. Unless the landowner is required to exhaust administrative remedies, he can challenge the zoning restriction as an as-applied taking of property by bringing an injunction action to restrain the municipality from enforcing the zoning ordinance against his land.[2] Courts will not grant an injunction to enjoin threatened legislative action that may injuriously affect a landowner's property because they will not enjoin a threatened harm.[3] A plaintiff can bring an injunction action only to challenge "illegal" governmental action, and the governing body must act in some illegal way before a court will grant injunctive relief. Zoning ordinances claimed to be a taking as applied to a landowner's property are one example of an "illegal" zoning action. A landowner may also bring an injunction to restrain a municipality from enforcing a zoning ordinance that is illegal for other reasons, such as a failure to provide a required statutory notice and hearing.[4]

Section 8 of the Standard Zoning Act authorized municipalities to bring "appropriate action or proceedings" to prevent a violation of the Act or a zoning ordinance. The state zoning acts usually include this provision, and the courts

[1] *See* Company, USA v. State Highway Admin., 731 A.2d 948 (Md. App. 1999) (collateral attack on zoning ordinance not available in condemnation proceedings).

[2] Phillips v. City of Homewood, 50 So. 2d 267 (Ala. 1951); Bama Invs., Inc. v. Metropolitan Dade County, 349 So. 2d 207 (Fla. App. 1977); 2700 Irving Park Bldg. Corp. v. City of Chicago, 69 N.E.2d 827 (Ill. 1946). *See* §§ 8.08–8.10. *But see* Tahoe Keys Prop. Owners' Ass'n v. State Water Resources Bd., 28 Cal. Rptr. 2d 734 (Cal. App. 1994) (denying preliminary injunction when damages would compensate plaintiffs and injunction would cause serious harm).

[3] Citizens for Orderly Dev. & Env't v. City of Phoenix, 540 P.2d 1239 (Ariz. 1975); Shellburne, Inc. v. Buck, 240 A.2d 757 (Del. 1968); Popisil v. Anderson, 527 N.Y.S.2d 819 (App. Div. 1988). *See also* Adams v. City of Fort Wayne, 423 N.E.2d 647 (Ind. App. 1981).

[4] Pyramid Corp. v. DeSoto County Bd. of Supvrs., 366 F. Supp. 1299 (N.D. Miss. 1973).

have held that it authorizes injunction actions to enforce zoning ordinances. Most courts interpret this provision liberally. They allow injunction actions to enforce the ordinance without proof of the irreparable injury courts usually require for injunctive relief.[5] Nor do the courts apply the rule that an injunction cannot issue to enjoin the violation of a crime.[6] This rule could apply because the Standard Act and state zoning acts make the violation of the Act or a zoning ordinance a misdemeanor. The courts apply the usual balancing of equities rule in actions to enforce zoning ordinances, although some courts do not balance equities if the landowner acted intentionally or in bad faith.[7]

Although the Standard Act did not authorize injunctions by private citizens to enforce zoning ordinances, most state zoning statutes include this authority.[8] A private citizen who brings an injunction action to enforce a zoning ordinance must show injury and special damage. Courts usually find the necessary injury and damage when the injunction is brought by neighboring landowners against a zoning violator.[9] In one case, a Florida court issued an order to demolish a building that had been constructed in violation of a comprehensive plan.[10]

§ 8.16 Declaratory Judgment.

The declaratory judgment is widely used as a judicial remedy in zoning cases. Plaintiffs usually bring an action for a declaratory judgment and may join it with an injunction as an alternative remedy. Declaratory judgment actions are fairly "civilized." The parties can obtain a resolution of their dispute without the disruptive effect that an award of monetary or injunctive relief may cause. Declaratory judgment actions are also on an expedited calendar in many jurisdictions. The parties can obtain a final decision on the merits much earlier. The plaintiff may also be able to obtain a temporary restraining order or preliminary injunction if a prayer for an injunction is joined with the prayer for declaratory relief.

---

[5] Culbertson v. Board of County Comm'rs, 41 P.3d 642 (Utah 2002).

[6] Johnson v. Murzyn, 469 A.2d 1227 (Conn. App. 1984); Joy v. Anne Arundel County, 451 A.2d 1237 (Md. App. 1982); San Miguel v. City of Windcrest, 40 S.W.3d 104 (Tex. App. 2000) (injury need not be shown and violator can be required to comply with ordinance); Utah County v. Baxter, 635 P.2d 61 (Utah 1981). See Utah Code Ann. § 17-27-1002(1)(b) (codifying *Baxter*).

[7] City of East Providence v. Rhode Island Hosp. Trust Nat'l Bank, 505 A.2d 1143 (R.I. 1986); Radach v. Gunderson, 695 P.2d 128 (Wash. App. 1985).

[8] *See* Little Joseph Realty, Inc. v. Town of Babylon, 363 N.E.2d 1163 (N.Y. 1977). *But see* City of Houston v. Tri-Lakes Ltd., 681 So.2d 104 (Miss. 1996) (private citizen cannot bring criminal proceedings).

[9] Hargreaves v. Skrbina, 662 P.2d 1078 (Colo. 1983) (must balance equities); Barton v. H.D. Riders Motorcycle Club, Inc., 550 A.2d 91 (N.H. 1988); Hill Homeowners Ass'n v. City of Passaic, 384 A.2d 172 (N.J. App. Div. 1978); Torbett v. Anderson, 564 S.W.2d 676 (Tenn. App. 1978).

[10] Pinecrest Lakes, Inc. v. Shidel, 705 So.2d 191 (Fla. App. 2001).

Section 2 of the Uniform Declaratory Judgment Act authorizes a declaratory judgment action to challenge zoning and other municipal ordinances. The Act has been widely adopted. Section 2 provides:

Any person . . . whose rights, status or other legal relations are affected by a . . . municipal ordinance . . . may have determined any question of construction or validity arising under the . . . ordinance . . . and obtain a declaration of rights, status or other legal relations thereunder.

The declaratory judgment is especially useful in zoning litigation because it authorizes a declaration of rights even though the plaintiff has not suffered an actual harm. A justiciable controversy is required,[1] and courts may impose a standing requirement. For example, a court may not allow a plaintiff to bring a declaratory judgment to challenge a zoning ordinance as facially unconstitutional if he has not been detrimentally affected by a permit denial or other adverse action.[2]

One court allowed a plaintiff to bring a declaratory judgment action claiming a special exception requirement that applied to its stores was facially invalid, even though it had not applied for or been denied a special exception.[3] The court noted the plaintiff was engaged in the business of obtaining suitable sites for its stores. It held the special exception requirement injured the plaintiff's business because it had to obtain a special exception before it could operate a store at a location it considered appropriate.

If the justiciability requirement is met, the declaratory judgment is available in a wide range of zoning controversies. Plaintiffs may bring declaratory judgment actions to make a facial attack on a zoning ordinance,[4] to challenge the constitutionality of a zoning restriction as applied to their land[5] and to secure

---

[1] Alameda County Land Use Ass'n v. City of Hayward, 45 Cal. Rptr. 2d 752 (Cal. App. 1995); Condiotti v. Board of County Comm'rs, 983 P.2d 184 (Colo. App. 1999) (comprehensive plan amendment held justiciable); County Comm'rs v. Days Cove Reclamation Co., 713 A.2d 351 (Md. App. 1998) (imminent amendment of plan held justiciable); Karches v. Cincinnati, 526 N.E.2d 1350 (Ohio 1988).

[2] City of Scottsdale v. Arizona Sign Ass'n, Inc., 564 P.2d 922 (Ariz. App. 1977) (dismissing challenge to architectural review ordinance when no permit issued or denied under ordinance); United Bank of Denver v. Reed, 635 P.2d 922 (Colo. App. 1981); Northeast Plaza Assocs. v. President & Comm'rs, 526 A.2d 963 (Md. 1987); Woods v. City of Newton, 208 N.E.2d 508 (Mass. 1965); Allen v. Coffel, 488 S.W.2d 671 (Mo. App. 1972); Ewing v. City of Springfield, 449 S.W.2d 681 (Mo. App. 1970); Southern Nat'l Bank v. City of Austin, 582 S.W.2d 229 (Tex. Civ. App. 1979). *But see* Village Creek Property Owners' Ass'n v. Town of Edenton, 520 S.E.2d 793 (N.C. App. 1999) (no special damage or standing requirement).

[3] Board of Supvrs. v. Southland Corp., 297 S.E.2d 718 (Va. 1982).

[4] Bombero v. Planning & Zoning Comm'n, 591 A.2d 390 (Conn. 1991) (certiorari not available).

[5] G.S.T. v. City of Avon Lake, 357 N.E.2d 38 (Ohio 1976); Davis v. Pima County, 590 P.2d 459 (Ariz. App.1978); Agins v. City of Tiburon, 598 P.2d 25 (Cal. 1979), *aff'd on other grounds,* 447 U.S. 255 (1980); Village Creek Property Owners' Ass'n v. Town of Edenton, 520 S.E.2d

an interpretation of a zoning ordinance.[6] A declaratory judgment is not available to test the constitutionality of a zoning map amendment as applied to an individual property if the amendment is characterized as an administrative or quasi-judicial action.[7] Nor is a declaratory judgment available when the zoning statute provides for an alternate and exclusive method of judicial review.[8] In the typical case in which this rule applies, review by way of mandamus or certiorari is available from decisions of the board of adjustment or planning commission.[9]

§ 8.17   Judicial Relief.

Landowner plaintiffs who are successful in zoning litigation quite understandably want a specific judicial remedy that compels the municipality to approve the use they proposed for their land. Specific judicial relief is available in mandamus, in which a court can compel the issuance of a building permit or the exercise of other nondiscretionary acts. A court can also grant specific relief in an appeal or certiorari action that challenges an administrative or quasi-judicial decision by a zoning agency.

Injunction actions present more difficult problems, especially in as-applied taking cases. If a court holds that a zoning restriction is a taking as applied to a property, the usual remedy is a decree invalidating the restriction and ordering the municipality to rezone the property. The court will not order the municipality to rezone the property for a use the court considers appropriate. The municipality may adopt a less restrictive zoning classification for the property that still does not allow the plaintiff's proposed use. The plaintiff must sue again, and the municipality may be able to repeat this strategy even if it loses a second or third time. The majority rule is that specific judicial relief that compels a rezoning is not available in as-applied taking cases.

---

793 (N.C. App. 1999) (claim that conditional rezoning invalid); Driscoll v. Austintown Assocs., 328 N.E.2d 395 (Ohio 1975).

[6] City of Coral Gables v. Hunter, 213 So. 2d 467 (Fla. App. 1968); Thompson v. Hancock County, 531 N.W.2d 181 (Iowa 1995); Rogers v. Town of Norfolk, 734 N.E.2d 1143 (Mass. 2000); Mt. Plainsboro Limited Partnership v. Township of Plainsboro, 719 A.2d 1285 (N.J. App. Div. 1998); 1000 Friends of Or. v. Board of County Comm'rs, 564 P.2d 1080 (Or. App. 1977).

[7] Snyder v. City of Lakewood, 542 P.2d 371 (Colo. 1975); Deffenbaugh Indus., Inc. v. Potts, 802 S.W.2d 520 (Mo. App. 1990). *See also* Taylor v. Swanson, 187 Cal. Rptr. 111 (Cal. App. 1982) (must use administrative mandate).

[8] Farmer's Stone Prods. Co. v. Hoyt, 950 S.W.2d 673 (Mo. App. 1997); Goldstein v. Upper Merion Twp., 403 A.2d 211 (Pa. Commw. 1979).

[9] Livingston Rock & Gravel Co. v. County of Los Angeles, 272 P.2d 4 (Cal. 1954); Contris v. Richmond County, 235 S.E.2d 19 (Ga. 1977); Master Disposal, Inc. v. Village of Menomonee Falls, 211 N.W.2d 477 (Wis. 1973).

§ 8.18   Specific Relief Not Available.

Under the majority rule, a court that holds a zoning restriction invalid in an injunction action can only grant a decree that invalidates the restriction and orders the municipality to rezone. *City of Conway v. Housing Auth.*[1] states the rationale for this rule. The court noted that courts in that state do not have the power to review zoning ordinances "in a de novo manner" and added:

> [I]t follows that the power of the court to review the action of the municipalities is limited to determining whether or not such action was arbitrary, capricious, or wholly inequitable. The judiciary has no right or authority to substitute its judgment for that of the legislative branch of government . . . . Courts are not super zoning commissions and have no authority to classify property according to zones.[2]

Although a court may not order a rezoning under this rule, it may order the municipality to rezone in a constitutional manner.[3] A court may also issue an order reinstating a prior zoning classification if it holds that a downzoning to a less intensive classification is unconstitutional.[4] Courts may also refuse to order a rezoning only in cases in which a constitutionally acceptable zoning alternative is not clear from the facts. On this state of the record, a court has no basis on which to order a rezoning.[5]

§ 8.19   Specific Relief Available.

A number of courts provide specific injunctive relief to successful plaintiffs in as-applied taking cases. Some courts will grant an order that frees the plaintiff's land from any zoning restrictions. In *City of Atlanta v. McLennan*,[1] the court held a trial court should give a municipality a reasonable time to adopt a rezoning that meets constitutional requirements. The trial court could declare the "property free of all zoning restrictions" if the municipality did not act. The court believed

---

[1] 584 S.W.2d 10 (Ark. 1979).

[2] *Id.* at 13. *See also* Mehlhorn v. Pima County, 978 P.2d 117 (Ariz. App. 1999); Guhl v. Holcomb Bridge Rd. Corp., 232 S.E.2d 830 (Ga. 1977); Lenette Realty & Inv. Co. v. City of Chesterfield, 35 S.W.3d 399 (Mo. App. 2001); Hart v. City of Albuquerque, 975 P.2d 366 (N.M. App. 1999); Emjay Props. v. Town of Brookhaven, 347 N.Y.S.2d 736 (Sup. Ct. 1973); City of Rusk v. Cox, 665 S.W.2d 233 (Tex. App. 1984) (may not enjoin future rezoning).

[3] Guhl v. Holcomb Bridge Rd. Corp., 232 S.E.2d 830 (Ga. 1977).

[4] H. Dev. Corp. v. City of Yonkers, 407 N.Y.S.2d 573 (App. Div. 1978).

[5] Seiler v. City of Granite City, 625 N.E.2d 1170 (Ill. App. 1993) (no specific proposal); Sedney v. Lloyd, 410 A.2d 616 (Md. 1980); Garrett v. City of Oklahoma City, 594 P.2d 764 (Okla. 1979). *See also* Alexander v. DeKalb County, 444 S.E.2d 743 (Ga. 1994) (when criminal contempt appropriate).

[1] 226 S.E.2d 732 (Ga. 1976). *See also* State ex rel. Nagawicka Island Corp. v. City of Delafield, 343 N.W.2d 816 (Wis. App. 1983).

this remedy would encourage municipalities to adopt a constitutionally acceptable zoning classification. The disadvantage of this remedy is that it leaves the property unregulated.

An alternative specific remedy relies on the tendency in as-applied taking cases to litigate the suitability of the use proposed by the landowner for the property as well as the uses allowed by the zoning ordinance. A trial court could order the municipality to allow the landowner's proposed use if the proof at the trial shows that it is suitable for its site. An order of this type is no different from an order entered in any case in which a court grants relief based on the facts proved by a successful plaintiff.

Sinclair Pipe Line Co. v. Village of Richton Park[2] adopted a specific remedy of this type:

> [I]t is appropriate for the court to avoid these difficulties by framing its decree with reference to the record before it, and particularly with reference to the evidence offered at trial. . . . In such cases the relief awarded may guarantee that the owner will be allowed to proceed with that use without further litigation and that he will not proceed with a different use.[3]

The court held this relief did not go "beyond the realm of adjudication." The court merely awarded the plaintiff specific relief comparable to the relief available in actions for mandamus and the review of administrative decisions. A number of other courts have held that specific judicial relief of this type is available in zoning cases.[4] In all of these cases, the evidence showed that the use proposed by the plaintiff was the only reasonable use of the land in the area in which it was located.

The Virginia and Florida courts authorize a similar specific remedy when a plaintiff proves that a zoning restriction is a taking as applied to his property. Although the details vary slightly, both courts authorize the trial court to grant a negative injunction rather than an order directing the municipality to rezone. In Florida, the trial court may enjoin the adoption of any zoning classification more restrictive than the use proposed by the plaintiff.[5] In Virginia, the trial court

---

[2] 167 N.E.2d 406 (Ill. 1960). *Accord* Schwartz v. City of Flint, 395 N.W.2d 678 (Mich. 1986).

[3] 167 N.E.2d at 411.

[4] Bryan v. Salmon Corp., 554 S.W.2d 912 (Ky. App. 1977); Trustees Under Will of Pomeroy v. Town of Westlake, 357 So. 2d 1299 (La. App. 1978); Board of County Comm'rs v. Oak Hill Farms, Inc., 192 A.2d 761 (Md. 1963); Vigilant Invs. Corp. v. Town of Hempstead, 312 N.Y.S.2d 1022 (App. Div. 1970); Union Oil Co. of Cal. v. City of Worthington, 405 N.E.2d 277 (Ohio 1980); Lynch v. City of Oklahoma City, 629 P.2d 1289 (Okla. App. 1981); Campbell v. Nance, 555 S.W.2d 407 (Tenn. App. 1976). *See also* Dobson Jamaica Realties v. Town of Brookhaven, 409 N.Y.S.2d 590 (Sup. Ct. 1978) (discriminatory zoning to delay developer).

[5] City of Miami Beach v. Weiss, 217 So. 2d 836 (Fla. 1969); Burritt v. Harris, 172 So. 2d 820 (Fla. 1965).

may grant an injunction prohibiting any municipal action disallowing the plaintiff's use, although the municipality may impose reasonable conditions. If the municipality refuses to comply, the court can make the injunction permanent.[6]

When a court reviews a decision by a zoning board or planning commission in an appeal or certiorari action, judicial review is on the record and the court may order specific relief if the right to such relief is clearly demonstrated.[7] When the board or commission has denied a variance or conditional use, for example, the court can order its approval. A court should remand an appeal to the board or commission if the right to specific relief is not shown.[8]

Some states require the adoption of a comprehensive plan and require zoning to be consistent with the plan. If the zoning that applies to a tract of land is inconsistent with the plan, a court in these states may order the municipality to rezone the tract so that its zoning is consistent with the comprehensive plan.[9]

§ 8.20   Inverse Condemnation.

Inverse condemnation is a remedy a landowner may bring to enforce the taking clause that is included in the federal and most state constitutions. The landowner's condemnation action is "inverse" or "reverse" because he claims a government entity has taken his property but has not paid him the compensation to which he is entitled. Inverse condemnation is an implied constitutional remedy and is self-executing under the federal and most state constitutions. A statute that authorizes the remedy is not required.

The U.S. Supreme Court holds a landowner may bring an inverse condemnation action to secure an award of compensation when a land use regulation is a taking of property.[1] Some state courts have also granted an inverse condemnation remedy. A plaintiff can elect to sue under either the federal or a state constitution or both in state court.

---

[6] City of Richmond v. Randall, 211 S.E.2d 56 (Va. 1975). *But see* Town of Jonesville v. Powell Valley Village Ltd. Partnership, 487 S.E.2d 207 (Va. 1997) (contra, where town previously unzoned). *See also* Board of Supervisors of James City County v. Rowe, 216 S.E.2d 199 (Va. 1975).

[7] *See* American Planning Association, Growing Smart Legislative Guidebook: Model Statutes for Planning and Management of Change § 10-617 (S. Meck ed. 2002) (authorizing definitive relief when land use decision based on record or record appeal is reversed).

[8] Bogue v. Zoning Bd. of Appeals, 345 A.2d 9 (Conn. 1975); Citizens Ass'n of Georgetown v. District of Columbia Bd. of Zoning Adjustment, 403 A.2d 737 (D.C. 1979); Duggan v. County of Cook, 324 N.E.2d 406 (Ill. 1975); Framingham Clinic v. Zoning Bd. of Appeals, 415 N.E.2d 840 (Mass. 1981); Pfile v. Zoning Bd. of Adjustment, 298 A.2d 598 (Pa. Commw. 1972).

[9] § 6.33.

[1] § 8.25

§ 8.21   State Cases: Remedy Available.

Several state cases hold an inverse condemnation remedy for a temporary taking is available in land use cases, and some authorized a state remedy even after the Supreme Court held an inverse condemnation remedy was available under the federal constitution..[1] In many of these cases, a municipality adopted highly restrictive zoning or refused to allow the development of a property and took these actions to depress its value prior to acquisition or to prevent its development.[2] In *Mattoon v. City of Norman*,[3] for example, the plaintiff's land was flooded when the city failed to maintain flood drainage channels. The city then adopted a floodplain ordinance restricting development on plaintiff's land. The plaintiff claimed the city adopted the ordinance to avoid the expense of maintaining the drainage system. Although it held that "a valid enactment of a floodplain ordinance is not a per se taking," the court overruled a demurrer to plaintiff's complaint and held that it stated an action in inverse condemnation.

Other cases approved an inverse condemnation remedy for land use ordinances that imposed severe land use restrictions to preserve open space or vulnerable environmental areas. In *Corrigan v. City of Scottsdale*,[4] the court held the plaintiff was entitled to receive "monetary damages" under the state constitution for a land use ordinance that severely restricted development in a hillside area. Another court held that the reclassification of plaintiff's land to a high flood danger district that precluded any development was a taking that required compensation for the fair market value of her property.[5]

Some of the state courts have held that landowners in taking cases are entitled only to actual losses proved to a reasonable certainty, as in tort cases.[6] This

---

[1] Poirier v. Grand Blanc Twp. (I), 423 N.W.2d 351 (Mich. App. 1988); Whitehead Oil Co. v. City of Lincoln (III), 515 N.W.2d 401 (Neb. 1994); PDR Dev. Corp. v. City of Santa Fe, 900 P.2d 973 (N.M. App. 1995). *But see* Cannone v. Noey, 867 P.2d 797 (Alaska 1994) (normal decision making delay not compensable). *See also* Chesterfield Village, Inc. v. City of Chesterfield, 64 S.W.3d 315 (Mo. 2002)(inverse condemnation claim barred by res judicata because not asserted at time suit brought to declare zoning unconstitutional).

[2] Burrows v. City of Keene, 432 A.2d 15 (N.H. 1981); Scheer v. Township of Evesham, 445 A.2d 46 (N.J. App. Div. 1982); Rippley v. City of Lincoln, 330 N.W.2d 505 (N.D. 1983). For similar pre-*San Diego Gas* cases see Peacock v. County of Sacramento, 77 Cal. Rptr. 391 (Cal. App. 1969); Ventures in Prop. I v. City of Wichita, 594 P.2d 671 (Kan. 1979); City of Austin v. Teague, 570 S.W.2d 389 (Tex. 1978). *See* § 2.23.

[3] 617 P.2d 1347 (Okla. 1980), *distinguished in* April v. City of Broken Arrow, 775 P.2d 1347 (Okla. 1989). *See also* Kraft v. Malone, 313 N.W.2d 758 (N.D. 1981).

[4] 720 P.2d 513 (Ariz. 1986).

[5] Buegel v. City of Grand Forks, 475 N.W.2d 133 (N.D. 1991); Annicelli v. Town of South Kingston, 463 A.2d 133 (R.I. 1983). *See also* Minch v. City of Fargo, 297 N.W.2d 785 (N.D. 1980) (taking of vested right), *on remand,* 322 N.W.2d 71 (N.D. 1983) (vested right not found); Zinn v. State, 334 N.W.2d 67 (Wis. 1983).

[6] Corrigan v. City of Scottsdale, 720 P.2d 513 (Ariz. 1986); Poirier v. Grand Blanc Township

measure of compensation does not appear consistent with the compensation remedy required by the Supreme Court.[7]

§ 8.22 State Cases: Remedy Not Available.

Several state courts hold an inverse condemnation remedy is not available when a court holds that a land use regulation is a taking of property.[1] An action in inverse condemnation under the federal constitution is available in these states, but plaintiffs must be able to show a taking under the federal constitution to invoke the federal remedy.

§ 8.23 Tort Liability.

Local governments historically were liable in tort when they exercised proprietary functions but were immune from liability when they exercised governmental functions. Zoning and planning fell in the governmental category.[1] Court decisions in practically all the states have abolished the governmental-proprietary distinction. The present basis for local government tort liability varies, but local governments are usually liable in tort in the exercise of ministerial functions but immune from liability in the exercise of discretionary functions.[2] Some state statutes authorizing tort suits against municipalities and their officials also apply in zoning actions.[3] Statutes may also confer an immunity in tort for

(II), 481 N.W.2d 762 (Mich. App. 1992); City of Austin v. Teague, 570 S.W.2d 389 (Tex. 1978). *See also* Miller Bros. v. Department of Nat. Resources, 513 N.W.2d 217 (Mich. App. 1994) (measure of compensation for loss of oil and gas rights).

[7] § 8.26.

[1] Agins v. City of Tiburon, 598 P.2d 25 (Cal. 1979), *aff'd on other grounds,* 447 U.S. 255 (1980); Snyder v. City of Lakewood, 542 P.2d 371 (Colo. 1975); Dade County v. National Bulk Carriers, Inc., 450 So. 2d 213 (Fla. 1984); Van Duyne v. City of Crest Hill, 483 N.E.2d 1307 (Ill. App. 1985) (plaintiff purchased with knowledge of zoning); Jack v. City of Olathe, 781 P.2d 1069 (Kan. 1989) (refusing to imply remedy from statute); Kraiser v. Horsham Twp., 455 A.2d 782 (Pa. Commw. 1983).

[1] Paedae v. Escambia County, 709 So.2d 575 (Fla. App. 1998) (no liability for governmental function of issuing or refusing to issue permits); City of Rochester Hills v. Six Star, Ltd., 423 N.W.2d 322 (Mich. App. 1988) (enforcement of zoning ordinance); Baucom's Nursery Co. v. Mecklenburg Cty., 366 S.E.2d 558 (N.C. App. 1988) (adoption and enforcement of zoning ordinance).

[2] Village of Bloomingdale v. C.D.G. Enters., 732 N.E.2d 633 (Ill. App. 2000) (no exception to statutory immunity for actions based on corrupt or malicious motives); Willow Creek Ranch, L.L.C. v. Town of Shelby, 611 N.W.2d 693 (Wis. 2000) (enforcing a zoning ordinance immune as discretionary legislative act).

[3] Ga. Code Ann. §§ 36-33-4, 36-33-1(b). *See* City of Buford v. Ward, 443 S.E.2d 279 (Ga. App. 1994) (cause of action shown under statute when condition on certificate of occupancy not authorized by law); Staubes v. City of Folly Beach, 500 S.E.2d 160 (S.C. App. 1998) (under act providing exception to immunity, complaint stated claim for gross negligence in revocation of building permit). *See also* 65 Ill. Comp. Stat. 5/11-12-8 (monetary liability for wilful failure to act on subdivision plat in time prescribed.)

actions taken under a land use regulation unless there is wilful misconduct or bad faith.[4]

The courts have classified many land use control functions, such as subdivision and site plan review and rezonings, as discretionary.[5] Tort liability can arise in the exercise of discretionary functions if a court finds an interference with contractual relations, even though a developer has not acquired a vested right. An example is a rezoning to block a housing project after the developer enters into a contract for governmental financial assistance.[6] Actions not requiring the exercise of discretion, such as the issuance of a building permit to which an applicant is entitled, are nondiscretionary.[7] A court may impose liability for the negligent exercise of a discretionary function,[8] and deny liability for the exercise

---

[4] Cal. Gov't Code § 821.2, *applied in* Brown v. City of Los Angeles, 73 Cal. Rptr. 364 (Cal. App. 1968) (no liability for erroneous issuance of enforcement notice); Conn. Gen. Stat. § 52-557n(b)(7); Ga. Code Ann. § 51-1-2, *applied in* Dyches v. McCorkle, 441 S.E.2d 518 (Ga. App. 1994) (no liability for denial of subdivision application); 745 Ill. Comp. Stat. Ann. 10/2-104 (injury caused by denial or failure to issue permit), applied in Village of Blommingdale v. CDG Enters., Inc., 752 N.E.2d 1090 (Ill. 2001) (failure to rezone; no exception for wilful conduct).N.J. Stat. Ann. §§ 59:2-5, 59:3-6.

[5] City of Seymour v. Onyx Paving Co., 541 N.E.2d 951 (Ind. App. 1989) (enforcement of zoning ordinance); Veling v. Borough of Ramsey, 228 A.2d 873 (N.J. App. Div. 1967) (zoning amendment); Della Villa v. Constantino, 668 N.Y.S.2d 724 (App. Div. 1998) (numerous acts); C & D Partnership v. City of Gahanna, 747 N.E.2d 303 (Ohio 1984) (subdivision approval); Hodges v. Reid, 836 S.W.2d 120 (Tenn. App. 1992); Young v. Jewish Welfare Fed'n, 371 S.W.2d 767 (Tex. Civ. App. 1963) (site plan review); Grader v. City of Lynwood, 767 P.2d 952 (Wash. App. 1989) (zoning ordinance interpretation held quasi-judicial); Willow Creek Ranch, LLC v. Town of Shelby, 611 N.W.2d 693 (Wis. 2000) (veto of permit and enforcement of ordinance). *See also* Trianon Park Condo. Ass'n v. City of Hialeah, 468 So. 2d 912 (Fla. 1985) (enforcement of regulatory laws); Snyder v. City of Minneapolis, 441 N.W.2d 781 (Minn. 1989) (no discretionary immunity when applicant did not have knowledge of restriction on property); Alger v. City of Mukilteo, 730 P.2d 1333 (Wash. 1987) (appearance of fairness doctrine). *But see* Win-Tasch Corp. v. Town of Merrimack, 411 A.2d 144 (N.H. 1980) (no immunity if municipality acts in bad faith). *Compare* Loveland v. Orem City Corp., 746 P.2d 763 (Utah 1987) (subdivision review held governmental).

[6] Mesolella v. City of Providence, 508 A.2d 661 (R.I. 1986). *See also* River Park, Inc. v. City of Highland Park, 667 N.E.2d 499 (Ill. App. 1996). *Compare* Pleas v. City of Seattle, 774 P.2d 1158 (Wash. 1989) (city liable in tort for abuse of zoning process).

[7] Winters v. City of Commerce City, 648 P.2d 175 (Colo. App. 1982) (denial of building permit); Alger v. City of Mukilteo, 730 P.2d 1333 (Wash. 1987) (permit revocation);Sundberg v. Evans, 897 P.2d 1285 (Wash. App. 1995) (providing information on zoning restrictions nondiscretionary). Sundberg v. Evans, 897 P.2d 1285 (Wash. App. 1995) (providing information on zoning restrictions nondiscretionary). *See also* J. Gregcin, Inc. v. City of Dayton, 593 P.2d 1231 (Or. App. 1979) (failure to comply with subdivision statute), *confirmed on remand,* 615 P.2d 419 (Or. App. 1980); Cox v. City of Lynwood, 863 P.2d 578 (Wash. App. 1993) (interpreting statute providing cause of action for unlawful denial of building permit).

[8] Pickle v. Board of Cty. Comm'rs, 764 P.2d 262 (Wyo. 1988) (water and septic tank system failure).

of a nondiscretionary function if the tort liability statute expressly makes the function immune.[9] Damages are also available for tortious interference with prospective contractual relationships.[10]

Tort liability may also arise when a landowner suffers damage when she relies on an action by a municipality or its official that turns out to be incorrect. For example, a municipality may mistakenly issue and then revokes a building permit after the permit holder has relied on it by proceeding with construction.[11] Some courts deny tort liability in these cases because of the rule that a municipality is not liable for negligence in the performance of duties owed to the general public as a whole rather than to a particular individual.[12] Other courts impose liability in these cases. Some apply ordinary principles of tort law to these claims because they believe that the abolition of tort immunity in the exercise of governmental functions abolished the public duty rule.[13]

Other courts adhere to the public duty rule but find liability if there is a "special relationship" between the public agency and the person harmed.[14] Courts apply the special relationship rule to find liability to a third party who was clearly protected by a land use ordinance.[15] The causation rule is also applied, and courts deny liability if the municipality was not the cause of the damage for which suit is brought.[16]

Landowners argued for tort liability based on exceptions to the public duty rule in other cases in which they suffered damage from the implementation of municipal regulations. One court denied liability under the public duty rule when a plaintiff sued for damages caused by excessive water run-off from an adjacent development allegedly caused by improper enforcement of a county development ordinance.[17] Other courts denied liability when a landowner was unable to carry

[9] Johnson v. County of Essex, 538 A.2d 448 (N.J.L. Div. 1987). *But see* Lutheran Day Care v. Snohomish Cty., 829 P.2d 746 (Wash. 1992).

[10] L.A. Ray Realty v. Town Council, 698 A.2d 202 (R.I. 1997).

[11] *See also* § 6.17.

[12] Biser v. Deibel, 739 A.2d 948 (Md. App. 1999) (no express assurance by official); Allen v. City & County of Honolulu, 571 P.2d 328 (Haw. 1977); Hunter v. City of Cleveland, 564 N.E.2d 718 (Ohio App. 1988) (improper reliance).

[13] Dykeman v. State, 593 P.2d 1183 (Or. App. 1979). *See also* Adams v. State, 555 P.2d 235 (Alaska 1976).

[14] Taylor v. Stevens County, 759 P.2d 447 (Wash. 1988). *See also* Frustuck v. City of Fairfax, 28 Cal Rptr. 357 (Cal. App. 1963); 41 A.L.R.4th 99 (1985). *But see* Myers v. Moore Engineering, Inc., 42 F.3d 452 (8th Cir. 1994); Cootey v. Sun Inv. Co., 718 P.2d 1086 (Hawaii 1986).

[15] Charlie Brown Constr. Co. v. City of Boulder City, 797 P.2d 946 (Nev. 1990).

[16] Kuriakuz v. West Bloomfield Township, 492 N.W.2d 797 (Mich. App. 1992) (no liability for water damage from adjacent development based solely on omission in approving site plan).

[17] Pepper v. J.J. Welcome Constr. Co., 871 P.2d 601 (Wash. App. 1994). *See also* Stillwater Condominium Ass'n v. Town of Salem, 668 P.2d 38 (N.H. 1995) (no duty to enforce subdivision regulations).

out a land use for which she had received a municipal permit on advice that the development was permitted.[18]

D. FEDERAL REMEDIES.

§ 8.24 Inverse Condemnation.

§ 8.25 When Available.

After passing up two opportunities to resolve the inverse condemnation remedy problem, the Supreme Court finally held in *First English Evangelical Lutheran Church v. County of Los Angeles*[1] that an inverse condemnation remedy is available in land use taking cases. A forest fire destroyed a large portion of a watershed in which plaintiff's campground buildings were located. The county then adopted an interim ordinance prohibiting the construction or reconstruction of any building in a flood protection area that included the plaintiff's property. The plaintiff brought an inverse condemnation action for compensation in state court and claimed that the interim ordinance denied it "all use" of its property. The California trial and appellate courts struck those portions of the complaint in which the plaintiff asked for compensation. They did not decide the taking issue.

The Supreme Court, in an opinion by then Justice Rehnquist, held an inverse condemnation was available. His opinion did not contain the discussion of policy reasons for the inverse condemnation remedy found in Justice Brennan's dissent in *San Diego Gas & Elec. Co. v. San Diego,*[2] where the majority refused to decide the inverse condemnation issue, and Justice Brennan argued in dissent that inverse condemnation should be available. Neither did *First English* elaborate on the rules for measuring compensation, or for determining the period of time during which a temporary taking should be held to have occurred.

The Court confirmed the rule it had adopted in earlier cases, that the taking clause is self-executing and requires compensation when a government takes property. The Court held a taking may occur without "formal proceedings" and rejected a claim that allowing an inverse condemnation remedy in land use taking cases would inhibit land use planning. Compensation is required in land use taking cases because invalidation of the ordinance is not a "sufficient remedy."

---

[18] Lehman v. City of Louisville, 857 P.2d 455 (Colo. App. 1993) (plaintiffs unable to carry out home occupation after renovating building in reliance on advice that use was permitted); Brady Dev. Co. v. Town of Hilton Head Island, 439 S.E.2d 366 (S.C. 1993) (developer unable to get water service after permit issued; also assumed risk). *See also* Millerick v. Village of Tinley Park, 652 N.E.2d 17 (Ill. App. 1995) (no special duty when officials incorrectly advised about soil condition of property).

[1] 482 U.S. 304 (1987).

[2] 450 U.S. 621 (1981).

The Court held a landowner can receive compensation for the temporary interference with use that occurred while the ordinance was in effect but cannot demand compensation for a permanent taking:

> Once a court determines that a taking has occurred, the government retains the whole range of functions already available — amendment of the regulation, withdrawal of the invalidated regulation, or exercise of eminent domain. . . . [But] no subsequent action by the government can relieve it of the duty to provide compensation for the period during which the taking was effective.[3]

The Court limited the availability of the inverse condemnation remedy to the "facts presented," and noted the plaintiff claimed the ordinance denied it "all use" of its property. Several references to the denial of the "all use" claim appear throughout the decision. These statements could mean that compensation is available only if a court holds a land use regulation denies a landowner "all use" of his property. Most land use regulations do not fall in this category. They permit some uses but prohibit others. A zoning ordinance that permits single-family but prohibits multifamily uses is an example. Compensation would not be payable if a court held the multifamily prohibition was a taking because the single-family restriction did not deny the property owner "all use" of his property.

The Court's holding in *First English* is limited to the compensation remedy. It did not hold the interim moratorium was a taking. It remanded the case for a decision on the merits and indicated that the denial of "all use" under the moratorium might be constitutional as part of the government's authority to adopt safety regulations. The Court also held it did not have to deal with the "quite different questions" raised by normal delays in obtaining building permits, zoning changes, variances, "and the like," which were not before it. On remand the California court held the ordinance constitutional.[4] The Supreme Court has now held a moratorium adopted to provide time to prepare a comprehensive plan was not a categorical per se taking. It held that the prohibition on development during the time the moratorium was in effect was not a facial taking.[5]

§ 8.26 Availability and Measure of Compensation.

Some state cases have denied compensation by applying the dictum in *First English* that compensation is not payable unless the landowner has been denied "all use" of her property.[1] These cases mean compensation is not payable in

---

[3] *Id.* at 421.

[4] § 12.09.

[5] Tahoe-Sierra Preservation Council, Inc. v. Tahoe Regional Planning Agency, 535 U.S. 302 (2002).

[1] Cline v. City of Clarksville, 746 S.W.2d 56 (Ark. 1988); Cobb Cty. v. McColister, 413 S.E.2d 441 (Ga. 1992); Lake Forest Chateau v. City of Lake Forest, 549 N.E.2d 336 (Ill. 1990); The Shopco Group v. City of Springdale, 586 N.E.2d 145 (Ohio App.), *cause dismissed,* 563 N.E.2d

the common case in which a court holds unconstitutional a zoning restriction that allows the landowner to put the property to some use, such as single-family residential development. However, some courts do not require a denial of all use of the property.[2]

The Supreme Court has held that the rental value of property during a temporary taking is the correct measure of compensation.[3] The court of appeals in *Wheeler v. City of Pleasant Grove (III)*[4] adopted the rental value standard. The city adopted an ordinance prohibiting apartments in the city when strong community opposition arose after plaintiffs obtained a building permit for an apartment project. The court held a property owner's loss in a temporary taking case is the injury to the property's potential for producing an income or profit as measured by the rate of return on the loss in market value caused by the regulatory restriction. The court did not award compensation for lost profits or increased development costs as this would be a double recovery for losses reflected in the loss in market value. The court also held an increase in value that occurred while the building prohibition was in effect should not be considered. The court of appeals reaffirmed its earlier holding in later appeal after the district court refused to award compensation on remand.[5] It awarded compensation at the market rate of return for the temporary taking period on plaintiff's 25 percent equity in the "complex," which they had the right to control.

Wheeler did not consider the uncertainty that the project proposed by the developer might not have been constructed. This may be incorrect.[6] Courts do

302 (Ohio 1992); Miller & Son Paving, Inc. v. Plumstead Township, 717 A.2d 483 (Pa. 1998); Stoner v. Township of Lower Merion, 587 A.2d 879 (Pa. Commw. 1991) (refusal to approve subdivision); Staubes v. City of Folly Beach, 500 S.E.2d 160 (S.C. App. 1998). *See also* McCutchan Estates Corp. v. Evansville-Vanderburgh Cty. Airport Auth. Dist., 580 N.E.2d 339 (Ind. App. 1991) (nine month administrative delay in subdivision approval). *Contra* Whitehead Oil Co. v. City of Lincoln (III), 515 N.W.2d 401 (Neb. 1994).

[2] Cannone v. Noey, 867 P.2d 797 (Alaska 1994); Poirier v. Grand Blanc Tp., 423 N.W.2d 351, 352–53 (Mich. App. 1988). *See also* Steinbergh v. City of Cambridge, 604 N.E.2d 1269 (Mass. 1992); Clay County By & Through County Comm'n v. Bogue, 988 S.W.2d 102 (Mo. App. 1999)/

[3] Kimball Laundry Co. v. United States, 338 U.S. 1 (1949). *See also* Lopes v. City of Peabody, 718 N.E.2d 846 (Mass. 1999) (property owner entitled to reimbursement of real estate taxes paid during temporary taking period)..

[4] 833 F.2d 267 (11th Cir. 1987). *See also* Nemmers v. City of Dubuque, 764 F.2d 502 (8th Cir. 1985) (downzoning; court applied similar compensation measure); Whitehead Oil Co. v. City of Lincoln (III), 515 N.W.2d 401 (Neb. 1994).

[5] Wheeler v. City of Pleasant Grove (IV), 896 F.2d 1347 (11th Cir. 1990).

[6] *See* Goss v. City of Little Rock, 151 F.3d 861 (8th Cir. 1998) (failure to rezone property without dedication requirement not compensable); Corn v. City of Lauderdale Lakes, 771 F. Supp. 1557 (S.D. Fla. 1991), *aff'd and rev'd in part and remanded*, 997 F.2d 1369 (11th Cir. 1993). *See also* Walcek v. United States, 303 F.3d 1356 (Fed. Cir. 2002) (need not adjust value of property for inflation).

not usually compensate for lost profits on uncertainties. They usually pay compensation on the fair market value of land for its "highest and best" use. Under this approach, the court should have considered alternative uses for the property that qualified as its highest and best use. This test does not mean that the land would have been valued at its existing use. Courts may consider a potential use of the land that probable zoning change would allow if the use is not speculative.

A federal district court adopted a formula in a substantive due process case for computing damages in situations of uncertainty when the issue was the probability that a subdivision would be approved.[7] The Court of Federal Claims awarded compensation for the denial of a permit to develop wetlands based on a land development cost approach as a method for determining market value. This approach considers the predicted sales revenue from selling a property as offset by the costs of development during that time.[8] The Eleventh Circuit has held that a market value test is to be used when there is a permanent taking of property. In cases of a partial taking, a modified market value test is applied that subtracts the market value of the property as restricted by the regulation from the market value without the regulation in place.[9]

§ 8.27 Trial by Jury.

In *City of Monterey v. Del Monte Dunes*,[1] the Supreme Court held that plaintiffs in § 1983 cases are entitled to a jury trial. It reserved judgment on whether a jury trial is required in inverse condemnation actions. The Court based its holding on the Seventh Amendment, which guarantees a right to trial by jury in actions at law, by holding that an action under § 1983 that seeks legal relief falls in this category. It held a jury trial is available on the second prong of the *Agins* test, which finds a taking if a land use regulation deprives a landowner of all economically viable use of his land. This prong raises fact-bound issues that juries can decide.

The Court then stated that whether a jury trial must be had on the first prong of the *Agins* takings test, which asks whether a land use regulation serves a legitimate governmental interest, is a "more difficult" question. It held this issue can properly be submitted to a jury in some circumstances, and that the first prong issue was legitimately submitted to the jury. The Court then held it was

---

[7] Herrington v. County of Sonoma, 790 F. Supp. 909 (N.D. Cal. 1991, aff'd, 12 F.3d 901 (9th Cir. 1993). *See also* City of Austin v. Teague, 570 S.W.2d 389 (Tex. 1978).

[8] Cooley v. United States, 45 Fed. Ct. 438 (2000) (also considering effect on valuation of presence of developers in the buyers' market).

[9] A.A. Profiles, Inc. v. City of Fort Lauderdale, 253 F.3d 546 (11th Cir. 2001). *See also* SDDS, Inc. v. State, 650 N.W.2d 1 (2002) (interest difference on present value of cash flow with and without delay in use for landfill).

[1] 526 U.S. 687 (1999). *See* § 2.13.

not offering a "precise demarcation" of the role of judge and jury in deciding first prong questions. A "broad challenge" to a land use regulation, or a claim that a regulation was unreasonable as applied, might well be for the judge. First prong issues were for the jury in this case because the "questions were whether the government had denied a constitutional right in acting outside the bounds of its authority."[2]

Although *Del Monte* provides guidelines on the right to a jury trial in inverse condemnation cases, its practical importance is limited. Plaintiffs must bring as-applied takings cases in state courts in most instances,[3] and state courts are not bound by the Seventh Amendment.[4]

§ 8.28 Section 1983 of the Federal Civil Rights Act.

§ 8.29 Scope of the Statute.

Section 1983 of the federal Civil Rights Act of 1871 provides:

Every person who, under color of any statute, ordinance, regulation, custom or usage, of any State . . ., subjects, or causes to be subjected, any citizen of the United States or other person within the jurisdiction thereof to the deprivation of any rights, privileges or immunities secured by the Constitution and laws, shall be liable to the party injured in an action at law, suit in equity, or other proper proceeding for redress.

Section 1983 authorizes a cause of action for the violation of any constitutional right, including substantive due process and equal protection violations.

Section 1983 assumed new importance in land use cases after the U.S. Supreme Court held, in *Monell v. Department of Social Serv.*,[1] that municipalities can be sued under § 1983. Section 1983 is not available in unconsented actions against the state.[2] The Civil Rights Attorney's Fees Award Act[3] authorizes prevailing plaintiffs and defendants to recover attorney's fees in § 1983 actions.

In *Maine v. Thiboutot*,[4] the Supreme Court held that the phrase "and laws" in § 1983 applies to any federal law. This decision opened up the possibility for § 1983 land use actions based on federal land use legislation, such as the National Coastal Zone Management Act. The Court limited *Thiboutot* in later

---

[2] *See* Buckles v. King County, 191 F.3d 1127 (9th Cir. 1999) (spot zoning case distinguishing *Del Monte* and holding legitimacy of governmental interest was for the court).

[3] § 2.36.

[4] County of El Dorado v. Schneider, 237 Cal. Rptr. 51 (Cal. App. 1987).

[1] 436 U.S. 658 (1978).

[2] Quern v. Jordon, 440 U.S. 332 (1979).

[3] 42 U.S.C. § 1988.

[4] 448 U.S. 1 (1980).

decisions. It held a § 1983 action cannot be brought to enforce nonsubstantive declarations of statutory policy.[5] Nor may § 1983 be used to enforce a federal statute that contains its own specific remedy.[6]

The Supreme Court has held that property rights are one of the "rights" protected by § 1983.[7] Landowners do not usually have difficulty showing that they have property rights protected under § 1983,[8] especially when they claim that a land use regulation unconstitutionally restricts the use of their property.[9]

An intent to violate the constitution is not required for liability under § 1983,[10] but procedural due process liability attaches only for intentional and not for negligent deprivations.[11]

§ 8.30   Land Use Cases Not Actionable Under § 1983.

Though the § 1983 remedy is available for any violation of the federal constitution, some lower federal courts hold a cause of action does not lie under § 1983 even though the plaintiffs claimed a land use decision violated the constitution. In most of these cases, the municipality denied the plaintiff a land use permit or other land use approval and the plaintiff made a substantive due process claim. *Creative Env'ts, Inc. v. Estabrook*[1] is a leading case. The plaintiff claimed a municipality violated the due process clause when it rejected the plaintiff's subdivision application for erroneous reasons and by misapplying state law and local regulations including a vague environmental study regulation and a misinterpretation of open space requirements. The court disagreed:

> But were such a theory to be accepted, any hope of maintaining a meaningful separation between federal and state jurisdiction in this and many other areas of law would be jettisoned. Virtually every alleged legal or procedural error of a local planning authority or zoning board of appeal could be brought to a federal court on the theory that the erroneous application of state law amounted to a taking of property without due process. Neither Congress nor the courts have, to date, indicated that section 1983 should have such a reach.[2]

---

[5] Pennhurst State School & Hosp. v. Halderman, 451 U.S. 1 (1981), *extended in* Suter v. Artist M., 503 U.S. 347 (1992). *See also* Gonzaga Univ. v. Doe, 536 U.S. 273 (2002) (right of action not found).

[6] Middlesex County Sewerage Auth. v. National Sea Clammers Ass'n, 453 U.S. 1 (1981).

[7] Lynch v. Household Fin. Corp., 405 U.S. 538 (1972).

[8] McCulloch v. City of Glasgow, 620 F.2d 47 (5th Cir. 1980).

[9] *See also* §§ 2.42, 2.44 (whether landowner must have entitlement to property in due process cases).

[10] Monroe v. Pape, 365 U.S. 167 (1961).

[11] Daniels v. Williams, 474 U.S. 327 (1986) (negligent deprivations not covered); Hudson v. Palmer, 468 U.S. 517 (1984) (intentional deprivations covered).

[1] 680 F.2d 822 (1st Cir. 1982).

[2] *Id.* at 861.

The court held the plaintiff's claim was too typical of a "run of the mill" land use dispute to give rise to a due process violation, and that a conventional planning dispute does not implicate the federal constitution. Giving a state law claim a constitutional label does not create a cause of action under § 1983.The court indicated it would hold differently in cases of "egregious" behavior or where there was a "gross abuse of power, invidious discrimination, or fundamentally unfair procedures." Other circuits have followed *Creative Environments*,[3] but the Supreme Court has not considered this issue in a land use case.

§ 8.31   Color of Law, Policy, and Custom.

Section 1983 makes a violation of the constitution actionable only if carried out under "color of any statute, ordinance, regulation, custom, or usage" of a governmental entity. The "color of law" requirement is similar to the "state action" requirement the courts apply in fourteenth amendment cases and usually is not troublesome in § 1983 land use litigation.[1]

Monell refused to adopt a respondeat superior theory of municipal liability under § 1983. It interpreted the "custom and usage" requirement in § 1983 to mean that local governments are liable only for actions that are "official policy" or "visited pursuant to a governmental custom," but did not fully explain these terms. The custom or usage requirement is not a problem in most land use cases because a governmental body, such as the legislative body, usually is responsible for the governmental action.[2] More difficult problems arise in § 1983 cases that challenge the action of a zoning official.

There must be an act by a municipal policymaker to establish municipal liability. The Supreme Court had earlier defined a policy as a deliberate choice to follow a course of action from among various alternatives.[3] In *Pembaur v. City of Cincinnati*,[4] a plurality held a policy includes unwritten as well as formal plans of action, and that a single action is enough to establish policy. The plurality then narrowed municipal liability by holding municipal liability can attach only for an "official policy" made by an authorized decision maker. A majority of the Court found an official policy in a state statute that clearly delegated to a

---

[3] Gardner v. City of Baltimore Mayor & City Council, 959 F.2d 63 (4th Cir. 1992); Chesterfield Dev. Corp. v. City of Chesterfield, 963 F.2d 1102 (8th Cir. 1992); Coniston Corp. v. Village of Hoffman Estates, 844 F.2d 461 (7th Cir. 1988); Hynes v. Pasco County, 801 F.2d 1269 (11th Cir. 1986); Smith v. City of Picayune, 795F.2d 482 (5th Cir. 1986).

[1] *But see* Fantasy Book Shop v. City of Boston, 531 F. Supp. 821 (D. Mass. 1982).

[2] Video Int'l Prods., Inc. v. Warner-Amex Cable Communications, Inc., 858 F.2d 1075 (5th Cir. 1988) (board of adjustment); Bateson v. Geisse, 857 F.2d 1300 (9th Cir. 1988) (governing body); Altaire Bldrs., Inc. v. Village of Horseheads, 551 F. Supp. 1066 (W.D.N.Y. 1982).

[3] City of Oklahoma v. Tuttle, 471 U.S. 808 (1985) (municipalities not liable for random acts by low-level city employees).

[4] 475 U.S. 469 (1986).

county prosecutor the authority to order a break-in to carry out arrests, but a majority could not agree on a further elaboration of the official policy requirement. Several land use cases applied *Pembaur*.[5]

City of St. Louis v. Praprotnik,[6] a public employee discharge case decided after *Pembaur*, was again a plurality decision. The plurality confirmed a statement in *Pembaur* that the identification of policymaking officials is a matter of state law. It was "confident" that state or local law "will always direct a court to some official or body that has the responsibility for making law or setting policy." The plurality added that an official's action is not final policy when it is constrained by "policies not of his making" or subject to review by authorized policymakers unless these policymakers ratify his decision.

The Court confirmed the *Pembaur* and *Praprotnik* plurality decisions in *Board of County Comm'rs v. Brown*,[7] an excessive force case. However, ambiguities in these decisions have made it difficult for courts to determine when a "custom or policy" exists in land use cases. A court is likely to find a custom or policy when a local agency with final authority, such as a board of adjustment[8] or legislative body,[9] has affirmed an official decision. When an official decision is appealable but has not been appealed, courts are likely to reach a contrary decision.[10]

§ 8.32 Fault and Causation.

The Supreme Court's holding that courts should interpret § 1983 against a "background of tort liability"[1] means that a plaintiff who has suffered a constitutional violation must show that government was at fault and that it caused the violation. As the Court has explained, fault and causation do not present a problem when the municipal action itself violated federal law or directed or authorized the deprivation of federal rights.[2] For this reason, fault and causation

---

[5] 805 F.2d 81 (2d Cir. 1986). Lake Nacimiento Ranch Co. v. County of San Luis Obispo, 841 F.2d 872 (9th Cir. 1987); Sullivan v. Town of Salem, 805 F.2d 81 (2d Cir. 1986). *See also* Coogan v. City of Wixom, 820 F.2d 170 (6th Cir. 1987).

[6] 485 U.S. 112 (1988).

[7] 520 U.S. 397 (1997).

[8] Bannum, Inc. v. City of Ft. Lauderdale, 901 F.2d 989 (11th Cir. 1990). *See also* Burkhart Advertising, Inc. v. City of Auburn, 786 F. Supp. 721 (N.D. Ind. 1991) (mayor signed ordinance).

[9] Browning-Ferris Indus., Inc. v. City of Maryland Heights, 747 F. Supp. 1340 (E.D. Mo. 1990) (council ratification); Lutheran Day Care v. Snohomish Cty., 829 P.2d 746 (Wash. 1992) (council denial of conditional use).

[10] Kawaoka v. City of Arroyo Grande, 17 F.3 d1227 (9th Cir. 1994) (racially discriminatory statements); Arroyo Vista Partners v. County of Santa Barbara, 732 F. Supp. 1046 (C.D. Cal. 1990) (ward courtesy system); Carr v. Town of Dewey Beach, 730 F. Supp. 591 (D. Del. 1990).

[1] Monroe v. Pape, 365 U.S. 167, 187 (1961).

[2] Board of County Comm'rs v. Brown, 520 U.S. 397 (1997). *See also* Tahoe-Sierra Preservation Council, Inc. v. Tahoe Regional Planning Agency, 535 U.S. 302 (2002) (Rehnquist, C.J., dissenting; agency was moving force behind and caused injury imposed by moratorium).

are not a problem in most land use cases because a legislative or administrative body is usually responsible for the constitutional deprivation.[3]

Fault and causation problems can arise if it is not clear whether the municipal conduct caused the constitutional deprivation. *Westborough Mall, Inc. v. City of Cape Girardeau (I)*[4] is an example. The court held the plaintiff's inability to build its shopping center was caused by financial problems and the plaintiff's poor business sills, not the city's reversion of its commercial zoning.

§ 8.33   Exhaustion and Adequacy of State Remedies.

The Supreme Court does not require exhaustion of administrative remedies in § 1983 actions.[1] This rule is qualified by *Parratt v. Taylor*.[2] *Parratt* held that the plaintiff could not bring a § 1983 procedural due process action in federal court for the negligent loss of a hobby kit by prison officials because post-deprivation state tort remedies provided an adequate remedy. The Court held that a state need not provide a pre-deprivation hearing when a loss is caused by "a random and unauthorized act by a state employee" because the state cannot "predict precisely" in these cases when a loss will occur. Negligence claims are no longer actionable under § 1983, but the *Parratt* holding on post-deprivation state remedies is still good law in procedural due process cases.

The Court qualified *Parratt* in *Logan v. Zimmerman Brush Co.*[3] A state court dismissed the plaintiff's fair employment practice claim before a state agency because the agency did not convene a hearing in the required statutory time period. The Court held that the plaintiff's right to use the state statutory procedures was protected by the due process clause. He did not have to use post-deprivation state tort remedies because the deprivation was caused by the "state system itself." The plaintiff challenged the "established state procedure," not the state agency's error.

The *Parratt-Logan* distinction is difficult to apply in land use cases. In a zoning variance case, for example, a procedural due process violation is both a "random

---

[3] Bannum v. City of Louisville, 958 F.2d 1354 (6th Cir. 1992) (inability to comply with zoning ordinance caused recission of contract); Bateson v. Geisse, 857 F.2d 1300 (9th Cir. 1988) (wrongful withholding of building permit); Schneider v. City of Ramsey, 800 F. Supp. 815 (D. Minn. 1992) (plaintiff voluntarily closed bookstore rather than face prosecution).

[4] Westborough Mall, Inc. v. City of Cape Girardeau (IV), 953 F.2d 345 (8th Cir. 1991). *See also* Muckway v. Craft, 789 F.2d 517 (7th Cir.1986) (refusal to enforce zoning ordinance); Roma Constr. Co. v. Russo, 906 F. Supp.78 (D. R.I. 1995) (bribe); B. Street Commons, Inc. v. Board of County Comm'rs, 835 F. Supp. 1266 (D. Colo. 1993) (ill-considered business acts).

[1] Patsy v. Florida Bd. of Regents, 457 U.S. 496 (1982). *See* Scudder v. Town of Greendale, 704 F.2d 999 (7th Cir. 1983).

[2] 451 U.S. 527 (1981). *See* Littlefield v. City of Afton, 785 F.2d 596 (8th Cir. 1986). *See also* § 2.32.

[3] 455 U.S. 422 (1982).

and unauthorized" act by the zoning board that triggers *Parratt* and an application of "established state procedure" that triggers *Logan*. One court applied *Parratt* to dismiss a § 1983 case in which the plaintiff sued a municipality after it issued a stop construction order.[4] The order was issued because the zoning enforcement officer made a mistake when he issued the building permit. The court held that a post-deprivation state remedy was adequate because the "alleged default" was like the negligent loss in *Parratt*. The court held that *Logan* rather than *Parratt* applied in a similar case because it held that "the effect on plaintiff of the established state procedures" created the constitutional deprivation.[5]

The Supreme Court substantially qualified *Parratt* in *Zinermon v. Burch*[6] and held that the *Parratt* rule applies only to procedural due process claims. Plaintiff in *Zinermon* brought a § 1983 action in which he claims a procedural due process violation based on his claim that his admission to a state mental health facility was not voluntary. The Court held that the *Parratt* bar is not absolute. Instead, a court must apply a balancing test in which it first identifies the risk involved and then evaluates the effectiveness of pre-deprivation safeguards in relationship to the risk identified. The Court held that the risk in *Zinermon* was predictable, the state could have provided pre-deprivation process and state officials had the authority to make this process available.

Zinermon should mean that *Parratt* should not bar most land use cases in which procedural due process claims are made. The risk of a procedural deprivation is predictable in the decision-making process, and adequate procedures are authorized. One court held that *Zinermon* does not change the *Parratt* rules,[7] and courts have also held a pre-deprivation hearing was not required when adequate post-deprivation procedures were available.[8] Other cases relied on *Zinermon* to hold a pre-deprivation hearing should have been provided,[9] or have held a pre-deprivation hearing was required because the plaintiff was challenging an established procedure or policy.[10]

---

[4] Albery v. Reddig, 718 F.2d 245 (7th Cir. 1983). *Accord* Lake Naciemento Ranch Co. v. County of San Luis Obispo, 841 F.2d 772 (9th Cir. 1987) (bias in decision making); Rymer v. Douglas County, 764 F.2d 796 (11th Cir. 1985) (error in issuing building permit); G.M. Eng'rs & Assocs., Inc. v. West Bloomfield Township, 922 F.2d 328 (6th Cir. 1990).

[5] Vari-Build, Inc. v. City of Reno, 596 F. Supp. 673 (D. Nev. 1984). *Accord* Sullivan v. Town of Salem, 805 F.2d 81 (2d Cir. 1986).

[6] 494 U.S. 113 (1990).

[7] New Burnham Prairie Homes, Inc. v. Village of Burnham, 910 F.2d 1474 (7th Cir. 1990).

[8] DeBlasio v. Zoning Bd. of Adjustment, 53F.3d 592 (3d Cir. 1995); Burnham v. City of Salem, 101 F. Supp.2d 26 (D. Mass. 2000); Henniger v. Pinellas County, 7 F. Supp.2d 1334 (M.D. Fla. 1998); Boudwin v. Great Bend Township, 921 F. Supp. 1326 (M.D. Pa. 1996).

[9] Weinberg v. Whatcom County, 241 F.3d 746 (9th Cir. 2001) (pre-deprivation hearing required on vacation of short plats); Lanmar Corp. v. Rendine, 811 F. Supp. 47 (D.R.I. 1993).

[10] Macene v. MJW, Inc., 951 F.2d 700 (6th Cir. 1991); Independent Coin Payphone Ass'n, Inc. v. City of Chicago, 863 F. Supp. 744 (N.D. Ill. 1994); Koncelik v. Town of East Hampton, 781 F. Supp. 152 (E.D.N.Y. 1991).

§ 8.34   Immunities.

§ 8.35   Legislative Bodies.

Though § 1983 does not expressly provide for immunities of any kind, the Supreme Court has implied the common law immunities the courts recognized when Congress enacted the statute. In *Tenney v. Brandhove*,[1] the Supreme Court held state legislators are absolutely immune from liability under § 1983 because absolute immunity confers a benefit to the "public good":

> The [legislative] privilege would be of little value if . . . [legislators] could be subjected to the cost and inconvenience and distractions of a trial upon a conclusion of the pleader, or to the hazard of judgment against them based upon a jury's speculation as to motives. . . . Self-discipline and the voters must be the ultimate reliance for discouraging or correcting . . . [legislative] abuses.[2]

In *Lake Country Estates, Inc. v. Tahoe Regional Planning Agency*,[3] the Court extended the absolute immunity of state legislators to members of a bi-state regional planning agency. It noted that alternative remedies were available, including a suit against the regional planning agency. The Court limited legislative immunity to officials "acting in a field where legislators traditionally have power to act" who did not usurp judicial or executive authority.

Finally, in *Bogan v. Scott-Harris*,[4] the Supreme Court held that local legislators are entitled to absolute immunity in § 1983 cases. A city administrator prepared termination charges against a temporary employee based on a complaint that the employee made racial and ethnic slurs. The council later accepted a settlement that suspended the employee without pay for 60 days, although the mayor later reduce this punishment. While the charges against the employee were pending, the mayor prepared a budget that eliminated a number of positions, including the position of the agency administrator who brought the charges. When the council adopted the budget, the administrator filed suit.

The Court held it was the "pervasive view" at common law, at the time § 1983 was adopted, that local legislators were absolutely immune from liability. Judicial interference, distorted by the fear of personal liability, should not be allowed

---

[1] 341 U.S. 367 (1951).

[2] *Id.* at 377–78.

[3] 440 U.S. 391 (1979).

[4] 523 U.S. 44 (1998). For earlier federal court cases holding accord see Orange Lake Assocs. v. Kirkpatrick, 21 F.3d 1214 (2d Cir. 1994); Shoultes v. Laidlaw, 886 F.2d 114 (6th Cir. 1989); Baytree of Inverrary Realty Partners v. City of Lauderhill, 873 F.2d 1407 (11th Cir. 1989); Culebras Enters. Corp. v. Rivera Rios, 813 F.2d 506 (1st Cir. 1987); Kuzinich v. County of Santa Clara, 689 F.2d 1345 (9th Cir. 1982); Bruce v. Riddle, 631 F.2d 272 (4th Cir. 1980).; Gorman Towers, Inc. v. Bogoslavsky 626 F.2d 607 (8th Cir. 1980) (downzoning).

to inhibit the exercise of legislative discretion. At the local level, the Court noted, the time and energy necessary to defend against a lawsuit were of particular concern because part-time legislators are common. In addition, deterrents to legislative abuse are greater at the local level because municipalities are liable for constitutional violations, and there is the electoral check on governmental abuse.

The Court then held that the ordinance eliminating the positions was legislative. Whether an act is legislative turns, not on the motive of the legislators, but on whether the act was "formally legislative" and within the "traditional sphere of legislative activity." In this case the act was legislative because it was a "discretionary, policymaking decision" that could well have prospective effect.

Governing bodies at the municipal level can exercise administrative as well as legislative functions. Prior to the *Bogan* decision the federal courts had adopted tests to determine whether an action by a legislative body was legislative or administrative. Courts usually held the adoption and amendment of zoning ordinances is a legislative act,[5] but the decision on absolute immunity is more difficult when the legislative body acts in an administrative capacity, as when it decides whether to issue a special permit. Courts have adopted traditional tests in these cases that hold a decision is legislative if its purpose is to establish a general policy and is administrative if it singles out specific individuals and treats them differently from others.[6] In a number of cases, courts held the actions of a governing body were administrative.[7] The Supreme Court's recent *Bogan* decision may have qualified this test because it adopted a different test for deciding when a governing body's action is legislative.[8]

---

[5] Ira Iglesia de la Biblia Abierta v. Banks, 129 F.3d 899 (7th Cir. 1997) (rezoning of single tract held legislative); Acierno v. Cloutier, 40 F.3d 597 (3d Cir. 1994); 2BD Ltd. Partnership v. County Comm'rs, 896 F. Supp. 528 (D. Md. 1995); *See also* Brown v. Crawford County, 960 F.2d 1002 (11th Cir. 1992).

[6] Crymes v. DeKalb County, 923 F.2d 1482 (11th Cir. 1991); Haskell v. Washington Township, 864 F.2d 1266 (6th Cir. 1988) (remanding to determine whether adoption of zoning ordinance administrative); Cutting v. Muzzey, 724 F.2d 249 (1st Cir. 1984); Scott v. Greenville County, 716 F.2d 1409 (4th Cir. 1983);

[7] Corn v. City of Lauderdale Lakes, 997 F.2d 1369 (11th Cir. 1993) (no immunity for denial of site plan); Crymes v. DeKalb County, 923 F.2d 1482 (11th Cir. 1991) (permit denial); Bateson v. Geisse, 857 F.2d 1300 (9th Cir. 1988) (permit withheld); Scott v. Greenville County, 716 F.2d 1409 (4th Cir. 1983) (building permit application); Keys Youth Servs., Inc. v. City of Olathe, 38 F. Supp. 2d 914 (D. Kan. 1999) (denial of conditional use permit not legislative); Homeowner/ Contractor Consultants, Inc. v. Ascension Parish Planning & Zoning Comm'n, 32 F. Supp. 2d 384 (M.D. La. 1999) (denial of subdivision plat not legislative). *But see* § 8.35 (suggesting absolute immunity if function adjudicatory).

[8] *See* Kamplain v. Curry County Bd. of Comm'rs, 159 F.3d 1248 (10th Cir. 1998) (discussing rule for determining legislative immunity); Maynard v. Beck, 741 A.2d 866 (R.I. 1999) (immunity granted to town planner and planning commission members who advised legislative body on zoning amendment).

§ 8.36   Land Use Agencies and Officials.

Land use agencies and officials are absolutely immune from liability under § 1983 if they exercise adjudicatory functions, but otherwise they have only a qualified good faith immunity. Absolute immunity is based on a Supreme Court case, *Butz v. Economou*.[1] The Court conferred absolute immunity on federal officials who initiated an adjudicatory proceeding against the plaintiff. The Court held that there may be "exceptional situations where it is demonstrated that absolute [executive] immunity is essential for the conduct of the public business." Adjudication by agencies is "functionally comparable" to adjudication by judges and should enjoy the absolute immunity judges enjoy.

The absolute immunity established by *Butz* should apply when land use agencies exercise adjudicatory functions.[2] Planning board members have also been given an absolute legislative immunity when they acted legislatively.[3] The courts have granted only a qualified good faith immunity to executive actions in the enforcement and implementation of land use regulation.[4]

Land use agencies and officials that have qualified good faith immunity are subject to immunity rules adopted by the Supreme Court, although the Court has not considered the immunity question in a land use case. The Court first adopted a two-part test that required both subjective and objective good faith.[5] It dropped the subjective part of the test in *Harlow v. Fitzgerald*[6] and restated the objective good faith test as a more protective formula:

> [G]overnment officials performing discretionary functions generally are shielded from liability insofar as their conduct does not violate clearly established statutory or constitutional rights of which a reasonable person would have known.[7]

---

[1] 438 U.S. 478 (1978).

[2] Buckles v. King County, 191 F.3d 1127 (9th Cir. 1999) (absolute immunity extended to members of Growth Management Hearings Board). Bass v. Attardi, 868 F.2d 45 (3d Cir. 1989) (members of planning board absolutely immune). Immunity denied: Cutting v. Mazzey, 724 F.2d 259 (1st Cir. 1984) (planning board merely decided to insist on completion of road before granting approval of proposed subdivision); Rodriguez v. Village of Larchmont, 608 F. Supp. 467 (S.D.N.Y. 1985) (board of zoning appeals held to exercise only administrative functions). *See also* Shoultes v. Laidlaw, 886 F.2d 114 (6th Cir. 1989) (prosecutorial immunity granted to city attorney brought civil injunction to enforce zoning ordinance).

[3] Fralin & Waldron, Inc. v. County of Henrico, 474 F. Supp. 1315 (E.D. Va. 1979) (recommendation of legislative action to local legislative body). *See also* Hernandez v. City of Lafayette, 643 F.2d 1188 (5th Cir. 1981) (mayor who vetoed rezoning held entitled to legislative immunity).

[4] Sullivan v. Town of Salem, 805 F.2d 81 (2d Cir. 1986) (refusal to issue occupancy certificates); Tahoe-Sierra Preservation Council v. Tahoe Regional Planning Agency, 638 F. Supp. 126 (D. Nev. 1986) (implementation of regional plan).

[5] Scheuer v. Rhodes, 416 U.S. 232 (1974). *See also* Pierson v. Ray, 386 U.S. 547 (1967).

[6] 457 U.S. 800 (1982).

[7] *Id.* at 818.

The Court also held that an official's conduct must meet a standard of "objective legal reasonableness."

Davis v. Scherer[8] elaborated the *Harlow rule*. The Court held that a mere violation of a state statute or regulation, standing alone, is not enough to defeat good faith immunity. Immunity is unavailable only if the defendant violated a clearly established constitutional right. Land use cases have applied *Harlow*.[9]

The Supreme Court further clarified official immunity in *Anderson v. Creighton*.[10] Plaintiff claimed that police officers had conducted a warrantless search. The Court held that even though the courts had previously recognized a constitutional right to be protected from a warrantless search without probable cause, the question was whether it was unconstitutional in this case under all the circumstances. This fact-specific inquiry requires the courts to determine whether a reasonable officer could have believed that a warrantless search was constitutional in light of the clearly established law and the available facts. The Court added that whether a defendant acted reasonably is determined by the "contours" of a constitutional right. It gave very little guidance on this question, but held that "the very action in question [need not have] been previously held unlawful," but that "in light of preexisting law the unlawfulness must be apparent."[11] Because so many land use actions brought under § 1983 are fact-specific, *Creighton* should lead to an expansion of official immunity in land use § 1983 actions.

The Supreme Court has not indicated what it takes to make a rule of law clearly established, and the courts disagree on what is required. It is not clear, for example, whether case law must be available in the jurisdiction, or whether there must be a substantial number of cases that establish the constitutional right.[12]

---

[8] 468 U.S. 183 (1984). *See also* Hunter v. Bryant, 502 U.S. 224 (1991).

[9] Desert Outdoor Advertising v. City of Moreno Valley, 103 F.3d 814 (9th Cir. 1996) (licensing scheme for signs); Acierno v. Cloutier, 40 F.3d 597 (3d Cir. 1994) (right to develop not clearly established); Rappa v. New Castle County, 18 F.3d 1043 (3d Cir. 1994) (qualified immunity in facial attack on sign restrictions); Culebras Enters. Corp. v. Rivera Rios, 813 F.2d 506 (1st Cir. 1987) (moratorium); Kaplan v. Clear Lake City Water Auth., 794 F.2d 1059 (5th Cir. 1986) (refusal to provide water and sewer service); Negin v. City of Mentor, 601 F. Supp. 1502 (N.D. Ohio 1985).

[10] 483 U.S. 635 (1987), noted in The Supreme Court: 1986 Term: Leading Cases, 101 Harv. L. Rev. 101, 220 (1987).

[11] 228 483 U.S. at 639. *See* Centerfold Club, Inc. v. City of St. Petersburg, 969 F. Supp. 1288 (M.D. Fla. 1997) (applying rule and finding immunity). *See also* Siegert v. Gilley, 500 U.S. 226 (1991) (must decide whether there is constitutional violation before deciding immunity defense).

[12] Daugherty v. Campbell, 935 F.2d 780 (6th Cir. 1991) (visual body search; can look to Supreme Court and circuit decisions); Walnut Props., Inc. v. City of Whittier, 861 F.2d 1102 (9th Cir. 1988) (adult use regulation; not enough cases to establish constitutional right); LeClair v. Hart, 800 F.2d 692 (7th Cir. 1986) (search and seizure; no immunity when lower courts but not Supreme Court had decided question).

The courts found that land use agencies and officials acted in good faith when no clearly established right was violated.[13] They denied good faith immunity in cases in which zoning officials arbitrarily withheld building permits or arbitrarily enforced a zoning ordinance.[14] Some of these cases are post-*Creighton* but did not make the fact-specific inquiry required by that decision.

§ 8.37 Local Governments.

Owen v. City of Independence[1] held that municipalities are not immune from liability in a § 1983 action. A police chief brought an action claiming he was terminated by the city without the procedural due process required by the federal constitution. The Court held there was no general municipal immunity at the time Congress enacted § 1983, either for proprietary as distinguished from governmental activities or for discretionary as distinguished from ministerial actions. It did not limit its decision to procedural due process violations but held that it applied to all "constitutional violations":

[A] municipality has no "discretion" to violate the Federal Constitution; its dictates are absolute and imperative. And when a court passes judgment on the municipality's conduct in a § 1983 action, it does not seek to second-guess the reasonableness of the city's decision nor to interfere with the local government's resolution of competing policy considerations. Rather, it looks only to whether the municipality has conformed to the requirements of the Federal Constitution and statutes.[2]

Although *Owen* held that municipalities are not immune under § 1983, it does not impose absolute liability. As the statement just quoted indicates, plaintiffs must still show a violation of the federal Constitution.

---

[13] Meadow Briar Home for Children, Inc. v. Gunn, 81 F.3d 521 (5th Cir. 1996) (Fair Housing Act); Zahra v. Town of Southold, 48 F.3d 674, 686 (2d Cir. 1995) (building permit revoked); Acierno v. Cloutier, 40 F.3d 597 (3d Cir. 1994); Walnut Properties, Inc. v. City of Whittier (II), 861 F.2d 1102 (9th Cir. 1988) (adult business zoning); Culebras Enters. Corp. v. Rivera Rios, 813 F.2d 506 (1st Cir. 1987); Kaplan v. Clear Lake City Water Auth., 794 F.2d 1059 (5th Cir. 1986); Keys Youth Servs., Inc. v. City of Olathe, 38 F. Supp. 2d 914 (D. Kan. 1999) (immunity granted on Fair Housing Act and constitutional claims). *But see* Dubuc v. Green Oak Township, 958 F. Supp. 1231 (E.D. Mich. 1997) (retaliation for exercise of free speech; no immunity).

[14] Blanche Road Corp. v. Bensalem Township, 57 F.3d 253 (3d Cir. 1995); Brady v. Town of Colchester, 863 F.2d 205 (2d Cir. 1988); Bateson v. Geisse, 857 F.2d 1300 (9th Cir. 1988) (because "contours" of substantive due process clear); TLC Dev., Inc. v. Town of Branford, 855 F. Supp. 555 (D. Conn. 1994) (denial of site plan); Mission Springs, Inc. v. City of Spokane, 954 P.2d 250 (Wash. 1998).

[1] 445 U.S. 622 (1980).

[2] *Id.* at 649.

§ 8.38 Damages.

Section 1983 provides that parties sued under the statute "shall be liable to the party injured in an action at law." This provision authorizes an award of compensatory damages. The rule for damages in a § 1983 action is not the same as the rule for damages in a takings case. The Supreme Court has held that the common law of torts provides an analogy for damages in § 1983 cases but requires careful adaptation when a constitutional right does not have a tort analogy.[1] Punitive damages are not available against local governments[2]. Courts may award punitive damages against local officials,[3] but the facts have not usually justified an award of punitive damages in land use cases.[4]

In *Carey v. Piphus*,[5] the Supreme Court rejected a claim that a court should presume damages when a plaintiff proves a procedural due process violation. Elementary and secondary school students brought a § 1983 action claiming they were denied procedural due process when they were temporarily suspended. The Court held that the defendant was liable only for nominal, not compensatory, damages because there was no proof that the students would not have been suspended if procedural due process requirements had been observed. *Carey* also applies to substantive due process violations.[6] This case means that damages are not available in a land use case unless the due process violation affected the outcome of the decision.

The Supreme Court has held that compensation is payable in land use cases for temporary takings in an inverse condemnation action brought directly under the federal constitution.[7] The Court did not indicate whether a plaintiff could recover compensation for a taking under § 1983, but compensation should be available in a § 1983 action as well.[8]

Damages are available in a § 1983 action for constitutional violations other than violations of the taking clause. Justice Brennan noted, for example, that substantive due process violations not actionable under the taking clause are actionable under § 1983.[9] Only a few cases have considered the damages

---

[1] Memphis Community School Dist. v. Stachura, 477 U.S. 299 (1986); Carey v. Piphus, 435 U.S. 247 (1978).

[2] City of Newport v. Fact Concerts, Inc., 453 U.S. 247 (1981).

[3] Smith v. Wade, 461 U.S. 30 (1983).

[4] Johansen v. City of Bartlesville, 862 F.2d 1423 (10th Cir. 1988); Creekside Assocs. v. City of Wood Dale, 684 F. Supp. 201 (N.D. Ill. 1988).

[5] 435 U.S. 247 (1978).

[6] Memphis Community School Dist. v. Stachura, 477 U.S. 299 (1986).

[7] § 8.25.

[8] Wheeler v. City of Pleasant Grove (II), 833 F.2d 267 (11th Cir. 1987).

[9] San Diego Gas & Elec. Co. v. City of San Diego, 450 U.S. 621, 656 n.23 (1981) (dissenting opinion).

question. In *Heritage Homes of Attleboro, Inc. v. Seekonk Water Dist. (II),*[10] the district delayed a housing project that was to be open to minorities by refusing to supply water. The court awarded compensatory damages equal to the difference between the cost of connecting to the district, and the cost the developer incurred to drill individual wells. It denied damages for the developer's inability to use its assets while the project was delayed. The developer did not provide evidence on the applicable interest rate, and did not show that the appreciation in the value of its property was less than what interest on its assets would have earned.

In *Herrington v. County of Sonoma,*[11] the court adopted a formula to calculate damages resulting from delay in the approval of a subdivision. It multiplied the property's maximum value, assuming its approval by one-third, which was the court's calculation of the probability of approval. It subtracted the undeveloped value of the property from that figure and multiplied the difference by the interest rate and the length of the delay. It then added any increased development costs were likely to have resulted from the delay. This is a reasonable approach to calculating damages that takes the probabilities of approval into account.

§ 8.39 Implied Constitutional Cause of Action.

The Supreme Court has recognized an implied cause of action to enforce some of the constitutional rights that are protected by the federal constitution. The action is known as a *Bivens* action for the search and seizure case that created it.[1] The Court has also approved a *Bivens* action brought under the equal protection clause[2] but has not decided whether it is available to enforce the fourteenth amendment. The Court has indicated that whether a *Bivens* action is available depends on whether damages are appropriate, whether there are special concerns "counseling hesitation," and whether Congress has provided an alternative remedy explicitly declared to be a substitute and which is equally effective.[3]

Carlson v. Green[4] held an alternative remedy under the Federal Tort Claims Act was not an effective substitute for a *Bivens* action brought to enforce the

---

[10] 648 F.2d 761 (1st Cir. 1981). *See also* Wheeler v. City of Pleasant Grove (II), 833 F.2d 267 (11th Cir. 1987) (taking); Cordeco Dev. Corp. v. Santiago Vasquez, 539 F.2d 256 (1st Cir.1976).

[11] 790 F. Supp. 909 (N.D. Cal. 1991) *aff'd,* 12 F.3d 901 (9th Cir. 1993). *But see* SMD, L.L.P. v. City of Boswell, 555 S.E.2d 813 (Ga. App. 2001) (damages not awarded to company in business of obtaining and selling permits that had never erected a billboard).

[1] Bivens v. Six Unknown Named Agents of the Fed. Bur. of Narcotics, 403 U.S. 388 (1971). *Compare* Kelley Prop. Dev. Co. v. Town of Lebanon, 627 A.2d 909 (Conn. 1993) (rejecting state *Bivens* action in zoning cases), *with* Old Tuckaway Assocs. Ltd. Partnership v. City of Greenfield, 509 N.W.2d 323 (Wis. App. 1993) (contra).

[2] Davis v. Passman, 442 U.S. 228 (1979) (action against congressman).

[3] *Id.* at 245–47.

[4] 446 U.S. 14 (1980). *See also* Bush v. Lucas, 462 U.S. 367 (1983) (*Bivens* action held unavailable).

eighth amendment's guarantee against cruel and unusual punishment. The court cited legislative history to the Tort Claims Act indicating Congress believed that a *Bivens* action was an alternative remedy. The court also noted that punitive damages were available in a *Bivens* action but not under the Act.

Some federal courts approved a *Bivens* action in land use cases prior to the Supreme Court decision holding that local governments are liable under § 1983.[5] Later federal court cases held the availability of a § 1983 action in land use cases precludes a *Bivens* action.[6] The *Carlson* decision casts doubt on these cases because punitive damages are not available against local governments in § 1983 actions. The lower federal courts are divided on whether a *Bivens* action is available to enforce the fourteenth amendment, on which land use cases are often based.[7] Neither the relationship between *Bivens* actions and an action to secure compensation under the taking clause is clear.

§ 8.40   Removal to Federal Court.

In *City of Chicago v. International College of Surgeons*,[1] the Supreme Court held a defendant could remove from state to federal district court a § 1983 case in which the plaintiff alleged federal constitutional claims arising out of the city's refusal to allow the plaintiff to demolish an historic building. Removal from state to federal district court is governed by federal statute, which permits removal of "any civil actions brought in a State court of which the district courts of the United States have original jurisdiction."[2] Whether removal is proper thus depends on whether the action could originally have been filed in federal court.

The city denied a permit to demolish all but the facades of historic buildings owned by the plaintiff to allow construction of a high-rise condominium tower, and then refused to give an exception that allows demolition in cases of economic hardship. The College filed suit in state court for appellate review under the state administrative procedures act and made federal constitutional claims. The city removed both lawsuits to federal district court, which took jurisdiction.

The Supreme Court held the College had made claims under the federal constitution, and that a party is allowed to remove a federal claim to federal court even though the state law, as in this case, creates the cause of action in which

---

[5] Gordon v. City of Warren, 579 F.2d 386 (6th Cir. 1978).

[6] Rogin v. Bensalem Twp., 616 F.2d 680 (3d Cir. 1980). *See also* Monell v. Department of Social Servs., 436 U.S. 658, 713 (1978) (Justice Powell, concurring). *But see* Ocean Acres Ltd. Partnership v. Dare County Bd. of Health, 514 F. Supp. 1117 (E.D.N.C. 1981), *aff'd on other grounds,* 707 F.2d 103 (4th Cir. 1983).

[7] For discussion of these decisions in a land use case, *see* Rogin v. Bensalem Twp., 616 F.2d 680 (3d Cir. 1980).

[1] 522 U.S. 15 (1998).

[2] 28 U.S.C. § 1441(a).

the federal claim is made. The Court rejected an argument the case was not a "civil action" entitled to removal because it contained state law claims that required "on-the-record"' review of the permit denial decisions. The federal court's jurisdiction arose from the federal claims, not the state law claims.[3] The decision suggests an as-applied takings claim that could not be brought initially in federal court under the ripeness rules[4] could be removed to a federal court by a municipality.

§ 8.41 Abstention.

A number of doctrines that limit federal court jurisdiction apply to land use cases. Under the ripeness rules a plaintiff must usually bring an as-applied takings claim in state rather than federal court.[1] A federal court may also decide not to hear a land use case under the *Rooker-Feldman* doctrine.[2]

Abstention is another basis for declining federal jurisdiction. Federal district courts may abstain from hearing a case that raises federal constitutional law questions under several abstention doctrines adopted by the U.S. Supreme Court. The abstention doctrine applies to land use cases in which plaintiffs allege violations of the federal constitution, including inverse condemnation actions, § 1983 actions, and implied causes of action based on the federal constitution. Though the Supreme Court has frequently stated that abstention is the exception rather than the rule,[3] the federal courts often abstain in land use cases.

Federal courts may abstain in actions for damages as well as actions for equitable relief, but a federal court may only stay an action for damages if it decides to abstain. It may not dismiss or remand a damages actions.[4] When a plaintiff presents its case in state court after a federal court has abstained, it may not return to federal court unless it has preserved its claim in state court.[5]

§ 8.42 *Younger* Abstention.

In *Younger v. Harris*,[1] the Supreme Court applied principles of federal comity embraced in "Our Federalism" to hold that federal courts should abstain from

---

[3] *See* Freeman v. Burlington Broadcasters, Inc., 204 F.3d 311 (2d Cir. 2000) (upholding removal of preemption claim under federal telecommunications act); Hanna v. City of Chicago, 212 F. Supp.2d 856 (N.D. Ill. 2002) (upholding removal of zoning challenge).

[4] §§ 2.24–2.33.

[1] §§ 2.24–2.33

[2] § 2.34.

[3] Colorado River Water Conservation Dist. v. United States, 424 U.S. 800 (1976).

[4] Quackenbush v. Allstate Ins. Co., 517 U.S. 706 (1996). *See* Carroll v. City of Mount Clemens, 139 F.3d 1072 (6th Cir. 1998).

[5] England v. Louisiana State Bd. of Medical Examiners, 375 U.S. 411 (1964).

[1] 401 U.S. 31 (1971).

enjoining pending state criminal proceedings. Abstention is appropriate if the plaintiff can make an adequate federal defense in the state proceedings, and if abstention does not cause the plaintiff irreparable injury. The Court indicated that a plaintiff would suffer irreparable injury if there was bad faith or harassment in the state proceedings, or if a state statute was flagrantly and patently unconstitutional.[2] The Court has extended *Younger* abstention to pending state civil proceedings that implicate important state interests[3] and to state administrative proceedings,[4] which include local administrative zoning proceedings. These extensions of the doctrine should lead courts to apply it more often in land use cases.

Younger abstention is required even if the federal action was filed first if "proceedings of substance" on the merits in federal court have not occurred when a later state action is filed.[5] Courts must dismiss and may not stay a federal action if they abstain under *Younger*.[6] However, a court must grant a stay if the action is for damages.[7]

New Orleans Public Serv. v. City of New Orleans[8] indicates the Supreme Court will not apply *Younger* abstention to legislative zoning actions that are under review in state courts.[9] The New Orleans city council refused a rate increase to a utility to cover the costs of a nuclear power plant. After the utility sought review of the order in state court, it sued in federal court claiming the order was preempted by federal legislation.

The Court held that *Younger* abstention does not apply when state court proceedings are pending to review legislative and executive action. The council's legislative action was complete and could be challenged in federal court, and it was not necessary to abstain to avoid disrupting state judicial proceedings. This case, the Court noted, was analogous to a facial challenge to a zoning ordinance,

---

[2] Exceptions not applied: Community Treatment Centers v. City of Westland, 970 F. Supp. 1197 (E.D. Mich. 1997); Wandyful Stadium v. Town of Hempstead, 939 F. Supp. 585 (E.D.N.Y. 1997); Danish News Co. v. City of Ann Arbor, 517 F. Supp. 86 (E.D. Mich. 1981) (significant delay in state proceedings held not to be irreparable harm), *aff'd mem.*, 751 F.2d 384 (6th Cir. 1984).

[3] Middlesex County Ethics Comm. v. Garden State Bar Ass'n, 457 U.S. 423 (1982). *See* Parkowners Ass'n v. City of Montclair, 211 F.3d 1144 (9th Cir. 2000) (*Younger* abstention does not apply if state court proceeding dismissed).

[4] Ohio Civil Rights Comm'n v. Dayton Christian Schools, Inc., 477 U.S. 619 (1986).

[5] Hicks v. Miranda, 422 U.S. 322 (1975). *See* Adult World Bookstore v. City of Fresno, 758 F.2d 1348 (9th Cir. 1985); Ciotti v. County of Cook, 712 F.2d 312 (7th Cir. 1983).

[6] Colorado River Water Conservation Dist. v. United States, 424 U.S. 800 (1976).

[7] Night Clubs v. City of Fort Smith, 163 F.3d 475 (8th Cir. 1998). *See* Quackenbush v. Allstate Ins. Co., 517 U.S. 706 (1996).

[8] 491 U.S. 350 (1989).

[9] *See* Night Clubs, Inc. v. City of Ft. Smith, 163 F.3d 475 (8th Cir. 1998) (*Younger* applies to refusal to issue business license; held judicial).

which should not be brought in state court. This statement is surprising. The Court apparently meant that a federal court should not abstain when a landowner makes a facial challenge to zoning in federal court even though a facial challenge is pending in a state court.

Courts apply the multi-factor *Younger* abstention doctrine to decide whether they should abstain in land use cases.[10] Issues that are often determinative is whether the plaintiff could litigate the constitutional issues in state court,[11] and whether the plaintiff would suffer irreparable harm.[12] The courts have held that zoning implicates an important state interest that deserves abstention in land use case.[13]

§ 8.43 *Pullman* Abstention.

In *Railroad Comm'n of Texas. v. Pullman Co.*,[1] the plaintiffs brought a suit in equity in which they claimed that a state agency order was racially discriminatory and unauthorized by the state statute. The Court held abstention was appropriate. It noted the plaintiffs raised substantial federal constitutional questions and held:

> [The complaint] touches a sensitive area of social policy upon which the federal courts ought not to enter unless no alternative to its adjudication is open. Such constitutional adjudication plainly can be avoided if a definitive ruling on the state issue would terminate the controversy.[2]

The Supreme Court has indicated when *Pullman* abstention is appropriate because a state law question is unsettled.[3] A state or local law must be "fairly

---

[10] Abstention granted: San Remo Hotel v. City & County of San Francisco, 145 F.3d 1095 (9th Cir. 1998); (rejecting claim because abstention would have been granted). Abstention denied: Sullivan v. City of Pittsburgh, 811 F.2d 171 (3d Cir. 1987); Oxford-House Evergreen v. City of Plainfield, 769 F. Supp. 1329 (D.N.J. 1991).

[11] Abstention granted: Night Clubs v. City of Fort Smith, 163 F.3d 475 (8th Cir. 1998); World Famous Drinking Emporium, Inc. v. City of Tempe, 820 F.2d 1079 (9th Cir. 1987). Abstention denied: Wiener v. County of San Diego, 23 F.3d 263 (9th Cir. 1994); Community Treatment Centers v. City of Westland, 970 F. Supp. 1197 (E.D. Mich. 1997). *See also* Casa Marie, Inc. v. Superior Court, 988 F.2d 252 (1st Cir. 1993).

[12] Harm found: Sullivan v. City of Pittsburgh, 811 F.2d 171 (3d Cir. 1987); United States v. Commonwealth of Puerto Rico, 764 F. Supp. 220 (D.P.R. 1991). Harm not found: Central Ave. News, Inc. v. City of Minot, 651 F.2d 565 (8th Cir. 1981); Danish News Co. v. City of Ann Arbor, 517 F. Supp. 86 (E.D. Mich. 1981), *aff'd mem.*, 751 F.2d 384 (6th Cir. 1984).

[13] San Remo Hotel v. City & County of San Francisco, 145 F.3d 1095 (9th Cir. 1998); Rodriguez v. County of Hawaii, 823 F. Supp. 798 (D. Haw. 1993); Naked City, Inc. v. Aregood, 667 F. Supp. 1246 (N.D. Ind. 1987). *But see* Glen-Gery Corp. v. Lower Heidelberg Township, 608 F. Supp. 1002 (E.D. Pa. 1985).

[1] 312 U.S. 496 (1971).

[2] *Id.* at 498.

[3] Hawaii Hous. Auth. v. Midkiff, 467 U.S. 2291 (1984) (summarizing Supreme Court decisions).

subject" to an interpretation that will make a decision on the federal constitutional questions unnecessary and must be uncertain and obviously susceptible of a limiting construction. A bare though unlikely possibility that this will occur is not enough.

The federal courts of appeals have adopted different multi-factor tests based on the *Pullman* decision to determine when *Pullman* abstention applies.[4] In the Ninth Circuit, an emphasis on the "sensitive social policy" factor has led to frequent abstention in land use cases.[5]

Federal courts have abstained under *Pullman* abstention in a number of land use cases when state law was unsettled.[6] *Kollsman v. City of Los Angeles*,[7] a Ninth Circuit case, illustrates these decisions. The state law question was whether the plaintiff's subdivision was deemed approved because the city did not make a "completeness" determination within the required statutory time period. The court held that the answer to this question depended on interlocking state statutes whose interpretation was unsettled and noted that the plaintiff and the city disagreed on their interpretation. The dissent believed the state statutes were clear and that the only issue before the court was factual.

The federal courts have refused to abstain under *Pullman* abstention in land use cases when state law questions were settled.[8] They often refuse to abstain in first amendment land use cases, and some of these cases hold that abstention is less appropriate when first amendment issues are raised.[9] Courts that refuse

---

But see Corder v. City of Sherwood, 579 F. Supp. 1042 (E.D. Ark. 1984) (court abstained though state law questions not clearly unsettled); Kent Island Joint Venture v. Smith, 452 F. Supp. 455 (D. Md. 1978) (same).

[4] Palmer v. Jackson, 617 F.2d 424 (5th Cir. 1980) (two-factor test); George v. Parratt, 602 F.2d 818 (8th Cir. 1979) (three-factor test).

[5] *See* Canton v. Spokane School Dist. No. 81, 498 F.2d 840 (9th Cir. 1974) (as part of three-factor test).

[6] San Remo Hotel v. City & County of San Francisco, 145 F.3d 1095 (9th Cir. 1998); Chez Sez III Corp. v. Township of Union, 945 F.2d 628 (3d Cir. 1991); Pearl Inv. Co. v. City & County of San Francisco, 774 F.2d 1460 (9th Cir. 1985); Caleb Stowe Assocs. v. Albemarle County, 724 F.2d 1079 (4th Cir. 1984); Hill v. City of El Paso, 437 F.2d 352 (5th Cir. 1971); Adams Outdoor Advertising v. City of Holland, 883 F. Supp. 207 (W.D. Mich. 1995); International Eateries of America v. Board of County Comm'rs, 838 F. Supp. 580 (S.D. Fla. 1993).

[7] 737 F.2d 830 (9th Cir. 1984). *See also* C-Y Dev. Co. v. City of Redlands, 703 F.2d 375 (9th Cir. 1983).

[8] International College of Surgeons v. City of Chicago, 153 F.3d 356 (7th Cir. 1998); Urbanizadora Versalles, Inc. v. Rivera Rios, 701 F.2d 993 (1st Cir. 1983); Nasser v. City of Homewood (I), 671 F.2d 432 (11th Cir. 1982); Donohue Constr. Co. v. Montgomery County Council, 567 F.2d 603 (4th Cir. 1977); Currier Bldrs., Inc. v. Town of York, 146 F. Supp.2d 71 (D. Me. 2001) (growth ordinance); People Tags, Inc. v. Jackson County Legislature, 636 F. Supp. 1345 (W.D. 1986) (adult use zoning); Rasmussen v. City of Lake Forest, 404 F. Supp. 148 (N.D. Ill. 1975) (strong statement disfavoring abstention).

[9] Cinema Arts, Inc. v. Clark County, 722 F.2d 579 (9th Cir. 1983); People Tags, Inc. v. Jackson

to abstain under *Pullman* abstention sometimes point out that federal as well as state courts can apply state law to difficult facts.[10]

"Mirror image" abstention problems arise frequently in *Pullman* abstention cases when a defendant asks the federal court to abstain so that a state court can interpret a state constitutional provision that parallels a provision in the federal constitution. The taking clause is an example. The federal courts have not allowed mirror image abstention,[11] following a Supreme Court decision holding that *Pullman* abstention is not appropriate to allow a state court to interpret a parallel state constitutional provision.[12]

§ 8.44 *Burford* Abstention.

A Supreme Court case, *Burford v. Sun Oil Co.*,[1] established a third abstention category. The Court held that abstention was appropriate in an action in equity brought to challenge a state agency's oil drilling order. The Court noted that the state agency adopted the order in a complex state regulatory program. It held that federal court intervention would lead to conflicts in the interpretation of the state law that would endanger state policies. The Court also emphasized that the state had provided "adequate and expeditious" judicial review of state agency decisions to a single state court. *Burford* abstention requires dismissal of the federal court proceeding. A stay is required if the action is for damages.[2]

The Court extended *Burford* abstention in *Colorado River Water Conservation Dist. v. United States*.[3] It stated in dictum:

> Abstention is also appropriate where there have been presented difficult questions of state law bearing on policy problems of substantial public import whose importance transcends the result in the case then at bar. . . . It is enough that exercise of federal review of the question . . . would be disruptive of state efforts to establish a coherent policy with respect to a matter of substantial public concern. . . .[4]

The Court stressed that in *Burford* the state "had established its own elaborate review system."

County Legislature, 636 F. Supp. 1345 (W.D. Mo. 1986); Amico v. New Castle County, 553 F. Supp. 738 (D. Del. 1982). *See also* Pearl Inv. Co. v. City & County of San Francisco, 774 F.2d 1460 (9th Cir. 1985).

[10] Heritage Farms, Inc. v. Solebury Twp., 671 F.2d 743 (3d Cir.).

[11] Pearl Inv. Co. v. City & County of San Francisco, 774 F.2d 1460 (9th Cir. 1985); Northern Va. Law School, Inc. v. City of Alexandria, 680 F. Supp. 222 (N.D. Va. 1988).

[12] Hawaii Hous. Auth. v. Midkiff, 467 U.S. 229, 237 n.4 (1984).

[1] 319 U.S. 315 (1942).

[2] Quackenbush v. Allstate Ins. Co., 517 U.S. 706 (1996).

[3] 424 U.S. 800 (1976).

[4] *Id.* at 814.

New Orleans Public Serv. v. City of New Orleans[5] indicates that the Supreme Court views *Burford* abstention less favorably. The Court held that *Burford* abstention did not apply to a case brought in federal court that claimed a city council rate order was preempted by a federal statute. The Court noted the *Burford* doctrine does not necessarily require abstention whenever there is a complex state regulatory system or even when there is a potential for conflict with state law and policy. *Burford* abstention did not apply in this case because the federal claim turned on federal preemption and required only a facial review of the council's rate order. The Court would presumably reach the same result when a facial constitutional challenge is brought to a zoning ordinance.

The federal courts have not usually abstained under *Burford* abstention in land use cases.[6] They emphasize that local land use regulation is piecemeal and fragmented, that it is not state policy, and that judicial review is not concentrated in a single court.[7] The courts also hold that *Burford* abstention is disfavored in first amendment and other civil rights cases.[8]

Burford and *Pullman* abstention overlap. Almost all *Burford* abstention cases are potential *Pullman* abstention cases because they can raise unsettled state law questions. The Fourth Circuit has held that *Burford* abstention applies when federal claims stem solely from a construction of state or local land use or zoning laws.[9]

§ 8.45 *Colorado River* Abstention.

The Supreme Court adopted another ground for abstention in *Colorado River Conserv. Dist. v. United States*.[1] Where there are concurrent state proceedings,

---

[5] 491 U.S. 350 (1989). *See also* Quackenbush v. Allstate Ins. Co., 517 U.S. 706 (1996) (reviewing basis for *Burford* abstention and noting that abstention on this basis "only rarely"granted).

[6] International College of Surgeons v. City of Chicago, 153 F.3d 356 (7th Cir. 1998); Ixzzo v. Borough of River Edge, 843 F.2d 765 (3d Cir. 1988); Urbanizadora Versalles, Inc. v. Rivera Rios, 701 F.2d 993 (1st Cir. 1983); Nasser v. City of Homewood (I), 671 F.2d 432 (11th Cir. 1982); Santa Fe Land Imp. Co. v. City of Chula Vista, 596 F.2d 838 (9th Cir. 1979); MacNamara v. County Council, 738 F. Supp. 134 (D. Del.), *aff'd without opinion*, 922 F.2d 832 (3d Cir. 1990) (citing this treatise); People Tags, Inc. v. Jackson County Legislature, 636 F. Supp. 1345 (W.D. Mo. 1986).

[7] Heritage Farms, Inc. v. Solebury Twp., 671 F.2d 743 (3d Cir. 1982); Rancho Palos Verdes Corp. v. City of Laguna Beach, 547 F.2d 1092 (9th Cir. 1976); Lerner v. Town of Islip, 272 F. Supp. 664 (E.D.N.Y. 1967).

[8] United States v. Commonwealth of Puerto Rico, 764 F. Supp. 220 (D.P.R. 1991) (Fair Housing Act); Amico v. New Castle County, 553 F. Supp. 738 (D. Del. 1982); Riccobono v. Whitpain Twp., 497 F. Supp. 1364 (E.D. Pa. 1980).

[9] Pomponio v. Fauquier County Bd. of Supvrs., 21 F.3d 1319 (4th Cir. 1994). *See also* Corder v. City of Sherwood, 579 F. Supp. 1042 (E.D. Ark. 1984) (combined *Pullman-Burford* abstention).

[1] 424 U.S. 800 (1976).

the Court reasoned that "wise judicial administration" might justify abstention. Courts were to consider the inconvenience of the federal forum, the desirability of avoiding piecemeal litigation and the order in which jurisdiction was obtained in the concurrent forums. A later Supreme Court case[2] modified the final factor by holding that priority should be measured by how much progress has been made in each forum and adding as another factor the probable inadequacy of the state court proceeding to protect the plaintiff's rights. The federal courts have applied the *Colorado River* abstention factors in land use cases.[3]

E. SLAPP SUITS.

§ 8.46 SLAPP Suits.

SLAPP suits, an acronym for "Strategic Lawsuits Against Public Participation," are suits filed by a land developer against opponents to a proposed development. To retaliate against the opposition, the developer sues for defamation, interference with business relationships, or on some similar theory for damages. Damages claimed usually average several million dollars, and the threat of liability may be enough to scare opponents into silence.

The great majority of SLAPP suits never make it to trial, and defendants usually prevail in those that are tried. Defendants can claim first amendment right to petition defense under the *Noerr-Pennington* doctrine that courts often recognize.[1] In *Baltimore Scrap Corp. v. The David J. Joseph Co.*,[2] for example, the court held the defendant scrap metal company was privileged to launch a concerted effort to delay approval of the plaintiff's zoning application and its entry into the market. Though many of the defendant's actions were reprehensible, they did not amount to a sufficient fraud or sham to deny defendants immunity under the first amendment.[3] SLAPP plaintiffs may also face

---

[2] Moses H. Cone Mem. Hosp. v. Mercury Constr. Corp., 460 U.S. 1 (1983).

[3] Abstention denied: Lake Lucerne Civic Ass'n v. Dolphin Stadium Corp., 878 F.2d 1360 (11th Cir. 1989); Tovar v. Billmeyer, 609 F.2d 1291 (9th Cir. 1990); Giulini v. Blessing, 654 F.2d 189 (2d Cir. 1981); Deja Vu of Kentucky, Inc. v. Lexington-Fayette Urban County Gov't, 194 F. Supp.2d 606 (E.D. Ky. 2002); Skipper v. Hambleton Meadows Architectural Review Comm., 996 F. Supp. 478 (D. Md. 1998) (Fair Housing Act claim). *See also* Baskin v. Bath Twp. Bd. of Zoning Appeals, 15 F.3d 569 (6th Cir. 1994) (parallel state proceeding not pending).

Abstention granted: Marcus v. Township of Abington, 1993 U.S. Dist. LEXIS 18156 (E.D. Pa. 1993); Oxford-House Evergreen v. City of Plainfield, 769 F. Supp. 1329 (D.N.J. 1991); Bible Truth Crusade v. City of Bloomington, 709 F. Supp. 849 (C.D. Ill. 1989); Stephens v. Cobb Cty., 684 F. Supp. 703 (N.D. Ga. 1988).

[1] § 5.55 (*Noerr-Pennington* Doctrine)

[2] 237 F.3d 394 (4th Cir. 2001)

[3] *Id.* at 403. *See also* Barnes Foundation v. Township of Lower Merion, 242 F.3d 151 (3rd Cir. 2001) (doubting *Noerr-Pennington* defense in civil rights action); Manistee Town Center v. City of Glendale, 227 F.3d 1090 (9th Cir. 2000) (lobbying of another governmental entity protected);

court-imposed sanctions under Rule 11 of the Federal Rules of Civil Procedure and state counterparts.[4]

The sham exception to the *Noerr-Pennington* doctrine that protects free speech rights in a SLAPP suit does not apply if a defendant's actions were objectively baseless and subjectively intended to interfere with the business relationships of a competitor.[5] In *Pound Hill Corp. v. Perl,*[6] for example, a plaintiff developer sought to amend a local zoning ordinance to allow a residential development. After the ordinance was amended, a defendant religious organization that had unsuccessfully sought to purchase the land prior to its sale began a vigorous campaign to frustrate the developer's efforts to retain the zoning approval. Summary judgment for the defendant was vacated because there was an issue of fact whether the defendant's petitioning was baseless under the *Noerr-Pennington* doctrine.[7]

SLAPP plaintiffs may also face heightened pleading requirements that make it easier for a defendant to succeed in a motion to dismiss.[8] In addition, plaintiffs

---

Nestor Colon & Sucesores, Inc. v. Custodio, 964 F.2d 32 (1st Cir. 1992); Gorman Towers v. Bogoslavsky, 626 F.2d 607 (8th Cir. 1980) (attempting to overrule board decision protected); Virginia Inn Management et al. v. Somerset Hotel Ass'n, 19 F.Supp 422 (W.D. Pa. 1998) (challenge to development not baseless); King v. Township of East Lampeter et al., 17 F.Supp 2d 394 (E.D. Pa. 1998), (taking photographs and testifying against plaintiff protected), *aff'd without opinion,* 182 F.3d 903 (3rd Cir. 1999); Fischer Sand and Aggregate Co. v. City of Lakeville, 874 F. Supp. 957 (D. Minn. 1994); Westfield Partners Ltd. v. Hogan, 740 F. Supp. 523 (N.D. Ill. 1990) (petitioning for zoning change privileged); Zeller v. Consolini, 758 A.2d 376 (Conn. App. 2000) (same); Eastern Ky. Resources, Inc. v. Arnett, 892 S.W.2d 617 (Ky. App. 1995) (seeking declaratory judgment protected); Fraser et al. v. Bovino et al., 721 A.2d 20 (N.J. App. Div. 1998) (challenge to development); Alfred Weissman Real Estate, Inc. V. Big V Supermarkets, Inc., 707 N.Y.S.2d 647 (App. Div. 2000) (engaging in the political process protected); Cove Road Dev. v. Western Cranston Industrial Park Assocs., 674 A.2d 1234 (R.I. 1996) (appealing zoning decision protected).

[4] Westfield Partners, Ltd. v. Hogan, 744 F. Supp. 189 (N.D. Ill. 1990); Gordon v. Marrone, 616 N.Y.S.2d 98 (App. Div. 1994).

[5] Professional Real Estate Investors, Inc. v. Columbia Pictures Industries, Inc., 508 U.S. 49 (1993).

[6] 668 A.2d 1260 (R.I. 1996).

[7] *Id* at 1264. *See also* Landmarks Holding Corp. v. Bermant, 664 F.2d 891 (2d Cir. 1981) (baseless litigation not protected) Livingston Downs Racing Ass'n v. Jefferson Downs Corp., 192 F.Supp.2d 519 (M.D. La. 2001) (genuine dispute on motivation); Randy's Sanitation v. Wright County, 65 F. Supp. 2d 1017 (D.C. Minn. 1999);Protect Our Mountain Env't, Inc. (POME) v. District Ct., 677 P.2d 1361 (Colo. 1984). *Contra* Londono v. Turkey Creek, 609 So. 2d 14 (Fla. 1992).

[8] Virginia Vermiculite, Ltd. v. W.R. Grace & Co., 144 F.Supp.2d 558 (W.D. Va. 2001) (claim not proved);Miness v. Alter, 691 N.Y.S.2d 171 (App. Div. 1999) (truthful accusations not actionable); Wampler v. Higgins, 752 N.E.2d 962 (Ohio 2001) (expressions of opinion are protected); Sturgeon v. Retherford Publications, 987 P.2d 1218 (Okla. App. 1999) (dismissing action when defamatory statements absent from record); Swerdlick v. Koch, 721 A.2d 849 (R.I. 1998) (surveillance and complaints to zoning official not actionable); Schmalenberg v. Tacoma News, 943 P.2d 350 (Wash. App. 1997) (statements did not cause injury).

who are public figures must prove with "convincing clarity" that defendants acted with actual malice. Some courts have held that land-use developer plaintiffs who participate in the public approval process are public figures who must prove actual malice.[9]

Defendants have also brought counterclaims, called SLAPPbacks, against plaintiffs who bring SLAPP suits. These suits are based on theories such as malicious prosecution, abuse of process, or a violation of constitutional rights, and often are successful.[10] In some instances, however, a defendant's conduct precludes a SLAPPback counterclaim or a dismissal under a SLAPP theory if there is an issue of fact whether the defendant acted in good faith or with actual malice.[11]

§ 8.47 Anti-SLAPP Statutes.

Several states have adopted statutes limiting SLAPP suits. These statutes typically fall into two categories. Most of the statutes provide for a defendant's special motion to strike with a stay of discovery upon filing of the motion, but the court may order discovery for good cause shown.[1] Statutes that provide for

---

[9] Carr v. Forbes, 259 F.3d 273 (4th Cir. 2001) (engineer who developed privately financed infrastructure projects is public figure);Okun v. Superior Court of Los Angeles, 629 P.2d 1369 (Cal.1981) (asserting that a developer is corrupt is not an assertion of crime but rather an expression of opinion); Pullum v. Johnson, 647 So.2d 254 (Fla. App. 1994) (actual malice standard for public figures applies to plaintiff who campaigned for ordinance); City of New Haven v. Reichhart, 748 N.E.2d 374 (Ind. 2001) (counterclaim dismissed; plaintiff had probable cause for suit); Lobiondo v. Schwartz, 733 A.2d 516 (N.J. App. Div. 1999) (ill will and spiteful motivation are irrelevant for establishing actual malice); 600 W. 15th St. Corp. v. Von Gutfield, 603 N.E.2d 930 (N.Y. 1992) (reasonable listener standard); SRW Assocs. v. Bellport Beach Property Owners, 517 N.Y.S.2d 741 (App. Div. 1987) (malice not sole factor); Clardy v. Cowles, 912 P.2d 1078 (Wash. App. 1996) (developer who sent letters to residents to influence sentiments about controversy is limited-purpose public figure.

[10] Leonardini v. Shell Oil Co., 264 Cal. Rptr. 883 (Cal. App. 1989) (upholding damage award in SLAPPback suit); Levin v. King, 648 N.E.2d 1108 (Ill. App. 1995) (plaintiff's suit dismissed; special injury not shown); Baglini v. Lauletta, 768 A.2d 825 (N.J. App. Div. 2001) (instituting a defamation suit against opponents of a development may constitute malicious use of process).

[11] Pisello v. Town of Brookhaven, 933 F.Supp 202 (E.D. N.Y. 1996) (municipal defendant who enforced zoning laws arbitrarily and issued a highly critical press release about plaintiff who suffered financial harm not entitled to judgment on the pleadings); Pellegrino Food Prods. Co. v. City of Warren, 136 F.Supp.2d 391 (W.D. Pa. 2000) (plaintiff's allegations against certain municipal defendants sufficient to establish § 1983 claim); Vittands v. Sudduth, 730 N.E.2d 325 (Mass. App. 2000) (refusing to dismiss counterclaim for abuse of process); Gill Farms, Inc., v. Darrow, 682 N.Y.S.2d 306 (App. Div. 1998) (refusing summary judgment on SLAPP theory because of issue of fact concerning outrageous conduct by defendant's part); Mission Springs, Inc. v. City of Spokane, 954 P.2d 250 (Wash. 1998) (failure to issue grading permit actionable when developer entitled to permit and no lawful delay in issuance).

[1] Cal. Code Civ. Proc. § 425.16, *applied in* Rosenaur v. Scherer, 105 Cal. Rptr. 2d 674 (Cal.

a motion to strike allow SLAPP suits to be dismissed during the pretrial pleading stages without going to trial. A motion to strike will generally be granted unless the plaintiff can prove that the defendant's petitioning was devoid of factual support and that the baseless petitioning caused actual injury.[2] A smaller group of statutes provide for an immunity defense in lieu of a motion to strike.[3] In these states, there are no special provisions to dispose of SLAPP suits during the pretrial phases. The statutes provide that SLAPP defendants who exercise their right to petition in connection with a public or governmental issue are immune from civil liability unless the defendant knowingly communicated false information or communicated with a reckless disregard for the truth.[4]

App. 2001) (motion to strike granted for defendants who voiced opposition to initiative to change zoning designation); Ludwig v. Superior Court, 43 Cal. Rptr.2d 350 (Cal. App. 1995) (recruiting and encouraging agents to oppose development protected; economic motive of defendant not disqualifying); Dixon v. Superior Ct., 36 Cal. Rptr. 2d 687 (Cal. App. Ct. 1994) (statements on matter of public concern, even if malicious, entitled to absolute immunity); Wilcox v. Superior Ct., 33 Cal. Rptr. 2d 446 (Cal. App. 1994) (requesting contributions for a lawsuit protected); Del. Code Ann. tit. 10, §§ 8136 et seq.; Fla. Stat. § 57.105, § 768.295; Ga. Code Ann. § 9-11-11.1, *applied in* Denton v. Browns Mill Dev. Co., 561 S.E.2d 431 (Ga. 2002) (trespass claim not within statute); Metzler v. Rowell, 547 S.E.2d 311 (Ga. App. 2001) (defendant's conduct protected); Ind. Code § 34-7-7-1 et seq.; La. Code Civ. Proc. Ann. Art. 971; Mass. Gen. Laws Ann. ch. 231, § 59, *applied in* Baker v. Parsons, 750 N.E.2d 953 (Mass. 2001) (petitioning activity that has any reasonable factual support or arguable basis in law is protected under statute); Me. Rev. Stat. Ann. tit. 14, § 556, *applied in* Morse Brothers v. Webster, 772 A.2d 842 (Me. 2001) (defendants' opposition not frivolous); Minn. Stat. § 554.01 et seq.; Neb. Rev. Stat. Ann. § 25-21,241 et seq.; N.Y. Civ. Rights Law § 70-a, N.Y. C.P.L.R. 3211(g), 3212 (h), *applied in* Yeshiva Chofetz Chaim Radin, Inc. v. Village of New Hempstead, 98 F. Supp. 2d 347 (S.D.N.Y. 2000) (misuse of power not protected). See Opinion of Justices, 641 A.2d 1012 (N.H. 1994) (proposed anti-SLAPP statute unconstitutional for denying right to trial by jury); Shaari v. Harvard Student Agencies, Inc., 691 N.E.2d 925 (Mass. 1998) (Massachusetts defamation law allowing recovery for malicious but truthful statements held unconstitutional violation of the first amendment).

[2] Mass. Gen. Laws Ann. ch. 231, § 59H; Me. Rev. Stat. Ann. tit. 14, § 556.

[3] Nev. Rev. Stat. Ann. § 41.637, § 41.650; Okla. Stat. tit. 12 § 1443.1; Tenn. Code Ann. § 4-21-1001 et seq.; Wash. Rev. Code Ann. § 4.24.500 et seq., *applied in* Right-Price Recreation, LLC v. Connells Prairie Community Council, 46 P.3d 789 (Wash. 2002) (defendants immune because actual malice not shown); Gilman v. MacDonald, 875 P.2d 897 (Wash. App. 1994) (same).

[4] Nev. Rev. Stat. Ann. § 41.637 (defendant's actual malice exception implicit in definition of "good faith communication in furtherance of the right to petition."); Okla. Stat. tit. 12 § 1443.1 (exception if defendant falsely imputes crime to a public official); Tenn. Code Ann. § 4-21-1003 (b) et seq. (public figure plaintiffs must prove defendant knowingly communicated false information or acted with reckless disregard for truth; if not public figures must only prove defendant acted negligently); Wash. Rev. Code Ann. § 4.24.520 (defendant's actual malice exception implicit in good faith communication requirement). *See also* R.I. Gen. Laws § 9-33-1 et seq. (authorizing motion to assert immunity and codifying sham exception), *applied in* Global Waste Recycling v. Mallette, 762 A.2d 1208 (R.I. 2000) (statements made to newspaper protected); Hometown Props. v. Fleming, 680 A.2d 56 1996 (R.I. 1996) (defendant's communications with various officials protected).

Several statutes from both groups allow intervention by a state or local government entity to support a party claiming a lawful right to exercise the right of petition or free speech.[5] Most Anti-SLAPP statutes also have a public concern requirement that excludes private disputes from dismissal under a SLAPP theory. Courts have given different interpretations of what constitutes a matter of public concern.[6] Nearly all statutes provide that a prevailing defendant may recover costs, attorneys fees and compensatory and punitive damages.[7] Conversely, many statutes provide that a plaintiff may recover attorney's fees if the defendant's motion to strike is frivolous or intended to cause delay.[8]

---

[5] Mass. Gen. Laws Ann. ch. 231, § 59H; Me. Rev. Stat. Ann. tit. 14, § 556; Minn. Stat. § 554.02 Subd. 2(4); R.I. Gen. Laws § 9-33-3; Tenn. Code Ann. § 4-21-1004; Wash. Rev. Code Ann. § 4.24.520.

[6] Briggs v. Eden Council For Hope & Opportunity, 969 P.2d 564 (Cal. 1999) (defendant claiming protection of anti-SLAPP statute need not allege statement concerned issue of public significance); Averill v. Superior Court, 50 Cal. Rptr. 2d 62 (Cal. App. 1996) (private conversations about issues of public concern protected). *But See* Harfenes v. Sea Gate Association, 647 N.Y.S.2d 329 (Sup. Ct. 1995) (only defendants in SLAPP suit have cause of action under anti-SLAPP law).

[7] Ketchum v. Moses, 17 P.3d 735, (Cal. 2001) (fee enhancement not proper); Coltrain v. Shewalter, 77 Cal. Rptr. 2d 600 (Cal. App. 1998) (fee award upheld); West Branch Conservation Association et al. v. Planning Board of the Town of Clarkstown, 636 N.Y.S.2d 61 (App. Div. 1995) (award of fees discretionary).

[8] Cal. Code Civ. Proc. § 425.16(c)); Fla. Stat. § 57.105(3); Ind. Code § 34-7-7-8; La. Code Civ. Proc. Ann. Art. 971B; Neb. Rev. Stat. Ann. § 25-21,244(1) (plaintiff must prove defendant's knowledge of falsity or reckless disregard for truthfulness of speech); Tenn. Code Ann. § 4-21-1004(b) (if intervening government agency fails to establish defendant's immunity); Wash. Rev. Code Ann. § 4.24.520 (same).

REFERENCES

Books

J. Delaney, S. Abrams & F. Schnidman, Land Use Practice & Forms: Handling the Land Use Case (1997 & Supps.)

How to Litigate a Land Use Case (ABA, L. Smith ed. 2000).

S. Nahmod, Civil Rights and Civil Liberties Litigation: The Law of 1983 (3d ed. 1991).

G. Pring & P. Canan, SLAPPs: Getting Sued for Speaking Out (1996).

M. Schwartz & J. Kirklin, Section 1983 Litigation: Claims, Defenses, and Fees (2d ed. 1991).

Articles

Alexander, Constitutional Torts, the Supreme Court, and the Law of Noncontradiction: An Essay on *Zinernon v. Burch,* 87 Nw. L. Rev. 576 (1993).

Arco, Barbara, When Rights Collide: Reconciling the First Amendment Rights of Opposing Parties in Civil Litigation, 52 U. Miami L. Rev. 587 (1998).

Ayer, The Primitive Law of Standing in Land Use Disputes: Some Notes from a Dark Continent, 55 Iowa L. Rev. 344 (1969).

Benson & Merriam, Identifying and Beating a Strategic Lawsuit Against Public Participation, 3 Duke Envtl. L. & Pol'y F. 17 (1993).

Blaesser, Closing the Federal Courthouse Door on Property Owners: The Ripeness and Abstention Doctrines in Section 1983 Land Use Cases, 2 Hofstra Prop. L.J. 73 (1989).

Borth, Municipal Tort Liability for Erroneous Issuance of Building Permits: A National Survey, 58 Wash. L. Rev. 537 (1983).

Braun, Increasing SLAPP Protection: Unburdening the Right of Petition in California, 32 U.C. Davis L. Rev. 965 (1999).

Brown, Correlating Municipal Liability and Official Immunity Under Section 1983, 1989 U. Ill. L. Rev. 625.

Capistrano, Enforcing Federal Rights: The Law of Section 1983, 33 Clearinghouse Rev. 217, 393 (1999).

Cook & Merriam, Recognizing a SLAPP Suit and Understanding its Consequences, 19 Zoning & Plan. L. Rep. 33 (1996).

Cushman, Municipal Liability Under § 1983: Toward a New Definition of Municipal Policymaker, 34 B.C. L. Rev. 693 (1993).

Freiman, The Problem of Qualified Immunity: How Conflating Microeconomics and Law Subverts the Constitution, 34 Idaho L. Rev. 61 (1997).

Glover & Jimison, S.L.A.P.P. Suits: A First Amendment Issue and Beyond, 21 N.C. Cent. L.J. 122 (1995).

Hyson, The Problem of Relief in Developer-Initiated Exclusionary Zoning Litigation, 12 Urb. L. Ann. 21 (1976).

Jeffries, Disaggregating Constitutional Torts, 110 Yale L.J. (2000).

Kendall, Dowling & Schwartz. Choice of Forum and Finality Ripeness: The Unappreciated Hot Topic in Regulatory Takings Cases, 33 Urb. Law. 405 (2001).

Kovacs, Accepting the Relegation of Takings Claims to State Courts: The Federal Courts' Misguided Attempts to Avoid Preclusion Under Williamson County, 26 Ecology L.Q. 1 (1999).

LaRusso, "Paying for the Change,": *First English Evangelical Church of Glendale v. County of Los Angeles* and the Calculation of Interim Damages for Regulatory Takings, 17 B.C. Envtl. Aff. L. Rev. 551 (1990).

Lyman, Finality Ripeness in Federal Land Use Cases From *Hamilton Bank* to *Lucas,* 9 J. Land Use & Envtl. L. 101 (1994).

Mandelker, Inverse Condemnation: The Constitutional Limits of Public Responsibility, 1966 Wis. L. Rev. 3.

McCann, The Interrelationship of Immunity and the *Prima Facie* Case in Section 1983 and *Bivens* Actions, 21 Gonz. L. Rev. 115 (1985-86).

McNamara, Inverse Condemnation: A "Sophistic Miltonian Serbonian Bog," 31 Baylor L. Rev. 443 (1977).

Morgan, Exhaustion of Administrative Remedies as a Municipal Defense to Inverse Condemnation Actions, in Proceedings of the Institute on Planning, Zoning, and Eminent Domain ch. 9 (1985).

Oren, Signing Into Heaven: *Zinermon v. Burch,* Federal Rights, and State Remedies Thirty Years After *Monroe v. Pape,* 40 Emory L.J. 1 (1991).

Overstreet, The Ripeness Doctrine of the Taking Clause: A Survey of Decisions Showing Just How Far Federal Courts Will Go to Avoid Adjudicating Land Use Cases, 10 J. Envtl. & Land Use L. 91 (1994).

Potter, Strategic Lawsuits Against Public Participation and Petition Clause Immunity, 31 Envtl. L. Rep. 10852 (2001).

Prahl, The Rezoning Dilemma: What May a Court Do With an Invalid Zoning Classification?, 25 S.D.L. Rev. 116 (1980).

Roberts, Procedural Implications of Williamson/First English in Regulatory Takings Legislation: Reservations, Removal, Diversity, Supplemental Jurisdiction, *Rooker-Feldman,* and Res Judicata, 31 Envt. L. Rep. 10350 (2001).

Rosen, The *Bivens* Constitutional Tort: An Unfulfilled Promise, 67 N.C.L. Rev. 337 (1989).

Sills, Jennifer E., SLAPPs (Strategic Lawsuits Against Public Participation): How can the Legal System Eliminate Their Appeal?, 25 Conn. L. Rev. 547 (1993).

Stein, Pinpointing the Beginning and Ending of a Temporary Regulatory Taking, 70 Wash. L. Rev. 953 (1995).

Young, Federal Court Abstention and State Administrative Law From *Burford* to *Ankenbrandt:* Fifty Years of Judicial Federalism Under *Burford v. Sun Oil Co.* and Kindred Doctrines, 42 DePaul L. Rev. 859 (1993).

Student Work

Note, Beyond Invalidation: The Judicial Power to Zone, 9 Urb. L. Ann. 159 (1975).

Note, Exhaustion of Remedies in Zoning Cases, 1964 Wash. U.L.Q. 368.

Note, From *Parratt* to *Zinermon:* Authorization, Adequacy, and Immunity in a System Analysis of State Procedure, 11 Cardozo L. Rev. 831 (1990).

Note, The Legal Literature on SLAPPs: A Look Behind the Smoke Nine Years After Professors Pring and Canan First Yelled "Fire!", 9 U. Fla. J.L. & Pub. Pol'y 85 (1997).

Note, Qualifying Immunity in Section 1983 & *Bivens* Actions, 71 Tex. L. Rev. 123 (1992).

Note, Reforming SLAPP Reform: New York's Anti-SLAPP Statute, 70 N.Y.U.L. Rev. 1324 (1995).

Note, Standing to Challenge Exclusionary Land Use Control Devices in Federal Courts After *Warth v. Seldin,* 29 Stan. L. Rev. 323 (1977).

Notes and Comments, Paying the Price: It's Time to Hold Municipalities Liable for Punitive Damages Under § 1983, 10 J.L. & Pol'y 189 (2001).

Comment, The Public Duty Doctrine and Municipal Liability for Negligent Administration of Zoning Codes, 20 Seattle U. L. Rev. 803 (1997).

Comment, SLAPP Suits: Weaknesses in First Amendment Law and in the Courts' Responses to Frivolous Litigation, 39 UCLA L. Rev. 979 (1992).

Casenote, Characterization of Land Use Decisions: A Zone of Uncertainty, 37 Vill. L. Rev. 663 (1992).

Case Note, *City of Chicago v. International College of Surgeons*: The Interplay Between Supplemental Jurisdiction and Cross-System Appeals, and the Impact on Federalism, 50 Mercer L. Rev. 1137 (1999).

Case Note, Federal Jurisdiction—Expanding Supplemental Jurisdiction Over Appeals From Non-Federal Administrative Agencies, 72 Temp. L. Rev. 529 (1999).

Chapter 9

RESIDENTIAL DEVELOPMENT CONTROLS

Synopsis

§ 9.01   An Introductory Note.

A. SUBDIVISION CONTROL.

§ 9.02   History and Purpose.
§ 9.03   Enabling Legislation.
§ 9.04   The Subdivision Control Process.
§ 9.05   Definition of "Subdivision."
§ 9.06   Relationship to Zoning.
§ 9.07   Vested Rights.
§ 9.08   Enforcement.
§ 9.09   Scope of Authority: Discretion to Approve or Reject.
§ 9.10   Variances and Waivers.
§ 9.11   Exactions.
§ 9.12   The Takings Issue.
§ 9.13   *Nollan* and What It Means: Applying the Nexus Test.
§ 9.14   *Dolan* and What It Means.
§ 9.15   On-Site Streets and Improvements.
§ 9.16   Off-Site Streets and Improvements.
§ 9.17   Parks and Schools.
§ 9.18   Statutory Authority.
§ 9.19   The Takings Issue.
§ 9.20   Impact Fees.
§ 9.21   Statutory Authority.
§ 9.22   The Takings Issue.
§ 9.23   Linkage Programs.

B. PLANNED UNIT DEVELOPMENT.

§ 9.24   The Land Use Problem.
§ 9.25   The Planned Unit Development Review Process.
§ 9.26   Under the Standard Zoning Act.
§ 9.27   Regulatory Techniques.
§ 9.28   Discretion to Approve or Reject.
§ 9.29   Amendments to Development Plans.
§ 9.30   Planned Unit Development Legislation.

§ 9.01   An Introductory Note.

In addition to the zoning ordinance, municipalities also have land use controls that apply primarily to residential development. These include subdivision control and planned unit development regulations. Subdivision controls are authorized

(5th Ed.—02/03)

by separate enabling legislation and are contained in a separate ordinance. They apply design, public facility and related requirements to new subdivisions, and often require developers to dedicate land for on-site and off-site facilities. Planned unit development regulations provide an administrative process for the comprehensive review of new development projects as a single entity. These projects are often limited to residential use, but they may also contain commercial and office uses. Planned development regulations are usually contained in the zoning ordinance and are not usually specifically authorized by legislation. This chapter discusses these controls, including a discussion of impact fees that are often demanded from developers in the development approval process.

A. SUBDIVISION CONTROL.

§ 9.02 History and Purpose.

States first enacted subdivision control legislation toward the close of the nineteenth century to remedy land conveyancing problems. Land historically had been conveyed by its legal description, a confusing and unreliable method that often led to boundary disputes. Land developers began to plat land they intended to develop into lots and blocks so that they could avoid conveyancing difficulties by conveying individual lots within the plat. Early subdivision laws required the recording of subdivision plats in the local records office, after which the conveyance of lots within the subdivision could be made "with reference" to the plat.

Subdivision control legislation was next amended to remedy problems in street planning. Street systems in early subdivisions often were not aligned with existing streets. To remedy this problem, some states amended their subdivision control legislation to require subdivision plats to comply with the municipal street plan.

The Standard City Planning Enabling Act used these early subdivision platting statutes as a model for subdivision control enabling legislation which was included in the Act. The Standard Act authorized subdivision control ordinances to require streets and other necessary improvements, access to the subdivision, and limitations on density. Most state subdivision control legislation is based on the Standard Act or on two similar statutory models proposed somewhat later.[1] Some modern subdivision control statutes add to these requirements. They require additional on-site improvements, prohibit subdivisions in floodplains and environmentally sensitive areas, and authorize the approval of subdivisions only if public facilities are adequate.

Subdivision controls apply when land is subdivided for development and usually apply only to residential development. They do not usually apply to

---

[1] E. Bassett, F. Williams, A. Bettman & R. Whitten, Model Laws for Planning Cities, Counties and States 39–47, 84–88 (1935).

nonresidential and multifamily residential development because this type of development usually occurs on unsubdivided land. Subdivision controls do not regulate the use of land. They require compliance with design and public facility standards and the provision of streets and other public improvements that are necessary for the subdivision. They may also require subdividers to dedicate land or make monetary payments for off-site improvements when the subdivision creates a need for them. Subdivision controls may contain restrictions that duplicate the zoning ordinance, such as a prohibition on the development of unsuitable land or a minimum lot size requirement.

Many states also have public health programs that affect subdivision development. They authorize state health and environmental agencies to regulate on-site wells and on-site sewage disposal through septic tanks and similar facilities.[2]

§ 9.03   Enabling Legislation.

Sections 13 and 14 of the Standard Planning Act provided the legislative enabling authority for subdivision control:

§ 13. Whenever a planning commission shall have adopted a major street plan . . . [on file in the county recorder's office], then no plat of a subdivision of land shall be filed or recorded until it shall have been approved by such planning commission. . . .

§ 14. Before exercising . . . [subdivision control] powers . . . the planning commission shall adopt regulations governing the subdivision of land within its jurisdiction. Such regulations may provide for the proper arrangement of streets in relation to other existing or planned streets and to the master plan, for adequate and convenient open spaces for traffic, utilities, access of firefighting apparatus, recreation, light and air, and for the avoidance of congestion of population, including minimum width and areas of lots.

Such regulations may include provisions as to the extent to which streets and other ways shall be graded and improved and to which water and sewer and other utility mains, piping, or other facilities shall be installed as a condition precedent to the approval of the plat. . . .

This legislation contains several important elements. The authority to approve subdivisions is granted to the planning commission. Many state statutes follow this model,[1] but some states grant approval authority to the local governing body.[2] In other states, the governing body may delegate the authority to approve

---

[2] Md. Envt. Code Ann. § 9-204; N.H. Rev. Stat. Ann. § 485:30. *See* Erb v. Maryland Dep't of the Envt., 676 A.2d 1017 (Md. App. (1996) (denial of permit for on-site septic tank held not a taking). *See also* Mich. Comp. Laws Ann. § 560.109a (no approval of subdivision of less than one acre unless public water and approved on-site sewer).

[1] Marx v. Zoning Bd. of Appeals, 529 N.Y.S.2d 330 (App. Div. 1988).

[2] Cal. Gov't Code § 66411.

subdivisions to the planning commission.[3] The planning commission must "adopt regulations" governing the subdivision of land. These regulations implement standards contained in the subdivision control ordinance.

The Standard Act authorized the adoption of a subdivision control ordinance after the municipality had adopted a master street plan. Other statutes go further and require subdivisions to be consistent with the local comprehensive plan.[4] In *Board of County Comm'rs v. Gaster,*[5] the court held the board could disapprove a subdivision that did not comply with the comprehensive plan even though it met all zoning requirements.

Subdivision control legislation defines the scope of subdivision control authority. The Standard Planning Act authorized subdivision controls for streets and other improvements and included the authority to impose controls "for the avoidance of congestion of population."[6] Most subdivision control statutes contain comparable provisions,[7] and some extend the scope of subdivision control authority. California authorizes the denial of a subdivision if the "site is not physically suitable" for the type or density of development or if the "design of the improvements is likely to cause substantial environmental damage."[8] Other states authorize the denial of a subdivision because of flooding or other environmental effects.[9]

Section 12 of the Standard Act authorized municipalities to regulate subdivisions in an extraterritorial area five miles beyond the municipal limits, most states

---

[3] N.J. Stat. Ann. § 40:55D-37.

[4] Cal. Gov't Code § 66474(a); 65 Ill. Comp. Stat. Ann. 5/11-12-8 (official map). *See* Families Unafraid to Uphold Rural El Dorado County v. Board of Supervisors, 74 Cal. Rptr. 2d 1 (Cal. App. 1998); Board of County Comm'rs v. Condor, 927 P.2d 1339 (Colo. 1996); Lake City Corp. v. City of Mequon, 558 N.W.2d 100 (Wis. 1997); Mont. Rev. Code Ann. § 76-1-606 (subdivision regulations must be consistent with adopted growth policy).

[5] 401 A.2d 666 (Md. 1979).

[6] §§ 3.05, 3.12

[7] Colo. Rev. Stat. § 30-28-133; N.J. Stat. Ann. § 40:55D-38.

[8] Cal. Gov't Code § 66474. *See* Topanga Ass'n for a Scenic Community v. County of Los Angeles, 263 Cal. Rptr. 214 (Cal. App. 1989) (statute requires independent environmental review); Sequoyah Hills Homeowners Ass'n v. City of Oakland, 29 Cal. Rptr. 2d 182 (Cal. App. 1994) (upholding approval based on compliance with plan policies).

[9] Ariz. Rev. Stat. Ann. § 9-463.01(C)(4); Mont. Code Ann. § 76-3-608(3); Burrell v. Lake County Plan Comm'n, 624 N.E.2d 526 (Ind. App. 1993) (upholds rejection because of septic tank leaching and increased flooding and drainage problems); Manthe v. Town Bd., 555 N.W.2d 167 (Wis. App. 1996) (upholds ordinance requiring public sewer service). *See also* American Planning Association, Growing Smart Legislative Guidebook: Model Statutes for Planning and Management of Change § 9-301(S. Meck ed. 2002) (proposed subdivision control enabling legislation.

confer the power to control subdivisions in extraterritorial areas,[10] and the courts have upheld this authority.[11]

§ 9.04 The Subdivision Control Process.

Most subdivision control ordinances authorize a standard subdivision review process. The process may begin with a preapplication conference in which the reviewing agency considers a sketch and general map of the subdivision and provides guidance on subdivision control requirements. Submission of a preliminary plat follows and is the first formal step in the approval of a subdivision. The preliminary plat contains all of the detailed elements the subdivision ordinance requires for approval of the final plat. The right to subdivide may vest after the preliminary plat is approved.[1] The subdivider may usually begin the construction of improvements after the preliminary plat is approved, and the municipality may require a bond as surety for their completion prior to final approval.[2]

Final approval of the subdivision comes next. Before the final plat is approved, the subdivider must obtain a certification that subdivision improvements are properly completed. Some municipalities require submission of two plats at this stage. One is called an "engineering plat" and is used internally to determine whether the required improvements have been completed. The second is a "plat for record," which shows necessary land title and boundary information. This plat is recorded after it is approved, and lots in the subdivision may then be offered for sale.

§ 9.05 Definition of "Subdivision."

Section 1 of the Standard Act defines a subdivision as a division of a lot for the "purpose of sale or building development," and this definition has been adopted in some statutes, as in the Connecticut statute discussed below. Many subdivision control statutes define a subdivision as a division of land into a minimum number of lots.[1] This type of statutory definition excludes developments on individual lots from the subdivision control ordinance[2] and encourages evasion by builders who build only a few homes at a time.[3] The courts have

---

[10] *E.g.*, Kan. Stat. Ann. §§ 12-749, 12-750.

[11] Petterson v. City of Naperville, 137 N.E.2d 371 (Ill. 1956). *See* City of Carlsbad v. Caviness, 346 P.2d 310 (N.M. 1959) (does not include zoning power). *See also* §§ 4.22, 4.23.

[1] § 9.07.

[2] *See* the Standard Act, § 14.

[1] Conn. Gen. Stat. § 8-18 (three or more); Mass. Gen. L. ch. 41, § 81L (two or more). *See* Ahearn v. Town of Wheatland, 39 P.3d 409 (Wyo. 2002) (ordinance providing abbreviated procedure for resubdivision held consistent with statute).

[2] Vinyard v. St. Louis County, 399 S.W.2d 99 (Mo. 1966).

[3] *See* State ex rel. Dreher v. Fuller, 849 P.2d 1045 (Mont. 1993) (rebuttable presumption of evasion authorized by state statute and does not violate due process).

held that the sale of land for condominium development is not a subdivision, but some subdivision control statutes include these developments.[4]

Some statutes, as in Connecticut, define a subdivision as a division of land for the "purpose . . . of sale or building development."[5] When landowners have sold lots for residential development without formally subdividing, some courts have held that the land was not sold "singly or collectively for residential purposes" or that the landowner did not hold himself out as a subdivider.[6] Most courts hold that a subdivision control ordinance cannot modify the "subdivision" definition which is in the statute.[7]

Subdivision control legislation usually contains exemptions from subdivision control regulation. The subdivision of land for agricultural use is one example.[8] Other statutes exempt the subdivision of small tracts if no additional streets are created.[9]

§ 9.06 Relationship to Zoning.

Some subdivision control legislation provides that subdivisions must comply with the zoning ordinance.[1] Even if the subdivision control legislation does not contain this requirement, a municipality may reject a subdivision if it does not comply with the zoning ordinance[2] or may require zoning compliance in its subdivision control ordinance.[3] Subdivision review cannot be used to amend the

---

[4] Gerber v. Town of Clarkstown, 356 N.Y.S.2d 926 (Sup. Ct. 1974). *See* Cal. Gov't Code § 66426 (included); N.H. Rev. Stat. Ann. § 672:14 (same). *Accord*, Town of York v. Cragin, 541 A.2d 932 (Me. 1988); Cohen v. Town of Henniker, 593 A.2d 1145 (N.H. 1991). *But see* County of Montgomery v. Deer Creek, Inc., 691 N.E.2d 185 (Ill. App. 1998) (conversion to condominium development held a subdivision).

[5] Conn. Gen. Stat. § 8-18. *See* State *ex rel.* Udall v. Cresswell, 960 P.2d 818 (N.M. App. 1998) (division of land to create security interest to finance sale held a subdivision).

[6] Slavin v. Ingraham, 339 N.E.2d 157 (N.Y. 1975). *See also* State ex rel. Anaya v. Select W. Lands, Inc., 613 P.2d 425 (N.M. App. 1979); Herrick v. Ingraham, 363 N.Y.S.2d 665 (App. Div. 1975).

[7] Penobscot, Inc. v. Board of County Comm'rs, 642 P.2d 915 (Colo. 1982); Peninsula Corp. v. Planning & Zoning Comm'n, 199 A.2d 1 (Conn. 1964); State v. Visser, 767 P.2d 858 (Mont. 1988) (exemption); Dearborn v. Town of Milford, 411 A.2d 1132 (N.H. 1980); Martorano v. Board of Comm'rs, 414 A.2d 411 (Pa. Commw. 1980). *Contra* Delaware Midland Corp. v. Incorporated Village of Westhampton Beach, 359 N.Y.S.2d 944 (Sup. Ct. 1974), *aff'd*, 355 N.E.2d 302 (N.Y. 1976).

[8] N.J. Stat. Ann. § 40:55D-7 (over five acres).

[9] Cal. Gov't Code § 66426. *See* Urban v. Planning Bd. of Manasquan, 592 A.2d 240 (N.J. 1991) (subdivision of nonconforming lots). *But see* Sugarman v. Lewis, 488 A.2d 709 (R.I. 1985).

[1] N.J. Stat. Ann. § 40:55D-38(b)(1).

[2] Krawski v. Planning & Zoning Comm'n, 575 A.2d 1036 (Conn. App. 1990); People v. City of Park Ridge, 166 N.E.2d 635 (Ill. App. 1960); Loveless v. Yantis, 513 P.2d 1023 (Wash. 1973).

[3] Benny v. City of Alameda, 164 Cal. Rptr. 776 (Cal. App. 1980). *See also* Town of Sun Prairie v. Storms, 327 N.W.2d 642 (Wis. 1983) (may include minimum lot size requirement in subdivision ordinance).

zoning ordinance because this would usurp the local zoning authority.[4] Compliance with the zoning ordinance is not sufficient when the subdivision control ordinance imposes additional requirements.[5]

§ 9.07 Vested Rights.

Vested rights problems arise under subdivision controls as well as zoning ordinances.[1] The mere recording of a plat without street dedications does not create a vested right that exempts the subdivider from complying with subdivision control requirements that are adopted later.[2] The approval of a preliminary plat does not create a vested right in the absence of statutory authority that gives it this effect.[3] A minority rule protects the subdivider from changes in lot sizes made after the date of application for subdivision approval.[4] Substantial construction in reliance on a subdivision approval will vest the landowner's rights to proceed under regulations in effect at that time.[5]

Some statutes require the approval of a final plat if it meets the requirements imposed when the municipality approved the preliminary plat.[6] The courts hold that the approval of a final plat that meets these requirements is a ministerial act they can mandate under these statutes, and that the approving agency may not impose additional requirements as the basis for final approval.[7]

Though the Standard Act did not protect an approved subdivision against subsequent changes in a zoning ordinance,[8] some subdivision control statutes

---

[4] Cristofaro v. Town of Burlington, 584 A.2d 1168 (Conn. 1991); Shapiro v. Town of Oyster Bay, 211 N.Y.S.2d 414 (Sup. Ct. 1961), aff'd, 249 N.Y.S.2d 663 (App. Div. 1964); Goodman v. Board of Comm'rs, 411 A.2d 838 (Pa. Commw. 1980); Snyder v. Zoning Bd., 200 A.2d 222 (R.I. 1964).

[5] Shoptaugh v. Board of County Comm'rs, 543 P.2d 524 (Colo. App. 1976); Popular Refreshments, Inc. v. Fuller's Milk Bar, Inc., 205 A.2d 445 (N.J. App. Div. 1964).

[1] §§ 6.12–6.23. See also McFillan v. Berkeley County Planning Comm'n, 438 S.E.2d 801 (W. Va. 1993) (applies nonconforming use principles to subdivision regulation).

[2] Blevens v. City of Manchester, 170 A.2d 121 (N.H. 1961); Lake Intervale Homes, Inc. v. Parsippany-Troy Hills, 147 A.2d 28 (N.J. 1958); In re McCormick Mgt. Co., 547 A.2d 1319 (Vt. 1988). But see Board of County Comm'rs v. Goldenrod Corp., 601 P.2d 360 (Colo. App. 1979).

[3] Boutet v. Planning Bd., 253 A.2d 53 (Me. 1969).

[4] Robinson v. Lintz, 420 P.2d 923 (Ariz. 1966); Smith v. Winhall Planning Comm'n, 436 A.2d 760 (Vt. 1981. But see In re Appeal of Taft Corners Ass'n, Inc., 758 A.2d 804 (Vt. 2000) (issuance of subdivision permit does not affect zoning permit requirements).

[5] Morganstern v. Town of Rye, 794 A.2d 782 (N.H. 2002); Ellington Constr. Corp. v. Zoning Bd., 566 N.E.2d 128 (N.Y. 1990). See also N.H. Rev. Stat. Ann. § 674:39.

[6] Cal. Gov't Code § 66458; Pa. Stat. Ann. tit. 53, § 10508(4). See Golden State Homebuilding Assocs. v. City of Modesto, 31 Cal. Rptr. 2d 572 (Cal. App. 1994).

[7] Youngblood v. Board of Supvrs., 586 P.2d 556 (Cal. 1979); Hakim v. Board of Comm'rs, 366 A.2d 1306 (Pa. Commw. 1976).

[8] R.A. Vachon & Son v. City of Concord, 289 A.2d 646 (N.H. 1972). See also Dawe v. City

protect the subdivider against future zoning and other changes in land use regulations. The Pennsylvania statute, which is typical, protects the subdivider for five years after preliminary or final approval of a subdivision plat from any "subsequent change or amendment in the zoning, subdivision or other governing ordinance or plan."[9] Other statutes provide similar protection.[10] These statutes protect against changes in local but not state land use requirements and regulations.[11]

§ 9.08 Enforcement.

The enforcement of subdivision control ordinances is difficult because evasion of the ordinance is difficult to control. The Standard Planning Act required the approval of a subdivision before it could be recorded. The Act did not require the approval of a subdivision if the subdivider did not wish to record it. The Act attempted to prevent evasion by authorizing a monetary penalty whenever a landowner sold "by reference to or exhibition" of a plat for a subdivision that was not approved under the subdivision control ordinance.[1] This sanction does not prevent evasion because a landowner can subdivide her land and sell lots by the legal description without going through the subdivision approval process.

Some statutes avoid this problem by requiring the approval of all subdivisions under the subdivision control ordinance, whether or not they are recorded.[2] To make this requirement effective, the statute should include a broad definition of the subdivisions subject to regulation.[3] The Standard Act authorized municipalities to enjoin the sale of lots in an unapproved subdivision.[4]

---

of Scottsdale, 581 P.2d 1136 (Ariz. 1978). *But see* Western Land Equities, Inc. v. City of Logan, 617 P.2d 388 (Utah 1980), discussed in § 6.16. *Compare* Wood v. North Salt Lake, 390 P.2d 858 (Utah 1964).

[9] Pa. Stat. Ann. tit. 53, § 10508(4). *See also* Wash. Rev. Code 58.17.033 (subdivision to be considered under subdivision, zoning and other land use ordinances at time completed application for preliminary plat approval submitted); Friends of the Law v. King County, 869 P.2d 1056 (Wash. 1994) (interprets statute extending common law vested rights doctrine to subdivisions).

[10] Conn. Gen. Stat. § 8-26a; Mass. Gen. L. ch. 40A, § 6; N.J. Stat. Ann. § 40:55D-49; N.Y. Gen. City Law § 83-a; N.Y. Town Law § 265-a; N.Y. Village Law § 7-708; Va. Code § 15.2-2307. *See* Ellington Constr. Corp. v. Zoning Bd., 566 N.E.2d 128 (N.Y. 1990) (sufficient expenditures to vest rights under law).

[11] Island Props., Inc. v. Martha's Vineyard Comm'n, 361 N.E.2d 385 (Mass. 1977); Ocean Acres v. State, 403 A.2d 967 (N.J. App. Div. 1979).

[1] Standard Planning Act § 16. *See* Commonwealth v. Fisher, 350 A.2d 428 (Pa. Commw. 1976) (penalty not a restraint on alienation).

[2] Conn. Gen. Stat. § 8-25.

[3] § 9.05.

[4] *See* N.Y. Town Law § 268(2). *See also* Lake Cty. v. Truett, 758 S.W.2d 529 (Tenn. App. 1988) (court will not compel compliance or posting of bond).

A sanction that goes too far may be invalid. An example is a statute or ordinance that prohibits the sale or conveyance of land in a subdivision until it is approved in the subdivision control process and recorded. Provisions of this type have been held invalid as a restraint on alienation.[5] A milder and often effective sanction authorizes the denial of building permits for dwellings in subdivisions that are not approved under the subdivision control ordinance.[6] This sanction may create problems because it places the penalty for lack of compliance on the buyer of a lot in an unapproved subdivision. The courts have refused to authorize the withholding of a building permit from an innocent purchaser in this situation.[7]

A subdivision control statute may prohibit the issuance of a building permit except on a lot abutting a street that is "suitably improved" to the satisfaction of the municipality.[8] This sanction allows the municipality to use the leverage of street improvements to compel compliance with the subdivision control ordinance. Opportunities for evasion remain if the statute or ordinance exempts construction along an existing street or highway. A builder can build one house at a time along an improved street or highway without subdivision approval.[9]

§ 9.09 Scope of Authority: Discretion to Approve or Reject.

Courts tend to construe subdivision control legislation based on the Standard Act and subdivision control ordinances strictly. A subdivision must be approved if it complies with the subdivision regulations.[1] They reverse subdivision disapprovals if the reason for disapproval is not authorized by the Standard Act or the subdivision control ordinance and invalidate requirements in subdivision control ordinances if they are not authorized by the Standard Act.[2] Courts take

---

[5] Kass v. Lewin, 104 So. 2d 572 (Fla. 1958).

[6] Wash. Rev. Code Ann. § 58.17.210.

[7] Keizer v. Adams, 471 P.2d 983 (Cal. 1970); State ex rel. Craven v. City of Tacoma, 385 P.2d 372 (Wash. 1963).

[8] Brous v. Smith, 106 N.E.2d 503 (N.Y. 1952) (upholding requirement).

[9] *See also* State v. Baker, 618 P.2d 997 (Or. App. 1980) (criminal prosecution); 77 A.L.R.3d 1058 (1977).

[1] Plan Comm'n of Harrison County v. Aulbach, 748 N.E..2d 926 (Ind. App. 2001).

[2] Richardson v. City of Little Rock Planning Comm'n, 747 S.W.2d 115 (Ark. 1988); Board of County Comm'rs v. Condor, 927 P.2d 1339 (Colo. 1996) (remanding case); Dosmann v. Area Plan Comm'n, 312 N.E.2d 880 (Ind. App. 1974); Snyder v. Owensboro, 528 S.W.2d 663 (Ky. 1975); Sealand Sisters, Inc. v. Planning Bd., 737 N.E.2d 503 (Mass. App. 2000); O'Dell v. City of Eagan, 348 N.W.2d 792 (Minn. App. 1984); J.E.D. Assocs. v. Town of Sandown, 430 A.2d 129 (N.H. 1981); Green Meadows at Montville, L.L.C. v. Planning Bd., 746 A.2d 1009 (N.J. App. Div. 2000); Pizzo Mantin Group v. Township of Randolph, 645 A.2d 89 (N.J. 1994); Goodman v. Board of Comm'rs, 411 A.2d 838 (Pa. Commw. 1980); Board of Supervisors v. Countryside Inv. Co., L.C., 522 S.E.2d 610 (Va. 1999) (ordinance requiring lots to comply with zoning code and prohibiting unsuitable subdivisions held not authorized by subdivision statute); Carlson v. Town

a more generous view of local subdivision control powers in states where the statute is broader than the Standard Act[3] or if they are asked to imply authority to impose physical requirements on development.[4] The subdivision control process may be either legislative or quasi-judicial depending upon how much discretion the ordinance confers on the decision agency. A court can mandamus the approval of a subdivision if the reason for disapproval is not authorized by the statute or the ordinance.[5] Courts will require adherence to quasi-judicial procedures if they hold the approval process is quasi-judicial.[6]

The strict view of the scope of subdivision control authority is illustrated by *Smith v. City of Mobile*.[7] The planning commission rejected a subdivision because it was "out of character" with other lots in the area. The subdivision ordinance provided that "[t]he size, width, depth, shape and orientation of lots . . . shall be appropriate to the location of the subdivision." The court held that this provision did not authorize the rejection of a subdivision for the reason given by the commission. "[T]he exercise of . . . discretion must be guided and limited

of Beaux Arts Village, 704 P.2d 663 (Wash. App. 1983); Hoepker v. City of Madison Plan Comm'n, 563 N.W.2d 145 (Wis. 1997) (cannot condition subdivision approval on consent to annexation); 11 A.L.R.2d 524 (1960). *See also* Reynolds v. City Council, 680 P.2d 1350 (Colo. App. 1984); Moscowitz v. Planning & Zoning Comm'n, 547 A.2d 569 (Conn. App. 1988); Equicor Dev., Inc. v. Westfield-Washington Township Plan Comm'n, 758 N.E.2d 34 (Ind. 2001) (agency estopped from denying approval because applicant relied on failure to indicate defect in application); Lee v. Maryland Nat'l Capital Park & Plan. Comm'n, 668 A.2d 980 (Md. App. 1995); C.F.T. Dev., L.L.C. v. Board of County Comm'rs, 32 P.3d 784 (N.M. App. 2001) (can reject subdivision because of inadequate septic tank disposal despite contrary recommendation from state agency). *But see* Serpa v. County of Washoe, 901 P.2d 690 (Nev. 1995) (can deny subdivision if inconsistent with county water-use plan). *Compare* Urrutia v. Blaine County, 2 P.3d 738 (Idaho 2000) (cannot rely completely on comprehensive plan to deny subdivision application).

[3] Smith v. Zoning Bd. of Appeals, 629 A.2d 1089 (Conn. 1993) (historic factors); Carruthers v. Board of Supervisors, 646 N.W.2d 867 (Iowa App. 2002) (statute requires consideration of "balance of interests");Durant v. Town of Dunbarton, 430 A.2d 140 (N.H. 1981); Jones v. Town of Woodway, 425 P.2d 904 (Wash. 1967). *See also* Carmel Valley View, Ltd. v. Board of Supvrs., 130 Cal. Rptr. 249 (Cal. App. 1976).

[4] North Landers Corp. v. Planning Bd., 416 N.E.2d 934 (Mass. 1981) (adequate access); Emerald Lakes, Inc. v. South Russell Planning Comm'n, 598 N.E.2d 60 (Ohio App. 1991) (allowing rejection of plat for inadequate groundwater supplies).

[5] El Dorado at Santa Fe, Inc. v. Board of County Comm'rs, 551 P.2d 1360 (N.M. 1976). *See* § 8.14.

[6] Guilford Financial Servs. v. City of Brevard, 563 S.E.2d 27 (N.C. App. 2002).

[7] 374 So. 2d 305 (Ala. 1979). *See also* Irwin v. Planning & Zoning Comm'n, 694 A.2d 809 (Conn. App. 1997) (reversing denial); Sonn v. Planning Comm'n, 374 A.2d 159 (Conn. 1976); Christopher Estates, Inc. v. Parish of East Baton Rouge, 413 So. 2d 1336 (La. App. 1982); State ex rel. Schaefer v. Cleveland, 847 S.W.2d 867 (Mo. App. 1993); Kaufman v. Planning & Zoning Comm'n, 298 S.E.2d 148 (W. Va. 1982). *But see* Fleckinger v. Jefferson Parish Council, 510 So. 2d 429 (La. App. 1987); City of Jackson v. Ridgway, 258 So. 2d 439 (Miss. 1972).

by clearly drawn standards which can be uniformly applied."[8] The court granted a writ of mandamus that compelled the municipality to approve the subdivision.

Scope of authority questions also arise when municipalities attempt to use subdivision controls for growth management or fiscal purposes. A few states expressly authorize the disapproval of a subdivision when public facilities are inadequate[9] or when the subdivision would be "scattered or premature" because of service inadequacies or health problems.[10] In the absence of statutory authority, the courts have usually overturned subdivision disapprovals for growth management or fiscal reasons. In *Interladco, Inc. v. Billings,*[11] the court overturned a subdivision denial when the record indicated that the county "did not want a development of single-family residences isolated from other developed urban areas, even though their subdivision regulations had no such restrictions." Nor may a municipality reject a subdivision because it imposes a burden on school or other public facilities if the statute or ordinance does not authorize this reason for disapproval.[12]

Courts easily uphold subdivision disapprovals based on inadequate access or other problems relating to the street system.[13] *Forest Constr. Co. v. Planning & Zoning Comm'n*[14] is a typical case. The commission rejected a subdivision because it provided only one access for 110 lots, causing all traffic from the subdivision to enter one street intersection. The court held that the denial was within the commission's authority to reject subdivisions that would be hazardous to the health and welfare of the community. A municipality may also reject a

---

[8] 374 So. 2d at 309. *See also* Ghent v. Planning Comm'n, 594 A.2d 5 (Conn. 1991); Hixon v. Walker County, 468 S.E.2d 744 (Ga. 1996).

[9] Md. Envt. Code Ann. § 9-512.

[10] N.H. Rev. Stat. Ann. § 674:36(II)(a). *See* Zukis v. Town of Fitzwilliam, 604 A.2d 956 (N.H. 1992); Garipay v. Town of Hanover, 351 A.2d 64 (N.H. 1976) (upholding denial under statute authorizing denial to prevent scattered development). *But see* Ettlingen Homes, Inc. v. Town of Derry, 681 A.2d 97 (N.H. 1996) (may not reject subdivision because of inadequate schools).

[11] 538 P.2d 496 (Colo. App. 1975).

[12] Beach v. Planning & Zoning Comm'n, 103 A.2d 814 (Conn. 1954); Baltimore Planning Comm'n v. Victor Dev. Co., 275 A.2d 478 (Md. 1971).

[13] Raybestos-Manhattan, Inc. v. Planning & Zoning Comm'n, 442 A.2d 65 (Conn. 1982); Oakes Constr. Co. v. City of Iowa City, 304 N.W.2d 797 (Iowa 1981); Burke & McCaffrey, Inc. v. City of Merriam, 424 P.2d 483 (Kan. 1967); North Landers Corp. v. Planning Bd., 416 N.E.2d 934 (Mass. 1981); Mac-Rich Realty Constr., Inc. v. Planning Bd., 341 N.E.2d 916 (Mass. App. 1976); Batch v. Town of Chapel Hill, 387 S.E.2d 655 (N.C. 1990) (citing treatise); Prudential Trust Co. v. City of Laramie, 492 P.2d 971 (Wyo. 1972). *See also* Isla Verda Internat'l Holdings v. City Camas, 49 P.3d 867 (Wash. 2002) (upholding condition to subdivision approval requiring secondary access for emergency vehicles).

[14] 236 A.2d 917 (Conn. 1967).

subdivision because of drainage and fire hazard problems.[15] The disapproval of a subdivision can raise taking of property problems.[16]

Municipalities sometimes reject a subdivision because it has unacceptable off-site impacts. A rejection for this reason raises statutory authority and taking of property problems. In *Pearson Kent Corp. v. Bear*,[17] the commission rejected a subdivision, "not because it regarded the plan itself as intrinsically not acceptable," but because it would cause traffic congestion that would create danger to nearby residents. The court held that although the local charter and subdivision control law were "addressed to approval or disapproval internal to the subdivision," the commission was not prevented from considering "the impact of the proposed development on adjacent territory and property within its jurisdiction."

The court took a somewhat different view of this problem in *Baker v. Planning Bd.*,[18] which was decided under a similar statute. An area of a proposed subdivision served as a retention pond in which water accumulated during heavy rains and snowstorms. The drainage system that would serve the subdivision was adequate, but the municipality refused to approve the subdivision. It stated that the development of the subdivision would destroy the retention pond, which would overtax a downstream drainage system and require public expenditure for its improvement.

The court held the statute did not authorize the disapproval of the subdivision for these reasons and suggested a taking problem. It noted that "a planning board may not exercise its authority to disapprove a plan so that a town may continue to use the owner's land as a water storage area and thereby deprive the owner of the reasonable use of it."

---

[15] Shoptaugh v. Board of County Comm'rs, 543 P.2d 524 (Colo. App. 1976); Brown v. City of Joliet, 247 N.E.2d 47 (Ill. App. 1969); Hamilton v. .Planning Bd., 345 N.E.2d 906 (Mass. App. 1976); Christianson v. Gasvoda, 789 P.2d 1234 (Mont. 1990) (drainage and flooding); El Shaer v. Planning Bd., 592 A.2d 565 (N.J. App. Div. 1991) (same). *See also* Sansoucy v. Planning Bd., 246 N.E.2d 811 (Mass. 1969) (underground utility lines).

[16] Smith v. Town of Wolfeboro, 615 A.2d 1252 (N.H. 1992) (finding no taking under nuisance exception to Supreme Court's *Lucas* decision); McFillan v. Berkeley County Planning Comm'n, 438 S.E.2d 801 (W. Va. 1993) (no taking; expansion of mobile home park denied). *See* § 2.12.

[17] 271 N.E.2d 218 (N.Y. 1971). *See also* North Landers Corp. v. Planning Bd., 416 N.E.2d 934 (Mass. 1981); Garipay v. Town of Hanover, 351 A.2d 64 (N.H. 1976). *But see* Ettlingen Homes, Inc. v. Town of Derry, 681 A.2d 97 (N.H. 1996) (may not reject subdivision because of inadequate schools).

[18] 228 N.E.2d 831 (Mass. 1967). *See also* Wood Bros. Homes v. City of Colorado Springs, 568 P.2d 487 (Colo. 1977); Sowin Assocs. v. Planning & Zoning Comm'n, 580 A.2d 91 (Conn. App. 1990); Florham Park Inv. Assocs. v. Planning Bd., 224 A.2d 352 (N.J.L. Div. 1966); De Leo v. Lecraw, 334 N.Y.S.2d 912 (App. Div. 1972).

§ 9.10   Variances and Waivers.

Subdivision control ordinances may contain provisions authorizing variances from or waivers of requirements contained in the ordinance. Some statutes authorize variances or exceptions,[1] and a variance provision in a subdivision control ordinance may require statutory authority.[2] The criteria for subdivision control variances are similar to those for zoning variances.[3] However, the cases and statutes may give planning boards more flexibility in granting variances or waivers under subdivision ordinances.[4] *Baum v. Lunsford*,[5] a typical case, assumed a hardship variance from the subdivision ordinance required a lesser burden of proof than a zoning hardship variance, but held a landowner was not entitled to a variance simply to prevent a financial loss.

§ 9.11   Exactions.

Subdivision control ordinances often require uncompensated exactions from subdividers. A subdivision exaction is an internal subdivision improvement, a dedication of land for a public facility, or a fee in lieu of dedication that the municipality can use to provide a public facility. Municipalities may require exactions for off-site streets and other improvements and for parks and schools, which may or may not be on-site. Subdivision control ordinances authorize an in-lieu fee rather than a dedication of land within the subdivision because a subdivision may not be large enough to provide a site for public facilities, because the municipality may prefer to locate them elsewhere, or to give the subdivider the option of paying a fee rather than dedicating land. The impact fee is another type of exaction. It is usually levied as a condition to the issuance of building permits to pay for off-site facilities such as water and sewage treatment facilities. Exactions are an important and highly contentious issue in land use law. Their use and cost has increased as local governments find themselves financially pressed to find revenues for necessary capital facilities.

---

[1] Mass. Gen. Laws ch. 41, § 81R; Minn. Stat. Ann. § 462.358(6); N.J. Stat. Ann. § 40:55D-51(a); Pa. Stat. Ann. tit. 53, § 10512.1(a) (undue hardship, not contrary to public interest and purpose and intent of ordinance).

[2] South E. Prop. Owners & Residents Ass'n v. City Plan Comm'n, 244 A.2d 394 (Conn. 1968).

[3] §§ 6.40-6.52.

[4] York v. Town of Ogunquit, 769 A.2d 172 (Me. 2001) (upholding variance); Caruso v. Planning Bd., 238 N.E.2d 872 (Mass. 1968); Meyer v. Planning Bd. of Westport, 558 N.E.2d 994 (Mass. App. 1990) (upholding waiver and explaining differences from zoning variance); Smith v. Township Comm., 244 A.2d 145 (N.J. App. Div. 1968); Ruf v. Buckinham Township, 765 A.2d 1166 (Pa. Commw. 2001) (refusal to grant modification for roadway widening and stormwater control reversed).

[5] 365 S.E.2d 739 (Va. 1988). *See also* Arrigo v. Planning Bd., 429 N.E.2d 355 (Mass. App. 1981); Van Landschoot v. City of Mendota Heights, 336 N.W.2d 503 (Minn. 1983); Garden State Homes, Inc. v. Heusner, 400 N.Y.S.2d 598 (App. Div. 1977);Amato v. Randolph Township, 457 A.2d 1188 (N.J. App. Div.) (remanding grant of variance).

The principal questions raised by subdivision exactions and impact fees are whether the municipality has the statutory authority to impose them and whether they are a taking of property. Whether a court will find the necessary statutory authority for a subdivision exaction depends on how broadly it interprets the subdivision control statute, which does not usually authorize exactions. Impact fees present an additional statutory authority problem if a court holds the fee is a tax, because most states do not authorize municipalities to levy this type of tax. Controversy over exactions has led a number of states to adopt statutes that determine how exactions may be used in the land development process. Municipalities may also be able to impose subdivision exactions and impact fees under their home rule powers.[1]

§ 9.12 The Takings Issue.

In the decades before the Supreme Court changed the takings tests that apply to exactions, the state courts had adopted a variety of tests[1] to decide whether a subdivision control exaction is a taking of property, These tests require a showing that the exaction is "reasonably related" to a need created by the subdivision, that there is a "rational nexus" between the exaction and that need, or that the exaction is "specifically and uniquely attributable" to the subdivision. The differences between these tests are semantic. All require a reasonable relationship between the exaction and a need for facilities created by the subdivision, and they differ only in the degree to which this relationship must be shown. The text uses the term "nexus test" to describe the various tests the state courts apply to exactions.

The nexus test is an example of the cost internalization theory that justifies zoning restrictions. Zoning internalizes costs by prohibiting development that imposes external costs on adjacent land uses. An example is a zoning ordinance that prohibits industrial uses in residential zoning districts. The nexus test internalizes costs by requiring subdividers to contribute to public improvements when the subdivision creates the need for them. The Supreme Court has adopted a "rough proportionality" test for exactions under the federal constitution which is more stringent than the nexus test adopted by the state courts. They may still apply a less stringent state takings test, but they often consider the Supreme Court tests because the federal constitution is enforceable in state courts.

§ 9.13 *Nollan* and What It Means: Applying the Nexus Test.

In *Nollan v. California Coastal Comm'n*,[1] the first Supreme Court exaction case, the Court held a California coastal permit condition that required an

---

[1] § 4.25.

[1] *See also* applying now-discredited right-privilege distinction, Ridgefield Land Co. v. City of Detroit, 217 N.W.2d 58 (Mich. 1926) (dismissing taking objection by holding right to subdivide is a privilege); Mid-Continent Bldrs., Inc. v. Midwest City, 539 P.2d 1377 (Okla. 1975) (same).

[1] 483 U.S. 625 (1987), discussed in § 2.11.

easement to cross the beach of a beachfront house was a taking. The Court held the "essential nexus" between the permit condition and the justification for the condition was lacking. It also held it would closely examine a government regulation to determine whether it "substantially" advanced a "legitimate" governmental interest, as required by the taking clause.

The Court cited a long line of state exaction cases with approval, but its formulation of the nexus test appears more stringent than the nexus test the state courts apply. However, the Court did not hold the coastal permit exaction requirement facially unconstitutional, but held only that the exaction requirement in that case was a taking of property as applied. The Court also indicated it would uphold a wide variety of coastal permit exactions, including a condition that required a coastal property owner to provide a viewpoint access if this was necessary to remedy the impact her development had on coastal views.

The *Nollan* nexus requirement for exactions has not been difficult to meet in most cases, especially when the exaction was imposed comprehensively as part of a regulatory scheme.[2] The *Nollan* test will invalidate an exaction when a nexus between the exaction and the regulatory purpose it is intended to implement is clearly lacking. In one post-*Nollan* case, for example,[3] the city demanded that a property owner dedicate land for the improvement of an imperfect street alignment as a condition to a permit for the renovation of a residential structure for office use. The court held there was no nexus between the renovation and the dedication, which was required to implement a general plan requirement for the realignment of the street. *Nollan* has also led courts to find a taking when an access dedication requirement is not related to the development of the landowner's property.[4]

§ 9.14 *Dolan* and What It Means.

The Supreme Court elaborated on the *Nollan* standards for exactions in *Dolan v. City of Tigard.*[1] The Court invalidated a condition to a building permit to

---

[2] Leroy Land Co. v. Tahoe Regional Planning Agency, 939 F.2d 696 (9th Cir. 1991) (environmental mitigation); Gardner v. New Jersey Pinelands Comm'n, 593 A.2d 251 (N.J. 1991) (upholding exaction requiring restriction of housing in agricultural area of New Jersey Pinelands to agricultural use with option to build five clustered homes); Schoonover v. Klamath Cty., 806 P.2d 156 (Or. App. 1991) (requiring annexation to fire district for fire protection); Town of Flower Mound v. Stafford Estates Ltd. Partnership, 71 S.W.3d 18 (Tex. App. 2002).

[3] Rohn v. City of Vasalia, 263 Cal. Rptr. 319 (Cal. App. 1989). *See also* Jones Ins. Trust v. City of Ft. Smith, 731 F. Supp. 912 (D. Or. 1992) (convenience store did not create enough traffic to justify street widening).

[4] Surfside Colony, Ltd. v. California Coastal Comm'n, 277 Cal. Rptr. 371 (Cal. App. 1991) (beach access); Paradyne Corp. v. State Dep't of Transp., 528 So. 2d 291 (Fla. App. 1988) (access for adjoining property owner); Luxembourg Group, Inc. v. Snohomish County, 887 P.2d 446 (Wash. App. 1995) (access to landlocked lot); Unlimited v. Kitsap County, 750 P.2d 651 (Wash. App. 1988) (same).

[1] 512 U.S. 374 (1994). *See* § 2.12

expand plaintiff's building that required the dedication of land for within a floodplain to improve a storm drainage system and provide a pedestrian-bicycle path. The Court adopted a "rough proportionality" test for exactions which it indicated was stricter than the nexus test adopted by most state courts. Some courts have held, however, that the difference between the *Dolan* test and the reasonable relationship test is only a matter of degree.[2] *Dolan* also placed the burden to prove the constitutionality of exactions on government agencies and indicated that the decision to impose the dedication on the building permit was adjudicative. Cases applying *Dolan* are discussed in subsequent sections in this chapter.

The Supreme Court held later in *City of Monterey v. Del Monte Dunes*[3] that "we have not extended the rough-proportionality test of *Dolan* beyond the special context of exactions — land-use decisions conditioning approval of development on the dedication of property to public use." This holding may mean the *Dolan* rough proportionality test does not apply to exactions in the form of impact fees.[4]

§ 9.15 On-Site Streets and Improvements.

The Standard Planning Act requires subdividers to provide streets and other improvements within the subdivision. Subdivision control statutes usually authorize[1] and subdivision control ordinances usually contain these requirements. The courts have applied the nexus test to reject takings claims to these exactions. *Blevens v. City of Manchester*[2] is an early leading case:

> Since the subdivider of land creates the need for local improvements which are of special benefit to the subdivision, it is considered reasonable that he should bear the cost rather than the municipality and the general taxpayer.[3]

The court rejected an argument the exaction was discriminatory because it did not apply to lots adjacent to the subdivision. It applied the usual zoning rule that does not require every "lot of land" to be regulated to the same degree.[4]

---

[2] Home Builders Ass'n of Central Arizona v. City of Scottsdale, 930 P.2d 993 (Ariz. 1997). Lincoln City Chamber of Commerce v. City of Lincoln City, 991 P.2d 1080 (Or. App. 1999) (upholding requirement that developer must provide city with "rough proportionality" report).

[3] 526 U.S. 687 (1999).

[4] *See* § 9.22.

[1] Cal. Gov't Code § 66475; Minn. Stat. Ann. § 462.358(2b).

[2] 170 A.2d 121 (N.H. 1961). *See also* Coastland Corp. v. County of Currituck, 734 F.2d 175 (4th Cir. 1984) (road access); Brous v. Smith, 106 N.E.2d 503 (N.Y. 1952) (streets); City of Bellefontaine Neighbors v. J.J. Kelly Realty & Bldg. Co., 460 S.W.2d 298 (Mo. App. 1970) (sewers and sidewalks); Crownhill Homes, Inc. v. City of San Antonio, 433 S.W.2d 448 (Tex. Civ. App. 1968) (water mains).

[3] *Id.* at 122–23.

[4] *Accord* Pengilly v. Multnomah County, 810 F. Supp. 1111 (D. Or. 1992).

§ 9.16   Off-Site Streets and Improvements.

Subdivision control requirements for internal improvements are expressly authorized by the Standard Planning Act and the state statutes that adopted it. Land dedications and fees for off-site streets and similar facilities raise more difficult statutory authority problems because they are not usually authorized by subdivision control legislation. A common example is the dedication of land in the subdivision for the widening of a street that is off-site but adjacent to the subdivision.

Divan Bldrs., Inc. v. Planning Bd. [1] is a leading case holding that a subdivision control act based on the Standard Act included implied statutory authority for off-site exactions. The municipality required a subdivider to contribute to the cost of improving a downstream drainage facility that carried drainage from the subdivision. The court agreed with a law review commentator that both off-site and on-site improvements were "a legitimate expense of subdividing which ought to be borne in the first instance by the developer." New Jersey legislation now authorizes exactions for off-site improvements "necessitated or required" by the subdivision. [2] The supreme court has held that the statute does not authorize developer contributions for municipality-wide road improvements based on the anticipated impact that new subdivisions would have on the municipality's road network. [3] Other states also have statutes authorizing dedications for off-site facilities, including roads. [4] These statutes usually enact the nexus test for exactions required under the taking clause. [5]

Some courts hold there is no implied statutory authority to require exactions for off-site improvements. [6] These holdings may reflect a belief that an off-site subdivision exaction would be a taking of property. *Arrowhead Dev. Co. v.*

---

[1] 334 A.2d 30 (N.J. 1975). *Accord* City of Mobile v. Waldon, 429 So. 2d 945 (Ala. 1983); KBW, Inc. v. Town of Bennington, 342 A.2d 653 (N.H. 1975). *See also* Sullivan v. Planning Bd., 645 N.E.2d 703 (Mass. App. 1995) (statute prohibiting dedication for public way applies only if dedication unrelated to adequate access and safety of subdivision); City of Stafford v. Gullo, 886 S.W.2d 524 (Tex. App. 1994) (no authority in ordinance).

[2] N.J. Stat. Ann. § 40:55D-32.

[3] New Jersey Bldrs. Ass'n v. Mayor & Twp. Comm., 528 A.2d 555 (N.J. 1987). *See also* Baltica Constr. Co. v. Planning Bd., 537 A.2d 319 (N.J. App. Div. 1988) (may consider benefit to abutting landowners from off-site water line).

[4] N.C. Gen. Stat. § 160A-372, applied in Buckland v. Town of Haw River, 541 S.E.2d 497 (N.C. App. 2000); Wash. Rev. Code Ann. § 58.17.110. *See also* § 9.18.

[5] Luxembourg Group v. Snohomish County, 887 P.2d 446 (Wash. App. (1995) (disapproving dedication of road not required by subdivision).

[6] Cherry Hills Resort Dev. Co. v. Cherry Hills Village (II), 790 P.2d 827 (Colo. 1990); Briar W., Inc. v. City of Lincoln, 291 N.W.2d 730 (Neb. 1980); Meixsell v. Ross Twp. Bd. of Supvrs., 623 A.2d 429 (Pa. Commw. 1993); Hylton Enters. v. Board of Supvrs., 258 S.E.2d 577 (Va. 1979). *See also* Cupp v. Board of Supvrs., 318 S.E.2d 407 (Va. 1984).

Livingston County Rd. Comm'n[7] illustrates these cases. The county required a subdivider to open an access to a public road, remove a hill that was a sight obstruction on the road, and regrade and resurface the road. The hill was not on the subdivision site. The court held that a provision in the subdivision control act that authorized subdividers to provide "drives which enter county roads and streets" did not authorize the county to require removal of the hill. It rejected an argument that the sight obstruction was a problem "solely attributable" to the subdivision. It noted that the same argument could be made "to justify . . . road widening and all other public services made necessary by the existence of a new residential community."

If there is statutory authority for an off-site facility exaction, the next question is whether it meets the nexus test. Courts upheld these exactions pre-*Nollan* if they met the nexus test.[8] *Lampton v. Pinaire*[9] is a typical case. It held a dedication of land for adjacent streets was not a taking because it was "based on the reasonably anticipated burdens to be caused by the development." The nexus test prohibits exactions for facilities that benefit only the general public.[10] Some courts find a taking under this rule when a municipality requires a dedication of land for a major highway designated in a comprehensive plan. The court may hold the dedication unconstitutional as a "land banking" operation and award compensation if it believes the dedication was an improper alternative to the use of eminent domain.

The courts usually upheld street widening dedications post-*Nollan* and before *Dolan*. They deferred to the judgment of the municipality that the dedication was needed and found that a nexus existed.[11] The cases have not yet fully

---

[7] 323 N.W.2d 702 (Mich. 1982).

[8] Wald Corp. v. Metropolitan Dade County, 338 So. 2d 863 (Fla. App. 1976); Land/Vest Props., Inc. v. Town of Plainfield, 379 A.2d 200 (N.H. 1977). Exaction invalidated: Lee County v. New Testament Baptist Church, 507 So. 2d 626 (Fla. App. 1987); Coates v. Planning Bd., 445 N.E.2d 642 (N.Y. 1983); Miller v. City of Port Angeles, 691 P.2d 229 (Wash. App. 1984). *See also* Ayres v. City Council, 207 P.2d 1 (Cal. 1947) (upholding dedication for street widening but basis for holding now questionable).

[9] 610 S.W.2d 915 (Ky. 1980). *See* Curtis v. Town of South Tomaston, 708 A.2d 657 (Me. 1998) (upholding dedication of fire pond and dedication to maintain and use). *But see* Lexington-Fayette Urban County Gov't v. Schneider, 849 S.W.2d 557 (Ky. App. 1993) (dedication for bridge did not meet *Lampton* test).

[10] Liberty v. California Coastal Comm'n, 170 Cal. Rptr. 247 (Cal. App. 1981); Schwing v. City of Baton Rouge, 249 So. 2d 304 (La. App.1971); Vrabel v. Mayor & Council, 601 A.2d 229 (N.J. App. 1991).

[11] Dedication upheld: Pengilly v. Multnomah County, 810 F. Supp. 1111 (D. Or. 1992) (dedication held to mitigate cumulative impact of residential development on road); Copeland v. City of Chattanooga, 866 S.W.2d 565 (Tenn. App. 1993) (dedication of right-of-way along adjacent road in conditional zoning approval); *See also* Department of Transp. v. Lundberg, 825 P.2d 641 (Or. 1992) (sidewalk dedication requirement valid and evidence of value in condemnation); Pitcher v. Heidelberg Township Bd. of Supervisors, 637 A.2d 715 (Pa. Commw. 1994) (upholding road improvement condition).

considered the implications of *Dolan* for street and highway dedications. They have held the Supreme Court intended *Dolan* to apply to land dedications even if they are an application of standards contained in an ordinance of the governing body.[12] They have also held the *Dolan* rough proportionality test is not a sharp or "seismic" departure from prior takings law.[13] The courts have applied *Dolan* to uphold or reject municipal findings intended to support street dedications.[14]

Most of the dedications considered by the courts were required from new residential subdivision developments, and the dedication could be determined because the extent of the development was known. More difficult problems may arise if a dedication of land is required as a condition to a rezoning because the rezoning changes the land uses permitted on the land but does not always determine how much and what kind of development can occur. In these cases, the court may disapprove the dedication, because it is based on speculative assumptions concerning the development that will occur and the highway needs it will create.[15]

§ 9.17　Parks and Schools.

§ 9.18　Statutory Authority.

Park and school exactions can raise serious statutory authority questions because the Standard Planning Act was less explicit in its requirements for these

---

[12] Amoco Oil Co. v. Village of Schaumburg, 661 N.E.2d 380 (Ill. App. 1996); Schultz v. City of Grants Pass, 884 P.2d 569 (Or. App. 1994).

[13] Amoco Oil Co. v. Village of Schaumburg, 661 N.E.2d 380 (Ill. App. 1996); Art Piculell Group v. Clackamas County, 922 P.2d 1227 (Or. App. 1996).

[14] Dedication valid: Dowerk v. Charter Township of Oxford, 592 N.W.2d 724 (Mich. App. 1999) (upgrading of access road); Kottschade v. City of Rochester, 537 N.W.2d 301 (Minn. App. 1995); McClure v. City of Springfield, 28 P.3d 1222 (Or. App. 2001) Nelson v. City of Lake Oswego, 869 P.2d 350 (Or. App. 1994) (drainage easement requirement as condition to permit to build house); Sparks v. Douglas County, 904 P.2d 738 (Wash. 1995) (street widening dedication as condition to subdivision approval). Dedication invalid: Amoco Oil Co. v. Village of Schaumburg, 661 N.E.2d 380 (Ill. App. 1996) (special use permit; 20 percent of property dedicated); Burton v. Clark County, 958 P.2d 343 (Wash. App. 1998) (no showing that related road will be built that will allow exacted road to remedy traffic conditions). *But see* Art Piculell Group v. Clackamas County, 922 P.2d 1227 (Or. App. 1996) (may give greater weight to subdivision benefits in appropriate cases; *Dolan* does not preclude quantification). *See also* Benchmark Land Co. v. City of Battle Ground, 49 P.3d 680 (Wash. 2002) (invalidating condition requiring construction of street improvements because not required by subdivision); Snider v. Board of County Comm'rs, 932 P.2d 704 (Wash. App. 1997) (requiring owner of land to obtain right of way to satisfy dedication does not violate *Dolan*).

[15] Goss v. City of Little Rock, 151 F.3d 861 (8th Cir. 1998) (may not demand dedication for street widening as condition to rezoning based on possibility of future development when no present plans for such development); Schultz v. City of Grants Pass, 884 P.2d 569 (Or. App. 1994) (dedication must be limited to impact of lot split and not worst case scenario of development of 15 to 17 homes).

facilities. Section 13 of the Act provided only that subdivision regulations "may provide . . . for adequate and convenient open spaces . . . for light and air." The statutory authority problem is even more troublesome when subdivision control ordinances authorize or require in-lieu fees for park and school sites rather than the dedication of land within the subdivision. A subdivider can argue the in-lieu fee is a tax which the statutes do not authorize.

Although a number of cases hold that land dedications and in-lieu fees for parks and schools are within the statutory authority conferred by subdivision control legislation based on the Standard Act,[1] several courts hold to the contrary.[2] The cases have divided in resolving the tax objection. Cases that find a lack of statutory authority often characterize the in-lieu fee as an unauthorized tax.[3] One case avoided the tax problem by holding that the in-lieu fee was simply "imposed on the transaction of obtaining plat approval."[4] Home rule authority may also authorize exactions for parks or schools.[5]

Several states have adopted statutes that authorize dedications and in-lieu fees for park and school sites.[6] These statutes usually codify the nexus test for exactions.

§ 9.19　The Takings Issue.

The state courts applied the nexus test to land dedications for parks and schools in a group of leading cases on park and school dedications decided pre-*Nollan*. An Illinois case, *Pioneer Trust & Sav. Bank v. Village of Mount Prospect*,[1]

---

[1] Trent Meredith, Inc. v. City of Oxnard, 170 Cal. Rptr. 685 (Cal. App. 1981); Cimarron Corp. v. Board of City Comm'rs, 563 P.2d 946 (Colo. 1977); Crucil v. Carson City, 600 P.2d 216 (Nev. 1979); Jenad, Inc. v. Village of Scarsdale, 218 N.E.2d 673 (N.Y. 1966); Jordan v. Village of Menomonee Falls, 137 N.W.2d 442 (Wis. 1965), *appeal dismissed,* 385 U.S. 4 (1966).

[2] City of Montgomery v. Crossroads Land Co., 355 So. 2d 363 (Ala. 1978); Admiral Dev. Corp. v. City of Maitland, 267 So. 2d 860 (Fla. App. 1972); Coronado Dev. Co. v. City of McPherson, 368 P.2d 51 (Kan. 1962); Eyde Constr. Co. v. Charter Twp. of Meridian, 386 N.W.2d 687 (Mich. App. 1986) (recreation land); West Park Ave., Inc. v. Township of Ocean, 224 A.2d 1 (N.J. 1966). *See* Grand Land Co. v. Township of Bethlehem, 483 A.2d 818 (N.J. App. Div. 1984).

[3] Haugen v. Gleason, 359 P.2d 108 (Or. 1961).

[4] Jenad, Inc. v. Village of Scarsdale, 218 N.E.2d 673 (N.Y. 1966). *Accord* Call v. City of West Jordan, 606 P.2d 217 (Utah 1979).

[5] City of College Station v. Turtle Rock Corp., 680 S.W.2d 802 (Tex. 1984).

[6] Cal. Gov't Code § 66477, *upheld in* Associated Home Bldrs. of Greater E. Bay, Inc. v. City of Walnut Creek, 484 P.2d 606 (Cal.) (questionable authority under *Dolan*); Colo. Rev. Stat. § 30-28-133(4)(a); Mont. Code Ann. § 76-3-621; N.Y. Town Law § 277(4);Wash. Rev. Code § 58.17.110.

[1] 176 N.E.2d 799 (Ill. 1961). Applying *Pioneer* test: Aunt Hack Ridge Estates, Inc. v. Planning Comm'n, 273 A.2d 880 (Conn. 1970) (fee for parks upheld); Schwing v. City of Baton Rouge, 249 So. 2d 304 (La. App. 1971) (road widening invalidated).

adopted the most restrictive version of the nexus test to invalidate a land dedication for park and school sites. The court held a municipality can require a subdivider to assume only those costs "specifically and uniquely attributable" to the subdivision. Later Illinois cases upheld in-lieu fees for parks and schools in cases that either distinguished or claimed to apply the *Pioneer* test.[2]

Cases in other states applied a more relaxed reasonableness test to uphold park and school exactions. *Jordan v. Village of Menomonee Falls,*[3] a Wisconsin case, is typical. The court believed the uniquely attributable test placed too great a burden on municipalities. It held a "reasonable basis" for attributing a need for parks and schools to a subdivision could be found if a number of approved subdivisions approved over several years were responsible for bringing a "considerable number of people" into the community.

Elsewhere in the opinion, the court indicated it would apply the police power "reasonableness" test to subdivision exactions. It stated that a municipality could require exactions in return for the benefits the subdivider received from selling land in the subdivision for home building lots. Exactions are justified if they meet a municipal demand that would not have occurred "but for the influx of people into the community to occupy the subdivision lots." Later cases followed *Menomonee Falls* pre-*Nollan*, sometimes with modifications.[4]

State courts may continue to apply these cases post-*Nollan* and *Dolan*. They must also apply the Supreme Court exaction decisions if a landowner relies on them.[5] In an interesting Maryland case, the court held the dedication of private open space within a subdivision was not a taking.[6]

§ 9.20 Impact Fees.

Municipalities may levy impact fees on new development as an alternative to subdivision exactions. The fee is often levied either when a building permit is issued or as a facility connection charge. If impact fees are not levied in the subdivision control process, they can be levied against developments that do not

---

[2] Krughoff v. City of Naperville, 369 N.E.2d 892 (Ill. 1977); Board of Educ. v. Surety Devs., Inc., 347 N.E.2d 149 (Ill. 1975).

[3] 137 N.W.2d 442 (Wis. 1965), *appeal dismissed,* 385 U.S. 4 (1966).

[4] Home Bldrs. Ass'n v. City of Kansas City, 555 S.W.2d 832 (Mo. 1977); Billings Props., Inc. v. Yellowstone County, 394 P.2d 182 (Mont. 1964); Collis v. City of Bloomington, 246 N.W.2d 19 (Minn. 1976); Patenaude v. Town of Meredith, 392 A.2d 582 (N.H. 1978); Jenad, Inc. v. Village of Scarsdale, 218 N.E.2d 673 (N.Y. 1966); City of College Station v. Turtle Rock Corp., 680 S.W.2d 802 (Tex. 1984); Call v. City of West Jordan, 614 P.2d 1257 (Utah 1980); Coulter v. City of Rawlings, 662 P.2d 888 (Wyo. 1983); 43 A.L.R.3d 864 (1972).

[5] *See* § 9.22 (applying Supreme Court decisions to impact fees).

[6] City of Annapolis v. Waterman, 745 A.2d 1000 (Md. 2000) (dedication of private recreational space not taking). *See also* Isla Verde Internat'l Holdings, Inc. v. City of Camas, 43 P.3d 867 (Wash. 2002) (open space dedication required held to be impact fee subject to impact fee statute).

require subdivision approval, such as multifamily housing. A municipality may also levy an impact fee as a condition to the approval of a subdivision. Municipalities can levy impact fees for any kind capital improvement, including roads, parks, and water and sewer facilities. Impact fees are also used to expand or improve these facilities.

§ 9.21 Statutory Authority.

Impact fees, like subdivision control exactions, raise a statutory authority problem, and some courts hold impact fees are not authorized by statute if there is no explicit statutory authority.[1] Developers can claim that impact fees are taxes that are not authorized by the state's tax legislation. A number of cases have taken this position,[2] but other cases uphold impact fees under legislation that authorizes municipalities to levy user charges for the maintenance and construction of capital facilities.[3] As the court pointed out in *Contractors & Bldrs. Ass'n of Pinellas County v. City of Dunedin*,[4] a municipality may levy user charges to create a capital fund for public improvements rather than fund them through bond issues that are retired through user charges.

---

[1] Board of County Commr's v. Bainbridge, Inc., 929 P.2d 691 (Colo. 1997) (can't levy impact fee for schools in addition to subdivision fee authorized by statute); Thompson v. Village of Newark, 768 N.E.2d 856 (Ill. App. 2002) (planning statute did not confer authority on non-home rule municipality).

[2] Home Bldrs. Ass'n of Cent. Ariz. v. Riddel, 510 P.2d 376 (Ariz. 1973); Rancho Colorado, Inc. v. City of Bloomfield, 586 P.2d 659 (Colo. 1978); State v. City of Port Orange, 650 So. 2d 1 (Fla. 1994) (transportation utility fee); Idaho Bldg. Contractors Ass'n v. City of Coeur D'Alene, 890 P.2d 326 (Idaho 1995); Home Builders Ass'n v. City of West Des Moines, 444 N.W.2d 339 (Iowa 2002); Lloyd E. Clarke, Inc. v. City of Bettendorf, 158 N.W.2d 125 (Iowa 1968); Eastern Diversified Properties, Inc. v. Montgomery County, 570 A.2d 850 (Md. 1990); Greater Franklin Developers Ass'n, Inc. v. Town of Franklin, 730 N.E.2d 900 (Mass. App. 2000) (school impact fee held tax); Country Joe, Inc. v. City of Eagan, 560 N.W.2d 681 (Minn. 1997) (road connection fee); Douglas County Contractors Ass'n v. Douglas County, 929 P.2d 253 (Nev. 1996); Sams Land Co. v. City of Soap Lake, 23 P.3d 477 (Wash. 2000) (standby fee imposed on vacant, unimproved, uninhabited lots abutting but unconnected to its water and sewer lines held a tax); Hillis Homes, Inc. v. Snohomish County, 650 P.2d 193 (Wash. 1982). *See also* Building Industry Ass'n v. City of Westlake, 660 N.E.2d 501 (Ohio App. 1995) (invalidating park and recreation fee).

[3] City of Arvada v. City & County of Denver, 663 P.2d 611 (Colo. 1983); Hartman v. Aurora San. Dist., 177 N.E.2d 214 (Ill. 1961); Waters Landing Ltd. Partnership v. Montgomery County, 650 A.2d 712 (Md. 1994) (development impact tax); Lechner v. City of Billings, 797 P.2d 191 (Mont. 1990); Ford v. Georgetown County Water & Sewer dist., 532 S.E.2d 873 (S.C. 2000) (water and sewer fee); Home Bldrs. Ass'n v. Provo City, 503 P.2d 451 (Utah 1972); Tidewater Ass'n of Homeowners v. City of Virginia Beach, 400 S.E.2d 523 (Va. 1991); Robes v. Town of Hartford, 636 A.2d 342 (Vt. 1993) (fee for expansion of sewage system); Coulter v. City of Rawlings, 662 P.2d 888 (Wyo. 1983). *See also* Centex Real Estate Corp. v. City of Vallejo, 24 Cal. Rptr. 2d 48 (Cal. App. 1993) (excise tax); Cherry Hill Farms, Inc. v. City of Cherry Hills Village, 670 P.2d 779 (Colo. 1983) (same).

[4] 329 So. 2d 314 (Fla. 1976). *Cf.* City of Boca Raton v. State, 595 So. 2d 25 (Fla. 1992) (home rule government may levy special assessment under home rule powers).

Almost half the states have adopted legislation authorizing impact fees.[5] Some of these statutes have codified the nexus test. The California legislation, which is typical, authorizes fees imposed on development projects and requires the municipality to identify the uses to which the fee will be put. There must be "a reasonable relationship between the fee's use and the type of development project on which the fee is imposed."[6] The statute expressly states that its purpose is to codify existing "constitutional and decisional" law.[7] One of the most elaborate impact fee statutes is the Texas law.[8] The statute enacts the nexus test by authorizing impact fees to fund capital improvements "necessitated by and attributable to . . . new development."[9]

Many of these statutes include requirements that help demonstrate that the required nexus exists. These include a statutory identification of the facilities for which municipalities may impose fees, the identification of service deficiencies and service and benefit areas, and fee calculation methodologies that apportion the impact fees fairly. Some statutes require a capital improvements plan as a condition to levying fees. These requirements help to establish strong spatial, benefit and earmarking relationships. Accounting requirements and time limits for expenditures help ensure that fees will be used for their intended purpose.

The cases have upheld impact fees levied under statutory authority when they meet the statutory nexus test.[10] For example, the Illinois court upheld a road

---

[5] *E.g.,* Ariz. Rev. Stat. § 11.1101 et seq. (counties); 9-563.05 (cities); Ga. Code Ann. § 36-71-1 et seq. Idaho Code § 67-8201 et seq.; 605 Ill. Comp. Stat. Ann. § 5/5-901 et seq.; Ind. Code Ann. § 36-7-4-1311 et seq.; Nev. Rev. Stat. §§ 278B.010 et seq.; N.H. Rev. Stat. Ann. § 674:21(V); N.J. Stat. Ann. § 40: 55D-42; N.M. Stat. Ann. §§ 5-8-1 et seq.; Or. Rev. Stat. §§ 223.297 et seq.; Pa. Stat. Ann. tit. 53, § 10501-A et seq.; R.I. Gen. Stat. § 45-33-47; Vt. Stat. Ann. tit. 24, §§ 5200 et seq.; Va. Code Ann. §§ 15.2-2307 et seq.;Wash. Rev. Code § 82.02.050 et seq..*See* Home Builders Ass'n v. City of Apache Junction, 11 P.3d 1032 (Ariz. App. 2000) (statute does not include public schools); Board of County Comm'rs v. Bainbridge, Inc., 929 P.2d 691 (Colo. 1997) (no authority to levy additional school impact fee); Cherokee County v. Great Atlanta Homebuilders Ass'n, Inc., 566 S.E.2d 470 (Ga. App. 2002) (may levy fee only in unincorporated areas); Southern Nevada Homebuilders Ass'n v. City of North Las Vegas, 913 P.2d 1276 (Nev. 1996) (fees limited to those authorized by statute). *See also* American Planning Association, Growing Smart Legislative Guidebook: Model Statutes for Planning and Management of Change § 6-101 (S. Meck ed. 2002) (model impact fee legislation).

[6] Cal. Gov't Code §§ 66001(3).

[7] *Id.* § 66005(c).

[8] Tex. Local Gov't Code §§ 395.001–395.080.

[9] Tex. Local Gov't Code §§ 395.001, 395.014, 395.015.

[10] Held valid: Robes v. Town of Hartford, 636 A.2d 342 (Vt. 1993) (upholding fee for sewage service expansion). Trimen Dev. Co. v. King County, 877 P.2d 187 (Wash. 1994) (fee reasonably necessary as result of proposed development as required by statute). Held invalid: Shapell Indus. v. Governing Bd., 1 Cal. Rptr. 2d 818 (Cal. App. 1991) (school development fee); Vintage Constr. Co. v. City of Bothell, 922 P.2d 828 (Wash. App. 1996) (no individualized determination), *aff'd on basis of court of appeals opinion,* 959 P.2d 1090 (Wash. 1998).

impact fee that adopted the "specifically and uniquely attributable" standard and held the fee could be predetermined by ordinance and need not be calculated for each proposed development.[11] The Arizona court upheld a fee adopted by the city council that provided capital improvements funds needed to provide water supply.[12] It held the fee satisfied a statutory requirement that fees must "result in a beneficial use to the development," which it held was a codification of the constitutional nexus test.[13] The principal claim was that water supply plans were too speculative to provide the necessary statutory benefit, but the court applied the presumption of constitutionality to reject this challenge.

§ 9.22   The Takings Issue.[1]

Courts prior to *Nollan* had applied the nexus test to uphold impact fees,[2] and continued to do so after the Supreme Court decided *Nollan*.[3] Post-*Dolan*, the first issue courts must face is whether *Dolan,* which was a land dedication case, also applies to impact fees. Some courts have held after *Dolan* that its rough proportionality rule does not apply to impact fees, reflecting the view that this case and *Nollan* treated land dedications as the equivalent of a physical occupation by government and limited to this situation.[4] The Supreme Court has

---

[11] Northern Ill. Home Bldrs. Ass'n v. County of DuPage, 649 N.E.2d 384 (Ill. 1995).

[12] Home Builders Ass'n of Central Arizona v. City of Scottsdale, 930 P.2d 993 (Ariz. 1997).

[13] *Accord* Ehrlich v. City of Culver City, 911 P.2d 429 (Cal.1996) ("reasonable relationship" standard of statute codifies *Dolan* test). *See* § 9.22.

[1] For cases considering equal protection and other objections to connection fees *see* holding valid: Loup-Miller Constr. Co. v. City & County of Denver, 676 P.2d 1170 (Colo. 1984); Home Builders Ass'n v. City of West Des Moines, 644 N.W.2d 339 (Iowa 2002); Meglino v. Township Comm., 510 A.2d 1134 (N.J. 1986); Amherst Bldrs. Ass'n v. City of Amherst, 402 N.E.2d 1181 (Ohio 1980); Oregon State Homebuilders Ass'n v. City of Tigard, 604 P.2d 886 (Or. App. 1979); Tidewater Ass'n of Homeowners v. City of Virginia Beach, 400 S.E.2d 523 (Va. 1991). Invalid: Patterson v. Alpine Village, 663 P.2d 95 (Utah 1983).

[2] Contractor & Bldrs. Ass'n of Pinellas County v. City of Dunedin, 329 So. 2d 314 (Fla. 1976); Hartman v. Aurora San. Dist., 177 N.E.2d 214 (Ill. 1961); Hayes v. City of Albany, 490 P.2d 1018 (Or. App. 1971). *See also* J.W. Jones Cos. v. City of San Diego, 203 Cal. Rptr. 580 (Cal. App. 1984) (upholding facilities benefit assessment in growth management area); Banberry Dev. Corp. v. South Jordan City, 631 P.2d 899, 903 (Utah 1981); Home Builders Ass'n v. City of North Logan, 983 P.2d 561 (Utah 1999) (applying *Banberry*); Home Builders Ass'n of Utah v. City of American Fork, 973 P.2d 425 (Utah 1999 (same).

[3] Tahoe Keys Prop. Owners' Ass'n v. State Water Resources Bd., 28 Cal. Rptr. 2d 734 (Cal. App. 1994) (environmental mitigation fee as condition to building permits); St. John's County v. Northeast Florida Builders Ass'n, 583 So. 2d 635 (Fla. 1991) (fee on residential development for schools and requiring earmarking of funds); City of Key West v. R.L.J.S. Corp., 537 So. 2d 641 (Fla. App. 1989) (fee valid though developer cannot pass on cost of fee to consumers).

[4] Commercial Builders of Northern California v. City of Sacramento, 941 F.2d 872 (9th Cir. 1991); McCarthy v. City of Leawood, 894 P.2d 836, (Kan. 1995) (impact fee). *Accord* Clajon Prod. Corp. v. Petera, 70 F.3d 1566 (10th Cir. 1995) (upholding hunting regulation); Harris v. City of Wichita, 862 F. Supp. 287 (D. Kan. 1994) (upholding airport overlay regulations) *aff'd*

indicated the *Dolan* rough proportionality rule is limited to physical dedications and does not extend to impact fees.[5] However, the statement was dictum, and not all courts agree it means that *Dolan* does not apply to impact fees..[6]

A related issue is whether *Dolan,* which invalidated exactions imposed as a condition to a building permit, is limited to impact fees imposed adjudicatively in the permit or development approval process, or whether it also applies to impact fees imposed legislatively without an individualized determination. The California Supreme Court provided a test for determining when an exaction is imposed legislatively or adjudicatively in *Ehrlich v. City of Culver City.*[7] After the plaintiff demolished a private recreational facility, the city approved an office building on the site subject to a condition that the plaintiff pay a recreational mitigation fee to be used for additional recreational facilities to replace those lost when plaintiff demolished his facility. The city also required payment of an art-in-public-places fee. A majority agreed the fee was adjudicative. The plurality emphasized the city exercised discretionary power when it imposed the fee rather than relying on a legislative mandate or formula. It held the *Dolan* rough proportionality rule applies only in cases of "regulatory leveraging." These are cases where a municipality can impose "land-use conditions in individual cases, authorized by a permit scheme which by its nature allows for both the discretionary deployment of the police power and an enhanced potential for its abuse." A later California case similarly held an impact fee was legislative, noting the basis for the *Dolan* heightened scrutiny approach was the discretionary use of the police power in the imposition of land use conditions in individual cases. The fee was also applied through generally applicable legislation that applied equally to all covered uses.[8] The courts have applied these or similar tests when deciding whether a fee has been imposed legislatively or adjudicatively.[9]

---

without opinion, 74 F.3d 1249 (10th Cir. Kan. 1996). *Contra* Ehrlich v. City of Culver City, 911 P.2d 429 (Cal. 1996) (when impact fee adjudicative).

[5] *See* § 2.03.

[6] Holding *Dollan* does not apply: Home Builders Ass'n of N. California v. City of Napa, 108 Cal. Rptr. 2d 60 (Cal. App. 2001) (heightened judicial review does not apply to mandatory set-aside affordable housing ordinance); Krupp v. Breckenridge Sanitation Dist., 1 P.3d 178 (Colo. App. 1999) (*Nollan/Dolan* tests do not apply to sewer connection fee levied by sanitation district). *Holding contra*: Clark v. City of Albany, 904 P.2d 185 (Or. App. 1995) (applying *Dolan* where permit conditions required the landowner to expend money on improvements for the public benefit); Home Builders Ass'n of Dayton v. City of Beavercreek, 729 N.E.2d 349 (Ohio 2000) (applying *Dolan* to uphold roadway exaction).

[7] 911 P.2d 429, 439 (Cal. 1996) (applying *Dolan* to impact fee statute to save statute's constitutionality).

[8] San Remo Hotel, L.P. v. City & County of San Francisco, 41 P.3d 87 (Cal. 2002) (upholding fee as alternative to construction of affordable housing units as condition to conversion of residential hotel to tourist use).

[9] Home Builders Ass'n of Central Arizona v. City of Scottsdale, 930 P.2d 993 (Ariz. 1996)

Whether a fee is legislative or adjudicative determines the standard of judicial review the courts apply when determining the constitutionality of the fee. If the fee is legislative, an individualized determination of rough proportionality is not required, and courts apply a rational basis review similar to that applied under the equal protection clause.[10] If the fee is adjudicative, an individual determination of rough proportionality is required, and courts apply a heightened scrutiny similar to the intermediate scrutiny standard of judicial review applied under the equal protection clause. Courts have upheld legislative impact fees[11] and have also upheld adjudicative impact fees under these judicial review standards.[12]

Different principles apply if an impact fee is held to be a tax. A tax is not subject to the takings clause and may be levied throughout a jurisdiction without a showing of special benefit.[13]

§ 9.23 Linkage Programs.

A number of cities have adopted exaction programs that require downtown office and commercial developers to provide housing for lower-income groups or contribute to a municipal fund for the construction of such housing.[1] Linkage programs satisfy the nexus test only if the municipality can show that downtown development contributes to the housing problem the linkage exaction is intended to remedy.

In *Commercial Builders of Northern California v. City of Sacramento*,[2] the

---

(fee held legislative); Krupp v. Breckenridge Sanitation Dist., 19 P.3d 687 (Colo. 2001) (applying statute that makes *Dolan* test inapplicable to legislatively mandated fees); Curtis v. Town of South Thomaston, 708 A.2d 657, 660 (Me. 1998) (legislative nature of exaction only one factor in applying *Dolan*); Rogers Machinery, Inc. v. Washington County, 45 P.3d 963 (Or. App. 2002) (fee held legislative when calculated according to legislatively set formula that does not require exercise of discretion); Schultz v. City of Grants Pass, 884 P.2d 569 (Or. App. 1994) (dedication imposed on a landowner is adjudicative though required by the provisions of the local ordinance).; (town acted adjudicatively when it selectively applied legislatively-enacted standards).

[10] Home Builders Ass'n of Central Arizona v. City of Scottsdale, 930 P.2d 993 (Ariz. 1996); San Remo Hotel, L.P. v. City & County of San Francisco, 41 P.3d 87 (Cal. 2002). *See* § 2.45.

[11] Home Builders Ass'n of Central Arizona v. City of Scottsdale, 930 P.2d 993 (Ariz. 1996); San Remo Hotel, L.P. v. City & County of San Francisco, 41 P.3d 87 (Cal. 2002). *See also* F & W Assocs. v. County of Somerset, 648 A.2d 482 (N.J. App. Div. 1994) (upholding traffic impact fee under state rational nexus test post-*Dolan*). *But see* Volusia County v. Aberdeen at Ormond Beach, L.P., 760 So.2d 126 (Fla. 2000) (invalidating impact fee for schools levied on age-restricted community under rational basis rule of state need-benefit test);

[12] Home Builders Ass'n of Dayton v. City of Beavercreek, 729 N.E.2d 349 (Ohio 2000). *See* Ehrlich v. City of Culver City, 911 P.2d 429 (Cal. 1996) (remanding to determine amount of fee).

[13] Volusia County v. Aberdeen at Ormond Beach, L.P., 760 So.2d 126 (Fla. 2000). *See also* Home Builders Ass'n v. City of West Des Moines, 644 N.W.2d 339 (Iowa 2002) (discussing but rejecting minority view that a tax is a taking if confiscatory).

[1] § 7.28.

[2] 941 F.2d 872 (9th Cir. 1991). *See also* Terminal Plaza Corp. v. City & County of San Francisco,

Ninth Circuit upheld, pre-*Dolan,* a linkage fee imposed as a condition to building permits for certain kinds of nonresidential buildings. The fee was based on a study of the need for lower-income housing, and the amount of fee required to offset the effect of nonresidential use on such housing. The court held *Nollan* did not mean a development must be "directly responsible" for the "social ill in question." The fee was reasonably related to a legitimate purpose, was based on careful study and conservatively assessed only part of the need for lower-income housing to developers.

Post-*Dolan* a court must also decide whether a linkage fee is a legislative fee subject to the rational basis test, or an adjudicative fee that requires an individualized determination and must satisfy the heightened judicial scrutiny requited by *Dolan.* The California Supreme Court held a linkage fee imposed as a condition to the conversion of a residential hotel to tourist use was a legislative fee that satisfied the rational basis test.[3]

B. PLANNED UNIT DEVELOPMENT.

§ 9.24 The Land Use Problem.

Developers often plan and build residential developments as a single project that may include single-family and multifamily dwellings and even office and commercial uses if the development is large enough in scale. Projects of this type are called planned unite developments. They can range from very small developments of a few acres to very large developments that may be independent new towns called master planned communities.

The application of conventional zoning to planned unit developments presents a number of problems. If a development includes single-family and multifamily dwellings it will require two or more zoning districts, which makes it impossible to adopt a single set of land use controls for the entire project. The zoning ordinance also provides a "cookie cutter" pattern of minimum lot sizes and setbacks because its site regulations apply to individual lots. They do not allow the variety in design that a planned unit development can provide if it is planned as an entity. In addition, developers may have to build on all of the site and destroy natural and environmentally important areas.

---

223 Cal. Rptr. 379 (Cal. App. 1986) (upholding exaction for affordable housing from hotel owners who planned to convert residential hotels to another use). *But see* Nunziato v. Planning Bd., 541 A.2d 1105 (N.J. App. Div. 1988) (fee for affordable housing negotiated to induce approval of building held invalid); San Telmo Assocs. v. City of Seattle, 735 P.2d 673 (Wash. 1987) (ordinance requiring owners to replace demolished low-income housing or pay fee for replacement housing held a tax and probably unconstitutional). *See also* Sintra, Inc. v. City of Seattle, 829 P.2d 765 (Wash. 1992) (remanding taking claim on ordinance held invalid in *San Telmo*).

[3] San Remo Hotel, L.P. v. City & County of San Francisco, 41 P.3d 87 (Cal. 2002).

Planned unit development (PUD) regulation can remedy these problems by providing a set of standards for the approval of a comprehensive PUD development plan in an administrative review process. Because the development is planned and reviewed as an entity, the developer can achieve better site planning by varying lot sizes, setbacks, and other site development requirements. She can also built at higher densities in some parts of the development in return for the preservation of open and natural areas elsewhere. The municipality can approve the PUD plan as an integrated set of land use controls that applies to the entire development.

In the simplest form of planned unit development, sometimes known as a cluster zoning or a density transfer PUD, densities and uses in the development are not changed. This type of PUD is usually limited to single-family dwellings. The ordinance allows an increase in single-family densities in one part of the PUD in return for compensating open space provided elsewhere in the development. More complex PUDs include a mixture of residential types without an increase in density, or a residential-type mixture with a density increase. The mixed-use concept is carried further if the PUD includes commercial and office development. The mix of uses in a PUD, and whether there is a need for a density increase or change in the zoned use, will determine whether a PUD can be approved administratively or whether a legislative approval is required.

§ 9.25   The Planned Unit Development Review Process.

PUD regulations authorize a review process that closely resembles subdivision and site plan review,[1] but the PUD approval standards usually confer more discretion on the reviewing agency. Although PUD regulations can either be in the zoning or subdivision control ordinance, they must be in the zoning ordinance if density or use changes are authorized, and inclusion in the zoning ordinance is common. The zoning ordinance may authorize a review process in which planned unit developments are reviewed on an individual basis. The ordinance may also require the governing body to adopt a new PUD zoning district for a proposed PUD before it can be reviewed and approved, which it can adopt as a floating zone.[2] A PUD can also be approved as a special exception.[3]

The governing body may have to participate in the review of a PUD if density or use changes are required, but it can delegate PUD review to the planning commission once it makes these changes. In the typical PUD review process, the developer submits a preliminary and then a final development plan for review by the approving agency. A variant of this process requires the submission of an outline concept plan prior to the submission of a preliminary plan. The outline

---

[1] §§ 6.66, 9.04.

[2] § 6.61.

[3] §§ 6.53–6.59.

plan is a schematic map of the project.[4] It provides a basis on which the governing body can approve uses and densities before the developer submits a detailed preliminary plan. A final plan is submitted for approval after the developer has obtained approval of the preliminary plan that must comply with the approved preliminary plan. The ordinance may provide that the approved final plan supersedes and takes the place of the zoning and subdivision regulations that previously applied to the area covered by the plan.[5]

The criteria for planned unit development approval usually cover all aspects of the planned unit development, including access, circulation, land uses, densities, and site development restrictions. The ordinance may also contain criteria covering project design and the provision of common open space. Ordinance criteria must provide enough guidance to avoid delegation of power problems.[6] Because the ordinance governs the design details of PUDs, a court may hold the ordinance criteria inadequate if they do not contain clear design and approval criteria.[7] Courts have rejected arguments that the approval of a PUD was invalid because it was inconsistent with a local comprehensive plan and that PUD approvals were invalid as spot zoning.[8] The comprehensive plan rulings were made in states that do not require land use controls to be consistent with the local comprehensive plan.

Some review standards contained in PUD ordinances have not received judicial approval. In *Soble Constr. Co. v. Zoning Hearing Bd.*,[9] the ordinance required the developer to "demonstrate that a sufficient market" existed for its PUD. The court invalidated the requirement because it was an improper attempt to zone "for the purpose of limiting competition."

There is always a fine balance between improving certainty and restricting flexibility in the PUD approval process. An ordinance can inject more certainty into the PUD approval process if it contains minimum development standards,

---

[4] *See* Approval of Request for Amendment to Frawley Planned Unit Dev., 638 N.W.2d 552 (S.D. 2002) (upholding interpretation that concept plan required).

[5] *See* Pa. Stat. Ann. tit. 53, § 10711, applied in Kang v. Supervisors of Township of Spring, 776 A.2d 324 (Pa. Commw. 2001) (cannot grant conditional use after plan approved); Alta Vita Condominium Ass'n v. Zoning Hearing Bd., 736 A.2d 724 (Pa. Commw. 1999).

[6] Held adequate: Tri-State Generation & Transmission Co. v. City of Thornton, 647 P.2d 670 (Colo. 1982); Zanin v. Iacono, 487 A.2d 780 (N.J.L. Div. 1984); Appeal of Moreland, 497 P.2d 1287 (Okla. 1972). Held inadequate: Harnett v. Board of Zoning, Subdivision & Bldg. Appeals, 350 F. Supp. 1159 (D. St. Croix 1972); City of Miami v. Save Brickell Ave., Inc., 426 So. 2d 1100 (Fla. App. 1983).

[7] Beaver Meadows v. Board of County Comm'rs, 709 P.2d 928 (Colo. 1985).

[8] Moore v. City of Boulder, 484 P.2d 134 (Colo. App. 1971); North Hempstead v. Village of North Hills, 324 N.E.2d 566 (N.Y. 1975); Cheney v. Village 2 at New Hope, Inc., 241 A.2d 81 (Pa. 1968); Wiggers v. County of Skagit, 596 P.2d 1345 (Wash. App. 1979).

[9] 329 A.2d 912 (Pa. Commw. 1974).

limits the location of PUDs and clearly specifies the zoning bonuses that are allowed, but more specific criteria will necessarily limit the flexibility.

§ 9.26   Under the Standard Zoning Act.

Planned unit developments (PUDs) are residential developments that can include multifamily and single-family dwellings and that may also include complementary commercial facilities. The entire development is reviewed at one time, and subdivision is not necessary to trigger the review process. Planned unit development regulations borrow from zoning and subdivision controls. Like the zoning ordinance, planned unit development regulations regulate land use, density, and the development of the site. They may also contain internal design and thoroughfare requirements similar to those contained in subdivision control ordinances.

Planned unit development regulations present several statutory authority problems under the Standard Zoning Act, which most states adopted. The Standard Act did not confer the review powers commonly exercised under planned unit development regulations by zoning agencies such as the planning commission and board of adjustment. Nor did the Standard Act authorize the case-by-case review that is typical under PUD regulations.

The uniformity requirement presents another problem. The Standard Act and state zoning acts require uniform zoning regulations for each zoning district. Some commentators argued that the uniformity requirement limited zoning districts to the single-use districts that are traditional in zoning practice. Under this interpretation, the uniformity requirement would prohibit zoning districts with the mixed uses allowed by planned unit development regulations.

Despite these problems, the Standard Zoning Act has not been a major barrier to the adoption of planned unit development regulations. The courts have rejected claims that planned unit development regulations are not authorized by the standard form of zoning legislation. In *Chrinko v. South Brunswick Twp. Planning Bd.*,[1] the court upheld a density transfer PUD ordinance for residential subdivisions that did not authorize density increases:

> Although the state zoning law does not in so many words empower municipalities to provide an option to developers for cluster or density zoning, such an ordinance reasonably advances the legislative purposes of securing open spaces, preventing overcrowding and undue concentration and promoting the general welfare.[2]

---

[1] 187 A.2d 221 (N.J.L. Div. 1963).

[2] *Id.* at 225.

Chrinko also rejected a uniformity objection to the density transfer ordinance and noted that the ordinance "accomplishes uniformity because the option is open to all developers."[3]

The courts have approved the inclusion of PUD regulations in zoning ordinances,[4] and inclusion in the subdivision control ordinance is another possibility. In *Prince George's County v. M & B Constr. Co.*,[5] the court held that the authority to approve a density transfer PUD was properly delegated to the planning commission in the exercise of its subdivision control powers.

The court held the bargaining and negotiation that occurs in the PUD review process is not invalid as contract zoning in *Rutland Envtl. Protection Ass'n v. Kane County*:[6]

> Since the overall aims of . . . [PUD] zoning cannot be accomplished without negotiations and because conferences are indeed mandated by the regulatory ordinance, the conduct of the . . . county cannot be read as contributing to contract zoning.[7]

§ 9.27 Regulatory Techniques.

The planned unit development regulations may require a PUD rezoning by the legislative body,[1] but once a rezoning has been adopted the planning commission may have the authority to review a PUD to determine whether it complies with the criteria contained in the ordinance. In *Cheney v. Village 2 at New Hope, Inc.*,[2] the legislative body rezoned a large tract of land from low density residential to a PUD. The planning commission then approved a plan for the PUD, and building permits were issued. The ordinance rezoning to the PUD specified allowable uses, maximum densities and heights, and a minimum distance between buildings. The state had a zoning act based on the Standard Act, and the court held it authorized the creation of a zoning district with this mixture of uses.

The court approved the delegation of authority to the commission to approve PUDs. even though the zoning statute did not specifically authorize this delegation. It held the flexibility needed in the administration of PUD regulations required a delegation to the planning commission as the most appropriate zoning

---

[3] *See also* Orinda Homeowners Comm. v. Board of Supvrs., 90 Cal. Rptr. 88 (Cal. App. 1970).

[4] Dupont Circle Citizens Ass'n v. District of Columbia Zoning Comm'n, 355 A.2d 550 (D.C. App. 1976).

[5] 297 A.2d 683 (Md. 1972).

[6] 334 N.E.2d 215 (Ill. App. 1975).

[7] *Id.* at 219.

[1] North Hempstead v. Village of North Hills, 324 N.E.2d 566 (N.Y. 1975) (floating zone).

[2] 241 A.2d 81 (Pa. 1968). Sheridan Planning Comm'n v. Board of Sheridan County Comm'rs, 924 P.2d 988 (Wyo. 1996).

agency to carry out the review process. Notice, however, that the ordinance specifically designated the uses, densities and site development standards that applied to approved PUDs. *Lutz v. City of Longview*[3] invalidated a PUD ordinance that delegated to the planning commission the authority to approve a PUD as a floating zone. The court distinguished *Cheney* because in that case the legislative body rezoned the land for a PUD and the ordinance delegated only the review of project details to the planning commission.

Whether the PUD review process is considered legislative or adjudicative and quasi-judicial may determine which local agency can be delegated the authority to review PUD applications. Delegation of PUD review authority to the legislative body does not necessarily mean a court will characterize the PUD review process as legislative. A court could hold the PUD review process is quasi-judicial if the PUD ordinance contains criteria the legislative body applies in the review of PUD applications.

Whether the PUD review process is held to be legislative or quasi-judicial may depend on how extensively the governing body changes the zoning regulations. In *Peachtree Dev. Co. v. Paul*,[4] the governing body approved a PUD that significantly departed from the single-family zoning regulations. It included multifamily and commercial uses at higher densities than the zoning regulations allowed. The court held the PUD approval was a legislative act subject to referendum, and that "the board's action was the functional equivalent of altering the zoning classification of a sizeable section of . . . [the] Township." Other cases upheld the delegation of PUD review to a board of zoning adjustment or governing body as a special exception because they characterized the PUD review process as adjudicative.[5]

An important question is whether the PUD review procedure can be made mandatory. A Florida court invalidated a rezoning for a PUD initiated by a county that included a detailed site plan showing buildings, uses and densities.[6] The court held that planned unit development is a voluntary procedure intended to provide development flexibility not available in the usual zoning district, and that it cannot be forced on a developer who simply wants her land rezoned.

---

[3] 520 P.2d 1374 (Wash. 1974).

[4] 423 N.E.2d 1087 (Ohio 1981). *See also* State *ex rel.* Helujon, Ltd. v. Jefferson County, 964 S.W.2d 531 (Mo. App. 1998) (held legislative); Todd-Mart, Inc. v. Town Bd. of Webster, 370 N.Y.S.2d 683 (App. Div. 1975); City of Waukesha v. Town Bd., 543 N.W.2d 515 (Wis. App. 1995) (cannot approve PUD through conditional use procedure when districts where PUDs allowed not legislatively designated).Sheridan Planning Comm'n v. Board of Sheridan County Comm'rs, 924 P.2d 988 (Wyo. 1996).

[5] Chandler v. Kroiss, 190 N.W.2d 472 (Minn. 1971); Appeal of Moreland, 497 P.2d 1287 (Okla. 1972); Mullin v. Planning Bd., 456 N.E.2d 780 (Mass. App. 1983) (planning commission). *Compare* Cetrulo v. City of Park Hills, 524 S.W.2d 628 (Ky. 1975).

[6] Porpoise Point Pt'ship v. St. John's Cty., 532 So. 2d 727 (Fla. App. 1988).

A municipality may create taking problems in the PUD review process if a density increase available under the PUD ordinance is spurious. This problem arises if a municipality downzones the residential densities permitted as-of-right in the PUD and then offers a bonus that restores the original densities if the PUD developer dedicates common open space. The developer can attack the downzoning as unconstitutional or claim that the land dedication is a taking of property because the density bonus is spurious. One court approved this use of downzoning in the PUD process.[7]

§ 9.28 Discretion to Approve or Reject.

The courts apply the usual arbitrary and capricious judicial review standard when they review administrative and legislative PUD approvals and denials. They review these decisions carefully because PUD ordinances usually contain detailed criteria for PUD approval, and may uphold or reject decisions to deny[1] or approve[2] PUD projects.

A court will reverse a PUD denial that is based on criteria not contained in the PUD ordinance. In *RK Dev. Corp. v. City of Norwalk*,[3] the governing body

---

[7] Mountcrest Estates, Inc. v. Mayor & Twp. Comm., 232 A.2d 674 (N.J. App. Div. 1967).

[1] Upholding denial: City of Tuscaloosa v. Bryan, 505 So. 2d 330 (Ala. 1987); Dore v. County of Ventura, 28 Cal. Rptr. 2d 299 (Cal. App. 1994); Ford Leasing Dev. Co. v. Board of County Comm'rs, 528 P.2d 237 (Colo. 1974); Whitesell v. Kosciusko Cty. Bd. of Zoning Appeals, 558 N.E.2d 889 (Ind. App. 1990); Croteau v. Planning Bd., 663 N.E.2d 583 (Mass. App. 1996); Coronet Homes, Inc. v. McKenzie, 439 P.2d 219 (Nev. 1968); C.C. & J. Enters., Inc. v. City of Asheville, 512 S.E.2d 766 (N.C. App. 1999) (cannot deny application that meets ordinance standards because of noncompliance with statement of intent); Board of Supvrs. v. West Chestnut Realty Corp., 532 A.2d 942 (Pa. Commw. 1987). Reversing denial: Woodhouse v. Board of Comm'rs, 261 S.E.2d 882 (N.C. 1980) (applicant satisfied ordinance criteria); West v. Mills, 380 S.E.2d 917 (Va. 1989); Old Tuckaway Assocs. Ltd. Partnership v. City of Greenfield, 509 N.W.2d 323 (Wis. App. 1993).

[2] Upholding rezoning: Moore v. City of Boulder, 484 P.2d 134 (Colo. App. 1971); Davis v. City of Leavenworth, 802 P.2d 494 (Kan. 1991);State ex rel. Helujon, Ltd. v. Jefferson County, 964 S.W.2d 531 (Mo. App. 1998) (upholding PUD rezoning though county considered economic benefits); Huntzicker v. Washington County, 917 P.2d 1051 (Or. App. 1996) (approval complied with plan); Petersen v. City of Clemson, 439 S.E.2d 317 (S.C. App. 1993) (same); Smith v. Georgetown County Council, 355 S.E.2d 864 (S.C. App. 1987); McCallen v. City of Memphis, 786 S.W.2d 633 (Tenn. 1990). Reversing or remanding approval: Cathedral Park Condominium Comm. v. District of Columbia Zoning Comm'n, 743 A.2d 1231 (D.C. App. 2000) (remanding approval for failure to give adequate attention to density and open space problems); Blagden Alley Ass'n v. District of Columbia Zoning Comm'n, 590 A.2d 139 (D.C. App. 1991) (remanding approval); BECA of Alexandria, L.L.P. v. County of Douglas, 607 N.W.2d 459 (Minn. App. 2000) (reversing approval of PUD with severely restrictive conditions); Springville Citizens for a Better Envt. v. City of Springville, 979 P.2d 332 (Utah 1999) (remanding because city violated mandatory provisions of ordinance in its approval); Citizens for Mount Vernon v. City of Mount Vernon, 947 P.2d 1208 (Wash. 1997) (cannot approve PUD that is inconsistent with underlying zone).

[3] 242 A.2d 781 (Conn. 1968). See also DeMaria v. Enfield Planning & Zoning Comm'n, 271 A.2d 105 (Conn. 1970); Hall v. Korth, 244 So. 2d 766 (Fla. App. 1971); LaSalle Nat'l Bank v. County of Lake, 325 N.E.2d 105 (Ill. App. 1975); Woodhouse v. Board of Comm'rs, 261 S.E.2d 882 (N.C. 1980); Mullins v. City of Knoxville, 665 S.W.2d 393 (Tenn. App. 1983).

denied a PUD because of "[t]he safety for the sake of the children up there; the welfare of the community and also the health hazards." The PUD contained specific site development standards for PUD applications but did not contain criteria authorizing denial for any of these reasons.

The court held that the denial was illegal because the ordinance did not prohibit PUDs for "any reason" given by the governing body. It was not entitled to substitute "pure discretion" for "a discretion controlled by fixed standards." The reasons given by the governing body were vague and uncertain and did not indicate how the applicant failed to comply with the ordinance.

Planned unit development regulations often contain clauses that specify the purposes served by planned unit developments. In *Dupont Circle Citizens Ass'n v. District of Columbia Zoning Comm'n*,[4] the ordinance contained a purpose clause stating that planned unit developments must provide an environment and amenities "superior" to what the zoning regulations could provide. This type of purpose clause is sometimes included in PUD ordinances. The court held the purpose clause did not enact a "comparison" test on which the commission had to make findings of fact in the adjudicative PUD review procedures. It could support its conclusion that a PUD met the purposes specified in the ordinance with "subsidiary findings of basic facts on material issues" raised by the PUD application.

§ 9.29   Amendments to Development Plans.

Problems can arise during the development of a PUD that require changes in the final development plan. The courts have held that major changes in the plan cannot be made administratively but require the same review procedure used to approve the PUD initially.[1] The PUD ordinance can resolve uncertainties in the amendment process by distinguishing between minor and major changes and providing that minor changes can be made administratively.[2] If the PUD was approved as a special exception, amendments to the plan can be made in the special exception process if the amendment does not authorize a use change that requires a rezoning.[3]

---

[4] 426 A.2d 327 (D.C. App. 1981). *See also* Smith v. Georgetown County Council, 355 S.E.2d 864 (S.C. App. 1987).

[1] Millbrae Ass'n for Residential Survival v. City of Millbrae, 69 Cal. Rptr. 251 (1968); City of New Smyrna Beach v. Andover Dev. Corp., 672 So.2d 618 (Fla. App. 1996).

[2] Bailey v. Zoning Bd. of Adjustment, 801 A.2d 492 (Pa. 2002) (ordinance authorized policy allowing planning commission approval of de minimis changes without council approval, but policy held not to be within this authority).

[3] Chandler v. Kroiss, 190 N.W.2d 472 (Minn. 1971). *See* McCarty v. City of Kansas City, 671 S.W.2d 790 (Mo. App. 1984) (use change requires rezoning). *Cf.* Gray v. Trustees, Monclova Twp., 313 N.E.2d 366 (Ohio 1974) (invalidating legislative amendment); Frankland v. City of Lake Oswego, 517 P.2d 1042 (Or. 1973) (sketch plan binds developer). *See* Foggy Bottom Ass'n v. District of Columbia Zoning Comm'n, 639 A.2d 578 (D.C. App. 1994) (upholding plan amendment deleting mini-park requirement).

§ 9.30 Planned Unit Development Legislation.

Several states have adopted legislation that authorizes planned unit development regulations.[1] Some of this legislation merely authorizes regulations that can provide for planned unit developments, but some contain detailed requirements for PUD ordinances. Some statutes authorize the approval of density transfer planned unit developments in the subdivision control or zoning process.[2]

Model legislation proposed in 1965 contained detailed enabling authority for planned unit development regulation intended to remedy problems that could arise under the Standard Zoning Act.[3] A few states adopted laws based on the model legislation.[4] Extensive detailed provisions contained in the model legislation have led to unexpected restraints on local PUD regulations. The cases divide, for example, on whether municipalities can enact PUD ordinances that do not comply with the model legislation.[5] Detailed review standards in the model legislation are similar to the standards contained in many PUD ordinances. The Pennsylvania Commonwealth Court held a municipality may reject a plan that satisfies the statutory standards if the circumstances are "so exceptional as to support the conclusion that the plan . . . would not be in the public interest."[6]

---

[1] Colo. Rev. Stat. § 24-67-101 et seq.; Conn. Gen. Stat. § 8-2; Idaho Code § 67-6515; 65 Ill. Comp. Stat. Ann. 5/11-13-1.1 (may classify as special use); Mass. Ann. Laws ch. 40A, § 9 (special permit); Miss. Code Ann. § 19-5-10 (authorizes development agreement authorizing master planned community to be governed by its master plan in lieu of county ordinances); Mont. Code Ann. § 76-3-504(2) (authorizing subdivision regulations that promote cluster development); Neb. Rev. Stat. § 19-4401; Nev. Rev. Stat. Ann. § 278A.010; Ohio Rev. Code, §§ 303.22, 519.021. *See* Glenbrook Homeowners Ass'n v. Glenbrook County, 901 P.2d 132 (Nev. 1995) (assurances required for open space). *See also* American Planning Association, Growing Smart Legislative Guidebook: Model Statutes for Planning and Management of Change § 8-303 (S. Meck ed. 2002) (model legislation for planned unit developments).

[2] Mich. Comp. Laws §§ 125.216h, 125.286h,125.584f, N.Y. Town Law § 278 (subdivision).

[3] Babcock, Krasnowiecki & McBride, "The Model State Statute", 114 U. Pa. L. Rev. 140 (1965).

[4] Mich. Comp. Laws §§ 125.216c et seq., 125.286c et seq., 125.584b et seq.; N.J. Stat. Ann. §§ 40:55D-39, 40:55D-40, 40:55D-45; Pa. Stat. Ann. tit. 53, §§ 10701–10711.

[5] *Compare* Niccollai v. Planning Bd., 372 A.2d 352 (N.J. App. Div. 1977) *with* Raum v. Board of Supvrs., 342 A.2d 450 (Pa. Commw. 1975). *See also* Township of Middleton v. Abel, 297 A.2d 525 (Pa. Commw. 1972) (concept plan not authorized); Carlson v. Town of Smithfield, 723 A.2d 1129 (R.I. 1999) (statute does not preclude approval by zoning board).

[6] Michaels Dev. Co. v. Benzinger Twp. Bd. of Supvrs., 413 A.2d 743 (Pa. Commw. 1980); Doran Inv. Co. v. Muhlenberg Twp., 309 A.2d 450 (Pa. Commw. 1973).

REFERENCES

Books and Monographs

R. Alterman, ed., Private Supply of Public Services: Evaluation of Real Estate Exactions, Linkage, and Alternative Land Policies (1988).

F. Bair, Intensity Zoning: Regulating Townhouses, Apartments and Planned Developments, American Planning Ass'n, Planning Advisory Serv. Rep. No. 314 (1976).

B. Blaesser, Discretionary Land Use Controls (1997).

R. Burchell, ed., Frontiers of Planned Unit Development (1973).

J. Frank, Development Exactions (1987).

R. Freilich & M. Shultz, Model Subdivision Regulations (2d Ed. 1995).

F. James & R. Rhodes, eds., Development Exactions (1987).

J. Leithe & M. Montavon, Impact Fee Programs: A Survey of Design and Administrative Issues (Government Finance Officers Ass'n, 1990).

D. Listokin & C. Walker, The Subdivision and Site Plan Handbook (1989).

D. Merrian, D. Brower & P. Tegeler, eds., Inclusionary Zoning Moves Downtown (1985).

J. Nichols, The Calculation of Proportionate-Share Impact Fees, American Planning Ass'n, Planning Advisory Serv. Rep. No. 409 (1988).

W. Sanders, The Cluster Subdivision: A Cost-Effective Approach, American Planning Ass'n, Planning Advisory Serv. Rep. No. 356 (1981).

T. Snyder & M. Stegman, Paying for Growth: Using Development Fees to Finance Infrastructure (1986).

F. So, D. Mosena & F. Bangs, Planned Unit Development Ordinances, American Planning Ass'n, Planning Advisory Serv. Rep. No. 291 (1973).

Articles

Alterman, Evaluating Linkage and Beyond: Letting the Windfall Recapture Genie out of the Exactions Bottle, 34 Wash. U.J. Urb. & Contemp. L. 51 (1988).

Ansson, *Dolan v. Tigard's* Rough Proportionality Standard: Why This Standard Should Not be Applied to an Inverse Condemnation Claim Based Upon Regulatory Denial, 10 Seton Hall Const. L.J. 417 (2000).

Blaesser & Kentopp, Impact Fees: The Second Generation, 38 Wash. U.J. Urb. & Contemp. L. 55 (1990).

Brooker & Cole, Automatic Approval Statutes: Escape Hatches and Pitfalls, 29 Urb. Law. 439 (1997).

Callies & Tappendorf, Unconstitutional Land Development Conditions and the Development Agreement Solution: Bargaining for Public Facilities After Nollan and Dolan, 51 Case West. L. Rev. 663 (2001).

Cholewa & Edmonds, Federalism and Land Use After *Dolan*: Has the Supreme Court Taken Takings from the States, 28 Urb. Law. 401 (1996).

Cordes, Legal Limits on Development Exactions: Responding to *Nollan* and *Dolan,* 15 N. Ill. U.L. Rev. 513 (1995).

Delaney, Impact Fees, Housing Costs, and Housing Affordability, 1 U. Fla. J.L. & Pub. Pol'y 87 (1987).

Denbo, Development Exactions: A New Way to Fund State and Local Government Infrastructure Improvements and Affordable Housing?, 23 Real Estate L.J. 7 (1994).

Ethier & Howard, Development Excise Taxes: An Exercise in Cleverness and Imagination, Land Use L. & Zoning Dig., Vol. 42, No. 2, at 3 (1990).

Faus, Exactions, Impact Fees, and Dedications—Local Government Responses to Nollan/Dolan Takings Law Issues, 29 Stetson L. Rev. 675–708 (2000).

Fennell, Hard Bargains and Real Steals: Land Use Exactions Revisited, 86 Iowa L. Rev. 1 (2000).

Freis & Reyniak, Putting Takings Back Into the Fifth Amendment: Land Use Planning After *Dolan v. City of Tigard,* 21 Colum. J. Envtl. L. 103 (1996).

Gudder, A Primer on Planned Unit Development, 21 Zon. & Plan. Rep. 18,25 (1998).

Henning, Mitigating Price Effects with a Housing Linkage Fee, 78 Calif. L. Rev. 721 (1990).

Holloway & Guy, The Impact of a Federal Takings Norm on Fashioning a Means-End Fit Under Takings Provisions of State Constitutions, 8 Dick. J. Envtl. L. & Pol'y 143 (1999).

Holloway & Guy, A Limitation on Development Impact Exactions to Limit Social Policy-Making: Interpreting the Takings Clause to Limit Land Use Policy-Making for Social Welfare Goals of Urban Communities, 9 Dick. J. Envtl. L. & Pol'y 1 (2000).

Krasnowiecki, The Pennsylvania Uniform Planned Community Act, 106 Dick. L. Rev. 463 (2002).

Leitner & Schoettle, A Survey of State Impact Fee Enabling Legislation, 25 Urb. Law. 491 (1993).

Lytton, Linkage: An Evaluation and Exploration, 21 Urb. Law. 413 (1989).

Merrill & Lincoln, Linkage Fees and Fair Share Regulations: Law and Method, 25 Urb. Law. 223 (1993).

Morgan, Development Exactions: Avoiding and Defending *Dolan* Challenges, Land Use L. & Zoning Dig., Vol. 52, No. 9, at 3 (2000).

Morgan, Exactions as Takings: Tactics for Dealing With *Dolan,* Land Use L. & Zoning Dig., Vol. 46, No. 9, at 3 (1994).

Morgan, Shortlidge & Watson, Right-of-Way Exactions and Rough Proportionality, Municipal Lawyer, Vol. 40, No. 1, at 28 (1999).

Morgan, State Impact Fee Legislation: Guidelines for Analysis, Land Use L. & Zoning Dig., Vol. 42, No. 3, at 3 & No. 4, at 3 (1990).

Reynolds, Local Subdivision Regulation: Formulaic Constraints in an Age of Discretion, 24 Ga. L. Rev. 525 (1990).

Reznik, The Distinction Between Legislative and Adjudicative Decisions in Dolan v. City of Tigard, 75 N.Y.U.L. Rev. 242 (2000).

Romero, Two Constitutional Theories for Invalidating Extortionate Exactions, 78 Neb. L. Rev. 348 (1999).

Schukoske, Housing Linkage: Regulating Development Impact on Housing Costs, 76 Iowa L. Rev. 1011 (1991).

Schultz & Kelly, Subdivision Improvement Requirements and Guarantees: A Primer, 28 Wash. U.J. Urb. & Contemp. L. 3 (1985).

Sternlieb, Burchell, Hughes & Listokin, Planned Unit Development Legislation: A Summary of Necessary Considerations, 7 Urb. L. Ann. 71 (1974).

Stroud & Trevarthen, Defensible Exactions After *Nollan v. California Coastal Commission* and *Dolan v. City of Tigard,* 25 Stetson L. Rev. 719 (1996).

Sullivan, *Dolan* and Municipal Risk Assessment, 12 J. Envtl. L. & Litigation 1 (1997).

Symposium, Development Impact Fees, 54 J. Am. Plan. Ass'n 3 (1988).

Symposium, Exactions: A Controversial New Source for Municipal Funds, 50 Law & Contemp. Prob. 1 (1987).

Symposium, Planned Unit Development, 114 U. Pa. L. Rev. 3 (1965).

White, Development Fees and Exemptions for Affordable Housing: Tailoring Regulations to Achieve Multiple Public Objectives, 6 J. Land Use & Envt'l L. 25 (1990).

Ziegler, Development Exactions and Permit Decisions: *Nolan, Dolan,* and *Del Monte Dunes,* 34 Urb. Law. 155 (2002).

Student Work

Note, Child Care Linkage: Addressing Child Care Needs Through Land Use Planning, 26 Harv. J. Legis. 591 (1989).

Note, The Distinction Between Legislative and Adjudicative Decisions in *Dolan v. City of Tigard*, 75 N.Y.U.L. Rev. 242, 253–259 (2000).

Note, Exactions for Transportation Corridors After *Dolan v. City of Tigard*, 29 Loy. L.A.L. Rev. 247 (1995).

Note, Land Subdivision Control, 65 Harv. L. Rev. 1226 (1952).

Note, Protecting Property Rights With Strict Scrutiny: An Argument for the "Specifically and Uniquely Attributable" Standard, 25 Fordham Urb. L.J. 575 (1998).

Note, Taking Sides: The Burden of Proof Switch in *Dolan v. City of Tigard*, 71 N.Y.U. L. Rev. 1301 (1996).

Note and Comment, The Scope of the Supreme Court's Heightened Scrutiny Takings Doctrine and its Impact on Development Exactions, 20 Whittier L. Rev. 181 (1998).

Comment, Exactions, Severability, and Takings: When Courts Should Sever Unconstitutional Conditions From Development Permits, 27 B.C. Envtl. Aff. L. Rev. 279 (2000).

Comment, A Poor Relation? Regulatory Takings after *Dolan v. City of Tigard*, 63 U. Chi. L. Rev. 199 (1996).

Chapter 10

GROWTH MANAGEMENT AND THE CONTROL OF PUBLIC FACILITIES

Synopsis

§ 10.01   An Introductory Note.

A. GROWTH MANAGEMENT PROGRAMS

§ 10.02   What These Programs Do.
§ 10.03   The Legal Problems.
§ 10.04   *Timing and Phasing Programs: Ramapo.*
§ 10.05   Adequate Public Facilities and Concurrency Requirements.
§ 10.06   Development Quotas: *Petaluma.*
§ 10.07   Urban Growth Boundaries and Service Areas.
§ 10.08   Exclusion and The Right to Travel.
§ 10.09   Public Utilities and Service as a Growth Management Control.
§ 10.10   Service Refusals: The Duty to Serve.
§ 10.11   The Takings Issue.

B. CORRIDOR PRESERVATION

§ 10.12   The Corridor Preservation Problem.
§ 10.13   Corridor Preservation Legislation.
§ 10.14   The Takings Issue.

§ 10.01   An Introductory Note.

Traditional zoning is not effective as growth management. The zoning map indicates areas for future development but does not include timing and phasing controls. Development can occur at any location where it is permitted. The overzoning typical of many communities contributes to this problem. The zoning map may designate areas for development far in excess of reasonable projections, and development may occur anywhere within these areas. Some areas are developed prematurely, new development is scattered, and environmental areas are damaged.

Growth management is also limited by the weak link provided by state planning legislation between the provision of public facilities and land development. The Standard Planning Act requires public facility locations to be consistent with the comprehensive plan, but a two-thirds vote of the governing body can override this requirement.[1]

---

[1] § 3.07.

(5th Ed.—02/03)

Growth management programs arose to correct these problems by providing control over the rate of growth, the provision of necessary public facilities and the location of new development to implement growth management strategies. Though usually adopted at the local government level, some states, such as Florida, Oregon, and Washington have state land use systems that include growth management controls. This chapter reviews the legal problems of local growth management programs.

A. GROWTH MANAGEMENT PROGRAMS

§ 10.02 What These Programs Do.

Growth management programs take many forms. One method is to link the existing comprehensive plan and zoning systems so that they can manage growth more effectively. Some states require growth management plans and regulatory strategies to implement the plan.[1] Under this approach, zoning and other land use control techniques are used to implement growth strategies contained in the comprehensive plan.

Communities have also adopted a range of programs to manage growth that may or may not be based on a comprehensive plan. One type of program controls the timing and phasing of new development, often by making adequate public facilities a condition to development approval.[2] Other communities have adopted annual quotas on new development, though quotas are no longer commonly used. Moratoria on new development,which were discussed in Chapter 6,[3] limits on the extension of public facility services, such as sewer service, and the adoption of service tiers and areas are other strategies that are concerned with the provision of adequate public services and facilities.

Another method is to identify specific areas in which new development is allowed. One example is the adoption of urban growth or urban service boundaries. New development is allowed inside but not outside the boundaries. The Oregon and Washington state land use program require urban growth boundaries, and municipalities have adopted urban growth boundaries in other states. An urban growth boundary may also limit the growth of existing communities and provide for the dispersal of new development to outlying urban centers.

Land use control techniques that can reserve land for necessary public facilities before they are built are also an important element in growth management

---

[1] § 3.10.

[2] Fla. Stat. Ann. § 161.3180 (requiring provision of public facilities to be concurrent with new development).

[3] §§ 6.06–6.11.

programs. The municipal official map and related land use controls can be used for this purpose.

§ 10.03   The Legal Problems.

Timing, phasing, and quota controls present several legal problems. Statutory authority is a problem because the Standard Zoning Act did not authorize land use controls of this type.[1] An equal protection problem arises because these programs allow development at different times in different areas of the community. Growth management programs also raise exclusionary zoning issues. They have an exclusionary effect if they do not make enough land available to meet market demand for affordable housing.

The takings issue is critical in growth management programs. A takings problem arises when a growth management program temporarily or permanently prohibits development. The Supreme Court's *Lake Tahoe* decision,[2] which dealt with the constitutionality of moratoria, also provides guidance on the constitutionality of growth management programs that delay development. The Court held a delay in development during a moratorium is not a categorical per se facial taking. It left open the possibility a moratorium could be a taking as applied, and held courts should apply the *Penn Central* balancing test to decide this question.

§ 10.04   *Timing and Phasing Programs: Ramapo.*

A timing and phasing program links the approval of new development with the provision of public services and facilities. This is usually done through the adoption of adequate public facilities and concurrency requirements discussed in the next section. *Golden v. Planning Bd. of Town of Ramapo*[1] is a leading New York case that upheld the validity of a unique and special program of this type that was based on a comprehensive plan. The case was decided before *Penn Central*, so its relevance under today's takings law is not clear. The town later abandoned the program because of difficulties in implementation.

The Town of Ramapo is located near New York City, on the New Jersey border. A New York town, like a Midwestern township, includes unincorporated and incorporated areas. Ramapo adopted a comprehensive plan that projected its future development and included an eighteen-year capital improvements program. The plan contemplated the development of all the land in the town within the eighteen-year period adopted for the capital facilities program. A

---

[1] *See* Boulder Bldrs. Group v. City of Boulder, 759 P.2d 752 (Colo. 1988) (growth management program authorized by constitutional home rule provision). *See also* § 4.25.

[2] Tahoe-Sierra Preservation Council v. Tahoe Regional Planning Agency, 535 U.S. 302. *See* § 6.08.

[1] 285 N.E.2d 291 (N.Y. 1975).

downzoning was not necessary because the town was zoned for very low residential densities. One-half of the zoned area was zoned for large residential lots, and the growth management program complemented the extensive large-lot zoning. Several incorporated villages within the town were not included.

The town also adopted an innovative amendment to its zoning ordinance to implement the program. It required all residential development, except individual single-family dwellings, to apply for and receive a special permit from the governing body. A developer could obtain a development permit if he acquired a designated number of points based on the availability of five essential services, not all of them controlled by the town. Though the decision did not indicate the basis on which the town awarded points, they varied depending on a development's distance from a public facility. More points were awarded if the development was closer to a facility. The program did not include multifamily development and did not apply to industrial and commercial development.

The program contained a number of remedial features. The town could issue a permit vesting development rights at a future time when public services became available. The ordinance authorized variances from the permit requirement. A developer could advance the time for development by providing enough of the designated facilities to acquire the necessary points. Landowners could also apply to the town for reductions in property tax assessments on land restricted from development under the growth management program.

The plaintiffs claimed the program was facially invalid because it was unauthorized by the zoning statute and unconstitutional. The court held the town zoning act, which was based on the Standard Zoning Act, authorized the growth management program. The power to "restrict and regulate" conferred by the act included the authority to direct the growth of population within the township for growth management purposes. "[T]he matrix of land use restrictions" which are common to the "enumerated powers" provided the authority to determine how development would proceed even though it would be diverted from "its natural course." The court's holding on the statutory authority question validated the residential development permit requirement, which was a notable variation from standard zoning practice.

The court held the growth management program constitutional in an elaborate opinion that was influenced by the decision to attack the program facially. It court noted a plaintiff could attack the constitutionality of the growth management ordinance as applied in a later proceeding. It rejected a claim the growth management program was exclusionary by noting that "the power to zone under current law is vested in local municipalities" and by deferring to the town's legislative judgment. The court was impressed by the comprehensive planning on which the growth management program was based, and viewed the plan as a rational and planned effort to "maximize population density consistent with orderly growth."

The court did not consider the extensive large-lot zoning the growth management program reinforced because the plaintiffs did not attack it, but noted in a footnote that a "compelling need" had not been advanced for the large-lot zoning. The town had made provision for low-and moderate-income housing, the court believed, and it noted this housing would help remedy lower-income housing problems in the town. It apparently was not aware that only a minimal amount of lower-income housing was available or contemplated, most of it for the elderly.

The court summed up the exclusionary issues by noting it would not "countenance . . . under any guise . . . [any] community efforts at immunization or exclusion." It held that

[w]hat segregates permissible from impermissible restrictions, depends in the final analysis upon the purpose of the restrictions and their impact in terms of both the community and the general public interest. . . . The line of demarcation between the two is not a constant, but will be found to vary with prevailing circumstances and conditions. . . .[2]

The New York court struck down exclusionary zoning in a later case.[3] A New Hampshire statute authorizes the timing of development but contains protections against the adoption of exclusionary programs.[4]

The court approached the takings claim by noting that growth management "restrictions threaten to burden individual parcels for as long as a full generation" and that it did not view these restrictions as a "temporary expedient." It noted that "[e]very restriction on the use of property entails hardships for some individual owners," but concluded that

[the restrictions] are not, however, absolute. The . . . [ordinance requirements] contemplate a definite term, as the development points are designed to operate for a maximum period of 18 years and during that period, the Town is committed to the construction and installation of capital improvements.[5]

---

[2] *Id.* at 302.

[3] §§ 7.14–7.18.

[4] N.H. Rev. Stat. § 674:22 (requires master plan and capital improvement ordinance., and growth management process must also "assess and balance community development needs and consider regional development needs"), codifying Beck v. Town of Raymond, 394 A.2d 847 (N.H. 1978). *See* Rancourt v. Town of Barnstead, 523 A.2d 55 (N.H. 1986) (rejecting growth rate in plan and holding growth control ordinance must be based on "reasonable rate of increase" in municipal services.) *See also* Caspersen v. Town of Lyme, 661 A.2d 759 (N.H. 1995) (50-acre minimum lot size ordinance not a growth control subject to the statute); Stoney-Brook Dev. Corp. v. Town of Fremont, 474 A.2d 561 (N.H. 1984); N.H. Rev. Stat. § 674:23 (authorizing interim growth controls).

[5] *Id.* at 304.

The court pointed out some land would be available for development before the close of the eighteen-year capital program, and that developers could accelerate the development of their land by providing the necessary public facilities.

The extensive planning that preceded the adoption of the growth management ordinance was an important factor in the case, as were the remedial measures available to developers. The court could uphold the growth management program as an interim measure because all of the municipality was committed to development. The *Ramapo* decision does not support growth management programs in communities that do not make this commitment. Ramapo's comparatively small size made this commitment possible. Larger communities may not be able to commit all of their area to development and may require restrictive zoning in areas not designated for development to implement a growth management program. The *Ramapo* case did not have to consider the constitutionality of this kind of zoning.

How the Ramapo program would be treated under modern takings law is not clear. The Supreme Court in *Lake Tahoe* was sensitive to the time issue and indicated a moratorium of over one year might be unconstitutional. It is not clear that a commitment to the development of a community at the end of a long 18-year period would overcome a claim that so long a delay is a taking. Neither is it clear that the purpose of a timing program, which was so important in *Ramapo*, would be a factor in a decision under the *Penn Central* takings factors.

§ 10.05 Adequate Public Facilities and Concurrency Requirements.

Adequate public facilities (APF) and concurrency requirements are another method of securing the provision of public services and facilities when new development is approved. An adequate public facilities ordinance conditions the approval of new development on the availability of adequate services, which are usually measured by level-of-service standards for traffic, school and other services. It is usually administered on a case-by-case basis, does not usually time or direct development to priority areas, and may or may not be based on a comprehensive plan. Unlike the Ramapo plan, the level-of-service standards are usually limited to one or two services and are based on performance standards rather than designated points. For example, a level-of-service standard for highways would be measured by the level of traffic congestion. A statute can authorize the adoption of adequate public facilities ordinances.[1]

Though an APF requirement is presumably safe from a facial attack, a landowner could attack a permit denial as a taking if the denial did not allow the property owner to put his property to an economically productive use for

---

[1] Md. Code Ann. Art. 66B, § 10.1(a)(1); N.H. Rev. Stat. §§ 674:21–674:22.

a substantial period of time.[2] Problems may also arise in determining when facilities are adequate. For example, a court may disagree with the selection of the service area in which the municipality evaluated the adequacy of public facilities.[3]

Florida and Washington State have a concurrency requirement as part of their state land use programs that is similar to what is required by an APF ordinance. In Florida, the mandatory comprehensive plan must include a capital facilities element that includes standards for adequate public facilities.[4] The statute also contains a concurrency requirement for seven public facilities.[5] Washington State's program contains a concurrency requirement for transportation facilities and requires the mandatory plan to specify transportation service levels.[6] The American Planning Association's model legislation also contains a provision for a concurrency and adequate public facilities requirement.[7]

§ 10.06   Development Quotas: *Petaluma*.

Quotas on new development, usually applied on an annual basis, are occasionally found in growth management programs. The courts have upheld these programs. A California court upheld against a facial taking attack two ordinances that regulated growth by encouraging development in cities, and by regulating the rate, distribution, quality and type of residential development on an annual basis, with periodic reviews. It noted that "[c]ourts have long recognized the legitimacy of such ordinances."[1] A Colorado court held an ordinance establishing an annual quota system for new building permits, based on a formula against which each development application is tested and scored, was authorized by the

---

[2] *But see* Albany Area Builders Ass'n v. Town of Clifton Park, 576 N.Y.S.2d 932 (App. Div, 1991) (upholding an ordinance that limited the number of building permits that could be approved in a development area to 20 percent of the total units approved for any one project to remedy congested traffic conditions).

[3] Maryland-National Capital Park & Planning Comm'n v. Rosenberg, 307 A.2d 704 (Md. 1973) (schools would be adequate if school service boundaries were redefined). *See also* Annapolis Market Place, L.L.C. v. Parker, 802 A.2d 1029 (Md. 2002) (interpreting ordinance to require inclusion of facility in county capital improvement program or state transportation program, except for on-site facilities to be provided by developer).

[4] Fla. Stat. Ann. § 163.3177(3)(a)(3).

[5] *Id.* § 163.3180(1)(a).

[6] Wash. Rev. Code § 36.70A.070(6). *For discussion see* Sammamish County Council v. City of Bellevue, 29 P.3d 728 (Wash. App. 2001).

[7] American Planning Association, Growing Smart Legislative Guidebook: Model Statutes for Planning and Management of Change § 8-603 (S. Meck ed. 2002).

[1] Long Beachfront Equities, Inc. v. County of Ventura, 282 Cal. Rptr. 877 (Cal. App. 1991) (as-applied taking and other claims not ripe).

enabling act. The act authorized the regulation of population density and the phased development of services and facilities.[2]

Construction Indus. Ass'n of Sonoma County v. City of Petaluma[3] is the best-known case upholding a development control program that contained an explicit annual quota on residential development. Petaluma is a self-sufficient community forty miles north of San Francisco and is part of the metropolitan Bay Area housing market. Petaluma grew dramatically in the years before it adopted its quota program.

The Petaluma program imposed an annual development quota of 500 dwelling units but exempted projects with four units or less. It included a Residential Development Control System, modeled on the Ramapo point system, under which it allocated the annual residential development quota. The Petaluma point system was elaborate and awarded points for good environmental and architectural design, for providing certain recreational facilities, and for providing low-and moderate-income dwellings in compliance with the city's housing policy. This policy allocated eight to twelve percent of the annual quota to low-and moderate-income housing.

The Court of Appeals held the program did not violate substantive due process. It assumed the quota would limit supply below anticipated market demand and would cause a housing shortfall in the region, with a consequent decline in regional housing quality and choice and a loss in mobility. The court noted, however, that the quota would not create this problem in Petaluma and would increase the number of lower-income housing units in that city. It held it was "unnecessary" to consider the city's claim that the program would prevent the overtaxing of "available water and sewage facilities."

The court noted the Petaluma program might be exclusionary but that all land use regulation can have this "purpose and effect." The city could justify any exclusionary effect by showing that the program had a "rational relationship to a *legitimate state interest.*" Due process rights are not violated simply because "a local entity exercises in its own self-interest the police power lawfully delegated to it by the state." In a footnote, the court pointed out that the Petaluma

---

[2] Wilkinson v. Board of County Comm'rs, 872 P.2d 1269 (Colo. App. 1994) (also upholding denial of development application under ordinance and dismissing taking claim as unripe). *See also* Giuliano v. Town of Edgartown, 531 F. Supp. 1076 (D. Mass. 1982) (upholding regulation on timing of development); Sturges v. Town of Chilmark, 402 N.E.2d 1346 (Mass. 1980) (holding ordinance limiting annual rate of growth on Martha's Vineyard for ten years so town could study problems resulting from subsoil conditions authorized by statute and not a due process violation); Albany Area Builders Ass'n v. Town of Clifton Park, 576 N.Y.S.2d 932 (App. Div. 1991) (upholding ordinance limiting building permits in 10% of town to 20% units approved in project to remedy traffic problems; ordinance effective for five years or until interchange completed).

[3] 522 F.2d 897 (9th Cir. 1975).

program's lower-income housing goals made it inclusionary rather than exclusionary.

Petaluma still has the annual development quota program. A California statute adopted after *Petaluma* provides that any ordinance that limits the number of residential building permits or buildable lots "is presumed to have an impact on the supply of residential units" in the municipality and in the territory outside its jurisdiction.[4] In an action challenging such an ordinance, a municipality has the burden to show that it "is necessary for the protection of the public health, safety or welfare" of the municipality.[5]

Courts will strike down a development quota they find arbitrary. *City of Boca Raton v. Boca Villas Corp.*[6] held an absolute quota on municipal growth violated substantive due process. It noted that the cap was supported only by after-the-fact studies, that the planning department was not consulted, and that the planning director testified that the quota was unnecessary. It held that the quota was not justified by inadequacies in public services subject to the city's control or by environmental problems.

§ 10.07   Urban Growth Boundaries and Service Areas.

An urban growth boundary (UGB) is a boundary that is placed around an urbanized area that marks the limits of urban growth. The UGB is a widely-used growth management technique, and several state statutes and land use programs require their adoption.[1] Maryland authorizes local governments to designate growth areas that are eligible for priority funding in state programs.[2]

---

[4] Cal. Evid. Code § 669.5. *See* Building Indus. Ass'n v. City of Camarillo, 718 P.2d 68 (Cal.1968) (applies to ordinance adopted by initiative). *See also* Cal. Gov't Code §§ 65302.8, 65863.6.

[5] *See also* William S. Hart Union High Sch. Dist. v. Regional Planning Comm'n, 277 Cal. Rptr. 645 (Cal. App. 1991) (denial of rezoning because of inadequate school facilities); Lee v. City of Monterrey Park, 219 Cal. Rptr. 309 (Cal. App. 1985) (complaint that initiative ordinance that adopted annual building quota violated California's exclusionary zoning rule stated cause of action).

[6] 371 So. 2d 154 (Fla. App. 1979). *Compare* Innkeepers Motor Lodge, Inc. v. City of New Smyrna Beach, 460 So. 2d 379 (Fla. App. 1984) (accord) *with* City of Hollywood v. Hollywood, Inc., 432 So. 2d 1332 (Fla. App. 1983) (upholding density cap for area of city). *See also* Begin v. Town of Sabbatus, 409 A.2d 1269 (Me. 1979) (invalidating slow-growth ordinance limited to mobile homes).

[1] Me. Rev. Stat. Ann. tit. 30-A, § 4326(3)(A); Tenn. Code Ann. § 6.58-101 et seq. (requires local governments to establish urban growth boundaries); Wash. Rev. Code Ann. § 36.70A.110. *See also* Utah Code Ann. §§ 11.38-101 to 11-38-203 (establishes state Quality Growth Commission that may assist local governments in identifying quality growth areas); American Planning Association, Growing Smart Legislative Guidebook: Model Statutes for Planning and Management of Change 6-94 to 6-103 (S. Meck ed. 2002) (discussing provisions in model legislation authorizing urban growth boundaries).

[2] Md. State Finance and Procurement Code Ann. § 5.7B-03.

The Oregon UGB program has been in place longest. The state land use program mandates the preparation of local comprehensive plans and their review by a state Land Conservation and Development Commission (LCDC) for compliance with state planning goals. The Urbanization Goal 14 requires the adoption of an Urban Growth Boundary (UGB) by municipalities. The UGB must also be approved by LCDC. New urban development generally can occur only within a UGB.

There have been no reported takings challenges to urban growth boundaries. Oregon has a comprehensive agricultural zoning program that supports the retention of land outside UGBs in non-urban use.[3] The cases have considered issues arising from the designation and amendment of UGBs.[4] The Urbanization Goal lists a number of factors municipalities must consider in designating and amending UGBs, particularly need factors that require consideration of the need for population growth, housing, employment opportunities and livability. In an interesting case, *Benjfran Dev., Inc. v. Metropolitan Serv. Dist.*,[5] the court held the economic development objectives of Goal 9 and a complementary statute did not prevail over and preempt the factors municipalities were required to consider under Goal 14. It held that economic development was not a per se need that required the amendment of a UGB boundary. The District, which has the authority to review UGBs in the Portland area, rejected a proposed amendment of 500 acres to provide for an industrial park because need had not been shown as required by the Goal, and the court affirmed.

§ 10.08   Exclusion and The Right to Travel.

Affordable housing and exclusion problems have been an issue in growth management programs. Both the *Ramapo* and *Petaluma* cases, for example, considered arguments that the growth management programs under review in those cases were exclusionary. New Jersey's *Mt. Laurel (I)*[1] fair share housing case stated that municipalities must include an up-front provision for low-and

---

[3] § 12.10.

[4] D.S. Parklane Dev., Inc. v. Metro, 994 P.2d 1205 (Or. App. 2000) (reversing decision to expand Portland UGB); Collins v. Land Conservation & Dev. Comm'n, 707 P.2d 599 (Or. App. 1985) (cannot include hillsides in UGB that are not urbanizable); Willamette Univ. v. Land Conservation and Dev. Comm'n, 608 P.2d 1178 (Or. App. 1980) (UGB must be based solely on determination of future growth needs, and not irrelevant political boundaries). City of Redmond v. Central Puget Sound Growth Mgt. Hearings Bd., 959 P.2d 1091 (Wash. 1998) (inclusion of agricultural land); King County v. Central Puget Sound Growth Mgt. Hearings Bd., 979 P.2d 374 (Wash. 1999) (reviewing designation of urban growth area)..

[5] 767 P.2d 467 (Or. App. 1989), *confirmed by* Port of St. Helens v. Land Conservation & Dev. Comm'n, 996 P.2d 1014 (Or. App. 2000).

[1] Southern Burlington County NAACP v. Township of Mt. Laurel (I), 336 A.2d 713 (N.J.), discussed in § 7.09.

moderate-income housing in growth management programs.[2] States and municipalities have also adopted inclusionary zoning programs that can help remedy problems of exclusion in growth management programs.[3]

The right to travel protected by the federal constitution could also limit the exclusionary effects of growth management programs. Beginning with *Shapiro v. Thompson*,[4] which invalidated a state residence requirement for welfare assistance, the U.S. Supreme Court struck down a number of residence restrictions that prevented nonresidents of a state from voting or from receiving necessary social services.[5] However, the Supreme Court has indicated the right to interstate travel does not present a serious obstacle to land use programs. It rejected a right-to-travel objection in its *Belle Terre*[6] decision, which upheld a zoning ordinance that limited the number of unrelated individuals who could occupy single-family dwellings. The Court noted the ordinance was not "aimed at transients" and did not implicate a fundamental constitutional right, such as the right to vote.

In *CEEED v. California Coastal Zone Conservation Comm'n*,[7] the court rejected a right-to-travel objection to the California coastal permit program that restricted growth in coastal areas. The court applied the Supreme Court's right-to-travel cases and held the coastal permit program did not interfere with the right to travel because "[i]t is not discriminatory; it imposes no durational residence requirement; it exacts no penalty for exercising the right to travel or to select one's place of residence. In short, it has no chilling effect on an individual's freedom of movement."[8]

---

[2] *See also* Griffin Homes, Inc. v. Superior Ct., 274 Cal. Rptr. 456 (Cal. App. 1990) (development quota program does not conflict facially with state policy goals relating to the provision of affordable housing.

[3] §§ 7.26–7.31.

[4] 394 U.S. 618 (1969).

[5] Saenz v. Roe, 526 U.S. 489 (1999); Memorial Hosp. v. Maricopa County, 415 U.S. 250 (1974); Dunn v. Blumstein, 405 U.S. 330 (1972). *But see* Zobel v. Williams, 457 U.S. 55 (1982); Sosna v. Iowa, 419 U.S. 393 (1975).

[6] Village of Belle Terre v. Boraas, 416 U.S. 1 (1974), discussed in § 5.03.

[7] 118 Cal. Rptr. 315 (Cal. App. 1974).

[8] *Id.* at 333. *See also* Associated Home Bldrs. of Greater Eastbay, Inc. v. City of Livermore, 557 P.2d 473 (Cal. 1976); Northern Ill. Home Bldrs. Ass'n v. County of DuPage, 649 N.E.2d 384 (Ill. 1995) (rejecting claim that roadway impact fee violated right to travel). *See* Smith v. Lower Merion Twp., 1991 U.S. Dist. Lexis 11100 (E.D. Pa. 1991) (extensive discussion of right to travel doctrine as applied to land use regulation).

§ 10.09   Public Utilities and Service as a Growth Management Control.

§ 10.10   Service Refusals: The Duty to Serve.

Many growth management programs allow the approval of new development only if adequate public utilities, such as sewer and water, are available. The Ramapo growth management program is an example.[1] A landowner whose development is disapproved because public utilities are unavailable may decide to bring an action to compel the extension of public utilities to his land.

A refusal to extend a public utility service to a landowner who wants to be served by the utility raises an equal protection problem. The municipality must have a justifiable reason for the refusal to extend service. Courts usually uphold municipal refusals to extend services within their boundaries when the refusal is based on utility-related reasons, such as inadequate financial resources or inadequate capacity.[2] The courts have also held that municipal utilities may exercise discretion in deciding whether to extend utility service to areas outside municipal boundaries. Courts may compel an extension of service if the municipal utility has held itself out to provide service by extending service generally in the extraterritorial area.[3]

Whether a municipality can deny public utility service extensions to implement a growth management program raises a more troublesome question. An early New Jersey case held that a municipality could not condition the extension of utility services on an agreement by a developer to increase lot sizes to conform to municipal planning policies.[4] *Robinson v. City of Boulder*[5] disapproved a refusal to extend utility services to implement a growth management program. The city and the surrounding county adopted a joint comprehensive plan, and the city established itself as the sole provider of utility services in an extraterritorial area outside the city. When a landowner in this area applied for an extension of utility services the city refused, claiming that development in the area would conflict with the growth management policies of the comprehensive plan.

The court held the city's refusal to provide utility services was unauthorized. Boulder had held itself out as the sole provider of utility services in the area

---

[1] § 10.04.

[2] Lawrence v. Richards, 88 A. 92 (Me. 1913); Rose v. Plymouth Town, 173 P.2d 285 (Utah 1946); 41 A.L.R.2d 1222 (1956). *Compare* Clark v. Board of Water & Sewer Comm'rs, 234 N.E.2d 893 (Mass. 1968). *But see* Council of Middletown Twp. v. Benham, 523 A.2d 311 (Pa. 1987).

[3] Delmarva Enters. v. Mayor & Council, 282 A.2d 601 (Del. 1971); Denby v. Brown, 199 S.E.2d 214 (Ga. 1973); Mayor & Council v. Goldberg, 264 A.2d 113 (Md. 1970); Okemo Trailside Condos. v. Blais, 380 A.2d 84 (Vt. 1977).

[4] Reid Dev. Corp. v. Parsippany-Troy Hills Twp., 107 A.2d 20 (N.J. App. Div. 1954).

[5] 547 P.2d 228 (Colo. 1976).

and had a duty to provide service on an equal basis to all landowners. It could not refuse service for reasons not related to utility concerns. The court did not consider the impact of the growth management plan on the city's duty to provide extraterritorial service because the city did not have extraterritorial planning and zoning powers. The county had those powers in the extraterritorial area but was not responsible for the provision of utility service.

The court reached a contrary result in *Dateline Bldrs., Inc. v. City of Santa Rosa.*[6] A developer planned to build a housing project that was adjacent to a city trunk sewer line outside the city's boundaries. The city refused to provide service because the project was outside the area designated for growth in a joint city-county growth management plan. The court upheld the denial. It rejected arguments by the developer that the city, as the only supplier, "could not act beyond its boundaries and could not use sewer hookup as a planning device." It held that the denial was "a necessary and proper exercise" of the police power in aid of the growth management plan.[7]

§ 10.11   The Takings Issue.

A takings problem can arise if a municipality refuses to provide public services in order to prevent development to implement a growth management program. The problem again is that a prohibition on development until the municipality can provide services may create a takings problem. Though the delay is not a per se categorical facial taking under the Supreme Court's *Lake Tahoe* decision,[1] an as-applied takings claim is again possible.

Charles v. Diamond,[2] an early New York case, considered this problem. A village ordinance required developers to connect with the village sewage system. The village granted a connection permit to a developer, but the state environmental department prohibited connection until the village corrected deficiencies in the system. The necessary steps to correct these deficiencies were delayed under a series of consent orders, and the system was still deficient when the developer brought suit claiming the delay was a taking of its property.

---

[6] 194 Cal. Rptr. 258 (Cal. App. 1983)., *followed in* County of Del Norte v. City of Crescent City, 84 Cal. Rptr.2d 179 (Cal. App. 1999). *See also* First Peoples Bank of New Jersey v. Township of Medford, 599 A.2d 1248 (N.J. 1991) (refusal to extend sewer service when reasonable attempt made to meet sewage treatment needs); Brennan Woods Ltd. Partnership v. Town of Williston, 782 A.2d 1230 (Vt. 2001) (may use sewer service allocations to phase growth under zoning ordinance); Town of Beloit v. Public Serv. Comm'n, 148 N.W.2d 661 (Wis. 1967).

[7] *See also* Town of Rocky Mount v. Wenco, Inc., 506 S.E.2d 17 (Va. 1998) (provision of sewer service to retail store to allow development in highway corridor held to be planning decision; holding out rule did not apply).

[1] § 6.08.

[2] 360 N.E.2d 1295 (N.Y. 1977).

The court held service difficulties could justify only temporary restrictions on development. It cited *Ramapo*[3] and noted the municipality "must be committed firmly to the construction and installation of the necessary improvements." An extensive delay was justified

> only if the remedial steps are of sufficient magnitude to require extensive preparations, including preliminary studies, applications for assistance to other governmental entities, the raising of large amounts of capital, and the letting of work contracts.[4]

The court remanded the case for trial because the record was not sufficiently developed to decide the constitutional issues. The issues are similar to the issues raised by development moratoria, but this case was decided before *Penn Central,* and the question is whether even a "firm" commitment to the provision of services would justify an extensive delay under the Supreme Court's takings rules.

B. CORRIDOR PRESERVATION

§ 10.12   The Corridor Preservation Problem.

Comprehensive plans do not contain legally enforceable land use restrictions and cannot prohibit the development of land the plan designates for public facilities, such as streets, highways and parks. Agencies must plan and designate land for these facilities in advance of their acquisition, but development may occur in planned corridors or on planned sites unless controls are available to reserve this land during the interim period prior to its acquisition. This kind of control can assist growth management and public facility improvement programs by protecting land planned for public facilities until the time public agencies are ready to acquire it. The reservation of land for highways in planned highway corridors, called corridor preservation, is the most common use of the power to preserve land from development in advance of its acquisition.

§ 10.13   Corridor Preservation Legislation.

The most common corridor preservation legislation is the municipal official map.[1] To implement planning for streets and public facilities, the Standard Planning Act authorized municipalities to adopt an official map that designated land reserved for acquisition for these facilities.[2] The Standard Planning Act's

---

[3] § 10.04.

[4] 360 N.E.2d at 1301.

[1] Nigro v. Planning Bd. of Saddle River, 584 A.2d 1350 (N.J. 1991) (reviewing function of official maps as a planning technique); Romaz Props., Ltd. v. McGowan, 657 N.Y.S.2d 942 (App. Div. 1997) (reversing refusal to remove land from official map).. *See also* Utah Code Ann. § 17-27-404(3) (county may adopt six-month development moratorium in area proposed as highway or transportation corridor).

[2] Standard Planning Act §§ 21–25.

provision for official maps was based on earlier legislation adopted in New York and other states. The Act required compensation to landowners whose land was reserved for future streets, denied compensation for any buildings built in mapped streets, and did not contain a variance provision. It authorized the local governing body to set a time limit on an official map reservation. Some official map legislation is based on the Standard Planning Act model. [3]

Two model acts published after the Standard Planning Act also included legislative authority for official maps. The model acts differ in detail, but their statutory authority for official maps is similar. The model acts rely on the police power and do not authorize compensation to landowners whose land is reserved for acquisition in an official map. The acts prohibit the development of land reserved on an official map unless the municipality grants a variance. [4] The model acts make the adoption of a street plan an explicit or implicit condition for the adoption of an official street map. Some official map legislation that authorizes official maps is based on one of the model acts. [5] Official map legislation in other states is similar to but not based directly on the model acts. [6] The model acts and most state official map acts do not designate a time limit for an official map reservation.

Some subdivision control statutes and ordinances also authorize the reservation of land for acquisition for a public facility. They may also prohibit the development of the land during the reservation period. [7]

A number of states authorize the state transportation agency to adopt maps for transportation corridors or for the location of future highway rights-of-way. [8] Unlike municipal official map law, these laws do not authorize the mapping of a corridor in which the statute prohibits development. Instead, a comprehensive state mapping law will require public hearings and comments on planned

---

[3] Colo. Rev. Stat. §§ 31-23-220 to 31-23-224; Pa. Stat. Ann. tit. 53, §§ 22777–22779.

[4] Mill Realty Assocs. v. Zoning Bd. of Review, 721 A.2d 887 (R.I. 1998) (upholding exception to allow construction of unimproved gravel road).

[5] Del. Code Ann. tit. 22, § 704; Md. Ann. Code art. 66B, § 6.01; Mass. Gen. Laws Ann. ch. 41, §§ 81E-81J; N.Y. Gen. City Law §§ 26, 29, 33–36.

[6] La Rev. Stat. Ann. § 33:116; Okla. Stat. Ann. tit. 11, 47-121 to 47-123 (building or setback line on streets); S.C. Code Ann. §§ 6-7-1210 to 6-7-1280.

[7] Ala. Code §§ 11-52-50 to 11-52-54. On the takings issue, see Ventures in Prop. I v. City of Wichita, 594 P.2d 671 (Kan. 1979); Howard County v. JJM, Inc., 482 A.2d 908 (Md. 1984). See also Batch v. Town of Chapel Hill,387 N.E.2d 655 (N.C. 1990) (upholding refusal to approve subdivision because subdivider would not reserve land for highway shown on comprehensive plan).

[8] Calif. State Highways Code §§ 740–742; 605 Ill. Comp. Stat. 5/4-510; Neb. Rev. Stat. §§ 39-1311 to 39-1311.05; N.H. Rev. Stat. Ann §§ 230-a:1 to 230-a:14; N.J. Stat. Ann. §§ 27:7-66, 27:7-67; Ohio Rev. Code Ann. § 5511.01. See also Del. Code Ann. tit. 17, § 145 (local comprehensive plans must incorporate state corridor designations); Utah. Code Ann.§ 72-5-401 et seq. (authorizes cooperative corridor preservation program by state transportation agency and local governments).

corridors, the preparation and recording of official maps of the corridors, and local government referral to the state transportation agency of any application to develop land within the corridor. The state transportation agency must then find either that the development proposal has an impact on the preservation of the corridor or does not have an impact. If the proposed development is found to have an impact on the corridor, the state transportation agency must negotiate with the developer either for the purchase of its land or for a modification in development plans that will protect the corridor.

The American Planning Association has proposed a model municipal official map law as part of its model legislation. It is based on state transportation corridor legislation, and provides a number of options to the municipality when a landowner applies for a permit that can avoid a severe restriction on the development of property yet preserve the official map designation.[9]

§ 10.14　The Takings Issue.

Like moratoria,[1] an official map or state transportation law can present an as-applied takings problem if a landowner is not able to make any use of her property for a period of time.[2] The takings issue is complicated, however, because a landowner can also argue a prohibition on development under these laws is an improper attempt to depress property values prior to the time the land is acquired, which courts hold to be a taking of property.[3]

One group of cases decided before the Supreme Court's 1987 taking trilogy held official map legislation was a taking. *Lomarch Corp. v. Mayor & Common Council*[4] is typical. The court held unconstitutional a statute requiring subdividers

---

[9] American Planning Association, Growing Smart Legislative Guidebook: Model Statutes for Planning and Management of Change § 7-501 (S. Meck ed. 2002)

[1] *But see* Headley v. City of Rochester, 5 N.E.2d 198 (N.Y. 1936) (cannot raise taking claim if did not request variance from map); State ex rel. Miller v. Manders, 86 N.W.2d 469 (Wis. 1957) (same).

[2] Ward v. Bennett, 625 N.Y.S.2d 609 (App. Div. 1995) (reinstating complaint for taking when official map reservation existed for 50 years and landowner denied all economically viable use of land). *But cf.* State of Delaware v. Booker, 1992 Del. Super. LEXIS 366 (Del. Super. 1992); Meixsell v. Ross Twp. Bd. of Supvrs., 623 A.2d 429 (Pa. Commw. 1993) (dictum, can require setback for future road widening if state to condemn land at later date). *See* §§ 6.06–6.11 (moratoria).

[3] § 2.35. *See* People ex rel. Department of Transp. v. Diversified Prods. Co. III, 17 Cal. Rptr. 2d 676 (Cal. App. 1993) (de facto taking by state found when city and state cooperated in preventing development of property in transportation corridor).

[4] 237 A.2d 881 (N.J. 1968). *See also* Urbanizadora Versalles, Inc. v. Rivera Rios, 701 F.2d 993 (1st Cir. 1983) (invalidating official map reservation for highway that was in effect for 14 years); Jensen v. City of New York, 369 N.E.2d 1179 (N.Y. 1977) (reservation made property "virtually unsalable"); Miller v. City of Beaver Falls, 82 A.2d 34 (Pa. 1951) (invalidating reservation for parks and playgrounds although reservation for streets previously upheld).

to reserve land shown on an official map for park and playground use. The reservation was effective for one year. The court held the reservation amounted to a unilateral option to reserve the land and was constitutional only if the municipality compensated the landowner. The court relied on an earlier New Jersey case, now discredited in that state,[5] which invalidated a zoning ordinance restricting development in a wetland because it conferred a benefit on the general public. In addition, the decision is inconsistent with the Supreme Court's decision in *Lake Tahoe*, that a prohibition on development during a moratorium is not a per se taking.[6] The compensation requirement for official map reservations is codified in the New Jersey subdivision control legislation.[7]

However, the New Jersey Appellate Division distinguished *Lomarch* in *Kingston E. Realty Co. v. State*,[8] and upheld a state corridor preservation law under which the state was mandated to acquire a property if a landowner in a corridor applied for a building permit. The court held a temporary taking of plaintiff's property did not occur during the time the statute stayed issuance of a building permit while the state agency was allowed to consider acquisition. The court distinguished *Lomarch* because the reservation in *Kingston* was for a considerably shorter period of time and was not a blanket reservation. It held that "similar measures," such as zoning moratoria, "have been recognized under narrow circumstances as reasonable regulations in the exercise of governmental police powers." The court noted the highway reservation was "reasonably designed to reduce the cost of public acquisition."

Kingston was also decided before the 1987 takings trilogy, and the status of official map and corridor preservation laws under the Supreme Court's present takings doctrine is unclear. A post-trilogy Florida decision in *Palm Beach County v. Wright*[9] is consistent with the Supreme Court's decision in *Lake Tahoe* that a moratorium is not a facial taking. It held an unrecorded county thoroughfare map adopted as part of the mandatory county plan was not a facial taking even though it prohibited all development in a transportation corridor that would impede future highway construction. The court noted that owners adjacent to transportation corridors would most likely benefit from planned road construction, and that the thoroughfare map limited development only to the extent

---

[5] *See* New Jersey Bldrs. Ass'n v. Department of Envt'l Protection, 404 A.2d 320 (N.J. App. Div. 1979).

[6] § 6.08.

[7] N.J. Stat. Ann. § 40:55D-44.

[8] 330 A.2d 40 (N.J. App. Div. 1975). Contra Lackman v. Hall, 364 A.2d 1244 (Del. Ch. 1976).

[9] 641 So. 2d 50 (Fla. 1994) (applying state law), *and distinguishing* Joint Ventures, Inc. v. Department of Transp., 563 So. 2d 622 (Fla. 1990) (invalidating state corridor mapping law as violation of due process). *See also* Rochester Bus. Inst. v. City of Rochester, 267 N.Y.S.2d 274 (App. Div. 1966) (applying balancing test to uphold street-widening reservation on official map that increased construction costs by six percent).

necessary to ensure future land use compatible with the planned highway. The thoroughfare map did not finally designate highway locations within the transportation corridor, and the court noted the county as a permitting authority "has the flexibility to ameliorate some of the hardships of a person owning land within the corridor." The court indicated the taking issue should be determined on an as-applied basis as individual owners made application for development within the transportation corridor. *Palm Beach County* suggests a corridor preservation law may survive a takings attack when, as in the American Planning Association's model, it provides alternatives that can avoid a severe restriction on development that can also preserve a highway corridor from damaging development.

REFERENCES

Books and Monographs

J. DeGrove, Planning & Growth Management in the States (1992).

G. Easley, Staying Inside the Lines: Urban Growth Boundaries, American Planning Ass'n, Planning Advisory Serv. Rep. No. 440 (1992).

R. Freilich, From Sprawl to Smart Growth (1999).

R. Einsweiler & D. Miness, Managing Community Growth and Change in Urban, Suburban, and Rural Settings (Lincoln Institute of Land Policy, 1992).

E. Kelly, Community Growth: Policies, Techniques, and Impacts (1993).

E. Kelly, Planning, Growth, and Public Facilities: A Primer for Local Officials, American Planning Ass'n, Planning Advisory Serv. Rep. No. 447 (1993).

D. Mandelker & B. Blaesser, Corridor Preservation: Study of Legal and Institutional Barriers (Federal Highway Admin., 1996).

A. Nelson & J. Duncan, Growth Management Principles and Practices (1995).

D. Porter, Managing Growth in America's Communities (1997).

D. Porter ed., Performance Standards for Growth Management, American Planning Ass'n, Planning Advisory Serv. Rep. No. 461 (1996).

D. Porter, Profiles in Growth Management (1996).

S.M. White, Adequate Public Facilities Ordinances and Transportation Management, American Planning Ass'n, Planning Advisory Serv. Rep. No. 465 (1996).

Articles

Blaesser & Mandelker, Official Maps in Modernizing State Planning Legislation: The Growing Smart Papers, Vol. 2, at 153, American Planning Ass'n, Planning Advisory Serv. Rep. Nos. 480–481 (1998).

Burchell, & Shad, The Evolution of the Sprawl Debate in the United States, 5 West-Northwest 137 (1999).

Buzbee, Sprawl's Dynamics: A Comparative Institutional Analysis Critique, 35 Wake Forest L. Rev. 509 (2000).

Chinn & Garvin, Designing Development Allocation Systems, Land Use L. & Zoning Dig., Vol. 44, No. 2, at 3 (1992).

Freilich & White, Transportation Congestion and Growth Management: Comprehensive Approaches to Resolving America's Major Quality of Life Crisis, 24 Loyola L.A.L. Rev. 915 (1991).

Kelly, Piping Growth: The Law, Economics and Equality of Sewer and Water Connection Policies, Land Use L. & Zoning Dig., Vol. 36, No. 7, at 3 (1984).

Kushner, Growth Management and the City, 12 Yale L. & Pol'y Rev. 68 (1994).

LeGates, The Emergence of Flexible Growth Management Systems in the San Francisco Bay Area, 24 Loyola L.A.L. Rev. 1035 (1991).

Mandelker, Interim Development Controls in Highway Programs: The Taking Issue, 4 J. Land Use & Envtl. L. 167 (1989).

Mandelker, Managing Space to Manage Growth, to be found at 23 Wm. & Mary Envtl. L. & Pol'y Rev. 801 (1999).

Morris & Schwab, Adequate Public Facilities Ordinances, Zoning News, May 1991, at 1.

Porter, Do State Growth Management Acts Make a Difference? Local Growth Management Measures Under Different State Growth Policies, 24 Loyola L.A.L. Rev. 1015 (1991).

Salkin, The Smart Growth Agenda: A Snapshot of State Activity at the Turn of the Century, 32 St. Louis U. Pub. L. Rev. 271 (2002).

Steiner, Florida's Transportation Concurrency: Are the Current Tools Adequate to Meet the Need for Coordinated Land Use and Transportation Planning, 12 U. Fla. J.L. & Pol'y 269 (2001).

Stone, The Prevention of Urban Sprawl Through Utility Extension Control, 14 Urb. Law. 357 (1982).

Stroud, State Review and Certification of Local Plans in Modernizing State Planning Legislation: The Growing Smart Papers, Vol. 1, at 85, American Planning Ass'n, Planning Advisory Serv. Rep. Nos. 462–463 (1996).

Thomas & Payne, Long-Range Highway Corridor Preservation: Issues, Methods and Model Legislation, 13 BYU J. Pub. L. 1 (1998).

Walsh & Pearce, The Concurrency Requirement of the Washington State Growth Management Act, 16 U. Puget Sound L. Rev. 1025 (1993).

Weaver, Concurrency, Concurrency Alternatives, Infrastructure, Planning and Regional Solution Issues, 12 U. Fla. J.L. & Pol'y 251 (2001).

Witten, Carrying Capacity and the Comprehensive Plan: Establishing and Defending Limits to Growth, 28 B.C. Envtl. Aff. L. Rev. 583 (2001).

Student Work

Note, Phased Zoning: Regulation of the Tempo and Sequence of Land Development, 26 Stan. L. Rev. 585 (1974).

Note, Public Utility Land Use Control on the Urban Fringe, 63 Iowa L. Rev. 889 (1978).

Note, Sometimes There's Nothing Left to Give: The Justification for Denying Water Service to New Consumers to Control Growth, 44 Stan. L. Rev. 429 (1992).

Note, A Zoning Program for Phased Growth: Ramapo Township's Time Controls on Residential Development, 47 N.Y.U. L. Rev. 723 (1972).

Comment, A Constitutionally Valid Justification for the Enactment of No-Growth Ordinances: Integrating Concepts of Population Stabilization and Sustainability, 19 U. Hawaii L. Rev. 93 (1997).

Comment, Wrong Turns: A Critique of the Supreme Court's Right to Travel Cases, 21 Wm. Mitchell L. Rev. 457 (1995).

Chapter 11

AESTHETICS, SIGN REGULATION AND HISTORIC PRESERVATION

Synopsis

§ 11.01　The Aesthetic Regulation Problem.
§ 11.02　Aesthetics as a Regulatory Purpose.
§ 11.03　The Early Period.
§ 11.04　The Minority View: Aesthetics as a Factor in Land Use Regulation.
§ 11.05　The Majority View: Aesthetics Alone as a Regulatory Purpose.

A. SIGN CONTROLS.

§ 11.06　Local, State and Federal Regulation.
§ 11.07　Sign Regulation on Highways and Streets: The Takings Issue.
§ 11.08　Billboard Exclusions.
§ 11.09　Exemption for On-Premise Signs.
§ 11.10　Controls on the Display of Signs.
§ 11.11　Nonconforming Signs.
§ 11.12　Free Speech Issues.
§ 11.13　*Metromedia*.
§ 11.14　*Taxpayers for Vincent*.
§ 11.15　*Ladue*: Residential Signs.
§ 11.16　*Lorillard*: Restrictions on Location.
§ 11.17　What These Cases Decided: Standing, Aesthetics and Content Neutrality.
§ 11.18　Time, Place and Manner Restrictions.
§ 11.19　Prohibition, Classification and Exemption of Off-Premise and On-Premise Signs.
§ 11.20　Portable Signs.
§ 11.21　Content-Based Sign Definitions.
§ 11.22　For Sale Signs.
§ 11.23　Political, Campaign and Temporary Signs.

B. ARCHITECTURAL DESIGN REVIEW.

§ 11.24　The Design Review Ordinance.
§ 11.25　Constitutionality.

C. HISTORIC PRESERVATION.

§ 11.26　The Historic Preservation Problem.
§ 11.27　Historic Districts.
§ 11.28　Enabling Legislation and Ordinances.
§ 11.29　Constitutionality of Historic Districts.
§ 11.30　Delegation of Power and Vagueness.
§ 11.31　Interim Controls.
§ 11.32　The Takings Issue.
§ 11.33　Historic Landmarks.
§ 11.34　Enabling Legislation and Ordinances.
§ 11.35　The Takings Issue.
§ 11.36　Maintenance and Repair.

(5th Ed.—02/03)

§ 11.37   Religious Uses.
§ 11.38   Transfer of Development Rights.

§ 11.01   The Aesthetic Regulation Problem.

Although aesthetic values underlie much traditional land use regulation, such as the separation of incompatible uses, a number of land use controls are more clearly intended to achieve aesthetic purposes. Architectural design review for residential dwellings is one example. Sign regulation falls in the aesthetic category because it regulates the impact of signs on the visual environment. Historic preservation has an aesthetic basis, but it is more tenuous. Historic areas and landmarks can have historic value because of their architectural merit, but some historic areas and landmarks are treasured because of their historic associations despite their lack of aesthetic value.

A substantive due process issue underlies all types of aesthetic regulation. Courts must determine whether aesthetic regulation is a proper exercise of the police power under the due process clause. Though the early cases struck down aesthetic land use regulations, a majority of courts now hold that aesthetics alone is a legitimate government purpose in land use regulation.

The substantive due process problem is eased for aesthetic land use controls based on the compatibility principle that supports zoning. Historic district controls are one example. They maintain the architectural and visual compatibility of the historic environment. Sign regulation is another. It prohibits signs that are visually incompatible in their environment or impose restrictions that ensure visual compatibility. The zoning analogy supports the constitutionality of this type of aesthetic regulation. Equal protection problems are not serious in aesthetic regulation.[1] They arise principally under sign regulations that provide different regulations for different types of signs, but most courts uphold these classifications.

Takings problems arise under aesthetic controls but are not serious when they regulate the design and exterior appearance of buildings rather than the development of land. More serious takings problems are raised by historic district and landmark preservation ordinances. Restrictions imposed under these ordinances can leave a landowner without an economically viable use of her land. An example is a refusal to allow the demolition of an uneconomic landmark and its replacement with another building.

Important free speech issues under violate the free speech clause of the federal constitution arise in sign regulation. The Supreme Court has not decided a

---

[1] §§ 2.44–2.48

majority opinion that clearly delineates the free speech doctrine that applies to sign regulations, and this failure has created a number of problems in the application of the free speech clause to signs.

§ 11.02   Aesthetics as a Regulatory Purpose.

§ 11.03   The Early Period.

An early New Jersey case illustrates the view, prevailing generally before 1930, that aesthetics is not a legitimate purpose in land use control. In *City of Passaic v. Paterson Bill Posting, Adv. & Sign Painting Co.*,[1] the court invalidated a statute that imposed setback and height restrictions on signs. It held:

> Aesthetic considerations are a matter of luxury and indulgence rather than of necessity, and it is necessity alone which justifies the exercise of the police power to take private property without compensation.[2]

Some early decisions that held billboard controls constitutional avoided the aesthetic purpose problem by finding a number of evils and dangers that justified the regulation of billboards. Criminal or immoral activities might occur behind them, or they might collapse and cause injury.[3] These evils and dangers no longer provide a basis for upholding billboard regulation. Billboards are made of sturdier and lightweight materials and are usually some distance from the ground.

§ 11.04   The Minority View: Aesthetics as a Factor in Land Use Regulation.

A minority of courts hold that aesthetics is an appropriate governmental purpose in land use regulation if it advances other legitimate governmental purposes. In *Village of Hudson v. Albrecht, Inc.*,[1] for example, the court held a local legislative body may take aesthetic factors into account when it adopts zoning regulations. It upheld the constitutionality of a design review ordinance and noted that it reflected "a concern for the monetary interests of protecting real estate from impairment and destruction of value" in addition to promoting aesthetic values.

The rule that aesthetics may be a factor in land use regulation is a fiction. The additional governmental purposes courts require to support an aesthetic regulation derive from its aesthetic purposes. The minority view upholds an ordinance that prohibits billboards, for example, because it prevents negative impacts on property values in addition to improving the visual quality of the environment. But billboards have a negative impact on property values only

---

[1] 62 A. 267 (N.J. Err. & App. 1905); 21 A.L.R.3d 1222 (1968).

[2] *Id.* at 268.

[3] St. Louis Gunning Adv. Co. v. City of St. Louis, 137 S.W. 929 (Mo. 1911).

[1] 458 N.E.2d 852 (Ohio 1984).

because they are aesthetically objectionable in the visual environment in which they are prohibited.

The relationship between aesthetic purposes and the protection of property values is acknowledged in cases that recognize a "coalescence" of economic and aesthetic values that supports aesthetic regulation. This view is best expressed in *United Adv. Corp. v. Borough of Metuchen*,[2] a leading New Jersey case that upheld an ordinance prohibiting billboards in a suburban community:

> There are areas in which aesthetics and economics coalesce, areas in which a discordant sight is as hard an economic fact as an annoying odor or sound. We refer not to some sensitive or exquisite preference but to concepts of congruity held so widely that they are inseparable from the enjoyment and hence the value of property.[3]

New Jersey has now adopted the majority view and holds that zoning and billboard control ordinances "may accommodate aesthetic concerns."[4]

§ 11.05 The Majority View: Aesthetics Alone as a Regulatory Purpose.

A clear majority of courts hold that aesthetics alone is a legitimate governmental purpose in land use regulation.[1] An important dictum in a U.S. Supreme Court urban renewal decision was a major factor in the judicial adoption of the "aesthetics alone" view. The Court wrote:

> The concept of the public welfare is broad and inconclusive. . . . The values it represents are spiritual as well as physical, aesthetic as well as monetary. It is within the power of the legislature to determine that the community should be beautiful as well as healthy, spacious as well as clean, well-balanced as well as carefully patrolled.[2]

---

[2] 198 A.2d 447 (N.J. 1964). Adopting minority view: Figarsky v. Historic Dist. Comm'n, 368 A.2d 163 (Conn. 1976); Mayor & City Council v. Mano Swartz, Inc., 299 A.2d 828 (Md. 1973); Naegele Outdoor Adv. Co. v. Village of Minnetonka, 162 N.W.2d 206 (Minn. 1968); City of Houston v. Johnny Frank's Auto Parts, Inc., 480 S.W.2d 774 (Tex. Civ. App. 1972).

[3] 198 A.2d at 449.

[4] State v. Miller, 416 A.2d 821 (N.J. 1980), discussed in § 11.05.

[1] Donrey Communications Co. v. City of Fayetteville, 660 S.W.2d 900 (Ark. 1983); Metromedia, Inc. v. City of San Diego, 610 P.2d 407 (Cal. 1980), *rev'd on other grounds,* 453 U.S. 490 (1981); Kucera v. Liza, 69 Cal. Rptr. 2d 582 (Cal. App. 1997) (upholding view and sunlight preservation ordinance); City of Lake Wales v. Lamar Adv. Ass'n, 414 So. 2d 1030 (Fla. 1982); John Donnelly & Sons v. Outdoor Adv. Bd., 339 N.E.2d 709 (Mass. 1975); Asselin v. Town of Conway, 628 A.2d 247 (N.H. 1993); Cromwell v. Ferrier, 225 N.E.2d 748 (N.Y. 1967); State v. Jones, 290 S.E.2d 675 (N.C. 1982); Oregon City v. Hartke, 400 P.2d 255 (Or. 1965); State v. Smith, 618 S.W.2d 474 (Tenn. 1981); Town of Sandgate v. Colehamer, 589 A.2d 1205 (Vt. 1990). *See* Tahoe Reg'l Planning Agency v. King, 285 Cal. Rptr. 335 (Cal. App. 1991) (*Nollan* decision does not erode legitimacy of aesthetics as a regulatory purpose).

[2] Berman v. Parker, 348 U.S. 26, 33 (1954).

State v. Miller,[3] a sign ordinance case, illustrates the cases that adopt the aesthetics alone view. The court held:

> Consideration of aesthetics in municipal land use planning is no longer a matter of luxury and indulgence. . . . The development and preservation of natural resources and clean, salubrious neighborhoods contribute to psychological and emotional stability and well-being as well as stimulate a sense of civic pride.[4]

The view that, aesthetics alone is a legitimate governmental purpose in land use regulation resolves the substantive due process problem raised by facial attacks on aesthetic controls. Courts must still determine whether aesthetic controls properly advance aesthetic purposes as applied.[5]

A. SIGN CONTROLS.

§ 11.06 Local, State and Federal Regulation.

Signs divide into a number of categories depending on their location, type, and purpose. One classification distinguishes between on-premise signs that advertise a business conducted on the premises and off-premise signs that carry general commercial advertising. Signs are also distinguished depending by whether they carry commercial or noncommercial messages, and whether they are freestanding or attached to the walls or roof of a building. Billboards are an example of freestanding, off-premise signs.

Municipalities may adopt sign controls as part of their zoning ordinance[1] or as a separate ordinance. The courts have found the necessary implied authority to enact sign regulations in either format.[2]

The federal Highway Beautification Act is an important factor in sign regulation. It requires states to regulate signs along interstate and primary federal

---

[3] 416 A.2d 821 (N.J. 1980).

[4] *Id.* at 824.

[5] *Compare* Asselin v. Town of Conway, 607 A.2d 132 (N.H. 1992) (ordinance allowing reader-boards for nightly entertainment uses but not restaurants violates equal protection under state's strict judicial review standard), *with* Caroll Sign Co. v. Adams County Zoning Hearing Bd., 606 A.2d 1250 (Pa. Commw. 1992) (ordinance banning billboards but allowing on-site signs upheld).

[1] City of Walnut Grove v. Questco, Ltd., 564 S.E.2d 445 (Ga. 2002) (invalidating sign ordinance for failure to follow statutory procedures for zoning ordinance).

[2] Outdoor Systems v. City of Mesa, 819 P.2d 44 (Ariz. 1991) (statutory authority to regulate billboards includes authority to prohibit off-site billboards); Whiteco Outdoor Advertising v. City of Tucson, 972 P.2d 647 (Ariz. App. 1999) (sign ordinance not part of zoning ordinance); City of Escondido v. Desert Outdoor Adv., 505 P.2d 1012 (Cal. 1973); Strazzulla v. Building Inspector, 260 N.E.2d 163 (Mass. 1970); Town of Boothbay v. National Adv. Co., 347 A.2d 419 (Me. 1975); Adams Outdoor Advertising, Inc. v. City of Holland, 625 N.W.2d 377 (Mich. 2000) (upholding billboard prohibition in zoning ordinance under zoning act); Transylvania County v. Moody, 565 S.E.2d 720 (N.C. App. 2002) (may regulate signs under police power authority).

highways.[3] The Act prohibits all signs within 660 feet of the edge of the highway and all signs visible from the edge of the highway in rural areas, except in zoned or unzoned commercial and industrial areas.[4] Federal regulations allow municipalities to rezone for commercial uses to allow the display of signs if done as part of a comprehensive zoning and not solely to permit outdoor advertising structures.[5] On-premise signs, such as signs advertising activities on the premises, are exempt from the statutory prohibition.

All states have enacted legislation that implements the federal requirements and that authorizes state highway agencies to control signs along federal highways in a permit program. States that do not comply with the federal statute's requirements for sign control may lose ten percent of their federal highway funds.

Many of the state sign control laws authorize the municipal regulation of signs along federal highways. The courts have relied on this grant of authority to hold the state sign control legislation does not preempt municipal control of signs.[6] A local ordinance or permit may be preempted by a more stringent state law.[7]

§ 11.07 Sign Regulation on Highways and Streets: The Takings Issue.

The courts rely on aesthetics, the protection of tourism, and traffic safety improvement to uphold sign controls on streets and highways.[1] They rely on

---

[3] 23 U.S.C. § 131. *See* Subdivision Servs. Bd. v. Zoning Hearing Bd., 784 A.2d 850 (Pa. Commw. 2001) (reversing municipal denial of permit to erect billboard on turnpike).

[4] State *ex rel.* Straatmann Enters., Inc. v. County of Franklin, 4 S.W.2d 641 (Mo. App. 1999) (conditional use permit authorizing commercial activity is not commercial zoning).

[5] L & W Outdoor Adv. Co. v. State, 539 N.E.2d 497 (Ind. App. 1989) (rezoning held invalid); Naegele Outdoor Advertising v. Hunt, 465 S.E.2d 549 (N.C. App. 1995) (rezoning upheld); Kunz & Co. v. State, 913 P.2d 765 (Utah App. 1996) (rezoning held invalid).

[6] Libra Group, Inc. v. State, 805 P.2d 409 (Ariz. App. 1991); Lamar-Orlando Outdoor Adv. v. City of Ormond Beach, 415 So. 2d 1312 (Fla. App. 1982); City of Doraville v. Turner Communications Co., 223 S.E.2d 798 (Ga. 1976); Scadron v. City of Des Plaines, 606 N.E.2d 1154 (Ill. 1992) (home rule municipality); PNA AOA Media, L.L.C. v. Jackson County, 554 S.E.2d 657 (N.C. App. 2001) (moratorium not preempted). *But see* National Adv. Co. v. Missouri State Hwy. & Transp. Comm'n, 862 S.W.2d 953 (Mo. App. 1993) (sign in commercial area had state permit).

[7] National Adv. Co. v. Department of Hwys., 751 P.2d 632 (Colo. 1988) (state law preempts less restrictive local ordinance and city's issuance of permit does not estop state denial); Chancellor Media Whiteco Outdoor Corp. v. Department of Transportation, 796 So.2d 547 (Fla. App. 2001) (state law preempts local nonconforming use ordinance); Southeastern Displays, Inc. v. Ward, 414 S.W.2d 573 (Ky. 1967); State *ex rel.* Whiteco Indus. v. Bowers, 965 S.W.2d 203 (Mo. App. 1998 (local ordinance inconsistent with state act but state act does not preempt building permit requirement, and noting new law authorizing local regulation of signs on highways); State ex rel. Missouri Hwy. & Transp. Comm'n v. Alexian Bros., 848 S.W.2d 472 (Mo. 1993) (state can remove sign permitted by city in residential area).

[1] E.B. Elliott Adv. Co. v. Metropolitan Dade County, 425 F.2d 1141 (5th Cir. 1970); Yarbrough

the traffic improvement justification even though studies on the effect of signs on traffic safety are inconclusive.[2] *Metromedia, Inc. v. City of San Diego*[3] is a leading case. The court held "as a matter of law . . . [that] an ordinance which eliminates billboards designed to be viewed from the streets and highways reasonably relates to traffic safety." It added a resolution of the traffic safety controversy was a matter of legislative judgment the court should not disturb unless it was unreasonable.

Sign regulations along streets and highways can create a takings problem. Most of the takings cases arose under state statutes that adopted the outdoor advertising controls required by the federal Highway Beautification Act.[4] Cases rejecting takings claims because only the right to display on-premise signs is protected by the takings clause,[5] or because public funds that constructed the highway created the opportunity to display signs,[6] are questionable under recent Supreme Court takings decisions.

However, the courts easily rejected takings claims against sign controls on streets and highways under the more traditional takings tests. One court held an ordinance prohibiting off-premise billboards with commercial advertising was not a taking because the "only damages" were lost business opportunities and a reduction in the value of the signs.[7] The courts also held the exclusion of billboards from a municipality was not a substantial limitation on use that amounted to a taking of property.[8] Some cases applied a balancing test, and held limitations on the use of property imposed by sign controls were justified by their regulatory purposes.[9] Other courts upheld billboard prohibitions against

v. Arkansas State Hwy. Comm'n, 539 S.W.2d 419 (Ark. 1976); Moore v. Ward, 377 S.W.2d 881 (Ky. 1964); Transylvania County v. Moody, 565 S.E.2d 720 (N.C. 2002); Newman Signs, Inc. v. Hjelle, 268 N.W.2d 741 (N.D. 1978); Markham Adv. Co. v. State, 439 P.2d 249 (Wash. 1968); 81 A.L.R.3d 564 (1977).

[2] Railway Express Agency v. City of New York, 336 U.S. 106 (1949).

[3] 610 P.2d 407 (Cal. 1980), *rev'd on other grounds*, 453 U.S. 490 (1981). *Accord* Robert L. Rieke Bldg. Co. v. City of Overland Park, 657 P.2d 1121 (Kan. 1983); Sun Oil Co. v. City of Madison Heights, 199 N.W.2d 525 (Mich. App. 1972); Hilton v. City of Toledo, 405 N.E.2d 1047 (Ohio 1980).

[4] § 11.06.

[5] Kelbro, Inc. v. Myrick, 30 A.2d 527 (Vt. 1943). *Accord* Moore v. Ward, 377 S.W.2d 881 (Ky. 1964); Ghaster Props., Inc. v. Preston, 200 N.E.2d 328 (Ohio 1964).

[6] Churchill & Tait v. Rafferty, 32 Philippines 580 (1915). *Accord* New York State Thruway Auth. v. Ashley Motor Court, Inc., 176 N.E.2d 566 (N.Y. 1961) (dismissing takings objection to sign controls on Thruway).

[7] Jackson v. City Council, 659 F. Supp. 470 (W.D. Va. 1987).

[8] Town of Boothbay v. National Adv. Co., 347 A.2d 419 (Me. 1975); Modjeska Sign Studies, Inc. v. Berle, 373 N.E.2d 255 (N.Y. 1977).

[9] Yarbrough v. Arkansas State Hwy. Comm'n, 539 S.W.2d 419 (Ark. 1976); Newman Signs, Inc. v. Hjelle, 268 N.W.2d 741 (N.D. 1978).

takings claims as "a use restriction . . . [that] is in essence a zoning of property adjacent to highways."[10] State statutes may prohibit signs along highways as public nuisances. The courts upheld these statutes under the authority of the state to declare billboards a nuisance under the police power.[11]

Sign regulations should be able to survive takings claims under the Supreme Court's recent takings decisions. Cases upheld sign regulations against takings objections after the Supreme Court's 1987 takings trilogy. They held sign regulation advances legitimate governmental purposes[12] and does not deprive the sign owner of all economically viable use.[13] The Fourth Circuit Court of Appeals adopted a multi-factor takings test based on the Court's 1987 trilogy that modifies the takings tests it previously applied.[14]

A holding a sign regulation denies a landowner all economically productive use under the Supreme Court's *Lucas* decision is unlikely. *Outdoor Sys., Inc. v. City of Mesa*[15] is an example. The court upheld a regulation requiring the removal of a nonconforming sign when vacant land is developed. It rejected a *Lucas* by the landowner because the lot would still have value after the nonconforming sign was removed. There was no taking of the sign companies' leasehold interests in displaying the sign. The ordinance did not affect these interests, and they would have remedies under state law when it compelled the removal of the nonconforming signs.[16]

§ 11.08   Billboard Exclusions.

Municipalities may adopt sign regulations that totally exclude billboards from their area. Billboard exclusions present a substantive due process problem in aesthetic control. Courts easily uphold billboard exclusions in rural areas because they protect the visual integrity of the rural landscape,[1] and in residential areas

---

[10] Mississippi State Hwy. Comm'n v. Roberts Enters., 304 So. 2d 637 (Miss. 1974).

[11] Opinion of the Justices, 169 A.2d 762 (N.H. 1961); 38 A.L.R.3d 647 (1971) (civil nuisance).

[12] Outdoor Sys., Inc. v. City of Mesa, 997 F.2d 604 (9th Cir. 1993) (upholding requirement for removal of nonconforming signs when vacant lot developed).

[13] National Adv. Co. v. Village of Downers Grove, 561 N.E.2d 1300 (Ill. App. 1990) (emphasizing sign owner is only lessee); Summey Outdoor Adv., Inc. v. County of Henderson, 386 S.E.2d 439 (N.C. App. 1989).

[14] Georgia Outdoor Adv. Co. v. City of Waynesville (II), 900 F.2d 783 (4th Cir. 1990) (applying Supreme Court's "whole parcel" rule).

[15] 997 F.2d 604 (9th Cir. 1993).

[16] *See also accord* Wilson v. City of Louisville, 957 F. Supp. 948 (W.D. Ky. 1997) (restrictions on freestanding signs limiting size, height and hours of display); Adams Outdoor Advertising v. City of East Lansing, 614 N.W.2d 634 (Mich. 2000) (upholding prohibition on rooftop signs). *See also* Outdoor Graphics, Inc. v. City of Burlington, 103 F.3d 690 (8th Cir. 1996) (upholding amortization requirement under *Penn Central* tests).

[1] Moore v. Ward, 377 S.W.2d 881 (Ky. 1964) (statute adopting federal Act's prohibition on billboards adjacent to highways).

because they protect residential neighborhoods.[2] A billboard exclusion from industrial and commercial areas is not as easy to justify because these areas are not always attractive. However, a Massachusetts case[3] upheld a billboard prohibition in a suburban Boston community, and held the enhancement of the environment was as important in urban as in rural areas. "Urban residents are not immune to ugliness."[4]

Whether a large city can constitutionally exclude billboards also is a difficult problem. In *Metromedia, Inc. v. City of San Diego*,[5] the court rejected an argument that an ordinance excluding billboards from the city was unconstitutional because a municipality may not use the police power to "prohibit completely" a business that is not a public nuisance. The court held that the rule that a municipality may regulate but not prohibit a land use was a "verbal formula" that "conflicts with reality and with current views of the police power." It rejected an argument that San Diego could not prohibit billboards because it is a large city and refused to adopt a rule "that a city's police power diminishes as its population grows."[6]

These cases indicate that courts will review sign ordinances to determine whether they advance aesthetic objectives as they are applied in addition to determining whether they are facially constitutional. As the New York court held in a case upholding an ordinance that restricted the display of business signs, an aesthetic regulation "must bear *substantially* on the economic, social and cultural patterns of the community or district."[7]

§ 11.09   Exemption for On-Premise Signs.

Sign ordinances that prohibit off-premise billboards usually allow on-premise business signs. A court could hold that the on-premise sign exemption violates equal protection because the aesthetic impact of a sign does not depend on its

---

[2] Naegele Outdoor Adv. Co. v. Village of Minnetonka, 162 N.W.2d 206 (Minn. 1968).

[3] John Donnelly & Sons v. Outdoor Adv. Bd., 339 N.E.2d 709 (Mass. 1975). *Accord* Town of Boothbay v. National Adv. Co., 347 A.2d 419 (Me. 1975); United Adv. Corp. v. Borough of Metuchen, 198 A.2d 447 (N.J. 1964); Suffolk Outdoor Adv. Co. v. Hulse, 373 N.E.2d 263 (N.Y. 1977); 81 A.L.R.2d 486 (1977). *See also* Oregon City v. Hartke, 400 P.2d 255 (Or. 1965) (junkyard exclusion).

[4] 339 N.E.2d at 720.

[5] 610 P.2d 407 (Cal. 1980), *rev'd on other grounds,* 453 U.S. 490 (1981).

[6] *Contra* Combined Communications Corp. v. City & Council of Denver, 542 P.2d 79 (Colo. 1975). *See also* Metromedia, Inc. v. City of Des Plaines, 326 N.E.2d 59 (Ill. App. 1975); Stoner McCray Sys. v. City of Des Moines, 78 N.W.2d 843 (Iowa 1956).

[7] People v. Goodman, 290 N.E.2d 139, 141 (N.Y. 1972) (emphasis in original). *See also* Temple Baptist Church, Inc. v. City of Albuquerque, 646 P.2d 565 (N.M. 1982); Sun Oil Co. v. City of Upper Arlington, 379 N.E.2d 266 (Ohio App. 1977) (sign must be "patently offensive" to surrounding area). *Compare* Norate Corp. v. Zoning Bd. of Adjustment, 207 A.2d 890 (Pa. 1965).

location. On-premise signs can be as visually unattractive as off-premise billboards. One court adopted this view,[1] but the overwhelming majority hold that on-premise sign exemptions are constitutional.[2] As one court noted, an exemption for on-premise signs is justified because these signs advance the business or industry on the premises while off-premise signs do not.[3] An exemption for on-premise signs, such as signs advertising activities conducted on the premises, may present constitutional problems under the free speech clause.[4]

§ 11.10 Controls on the Display of Signs.

Sign ordinances contain controls that regulate the display of on-premise and off-premise signs, such as controls on spacing, height, and size, and the number of signs a business can display. Sign ordinances may also control features such as flashing lights, banners, and changeable copy and prohibit certain types of signs, such as roof and portable signs.

The cases have upheld controls on the display of signs. Early cases held that municipalities could limit the size of signs to protect the public from falling billboards.[1] The recent cases apply the presumption of constitutionality and the aesthetics alone rule to uphold controls on the display of signs such as height, size, and setback regulations and restrictions on the number of signs a business is allowed.[2] *Westfield Motor Sales Co. v. Town of Westfield*[3] is an illustrative case that upheld a restriction on the size of an automobile dealership's signs. The court recognized the right of a business to advertise but held that a municipality may perceive that a "plethora" of signs "may have an undesirable cumulative effect on the community."

---

[1] Metromedia, Inc. v. City of Des Plaines, 326 N.E.2d 59 (Ill. App. 1975).

[2] Metromedia, Inc. v. City of Pasadena, 30 Cal. Rptr. 731 (Cal. App. 1963) City of Lake Wales v. Lamar Adv. Ass'n, 414 So. 2d 1030 (Fla. 1982); Donnelly Adv. Corp. v. City of Baltimore, 370 A.2d 1127 (Md. 1977); State Dep't of Roads v. Popco, Inc., 528 N.W.2d 281 (Neb. 1995) (upholding distinction between on-premise and off-premise signs required by federal Highway Beautification Act); Summey Outdoor Adv., Inc. v. County of Henderson, 386 S.E.2d 439 (N.C. App. 1989); Landau Adv. Co. v. Zoning Bd. of Adjustment, 128 A.2d 559 (Pa. 1957).

[3] United Adv. Corp. v. Borough of Metuchen, 198 A.2d 447 (N.J. 1964).

[4] 23 U.S.C. § 131(c). *See* §§ 11.13, 11.18.

[1] St. Louis Poster Adv. Co. v. City of St. Louis, 249 U.S. 269 (1919). *See also* Board of Adjustment v. Osage Oil & Transp. Co., 522 S.W.2d 836 (Ark. 1975).

[2] Village of Skokie v. Walton on Dempster, Inc., 456 N.E.2d 293 (Ill. App. 1983); Temple Baptist Church, Inc. v. City of Albuquerque, 646 P.2d 565 (N.M. 1982); People v. Goodman, 290 N.E.2d 139 (N.Y. 1972); 56 A.L.R.3d 1207 (1974); Sun Oil Co. v. City of Arlington, 379 N.E.2d 266 (Ohio App. 1977). *See also* Merritt v. Peters, 65 So. 2d 861 (Fla. 1953); State v. Diamond Motors, Inc., 429 P.2d 825 (Haw. 1967).

[3] 324 A.2d 113 (N.J.L. Div. 1974). *But see* Art Van Furniture Co. v. City of Kentwood, 437 N.W.2d 380 (Mich. App. 1989) (cannot restrict wall sign size for single occupant of building but allow larger wall signs if building occupied by multiple occupants).

The courts have upheld limitations on illumination, movement, and color[4] and prohibitions on searchlights and windblown signs.[5] They universally uphold ordinances that prohibit projecting signs or limit the extent to which they can project.[6] The authority to regulate projecting signs derives from the authority of municipalities to regulate public streets.

Rent-A-Sign v. City of Rockford[7] held traffic safety and aesthetic considerations justified an ordinance that limited the time periods during which portable signs could be displayed. The court held that the city could place time limitations on portable signs because they are designed to attract attention to temporary events rather than to inform. Most courts uphold restrictions on roof signs.[8]

§ 11.11 Nonconforming Signs.

The case law that determines the extent to which municipalities can regulate nonconforming uses applies to nonconforming signs, including the case law that approves the amortization of nonconforming uses after a reasonable amortization period.[1] The amortization of nonconforming signs by municipalities is affected by provisions in the federal Highway Beautification Act,[2] which has always required compensation for the removal of nonconforming signs on federal highways. Congress amended the Act in 1978 to require compensation "whether or not" the sign was removed under the Act.[3] This amendment was intended to prohibit the municipal amortization of nonconforming signs.[4] The federal

---

[4] City of Fayetteville v. S & H, Inc., 547 S.W.2d 94 (Ark. 1977); Schaffer v. City of Omaha, 248 N.W.2d 764 (Neb. 1977); Asselin v. Town of Conway, 628 A.2d 247 (N.H. 1993) (illumination); Hilton v. City of Toledo, 405 N.E.2d 1047 (Ohio 1980); Kenyon Peck, Inc. v. Kennedy, 168 S.E.2d 117 (Va. 1969). *Contra* In re Appeal of Ammon R. Smith Auto Co., 223 A.2d 683 (Pa. 1966). *But see* Capalbo v. Planning & Zoning Bd., 547 A.2d 528 (Conn. 1988) (statute did not authorize regulation of color); 30 A.L.R.5th 549 (regulations relating to illuminated signs).

[5] *See* Robert L. Rieke Bldg. Co. v. City of Overland Park, 657 P.2d 1121 (Kan. 1983) (search-lights); Goodman Toyota, Inc. v. City of Raleigh, 306 S.E.2d 192 (N.C. App. 1983) (windblown signs).

[6] McMahan's Furn. Co. v. City of Pacific Grove, 33 Cal. Rptr. 476 (Cal. App. 1963); People ex rel. Herman Armanetti, Inc. v. City of Chicago, 112 N.E.2d 616 (Ill. 1953); State v. Sanguinetti, 449 A.2d 922 (Vt. 1982); 80 A.L.R.3d 687 (1977).

[7] 406 N.E.2d 943 (Ill. App. 1980).

[8] General Outdoor Adv. Co. v. Department of Pub. Works, 193 N.E. 799 (Mass. 1935). *Contra* Mayor & City Council v. Mano Swartz, Inc., 299 A.2d 828 (Md. 1973).

[1] §§ 5.78–5.86.

[2] § 11.06.

[3] 23 U.S.C. § 131(g). *See* Donnelly Adv. Corp. v. City of Baltimore, 370 A.2d 1127 (Md. 1977) (decided prior to amendment).

[4] Root Outdoor Adv. v. City of Ft. Collins, 788 P.2d 149 (Colo. 1990) (five-year amortization ordinance does not comply with statutory compensation requirement). *But see* Ackerley Communi-

compensation requirement does not preempt ordinances that amortize signs,[5] but the federal highway agency can withhold ten percent of a state's highway funds if a municipality removes a nonconforming sign through amortization.[6]

A substantial number of states have adopted statutes to comply with the federal compensation requirement. By requiring the payment of compensation for the removal of lawfully erected signs, they prohibit municipal amortization of nonconforming signs on highways covered by the federal act or all nonconforming signs.[7] In *Metromedia,*[8] the court held a state statute requiring compensation for the removal of nonconforming signs on federal highways preempted municipal amortization of nonconforming signs on these highways. The statute required the preemption of municipal ordinances when this was necessary to protect the receipt of federal highway funds. The court also held a compensation requirement for nonconforming signs that applied only to federal highways did not violate equal protection.

The courts have upheld methods short of amortization for the removal of nonconforming signs. A municipality may condition an application for new development on the removal of a nonconforming sign.[9] A taking does not occur if an ordinance requires a billboard to be lowered to conform with height restrictions.[10]

---

cations, Inc. v. City of Seattle, 602 P.2d 1177 (Wash. 1979) (federal act does not require compensation for removal of nonconforming signs in industrial and commercial areas). *Contra Metromedia,* note 8, *infra.*

[5] National Adv. Co. v. City of Ashland, 678 F.2d 106 (9th Cir. 1982).

[6] 23 U.S.C. § 131(b) (applies to all violations of statute).

[7] Cal. Bus. & Prof. Code § 5412; Fla. Stat. Ann. § 479.15(2); Idaho Code § 40-1910A; Iowa Code Ann. § 306C.24(2); Md. Transportation Code Ann. § 8-745; Mich. Comp. Laws Ann. § 252.304; Miss. Code Ann. § 49-23-17; N.D. Cent. Code § 24-17-05; N. Mex. Stat. Ann. § 42A-1-34.

[8] Metromedia, Inc. v. City of San Diego, 610 P.2d 407 (Cal. 1980), *rev'd on other grounds,* 453 U.S. 490 (1981). *But see* Whiteco Outdoor Advertising v. City of Tucson, 972 P.2d 647 (Ariz. App. 1999) (statute does not prohibit removal of bottom-mounted lighting fixtures); Suffolk Outdoor Adv. Co. v. Town of Southampton, 455 N.E.2d 1245 (N.Y. 1983) (federal statute does not preempt local ordinance requiring amortization).

[9] Outdoor Systems, Inc. v. City of Mesa, 819 P.2d 44 (Ariz. 1991) (holding *Nollan* does not apply). *See* Outdoor Sys., Inc. v. City of Mesa, 997 F.2d 604 (9th Cir. 1993) (ordinance upheld in state case not a taking of property); Circle K Corp. v. City of Mesa, 803 P.2d 457 (Ariz. App. 1990) (can condition permit for new nonconforming sign on removal of existing nonconforming sign). *But see* Ariz. Rev. Stat. Ann. § 9-462.02(B), 11-830(F) (prohibiting ordinances of this type). *See also* Naegele Outdoor Advertising Co. v. City of Lakeville, 532 N.W.2d 249 (Minn. App. 1995) (requirement for removal of nonconforming sign when lease terminated by owner of property held not a taking).

[10] National Adv. Co. v. Board of Adj., 800 P.2d 1349 (Colo. App. 1990). *See* Barron Chevrolet Co. v. Town of Danvers, 646 N.E.2d 89 (Mass. 1995) (change in sign panels does not remove sign from protection of nonconforming use statute).

§ 11.12 Free Speech Issues.

Free speech issues are critically important in sign regulation. Ordinances that regulate signs raise free speech problems because messages on signs are a form of speech. Signs with political and ideological messages are protected by the free speech clause as noncommercial speech. The free speech clause also protects signs with commercial messages, although the U.S. Supreme Court does not give commercial speech as much protection as noncommercial speech. The effect of the free speech clause on the constitutionality of sign ordinances is dramatic: it reverses the presumption of constitutionality the courts usually apply to police power regulations. The burden on municipalities to show that sign ordinances are justified by the usual governmental interests, such as traffic safety and aesthetics, is heavier.[1]

§ 11.13 *Metromedia.*

Metromedia, Inc. v. City of San Diego,[1] which considered a comprehensive sign regulation ordinance adopted by the city, is the leading case on the application of the free speech clause of the federal constitution to sign regulation. San Diego adopted a sign ordinance that prohibited off-premise commercial billboards but exempted on-premise signs that identified the business conducted on the premises. The ordinance also exempted twelve categories of signs, including governmental real estate and temporary political signs. A majority of the Justices upheld the billboard ban but invalidated the ordinance for other violations of the free speech clause, but a majority did not agree on the reasons why the ordinance was unconstitutional. A plurality opinion by four of the Justices attracted the most support in the Court, and deserves discussion because it has influenced state and federal court decisions.

The Court applied the *Central Hudson*[2] test, that required the city to show the ordinance would "directly advance" its interests in traffic safety and aesthetics. The *Metromedia* plurality approved both as a basis for upholding the city's ordinance. It seemed to accept traffic safety as a per se justification, noting the California Supreme Court held as a matter of law that an ordinance prohibiting billboards "designed to be viewed from streets and highways reasonably relates to traffic safety." The plurality agreed, holding it would "likewise hesitate to disagree with the accumulated, common-sense judgments of local lawmakers" and many courts that billboards "are real and substantial hazards to traffic safety."

The California Supreme Court had accepted aesthetics alone as a sufficient basis for upholding the San Diego ordinance, though it also noted that aesthetic

---

[1] *See* § 2.50, discussing standards of judicial review..

[1] 453 U.S. 490 (1981).

[2] § 2.50.

and economic justifications were identical because the state relied on its scenery to attract traffic and commerce. The Metromedia plurality went further, holding it was not "speculative to recognize that billboards, by their very nature, wherever located and however constructed, can be perceived as an esthetic harm."

The plurality then rejected an argument that the ordinance undercut the city's interest in aesthetics because it permitted on-site signs with commercial advertising. It held a ban on off-site commercial advertising was related to the city's traffic and safety objectives, that the off-site commercial advertising was more acute, and that the city could exempt on-site commercial advertising because it could "reasonably conclude" that its interest in allowing on-site commercial advertising was stronger than it's interest in traffic safety and aesthetics. Justice Stevens concurred in this part of the plurality opinion, which thus had a majority of the Court.

However, the plurality invalidated the provision in the ordinance that allowed commercial but prohibited commercial signs on-site. It noted its cases had always given noncommercial speech a greater degree of protection than commercial speech. The city did not explain why allowing noncommercial as well as commercial messages on site would threaten traffic safety and the city's aesthetic interests, and it could not conclude that the communication of commercial information on site was of greater value than the communication of noncommercial information.

The plurality invalidated the twelve exceptions for noncommercial signs contained in the ordinance. It held the city could distinguish between the relative value of commercial speech, but could not evaluate or distinguish between the "various communicative interests" of noncommercial speech. "With respect to noncommercial speech, the city may not choose the appropriate subjects for public discourse."

The plurality also held the sign exemptions did not meet the requirements for a reasonable time, place and manner regulation. The parties stipulated there were no alternative channels of communication for the noncommercial signs that where not included in the exemptions. In addition, "[i]t is apparent as well that the ordinance distinguishes in several ways between permissible and impermissible signs at a particular location by reference to their content."

Because the dominant opinion in *Metromedia* was written by four Justices no longer on the Court, its value as precedent may be limited. However, most federal circuits have adopted the *Metromedia* plurality opinion as the basis for deciding free speech problems raised by sign regulation,[3] and the state courts have also relied on the *Metromedia* plurality.

---

[3] *E.g.* Lavey v. City of Two Rivers, 171 F.3d 1110 (7th Cir. 1999); Ackerley Communications v. Krochalis, 108 F.3d 1095 (9th Cir. 1997) (rejecting claim that later cases undermined *Metromedia*); Outdoor Graphics v. City of Burlington, 103 F.3d 690 (8th Cir. 1996) (favorably

§ 11.14 *Taxpayers for Vincent.*

Members of City Council v. Taxpayers for Vincent,[1] the Court upheld in a 6-3 decision a Los Angeles ordinance that prohibited the posting of signs on public property in an action brought by a candidate for public office whose political signs were removed by the city. It held the ordinance did not violate the free speech clause because it was a viewpoint-neutral time, place, and manner regulation.[2] If the Court meant that sign regulation need only be viewpoint-neutral and did not have to be content-neutral, this holding would overrule that part of the plurality decision in *Metromedia* that invalidated part of the San Diego ordinance because it violated content neutrality.

The Court confirmed the holding in *Metromedia,* that aesthetics is a substantial governmental interest that justifies the restrictions a sign ordinance imposes on free speech:

These [aesthetic] interests are both psychological and economic. The character of the environment affects the quality of life and the value of property in both residential and commercial areas.[3]

The Court upheld the prohibition on signs on public property because it was no greater than necessary to advance these interests. It held the "substantive evil" of visual blight was not a "possible byproduct" of the activity but was created by signs as a "medium of expression." The Court also held the city was not required to adopt a less restrictive alternative than prohibition, such as an exemption for political and perhaps other signs. It indicated these exemptions might be unconstitutional as discrimination against the content of speech and could defeat the objective of combating visual blight.

Finally, the Court held that the ordinance was not invalid because alternative means of communication were inadequate. Individuals could speak and distribute literature at places where the ordinance prohibited signs on public property. In an important footnote it added:

Although the Court has shown special solicitude for forms of expression that are much less expensive than feasible alternatives and hence may be important to a large segment of the citizenry, . . . this solicitude has practical boundaries.[4]

---

citing *Metromedia*); National Advertising Co. v. Town of Niagra, 942 F.2d 145 (2d Cir.1991); Naegele v. City of Durham, 844 F.2d 172 (4th Cir. 1988). *Contra* Rappa v. Newcastle County, 18 F.3d 1043 (3rd Cir. 1994).

[1] 466 U.S. 789 (1984).

[2] United States v. O'Brien, 391 U.S. 367 (1968). *See* § 2.50.

[3] 466 U.S. at 817.

[4] *Id.* at 812 n.30.

The Court held the ordinance constitutional even though it did not prohibit signs on private property. It justified this exemption because private property owners would keep the posting of signs on their property within reasonable limits. By not extending the prohibition to private property, the city also left open a "significant opportunity to communicate by means of temporary signs." This limitation of the sign prohibition to a public forum limits the value of the case as precedent for sign regulation on private property.

§ 11.15 *Ladue*: Residential Signs.

In City of *Ladue v. Gilleo*,[1] an exclusive St. Louis residential suburb prohibited homeowners from displaying any signs on residential property except for residence identification, "for sale," and safety hazard warning signs. It permitted commercial business, churches, and nonprofit organizations to display signs not allowed at residences. The Court held the ordinance violated the free speech clause in a case brought by a homeowner prohibited from displaying in her window an 8 ½ by 11 inch sign stating "For Peace in the Gulf."

The Court accepted the city's statement the ordinance was free of content or viewpoint discrimination, but held Ladue's interest in minimizing visual clutter was not a sufficient "compelling" reason for prohibiting residential message signs completely. Ladue had "almost completely foreclosed" a venerable, unique, and important means of communication to political, religious, or personal messages. The Court also indicated the exemptions from the residential sign prohibitions in the Ladue ordinance "undermined the credibility" of "the City's aesthetic interest in eliminating outdoor signs."

The Court held the prohibition on residential message signs was not a "time, place, or manner" regulation because residents did not have alternative means to convey their messages. It held that displaying a sign from a residence carried a "quite distinct" message because it provides information about the identity of the speaker. In addition, residential signs are "an unusually cheap and convenient form of communication." Respect for individual liberty in the home, the Court concluded, has long been part of our culture and law. It suggested Ladue could adopt "more temperate measures" to meet its regulatory needs, and noted that not every kind of sign must be permitted in residential areas.

§ 11.16 *Lorillard*: Restrictions on Location.

Lorillard Tobacco Co. v. Reilly,[1] in an opinion by Justice O'Connor joined throughout by at least five Justices, invalidated a Massachusetts regulation that

---

[1] 512 U.S. 43 (1994), relying especially on Linmark Assocs. v. Township of Willingboro, discussed in § 11.22. *See* City of Forest Park v. Pelfrey, 669 N.E.2d 863 (Ohio App. 1995) (invalidating ordinance prohibiting message wall signs in residential areas).

[1] 533 U.S. 525 (2001).

prohibited the advertising of tobacco products within 1000 feet of a school or playground. It held the restrictions applied to cigarette advertising were pre-empted by a federal statute, and that the restrictions applied to cigar and smokeless tobacco advertising violated the First Amendment. The Court rejected a suggestion that it abandon the *Central Hudson* tests for regulations that affect commercial speech, but held the regulation violated those tests.

It held the regulation substantially advanced a governmental interest because there had been a substantial increase in underage use of these products, and suppressing advertising for these products would reduce their use. However, the Court held the regulation was more extensive than necessary to advance that interest. The regulation, together with other zoning restrictions, would almost completely ban advertising truthful information for these product in three of the largest cities in the state.

The Court held the breadth of the regulation and the process by which it was adopted did not show a "careful calculation" of the speech interests involved. The uniformly broad sweep of the regulation did not show sufficient tailoring, because its effect would vary by place and would have a substantial impact on commercial speech in major metropolitan areas. In addition, the range of communication restricted was too broad. The Court noted, for example, that the restriction on signs of any size was ill-suited to target the problem of highly visible billboards, and that the regulation prohibited advertising directed to adults as well as children. The Court noted its holding did not apply to sign regulations that applied equally to all signs, but its cautionary holding on the extent of sign regulation as it affects free speech could apply even to sign regulations not directed toward a particular product.

§ 11.17   What These Cases Decided: Standing, Aesthetics and Content Neutrality.

These Supreme Court cases clarified a number of free speech issues in the regulation of signs. Standing to sue is one of them. Standing rules require a litigant to show that her own constitutional rights have been violated, but first amendment cases are an exception. In *Metromedia,* for example, the Court decided a case brought by owners of commercial signs in which they successfully attacked ordinance requirements that applied to noncommercial signs. This exception to standing requirements is based on the Supreme Court's overbreadth doctrine. It holds a plaintiff may claim a law is facially invalid if it violates the first amendment rights of others not before the court, even though the plaintiff cannot assert their claims.[1] The reason for the doctrine is that the "very existence

---

[1] Members of City Council v. Taxpayers for Vincent, 466 U.S. 789 (1984) (must be substantial danger that statute will significantly compromise recognized first amendment rights of others); Broadrick v. Oklahoma, 413 U.S. 601 (1973) (overbreadth must be "real and substantial").

of some broadly written statutes may have such a deterrent effect on free expression that they should be subject to challenge even by a party whose own conduct may be unprotected."[2] The courts have applied this doctrine to allow plaintiffs to claim a sign ordinance is facially invalid because regulations that affect parties not before the court are content-based, or confer too much discretion on decision makers.[3]

The Court has also made it clear that "common sense" justifies aesthetic and traffic safety interests as a basis for sign regulation. Problems remain because the *Metromedia* appeal was from a summary judgment decided on stipulated facts admitting the aesthetic effects of the ordinance, so that the Court did not reach the question of how aesthetic impact should be determined when facts are not stipulated. The cases have considered this question, and have held the aesthetic effect of a sign ordinance need be tested only by its effect on a broad category of speech, not on an individual plaintiff's signs.[4]

Content neutrality remains an important if somewhat unsettled issue in sign regulation. *Metromedia* invalidated the sign exemptions in the San Diego ordinance because they were not content-neutral, but the Court did not decide either the *Ladue*[5] or *Lorillard* cases on content neutrality grounds, even though the ordinances in those cases would seem to have violated the content neutrality requirement. Nevertheless, content neutrality remains a key free speech issue in those circuits that accept the *Metromedia* plurality's opinion.

§ 11.18 Time, Place and Manner Restrictions.

The courts have usually upheld time, place and manner restrictions on commercial signs,[1] such as size, height, number and similar restrictions. *Donrey*

---

[2] Thornhill v. Alabama, 310 U.S. 88, 97–98 (1940).

[3] *See, e.g.,* North Olmsted Chamber of Commerce v. City of North Olmsted, 86 F. Supp. 2d 755, (N.D. Ohio 2000) (accepting third party claims in a sign regulation free speech case). *But see* Members of City Council v. Taxpayers for Vincent, 466 U.S. 789 (1984) (rejecting overbreadth claim because no showing that other parties would suffer different injury), *distinguished in* Sugarman v. Village of Chester, 192 F. Supp.2d 282 (S.D.N.Y. 2002). *See also* Harp Advertising Ill., Inc. v. Village of Chicago Ridge, 9 F.3d 1290 (7th Cir. 1993) (plaintiff did not have standing because size limit on signs prevented display of its billboards, and plaintiff did not challenge size limit).

[4] Lavey v. City of Two Rivers, 171 F.3d 1110, 1115 n.18 (7th Cir. 1999); Ackerley Communications of the Northwest v. Krochalis, 108 F.3d 1095 (9th Cir. 1997); Outdoor Systems, Inc. v. City of Lenexa, 67 F. Supp.2d 1241 (D. Kan. 1999). *See also* United States v. Edge Broadcasting Co., 509 U.S. 418 (1993); Members of City Council v. Taxpayers for Vincent, 466 U.S. 789 (1984).

[5] *See* 512 U.S. at 49, Justice O'Connor concurring (would have held ordinance discriminated on the basis of content).

[1] American Federated General Agency, Inc. v. City of Ridgeland, 72 F. Supp. 2d 695 (S.D. Miss. 1999) (prohibition on building sign); Ad Craft, Inc. v. Board of Zoning Appeals, 693 N.E.2d 110 (Ind. App. 1998) (upholding permit requirement). *Cf.* Jim Gall Auctioneers, Inc. v. City of

Communications Co. v. City of Fayetteville[2] is a typical case. The court upheld a sign ordinance that limited the size of the plaintiff's signs to seventy-five square feet and that prevented the plaintiff from using the standard 300-square-foot poster the sign industry uses. The court held the ordinance did not "eliminate billboards as a channel of communications" even though a sign that complied with the ordinance cost fifty percent more than the standard industry sign. Courts have also upheld ordinances restricting the height[3] and number[4] and illumination[5] of signs. However, ordinances restricting or prohibiting price information on signs violate the free speech clause because this type of ordinance is not content-neutral..[6]

The Supreme Court indicated in the *Ladue* case it would approve "moderate" regulations of signs in residential areas, and courts since that case have upheld reasonable regulations on signs in residential districts.[7] *Long Island Bd. of*

Coral Gables, 210 F.3d 1331 (11th Cir. 2000) (upholding ordinance prohibiting auctions of third-party goods in residential areas); People v. Target Advertising, Inc., 708 N.Y.S.2d 597 (Sup. Ct. 2000) (upholding ordinance barring the operation of vehicles solely for the purpose of displaying commercial advertising).

[2] 660 S.W.2d 900 (Ark. 1983). *Accord* Outdoor Systems, Inc. v. City of Mesa, 997 F.2d 604 (9th Cir. 1993); South-Suburban Housing Center v. Greater South Suburban Bd. of Realtors, 935 F.2d 868 (7th Cir. 1991). *But see* Real Estate Bd. of Metropolitan St. Louis v. City of Jennings, 808 S.W.2d 7 (Mo. App. 1991).

[3] City of Albuquerque v. Jackson, 684 P.2d 543 (N.M. App. 1984).

[4] South-Suburban Housing Center v. Greater South Suburban Bd. of Realtors, 935 F.2d 868 (7th Cir. 1991); Bender v. City of Saint Ann, 816 F. Supp. 1372 (E.D. Mo. 1993), *aff'd on other grounds,* 36 F.3d 57 (8th Cir. 1994); Williams v. City & County of Denver, 622 P.2d 542 (Colo. 1981); City of Sunrise v. D.C.A. Homes, Inc., 421 So. 2d 1084 (Fla. App. 1982).

[5] Ellen Media Co. v. City of Tucson, 7 P.3d 136 (Ariz. App. 2000) (upholding ordinance requiring top-mounted lights on billboards); Wallace v. Brown County Area Plan Comm'n, 689 N.E.2d 491 (Ind. App. 1998) (upholding ban on neon signs). Asselin v. Town of Conway, 628 A.2d 247 (N.H. 1993) (upholding ordinance prohibiting internally lit sign). *But see* State v. Calabria, 693 A.2d 949 (N.J. App. Div. 1997) (neon sign prohibition violates free speech); *See also* State v. Schad, 733 A.2d 1159 (N.J. 1999) (interior visual displays held to be signs covered by ordinance).

[6] H & H Operations, Inc. v. City of Peachtree City, 283 S.E.2d 867 (Ga. 1981); People v. Mobil Oil Corp., 397 N.E.2d 724 (N.Y. 1979). *See* Virginia State Bd. of Pharmacy v. Virginia Citizens Consumer Council, 425 U.S. 748 (1976).*But see* Suburban Lodges of America, Inc. v. City of Columbus Graphics Comm'n, 761 N.E.2d 1060 (Ohio App. 2000) (on-premises signs directed toward freeways and interstate highways may only include business logo and language identifying use or activity by name, street address, and principal product or principal service being advertised; may not include weekly rates).

[7] Kroll v. Steere, 759 A.2d 541 (Conn. App. 2000) (upholding size limitation on signs displayed on residential property); City of Rochester Hills v. Schultz, 592 N.W.2d 69 (Mich. 1999) (remanding for proof that regulation prohibiting home occupation signs while allowing noncommercial and temporary signs advanced governmental purpose); United Property Owners Ass'n v. Borough of Belmar, 777 A.2d 950 (N.J. App. Div. 2001) (upholding prohibition on commercial signs in residential areas); Spriggs v. South Strabane Township Zoning Hearing Bd., 786 A.2d 333 (Pa. Commw. 2001) (upholding ordinance prohibiting billboards and limiting size of signs in residential districts as applied to prohibit oversized text from bible on fence).

Realtors v. Incorporated Village of Massapequa Park[8] is an example. The court upheld an ordinance that allowed only one sign on residential property in addition to one identification sign; regulated their height, size and duration; required the removal of existing signs after property was transferred; and prohibited off-site commercial advertising. It held the ordinance advanced the village's interests in aesthetics and traffic safety and was no more extensive than necessary to serve those interests. It noted courts had upheld similar ordinances adopted to further aesthetic and traffic safety, and that the ordinance did not prevent the Board from displaying real estate signs or conveying its message.

§ 11.19   Prohibition, Classification and Exemption of Off-Premise and On-Premise Signs.

Metromedia sent mixed signals on how far municipalities can go in prohibiting off-premise signs. The Court upheld the ban on off-premise commercial signs but left open the constitutionality of a total prohibition on all off-premise signs, including noncommercial signs. Since *Metromedia* courts have upheld ordinances banning all types of signs when the ban was limited to selected areas, such as an urban renewal area,[1] an historic district,[2] and a retail commercial district.[3] Courts have also upheld ordinances prohibiting signs near highways, including signs prohibited by state legislation adopted to implement the federal Highway Beautification Act.[4] Cases that upheld restrictions on advertising for liquor and tobacco products[5] may now be questionable. under the Supreme Court's *Lorillard* decision.[6]

---

[8] 277 F.3d 622 (2d Cir. 2002).

[1] Donnelly Advertising Co. v. City of Baltimore, 370 A.2d 1127 (Md. 1977).

[2] Messer v. City of Douglasville, 975 F.2d 1505 (11th Cir. 1992). *See also* Burke v. City of Charleston, 893 F. Supp. 589 (D.S.C. 1995) (upholding ordinance requiring removal of mural from wall in historic district).

[3] Rzadkowolski v. Lake Orion, 845 F.2d 653 (6th Cir. 1988).

[4] National Advertising Co. v. Denver, 912 F.2d 405 (10th Cir. 1990); Naegele Outdoor Advertising, Inc. v. City of Durham, 844 F.2d 172 (4th Cir. 1988); Wheeler v. Commissioner of Highways, 822 F.2d 586 (6th Cir. 1987); Major Media of the Southeast, Inc. v. City of Raleigh, 792 F.2d 1269 (4th Cir. 1986) (and public parks); Infinity Outdoor, Inc. v. City of New York, 165 F. Supp.2d 403 (S.D.N.Y. 2001); Rodriguez v. Solis, 2 Cal. Rptr. 2d 50 (Cal. App. 1991); U.S. Outdoor Advertising Co., Inc. v. Indiana Dep't of Transp., 714 N.E.2d 1244 (Ind. App. 1999); Barber v. Texas Dep't of Transp, 49 S.W.3d 12 (Tex. App. 2001 (upholding law prohibiting display of ideological speech on private property).

[5] Penn Advertising of Baltimore, Inc. v. Mayor & Council, 63 F.3d 1318 (4th Cir. 1995), *modified & adhered to,* 101 F.3d 332 (4th Cir. 1996) (cigarettes); Anheuser-Busch, Inc. v. Schmoke, 63 F.3d 1305 (4th Cir. 1995), *adhered to on remand,* 101 F.3d 325 (4th Cir. 1996) (liquor).

[6] Eller Media Co. v. City of Cleveland, 161 F. Supp.2d 796 (N.D. Ohio 2001) (invalidating post-*Lorillard* an ordinance prohibiting advertising of alcohol in a large portion of Cleveland's densely populated areas). *See* § 11.17.

The courts have also followed *Metromedia* by upholding ordinances that prohibit off-premise commercial signs when on-premise signs are allowed.[7] Prohibitions on both off-premise commercial and noncommercial signs are more of a problem because noncommercial speech is affected. Some courts upheld city-wide prohibitions on commercial and noncommercial signs when both commercial and noncommercial messages were allowed on-premise,[8] but other courts have disagreed.[9] The Eleventh Circuit solved this problem by holding that all noncommercial signs are on-premise signs.[10] This holding means an ordinance that prohibits off-premise signs will only prohibit commercial speech.

Adopting regulations for off-premise and on-premise signs is complicated by the problems presented by a definition of an off-premise sign, usually called a billboard. A typical definition is a sign that advertises goods and services not sold on the premises. Objectors can argue that this definition is content-based because it is necessary to look at a sign and examine its message to determine whether it conforms to the definition in the ordinance. Though some courts took this view[11] the Supreme Court rejected it,[12] and courts have held this definition is not content-based because it only regulates signs by location.[13]

[7] Outdoor Systems, Inc. v. City of Mesa, 997 F.2d 604 (9th Cir. 1993); National Adv. Co. v. City & Cty. of Denver, 912 F.2d 405 (10th Cir. 1990); National Adv. Co. v. City of Orange, 861 F.2d 246 (9th Cir. 1988); Major Media of the Southeast, Inc. v. City of Raleigh, 792 F.2d 1269 (4th Cir. 1986); Outdoor Systems, Inc. v. City of Merriam, 67 F. Supp.2d 1258 (D. Kan. 1999); National Adv. Co. v. City of Bridgeton, 626 F. Supp. 837 (E.D. Mo. 1985) (Street Graphics Model Ordinance). *But see* National Adv. Co. v. Town of Babylon, 900 F.2d 551 (2d Cir. 1990). *See also* Lavey v. City of Two Rivers, 171 F.3d 1110 (7th Cir. 1999) (upholding ordinance placing more restrictions on off-premise than on-premise signs). (failure to show governmental interests advanced); Ackerley Communications v. Krochalis, 108 F.3d 1095 (9th Cir. 1997); City of Lakewood v. Colfax Unlimited Ass'n, 634 P.2d 52 (Colo. 1981) (invalidating classification of commercial signs). *Compare* Pigg v. State Dep't of Hwys., 746 P.2d 961 (Colo. 1987). *But see* Discovery Network, Inc. v. City of Cincinnati, 507 U.S. 410 (1993) (striking ordinance discriminating against commercial newsracks but distinguishing *Metromedia*).

[8] Georgia Outdoor Advertising, Inc. v. Waynesville, 833 F.2d 43 (4th Cir. 1987) (though plaintiff argued that only prohibition on off-site commercial speech was invalid); Wheeler v. Commissioner of Highways, 822 F.2d 586 (6th Cir. 1987). *But see* Ackerley Communications v. City of Cambridge, 88 F.3d 33 (1st Cir. 1996).

[9] National Advertising Co. v. Orange, 861 F.2d 246 (9th Cir. 1988).

[10] Southlake Property Associates, Ltd. v. City of Morrow, 112 F.3d 1114 (11th Cir. 1997). *But see* Union City Bd. of Zoning Appeals v. Justice Outdoor Displays, 467 S.E.2d 875 (Ga. 1996) (disagreeing with *Southlake*).

[11] Ackerley Communications, Inc. v. City of Cambridge, 88 F.3d 33, 37 n.7 (1st Cir. 1996); Burkhart Advertising, Inc. v. City of Auburn, 786 F. Supp. 721 (N.D. Ind. 1991).

[12] Hill v. Colorado, 530 U.S. 703, 722 (2000) ("We have never held, or suggested, that it is improper to look at the content of an oral or written statement in order to determine whether a rule of law applies to a course of conduct," upholding statute prohibiting picketing with signs near health facility).

[13] Messer v. City of Douglasville, 975 F.2d 1505 (11th Cir. 1992). *Accord,* Wheeler v. Commis-

A free speech problem also arises from the holding by the *Metromedia* plurality that invalidated a provision allowing on-premise commercial but prohibiting on-premise noncommercial signs. This problem is easily solved by a "substitution" clause.[14] This clause allows all signs permitted by the ordinance to contain both commercial and noncommercial messages.

More difficult problems are presented by the *Metromedia* plurality holding that the 12 exemptions in the San Diego ordinance violated the free speech clause because they were content-based and improperly distinguished among noncommercial messages. This holding is questionable; some of these exemptions, such as the exemption of for sale signs, are required by Supreme Court decisions. *Vincent* also undercuts the plurality holding if *Vincent* means only viewpoint, not content, neutrality is necessary. The ordinance upheld in *Vincent* contained some of the same exemptions contained in the San Diego ordinance, but the Court did not discuss them. Some courts have struck down[15] ordinances containing exemptions similar to those held invalid by the *Metromedia* plurality, but some have been troubled by the *Metromedia* plurality holding and have upheld similar exemptions.[16]

When an ordinance clearly discriminated against noncommercial speech, it was struck down.[17] The courts have also invalidated sign ordinances that prohibit

---

sioner of Highways, 822 F.2d 586, 591 (6th Cir. 1987). *See also* National Advertising Co. v. City & County of Denver, 912 F.2d 405 (10th Cir. 1990) (Supreme Court has provided "ample guidance" on the common-sense distinction between commercial and noncommercial speech). Accord, Major Media of the Southeast, Inc. v. City of Raleigh, 792 F.2d 1269, 1272 (4th Cir. 1986) (and holding that codification of these terms is unnecessary).

[14] Outdoor Sys., Inc. v. City of Mesa, 997 F.2d 604 (9th Cir. 1993) (upholding distinction between offsite and onsite commercial signs); Wheeler v. Commissioner of Hwys., 822 F.2d 586 (6th Cir. 1987) (ordinance allowed signs relating to any "activity" on-premises); Major Media of the Southeast, Inc. v. City of Raleigh, 792 F.2d 1269 (4th Cir. 1986); City & County of San Francisco v. Eller Outdoor Adv., 237 Cal. Rptr. 815 (1987) (also upholds exemptions); Gannett Outdoor Co. v. City of Troy, 409 N.W.2d 719 (Mich. App. 1987).

[15] Foti v. City of Menlo Park, 146 F.3d 629 (9th Cir. 1998); Dimitt v. City of Clearwater, 985 F.2d 1565 (11th Cir. 1993) (ordinance limiting permit exemptions to governmental flags); National Advertising Co. v. Town of Niagra, 942 F.2d 945 (2d Cir. 1991); National Adv. Co. v. City of Orange, 861 F.2d 246 (9th Cir. 1988) (exemptions similar to those invalidated in *Metromedia*); Village of Schaumburg v. Jeep Eagle Sales Corp., 676 N.E.2d 200 (Ill. App. 1996) (flags). *See also* Rappa v. New Castle County, 18 F.3d 1043 (3d Cir. 1994) (striking down exemptions in state outdoor advertising law but refusing to apply *Metromedia*). *See* 2002 A.L.R.5th 9 (2002).

[16] Lavey v. City of Two Rivers, 171 F.3d 1110 (7th Cir. 1999); Messer v. City of Douglasville, 975 F.2d 1505 (11th Cir. 1992); National Adv. Co. v. Town of Babylon, 900 F.2d 551 (2d Cir. 1990) (exemption of "for sale" sign); Scadron v. City of Des Plaines, 734 F. Supp. 1437 (N.D. Ill. 1990), *aff'd without opinion,* 989 F.2d 502 (7th Cir. 1992).

[17] Desert Outdoor Advertising v. City of Moreno Valley, 103 F.3d 814 (9th Cir. 1996) (noncommercial messages restricted to certain areas of city but onsite commercial messages allowed anywhere); Matthews v. Town of Needham, 764 F.2d 58 (1st Cir. 1985) (ordinance prohibiting political signs but allowing commercial signs invalid).

noncommercial messages entirely.[18]

§ 11.20 Portable Signs.

Sign ordinances that regulate portable signs can present difficult problems under the free speech clause. Several cases struck down ordinances that prohibited portable signs or limited the time periods for their display.[1] These cases held the municipality did not show that portable signs are aesthetically offensive or that inherent aesthetic differences between portable and permanent signs require more stringent portable sign regulations. The courts also held that less restrictive alternatives, such as safety regulations, could eliminate the dangers created by portable signs.

Cases decided since the Supreme Court's *Vincent* decision have taken a more favorable view of restrictions on portable signs.[2] *Harnish v. Manatee County*,[3] which upheld an ordinance that prohibited portable signs, is an example. The court held that the prohibition reached no further than necessary to accomplish the county's aesthetic objective and that the county had the discretion to determine how much aesthetic protection was necessary and how to achieve that protection. The court noted that the county had "an aesthetically appealing and fragile environment" and had sponsored workshops in which residents complained about "inherently ugly" portable signs. In some of the cases that invalidated portable sign restrictions, the municipality had not made a strong factual case for the aesthetic regulation of portable signs.

Harnish concluded that the constitution did not require a court to speculate on how a municipality should narrowly tailor its regulations to achieve a governmental objective while leaving alternative means of communication available. This holding weakens the presumption reversal that occurs in free speech cases because it reduces the municipal burden to show that a sign ordinance affects free speech no more than necessary to accomplish the governmental interests it serves.

§ 11.21 Content-Based Sign Definitions.

It has been common in sign ordinances to define signs by their content. For example, an ordinance may define a directional sign as "a sign indicating only

---

[18] Pica v. Sarno, 907 F. Supp. 795 (D.N.J. 1995) (ordinance prohibited signs promoting "interests of any person").

[1] Dills v. City of Marietta, 674 F.2d 1377 (11th Cir. 1982); Dills v. Cobb County, 593 F. Supp. 170 (N.D. Ga. 1984), *aff'd per curiam,* 755 F.2d 1473 (11th Cir. 1985); Risner v. City of Wyoming, 383 N.W.2d 226 (Mich. App. 1985).

[2] City of Hot Springs v. Carter, 836 S.W.2d 863 (Ark. 1992).

[3] 783 F.2d 1535 (11th Cir. 1986). *Accord* Lindsay v. City of San Antonio, 821 F.2d 1103 (5th Cir. 1987); Barber v. Municipality of Anchorage, 776 P.2d 1036 (Alaska 1989).

the direction of pedestrian and vehicular circulation routes on the lot on which the sign is located." Other examples are definitions of real estate, construction and identification signs. Courts have followed the *Metromedia* plurality holding that content-based regulations are unconstitutional, and have struck down sign regulations of this type because they are content-based.[1] Municipalities must find alternate ways of defining and permitting this type of sign.

§ 11.22   For Sale Signs.

In *Linmark Assocs. v. Township of Willingboro*,[1] the Supreme Court struck down an ordinance that banned for sale signs in the community to reduce residential turnover and prevent panic selling by white homeowners that would impair racial integration. It rejected a claim the ordinance was constitutional as a time, place, and manner regulation even though it viewed the prohibition as a restriction on commercial speech. It held the purpose of the ban was to restrict the content of expression on a matter of vital concern to the community. The Court concluded that alternative means of communicating information on the sale of homes were unsatisfactory and that the evidence did not support the township's claim that the purpose of the ordinance was to prevent panic selling.[2] In *Metromedia*, however, the plurality opinion invalidated an exemption to the ordinance that permitted the display of real estate signs because it was content-based. Some courts have followed that decision.[3]

---

[1] Savago v. Village of New Paltz, 214 F. Supp.2d 252 (N.D.N.Y. 2002); Granite State Outdoor Advertising, Inc. v. City of Clearwater, 213 F. Supp.2d 1312 (M.D. Fla. 2002); King Enters., Inc. v. Thomas Township, 215 F. Supp.2d 891 (E.D. Mich. 2002); North Olmsted Chamber of Commerce v. City of North Olmsted, 86 F. Supp.2d 755 (N.D. Ohio 2000) (invalidating numerous content-based regulations); Young v. City of Roseville, 78 F. Supp.2d 970 (D. Minn. 1999) (regulation of flags held content-based). *See also* Flying J Travel Plaza v. Transportation Cabinet, Dep't of Highways, 928 S.W.2d 344 (Ky. 1996) (invalidating prohibition of signs with flashing, moving or intermittent lights except time, date, temperature or weather signs with limits on cycling). *But see* American Legion Post 7 v. City of Durham, 239 F.3d 601 (4th Cir. 2001) (upholding ordinance regulating size of flags).

[1] 431 U.S. 85 (1977). *Accord* Citizens United for Free Speech II v. Long Beach Township Bd. of Comm'rs, 802 F. Supp. 1223 (D.N.J. 1992) (prohibiting "for rent" signs during summer months); Greater Baltimore Bd. of Realtors v. Huges, 596 F. Supp. 906 (D. Md. 1984); Daugherty v. City of East Point, 447 F. Supp. 290 (N.D. Ga. 1978); City of Chicago v. Gordon, 497 N.E.2d 442 (Ill. App. 1986); Berg Agency v. Township of Maplewood, 395 A.2d 261 (N.J.L. Div. 1978). *But see* South Suburban Housing Center v. Greater South Suburban Bd. of Realtors, 935 F.2d 868 (7th Cir. 1991) (ban allowed when ban justified by aesthetic interests of municipalities).

[2] *See also* Cleveland Area Bd. of Realtors v. City of Euclid, 88 F.3d 382 (6th Cir. 1996) (invalidating ordinance limiting for-sale signs to windows); Burkow v. City of Los Angeles, 119 F. Supp. 2d 1076 (C.D. Cal. 2000) (invalidating ordinance prohibiting only "for sale" signs on vehicles)

[3] § 11.21.

§ 11.23   Political, Campaign and Temporary Signs.

Because the protection of political speech is one of the primary purposes of the free speech clause, the courts are especially sensitive to restrictions on the display of political and campaign messages. For example, they uphold limitations on the size of signs only if they are not too restrictive.[1] *Vincent*[2] upheld an ordinance that prohibited the posting of all signs, including political signs, on public property, but the courts strike down ordinances that prohibit the display of political signs throughout the community[3] or on residential property.[4] They hold this restriction improperly suppresses an important medium of communication, and that alternative measures can remedy the problems the display of these signs creates

The courts have also struck down ordinances that limit the display of political signs to brief periods of time.[5] They held the time limit was unnecessarily restrictive, that alternative means of communication were not available, and that the ordinances discriminated against political speech because they did not place similar restrictions on other signs. The courts agree that ordinances limiting the period of time a sign can be displayed before an election are unconstitutional. However, some courts have more recently approved time limits on the display of political signs requiring their removal after a period of time.[6]

---

[1] Baldwin v. Redwood City, 540 F.2d 1360 (9th Cir. 1976); Davis v. City of Green, 665 N.E.2d 753 (Ohio App. 1996) (upholds size restriction). *See also* Brayton v. City of New Brighton, 519 N.W.2d 243 (Minn. App. 1994) (upholding ordinance with same regulations for campaign and opinion signs); Verilli v. City of Concord, 548 F.2d 262 (9th Cir. 1977) (invalidating ordinance requiring signs to be freestanding).

[2] § 11.14.

[3] Matthews v. Town of Needham, 764 F.2d 58 (1st Cir. 2002); Runyon v. Fasi, 762 F. Supp. 949 (D. Hawaii 1991). *See also* Peltz v. City of South Euclid, 228 N.E.2d 320 (Ohio 1967).

[4] Arlington Political Republican Comm. v. Arlington County, 983 F.2d 587 (4th Cir. 1993); Matthews v. Town of Needham, 764 F.2d 58 (1st Cir. 1985); Martin v. Wray, 473 F. Supp. 1131 (E.D. Wis. 1979); Goward v. City of Minneapolis, 456 N.W.2d 460 (Minn. App. 1990); City of Euclid v. Mabel, 484 N.E.2d 249 (Ohio App. 1984). *See also* Runyon v. Fasi, 762 F. Supp. 280 (D. Haw. 1991) (ordinance totally prohibiting political signs held invalid); Tauber v. Town of Longmeadow, 695 F. Supp. 1358 (D. Mass. 1988) (same); Collier v. City of Tacoma, 854 P.2d 1046 (Wash. 1993) (signs prohibited in residential yards and parking strips). *See also* the Supreme Court's *Ladue* decision, discussed in § 11.15.

[5] Whitton v. City of Gladstone, 54 F.3d 1400 (8th Cir. 1995); Outdoor Systems, Inc. v. City of Lenaxa, 67 F. Supp.2d 1231 (D. Kan. 1999); Orazio v. Town of North Hempstead, 426 F. Supp. 1144 (E.D.N.Y. 1977); Knoeffler v. Town of Mankakating, 87 F. Supp. 2d 322 (S.D.N.Y. 2000); Union City Bd. of Zoning Appeals v. Justice Outdoor Displays, Inc., 467 S.E.2d 875 (Ga. 1996); Van v. Travel Information Council, 628 P.2d 1217 (Or. 1981).

[6] Messer v. Douglasville, 975 F.2d 1505 (11th Cir. 1992) (removal in 10 days); Brayton v. City of New Brighton, 519 N.W.2d 243 (Minn. App. 1994) (campaign season); Collier v. City of Tacoma, 854 P.2d 1046 (Wash. 1993) (suggesting seven-day removal requirement is acceptable). *See also* City of Waterloo v. Markham, 600 N.E.2d 1320 (Ill. App. 1992) (upholding 90-day limit

The difficulty is that isolating political and campaign signs for regulation necessarily requires not only a definition of the sign that is content-based, but also the adoption of regulations that apply only to these signs. This type of regulation may violate the free speech clause. For example, in *Whitton v. City of Gladstone*[7] the ordinance prohibited the display of political signs more then seven days before an election and their external illumination, and held political candidates vicariously responsible for their placement, erection and removal. The ordinance did not impose these requirements on other signs. The court held these were content-based regulations that failed strict scrutiny review, because there was no compelling reason for applying them to political signs but not to other signs. The court suggested the city could deal with aesthetic and traffic safety problems by regulating the construction of the signs, the amount of signage, and the length of time a temporary political sign could remain before it had to be removed or replaced. Sign regulations have been held constitutional when they apply to all temporary signs and do not identify political or campaign signs for selective treatment.[8]

B. ARCHITECTURAL DESIGN REVIEW.

§ 11.24   The Design Review Ordinance.

Architectural design review is an important element in land use regulation, and many municipalities have adopted architectural design review ordinances. Most of these ordinances apply to single-family residences, but they may also apply to nonresidential buildings. They usually create a design review board with the authority to approve or disapprove the design of a residential dwelling.[1]

Appearance codes were the earliest type of architectural design review ordinances. They contain a set of standards the board applies in the design review process. One type of appearance code adopts an "anti-look-alike" requirement for residential dwellings by providing that a new dwelling may not be too similar to existing dwellings in the area. Conversely, an appearance code can provide that new dwellings may not differ too much from existing dwellings, a "look-alike" requirement that is a variant of the "compatibility" standard. If the

---

on temporary and political signs). *But see* Whitton v. City of Gladstone, 54 F.3d 1400 (8th Cir. 1995) (invalidating seven-day removal requirement because not applicable to other signs); City of Painesville Bldg. Dep't v. Dworken & Bernstein Co., 733 N.E.2d 1152 (Ohio 2000) (invalidating ordinance prohibiting political signs for a period of seventeen days before an election and two days after).

[7] 54 F.3d 1499 (8th Cir. 1995).

[8] Sugarman v. Village of Chester, 192 F. Supp.2d 282 (S.D.N.Y. 2002).

[1] Diller & Fisher Co. v. Architectural Review Bd., 587 A.2d 674 (N.J.L. Div. 1991) (creation of architectural review board not authorized by zoning legislation). *See* American Planning Association, Growing Smart Legislative Guidebook: Model Statutes for Planning and Management of Change § 9-301 (S. Meck ed. 2002) (model legislation for design review).

ordinance contains both requirements, it legislates against monotony in residential design but also prohibits excessive departures from the design standard established by dwellings in the neighborhood. Architectural design review ordinances can also provide more comprehensive design standards that differ from appearance codes by including design standards that cover a variety of exterior elements, such as materials, orientation, and facade.

Design review ordinances may have an exclusionary effect in upper-income residential suburbs. By requiring variety in residential design, they can effectively exclude mass-produced residential development that uses standard or slightly varied residential design patterns.

Courts review decisions made by design review boards to determine whether they are supported by substantial evidence and properly apply the review criteria in the ordinance.[2] A California court held a design review ordinance did not require review of tenant selection in a retail development.[3]

§ 11.25   Constitutionality.

A group of early leading cases that considered the constitutionality of appearance codes dominates the case law on architectural design review. Most of these cases were decided before a majority of the courts adopted the rule that aesthetics alone is a proper purpose in land use regulation. These cases also arose in residential suburbs, some of them upper-income, and this physical setting affected the court decisions that approved design review. They upheld architectural design review as a measure that protected property values in established neighborhoods. This holding is an example of the minority view on the role of aesthetics in land use regulation, which upholds aesthetic regulation if it advances other legitimate government interests.[1]

A few cases struck down architectural design review ordinances, and some refused to recognize the protection of aesthetic values as a legitimate regulatory purpose.[2] In some of the states where the decisions were unfavorable, the court later adopted a more receptive view of the role of aesthetics in land use regulation. Other cases struck down architectural design review ordinances as an improper

---

[2] Breneric Assocs. v. City of Del Mar, 81 Cal. Rptr. 2d 324 (Cal. App. 1998) (upholding denial of permit for addition to residence because inconsistent with existing structure and surrounding neighborhood); Peterson Outdoor Advertising v. City of Myrtle Beach, 489 S.E.2d 630 (S.C. 1997) (board improperly applied criteria in design review ordinance for signs).

[3] 119 Friends of Davis v. City of Davis, 100 Cal. Rptr. 2d 413 (Cal. App. 2000).

[1] § 11.04. See Coscan Washington, Inc. v. Maryland-National Capital Park & Planning Com., 590 A.2d 1080 (Md. App. (1991) (upholding requirement that certain percentage of residential units be built with brick); County of Wright v. Kennedy, 415 N.W.2d 728 (Minn. App. 1987) (upholding mobile home roof pitch requirement); 41 A.L.R.3d 1397 (1972).

[2] City of West Palm Beach v. State, 30 So. 2d 491 (Fla. 1947); Piscitelli v. Township Comm., 248 A.2d 274 (N.J.L. Div. 1968); Board of Supvrs. v. Rowe, 216 S.E.2d 199 (Va. 1975).

delegation of power or held that they were unconstitutionally vague.[3] The delegation of power holdings clearly indicate a deeper judicial hostility to any use of design review powers for aesthetic purposes.

State ex rel. Saveland Park Holding Corp. v. Wieland[4] is an early leading case upholding an architectural design review ordinance adopted by an upper-income suburb of Milwaukee, Wisconsin. The ordinance provided a building permit could issue only if a special building board found that the "exterior architectural appeal and functional plan" of a proposed structure was not "so at variance" with structures built or planned "in the immediate neighborhood . . . as to cause a substantial depreciation in the property values of said neighborhood." This ordinance legislated a look-alike requirement, which the court sustained as a measure for protecting property values. It relied on *Berman v. Parker,*[5] which the U.S. Supreme Court had just decided, and noted that the law on aesthetic purposes in zoning was evolving toward a more positive view. The court rejected a delegation of power objection to the ordinance.

State ex rel. Stoyanoff v. Berkeley[6] is a more recent but similar case. An upper-income suburb in the St. Louis, Missouri, area created an architectural review board to review building plans. It was to determine "whether the proposed structure will conform to proper architectural standards in appearance and design, and will be in general conformity with the style and design of surrounding structures and conducive to the proper architectural development of the City," and it was required to disapprove the application "if it determines that the proposed structure will constitute an unsightly, grotesque or unsuitable structure in appearance, detrimental to the welfare of surrounding property or residents."This is a "look-alike" requirement. implemented through the application of architectural design standards.

The board denied the plaintiffs a permit for a residence in the shape of a pyramid with a flat top and windows at the corners. They brought suit claiming that the ordinance was facially unconstitutional. The court held the state zoning act authorized the ordinance and rejected a delegation of power objection. It held the ordinance constitutional and relied on the protection of property rationale adopted in *Saveland.* The court noted that homes in the area were "two-story houses of conventional architectural design, such as Colonial, French Provincial or English." It held that "[t]he intrusion into this neighborhood of . . . [an]

---

[3] Waterfront Estates Dev., Inc. v. City of Palos Hills, 597 N.E.2d 641 (Ill. App. 1992); Pacesetter Homes v. Village of Olympia Fields, 244 N.E.2d 369 (Ill. App. 1968); Morristown Rd. Assocs. v. Mayor & Common Council, 394 A.2d 157 (N.J.L. Div. 1978). *See also* cases cited in note 98. *Contra* Novi v. City of Pacifica, 215 Cal. Rptr. 439 (Cal. App. 1985) (ordinance held not vague).

[4] 69 N.W.2d 217 (Wis.1955).

[5] § 11.05.

[6] 458 S.W.2d 305 (Mo. 1970). *Accord* Reid v. Architectural Bd. of Review, 192 N.E.2d 74 (Ohio App. 1963).

unusual, grotesque and nonconforming structure would have a substantial adverse effect on market values of other homes in the area."

In *Village of Hudson v. Albrecht, Inc.*,[7] the owner of a retail store brought suit claiming that an architectural review ordinance that contained look-alike and anti-look-alike requirements was facially unconstitutional. The court upheld the ordinance. It noted the "evolving trend" to grant "a more significant role" to aesthetic considerations and held that "aesthetic considerations may be taken into account by the legislative body in enacting zoning legislation." The court held the ordinance reflected an appropriate concern with the protection of property values and was not an improper delegation of legislative power.

A court that upholds an architectural design review ordinance because it protects property values may hold that a design review board cannot reject an architectural design unless it is incompatible with existing development in the community. In *Hankins v. Borough of Rockleigh*,[8] the ordinance required an "architectural style conforming with the existing residential structures and with the rural surroundings of the Borough." It prohibited modern flat roofs. The court reversed a borough council decision that refused to approve a dwelling with a partial flat roof. The court noted that the community was extremely small, that about half the structures in the community did not comply with the ordinance, and that there were several flat-roof buildings in the vicinity of the proposed flat-roof dwelling. The court held the ordinance unreasonable "in light of the actual physical development of the community."

Architectural design review ordinances may raise a free speech problem. The courts could protect architectural design as a form of commercial speech and hold that architectural design review places an excessive restriction on architectural expression. Architectural design review does more than regulate the time, place, and manner of architectural expression because it may totally exclude an architectural style. The courts could hold that the total exclusion of an architectural style is invalid as a prohibition on the content of commercial speech.

C. HISTORIC PRESERVATION.

§ 11.26 The Historic Preservation Problem.

The historic preservation movement began with the designation of historic districts for "showplace areas" containing buildings of historic architectural merit. Beacon Hill in Boston and the French Quarter in New Orleans are examples. Historic preservation now has much broader objectives. Municipalities designate areas as historic districts if they have historic associations or distinctive "period style" buildings worth preserving, even though they are more recent and do not

---

[7] 458 N.E.2d 852 (Ohio 1984).

[8] 150 A.2d 63 (N.J. App. Div. 1959).

have historic associations. Nineteenth century Victorian residential neighborhoods are an example. Historic preservation also includes municipal programs
for the designation and preservation of historic landmarks not located in historic
districts.

Historic preservation serves different purposes than zoning. As one court
pointed out, zoning regulates land use, density, and location. Historic preservation
is concerned with "the preservation of the exterior of buildings having historic
or architectural merit."[1] Historic preservation ordinances also prohibit the
demolition and require the maintenance of historic structures. These differences
in the controls included in historic preservation ordinances create different
constitutional problems than zoning.

The majority rule that aesthetics alone is a proper purpose in land use regulation
supports the regulatory purposes of historic preservation. As the Supreme Court
noted in *Penn Central*,[2] the "States and cities may enact land use restrictions
and controls to enhance the quality of life by preserving the character and
desirable aesthetic features of a city." The state courts have also held that historic
preservation controls advance a legitimate governmental purpose.

The federal government has undertaken a number of historic preservation
initiatives. The most important federal legislation is the National Historic
Preservation Act of 1966.[3] This act authorizes the Secretary of the Interior to
maintain a National Register of Historic Places, which includes historic areas,
sites, and buildings.[4] Municipalities often rely on National Register designations
as the basis for making local designations of historic districts and landmarks.

The act requires federal agencies to take into account the effect of federal
"undertakings" on historic districts, sites, and buildings listed on the National
Register.[5] The Act establishes an Advisory Council on Historic Preservation that
may comment on any federal undertaking that will have an adverse effect on
a listed historic area or property. The Council's comments are advisory and do
not bind the federal agency.

§ 11.27 Historic Districts.

§ 11.28 Enabling Legislation and Ordinances.

Although a court can imply the authority to designate historic districts from
a zoning enabling act,[1] most states have enacted legislation that authorizes the

---

[1] Mayor & Aldermen v. Anne Arundel County, 316 A.2d 807 (Md. 1974).

[2] § 2.07.

[3] 16 U.S.C. §§ 470a–470m.

[4] 16 U.S.C. § 470a.

[5] 16 U.S.C. § 470f.

[1] City of Santa Fe v. Gamble-Skogmo, Inc., 389 P.2d 13 (N.M. 1964).

designation of historic districts and their regulation. Some legislation applies to both historic districts and landmarks Most of these statutes simply include historic preservation as a permissible objective in zoning and other land use controls.[2] Other statutes authorize the designation of historic districts and the adoption of historic district regulation but leave most of the implementation details to municipalities.[3]

Some historic district enabling legislation is more detailed. It authorizes local governments to establish historic district commissions and designate historic districts and specifies the regulatory powers and procedures that are necessary for historic district regulation.[4] This legislation typically authorizes the commission to conduct a study of historic areas and make recommendations for their preservation. The governing body is authorized to act on these recommendations by designating historic districts.[5] Once an historic district is designated, owners of buildings in the district must secure a "certificate of appropriateness" from the commission for the exterior alteration or demolition of structures, and owners of land must secure a certificate for new construction. Some statutes authorize the commission to approve construction on nearby property that affects the historic district. The historic district is an overlay on the zoning ordinance, and the legislation should provide that it does not affect the zoning regulations.

Historic district ordinances implement the enabling legislation. The ordinance typically includes a purpose clause, establishes the commission, and designates the boundaries of historic districts. It also specifies the procedures and criteria for the issuance of certificates of appropriateness and includes controls on the demolition and exterior alteration of buildings within the district, whether or not they are individually of historic merit.[6] Controls on new construction, maintenance, and repair also are usually included. Under some ordinances, the commission may only delay a proposal that requires a certificate of

---

[2] Neb. Rev. Stat. § 23-114.03(14); N.M. Stat. Ann. § 3-22-2; N.Y. Gen. Mun. Law §§ 96-a; 119-dd.

[3] Miss. Code Ann. §§ 39-13-3 to 39-13-9; Mo. Stat. Ann. § 253.415;Neb. Rev. Stat. §§ 14-2001 to 14-2004. *See* Portsmouth Advocates, Inc. v. City of Portsmouth, 587 A.2d 600 (N.H. 1991) (change of historic district boundary to less restrictive district upheld).

[4] Conn. Gen. Stat. § 8-2j; Ga. Code Ann. §§ 44-10-20 to 44-10-31; 65 Ill. Comp. Stat. Ann. 5/11-48.2-1 to 11-48.2-7; Mass. Gen. L. ch. 40C; Pa. Stat. Ann. tit. 53, §§ 8001–8006. *See also* American Planning Association, Growing Smart Legislative Guidebook: Model Statutes for Planning and Management of Change § 9-301(S. Meck ed. 2002).

[5] *See* Heithaus v. Planning & Zoning Comm'n, 779 A.2d 750 (Conn. 2001) (upholding denial of application for historic district overlay zone).

[6] *See* Trustees of Union College v. Members of the Schenectady City Council, 690 N.E.2d 862 (N.Y. 1998) (city may not deny educational use the opportunity to apply fora special permit in an historic district).

appropriateness if it decides to reject it. Appeals are usually provided to the legislative body or the board of zoning adjustment.[7]

§ 11.29 Constitutionality of Historic Districts.

The courts have upheld historic district designations against substantive due process objections,[1] but the rationale for the decisions varies. These cases accept the role of aesthetics in land use regulation, but the sense in which they use the term "aesthetic" is not always clear. Historic district designations implement aesthetic purposes when the buildings in the district have attractive architectural qualities, but they also implement aesthetic objectives even when the buildings in an historic district are not architecturally attractive. In this situation, the designation prevents the intrusion of incompatible uses in an area that has a unifying historic architectural theme.

Some of the early historic district cases, though not fully embracing an aesthetic rationale, were influenced by the historic and attractive appearance of "showplace" historic settlements. In *Opinion of the Justices,*[2] the court upheld legislation designating the town of Nantucket as an historic district. It noted that "the sedate and quaint appearance of the old island town has to a large extent still remained unspoiled." Similar considerations influenced decisions upholding historic district designations of Beacon Hill in Boston and the French Quarter in New Orleans.[3] The unifying character of well-established historic districts justifies controls covering architectural details, such as the design of window panes,[4] and refusals to allow building projects that interfere with the historic design of buildings in the district.

Cases upholding historic district designations for areas that do not have venerable and "quaint" architectural features rely on broader justifications. *A-S-P Assocs. v. City of Raleigh*[5] is an example. The city designated as an historic district "the only intact nineteenth century neighborhood remaining in Raleigh

---

[7] Farash Corp. v. City of Rochester, 713 N.Y.S.2d 423 (App. Div. 2000) (upholding denial of certificate of appropriateness to demolish).

[1] Van Horn v. Town of Castine, 167 F. Supp.2d 103 (D. Mass. 2001).

[2] 128 N.E.2d 557 (Mass. 1955).

[3] Maher v. City of New Orleans, 516 F.2d 1051 (5th Cir. 1975; Figarsky v. Historic Dist. Comm'n, 368 A.2d 163 (Conn. 1976) (New England town green); City of New Orleans v. Pergament, 5 So. 2d 129 (La. 1941); Opinion of the Justices, 128 N.E.2d 563 (Mass. 1955).

[4] Harris v. Old King's Highway Regional Historic Dist. Comm'n, 658 N.E.2d 972 (Mass. (1996) (conversion of garage); Globe Newspaper Co. v. Beacon Hill Architectural Comm'n, 659 N.E.2d 710 (Mass. 1996) (statute authorizes ban on street furniture on Beacon Hill); Parker v. Beacon Hill Arch. Ass'n, 536 N.E.2d 1108 (Mass. 1989) (additional floor on rowhouse); Anderson v. Old King's Hwy. Regional Historic Dist., 493 N.E.2d 188 (Mass. 1986) (change in siding); City of Santa Fe v. Gamble-Skogmo, Inc., 389 P.2d 13 (N.M. 1964) (window pane).

[5] 258 S.E.2d 444 (N.C. 1979).

. . . composed predominantly of Victorian houses." The neighborhood was in a state of decline but was undergoing revitalization. Although it did not fully approve aesthetic purposes as the sole justification for the designation, the court upheld it because it implemented the "general welfare" by achieving a number of regulatory objectives. They included the provision of a visual and educational medium, incentives to revitalization, fostering architectural creativity by preserving outstanding architectural examples from the past, and promoting tourism.[6]

§ 11.30   Delegation of Power and Vagueness.

Delegation of power objections to historic district ordinances are similar to those made to architectural design review ordinances.[1] As in the design review cases, the objection is that the standards for granting certificates of appropriateness are too subjective aesthetically to meet delegation of power requirements. The courts rejected delegation of power objections in practically all of the historic district cases. The *A-S-P* case[2] contains the most careful review of the delegation of power problem. The court upheld the standards provided for the review of exterior changes to buildings in the historic district. It noted that the presence of members with experience and interest in architecture on the historic district commission minimized delegation of power problems. The court also adopted the rule accepted by a minority of courts, that the availability of adequate procedural safeguards in the ordinance diminished any delegation of power problems the ordinance created.[3]

The historic district ordinance provided an "incongruity" standard for the review of exterior building changes. The court characterized this standard as "contextual" and added the following comments:

> [T]he standard of "incongruity" must derive its meaning, if any, from the total physical environment of the historic district. . . . Although the neighborhood encompassed by the Historic District is to a considerable extent an architectural melange, that heterogeneity of architectural style is not such as to render the standard of "incongruity" meaningless.[4]

---

[6] *See also* Bohannan v. City of San Diego, 106 Cal. Rptr. 333 (Cal. App. 1973); City of Santa Fe v. Gamble-Skogmo, Inc., 389 P.2d 13 (N.M. 1964).

[1] § 11.25.

[2] A-S-P Assocs . v. City of Raleigh, 258 S.E.2d 444 (N.C. 1979). *See* § 11.29. *Accord* Mayes v. City of Dallas, 747 F.2d 323 (5th Cir. 1984) (facade and landscape standards); Burke v. City of Charleston, 893 F. Supp. 589 (D.S.C. 1995); South of Second Assocs. v. Georgetown, 580 P.2d 807 (Colo. 1978); Town of Deering ex rel. Bittenbender v. Tibbetts, 202 A.2d 232 (N.H. 1964). *Contra* City of Mobile v. Weinacker, 720 So.2d 953 (Ala. Civ. App. 1998) (signs; no standards in ordinance and design guidelines vague);

[3] § 6.02.

[4] 258 S.E.2d at 454.

§ 11.31   Interim Controls.

Interim controls are necessary during the time a legislative body is considering an historic district for designation. The ordinance usually authorizes the legislative body during this period to prohibit the demolition of historic buildings and to prevent building exterior changes that are inconsistent with the district's historic character. *City of Dallas v. Crownrich*[1] upheld interim controls of this type. After a landowner applied for a building permit for an apartment building, the city council adopted a resolution prohibiting the issuance of building permits in the area while they considered it for designation as an historic district. The court held that the landowner was not entitled to a writ of mandamus to compel the issuance of the permit because the city's statutory zoning and home rule powers conferred the authority to adopt the moratorium resolution. Interim controls are not likely to create a takings problem under the Supreme Court's *Lucas* decision if the landowner can make an economically viable use of the property during the interim period.

§ 11.32   The Takings Issue.

Historic district regulations can raise a takings problem. It is not troublesome when an historic district commission refuses to allow a change in the exterior features of a building. The property owner is not denied permission to build, only to build in a certain style.[1] More difficult takings questions arise when a commission denies a permit to build a new building, prohibits the demolition of a building, or requires its maintenance and repair.

However, the Supreme Court's *Penn Central* decision[2] suggests the comprehensive application of historic preservation regulations to an entire district may avoid a takings claim. The Court upheld a refusal to allow the construction of an office tower on Grand Central Station, an historic landmark. The station owners made the argument that the land mark law "is inherently incapable of producing the fair and equitable distribution of benefits and burdens of governmental action which is characteristic of zoning laws and historic-district legislation."[3] The Court did not dispute this principle, which was an apparent reference to the average reciprocity of advantage principle[4] that supports the constitutionality of land use regulations such as historic districts.

---

[1] 506 S.W.2d 654 (Tex. Civ. App. 1974). *But see* Southern Nat'l Bank v. City of Austin, 582 S.W.2d 229 (Tex. Civ. App. 1979).

[1] Van Horn v. Town of Castine, 167 F. Supp.2d 103 (D. Mass. 2001) (denial of permission to reconstruct porch; no economic damage asserted).

[2] § 2.07.

[3] *Penn Central*, 438 U.S. at 133.

[4] § 2.15.

A case decided one year after *Penn Central*, *A-S-P Assocs. v. City of Raleigh*,[5] held a certificate of appropriateness requirement in an historic district ordinance was reasonable as applied to a landowner who planned to build an office building on a vacant lot. The court held the comprehensive regulation of development in historic districts is necessary for their preservation and that the preservation of the historic setting for historic buildings is just as important as the preservation of the buildings. It noted that "this 'tout ensemble' doctrine, as it is now termed, is an integral and reasonable part of effective historic district preservation." The court noted the ordinance did not prohibit property owners from erecting new structures but only prohibited structures that were "incongruous with the historic aspects of the Historic District." It held that property owners in historic districts might not be able to develop their land for its most profitable use, but that this depreciation in value was not a taking.

Takings problems also arise in historic districts when a municipality refuses to allow the demolition of an historic building so that the owner can develop the site for a more intensive use. *Maher v. City of New Orleans*[6] held a refusal to allow the demolition of a Victorian cottage in the New Orleans French Quarter so that its owner could erect a seven-apartment complex was not a taking. The court applied traditional takings theory, and held the landowner had not shown the refusal to allow demolition totally diminished the value of the property. The court rejected a facial takings attack on a provision in the ordinance that required the reasonable maintenance and repair of buildings in the historic district. It indicated this requirement might be a taking as applied if the expense of maintaining a building was unreasonable.

This was the decision in *Lafayette Park Baptist Church v. Scott (I)*.[7] A board of adjustment upheld a decision by a landmarks commission that denied permission to demolish a substandard building in an historic district. The board found the building was in need of extensive rehabilitation but had not degenerated structurally beyond the feasible limits for rehabilitation, considering its historic and architectural significance. The court reversed because it found that restoration was not economically feasible. It held the effect of the demolition on the historic district was a "legitimate consideration" but could not be the "sole basis" for refusing to allow demolition. Voluntary restoration actions by other property owners in the district "did not warrant imposing similar conduct on another

---

[5] 258 S.E.2d 444 (N.C. 1979). *See also* Figarsky v. Historic Dist. Comm'n, 368 A.2d 163 (Conn. 1976) (no showing that taking occurred); Rebman v. City of Springfield, 250 N.E.2d 282 (Ill. App. 1969) (noting that creation of historic district enhanced value of property).; § 11.29

[6] 516 F.2d 1051 (5th Cir. 1975. *See also* First Presbyterian Church v. City Council, 360 A.2d 257 (Pa. Commw. 1976).

[7] 553 S.W.2d 856 (Mo. App. 1977). *See also* Lafayette Park Baptist Church v. Board of Adjustment (II), 599 S.W.2d 61 (Mo. App. 1980) (upholding refusal to allow demolition when board on remand found rehabilitation economically feasible); § 11.35

landowner or precluding his effective use of the property." This case is consistent with the holding in the Supreme Court's *Lucas* decision that a restriction on property that denies a landowner all economically viable uses is a taking per se.

§ 11.33 Historic Landmarks.

Many municipalities have adopted ordinances for the preservation of historic landmarks located outside historic districts. Since *Penn Central*,[1] which upheld the New York City landmarks preservation law, the courts have accepted the aesthetic and other regulatory purposes served by historic landmark preservation.

§ 11.34 Enabling Legislation and Ordinances.

Fewer states have adopted historic landmark legislation, which may authorize historic landmark regulation in a separate ordinance[1] or in the zoning ordinance.[2] Historic landmark preservation statutes and ordinances authorize landmark designation[3] and include regulatory controls similar to those that are adopted for historic districts.[4] Historic landmark owners must obtain a certificate of appropriateness for exterior alteration, demolition, and new construction. The repair and rehabilitation of historic landmarks is usually required. The statute or ordinance may authorize variances from restrictions on historic landmarks that do not allow the owner a reasonable return.

Landmark preservation laws also raise delegation of power and interim control problems.[5] The courts have held the standards provided for historic landmark designation are not an unconstitutional delegation of legislative power.[6] Absent

---

[1] § 2.07

[1] Cal. Gov't Code §§ 25373, 37361; La. Rev. Stat. §§ 25:751 to 25:767.

[2] 55 Ill. Comp. Stat. Ann. 5/5-30004; N.J. Stat. Ann. § 40:55D-65(i). *See* Reiter v. City of Beloit, 947 P.2d 425 (Kan. 1997) (upholding zoning change for commercial use adjacent to historic residence); Estate of Neuberger v. Township of Middletown, 521 A.2d 1336 (N.J. App. Div. 1987).

[3] Mastroianni v. Strada, 571 N.Y.S.2d 55 (App. Div. 1991) (upholding designation of historic home); Handicraft Block Ltd. Partnership v. City of Minneapolis, 611 N.W.2d 16 (Minn. App. 2000) (designation held quasi-judicial); Schubert Organization, Inc. v. Landmarks Preservation Comm'n, 570 N.Y.S.2d 504 (App. Div. 1991) (upholding designation of theaters in Manhattan theater district).

[4] § 11.28. *See also* American Planning Association, Growing Smart Legislative Guidebook: Model Statutes for Planning and Management of Change § 9-301(S. Meck ed. 2002).

[5] *See* §§ 11.30–11.31.

[6] Citizens Comm. to Save Historic Rhodes Tavern v. District of Columbia Dep't of Hous. & Community Dev., 432 A.2d 710 (D.C. App. 1981) (held not vague claim); Lafayette Park Baptist Church v. Board of Adjustment (II), 599 S.W.2d 61 (Mo. App. 1980); County of Stutsman v. State Historical Soc'y, 371 N.W.2d 321 (N.D. 1985). *Contra* Texas Antiquities Comm. v. Dallas County Community College Dist., 554 S.W.2d 924 (Tex. 1977).

statutory authority, a municipality may not delay the demolition of an historic building,[7] or designate the interior of a building as a landmark.[8]

§ 11.35 The Takings Issue.

Historic landmark preservation creates takings problems similar to those raised by historic districts, but they are more difficult because historic landmark preservation outside historic districts does not confer an average reciprocity of advantage. *Maher v. City of New Orleans*[1] and *Penn Central Transportation Co. v. New York City*[2] are the principal cases that considered a takings problem created by historic landmark regulation. *Maher* held a refusal to allow demolition was not a taking when it did not totally diminish the value of the property. This is still acceptable takings doctrine, and other courts have applied it to uphold refusals to allow demolition.[3]

In *Penn Central,* the U.S. Supreme Court held the city landmarks commission's rejection of a high-rise office building over Grand Central Terminal, which it had designated as an historic landmark, was not a taking. The Court held the Terminal owners did not have an expectation in the development of the airspace over the Terminal that was protected under the takings clause. It also held the burdens imposed on the Terminal owners by the landmark designation were offset by benefits the landmark law conferred on them by improving the "quality of life" in the city.

The Court held the landmark designation did not interfere with the present use of the Terminal and noted that the Terminal's owners conceded that it earned a reasonable return. Nor had they applied for approval of a less intrusive structure in the Terminal's airspace. *Penn Central* does not control the more typical case,

---

[7] People ex rel. Marbro Corp. v. Ramsey, 171 N.E.2d 246 (Ill. App. 1960). *See also* Lawrence Preservation Alliance, Inc. v. Allen Realty, Inc. (II), 819 P.2d 138 (Kan. App. 1991) (failure to give notice of hearing on demolition held arbitrary); Keystone Assocs. v. Moerdler, 224 N.E.2d 700 (N.Y. 1966).

[8] United Artists Theater Circuit, Inc. v. City of Philadelphia, 635 A.2d 612 (Pa. 1993).

[1] 516 F.2d 1051 (5th Cir. 1975), (court noted Maher did not show sale of the property was impracticable, that commercial rental could not provide reasonable rate of return, or that other potential use of property was foreclosed), discussed in § 11.30.

[2] 438 U.S. 104 (1978), discussed in § 2.07.

[3] Rector, Wardens & Vestry of St. Bartholomew's Ch. v. City of New York, 914 F.2d 348 (2d Cir. 1990); MB Assocs. v. District of Columbia Dep't of License, Investigation & Inspection, 456 A.2d 344 (D.C. App. 1982); 900 G Street Assocs. v. Department of Hous. & Community Dev., 430 A.2d 1387 (D.C. App. 1981); Lubelle v. Rochester Preserv. Bd., 551 N.Y.S.2d 127 (App. Div. 1990). *See also* Allen Realty, Inc. v. City of Lawrence (I), 790 P.2d 948 (Kan. App. 1990) (temporary denial of demolition permit not a taking); Historic Albany Found. v. Coyne, 558 N.Y.S.2d 986 (App. Div. 1990) (upholding submission of development plan as condition to demolition); State *ex rel.* BSW Dev. Group v. City of Dayton, 699 N.E.2d 1271 (Ohio 1998) (building structurally sound and was in use several years before denial of demolition permit).

in which an historic landmark owner would like to demolish an historic landmark and build a more intensive structure on the landmark site.[4] In addition, *Lucas* now requires courts to find a per se taking if a restriction on an historic landmark leaves a landowner without a reasonable use of the property. This problem did not arise in *Penn Central.* Standard takings rules apply if a per se taking does not occur. Cases since *Lucas* have reversed refusals to demolish historic landmark structures when there was proof that renovation of the structure would be economically feasible, or when there were profitable alternatives to demolition.[5] A court of appeals has upheld the denial of building permits to build townhouses on the site of an historic landmark.[6] The property was not denied all economically beneficial use under the *Lucas* per se takings rule, and there was no taking under the *Penn Central* multi-factor takings test.

§ 11.36 Maintenance and Repair.

Maher indicated a requirement for the maintenance of an historic building could raise an as-applied takings problem, and several cases have considered this question. *Lafayette Park Baptist Church v. Scott (I)*[1] is an influential decision. A board of adjustment refused to allow the demolition of an historic building that was in a serious state of disrepair. The building was located in an historic district. The court reversed and held an historic district ordinance "must be interpreted to authorize demolition when the condition of the structure is such that the economics of restoration preclude the landowner from making any reasonable economic use of the property." This case is consistent with the holding in the Supreme Court's *Lucas* decision that a restriction on property that denies a landowner all economically viable uses is a taking per se. It is also consistent with decisions that upheld a takings objection to maintenance and repair requirements in housing codes.[2] Other cases applied the *Lafayette (I)* rule to strike

---

[4] *Accord* United Artists Theater Circuit, Inc. v. City of Philadelphia, 635 A.2d 612 (Pa. 1993) (designation of theater as historic landmark; applying *Penn Central* and Pennsylvania takings law).

[5] Keeler v. Mayor & City Council, 940 F. Supp. 879 (D. Md. 1996) (taking when no economically feasible rehabilitation plan possible); Park Home v. City of Williamsport, 680 A.2d 835 (Pa. 1996) (upheld; owners did not consider sale of property as alternative to demolition); City of Pittsburgh, Historic Review Comm'n v. Weinberg, 676 A.2d 207 (Pa. 1996) (cost of renovation would not exceed value after renovation, owner knew of historic designation when bought property and could sell it for a profit).

[6] District Intown Props. Ltd. Partnership. v. District of Columbia, 198 F.3d 874 (D.C. Cir. 1999).

[1] 553 S.W.2d 856 (Mo. App. 1977), also discussed in § 11.32. *See also* Lafayette Park Baptist Church v. Board of Adjustment (II), 599 S.W.2d 61 (Mo. App. 1980) (upholding refusal to allow demolition when board on remand found rehabilitation economically feasible).

[2] City of St. Louis v. Brune, 515 S.W.2d 471 (Mo. 1974).

down refusals to allow the demolition of substandard historic buildings outside historic districts.[3]

§ 11.37   Religious Uses.

Takings problems also arise when municipalities apply historic landmark ordinances to religious uses. The takings problem is complicated because religious uses are not-for-profit, so a takings test that turns on a denial of all economically beneficial use is not helpful.

Two New York cases decided before the Supreme Court's 1987 takings trilogy were the first important decisions that considered the validity of an historic designation as applied to religious property. In the first case, *Lutheran Church in Am. v. City of New York*,[1] the court held invalid the city's refusal to allow demolition of an historic landmark the church found inadequate and its replacement with an office building because the refusal "would prevent or seriously interfere with the carrying out of the charitable purpose." Here the proof of "economic hardship . . . [was] substantially unchallenged." The court held the city had attempted to "add this property to the public use by purely and simply invading the owner's right to own and manage." The court noted the landmark law's guarantee of a reasonable return did not apply to landmarks owned by religious groups.

The New York court rejected a takings claim in *Society for Ethical Culture v. Spatt*,[2] a case similar to *Lutheran Church* decided after *Penn Central*. The court distinguished *Lutheran Church* by holding that "landmark designations, if not unreasonable, are not an undue imposition under the police power." The Society had not shown the "compelling circumstances" present in *Lutheran Church* and had not shown the only solution to the building's inadequacy was demolition of the protected facade. The Society complained instead "that the landmark stands as an effective bar against putting the property to its most lucrative use." The court held the constitution does not guarantee a landowner the most beneficial use of its property.

Later takings cases also considered claims that a landmark designation violated the free exercise of religion clause in the federal constitution. An important post-1987 Second Circuit case rejected a takings claim in a case, similar to *Spatt*,

---

[3] Foundation for San Francisco's Architectural Heritage v. City & County of San Francisco, 165 Cal. Rptr. 401 (Cal. App. 1980); Citizens Comm'n to Save Historic Rhodes Tavern v. District of Columbia Dep't of Hous. & Urban Dev., 432 A.2d 710 (D.C. App. 1981); Broadview Apts. Co. v. Commission for Historical & Architectural Preservation, 433 A.2d 1214 (Md. App. 1981); State v. Erickson, 301 N.W.2d 324 (Minn. 1981). *But see* Mayor & Aldermen v. Anne Arundel County, 316 A.2d 807 (Md. 1974).

[1] 316 N.E.2d 305 (N.Y. 1974).

[2] 415 N.E.2d 922 (N.Y. 1980). *See also* Manhattan Club v. Landmarks Preservation Comm'n, 273 N.Y.S.2d 848 (Sup. Ct. 1966).

where New York City denied a church permission to demolish a "community house" and build an office tower on the site.[3] The court applied the *Spatt* test and found the church could still make use of the building and had exaggerated repair costs. The court also held there was no violation of the Free Exercise of Religion clause of the federal constitution. It relied heavily on the Supreme Court's decision in *Employment Div., Dep't of Human Resources v. Smith,*[4] which held the Free Exercise clause does not prohibit compliance with a valid and neutral law that is generally applicable.

The Supreme Court denied certiorari in the Second Circuit decision[5] and on the same day remanded for reconsideration, in light of *Smith,* a Washington Supreme Court decision that had taken a contrary position on the Free Exercise issue.[6] The Washington case held a landmark law that required a church to secure approval of a change in its facade interfered with the practice of religion. Aesthetic and cultural interests in preservation were not sufficiently compelling state interests to overcome the religious infringement. These actions indicate the Court favors the Second Circuit holding, and reads its *Smith* decision to mean that landmark designation laws do not present a Free Exercise problem. Nevertheless, on remand, the Washington Supreme Court reaffirmed its holding that the landmark designation violated the free exercise clause in both the federal and state constitutions.[7]

The California Supreme Court held that statutes allowing religious organizations to exempt themselves from landmark designation did not violate the First Amendment Establishment Clause.[8] The court held that landmark designation was a potential burden on religious uses. The court also held the exemption did not constitute an unconstitutional advancement of religion by the state just because a property may be used to propagate a religious message. It was also irrelevant that the owner of the religious landmark might enjoy an economic advantage over secular owners of landmark properties.

---

[3] Rector, Wardens & Vestry of St. Bartholomew's Ch. v. City of New York, 914 F.2d 348 (2d Cir. 1990).*See also* First Church of Christ, Scientist v. Historic District Comm'n, 738 A.2d 224 (Conn. Super.), *aff'd on basis of trial court opinion,* 737 A.2d 989 (Conn. App. 1999) (upholding denial of permit to place vinyl siding on historic church).

[4] 494 U.S. 872 (1990).

[5] 499 U.S. 905 (1991).

[6] First Covenant Ch. v. City of Seattle, 787 P.2d 1352 (Wash. 1990), *vacated and remanded,* 499 U.S. 901 (1991), *adhered to on remand,* 840 P.2d 174 (Wash. 1992).

[7] First Covenant Church of Seattle v. City of Seattle, 840 P.2d 174 (Wash. 1992). *Accord* Keeler v. Mayor & City Council, 940 F. Supp. 879 (D. Md. 1996); *Accord* Society of Jesus v. Boston Landmarks Comm'n, 564 N.E.2d 571 (Mass. 1990) (designation of church interior as religious landmark violates state constitutional provision protection religious worship); First United Methodist Church v. Hearing Examiner for Seattle Landmarks Preservation Bd., 916 P.2d 374 (Wash. 1996).

[8] East Bay Asian Local Development Corp. v. State of California, 13 P.3d 1122 (Cal. 2000).

§ 11.38 Transfer of Development Rights.

Municipalities have adopted a land use control technique known as the transfer of development rights (TDR) to resolve the takings problem created by historic landmark preservation. A TDR program for historic landmark preservation is quite simple. Historic landmark buildings are often undersized for their site and do not use up the building densities permitted by the zoning ordinance. A TDR program transfers unused densities at landmark sites to transfer sites or areas designated by the municipality, which may be nearby or in other areas of the municipality. Under one variant, the owner of the transfer site purchases the unused development rights at the landmark site from the landmark owner. This payment provides the compensation necessary to avoid a takings objection. Under another variant, the municipality creates an agency with the authority to acquire development rights from landmark owners. The agency later sells these rights to landowners at transfer sites.

TDR programs present a number of constitutional problems. A municipality may need to downzone the transfer sites in order to make the purchase of development rights at these sites attractive. A court could hold that a downzoning for this purpose is unconstitutional.[1] A TDR program may also violate the statutory requirement that zoning regulations must be uniform within zoning districts. Developers at transfer site areas build at existing zoning densities without purchasing development rights but build more intensively if development rights are purchased. An answer to the uniformity objection is that transfer site areas where landowners can purchase development rights are similar to planned unit developments, where uses and densities are mixed. The courts have rejected uniformity objections to regulations that allow planned unit developments.[2] The purchaser of development rights at a transfer site also secures an increase in the zoning density previously allowed on her property. This density increase may be an unconstitutional spot zoning.[3]

Takings problems also arise in TDR programs when an historic landmark owner claims the sale of his development rights does not compensate him for the restrictions the landmark designation imposes on his property. The most important of these cases arose in New York City, which has a TDR program for historic landmarks. *Fred F. French Inv. Co. v. City of New York*[4] was the first case. It applies to, though it did not involve, the use of TDRs for historic landmarks. The city adopted an amendment to its zoning ordinance that classified

---

[1] §§ 6.36–6.38.

[2] § 9.26.

[3] §§ 6.28–6.35. *See* Dupont Circle Citizens Ass'n v. District of Columbia Zoning Comm'n, 355 A.2d 550 (D.C. App. 1976) (approving TDR transfer).

[4] 350 N.E.2d 381 (N.Y.) (explaining that ordinance was invalidated as deprivation of property without due process of law).

two private parks in a multifamily complex as parks open to public use. The court found a taking, but the city argued its TDR program resolved the takings objection. Under this program, the owner of the development rights on the restricted park site could transfer them to an area in midtown Manhattan. The program allowed limited density increases in the transfer area as-of-right, but additional density increases required a public hearing and municipal approval.

The court noted that development rights "are a potentially valuable and even a transferable commodity" that a court should not disregard when it considers a takings claim. But it believed the TDR program did not resolve the takings objection to the ordinance that restricted the use of the park:

> But severed, the development rights are a double abstraction until they are actually attached to a receiving parcel, yet to be identified, acquired, and subject to the contingent approvals of administrative agencies, events which may never happen because of the contingencies of the market and the contingencies and exigencies of administrative action.[5]

The court summarized its holding by noting the severance of the development rights "rendered their value so uncertain and contingent, as to deprive the property owner of their practical usefulness, except under rare and perhaps coincidental circumstances." The court was sympathetic to TDR programs that protected an owner's development rights in his property and suggested that "just compensation . . . instantly and in money" would avoid a takings problem.

The New York court next considered the takings problems created by a TDR program for historic landmarks in its decision in the *Penn Central* case.[6] The TDR program authorized the transfer of development rights from the Terminal to sites in the immediate vicinity. The court noted the value of the transferred rights might not equal the value of the development rights at the original site. It did not find this possibility fatal because land use regulation always diminishes the value of property. Diminution in value is unconstitutional only if a land use regulation does not allow any reasonable use. Transferred development rights need only provide "reasonable compensation."

The court also noted the landmark preservation ordinance allowed the continued productive use of the Terminal. "In addition, the development rights were made transferable to numerous sites in the vicinity of the terminal, several owned by Penn Central, and at least one or two" were suitable for office building construction. The court distinguished *French* because the transferred development rights in that case were left in "legal limbo."[7]

---

[5] *Id.* at 388.

[6] 366 N.E.2d 1271 (N.Y. 1977).

[7] *See also* A Local & Regional Monitor v. City of Los Angeles, 16 Cal. Rptr. 2d 358 (Cal. App. 1993) (upheld density transfer authorized by agreement with city); City of Hollywood v. Hollywood, Inc., 432 So.2d 1332 (Fla. App. 1983) (upholding up TDR transfer in development

The Supreme Court gave little attention to the TDR program because it held a taking had not occurred.[8] It indicated the transferred development rights might not have avoided a takings objection, but that they could mitigate whatever financial burden the landmark designation imposed.

Several states now authorize TDR programs. A statute may simply provide the authority for TDR without providing detailed requirements for its implementation.[9] Other statutes contain quite detailed requirements for TDR programs.[10] For example, the Illinois law establishes the development right as the density allowed under the zoning ordinance, and requires the execution of a conservation easement against the landmark and in favor of the municipality before the TDR option can be exercised.[11] New York has adopted a TDR statute for the preservation of historic resources that has a number of safeguards.[12] For example, a TDR ordinance must be adopted in accordance with a comprehensive plan, the receiving district must have adequate public facilities and other resources to accommodate the transferred development rights, the impact of TDR on affordable housing must be considered, and the local government must produce a generic environmental impact statement on the receiving area under its state environmental assessment law and keep it updated. Procedures are specified in detail, a TDR development bank is authorized and the assessed value of property must be adjusted for the transfer.

---

project on coast); W.J.F. Realty Corp. v. State, 672 N.Y.S.2d 1007 (Sup. Ct. 1998) (upholding TDR program in Pine Barrens), *affirmed for reasons stated by trial court*, 710 N.Y.S.2d 249 (App. Div. 1999).

[8] 438 U.S. 104 (1978). *See* § 2.07. *See also* Suitum v Tahoe Regional Planning Agency, 520 U.S. 725 (takings claim against TDR program held not ripe).

[9] Idaho Code § 67-4619.

[10] Ariz. Rev. Stat. Ann. § 9-462.01(12);P.R. Laws Ann. tit. 21, § 4622; S.D. Codified Laws § 1.19B-26;Tenn. Code Ann. § 3-7-101(a)(2); Wash. Rev. Code § 36.70A.090 (comprehensive plan should provide for innovative techniques including TDRs). *See also* American Planning Association, Growing Smart Legislative Guidebook: Model Statutes for Planning and Management of Change § 9-401 (S. Meck ed. 2002) (model TDR statute).

[11] 65 Ill. Comp. Stat. Ann. § 5/11-48.2-1 to 48.2-7.

[12] N.Y. Gen. City Law § 20-f; N.Y. Town Law § 261-a.

REFERENCES

Books and Monographs

J. Costonis, Icons and Aliens: Law, Aesthetics, and Environmental Change (1989).

T. Daniels & D. Bowers, Holding Our Ground: Protection America's Farms and Farmland (1997).

C. Duerksen, Aesthetics and Land Use Controls, American Planning Ass'n, Planning Advisory Serv. Rep. No. 399 (1986).

C. Duerksen & R.M. Gobel, Aesthetics, Community Character, and the Law, American Planning Ass'n, Planning Advisory Serv. Rep. No. 489/490 (1999).

C. Floyd & P. Shedd, Highway Beautification: The Environmental Movement's Greatest Failure (1979).

P. Glassford, Appearance Codes for Small Communities, American Planning Ass'n, Planning Advisory Serv. Rep. No. 379 (1983).

F. James & D. Gale, Zoning for Sale: A Critical Analysis of Transferable Development Rights Programs (Urban Institute, 1977).

E. Kelly & G. Raso, Sign Regulations for Small and Midsize Communities: A Planners Guide and A Model Ordinance, American Planning Ass'n, Planning Advisory Serv. Rep. No. 419 (1989).

Mandelker, Sign Regulation and Free Speech: Spooking the Doppelganger in Trends in Land Use Law from A to Z Ch. 3 (American Bar Ass'n, P. Salkin ed. 2001).

D. Mandelker & W. Ewald, Street Graphics and the Law (1988).

M. Morris, Innovative Tools for Historic Preservation (American Planning Ass'n, Planning Advisory Serv., Rep. No. 438, 1992).

Morrison, Sign Regulation, in Protecting Free Speech and Expression: The First Amendment and Land Use Law (American Bar Ass'n, D. Mandelker & R. Rubin eds. 2001).

R. Olshansky, Planning for Hillside Development, American Planning Ass'n, Planning Advisory Serv. Rep. No. 466 (1997).

R. Pruetz, Saved by Development (1997) (nationwide review of TDR programs).

R. Roddewig, Preparing a Historic Preservation Ordinance, American Planning Ass'n, Planning Advisory Serv. Rep. No. 374 (1983).

Articles

Ashe, Reflecting the Best of Our Aspirations: Protecting Modern and Post-Modern Architecture, 15 Cardozo Arts & Ent. L.J. 69 (1997) (has summaries of historic preservation ordinances in several cities).

Babcock & Theriaque, Landmarks Preservation Ordinances: Are the Religious Clauses Violated by Their Application to Religious Properties?, 7 J. Land Use & Envt'l L. 165 (1992).

Bowers, Historic Preservation Law Concerning Private Property, 30 Urb. Law. 405 (1998).

Breitel, A Judicial View of Transferable Development Rights, Land Use L. & Zoning Dig., Vol. 30, No. 2, at 5 (1978).

Callies, Historic Preservation Law in the United States, 32 Envt. L. Reptr. 10348 (2002).

Carmella, Houses of Worship and Religious Liberty: Constitutional Limits to Landmark Preservation and Architectural Review, 36 Vill. L. Rev. 401 (1991).

Costonis, The Chicago Plan: Incentive Zoning and the Preservation of Urban Landmarks, 85 Harv. L. Rev. 574 (1972).

Costonis, Development Rights Transfer: An Exploratory Essay, 83 Yale L.J. 75 (1973).

Costonis, Law and Aesthetics: A Critique and Reformulation of the Dilemmas, 80 Mich. L. Rev. 355 (1982).

Duerksen, Drafting and Administering Historic Preservation Ordinances, 8 Zoning & Plan. L. Rep. 97, 105 (1985).

Dukeminier, Zoning for Aesthetic Objectives: A Reappraisal, 20 Law & Contemp. Probs. 218 (1955).

Floyd, The Takings Issue in Billboard Control, 3 Wash. U.J.L. & Pol'y 357 (2000).

Gerard, Election Signs and Time Limits, 3 Wash. U. J.L. & Pol'y 379 (2000).

Gerstenblith, Architect as Artist: Artist's Rights and Historic Preservation, 12 Cardozo Arts & Ent. L.J. 431 (1994).

Gold, The Welfare Economics of Historic Preservation, 8 Conn. L. Rev. 348 (1976).

Homer, Landmarking Religious Institutions: The Burden of Rehabilitation and the Loss of Religious Freedom, 28 Urb. Law. 327 (1996).

Juergensmeyer, Nicholas & Leebrick, Transferable Development Rights and Alternatives After *Suitum*, 30 Urb. Law. 441 (1998).

Karp, The Evolving Meaning of Aesthetics in Land-Use Regulation, 15 Colum. J. Envtl. L. 307 (1990).

Linder, New Directions for Preservation Law: Creating an Environment Worth Experiencing, 20 Envt'l L. 4 (1990).

Marcus, Air Rights in New York City: TDR, Zoning Lot Merger and the Well-Considered Plan, 50 Brooklyn L. Rev. 867 (1984).

Marcus, The Grand Slam Grand Central Terminal Decision: A Euclid for Landmarks, Favorable Notice for TDR and a Resolution of the Regulatory Taking Impasse, 7 Ecology L.Q. 731 (1978).

Merriam, Making TDR Work, 56 N.C.L. Rev. 77 (1978).

Miller, Transferable Development Rights in the Constitutional Landscape: Has Penn Central Failed to Weather The Storm? 39 Nat. Resources J. 459 (1999).

Netherton, The Due Process Issue in Zoning for Historic Preservation, 19 Urb. Law. 77 (1987).

Netter & Barry, Zoning for Historic Preservation, 13 Zon. & Plan. L. Rep. 9 (1990).

Nivala, The Future For Our Past: Preserving Landmark Preservation, 5 N.Y.U. Envtl. L.J. 83 (1996).

Poole & Kobert, Architectural Appearance Review Regulations and the First Amendment: The Constitutionally Infirm "Excessive Difference" Test, 12 Zoning & Plan. L. Rev. 89 (1989).

Symposium, Preserving, Conserving, and Reusing Historic Properties, 12 Urb. Law. 1 (1980).

Weinstein, The Myth of Ministry v. Mortar: A Legal and Policy Analysis of Landmark Designation of Religious Institutions, 65 Temp. L. Rev. 91 (1992).

Williams, Subjectivity, Expression and Privacy: Problems of Aesthetic Regulation, 62 Minn. L. Rev. 1 (1977).

Ziegler, The Transfer of Development Rights, 18 Zon. & Plan. L. Rep. 61, 69 (1995).

Ziegler, Visual Environment Regulation and Derivative Human Values: The Emerging Rational Basis for Modern Aesthetic Doctrine, 9 Zoning & Plan. L. Rep. 17 (1986).

Student Work

Note, Applying Historic Preservation Ordinances to Church Property: Protecting the Past and Preserving the Constitution, 63 N.C.L. Rev. 404 (1985).

Note, Architectural Expression: Police Power and the First Amendment, 16 Urb. L. Ann. 273 (1979).

Note, Architecture, Aesthetic Zoning, and the First Amendment, 28 Stan. L. Rev. 179 (1975).

Note, Banking on TDRs: The Government's Role as Banker of Transferable Development Rights, 73 N.Y.U. L. Rev. 1329 (1998).

Note, Banning Portable Signs for Aesthetic Reasons, 17 Stetson L. Rev. 829 (1988).

Note, Caught Between Scalia and the Deep Blue Lake: The Takings Clause and Transferable Development Rights Programs, 83 Minn. L. Rev. 815 (1999).

Note, Development Rights Transfer and Landmarks Preservation Providing a Sense of Orientation, 9 Urb. L. Ann. 131 (1975).

Note, Free Exercise, Free Expression, and Landmarks Preservation, 91 Colum. L. Rev. 181 (1991).

Note, Historic Districts: Preserving City Neighborhoods for the Privileged, 60 N.Y.U. L. Rev. 64 (1985).

Note, Landmarks as Cultural Property: An Appreciation of New York City, 44 Rutgers L. Rev. 427 (1992).

Note, Making Sense of Billboard Law: Justifying Prohibitions and Exemptions, 88 Mich. L. Rev. 2482 (1990).

Note, *Members of the City Council v. Taxpayers for Vincent:* The Constitutionality of Prohibiting Temporary Sign Posting on Public Property to Advance Local Aesthetic Concerns, 34 DePaul L. Rev. 197 (1984).

Note, Municipal Regulation of Political Signs: Balancing First Amendment Rights Against Aesthetic Concerns, 45 Drake L. Rev. 767 (1997).

Note, Preservation of Historic Landmarks, 92 Harv. L. Rev. 222 (1978).

Note, Preserving the Past: Historic Preservation Regulations and the Taking Clause, 34 Wash. U.J. Urb. & Contemp. L. 297 (1988).

Note, Religious Landmark Preservation Under the First and Fifth Amendments: *St. Bartholomew's Church v. City of New York,* 65 St. John's L. Rev. 553 (1991).

Note, A Sense of Time and Place: The Past, Present, and Future of the Seattle Landmarks Preservation Ordinance, 17 Va. Envtl. L.J. 415 (1998).

Note, The Unconstitutionality of Transferable Development Rights, 84 Yale L.J. 1001 (1975).

Note, Unsightly Politics: Aesthetics, Sign Ordinances, and Homeowners' Speech in *City of Ladue v. Gilleo,* 20 Harv. Envtl. L. Rev. 473 (1996).

Note, You Can't Build That Here: The Constitutionality of Aesthetic Zoning and Architectural Review, 58 Fordham L. Rev. 1013 (1990).

Comment, Beyond the Eye of the Beholder: A New Majority of Jurisdictions Authorize Aesthetic Regulation, 48 UMKC L. Rev. 125 (1980).

Comment, Billboard Regulation After *Metromedia* and *Lucas,* 31 Hous. L. Rev. 1555 (1995).

Comment, Florida's Local Historic Preservation Ordinances: Maintaining Flexibility While Avoiding Vagueness Claims, 25 Fla. St. U. L. Rev. 1017 (1998).

Comment, For Whom the Bell Tolls: Religious Properties as Landmarks Under the First Amendment, 8 Pace Envt'l L. Rev. 579 (1991).

Comment, The Free Exercise Clause and Historic Preservation Law: Suggestions For a More Coherent Free Exercise Analysis, 72 Tul. L. Rev. 1767 (1998).

Comment, From *Penn Central* to *United Artists' I & II,* The Rise to Immunity of Historic Preservation Designation From Successful Challenges, 22 B.C. Envtl. Aff. L. Rev. 593 (1995).

Comment, Past, Present, and Future Constitutional Challenges to Transferable Development Rights, 74 Wash. L. Rev. 825 (1999).

Comment, San Francisco's Downtown Plan: Environmental and Urban Design Values in Central Business District Regulation, 12 Ecology L.Q. 511 (1985).

Comment, Strange Brew: The State of Commercial Speech Jurisprudence Before and After (44 Liquormart, Inc. v. Rhode Island), 47 Case W. Res. L. Rev. 681 (1997).

Comment, Transferable Development Rights, TRPA, and Takings: The Role of TDRs in the Constitutional Takings Analysis, 30 McGeorge L. Rev. 201 (1998).

Comment, Zoning Law: Architectural Expression and the First Amendment, 76 Marq. L. Rev. 439 (1993).

Chapter 12

ENVIRONMENTAL LAND USE REGULATION

Synopsis

A. ENVIRONMENTAL LAND USE PROGRAMS

§ 12.01   An Overview.
§ 12.02   Slope and View Protection Ordinances.
§ 12.03   Groundwater Protection.
§ 12.04   Critical Area Controls.

B. WETLANDS.

§ 12.05   State and Local Programs.
§ 12.06   Clean Water Act Permit.
§ 12.07   The Takings Issue.

C. FLOODPLAINS.

§ 12.08   State and Local Programs.
§ 12.09   The Takings Issue.

D. PRESERVATION OF AGRICULTURAL LAND.

§ 12.10   Federal, State and Local Programs.
§ 12.11   Right-to-Farm Laws.
§ 12.12   Agricultural Zoning.
§ 12.13   The Takings Issue.

E. COASTAL SETBACK LEGISLATION.

§ 12.14   National and State Programs.
§ 12.15   The Takings Issue.

E. TRANSFER OF DEVELOPMENT RIGHTS.

§ 12.16   Transfer of Development Rights.

A. ENVIRONMENTAL LAND USE PROGRAMS

§ 12.01   An Overview.

Federal, state, and local governments have adopted a number of regulatory programs for the protection of environmental and natural resource areas. They include wetland and floodplain regulation and zoning for the protection of agricultural land. Though these programs are similar because they apply to environmentally important areas, they serve different regulatory purposes. Wetland regulation imposes restrictive controls in wetland areas to preserve their environmental function by keeping them free from development. Floodplain regulation imposes restrictive controls on development in floodways and adjacent floodplains to prevent loss of life and property damage from flooding. Agricultural zoning restricts nonagricultural development to preserve agricultural areas.

(5th Ed.—02/03)

12–1

Ordinances that restrict development on hillside slopes to control erosion are another example, as are view protection ordinances.

Unlike traditional zoning, there is a strong state and federal presence in environmental land use regulation. Federal and state intervention varies with the environmental resource that is protected. A federal program administered under the Clean Water Act requires dredge and fill permits for development in wetland areas. A federal flood insurance program has encouraged the enactment of floodplain regulations by municipalities throughout the country. Many states have regulatory programs for wetlands and floodplains, and they often authorize local regulation that complies with state statutory criteria. Agricultural zoning is usually included in local zoning ordinances, and many states have related agricultural land protection programs.

The National Coastal Zone Management Act[1] provides funding for state coastal management programs. The statute authorizes land use controls in state programs, and several coastal states have incorporated wetlands and floodplain regulation in their coastal programs. States have also adopted beachfront management statutes that require setbacks in coastal areas.

Environmental land use regulation presents important taking problems. These programs had raised taking problems under the harm-benefit rule, which invalidates regulations that provide regulatory benefits for the general public but concentrate their development restrictions on a limited number of landowners. The Supreme Court rejected the harm-benefit rule in the *Lucas* case,[2] but adopted a rule that a land use regulation is a per se taking if it leaves a landowner without an economically beneficial use of her land. The per se takings rule could invalidate environmental land use regulations because they often impose severe restrictions on the development of property. However, the Supreme Court in *Lake Tahoe*[3] indicated the *Lucas* rule would be confined to "rare" cases, and that the multifactor *Penn Central* takings rule would apply in most cases.

Penn Central's "whole parcel" rule[4] is an important issue in environmental land use regulation takings cases. Environmental requirements will often affect only part of the property, as when part of a property is wetlands covered by restrictive wetlands regulations. The ability to develop the remainder of the property may avoid a successful takings claim.

---

[1] 16 U.S.C. §§ 1451–1474.

[2] § 2.21.

[3] Tahoe-Sierra Preservation Council, Inc. v. Tahoe Regional Planning Agency, 535 U.S. 302 (2002).

[4] § 2.17.

§ 12.02   Slope and View Protection Ordinances.

Regulations that protect slopes from development and that protect views serve important environmental values. The control of development on steep slopes is essential to prevent landslides, control the risk of fire, and prevent erosion and drainage problems. Hillside development ordinances may include a variety of regulations. They can include regrading and re-engineering requirements, grading improvements, setbacks from ridge lines, and restrictions on the removal of vegetation and forest to protect natural resources. The ordinance may also reduce densities or prohibit development altogether in some areas in order to protect hillside slopes from disturbance.

Ordinances of this type present potential takings problems, though a taking should not occur if a reasonable use of the property is possible despite the restrictions. The courts have no difficulty finding that slope protection serves a legitimate governmental purpose. A takings claim based on economic lass is also not likely to succeed. Land use restrictions on hillsides usually require a less intensive use of the property or less development of the property, leaving the owner with a residual economically beneficial use. Courts can rely on the whole parcel rule, or find an economically beneficial residual use, even when development is completely prohibited.[1]

Municipalities also adopt land use regulations that protect views. One common type of regulation protects viewsheds, such as views of hills and mountains, usually by limiting the height of buildings, structures and trees. Preserving view corridors is another type of view protection, usually in urban areas, where a municipality limits height and bulk to protect views of important buildings, such as a state capitol. View protection ordinances do not have the safety and resource protection objectives that reinforce slope protection, but the courts have accepted their aesthetic purpose, and have not found a taking because the ordinances leave the landowners with an economically beneficial use of their property.[2]

---

[1] Rejecting takings claims: Seldon v. City of Manitou Springs, 745 P.2d 229 (Colo. 1987) (economic impact not considered); Kelly v. Tahoe Regional Planning Agency, 855 P.2d 1027 (Nev. 1993) (upholding regulations that temporarily prohibited development because of erosion hazard and runoff potential); Anello v. Zoning Bd. of Appeals, 678 N.E.2d 870 (N.Y. 1997) (applying notice rule to defeat investment-backed expectations); Jones v. Zoning Hearing Bd., 578 A.2d 1369 (Pa. Commw. 1990) (upholding bufferyards adopted to preserve woodlands, streams and steep slopes); *In re* Interim Bylaw, Waitsfield, 742 A.2d 742 (Vt. 1999) (upholding ordinance prohibiting one-or two-family dwelling units at elevations at or above 1700 feet in forest reserve district; agricultural and forestry uses still possible). *Contra* Corrigan v. City of Scottsdale, 720 P.2d 528 (Ariz. App. 1985) (ordinance prohibited development on steep slopes), *aff'd in part and vacated in part on other grounds,* 720 P.2d 513 (Ariz. 1986). *See* Va. Code Ann. § 15.2-2295.1 (regulation of construction on mountain ridges).

[2] Echevarrieta v. City of Rancho Palos Verdes, 103 Cal. Rptr. 2d 165 (Cal. App. 2001) (requiring property owner to trim trees under view preservation ordinance held not a taking; diminution in

§ 12.03   Groundwater Protection.

Land use regulations can protect groundwater supplies. This can be done through an overlay zone for groundwater protection areas that have more restrictive land use requirements to protect groundwater sources. The ordinance can prohibit development that is a threat to groundwater, and can require lower densities in areas near groundwater sources to limit development that can aggravate water pollution through surface runoff. Courts will uphold large lot zoning that is adopted for this purpose.[1] The preservation objective served by the ordinance is clearly legitimate, and the ordinance leaves the landowner with an economically beneficial use of her land.

§ 12.04   Critical Area Controls.

A related land use program that can protect environmental areas is the adoption of land use controls for critical areas. The American Law Institute's Model Land Development Code first proposed this program in 1976.[1] Under its proposal, a state agency can designate an environmental area as a critical area, and then adopt guidelines that local governments must apply in their land use regulations. Florida adopted this proposal.[2] The state agency designates critical areas and then adopts criteria for development in critical areas that the local government must follow.

Other states have adopted legislation based on the ALI model that authorizes either the state or local governments to designate critical areas.[3] For example, the Washington State growth management legislation requires local governments to designate critical areas and protect their functions.[4] A few other states have designated particular environmental areas as areas that require special attention through land use regulation.[5]

---

value questionable); Land Mark Land Co., Inc. v. City & County of Denver, 728 P.2d 1281 (Colo. 1986). *See also* Kucera v. Liza, 69 Cal. Rptr. 2d 582 (Cal. App. 1997) (upholding view and sunlight preservation ordinance imposing height limit on trees as valid under substantive due process).

[1] Moviematic Indus. Corp. v. Board of County Comm'rs, 349 So.2d 667 (Fla. App. 1977); Security Mgt. Corp. v. Baltimore County, 655 A.2d 1326 (Md. App. 1995) (upholding five-acre zoning adopted to prevent unsuitable development that would contaminate watershed); § 5.31

[1] § 7-201.

[2] Fla. Stat. Ann. § 390.05. *See* Askew v. Cross Key Waterways, 372 So.2d 913 (Fla. 1978) (holding earlier version of law unconstitutional as invalid delegation of power). *See also* American Planning Association, Growing Smart Legislative Guidebook: Model Statutes for Planning and Management of Change §§ 5-201 to 5-214 (S. Meck ed. 2002) (model critical area legislation based on but making revisions in ALI model).

[3] Colo. Rev Stat § 24-65.1-201 et seq. (local designation of areas of state interest); Minn. Stat. Ann. § 116G.01 et seq. (state designation); Nev. Rev. Stat. §§ 321.755, 321.770 (state authority); Wyo. Stat. §§ 9-8-102(a)(i), 9-8-202(a)(ix) (state agency).

[4] Wash. Rev. Code §§ 36.70.060, 35.70.172, 36.70A.170.

[5] Md. Nat. Res. Code Ann. §§ 8-1801 et seq, (Chesapeake Bay);1977 Mass. Acts, Ch. 831 (Martha's Vineyard); N.Y. Exec. Law §§ 800–820 (Adirondack Park); N.J. Stat. Ann. §§ 13.18A-1 et seq. (Pinelands); Va. Code §§ 10.1-2100 et seq. (Chesapeake Bay).

Critical area regulations will vary depending on the type of area, and may designate areas where development can be allowed to occur as well as areas in which development is restricted.[6] The decision on how land within a critical area is designated is critical, and will require joint participation by the state agency and the local government if both share in the administration of the program.[7]

B. WETLANDS.

§ 12.05   State and Local Programs.

Regulatory programs for wetlands are intended to preserve the many important environmental functions these areas serve. As transitional "marshy" areas between land and bodies of water, wetlands help preserve water quality by slowing water flow and allowing sediment to settle. They also stabilize water tables by retaining water during dry periods and holding it back during floods. Wetlands are important resources for environmental diversity and provide an important habitat for many forms of wildlife.

A number of states, especially the Great Lakes and eastern states, have legislation that regulates development in coastal wetlands, and some also have inland wetlands legislation.[1] Legislation in some states applies to "shoreland" areas, which include wetlands. This legislation usually requires permits for dredging, filling, the alteration of wetlands or for any development in wetlands. These activities are necessary for housing and other development. Other statutes authorize the state agency to adopt land use regulations that specify permitted uses in wetlands and authorize permits only for developments that are allowed by these regulations.

A number of wetland statutes require local governments to adopt wetland regulations that are consistent with the state statute, and which the state agency must approve. These regulations are sometimes included in the zoning ordinance. The state agency in some states can adopt regulations for a local government if it fails to adopt them. Local wetland ordinances usually allow only limited uses in wetlands areas, such as recreational and other natural uses of the land, and do not allow major structural development.

---

[6] See New Jersey Bldrs. Ass'n v. Department of Envtl. Protection, 404 A.2d 320 (N.J. App. Div. 1979) (upholding boundary of critical area in Pinelands to protect water quality and holding a taking had not occurred).

[7] Maryland critical area program for Chesapeake Bay: Bucktail, LLC v. County Council, 723 A.2d 440 (Md. 1999) (remanding decision on denial of growth allocation in critical area); White v. North, 675 A.2d 1023 (Md. App. 1996) (upholding redesignation of land because of mistake in original designation); North v. Kent Island Ltd. Partnership, 664 A.2d 34 (Md. App. 1995) (state agency role limited to review of local amendments for compliance with state act).

[1] Conn. Gen. Stat. §§ 22a-28 to 22a-45; Fla. Stat. Ann. §§ 373.414; Mass. Gen. Laws ch. 130, § 105; ch. 131, § 40; Mich. Comp. Laws Ann. § 324.30301–30323; N.H. Rev. Stat. Ann. §§ 483-B:1 to 483-B:19; N.Y. Envtl. Conserv. Law §§ 25-0101 to 25-0601; 71-2501 to 71-2507.

State wetland statutes provide criteria for the issuance of permits for regulated activities in wetlands.[2] Some statutes authorize the state agency to consider the "public interest" or the "policy" of the act. Other statutes contain "factors" the state agency must consider when it decides whether to issue a permit. These factors typically include the environmental impact of the development, whether alternatives are available, and the suitability of the activity for the wetlands.

State wetland statutes may preempt local wetland ordinances if the statute does not expressly allow local regulation. Whether a court finds local regulation preempted if the statute does not authorize it depends on its view of the state regulatory responsibilities conferred by the state legislation. *Golden v. Board of Selectmen*[3] held a state wetland statute did not preempt a local wetland ordinance because each conferred "a separate and distinct type of authority."

The courts have implied the authority to adopt local wetland regulations from the standard zoning enabling act.[4] A related question is whether state wetland legislation is unconstitutional as an infringement on local home rule. The courts have held that similar environmental land use legislation serves state interests and does not interfere with local home rule autonomy.[5]

§ 12.06 Clean Water Act Permit.

Section 404 of the federal Clean Water Act[1] requires permits from the U.S. Army Corps of Engineers for the discharge of dredge and fill material in the "waters of the United States." The act also gives the Environmental Protection Agency (EPA) a veto authority over Corps permits.[2] Dredge and fill material permits are required for development in wetlands, which usually require dredging and filling activities. The Supreme Court upheld a Corps regulation that defined

---

[2] Sampieri v. Inland Wetlands Agency, 628 A.2d 1286 (Conn. 1993) (interpreting "feasible and prudent alternative" requirement); Avatar Dev. Corp. v. State, 723 So.2d 199 (Fla. 1998) (statute held not to be unconstitutional delegation of power); MacGibbon v. Board of Appeals, 340 N.E.2d 487 (Mass. 1976) (reversing denial of permit); Murphy v. Board of Envt'l Protection, 615 A.2d 255 (Me. 1992) (all statutory standards apply to review of permit for development adjacent to coastal wetlands); Friends of the Crystal River v. Kuras Props., 554 N.W.2d 528 (Mich. App. 1996) (upholding grant of permit).

[3] 265 N.E.2d 573 (Mass. 1970). *Contra* Lauricella v. Planning & Zoning Bd., 342 A.2d 374 (Conn. Sup. 1974).

[4] Morland Dev. Co. v. City of Tulsa, 596 P.2d 1255 (Okla. 1979) (concurring opinion).

[5] CEEED v. California Coastal Zone Conservation Comm'n, 118 Cal. Rptr. 315 (Cal. App. 1974) (coastal permit legislation); Pope v. City of Atlanta, 418 F. Supp. 665 (Ga. 1977) (floodplains). *See also* Town of Monroe v. Carey, 412 N.Y.S.2d 939 (Sup. Ct. 1977).

[1] 33 U.S.C. § 1444(a). *See also* Wetlands Executive Order 11,990 (May 24, 1977) (federal agency new construction not allowed unless no practicable alternative and all practicable mitigation measures have been taken). *See* City of Carmel-by-the-Sea v. United States Dep't of Transp., 123 F.3d 1142 (9th Cir. 1997) (proposed highway complied with Order).

[2] 33 U.S.C. §§ 1444(b), 1444(c).

the "waters of the United States" to include "saturated" wetlands adjacent to bodies of water even though the wetlands are not inundated by the adjacent water body.[3] Corps jurisdiction over "isolated" wetlands is less clear.[4]

The Clean Water Act does not contain criteria for the Corps' permit review, but Corps regulations provide for a "public interest" review in which it must balance the harms and benefits of a proposed dredging and filling activity. These regulations apply to wetlands.[5] In addition, EPA regulations provide an alternate site not in a wetlands is presumptively available for a use proposed in a wetlands that is not water-dependent.[6] The courts have reversed Corps decisions to grant permits when it did not take these factors into account.[7]

EPA has also adopted a water dependency rule. It provides a "practicable" alternate location is presumed available, when a proposed use is not water-dependent, if the alternate site would cause less damage to wetlands.[8] This regulation would usually apply to housing development. A court of appeals upheld the regulation, and held the availability of alternate sites should be considered at the time a permit applicant entered the market.[9]

The issuance of a dredge and fill permit under the Clean Water Act requires an environmental review under the National Environmental Policy Act (NEPA), and the preparation of an environmental impact statement if the development authorized by the permit will have significant environmental effects.[10]

The Supreme Court has held the statutory permit requirement is not a taking.[11] A taking occurs only when a permit denial prevents an economically viable use of the land. The landowner must sue for compensation in these cases in the Court of Federal Claims.

§ 12.07 The Takings Issue.

Wetlands regulation presents a potentially difficult takings problem because a restriction on or denial of development in a wetland means the landowner the

---

[3] United States v. Riverside Bayview Homes, Inc., 474 U.S. 121 (1986).

[4] Solid Waste Agency v. United States Army Corps of Eng'rs, 531 U.S. 159 (2001) (jurisdiction does not extend to non-navigable, isolated, intrastate gravel pit).

[5] 33 C.F.R. § 320.4.

[6] 40 C.F.R. § 230.10. *See* Bersani v. Robichard, 850 F.2d 36 (2d Cir. 1988) (applying test and holding EPA could consider alternate sites).

[7] Van Abbema v. Fornell, 807 F.2d 633 (7th Cir. 1986); Hough v. Marsh, 557 F. Supp. 74 (D. Mass. 1982). *But see* Mall Props. v. Marsh, 672 F. Supp. 561 (D. Mass. 1987) (may not consider socioeconomic effects), *appeal dismissed*, 841 F.2d 440 (1st Cir. 1988).

[8] 40 C.F.R. § 230.10.

[9] Bersani v. EPA, 850 F.2d 36 (2d Cir. 1988) (shopping center).

[10] 42 U.S.C. § 4332.*See* Sierra Club v. Sigler, 695 F.2d 957 (5th Cir. 1983) (inadequate impact statement tainted decision making process for permit).

[11] United States v. Riverside Bayview Homes, Inc., 474 U.S. 121 (1986).

landowner must maintain the wetlands in its natural state. Early cases were divided. There was authority that a wetlands restriction is a taking,[1] but *Just v. Marinette County*[2] was the leading pre-trilogy state case holding a regulation restricting a wetland to passive uses was not a taking. The court reformulated the harm-benefit rule to reach its decision, holding that "we have a restriction on the use of a citizen['s] property, not to secure a benefit for the public, but to prevent a harm from the change in the natural character of the citizens' property."[3] The *Just* decision attracted criticism because it inverted the harm-benefit theory of the taking clause, but other courts followed it.[4] The status of *Just* since the Supreme Court rejected the harm-benefit rule in *Lucas* is not clear.

Wetlands regulations have presented a more serious takings problem since the Supreme Court's *Lucas* decision,[5] which held a land use regulation is a taking if it prevents any economically beneficial use of the land. Wetlands regulations often allow only passive recreational uses in order to protect the wetlands ecology. A court might hold a per se taking occurs in these cases because these uses are not economically beneficial.[6] This result is not inevitable. As the cases below show, wetlands regulations often allow economically beneficial uses. The *Penn Central* takings tests would then apply.

State courts since *Lucas* rejected per se takings claims when they found the landowner was still able to make economically beneficial use of his property,[7]

---

[1] Bartlett v. Zoning Comm'n, 282 A.2d 907 (Conn.1971); State v. Johnson, 265 A.2d 711 (Me. 1970).

[2] 201 N.W.2d 761 (Wis. 1972). *See* Zealy v. City of Waukesha, 548 N.W.2d 528 (Wis. 1996) (continuing validity of *Just* not considered).

[3] *Id.* at 767–68.

[4] Manor Dev. Corp. v. Conservation Comm'n, 433 A.2d 999 (Conn. 1980); Graham v. Estuary Props., Inc.,399 So. 2d 1374 (Fla. 1981); Carter v. South Carolina Coastal Council, 314 S.E.2d 327 (S.C. 1984); Chokecherry Hills Estates v. Deuel County, 294 N.W.2d 654 (S.D. 1980); 46 A.L.R.3d 1422 (1972). *See also* Candlestick Props., Inc. v. San Francisco Bay Conservation & Dev. Comm'n, 89 Cal. Rptr. 897 (Cal. App. 1970); Glisson v. Alachua Cty., 558 So. 2d 1030 (Fla. App. 1990) (dismissing facial taking claim; existing uses preserved and transfer of development rights available); Namon v. State Dep't of Envtl. Reg., 558 So. 2d 504 (Fla. App. 1990) (taking not found; landowner had only unilateral expectation); Potomac Sand & Gravel Co. v. Governor of Md., 293 A.2d 241 (Md. 1972) (dredge and fill prohibition upheld under nuisance theory); Milardo v. Coastal Resources Mgt. Council, 424 A.2d 266 (R.I. 1981).

[5] § 2.21.

[6] Vatalaro v. Department of Envtl. Regulation, 601 So. 2d 1223 (Fla. App. 1992) (permit denial held a taking pre-*Lucas*; state agency offered only passive recreational use).

[7] R & Y, Inc. v. Municipality of Anchorage, 34 P.3d 289 (Alaska 2001)(rejecting takings claim under state takings test similar to *Penn Central*); State of Florida v. Burgess, 772 So.2d 540 (Fla. App. 2000) (no denial of economically viable use as owner could use land for recreational purpose for which it was bought); FIC Homes of Blackstone, Inc. v. Conservation Comm'n, 673 N.E.2d 61 (Mass. App. 1996) (lot may be devoted to beneficial woodland, wetland, and recreational purposes); Gazza v. New York State Dep't of Envtl. Conservation, 679 N.E.2d 1035 (N.Y. 1997)

or that the loss of all economically beneficial use was not proved.[8] Two other takings doctrines play an important role in wetlands takings cases and may defeat a takings claim. One, known as the whole parcel rule, determines the parcel of land the court must consider when a landowner argues a taking has occurred. Wetlands may occupy only a portion of the property affected by a regulation, and a court must decide whether it is to consider all or only the wetlands part of the property in its takings decision. This problem also arises when a landowner owns several properties, and not all of them are affected by the wetlands regulation. Courts rejected takings claims when they adopted a broad definition of the parcel taken and an economically beneficial use could be made on that part of the property that was not subject to the wetlands restriction.[9]

The second doctrine is based on the rule that a landowner's investment-backed expectations are a factor courts must consider under the *Penn Central* multifactor takings test.[10] Courts interpreted this factor to include a notice rule. Under this rule, they rejected a takings claim in wetlands cases when a landowner did not have investment-backed expectations because she had notice a restrictive land use regulation applied to her property.[11] Cases in the Court of Federal Claims and its appellate Federal Circuit applied the whole parcel and notice rules under the *Lucas* and *Penn Central* takings tests to claims the denial of a dredge and

---

(recreational use); Mock v. Department of Envtl. Resources, 623 A.2d 940 (Pa. Commw. 1993) (only denied the specific project under consideration), *aff'd without opinion,* 667 A.2d 212 (Pa. 1995).

[8] MC Assocs. v. Town of Cape Elizabeth, 773 A.2d 439 (Me. 2001) (appraisal did not establish property values). Takings claim not ripe: Zerbetz v. Municipality of Anchorage, 856 P.2d 777 (Alaska 1993) (designation of coastal wetlands; plaintiff had not made application for development permission); Gil v. Inland Wetlands & Watercourses Agency, 593 A.2d 1268 (Conn. 1993) (may approve more modest proposal); Lopes v. City of Peabody, 629 N.E.2d 1312 (Mass. 1994) (remanding to decide whether taking had occurred); Alegria v. Keeney, 687 A.2d 1249 (R.I. 1997) (landowner made only one permit application).

[9] Walcek v. United States, 49 Fed. Cl. 248 (2001) (no taking; segmentation not allowed: property contiguous and unsubdivided; purchased over a month or two, maintained as single parcel in same ownership with intent to develop as whole); FIC Homes of Blackstone, Inc. v. Conservation Comm'n, 673 N.E.2d 61 (Mass. App. 1996); K & K Constr., Inc. v. Department of Natural Resources, 575 N.W.2d 531 (Mich. 1998) (but remanding to determine whether taking had occurred under *Penn Central* tests); R.W. Docks & Slips v. State, 628 N.W.2d 781 (Wis. 2001) (upholding denial of permit for additional boat slips when property as whole considered). Pre-*Lucas* cases holding no taking under rule: Deltona Corp. v. United States, 657 F.2d 1184 (Ct. Cl. 1991); State v. Schindler, 604 So.2d 565 (Fla. App. 1992); Moskow v. Comm'r, 427 N.E.2d 750 (Mass. 1981); American Dredging Co. v. State, Dep't of Environmental Protection, 404 A.2d 42 (N.J. App. Div.1979). *See* § 2.19.

[10] § 2.05.

[11] *E.g.,* FIC Homes of Blackstone, Inc. v. Conservation Comm'n, 673 N.E.2d 61 (Mass. App. 1996); Claridge v. New Hampshire Wetlands Bd., 485 A.2d 287 (N.H. 1984); Gazza v. New York State Dep't of Envtl. Conservation, 679 N.E.2d 1035 (N.Y. 1997; Alegria v. Keeney, 687 A.2d 1249 (R.I. 1997). *See* § 2.16.

fill permit under the federal Clean Water Act was a taking, and usually rejected these claims.[12] In some of these cases, the court held notice of a restrictive wetlands regulation before purchase was an absolute bar to a takings claim. Some of these cases also applied the rule from *Lucas* that a taking does not occur, even if a land use regulation denies all economically beneficial use of the land, if the regulation "inheres in the title." These cases held that a law existing at the time of purchase defeated the takings claim because it inhered in the title.[13]

The Supreme Court's decision in *Palazzolo v. State of Rhode Island*[14] provided additional interpretation of the *Lucas* per se takings rule and the scope of the notice rule in takings cases. The Court clarified the notice rule by holding the purchase of land after a restrictive regulation was adopted under which an application to develop the property is denied is not an absolute bar to a takings claim. It also indicated an existing land use regulation is not part of a landowner's inherent title that defeats a *Lucas* per se takings claim. However, a controlling concurring opinion by Justice O'Connor held the regulatory environment at the time of purchase is a factor courts should consider when they decide whether a landowner has investment-backed expectations that required consideration under the *Penn Central* multifactor takings test. A majority of the Court endorsed Justice O'Connor's concurring opinion in its *Lake Tahoe* decision.[15]

The Court in *Palazzolo* also decided a per se taking had not occurred under *Lucas* because development allowed on the uplands portion of the property had a value of $200,000. It remanded the case for a decision under the *Penn Central* multifactor takings test. Though the Court did not consider the whole parcel problem in *Palazzolo*, it endorsed that principle in *Lake Tahoe*. That case held

---

[12] Taking found: Florida Rock Indus. v. United States, 18 F.3d 1560 (Fed. Cir. 1994), *on remand,* 45 Fed. Cl. 21 (1999), *cross-appeal dismissed for lack of jurisdiction,* 243 F.3d 555 (Fed. Cir. 2000); Loveladies Harbor, Inc. v. United States, 28 F.3d 1171 (Fed. Cir. 1994) (affirming award of compensation); Bowles v. United States, 31 Fed. Cl. 37 (1994); Taking not found: Good v. United States, 189 F.3d 1355 (Fed. Cir. 1999) (landowner did not have investment-backed expectations under notice rule);Forest Props., Inc. v. United States, 177 F.3d 1360 (Fed. Cir. 1999) (parcel treated as whole still had economic value); Breakwater Farms Joint Venture v. United States, 35 Fed. Cl. 232 (1996) (no taking when residual land had value); Ciampitti v. United States, 22 Cl. Ct. 310 (1991) (knowledge of permit requirement defeated takings claim); Formanek v. United States, 18 Cl. Ct. 785 (1989) (also holding that offers of purchase by conservation organizations are not basis for summary judgment for government); Beure-Co. v. United States, 16 Cl. Ct. 42 (1989). *See also* Palm Beach Isles Assocs. v. United States, 208 F.3d 1374 (Fed. Cir. 2000) (remanding to determine whether navigational servitude defense available to government); Tabb Lakes, Ltd. v. United States, 10 F.3d 796 (Fed. Cir. 1993) (cease and desist order under federal law that stopped filling of wetlands not a taking when plaintiff could have developed land by obtaining a permit).

[13] Kim v. City of New York, 681 N.E.2d 312 (N.Y. 1997).

[14] Palazzolo v. State of Rhode Island, 533 U.S. 606 (2001).

[15] Tahoe-Sierra Preservation Council, Inc. v. Tahoe Regional Planning Agency, 535 U.S. 302 (2002).

the period of time during which property is prohibited from development under a moratorium is not a per se taking. The Court did not consider how courts should apply the whole parcel rule in cases, like wetlands cases, where the issue is how to define the geographic unit of the property for purposes of applying the takings clause. However, the Court's endorsement of the whole parcel rule as a takings principle means courts can continue to apply it in wetlands takings cases. The Court in *Lake Tahoe* also indicated that cases in which a *Lucas* per se taking would be found would be "rare."

C. FLOODPLAINS.

§ 12.08   State and Local Programs.

Floodplain regulation is a restrictive land use control that prohibits or limits development in areas subject to flooding. Floodplain regulation usually distinguishes between the floodway and the flood fringe. The floodway is the unobstructed part of the floodplain consisting of the stream channel and overbank areas capable of carrying a flood discharge. The floodway is intended to carry deep and fast-moving water. The adjacent flood fringe is intended to carry shallow and slow-moving water. Structural development is not usually permitted in the floodway. Open nonstructural uses are permitted, such as agricultural and recreational uses. Structural development is permitted in the flood fringe, often as a special permit use, if it is elevated above expected flood levels or protected from flood damage. Development in floodplains increases the flooding danger by diminishing the carrying capacity of the floodplain. This causal relationship between floodplain development and flood danger provides an important basis for upholding restrictive floodplain regulations against taking objections.

The National Flood Insurance Act[1] has stimulated the widespread enactment of state and local floodplain regulation. The act establishes a national program of federal flood insurance and requires the federal agency that administers the act to adopt criteria for state and local floodplain regulations.[2] Owners of property in a floodplain may obtain federal insurance only if their municipality has adopted a federally-approved ordinance. After an approved floodplain ordinance is adopted, the purchase of federal insurance is required for the receipt of direct federal financial assistance and for loans from private financial institutions regulated or insured by the federal government.[3]

---

[1] 42 U.S.C. §§ 4001–4028.

[2] 42 U.S.C. § 4102(c). *See* Adolph v. Federal Emergency Mgt. Agency, 854 F.2d 732 (5th Cir. 1988) (upholds local regulations adopted to comply with federal act). *See also* Floodplain Management Order, Executive Order 11,988 (May 24, 1977) (federal agencies proposing actions in floodplains must consider "alternatives to avoid adverse effects and incompatible development in the floodplain"); Dangerfield Island Protective Soc'y v. Babbitt, 40 F.3d 342 (D.C. Cir. 1994) (agency properly rejected no-build alternative and mitigated environmental impacts).

[3] 42 U.S.C. § 4012a.

A large number of states have legislation authorizing floodplain regulation.[4] This legislation usually authorizes the direct state regulation of floodplains. It may also mandate or authorize local governments to adopt floodplain regulations that comply with criteria included in the statute. The legislation may authorize a state agency to adopt floodplain regulations for a locality if it does not adopt regulations that comply with state legislative requirements. The state agency may compel the adoption of a local floodplain ordinance if the state statute requires one.[5]

The typical state floodplain statute contains authority to survey and map floodplain areas, provisions for the control of existing structures, authority to issue permits for new development, and standards for permit review. Some statutes authorize subdivision review. If the statute requires or authorizes the adoption of local ordinances, it will also contain criteria for local regulations. A municipality may adopt floodplain regulations in a separate ordinance or as an overlay district that is part of the zoning ordinance.

Some state zoning statutes authorize the adoption of floodplain regulations.[6] A court can imply the authority to adopt floodplain regulations from the zoning act if express authority is not granted.[7] Some state subdivision control acts authorize the disapproval of subdivisions that will create flooding dangers.[8]

§ 12.09 The Takings Issue.

Most courts have taken a favorable view of floodplain regulation under the takings clause.[1] *Turnpike Realty Co. v. Town of Dedham*[2] is a typical case. The court upheld a floodplain ordinance that allowed only passive uses and prohibited any building or structure, even though these restrictions allegedly reduced the value of the property from $431,000 to $53,000. The court noted that floodplain regulation protects individuals who might choose to build in floodplains despite the flood danger, protects other landowners from floodplain development, and protects the "entire community from individual choices of land use which require subsequent public expenditures for public works and disaster relief." It held these regulatory purposes satisfied the usual substantive due process tests. The court

---

[4] Ariz. Rev. Stat. Ann. §§ 48-3601 to 48-3615; Iowa Code Ann. § 455B.276; Minn. Stat. Ann. §§ 103F.101-103F.155; N.C. Gen. Stat. § 143-215.54; Wash. Rev. Code Ann. §§ 86.12.200, 86.12.210; Wis. Stat. Ann. § 87.30.

[5] County of Ramsey v. Stevens, 283 N.W.2d 918 (Minn. 1979).

[6] Conn. Gen. Stat. § 8-2; Iowa Code Ann. § 414.3; Minn. Stat. Ann. § 394.25.

[7] Turnpike Realty Co. v. Town of Dedham, 284 N.E.2d 891 (Mass. 1972).

[8] § 9.03.

[1] *But see* Dooley v. Town Plan & Zoning Comm'n, 197 A.2d 770 (Conn. 1964), qualified in Brecciaroli v. Connecticut Comm'r of Envtl. Protection, 362 A.2d 948 (Conn. 1975).

[2] 284 N.E.2d 891 (Mass. 1972).

also held the ordinance did not deprive the landowner of all of the use of its land because it allowed a number of passive uses. The court balanced the restrictions the ordinance imposed on the property "against the potential harm to the community from overdevelopment of a flood plain area." It applied standard taking law to hold a taking had not occurred even though the ordinance substantially diminished the value of the property.[3]

A number of cases that rejected taking objections to floodplain regulations emphasized the dangers that flooding creates.[4] *Penn Central's*[5] generous interpretation of the harm-benefit rule also influenced the floodplain regulation cases. *Krahl v. Nine Mile Creek Watershed Dist.*[6] is an example. A landowner denied a permit to construct a building in a floodplain brought an action challenging the floodplain regulation as a taking. The court observed the filling necessary for the building would create a flood danger, noted that a number of nonstructural uses of the land were allowed, and applied a balancing test to uphold the regulation. The court also noted the restrictions on the land were not permanent and would be modified once permanent flood control facilities were constructed. The court cited *Penn Central* for the proposition that "this is not a case where a property owner is burdened with a restriction without receiving a reciprocal benefit in his favor."

In *First English Evangelical Lutheran Church v. County of Los Angeles*,[7] the U.S. Supreme Court remanded a case that claimed a moratorium on development in a floodplain was a taking. It left open the question whether the county "might avoid" a conclusion that the moratorium was a taking by a showing that the denial of "all use" under the moratorium "was insulated as a part of the State's authority to enact safety regulations."

On remand, the California Court of Appeals held the floodplain moratorium was not a taking.[8] The court held the moratorium substantially advanced the preeminent state interest in public safety and did not deny the landowner all use

---

[3] Following *Dedham:* S. Kemble Fischer Realty Trust v. Board of Appeals, 402 N.E.2d 100 (Mass. App. 1980); Dur-Bar Realty Co. v. City of Utica, 394 N.Y.S.2d 913 (App. Div. 1977).

[4] Turner v. County of Del Norte, 101 Cal. Rptr. 93 (Cal. App. 1972); Foreman v. State, 387 N.E.2d 455 (Ind. App. 1979); Subaru of N.E. v. Board of Appeals, 395 N.E.2d 880 (Mass. App. 1979). *See also* Fortier v. City of Spearfish, 433 N.W.2d 228 (S.D. 1988) (upholding purpose of ordinance). *But see* Sturdy Homes, Inc. v. Township of Redford, 186 N.W.2d 43 (Mich. App. 1971) (flood danger not found on property).

[5] § 2.05.

[6] 283 N.W.2d 538 (Minn. 1979). *Accord and also applying Penn Central,* Responsible Citizens in Opposition to the Flood Plain Ordinance v. City of Asheville, 302 S.E.2d 204 (N.C. 1983). *See also* Usdin v. State, 414 A.2d 280 (N.J.L. Div. 1980), *aff'd,* 430 A.2d 949 (N.J. App. Div. 1981); Maple Leaf Invs., Inc. v. State, 565 P.2d 1162 (Wash. 1977) (applied balancing test).

[7] 482 U.S. 304 (1987).

[8] First English Evangelical Lutheran Ch. v. County of Los Angeles, 258 Cal. Rptr. 893 (1989).

of his property. The court also held the moratorium had been imposed for a reasonable time while a study could be done to determine what uses, if any, were compatible with public safety. Other courts upheld floodplain regulations post-*First English.*[9]

The Supreme Court rejected the harm-benefit rule in *Lucas,* and balancing the public interest against the economic loss to a landowner is not permissible if a floodplain regulation is a taking per se, because it denies all economically viable use of a property. The Court did indicate in *Lucas* that a restriction on the use of land to prevent flooding would fall within the nuisance exception to the per se rule, so that this rule would not apply.[10] In addition, traditional taking doctrine will apply if some use is possible. This is likely if the floodplain does not include all of the property. The court can then apply the whole parcel rule to hold that an economic use of the remainder is possible and can recognize passive uses as economically viable.[11]

D.   PRESERVATION OF AGRICULTURAL LAND.

§ 12.10   Federal, State and Local Programs.

The threat to agriculture from urban development has encouraged the adoption of federal, state and local programs for the preservation of agricultural land. Congress adopted a Farmland Policy Protection Act[1] in response to a national study of agricultural land published in 1981. The Department of Agriculture, in cooperation with other federal agencies, adopts criteria to identify the effects of federal programs on the conversion of farmland to nonagricultural use. Federal agencies are to consider the adverse effects of federal programs on farmland preservation, consider alternative actions that could lessen such adverse effects, assure that federal programs are compatible with state, local and private farmland protection programs if this is practicable. However, the statute expressly provides the federal government may not regulate the use of private or non-federal land.[2]

---

[9] McDougal v. County of Imperial, 942 F.2d 668 (9th Cir. 1991); McElwain v. County of Flathead, 811 P.2d 1267 (Mont. 1991), April v. City of Broken Arrow, 775 P.2d 1347 (Okla. 1989).

[10] *See* Powers v. Skagit County, 835 P.2d 230 (Wash. App. 1992) (remanding taking challenge to floodplain regulation for trial under *Lucas* rules).

[11] Leonard v. Town of Broomfield, 666 N.E.2d 1300 (Mass. 1996) (also holding landowner had no investment-backed expectations because had constructive notice of floodplain map). *See also* Bonnie Briar Syndicate, Inc. v. Town of Mamaroneck, 721 N.E.2d 971 (N.Y. 1999) (upholding zoning for recreational use to further objectives of open space, recreation and flood control).

[1] 7 U.S.C. §§ 4201–4209. *See also* 7 U.S.C. § 4203 (federal agencies must bring programs, authorities and administrative activities into compliance with act).

[2] 7 U.S.C. § 4208(a).

Real property tax preference programs are the most common agricultural preservation programs at the state level, and all states have adopted them.[3] These programs reduce local real property taxes on agricultural land by reducing property assessments. The reduction may be mandatory or voluntary. The property assessment reduction is deferred under some laws and recaptured when the land is developed for nonagricultural uses. Agricultural zoning, which restricts land to agricultural uses, is less common, but local governments have used it extensively in some states.[4] It may be linked to a property tax preference.

Property tax preferences and agricultural zoning are not the only state and local agricultural preservation programs. The subdivision of land for agricultural purposes is frequently exempted by statute from subdivision controls.[5] Several states have authorized the creation of voluntary agricultural districts.[6] The New York law is a leading example.[7] Agricultural district laws protect agricultural land from local ordinances that hinder farming and limit governmental activities that are detrimental to agriculture, such as public investment for nonagricultural development, public land acquisition, and municipal annexations.

§ 12.11   Right-to-Farm Laws.

All states have adopted right-to-farm (RTF) laws. One type of law is modeled on a provision in New York's agricultural district law. It prohibits local governments from enacting any ordinances "which would unreasonably restrict or regulate farm structures or farming practices."[1] Another type of RTF law modifies traditional common law nuisance principles as applied to farming. The purpose of these RTF laws is to prevent nuisance suits against farming brought by nonagricultural users of land who move into agricultural areas. The laws vary, but the North Carolina law is typical. It provides that no "agricultural . . . operation . . . shall be or become a nuisance, public or private, by any changed conditions in or about the locality thereof after the same has been in operation for more than one year."[2] The laws define the agricultural operations they cover,

---

[3] *E.g.*, Ariz. Stat. Ann. §§ 42-12004, 42-15004; Iowa Code Ann. § 441.21; W.Va. Code § 22-1A-10.

[4] § 12.12.

[5] *See* Hopewell Twp. Bd. of Supvrs. v. Golla, 452 A.2d 1337 (Pa. 1982).

[6] Md. Code Ann., Agric. §§ 2-501 to 2-516; Minn. Stat. Ann. §§ 473H.01-473H.18; N.J. Stat. Ann. §§ 4:1C-1 to 4:1C-55; Utah Code Ann. §§ 17-41-101 to 17-41-406.

[7] N.Y. Agric. & Mkts. Law §§ 301–307. *See* Town of Lysander v. Hafner, 759 N.E.2d 356 (N.Y. 2001) (use of mobile homes to house migrant farm workers protected from local zoning ordinance).

[1] N.Y. Agric. & Mkts. Law § 305(2)(a).

[2] N.C. Gen. Stat. § 106-701. *See also* Ga. Code Ann. § 41-1-7; Ind. Code Ann. § 32-30-6-9. *See* Township of Richmond v. Erbes, 489 N.W.2d 504 (Mich. App. 1992) (assembling wood products not covered by law). *But see* Steffens v. Keeler, 503 N.W.2d 675 (Mich. App. 1993)

and some apply only to commercial operations. When a statute protects only against nuisance suits from "nonagricultural activities," the courts have held that agricultural operations are still subject to nuisance suits brought by other agricultural uses.[3]

To be protected under an RTF law, a farm must be in existence before the establishment of a conflicting non-agricultural use.[4] Like the North Carolina law, most right-to-farm laws also include an "establishment' period, usually one year, to qualify for protection under the statute.[5] There usually also is a distance requirement that requires agricultural uses to be a prescribed distance from non-agricultural uses to trigger the protection of the statute.[6] Agricultural operations change with time, and changes after neighboring non-agricultural uses are established may remove the protection of an RTF law. Some statutes define a change in operations that is disqualifying.[7]

Another common requirement, imposed in varying degrees by all RTF laws, is that the agricultural use must not be run negligently,[8] or that it must be operated in accordance with Generally Accepted Agricultural Management Practices (GAAMPS).[9] Most RTF laws put the burden of persuasion on the plaintiff neighbor who brings a nuisance suit to show that the agricultural use is either negligently operated or does not comply with GAAMPs.[10]

(defendant protected because surrounding area agricultural when defendant began operation). *Compare* Rancho Viejo, LLC v. Tres Amigos Viejos, LLC, 123 Cal. Rptr.2d 479 (Cal. App. 2002) (law precludes action in trespass), *with* Buchanan v. Simplot Feeders Ltd. Partnership, 952 P.l2d 610 (Wash. 1998) (contra).

[3] Crea v. Crea. 16 P.3d 922 (Idaho 2000); Buchanan v. Simplot Feeders Ltd. Partnership, 952 P.l2d 610 (Wash. 1998). *Contra* Souza v. Lauppe, 69 Cal. Rptr.2d 494 (Cal. App. 1997).

[4] Swedenberg v. Phillips, 562 So. 2d 170 (Ala. 1990) (law not applicable when plaintiffs residing on land before agricultural operation began); Herrin v. Opatut, 281 S.E.2d 575 (Ga. 1981) (nonagricultural use established first); Jerome Twp. v. Melchi, 457 N.W.2d 52 (Mich. App. 1989) (agricultural use not protected that began after land zoned residential).

[5] Holubec v. Brandenburger, 58 S.W.2d 201 (Tex. App. 2001) (feedlot operation not established for one year). *But see* Tenn. Code Ann. § 43-26-103 (no establishment period)

[6] Mich. Comp. Laws § 286.473(3) (one mile).

[7] Fla. Stat. Ann. § 823.14(5) (may not "change to a more excessive farm operation with regard to noise, odor, dust, or fumes where the existing farm operation is adjacent to an established homestead or business), *explained and remanded*, Pasco Cty. v. Tampa Farm Serv., 573 So. 2d 909 (Fla. App. 1990); Ind. Code Ann. §§ 32-30-6-9 (no change in hours or type of operation and not a nuisance at time it began), explained and remanded; Laux v. Chapin Land Assocs., Inc., 550 N.E.2d 100 (Ind. App. 1990); Mich. Comp. Laws § 286.473(3) (adoption of new technology or change in type of farm product produced does not remove protection of statute).

[8] Iowa Code Ann. § 352.11(1)(a). *See also* Ark. Code Ann. § 2-4-106 (authorizing nuisance suit against agricultural uses that pollute streams or other bodies of water that cross a plaintiff's land).

[9] Minn. Stat. Ann. § 561.19.

[10] La. Rev. Stat. Ann. § 3:3604.

How RTF laws affect the application of zoning ordinances to agricultural operations is another important question. If the zoning ordinance applies, and prohibits agricultural uses, the protection provided by the RTF law will be lost. Some RTF statutes specifically preempt local zoning.[11] Many RTF laws also provide that a local ordinance may not make an agricultural operation protected by the law a nuisance.[12] This type of law does not preempt the local zoning ordinance.[13]

The Iowa Supreme Court held the statutory immunity from nuisance suits conferred by its RTF law was a taking without compensation. It held the immunity created an easement over the land of others by allowing the protected agricultural use to carry out activities that would otherwise be a nuisance.[14] This decision makes laws of this type unconstitutional, but may be consistent with Supreme Court decisions holding that exactions in the form of compelled dedications of land are a taking.[15]

§ 12.12   Agricultural Zoning.

Agricultural zoning is either exclusive or nonexclusive.[1] Exclusive agricultural zoning only allows agricultural uses and prohibits or restricts the approval of non-farm dwellings.[2] The ordinance can adopt a performance definition of agricultural use and permit non-farm dwellings only after an individual review to determine whether the performance criteria are satisfied. Oregon has the most comprehensive agricultural land preservation programs in the country. The state planning goal requires the preservation of agricultural land and contains factors that determine its conversion to nonagricultural use. Complementary state legislation authorizes Exclusive Farm Use (EFU) zones in which new farm and non-farm uses are regulated, an 80-acre lot size is mandatory, and exacting

---

[11] Mich. Comp. Laws. § 286.474(6) (local government shall not adopt ordinance that conflicts with this act or generally accepted agricultural and management practices), applied in Travis v. Preston, 643 N.W.2d 235 (Mich. App. 2002); N.J. Stat. Ann. § 4:1C-9, applied in Franklin v. Hollander, 796 A.2d 874 (N.J. 2002); N.C. Gen. Stat. § 16-701(d).

[12] Ala. Code § 6-5-127. *See* Town of North Kingston v. Albert, 767 A.2d 659 (R.I. 2001) (interpreting law to preclude application of local regulation of earth removal to prohibit use protected under RTF law).

[13] Ammirata v. Zoning Bd. of Appeals, 782 A.2d 1285 (Conn. App. 2001) (statute does not preempt zoning ordinance).

[14] Bormann v. Board of Supervisors, 584 N.W.2d 309 (Iowa 1998) (holding right-to-farm law unconstitutional).

[15] §§ 2.11, 2.12.

[1] Thorp v. Town of Lebanon, 612 N.W.2d 59 (Wis. 2000) (equal protection claim stated because town rezoned agricultural land without examining its suitability to the zoned usage but rejecting substantive and procedural due process claims; citing this treatise).

[2] Wash. Rev. Code Ann. § 36.70A.177(2)(a) (may regulate density of development in agricultural zones and restrict or prohibit non-farm uses).

statutory standards govern reclassification. Land in EFU zones receives preferential property tax assessment.[3]

Nonexclusive agricultural zoning allows non-farm dwellings as-of-right or as a conditional use in agricultural zones, though agricultural uses are preferred. The as-of-right ordinances may require a large lot for a single-family dwelling that can range from ten to 640 acres.[4] Conditional use zoning allows non-farm dwellings as a conditional use if they meet criteria based on the compatibility of the dwelling with surrounding agricultural uses.[5]

Area-based allocation is another form of as-of-right nonexclusive agricultural zoning for non-farm dwellings. Under one variant, the ordinance allows one non-farm dwelling unit for a specified number of farm acres. A one-hundred-acre farm, for example, is allowed two non-farm dwellings if the ordinance allows one non-farm dwelling for each fifty farm acres. Another alternative provides a sliding scale allocation under which the number of non-farm dwellings permitted per acre decreases as farm size increases.

In *Boundary Drive Assocs. v. Shrewsbury Twp. Bd. of Supvrs.*,[6] the Pennsylvania Supreme Court applied substantive due process analysis under state law that balances the public interest against the impact of a regulation on property rights and upheld an area-based allocation ordinance. The ordinance included an area-based sliding scale that increased the number of single-family dwellings allowed as the size of the farm increased, but the number of dwellings allowed did not increase in linear proportion to the increase in farm size. As a result, the ordinance allowed a greater residential density on small farms than it did on large farms. The court upheld the ordinance as applied to a thirty-nine-acre farm.

The court was skeptical about the utility of a linear area-based allocation. If it allowed one dwelling unit for each farm acre it would allow one hundred homes on each one-hundred-acre farm. This would not help preserve agricultural land. The court also held that the ordinance was not discriminatory even though it allowed a greater residential density on smaller farms. This density differential helped preserve the larger, more workable, farms, but allowed more density on smaller farms that were not economically viable.

---

[3] Or. Rev. Stat. §§ 215.203, 215.263; 215.780. *See* Lane County v. Land Conserv. & Dev. Comm'n, 942 P.2d 278 (Or 1997) (upholding rule providing stringent requirements for non-farm use); Dorvinen v. Crook County, 957 P.2d 180 (Or. App. 1998) (prohibiting division of farmland into parcels that violate statutory minimum); Still v. Board of County Comm'rs, 600 P.2d 433 (Or. App.1979) (reversing approval of 30-lot subdivision). *See also* Wis. Stat. Ann. §§ 91.71–91.80 (authorizing county agricultural zoning and property tax preferences).

[4] Vt. Stat. Ann. tit.24m § 4407(1)(A) (25 acres).

[5] Whitted v. Canyon County Board of Comm'rs, 44 P.3d 1173 (Idaho 2002) (upholding conditional use for subdivision of farmland into residential lots).

[6] 491 A.2d 86 (Pa. 1985), *distinguishing* Hopewell Twp. Bd. of Supvrs. v. Golla, 452 A.2d 1337 (Pa. 1982).

§ 12.13   The Takings Issue.

Agricultural zoning can present a takings issue if it prohibits non-farm development or restricts the density of development in agricultural zones. The Supreme Court's decision in *Agins v. City of Tiburon*,[1] which dismissed a facial takings attack on an open space zoning ordinance, provides support for the constitutionality of agricultural zoning under the takings clause. The Court held the open space ordinance advanced "legitimate governmental goals," and noted that California legislation required open space plans that would discourage "the premature and unnecessary conversion of open-space land to urban uses." The Court also held the zoning ordinance was adopted to protect the residents of the municipality from the "ill effects of urbanization." and that "[s]uch governmental purposes have long been recognized as legitimate." Agricultural zoning serves similar purposes, and courts have had no difficulty holding agricultural zoning as serving a legitimate governmental purpose.[2]

The courts have upheld large lot requirements for residential lots in agricultural districts as a legitimate means of preserving agricultural land by discouraging residential development.[3] They have also upheld large lot requirements in agricultural zones against takings claims based on a loss of property value, because some value remained in the property under the agricultural zoning.[4] Takings problems are mitigated when the ordinance allows some non-agricultural use of the property, such as the clustering of a minimum number of homes or the construction of residential dwellings.[5]

---

[1] 447 U.S. 255 (1980), discussed in § 2.08.

[2] Mays v. Board of Trustees, 2002 Ohio App. LEXIS 3347 (Ohio App. 2002) (20-acre lot minimum); Gardner v. New Jersey Pinelands Comm'n, 593 A.2d 251 (N.J. 1991) (upholding agricultural use restrictions in Pinelands).

[3] Kirk v. Zoning Hearing Bd., 713 A.2d 1226 (Pa. Commw. 1998) (one or 1 ½ acres depending on whether public services available).

[4] Gisler v. County of Madera, 112 Cal. Rptr. 919 (Cal. App. 1974) (18 acres); County of Ada v. Henry, 668 P.2d 994 (Idaho 1983) (160 acres; property owners were properly charged with notice of restriction when they bought property). *See also* North Sacramento Land Co. v. City of Sacramento, 189 Cal. Rptr. 739 (Cal. App. 1983) (upholding open space ordinance); Cordorus Twp. v. Rodgers, 492 A.2d 73 (Pa. Commw. 1985) (court held fifty-acre lot size requirement did not violate substantive due process even though it reduced value of property by two-thirds); Chevron Oil Co. v. Beaver County, 449 P.2d 989 (Utah 1969) (upholding grazing ordinance). *Contra* Nagawicka Island Corp. v. City of Delafield, 343 N.W.2d 816 (Wis. App. 1983) (three-acre agricultural zoning totally prohibited development on lake island).

[5] Daddario v. Cape Cod Comm'n, 681 N.E.2d 833 (Mass. 1997) (no taking when less extensive sand and gravel operations than those proposed would be allowed, and when ordinance allowed alternative uses such as residential use); Bell River Assocs. v. China Charter Township, 565 N.W.2d 695 (Mich. App. 1997); Gardner v. New Jersey Pinelands Comm'n, 593 A.2d 251 (N.J. 1991);.Appeal of Realen Valley Forge Greene Assocs, 799 A.2d 938 (Pa. Commw. 2002);

Several cases, especially in Illinois, considered claims that exclusive agricultural zoning and large lot zoning requirements were a taking as applied to a particular property.[6] In some of these cases, the municipality refused to rezone the land to a nonagricultural use. The courts evaluate an as-applied taking claim by determining whether the agriculturally zoned land is suitable for productive agricultural use and whether the agricultural use is reasonable in view of the surrounding uses in the area. Courts that uphold agricultural zoning against as-applied taking claims also rely on its consistency with a comprehensive plan. If an agricultural use is viable, a landowner should not be able to argue a per se taking has occurred under the *Lucas* case[7] because she has been deprived of all economically beneficial use of her land.[8]

E. COASTAL SETBACK LEGISLATION.

§ 12.14 National and State Programs.

A number of states along the nation's coasts and lakes have enacted coastal setback legislation. The adoption of coastal setback legislation is encouraged by the National Coastal Zone Management Act (CZMA), which provides federal funding for coastal management programs in the coastal and Great Lakes states. The protection of beaches and dunes and the prevention of development in erosion-prone areas are among the policies adopted as the basis for state coastal programs that are funded by the Act.[1]

Setback legislation adopted by the coastal and Great Lakes states is usually enacted to control erosion, though there may be other purposes, such as a reduction in the loss of lives and property from coastal hazards.[2] The statute

---

[6] As-applied taking not found: Racich v. County of Boone, 625 N.E.2d 1095 (Ill. App. 1993) (upholding rating system applied to determine when agricultural land should be developed); Harvard State Bank v. County of McHenry, 620 N.E.2d 1360 (Ill. App. 1993); Vanderburgh County. v. Rittenhouse, 575 N.E.2d 663 (Ind. App. 1991); Smythe v. Butler Twp., 620 N.E.2d 901 (Ohio App. 1993); Joyce v. City of Portland, 546 P.2d 1100 (Or. App. 1976); Petersen v. Dane County, 402 N.W.2d 376 (Wis. App. 1987). *Contra* Pierson v. Henry County, 417 N.E.2d 234 (Ill. App. 1981); Smeja v. County of Boone, 339 N.E.2d 452 (Ill. App. 1975). *See also* Barrett v. Poinsett Cty., 811 S.W.2d 324 (Ark. 1991) (can prohibit landfill on agricultural land); Nagatani Bros. v. Skagit County Bd. of Comm'rs, 728 P.2d 1104 (Wash. App. 1986) (subdivision denial on residentially-zoned land to preserve adjacent agricultural area held invalid).

[7] § 2.09.

[8] Nelson v. Benton County, 839 P.2d 233 (Or. App. 1992) (rejecting per se taking argument based on denial of non-farm dwelling; *Nollan* exaction rule does not apply); Mays v. Board of Trustees, 2002 Ohio App. LEXIS 3347 (Ohio App. 2002)

[1] 16 U.S.C. § 1452.

[2] *E.g.*, Fla. Stat. Ann. §§ 161.041, 161.053; Md. Nat. Res. Code § 8-1102; Me. Rev. Stat. Ann. tit. 38, §§ 480-A et seq.; Mich. Comp. Laws § 34.3211 (state environmental agency to identify high risk coastal erosion areas and approve local zoning that regulates coastal erosion); S.C. Code

usually authorizes a state agency to administer the law, though it may also provide for local participation under state agency supervision. It may authorize the establishment of a fixed coastal set back line, or a floating setback that is established when a landowner makes an application for a development permit. It may prohibit any permanent development or structure seaward of the setback area, or may allow development only when the permitting agency finds that it will not have a detrimental effect on the coastal area. Non-structural uses, such as recreation, are usually allowed.

§ 12.15   The Takings Issue.

State coastal setback legislation can present a serious taking problem because a development restriction or permit denial under these statutes can result in an almost total prohibition on the use of property. The Supreme Court's decision in *Lucas v. South Carolina Coastal Comm'n*[1] held the South Carolina beach setback law was a taking per se because the state agency denied the landowner all economically beneficial use of his property by refusing to approve residential development within the setback line. Cases prior to *Lucas* had divided on the constitutionality of coastal setback and dune control legislation.[2] The holdings in these cases require reconsideration under the *Lucas* decision. Courts can find a taking has not occurred if development is possible outside the protected area, if a refusal to allow development does not totally prohibit all economically viable use, or if the development restriction is held to be a "background principle" of state property law.[3] The *Lucas* decision may now also be of less importance. The Court held in its *Lake Tahoe* decision that cases in which a taking would be found under *Lucas* are rare.[4]

---

§§ 48-39-250 et seq.; Tex. Nat. Res. Code §§ 61.012, 61.013 (public beaches); Va. Code Ann. §§ 28.2-1400 et seq. *See* Island Harbor Beach Club, Ltd. v. Department of Natural Resources, 495 So. 2d 209 (Fla. App. 1986). (upholding establishment of setback line); Topliss v. Planning Comm'n, 842 P.2d 648 (Hawaii App. 1993) (reversing denial of permit in shoreline special management area). *See also* Cal. Pub. Res. Code § 30253(2) (coastal act policy on coastal erosion); Conn. Gen. Stat. § 22a-109 (municipal zoning commissions to review coastal site plans for conformity with coastal regulations).

[1] 505 U.S. 1003 (1992). *See* § 2.09.

[2] Held constitutional: Hirtz v. State, 773 F. Supp. 6 (S.D. Tex. 1991) (public beaches); McNulty v. Town of Indialantic, 727 F. Supp. 604 (M.D. Fla. 1989) (applying nuisance exception and rule that landowner had knowledge of regulatory system). Held unconstitutional: Seichner v. Town of Islip, 439 N.E.2d 352 (N.Y. 1982) (dune district ordinance); Annicelli v. Town of South Kingstown, 463 A.2d 133 (R.I. 1983) (shoreline high flood danger district).

[3] Oceco Land Co. v. Department of Natural Resources, 548 N.W.2d 702 (Mich. App. 1996) (refusal of development held not a taking under sand dune protection act because landowner could build on alternative site on property); Stevens v. City of Cannon Beach, 854 P.2d 449 (Or. 1993) (denial of permits for seawall justified by "background principles" of state property law and nuisance; economically viable use of property not prohibited)

[4] Tahoe-Sierra Preservation Council, Inc. v. Tahoe Regional Planning Agency, 535 U.S. 302 (2002).

Some courts had applied the notice rule to hold a taking did not occur when a property owner bought or acquired land after a coastal setback law was adopted.[5] The Supreme Court rejected the rule that purchase with notice is an absolute bar to a takings claim in its *Palazzolo* decision, but courts may still consider purchase after the enactment of a law as a factor in a takings case.

E.   TRANSFER OF DEVELOPMENT RIGHTS.

§ 12.16   Transfer of Development Rights.

Transfer of development rights (TDR) programs have been proposed and adopted as a method for protecting natural resource areas. As in TDR programs for historic landmarks, they authorize the sale of unused development rights in protected natural resource areas to landowners in receiving areas, who may utilize the transferred development rights for more intensive development. Montgomery County, Maryland, adopted a successful TDR program for its agriculturally zoned areas,[1] and state legislation authorizes a TDR program to implement land use regulations for the preservation of land in the New Jersey Pinelands.[2] A county development bank established to administer the Pinelands TDR program has been upheld.[3] Some states specifically authorize transfer of development rights programs for natural resource areas.[4]

The constitutional problems raised by TDR programs in natural resource areas are the same as those raised by TDR programs for historic landmarks.[5] Courts have upheld TDR programs adopted to preserve land in agricultural and natural resource areas.[6] The New Jersey Supreme Court relied on the availability of a

---

[5] Wooten v. South Carolina Coastal Comm'n, 510 S.E.2d 716 (S.C. 1999); City of Virginia Beach v. Bell, 498 S.E.2d 414 (Va. 1998). *See* § 2.16 (discussing notice rule as application of investment-backed expectations takings factor).

[1] *See* Md. Ann. Code art. 66B, § 11.01 (authorizing TDR programs).

[2] N.J. Stat. Ann. §§ 13:18A-1 to 13:18A-29. *See also* N.J. Stat. Ann. §§ 4:1C-49 to 4:1C-55 (State Transfer of Development Rights Bank Act).

[3] Matlack v. Board of Chosen Freeholders, 466 A.2d 83 (N.J.L. Div. 1983), *aff'd per curiam*, 476 A.2d 1262 (N.J. App. Div. 1984).

[4] *E.g.*, Ga. Code Ann. § 36-66A-1 et seq.; Mich. Comp. Laws Ann. §§ 125.593-125.595 (agricultural land); N.Y. General City Law § 20-f; N.Y. Town Law § 261-a; N.Y. Village Law § 7-101; Tenn. Code Ann. § 13-7-101(a)(2). *See also* § 11.38.

[5] § 11.38.

[6] Barancik v. County of Marin, 872 F.2d 834 (9th Cir. 1988) (upholding TDR program as rationally related to goal of agricultural preservation); Aptos Seascape Corp. v. County of Santa Cruz, 188 Cal. Rptr. 191 (Cal. App. 1982) (compensating densities on-site and off-site for restrictions on beachfront); Glisson v. Alachua Cty., 558 So. 2d 1030 (Fla. App. 1990) (TDR program a factor in dismissing facial taking claim against wetlands regulations); City of Hollywood v. Hollywood, Inc., 432 So.2d 1332 (Fla. App. 1982) (on-site compensating densities to preserve beachfront); W.J.F. Realty Corp. v. State, 672 N.Y.S.2d 1007 (Sup. Ct. 1998) (upholding TDR program in Pine Barrens).

TDR program when upholding the constitutionality of agricultural zoning in the Pinelands.[7]

The Maryland court invalidated the Montgomery County TDR program because the county had not properly adopted it.[8] The court held the zoning ordinance improperly delegated to the planning board an unlimited authority it did not have to designate receiving parcels and determine the increased density allowable on these parcels. It suggested the proper procedure was to designate receiving areas as subclassifications in designated zoning districts. The county has now implemented the court's suggestion.

---

[7] Gardner v. New Jersey Pinelands Comm'n, 593 A.2d 251 (N.J. 1991).

[8] West Montgomery County Citizens Ass'n v. Maryland-Nat'l Capital Park & Planning Comm'n, 522 A.2d 1328 (Md. 1987).

REFERENCES

Books and Monographs

Berry, Areas of Critical State Concern in Modernizing State Planning Legislation: The Growing Smart Papers, Vol. 1, at 105, American Planning Ass'n, Planning Advisory Serv. Rep. Nos. 462–463 (1996).

C. Duerksen & R.M. Gobel, Aesthetics, Community Character, and the Law, Planning Advisory Serv. Rep. No. 489/490 (1999).

M. Jaffe & F. DiNovo, Local Groundwater Protection (1987).

L. Malone, Environmental Regulation of Land Use. (supplemented periodically)

National Agricultural Lands Study, The Protection of Farmland: A Reference Guidebook for State and Local Governments (1981).

R. Olshanksy, Planning for Hillside Development, American Planning Ass'n, Planning Advisory Serv. Rep. No. 466 (1996).

Regulations for Flood Plains, American Planning Ass'n, Planning Advisory Serv. Rep. No. 277 (1972).

D. Thurow, W. Toner & D. Erley, Performance Controls for Sensitive Lands, American Planning Ass'n, Planning Advisory Serv. Rep. No. 307 (1975).

Articles

Ausness, Wild Dunes and Serbonian Bogs: The Impact of the *Lucas* Decision on Shoreline Protection Programs, 70 Denver L.J. 437 (1993) (contains citations to state statutes).

Ausness, Regulatory Takings and Wetland Protection in the Post-*Lucas* Era, 30 Land & Water L. Rev. 349 (1995).

Babcock, Has the U.S. Supreme Court Finally Drained the Swamp of Takings Jurisprudence? The Impact of *Lucas v. South Carolina Coastal Council* on Wetlands and Coastal Barrier Beaches, 19 Harv. Envtl. L. Rev. 1 (1995).

Burgess-Jackson, The Ethics and Economics of Right-to-Farm Statutes, 9 Harv. J.L. & Pub. Pol'y 481 (1986).

Cordes, Takings, Fairness and Farmland Preservation, 60 Ohio St. L.J. 1033 (1999).

DeGrove, Critical Area Programs in Florida: Creative Balancing of Growth and the Environment, 34 Wash. U.J. Urb. & Contemp. L. 51 (1988).

Duerksen, Tree and Vegetation Protection Ordinances, 16 Zoning & Plan. L. Rep. 169 (1993); 17 *id.* 1.

Duncan, Toward a Theory of Broad-Based Planning for the Preservation of Agricultural Land, 24 Nat. Resources J. 591 (1984).

Geier, Agricultural Districts and Zoning: A State-Local Approach to a National Problem, 8 Ecology L.Q. 655 (1980).

Grossman & Fischer, Protecting the Right to Farm: Statutory Limits on Nuisance Actions Against the Farmer, 1983 Wis. L. Rev. 95.

Guy & Holloway, Policy Coordination and the Takings Clause: The Coordination of Natural Resource Programs Imposing Multiple Burdens on Farmers and Landowners, 8 J. Land Use & Envtl. L. 175 (1992).

Hand, Right-To-Farm Laws: Breaking New Ground in the Preservation of Farmland, 45 U. Pitt. L. Rev. 289 (1984).

Hartzell, Agricultural and Rural Zoning in Pennsylvania — Can You Get From Here to There?, 10 Vill. Envtl. L.J. 245 (1999).

Holloway & Guy, Rethinking Local and State Agricultural Land Use and Natural Resource Policies: Coordinating Programs to Address the Interdependency and Combined Losses of Farms, Soils, and Farmland, 5 J. Land Use & Envtl. L. 379 (1990).

Houlahan, Comparison of State Construction Setbacks to Manage Development in Coastal Hazard Areas, 17 Coastal Mgt. 219 (1989).

Johnson, Defining the Property Interest: A Vital Issue in Wetlands Taking Analysis After *Lucas,* 14 J. Energy, Natural Resources & Envtl. L. 1 (1994).

Johnston & Madison, From Landmarks to Landscapes: A Review of Current Practice in the Transfer of Development Rights, 63 J. Am. Plan. Ass'n 365 (1997).

McGilvray, Anderson & West, Managing Coastal Development: An Evaluation of the Transfer of Development Rights Approach, 13 Coastal Zone Mgt. J. 25 (1985).

Pivo, Small & Wolfe, Rural Cluster Zoning: Survey and Guidelines, Land Use L. & Zoning Dig., Vol. 42, No. 9, at 3 (1990).

Popp, A Survey of Governmental Response to the Farmland Crisis: States' Application of Agricultural Zoning, 11 U. Ark. Little Rock L.J. 515 (1988-89).

Rasche, Protecting Agricultural Lands in Oregon: An Assessment of the Exclusive Farm Use System, 77 Or. L. Rev. 993 (1998).

Rose, Farmland Preservation Policy and Programs, 24 Nat. Resources J. 591 (1984).

Spahn, The Beach and Shore Preservation Act: Regulating Coastal Construction in Florida, 24 Stetson L. Rev. 353 (1995).

Strong, Transfer of Development Rights to Protect Water Resources, Land Use L. & Zoning Dig., Vol. 50, No. 9, at 3 (1998).

Tarlock, Prevention of Groundwater Contamination, 8 Zoning & Plan. L. Rep. 121 (1985).

Titus, Rising Seas, Coastal Erosion, and the Takings Clause: How to Save Wetlands and Beaches Without Hurting Property Owners, 57 Md. L. Rev. 1279 (1998).

Vandlik, Waiting for Uncle Sam to Buy the Farm. . .Forest, or Wetland? A Call For New Emphasis on State and Local Land Use Controls in Natural Resource Protections, 8 Fordham Envtl. L.J. 691 (1997).

Weinstein, Revisiting the National Flood Insurance Program, Land Use L. & Zoning Dig., Vol. 48, No. 10, at 3 (1996).

White, Beating Plowshares Into Townhomes: The Loss of Farmland and Strategies For Slowing Its Conversion to Nonagricultural Uses, 28 Envtl. L. 113 (1998).

Williams, Scenic Protection as a Legitimate Goal of Public Regulation, 38 W.U.J. Urb. & Contemp. L. 3 (1990).

Student Work

Note, The Chesapeake Bay Preservation Act: Does Land Use Regulation Protect Interstate Resources?,31 Wm. & Mary L. Rev. 735 (1990).

Note, Farmland and Open Space Preservation in Michigan: An Empirical Analysis, 19 U. Mich. J.L. Ref. 1107 (1986).

Note, Preserving New Jersey's Forestland Through the Farmland Assessment Act, 17 Rutgers L.J. 155 (1985).

Note, The Right to Farm: Hog-Tied and Nuisance-Bound, 73 N.Y.U. L. Rev. 1694 (1998).

Comment, Ecosystem Communities: Zoning Principles to Promote Conservation and the Economy, 35 Santa Clara L. Rev. 1309 (1995).

Comment, Evaluating Farmland Preservation Through Suffolk County, New York's Purchase of Development Rights Program, 18 Pace Envtl. L. Rev. 197 (2000).

Comment, Florida's Local Historic Preservation Ordinances: Maintaining Flexibility While Avoiding Vagueness Claims, 25 Fl. St. U.L. Rev. 1017 (1998).

Comment, Preserving Our Heritage: Tools to Cultivate Agricultural Preservation in New York State, 17 Pace L. Rev. 591 (1997).

Comment, Transferable Development Rights and the Deprivation of All Economically Beneficial Use: Can TDRs Salvage Regulations That Would Otherwise Constitute a Taking? 34 Idaho L. Rev. 679 (1998).

Comment, Trophy Homes and Other Alpine Predators: The Protection of Mountain Views Through Ridge Line Zoning, 25 B.C. Envtl. Aff. L. Rev. 913 (1998).

Comment, Wisconsin's Shoreland Management Program: An Assessment With Implications for Effective Natural Resources Management and Protection, 1999 Wis. L. Rev. 273–346.

Casenote, Zoning and Planning — Innovative Zoning for the Preservation of Agricultural Land, 59 Temple L.Q. 861 (1986).

Notes on a Bibliography

Treatises. Several multi-volume treatises on land use law are available. These include: Williams, *American Planning Law: Land Use and the Police Power* (John M. Taylor, Revision Author); Rohan, *Zoning and Land Use Controls* (Eric Damian Kelly, Revision Author); Anderson, *American Law of Zoning*, (Kenneth Young, Revision Author); Yokley, Zoning Law and Practice (Douglas MacGregor, Revision Author); and Rathkopf, *The Law of Zoning and Planning* (Edward J. Ziegler, Revision Author); and Kmiec, *Zoning and Planning Deskbook*. These treatises are updated regularly with revised chapters and supplementary material.

Periodicals. There is only one university-based law review that specializes in land use law, the Journal of Land Use and Environmental Law, published at Florida State University. Land use law articles are published frequently in The Urban Lawyer (official publication of the State and Local Government Law Section of the American Bar Association). The Planning and Law Division of the American Planning Association publishes a newsletter that reviews recent cases of interest and contains other articles and features.

Two monthly periodicals are devoted entirely to land use law. The American Planning Association publishes the *Land Use Law and Zoning Digest.* Each issue contains a lead article and digests of recent cases and legislation. APA also publishes a monthly *Zoning News* that reports on new developments in zoning around the country. West Group publishes a monthly *Zoning and Planning Law Report* that contains a lead article and reports on recent court decisions.

West Group also publishes an annual *Land Use and Environment Law Review,* that contains leading articles on land use law published in the law reviews during the previous year, and an annual *Zoning and Planning Law Handbook.* The *Handbook* contains articles from the law reviews and new material on current land use law topics. The *Journal of the American Planning Association* occasionally carries articles on land use law and practice.

Several journals are devoted to environmental law. Of these, the *Ecology Law Quarterly, Environmental Law, The Harvard Environmental Law Review,* and the *Natural Resources Journal* are most likely to carry articles on land use law. Another journal, *Coastal Management,* carries articles on legal problems in coastal zone management programs, including land use programs.

Services. The American Planning Association publishes a monthly *Planning Advisory Service.* Each issue is a report on a land use or planning topic. Attention is given on a periodic basis to land use control problems and techniques. Two services in the environmental law field are of interest. The *Environmental Law Reporter* is published monthly by the Environmental Law Institute and contains articles, judicial decisions and case abstracts. The *Environment Reporter,* published by the Bureau of National Affairs, reviews recent developments in the field and includes the full text of selected decisions.

Bibliographies. The *Journal of Planning Literature* reviews recent periodical literature on planning and land use and also publishes bibliographies on land use topics.

TABLE OF CASES

A

A Local & Regional Monitor v. Los Angeles, City of, 16 Cal. Rptr. 2d 358 (Cal. App. 1993) 11.38n7

A.A. Profiles, Inc. v. Fort Lauderdale, City of, 253 F.3d 546 . . . . 8.26n9

A.A. Profiles, Inc. v. Ft. Lauderdale, City of, 850 F.2d 1483 (11th Cir. 1988) . . . 2.30n3, n13; 6.36n1

Abbeville Arms v. Abbeville, City of, 257 S.E.2d 716 (S.C. 1979) 6.16n6; 6.17n2

Abbott House v. Tarrytown, 312 N.Y.S.2d 841 (App. Div. 1970) 5.10n1

Abdella v. Smith, 149 N.W.2d 537 (Wis.1967) . . . 4.04n1

Abel v. Zoning Bd. of Appeals, 374 A.2d 227 (Conn. 1977) 6.48n2

Aberdeen, City of v. Herrmann, 301 N.W.2d 674 (S.D. 1981) 5.20n1

ABN 51st Street Partners v. New York, City of, 724 F. Supp. 1142 (S.D.N.Y. 1989) 6.05n18

Aboud v. Wallace, 463 N.Y.S.2d 572 (App. Div. 1983) 5.79n9

Abram v. Fayetteville, City of, 661 S.W.2d 371 (Ark. 1983) 6.57n15

Abrams v. Gearhart, 184 N.E.2d 411 (Ohio App. 1961) 8.02n9

A.C.E. Equip. Co. v. Erickson, 152 N.W.2d 739 (Minn. 1967) 4.25n2

Acierno v. Cloutier, 40 F.3d 597 (3d Cir. 1994) . . 8.35n5; 8.36n9, n14

Acierno v. Folsom, 337 A.2d 309 (Del. 1975) . . . 6.73n1

Ackerley Communications v. Cambridge, City of, 88 F.3d 33 (1st Cir. 1996) 11.19n8

Ackerley Communications v. Krochalis, 108 F.3d 1095 (9th Cir. 1997) 11.13n3; 11.19n7

Ackerley Communications, Inc. v. Cambridge, City of, 88 F.3d 33 (1st Cir. 1996) 11.19n11

Ackerley Communications, Inc. v. Seattle, City of, 602 P.2d 1177 (Wash. 1979) 11.11n4

Ackerley Communications of the Northwest v. Krochalis, 108 F.3d 1095 (9th Cir. 1997) 11.17n4

Ackerman v. Port of Seattle, 348 P.2d 64 (Wash. 1960) 5.39n8

Ackman v. Board of Adjustment, 596 N.W.2d 96 (Iowa 1999) 6.05n10; 6.56n4

Acorn Corp. v. Zoning Hearing Bd., 523 A.2d 436 (Pa. Commw. 1987) 8.06n1

Act I, Inc. v. Zoning Hearing Bd., 704 A.2d 732 (Pa. Commw. 1997) 5.08n8

Ad Craft, Inc. v. Board of Zoning Appeals, 693 N.E.2d 110 (Ind. App. 1998) 11.18n1

Ad + Soil, Inc. v. County Comm'rs, 513 A.2d 893 (Md.1986) 6.50n3

Ada, County of v. Henry, 668 P.2d 994 (Idaho 1983) 12.13n4

Adams v. Brian, 212 So. 2d 128 (La. App. 1968) 6.05n16

Adams v. Cowart, 160 S.E.2d 805 (Ga. 1968) . . . 5.26n1

Adams v. DelMonte, 707 A.2d 1061 (N.J. App. Div. 1998) 5.20n3

Adams v. Fort Wayne, City of, 423 N.E.2d 647 (Ind. App. 1981) 8.15n3

Adams v. State, 555 P.2d 235 (Alaska 1976) 8.23n13

Adams Outdoor Advertising v. East Lansing, 483 N.W.2d 38 (Mich. 1992) 4.25n2

Adams Outdoor Advertising v. East Lansing, City of, 614 N.W.2d 634 . . . . 5.84n8; 11.07n16

Adams Outdoor Advertising v. Holland, City of, 600 N.W. 2d 339 (Mich. App. 1997) 4.25n6

Adams Outdoor Advertising v. Holland, City of, 600 N.W.2d 339 (Mich. App. 1999) 4.24n2

Adams Outdoor Advertising v. Holland, City of, 883 F. Supp. 207 (W.D. Mich. 1995) 8.43n6

Adams Outdoor Advertising, Inc. v. Holland, City of, 625 N.W.2d 377 . . . . 11.06n2

Adcock v. King, 520 S.W.2d 418 (Tex. Civ. App. 1975) 5.80n11

Adelman v. Baldwin, Town of, 750 A.2d 577 . . . 6.33n2; 6.58n1; 6.71n9

Admiral Dev. Corp. v. Maitland, City of, 267 So. 2d 860 (Fla. App. 1972) 9.18n2

Adolph v. Federal Emergency Mgt. Agency, 854 F.2d 732 (5th Cir. 1988) 12.08n2

Adolphson v. Zoning Bd. of Appeals, 535 A.2d 799 (Conn. 1988) 6.50n6

Adoption of (see name of party)

Ad+ Soil, Inc. v. County Commissioners 513 A.2d 893 (Md. 1986) 4.30n11

Adult World Bookstore v. Fresno, City of, 758 F.2d 1348 (9th Cir. 1985) 8.42n5

Advocacy Center for Persons With Disabilities, Inc. v. Woodlands Estates Ass'n, Inc. 192 F. Supp.2d 1344 . . . . 5.12n7

Aegerter v. Delafield, City of, 174 F.3d 886 (7th Cir. 1999) 4.42n5, n14

Aesthetics, Sign Ordinances, and Homeowners' Speech in City v. Gilleo, 20 Harv. Envtl. L. Rev. 473 (1996)

A.F.M., Ltd. v. Medford, City of, 704 N.E.2d 184 (Mass. 1999) 5.63n8

Agins v. Tiburon, City of 2.08

Agins v. Tiburon, City of, 447 U.S. 255 (1980) . . 2.11n2; 2.23n2

Agins v. Tiburon, City of, 447 U.S. 266 (1980) . . 6.09n5

Agins v. Tiburon, City of, 477 U.S. 255 (1980) . . 2.22n1

Agins v. Tiburon, City of, 598 P.2d 25 (Cal. 1979) 8.14n2

Agins v. Tiburon, City of, 598 P.2d 25 (Cal. 1979), *aff'd on other grounds,* 447 U.S. 255 (1980) . . 8.16n5; 8.22n1

Agins v. Tiburon, City of 447 U.S. 255 (1980) . . . 2.25n1; 12.13n1

Agripost Inc. v. Miami-Dade County, 195 F.3d 1225 (11th Cir. 1999) 2.34n4

Ahearn v. Wheatland, Town of, 39 P.3d 409 . . . . 9.05n1

Ahearn v. Zoning Bd. of Appeals, 551 N.Y.S.2d 392 (App. Div. 1990) 6.74n12

Ahmed v. Washington, 262, State of . . . 2.34n3

AIA Mobile Home Park v. Brevard County, 246 So. 2d 126 (Fla. App. 1971) 4.35n1

Ailes v. Decatur County Area Planning Comm'n, 448 N.E.2d 1057 (Ind. 1983) 5.85n1

A.J. Aberman, Inc. v. New Kensington, City of, 105 A.2d 586 (Pa. 1954) 6.18n2

Alachua County v. Eagle's Nest Farms, Inc., 473 So. 2d 257 (Fla. App. 1985) 6.03n3

Alameda, City of v. Van Horn, 219 Cal. Rptr. 764 (Cal. App. 1985) 5.37n3

Alameda County Land Use Ass'n v. Hayward, City of, 45 Cal. Rptr. 2d 752 (Cal. App. 1995) 3.08n1; 8.16n1

Alaska Airlines, Inc. v. Long Beach, City of, 951 F.2d 977 (9th Cir. 1991) 4.43n3

Albano v. Mayor & Twp. Comm., 476 A.2d 852 (N.J. App. Div. 1984) 5.31n5

Albany Area Builders Ass'n v. Clifton Park, Town of, 1991) 10.05n2

Albany Area Builders Ass'n v. Clifton Park, Town of, 576 N.Y.S.2d 932 (App. Div. 1991) . . 10.06n2

Albery v. Reddig, 718 F.2d 245 (7th Cir. 1983) . . 8.33n4

Albright v. Portage, City of, 470 N.W.2d 657 (Mich. App. 1991) 6.82n7

Albuquerque, City of v. Jackson, 684 P.2d 543 (N.M. App. 1984) 11.18n3

Aldom v. Borough of Roseland, 127 A.2d 190 (N.J. 1956) 6.74n10

Alegria v. Keeney, 687 A.2d 1249 (R.I. 1997) . . . 12.07n8, n11

Alexander v. DeKalb County, 444 S.E.2d 743 (Ga. 1994) 8.18n5

Alexander v. Hampstead, 525 A.2d 276 (N.H. 1987) 5.74n2

Alexander v. Hampstead, Town of, 525 A.2d 276 (N.H. 1987) 6.05n4

Alexander v. Minneapolis, City of, 125 N.W.2d 583 (Minn. 1963) 6.11n3

Alexander v. Minneapolis, City of, 928 F.2d 278 (8th Cir. 1991) 5.63n2; 5.65n5

Alexander's Department Stores v. Borough of Paramus, 592 A.2d 1168 (N.J. 1991) . . . 7.12n8

Alfred Weissman Real Estate, Inc. v. Big 5.55n6; 8.46n3

Alger v. Mukilteo, City of, 730 P.2d 1333 (Wash. 1987) 8.23n5, n7

Ali v. Los Angeles, City of, 91 Cal. Rptr.2d 458 (Cal. App. 1999) 2.22n9

Alleged Contempt of (see name of party)

Allegheny West Civic Council v. Zoning Bd. of Adjustment, 716 A.2d 600 (Pa. 1998) . . 5.19n3

Allegheny West Civic Council, Inc. v. Zoning Bd. of Adjustment, 689 A.2d 225 (Pa. 1997) . . 6.45n2

Allen v. City & County of Honolulu, 571 P.2d 328 (Haw. 1977) 6.13n2; 8.23n12

Allen v. Coffel, 488 S.W.2d 671 (Mo. App. 1972) 8.05n2; 8.13n6; 8.16n2

Allen v. Iranon, 283 F.3d 1070 . . . . . . 2.51n3

Allen v. St. Tammany Parish Police Jury, 690 So.2d 150 . . . . 8.14n1

Allen Plywood, Inc. v. Planning & Zoning Comm'n, 480 A.2d 584 (Conn. App. 1984) . . . 6.66n10

Allen Realty, Inc. v. Lawrence (I), City of, 790 P.2d 948 (Kan. App. 1990) 11.35n3

Allendale Congregation of Jehovah's Witnesses v. Grosman, 152 A.2d 569 (N.J. 1959) . . 6.57n15

Allied Structural Steel Co. v. Spannaus, 438 U.S. 234 (1978) 2.52n3

Allison v. Smith, 695 P.2d 791 (Colo. App. 1984) 4.09n2; 4.10n2

Allison v. Washington County, 548 P.2d 188 (Or. App. 1976) 6.82n6

Allred v. Raleigh, City of, 173 S.E.2d 533 (N.C. App. 1970), *rev'd on other grounds,* 178 S.E.2d 432 (N.C. 1971) 5.02n4

Alluis v. Marion County 3.18n4

Alluis v. Marion County, 668 P.2d 1242 (Or. App. 1983) 6.33n4

Almeida v. Zoning Bd. of Review, 606 A.2d 1318 (R.I. 1992) 6.17n1

Almquist v. Marshan, Town of, 245 N.W.2d 819 (Minn. 1976) 6.07n1; 6.11n3

Alperin v. Mayor & Twp. Comm., 219 A.2d 628 (N.J. 1966) 6.51n9

Alpine Christian Fellowship v. County Comm'rs, 870 F. Supp. 991 (D. Colo. 1994) 6.57n8

Alsensas v. Brecksville, 281 N.E.2d 21 (Ohio App. 1972) 2.36n5

Alta, Town of v. Ben Hame Corp., 836 P.2d 797 (Utah 1992) 5.19n3

Alta Vita Condominium Ass'n v. Zoning Hearing Bd., 736 A.2d 724 (Pa. Commw. 1999) . . . 9.25n5

Altaire Bldrs., Inc. v. Horseheads, Village of, 551 F. Supp. 1066 (W.D.N.Y. 1982) 8.31n2

Aluminum Co. of Am. v. Lipke, 320 S.W.2d 751 (Ark. 1959) 6.57n14

Alumni Control Bd. v. Lincoln, City of, 137 N.W.2d 800 (Neb. 1965) 6.42n1; 6.48n2

Alviani v. Dixon, 775 A.2d 1234 . . . . . 6.56n5

Amato v. Randolph Township, 457 A.2d 1188 (N.J. App. Div.) 9.10n5

Ambassador Books & Video, Inc. v. Little Rock, City of, 20 F.3d 585 (8th Cir. 1994) 5.64n1

Ambassador Books & Video, Inc. v. Little Rock, City of, 20 F.3d 858 (8th Cir. 1994) 5.63n4

Amberley Swim & Country Club v. Zoning Bd. of Appeals, 191 N.E.2d 364 (Ohio App. 1963) . . . 6.47n5

Ambler Realty Co. v. Euclid, Village of, 272 U.S. 365 (1926) 2.45n2

Amcon Corp. v. Eagan, City of, 348 N.W.2d 66 (Minn. 1984) 6.33n3; 8.11n16

American Airlines v. Hempstead, Town of, 398 F.2d 369 (2d Cir. 1969) 4.43n3

American Dredging Co. v. State, Dep't of Environmental Protection, 404 A.2d 42 (N.J. App. Div.1979) 12.07n9

American Federated General Agency, Inc. v. Ridgeland, City of, 72 F. Supp. 2d 695 (S.D. Miss. 1999) 11.18n1

American Legion Post 7 v. Durham, City of, 239 F.3d 601 . . . . 11.21n1

American Nat'l Bank & Trust Co. v. Chicago, City of, 311 N.E.2d 325 (Ill. App. 1974) 6.16n2

American Oil Co. v. Board of Appeals, 310 A.2d 796 (Md. 1973) 5.47n5

American Oil Co., State ex rel. v. Bessent, 135 N.W.2d 317 (Wis. 1965) 5.36n1

American Oil Co., State ex rel. v. Bessent 135 N.W.2d 317 (Wis. 1965) 2.46n5

American Savings and Loan Association v. Marin, County of, 653 F.2d 364 (9th Cir. 1980) 2.19n4

American Tower Corp. v. Common Council, 557 S.E.2d 752 . . . . 6.55n3

American Tower LP v. Huntsville, City of, 295 F.3d 1203 . . . . 4.42n14

Amerikohl Mining Co. v. Zoning Hearing Bd., 597 A.2d 219 (Pa. Commw. 1991) 6.74n3

Ames v. Painter, Town of, 389 S.E.2d 702 (Va. 1990) 6.56n2

Ames, City of v. Story County, 392 N.W.2d 145 (Iowa 1986) 4.38n7

Amherst Bldrs. Ass'n v. Amherst, City of, 402 N.E.2d 1181 (Ohio 1980) 9.22n1

Amherst Growth Study Comm'n, Inc. v. Board of Appeals, 296 N.E.2d 717 (Mass. App. 1973) . . 8.03n1; 8.06n1

Amherst, Town of v. Omnipoint Communications Enters., 173 F.3d 9 (1st Cir. 1999) . . . 4.42n7

Amico v. New Castle County, 553 F. Supp. 738 (D. Del. 1982) 8.43n9; 8.44n8

Ammirata v. Zoning Bd. of Appeals, 782 A.2d 1285 . . . . 12.11n13

Ammon R. Smith Auto Co., In re Appeal of , 223 A.2d 683 (Pa. 1966) 11.10n4

Amoco Oil Co. v. Minneapolis, City of, 395 N.W.2d 115 (Minn. App. 1986) 6.56n8

Amoco Oil Co. v. Schaumburg, Village of, 661 N.E.2d 380 (Ill. App. 1996) . . . 9.16n12, n13, n14

Amwest Investments, Ltd. v. Aurora, City of, 701 F. Supp. 1508 (D. Colo. 1988) 2.30n13

An Essay on Zinernon v. Burch, 87 Nw. L. Rev. 576 (1993)

Anaya, State ex rel. v. Select W. Lands, Inc., 613 P.2d 425 (N.M. App. 1979) 9.05n6

Anderson v. Board of Adjustment for Zoning Appeals, 931 P.2d 517 (Colo. App. 1996) 5.79n9

Anderson v. Board of Appeals of Chesapeake Beach, 322 A.2d 220 (Md. App. 1974) 6.42n1

Anderson v. Charter Township of Ypsilanti, 266 F.3d 487 . . . . 2.34n3

Anderson v. City Council, 40 Cal. Rptr. 41 (Cal. App. 1964) 6.21n6

Anderson v. Creighton 8.36

Anderson v. Douglas County, 4 F.3d 574 (8th Cir. 1993) 2.39n6; 2.42n10; 2.47n1

Anderson v. Island County, 501 P.2d 594 (Wash. 1972) 6.29n5; 8.04n1

Anderson v. Issaquah, City of, 851 P.2d 754 (Wash. App. 1993) 6.05n23

Anderson v. Old King's Hwy. Regional Historic Dist., 493 N.E.2d 188 (Mass. 1986) 11.29n4

Anderson v. Paragould, City of, 695 S.W.2d 851 (Ark. App. 1985) 5.81n7

Anderson v. Peden, 587 P.2d 59 (Or. 1978) 6.54n1; 6.56n15

Anderson v. Seattle, City of, 390 P.2d 994 (Wash. 1964) 5.74n3

Andover Dev. Corp. v. New Smyrna Beach, City of, 328 So. 2d 231 (Fla. App. 1972) 6.83n1

Andrus v. Allard 444 U.S. 51 (1979) 2.18n1

Anello v. Zoning Bd. of Appeals, 678 N.E.2d 870
(N.Y. 1997) 12.02n1
Anheuser-Busch, Inc. v. Schmoke, 63 F.3d 1305 (4th
Cir. 1995) 11.19n5
Animas Valley Sand & Gravel, Inc. v. Board of
County Comm'rs, 38 P.3d 59 . . . . . 2.19n1
Annapolis, City of v. Waterman, 745 A.2d 1000 . .
9.19n6
Annapolis Market Place, L.L.C. v. Parker, 802 A.2d
1029 . . . . 10.05n3
Annicelli v. South Kingston, Town of, 463 A.2d 133
(R.I. 1983) 8.21n5
Annicelli v. South Kingstown, Town of, 463 A.2d 133
(R.I. 1983) 12.15n2
The Ansley House, Inc. v. Atlanta, City of, 397 S.E.2d
419 (Ga. 1990) 5.81n2, n5
Ansson, Dolan v. Tigard's Rough Proportionality
Standard
Anza Parking Corp. v. Burlingame, City of, 241 Cal.
Rptr. 175 (Cal. App. 1987) 6.59n4
Appalachian Poster Advertising, Inc. v. Zoning Bd. of
Adjustment, 278 S.E.2d 321 (N.C. App. 1981)
. . . . 5.80n6
Appeal of (see name of party)
Appeal of Estate of (see name of party)
Application of (see name of applicant)
Applied Chem. Tech., Inc. v. Merrimack, Town of,
490 A.2d 1348 (N.H. 1985) 4.30n4
April v. Broken Arrow, City of, 775 P.2d 1347 (Okla.
1989) 8.09n4; 8.21n3; 12.09n9
Aptos Seascape Corp. v. Santa Cruz, County of, 188
Cal. Rptr. 191 (Cal. App. 1982) 12.16n6
Aragon & McCoy v. Albuquerque Nat'l Bank, 659
P.2d 306 (N.M. 1983) 6.15n4
Arant v. Board of Adjustment, 126 So. 2d 100 (Ala.
1961) 6.50n7
Archdiocese of Portland v. Washington, County of
458 P.2d 682 (Or. 1969) 6.56n6
Area Plan Comm'n v. Wilson, 701 N.E.2d 856 (Ind.
App. 1998) 6.57n4, n13
Aries Dev. Co. v. California Coastal Zone Conserva-
tion Comm'n, 122 Cal. Rptr. 315 (Cal. App. 1975)
. . . . 6.18n1
Arithmetic, Matter of
Arizona v. Owens, 562 P.2d 738 (Ariz. App. 1977)
. . . . 6.05n21
Arizona v. Zack, 674 P.2d 329 (Ariz. App. 1983)
. . . . 6.05n3
Arkansas Release Guidance Found. v. Needler, 477
S.W.2d 821 (Ark. 1972) 4.08n3
Arkules v. Board of Adjustment, 728 P.2d 657 (Ariz.
App. 1986) 6.41n10
Arlington Heights, Village of v. Metropolitan Hous.
Dev. Corp 2.45

Arlington Heights, Village of v. Metropolitan Housing
Dev. Corp 7.02
Arlington Political Republican Comm. v. Arlington
County, 983 F.2d 587 (4th Cir. 1993) . . . . . .
11.23n4
Armendirez v. Penman, 76 F.3d 1311 (9th Cir. 1996)
. . . . 2.44n1
Armory Park Neighborhood Ass'n v. Episcopal Com-
munity Serv., 712 P.2d 914 (Ariz. 1985) . . . .
4.08n3; 4.10n2
Armour & Co., Inc. v. Inver Grove Heights, 2 F.3d
176 (8th Cir. 1993) 2.23n2
Armstrong v. United States, 364 U.S. 40 (1960) . .
2.08n7
Arnel Dev. Co. v. Costa Mesa, City of, 620 P.2d 565
(Cal. 1980) 6.83n5
Arnel Dev. Co. v. Costa Mesa, City of 178 Cal. Rptr.
723 (Cal. App. 1981) 6.83n7
Arnel Dev. Co. v. Costa Mesa, City of 620 P.2d 565
(Cal. 1980) 6.26n6
Arnold v. Prince George's County, 311 A.2d 223 (Md.
1973) 3.21n2
Arnold Bernhard & Co. v. Planning & Zoning
Comm'n, 479 A.2d 801 (Conn. 1984) . . . . . .
6.07n1; 6.09n2
Aronovitz v. Metropolitan Dade County, 290 So. 2d
536 (Fla. App. 1974) 6.37n8
Aronson v. Sharon, Town of 195 N.E.2d 341 (Mass.
1965) 5.32n4
Arrigo v. Planning Bd., 429 N.E.2d 355 (Mass. App.
1981) 9.10n5
Arrington v. Dickerson, 915 F.Supp 1516 (M.D. Ala
1996) 2.51n3
Arrowhead Dev. Co. v. Livingston County Rd.
Comm'n 323 N.W.2d 702 (Mich. 1982) . . . . .
9.16n7
Arroyo Vista Partners v. Santa Barbara, County of,
732 F. Supp. 1046 (C.D. Cal. 1990) . . 2.51n9;
8.31n10
Art Neon Co. v. City & County of Denver, 488 F.2d
118 (10th Cir. 1973) . . 5.84n6; 5.86n1, n5, n6
Art Piculell Group v. Clackamas County, 922 P.2d
1227 (Or. App. 1996) 9.16n13, n14
Art Van Furniture Co. v. Kentwood, City of, 437
N.W.2d 380 (Mich. App. 1989) 11.10n3
Arthur v. Toledo, City of, 782 F.2d 565 (6th Cir. 1986)
. . . . 7.05n4
Arthur Land Co., LLC v. Ostego County, 645 N.W.2d
50 . . . . 6.25n3
Arthur Whitcomb, Inc. v. Carroll, Town of, 686 A.2d
743 (N.H. 1996) 4.30n10
Arvada, City of v. City & County of Denver, 663 P.2d
611 (Colo. 1983) 9.21n3
Arverne Bay Constr. Co. v. Thatcher 15 N.E.2d 587
(N.Y. 1938) 5.17n5

Ash Grove Cement Co. v. Jefferson County, 943 P.2d 85 (Mont. 1997) 3.13n1

Asian Americans for Equality v. Koch, 514 N.Y.S.2d 939 (App. Div. 1987) 4.25n1

Asian Americans for Equality v. Koch 527 N.E.2d 265 (N.Y. 1988) 7.17n1

Askew v. Cross Key Waterways, 372 So.2d 913 (Fla. 1978) 12.04n2

Aspen, City of v. Marshall, 912 P.2d 56 (Colo. 1996) 6.15n1

Aspen Hill Venture v. Montgomery County Council, 289 A.2d 303 (Md. App. 1972) 2.46n6

Asselin v. Conway, Town of, 607 A.2d 132 (N.H. 1992) 11.05n5

Asselin v. Conway, Town of, 628 A.2d 247 (N.H. 1993) . . . 6.05n11; 11.05n1; 11.10n4; 11.18n5

Associated Home Bldrs. of Greater E. Bay, Inc. v. Walnut Creek, City of, 484 P.2d 606 (Cal.) . . . 9.18n6

Associated Home Bldrs. of Greater Eastbay, Inc. v. Livermore, City of, 557 P.2d 473 (Cal. 1976) . . 10.08n8

Associated Home Bldrs. of Greater Eastbay, Inc. v. Livermore, City of 557 P.2d 473 (Cal. 1976) . . 6.10n5; 6.83n3; 7.24n1

Association for Preservation of 1700 Block of N St., N.W., & v. District of Columbia Bd. of Zoning Adjustment, 384 A.2d 674 (D.C. App. 1978) . . 6.50n5

Association of Relatives & Friends of AIDS Pations v. Regulations and Permits Admin., 740 F. Supp. 95 (D.P.R. 1990) 5.13n1

A.T. & G., Inc. v. Zoning Bd. of Review, 322 A.2d 294 (R.I. 1974) 5.81n8

AT & T Wireless PCS, Inc. v. City Council, 155 F.3d 423 (4th Cir. 1998) 4.42n6, n9, n12, n14, n15

AT&T Wireless PCS, Inc. v. Leafmore Forest Condominium Ass'n of Owners, 509 S.E.2d 374 (Ga. App. 1998) 8.04n4

Atherton, Town of v. Superior Court, 324 P.2d 328 (Cal. App. 1958) 4.28n2; 4.39n1

Athey v. Peru, City of, 317 N.E.2d 294 (Ill. App. 1974) 6.72n2

Atlanta, City of v. McLennan 226 S.E.2d 732 (Ga. 1976) 8.19n1

Atlanta, City of v. Tap Assocs., 544 S.E.2d 433 . . 6.25n3

Atlanta, City of v. Wansley Moving & Storage Co., 267 S.E.2d 234 (Ga. 1980) 8.14n10

Atlantic Richfield Co. v. Franklin Zoning Hearing Bd., City of, 465 A.2d 98 (Pa. Commw. 1983) 6.56n10, n11

Aunt Hack Ridge Estates, Inc. v. Planning Comm'n, 273 A.2d 880 (Conn. 1970) 9.19n1

Austin v. City & County of Honolulu, 840 F.2d 678 (9th Cir. 1988) 2.31n3

Austin, City of v. Teague, 570 S.W.2d 389 (Tex. 1978) 8.21n2, n6; 8.26n7

Austin Indep. School Dist. v. Sunset Valley, City of, 502 S.W.2d 670 (Tex. 1973) 4.28n2

Avalon v. Residential Care Homes 5.09n4

Avalon Home & Land Owners Ass'n v. Borough of Avalon, 543 A.2d 950 (N.J. 1988) . . . 5.80n1

Avatar Dev. Corp. v. State, 723 So.2d 199 (Fla. 1998) 12.05n2

Avco Community Devs., Inc. v. South Coast Regional Comm'n 553 P.2d 546 (Cal. 1976) . . . 6.15n2

Averill v. Superior Court, 50 Cal. Rptr. 2d 62 (Cal. App. 1996) 8.47n6

AVR, Inc. v. St. Louis Park, City of, 585 N.W.2d 411 (Minn. App. 1998) 5.86n5, n7

Ayres v. City Council, 207 P.2d 1 (Cal. 1947) . . . 9.16n8

Ayres v. City Council 207 P.2d 1 (Cal. 1949) . . . 4.25n5

B

B. Street Commons, Inc. v. Board of County Comm'rs, 835 F. Supp. 1266 (D. Colo. 1993) . . 8.32n4

B & W Mgt., Inc. v. Tasea Inv. Co., 451 A.2d 879 (D.C. App. 1982) 4.09n3

Baby Dolls Topless Saloons, Inc. v. Dallas, City of, 295 F.3d 471 . . . . 5.63n3; 5.65n2

Baby Tam & Co. v. Las Vegas, City of, 154 F.3d 1097 (9th Cir. 1998) 6.57n8, n12

Baby Tam & Co. v. Las Vegas II, City of, 199 F.3d 111 . . . . 6.57n8

Backer v. Sullivan's Island, Town of, 310 S.E.2d 433 (S.C. 1983) 5.18n8

Baddour v. Long Beach, City of, 18 N.E.2d 18 (N.Y. 1938) 5.19n6

Badger v. Ferrisburgh, Town of, 712 A.2d 911 (Vt. 1998) 5.81n7

Badger v. Frerrisburgh, Town of, 712 A.2d 911 (Vt. 1998) 5.81n3

Badke, State ex rel. v. Village Bd., 494 N.W.2d 408 (Wis. 1993) 6.76n11, n13

Baer v. Brookhaven, Town of, 537 N.E.2d 619 (N.Y. 1989) 5.05n2

Baggett v. Montgomery, City of, 160 So. 2d 6 (Ala. 1963) 5.39n7

Baglini v. Lauletta, 768 A.2d 825 . . . . . 8.46n10

Bagnall v. Beverly Shores, Town of, 726 N.E.2d 782 . . . . 8.04n4

Bailey v. Zoning Bd. of Adjustment, 801 A.2d 492 . . . . 9.29n2

Baker v. Chartiers Tp. Zoning Hearing Bd., 677 A.2d 1274 (Pa. Commw. 1996) 6.29n12

Baker v. Connell, 488 A.2d 1303 (Del. 1985) . . . 6.45n2; 6.50n2

Baker v. Coxe, 230 F.3d 470 . . . . 2.51n6

Baker v. Metropolitan Dade County, 774 So.2d 14 . . . . 6.58n1

Baker v. Milwaukee, City of 533 P.2d 772 (Or. 1975) 3.15n3

Baker v. Milwaukie, City of 533 P.2d 772 (Or. 1975) 6.33n9

Baker v. Parsons, 750 N.E.2d 953 . . . . . 8.47n1

Baker v. Planning Bd. 228 N.E.2d 831 (Mass. 1967) 9.09n18

Baker; State v. , 405 A.2d 368 (N.J. 1979) 5.05n2

Baker; State v. , 618 P.2d 997 (Or. App. 1980) . . 9.08n9

Bakken v. Council Bluffs, City of, 470 N.W.2d 34 (Iowa 1991) 8.09n7

Baldwin v. Redwood City, 540 F.2d 1360 (9th Cir. 1976) 11.23n1

Ballenger v. Door County, 388 N.W.2d 624 (Wis. App. 1986) 6.30n1

Baltica Constr. Co. v. Planning Bd., 537 A.2d 319 (N.J. App. Div. 1988) 9.16n3

Baltimore Planning Comm'n v. Victor Dev. Co., 275 A.2d 478 (Md. 1971) 9.09n12

Baltimore Scrap Corp. v. David J. Joseph Co., 81 F. Supp.2d 602 . . . . 5.55n6

Baltimore Scrap Corp. v. The David J. Joseph Co. 237 F.3d 394 . . . . 8.46n2

Baltis v. Westchester, Village of, 121 N.E.2d 495 (Ill. 1954) 4.35n1

Bama Invs., Inc. v. Metropolitan Dade County, 349 So. 2d 207 (Fla. App. 1977) . . 8.13n8; 8.15n2

Bamber v. United States, 45 Fed. Cl. 162 (1999) . . 2.08n8

Banberry Dev. Corp. v. South Jordan City, 631 P.2d 899 (Utah 1981) 9.22n2

Bangs v. Wells, Town of, 760 A.2d 632 . . 5.26n3

Bank of the Orient v. Tiburon, Town of, 269 Cal. Rptr. 690 (Cal. App. 1990) 6.07n4

Bankoff v. Board of Adjustment, 875 P.2d 1138 (Okla. 1994) 6.16n4; 6.56n8

Banks v. Bethany, City of, 541 P.2d 178 (Okla. 1975) 6.43n2

Bannum v. Louisville, City of, 958 F.2d 1354 (6th Cir. 1992) 8.32n3

Bannum, Inc. v. Columbia, City of, 516 S.E.2d 439 (S.C. 1999) 5.09n2

Bannum, Inc. v. Fort Lauderdale, City of, 157 F.3d 819 (11th Cir. 1998) . . 2.47n2; 2.48n3; 5.09n2, n4

Bannum, Inc. v. Ft. Lauderdale, City of, 901 F.2d 989 (11th Cir. 1990) 8.31n8

Bannum, Inc. v. Louisville, City of, 958 F.2d 1354 (6th Cir. 1992) 2.48n2; 5.09n4

Bannum, Inc. v. St. Charles, City of, 2 F.3d 267 (8th Cir. 1993) 2.48n3; 5.09n4

Barancik v. Marin, County of, 872 F.2d 834 (9th Cir. 1988) 12.16n6

Barbara Realty Co. v. Zoning Bd. of Review, 128 A.2d 342 (R.I. 1957) 6.73n1

Barbarino Realty & Dev. Co. v. Planning & Zoning Comm'n, 610 A.2d 1205 (Conn. 1992) 6.05n16

Barbaro v. Wroblewski, 689 N.E.2d 1369 (Mass. App. 1998) 6.56n14

Barber v. Municipality of Anchorage, 776 P.2d 1036 (Alaska 1989) 11.20n3

Barber v. Texas Dep't of Transp, 49 S.W.3d 12 . . 11.19n4

Barbulean v. Newburgh, City of, 640 N.Y.S.2d 935 (Sup. Ct. 1996) 6.57n2

Barnes Foundation v. Township of Lower Merion, 242 F.3d 151 . . . . 8.46n3

Barnes Foundation v. Township of Lower Merion, 982 F. Supp. 970 (E.D. Pa. 1997) 7.03n6

Barnhill v. North Myrtle Beach, City of, 511 S.E.2d 361 (S.C. 1999) 4.31n7

Barnum, City of v. Carlton, County of, 386 N.W.2d 770 (Minn. App. 1986) 6.56n12

Barolomeo v. Paradise Valley, Town of, 631 P.2d 564 (Ariz. App. 1981) 5.17n8

Barre Mobile Home Park v. Petersham, Town of 592 F. Supp. 633 (D. Mass. 1984), *aff'd* . . . *5.24n1*

Barrett v. Poinsett Cty., 811 S.W.2d 324 (Ark. 1991) 12.13n6

Barrett v. Union Twp. Comm., 553 A.2d 62 (N.J. App. Div. 1989) 6.74n9

Barrington Hills, Village of v. Hoffman Estates, Village of 410 N.E.2d 37 (Ill. 1980) . . 8.07n3

Barron Chevrolet Co. v. Danvers, Town of, 646 N.E.2d 89 (Mass. 1995) 11.11n10

Bartle v. Zoning Bd. of Adjustment, 137 A.2d 239 (Pa. 1958) 4.25n4

Bartlett v. Zoning Comm'n, 282 A.2d 907 (Conn.1971) 12.07n1

Barton v. H.D. Riders Motorcycle Club, Inc., 550 A.2d 91 (N.H. 1988) 8.15n9

Barton Contr'g Co. v. Afton, City of, 268 N.W.2d 712 (Minn. 1978) 6.68n3; 6.70n10

Bartram v. Zoning Comm'n of City of Bridgeport, 68 A.2d 308 (Conn. 1949) 6.30n3

Bartsch v. Planning & Zoning Comm'n 506 A.2d 1093 (Conn. App. 1986) 6.64n5

Baskin v. Bath Twp. Bd. of Zoning Appeals, 15 F.3d 569 (6th Cir. 1994) 8.45n3

Bass v. Attardi, 868 F.2d 45 (3d Cir. 1989) . . . .
8.36n2

Bass River Assocs. v. Mayor of Bass River Twp., 573
F. Supp. 205 (D.N.J. 1983), aff'd, 743 F.2d 159 (3d
Cir. 1984) 6.15n1

Batch v. Chapel Hill, Town of, 387 S.E.2d 655 (N.C.
1990) 9.09n13

Batch v. Chapel Hill, Town of,387 N.E.2d 655 (N.C.
1990) 10.14n7

Bateman v. W. Bountiful, City of 89 F.3d 704 . . .
2.44n1

Bateman v. West Bountiful, City of, 89 F.3d 704 (10th
Cir. 1996) 2.30n6; 2.31n2

Bates; State v. , 305 N.W.2d 426 (Iowa 1981) . . .
5.82n4

Bateson v. Geisse, 857 F.2d 1300 (9th Cir. 1988)
. . . . 2.31n1; 2.39n7; 2.42n7; 8.31n2;
8.32n3; 8.35n7; 8.37n1

Battagliani v. Red River, Town of, 669 P.2d 1082
(N.M. 1983) 5.83n2

Baucom's Nursery Co. v. Mecklenburg Cty., 366
S.E.2d 558 (N.C. App. 1988) 8.23n1

Baudier; State v. , 334 So. 2d 197 (La. 1976) . . .
5.20n1

Bauer v. Waste Management, 662 A.2d 1179 (Conn.
1995) 2.16n4; 2.35n2

Baum v. City & County of Denver, 363 P.2d 688
(Colo. 1961) 8.11n8

Baum v. Lunsford 365 S.E.2d 739 (Va. 1988) . . .
9.10n5

Baxter v. Belleville, City of, 720 F. Supp. 720 (S.D.
Ill. 1989) 5.13n1

Baxter v. Preston, City of 768 P.2d 1340 (Idaho 1989)
. . . . 5.79n11

Bay Area Addiction & Research, Inc. v. Antioch, City
of, 179 F.3d 715 (9th Cir. 1999) 5.16n2

Bay Area Addiction Research & Treatment Inc. v.
Antioch, City of, 179 F.3d 725 (9th Cir. 1999)
. . . . 5.12n11

Baylis v. Baltimore, City of, 148 A.2d 429 (Md. 1959)
. . . . 6.63n1

Baytree of Invarerray Realty Partners v. Lauderhill,
City of, 873 F.2d 1407 (11th Cir. 1989) . . . . .
7.04n4

Baytree of Inverarry Realty Partner v. Lauderhill, City
of, 873 F.2d 1407 (11th Cir. 1989) . . 6.25n11

Baytree of Inverrary Realty Partners v. Lauderhill,
City of, 873 F.2d 1407 (11th Cir. 1989) . . . . .
8.35n4

Baytree of Inverrary Realty Ptn. v. Lauderhill, City of,
873 F.2d 1407 (11th Cir. 1989) 7.02n4

BCT Partnership v. Portland, City of, 881 P.2d 176
(Or. App. 1994) 6.53n2

Beach v. Planning & Zoning Comm'n, 103 A.2d 814
(Conn. 1954) 9.09n12

Beacon Falls, Town of v. Posick, 549 A.2d 656 (Conn.
App. 1988) 4.30n6

Beacon Falls, Town of v. Posick, 563 A.2d 285 (Conn.
1989) 5.37n2

Beacon Hill Farm Assocs. II, Ltd. Partnership v.
Loudoun County Bd. of Supervisors, 875 F.2d
1081 (4th Cir. 1989) 2.32n5

Beasley v. Potter, 493 F. Supp. 1059 (W.D. Mich.
1980) 2.53n3; 7.03n5

Beaudoin v. Rye Beach Village Dist., 369 A.2d 618
(N.J. 1976) 6.50n5

Beaufort Realty Co., Inc. v. Beaufort County, 551
S.E.2d 588 . . . . 8.06n1

Beaver Gasoline Co. v. Zoning Hearing Bd . . . .
5.37

Beaver Meadows v. Board of County Comm'rs, 709
P.2d 928 (Colo. 1985) 9.25n7

BECA of Alexandria, L.L.P. v. Douglas, County of,
607 N.W.2d 459 . . . . 9.28n2

Beck v. Crisp County Bd. of Zoning Appeals, 472
S.E.2d 558 (Ga. App. 1996) 6.76n14

Beck v. Raymond, Town of, 394 A.2d 847 (N.H.
1978) 10.04n4

Becker v. Hampton Falls, Town of, 374 A.2d 653
(N.H. 1977) 5.19n11

Bedford, Town of v. Mount Kisco, Village of, 306
N.E.2d 155 (N.Y. 1973) 6.33n7

Beechwood Village, City of v. Council of & City of
St. Matthews, 574 S.W.2d 322 (Ky. 1978) . . .
6.31n2

Beeshos Restaurant, Inc. v. State Liquor Auth., 281
N.Y.S.2d 720 (Sup. Ct. 1967) 6.21n1

Beford, City of v. Board of Elections, 577 N.E.2d 645
(Ohio 1991) 4.24n7

Begin v. Inhabitants of Town of Sabattus, 409 A.2d
1269 (Me. 1979) 5.21n1

Begin v. Sabbatus, Town of, 409 A.2d 1269 (Me.
1979) 10.06n6

Behavioral Health Agency of Cent. Ariz.
(BHACA) v. Casa Grande, City of, 708 P.2d 1317
(Ariz. App. 1985) 5.08n3, n11

Belanger v. Nashua, City of, 430 A.2d 166 (N.H.
1981) 6.41n2; 6.49n1

Bell v. Elkhorn, City of, 364 N.W.2d 144 (Wis. 1985)
. . . . 3.14n1; 6.26n5; 6.29n11

Bell v. Planning & Zoning Comm'n, 391 A.2d 154
(Conn. 1978) 8.03n1

Bell v. Waco, City of, 835 S.W.2d 211 (Tex. App.
1992) 5.36n11

Bell Atlantic Mobile Systems, Inc. v. Borough of
Clifton Heights, 661 A.2d 909 (Pa. Commw. 1995)
. . . . 8.14n5

Bell River Assocs. v. China Charter Township, 565
N.W.2d 695 (Mich. App. 1997) 12.13n5

Bella Vista Apartment Co. v. Bennett, 678 N.E.2d 198 (N.Y. 1997) 6.42n1

Belle Harbor Realty Corp. v. Kerr, 323 N.E.2d 697 (N.Y. 1974) 6.10n3

Belle Terre in Moore v. East Cleveland, City of . . 5.04

Belle Terre, Village of v. Boraas 5.04

Belle Terre, Village of v. Boraas, 416 U.S. 1 (1974) 10.08n6

Belle Terre, Village of v. Boraas 416 U.S. 1 (1974) 2.45n1

Bellefontaine Neighbors, City of v. J.J. Kelly Realty & Bldg. Co., 460 S.W.2d 298 (Mo. App. 1970) 9.15n2

Bellemeade Co. v. Priddle, 503 S.W.2d 734 (Ky. 1974) 6.61n3

Belleville v. Parrillo's, Inc 5.79

Bellevue, City of v. East Bellevue Community Council, 983 P.2d 602 (Wash. 1999) 6.33n3

Bellhaven Imp. Ass'n v. Jackson, City of, 507 So. 2d 41 (Miss. 1987) 8.06n2

Bello v. Walker, 840 F.2d 1124 (3d Cir. 1988) . . . 2.22n5

Beloit, Town of v. Public Serv. Comm'n, 148 N.W.2d 661 (Wis. 1967) 10.10n6

Belvoir Farms Homeowners Ass'n, Inc. v. North, 734 A.2d 227 (Md. 1999) 6.45n3, n5

Ben Lomond, Inc. v. Idaho Falls, City of, 448 P.2d 209 (Idaho 1968) 6.16n3

Ben Lomond, Inc. v. Municipality of Anchorage, 761 P.2d 119 (Alaska 1988) 8.09n5

Benchmark Land Co. v. Battle Ground, City of, 49 P.3d 680 . . . . 9.16n14

Bender v. Saint Ann, City of, 816 F. Supp. 1372 (E.D. Mo. 1993), *aff'd on other grounds,* 36 F.3d 57 (8th Cir. 1994) 11.18n4

Bender v. St. Ann, City of, 36 F.3d 57 (8th Cir. 1994) 2.42n10

Benenson v. United States, 548 F.2d 939 (Ct. Cl. 1977) 2.23n4

Benesh v. Township of Frenchtown, 228 N.W.2d 459 (Mich. App. 1975) 4.18n2

Benjfran Dev., Inc. v. Metropolitan Serv. Dist. 767 P.2d 467 (Or. App. 1989) 10.07n5

Bennett v. City Council, 973 P.2d 871 (N.M. App. 1999) 6.70n12

Bennett v. Sullivan's Island Bd. of Adjustment, 438 S.E.2d 273 (S.C. App. 1993) 6.48n2

Bennion v. Sundance Dev. Corp., 897 P.2d 1232 (Utah App. 1997) 8.11n15

Benny v. Alameda, City of, 164 Cal. Rptr. 776 (Cal. App. 1980) 9.06n3

Benson v. DeSoto, City of, 510 P.2d 1281 (Kan. 1973) 6.16n5

Benson v. Zoning Bd. of Appeals, 27 A.2d 389 (Conn. 1942) 5.46n1

Bentley v. Chastain, 249 S.E.2d 38 (Ga. 1978) . . . 6.52n8

Berea, City of v. Wren, 818 S.W.2d 274 (Ky. 1991) 6.17n2

Berenson v. New Castle, Town of 7.15

Berenson in Suffolk Hous. Serv. v. Brookhaven, Town of 7.16

Berg Agency v. Township of Maplewood, 395 A.2d 261 (N.J.L. Div. 1978) 11.22n1

Berger v. State, 364 A.2d 993 (N.J. 1976) 5.10n1

Berman v. Board of Comm'rs, 608 A.2d 585 (Pa. Commw. 1992) 5.32n9

Berman v. Parker 5.04; 11.25n5

Berman v. Parker, 348 U.S. 26 (1954) . . 11.05n2

Berman v. Parker 348 U.S. 26 (1954) . . . 5.04n3

Bernardsville Quarry v. Borough of Bernardsville, 608 A.2d 1377 (N.J. 1992) 5.40n2

Bersani v. EPA, 850 F.2d 36 (2d Cir. 1988) 12.06n9

Bersani v. Robichard, 850 F.2d 36 (2d Cir. 1988) 12.06n6

Bethel Evangelical Lutheran Ch. v. Morton, Village of, 559 N.E.2d 533 (Ill. App. 1990) . . 5.69n2

Better Envt. v. Springville, City of, 979 P.2d 332 (Utah 1999) 9.28n2

Beure-Co. v. United States, 16 Cl. Ct. 42 (1989) . . 12.07n12

Bevan v. Brandon Township, 475 N.W.2d 37 (Mich. 1991) 2.19n1

Beverly Bank v. Illinois Department of Transportation, 579 N.E.2d 815 (Ill. 1991) 8.09n7

Beyer v. Burns, 567 N.Y.S.2d 599 (Sup. Ct. 1991) 6.61n2; 6.63n4

Bi-County Dev. Corp. v. Mayor & Council, 540 A.2d 927 (N.J.L. Div. 1988) 7.12n9

Bi-County Dev. of Clinton, Inc. v. Borough of High Bridge, 805 A.2d 433 . . . . 7.13n7

Bibco Corp. v. Sumter, City of, 504 S.E.2d 112 (S.C. 1998) 5.21n3; 5.26n6

Bible Truth Crusade v. Bloomington, City of, 709 F. Supp. 849 (C.D. Ill. 1989) 8.45n3

Biblia Abierta v. Banks, 129 F.3d 899 (7th Cir. 1997) 8.35n5

Bickerstaff Clay Prods. Co. v. Harris County, 89 F.3d 1481 (11th Cir. 1996) 2.40n3

Bickerstaff Clay Prods. Co., Inc. v. Harris County, 89 F.3d 1481 . . . . 2.31n2

Bieger v. Moreland Hills, Village of, 209 N.E.2d 218 (Ohio App. 1965) 8.13n11

Bielunski v. Tousignant, 149 N.E.2d 801 (Ill. App. 1958) 4.40n1

Bierman v. Township of Taymouth, 383 N.W.2d 235 (Mich. App. 1985) 6.54n4

Big Creek Lumber Co. v. San Mateo, County of, 37 Cal. Rptr. 2d 159 (Cal. App. 1995) . . . 4.31n3

Big Creek Lumber Co. v. San Mateo, County of 37 Cal. Rptr. 2d 159 (Cal. App. 1995) 4.31n6

Big Train Constr. Co. v. Parish of St. Tammany, 446 So. 2d 889 (La. App. 1984) 8.14n9

Bigelow v. Virginia, 421 U.S. 809 (1975) 2.50n1

Bigwood v. Wahpeton, City of, 565 N.W.2d 498 (N.D. 1997) 6.29n12

Billings Props., Inc. v. Yellowstone County, 394 P.2d 182 (Mont. 1964) 9.19n4

Bird v. Colorado Springs, City of, 489 P.2d 324 (Colo. 1971) 6.37n5

Birmingham, City of v. Morris, 396 So. 2d 53 (Ala. 1981) 2.46n6; 5.35n4

Biser v. Deibel, 739 A.2d 948 (Md. App. 1999) . . 8.23n12

Bittinger v. Corporation of Bolivar, 395 S.E.2d 554 (W.Va. 1990) 4.16n1

Bituminous Materials v. Rice County, 126 F.3d 1068 (8th Cir. 1997) 2.40n6

Bivens v. Six Unknown Named Agents of the Fed. Bur. of Narcotics, 403 U.S. 388 (1971) 8.39n2

Bixler v. LaGrange County Bldg. Dep't, 730 N.E.2d 818 . . . . 8.11n15

Bixler v. Pierson, 188 So. 2d 681 (Fla. App. 1966) 5.80n10

Bjarnson v. Kitsap County, 899 P.2d 1290 . . . . . 6.31n6

Bjarnson v. Kitsap, County of, 899 P.2d 1290 (Wash. App. 1995) 6.33n2

Black v. Summers, 542 N.Y.S.2d 837 (App. Div. 1989) 6.66n11

Black v. Waukesha, City of, 371 N.W.2d 389 (Wis. 1985) 6.51n9

Black Jack; United States v. , 508 F.2d 1179 (8th Cir. 1974) 7.05n5

Black Prop. Owners Ass'n v. Berkeley, City of, 28 Cal. Rptr. 2d 305 (Cal. App. 1994) . . 3.22n10

Blagden Alley Ass'n v. District of Columbia Zoning Comm'n, 590 A.2d 139 (D.C. App. 1991) 7.28n1; 9.28n2

Blake v. Phoenix, City of, 754 P.2d 1368 (Ariz. 1988) 5.79n4

Blaker v. Planning & Zoning Comm'n, 562 A.2d 1093 (Conn. 1989) 6.71n3

Blanche Road Corp. v. Bensalem Township, 57 F.3d 2 . . . . 2.32n3

Blanche Road Corp. v. Bensalem Township, 57 F.3d 253 (3d Cir. 1995) 8.37n1

Blank v. Lake Clarke Shores, Town of, 161 So. 2d 683 (Fla. 1964) 5.17n8

Blevens v. Manchester, City of, 170 A.2d 121 (N.H. 1961) 9.07n2

Blevens v. Manchester, City of 170 A.2d 121 (N.H. 1961) 9.15n2

Blitz v. New Castle, Town of 463 N.Y.S.2d 832 (App. Div. 1983) 7.15n2

Blommingdale, Village of v. CDG Enters., Inc., 752 N.E.2d 1090 . . . . 8.23n4

Bloomingdale, Village of v. C.D.G. Enters., 732 N.E.2d 633 . . . . 8.23n2

Blue Canary Corp. v. Milwaukee, City of, 251 F.3d 1121 . . . . 6.57n4

Blue Canary Corp. v. Milwaukee (II), City of, 270 F.3d 1156 . . . . 5.65n2

Bluffs Dev. Co. v. Board of Adjustment, 499 N.W.2d 12 (Iowa 1993) 6.74n6

Blumberg v. Hill, 119 N.Y.S.2d 855 (Sup. Ct. 1953) 8.03n1

Board of Adjustment v. Henderson Union Ass'n, 374 A.2d 3 (Del. 1977) 6.52n3

Board of Adjustment v. Kwik-Check Realty, Inc., 389 A.2d 1289 (Del. 1978) 6.48n8

Board of Adjustment v. Levinson, 244 S.W.2d 281 (Tex. Civ. App. 1951) 5.20n5

Board of Adjustment v. Osage Oil & Transp. Co., 522 S.W.2d 836 (Ark. 1975) 11.10n1

Board of Adjustment v. Patel, 887 S.W.2d 90 (Tex. App. 1994) 6.04n2

Board of Adjustment v. Shanbour, 435 P.2d 569 (Okla. 1968) 6.50n6

Board of Adjustment v. Willie, 511 S.W.2d 591 (Tex. Civ. App. 1974) 6.42n5

Board of Adjustment v. Winkles, 832 S.W.2d 803 (Tex. App. 1992) 5.86n5

Board of Adjustments v. Brown, 969 S.W.2d 214 (Ky. App. 1998) 5.79n4

Board of Appeals v. Housing Appeals Comm., 357 N.E.2d 936 (Mass. App. 1976) 7.31n9

Board of Appeals of Hanover v. Housing Appeals Comm., 294 N.E.2d 393 (Mass. 1973) 4.25n9

Board of Child Care v. Harker, 561 A.2d 219 (Md. 1989) 5.10n1

Board of Comm'rs v. Toll Bros., 607 A.2d 824 (Pa. Commw. 1992) 6.22n4

Board of Coop. Educ. Serv. v. Gaynor, 303 N.Y.S.2d 183 (Sup. Ct. 1969) 4.28n2

Board of County Commr's v. Bainbridge, Inc., 929 P.2d 691 (Colo. 1997) 9.21n1, n5

Board of County Comm'rs v. Brown, 520 U.S. 397 (1997) 8.32n2

Board of County Comm'rs v. Brown 520 U.S. 397 (1997) 8.31n7

Board of County Comm'rs v. Condor, 927 P.2d 1339 (Colo. 1996) 9.03n4; 9.09n2

Board of County Comm'rs v. Gaster 401 A.2d 666 (Md. 1979) 9.03n5

Board of County Comm'rs v. Goldenrod Corp., 601 P.2d 360 (Colo. App. 1979) . . 8.11n19; 9.07n2

Board of County Comm'rs v. H. Manny Holtz, Inc., 501 A.2d 489 (Md. App. 1985) 6.64n5

Board of County Comm'rs v. Kokomo City Planning Comm'n, 310 N.E.2d 877 (Ind. App. 1974), rev'd on other grounds, 330 N.E.2d 92 (Ind. 1975) . . 4.23n1

Board of County Comm'rs v. Las Vegas, City of, 622 P.2d 695 (N.M. 1980) 3.15n7

Board of County Comm'rs v. Martin, 856 P.2d 62 (Colo. App. 1993) 4.31n1

Board of County Comm'rs v. Oak Hill Farms, Inc., 192 A.2d 761 (Md. 1963) 8.19n4

Board of County Comm'rs v. Olathe, City of, 952 P.2d 1302 (Kan. 1998) 6.29n2

Board of County Comm'rs. v. Snyder, 627 So. 2d 469 (Fla. 1993) 3.15n5; 3.17n1

Board of County Comm'rs v. Thornton, City of, 629 P.2d 605 (Colo. 1981) 4.25n3; 8.07n4

Board of County Comm'rs v. Webber, 658 So. 2d 1069 (Fla. App. 1995) 6.70n13; 6.76n10

Board of County Supvrs. v. Carper, 107 S.E.2d 390 (Va. 1959) 5.32n5

Board of Cty. Comm'rs v. East Prince Frederick Corp., 559 A.2d 822 (Md. App. 1989) 2.52n3

Board of Cty. Comm'rs v. Teton Cty. Youth Servs., 652 P.2d 400 (Wyo. 1982) 6.70n4

Board of Educ. v. Houghton, 233 N.W. 834 (Minn. 1930) 4.39n1

Board of Educ. v. Idle Motors, Inc., 90 N.E.2d 121 (Ill. App. 1950) 8.14n13

Board of Educ. v. Surety Devs., Inc., 347 N.E.2d 149 (Ill. 1975) 9.19n2

Board of Regents v. Tempe, City of, 356 P.2d 399 (Ariz. 1960) 4.27n1

Board of Selectmen v. Monson, 247 N.E.2d 364 (Mass. 1969) 5.81n16

Board of Supervisors v. Countryside Inv. Co., L.C., 522 S.E.2d 610 (Va. 1999) 9.09n2

Board of Supervisors v. McDonald's Corp., 544 So.2d 334 . . . . 6.56n15

Board of Supervisors v. Omni Homes, Inc., 481 S.E.2d 460 (Va. 1997) 2.16n8

Board of Supervisors v. Snell Constr. Corp., 202 S.E.2d 889 (Va. 1974) 6.38n1

Board of Supervisors v. Stickley, 556 S.E.2d 748 . . . . 6.56n5

Board of Supervisors of James City County v. Rowe, 216 S.E.2d 199 (Va. 1975) 8.19n6

Board of Suplers v. Hillman. 211 S.E.2d 48 (Va. 1975) 3.17n2

Board of Supvrs. v. DeGroff Enters., 198 S.E.2d 600 (Va. 1973) 7.27n4

Board of Supvrs. v. Horne, 215 S.E.2d 453 (Va. 1975) 6.07n1

Board of Supvrs. v. Jackson, 269 S.E.2d 381 (Va. 1980) 3.18n4; 6.33n1

Board of Supvrs. v. Medical Structures, Inc., 192 S.E.2d 799 (Va. 1972) 6.16n7

Board of Supvrs. v. Rowe, 216 S.E.2d 199 (Va. 1975) 8.11n8; 11.25n2

Board of Supvrs. v. Rowe 216 S.E.2d 199 (Va. 1975) 5.36n8; 5.71n4

Board of Supvrs. v. Snell Constr. Corp . . . 6.38

Board of Supvrs. v. Southland Corp 6.54

Board of Supvrs. v. Southland Corp., 297 S.E.2d 718 (Va. 1982) 8.16n3

Board of Supvrs. v. West Chestnut Realty Corp., 532 A.2d 942 (Pa. Commw. 1987) 9.28n1

Board of Township Trustees v. Funtime, Inc., 563 N.E.2d 717 (Ohio 1990) 4.16n2

Board of Trustees v. Fox, 492 U.S. 469 (1989) . . . 2.50n4

Board of Trustees v. Garrett, 531 U.S. 356 . . . . . 2.48n4

Board of Zoning Adjustment v. Murphy, 438 S.E.2d 134 (Ga. App. 1994) 6.59n4

Board of Zoning Adjustment v. Summers, 814 So.2d 851 . . . . 6.48n14

Board of Zoning Appeals v. CasLin Systems, Inc., 501 S.E.2d 397 (Va. 1998) 6.16n8

Board of Zoning Appeals v. Decatur, Ind. Congregation of Jehovah's Witnesses, 117 N.E.2d 115 (Ind. 1954) 5.68n4

Board of Zoning Appeals v. Leinz, 702 N.E.2d 1026 (Ind. 1998) 5.78n1; 5.85n1

Boca Raton, City of v. Boca Villas Corp . . 10.06

Boca Raton, City of v. State, 595 So. 2d 25 (Fla. 1992) 4.25n8; 9.21n4

Boerne, City of v. Flores, 521 U.S. 507 (1997) . . . 5.70n3

Bogan v. Scott-Harris, 523 U.S. 44 (1998) 2.42n3

Bogert v. Washington Twp., 135 A.2d 1 (N.J. 1957) 5.31n4

Bogue v. Zoning Bd. of Appeals, 345 A.2d 9 (Conn. 1975) 8.19n8

Bohannan v. San Diego, City of, 106 Cal. Rptr. 333 (Cal. App. 1973) 11.29n6

Boise City v. Blaser, 572 P.2d 892 (Idaho 1977) . . . 6.21n3

Boivin v. Sanford, Town of, 588 A.2d 1197 (Me. 1991) 5.79n9

Boland v. Great Falls, City of, 910 P.2d 890 (Mont. 1996) 6.29n8

Boles v. Chattanooga, City of, 892 S.W.2d 416 (Tenn. App. 1994) 5.81n3

Bombero v. Planning & Zoning Comm'n, 591 A.2d 390 (Conn. 1991) 8.16n4

Bone v. Lewiston, City of, 693 P.2d 1046 (Idaho 1984) 3.15n5; 3.17n1, n3; 6.33n10

Bonge v. Madison, County of, 573 N.W.2d 448 (Neb. 1998) 8.09n4, n6

Bongiorno v. Planning Bd., 533 N.Y.S.2d 631 (App. Div. 1988) 6.66n10

Bonnell, Inc. v. Board of Adj., 791 P.2d 107 (Okla. Ct. App. 1989) 6.05n24

Bonnie Briar Syndicate, Inc. v. Mamaroneck, Town of, 721 N.E.2d 971 (N.Y. 1999) . . . 12.09n11

Bonnie Briar Syndicate, Inc. v. Mamaronek, Town of, 721 N.E.2d 971 (N.Y. 1999) 2.13n2

Boomer v. Atlantic Cement Co. 257 N.E.2d 870 (N.Y. 1970) 4.13n1

Boomhower v. Cerro Gordo County Bd. of Supvrs., 173 N.W.2d 95 (Iowa 1969) 8.08n1

Boos v. Barry, 485 U.S. 312 (1988) 5.61n1

Booth v. Board of Adjustment, 234 A.2d 681 (N.J. 1967) 8.03n2

Boothbay, Town of v. National Adv. Co., 347 A.2d 419 (Me. 1975) . . . 11.06n2; 11.07n8; 11.08n3

Bora v. Zoning Bd. of Appeals, 288 A.2d 89 (Conn. 1972) 6.51n5

Boreth v. Philadelphia Zoning Bd. of Adjustment, 151 A.2d 474 (Pa. 1959) 5.19n2

Bormann v. Board of Supervisors, 584 N.W.2d 309 (Iowa 1998) 12.11n14

Boron Oil Co. v. L.C. Kimple, 284 A.2d 744 (Pa. 1971) 6.18n4, n6

Borough of Cresskill v. Borough of Dumont, 104 A.2d 441 (N.J. 1954) 6.35n1

Borough of Fleetwood v. Zoning Hearing Bd., 649 A.2d 651 (Pa. 1994) 5.36n3

Borough of Glassboro v. Vallorisi, 529 A.2d 1028 (N.J. Ch. Div. 1987) 5.05n2

Borough of Glassboro v. Vallorisi, 568 A.2d 888 (N.J. 1990) 5.03n1

Borough of Roselle Park v. Township of Union, 272 A.2d 762 (N.J. 1970) 8.07n4

Bortz v. Troth, 59 A.2d 93 (Pa. 1948) . . . 4.06n6

Boss Capital, Inc. v. Casselberry, City of, 187 F.3d 1251 (11th Cir. 1999) . . 5.63n12, n16; 6.57n12

Bosse v. Portsmouth, City of, 226 A.2d 99 (N.H. 1967) 6.18n3; 6.29n9

Bossman v. Riverton, Village of, 684 N.E.2d 427 (Ill. App. 1997) 6.29n12

Bothwell v. Eagle, City of, 938 P.2d 1212 (Idaho 1997) 8.09n2

Boudwin v. Great Bend Township, 921 F. Supp. 1326 (M.D. Pa. 1996) 8.33n8

Boulder Bldrs. Group v. Boulder, City of, 759 P.2d 752 (Colo. 1988) 4.25n6; 10.03n1

Boundary Drive Assocs. v. Shrewsbury Twp. Bd. of Supvrs 12.12

Bourgeois v. Parish of St. Tammany, 628 F. Supp. 159 (E.D. La. 1986) 5.21n3

Bourne, Town of v. Plante, 708 N.E. 2d 103 (Mass. 1999) 4.27n1

Bourne, Town of v. Plante, 708 N.E.2d 103 (Mass. 1999) 4.27n1

Boutet v. Planning Bd., 253 A.2d 53 (Me. 1969) . . 9.07n3

Bove v. Donner-Hanna Coke Corp 4.04

Bowen v. Board of Appeals, 632 N.E.2d 858 (Mass. App. 1994) 6.66n11

Bowles v. United States, 31 Fed. Cl. 37 (1994) . . 12.07n12

Boyajian v. Gatzunis, 212 F.3d 1 . . . . . . 5.69n8

Boyds Civic Ass'n v. Montgomery County Council, 526 A.2d 598 (Md. 1987) 3.15n5

Boynton Beach, City of v. V.S.H. Realty, Inc., 443 So. 2d 452 (Fla. App. 1984) 6.66n11

BP America, Inc. v. Avon City Council, 753 N.E.2d 947 . . . . 5.36n11

Brackett v. Des Moines, City of, 67 N.W.2d 542 (Iowa 1954) 6.21n5

Bradley v. Trussville, City of, 527 So. 2d 1303 (Ala. Civ. App. 1988) 6.62n4

Bradley v. Zoning Bd. of Appeals, 334 A.2d 914 (Conn. 1973) 6.43n2

Brady v. Board of Appeals, 204 N.E.2d 513 (Mass. 1965) 8.14n11

Brady v. Colchester, Town of, 863 F.2d 205 (2d Cir. 1988) 2.39n7; 2.51n4; 8.37n1

Brady v. Superior Court, 19 Cal. Rptr. 242 (Cal. App. 1962) 5.19n6

Brady Dev. Co. v. Hilton Head Island, Town of, 439 S.E.2d 366 (S.C. 1993) 8.23n18

Bragdon v. Scott, 524 U.S. 624 (1998) . . . 5.12n3

Bragdon v. Vassalboro, Town of, 780 A.2d 299 . . 6.66n3

Brammer v. Housing Auth., 195 So. 256 (Ala. 1940) 4.03n1

Brandt v. Davis, 191 F.3d 887 (8th Cir. 1999) . . 2.47n3

Brandywine Park Condo. Council v. Members of City of Wilmington Zoning Bd. of Adjustment, 534 A.2d 286 (Del. Super. 1987) 8.05n2

Brant v. Custom Design Constructors Corp., 677 N.E.2d 92 (Ind. App. 1997) 8.14n1

Brayton v. New Brighton, City of, 519 N.W.2d 243 (Minn. App. 1994) 11.23n1, n6

Brazos Land, Inc. v. Board of County Comm'rs, 848 P.2d 1095 (N.M. App. 1993) 6.07n1

Breakwater Farms Joint Venture v. United States, 35 Fed. Cl. 232 (1996) 12.07n12

Breakzone Billiards v. Torrance, City of, 97 Cal. Rptr. 2d 467 . . . . 6.72n3

Breakzone Billiards v. Torrance, City of, 97 Cal. Rptr.2d 467 . . . . 6.73n5

Brecciaroli v. Connecticut Comm'r of Envtl. Protection, 362 A.2d 948 (Conn. 1975) 12.09n1

Bredberg v. Wheaton, City of, 182 N.E.2d 742 (Ill. 1962) 6.04n2

Bremner v. City & County of Honolulu, 28 P.2d 350 . . . . 8.02n4; 8.03n1

Breneric Assocs. v. Del Mar, City of, 81 Cal. Rptr. 2d 324 (Cal. App. 1998) 11.24n2

Brennan Woods Ltd. Partnership v. Williston, Town of, 782 A.2d 1230 . . . . 10.10n6

Brentwood Borough v. Cooper, 431 A.2d 1177 (Pa. Commw. 1981) 6.56n13

Bressman v. Gash, 621 A.2d 476 (N.J. 1993) 6.48n14

Briar W., Inc. v. Lincoln, City of, 291 N.W.2d 730 (Neb. 1980) 9.16n6

Bridger Canyon Property Owners' Ass'n v. Planning & Zoning Comm'n, 890 P.2d 1268 (Mont. 1995) 6.33n4

Bridgeton, City of v. St. Louis, City of, 18 S.W.2d 107 . . . . 4.38n3

Bridle Trails Community Club v. Bellevue, City of, 724 P.2d 1110 (Wash. App. 1986) . . . 8.13n6

Briggs v. Eden Council For Hope & Opportunity, 969 P.2d 564 (Cal. 1999) 8.47n6

Briggs v. Rolling Hills Estates, City of, 47 Cal. Rptr. 2d 29 (Cal. App. 1995) 6.05n16

Bright v. Evanston, City of, 139 N.E.2d 270 (Ill. 1957) 8.10n5

Bringle v. Board of Supvrs., 351 P.2d 765 (Cal. 1960) 6.51n9

Bristow v. Woodhaven, City of, 192 N.W.2d 322 (Mich. App. 1971) 7.23n1

Britton v. Chester, Town of 7.25

Broadrick v. Oklahoma, 413 U.S. 601 (1973) 11.17n1

Broadview Apts. Co. v. Commission for Historical & Architectural Preservation, 433 A.2d 1214 (Md. App. 1981) 11.36n3

Broadwater Farms Joint Venture v. United States, 35 Fed. Cl. 232 (1996) 2.19n3; 2.30n15

Broadway, Laguna, Vallejo Ass'n v. Board of Permit Appeals, 427 P.2d 810 (Cal. 1967) . . . 5.75n1; 6.42n5

Broderick v. Board of Appeal, 280 N.E.2d 670 (Mass. 1972) 6.39n2

Brookings, City of v. Winker, 554 N.W.2d 827 (S.D. 1996) 5.05n1

Brooks v. Fisher, 705 S.W.2d 135 (Tenn. App. 1985) 6.66n10

Brookside Poultry Farms, Inc., State ex rel. v. Jefferson County Bd. of Adjustment, 388 N.W.2d 593 (Wis. 1986) 8.02n9

Brookside Village, City of v. Comeau, 633 S.W.2d 790 . . . . 5.23n3

Brookside Village, City of v. Comeau, 633 S.W.2d 790 (Tex.1982) 5.26n6

Brookwood Area Homeowners Ass'n v. Anchorage, 702 P.2d 1317 (Alaska 1985) . . . 6.76n10, n17

Brougher v. Board of Pub. Works, 271 P. 487 (Cal. 1928) 4.25n6

Broughton Lumber Co. v. Columbia River Gorge Comn'n, 975 F.2d 616 (9th Cir. 1992) 2.24n2

Brous v. Planning Bd., 594 N.Y.S.2d 816 (App. Div. 1993) 6.51n8

Brous v. Smith, 106 N.E.2d 503 (N.Y. 1952) 9.08n8; 9.15n2

Broward County v. G.B.V. Internat'l, Inc., 787 So.2d 838 . . . . 8.13n6

Broward County v. Griffey, 366 So. 2d 869 (Fla. App. 1979) 6.63n1

Brown v. Crawford County, 960 F.2d 1002 (11th Cir. 1992) 8.35n5

Brown v. Davidson, Town of, 439 S.E.2d 206 (N.C. App. 1994) 6.72n1

Brown v. Fraser, 467 P.2d 464 (Okla. 1970) 6.48n2

Brown v. Joliet, City of, 247 N.E.2d 47 (Ill. App. 1969) 9.09n15

Brown v. Kansas Forestry, Fish & Game Comm'n, 576 P.2d 230 (Kan. App. 1978) 4.27n5

Brown v. Los Angeles, City of, 73 Cal. Rptr. 364 (Cal. App. 1968) 8.23n4

Brown v. Wimpress, 242 A.2d 157 (Md. 1968) . . 6.31n5

Browndale Int'l, Ltd. v. Board of Adjustment, 208 N.W.2d 121 (Wis. 1973) 5.08n3

Brownfield v. State, 407 N.E.2d 1365 (Ohio 1980) 4.27n5

Browning-Ferris Indus., Inc. v. Maryland Heights, City of, 747 F. Supp. 1340 (E.D. Mo. 1990) . . 8.31n9

Bruce v. Riddle, 631 F.2d 272 (4th Cir. 1980) . . . 8.35n4

Brunelle v. S. Kingston, Town of, 700 A.2d 1075 (R.I. 1997) 2.16n8

Bruni v. Farmington Hills, City of, 293 N.W.2d 609 (Mich. App. 1980) 8.10n1

Brunswick v. Inland Wetlands Comm'n, 617 A.2d 466 (Conn. App. 1992) 6.74n3

Bryan v. Madison, City of, 213 F.3d 267 . . . . . . 2.49n4

Bryan v. Salmon Corp., 554 S.W.2d 912 (Ky. App. 1977) 6.70n14; 8.19n4

Bryant v. Cleveland Township, 608 N.W.2d 101 . . 6.76n9

Bryant Woods Inn, Inc. v. Howard County, 124 F.3d 597 (4th Cir. 1997) 5.12n8

Bryniarski v. Montgomery County Bd. of Appeals, 230 A.2d 289 (Md. 1967) 8.02n9, n10

BSW Dev. Group, State ex rel. v. Dayton, City of, 699 N.E.2d 1271 (Ohio 1998) 11.35n3

Bucholz v. Omaha, City of, 120 N.W.2d 270 (Neb. 1963) 6.64n1

Buckel v. Board of Cty. Comm'rs, 562 A.2d 1297 (Md. App. 1989) 6.31n7

Buckelew v. Parker, Town of, 937 P.2d 368 (Ariz. App. 1997) 8.04n1

Buckeye Community Hope Foundation v. Cuyahoga Falls, City of, 263 F.3d 627 . . . . 6.80n5

Buckland v. Haw River, Town of, 541 S.E.2d 497 . . . . 9.16n4

Buckles v. King County, 191 F.3d 1127 (9th Cir. 1999) 6.36n1; 8.27n2; 8.36n2

Buckley v. Valeo, 424 U.S. 1 (1976) 2.24n2

Bucks, County of; Commonwealth v. , 302 A.2d 897 (Pa. Commw. 1973), *cert. denied,* 414 U.S. 1130 (1974) 7.07n5

Bucktail, LLC v. County Council, 723 A.2d 440 (Md. 1999) 12.04n7

Budget Inn of Daphne, Inc. v. Daphne, City of, 789 So.2d 154 . . . . 5.81n13

Buegel v. Grand Forks, City of, 475 N.W.2d 133 (N.D. 1991) 8.21n5

Buena Vista Gardens Apt. Ass'n v. San Diego Planning Dep't, City of, 220 Cal. Rptr. 732 (Cal. App. 1985) 3.22n5, n10

Buford, City of v. Ward, 443 S.E.2d 279 (Ga. App. 1994) 8.23n3

Builders Service Corp. v. Planning & Zoning Comm'n., 545 A.2d 530 (Conn. 1988) 2.11n3

Building Indus. Ass'n v. Camarillo, City of, 718 P.2d 68 (Cal.1968) 10.06n4

Building Indus. Ass'n. v. Oceanside, City of, 33 Cal. Rptr. 2d 137 (Cal. App. 1994) . 3.17n2; 7.27n1

Building Industry Ass'n v. Westlake, City of, 660 N.E.2d 501 (Ohio App. 1995) 9.21n2

Building Industry Legal Defense Foundation v. Superior Court, 85 Cal. Rptr.2d 828 (Cal. App. 1999) 6.07n4

Burbank, City of v. Burbank -Glendale- . . 4.43n5

Burbank, City of v. Lockheed Air Terminal 411 U.S. 624 . . . . 4.43n2

The Burden of Proof Switch in Dolan v. Tigard, City of, 71 N.Y.U. L. Rev. 1301 (1996)

Burford v. Sun Oil Co. 319 U.S. 315 (1942) 8.44n1

Burger King Corp., State ex rel. v. Oakwood, 594 N.E.2d 116 (Ohio App. 1991) 8.14n1

Burke v. Charleston, City of, 893 F. Supp. 589 (D.S.C. 1995) 11.19n2; 11.30n2

Burke v. Denison, 630 N.Y.S.2d 421 (App. Div. 1995) 6.05n6

Burke & McCaffrey, Inc. v. Merriam, City of, 424 P.2d 483 (Kan. 1967) 9.09n13

Burkett v. Texarkana, City of, 500 S.W.2d 242 (Tex. Civ. App. 1973) 6.28n1

Burkhart Advertising, Inc. v. Auburn, City of, 786 F. Supp. 721 (N.D. Ind. 1991) . 8.31n8; 11.19n11

Burkholder v. Twinsburg Township Bd. of Zoning Appeals, 701 N.E.2d 766 (Ohio App. 1997) . . . 6.48n5

Burkow v. Los Angeles, City of, 119 F. Supp. 2d 1076 . . . . 11.22n2

Burley, City of v. McCaslin Lumber Co., 693 P.2d 1108 (Idaho 1984) 6.48n13

Burley, City of v. McCaslin Lumber Co., 693 P.2d 1108 (Idaho App. 1984) 6.46n4; 8.07n1

Burlington, Town of v. Jencik, 362 A.2d 1338 (Conn. 1975) 6.51n4

Burlington, Town of v. Jencik 362 A.2d 1338 (Conn. 1975) 6.51n1

Burnham v. Salem, City of, 101 F. Supp.2d 26 . . . 8.33n8

Burrell v. Lake County Plan Comm'n, 624 N.E.2d 526 (Ind. App. 1993) 6.03n4; 9.03n9

Burritt v. Harris, 172 So. 2d 820 (Fla. 1965) 8.19n5

Burrows v. Keene, City of, 432 A.2d 15 (N.H. 1981) 8.21n2

Burstyn v. Miami Beach, City of, 663 F. Supp. 528 (S.D. Fla. 1987) 2.48n2

Burt; State v. , 127 N.W.2d 270 (Wis. 1964) 5.80n11

Burton v. Clark County, 958 P.2d 343 (Wash. App. 1998) 9.16n14

Bush v. Lucas, 462 U.S. 367 (1983) 8.39n5

Buskey v. Hanover, Town of, 577 A.2d 406 (N.H. 1990) 2.36n6

Buss v. Johnson, 624 N.W.2d 781 . . . . . 5.80n11

Butte, County of v. Bach, 218 Cal. Rptr. 613 (Cal. App. 1985) 5.20n4

Butters v. Hauser, 960 P.2d 181 (Idaho 1998) . . . 8.04n1

Button Gwinnett Landfill, Inc. v. Gwinnett Cty., 353 S.E.2d 328 (Ga. 1987) 6.03n3

Butz v. Economou 8.36

C

C & D Partnership v. Gahanna, City of, 747 N.E.2d 303 (Ohio 1984) 8.23n5

C & M Sand & Gravel v. Board of County Comm'rs, 673 P.2d 1013 (Colo. App. 1983) 6.03n3

C. Miller Chevrolet, Inc. v. Willoughby Hills, City of, 313 N.E.2d 400 (Ohio 1974) 6.49n1

C-Y Dev. Co. v. Redlands, City of, 703 F.2d 375 (9th Cir. 1983) 8.43n7

Cablevision ⎯ Div. of Sammons Communications, Inc. v. Zoning Hearing Bd., 320 A.2d 388 (Pa. Commw. 1974) 8.05n1

Cadiz Land Co. v. Rail Cycle, L.P., 99 Cal. Rptr.2d 378 . . . . 6.58n4

Cadoux v. Planning & Zoning Comm'n, 294 A.2d 582 . . . . 5.17n8

Calabria; State v. , 693 A.2d 949 (N.J. App. Div. 1997) 11.18n5

Caldwell v. Lambrou, 391 A.2d 590 (N.J. App. Div. 1978) 6.76n15

Caldwell v. Pima County, 837 P.2d 154 (Ariz. 1992) 5.36n1

Caleb Stowe Assocs. v. Albemarle County, 724 F.2d 1079 (4th Cir. 1984) 8.43n6

California Motor Transp., Inc. v. Trucking Unlimited, 404 U.S. 508 (1972) 5.55n3

California Retail Liquor Dealers Ass'n v. Midcal Aluminum Co 5.50

Call v. West Jordan, City of, 606 P.2d 217 (Utah 1979) 9.18n4

Call v. West Jordan, City of, 614 P.2d 1257 (Utah 1980) 9.19n4

Calton Homes, Inc. v. Council on Affordable Housing, 582 A.2d 1024 (N.J. App. Div. 1990) . . 7.12n9

Cam v. Marion County, 987 F. Supp. 854 (D. Or. 1997) 5.69n6

Camara v. Board of Adj., 570 A.2d 1012 (N.J. App. Div. 1990) 5.81n1

Camara v. Board of Adjustment, 570 A.2d 1012 (N.J. App. Div. 1990) 5.81n14

Camboni's, Inc. v. Du Page, County of, 187 N.E.2d 212 (Ill. 1962) 5.23n2

Cambridge Land Co. v. Township of Marshall, 560 A.2d 253 (Pa. Commw. 1989) 7.20n4

Camden Community Dev. Corp. v. Sutton, 5 S.W.3d 439 (Ark. 1999) 6.83n6

Cameron; State v. , 498 A.2d 1217 (N.J. 1985) . . 5.68n3; 6.05n4, n17

Cameron v. Zoning Agent of Bellingham, 260 N.E.2d 143 (Mass. 1970) 7.26n1

Camp v. Mendocino County Bd. of Supvrs., 176 Cal. Rptr. 620 (Cal. App. 1981) 3.22n7

Camp v. Warrington, 182 S.E.2d 419 (Ga. 1971) . . 4.03n3

Campbell v. City Council, 616 N.E.2d 445 (Mass. 1993) 5.10n2

Campbell v. Monroe County, 426 So. 2d 1158 (Fla. App. 1983) 5.21n2

Campbell v. Nance, 555 S.W.2d 407 (Tenn. App. 1976) 8.19n4

Canada's Tavern, Inc. v. Glen Echo, Town of, 271 A.2d 664 (Md. 1970) 5.81n7

Canal/Norcrest/Columbus Action Comm. v. Boise, City of, 39 P.3d 606 . . . . 8.09n2

Candlestick Props., Inc. v. San Francisco Bay Conservation & Dev. Comm'n, 89 Cal. Rptr. 897 (Cal. App. 1970) 12.07n4

Cannon v. Coweta Cty., 389 S.E.2d 329 (Ga. 1990) 5.23n4

Cannon v. Murphy, 600 N.Y.S.2d 965 (App. Div. 1993) 6.29n5

Cannone v. Noey, 867 P.2d 797 (Alaska 1994) . . . 2.21n2; 8.21n1; 8.26n2

Canton v. Spokane School Dist. No. 81, 498 F.2d 840 (9th Cir. 1974) 8.43n5

Capalbo v. Planning & Zoning Bd., 547 A.2d 528 (Conn. 1988) 11.10n4

Cape Ann Dev. Corp. v. City Council, 373 N.E.2d 218 (Mass. 1978) 5.48n2

Cappture Realty Corp. v. Board of Adjustment 313 A.2d 624 (N.J.L. Div. 1973), aff'd, 336 A.2d 30 (N.J. App. Div. 1975) 6.10n2

Capture Realty Corp. v. Board of Adjustment, 313 A.2d 624 (N.J.L. Div. 1973), aff'd, 336 A.2d 30 (N.J. App. Div. 1975) 6.11n5

Carana v. Kenai Peninsula Borough, 21 P.3d 833 . . . . 6.26n5

Carbonneau v. Exeter, Town of 6.45

Cardamone v. Whitpain Township Zoning Hearing Bd., 771 A.2d 103 . . . . 6.48n6, n13

Cardillo v. Council of South Bethany, 1991 Del. Super. Lexis 224 (Super. Ct. 1991) . . . 6.70n4

Cardinal Props. v. Borough of Westwood, 547 A.2d 316 (N.J. App. Div. 1988) 5.46n5

Care of Tenafly, Inc. v. Tenafly Zoning Bd. of Adjustment, 704 A.2d 1032 (N.J. App. Div. 1998) . . . 6.74n9

Carey v. Piphus 8.38n5

Carey v. Piphus, 435 U.S. 247 (1978) . . . 8.38n2

Carl Bolander & Sons v. Minneapolis, City of, 378 N.W.2d 826 (Minn. App. 1985) 2.23n6

Carl M. Freeman Assocs. v. State Roads Comm'n, 250 A.2d 250 (Md. 1969) 2.23n6

Carlino v. Whitpain Invs., 453 A.2d 1385 (Pa. 1982) 6.63n1

Carlsbad, City of v. Caviness, 346 P.2d 310 (N.M. 1959) 4.22n1; 9.03n11

Carlson v. Beaux Arts Village, Town of, 704 P.2d 663 (Wash. App. 1983) 9.09n2

Carlson v. Bellevue, City of, 435 P.2d 957 (Wash. 1968) 2.46n5

Carlson v. Green 8.39n4

Carlson v. Smithfield, Town of, 723 A.2d 1129 (R.I. 1999) 9.30n5

Carmel-by-the-Sea, City of v. United States Dep't of Transp., 123 F.3d 1142 (9th Cir. 1997) 12.06n1

Carmel Valley View, Ltd. v. Board of Supvrs., 130 Cal. Rptr. 249 (Cal. App. 1976) 9.09n3

Caroll Sign Co. v. Adams County Zoning Hearing Bd., 606 A.2d 1250 (Pa. Commw. 1992) 11.05n5

Carpenter v. Petal, City of, 699 So.2d 928 (Miss. 1997) 5.23n4

Carpenter v. Tahoe Regional Planning Agency, 804 F. Supp. 1316 (D. Nev. 1992) 2.16n9

Carpenter Outdoor Advertising Co. v. Fenton, City of, 251 F.3d 686 . . . . 2.40n6

Carr v. Dewey Beach, Town of, 730 F. Supp. 591 (D. Del. 1990) 8.31n10

Carr v. Forbes, 259 F.3d 273 . . . . 8.46n9

Carroll v. Hurst, 431 N.E.2d 1344 (Ill. App. 1982) 4.09n3

Carroll v. Mount Clemens, City of, 139 F.3d 1072 (6th Cir. 1998) 8.41n4

Carroll County Ethics Comm'n v. Lennon, 703 A.2d 1338 (Md. App. 1998) 6.74n11

Carron v. Board of County Comm'rs, 976 P.2d 359 (Colo. App. 1998) 6.61n3

Carruth v. Medera, City of, 43 Cal. Rptr. 855 (Cal. App. 1965) 6.23n4

Carruthers v. Board of Adjustment, 290 S.W.2d 340 (Tex. Civ. App. 1956) 5.31n5

Carruthers v. Board of Supervisors, 646 N.W.2d 867 . . . . 9.09n3

Carson v. Miller, 370 So. 2d 10 (Fla. 1979) 6.21n5

Carter v. South Carolina Coastal Council, 314 S.E.2d 327 (S.C. 1984) 12.07n4

Carty v. Ojai, City of, 143 Cal. Rptr. 506 (Cal. App. 1978) . . . 5.48n2; 6.12n1; 6.18n3; 6.37n9, n11

Caruso v. Planning Bd., 238 N.E.2d 872 (Mass. 1968) 9.10n4

Cary v. Rapid City, City of, 559 N.W.2d 891 (S.D. 1997) 6.04n4

Casa Marie, Inc. v. Superior Court, 988 F.2d 252 (1st Cir. 1993) 8.42n11

Casey v. Zoning Hearing Bd., 328 A.2d 464 (Pa. 1974) 6.16n3; 7.22n5

Caspersen v. Lyme, Town of, 661 A.2d 759 (N.H. 1995) 7.07n6; 10.04n4

Cass v. Board of Appeal, 317 N.E.2d 77 (Mass. 1974) 6.46n5

Caster v. West Valley City, 29 P.3d 22 . . 5.81n9

Cathedral Park Condominium Comm. v. District of Columbia Zoning Comm'n, 743 A.2d 1231 . . . 9.28n2

Catholic Bishop of Chicago v. Kingery, 20 N.E.2d 583 (Ill. 1939) 5.27n2

Catholic Family & Children's Servs., State ex rel. v. Bellingham, City of, 605 P.2d 788 (Wash. App. 1979) 5.08n7

Caudill v. Milford, Village of, 225 N.E.2d 302 (Ohio C.P. 1967) 5.46n4

Cavanaugh v. DiFlumera, 401 N.E.2d 867 (Mass. 1980) 6.43n4

C.B.H. Props., Inc. v. Rose, 613 N.Y.S.2d 913 (App. Div. 1994) 6.56n8

C.C. & J. Enters., Inc. v. Asheville, City of, 512 S.E.2d 766 (N.C. App. 1999) 9.28n1

Cederberg v. City of Rockford, 291 N.E.2d 249 (Ill. App. 1972) 6.63n1

CEEED v. California Coastal Zone Conservation Comm'n, 118 Cal. Rptr. 315 (Cal. App. 1974) 12.05n5

CEEED v. California Coastal Zone Conservation Comm'n 118 Cal. Rptr. 315 (Cal. App. 1974) . . 10.08n7

Celentano, Inc. v. Board of Zoning Appeals, 184 A.2d 49 (Conn. 1962) 6.41n8

Cellco Partnership v. Bellows, 692 N.Y.S.2d 203 (App. Div. 1999) 6.48n9, n11

Cellular Telephone Co. v. Oyster Bay, Town of, 166 F.3d 490 (2d Cir. 1999) . . . 4.42n11, n13, n15

Cellular Telephone Co. v. Zoning Bd. of Adjustment, 197 F.3d 64 (3d Cir. 1999) 4.42n8

Centerfold Club v. St. Petersburg, City of, 969 F. Supp. 1288 (M.D. Fla. 1997) 5.63n14

Centerfold Club, Inc. v. St. Petersburg, City of, 969 F. Supp. 1288 (M.D. Fla. 1997) 8.36n11

Centex Real Estate Corp. v. Vallejo, City of, 24 Cal. Rptr. 2d 48 (Cal. App. 1993) 9.21n3

Central Ave. Enters., Inc. v. Las Cruces, City of, 845 F. Supp. 1499 (D.N.M. 1994) 5.65n2

Central Ave. News, Inc. v. Minot, City of, 651 F.2d 565 (8th Cir. 1981) 8.42n12

Central Hudson Gas & Elec. Co. v. Public Serv. Comm'n 2.50

Central Motors Corp. v. Pepper Pike, City of, 653 N.E.2d 639 (Ohio 1995) 5.17n4; 5.35n2

Certain-Teed Prods. Corp. v. Paris Twp., 88 N.W.2d 705 (Mich. 1958) 6.03n3

Cetrulo v. Park Hills, City of, 524 S.W.2d 628 (Ky. 1975) 9.27n5

Challenge Exclusionary Land Use Control Devices in Federal C v. Seldin, 29 Stan. L. Rev. 323 (1977)

Challenge Exclusionary Land Use Devices in Federal Courts Af v. Seldin, 29 Stan. L. Rev. 323 (1977)

Champoux; State v. , 566 N.W.2d 763 (Neb.1997) 5.05n1

Chancellor Media Whiteco Outdoor Corp. v. Department of Transportation, 796 So.2d 547 . . . . . 11.06n7

Chandis Securities Co. v. Dana Point, City of, 60 Cal. Rptr.2d 481 (Cal. App. 1996) 6.82n9

Chandler v. Kroiss, 190 N.W.2d 472 (Minn. 1971) 9.27n5; 9.29n3

Chandler v. Pittsfield, Town of, 496 A.2d 1058 (Me. 1985) 6.03n3

Chanhassen Estates Residents Ass'n v. Chanhassen, City of 342 N.W.2d 335 (Minn. 1984) 6.75n1

The Chapel v. Solon, City of, 530 N.E.2d 1321 (Ohio 1988) 8.14n9

Chapman v. Board of Adjustment, 485 So. 2d 1161 (Ala. 1986) 6.50n1

Chapman v. Montgomery County Council 271 A.2d 156 (Md. 1970) 6.31n6

Charles v. Diamond 360 N.E.2d 1295 (N.Y. 1977) 10.11n2

Charlie Brown Constr. Co. v. Boulder City, City of, 797 P.2d 946 (Nev. 1990) 8.23n15

Charlie Brown of Chatham, Inc. v. Board of Adjustment, 495 A.2d 119 (N.J. App. Div. 1985) . . . 5.19n2

Charter Township of Canton v. Department of Soc. Servs., 340 N.W.2d 306 (Mich. App. 1983) . . . 6.05n10

Charter Twp. of Delta v. Dinolfo, 351 N.W.2d 831 (Mich. 1984) 5.05n2

Charter Twp. of Harrison v. Calisi, 329 N.W.2d 488 (Mich. App. 1982) 6.66n1

Chater v. Board of Appeals, 202 N.E.2d 805 (Mass. 1964) 6.48n16

Cheney v. Village 2 at New Hope, Inc 9.27

Cheney v. Village 2 at New Hope, Inc., 241 A.2d 81 (Pa. 1968) 9.25n8

Chernik v. McGowan, 656 N.Y.S.2d 392 (App. Div. 1997) 6.56n12

Cherokee, City of v. Tatro, 636 P.2d 337 (Okla. 1981) 8.13n15

Cherokee County v. Great Atlanta Homebuilders Ass'n, Inc., 566 S.E.2d 470 . . . . 9.21n5

Cherry Hill Farms, Inc. v. Cherry Hills Village, City of, 670 P.2d 779 (Colo. 1983) 9.21n3

Cherry Hill Township v. Oxford House, Inc., 621 A.2d 952 (N.J. App. Div. 1993) 5.08n2

Cherry Hills Resort Dev. Co. v. Cherry Hills Village, 757 P.2d 622 (Colo. 1988) 6.26n1

Cherry Hills Resort Dev. Co. v. Cherry Hills Village, City of, 757 P.2d 622 (Colo. 1988) . . . 6.26n7

Cherry Hills Resort Dev. Co. v. Cherry Hills Village (II), 790 P.2d 827 (Colo. 1990) 9.16n6

Cherry Hills Village, City of v. Trans-Robles Corp., 509 P.2d 797 (Colo. 1973) 6.37n8

Chesapeake, City of v. Gardner Enters., Inc., 482 S.E.2d 812 (Va. 1997) 5.79n3

Chesterfield, County of v. Windy Hill, Ltd., 559 S.E.2d 627 . . . . 4.33n2

Chesterfield Dev. Corp. v. Chesterfield, City of, 963 F.2d 1102 (8th Cir. 1992) 2.39n5; 8.30n3

Chesterfield, Town of v. Brooks, 489 A.2d 600 (N.H. 1985) 2.45n6; 5.23n2

Chesterfield Village, Inc. v. Chesterfield, City of, 64 S.W.2d 315 . . . . 8.21n1

Chevron Oil Co. v. Beaver County, 449 P.2d 989 (Utah 1969) 5.48n2; 12.13n4

Chez Sez III Corp. v. Township of Union, 945 F.2d 628 (3d Cir. 1991) 8.43n6

Chez Sez VIII, Inc. v. Poritz, 688 A.2d 119 (N.J. App. Div. 1997) 5.65n2

Chiavola, State ex rel. v. Oakwood, Village of, 886 S.W.2d 74 (Mo. App. 1994) 3.14n1

Chicago, City of v. Gordon, 497 N.E.2d 442 (Ill. App. 1986) 11.22n1

Chicago, City of v. International College of Surgeons

Chicago, City of v. International College of Surgeons 522 U.S. 15 (1998) 8.40n1

Chicago Heights, City of v. Living Word Outreach Full Gospel Church & Ministries, In, 749 N.E.2d 916 . . . . 6.54n7; 6.55n5; 6.58n2

Chicago Title & Trust Co. v. Lombard, Village of, 166 N.E.2d 41 (Ill. 1960) 5.46n1, n4

Chicago Title & Trust Co. v. Lombard, Village of, 166 N.E.2d 41 (Ill. App. 1961) 5.47n6

Children's Alliance v. Bellevue, City of, 950 F. Supp. 1491 (W.D. Wash. 1997) 5.12n5

Childress, State ex rel. v. Anderson, 865 S.W.2d 384 (Mo. App. 1993) 6.83n1

Chioffi v. Winooski, City of, 676 A.2d 786 (Vt. 1996) 2.22n9

Chioffi v. Winooski Zoning Bd., 556 A.2d 103 (Vt. 1989) 6.52n8

Chirichello v. Zoning Bd. of Adjustment, 397 A.2d 646 (N.J. 1979) 6.45n9; 6.48n2; 6.50n7

Chokecherry Hills Estates v. Deuel County, 294 N.W.2d 654 (S.D. 1980) 12.07n4

Chongris v. Board of Appeals, 811 F.2d 36 (1st Cir. 1987) 2.42n10

Chrinko v. South Brunswick Twp. Planning Bd. 187 A.2d 221 (N.J.L. Div. 1963) 9.26n1

Chrismon v. Guilford Cty., 370 S.E.2d 579 (N.C. 1988) 6.29n12; 6.64n1, n4

Christensen v. Carson, 533 N.W.2d 712 (S.D. 1995) 6.77n1

Christensen v. Yolo County Bd. of Supervisors, 995 F.2d 161 (9th Cir. 1993) 2.31n5

Christian Activities Council, Congregational v. Town Council, 735 A.2d 231 (Conn. 1999) . . 7.31n5

Christian Gospel Ch. v. City & Cty. of San Francisco, 896 F.2d 1221 (9th Cir. 1990) 6.57n13

Christianson v. Gasvoda, 789 P.2d 1234 (Mont. 1990) 9.09n15

Christine Bldg. Co. v. Troy, City of, 116 N.W.2d 816 (Mich. 1962) 3.22n11

Christopher Estates, Inc. v. Parish of East Baton Rouge, 413 So. 2d 1336 (La. App. 1982) 9.09n7

Christy v. Ann Arbor, City of, 824 F.2d 489 (6th Cir. 1987) 5.65n5

Christy's Realty Ltd. Partnership v. Kittery, Town of, 663 A.2d 59 (Me. 1995) 8.04n1

Chrobuck v. Snohomish County, 480 P.2d 489 (Wash. 1971) 6.29n10; 6.73n1

Chucta v. Planning & Zoning Comm'n, 225 A.2d 822 (Conn. 1967) 6.37n15

Chula Vista, City of v. Pagard, 171 Cal. Rptr. 738 (Cal. App. 1981) 5.05n2

Chung v. Sarasota County, 686 So.2d 1358 (Fla. App. 1996) 6.63n1

Church v. Islip, Town of, 168 N.E.2d 680 (N.Y. 1960) 6.64n1

Church v. St. Charles Parish, 767 So.2d 913 . . . . 5.81n9

Church of the Lukumi Babalu Aye v. Hialeah, City of, 508 U.S. 520 (1993) 5.69n2

Church of the Lukumi Babalu Aye, Inc. v. Hialeah, City of, 508 U.S. 520 (1993) 5.69n5

Churchill & Tait v. Rafferty, 32 Philippines 580 (1915) 11.07n6

Ciampitti v. United States, 22 Cl. Ct. 310 (1991) . 2.16n9; 2.19n2; 12.07n12

Cimarron Corp. v. Board of City Comm'rs, 563 P.2d 946 (Colo. 1977) 9.18n1

Cinema Arts, Inc. v. Clark County, 722 F.2d 579 (9th Cir. 1983) 8.43n9

Ciotti v. Cook, County of, 712 F.2d 312 (7th Cir. 1983) 8.42n5

Circle K Corp. v. Mesa, 803 P.2d 457 (Ariz. App. 1990) 5.84n8

Circle K Corp. v. Mesa, City of, 803 P.2d 457 (Ariz. App. 1990) 11.11n9

Circle Lounge & Grill, Inc. v. Board of Appeal 86 N.E.2d 920 (Mass. 1949) 5.46n2

Cities Service Oil Co., State ex rel. v. Board of Appeals, 124 N.W.2d 809 (Wis. 1963) 6.76n6

Citizens Ass'n of Georgetown v. District of Columbia Bd. of Zoning Adjustment, 403 A.2d 737 (D.C. 1979) 8.19n8

Citizen's Awareness Now v. Marakis, 873 P.2d 1117 (Utah 1994) 6.82n7

Citizens Coordinating Comm. on Friendship Heights, Inc. v. TKU Assocs., 351 A.2d 133 (Md. 1976) 8.06n2

Citizens for Mount Vernon v. Mount Vernon, City of, 947 P.2d 1208 (Wash. 1997) . 6.33n10; 9.28n2

Citizens for Orderly Dev. & Env't v. Phoenix, City of, 540 P.2d 1239 (Ariz. 1975) 8.15n3

Citizens for Quality Growth Petitioners' Comm. v. Steamboat Springs, City of, 807 P.2d 1197 (Colo. App. 1991) 6.82n7

Citizens Growth Mgt. Coalition of W. Palm Beach, Inc. v. West Palm Beach, Inc., City of, 450 So. 2d 204 (Fla. 1984) 8.03n1

Citizens United for Free Speech II v. Long Beach Township Bd. of Comm'rs, 802 F. Supp. 1223 (D.N.J. 1992) 11.22n1

City v. (see name of city)

City and County v. (see name of city and county)

City & Borough of Juneau v. Thibodeau 595 P.2d 626 (Alaska 1979) 6.48n3

City Council v. Lindsey Trusts, 520 S.E.2d 181 (Va. 1999) 5.78n4

City Council v. Trebor Constr. Corp., 254 So. 2d 51 (Fla. App. 1971) 8.13n7

City Council of Waltham v. Vinciullo, 307 N.E.2d 316 (Mass. 1974) 6.45n7

City & County of San Francisco v. Eller Outdoor Adv., 237 Cal. Rptr. 815 (1987) . . . 11.19n14

City News & Novelty, Inc. v. Waukesha, City of, 531 U.S. 278 . . . . 6.57n11

City Plan Comm'n v. Pielet, 338 N.E.2d 648 (Ind. App. 1975) 8.13n5

City Planning Comm'n of Greensburg v. Threshold, Inc., 315 A.2d 311 (Pa. Commw. 1974) 5.09n2

Civitans Care, Inc. v. Board of Adjustment, 437 So. 2d 540 (Ala. 1983) 5.08n11

Cizek v. Concerned Citizens of Eagle River Valley, 41 P.3d 140 . . . . 5.81n9

Cizek v. Concerned Citizens of Eagle River Valley, Inc., 41 P.3d 140 . . . . 1.13n2

Clackamas County v. Holmes, 508 P.2d 190 (Or. 1973) 6.18n4; 6.20n2, n3

Clajon Prod. Corp. v. Petera, 70 F.3d 1566 (10th Cir. 1995) 2.19n4; 2.21n6; 9.22n4

Clardy v. Cowles, 912 P.2d 1078 (Wash. App. 1996) 8.46n9

Claridge v. New Hampshire Wetlands Bd., 485 A.2d 287 (N.H. 1984) 2.16n6; 12.07n11

Clark v. Albany, City of, 904 P.2d 185 (Or. App. 1995) 9.22n6

Clark v. Asheboro, City of, 524 S.E.2d 46 (N.C. App. 1999) 6.56n8

Clark v. Board of Appeals, 204 N.E.2d 434 (Mass. 1965) 6.03n4

Clark v. Board of Water & Sewer Comm'rs, 234 N.E.2d 893 (Mass. 1968) 10.10n2

Clark v. Colorado Springs, City of, 428 P.2d 359 (Colo. 1967) 8.05n1

Clark v. Estes Park, Town of, 686 P.2d 777 (Colo. 1984) 4.34n1

Clark v. Hermosa Beach, City of, 56 Cal. Rptr. 2d 223 (Cal. App. 1996) 6.70n13

Clark v. Hermosa Beach, City of, 56 Cal. Rptr.2d 223 (Cal. App. 1996) 6.74n13

Clark v. International Horizons, Inc., 252 S.E.2d 488 (Ga. 1979) 6.15n3

Clark v. Shreveport, City of, 655 So. 2d 617 (La. App. 1995) 8.14n5

Clark, County of v. Doumani, 952 P.2d 13 (Nev. 1998) 6.33n10

Clarke v. Board of Zoning Appeals, 92 N.E.2d 903 (N.Y. 1950) 6.50n4

Clarke v. Morgan, 327 So. 2d 769 (Fla. 1976) . . . 6.03n1; 6.43n1; 6.50n1

Clawson v. Harborcreek Twp. Zoning Hearing Bd., 304 A.2d 184 (Pa. Commw. 1973) . . . 6.29n3

Clay County By & Through County Comm'n v. Bogue, 988 S.W.2d 102 (Mo. App. 1999) 8.26n2

Cleaver v. Board of Adjustment, 200 A.2d 408 (Pa. 1964) 3.14n1; 6.33n2

Cleburne, City of v. Cleburne Living Center, 473 U.S. 432 (1985) 5.08n4; 6.75n2

Cleburne, City of v. Cleburne Living Center 473 U.S. 432 (1985) 2.48n1; 5.09n3

Clements' Appeal, In re , 207 N.E.2d 573 (Ohio App. 1965) 6.02n4

Cleveland Area Bd. of Realtors v. Euclid, City of, 88 F.3d 382 (6th Cir. 1996) 11.22n2

Cleveland, City of v. Brook Park, City of 893 F. Supp. 742 (N.D. Ohio 1995) 4.43n5

Cleveland, City of v. Young, 111 So. 2d 29 (Miss. 1959) 5.19n10

Cline v. Clarksville, City of, 746 S.W.2d 56 (Ark. 1988) 8.26n1

Clinkscales v. Lake Oswego, City of, 615 P.2d 1164 (Or. App. 1980) 3.17n2; 6.33n10

CLR Corp. v. Henline, 702 F.2d 637 (6th Cir. 1983) 5.63n5

Clute, City of v. Linscomb, 446 S.W.2d 377 (Tex. Civ. App. 1969) 4.33n2

CMH Mfg. v. Catawba County, 994 F. Supp. 697 (W.D.N.C. 1998) 5.21n2

CMH Mfg., Inc. v. Catawba County, 994 F. Supp. 697 (W.D.N.C. 1998) 5.26n6

Coachella, City of v. Riverside County Airport Land Use Comm'n, 258 Cal. Rptr. 795 . . . . 8.14n1

Coalition Advocating Legal Housing Options v. Santa Monica, City of, 105 Cal. Rptr. 2d 802 . . . . . 5.19n9

Coastal Dev. of North Florida, Inc. v. Jacksonville, City of, 788 So. 2d 204 . . . . 3.22n4

Coastland Corp. v. Currituck, County of, 734 F.2d 175 (4th Cir. 1984) 9.15n2

Coates v. Planning Bd., 445 N.E.2d 642 (N.Y. 1983) 9.16n8

Cobb Cty. v. McColister, 413 S.E.2d 441 (Ga. 1992) 8.26n1

Cochran v. Planning Bd., 210 A.2d 99 (N.J.L. Div. 1965) 3.21n5

Cohen v. Des Plaines, City of, 8 F.3d 484 (7th Cir. 1993) 5.69n8; 6.57n13

Cohen v. Ford, 339 A.2d 175 (Pa. Commw. 1975) 4.32n1

Cohen v. Henniker, Town of, 593 A.2d 1145 (N.H. 1991) 9.05n4

Cole v. Board of Adjustment, 616 N.W.2d 483 . . . 6.52n5

Collard v. Incorporated Village of Flower Hill . . . 6.64

College Area Renters & Landlord Ass'n v. San Diego, City of, 50 Cal. Rptr. 2d 515 (Cal. App. 1996) 5.05n4

College Station, City of v. Turtle Rock Corp., 680 S.W.2d 802 (Tex. 1984) 4.25n7; 9.18n5; 9.19n4

Collier v. Tacoma, City of, 854 P.2d 1046 (Wash. 1993) 11.23n4, n6

Collins v. El Campo, City of, 684 S.W.2d 756 (Tex. App. 1984) 5.08n6

Collins v. Harker Heights, City of, 503 U.S. 115 (1992) 2.40n1

Collins v. Land Conservation & Dev. Comm'n, 707 P.2d 599 (Or. App. 1985) 10.07n4

Collins v. Spartanburg, City of, 314 S.E.2d 322 (S.C. 1984) 5.84n6

Collis v. Bloomington, City of, 246 N.W.2d 19 (Minn. 1976) 9.19n4

Collura v. Arlington, Town of, 329 N.E.2d 733 (Mass. 1975) 6.07n1; 6.09n2

Colonial Inv. Co. v. Leawood, City of, 646 P.2d 1149 (Kan. App. 1982) 6.16n6

Colorado Housing Ass'n v. Salida, City of, 977 F. Supp. 1080 (D. Colo. 1997) . . . . . . , 5.23n3

Colorado Leisure Prods., Inc. v. Johnson, 532 P.2d 742 (Colo. 1975) 6.34n4

Colorado Manufactured Housing Ass'n v. Pueblo County, 857 P.2d 507 (Colo. App. 1993) 8.06n2

Colorado River Conserv. Dist. v. United States . . 8.45

Colorado River Water Conservation Dist. v. United
    States 8.44
Colorado River Water Conservation Dist. v. United
    States, 424 U.S. 800 (1976) . . . 8.41n3; 8.42n6
Colorado Springs, City of v. Blanche, 761 P.2d 212
    (Colo. 1988) 5.68n3
Colorado Springs, City of v. Securecare Self Storage,
    Inc., 10 P.3d 1244 . . . . 6.66n10
Coltrain v. Shewalter, 77 Cal. Rptr. 2d 600 (Cal. App.
    1998) 8.47n7
Colt's Run Civic Ass'n v. Colts Neck Township
    Zoning Bd., 717 A.2d 456 (N.J. 1998) . . . . . .
    . . . . 5.19n3
Columbia, City of v. Omni Outdoor Adv., Inc . . .
    . . . . 5.53
Columbia Oldsmobile, Inc. v. Montgomery, City of,
    564 N.E.2d 455 (Ohio 1990) 2.36n6
Columbus v. Diaz-Verson, 373 S.E.2d 208 (Ga. 1988)
    . . . . 8.04n4
Columbus, City of; State v. , 209 N.E.2d 405 (Ohio
    1965) 5.39n8
Columbus Park Congregation of Jehovah's Witnesses,
    Inc. v. Board of Appeals, 182 N.E.2d 722 (Ill.
    1962) 6.57n14
Colwell v. Howard County, 354 A.2d 210 (Md. App.
    1976) 6.63n4; 6.66n2
Combined Communications Corp. v. City & Council
    of Denver, 542 P.2d 79 (Colo. 1975) . . . . . .
    . . . . 11.08n6
Comer v. Twin Falls, County of, 942 P.2d 557 (Idaho
    1997) 6.70n5
Comforti v. Manchester, City of, 677 A.2d 147 (N.H.
    1996) 5.79n9
Commercial Airfield, In re , 752 A.2d 13 . . . . . .
    . . . . 4.43n5
Commercial Builders of Northern California v. Sacra-
    mento, City of, 941 F.2d 872 (9th Cir. 1991) . .
    . . . . 9.22n4
Commercial Builders of Northern California v. Sacra-
    mento, City of 941 F.2d 872 (9th Cir. 1991) . .
    . . . . 9.23n2
Commercial Props., Inc. v. Peternel, 211 A.2d 514
    (Pa. 1965) 6.16n4
Commission v. (see name of opposing party)
Commissioner v. (see name of opposing party)
Commissioner of Internal Revenue (see name of
    defendant)
Committee for Responsible Dev. on 25th Street v.
    Mayor & City Council, 767 A.2d 906 . . 8.03n1
Committee for Sensible Land Use v. Garfield Twp.,
    335 N.W.2d 216 (Mich. App. 1983) . . 6.35n2
Commons v. Westwood Zoning Bd. of Adjustment
    410 A.2d 1138 (N.J. 1980) 6.47n4
Commonwealth v. (see name of defendant)

Commonwealth, Dep't of Gen. Servs. v. Ogontz Area
    Neighbors Ass'n, 483 A.2d 448 (Pa. 1984) . . .
    . . . . 4.38n8
Commonwealth, Dep't of Gen. Servs. v. Ogontz Area
    Neighbors Ass'n 483 A.2d 448 (Pa. 1984) . . . .
    . . . . 4.27n6
Commonwealth Edison Co. v. Warrenville, City of,
    680 N.E.2d 465 (Ill. App. 1997) 4.32n2
Commonwealth ex rel. (see name of relator)
Commonwealth of Pa., Bureau of Cors. v. Pittsburgh
'   City Council, City of, 532 A.2d 12 (Pa. 1987)
    . . . . 6.56n1
Commonwealth of Puerto Rico; United States v. , 764
    F. Supp. 220 (D.P.R. 1991) . . 8.42n12; 8.44n8
Communications Co. v. Fayetteville, City of 660
    S.W.2d 900 (Ark. 1983) 11.18n2
Communications in Local Land Use Decisions, Ex
    Parte , 15 B.C. Envtl. Aff. L. Rev. 181 (1987)
Community Communications Co. v. Boulder, City of
    . . . . 5.51
Community Treatment Centers v. Westland, City of,
    970 F. Supp. 1197 (E.D. Mich. 1997) . . . . . .
    . . . . 8.42n2, n11
Compana v. Clark Twp., 197 A.2d 711 (N.J. 1964)
    . . . . 6.09n1
Company, USA v. State Highway Admin., 731 A.2d
    948 (Md. App. 1999) 8.15n1
Comparo v. Woodbridge Twp., 222 A.2d 28 (N.J.
    App. Div. 1966) 6.22n7
Concerned Citizens v. Guilderland, Town of, 458
    N.Y.S.2d 13 (App. Div. 1982) 6.76n5
Concerned Citizens of Calaveras County v. Calaveras
    County Bd. of Supvrs., 212 Cal. Rptr. 273 (Cal.
    App. 1985) 3.22n9
Concerned Citizens of Murphys v. Jackson, 140 Cal.
    Rptr. 531 (Cal. App. 1977) 8.04n2
Concordia College Inst. v. Miller 93 N.E.2d 632 (N.Y.
    1950) 6.04n5
Condiotti v. Board of County Comm'rs, 983 P.2d 184
    (Colo. App. 1999) 8.16n1
Condor Corp. v. St. Paul, City of, 912 F.2d 215 (8th
    Cir. 1990) 4.43n5
Conetta v. Sarasota, City of, 400 So. 2d 1051 (Fla.
    App. 1981) 6.56n12
Congregation Beth Yitzchok of Rockland, Inc. v.
    Ramapo, Town of, 593 F. Supp. 655 (S.D.N.Y.
    1984) 5.69n2
Coniston Corp. v. Hoffman Estates, Village of, 844
    F.2d 461 (7th Cir. 1988) 2.39n3; 8.30n3
Coniston Corp. v. Hoffman Homes, Village of, 844
    F.2d 461 (7th Cir. 1988) 2.40n7
Connecticut Bank & Trust Co. v. Mularcik, 174 A.2d
    128 (Conn. 1961) 4.03n2

Connecticut Health Facilities, Inc. v. Zoning Bd. of Appeals, 613 A.2d 1358 (Conn. App. 1992) . . . 6.56n15

Conner v. Shellburne, Inc., 281 A.2d 608 (Del. 1971) 6.31n4

Conner v. Smith, 433 S.W.2d 911 (Tex. Civ. App. 1968) 4.03n3

Conniston Corp. v. Hoffman Estates, Village of, 844 F.2d 461 (7th Cir. 1988) 2.42n4

Consaul v. San Diego, City of, 8 Cal. Rptr. 2d 762 (Cal. App. 1993) 6.15n1

Conservatorship of (see name of party)

Consolidated Edison Co. of N.Y. v. Briarcliff Manor, Village of, 144 N.Y.S.2d 379 (Sup. Ct. 1955) . . 4.32n2

Consolidated Edison Co. of N.Y. v. Hoffman, 374 N.E.2d 105 (N.Y. 1978) 6.42n1

Consolidated Gov't of Columbus v. Barwick, 549 S.E.2d 73 . . . . 5.47n6

Consolidated Mgt., Inc. v. Cleveland, City of, 452 N.E.2d 1287 (Ohio 1983) 6.03n1

Construction Indus. Ass'n of Sonoma County v. Petaluma, City of 522 F.2d 897 (9th Cir. 1975) 10.06n3

Conti v. Fremont, City of, 919 F.2d 1385 (9th Cir. 1990) 2.47n1

Contractor & Bldrs. Ass'n of Pinellas County v. Dunedin, City of, 329 So. 2d 314 (Fla. 1976) . . 9.22n2

Contractors & Bldrs. Ass'n of Pinellas County v. Dunedin, City of 329 So. 2d 314 (Fla. 1976) . . 9.21n4

Contris v. Richmond County, 235 S.E.2d 19 (Ga. 1977) 8.16n9

Conway, City of v. Housing Auth., 584 S.W.2d 10 (Ark. 1979) 2.23n6

Conway, City of v. Housing Auth. 584 S.W.2d 10 (Ark. 1979) 8.18n1

Coogan v. Wixom, City of, 820 F.2d 170 (6th Cir. 1987) 8.31n5

Cook v. Price, City of, 566 F.2d 699 (10th Cir. 1977) 2.47n3

Cook v. Zoning Bd. of Adj., 776 P.2d 181 (Wyo. 1989) 6.68n3

Cook v. Zoning Hearing Bd., 408 A.2d 1157 (Pa. Commw. 1979) 6.39n2

Cook, County of v. Priester, 342 N.E.2d 41 (Ill. 1976) 8.07n1

Cook, County of v. Renaissance Arcade & Bookstore, 522 N.E.2d 73 . . . . 5.63n7

Cook, County of v. Renaissance Arcade & Bookstore, 522 N.E.2d 73 (Ill.) 5.86n1

Cook, County of v. Renaissance Arcade & Bookstore, 522 N.E.2d 73 (Ill. 1988) 5.64n1

Cook-Johnson Realty Co. v. Bertolini, 239 N.E.2d 80 (Ohio 1968) 6.82n3

Cooley v. United States, 45 Fed. Ct. 438 . . 8.26n8

Cooper v. Board of County Comm'rs, 614 P.2d 947 (Idaho 1980) 6.26n4

Cooper v. Board of Cty. Comm'rs, 614 P.2d 947 (Idaho 1980) 6.70n4

Cooper v. Sinclair, 66 So. 2d 702 (Fla. 1953) . . . 5.23n3

Cootey v. Sun Inv. Co., 718 P.2d 1086 (Hawaii 1986) 8.23n14

Copart Indus. v. Consolidated Edison Co., 362 N.E.2d 968 (N.Y. 1977) 4.02n6

Cope v. Cannon Beach, City of, 855 P.2d 1083 (Or. 1993) 5.17n1

Copechal v. Township of Bristol, 668 A.2d 1222 (Pa. Commw. 1995) 5.81n8

Copeland v. Chattanooga, City of, 866 S.W.2d 565 (Tenn. App. 1993) 9.16n11

Copperweld Corp. v. Independence Tube Corp., 467 U.S. 752 (1984) 5.56n4

Copple v. Lincoln, City of, 315 N.W.2d 628 (Neb. 1979) 8.13n4

Copple v. Lincoln, City of, 315 N.W.2d 628 (Neb. 1982) 6.25n2; 8.13n8

Copple v. Lincoln, City of 274 N.W.2d 520 (Neb. 1979) 6.74n6

Coppolino v. County Bd. of Appeals, 328 A.2d 55 (Md. 1974) 6.34n6; 6.37n7

Coral Gables, City of v. Carmichael, 256 So. 2d 404 (Fla. App. 1972) 6.82n5

Coral Gables, City of v. Hunter, 213 So. 2d 467 (Fla. App. 1968) 8.16n6

Coral Reef Nurseries, Inc. v. Babcock Co., 410 So. 2d 648 (Fla. App. 1982) 6.70n4

Cord Meyer Dev. Co. v. Bell Ray Drugs, Inc., 229 N.E.2d 44 (N.Y. 1967) 5.46n3

Cordeco Dev. Corp. v. Santiago Vasquez, 539 F.2d 256 (1st Cir.1976) 8.38n11

Corder v. Sherwood, City of, 579 F. Supp. 1042 (E.D. Ark. 1984) 8.43n3; 8.44n9

Cordorus Twp. v. Rodgers, 492 A.2d 73 (Pa. Commw. 1985) 12.13n4

Corey Outdoor Adv., Inc. v. Board of Zoning Adjustments, 327 S.E.2d 178 (Ga. 1985) 6.17n1

Cormier v. Danville Zoning Bd. of Adjustment, Town of, 710 A.2d 401 (N.H. 1998) 6.56n2

Corn v. Lauderdale Lakes, City of, 771 F. Supp. 1557 (S.D. Fla. 1991), aff'd 8.26n6

Corn v. Lauderdale Lakes, City of, 816 F.2d 1514 . . . . 2.31n2

Corn v. Lauderdale Lakes, City of, 997 F.2d 1369 (11th Cir. 1993) 2.39n6; 8.35n7

Cornell Univ. v. Bagnardi, 503 N.E.2d 509 (N.Y. 1986) 5.68n1, n2

Cornerstone Bible Ch. v. Hastings, City of, 948 F.2d 464 (8th Cir. 1991) 5.69n4

Cornerstone Bible Church v. Hastings, City of, 948 F.2d 464 (8th Cir. 1991) 2.48n2

Corning v. Ontario, Town of, 121 N.Y.S.2d 288 (Sup. Ct. 1953) 5.23n1

Coronado Dev. Co. v. McPherson, City of, 368 P.2d 51 (Kan. 1962) 9.18n2

Coronet Homes, Inc. v. McKenzie, 439 P.2d 219 (Nev. 1968) 9.28n1

Corporation of Presiding Bishop of Church of Jesus Christ of v. Porterville, City of, 203 P.2d 823 (Cal.) 5.68n1

Corporation Way Realty Trust v. Building Comm'r of Medford, 205 N.E.2d 718 (Mass. 1965) 6.55n4

Corpus Christi, City of v. Unitarian Church, 436 S.W.2d 923 (Tex. Civ. App. 1968) . . . 6.51n9

Corrigan v. Scottsdale, City of, 720 P.2d 513 (Ariz. 1986) 8.21n6

Corrigan v. Scottsdale, City of, 720 P.2d 528 (Ariz. App. 1985) 12.02n1

Corrigan v. Scottsdale, City of 720 P.2d 513 (Ariz. 1986) 8.21n4

Corsino v. Grover, 170 A.2d 267 (Conn. 1961) . . 8.11n16

Corthouts v. Newington, Town of, 99 A.2d 112 (Conn. 1953) 5.43n3

Coscan Washington, Inc. v. Maryland-National Capital Park & Planning Com., 590 A.2d 1080 . . . 11.25n1

Coscan Washington, Inc. v. Maryland-National Capital Park & Planning Comm'n, 590 A.2d 1080 (Md. App. 1991) 6.66n7

Costco Wholesale Corp. v. Orange County, 780 So.2d 198 . . . . 5.46n4

Cottonwood Christian Center v. Cypress Redev. Agency, 218 F. Supp.2d 1203 . . . . . . 5.69n6

Couf v. De Blaker, 652 F.2d 585 (5th Cir. 1981) 6.36n2

Coughlin v. Topeka, City of, 480 P.2d 91 (Kan. 1971) 6.30n1

Coulter v. Rawlings, City of, 662 P.2d 888 (Wyo. 1983) 9.19n4; 9.21n3

Council Bluffs, City of v. Cain, 342 N.W.2d 810 (Iowa 1983) 6.05n3

Council of Middletown Twp. v. Benham, 523 A.2d 311 (Pa. 1987) 10.10n2

Council of Middletown Twp. v. Benhjam, 523 A.2d 311 (Pa. 1987) 4.30n3

Council Rock School Dist. v. Wrightstown Township Zoning Hearing Bd., 709 A.2d 453 (Pa. Commw. 1998) 4.28n2

Country Club Estates v. Loma Linda, Town of, 281 F.3d 723 . . . . 5.29n4

Country Joe, Inc. v. Eagan, City of, 560 N.W.2d 681 (Minn. 1997) 9.21n2

Countrywalk Condominiums, Inc. v. Orchard Lake Village, City of, 561 N.W.2d 405 (Mich. App. 1997) 5.18n6

County v. (see name of county)

County Aviation, Inc. v. Tinicum Township, 9 F.3d 1539 (3rd Cir. 1993) 4.43n3

County Comm'rs v. Conservation Comm'n of Dartmouth, 405 N.E.2d 637 (Mass. 1980) . . 4.28n1

County Comm'rs v. Days Cove Reclamation Co., 713 A.2d 351 (Md. App. 1998) 8.16n1

County Comm'rs of Queen Anne's County v. Miles, 228 A.2d 450 (Md. 1967) 5.31n2

County Council v. Carl M. Freeman Assocs., 376 A.2d 860 (Md. 1977) 8.13n5

County Council v. District Land Corp., 337 A.2d 712 (Md. 1975) 6.15n1; 6.21n1, n4

County Mobilehome Positive Action Comm., Inc. v. San Diego, County of, 73 Cal. Rptr. 2d 409 (Cal. App. 1998) 6.23n5

Cove Road Dev. v. Western Cranston Industrial Park Assocs., 674 A.2d 1234 (R.I. 1996) . . . 8.46n3

Covington v. Apex, Town of, 423 S.E.2d 537 (N.C. App. 1992) 6.29n8

Covington Court, Ltd. v. Oak Brook, Village of, 77 F.3d 177 (7th Cir. 1996) 2.30n2

Cowan v. Kern, 363 N.E.2d 305 (N.Y. 1977) 6.52n5

Cowart v. Ocala, City of, 478 F. Supp. 744 (M.D. Fla. 1979) 7.03n5

Cox v. Lynnwood, City of, 863 P.2d 578 (Wash. App. 1993) 8.09n7, n8

Cox v. Lynwood, City of, 863 P.2d 578 (Wash. App. 1993) 8.23n7

Coyote Flats, L.L.C. v. Sanborn County Comm'n, 596 N.W.2d 347 (S.D. 1999) 6.56n4

C.R. Invs., Inc. v. Shoreview, Village of 304 N.W.2d 320 (Minn. 1981) 6.56n14

Crabtree v. City Auto Salvage Co., 340 S.W.2d 940 (Tenn. App. 1960) 4.09n3

Crann v. Town Plan & Zoning Comm'n, 282 A.2d 900 (Conn. 1971) 6.66n11

Craven, State ex rel. v. Tacoma, City of, 385 P.2d 372 (Wash. 1963) 9.08n7

Crawford v. Board of Educ., 458 U.S. 527 (1982) 6.80n3

Crea v. Crea. 16 P.3d 922 . . . . 12.11n3

Creative Country Day School, Inc. v. Montgomery County Board of Appeals, 219 A.2d 789 (Md. 1966) 5.27n3

Creative Env'ts, Inc. v. Estabrook 680 F.2d 822 (1st Cir. 1982) 8.30n1

Creekside Assocs. v. Wood Dale, City of, 684 F. Supp. 201 (N.D. Ill. 1988) 8.38n5

Crew, Development Agreements After Nollan v. California Coastal Commission, 22 Urb. Law. 23 (1990)

Cricklewood Hill Realty Assocs. v. Zoning Bd. of Adj., 558 A.2d 178 (Pa. Commw. 1989) 6.41n11

Crider v. Board of County Comm'rs, 246 F.3d 1285 . . . . 2.47n2

Crispin v. Scarborough, Town of, 736 A.2d 241 (Me. 1999) 6.70n7

Cristofaro v. Burlington, Town of, 584 A.2d 1168 (Conn. 1991) 9.06n4

Cromwell v. Ferrier, 225 N.E.2d 748 (N.Y. 1967) 11.05n1

Cromwell v. Ward, 651 A.2d 424 (Md. App. 1995) 6.41n1; 6.48n10

Crooked Creek Conserv. & Gun Club, Inc. v. Hamilton County N. Bd. of Zoning Appeals 677 N.E.2d 544 (Ind. App. 1997) 6.56n17

Cross v. Hall County 235 S.E.2d 379 (Ga. 1977) . 6.65n2

Croteau v. Planning Bd., 663 N.E.2d 583 (Mass. App. 1996) 9.28n1

Crowley v. Courville, 76 F.3d 47 (2d Cir. 1996) . . 2.47n3; 2.49n3

Crown Point, City of v. Lake County, 510 N.E.2d 684 (Ind. 1992) 4.38n3

Crownhill Homes, Inc. v. San Antonio, City of, 433 S.W.2d 448 (Tex. Civ. App. 1968) . . . 9.15n2

Crucil v. Carson City, 600 P.2d 216 (Nev. 1979) . 9.18n1

Cruz v. Cicero, Town of, 275 F.3d 579 . . 2.49n4

Crymes v. DeKalb County, 923 F.2d 1482 (11th Cir. 1991) 8.35n6, n7

Crystal, City of v. Fantasy House, Inc., 569 N.W.2d 225 (Minn. App. 1997) 5.63n1

Cty. of Monroe, Matter of , 530 N.E.2d 202 (N.Y. 1988) 4.38n3

Culbertson v. Board of County Comm'rs, 41 P.3d 642 . . . . 8.11n9; 8.15n5

Culebras Enters. Corp. v. Rivera Rios, 813 F.2d 506 (1st Cir. 1987) 8.35n4; 8.36n9, n14

Culinary Inst. of Am. v. Board of Zoning Appeals, 121 A.2d 637 (Conn. 1956) 6.45n10; 6.47n2

Cully Realty, Inc.; People v. , 442 N.Y.S.2d 847 (Misc. 1981) 5.20n5

Culp v. Seattle, City of, 590 P.2d 1288 (Wash. App. 1979) 5.08n12

Cumberland, County of v. Eastern Fed. Corp., 269 S.E.2d 672 (N.C. App. 1980) 5.86n2

Cumberland Farms, Inc. v. Groton, Town of, 719 A.2d 465 (Conn. 1998) 8.09n4, n5

Cummings v. Seattle, City of, 935 P.2d 663 (Wash. App. 1997) 6.48n2

Cunningham v. Kittery Planning Bd., 400 A.2d 1070 (Me. 1979) 8.10n2

Cuomo, Estate of v. Rush, 708 N.Y.S.2d 695 . . . . 5.81n7, n9

Cupp v. Board of Supvrs., 318 S.E.2d 407 (Va. 1984) 9.16n6

Curran v. Church Community Hous. Corp., 672 A.2d 453 (R.I. 1996) 7.31n10

Currey v. Kimple, 577 S.W.2d 508 (Tex. Civ. App. 1979) 8.13n6

Currier Bldrs., Inc. v. York, Town of, 146 F. Supp.2d 71 . . . . 8.43n8

Curtis v. South Thomaston, Town of, 708 A.2d 657 (Me. 1998) 9.22n9

Curtis v. South Tomaston, Town of, 708 A.2d 657 (Me. 1998) 9.16n9

Curtis Oil v. North Branch, City of, 364 N.W.2d 880 (Minn. App. 1985) 8.14n4

Custody of (see name of party)

Cutting v. Mazzey, 724 F.2d 259 (1st Cir. 1984) . . 7.02n4; 8.36n2

Cutting v. Muzzey, 724 F.2d 249 (1st Cir. 1984) . . 8.35n6

Cyclone Sand & Gravel Co. v. Zoning Bd. of Adjustment, 351 N.W.2d 778 (Iowa 1984) . . . 6.03n3

D

Dacy v. Ruidoso, Village of, 845 P.2d 793 (N.M. 1992) 6.64n5

Daddario v. Cape Cod Comm'n, 681 N.E.2d 833 (Mass. 1997) 8.09n3; 12.13n5

D'Addario v. Planning & Zoning Comm'n, 593 A.2d 511 (Conn. App. 1991) 6.25n7; 6.37n10

Dade County v. Inversiones Rafamar, S.A., 360 So. 2d 1130 (Fla. App. 1978) 3.17n2

Dade County v. Metro Imp. Corp., 190 So. 2d 202 (Fla. App. 1966) 8.13n5

Dade County v. National Bulk Carriers, Inc., 450 So. 2d 213 (Fla. 1984) 8.22n1

Daigle v. Continental Oil Co., 277 F. Supp. 875 (1967) 4.12n2

Dailey v. Lawton, City of 425 F.2d 1037 (10th Cir. 1970) 7.03n4

Dallas, City of v. Crownrich 506 S.W.2d 654 (Tex. Civ. App. 1974) 11.31n1

Dallen v. Kansas City, City of, 822 S.W.2d 429 (Mo. App. 1991) 5.71n4

Dalton v. City & County of Honolulu 6.34

Dalton v. City & County of Honolulu, 462 P.2d 199 (Haw. 1969) 8.04n4

Daly v. Town Plan & Zoning Comm'n, 191 A.2d 250 (Conn. 1963) 6.74n10

Damascus Community Church v. Clackamas County Bd. of Comm'rs, 573 P.2d 726 (Or. App. 1978) 6.56n1

Damurjian v. Board of Adjustment, 890 A.2d 655 (N.J. App. Div. 1997) 5.72n3

Dana-Robin Corp. v. Common Council 348 A.2d 560 (Conn. 1974) 6.74n4

Dangerfield Island Protective Soc'y v. Babbitt, 40 F.3d 342 (D.C. Cir. 1994) 12.08n2

Daniels v. Goose Creek, City of, 431 S.E.2d 256 (S.C. App. 1993) 6.21n6

Daniels v. Van Voris, 660 N.Y.S.2d 758 (App. Div. 1997) 6.32n2

Daniels v. Williams, 474 U.S. 327 (1986) 8.29n11

Danis Montco Landfill Co. v. Jefferson Twp. Zoning Comm'n, 620 N.E.2d 140 (Ohio App. 1993) . . 6.76n10

Danish News Co. v. Ann Arbor, City of, 517 F. Supp. 86 (E.D. Mich. 1981) 8.42n2

Danish News Co. v. Ann Arbor, City of, 517 F. Supp. 86 (E.D. Mich. 1981), aff'd mem., 751 F.2d 384 (6th Cir. 1984) 8.42n12

Danville-Boyle County Planning & Zoning Comm'n v. Prall, 840 S.W.2d 205 (Ky. 1992) 6.70n10

Dateline Bldrs., Inc. v. Santa Rosa, City of 10.10

Daugherty v. Campbell, 935 F.2d 780 (6th Cir. 1991) 8.36n12

Daugherty v. East Point, City of, 447 F. Supp. 290 (N.D. Ga. 1978) 11.22n1

Davidson County v. High Point, City of, 354 S.E.2d 280 (N.C. App. 1987) 4.34n1

Davis v. Albuquerque, City of, 648 P.2d 777 (N.M. 1982) 6.38n1

Davis v. Archdale, City of, 344 S.E.2d 369 (N.C. App. 1986) 8.04n3

Davis v. Bandon, City of, 805 P.2d 709 (Or. App. 1991) 6.07n4

Davis v. Blount County Beer Bd., 621 S.W.2d 149 (Tenn. 1981) 6.04n4

Davis v. Green, City of, 665 N.E.2d 753 (Ohio App. 1996) 11.23n1

Davis v. Leavenworth, City of, 802 P.2d 494 (Kan. 1991) 9.28n2

Davis v. Miller, 96 S.E.2d 498 (Ga. 1957) 4.03n1

Davis v. Passman, 442 U.S. 228 (1979) . . 8.39n3

Davis v. Pima County, 590 P.2d 459 (Ariz. App.1978) 8.16n5

Davis v. Princeton, City of, 401 N.W.2d 391 (Minn. App. 1987) 5.39n6

Davis v. Sails, 318 So. 2d 214 (Fla. App. 1975) . . 5.18n4

Davis v. Scherer 468 U.S. 183 (1984) . . . 8.36n8

Davis v. Zoning Bd., 754 N.E.2d 101 . . . 6.56n15

Davis County v. Clearfield City, 756 P.2d 704 (Utah App. 1988) 6.75n3

Davis Cty. v. Clearfield City, 756 P.2d 704 (Utah App. 1988) 6.56n9; 8.12n1; 8.14n4

Dawe v. Scottsdale, City of, 581 P.2d 1136 (Ariz. 1978) 9.07n8

Dawson v. Laufersweiler, 43 N.W.2d 726 (Iowa 1950) 4.07n1

Dawson Enters., Inc. v. Blaine County, 567 P.2d 1257 (Idaho 1977) 3.14n1

Daytona Rescue Mission, Inc. v. Daytona Beach, City of, 885 F. Supp. 1554 (M.D. Fla. 1995) 5.69n2

De Blasio v. Board of Zoning Adjustment, 53 F.2d 592 (3d Cir. 1995) 2.40n7

De Leo v. Lecraw, 334 N.Y.S.2d 912 (App. Div. 1972) 9.09n18

De Mars v. Zoning Comm'n, 115 A.2d 653 (Conn. 1955) 5.31n5

De Mull v. Lowell, City of, 118 N.W.2d 232 (Mich. 1962) 5.82n2

Deal Gardens, Inc. v. Board of Trustees, 226 A.2d 607 (N.J. 1967) 8.08n1; 8.11n5

Dearborn v. Milford, Town of, 411 A.2d 1132 (N.H. 1980) 9.05n7

Dearden v. Detroit, City of, 245 N.W.2d 700 (Mich. App. 1976) 4.27n7

Dearden v. Detroit, City of, 269 N.W.2d 139 (Mich. 1978) 4.38n8

Deardorf v. Board of Adjustment, 118 N.W.2d 78 (Iowa 1962) 6.44n3; 6.52n4

Dease v. Anaheim, City of, 826 F. Supp. 336 (C.D. Cal. 1993) 6.57n2

DeBlasio v. Zoning Bd. of Adjustment, 53 F.3d 592 (3d Cir. 1995) 2.39n5

deBottari v. Norco City Council, 217 Cal. Rptr. 790 (Cal. App. 1985) 6.33n3

DeCoals, Inc. v. Board of Zoning Appeals 284 S.E.2d 856 (W. Va. 1981) 5.41n1

Decuir v. Marksville, Town of, 426 So. 2d 766 (La. App. 1983) 6.30n1

Deep East Texas Regional Mental Health & Mental Retardat v. Kinnear, 877 S.W.2d 550 (Tex. App. 1994) 4.08n1

Deerfield Med. Center v. Deerfield Beach, City of, 661 F.2d 328 (5th Cir. 1981) 5.58n1

Deering ex rel. Bittenbender, Town of v. Tibbetts, 202 A.2d 232 (N.H. 1964) 11.30n2

DeFelice v. Zoning Bd. of Adjustment, 523 A.2d 1086 (N.J. App. Div. 1987) 6.51n6

Deffenbaugh Indus., Inc. v. Potts, 802 S.W.2d 520 (Mo. App. 1990) 8.16n7

Deighton v. City Council, 902 P.2d 426 (Colo. App. 1995) 6.07n2

Deja Vu of Kentucky, Inc. v. Lexington-Fayette Urban County Gov't, 194 F. Supp.2d 606 . . . 8.45n3

DeKalb County v. Publix Super Markets, 452 S.E.2d 471 (Ga. 1994) 8.14n5

DeKalb County v. Townsend Assocs., 252 S.E.2d 498 (Ga. 1979) 6.11n2

DeKalb Stone, Inc. v. DeKalb, County of, 106 F.3d 956 (11th Cir. 1997) 2.40n4

Del Mar, City of v. San Diego, City of, 183 Cal. Rptr. 898 (Cal. App. 1983) 7.24n1

Del Monte Dunes Ltd. v. Monterey, City of, 920 F.2d 1496 (9th Cir. 1990) 2.30n9

Del Norte, County of v. Crescent City, City of, 84 Cal. Rptr.2d 179 (Cal. App. 1999) 10.10n6

Delaware & Hudson Ry. Co.; Commonwealth v. , 339 A.2d 155 (Pa. Commw. 1975) 4.32n2

Delaware Midland Corp. v. Incorporated Village of Westhampton Beach, 359 N.Y.S.2d 944 (Sup. Ct. 1974), aff'd, 355 N.E.2d 302 (N.Y. 1976) 9.05n7

Delaware, State of v. Booker, 1992 Del. Super. LEXIS 366 (Del. Super. 1992) 10.15n2

Della Villa v. Constantino, 668 N.Y.S.2d 724 (App. Div. 1998) 8.23n5

Delmarva Enters. v. Mayor & Council, 282 A.2d 601 (Del. 1971) 10.10n3

Delta Biological Resources, Inc. v. Board of Zoning Appeals, 467 N.W.2d 164 (Wis. App. 1991) . . 6.54n1; 6.56n1

Deltona Corp. v. United States, 657 F.2d 1184 (Ct. Cl. 1981) 2.19n3

Deltona Corp. v. United States, 657 F.2d 1184 (Ct. Cl. 1991) 12.07n9

Delucchi v. Santa Cruz, County of, 225 Cal. Rptr. 43 . . . . 6.23n5

Delucchi v. Santa Cruz, County of, 225 Cal. Rptr. 43 (Cal. App. 1986) 6.62n2

Dema Realty Co., State ex rel. v. McDonald, 121 So. 613 (La.) 5.84n1

DeMaria v. Enfield Planning & Zoning Comm'n, 271 A.2d 105 (Conn. 1970) 9.28n3

Dempsey v. Newport Bd. of Adjustments, 941 S.W.2d 483 (Ky. App. 1997) 5.81n16

Denby v. Brown, 199 S.E.2d 214 (Ga. 1973) 10.10n3

Deniz v. Municipality of Guaynabo, 285 F.3d 142 . . . . 2.31n3

Denney v. Duluth, City of, 202 N.W.2d 892 (Minn. 1973) 6.82n7

Denning v. Maui, County of, 485 P.2d 1048 (Haw. 1971) 6.15n4

Denton v. Browns Mill Dev. Co., 561 S.E.2d 431 . . . . 8.47n1

DePaolo v. Ithaca, Town of, 694 N.Y.S.2d 235 (App. Div. 1999) 6.64n4

Department of Transp. v. Lundberg, 825 P.2d 641 (Or. 1992) 2.23n6; 9.16n11

Department of Transp., People ex rel. v. Diversified Prods. Co. III, 17 Cal. Rptr. 2d 676 (Cal. App. 1993) 10.15n3

Dep't of Transp., People ex rel. v. Diversified Props. Co. III 17 Cal. Rptr. 2d 676 (Cal. App. 1993) 2.23n3

Des Moines, City of v. Lohner, 168 N.W.2d 779 (Iowa 1969) 6.55n3

Des Plaines, City of v. Metropolitan San. Dist., 268 N.E.2d 428 (Ill. 1971) 4.36n1

Des Plaines, City of v. Trottner, 216 N.E.2d 116 (Ill. 1966), rev'd 5.05n5

Desert Outdoor Advertising v. Moreno Valley, City of, 103 F.3d 814 (9th Cir. 1996) 8.36n9; 11.19n17

Deshotel v. Calcasieu Parish Police Jury, 323 So. 2d 155 (La. App.), aff'd, 326 So. 2d 371 (La. 1976) 6.18n1

DeSimone v. Greater Englewood Hous. Corp. No. 1, 267 A.2d 31 (N.J. 1970) 6.43n4

Desmond v. City 5.17n2

Detroit, City of v. Volunteers of America, 426 N.W.2d 743 (Mich. App. 1988) 4.27n1

Detroit Edison Co. v. Township of Richmond, 388 N.W.2d 296 (Mich. App. 1986) 4.32n8

Detroit Osteopathic Hosp. Corp. v. Southfield, City of, 139 N.W.2d 728 (Mich. 1966) 6.55n4

Dettmar v. County Bd. of Zoning Appeals, 273 N.E.2d 921 (Ohio Misc. 1971) 5.19n3

Devaney v. Board of Zoning Appeals, 45 A.2d 828 (Conn. 1946) 6.03n1

Devaney v. Burlington, City of, 545 S.E.2d 763 . . 6.26n2

Develo-Cepts, Inc. v. Galveston, City of, 668 S.W.2d 790 (Tex. App. 1984) 8.02n10

Development Servs. Of America, Inc. v. Seattle, City of, 979 P.2d 387 (Wash. 1999) 1.13n2

Devita v. Napa, County of, 889 P.2d 1019 (Cal. 1995) 6.83n3

Dews v. Sunnyvale, Town of, 109 F. Supp. 2d 526 . . . . 7.05n6

Dexter v. Town Bd., 324 N.E.2d 870 (N.Y. 1975) 6.63n4

D.H.L. Assocs., Inc. v. O'Gorman, 199 F.3d 50 (1st Cir. 1999) 5.63n13

Di Salle v. Giggal, 261 P.2d 499 (Colo. 1953) . . . 5.72n1

Diamond v. Taft, City of, 215 F.3d 1057 . . . . . . 5.63n12

Diamond v. Taft, City of, 29 F. Supp. 2d 633 (E.D. Cal. 1998) 6.57n2

Diamond Motors, Inc.; State v. , 429 P.2d 825 (Haw. 1967) 11.10n2

DiBlasi v. Zoning Bd. of Appeals, 624 A.2d 372 (Conn. 1993) 5.79n9

Dick v. Williams, 452 S.E.2d 172 (Ga. App. 1994) 6.74n11

Diehl v. Lockard, 385 A.2d 550 (Pa. Super. 1978) 4.06n4

Diehl v. Mason County, 972 P.2d 543 (Wash. App. 1999) 3.22n1

Diehl, State ex rel. v. Helena, City of, 593 P.2d 458 (Mont. 1979) 5.48n2

Dill v. Brinkley, 1988 Tenn. App. LEXIS 118 (Tenn. App. 1988) 4.03n1

Diller & Fisher Co. v. Architectural Review Bd., 587 A.2d 674 (N.J.L. Div. 1991) 11.24n1

Dills v. Cobb County, 593 F. Supp. 170 (N.D. Ga. 1984), aff'd *11.20n1*

Dills v. Marietta, City of, 674 F.2d 1377 (11th Cir. 1982) 11.20n1

DiMas Corp. v. Hallie, Town of, 185 F.3d 823 (7th Cir. 1999) 5.63n4

Dimitt v. Clearwater, City of, 985 F.2d 1565 (11th Cir. 1993) 11.19n15

Dinan v. Board of Zoning Appeals, 595 A.2d 864 (Conn. 1991) 5.05n1

Disabatino v. New Castle County, 781 A.2d 687 . . 6.16n5

Discovery Network, Inc. v. Cincinnati, City of, 507 U.S. 410 (1993) 11.19n7

The Distinction Between Legislative and Adjudicative Decisio v. Tigard, City of, 75 N.Y.U.L. Rev. 242

District Intown Props. Ltd. Partnership. v. District of Columbia, 198 F.3d 874 (D.C. Cir. 1999) 11.35n6

District of Columbia Court of Appeals v. Feldman, 460 U.S. 4621 (1983) 2.34n1

Divan Bldrs., Inc. v. Planning Bd. 334 A.2d 30 (N.J. 1975) 9.16n1

Dixon v. Jacksonville, City of, 774 So.2d 763 . . . 6.33n3, n5

Dixon v. Superior Ct., 36 Cal. Rptr. 2d 687 (Cal. App. Ct. 1994) 8.47n1

DJL Restaurant Corp. v. New York, City of, 749 N.E.2d 186 . . . . 4.33n2

DLC Mgmt. Corp. v. Hyde Park, Town of, 163 F.3d 124 (2d Cir. 1998) 2.40n6

Dobson Jamaica Realties v. Brookhaven, Town of, 409 N.Y.S.2d 590 (Sup. Ct. 1978) . . . 8.19n4

Dodd v. Hood River County, 136 F.3d 1219 (9th Cir. 1998) 1.12n1; 2.33n2

Dodd v. Hood River County, 59 F.3d 852 (9th Cir. 1995) 2.31n6

Doe v. Butler, City of, 892 F.2d 315 (3d Cir. 1989) 5.06n2

Doe v. Butler, City of 892 F.2d 315 (3d Cir. 1989) 5.08n5

Doherty v. Chicago, City of, 75 F.3d 318 (7th Cir. 1996) 2.39n7

Dolan v. Tigard, City of 9.14

Dolan v. Tigard, City of 512 U.S. 374 (1994) . . . 2.12n1

Dolan v. Tigard, City of, 63 U. Chi. L. Rev. 199 (1996)

Dolan v. Zoning Bd. of Appeals, 242 A.2d 713 (Conn. 1968) 6.39n2

Donahue v. Zoning Bd. of Adjustment, 194 A.2d 610 (Pa. 1963) 6.34n1

Donnelly Adv. Corp. v. Baltimore, City of, 370 A.2d 1127 (Md. 1977) 11.09n2; 11.11n3

Donnelly Advertising Co. v. Baltimore, City of, 370 A.2d 1127 (Md. 1977) 11.19n1

Donohue Constr. Co. v. Montgomery County Council, 567 F.2d 603 (4th Cir. 1977) 8.43n8

Donrey Communications Co. v. Fayetteville, City of, 660 S.W.2d 900 (Ark. 1983) . 5.84n6; 11.05n1

Dooley v. Town Plan & Zoning Comm'n, 197 A.2d 770 (Conn. 1964) 12.09n1

Dooling's Windy Hill v. Zoning Bd. of Adjustment, 89 A.2d 505 (Pa. 1952) 6.03n2

Doran Inv. Co. v. Muhlenberg Twp., 309 A.2d 450 (Pa. Commw. 1973) 9.30n6

Doraville, City of v. Turner Communications Co., 223 S.E.2d 798 (Ga. 1976) 11.06n6

Dore v. Ventura, County of, 28 Cal. Rptr. 2d 299 (Cal. App. 1994) 9.28n1

Dorvinen v. Crook County, 957 P.2d 180 (Or. App. 1998) 12.12n3

Dosmann v. Area Plan Comm'n, 312 N.E.2d 880 (Ind. App. 1974) 9.09n2

Dougherty v. North Hempstead Bd. Of Zoning, Town of, 282 F.3d 83 . . . . 2.51n6

Dougherty County v. Webb, 350 S.E.2d 457 (Ga. 1986) 8.14n3

Douglas County Contractors Ass'n v. Douglas County, 929 P.2d 253 (Nev. 1996) . . . 9.21n2

Douglaston Civic Ass'n v. Galvin 324 N.E.2d 317 (N.Y. 1974) 8.06n6

Douglaston Civic Ass'n v. Klein, 416 N.E.2d 1040 (N.Y. 1980) 6.46n2

Dowerk v. Charter Township of Oxford, 592 N.W.2d 724 (Mich. App. 1999) 9.16n14

Downing v. Board of Zoning Appeals, 274 N.E.2d 542 (Ind. App. 1971) 8.13n13

Downtown Neighborhood Ass'n v. Albuquerque, City of, 783 P.2d 962 (N.M. App. 1989) . . . 6.46n5

Dowsey v. Kensington, Village of, 177 N.E. 427 (N.Y. App. 1937) 5.18n6

Doyle v. Amster, 594 N.E.2d 911 (N.Y. 1992) . . . 6.48n5; 6.50n4

Dreher, State ex rel. v. Fuller, 849 P.2d 1045 (Mont. 1993) 9.05n3

Driscoll v. Austintown Assocs., 328 N.E.2d 395 (Ohio 1975) 8.16n5

Drovers Bank of Chicago v. Hinsdale, Village of, 506 N.E.2d 899 (Ill. App. 1991) 8.09n8

Drovers Bank of Chicago v. Hinsdale, Village of, 566 N.E. 2d 899 (Ill. App. 1991) 8.09n4

D.S. Parklane Dev., Inc. v. Metro, 994 P.2d 1205 . . . . 10.07n4

Dsuban v. Union Township Zoning Bd. of Appeals, 748 N.E.2d 597 . . . . 6.41n8

Du Page County v. Halkier, 115 N.E.2d 635 (Ill. 1953) 5.32n3

Dublin, City of v. Finkes, 615 N.E.2d 690 (Ohio App. 1993) 5.78n3

Dubuc v. Green Oak Township, 958 F. Supp. 1231 (E.D. Mich. 1997) 8.36n14

Duckworth v. Bonney Lake, City of, 586 P.2d 860 (Wash. 1978) 5.23n1

Dufau v. United States 2.22n4

Dufau v. United States, 22 Cl. Ct. 156 (Cl. Ct. 1990) 2.22n4, n6

Duffcon Concrete Prods., Inc. v. Borough of Cresskill 5.42

Duggan v. Cook, County of, 324 N.E.2d 406 (Ill. 1975) 8.19n8

Duggins v. Walnut Grove, Town of, 306 S.E.2d 186 (N.C. App. 1981) 5.23n1

Duke & Co. v. Foerster, 521 F.2d 1277 (3d Cir. 1975) 5.55n2

Dull v. York County, 528 S.E.2d 447 . . . 4.30n12

Dunaway v. Austin, City of, 290 S.W.2d 703 (Tex. App. 1956) 4.10n2

Dunaway v. Marietta, City of, 308 S.E.2d 823 (Ga. 1983) 8.04n4

Duncan v. Midfield, Village of, 491 N.E.2d 692 (Ohio 1986) 6.48n5

Dunkin' Donuts of N.J., Inc. v. Township of North Brunswick Plan. Bd. 475 A.2d 71 (N.J. App. Div. 1984) 6.66n4

Dunn v. Blumstein, 405 U.S. 330 (1972) 10.08n5

Dunnett, In re , 776 A.2d 406 . . . . 6.44n4

DuPage, County of v. Harris, 231 N.E.2d 195 (Ill. App. 1967) 4.31n2

Dupont Circle Citizens Ass'n v. Barry, 455 A.2d 417 (D.C. App. 1983) 8.06n2

Dupont Circle Citizens Ass'n v. District of Columbia Bd. of Zoning Adjustment, 749 A.2d 1258 . . . 5.19n3

Dupont Circle Citizens Ass'n v. District of Columbia Zoning Comm'n, 355 A.2d 550 (D.C. App. 1976) 9.26n4; 11.38n3

Dupont Circle Citizens Ass'n v. District of Columbia Zoning Comm'n 426 A.2d 327 (D.C. App. 1981) 9.28n4

Duquesne Light Co. v. Upper St. Clair Twp., 105 A.2d 287 (Pa. 1954) 4.32n2

Dur-Bar Realty Co. v. Utica, City of, 394 N.Y.S.2d 913 (App. Div. 1977) 12.09n3

Durant v. Dunbarton, Town of, 430 A.2d 140 (N.H. 1981) 9.09n3

Durham, Town of v. White Enters., Inc., 348 A.2d 706 (N.H. 1975) 5.05n1

Dusdal v. Warren, City of, 196 N.W.2d 778 (Mich. 1972) 5.81n3

Dvorak v. Bloomington, City of, 702 N.E.2d 1121 (Ind. App. 1998) 5.05n2

Dvorak v. Bloomington, City of, 768 N.E.2d 490 . . . . 5.05n2

Dyches v. McCorkle, 441 S.E.2d 518 (Ga. App. 1994) 8.23n4

Dye v. Phoenix, City of, 542 P.2d 31 (Ariz. App. 1975) 6.31n4

Dykeman v. State, 593 P.2d 1183 (Or. App. 1979) 8.23n13

Dynasty Bldg. Corp. v. Borough of Upper Saddle River, 632 A.2d 544 (N.J. App. Div. 1993) . . . 7.12n7

E

E. Brooks Books v. Memphis, City of, 48 F.3d 220 (6th Cir. 1995) 5.64n1

E & G Enters. v. Mount Vernon, City of, 373 N.W.2d 693 (Iowa App. 1985) 5.48n2

Earth Movers of Fairbanks, Inc. v. Fairbanks North Star Borough, 865 P.2d 741 (Alaska 1993) . . . 5.46n3

East Bay Asian Local Development Corp. v. California, State of, 13 P.3d 1122 . . . . 11.37n8

East-Bibb Twiggs Neighborhood Ass'n v. Macon-Bibb County Planning & Zoning Comm'n, 896 F.2d 1264 (11th Cir. 1989) 2.31n3

East-Bibb Twiggs Neighborhood Ass'n v. Macon Bibb Planning & Zoning Corn., 896 F.2d 1264 . . . . 2.24n4

East Cape May Assocs. v. New Jersey Dep't of Envtl. Protection, 693 A.2d 114 (N.J. App. Div. 1997) 2.22n2

East Cleveland, City of; State v. , 153 N.E.2d 177 (Ohio App. 1958), aff'd, 160 N.E.2d 1 (Ohio 1959) 5.46n1

East Lake Partners v. Dover Planning Comm'n, City of, 655 A.2d 821 (Del. Super. 1995) . . 6.66n10

East Lampeter Township v. Lancaster, County of, 744 A.2d 359 (Pa. Commw. 1999) 6.25n2

East Providence, City of v. Rhode Island Hosp. Trust Nat'l Bank, 505 A.2d 1143 (R.I. 1986) 8.15n7

East Providence, City of v. Shell Oil Co., 290 A.2d 915 (R.I. 1972) 8.07n1

East Side Baptist Church v. Klein, 487 P.2d 549 (Colo. 1971) 5.68n4

East/West Venture v. Borough of Fort Lee, 669 A.2d 260 (N.J. App. Div. 1996) 7.12n8

Easter Seal Soc'y of New Jersey, Inc. v. Township of North Bergen, 798 F. Supp. 228 (D.N.J. 1992) 5.14n1

Eastern Diversified Properties, Inc. v. Montgomery County, 570 A.2d 850 (Md. 1990) . . . 9.21n2

Eastern Enterprises v. Apfel, 524 U.S. 498 (1998) 2.08n8

Eastern Ky. Resources, Inc. v. Arnett, 892 S.W.2d 617 (Ky. App. 1995) 8.46n3

Eastern R.R. Presidents' Conference v. Noerr Motor Freight Co., 365 U.S. 127 (1961) 5.55n1

Eastern Serv. Ctrs., Inc. v. Cloverland Farms Dairy, Inc., 744 A.2d 63 . . . . 5.36n3

Eastlake, City of v. Forest City Enters. 426 U.S. 668 (1976) 6.80n7

E.B. Elliott Adv. Co. v. Metropolitan Dade County, 425 F.2d 1141 (5th Cir. 1970) 11.07n1

Ebel v. Corona, City of, 767 F.2d 635 (9th Cir. 1985) 5.64n1

Eberhart v. Indiana Waste Sys., 452 N.E.2d 455 (Ind. App. 1983) 6.54n1

Eberle v. Dane County Bd. of Adjustment, 595 N.W.2d 730 (Wis. 1999) 2.22n9

Ebzery v. Sheridan, City of, 982 P.2d 1251 (Wyo. 1999) 6.18n8; 6.48n8

Echevarrieta v. Rancho Palos Verdes, City of, 103 Cal. Rptr. 2d 165 . . . . 6.05n16; 12.02n2

Eck v. Bismarck (II), City of, 302 N.W.2d 739 (N.D. 1981) 5.39n6

Economy Whsle. Co. v. Rodgers, 340 S.W.2d 583 (Ark. 1960) 6.02n1

Edge Broadcasting Co.; United States v. , 509 U.S. 418 (1993) 11.17n4

Edmonds, City of v. Oxford 5.06

Edmonds, City of v. Oxford House, Inc.

Edmonds, City of v. Oxford House, Inc. 514 U.S. 725 (1995) 5.14n3

Egg Harbor Assocs. (Bayshore Center), In re , 464 A.2d 1115 (N.J. 1983) 7.27n5

Ehlers-Renzi v. Connelly School of the Holy Child, 224 F.3d 283 . . . . 5.69n8

Ehrlich v. Culver City, City of 9.22

Ehrlich v. Culver City, City of, 911 P.2d 429 (Cal. 1996) 9.22n4, n12

Ehrlich v. Culver City, City of, 911 P.2d 429 (Cal.1996) 9.21n13

Eichlin v. Zoning Hearing Bd., 671 A.2d 1173 (Pa. Commw. 1996) 5.08n8

Eide v. Sarasota Cty., 895 F.2d 1326 (11th Cir. 1990) 2.32n4

Eisner v. Farrington, 209 N.Y.S.2d 673 (App. Div. 1961) 5.20n4

Ekern, State ex rel. v. Milwaukee, City of, 209 N.W. 860 (Wis. 1926) 4.25n2

El Dorado at Santa Fe, Inc. v. Board of County Comm'rs, 551 P.2d 1360 (N.M. 1976) 9.09n5

El Dorado, County of v. Schneider, 237 Cal. Rptr. 51 (Cal. App. 1987) 8.27n4

El Shaer v. Planning Bd., 592 A.2d 565 (N.J. App. Div. 1991) 9.09n15

Elderhaven, Inc. v. Lubbock, City of, 98 F.3d 175 (5th Cir. 1996) 5.13n2

Elias v. Brookhaven, Town of, 783 F. Supp. 758 (E.D.N.Y. 1992) 2.16n9

Elizabeth Lake Estates v. Waterford Twp., 26 N.W.2d 788 (Mich. 1947) 5.29n2

Elkhart County Bd. of Zoning Appeals v. Earthmovers, Inc., 631 N.E.2d 927 (Ind. App. 1994) 6.59n4

Ellen Media Co. v. Tucson, City of, 7 P.3d 136 . . 11.18n5

Eller Media Co. v. Cleveland, City of, 161 F. Supp.2d 796 . . . . 11.19n6

Ellick v. Board of Supvrs., 333 A.2d 239 (Pa. Commw. 1975) 7.22n5

Ellington Constr. Corp. v. Zoning Bd., 566 N.E.2d 128 (N.Y. 1990) 9.07n5, n10

Elliott v. Clawson, City of, 175 N.W.2d 821 (Mich. App. 1970) 6.82n1

Ellsworth v. Gercke, 156 P.2d 242 (Ariz. 1945) . . 5.68n3

Elysian Heights Residents Ass'n v. Los Angeles, City of, 227 Cal. Rptr. 226 (Cal. App. 1986) 6.58n3

Emerald Lakes, Inc. v. South Russell Planning Comm'n, 598 N.E.2d 60 (Ohio App. 1991) . . . 9.09n4

Emjay Props. v. Brookhaven, Town of, 347 N.Y.S.2d 736 (Sup. Ct. 1973) 8.18n2

Emond v. Board of Appeals, 541 N.E.2d 380 (Mass. App. 1989) 5.72n1

Employment Div., Dep't of Human Resources v. Smith 494 U.S. 872 (1990) 11.37n4

Employment Division v. Smith (II) 419 U.S. 872 (1990) 5.69n1

Encore Videos, Inc. v. San Antonio, City of 5.63n3

Energy Reserves Group, Inc. v. Kansas Power & Light Co., 459 U.S. 400 (1983) 2.52n3

England v. Louisiana State Bd. of Medical Examiners, 375 U.S. 411 (1964) 8.41n5

Englewood, City of v. Apostolic Christian Church, 362 P.2d 172 (Colo. 1961) 6.57n14

Englin v. Board of County Comm'rs . . . 5.35n2

Englin v. Board of County Comm'rs, 48 P.3d 39 . . . . 6.25n3

English v. Augusta Twp., 514 N.W.2d 172 (Mich. App. 1994) 7.23n5

Englund v. King County, 839 P.2d 339 . . 6.38n1

Ensco v. Dumas, 807 F.2d 743 (8th Cir. 1986) . . 4.41n1

Ensign Bickford Realty Corp. v. City Council 137 Cal. Rptr. 304 (Cal. App. 1977) 5.47n7

Ensign-Bickford Realty Corp. v. Zoning Comm'n, 715 A.2d 701 (Conn. 1998) 7.31n1

Enterprise Citizens Action Comm. v. Clark County Bd. of Comm'rs, 918 P.2d 305 (Nev. 1996) . . . 6.45n7

Environmental Coalition of Florida, Inc. v. Broward Cty., 586 So. 2d 1212 (Fla. App. 1991) 3.22n5

Environmental Council of Sacramento v. Board of Supvrs., 185 Cal. Rptr. 363 (Cal. App. 1982) . . 3.22n8

Environmental Law Fund, Inc. v. Corte Madera, Town of 122 Cal. Rptr. 282 (Cal. App. 1975) 8.11n14

Envision Realty, LLC v. Henderson, 182 F. Supp.2d 143 . . . . 2.31n1

Equicor Dev., Inc. v. Westfield-Washington Township Plan Comm'n, 758 N.E.2d 34 . . . . . . 9.09n2

Erb v. Maryland Dep't of the Envt., 676 A.2d 1017 . . . . 9.02n2

Erb v. Maryland Dep't of the Env't., 676 A.2d 1017 (Md. App. 1996) 2.09n3

Erdman v. Fort Atkinson, City of, 84 F.3d 960 (7th Cir. 1996) 5.13n2

Erickson; State v. , 301 N.W.2d 324 (Minn. 1981) 11.36n3

Erickson & Assoc. v. McLerban, 872 P.2d 1090 (Wash. 1994) 6.22n2

Ernest W. Hahn, Inc. v. Codding, 615 F.2d 830 (9th Cir. 1980) 5.55n6

Ernst v. Johnson County, 522 N.W.2d 599 (Iowa 1994) 5.81n3

Escondido, City of v. Desert Outdoor Adv., 505 P.2d 1012 (Cal. 1973) 11.06n2

Essex Leasing Co. v. Zoning Bd. of Appeals, 539 A.2d 101 (Conn. 1988) 5.81n7

Essex Leasing, Inc. v. Zoning Bd. of Appeals, 539 A.2d 101 (Conn. 1988) 5.81n6

Essick v. Shillam 32 A.2d 416 (Pa. 1943) 4.06n2

Est. of (see name of party)

Estate & Heirs of Sanchez v. Bernalillo, County of, 902 P.2d 550 (N.M. 1995) 2.21n1

Estate of (see name of party)

Eternalist Foundation, Inc. v. Platteville, City of, 593 N.W.2d 84 (Wis. App. 1999) 6.25n6

Ettinger v. City of Lansing, 546 N.W.2d 652 (Mich. App. 1996) 5.26n3

Ettlingen Homes, Inc. v. Derry, Town of, 681 A.2d 97 (N.H. 1996) 9.09n10, n17

Eubank v. Richmond, City of, 226 U.S. 137 (1912) 6.04n3

Euclid, City of v. Mabel, 484 N.E.2d 249 (Ohio App. 1984) 11.23n4

Euclid, Village of v. Ambler Realty Co . . . 5.02

Euclid, Village of v. Ambler Realty Co., 272 U.S. 365 (1926) 1.18n1; 4.02n7; 8.11n10

Euclid, Village of v. Ambler Realty Co 272 U.S. 365 (1926) 2.06n1

Even v. Parker, City of, 597 N.W.2d 670 (S.D. 1999) 6.20n4

Everett v. Paschall, 111 P. 879 (Wash. 1910) 4.08n2

Everett v. Snohomish Cty., 772 P.2d 992 (Wash. 1989) 4.38n8

Everson v. Zoning Bd. of Adjustment, 149 A.2d 63 (Pa. 1959) 6.51n2

Eves v. Zoning Bd. of Adjustment, 164 A.2d 7 (Pa. 1960) 3.15n8; 6.61n4

Evesham Twp. Zoning Bd. of Adjustment v. Evesham Twp. Council, 404 A.2d 1274 (N.J. 1979) 6.52n5

Ewing v. Carmel-by-the-Sea, City of, 286 Cal. Rptr. 382 (Cal. App. 1991) 5.18n1

Ewing v. Springfield, City of, 449 S.W.2d 681 (Mo. App. 1970) 8.16n2

Ex parte (see name of applicant)

Ex rel. (see name of relator)

Exactions for Transportation Corridors After Dolan v. Tigard, City of, 29 Loy. L.A.L. Rev. 247 (1995)

Excaliber Group, Inc. v. Minneapolis, City of, 116 F.3d 1216 (8th Cir. 1997) 5.64n3; 5.65n4

Exchange Invs., Inc. v. Alachua County, 481 So. 2d 1223 (Fla. App. 1985) 8.04n6

Executive 100, Inc. v. Martin Cty., 922 F.2d 1536 (11th Cir. 1991) 2.31n1

Exton Quarries, Inc. v. Zoning Bd. of Adjustment, 228 A.2d 169 (Pa. 1967) 5.42n3

Exxon Co., U.S.A. v. Township of Livingston, 489 A.2d 1218 (N.J. App. Div. 1985) 5.46n4

Exxon, Inc. v. Frederick, City of, 375 A.2d 34 (Md. 1977) 6.59n3

Eyde Constr. Co. v. Charter Twp. of Meridian, 386 N.W.2d 687 (Mich. App. 1986) 9.18n2

F

F & W Assocs. v. Somerset, County of, 648 A.2d 482 (N.J. App. Div. 1994) 9.22n11

Fabiano v. Boston, City of, 730 N.E.2d 311 . . . . 6.29n12

Fabyan v. Waukesha County Bd. of Adjustment, 632 N.W.2d 116 . . . . 6.54n8

Fafard v. Conservation Comm'n of Barnstable, 733 N.E.2d 66 . . . . 4.30n11

Fair Hous. Dev. Fund v. Burke, 55 F.R.D. 414 (E.D.N.Y. 1972) 7.07n5

Fair Housing Advocates Ass'n v. Richmond Heights, City of, 209 F.3d 626 . . . . 5.06n8

Fair Share Housing Center, Inc. v. Township of Cherry Hill, 802 A.2d 512 . . . . 7.13n5

Fairbairn v. Planning Bd., 360 N.E.2d 668 (Mass. App. 1977) 6.69n3; 6.70n4

Fairchild, In re , 616 A.2d 228 (Vt. 1992) 8.11n1; 8.14n1

Fairfax, County of v. Fleet Indus. Park Ltd. Pt'ship, 410 S.E.2d 669 (Va. 1991) 6.04n4

Fairfield, City of v. Superior Court of Solano County, 537 P.2d 375 (Cal. 1975) 6.73n3

Fallin v. Knox County Bd. of Comm'rs, 656 S.W.2d 338 (Tenn. 1983) 6.30n1

Fallon v. Baker, 455 S.W.2d 572 (Ky. 1970) 5.47n7

Familystyle of St. Paul, Inc. v. St. Paul, City of, 923 F.2d 91 (8th Cir. 1991) 5.15n1

Fantasy Book Shop v. Boston, City of, 531 F. Supp. 821 (D. Mass. 1982) 8.31n1

Farah v. Sachs, 157 N.W.2d 9 (Mich. App. 1968) 6.46n5

Farash Corp. v. Rochester, City of, 713 N.Y.S.2d 423 . . . . 11.28n7

Fargo, City of v. Harwood Twp., 256 N.W.2d 694 (N.D. 1977) 4.38n7

Farley v. Zoning Hearing Bd., 636 A.2d 1232 (Pa. Commw. 1994) 5.05n1; 6.05n16; 7.20n4

Farmers Branch, City of v. Hawnco, Inc., 435 S.W.2d 288 (Tex. Civ. App. 1968) 6.73n4

Farmer's Stone Prods. Co. v. Hoyt, 950 S.W.2d 673 (Mo. App. 1997) 8.16n8

Farr v. Board of Adjustment, 326 S.E.2d 382 (N.C. App. 1985) 5.19n8

Farrell v. Miami, City of, 587 F. Supp. 413 (S.D. Fla. 1984) 5.20n2

Farrington v. Zoning Bd. of Appeals, 413 A.2d 817 (Conn. 1979) 6.50n1; 6.52n5

Fasano v. Board of County Comm'rs, 507 P.2d 23 (Or. 1973) 6.29n1

Fasano v. Board of County Comm'rs 507 P.2d 23 (Or. 1973) 3.15n1; 6.26n1

Faulkner v. Chestertown, Town of, 428 A.2d 879 (Md. 1981) 6.05n15

Fayetteville, City of v. S & H, Inc., 547 S.W.2d 94 (Ark. 1977) 11.10n4

Fedorich v. Zoning Bd. of Appeals, 424 A.2d 289 (Conn. 1979) 5.22n2

Feezell; State v. , 400 S.W.2d 716 (Tenn. 1966) . . 4.02n8

Feldstein v. La Vale Zoning Bd., 227 A.2d 731 (Md. 1967) 5.79n4

Ferguson v. Board of County Comm'rs, 718 P.2d 1223 (Idaho 1986) 6.33n8

Ferguson v. Mill City, City of, 852 P.2d 205 (Or. App. 1983) 2.03n2

Fernley v. Board of Supvrs 7.21

Ferreira v. D'Asaro, 152 So. 2d 736 (Fla. App. 1963) 4.10n2

FIC Homes of Blackstone, Inc. v. Conservation Comm'n, 673 N.E.2d 61 (Mass. App. 1996) . . 2.16n9; 2.19n1; 12.07n7, n9, n11

Fields v. Sarasota Manatee Airport Auth., 953 F.2d 1299 (11th Cir. 1992) 2.33n1

Fifteen Fifty N. State Bldg. Corp. v. Chicago, City of, 155 N.E.2d 97 (Ill. 1959) 6.29n10

Fifth Ave. Corp. v. Washington County, 581 P.2d 50 (Or. 1978) 3.21n4; 8.10n6

Fifth Ave. Presbyterian Church v. New York, City of, 293 F.3d 570 . . . . 5.69n4

Fifty Years of Judicial Federalism Under Burford v. Sun Oil Co. and Kindred Doctrines, 42 DePaul L. Rev. 859 (1993)

Figarsky v. Historic Dist. Comm'n, 368 A.2d 163 (Conn. 1976) 11.04n2; 11.29n3; 11.32n5

Filangeri v. Foster, 684 N.Y.S.2d 50 (App. Div. 1999) 6.48n16

Finally, in Bogan v. Scott-Harris 523 U.S. 44 (1998) 8.35n4

Finch v. Durham, City of, 384 S.E.2d 8 (N.C. 1989) 2.16n8

Finch v. Durham, City of, 384 S.E.2d 9 (N.C. 1989) 6.37n9

First Assembly of God v. Alexandra, City of, 739 F.2d 942 (4th Cir. 1984) 6.57n15

First Assembly of God v. Collier County, 20 F.3d 419 (11th Cir. 1994) 2.42n10

First Assembly of God v. Collier County 20 F.3d 419 (11th Cir. 1994) 5.69n3

First Baptist Church v. Miami-Dade County, 768 So.2d 1114 . . . . 5.69n2; 6.57n15

First Church of Christ, Scientist v. Historic District Comm'n, 738 A.2d 224 (Conn. Super.), aff'd . . 11.37n3

First Covenant Ch. v. Seattle, City of, 787 P.2d 1352 (Wash. 1990), vacated 11.37n6

First Covenant Ch. v. Seattle, City of, 840 P.2d 174 (Wash. 1992) 5.69n6

First Covenant Church of Seattle v. Seattle, City of, 840 P.2d 174 (Wash. 1992) 11.37n7

First English Evangelical Church of Glendale v. Los Angeles and the Calculation of Interim Damages for Regul, 17 B.C. Envtl. Aff. L. Rev. 551 (1990)

First English Evangelical Lutheran Ch. v. Los Angeles, County of, 258 Cal. Rptr. 893 (1989) 12.09n8

First English Evangelical Lutheran Church v. Los Angeles, County of, 482 U.S. 304 (1987) 2.28n4

First English Evangelical Lutheran Church v. Los Angeles, County of 482 U.S. 304 (1987) 8.25n1; 12.09n7

First Nat'l Bank of Highland Park v. Vernon Hills, Village of, 371 N.E.2d 659 (Ill. App. 1977) . . . 3.15n7

First Nat'l Bank & Trust v. Rockford, City of, 361 N.E.2d 832 (Ill. App. 1977) 6.22n8

First Nat'l Bank & Trust Co. v. Evanston, City of, 197 N.E.2d 705 (Ill. 1964) 2.46n7

First Peoples Bank v. Medford, 599 A.2d 1248 (N.J. 1991) 2.22n7

First Peoples Bank of New Jersey v. Township of Medford, 599 A.2d 1248 (N.J. 1991) 10.10n6

First Presbyterian Church v. City Council, 360 A.2d 257 (Pa. Commw. 1976) 11.32n6

First United Methodist Church v. Hearing Examiner for Seattle Landmarks Preservation Bd., 916 P.2d 374 (Wash. 1996) 11.37n7

Fischer v. Kellenberger, 392 N.E.2d 733 (Ill. App. 1979) 6.09n2

Fischer Sand and Aggregate Co. v. Lakeville, City of, 874 F. Supp. 957 (D. Minn. 1994) . . . 8.46n3

Fiser v. Knoxville, City of, 584 S.W.2d 659 (Tenn. App. 1979) 6.72n1

Fisher v. Berkeley, City of, 475 U.S. 260 (1986) . . 5.52n2; 5.56n5

Fisher v. Berkeley, City of, 693 P.2d 261 (Cal. 1976) 6.05n4

Fisher; Commonwealth v. , 350 A.2d 428 (Pa. Commw. 1976) 9.08n1

Fisher v. Pilcher, 341 A.2d 713 (Del. Super. 1975) 6.57n1

Fisher v. Viola, 789 A.2d 782 . . . 5.31n3; 5.32n9

Fisher Buick, Inc. v. Fayetteville, City of, 689 S.W.2d 350 (Ark. 1985) 5.86n5

Fishman v. Palo Alto, City of, 150 Cal. Rptr. 326 (Cal. App. 1974) 6.82n8

Fisichelli v. Methuen, Town of, 956 F.2d 12 (1st Cir. 1992) 5.53n1

Fitanides v. Crowley, 467 A.2d 168 (Me. 1983) . . 6.03n4

Fitzgerrald v. Iowa City, City of 492 N.W.2d 659 (Iowa 1992) 5.39n5

Flavell v. Albany, City of, 25 Cal. Rptr. 2d 21 (Cal. App. 1993) 3.18n1

Fleckinger v. Jefferson Parish Council, 510 So. 2d 429 (La. App. 1987) 6.75n4; 9.09n7

Fleming v. Tacoma, City of, 502 P.2d 327 (Wash. 1972) 6.26n2; 6.72n5

Fletcher v. Porter, 21 Cal. Rptr. 452 (Cal. App. 1962) 6.07n3

the Flood Plain Ordinance v. Asheville, City of, 302 S.E.2d 204 (N.C. 1983) 12.09n6

Flora Realty & Inv. Co. v. Ladue, City of, 246 S.W.2d 771 (Mo.) 5.31n2

Florence, City of v. Turbeville, 121 S.E.2d 437 (S.C. 1961) 5.20n2

Florham Park Inv. Assocs. v. Planning Bd., 224 A.2d 352 (N.J.L. Div. 1966) 9.09n18

Florida Land Co. v. Winter Springs, City of, 427 So. 2d 170 (Fla. 1983) 6.82n3

Florida Power & Light Co. v. Dania, City of, 761 So.2d 1089 . . . . 8.13n16

Florida Rock Indus. v. United States, 18 F.3d 1560 (Fed. Cir. 1994) . . . 2.19n4; 2.21n5; 12.07n12

Florida Rock Indus. v. United States, 45 Fed. Cl. 21 (1999) 2.16n13

Florida Rock Props. v. Keyser, 709 So.2d 175 (Fla. App. 1998) 8.04n3

Florida, State of v. Burgess, 772 So.2d 540 . . . . . 12.07n7

Florka v. Detroit, City of, 120 N.W.2d 797 (Mich. 1963) 8.13n7

Flower Hill Bldg. Corp. v. Flower Hill, Village of, 100 N.Y.S.2d 903 (Sup. Ct. 1950) 5.29n2

Flower Mound, Town of v. Stafford Estates Ltd. Partnership, 71 S.W.3d 18 . . . . 9.13n2

Floyd v. County Council, 461 A.2d 76 (Md. App. 1983) 6.61n5

Flying J Travel Plaza v. Transportation Cabinet, Dep't of Highways, 928 S.W.2d 344 (Ky. 1996) 11.21n1

Flynn v. Zoning Bd. of Review, 73 A.2d 808 (R.I. 1950) 6.03n4

FM Props. Operating Co. v. Austin, City of, 93 F.3d 167 (5th Cir. 1996) 6.22n2

Fobe Assocs. v. Mayor & Council, 379 A.2d 31 (N.J. 1977) 6.41n2

Fogg v. South Miami, City of, 183 So. 2d 219 (Fla. App. 1966) 5.46n4

Foggy Bottom Ass'n v. District of Columbia Zoning Comm'n, 639 A.2d 578 (D.C. App. 1994) 9.29n3

Foley v. Harris, 286 S.E.2d 186 (Va. 1982) 4.09n2

Folsom Enters. v. Scottsdale, City of, 620 F. Supp. 1372 (D. Ariz. 1985) 6.16n1

Folsom Rd. Civic Ass'n v. Parish of St. Tammany, 407 So. 2d 1219 (La. 1981) 5.17n8

Fontana Unified School Dist. v. Rialto, City of, 219 Cal. Rptr. 254 (Cal. App. 1985) 8.14n3

Foran v. Zoning Bd. of Appeals, 260 A.2d 609 (Conn. 1969) 8.04n3

Ford v. Board of County Commr's, 924 P.2d 91 (Wyo. 1996) 3.13n3

Ford v. Georgetown County Water & Sewer 9.21n3

Ford Leasing Dev. Co. v. Board of County Comm'rs, 528 P.2d 237 (Colo. 1974) 9.28n1

Foreman v. State, 387 N.E.2d 455 (Ind. App. 1979) 12.09n4

Foreman v. Union Township Zoning Hearing Bd., 787 A.2d 1099 . . . . 5.64n1

Foreman, State ex rel. v. City Council, 205 N.E.2d 398 (Ohio 1965) 8.11n3

Forest City Daly Housing, Inc. v. North Hempstead, Town of, 175 F.3d 144 (2d Cir. 1999) 5.13n5; 5.16n3

Forest Constr. Co. v. Planning & Zoning Comm'n 236 A.2d 917 (Conn. 1967) 9.09n14

Forest Daly Housing, Inc. v. North Hempstead, Town of, 173 F.3d 144 (2d Cir. 1999) 5.12n11

Forest Park, City of v. Pelfrey, 669 N.E.2d 863 (Ohio App. 1995) 11.15n1

Forest Props., Inc. v. United States, 177 F.3d 1360 (Fed. Cir. 1999) 2.19n3; 12.07n12

Forestview Homeowners' Ass'n v. Cook, County of, 309 N.E.2d 763 (Ill. App. 1974) 3.15n6

Forman v. Eagle Thrifty Drugs & Mkts., Inc., 516 P.2d 1234 (Nev. 1974) 6.82n7

Formanek v. United States, 18 Cl. Ct. 785 (1989) 12.07n12

Forrest v. Evershed 164 N.E.2d 841 (N.Y. 1959) . . 6.45n8

Forseth v. Sussex, Village of, 199 F.3d 363 . . . . 2.32n2, n3

Forsyth County v. Shelton, 329 S.E.2d 730 (N.C. App. 1985) 5.81n3, n9

Fort Collins, City of v. Dooney, 496 P.2d 316 (Colo. 1972) 6.82n3

Fort Collins, City of v. Dooney 496 P.2d 316 (Colo. 1972) 6.82n4

Forte v. Borough of Tenafly 255 A.2d 804 (N.J. App. Div. 1969) 5.48n2

Fortier v. Spearfish, City of, 433 N.W.2d 228 (S.D. 1988) 12.09n4

Foster, State ex rel. v. Morgantown, City of, 432 S.E.2d 195 (W. Va. 1993) 6.82n1

Foti v. Menlo Park, City of, 146 F.3d 629 (9th Cir. 1998) 11.19n15

Foundation for San Francisco's Architectural Heritage v. City & County of San Francisco, 165 Cal. Rptr. 401 (Cal. App. 1980) 11.36n3

Four M Constr. Corp. v. Fritts, 543 N.Y.S.2d 213 (App. Div. 1989) 6.48n6

Four States Realty Co. v. Baton Rouge, City of, 309 So. 2d 659 (La. 1975) 6.37n6

421 Corp. v. Metropolitan Gov't of Nashville & Davidson County, 36 S.W.3d 469 . . . . 2.49n5

4. Zavala v. City & Cty. of Denver, 759 P.2d 664 (Colo. 1988) 5.05n1

Fox v. Polk County Bd. of Supervisors, 569 N.W.2d 503 (Iowa 1997) 6.29n11

Foxhall Community Citizens Ass'n v. District of Columbia Bd. of Zoning Adjustment, 524 A.2d 759 (D.C. App. 1987) 6.50n1

Fralin & Waldron, Inc. v. Henrico, County of, 474 F. Supp. 1315 (E.D. Va. 1979) 8.36n3

Framike Realty Corp. v. Hinck, 632 N.Y.S.2d 177 (App. Div. 1995) 6.56n9

Framingham Clinic v. Zoning Bd. of Appeals, 415 N.E.2d 840 (Mass. 1981) 8.19n8

Franchi v. Zoning Hearing Bd., 543 A.2d 239 (Pa. Commw. 1988) 5.20n3

Franchise Developers, Inc. v. Cincinnati, City of, 505 N.E.2d 966 (Ohio 1987 (zoning ordinance puts property owner on notice that property is subject 6.05n5

Franchise Devs., Inc. v. Cincinnati, City of, 505 N.E.2d 966 (Ohio 1987) 5.36n11

Frank v. Mobil Oil Corp., 296 A.2d 300 (Pa. Commw. 1973) 8.02n9

Frank v. Russell, 70 N.W.2d 306 (Neb. 1995) . . . 6.50n3

Frank Hardie Adv., Inc. v. Dubuque Zoning Bd. of Adjustment, City of, 501 N.W.2d 521 (Iowa 1993) 8.02n1

Frankland v. Lake Oswego, City of, 517 P.2d 1042 (Or. 1973) 9.29n3

Franklin v. Hollander, 796 A.2d 874 . . . 12.11n11

Franklin, City of v. Gerovac, 197 N.W.2d 772 (Wis. 1972) 5.81n16

Franklin County v. Leisure Props., Ltd., 430 So. 2d 475 (Fla. App. 1983) 6.16n5

Franklin County v. Webster, 400 S.W.2d 693 (Ky. 1966) 6.55n2

Franmor Realty Co. v. Le Boeuf, 104 N.Y.S.2d 247 (Sup. Ct. 1951), aff'd, 109 N.Y.S.2d 525 (App. Div. 1952) 5.81n8

Frazier v. Grand Lodge, City of, 135 F. Supp. 2d 845 . . . . 5.08n4

Fred F. French Inv. Co. v. New York, City of 350 N.E.2d 381 (N.Y.) 11.38n4

Fred McDowell, Inc. v. Board of Adjustment, 757 A.2d 822 . . . . 5.79n7

Frederick v. Zoning Hearing Bd., 713 A.2d 139 (Pa. Commw. 1998) 5.20n4

Frederico v. Moore, 395 N.Y.S.2d 535 (App. Div. 1977) 8.13n10

Freedman v. Lewis, 776 S.W.2d 212 (Tex. App. 1989) 4.03n3

Freedman v. Maryland, State of 380 U.S. 51 (1965) 6.57n6

Freedom Ranch, Inc. v. Board of Adjustment, 878 P.2d 380 (Okla. App. 1994) . . 2.48n3; 5.09n4

Freeman v. Burlington Broadcasters, Inc., 204 F.3d 311 . . . . 8.40n3

Freeport, Town of v. Brickyard Cove Assocs., 594 A.2d 556 (Me. 1991) 6.05n6

Fremont Twp. v. Greenfield, 347 N.W.2d 204 (Mich. App. 1984) 7.23n5

Fried v. Fox, 373 N.Y.S.2d 197 (Sup. Ct. 1975) . . 8.14n13

Friedman, Estate of v. Pierce County, 768 P.2d 462 (Wash. 1989) 8.09n6

Friedman, Estate of v. Pierce Cty., 752 P.2d 936 (Wash. App. 1988) 8.11n16

Friends of the Crystal River v. Kuras Props., 554 N.W.2d 528 (Mich. App. 1996) 12.05n2

Friends of the Law v. King County, 869 P.2d 1056 (Wash. 1994) 9.07n9

Fritts v. Ashland, City of, 348 S.W.2d 712 (Ky. 1961) 6.30n5

Fritz v. Kingman, City of, 957 P.2d 337 (Ariz. 1998) 6.82n7

Fritz v. Lexington-Fayette Urban County Gov't, 986 S.W.2d 456 (Ky. App. 1998) 6.33n1

Front Royal & Indus. Park Corp. v. Front Royal, Town of, 135 F.3d 275 (4th Cir. 1998) 2.33n1

Frustuck v. Fairfax, City of, 28 Cal Rptr. 357 (Cal. App. 1963) 8.23n14

Frye Constr., Inc. v. Monongahela, City of, 584 A.2d 946 (Pa. 1991) 8.11n9, n15

F.S. Plummer Co. v. Cape Elizabeth, Town of, 612 A.2d 856 (Me. 1992) 6.25n2; 6.33n1

Ft. Collins, City of v. Root Outdoor Adv., Inc., 788 P.2d 149 (Colo. 1990) 5.83n2

FTC v. Ticor Title Ins. Co., 504 U.S. 621 (1992) 5.53n7

Fuller v. New Orleans, City of, 311 So. 2d 466 (La. App. 1975) 5.81n7

Fulton County v. Bartenfeld, 363 S.E.2d 555 (Ga. 1988) 8.14n4

Fulton Cty. v. Bartenfeld, 363 S.E.2d 555 (Ga. 1988) 6.56n9

Furey v. Sacramento, City of, 592 F. Supp. 463 (E.D. Cal. 1984), *aff'd on other grounds,* 780 F.2d 1448 (9th Cir. 1986) 2.16n6

Furtney v. Simsbury Zoning Comm'n, 271 A.2d 319 (Conn. 1970) 3.14n1

Fusco v. Connecticut, State of, 815 F.2d 201 (2d Cir. 1987) 2.42n7

FW/PBS v. Dallas, City of, 493 U.S. 215 (1990) . . 5.65n3

FW/PBS v. Dallas, Inc., City of 493 U.S. 215 (1990) 6.57n7

G

Gackler Land Co. v. Yankee Springs Twp., 359 N.W.2d 226 (Mich. App. 1984) 5.23n4

Gackler Land Co. v. Yankee Springs Twp., 398 N.W.2d 393 (Mich. 1986) . . . 5.26n6; 6.20n1; 6.21n3

Gage's Appeal, In re , 167 A.2d 292 (Pa. 1961) . . 6.54n2

Gagliardi v. Pawling, Village of 18 F.3d 188 . . . . 2.51n6

Galanes v. Brattleboro, Town of, 388 A.2d 406 (Vt. 1978) 6.29n8

Galbraith v. Planning Dep't, 627 N.E.2d 850 (Ind. App. 1994) 8.09n2

Galliford v. Commonwealth, 430 A.2d 1222 (Pa. Commw. 1981) 5.19n11

Gallo v. Mayor & Township Council, 744 A.2d 1219 . . . . 6.70n5

Gallop Bldg.; State v. , 247 A.2d 350 (N.J. App. Div. 1968) 5.38n1

Galt v. Cook County, 91 N.E.2d 395 (Ill. 1950) . . 2.36n5

Gamble v. Eau Claire County, 5 F.3d 285 (7th Cir. 1993) 2.31n1

Gamble v. Escondido, City of, 104 F.3d 300 (9th Cir. 1997) 5.13n2

Gammoh v. Anaheim, City of, 86 Cal. Rptr.2d 194 (Cal. App. 1999) 5.63n9

Gangemi v. Zoning Bd. of Appeals Berninger . . . 6.51n8

Gannett Outdoor Co. v. Mesa, City of, 768 P.2d 191 (Ariz. App. 1989) 5.80n1

Gannett Outdoor Co. v. Troy, City of, 409 N.W.2d 719 (Mich. App. 1987) 11.19n14

Gara Realty, Inc. v. Zoning Bd. of Review, 523 A.2d 855 (R.I. 1987) 6.48n9

Garat v. Riverside, City of, 3 Cal. Rptr. 2d 504 (Cal. App. 1991) 3.22n5

Garcia v. Siffrin Residential Ass'n, 407 N.E.2d 1369 (Ohio 1980) 5.10n4

Garden State Farms, Inc. v. Bay, II, 390 A.2d 1177 (N.J. 1978) 4.31n2

Garden State Homes, Inc. v. Heusner, 400 N.Y.S.2d 598 (App. Div. 1977) 9.10n5

Gardner v. Baltimore, City of, 969 F.2d 63 (4th Cir. 1992) 2.40n6

Gardner v. Baltimore Mayor & City Council, City of, 959 F.2d 63 (4th Cir. 1992) 8.30n3

Gardner v. Harahan, 504 So. 2d 1107 (La. App. 1987) 6.03n1

Gardner v. New Jersey Pinelands Comm'n, 593 A.2d 251 (N.J. 1991) . 9.13n2; 12.13n2, n5; 12.16n7

Garipay v. Hanover, Town of, 351 A.2d 64 (N.H. 1976) 9.09n10, n17

Garner v. Du Page, County of, 133 N.E.2d 303 (Ill. 1956) 8.03n1; 8.04n6

Garrett v. Oklahoma City, City of, 594 P.2d 764 (Okla. 1979) 8.18n5

Garrow v. Teaneck Tryon Co., 94 A.2d 332 (N.J. 1953) 8.14n11

Gas 'N Shop, Inc. v. Kearney, City of, 539 N.W.2d 423 (Neb. 1995) 5.36n9

Gaslight Villa, Inc. v. Governing Body, City of Lansing, 518 P.2d 410 (Kan. 1974) . . . 5.09n2

Gatri v. Blane, 962 P.2d 367 (Hawaii 1998) 6.58n4

Gay v. Zoning Bd. of Appeals, 757 A.2d 61 . . . . 6.51n8

Gazza v. New York State Dep't of Envtl. Conservation, 679 N.E.2d 1035 . . . . 12.07n11

Gazza v. New York State Dept. of Envtl. Conservation, 679 N.E.2d 1035 (N.Y. 1997) . . . 2.16n8; 12.07n7

Geiben v. Pomfret Zoning Bd. of Appeals, Town of, 688 N.Y.S.2d 303 (App. Div. 1999) . . . 6.59n4

Geiger v. Zoning Hearing Bd., 507 A.2d 361 (Pa. 1986) 5.21n3

General Battery Corporation v. The Zoning Hearing Board of Alsace Township, 371 A.2d 1030 (Pa. Commw. 1977) 5.42n3

General Outdoor Adv. Co. v. Department of Pub. Works, 193 N.E. 799 (Mass. 1935) . . 11.10n8

George v. Parratt, 602 F.2d 818 (8th Cir. 1979) . . 8.43n4

Georgia Manufactured Hous. v. Spalding County, 148 F.3d 1304 (11th Cir. 1998) 5.21n2

Georgia Outdoor Adv. Co. v. Waynesville (II), City of, 900 F.2d 783 (4th Cir. 1990) . . . 11.07n14

Georgia Outdoor Adv. Co. v. Waynesville (II), City of 900 F.2d 783 (4th Cir. 1990) 5.84n9

Georgia Outdoor Advertising, Inc. v. Waynesville, 833 F.2d 43 (4th Cir. 1987) 11.19n8

Gerber v. Clarkstown, Town of, 356 N.Y.S.2d 926 (Sup. Ct. 1974) 9.05n4

Gerchen v. Ladue, City of, 784 S.W.2d 232 (Mo. App. 1989) 2.36n6

Gernatt v. Sardinia, Town of, 664 N.E.2d 1226 (N.Y. 1996) 6.70n5

Gernatt Asphalt Prods., Inc. v. Sardinia, Town of, 664 N.E.2d 1226 (N.Y. 1996) 7.15n1

Ghaster Props., Inc. v. Preston, 200 N.E.2d 328 (Ohio 1964) 11.07n5

Ghent v. Planning Comm'n, 594 A.2d 5 (Conn. 1991) 9.09n8

Ghent v. Zoning Comm'n, 600 A.2d 1010 (Conn. 1991) 6.74n14

Giambrone v. Aurora, City of, 621 N.E.2d 475 (Ohio App. 1993) 5.71n4

Gibson v. Riverside, County of, 181 F. Supp.2d 1057 . . . . 5.06n4

Giger v. Omaha, City of, 442 N.W.2d 182 (Neb. 1989) 6.62n4

Gil v. Inland Wetlands & Watercourses Agency, 593 A.2d 1268 (Conn. 1993) 12.07n8

Gil v. Inland Wetlands & Watercourses Agency, 593 A.2d 1368 (Conn. 1991) 2.16n2

Gilbert v. Cambridge, City of, 932 F.2d 51 (1st Cir. 1991) 2.30n15

Gill Farms, Inc. v. Darrow, 682 N.Y.S.2d 306 (App. Div. 1998) 8.46n11

Gillis v. Springfield, City of 3.18

Gillis v. Springfield, City of, 611 P.2d 355 (Or. App. 1980) 6.33n3

Gilman v. MacDonald, 875 P.2d 897 (Wash. App. 1994) 8.47n3

Gilmartin v. District of Columbia Bd. of Adj., 579 A.2d 1164 (D.C. App. 1990) 6.48n15

Gingell v. Board of County Comm'rs, 239 A.2d 903 (Md. 1968) 8.11n5

Gisler v. Madera, County of, 112 Cal. Rptr. 919 (Cal. App. 1974) 12.13n4

Giuliano v. Edgartown, Town of, 531 F. Supp. 1076 (D. Mass. 1982) 10.06n2

Giulini v. Blessing, 654 F.2d 189 (2d Cir. 1981) . . 8.45n3

Gladwyne Colony, Inc. v. Township of Lower Merion, 187 A.2d 549 (Pa. 1963) 6.64n3

Glascock v. Baltimore Cty., 581 A.2d 822 (Md. 1990) 4.28n1

Glen-Gery Corp. v. Lower Heidelberg Township, 608 F. Supp. 1002 (E.D. Pa. 1985) 8.42n13

Glenbrook Homeowners Ass'n v. Glenbrook County, 901 P.2d 132 (Nev. 1995) 9.30n1

Glendale, City of v. Aldabbagh, 939 P.2d 418 (Ariz. 1997) 5.81n10

Glengary-Gamlin Protective Ass'n v. Bonner County Bd. of Comm'rs, 675 P.2d 344 (Idaho App. 1983) 8.06n2

Glennon Heights, Inc. v. Central Bank & Trust, 658 P.2d 872 (Colo. 1983) 5.10n4

Glenview, Village of v. Velasquez, 463 N.E.2d 873 (Ill. App. 1984) 5.84n6

Glisson v. Alachua Cty., 558 So. 2d 1030 (Fla. App. 1990) 12.07n4; 12.16n6

Global Waste Recycling v. Mallette, 762 A.2d 1208 . . . . 8.47n4

Globe Newspaper Co. v. Beacon Hill Architectural Comm'n, 659 N.E.2d 710 (Mass. 1996) 11.29n4

Glocester, Town of v. Olivo's Mobile Home Court, Inc., 300 A.2d 465 (R.I. 1973) 5.21n1

G.M. Eng'rs & Assocs., Inc. v. West Bloomfield Township, 922 F.2d 328 (6th Cir. 1990) 2.40n8; 8.33n4

Godfrey v. Union County Board of Comm'rs, 300 S.E.2d 273 (N.C. App. 1983) 6.29n8

Goerke v. Township of Middletown, 205 A.2d 338 (N.J. 1964) 6.55n3

Goffinet v. Christian, County of, 357 N.E.2d 442 (Ill. 1976) 6.63n4

Goffinet v. Christian, County of 357 N.E.2d 442 (Ill. 1976) 6.65n3

Goldberg v. Rehoboth Beach, City of, 565 A.2d 936 (Del. Super. Ct.) 6.69n3; 6.70n2

Goldblatt v. Hempstead, Town of 369 U.S. 590 (1962) 2.04n4

Golden v. Board of Selectmen 265 N.E.2d 573 (Mass. 1970) 12.05n3

Golden v. Overland Park, City of, 584 P.2d 130 (Kan. 1978) 6.26n2

Golden v. Planning Bd. of Town of Ramapo . . . 3.20

Golden v. Planning Bd. of Town of Ramapo, 285 N.E.2d 291 (N.Y.1972) 6.11n5

Golden v. Planning Bd. of Town of Ramapo 285 N.E.2d 291 (N.Y. 1975) 10.04n1

Golden v. Planning Bd. of Town of Ramapo 285 N.E.2d 291 (N.Y.1972) 8.11n11

Golden v. St. Louis Park, City of, 122 N.W.2d 570 (Minn. 1963) 6.55n7

Golden Gate Corp. v. Narragansett, Town of, 359 A.2d 321 (R.I. 1976) . . 6.14n1; 6.72n5; 8.11n5

Golden State Homebuilding Assocs. v. Modesto, City of, 31 Cal. Rptr. 2d 572 (Cal. App. 1994) 9.07n6

Golden Triangle News, Inc. v. Corbett, 689 A.2d 974 (Pa. Commw. 1997) 5.65n5

Goldstein v. Upper Merion Twp., 403 A.2d 211 (Pa. Commw. 1979) 8.16n8

Gomez v. Zoning Bd. of Appeals, 740 N.Y.S.2d 139 . . . . 6.51n4

Gonzaga Univ. v. Doe 8.29n5

Good v. United States, 189 F.3d 1355 (Fed. Cir. 1999) 2.16n9, n13, n14; 12.07n12

Good Neighbors of South Davidson v. Denton, Town of, 559 S.E.2d 768 . . . . 6.29n12

Goode v. Dallas, City of, 554 S.W.2d 753 (Tex. Ct. App. 1977) 6.05n20

Goodell v. Humboldt County, 575 N.W.2d 486 (Iowa 1998) 4.24n4

Goodman v. Board of Comm'rs, 411 A.2d 838 (Pa. Commw. 1980) 9.06n4; 9.09n2

Goodman; People v. , 290 N.E.2d 139 (N.Y. 1972) 11.08n7; 11.10n2

Goodman Toyota, Inc. v. Raleigh, City of, 306 S.E.2d 192 (N.C. App. 1983) 5.84n6; 11.10n5

Goodrich v. Southampton, Town of, 355 N.E.2d 297 (N.Y. 1976) 6.29n5

Goodson Todman Ent. v. Town Bd. of Milan, 542 N.Y.S.2d 373 (App. Div. 1989) 6.76n3

Gordon v. Marrone, 616 N.Y.S.2d 98 (App. Div. 1994) 8.46n4

Gordon v. Warren, City of, 579 F.2d 386 (6th Cir. 1978) 8.39n6

Gorham v. Cape Elizabeth, Town of, 625 A.2d 898 (Me. 1993) 6.03n3

Gorieb v. Fox 5.71

Gorman Towers v. Bogoslavsky, 626 F.2d 607 (8th Cir. 1980) 8.46n3

Gorman Towers, Inc. v. Bogoslavsky 626 F.2d 607 (8th Cir. 1980) 8.35n4

Goss v. Little Rock, City of, 151 F.3d 861 (8th Cir. 1998) 8.26n6; 9.16n15

Gosselin v. Nashua, City of, 321 A.2d 593 (N.H. 1974) 6.15n4

Gouge v. Snellville, City of, 287 S.E.2d 539 (Ga. 1982) 6.05n3

Gould v. Santa Fe County, 37 P.3d 122 . . 6.41n9

Governor's Island Club, Inc. v. Gilford, Town of, 467 A.2d 246 (N.H. 1983) 6.46n4

Goward v. Minneapolis, City of, 456 N.W.2d 460 (Minn. App. 1990) 11.23n4

Grace Baptist Church v. Oxford, City of, 358 S.E.2d 372 (N.C. 1987) 5.77n2

Grace Community Church v. Planning & Zoning Comm'n, 622 A.2d 591 (Conn. App. 1993) . . . 6.57n13

Grader v. Lynwood, City of, 767 P.2d 952 (Wash. App. 1989) 8.23n5

Graff v. Chicago, City of, 9 F.3d 1309 (7th Cir. 1993) 6.57n12

Graham v. Connor, 490 U.S. 386 (1990) . . 2.40n1

Graham v. Estuary Props., Inc., 399 So. 2d 1374 (Fla.1981) 2.16n6

Graham v. Estuary Props., Inc.,399 So. 2d 1374 (Fla. 1981) 12.07n4

Graham Corp. v. Board of Zoning Appeals, 97 A.2d 564 (Conn. 1953) 6.18n3

Graham Court Assocs. v. Town Council, 281 S.E.2d 418 (N.C. App. 1981) 5.18n8

Graham Farms, Inc. v. Indianapolis Power & Light Co., 233 N.E.2d 656 (Ind. 1968) 4.32n2

Granby, Town of v. Landry, 170 N.E.2d 364 (Mass. 1960) 5.23n3

Grand Chute, Town of v. U.S. Paper Converters, Inc., 600 N.W.2d 33 (Wis. App. 1999) 6.66n2

Grand Land Co. v. Township of Bethlehem, 483 A.2d 818 (N.J. App. Div. 1984) 9.18n2

Grandview Baptist Church v. Zoning Bd. of Adjustment, 301 N.W.2d 704 (Iowa 1981) . . . 6.18n7

Granger v. Board of Adjustment 44 N.W.2d 399 (Iowa 1950) 5.80n3

Granger v. Woodford, Town of, 708 A.2d 1345 (Vt. 1998) 6.29n12

Granite State Outdoor Advertising, Inc. v. Clearwater, City of, 213 F. Supp.2d 1312 . . . . . 11.21n1

Grant v. Folly Beach, City of, 551 S.E.2d 229 . . . 6.17n1

Grant v. Mayor & City Council, 129 A.2d 363 (Md. 1957) 5.84n5

Grant v. Seminole, County of, 817 F.2d 731 (11th Cir. 1987) 2.47n2

Gray v. Trustees, Monclova Twp., 313 N.E.2d 366 (Ohio 1974) 9.29n3

Graziano v. Board of Adjustment, 323 N.W.2d 233 (Iowa 1982) 6.45n7; 6.48n2

Great Atlantic & Pacific Tea Co. v. Borough of Point Pleasant, 644 A.2d 598 (N.J. 1994) . . . 6.82n1

Great Atlantic & Pacific Tea Co. v. East Hampton, Town of, 997 F. Supp. 340 (E.D.N.Y. 1998) . . 5.36n5

Greater Baltimore Bd. of Realtors v. Huges, 596 F. Supp. 906 (D. Md. 1984) 11.22n1

Greater Franklin Developers Ass'n, Inc. v. Franklin, Town of, 730 N.E.2d 900 . . . . 9.21n2

Greater Yellowstone Coalition, Inc. v. Board of County Comm'rs, 25 P.3d 168 . . . . . . 6.29n5

Green v. Board of App., 529 N.E.2d 159 (Mass. App. 1988) 8.14n11

Green v. Castle Concrete Co., 509 P.2d 588 (Colo. 1973) 4.03n3; 4.09n3

Green v. County Council, 508 A.2d 882 (Del. Ch.) 6.33n3

Green v. County Council, 508 A.2d 882 (Del. Ch. 1986) 3.15n1

Green v. Hayward 552 P.2d 815 (Or. 1976) 6.33n6

Green Meadows at Montville, L.L.C. v. Planning Bd., 746 A.2d 1009 . . . . 9.09n2

Green Point Sav. Bank v. Board of Zoning Appeals, 24 N.E.2d 319 (N.Y. 1939) . . . 6.02n2; 6.55n4

Greenbelt, City of v. Bresler, 236 A.2d 1 (Md. 1967) 6.63n6

Greenbelt, City of v. Jaeger, 206 A.2d 694 (Md. 1965) 8.07n2

Greenberg v. State, 502 A.2d 522 (Md. App. 1986) 5.39n6

Greenbriar, Ltd. v. Alabaster, City of, 881 F.2d 1570 . . . . 2.30n4

Greenbriar, Ltd. v. Alabaster, City of, 881 F.2d 1570 (11th Cir. 1990) 2.30n6

Greene v. Blooming Grove, Town of, 879 F.2d 1061 (2d Cir. 1989) 2.47n2

Greenebaum v. Los Angeles, City of, 200 Cal. Rptr. 237 (Cal. App. 1984) 6.33n2

Greens at Fort Missoula, LLC v. Missoula, City of, 897 P.2d 1078 (Mont. 1995) 6.82n7

Gregory v. Harnett, County of, 493 S.E.2d 786 (N.C. App. 1997) 6.37n7

Grey Rocks Land Trust v. Hebron, Town of, 614 A.2d 1048 (N.H. 1992) 5.79n4; 6.45n2

Griffin v. Marin, County of, 321 P.2d 148 (Cal. App. 1958) 6.21n4

Griffin Dev. Co. v. Oxnard, City of, 199 Cal. Rptr. 739 (Cal. App. 1984) 5.18n8

Griffin Homes, Inc. v. Superior Ct., 274 Cal. Rptr. 456 (Cal. App. 1990) 8.14n3; 10.08n2

Griggs v. Allegheny County, 369 U.S. 84 (1961) . . 4.43n2

Griggs v. Allegheny, County of, 369 U.S. 84 (1962) 5.39n9

Grimes v. Conservation Comm'n, 703 A.2d 101 (Conn. 1997) 6.70n5

Grimpel Assocs. v. Cohalan, 361 N.E.2d 1022 (N.Y. 1977) 2.36n10; 6.37n7

Grimpel Assocs. v. Cohalan 361 N.E.2d 1022 (N.Y. 1977) 8.11n13

Griswold v. Homer, City of, 925 P.2d 1015 (Alaska 1996) 6.28n1; 6.29n10; 6.30n3; 6.33n2; 6.74n3

Gromme Resources Ltd., L.L.C. v. Parish of Jefferson, 234 F.3d 192 . . . . 5.12n1

Grosz v. Miami Beach, City of, 721 F.2d 729 (11th Cir. 1983) 5.69n2

Group House of Port Wash., Inc. v. Board of Zoning & Appeals, 380 N.E.2d 207 (N.Y. 1978) 5.08n10

Grover v. Golden Gate Gardens Apartments, 250 F.3d 1039 . . . . 5.12n8

Grubel v. MacLaughlin, 286 F. Supp. 24 (D.C.V.I. 1968) 5.43n2

Gruber v. Mayor & Twp. Comm., 186 A.2d 489 (N.J. 1962) 6.21n1

Gruber v. Raritan Twp., 186 A.2d 489 (N.J. 1962) 5.43n5

G.S.T. v. Avon Lake, City of, 357 N.E.2d 38 (Ohio 1976) 8.08n2; 8.10n4; 8.16n5

GTI Mobilnet v. Pascouet, 61 S.W.2d 599 . . . . . 4.06n1

Guardianship of (see name of party)

Guenther v. Zoning Bd. of Review, 125 A.2d 214 (R.I. 1956) 6.45n10

Guffey; State v. , 306 S.W.2d 552 (Mo. 1957) . . . 6.02n4

Guhl v. Holcomb Bridge Rd. Corp., 232 S.E.2d 830 (Ga. 1977) 8.18n2, n3

Guhl v. Holcomb Bridge Road Corp., 232 S.E.2d 830 (Ga. 1977) 2.37n7

Guilford Financial Servs. v. Brevard, City of, 563 S.E.2d 27 . . . . 9.09n6

Guillot v. Brooks, 651 So.2d 345 (La. App. 1995) 4.43n5

Guinanne v. City & County of San Francisco, 241 Cal. Rptr. 787 (1987) 6.11n6

Guinanne v. San Francisco, 241 Cal. Rptr. 787 (Cal. App. 1988) 2.22n2

Guinnane v. City & County of San Francisco, 241 Cal. Rptr. 787 (Cal. App. 1987) 2.23n5

Gulf House Ass'n v. Gulf Shores, Town of, 484 So. 2d 1061 (Ala. 1985) 8.04n4

Gulf Oil Corp. v. Board of Appeals, 244 N.E.2d 311 (Mass. 1969) 6.56n15

Gulf Oil Corp. v. Township Bd. of Supvrs., 266 A.2d 84 (Pa. 1970) 6.16n3; 6.21n6

Gullickson v. Stark County Bd. of County Comm'rs, 474 N.W.2d 890 (N.D. 1991) 6.47n2

Gumprecht v. Coeur D'Alene, City of, 661 P.2d 1214 (Idaho 1983) 4.25n2; 6.83n1

Gunthner v. Planning Bd., 762 A.2d 710 . . 6.74n3

Guy v. Brandon Twp., 450 N.W.2d 279 (Mich. App. 1989) 5.32n3

Gwinnett County v. Ehler Enters., Inc. 512 S.E.2d 239 (1999) 8.14n4

H

H. Dev. Corp. v. Yonkers, City of, 407 N.Y.S.2d 573 (App. Div. 1978) 8.18n4

H & H Bldrs., Inc. v. Borough Council, 555 A.2d 948 (Pa. Commw. 1989) 7.21n3; 7.22n6

H & H Operations, Inc. v. Peachtree City, City of, 283 S.E.2d 867 (Ga. 1981) 11.18n6

Haack v. Lindsay Light & Chem. Co., 66 N.E.2d 391 (Ill. 1946) 4.12n2

Haas v. Mobile, City of, 265 So.2d 564 (Ala. 1972) 6.64n1

Hadacheck v. Sebastian 239 U.S. 394 (1915) 2.04n2

Hadley v. Harold Realty Co., 198 A.2d 149 (R.I. 1964) 3.14n1, n4

Hager v. Louisville & Jefferson County Planning & Zoning Comm, 261 S.W.2d 619 (Ky. 1953) . . . 2.23n1

Hagfeldt v. Bozeman, City of, 757 P.2d 753 (Mont. 1988) 4.34n1; 4.38n3

Hailey, City of; State v. , 633 P.2d 576 (Idaho 1981) 6.76n18

Haines v. Phoenix, City of, 727 P.2d 339 (Ariz. App. 1986) 6.33n6

Hakim v. Board of Comm'rs, 366 A.2d 1306 (Pa. Commw. 1976) 9.07n7

Hale v. Osborn Coal Enters., Inc., 729 So.2d 853 (Ala. Civ. App. 1997) 6.63n1

Halfway House v. Waukegan, City of, 641 N.E.2d 1005 (Ill. App. 1994) 6.59n4

Halifax Area Council v. Daytona Beach, City of, 385 So. 2d 184 (Fla. App. 1980) 8.11n16

Hall v. Durham, City of, 372 S.E.2d 564 (N.C. 1988) 6.64n1

Hall v. Korth, 244 So. 2d 766 (Fla. App. 1971) . . 9.28n3

Hall v. Planning Comm'n, 435 A.2d 975 (Conn. 1981) 8.02n10

Hall Paving Co. v. Hall County, 226 S.E.2d 728 (Ga. 1976) 6.26n5

Hallie, Town of v. Eau Claire, City of 471 U.S. 34 (1985) 5.52n1

Hamer v. Ross, Town of, 382 P.2d 375 (Cal. 1963) 5.32n3

Hamilton Amusement Center, Inc. v. Poritz, 689 A.2d 201 (N.J. App. Div. 1997) 5.64n2

Hamilton Amusement Center, Inc. v. Poritz, 716 A.2d 1137 (N.J. 1998) 5.64n3

Hampton v. Richland County, 357 S.E.2d 463 (S.C. 1987) 6.26n5

Hancock v. Rouse, 437 S.W.2d 1 (Tex. Civ. App. 1969) 6.83n1

Handicraft Block Ltd. Partnership v. Minneapolis, City of, 611 N.W.2d 16 . . . . 8.13n6; 11.34n3

Hankins v. Borough of Rockleigh 150 A.2d 63 (N.J. App. Div. 1959) 11.25n8

Hanna v. Board of Adjustment, 183 A.2d 539 (Pa. 1962) 5.80n10

Hanna v. Chicago, City of, 212 F. Supp.2d 856 . . 8.40n3

Hansel v. Keene, City of, 634 A.2d 1351 (N.H. 1993) 6.66n10

Hansen Bros. Enters. v. Board of Supervisors, 907 P.2d 1324 (Cal. 1995) 5.79n7

Happy Valley, City of v. Land Conservation & Dev. Comm'n, 677 P.2d 43 (Or. App. 1984) 7.30n2

Harbor Carriers, Inc. v. Sausalito, City of, 121 Cal. Rptr. 577 (Cal. App. 1975) 4.32n2

Hardin County v. Jost, 897 S.W.2d 592 (Ky. App. 1995) 6.03n3

Harding v. Board of Zoning Appeals, 219 S.E.2d 324 (W. Va. 1975) 6.56n2

Harfenes v. Sea Gate Association, 647 N.Y.S.2d 329 (Sup. Ct. 1995) 8.47n6

Hargreaves v. Skrbina, 662 P.2d 1078 (Colo. 1983) 8.15n9

Harlen Assocs. v. Incorporated Village of Mineola, 273 F.3d 494 . . . . 2.49n4

Harlow v. Fitzgerald 457 U.S. 800 (1982) 8.36n6

Harmon City, Inc. v. Draper City, 997 P.2d 321 . . 5.35n2; 6.25n3

Harnett v. Board of Zoning, Subdivision & Bldg. Appeals, 350 F. Supp. 1159 (D. St. Croix 1972) 9.25n6

Harnish v. Manatee County 783 F.2d 1535 (11th Cir. 1986) 11.20n3

Harp Advertising Ill., Inc. v. Chicago Ridge, Village of, 9 F.3d 1290 (7th Cir. 1993) 11.17n3

Harper v. Summit County, 26 P.3d 193 . . 6.76n9

Harrell's Candy Kitchen, Inc. v. Sarasota-Manatee Airport Auth., 111 So.2d 439 (Fla. 1959) 5.39n6

Harrington Glen, Inc. v. Municipal Bd. of Adjustment, 243 A.2d 233 (N.J. 1968) 6.52n3

Harris v. Costa Mesa, City of, 31 Cal. Rptr. 2d 1 (Cal. App. 1994) 6.56n13

Harris v. Old King's Highway Regional Historic Dist. Comm'n, 658 N.E.2d 972 . . . . 11.29n4

Harris v. Riverside, County of, 904 F.2d 497 (9th Cir. 1990) 2.32n3; 2.42n6, n10

Harris v. Wichita, City of, 862 F. Supp. 287 (D. Kan. 1994) 5.39n7; 9.22n4

Harris v. Zoning Comm'n, 788 A.2d 1239 . . . . . 8.04n5

Harris Used Car Co. v. Anne Arundel County, 263 A.2d 520 (Md. 1970) 6.17n1

Harrison v. Indiana Auto Shredders Co., 528 F.2d 1107 (7th Cir. 1976) 4.10n1

Harrison Orthodox Minyan, Inc. v. Town Bd., 552 N.Y.S.2d 434 (App. Div. 1990) 6.57n14

Hart v. Albuquerque, City of, 975 P.2d 366 (N.M. App. 1999) 8.14n1; 8.18n2

Hart Bookstores, Inc. v. Edminsten, 612 F.2d 821 (4th Cir. 1979) 5.64n1

Hart Bookstores, Inc. v. Edmisten, 612 F.2d 821 (4th Cir. 1979) 5.63n4

Hartford Penn-Cann Serv. v. Zymblosky, 549 A.2d 554 (Pa. Super. 1988) 4.12n6

Hartley v. Colorado Springs, City of, 764 P.2d 1216 (Colo. 1988) 5.81n7

Hartman v. Aurora San. Dist., 177 N.E.2d 214 (Ill. 1961) 9.21n3; 9.22n2

Hartman v. Buckson, 467 A.2d 694 (Del. Ch. 1983) 6.63n1

Hartman, Lucas v. South Carolina Coastal Council

Hartnett v. Austin, 93 So. 2d 86 (Fla. 1956) 6.63n1

Harts Book Stores v. Raleigh, City of, 281 S.E.2d 761 (N.C. App. 1981) 6.56n11

Harvard Square Defense Fund v. Planning Bd., 540 N.E.2d 182 (Mass. App. 1989) 8.02n10

Harvard State Bank v. McHenry, County of, 620 N.E.2d 1360 (Ill. App. 1993) 12.13n6

Harvey v. Marion, Town of, 756 So.2d 835 . . . . 6.31n2

Haskell v. Washington Township, 864 F.2d 1266 (6th Cir. 1988) 8.35n6

Hatfield v. Fayetteville, City of, 647 S.W.2d 450 (1983) 5.86n2

Hattiesburg, City of v. Region XII Comm'n on Mental Health & Retardation, 654 So. 2d 516 (Miss. 1995) 4.27n7

Haugen v. Gleason, 359 P.2d 108 (Or. 1961) 9.18n3

Hausmann & Johnson, Inc. v. Berea Bd. of Bldg. Code Appeals, 320 N.E.2d 685 (Ohio App. 1974) . . . 6.63n4

Hawaii Hous. Auth. v. Midkiff, 467 U.S. 229 (1984) 8.43n12

Hawaii Hous. Auth. v. Midkiff, 467 U.S. 2291 (1984) 8.43n3

Hawkins v. Marin, County of, 126 Cal. Rptr. 754 (Cal. App. 1976) 6.58n3

Hay v. Stevens, 530 P.2d 37 (Or. 1975) . . 4.09n2

Hayden v. Port Townsend, City of, 613 P.2d 1164 (Wash. 1980) 6.31n2

Hayes v. Albany, City of, 490 P.2d 1018 (Or. App. 1971) 9.22n2

Hayes v. Miami, City of, 52 F.3d 918 (11th Cir. 1995) 2.47n2

Hays County v. Hays County Water Planning Partnership, 69 S.W.3d 253 . . . . 6.76n5

Hayward v. Gaston, 542 A.2d 760 (Del. 1988) . . . 4.27n5; 5.08n3; 5.10n4

Hazleton Area School Dist. v. Zoning Hearing Bd., 720 A.2d 220 (Pa. Commw. 1998) . . . 4.28n2

Hazleton Area School Dist. v. Zoning Hearing Bd., 778 A.2d 1205 . . . . 4.28n3

Headley v. Rochester, City of, 5 N.E.2d 198 (N.Y. 1936) 10.15n1

Healey v. New Durham Zoning Bd. of Adjustment, Town of, 665 A.2d 360 . . . . 6.16n6

Health Mgt., Inc. v. Union Township Bd. of Zoning Appeals, 692 N.E.2d 667 (Ohio App. 1997) . . . 6.56n15

Heath Twp. v. Sall, 502 N.W.2d 627 (Mich. 1993) 6.21n4

Hehir v. Bowers, 407 N.E.2d 149 (Ill. App. 1980) 6.50n6

Heidrich v. Lee's Summit, City of, 26 S.W.3d 179 . . . . 6.66n11

Heiney v. Sylvania Township Bd. of Zoning Appeals, 710 N.E.2d 725 (Ohio App. 1998) . . . 6.56n2

Heiss v. Casper Planning & Zoning Comm'n, City of, 941 P.2d 27 (Wyo. 1997) 6.56n2

Heithaus v. Planning & Zoning Comm'n, 779 A.2d 750 . . . . 11.28n5

Helicopter Assocs. v. Stamford, City of, 519 A.2d 49 (Conn. 1986) 4.31n2

Helmkamp v. Clark Ready Mix Co., 214 N.W.2d 126 (Iowa 1974) 4.12n1

Helsel, State ex rel. v. Board of County Comm'rs, 78 N.E.2d 694 (Ohio App. 1948) 4.36n1

Helujon, Ltd. v. Jefferson County, 964 S.W.2d 531 (Mo. App. 1998) 9.27n4; 9.28n2

Hemisphere Bldg. Co. v. Richton Park, Village of, 171 F.3d 437 (7th Cir. 1999) 5.13n5

Hemisphere Bldg. Co., Inc. v. Richton Park, Village of, 171 F.3d 437 (7th Cir. 1999) 5.13n2

Hemontolor v. Wilson County Bd. of Zoning Appeals, 883 S.W.2d 613 (Tenn. App. 1994) . . . 6.59n3

Hendel's Investor Co. v. Zoning Bd. of Appeals, 771 A.2d 182 . . . . 8.04n3

Henley v. Youngstown Bd. of Zoning Appeals, City of, 735 N.E.2d 433 . . . . 5.68n5

Henn v. Universal Atlas Cement Co 4.03

Henniger v. Pinellas County, 7 F. Supp.2d 1334 (M.D. Fla. 1998) 8.33n8

Henry v. Jefferson County Planning Comm'n, 148 F. Supp.2d 698 . . . . 7.03n5

Henry County v. The Jones Props., 539 S.E.2d 167 . . . . 6.25n4

Heritage Bldg. Group, Inc. v. Bedminster Township Bd. of Supervisors, 742 A.2d 708 (Pa. Commw. 1999) 7.20n4

Heritage Farms, Inc. v. Solebury Twp., 671 F.2d 743 (3d Cir.) 8.43n10

Heritage Farms, Inc. v. Solebury Twp., 671 F.2d 743 (3d Cir. 1982) 8.44n7

Heritage Homes of Attleboro, Inc. v. Seekonk Water Dist. (II) 8.38n10

Herman Armanetti, Inc., People ex rel. v. Chicago, City of, 112 N.E.2d 616 (Ill. 1953) . . . 11.10n6

Herman Glick Realty Co. v. St. Louis County, 545 S.W.2d 320 (Mo. App. 1977) 5.46n1

Hermanson v. Board of County Comm'rs, 595 P.2d 694 (Colo. App. 1979) 2.23n6

Hernandez v. Encinitas, City of, 33 Cal Rptr. 2d 875 (Cal. App. 1994) 3.10n9

Hernandez v. Encinitas, City of, 33 Cal. Rptr. 2d 875 (Cal. App. 1994) 3.22n8

Hernandez v. Lafayette, City of, 643 F.2d 1188 (5th Cir. 1981) 8.36n3

Herrick v. Ingraham, 363 N.Y.S.2d 665 (App. Div. 1975) 9.05n6

Herrin v. Opatut, 281 S.E.2d 575 (Ga. 1981) 12.11n4

Herrington v. Sonoma, County of, 790 F. Supp. 909 . . . . 8.26n7

Herrington v. Sonoma, County of, 857 F.2d 567 . . 2.24n4

Herrington v. Sonoma, County of, 857 F.2d 567 (9th Cir. 1988) 2.30n4, n12; 2.32n2; 2.42n10

Herrington v. Sonoma, County of 648 F.2d 761 (1st Cir. 1981) 8.38n11

Herrmann v. Board of Cty. Comm'rs, 785 P.2d 1003 (Kan. 1990) 4.27n5

Hertzberg v. Zoning Bd. of Adjustment, 721 A.2d 53 (Pa. 1998) 6.42n1; 6.48n13

Hessling v. Broomfield, City of, 563 P.2d 12 (Colo. 1977) 5.08n9

Hi-Top Steel Corp. v. Lehrer, 29 Cal. Rptr.2d 646 (Cal. App. 1994) 5.55n6

Hibernia Nat'l Bank v. New Orleans, City of, 455 So. 2d 1239 (La. App. 1984) 6.37n11

Hickerson v. New York, City of, 146 F.3d 99 (2d Cir. 1998) 5.63n10

Hickman, State ex rel. v. City Council, 690 S.W.2d 799 (Mo. App. 1985) 6.83n3

Hicks v. Miranda, 422 U.S. 322 (1975) . . 8.42n5

High Meadows Park v. Aurora, City of, 250 N.E.2d 517 (Ill. App. 1969) 6.54n4

Highland Park, City of v. Train, 519 F.2d 861 (7th Cir. 1977) 2.47n2

Highland Park Community Club v. Zoning Bd. of Adjustment, 475 A.2d 925 (Pa. Commw. 1984) 6.17n1

Hill v. Chester, Town of, 771 A.2d 559 . . 6.50n7

Hill v. Colorado, 530 U.S. 703 . . . . . . 11.19n12

Hill v. Conway, Town of, 193 F.3d 33 (1st Cir. 1999) 2.34n3

Hill v. El Paso, City of, 437 F.2d 352 (5th Cir. 1971) 8.43n6

Hill v. Zoning Hearing Bd., 626 A.2d 510 (Pa. 1993) 6.18n6

Hill Homeowners Ass'n v. Passaic, City of, 384 A.2d 172 (N.J. App. Div. 1978) 8.15n9

Hillis Homes, Inc. v. Snohomish County, 650 P.2d 193 (Wash. 1982) 9.21n2

Hills Dev. Co. v. Township of Bernards . . . 7.12

Hillsborough, Town of v. Smith, 167 S.E.2d 51 (N.C. App. 1969) 8.11n3

Hillsborough, Town of v. Smith, 170 S.E.2d 904 (N.C. 1969) 6.21n1

Hilton v. Toledo, City of, 405 N.E.2d 1047 (Ohio 1980) 11.07n3; 11.10n4

Hilton v. Wheeling, City of, 209 F.3d 1005 . . . . . 2.49n4

Hilton Head Island, Town of v. Fine Liquors, Ltd., 397 S.E.2d 662 (S.C. 1990) 4.33n2

Himelstein, Estate of v. Fort Wayne, City of, 898 F.2d 573 (7th Cir. 1990) 2.31n3

Hinman v. Planning & Zoning Comm'n, 214 A.2d 131 (Conn. C.P. 1965) 7.10n1

Hirt v. Polk Cty. Bd. of Comm'rs, 578 So. 2d 415 (Fla. App. 1991) 8.13n7

Hirtz v. State, 773 F. Supp. 6 (S.D. Tex. 1991) . . 12.15n2

Historic Albany Found. v. Coyne, 558 N.Y.S.2d 986 (App. Div. 1990) 11.35n3

Hixon v. Walker County, 468 S.E.2d 744 (Ga. 1996) 9.09n8

Hobart, Town of v. Collier, 87 N.W.2d 868 (Wis. 1958) 6.61n4

Hobbs v. Markey, 398 S.W.2d 54 (Ky. 1966) . . . 8.04n2

Hoberg v. Bellevue, City of, 884 P.2d 1339 (Wash. App. 1994) 6.50n6

Hochberg v. Borough of Freehold, 123 A.2d 46 (N.J. 1956) 6.74n8

Hock v. Board of Supvrs., 622 A.2d 431 (Pa. Commw. 1993) 5.32n9

Hodel v. Irving, 481 U.S. 704 (1987) . . . 2.18n1

Hodel v. Virginia Surface Mining & Reclamation Ass'n, 452 U.S. 264 (1981) 2.25n2

Hodge, State ex rel. v. Turtle Lake, Town of, 508 N.W.2d 603 (Wis. 1993) 6.76n15

Hodges v. Reid, 836 S.W.2d 120 (Tenn. App. 1992) 8.23n5

Hoehne v. San Benito, County of, 870 F.2d 529 (9th Cir. 1989) 2.30n12

Hoepker v. Madison Plan Comm'n, City of, 563 N.W.2d 145 (Wis. 1997) 9.09n2

Hoffman v. Kinealy, 389 S.W.2d 745 (Mo. 1965) 5.85n3

Hoffman Estates, Village of v. Flipside, Hoffman Estates, 455 U.S. 489 (1982) 6.05n2, n18

Hoffmaster v. San Diego, City of, 64 Cal. Rptr. 2d 684 (Cal. App. 1997) 3.22n10

Hofmeister v. Frank Realty Co., 373 A.2d 273 (Md. App. 1977) 6.54n1

Hoke v. Moyer, 865 P.2d 624 (Wyo. 1994) 8.04n1

Holbrook, Inc. v. Clark County, 49 P.3d 142 . . . . 2.42n5

Holiday Point Marina Partners v. Anne Arundel County, 707 A.2d 829 (Md. 1998) . . . 8.11n1

Hollingsworth v. Dallas, City of, 931 S.W.2d 699 (Tex. App. 1996) 4.25n7

Hollywood, City of v. Hollywood, Inc., 432 So. 2d 1332 (Fla. App. 1983) 10.06n6

Hollywood, City of v. Hollywood, Inc., 432 So.2d 1332 (Fla. App. 1982) 12.16n6

Hollywood, City of v. Hollywood, Inc., 432 So.2d 1332 (Fla. App. 1983) 11.38n7

Hollywood, Inc. v. Broward County, 431 So. 2d 606 (Fla. App. 1983) 4.25n8

Holmberg v. Ramsey, City of, 12 F.3d 140 (8th Cir. 1994) 5.63n5

Holmberg v. Ramsey, City of, 12 F.3d 149 (8th Cir. 1993) 5.63n11

Holmdel Bldrs. Ass'n v. Township of Holmdel, 583 A.2d 277 (N.J. 1990) 7.27n7

Holmes v. Maryland Reclamation Assocs., 600 A.2d 864 (Md. 1992) 4.30n4

Holmes v. Planning Bd. of Town of New Castle, 433 N.Y.S.2d 587 (Sup. Ct. 1980) . . 6.33n8; 6.66n7

Holmes v. Planning Bd. of Town of New Castle 433 N.Y.S.2d 587 (App. Div. 1980) 3.22n11

Holmgren v. Lincoln, City of, 256 N.W.2d 686 (Neb. 1977) 6.33n2

Holsheimer v. Columbia County, 890 P.2d 447 (Or. App. 1995) 5.20n1

Holt Civic Club v. Tuscaloosa, City of 439 U.S. 60 (1978) 4.23n2

Holt-Lock, Inc. v. Zoning & Planning Comm'n, 286 A.2d 299 (Conn. 1971) 8.10n1

Holubec v. Brandenburger, 58 S.W.2d 201 . . . . . 12.11n5

Homart Dev. Co. v. Planning & Zoning Comm'n, 600 A.2d 13 (Conn. App. 1991) 6.61n3

Home Bldrs. Ass'n v. Kansas City, City of, 555 S.W.2d 832 (Mo. 1977) 9.19n4

Home Bldrs. Ass'n v. Provo City, 503 P.2d 451 (Utah 1972) 9.21n3

Home Bldrs. Ass'n of Cent. Ariz. v. Riddel, 510 P.2d 376 (Ariz. 1973) 9.21n2

Home Bldrs. League of S. Jersey, Inc. v. Township of Berlin 7.07

Home Bldrs. League of S. Jersey, Inc. v. Township of Berlin, 405 A.2d 381 (N.J. 1979) 7.10n2; 8.02n12

Home Builders Ass'n v. Apache Junction, City of, 11 P.3d 1032 . . . . 9.21n5

Home Builders Ass'n v. North Logan, City of, 983 P.2d 561 (Utah 1999) 9.22n2

Home Builders Ass'n v. West Des Moines, City of, 444 N.W.2d 339 . . . . 9.21n2

Home Builders Ass'n v. West Des Moines, City of, 644 N.W.2d 339 . . . . 9.22n1, n13

Home Builders Ass'n of Central Arizona v. Scottsdale, City of, 930 P.2d 993 (Ariz. 1996) 9.22n9, n10, n11

Home Builders Ass'n of Central Arizona v. Scottsdale, City of, 930 P.2d 993 (Ariz. 1997) 9.14n2; 9.21n12

Home Builders Ass'n of Dayton v. Beavercreek, City of, 729 N.E.2d 349 . . . . 9.22n6, n12

Home Builders Ass'n of Maine, Inc. v. Eliot, Town of, 750 A.2d 566 . . . . 6.07n4

Home Builders Ass'n of N. California v. Napa, City of, 108 Cal. Rptr. 2d 60 . . . . . 7.27n5; 9.22n6

Home Builders Ass'n of Utah v. American Fork, City of, 973 P.2d 425 (Utah 1999 (same) . . 9.22n2

Home Depot U.S.A., Inc. v. Portland, City of, 10 P.3d 316 . . . . 5.36n6

Home Depot U.S.A., Inc. v. Rockville Centre, Village of, 743 N.Y.S.2d 541 . . . . 6.11n1

Homebuilders Ass'n of Dayton v. Beavercreek, City of, 729 N.E.2d 359 . . . . 2.35n1

Homeowner/Contractor Consultants, Inc. v. Ascension Parish Planning & Zoning Comm'n, 32 F. Supp. 2d 384 (M.D. La. 1999) 8.35n7

Hometown Props. v. Fleming, 680 A.2d 56 (R.I. 1996) 8.47n4

Honeck v. Cook, County of, 146 N.E.2d 35 (Ill. 1957) 5.31n2, n4

Hope v. Gainesville, City of, 355 So. 2d 1172 (Fla. 1978) 6.04n2

Hope, Inc. v. DuPage, County of, 738 F.2d 797 (7th Cir. 1984) 7.02n1

Hopengarten v. Board of Appeals, 459 N.E.2d 1271 (Mass. App. 1984) 6.59n4

Hopewell Twp. Bd. of Supvrs. v. Golla, 452 A.2d 1337 (Pa. 1982) 12.10n5; 12.12n6

Hopkins v. Zoning Hearing Bd., 423 A.2d 1082 (Pa. Commw. 1980) 5.08n7

Horizon Adirondack Corp. v. New York, State of, 388 N.Y.S.2d 235 (Ct. Cl. 1976) 6.37n11

Horizon Constr. Co. v. Newberg, City of, 834 P.2d 523 (Or. App. 1992) 6.71n6

Horizon House Develpmt'l Servs., Inc. v. Township of Upper Southampton, 804 F. Supp. 683 (E.D. Pa. 1992), aff'd 5.15n2

Horn v. Township of Hilltown, 337 A.2d 858 (Pa. 1975) 6.68n3; 6.71n11

Horn v. Ventura, County of, 596 P.2d 1134 (Cal. 1979) 6.68n2; 6.70n2; 8.11n7

Hot Springs, City of v. Carter, 836 S.W.2d 863 (Ark. 1992) 11.20n2

Hotel Coamo Springs, Inc. v. Hernandez Colon, 539 F. Supp. 1008 (D.P.R. 1982) 2.23n2

Hough v. Marsh, 557 F. Supp. 74 (D. Mass. 1982) 12.06n7

Hougham v. Lexington-Fayette Urban County Gov't, 29 S.W.3d 370 . . . . 6.71n3

Houser v. Board of Comm'rs, 247 N.E.2d 670 (Ind. 1969) 6.34n4

Housing Investors, Inc. v. Clanton, City of, 68 F. Supp.2d 1287 (M.D. Ala. 1999) 7.03n6

Houston v. Board of City Comm'rs, 543 P.2d 1010 (Kan. 1975) 2.46n6

Houston, City of v. Johnny Frank's Auto Parts, Inc., 480 S.W.2d 774 (Tex. Civ. App. 1972) 11.04n2

Houston, City of v. Tri-Lakes Ltd., 681 So.2d 104 (Miss. 1996) 8.15n8

Houston Petroleum Co. v. Automotive Prods. Credit Ass'n 87 A.2d 319 (N.J. 1952) 6.63n2

Hovson's, Inc. v. Township of Brick, 89 F.3d 1096 (3d Cir. 1996) 5.13n1

Howard v. Beavercreek, City of, 276 F.3d 802 . . . 5.13n1

Howard v. Garland, City of, 917 F.2d 898 (5th Cir. 1990) 2.47n2; 2.48n3

Howard v. Kinston, City of, 558 S.E.2d 221 . . . . 6.70n6

Howard County v. JJM, Inc., 482 A.2d 908 (Md. 1984) 10.14n7

Howard Cty. v. Potomac Elec. Power Co., 573 A.2d 821 (Md. 1990) 4.32n2

Howard Township Bd. of Trustees v. Waldo, 425 N.W.2d 180 (Mich. App. 1988) 6.16n6

Howard Twp. Bd. of Trustees v. Waldo, 425 N.W.2d 180 (Mich. App. 1988) 6.04n4

Howard W. Heck & Assocs. v. United States, 37 Fed. Cl. 245 (1997) 2.30n15

Howell Plaza, Inc. v. State Hwy. Comm'n, 284 N.W.2d 887 (Wis. 1979) 2.23n6

However, the Court, in Tahoe-Sierra Preservation Council v. Tahoe Regional Planning Agency . . 6.09n4

Howland Realty Co. v. Wolcott, 457 N.E.2d 883 (Ohio App. 1982) 8.10n1

H.R. Miller Co. v. Board of Supvrs. of Lancaster Twp., 605 A.2d 321 (Pa. 1992) 7.22n6

H.R.D.E., Inc. v. Zoning Officer, 430 S.E.2d 341 (W. Va. 1993) 6.21n4

Hubbard Broadcasting, Inc. v. Afton, City of, 323 N.W.2d 757 (Minn. 1982) 6.58n4

Hudson v. Palmer, 468 U.S. 517 (1984) 8.29n11

Hudson Canyon Constr., Inc. v. Cortlandt, Town of, 692 N.Y.S.2d 158 (App. Div. 1999) . . 6.66n11

Hudson, Village of v. Albrecht, Inc . 11.04; 11.25

Hudspeth v. Board of County Comm'rs of Routt, 667 P.2d 775 (Colo. App. 1983) 6.76n3

Huff v. Board of Zoning Appeals, 133 A.2d 83 (Md. 1957) 6.61n3

Hugham v. Lexington-Fayette Urban County Gov't, 29 S.W.3d 370 . . . . 6.33n2

Hughes v. Mayor & Comm'rs of City of Jackson, 296 So. 2d 689 (Miss. 1974) 6.31n7

Human Dev. Serv. of Porth Chester v. Zoning Bd. of Appeals, 493 N.Y.S.2d 481 (App. Div. 1985) . . . 6.48n5

Humble Oil & Refining Co., State ex rel. v. Wahner, 130 N.W.2d 304 (Wis. 1964) 6.15n1

Hunt v. Washington State Apple Advertising Comm'n 432 U.S. 333 (1977) 8.06n3

Hunter v. Bryant, 502 U.S. 224 (1991) . . . 8.36n8

Hunter v. Cleveland, City of, 564 N.E.2d 718 (Ohio App. 1988) 8.23n12

Hunter v. Erickson 393 U.S. 385 (1969) . . 6.80n1

Huntington v. Zoning Bd. of Appeals, 428 N.E.2d 826 (Mass. App. 1981) 6.51n6

Huntington Branch, NAACP v. Huntington, Town of 844 F.2d 926 (2d Cir. 1988), aff'd, 488 U.S. 15 (1988) 7.05n5

Huntington Health Care Partnership v. Zoning Bd. of Appeals, 516 N.Y.S.2d 99 (App. Div. 1987) . . 6.75n3

Huntington, Town of v. Town Bd. of Oyster Bay, 293 N.Y.S.2d 558 (Sup. Ct. 1968) 8.07n2

Huntzicker v. Washington County, 917 P.2d 1051 (Or. App. 1996) 9.28n2

Hurley v. Hollis, Town of, 729 A.2d 998 (N.H. 1999) 5.79n8

Husnander v. Barnstead, Town of, 660 A.2d 477 (N.H. 1995) 6.48n15

Hutchins, City of v. Prasifka, 450 S.W.2d 829 (Tex. 1970) 6.17n1

Hutchinson v. Huntington, City of, (1996) 2.22n3

Huttig v. Richmond Heights, City of, 372 S.W.2d 833 (Mo. 1963) 6.35n1

Hyde Park Co. v. Santa Fe City Council, 226 F.3d 1207 . . . . 2.42n7

Hyde Park Co. v. Santa Fe City Council, 226 F.3d1207 (10th Cir. 2000) 2.40n6

Hydraulic Press Brick Co. v. Council of City of Independence, 475 N.E.2d 144 (Ohio App. 1984) 6.56n8

Hyland v. Mayor & Twp. Comm., 327 A.2d 675 (N.J. App. Div. 1974) 6.37n7

Hylton Enters. v. Board of Supvrs., 258 S.E.2d 577 (Va. 1979) 9.16n6

Hynes v. Pasco County, 801 F.2d 1269 (11th Cir. 1986) 8.30n3

I

Idaho Bldg. Contractors Ass'n v. Coeur D'Alene, City of, 890 P.2d 326 (Idaho 1995) 9.21n2

Idaho Historic Preservation Council, Inc. v. City Council, 8 P.3d 646 . . . . 6.71n8

ILQ Investments, Inc. v. Rochester, City of, 25 F.3d 1413 (8th Cir. 1994) 5.63n2

ILQ Invs., Inc. v. Rochester, City of, 25 F.3d 1413 (8th Cir. 1994) 5.65n4

The Impact of Employment Division v. Smith, 7 B.Y.U. J. Pub. L. 395 (1993)

The Impact of Lucas v. South Carolina Coastal Council on Wetlands and Coastal Barri, 19 Harv. Envtl. L. Rev. 1 (1995)

Imperial Beach, City of v. Palm Ave. Books, 171 Cal. Rptr. 197 (Cal. App. 1981) 6.57n2

In re (see name of party)

Inc. v. Philadelphia, City of, 635 A.2d 612 (Pa. 1993) 11.34n8; 11.35n4

Inc. v. United States, 270 F.3d 1347 . . . 2.16n12

Incorporated Village of Island Park; United States v. , 888 F. Supp. 419 (E.D.N.Y. 1995) . . 7.04n1

Independence, City of v. Richards, 666 S.W.2d 1 (Mo. App. 1983) 6.05n21

Independent Coin Payphone Ass'n, Inc. v. Chicago, City of, 863 F. Supp. 744 (N.D. Ill. 1994) 8.33n10

Independent School Dist. No. 89 v. Oklahoma City, City of, 722 P.2d 1212 (Okla. 1986) . . 4.38n3

Indialantic, Town of v. Nance, 400 So. 2d 37 (Fla. App. 1981) 6.52n5

Indialantic, Town of v. Nance, 419 So. 2d 1041 (Fla. 1982) 6.46n4

Indiana Toll Rd. Comm'n v. Jankovich, 193 N.E.2d 237 (Ind. 1963) 5.39n8

Indio, City of v. Arryo, 191 Cal. Rptr. 565 (Cal. App. 1983) 6.57n2

Infinity Outdoor, Inc. v. New York, City of, 165 F. Supp.2d 403 . . . . 11.19n4

Inland Constr. Co. v. Bloomington, City of, 195 N.W.2d 558 (Minn. 1972) 6.56n13

Innkeepers Motor Lodge, Inc. v. New Smyrna Beach, City of, 460 So. 2d 379 (Fla. App. 1984) 10.06n6

Innovative Health Systems, Inc. v. White Plains, City of, 117 F.3d 37 (2d Cir. 1997) 5.12n11

Innovative Health Systems, Inc. v. White Plains, City of, 177 F.3d 37 (2d Cir. 1997) 5.16n2

Institute for Evaluation & Planning, Inc. v. Board of Adjustment, 637 A.2d 235 (N.J.L. Div. 1993) . . 5.79n9

Interladco, Inc. v. Billings 538 P.2d 496 (Colo. App. 1975) 9.09n11

International College of Surgeons v. Chicago, City of, 153 F.3d 356 (7th Cir. 1998) . . 8.43n8; 8.44n6

International Eateries of America v. Board of County Comm'rs, 838 F. Supp. 580 (S.D. Fla. 1993) . . 8.43n6

International Eateries of America, Inc. v. Broward County, 941 F.2d 1157 (11th Cir. 1991) 5.63n4

International Villages, Inc. of Am. v. Board of County Comm'rs, 585 P.2d 999 (Kan. 1978) . . 6.58n4

Interstate Power Co., Inc. v. Nobles County Bd. of Comm'rs, 617 N.W.2d 566 . . . . 6.16n4

Interstate Props., Inc. v. Pyramid Co., 586 F. Supp. 1160 (S.D.N.Y. 1984) 5.55n6

I'On, L.L.C. v. Mt. Pleasant, Town of, 526 S.E.2d 716 . . . . 6.82n1; 6.83n1

Iowa City, City of v. Hagen Electronics, Inc. 545 N.W.2d 530 (Iowa 1996) 8.11n16

Iowa Coal Mining Co. v. Monroe City, 494 N.W.2d 664 (Iowa 1993) 2.21n2

Iowa Coal Mining Co. Inc. v. Monroe County, 494 N.W.2d 664 (Iowa 1993) 3.14n1; 6.25n6

Iowa Wireless Servs. v. Moline, City of, 29 F. Supp.2d 915 (C.D. Ill. 1998) 4.42n14

Irvine v. Duval County Planning Comm'n, 495 So. 2d 167 (Fla. 1986) 6.56n1

Irvine, City of v. Irvine Citizens Against Overdevelopment, 30 Cal. Rptr. 2d 797 (Cal. App. 1994) . . 8.07n1

Irwin v. Planning & Zoning Comm'n, 694 A.2d 809 (Conn. App. 1997) 9.09n7

Irwin v. Planning & Zoning Comm'n, 711 A.2d 675 (Conn. 1998) 6.56n16

Isbell v. San Diego, 258 F.3d1108 (9th Cir. 2001), City of 5.63n6

Isla Verda Internat'l Holdings v. City Camas, 49 P.3d 867 . . . . 9.09n13

Isla Verde Internat'l Holdings, Inc. v. Camas, City of, 43 P.3d 867 . . . . 9.19n6

Islamic Center of Miss., Inc. v. Starkville, City of, 840 F.2d 293 (5th Cir. 1988) 5.69n4; 6.57n16

Island Harbor Beach Club, Ltd. v. Department of Natural Resources, 495 So. 2d 209 (Fla. App. 1986) 12.14n2

Island Props., Inc. v. Martha's Vineyard Comm'n, 361 N.E.2d 385 (Mass. 1977) 9.07n11

Islip, Town of v. Caviglia, 540 N.E.2d 215 (N.Y. 1989) 5.63n2; 5.64n1; 5.65n4

IT Corp. v. Solano County Bd. of Supvrs., 820 P.2d 1023 (Cal. 1991) 4.30n3, n7

Ithaca, City of v. Tompkins, County of, 355 N.Y.S.2d 275 (Sup. Ct. 1974) 4.37n3

Ivancovich v. Tucson, City of, 529 P.2d 242 (Ariz. App. 1975) 6.48n8

Ixzzo v. Borough of River Edge, 843 F.2d 765 (3d Cir. 1988) 8.44n6

Izaak Walton League of Am. v. Monroe County, 448 So. 2d 1170 (Fla. App. 1984) 6.73n3

J

J. Gregcin, Inc. v. Dayton, City of, 593 P.2d 1231 (Or. App. 1979) 8.23n7

J-Marion Co. v. Sacramento, County of, 142 Cal. Rptr. 723 (Cal. App. 1977) 6.64n1

Jachimek v. Superior Ct., 819 P.2d 487 (Ariz. 1991) 6.54n5

Jack v. Olathe, City of, 781 P.2d 1069 (Kan. 1989) 8.22n1

Jackson v. Auburn, City of, 41 F. Supp.2d 1300 (M.D. Ala. 1999) 7.03n5

Jackson v. City Council, 659 F. Supp. 470 (W.D. Va. 1987) 11.07n7

Jackson v. San Mateo, City of, 307 P.2d 451 (Cal. App. 1957) 6.47n2

Jackson v. Spaulding County, 462 S.E.2d 361 (Ga. 1995) 8.13n1

Jackson, City of v. Ridgway, 258 So. 2d 439 (Miss. 1972) 9.09n7

Jackson Court Condominiums, Inc. v. New Orleans, City of, 874 F.2d 1070 (5th Cir. 1989) 2.42n2

Jackson Ct. Condominiums, Inc. v. New Orleans, City of, 874 F.2d 1070 (5th Cir. 1989) 6.11n5

Jacksonville Beach, City of v. Grubbs, 461 So. 2d 160 (Fla. App. 1984) 3.17n2

Jacksonville Beach, City of v. Prom, 656 So.2d 581 (Fla. App. 1995) 3.18n4

Jacksonville, City of, Ex parte , 693 So.2d 465 (Ala. 1996) 6.37n7

Jacobs, Visconsi & Jacobs v. Lawrence, City of, 927 F.2d 111 (10th Cir. 1991) 5.54n5

Jacobs, Visconsi & Jacobs v. Lawrence, City of, 927 F.2d 1111 (10th Cir. 1991) . . . 2.40n8; 2.42n7

Jacobs, Visconsi & Jacobs Co. v. Lawrence, City of, 927 F.2d 1111 (10th Cir. 1991) 2.47n1; 5.54n3; 6.25n13

Jafay v. Board of County Comm'rs, 848 P.2d 892 (Colo. 1993) 6.37n2

Jaffe; Commonwealth v. , 494 N.E.2d 1342 (Mass. 1986) 5.03n1; 6.05n4

Jago-Ford v. Planning & Zoning Comm'n, 642 A.2d 14 (Conn. App. 1994) 6.70n8

Jakes, Ltd., Inc. v. Coates, City of, 284 F.3d 884 . . . . 5.63n2; 6.57n4

James v. Valtierra 402 U.S. 137 (1971) . . 6.80n2

James Emory, Inc. v. Twiggs County, 883 F. Supp. 1546 (M.D. Ga. 1995) 5.54n5

Janssen v. Holland Charter Bd. of Zoning Appeals, 651 N.W.2d 464 . . . . 6.47n2

J.B. Advertising Co. v. Sign Bd. of Appeals, 883 S.W.2d 443 (Tex. App. 1994) 6.05n11

J.E.D. Assocs. v. Sandown, Town of, 430 A.2d 129 (N.H. 1981) 9.09n2

Jefferson County v. Birmingham, City of, 55 So. 2d 196 (Ala. 1951) 4.37n1

Jefferson County v. O'Rorke, 394 So. 2d 937 (Ala. 1981) 5.38n1

Jeffrey Lauren Land Co. v. Livonia, City of, 326 N.W.2d 604 (Mich. 1982) 5.63n5

Jeffrey Lauren Land Co. v. Livonia, City of, 326 N.W.2d 604 (Mich. App. 1982) 6.57n4

Jehovah's Witness Assembly Halls of New Jersey, Inc. v. Jersey City, City of, 597 F. Supp. 972 (D.N.J. 1984) 5.68n1

Jehovah's Witnesses Assembly Hall v. Wollrich Twp., 532 A.2d 276 (N.J.L. Div. 1987) 5.68n3

Jenad, Inc. v. Scarsdale, Village of, 218 N.E.2d 673 (N.Y. 1966) 9.18n1, n4; 9.19n4

Jenkins v. Gallipolis, City of, 715 N.E.2d 196 (Ohio App. 1998) 8.04n6

Jenkins v. St. Tammany Parish Police Jury, 736 So.2d 1287 (La. 1999) 6.56n4

Jenney v. Durham, 707 A.2d 752 (Del. Super. 1997) 6.42n1; 6.45n2

Jennings v. Dade Cty., 1991 Fla. App. Lexis 1267 (Fla. App. 1991) 6.71n4

Jensen v. New York, City of, 369 N.E.2d 1179 (N.Y. 1977) 10.15n4

Jensen's, Inc. v. Dover, City of, 547 A.2d 277 (N.H. 1988) 5.25n1; 5.26n3

Jensen's, Inc. v. Plainville, Town of, 150 A.2d 297 (Conn. 1959) 5.23n1

Jerome Twp. v. Melchi, 457 N.W.2d 52 (Mich. App. 1989) 12.11n4

Jerry Harmon Motors, Inc. v. Farmers Union Grain Term. Ass'n, 337 N.W.2d 427 (N.D. 1983) . . . 4.04n1

Jesus Fellowship, Inc. v. Miami-Dade County, 752 So.2d 708 . . . . 6.56n8

Jim Gall Auctioneers, Inc. v. Coral Gables, City of, 210 F.3d 1331 . . . . 11.18n1

JJR, Inc. v. Seattle, City of, 891 P.2d 720 (Wash. 1997) 6.57n8

Jock v. Shire Realty, Inc., 684 A.2d 921 (N.J. App. Div. 1996) 6.74n13

Joe Horisk's Salvage Pool Systems of Ohio v. Strongsville, City of, 631 N.E.2d 1097 (Ohio App. 1993) 4.31n1

Johansen v. Bartlesville, City of, 862 F.2d 1423 (10th Cir. 1988) 8.38n5

John Corp. v. Houston, City of, 214 F.3d 573 . . . 2.32n2; 2.40n2

John Donnelly & Sons v. Outdoor Adv. Bd., 339 N.E.2d 709 (Mass. 1975) . . . 11.05n1; 11.08n3

Johnson v. Edgartown, Town of, 680 N.E.2d 37 (Mass. 1997) 5.31n7

Johnson v. Essex, County of, 538 A.2d 448 (N.J.L. Div. 1987) 8.23n9

Johnson v. Murzyn, 469 A.2d 1227 (Conn. App. 1984) 8.15n6

Johnson; State v. , 265 A.2d 711 (Me. 1970) 12.07n1

Johnson v. Township of Robinson, 359 N.W.2d 526 (Mich. 1984) 6.50n2

Johnson's Island v. Board of Twp. Trustees, 431 N.E.2d 672 (Ohio 1982) 8.11n19

Johnston v. Claremont, City of, 323 P.2d 71 (Cal. 1958) 6.82n7

Joint Ventures, Inc. v. Department of Transp., 563 So. 2d 622 (Fla. 1990) 10.15n9

Joliet, City of v. Snyder, 741 N.E.2d 1051 . . . . . 4.27n1

Jones v. Coconino, County of, 35 P.3d 422 . . . . . 5.79n8

Jones v. King County, 874 P.2d 853 (Wash. App. 1994) 2.21n2

Jones v. Los Angeles, City of, 295 P. 14 (Cal. 1930) 5.78n4

Jones; State v. , 290 S.E.2d 675 (N.C. 1982) 11.05n1

Jones; State v. , 865 P.2d 138 (Ariz. App. 1993) . . 6.05n17

Jones v. Woodway, Town of, 425 P.2d 904 (Wash. 1967) 9.09n3

Jones v. Zoning Hearing Bd., 578 A.2d 1369 (Pa. Commw. 1990) 12.02n1

Jones Ins. Trust v. Ft. Smith, City of, 731 F. Supp. 912 (D. Or. 1992) 9.13n3

Jonesville, Town of v. Powell Valley Ltd. Partnership, 487 S.E.2d 207 (Va. 1997) 8.14n1

Jonesville, Town of v. Powell Valley Village Ltd. Partnership, 487 S.E.2d 207 (Va. 1997) 3.16n1; 8.11n1; 8.19n6

Jordan v. Menomonee Falls, Village of, 137 N.W.2d 442 (Wis. 1965) 9.18n1

Jordan v. Menomonee Falls, Village of 137 N.W.2d 442 (Wis. 1965) 9.19n3

Jordan Partners v. Goehringer, 611 N.Y.S.2d 626 (App. Div. 1994) 8.14n1

Jorgensen v. Board of Adj., 336 N.W.2d 423 (Iowa 1983) 6.70n11

Joseph B. Simon & Co. v. Zoning Bd. of Adjustment, 168 A.2d 317 (Pa. 1961) 6.44n3

Josephson v. Autrey, 96 So. 2d 784 (Fla. 1957) . . 6.50n5

Joy v. Anne Arundel County, 451 A.2d 1237 (Md. App. 1982) 8.15n6

Joy Street Condominium Ass'n v. Board of Appeal, 688 N.E.2d 1363 (Mass. 1998) 6.45n2

Joyce v. Multnomah County, 835 P.2d 127 (Or. App. 1992) 8.09n3, n6

Joyce v. Portland, City of, 546 P.2d 1100 (Or. App. 1976) 12.13n6

JPI Partners v. Planning & Zoning Bd., 791 A.2d 552 . . . . 7.31n6

JSS Realty Co. v. Kittery, Town of, 177 F. Supp.2d 64 . . . . 6.36n1

JSS Realty Co., LLC v. Kittery, Town of, 177 F. Supp.2d 64 . . . . 2.53n3

Just v. Marinette County 201 N.W.2d 761 (Wis. 1972) 12.07n2

J.W. Jones Cos. v. San Diego, City of, 203 Cal. Rptr. 580 (Cal. App. 1984) 9.22n2

K

K" Care, Inc. v. Lac, Town of 5.13n4

K & K Constr., Inc. v. Department of Natural Resources, 575 N.W.2d 531 (Mich. 1998) 2.19n3; 12.07n9

Ka-Hur Enters., Inc. v. Zoning Bd. of Appeals, 676 N.E.2d 838 (Mass. 1997) 5.81n7

Kaelin v. Louisville, City of, 643 S.W.2d 590 (Ky. 1983) 6.70n4

Kaiser Aetna v. United States 444 U.S. 164 (1979) 2.18n2

Kaiser Hawaii Kai Dev. Co. v. City & Cty. of Honolulu, 777 P.2d 244 (Hawaii 1989) 6.83n1

Kaiser Hawaii Kai Development Company v. Honolulu, City and County of

Kali Bari Temple v. Board of Adjustment, 638 A.2d 839 (N.J. App. Div. 1994) 6.57n14

Kalimian v. Board of Zoning Appeals, 783 A.2d 506 . . . . 6.50n5

Kaloo v. Zoning Bd. of Appeals, 654 N.E.2d 493 (Ill. App. 1995) 6.15n4

Kamplain v. Curry County Bd. of Comm'rs, 159 F.3d 1248 (10th Cir. 1998) 8.35n8

Kang v. Supervisors of Township of Spring, 776 A.2d 324 . . . . 9.25n5

Kaplan v. Clear Lake City Water Auth., 794 F.2d 1059 (5th Cir. 1986) 6.10n4; 8.36n9, n14

Karam v. Department of Envtl. Protection, 723 A.2d 943 (N.J. 1999) 2.19n3

Karches v. Cincinnati, 526 N.E.2d 1350 (Ohio 1988) 8.16n1

Karches v. Cincinnati, City of, 526 N.E.2d 1350 (Ohio 1988) 8.11n16

Karlson v. Camarillo, City of, 161 Cal. Rptr. 260 (Cal. App. 1980) 6.34n2

Kasha v. Department of Transp. 782 A.2d 15 . . . 5.80n5

Kasparek v. Johnson County Bd. of Health, 288 N.W.2d 511 (Iowa 1980) 6.18n4

Kass v. Lewin, 104 So. 2d 572 (Fla. 1958) 9.08n5

Katobimar Realty Co. v. Webster, 118 A.2d 824 (N.J. 1955) 5.43n2

Katzin v. McShain, 89 A.2d 519 (Pa. 1952) 6.02n1

Kauai, County of v. Pacific Standard Life Ins. Co., 653 P.2d 766 (Haw. 1982) 2.16n4

Kauai, County of v. Pacific Stds. Life Ins. Co., 653 P.2d 766 (Haw. 1982) 6.15n1

Kaufman v. Planning & Zoning Comm'n, 298 S.E.2d 148 (W. Va. 1982) 9.09n7

Kaufman v. Zoning Comm'n, 653 A.2d 798 (Conn. 1995) 7.31n4

Kaufmann v. Planning Bd., 542 A.2d 457 (N.J. 1988) 6.48n11

Kavanewsky v. Zoning Bd. of Appeals 279 A.2d 567 (Conn. 1971) 6.37n16

Kawaoka v. Arroyo Grande, City of, 17 F.3d 1227 (9th Cir. 1994) 2.30n1

Kawaoka v. Arroyo Grande, City of, 73 F.3d 1227 (9th Cir. 1994) 7.03n5

KBW, Inc. v. Bennington, Town of, 342 A.2d 653 (N.H. 1975) 9.16n1

KCI Mgt., Inc. v. Board of Appeal, 764 N.E.2d 377 . . . . 6.66n2

Kee v. Pennsylvania Turnpike Comm'n, 722 A.2d 1123 (Pa. Commw. 1998) 4.27n6

Keeler v. Mayor & City Council, 940 F. Supp. 879 (D. Md. 1996) 11.35n5; 11.37n7

Keeler v. Mayor & Council, 949 F. Supp. 879 (D. Md. 1999) 5.69n6

Keeling v. Board of Zoning Appeals, 69 N.E.2d 613 (Ind. App. 1946) 5.68n5

Keith v. Volpe, 858 F.2d 467 (9th Cir. 1988) . . . 7.05n5

Keith v. Volpe, 858 F.2d 467 (9th Cir. 1988), cert. denied, 493 U.S. 813 (1989) 7.02n4

Keizer v. Adams, 471 P.2d 983 (Cal. 1970) 9.08n7

Kelber v. St. Louis Park, City of, 185 N.W.2d 526 (Minn. 1971) 5.35n2

Kelbro, Inc. v. Myrick, 30 A.2d 527 (Vt. 1943) . . 11.07n5

Keller v. Bellingham, City of, 600 P.2d 1276 (Wash. 1979) 5.79n7

Kelley v. Clackamas County, 973 P.2d 916 (Or. App. 1999) 6.48n2

Kelley v. John, 75 N.W.2d 713 (Neb. 1956) 6.82n7

Kelley Prop. Dev. Co. v. Lebanon, Town of, 627 A.2d 909 (Conn. 1993) 8.39n2

Kellogg v. Viola, Village of, 227 N.W.2d 55 (Wis. 1975) 4.04n1

Kelly v. Tahoe Regional Planning Agency, 855 P.2d 1027 (Nev. 1993) 2.16n8; 12.02n1

Kelly v. Zoning Bd. of Adjustment, 276 A.2d 569 (Pa. Commw. 1971) 6.37n7

Kelly v. Zoning Bd. of Appeals, 575 A.2d 249 (Conn. App. 1990) 6.46n4

Kempf v. Iowa City, City of, 402 N.W.2d 393 (Iowa 1987) 6.37n3

Kennedy v. Upper Milford Township Zoning Hearing Bd., 779 A.2d 1257 . . . . 6.76n5

Kennedy Park Homes Ass'n v. Lackawanna, City of, 436 F.2d 108 (2d Cir. 1970), *cert. denied*, 401 U.S. 1010 (1971) 7.03n3

Kenner, City of v. Normal Life of La., Inc., 483 So. 2d 903 (La. 1986) 5.08n11

Kenosha County Bd. of Adjustment; State v. , 577 N.W.2d 813 (Wis. 1998) 6.48n4

Kent v. Zoning Bd. of Review, 58 A.2d 623 (R.I. 1948) 6.41n10

Kent Island Joint Venture v. Smith, 452 F. Supp. 455 (D. Md. 1978) 8.43n3

Kentucky Institute for Educ. of the Blind v. Louisville, City of 4.26

Kenyon Peck, Inc. v. Kennedy, 168 S.E.2d 117 (Va. 1969) 11.10n4

Kessler-Allisonville Civic League, Inc. v. Marion County Bd. of Zoning Appeals, 209 N.E.2d 43 (Ind. App. 1965) 6.46n5

Ketchum v. Moses, 17 P.3d 735 . . . . . . 8.47n7

Kewseling v. Baltimore, City of, 151 A.2d 726 (Md. 1959) 5.19n5

Key Biscayne, Village of v. Tesaurus Holdings, Inc., 761 So.2d 397 . . . . 6.66n11

Key West, City of v. R.L.J.S. Corp., 537 So. 2d 641 (Fla. App. 1989) 6.13n1; 9.22n3

Keys Youth Servs. v. Olathe, City of, 52 F. Supp.2d 1284 (D. Kan. 1999) 5.06n5

Keys Youth Servs., Inc. v. Olathe, City of, 38 F. Supp. 2d 914 (D. Kan. 1999) 8.35n7; 8.36n14

Keystone Assocs. v. Moerdler, 224 N.E.2d 700 (N.Y. 1966) 11.34n7

Keystone Bituminous Coal Ass'n v. Benedictus 480 U.S. 470 (1987) 2.53n1

Keystone Bituminous Coal Ass'n v. DeBenedictis 480 U.S. 470 (1987) 2.05n3

Keystone Bituminous Coal Ass'n v. DeBenedictus 480 U.S. 470 (1987) 2.08n3

Keystone Outdoor Advertising v. Commonwealth, 687 A.2d 47 (Pa. Commw. 1996) 5.80n6

Khan v. Zoning Bd. of Appeals, 662 N.E.2d 783 (N.Y. 1996) 6.48n17

Kiges v. St. Paul, City of, 62 N.W.2d 363 (Minn. 1953) 6.21n3

Killington, Ltd. v. State, 668 A.2d 1278 (Vt. 1995) 8.09n3, n6

Kim v. New York, City of, 681 N.E.2d 312 (N.Y. 1997) 2.16n10; 12.07n13

Kimball Laundry Co. v. United States, 338 U.S. 1 (1949) 2.15n3; 8.26n3

Kimberlin v. Topeka, City of, 710 P.2d 682 (Kan. 1985) 5.39n6

Kindred Homes, Inc. v. Dean, 605 S.W.2d 15 (Ky. App. 1979) 3.22n4

King v. Township of East Lampeter 8.46n3

King County v. Central Puget Sound Growth Mgt. Hearings Bd., 979 P.2d 374 (Wash. 1999) 10.07n4

King Enters., Inc. v. Thomas Township, 215 F. Supp.2d 891 . . . . 11.21n1

Kings Cty. Farm Bur. v. Hanford, City of, 270 Cal. Rptr. 650 (Cal. App. 1990) 3.22n5

King's Mill Homeowners Ass'n v. Westminster, City of, 557 P.2d 1186 (Colo. 1976) . 6.31n3; 6.64n2

Kingsley v. Miller, 388 A.2d 357 (R.I. 1978) 8.11n7

Kinnard v. Carrier, 175 So.2d 920 (La. App. 1965) 5.81n12

Kinzli v. Santa Cruz, City of 818 F.2d 1449 . . . . 2.30n11

Kirby Forest Indus. v. United States, 467 U.S. 1 (1984) 2.16n6

Kirk v. Mabis, 246 N.W. 759 (Iowa 1933) 4.10n3

Kirk v. Zoning Hearing Bd., 713 A.2d 1225 (Pa. Commw. 1998) 5.32n9

Kirk v. Zoning Hearing Bd., 713 A.2d 1226 (Pa. Commw. 1998) 12.13n3

Kirkwood, City of v. Sunset Hills, City of, 589 S.W.2d 31 (Mo. App. 1979) 4.37n2

Kirsch v. Prince George's County, 626 A.2d 372 (Md. 1993) 2.48n2; 5.05n2

Kissinger v. Los Angeles, City of, 327 P.2d 10 (1958) 2.23n6

Klaeren v. Lisle, Village of, 737 N.E.2d 1099 . . . 6.70n7

Klawuhn v. Board of Zoning Adjustment, 952 S.W.2d 725 (Mo. App. 1997) 6.48n4

Kleck v. Zoning Bd. of Adjustment, 319 S.W.2d 406 (Tex. App. 1958) 6.56n15

Klein v. Hamilton County Bd. of Zoning Appeals, 716 N.E.2d 268 (Ohio App. 1999) 6.41n13

Klem v. Zoning Hearing Bd., 387 A.2d 667 (Pa. Commw. 1978) 6.61n4

Kletschka v. LeSueur Cty. Bd. of Comm'rs, 277 N.W.2d 404 (Minn. 1979) 6.70n3

Klien v. Township of Lower Macungie, 395 A.2d 609 (Pa. 1978) 5.19n4

Kline v. Harrisburg, City of, 68 A.2d 182 (Pa. 1949) 6.07n2

Knappett v. Locke, 600 P.2d 1257 (Wash. 1979) . . 1.13n1

Knipple v. Geistown Borough Zoning Hearing Bd., 624 A.2d 766 (Pa. Commw. 1993) . . . 6.41n10

Knoeffler v. Mankakating, Town of, 87 F. Supp. 2d 322 . . . . 11.23n5

Knowlton v. Browning-Ferris Indus. of Va., 260 S.E.2d 232 (Va. 1979) 5.79n9

Kohn v. Boulder, City of, 919 P.2d 822 (Colo. App. 1996) 6.13n1

Kollsman v. Los Angeles, City of 737 F.2d 830 (9th Cir. 1984) 8.43n7

Koncelik v. East Hampton, Town of, 781 F. Supp. 152 (E.D.N.Y. 1991) 8.33n10

Kopetzke v. San Mateo Bd. of Supvrs., County of, 396 F. Supp. 1004 (N.D. Cal. 1975) 6.10n4

Kopietz v. Zoning Bd. of Appeals, 535 N.W.2d 910 (Mich. App. 1995) 5.79n2; 6.03n3

Koppel v. Fairway, City of, 371 P.2d 113 (Kan. 1962) 6.69n4; 8.05n2

Korean American Legal Advocacy Found. v. Los Angeles, City of, 28 Cal. Rptr. 2d 530 (Cal. App. 1994) 4.33n2

Korean Buddhist Dae Won Sa Temple v. Zoning Bd. of Appeals, 953 P.2d 1315 (Hawaii 1998) 5.69n2; 6.48n15

Kosalka v. Georgetown, Town of, 752 A.2d 183 . . 6.03n3

Kosinski v. Lawlor, 418 A.2d 66 (Conn. 1979) . . . 8.14n8

Kosinski v. Lawlor 418 A.2d 66 (Conn. 1979) . . . 6.66n9

Kotrich v. DuPage, County of, 166 N.E.2d 601 . . 6.02n2

Kotrich v. DuPage, County of, 166 N.E.2d 601 (Ill. 1960) 6.54n1; 6.55n4

Kottschade v. Rochester, City of, 537 N.W.2d 301 (Minn. App. 1995) 9.16n14

Kovalik v. Planning & Zoning Comm'n 234 A.2d 838 (Conn. 1967) 6.74n2

Kozesnik v. Township of Montgomery 3.14

Kozesnik v. Township of Montgomery, 131 A.2d 1 (N.J. 1957) 5.43n2; 6.66n2

Kozesnsik v. Township of Montgomery, 131 A.2d 1 (N.J. 1957) 4.10n2

Kraft v. Malone, 313 N.W.2d 758 (N.D. 1981) . . . 8.21n3

Krahl v. Nine Mile Creek Watershed Dist., 283 N.W.2d 538 (Minn. 1979) 2.37n5

Krahl v. Nine Mile Creek Watershed Dist. 283 N.W.2d 538 (Minn. 1979) 12.09n6

Kraiser v. Horsham Twp., 455 A.2d 782 (Pa. Commw. 1983) 8.22n1

Kramer v. Board of Adjustment, 212 A.2d 153 (N.J. 1965) 6.73n3

Krause v. Royal Oak, City of, 160 N.W.2d 769 (Mich. App. 1968) 2.36n6; 2.46n6; 5.02n3

Krause v. Royal Oak, City of 160 N.W.2d 769 (Mich. App. 1968) 5.18n2

Krawski v. Planning & Zoning Comm'n, 575 A.2d 1036 (Conn. App. 1990) 9.06n2

Kremer v. Plainfield, City of, 244 A.2d 335 (N.J. 1968) 6.74n11

Kriener v. Turkey Valley Community School Dist., 212 N.W.2d 526 (Iowa 1973) 4.04n1

Kristensen v. Eugene Planning Comm'n, City of, 544 P.2d 591 (Or. App. 1976) 6.58n5

Kroll v. Steere, 759 A.2d 541 . . . . 11.18n7

Kropf v. Sterling Heights, City of 215 N.W.2d 179 (Mich. 1974) 7.23n2

Krughoff v. Naperville, City of, 369 N.E.2d 892 (Ill. 1977) 9.19n2

Krupp v. Breckenridge Sanitation Dist., 1 P.3d 178 (Colo. App. 1999) 9.22n6

Krupp v. Breckenridge Sanitation Dist., 19 P.3d 687 . . . . 9.22n9

KSC Realty Trust v. Freedom, Town of, 772 A.2d 321 . . . . 5.19n3

Kucera v. Liza, 69 Cal. Rptr. 2d 582 (Cal. App. 1997) 11.05n1; 12.02n2

Kuehne v. Town Council, 72 A.2d 474 (Conn. 1950) 6.30n3

Kunimoto v. Kawakami, 545 P.2d 684 (Haw. 1976) 4.27n5

Kunz & Co. v. State, 913 P.2d 765 (Utah App. 1996) 11.06n5

Kuriakuz v. West Bloomfield Township, 492 N.W.2d 797 (Mich. App. 1992) 8.23n16

Kurlanski v. Portland Yacht Club, 782 A.2d 783 . . 6.66n11

Kuzinich v. Santa Clara, County of, 689 F.2d 1345 (9th Cir. 1982) 2.47n3; 8.35n4

L

L & W Outdoor Adv. Co. v. State, 539 N.E.2d 497 (Ind. App. 1989) 11.06n5

La Mesa v. Tweed & Gambrell Planning Mill, 304 P.2d 803 (Cal. App. 1957) 5.86n1

La Mesa, City of v. Tweed & Gambrell Planing Mill, 304 P.2d 803 (Cal. App. 1956) 5.86n7

L.A. Ray Realty v. Town Council, 603 A.2d 311 (R.I. 1992) 6.83n1

L.A. Ray Realty v. Town Council, 698 A.2d 202 (R.I. 1997) 8.23n10

La Salle Nat'l Bank v. Chicago, City of 125 N.E.2d 609 (Ill. 1955) 5.73n1

LaBonta v. Waterville, City of, 528 A.2d 1262 (Me. 1987) 6.33n6

Lackman v. Hall, 364 A.2d 1244 (Del. Ch. 1976) 10.15n8

Ladue, City of v. Gilleo, 114 S. Ct. 2038 (1994) . . 2.50n7

Ladue, City of v. Gilleo 512 U.S. 43 (1994) 11.15n1

Lady J Lingerie, Inc. v. Jacksonville, City of, 176 F.3d 1358 (11th Cir. 1999) 6.57, n2

Lafayette, City of v. East Bay Mun. Utility Dist., 20 Cal. Rptr. 2d 658 (Cal. App. 1993) . . . 4.40n2

Lafayette, City of v. Louisiana Power & Light Co
. . . . 5.50
Lafayette Park Baptist Church v. Board of Adjustment
(II), 599 S.W.2d 61 (Mo. App. 1980) . . . . . .
11.32n7; 11.34n6; 11.36n1
Lafayette Park Baptist Church v. Scott (I) . . . . .
11.32
Lafayette Park Baptist Church v. Scott (I) 553 S.W.2d
856 (Mo. App. 1977) 11.36n1
Lage v. Zoning Bd. of Appeals, 172 A.2d 911 (Conn.
1961) 6.73n1
Lake Bluff Housing Partners v. S. Milwaukee, City of,
540 N.W.2d 189 (Wis. 1995) 8.14n5
Lake Bluff Housing Partners v. South Milwaukee,
City of, 525 N.W.2d 59 (Wis. App. 1994) . . . .
6.16n4
Lake Charles Harbor & Term. Dist. v. Calcasieu
Parish Police Jury, 613 So. 2d 1031 (La. App.
1993) 4.28n1
Lake City Corp. v. Mequon, City of, 558 N.W.2d 100
(Wis. 1997) 9.03n4
Lake Country Estates, Inc. v. Tahoe Regional Plan-
ning Agency 440 U.S. 391 (1979) 8.35n3
Lake Cty. v. Truett, 758 S.W.2d 529 (Tenn. App.
1988) 9.08n4
Lake Forest Chateau v. Lake Forest, City of, 549
N.E.2d 336 (Ill. 1990) 8.26n1
Lake Intervale Homes, Inc. v. Parsippany-Troy Hills,
147 A.2d 28 (N.J. 1958) 9.07n2
Lake Lucerne Civic Ass'n v. Dolphin Stadium Corp.,
878 F.2d 1360 (11th Cir. 1989) 8.45n3
Lake Naciemento Ranch Co. v. San Luis Obispo,
County of, 841 F.2d 772 (9th Cir. 1987) . . . .
8.33n4
Lake Nacimiento Ranch Co. v. San Luis Obispo,
County of, 841 F.2d 872 (9th Cir. 1987) . . . .
8.31n5
Lake Shore Drive Baptist Church v. Bayside Bd. of
Trustees, Village of, 108 N.W.2d 288 (Wis. 1961)
. . . . 5.68n3
Lake Wales v. Lamar Adv. Ass'n, 414 So. 2d 1030
(Fla. 1982) 11.09n2
Lake Wales, City of v. Lamar Adv. Ass'n, 414 So. 2d
1030 (Fla. 1982) 11.05n1
Lakeland Bluff v. Will, County of, 252 N.E.2d 765
(Ill. App. 1969) 5.23n2
Lakeland Lounge of Jackson, Inc. v. Jackson, City of,
973 F.2d 1255 (5th Cir. 1992) . . . 5.63n4, n5,
n15
Lakewood v. Olson, 2001 Wash. App. Lexis 2475
. . . . 5.81n13
Lakewood, City of v. Colfax Unlimited Ass'n, 634
P.2d 52 (Colo. 1981) 11.19n7
Lakewood Dev. Co. v. Oklahoma City, 534 P.2d 23
(Okla. App. 1975) 2.36n2; 5.35n2

Lakewood Estates, Inc. v. Deerfield Twp. Zoning Bd.
of Appeals, 194 N.W.2d 511 (Mich. App. 1977)
. . . . 5.25n2
Lakewood, Ohio Congregation of Jehovah's Witnesses, Inc. v. Lakewood, City of, 699 F.2d 303
(6th Cir. 1983) 5.69n2
Lamar Adv. Assocs. of E. Fla. v. Daytona Beach, City
of, 450 So. 2d 1145 (Fla. App. 1984) . . . . . .
5.84n6; 5.86n5
Lamar Adv. of South Ga., Inc. v. Albany, City of, 389
S.E.2d 216 (Ga. 1990) 5.85n4
Lamar Corp. v. Twin Falls, City of, 981 P.2d 1146
(Idaho 1999) 6.57n4
Lamar-Orlando Outdoor Adv. v. Ormond Beach, City
of, 415 So. 2d 1312 (Fla. App. 1982) . . . . . .
11.06n6
Lamb v. Monroe, City of, 99 N.W.2d 566 (Mich.
1959) 5.43n2
Lambros, Inc. v. Ocean Ridge, Town of, 392 So. 2d
993 (Fla. 1981) 5.37n6
Lampton v. Pinaire 610 S.W.2d 915 (Ky. 1980) . .
9.16n9
Lancaster, County of v. Mecklenburg County, 434
S.E.2d 604 (N.C. 1993) 6.68n3
Land Assocs. v. Metropolitan Airport Auth., 547 F.
Supp. 1128 (M.D. Tenn. 1982) 5.39n6
Land Mark Land Co., Inc. v. City & County of
Denver, 728 P.2d 1281 (Colo. 1986) . . 12.02n2
Land Use Planning After Dolan v. Tigard, City of, 21
Colum. J. Envtl. L. 103 (1996)
Land/Vest Props., Inc. v. Plainfield, Town of, 379
A.2d 200 (N.H. 1977) 9.16n8
Landau v. City Council, 767 P.2d 1290 (Kan. 1989)
. . . . 2.37n7
Landau Adv. Co. v. Zoning Bd. of Adjustment, 128
A.2d 559 (Pa. 1957) 11.09n2
Landgate, Inc. v. California Coastal Comm'n, 953
P.2d 1188 (Cal. 1998) 2.22n9
Landmark Land Co. v. Buchanan, 874 F.2d 717 (10th
Cir. 1989) 2.30n13, n14; 2.32n5; 2.42n10
Landmark Land Co. v. City & County of Denver, 728
P.2d 1281 (Colo. 1986) 5.74n2
Landmark Universal, Inc. v. Pitkin County Bd. of
Adjustment, 579 P.2d 1184 (Colo. App. 1978)
. . . . 6.50n6
Landmarks Holding Corp. v. Bermant, 664 F.2d 891
(2d Cir. 1981) 8.46n7
Landover Books, Inc. v. Prince George's Cty., 566
A.2d 792 (Md. App. 1989) 6.57n2
Lane County v. Land Conserv. & Dev. Comm'n, 942
P.2d 278 (Or 1997) 12.12n3
Lang v. Zoning Bd. of Adjustment, 733 A.2d 464 (N.J.
1999) 6.48n10, n14
Lange v. Woodway, Town of, 483 P.2d 116 (Wash.
1971) 8.10n1

Langer v. Planning & Zoning Comm'n, 313 A.2d 44 (Conn. 1972) 6.55n2

Language in Parker v. Brown 5.53

Lanmar Corp. v. Rendine, 811 F. Supp. 47 (D.R.I. 1993) 8.33n9

Lanner v. Board of Appeal, 202 N.E.2d 777 (Mass. 1964) 6.31n3

Lapid Laurel, L.L.C. v. Zoning Bd. of Adjustment, 284 F.3d 442 . . . . 5.12n8; 5.13n1

Largo, Town of v. Imperial Homes Corp., 309 So. 2d 571 (Fla. App. 1975) 6.16n5

Larkin v. Grendel's Den, Inc. 459 U.S. 116 (1982) 5.69n7

Larkin v. Michigan Dep't of Soc. Servs., State of, 89 F.3d 295 (6th Cir. 1996) 5.15n2

Larkin Co. v. Schwab, 151 N.E. 637 (N.Y. 1926) 6.02n3

Larsen v. Zoning Bd. of Adjustment, 672 A.2d 286 (Pa. 1996) 6.41n3; 6.44n3

Larsen v. Zoning Comm'n, 217 A.2d 715 (Conn. 1966) 5.31n4

Larson; State v. , 195 N.W.2d 180 (Minn. 1972) . . 5.23n3

LaRue v. Township of East Brunswick, 172 A.2d 691 (N.J. App. Div. 1961) 6.54n4

Las Cruces, City of v. Huerta, 692 P.2d 1331 (N.M. App. 1984) 6.57n13

Las Vegas, City of v. 1017 S. Main Corp., 885 P.2d 552 (Nev. 1994) 6.05n14

Las Virgnenes Homeowners Fed'n, Inc. v. Los Angeles, County of, 223 Cal. Rptr. 18 (Cal. App. 1986) 6.33n6

LaSalle Nat'l Bank v. Chicago, City of, 125 N.E.2d 609 (Ill. 1955) 5.74n3

LaSalle Nat'l Bank v. Cook, County of . . . 2.37

LaSalle Nat'l Bank v. Cook, County of, 340 N.E.2d 79 (Ill. 1975) 5.39n6

LaSalle Nat'l Bank v. Cook, County of, 340 N.E.2d 79 (Ill. App. 1975) 4.43n4

LaSalle Nat'l Bank v. DuPage, County of, 777 F.2d 377 (7th Cir. 1985) 5.54n3

LaSalle Nat'l Bank v. Evanston, City of, 312 N.E.2d 625 (Ill. 1974) 5.74n3

LaSalle Nat'l Bank v. Highland Park, City of, 189 N.E.2d 302 (Ill. 1963) 5.32n3

LaSalle Nat'l Bank v. Lake, County of, 325 N.E.2d 105 (Ill. App. 1975) 9.28n3

LaTrieste Restaurant v. Port Chester, Village of, 188 F.3d 65 (2d Cir. 1999) 2.47n3

Latrobe Speedway v. Zoning Hearing Bd., 720 A.2d 1197 (Pa. 1998) 5.81n12

Latrobe Speedway, Inc. v. Zoning Hearing Bd., 720 A.2d 127 (Pa. 1998) 5.81n5, n7

Lauderdale-by-the-Sea, Town of v. Meretsky, 773 So.2d 1245 . . . . 6.17n1

Lauderdale County Bd. of Educ. v. Alexander, 110 So. 2d 911 (Ala. 1959) 4.35n1

Lauricella v. Planning & Zoning Bd., 342 A.2d 374 (Conn. Sup. 1974) 12.05n3

Laux v. Chapin Land Assocs., Inc., 550 N.E.2d 100 (Ind. App. 1990) 12.11n7

LaVallee v. Britt, 383 A.2d 709 (N.H. 1978) 6.52n1

Lavey v. Two Rivers, City of, 171 F.3d 1110 (7th Cir. 1999) 11.13n3; 11.17n4; 11.19n7, n16

Lawler v. Redding, City of, 9 Cal. Rptr. 2d 392 (Cal. App. 1992) 4.40n2

Lawrence v. Richards, 88 A. 92 (Me. 1913) 10.10n2

Lawrence Preservation Alliance, Inc. v. Allen Realty, Inc., 819 P.2d 138 (Kan. App. 1991) . . 6.69n4

Lawrence Preservation Alliance, Inc. v. Allen Realty, Inc. (II), 819 P.2d 138 (Kan. App. 1991) 11.34n7

Layne v. Zoning Bd. of Adjustment, 460 A.2d 1088 (Pa. Commw. 1983) 5.36n9

Lazarus v. Northbrook, Village of, 199 N.E.2d 797 (Ill. 1964) 6.56n8

Leadville, City of v. Rood, 600 P.2d 62 (Colo. 1979) 5.71n2

League of Women Voters of Appleton, Inc. v. Outagamie County, 334 N.W.2d 887 (Wis. 1983) . . . 8.11n16

Leatherbury v. Gaylord Fuel Corp., 347 A.2d 826 (Md. 1975) 4.03n1

Leavitt v. Jefferson County, 875 P.2d 681 (Wash. App. 1994) 8.13n6

Lechner v. Billings, City of, 797 P.2d 191 (Mont. 1990) 9.21n3

LeClair v. Hart, 800 F.2d 692 (7th Cir. 1986) . . . 8.36n12

Leda Lanes Realty, Inc. v. Nashua, City of, 293 A.2d 320 (N.H. 1972) 6.66n11

Ledbetter v. Roberts, 98 S.E.2d 654 (Ga. App. 1957) 8.13n2

Lee v. District of Columbia Zoning Comm'n, 411 A.2d 635 (D.C. App. 1980) . . . 6.29n5; 6.30n2

Lee v. Maryland Nat'l Capital Park & Plan. Comm'n, 668 A.2d 980 (Md. App. 1995) 9.09n2

Lee v. Monterrey Park, City of, 219 Cal. Rptr. 309 (Cal. App. 1985) 10.06n5

Lee County v. New Testament Baptist Church, 507 So. 2d 626 (Fla. App. 1987) 9.16n8

Lee Cty. v. Morales, 557 So. 2d 652 (Fla. App. 1990) 6.37n15

Lehman v. Louisville, City of, 857 P.2d 455 (Colo. App. 1993) 8.23n18

Leisure Time Cruise Corp. v. Barnstable, Town of, 62 F. Supp.2d 202 (D. Mass 1999) 4.41n1

Lemir Realty Corp. v. Larkin, 181 N.E.2d 407 (N.Y. 1962) 6.55n7

Lenette Realty & Inv. Co. v. Chesterfield, City of, 35 S.W.3d 399 . . . . 6.25n4; 8.18n2

Lentine v. St. George, Town of, 599 A.2d 76 (Me. 1991) 6.05n7

Leonard v. Bothell, City of, 557 P.2d 1306 (Wash. 1976) 6.82n7

Leonard v. Broomfield, Town of, 666 N.E.2d 1300 (Mass. 1996) 12.09n11

Leonardini v. Shell Oil Co., 264 Cal. Rptr. 883 (Cal. App. 1989) 8.46n10

Lerner v. Islip, Town of, 272 F. Supp. 664 (E.D.N.Y. 1967) 8.44n7

Leroy Land Co. v. Tahoe Regional Planning Agency, 939 F.2d 696 (9th Cir. 1991) 9.13n2

Lesher Communications, Inc. v. Walnut Creek, City of, 262 Cal. Rptr. 337 (Cal. App. 1989) 6.83n5

Lesher Communications, Inc. v. Walnut Creek, City of, 802 P.2d 317 (Cal. 1990) 3.18n1

Leslie v. Toledo, City of, 423 N.E.2d 123 (Ohio 1981) 5.35n2

Lester v. Winthrop, Town of, 939 P.2d 1237 (Wash. App. 1997) 2.22n2

Letourneau, In re , 726 A.2d 31 (Vt. 1998) 5.71n2

Leverett v. Limon, Town of, 567 F. Supp. 471 (D. Colo. 1983) 2.42n9

Levin v. King, 648 N.E.2d 1108 (Ill. App. 1995) . 8.46n10

Levin v. Township of Parsippany-Troy Hills, 411 A.2d 704 (N.J.1980) 6.04n2

Levinson v. Montgomery County, 620 A.2d 961 (Md. App. 1993) 5.20n2

Levitt v. Incorporated Village of Sands Point, 160 N.E.2d 501 . . . . 5.31n2

Levitt v. Incorporated Village of Sands Point, 174 N.Y.S.2d 283 (Sup. Ct. 1958) 6.31n4

Lewis v. Atlantic Beach, City of, 467 So. 2d 751 (Fla. App. 1985) 5.81n3

Lewis v. Jackson, City of, 184 So. 2d 384 (Miss. 1966) 6.31n2

Lewis v. Swan, 716 A.2d 127 (Conn. App. 1998) 8.03n1

Lewiston, City of v. Knieriem, 685 P.2d 821 (Idaho 1984) 5.23n1

Lexington-Fayette Urban County Gov't v. Schneider, 849 S.W.2d 557 (Ky. App. 1993) 9.16n9

Liberty v. California Coastal Comm'n, 170 Cal. Rptr. 247 (Cal. App. 1981) 9.16n10

Liberty Nat'l Bank of Chicago v. Chicago, City of, 139 N.E.2d 235 (Ill. 1957) 6.35n1

Libra Group, Inc. v. State, 805 P.2d 409 (Ariz. App. 1991) 11.06n6

Licari v. Ferruzzi, 22 F.3d 344 . . . . . . 2.42n10

License of (see name of party)

L.I.F.E. Comm. v. Lodi, City of, 262 Cal. Rptr. 166 (Cal. App. 1989) 6.83n5

Life Concepts, Inc. v. Harden, 562 So. 2d 726 (Fla. App. 1990) 6.05n6

Life of the Land v. Land Use Comm'n, 594 P.2d 1079 (Haw. 1979) 8.06n2

Lim v. Long Beach, City of, 217 F.3d 1050 . . . . . 5.63n9

Limley v. Zoning Hearing Bd., 625 A.2d 54 (Pa. 1993) 5.79n9

Lince v. Bremerton, City of, 607 P.2d 329 (Wash. App. 1980) 6.83n1

Lincoln v. Zoning Bd. of Review, 201 A.2d 482 (R.I. 1964) 6.48n16

Lincoln City Chamber of Commerce v. Lincoln City, City of, 991 P.2d 1080 (Or. App. 1999) 9.14n2

Lincoln County v. Johnson 257 N.W.2d 453 (S.D. 1977) 4.38n6

Lincoln Heights Ass'n v. Township of Cranford Planning Bd., 714 A.2d 995 (N.J.L. Div. 1998) 6.74n6

Lindborg/Dahl Invs., Inc. v. Garden Grove, City of, 225 Cal. Rptr. 154 (Cal. App. 1986) . . . 6.66n11

Lindsay v. San Antonio, City of, 821 F.2d 1103 (5th Cir. 1987) 11.20n3

Lindsey v. Normet 2.45

Lindsey Creek Area Civic Ass'n v. Consolidated Gov't of Columbus, 292 S.E.2d 61 (Ga. 1982) 6.72n2; 8.06n1

Lindteigen v. Bismarck, City of, 565 N.W.2d 47 (N.D. 1997) 6.56n15

Lindy Homes, Inc. v. Sabatini, 453 A.2d 972 (Pa. 1982) 8.14n1

Linmark Assocs. v. Township of Willingboro 11.15n1

Linmark Assocs. v. Township of Willingboro 431 U.S. 85 (1977) 11.22n1

Linn County v. Hiawatha, City of, 311 N.W.2d 95 (Iowa 1981) 5.08n7

Lionel's Appliance Center, Inc. v. Citta. 383 A.2d 773 (N.J.L. Div. 1978) 6.66n4

Lionshead in Home Bldrs. League of S. Jersey, Inc. v. Township of Berlin 5.29

Lionshead Lake, Inc. v. Wayne Twp 5.29

Lionshead Woods Corp. v. Kaplan Bros., 595 A.2d 568 (N.J.L. Div. 1991) 6.05n22

Lisa's Party City, Inc. v. Henrietta, Town of, 185 F.3d 12 (2d Cir. 1999) 2.47n4

Lithonia Asphalt Co. v. Hall Cty. Planning Comm'n, 364 S.E.2d 860 (Ga. 1988) 5.41n2

Little v. Board of County Comm'rs, 631 P.2d 1282 (Mont. 1981) 3.16n5

Little v. Lawrenceville, City of, 528 S.E.2d 515 . . 6.74n15

Little v. Winborn, 518 N.W.2d 384 (Iowa 1994) . . 6.29n11

Little Falls Twp. v. Bardin, 414 A.2d 559 (N.J. 1979) 4.30n4

Little Joseph Realty, Inc. v. Babylon, Town of, 363 N.E.2d 1163 (N.Y. 1977) 4.13n2; 8.15n8

Littlefield v. Afton, City of, 785 F.2d 596 (8th Cir. 1986) 8.33n2

Littlefield v. Afton, City of, 785 F.2d 598 (8th Cir. 1986) 2.31n3

Litton Int'l Dev. Co. v. Simi Valley, City of, 616 F. Supp. 275 (C.D. Cal. 1985) 7.03n5

Livingston Builders, Inc. v. Township of Livingston, 707 A.2d 186 (N.J. App. Div.1998) . . . 7.13n1

Livingston Downs Racing Ass'n v. Jefferson Downs Corp., 192 F.Supp.2d 519 . . . . 8.46n7

Livingston Rock & Gravel Co. v. Los Angeles, County of, 272 P.2d 4 (Cal. 1954) . . . 8.16n9

Livonia, City of v. Department of Social Servs., 333 N.W.2d 151 (Mich. App. 1983) 5.10n4

Livonia, City of v. Department of Social Servs., 378 N.W.2d 402 (Mich. 1985) 4.25n1

LLEH, Inc. v. Wichita Falls, City of, 289 F.3d 359 . . . . 5.63n4

Lloyd E. Clarke, Inc. v. Bettendorf, City of, 158 N.W.2d 125 (Iowa 1968) 9.21n2

Lobiondo v. Schwartz, 733 A.2d 516 (N.J. App. Div. 1999) 8.46n9

Lockary v. Kayfetz, 917 F.2d 1150 (9th Cir. 1990) 6.10n4; 6.11n6

Loh v. Town Plan & Zoning Comm'n, 282 A.2d 894 (Conn. 1971) 6.61n5

Lomarch Corp. v. Mayor & Common Council 237 A.2d 881 (N.J. 1968) 10.15n4

Lomarch in Kingston E. Realty Co. v. State 330 A.2d 40 (N.J. App. Div. 1975) 10.15n8

Londono v. Turkey Creek, 609 So. 2d 14 (Fla. 1992) 8.46n7

Lone v. Montgomery County, 584 A.2d 142 (Md. App. 1991) 5.84n7

Lone v. Montgomery Cty., 584 A.2d 142 (Md. App. 1991) 5.86n1

Lone Star Indus., Inc. v. Department of Transp., 671 P.2d 511 (Kan. 1983) 3.21n2

Long Beach Equities, Inc. v. Superior Court of Ventura County, 282 Cal. Rptr. 877 (Cal. App. 1991) 2.16n3

Long Beach Equities, Inc. v. Ventura, County of, 282 Cal. Rptr. 877 (Cal. App. 1991) 8.09n1

Long Beachfront Equities, Inc. v. Ventura, County of, 282 Cal. Rptr. 877 (Cal. App. 1991) . . 10.06n1

Long Island Bd. of Realtors v. Incorporated Village of Massapequa Park 277 F.3d 622 . . . . 11.18n8

Long, State ex rel. v. Cardington, Village of, 748 N.E.2d 58 . . . . 6.76n6

Long, State ex rel. v. Council of Cardington, 748 N.E.2d 58 . . . . 8.14n11

Longwell v. Hodge, 297 S.E.2d 820 (W. Va. 1982) 4.33n2

Lopes v. Peabody, City of, 629 N.E.2d 1312 (Mass. 1994) 12.07n8

Lopes v. Peabody, City of, 718 N.E.2d 846 (Mass. 1999) 8.26n3

Loreto Dev. Co., Inc. v. Chardon, Village of, 695 N.E.2d 1151 (Ohio App. 1996) 5.36n6

Loretto v. Teleproinpter Manhattan CATV Corp., 458 U.S. 419 (1982) 2.24n6

Loretto v. Teleprompter Manhattan CATV Corp. 458 U.S. 419 (1982) 2.03n1

Lorillard Tobacco Co. v. Reilly, 533 U.S. 525 . . . 2.50n3

Lorillard Tobacco Co. v. Reilly 533 U.S. 525 . . . 11.16n1

Los Altos, City of v. Barnes, 5 Cal. Rptr.2d 77 (Cal. App. 1992) 6.05n12

Los Altos Hills, Town of v. Adobe Creek Props., Inc 5.37

Los Altos Hills, Town of v. Adobe Creek Props., Inc., 108 Cal. Rptr. 271 (Cal. App. 1973) . . 7.24n1

Los Angeles v. State Dep't of Health, 133 Cal. Rptr. 771 (Cal. App. 1976) 5.10n4

Los Angeles, City of v. Alameda Books, Inc. 5.62n1

Los Angeles, City of v. Gage 274 P.2d 34 (Cal. App. 1954) 5.84n3

Los Angeles, City of v. State, 187 Cal. Rptr. 893 (Cal. App. 1982) 4.25n5

Los Angeles, County of v. Los Angeles, City of, 28 Cal. Rptr. 32 (Cal. App. 1963) 4.28n1

Louisville, City of v. Fiscal Court, 621 S.W.2d 219 (Ky. 1981) 6.23n5

Louisville, City of v. McDonald, 470 S.W.2d 173 (Ky. 1971) 6.26n2

Loulis v. Parrott, 695 A.2d 1040 (Conn. 1997) . . . 8.11n4

Loundsbury v. Keene, City of, 453 A.2d 1278 (N.H. 1982) 5.85n2

Loup-Miller Constr. Co. v. City & County of Denver, 676 P.2d 1170 (Colo. 1984) 9.22n1

Love v. Board of City Comm'rs, 671 P.2d 471 (Idaho 1983) 6.33n5

Love Church v. Evanston, City of, 671 F. Supp. 508 (N.D. Ill. 1987) 5.68n2

Loveladies Harbor, Inc. v. United States, 28 F.3d 1171 (Fed. Cir. 1994) 2.19n4; 12.07n12

Loveland v. Orem City Corp., 746 P.2d 763 (Utah 1987) 8.23n5

Loveless v. Yantis, 513 P.2d 1023 (Wash. 1973) . .
9.06n2
Lovely v. Zoning Bd. of Appeals, 259 A.2d 666 (Me.
1969) 6.44n3; 6.45n7
Low v. Madison, Town of, 60 A.2d 774 (Conn. 1948)
. . . . 6.74n9
Lowell v. M & N Mobile Home Park, 916 S.W.2d 95
(Ark. 1996) 8.13n10
Loyola Fed. Sav. & Loan Ass'n v. Buschman, 176
A.2d 355 (Md. 1961) 5.74n2
Ltd. Partnership v. District of Columbia, 198 F.3d 874
(D.C. Cir. 1999) 2.19n3
Lubavitch Chabad House of Ill., Inc. v. Evanston, City
of, 445 N.E.2d 343 (Ill. App. 1982) . . 6.57n14
Lubbock, City of v. Austin, 628 S.W.2d 49 (Tex.
1982) 4.34n1
Lubbock Poster Co. v. Lubbock, City of, 569 S.W.2d
935 (Tex. Civ. App. 1978) . . . 5.84n6; 5.86n5
Lubelle v. Rochester Preserv. Bd., 551 N.Y.S.2d 127
(App. Div. 1990) 11.35n3
Lucas v. South Carolina Coastal Comm'n 505 U.S.
1003 (1992) 12.15n1
Lucas v. South Carolina Coastal Council, 503 U.S.
1003 (1992) 2.24n6
Lucas v. South Carolina Coastal Council, 505 U.S.
1003 (1992) 2.28n5; 2.30n10
Lucas v. South Carolina Coastal Council, 52 Md. L.
Rev. 162 (1993)
Lucas v. South Carolina Coastal Council, Colloquium,
10 Pace Envt'l L. Rev. 1 (1992)
Lucas v. South Carolina Coastal Council 505 U.S.
1003 (1992) 2.09n1; 4.02n5
Lucas Valley Homeowners Ass'n v. Marin, County of,
284 Cal. Rptr. 427 (Cal. App. 1991) . . 5.68n4
Lucky Stores, Inc. v. Board of Montgomery County,
312 A.2d 758 (Md. 1973) 5.47n7
Luczynski v. Temple, 497 A.2d 211 (N.J. Ch. Div.
1985) 5.23n4
Ludewig; State v. , 187 N.E.2d 170 (Ohio App. 1962)
. . . . 8.14n5
Ludlow, State ex rel. v. Guffey, 306 S.W.2d 552 (Mo.
1957) 6.55n3
Ludwig v. Superior Court, 43 Cal. Rptr.2d 350 (Cal.
App. 1995) 8.47n1
Luery v. Zoning Bd. of City of Stamford, 187 A.2d
247 (Conn. 1962) 6.29n9
Luger v. Brunsville, City of, 295 N.W.2d 609 (Minn.
1980) 6.39n1
Lum Yip Kee, Ltd. v. City & Cty. of Honolulu, 767
P.2d 815 (Hawaii 1989) 6.37n7, n11
Lutheran Church in Am. v. New York, City of 316
N.E.2d 305 (N.Y. 1974) 11.37n1
Lutheran Day Care v. Snohomish Cty., 829 P.2d 746
(Wash. 1992) 8.23n9; 8.31n9

Lutheran High School Ass'n v. Farmington Hills, City
of, 381 N.W.2d 417 (Mich. App. 1986) . . . . .
5.68n1
Lutz v. Longview, City of, 520 P.2d 1374 (Wash.
1974) 6.61n3
Luxembourg Group v. Snohomish County, 887 P.2d
446 . . . . 9.16n5
Luxembourg Group, Inc. v. Snohomish County, 887
P.2d 446 (Wash. App. 1995) 9.13n4
Lynch v. Household Fin. Corp., 405 U.S. 538 (1972)
. . . . 8.29n7
Lynch v. Oklahoma City, City of, 629 P.2d 1289
(Okla. App. 1981) 8.19n4
Lyons, Town of v. Bashor, 867 P.2d 159 (Colo. App.
1993) 5.78n4; 5.81n13
Lysander, Town of v. Hafner, 759 N.E.2d 356 . . .
12.10n7
Lytle Co. v. Clark, 491 F.2d 834 (10th Cir. 1974)
. . . . 5.81n8

M

M.A. Kravitz Co., In re , 460 A.2d 1075 (Pa. 1983)
. . . . 7.21n1
Mac-Rich Realty Constr., Inc. v. Planning Bd., 341
N.E.2d 916 (Mass. App. 1976) 9.09n13
MacDonald v. Board of County Comm'rs, 210 A.2d
325 (Md. 1965) 6.31n1
Macedonian Orthodox Church v. Planning Bd., 636
A.2d 96 (N.J. App. Div. 1994) 6.57n15
Macene v. MJW, Inc., 951 F.2d 700 (6th Cir. 1991)
. . . . 8.33n10
Macer v. New Orleans, City of 516 F.2d 1051 (5th Cir.
1975) 11.35n1
MacGibbon v. Board of Appeals, 340 N.E.2d 487
(Mass. 1976) 12.05n2
Mack T. Anderson Ins. Agency, Inc. v. Belgrade, City
of, 803 P.2d 648 (Mont. 1990) 5.23n1
MacKenzie v. Rockledge, City of, 920 F.2d 1554
(11th Cir. 1991) 2.40n6
MacLean v. Zoning Bd. of Adjustment, 185 A.2d 533
(Pa. 1962) 6.45n7
MacLeod v. Santa Clara, County of, 749 F.2d 541 (9th
Cir. 1984) 2.16n3
MacNamara v. County Council, 738 F. Supp. 134 (D.
Del.), aff'd 8.44n6
Macon Ass'n for Retarded Citizens v. Macon-Bibb
County Planning & Zoning Comm'n, 314 S.E.2d
218 (Ga.) 5.08n4; 5.10n1
Macon-Bibb County Hospital Auth. v. Madison, 420
S.E.2d 586 (Ga. App. 1992) 4.35n1
Macone v. Wakefield, Town of, 277 F.3d 1 . . . .
7.03n5; 7.05n6
MacQueen, State ex rel. v. Dunbar, City of, 278
S.E.2d 636 (W. Va. 1981) 6.82n1

Macri v. King County, 126 F.3d 1125 (9th Cir. 1997) 2.40n3

Madigan, State Liquor Control Boards v. Local Government

Madison, City of v. Clarke, 288 N.W.2d 312 (S.D. 1980) 6.03n1

Magnano v. Zoning Bd. of Appeals, 449 A.2d 148 (Conn. 1982) 5.81n3, n12

Maher v. New Orleans, City of, 516 F.2d 1051 . . 11.29n3

Maher v. New Orleans, City of 516 F.2d 1051 . . . 11.32n6

Maher v. Town Planning & Zoning Comm'n, 226 A.2d 397 (Conn. 1967) 8.13n12

Mahoney v. Walter, 205 S.E.2d 692 (W. Va. 1974) 4.12n6

Mahony v. Township of Hampton, 651 A.2d 525 (Pa. 1994) 5.36n1

Maider v. Dover, Town of, 306 N.E.2d 274 (Mass. App. 1974) 2.36n6

Maine v. Thiboutot 448 U.S. 1 (1980) . . . 8.29n4

Major Media of the Southeast, Inc. v. Raleigh, City of, 621 F. Supp. 1446 (E.D.N.C. 1985) . . . 5.86n2

Major Media of the Southeast, Inc. v. Raleigh, City of, 792 F.2d 1269 (4th Cir. 1986) . . . 11.19n4, n7, n13, n14

Malafronte v. Planning & Zoning Bd., 230 A.2d 606 (Conn. 1967) 6.30n1

Maldini v. Ambro, 330 N.E.2d 403 (N.Y.) 7.10n1

Mall Props. v. Marsh, 672 F. Supp. 561 (D. Mass. 1987) 12.06n7

Malone, In re , 592 F. Supp. 1135 (E.D. Mo. 1984) 7.05n2

Malone, In re , 592 F. Supp. 1135 (E.D. Mo. 1984), *aff'd mem.,* 794 F.2d 680 (8th Cir. 1986) 7.03n5; 7.04n4

Maloy v. Lewisville, City of, 848 S.W.2d 380 (Tex. App. 1993) 5.65n5

Manalapan Realty v. Tp. Committee, 658 A.2d 1230 (N.J. 1995) 3.16n5

Manalapan Realty, L.P. v. Township Comm., 658 A.2d 1230 (N.J. 1995) 3.18n1; 5.36n1

Manassas, City of v. Rosson, 294 S.E.2d 799 (Va.) 5.20n2

Manchester, Town of v. Phillips 180 N.E.2d 333 (Mass. 1962) 5.22n1

Manhattan Club v. Landmarks Preservation Comm'n, 273 N.Y.S.2d 848 (Sup. Ct. 1966) . . . 11.37n2

Manhattan Sepulveda, Ltd. v. Manhattan Beach, City of, 27 Cal. Rptr. 2d 565 (Cal. App. 1994) 5.80n11

Manistee Town Center v. Glendale, City of, 227 F.3d 1090 . . . . 8.46n3

Mann v. Mack, 202 Cal. Rptr. 296 (Cal. App. 1984) 6.05n16

Mann Media, Inc. v. Randolph County Planning Bd., 565 S.E.2d 9 . . . . 6.56n10

Manning v. East Tawas, City of, 593 N.W.2d 649 (Mich. App. 1999) 6.76n15

Manookian v. Blaine County, 735 P.2d 1008 (Idaho 1987) 6.74n3

Manor Dev. Corp. v. Conservation Comm'n, 433 A.2d 999 (Conn. 1980) 12.07n4

Manthe v. Town Bd., 555 N.W.2d 167 (Wis. App. 1996) 9.03n9

Maple Leaf Invs., Inc. v. State, 565 P.2d 1162 (Wash. 1977) 12.09n6

Marashlian v. Zoning Bd. of Appeals, 660 N.E.2d 369 (Mass. 1996) 8.04n2, n4

Marbro Corp., People ex rel. v. Ramsey, 171 N.E.2d 246 (Ill. App. 1960) 11.34n7

Marchese v. Norristown Borough Zoning Bd. of Adjustment, 277 A.2d 176 (Pa. Commw. 1971) 5.81n7

Marchi v. Scarborough, Town of, 511 A.2d 1071 (Me. 1986) 6.48n2, n4

Marcus v. Huntington, Town of 382 N.E.2d 1323 (N.Y. 1978) 5.40n3

Marcus v. Township of Abington, 1993 U.S. Dist. LEXIS 1815 (E.D. Pa. 1993) 8.45n3

Margate Motel, Inc. v. Gilford, Town of, 534 A.2d 717 (N.H. 1987) 6.48n4

Marggi v. Ruecker, 533 P.2d 1372 (Or. App. 1975) 6.34n2

Margolis v. District Court, 638 P.2d 297 (Colo. 1981) 6.26n10; 6.82n7

Marino v. Baltimore, City of, 137 A.2d 198 (Md. 1957) 6.50n5

Marion County v. Department of Community Affairs, 817 So.2d 1062 . . . . 5.26n2

Markham Adv. Co. v. State, 439 P.2d 249 (Wash. 1968) 11.07n1

Marks v. Chesapeake, City of, 883 F.2d 308 (4th Cir. 1989) 2.39n7; 6.75n3

Marmah, Inc. v. Greenwich, Town of, 405 A.2d 63 (Conn. 1978) 6.16n4; 6.73n1

Marracci v. Scappoose, City of, 552 P.2d 552 (Or. App. 1976) 3.15n5; 3.17n1; 6.33n10

Marriage of (see name of party)

Marris v. Cedarburg, City of, 498 N.W.2d 842 (Wis. 1993) 5.80n4; 6.73n1

Marshall v. Consumers' Power Co., 237 N.W.2d 266 (Mich. 1975) 4.03n1

Marshall v. Salt Lake City, 141 P.2d 704 (Utah 1943) 5.35n1

Martin v. Brentwood, City of, 200 F.3d 1205 . . . . . 2.47n3

Martin v. Corporation of Presiding Bishop, 747 N.E.2d 131 . . . . 5.70n8

Martin v. Hatfield, 308 S.E.2d 833 (Ga. 1983) . . . 6.64n1

Martin v. Township of Millcreek, 413 A.2d 764 . . 5.32n9

Martin v. Wray, 473 F. Supp. 1131 (E.D. Wis. 1979) 11.23n4

Martin County v. Yusem, 690 So.2d 1288 (Fla. 1997) 3.22n4

Martino v. Santa Clara Valley Water Dist., 703 F.2d 1141 (1983) 2.23n2

Martino v. Santa Clara Water Dist., 703 F.2d 1141 (9th Cir.1983) 2.24n6

Martorano v. Board of Comm'rs, 414 A.2d 411 (Pa. Commw. 1980) 9.05n7

Marty's Adult World of Enfield, Inc. v. Enfield, Town of, 20 F.3d 512 (2d Cir. 1994) 6.57n1

Marvin E. Neiberg Real Estate Co. v. St. Louis County, 488 S.W.2d 626 (Mo. 1973) . . 3.21n2

Marx v. Zoning Bd. of Appeals, 529 N.Y.S.2d 330 (App. Div. 1988) 9.03n1

Maryland-National Capital Park & Planning Comm'n v. Rosenberg, 307 A.2d 704 (Md. 1973) 10.05n3

Maryland-Nat'l Capital Park & Planning Comm'n v. Rockville, City of, 305 A.2d 122 (Md. 1973) . . 8.07n4

Maselbas v. Zoning Bd. of Appeals, 694 N.E.2d 1314 (Mass. App. 1998) 5.19n3

Mason City Center Assocs. v. Mason City, City of, 468 F. Supp. 737 (N.D. Iowa) 5.54n1

Massachusetts Feather Co. v. Aldermen of Chelsea, 120 N.E.2d 766 (Mass. 1954) 8.13n2

Massiello v. Town Board, 684 N.Y.S.2d 330 (App. Div. 1999) 8.04n2

Master Disposal, Inc. v. Menomonee Falls, Village of, 211 N.W.2d 477 (Wis. 1973) 8.16n9

Mastroianni v. Strada, 571 N.Y.S.2d 55 (App. Div. 1991) 11.34n3

Mathews v. Eldridge, 424 U.S. 319 (1976) 2.42n8; 6.70n1

Matlack v. Board of Chosen Freeholders, 466 A.2d 83 (N.J.L. Div. 1983), aff'd 12.16n3

Matter of (see name of party)

Matthew v. Smith, 707 S.W.2d 411 (Mo. 1986) . . 6.43n1; 6.44n3; 6.48n2

Matthews v. Board of Zoning Appeals, 237 S.E.2d 128 (Va. 1977) 6.07n1

Matthews v. Needham, Town of, 764 F.2d 58 . . . 11.23n3

Matthews v. Needham, Town of, 764 F.2d 58 (1st Cir. 1985) 11.19n17; 11.23n4

Mattoon v. Norman, City of 617 P.2d 1347 (Okla. 1980) 8.21n3

Mattson v. Chicago, City of, 411 N.E.2d 1002 (Ill. App. 1980) 6.21n5

Mavrantonis v. Board of Adjustment, 258 A.2d 908 (Del. 1969) 6.42n5

Mayes v. Dallas, City of, 747 F.2d 323 (5th Cir. 1984) 11.30n2

Mayhew v. Sunnyvale, Town of, 774 S.W.2d 284 (Tex. App. 1989) 3.15n9

Mayhew v. Sunnyvale, Town of, 964 S.W.2d 922 (Tex. 1998) . . 1.12n1; 2.16n8; 2.46n1; 5.31n2; 8.09n6

Maynard v. Beck, 741 A.2d 866 (R.I. 1999) 8.35n8

Mayor & Alderman v. Hudson, 774 So.2d 448 . . . 6.56n18

Mayor & Aldermen v. Anne Arundel County, 316 A.2d 807 (Md. 1974) 11.26n1; 11.36n3

Mayor & Board of Aldermen v. Hudson, 774 So.2d 448 . . . . 6.57n17

Mayor & City Council v. Crane, 352 A.2d 786 (Md. 1976) 6.23n5

Mayor & City Council v. Dembo, 719 A.2d 1007 . . . . 5.78n2

Mayor & City Council v. Dembo, Inc., 719 A.2d 1007 (Md. App. 1998) 5.81n16

Mayor & City Council v. Mano Swartz, Inc., 299 A.2d 828 (Md. 1973) 11.04n2; 11.10n8

Mayor & Council v. Clark, 516 A.2d 1126 (N.J. App. Div. 1986) 4.27n3

Mayor & Council v. Goldberg, 264 A.2d 113 (Md. 1970) 10.10n3

Mayor & Council v. Rollings Outdoor Adv., Inc., 475 A.2d 355 (Del. 1984) 5.84n6

Mayor of Annapolis v. Anne Arundel County 316 A.2d 807 (Md. 1974) 4.37n3

Mayor of Savannah v. Collins, 84 S.E.2d 454 (Ga. 1954) 4.36n1

Mays v. Board of Trustees, 2002 Ohio App. LEXIS 3347 . . . . 12.13n2, n8

Maysom Ltd. Partnership v. Mayfield, Village of, 645 N.E.2d 763 (Ohio App. 1994) 1.12n2

MB Assocs. v. District of Columbia Dep't of License, Investigation & I, 456 A.2d 344 (D.C. App. 1982) 11.35n3

MC Assocs. v. Cape Elizabeth, Town of, 773 A.2d 439 . . . . 8.09n1; 12.07n8

MC Props., Inc. v. Chatanooga, City of, 994 S.W.2d 132 (Tenn. App. 1999) 2.36n6

MC Props., Inc. v. Chattanooga, City of, 994 S.W.2d 132 (Tenn. App. 1999) 6.25n3

McCallen v. Memphis, City of, 786 S.W.2d 633 (Tenn. 1990) 8.13n5; 9.28n2

McCarthy v. Leawood, City of, 894 P.2d 836 (Kan. 1995) 9.22n4

McCarty v. Kansas City, City of, 671 S.W.2d 790 (Mo. App. 1984) 9.29n3

McCarty v. Macy & Co., 334 P.2d 156 (Cal. App. 1959) 4.12n2, n4

McClure v. Springfield, City of, 28 P.3d 1222 . . . 9.16n14

McCollum v. Berea, City of, 53 S.W.3d 106 . . . . 5.23n3

McCormick Mgt. Co., In re , 547 A.2d 1319 (Vt. 1988) 9.07n2

McCrann v. Town Plan. & Zoning Comm'n, 282 A.2d 900 (Conn. 1971) 6.66n1

McCulloch v. Glasgow, City of, 620 F.2d 47 (5th Cir. 1980) 8.29n8

McCutchan Estates v. Evansville-Vanderburgh County Airport, 580 N.E.2d 339 (Ind. App. 1991) 2.22n2

McCutchan Estates Corp. v. Evansville-Vanderburgh Cty. Airport Auth. Dist., 580 N.E.2d 339 (Ind. App. 1991) 8.26n1

McDonald v. Columbus, City of, 231 N.E.2d 319 (Ohio App. 1967) 4.39n4

McDonald, Sommer & Frates v. Yolo County 477 U.S. 340 (1986) 2.27n1

McDonald's Corp. v. Norton Shores, City of, 102 F. Supp. 2d 432 . . . . 2.49n4

McDonough, City of v. Tusk Partners, 492 S.E.2d 206 (Ga. 1997) 2.36n1

McDougal v. Imperial, County of, 942 F.2d 668 (9th Cir. 1991) 12.09n9

McElwain v. Flathead, County of, 811 P.2d 1267 (Mont. 1991) 12.09n9

McFillan v. Berkeley County Planning Comm'n, 438 S.E.2d 801 (W. Va. 1993) . . . 9.07n1; 9.09n16

McGowan v. Cohalan, 361 N.E.2d 1025 (N.Y. 1977) 2.36n10

McGowan v. Cohalan 361 N.E.2d 1025 (N.Y. 1977) 6.37n10

McHenry State Bank v. McHenry, City of, 46 N.E.2d 521 (Ill. App. 1983) 5.18n8

McKenzie v. White Hall, City of, 112 F.3d 313 (8th Cir. 1997) 2.31n1; 2.32n4

McKinstry v. Wells, 548 S.W.2d 169 (Ky. App. 1977) 6.70n14

McLaughlin v. Brockton, City of, 587 N.E.2d 251 (Mass. App. 1992) 5.79n2

McLean v. Soley, 270 Md. 208 (Md. 1973) 6.48n5

McMahan's Furn. Co. v. Pacific Grove, City of, 33 Cal. Rptr. 476 (Cal. App. 1963) 11.10n6

McMinn v. Oyster Bay, Town of, 488 N.E.2d 1240 (N.Y. 1985) 5.05n2

McNamara v. Borough of Saddle River, 166 A.2d 391 (N.J. 1960) 6.74n3

McNaughton v. Boeing, 414 P.2d 778 (Wash. 1966) 6.30n7

McNeil v. Avon, Town of, 435 N.E.2d 1043 (Mass. 1982) 5.72n3

McNeil v. Township of Plumstead, 522 A.2d 469 (N.J. App. Div. 1987) 5.37n2

McNulty v. Indialantic, Town of, 727 F. Supp. 604 (M.D. Fla. 1989) 2.16n9; 12.15n2

McPherson Landfill, Inc. v. Board of County Comm'rs, 49 P.3d 522 . . . . 2.21n2; 6.73n1

McQuail v. Shell Oil Co., 183 A.2d 572 (Del. 1962) 6.61n5

McShane v. Faribault, City of, 292 N.W.2d 253 (Minn. 1980) 5.39n8

McWhorter v. Winnsboro, City of, 525 S.W.2d 701 (Tex. Civ. App. 1975) 6.29n10

MD II Entertainment, Inc. v. Dallas, City of, 28 F.3d 492 (5th Cir. 1994) 5.64n2

Meadow Briar Home for Children, Inc. v. Gunn, 81 F.3d 521 (5th Cir. 1996) 8.36n14

Meadowland Regional Dev. Agency v. Hackensack Meadowlands Dev. Comm'n, 293 A.2d 192 (N.J. App. Div. 1972) 6.09n1

Mechem v. Santa Fe, City of, 634 P.2d 690 (N.M. 1981) 6.59n4

Media Art Co. v. Gates, City of, 974 P.2d 249 (Or. App. 1999) 6.57n4

Medici v. BPR Co., 526 A.2d 109 (N.J. 1987) . . . 6.41n5; 6.49n2

Megin Realty Corp. v. Baron, 387 N.E.2d 618 (N.Y. 1979) 2.36n6

Meglino v. Township Comm., 510 A.2d 1134 (N.J. 1986) 9.22n1

Mehlhorn v. Pima County, 978 P.2d 117 (Ariz. App. 1999) 8.18n2

Mehring v. Zoning Bd., 762 A.2d 1137 . . 6.56n8

Meixsell v. Ross Twp. Bd. of Supvrs., 623 A.2d 429 (Pa. Commw. 1993) 9.16n6; 10.15n2

Melucci v. Zoning Bd. of Review, 226 A.2d 416 (R.I. 1967) 6.56n2

Members of City Council v. Taxpayers for Vincent, 466 U.S. 789 (1984) 11.17n1, n3, n4

Members of City Council v. Taxpayers for Vincent 466 U.S. 789 (1984) 11.14n1

Members of the City Council v. Taxpayers for Vincent

Memorial Hosp. v. Maricopa County, 415 U.S. 250 (1974) 10.08n5

Memphis Community School Dist. v. Stachura, 477 U.S. 299 (1986) 8.38n2, n7

Menger v. Pass, 80 A.2d 702 (Pa. 1951) . . 4.03n4

Meredith Outdoor Advertising, Inc. v. Iowa Dep't of Transp., 648 N.W.2d 109 . . . . . . 5.80n6, n8

Merriam, City of v. Board of Zoning Appeals, 748 P.2d 883 (Kan. 1988) 6.48n2

Merrillville Bd. of Zoning Appeals, Town of v. Public Storage, Inc., 568 N.E.2d 1092 (Ind. App. 1991) 6.56n8

Merritt v. Peters, 65 So. 2d 861 (Fla. 1953) 11.10n2

Mesilla, Town of v. Las Cruces, Town of, 898 P.2d 121 (N.M. App. 1995) 8.07n3

Mesolella v. Providence, City of, 508 A.2d 661 (R.I. 1986) 8.23n6

Messer v. Chapel Hill, Town of, 479 S.E.2d 221 (N.C. App.) 8.09n6

Messer v. Chapel Hill, Town of, 479 S.E.2d 221 (N.C. App.), *vacated* *8.09n1, n8*

Messer v. Douglasville, 975 F.2d 1505 (11th Cir. 1992) 11.23n6

Messer v. Douglasville, City of, 975 F.2d 1505 (11th Cir. 1992) 11.19n2, n13, n16

Messer v. Snohomish Cty. Bd. of Adj., 578 P.2d 50 (Wash. App. 1978) 6.70n9

Messiah Baptist Ch. v. Jefferson, County of, 859 F.2d 820 (10th Cir. 1988) 5.69n2

Metro 500, Inc. v. Brooklyn Park, City of, 211 N.W.2d 358 (Minn. 1973) 5.46n5

Metro Realty v. El Dorado, County of, 35 Cal. Rptr. 480 (Cal. App. 1963) 6.09n1

Metromedia, Inc. v. Des Plaines, City of, 326 N.E.2d 59 (Ill. App. 1975) 11.08n6; 11.09n1

Metromedia, Inc. v. Pasadena, City of, 30 Cal. Rptr. 731 (Cal. App. 1963) 11.09n2

Metromedia, Inc. v. San Diego, City of, 610 P.2d 407 (Cal. 1980), *rev'd on other grounds,* 453 U.S. 490 (1981) 5.84n6; 11.05n1; 11.11n8

Metromedia, Inc. v. San Diego, City of 453 U.S. 490 (1981) 11.13n1

Metromedia, Inc. v. San Diego, City of 610 P.2d 407 (Cal. 1980), *rev'd on other grounds,* 453 U.S. 490 (1981) 5.86n1; 11.07n3; 11.08n5

Metropolitan Baptist Church v. District of Columbia Dep't of Consumer & Reg. Aff.. 718 A.2d 119 (D.C. 1998) 8.09n1

Metropolitan Bd. of Zoning Appeals v. McDonald's Corp., 481 N.E.2d 141 (Ind. App. 1985) 6.48n5

Metropolitan Dev. Comm'n v. Ching, Inc., 460 N.E.2d 1236 (Ind. App. 1984) 8.11n19

Metropolitan Dev. Comm'n v. Mullin, 399 N.E.2d 751 (Ind. App. 1979) 5.20n3

Metropolitan Dev. Comm'n v. Villages, Inc., 464 N.E.2d 367 (Ind. App. 1984) 5.08n11

Metropolitan Homes, Inc. v. Town Planning & Zoning Comm'n, 202 A.2d 241 (Conn. 1964) . . 5.31n4

Metropolitan Hous. Dev. Corp. v. Arlington Heights, Village of, 558 F.2d 1283 (7th Cir. 1977), *cert. denied,* 434 U.S. 1025 (1978) 7.05n2

Metropolitan Hous. Dev. Corp. v. Arlington Heights, Village of, 616 F.2d 1006 (7th Cir. 1980) 7.05n3

Metzger v. Brentwood (II), Town of 374 A.2d 954 (N.H. 1977) 5.72n3

Metzler v. Rowell, 547 S.E.2d 311 . . . . . 8.47n1

Meyer v. Planning Bd. of Westport, 558 N.E.2d 994 (Mass. App. 1990) 9.10n4

MFH Holding Co. v. New Jersey Dep't of Envtl. Protection, 713 A.2d 1096 (N.J.L. Div. 1997) . . 8.09n2

Miami Beach, City of v. Fleetwood Hotel, Inc., 261 So.2d 801 (1972) 4.24n6

Miami Beach, City of v. Lear, State ex rel., 175 So. 537 (Fla. 1937) 5.27n2

Miami Beach, City of v. Mr. Samuel's, Inc., 351 So. 2d 719 (Fla. 1977) 8.14n6

Miami Beach, City of v. Weiss, 217 So. 2d 836 (Fla. 1969) 8.19n5

Miami Beach, City of v. Wiesen, 86 So.2d 442 (Fla. 1956) 2.46n5

Miami, City of v. Save Brickell Ave., Inc., 426 So. 2d 1100 (Fla. App. 1983) 9.25n6

Miami-Dade County v. New Life Apostolic Church, 750 So.2d 738 . . . . 6.48n7

Miami Dolphins, Ltd. v. Metropolitan Dade Cty., 394 So. 2d 981 (Fla. 1981) 6.05n9

Michaels Dev. Co. v. Benzinger Twp. Bd. of Supvrs., 413 A.2d 743 (Pa. Commw. 1980) . . . 9.30n6

Mid-Continent Bldrs., Inc. v. Midwest City, 539 P.2d 1377 (Okla. 1975) 9.12n1

Middlesex & Boston St. Ry. v. Board of Aldermen, 359 N.E.2d 1279 (Mass. 1977) . 6.59n4; 7.27n4

Middlesex County Ethics Comm. v. Garden State Bar Ass'n, 457 U.S. 423 (1982) 8.42n3

Middlesex County Sewerage Auth. v. National Sea Clammers Ass'n, 453 U.S. 1 (1981) . . . 8.29n6

Midwest Fireworks Mfg. Co. v. Deerfield Township Board of Zoning Appeals, 743 N.E.2d 894 . . . . 8.04n3

Milardo v. Coastal Resources Mgt. Council, 424 A.2d 266 (R.I. 1981) 12.07n4

Miles v. Dade County Bd. of County Comm'rs, 260 So. 2d 553 (Fla. App. 1972) 6.30n1

Mill Realty Assocs. v. Zoning Bd. of Review, 721 A.2d 887 (R.I. 1998) 10.14n4

Millbrae Ass'n for Residential Survival v. Millbrae, City of, 69 Cal. Rptr. 251 (1968) 9.29n1

Miller v. Albuquerque, City of, 554 P.2d 665 (N.M. 1976) 6.31n2

Miller v. Bainbridge Island, City of, 43 P.3d 1250 . . . . 5.81n5

Miller v. Beaver Falls, City of, 82 A.2d 34 (Pa. 1951) 10.15n4

Miller v. Board of Adjustment, 521 A.2d 642 (Del. Super. 1986) 6.17n1

Miller v. Campbell County, 945 F.2d 348 (10th Cir. 1991) 2.40n3

Miller v. Council of City of Grants Pass, 592 P.2d 1088 (Or. App. 1979) 3.18n4; 6.33n4

Miller v. Dassler, 155 N.Y.S.2d 975 (Sup. Ct. 1956) 6.18n3

Miller v. Maloney Concrete Co., 491 A.2d 1218 (Md. App. 1985) 6.05n4, n21

Miller v. Port Angeles, City of, 691 P.2d 229 (Wash. App. 1984) 9.16n8

Miller; State v. , 416 A.2d 821 (N.J. 1980) 11.04n4

Miller; State v. 416 A.2d 821 (N.J. 1980) 11.05n3

Miller v. Tilton, Town of, 655 A.2d 409 (N.H. 1995) 6.37n13

Miller Bros. v. Department of Nat. Resources, 513 N.W.2d 217 (Mich. App. 1994) 8.21n6

Miller & Son Paving, Inc. v. Plumstead Township, 717 A.2d 483 (Pa. 1998) 2.22n9; 8.26n1

Miller & Son Paving, Inc. v. Wrightstown Twp., 451 A.2d 1002 (Pa. 1982) 5.71n2

Miller, State ex rel. v. Cain, 242 P.2d 505 (Wash. 1952) 2.46n6; 5.80n2, n10

Miller, State ex rel. v. Manders, 86 N.W.2d 469 (Wis. 1957) 10.15n1

Millerick v. Tinley Park, Village of, 652 N.E.2d 17 (Ill. App. 1995) 8.23n18

Milwaukie Company of Jehovah's Witnesses v. Mullen, 330 P.2d 5 (Or. 1958) . . . 5.68n1; 6.57n15

Minch v. Fargo, City of, 297 N.W.2d 785 (N.D. 1980) 8.21n5

Miness v. Alter, 691 N.Y.S.2d 171 (App. Div. 1999) 8.46n8

Mings v. Ft. Smith, City of, 701 S.W.2d 705 (Ark. 1986) 8.04n1

Miniat v. McGinnis, 762 S.W.2d 390 (Ark. 1988) 4.03n1

Minnesota v. Clover Leaf Creamery Co., 449 U.S. 456 (1981) 2.11n2

Minor v. Cochise County, 608 P.2d 309 (Ariz. 1980) 8.10n2

Minster v. Gray, Town of, 584 A.2d 646 (Me. 1990) 6.07n4

Mira Dev. Co. v. San Diego, City of, 252 Cal. Rptr. 825 (Cal. App. 1988) . . . 2.23n6; 6.33n3, n10

Miracle Mile Assocs. v. Rochester, City of, 617 F.2d 18 (2d Cir. 1980) 5.55n6

Miriam Homes, Inc. v. Board of Adjustment, 384 A.2d 147 (App. Div. 1976), aff'd mem., 384 A.2d 143 (N.J. 1978) 6.48n16

Mission Springs, Inc. v. Spokane, City of, 954 P.2d 250 (Wash. 1998) 8.37n1; 8.46n11

Mississippi State Hwy. Comm'n v. Roberts Enters., 304 So. 2d 637 (Miss. 1974) 11.07n10

Missouri Hwy. & Transp. Comm'n, State ex rel. v. Alexian Bros., 848 S.W.2d 472 (Mo. 1993) . . . 11.06n7

Missouri Rock, Inc. v. Winholtz, 614 S.W.2d 734 (Mo. App. 1981) 5.78n4

Mobil Oil Corp. v. Board of Adjustment, 283 A.2d 837 (Del. Super. 1971) 5.46n4

Mobil Oil Corp. v. Clawson, City of, 193 N.W.2d 346 (Mich. App. 1971) 6.03n4

Mobil Oil Corp.; People v. , 397 N.E.2d 724 (N.Y. 1979) 11.18n6

Mobil Oil Corp. v. Zoning Bd. of Appeals, 644 A.2d 401 (Conn. App. 1994) 6.56n15

Mobile, City of v. Waldon, 429 So. 2d 945 (Ala. 1983) 9.16n1

Mobile, City of v. Weinacker, 720 So.2d 953 (Ala. Civ. App. 1998) 6.05n4; 11.30n2

Mobile Home City of Chattanooga v. Hamilton County, 552 S.W.2d 86 (Tenn. App. 1976) . . . 5.23n3

Mobile Home Owners Protective Assoc. v. Chatham, Town of, 305 N.Y.S.2d 334 (App. Div. 1969) 5.23n3

Mock v. Department of Envtl. Resources, 623 A.2d 940 (Pa. Commw. 1993) 12.07n7

Modjeska Sign Studies, Inc. v. Berle, 373 N.E.2d 255 (N.Y. 1977) 11.07n8

Modjeska Sign Studios, Inc. v. Berle, 373 N.E.2d 255 (N.Y. 1977) 5.84n6

Modjeska Sign Studios, Inc. v. Berle 373 N.E.2d 255 (N.Y. 1977) 5.86n4

Mojica v. Gannett Co., 7 F.3d 552 (7th Cir. 1993) 7.04n1

Molnar v. Carver Bd. of Comm'rs, County of, 568 N.W.2d 177 (Minn. App. 1997) 6.56n15

Monell v. Department of Social Serv 8.29

Monell v. Department of Social Servs., 436 U.S. 658 (1978) 8.39n7

Monett, City of v. Buchanan, 411 S.W.2d 108 (Mo. 1967) 6.22n9

Money v. Zoning Hearing Bd., 755 A.2d 732 . . . 5.80n9

Monmouth Consol. Water Co., In re v. Board of Pub. Util. Comm'rs, 220 A.2d 189 (N.J. 1966) 4.32n5

Monroe v. Pape, 365 U.S. 167 (1961) . . 8.29n10; 8.32n1

Monroe, Town of v. Carey, 412 N.Y.S.2d 939 (Sup. Ct. 1977) 12.05n5

Montana Wildlife Fed'n v. Sager, 620 P.2d 1189 (Mont. 1980) 8.06n2

Montauk-Caribbean Airways, Inc. v. Hope, 784 F.2d 91 (2d Cir. 1986) 5.57n3

Monterey, City of v. Del Monte Dunes . . . 2.13

Monterey, City of v. Del Monte Dunes 526 U.S. 687 (1999) 8.27n1

Montgomery v. Sherburne, Town of, 514 A.2d 702 (Vt. 1986) 4.26n1

Montgomery, City of v. Crossroads Land Co., 355 So. 2d 363 (Ala. 1978) 9.18n2

Montgomery County v. Citizens Bldg. & Loan Ass'n, 316 A.2d 322 (Md. 1974) 8.11n2

Montgomery County v. Colesville Citizens Ass'n, 521 A.2d 770 (Md. App. 1987) 6.61n3

Montgomery County v. Woodward & Lothrop, Inc., 376 A.2d 483 (Md. 1977) 5.77n1

Montgomery County v. Woodward & Lothrop, Inc. 376 A.2d 483 (Md. 1977) 5.76n2

Montgomery, County of v. Deer Creek, Inc., 691 N.E.2d 185 (Ill. App. 1998) 9.05n4

Montgomery Crossing Assocs. v. Township of Lower Gwynedd, 758 A.2d 285 . . . . 5.37n5

Montgomery Cty. v. Woodward & Lothrop, 376 A.2d 483 (Md. 1977) 6.26n5

Moody v. Univ. Park, City of, 278 S.W.2d 912 (Tex. Civ. App. 1955) 6.74n12

Mooney v. Orchard Lake, Village of, 53 N.W.2d 308 (Mich. 1952) 6.57n14

Moore v. Boulder, City of, 484 P.2d 134 (Colo. App. 1971) 4.25n3; 7.26n1; 9.25n8; 9.28n2

Moore v. Costa Mesa, 886 F.2d 260 (9th Cir. 1989) 2.22n9

Moore v. Costa Mesa, City of, 886 F.2d 260 (9th Cir. 1989) 6.11n6

Moore v. Pettus, 71 So. 2d 814 (Ala. 1954) 5.80n3

Moore v. Rochester, City of, 427 A.2d 10 (N.H. 1981) 6.46n4

Moore v. Township of Raccoon, 625 A.2d 737 (Pa. Commw. 1993) 6.76n10, n17

Moore v. Ward, 377 S.W.2d 881 (Ky. 1964) 11.07n1, n5; 11.08n1

Moore Bldg. Co. v. Committee for the Repeal of Ordinance R(C)-88-13, 391 S.E.2d 587 (Va. 1990) 6.80n7

Moore, City of v. Atchison, Topeka & Santa Fe Ry. Co., 699 F.2d 507 (10th Cir. 1983) . . . 4.25n1

Morganstern v. Rye, Town of, 794 A.2d 782 . . . . 9.07n5

Morgran Co., Inc. v. Orange County, 818 So.2d 640 . . . . 6.23n6

Moriarty v. Planning Bd., 506 N.Y.S.2d 184 (App. Div. 1986) 6.66n3

Morland Dev. Co. v. Tulsa, City of, 596 P.2d 1255 (Okla. 1979) 8.11n7; 12.05n4

Moroney v. Mayor & City Council, 633 A.2d 1045 (N.J. App. Div. 1993) 2.21n4

Moroney v. Mayor & Council, 633 A.2d 1045 (N.J. App. 1993) 6.44n5

Morris v. Postma, 196 A.2d 792 (N.J. 1964) 6.15n1; 6.18n4

Morrison Homes Corp. v. Pleasanton, City of, 130 Cal. Rptr. 196 (Cal. App. 1976) 6.23n4

Morristown Rd. Assocs. v. Mayor & Common Council, 394 A.2d 157 (N.J.L. Div. 1978) . . 11.25n3

Morse v. San Luis Obispo, County of, 55 Cal. Rptr. 710 (Cal. App. 1967) 5.31n3

Morse v. Vermont Div. Of State Bldgs., 388 A.2d 371 (Vt. 1978) 4.27n1

Morse Brothers v. Webster, 772 A.2d 842 . . . . . 8.47n1

Moscow, Village of v. Skeene, 585 N.E.2d 493 (Ohio App. 1989) 5.22n2

Moscowitz v. Planning & Zoning Comm'n, 547 A.2d 569 (Conn. App. 1988) 9.09n2

Moses H. Cone Mem. Hosp. v. Mercury Constr. Corp., 460 U.S. 1 (1983) 8.45n2

Moskow v. Comm'r, 427 N.E.2d 750 (Mass. 1981) 12.07n9

Mossman v. Columbus, City of, 449 N.W.2d 214 (Neb. 1989) 5.80n3

Motel 6 Operating Ltd. Partnership v. Flagstaff, City of, 991 P.2d 272 (Ariz. App. 1999) . . . 5.79n5

Mounds View, City of v. Johnson, 377 N.W.2d 476 (Minn. App. 1985) 6.33n1

Mount Elliot Cemetery Ass'n v. Troy, City of, 171 F.3d 398 (6th Cir. 1999) 5.69n2

Mount Elliott Cemetery Ass'n v. Troy, City of, 171 F.3d 398 (6th Cir. 1999) . . 2.47n2, n3; 2.49n3

Mount Olive Complex v. Township of Mount Olive, 774 A.2d 704 . . . . 7.13n2

Mountain View Chamber of Commerce v. Mountain View, City of, 143 Cal. Rptr. 441 (Cal. App. 1978) 8.11n6, n17

Mountcrest Estates, Inc. v. Mayor & Twp. Comm 6.37

Mountcrest Estates, Inc. v. Mayor & Twp. Comm., 232 A.2d 674 (N.J. App. Div. 1967) . . 9.27n7

Moviematic Indus. v. Board of County Comm'rs, 349 So. 2d 667 (Fla. App. 1977) 6.37n15

Moviematic Indus. Corp. v. Board of County Comm'rs, 349 So.2d 667 (Fla. App. 1977) . . . 12.03n1

Mraz v. County Comm'rs, 433 A.2d 771 (Md. 1981) 6.29n1

M.S.W., Inc. v. Board of Zoning Appeals, 24 P.3d 175 . . . . 6.54n1

Mt. Elliott Cemetery Ass'n v. Troy, City of, 171 F.3d 398 (6th Cir. 1999) 7.23n5

Mt. Healthy School Dist. Bd Of Educ. v. Doyle, 429 U.S. 274 (1977) 2.51n3

Mt. Plainsboro Limited Partnership v. Township of Plainsboro, 719 A.2d 1285 (N.J. App. Div. 1998) 5.36n7; 8.16n6

Muckway v. Craft, 789 F.2d 517 (7th Cir. 1986) . . 2.47n3

Muckway v. Craft, 789 F.2d 517 (7th Cir.1986) . . 8.32n4

Mugler v. Kansas 123 U.S. 623 (1887) . . . 2.01n1

Mullin v. Planning Bd., 456 N.E.2d 780 (Mass. App. 1983) 9.27n5

Mullins v. Knoxville, City of, 665 S.W.2d 393 (Tenn. App. 1983) 9.28n3

Multiplex Corp. v. Hartz Mountain Indus., 564 A.2d 146 (N.J. App. Div. 1989) 8.02n11

Munch v. Mott, City of, 311 N.W.2d 17 (N.D. 1981) 8.03n1

Municipal Antitrust Immunity After City of Columbia v. Omni Outdoor Advertising, Inc., 67 Wash. L. Rev. 479 (1992)

Munroe v. East Greenwich, Town of, 733 A.2d 703 (R.I. 1999) 4.24n4

Murmur Corp. v. Board of Adjustment, 718 S.W.2d 790 (Tex. App. 1986) 5.86n1, n7

Murphy v. Board of Envt'l Protection, 615 A.2d 255 (Me. 1992) 12.05n2

Murphy v. Crosby, 298 N.E.2d 885 (Mass. App. 1973) 6.22n8

Murphy v. Zoning Comm'n, 148 F. Supp.2d 173 . . 5.70n4

Murrell v. Wolff, 408 S.W.2d 842 (Mo. 1966) . . . 6.21n5

Mutton Hill Estates, Inc. v. Oakland, Town of, 468 A.2d 989 (Me. 1983) 6.68n2

Mx Group, Inc. v. Covington, City of, 293 F.3d 326 . . . . 5.12n11

My Brother's Keeper v. Scott County, 621 N.W.2d 1121 (Ind. App. 1998) 5.08n1

Myers v. Moore Engineering, Inc., 42 F.3d 452 (8th Cir. 1994) 8.23n14

Myhre, State ex rel. v. Spokane, City of, 422 P.2d 790 (Wash. 1967) 6.62n3; 6.64n3

Myron v. Plymouth, City of, 562 N.W.2d 21 (Minn. App. 1997) 6.50n6

Myrtle Beach, City of v. Jual P. Corp., 543 S.E.2d 538 . . . . 5.81n3

Myrtle Beach, City of v. Juel P. Corp., 543 S.E.2d 538 . . . . 5.81n15

The Myth and Meaning of Justice Holmes' Opinion in Pennsylva v. Mahon, 106 Yale L.J. 613 (1996)

N

N. Las Vegas, City of v. Parde Constr. Co., 21 P.3d 8 . . . . 6.23n1

Nadeau; People v. , 227 Cal. Rptr. 644 (Cal. App. 1986) 6.57n4

Naegele v. Durham, City of, 844 F.2d 172 (4th Cir. 1988) 11.13n3

Naegele Outdoor Adv. Co. v. Minnetonka, Village of, 162 N.W.2d 206 (Minn. 1968) 5.82n5; 5.84n6; 5.86n5; 11.04n2; 11.08n2

Naegele Outdoor Advertising v. Hunt, 465 S.E.2d 549 (N.C. App. 1995) 11.06n5

Naegele Outdoor Advertising Co. v. Lakeville, City of, 532 N.W.2d 249 (Minn. App. 1995) 11.11n9

Naegele Outdoor Advertising, Inc. v. Durham, City of, 803 F. Supp. 1068 (M.D.N.C. 1992) . . 2.16n9

Naegele Outdoor Advertising, Inc. v. Durham, City of, 844 F.2d 172 (4th Cir. 1988) 11.19n4

Naegle Outdoor Advertising, Inc. v. Durham, City of, 803 F. Supp. 1068 (M.D.N.C. 1992) . . 2.31n4

Nagatani Bros. v. Skagit County Bd. of Comm'rs, 728 P.2d 1104 (Wash. App. 1986) 12.13n6

Nagawicka Island Corp. v. Delafield, City of, 343 N.W.2d 816 (Wis. App. 1983) 12.13n4

Nagawicka Island Corp., State ex rel. v. Delafield, City of, 343 N.W.2d 816 (Wis. App. 1983) . . . 8.19n1

Naierowski Bros. Inv. Co. v. Sterling Heights, City of, 949 F.2d 890 (6th Cir. 1992) 2.42n6

Naked City, Inc. v. Aregood, 667 F. Supp. 1246 (N.D. Ind. 1987) 8.42n13

Namon v. State Dep't of Envtl. Reg., 558 So. 2d 504 (Fla. App. 1990) 12.07n4

Napa Citizens for Honest Gov't. v. Napa County Bd. Of Supervisors, 100 Cal. Rptr. 2d 579 . . . . . . 3.22n5

Napierkowski v. Township of Gloucester, 150 A.2d 481 (N.J. 1959) 8.11n16

Narrowsview Preservation Ass'n v. Tacoma, City of, 526 P.2d 897 (Wash. 1974) 6.74n7

Nasser v. Homewood, City of, 671 F.2d 432 (11th Cir. 1982) 7.04n4

Nasser v. Homewood (I), City of, 671 F.2d 432 (11th Cir. 1982) 8.43n8; 8.44n6

Natale v. Ridgefield, Town of, 170 F.3d 258 (2d Cir. 1999) 2.39n5

National Adv. Co. v. Ashland, City of, 678 F.2d 106 (9th Cir. 1982) 5.83n1; 11.11n5

National Adv. Co. v. Babylon, Town of, 900 F.2d 551 (2d Cir. 1990) 11.19n7, n16

National Adv. Co. v. Board of Adj., 800 P.2d 1349 (Colo. App. 1990) 11.11n10

National Adv. Co. v. Bridgeton, City of, 626 F. Supp. 837 (E.D. Mo. 1985) 11.19n7

National Adv. Co. v. City & Cty. of Denver, 912 F.2d 405 (10th Cir. 1990) 11.19n7

National Adv. Co. v. Department of Hwys., 751 P.2d
632 (Colo. 1988) 11.06n7
National Adv. Co. v. Downers Grove, Village of, 561
N.E.2d 1300 (Ill. App. 1990) 11.07n13
National Adv. Co. v. Missouri State Hwy. & Transp.
Comm'n, 862 S.W.2d 953 (Mo. App. 1993) . . .
11.06n6
National Adv. Co. v. Monterey, County of, 464 P.2d
33 (Cal. 1970) 5.86n3
National Adv. Co. v. Orange, City of, 861 F.2d 246
(9th Cir. 1988) 11.19n7, n15
National Advertising Co. v. City & County of Denver,
912 F.2d 405 (10th Cir. 1990) 11.19n13
National Advertising Co. v. Denver, 912 F.2d 405
(10th Cir. 1990) 11.19n4
National Advertising Co. v. Department of Transp.,
932 P.2d 871 (Colo. App. 1997) 5.81n15
National Advertising Co. v. Downers Grove, Village
of, 561 N.E.2d 1300 (Ill. App. 1990) . . 2.16n8
National Advertising Co. v. Monterey, County of, 464
P.2d 33 (Cal. 1970) 5.86n6
National Advertising Co. v. Niagra, Town of, 942 F.2d
145 (2d Cir.1991) 11.13n3
National Advertising Co. v. Niagra, Town of, 942 F.2d
945 (2d Cir. 1991) 11.19n15
National Advertising Co. v. Orange, 861 F.2d 246 (9th
Cir. 1988) 11.19n9
National Amusements, Inc. v. Boston, City of, 560
N.E.2d 138 (Mass. App. 1990) . 6.37n9; 6.75n3
National Associated Props. v. Planning & Zoning
Comm'n, 658 A.2d 114 (Conn. App. 1995) . . .
7.31n4
National Black Child Dev. Inst. v. District of Colum-
bia Bd. of Adjustment, 483 A.2d 687 (D.C. App.
1984) 6.51n7
National Boatland, Inc. v. Farmington Hills Zoning
Bd. of Appeals, 380 N.W.2d 472 (Mich. App.
1985) 6.48n5
National Brick Co. v. Chicago, City of, 235 N.E.2d
301 (Ill. App. 1968) 8.11n18
National City, City of v. Wiener, 838 P.2d 223 (Cal.
1992) 5.63n4
National Land & Inv. Co. v. Kohn 215 A.2d 597 (Pa.
1965) 1.18n3; 5.32n6
National Soc'y of Professional Eng'rs v. United
States, 435 U.S. 679 (1980) 5.56n1
National Telecommunications Advisors v. Board of
Selectman, 27 F. Supp.2d 184 (D. Mass. 1998)
. . . . 4.42n4, n14
National Tower, L.L.C. v. Plainville Zoning Bd. of
Appeals, 297 F.3d 14 . . . . 4.42n3
Native Village of Eklutna v. Board of Adjustment, 995
P.2d 641 . . . . 6.56n16
Nattress v. Land Use Regulation Comm'n, 600 A.2d
391 (Me. 1991) 6.33n5

Nautilus of Exeter, Inc. v. Exeter, Town of, 656 A.2d
407 (N.H. 1995) 5.46n3
Naylor v. Township of Hellam, 717 A.2d 629 (Pa.
Commw. 1998) 6.09n2
Naylor v. Township of Hellam, 773 A.2d 770 . . .
6.07n1
Nazarko v. Conservation Comm'n, 717 A.2d 853
(Conn. App. 1998) 6.70n5
Nectow v. Cambridge., City of 277 U.S. 183 (1928)
. . . . 2.06n2
Negin v. Mentor, City of, 601 F. Supp. 1502 (N.D.
Ohio 1985) 8.36n9
Neighborhood Action Group v. Calaveras, County of
203 Cal. Rptr. 401 (Cal. App. 1984) . . 6.58n3
Neighborhood Env't v. Seattle, City of, 676 P.2d 1006
(Wash. 1984) 6.30n4
Neighbors for Livability v. Beaverton, City of, 35 P.3d
1122 . . . . 6.33n1
Neilson v. Zoning Hearing Bd., 786 A.2d 1050 . .
6.48n16
Nelson v. Benton County, 839 P.2d 233 (Or. App.
1992) 12.13n8
Nelson v. Donaldson, 50 So. 2d 244 (Ala. 1951) . .
6.41n8
Nelson v. Lake Oswego, City of, 869 P.2d 350 (Or.
App. 1994) 9.16n14
Nelson v. Seattle, City of, 395 P.2d 82 (Wash. 1964)
. . . . 5.53n4
Nelson v. Seattle, City of, 395 P.2d 82 (Wash. 1965)
. . . . 4.25n2
Nelson v. Selma, City of, 881 F.2d 836 (9th Cir. 1989)
. . . . 2.47n1
Nelson v. Selma, City of 881 F.2d 836 (9th Cir. 1989)
. . . . 6.75n4
Nemmers v. Dubuque, City of, 764 F.2d 502 (8th Cir.
1985) 8.26n4
Nemmers v. Dubuque (I), City of, 716 F.2d 1194 (8th
Cir. 1983) 6.16n6
Nernberg v. Pittsburgh, City of, 620 A.2d 692 (Pa.
Commw. 1993) 8.02n11
Ness v. Albert, 665 S.W.2d 1 (Mo. App. 1983) . .
4.09n3
Neston Colon Medina & Sucesores, Inc. v. Custodio,
964 F.2d 32 (1st Cir. 1992) 2.39n6
Nestor Colon Successors, Inc. v. Custodio, 964 F.2d
32 (1st Cir. 1992) 2.51n3
Nestor Colon & Sucesores, Inc. v. Custudio, 964 F.2d
32 (1st Cir. 1992) 8.46n3
Netluch v. Mayor & Council, 325 A.2d 517 (N.J.
1974) 6.72n4
Neuberger v. Portland, City of, 607 P.2d 722 (Or.
1980) 6.70n4; 6.71n3, n6
Neuberger v. Portland, City of 603 P.2d 771 (Or.
1979) 3.15n2; 6.26n8

Neuberger, Estate of v. Township of Middletown, 521 A.2d 1336 (N.J. App. Div. 1987) . . . 11.34n2

Neuzil v. Iowa City, 451 N.W.2d 159 (Iowa 1990) 6.37n8

Nevada Contrs. v. Washoe Cty., 792 P.2d 31 (Nev. 1990) 6.56n14

Nevel v. Schaumburg, Village of, 297 F.3d 673 . . 2.49n4

New Burnham Prairie Homes, Inc. v. Burnham, 910 F.2d 1474 (7th Cir. 1990) 7.05n6

New Burnham Prairie Homes, Inc. v. Burnham, Village of, 910 F.2d 1474 (7th Cir. 1990) 8.33n7

New Burnham Prairie Homes, Inc. v. Burnham, Village of, 910 F.2d 2474 (7th Cir. 1990) 2.47n1

New Castle Cty. Council v. BC Dev. Assocs., 567 A.2d 1271 (Del. 1989) 6.26n2

New England Brickmaster, Inc. v. Salem, Town of, 582 A.2d 601 (N.H. 1990) 6.66n4

New England LNG Co. v. Fall River, City of, 331 N.E.2d 536 (Mass. 1975) 4.32n5

New Haven, City of v. Allen County Bd. of Zoning Appeals, 694 N.E.2d 306 (Ind. App. 1998) . . . 8.07n2

New Haven, City of v. Reichhart, 748 N.E.2d 374 . . . . 8.46n9

New Jersey Bldrs. Ass'n v. Department of Envt'l Protection, 404 A.2d 320 (N.J. App. Div. 1979) 10.15n5; 12.04n6

New Jersey Bldrs. Ass'n v. Mayor & Twp. Comm., 528 A.2d 555 (N.J. 1987) 9.16n3

New Orleans, City of v. Board of Comm'rs, 640 So. 2d 237 (La. 1994) 4.39n3

New Orleans, City of v. Pergament, 5 So. 2d 129 (La. 1941) 11.29n3

New Orleans, City of v. State, 364 So. 2d 1020 (La. 1978) 4.27n1; 4.38n8

New Orleans Public Serv. v. New Orleans, City of 491 U.S. 350 (1989) 8.42n8; 8.44n5

New Par v. Saginaw, City of, 301 F.3d 390 . . . . 4.42n3, n12, n13

New Port Largo, Inc. v. Monroe County, 95 F.3d 1084 (11th Cir. 1996) 6.36n2

New Smyrna Beach, City of v. Andover Dev. Corp., 672 So.2d 618 (Fla. App. 1996) 9.29n1

New York, City of v. Hommes, 724 N.E.2d 368 (N.Y. 1999) 5.65n5

New York, City of v. 17 Vista Assocs., 642 N.E.2d 606 (N.Y. 1994) 6.23n5

New York State Thruway Auth. v. Ashley Motor Court, Inc., 176 N.E.2d 566 (N.Y. 1961) 11.07n6

New York Trap Rock Corp.; People v. , 442 N.E.2d 1222 (N.Y. 1982) 6.05n4, n21

Newark, City of v. Daley, 214 A.2d 410 (N.J. 1965) 5.20n6

Newark, City of v. University of Del., 304 A.2d 347 (Del. Ch. 1973) 4.27n5

Newark Milk & Cream Co. v. Parsippany-Troy Hills Twp., 135 A.2d 682 (N.J.L. 1957) . . . 5.43n5

Newbury Twp. Bd. of Twp. Trustees v. Lomak Petroleum (Ohio), Inc. 583 N.E.2d 302 (Ohio 1992) 4.31n4

Newman Signs, Inc. v. Hjelle, 268 N.W.2d 741 (N.D. 1978) 11.07n1, n9

Newport, City of v. Fact Concerts, Inc., 453 U.S. 247 (1981) 8.38n3

Nextel W. Corp. v. Unity Township, 282 F.3d 257 . . . . 4.42n5

Nextel West Corp. v. Unity Township, 282 F.3d 257 . . . . 4.42n1

the Nexus Test of Nollan v. California Coastal Commission, 12 Harv. Envtl. L.J. 231 (1988)

Niccollai v. Planning Bd., 372 A.2d 352 (N.J. App. Div. 1977) 9.30n5

Nichols v. Tullahoma Open Door, Inc., 640 S.W.2d 13 (Tenn. App. 1982) 5.10n4

Nicholson v. Connecticut Half-Way House, Inc . . 4.08

Nicholson v. Tourtellotte, 293 A.2d 909 (R.I. 1972) 6.62n2

Nicholson v. Zoning Bd. of Adjustment, 140 A.2d 604 (Pa. 1958) 6.51n4

Nickerson v. Zoning Bd. of Appeals, 761 N.E.2d 544 . . . . 8.04n6

Night Clubs v. Fort Smith, City of, 163 F.3d 475 (8th Cir. 1998) 8.42n7, n11

Night Clubs, Inc. v. Ft. Smith, City of, 163 F.3d 475 (8th Cir. 1998) 8.42n9

Nightclubs, Inc. v. Paducah, City of, 202 F.3d 84 . . . . 6.57n12

Nightclubs, Inc. v. Paducah, City of, 202 F.3d 884 . . . . 6.57n8

Nigro v. Planning Bd. of Saddle River, 584 A.2d 1350 (N.J. 1991) 10.14n1

900 G Street Assocs. v. Department of Hous. & Community Dev., 430 A.2d 1387 (D.C. App. 1981) 11.35n3

Noakes v. Gaiser, 315 P.2d 183 (Colo. 1957) 4.09n3

Noble Manor Co. v. Pierce County, 943 P.2d 1378 (Wash. 1997) 6.22n2

Nodell Inv. Corp. v. Glendale, City of, 254 N.W.2d 310 (Wis. 1977) 8.08n1

Nolan v. Taylorville, City of, 420 N.E.2d 1037 (Ill. App. 1981) 6.65n4

Nolden v. East Cleveland City Comm'n, 232 N.E.2d 421 (Ohio C.P. 1966) 5.29n1

Nollan v. California Coastal Comm'n, 483 U.S. 815 (1987) 2.16n7

Nollan v. California Coastal Comm'n, 483 U.S. 825 (1987) 2.04n5; 2.18n4; 2.39n2

Nollan v. California Coastal Comm'n 483 U.S. 625 (1987) 9.13n1

Nollan v. California Coastal Comm'n 483 U.S. 85 (1987) 2.11n1

Non-Profit Affordable Housing Network of N.J. v. New Jersey Council on Affordable Housing, 627 A.2d 1153 (N.J. App. Div. 1993) 7.12n9

Norate Corp. v. Zoning Bd. of Adjustment, 207 A.2d 890 (Pa. 1965) 11.08n7

Norbeck Village Joint Venture v. Montgomery County Council, 254 A.2d 700 (Md. 1969) . . . 5.31n3; 6.37n1

Norbeck Village Joint Venture v. Montgomery County Council 254 A.2d 700 (Md. 1969) . . . 3.20n1

Nordmarken v. Richfield, City of, 641 N.W.2d 343 . . . . 6.82n1

Normal Life of La., Inc. v. Jefferson Parish Dep't of Inspection & Code Enforcement, 483 So. 2d 1123 (La. App. 1986) 5.09n2

Normandy School Dist. v. Pasadena Hills, City of, 70 S.W.3d 488 . . . . 4.28n2

North v. Kent Island Ltd. Partnership, 664 A.2d 34 (Md. App. 1995) 12.04n7

North v. St. Mary's County, 638 A.2d 1175 (Md. App. 1994) 6.46n2

North Avenue Novelties, Inc. v. Chicago, City of, 88 F.3d 441 (7th Cir. 1996) 5.63n7, n15

North Georgia Mountain Cross Network, Inc. v. Blue Ridge, City of, 546 S.E.2d 850 . . . . . 6.21n6

North Hempstead v. North Hills, Village of, 324 N.E.2d 566 (N.Y. 1975) 9.25n8; 9.27n1

North Hempstead, Town of v. North Hills, Village of, 342 N.E.2d 566 (N.Y. 1975) . . 6.74n3; 8.07n2

North Kingston, Town of v. Albert, 767 A.2d 659 . . . . 12.11n12

North Landers Corp. v. Planning Bd., 416 N.E.2d 934 (Mass. 1981) 9.09n4, n13, n17

North Olmsted Chamber of Commerce v. North Olmsted, City of, 86 F. Supp. 2d 755 . . . 11.17n3

North Olmsted Chamber of Commerce v. North Olmsted, City of, 86 F. Supp.2d 755 . . . . . 11.21n1

North Sacramento Land Co. v. Sacramento, City of, 189 Cal. Rptr. 739 (Cal. App. 1983) . . 12.13n4

North Shore Steak House, Inc. v. Board of Appeals, 282 N.E.2d 606 (N.Y. 1972) . . 6.39n1; 6.56n8

North Shore Unitarian Universalist Soc'y v. Upper Brookville, Town of, 493 N.Y.S.2d 564 (App. Div. 1985) 7.16n2

Northeast Plaza Assocs. v. President & Comm'rs, 526 A.2d 963 (Md. 1987) 8.16n2

Northeastern Gas Co. v. Foster Twp. Zoning Hearing Bd., 613 A.2d 606 (Pa. 1992) 4.31n4

Northend Cinema, Inc. v. Seattle, City of, 585 P.2d 1153 (Wash. 1978) 5.63n5; 5.64n1

Northern Ili. Home Bldrs. Ass'n v. DuPage, County of, 649 N.E.2d 384 (Ill. 1995) 9.21n11; 10.08n8

Northern Maine Gen. Hosp. v. Ricker, 572 A.2d 479 (Me. 1990) 5.08n11

Northern Ohio Sign Contractors Ass'n v. Lakewood, City of, 513 N.E.2d 324 (Ohio 1987) . . 5.85n2

Northern Trust Bank/Lake Forest v. Lake, County of, 723 N.E.2d 1269 . . . . 2.37n6

Northern Va. Law School, Inc. v. Alexandria, City of, 680 F. Supp. 222 (N.D. Va. 1988) . . . 8.43n11

Northern Westchester Professional Park Assocs. v. Bedford, Town of, 458 N.E.2d 809 (N.Y. 1983) 2.36n2; 2.37n5

Northfield Dev. Co., Inc. v. Burlington, City of, 523 S.E.2d 743 (N.C. App) 5.26n3

Northville, Town of v. Sheridan, Village of, 655 N.E.2d 22 (Ill. App. 1995) . . . 4.23n3; 8.07n1

Northwest Residence, Inc. v. Brooklyn Center, City of, 352 N.W.2d 764 (Minn. App. 1984) 5.10n4

Northwestern Nat'l Life Ins. Co. v. Tahoe Reg'l Planning Agency, 632 F.2d 104 (9th Cir. 1980) 2.53n2

Northwestern Preparatory School; State v. , 37 N.W.2d 370 (Minn. 1949) 5.27n2

Northwestern Univ. v. Evanston, City of, 383 N.E.2d 964 (Ill. 1978) 8.11n12, n16

Northwood Homes, Inc. v. Moraga, Town of, 265 Cal. Rptr. 363 (Cal. App. 1989) 6.83n8

Northwood Props. Co. v. Perkins, 39 N.W.2d 25 (Mich. 1949) 5.29n2; 6.04n2

Nott v. Wolf, 163 N.E.2d 809 (Ill. 1960) . . 6.20n3

Nottingham Village, Inc. v. Baltimore County, 292 A.2d 680 (Md. 1972) 3.14n1

Nova Horizon, Inc. v. City Council, 769 P.2d 721 (Nev. 1989) 3.15n9; 6.33n10; 8.14n4

Novi v. Pacifica, City of, 215 Cal. Rptr. 439 (Cal. App. 1985) 11.25n3

Nucholls v. Board of Adjustment, 560 P.2d 556 (Okla. 1977) 6.39n1; 6.43n1

Nunes v. Bristol, Town of, 232 A.2d 775 (R.I. 1967) 4.34n1

Nunziato v. Planning Bd., 541 A.2d 1105 (N.J. App. Div. 1988) 9.23n2

Nyack, Village of v. Daytop Village, Inc., 583 N.E.2d 928 (N.Y. 1991) 5.10n1

O

O & G Indus. v. Planning & Zoning Comm'n, 655 A.2d 1121 (Conn. 1995) 8.11n16

Oak Forest Mobile Home Park v. Oak Forest, City of, 326 N.E.2d 473 (Ill. App. 1975) 5.24n3

Oakes Constr. Co. v. Iowa City, City of, 304 N.W.2d 797 (Iowa 1981) 9.09n13

Oakwood at Madison, Inc. v. Township of Madison 371 A.2d 1192 (N.J. 1977) 7.11n1

O'Banion v. Shively, State ex rel., 253 N.E.2d 739 (Ind. App. 1969) 4.33n2

O'Brien v. Saint Paul, City of, 173 N.W.2d 462 (Minn. 1969) 6.04n6

O'Brien; United States v. , 391 U.S. 367 (1968) . . 2.50n5; 11.14n2

Ocean Acres v. State, 403 A.2d 967 (N.J. App. Div. 1979) 9.07n11

Ocean Acres Ltd. Partnership v. Dare County Bd. of Health, 514 F. Supp. 1117 (E.D.N.C. 1981), *aff'd on other grounds,* 707 F.2d 103 (4th Cir. 1983) 8.39n7

Ocean Acres, Ltd. Partnership v. Dare County Bd. of Health, 707 F.2d 103 (4th Cir. 1983) . . 6.10n4

Ocean Cty. Bd. of Realtors v. Township of Long Beach, 599 A.2d 1309 (N.J.L. 1991) . . 5.05n2

Oceco Land Co. v. Department of Natural Resources, 548 N.W.2d 702 (Mich. App. 1996) . . 12.15n3

O'Connor v. Moscow, City of, 202 P.2d 401 (Idaho 1941) 5.81n13

Oconomowoc Residential Programs, Inc. v. Greenfield, City of, 23 F. Supp.2d 941 (E.D. Wis. 1998) 5.15n2

Odabash v. Mayor & Council of Borough of Dumont, 319 A.2d 712 (N.J. 1974) 6.37n8

O'Dell v. Eagan, City of, 348 N.W.2d 792 (Minn. App. 1984) 9.09n2

Ogden v. Premier Props., USA, Inc., 755 N.E.2d 661 . . . . 6.64n1

Ogo Assocs. v. Torrance, City of, 112 Cal. Rptr. 761 (Cal. App. 1974) 6.11n4; 6.37n17

Ogo Assocs. v. Torrance, City of 112 Cal. Rptr. 761 (Cal. App. 1974) 8.11n17

Ohio Civil Rights Comm'n v. Dayton Christian Schools, Inc., 477 U.S. 619 (1986) . . . 8.42n4

Oka v. Cole, 145 So. 2d 233 (Fla. 1962) . . 6.31n4

Okemo Trailside Condos. v. Blais, 380 A.2d 84 (Vt. 1977) 10.10n3

Oklahoma, City of v. Tuttle, 471 U.S. 808 (1985) 8.31n3

O'Ko'olau v. Pacarro, 666 P.2d 177 (Haw. App. 1983) 6.74n3

Okun v. Superior Court of Los Angeles, 629 P.2d 1369 (Cal.1981) 8.46n9

Olathe, City of v. Board of Zoning Appeals, 696 P.2d 409 (Kan. App. 1986) 6.48n4

Old Country Burgers v. Town Bd. of Oyster Bay, 553 N.Y.S.2d 843 (App. Div. 1990) 6.59n4

Old Town, City of v. Dimoulas, 803 A.2d 1018 . . 6.33n2

Old Tuckaway Assocs. Ltd. Partnership v. Greenfield, City of, 509 N.W.2d 323 (Wis. App. 1993) . . . 2.22n7; 8.39n2; 9.28n1

Oliver v. AT&T Wireless Servs., 90 Cal. Rptr.2d 491 (Cal. App. 1999) 4.09n3

Oliver v. Zoning Comm'n, 326 A.2d 841 (Conn. C.P. 1974) 5.08n9

Olley Valley Estates, Inc. v. Fussell, 208 S.E.2d 801 (Ga. 1974) 6.72n4

Ollinger v. Collins, 470 So. 2d 1183 (Ala. 1985) . . 5.79n7

O'Loane v. O'Rourke, 42 Cal. Rptr. 283 (Cal. App. 1965) 3.21n1; 6.82n6

Olon v. Commonwealth, 626 A.2d 533 (Pa. 1993) 4.27n6

Olp v. Brighton, Town of, 19 N.Y.S.2d 546 (Sup. Ct. 1940), *aff'd,* 29 N.Y.S.2d 956 (App. Div. 1941) 6.02n2

Olsen v. Baton Rouge, City of, 247 So. 2d 889 (La. App. 1971) 4.03n1

Olson v. Deadwood, City of, 480 N.W.2d 170 (S.D. 1992) 3.16n1

Olson v. Zoning Bd. of Appeal, 84 N.E.2d 544 (Mass. 1949) 5.19n10

Olszak v. New Hampton, Town of, 661 A.2d 768 (N.H. 1995) 6.45n7

O'Mara v. Council of City of Newark, 48 Cal. Rptr. 208 (Cal. App. 1965) 5.80n2

O'Mara v. Council of City of Newark, 48 Cal. Rptr. 208 (Cal. App. 1966) 8.11n3

Omnipoint Corp. v. Zoning Hearing Bd., 181 F. 3d 403 (3d Cir. 1999) 4.42n11

Omnipoint Corp. v. Zoning Hearing Bd., 181 F.3d 403 (3d Cir. 1999) 4.42n13

140 Riverside Drive v. Murdock, 95 N.Y.S.2d 860 (App. Div. 1950) 5.20n6

One Hundred Two Glenstone, Inc. v. Board of Adjustment, 572 S.W.2d 891 (Mo. App. 1978) 6.54n6

1902 Atlantic Ltd. v. United States, 26 Cl. Ct. 575 (Cl. Ct. 1992) 2.22n3, n5

119 Friends of Davis v. Davis, City of, 100 Cal. Rptr. 2d 413 . . . . 11.24n3

11126 Baltimore Blvd., Inc. v. Prince George's County, 58 F.3d 998 (4th Cir. 1995) . . 6.57n12

11.30. and Penn Central Transportation Co. v. New York City 438 U.S. 104 (1978) 11.35n2

1126 Baltimore Blvd., Inc. v. Prince George's County, 58 F.3d 988 (4th Cir. 1995) 6.57n8

1000 Friends of Or. v. Board of County Comm'rs, 564 P.2d 1080 (Or. App. 1977) 8.16n6

1000 Friends of Or. v. Land Conservation & Dev. Comm'n, 593 P.2d 1171 (Or. App. 1979) 8.06n2

1000 Friends of Oregon v. Wasco Cty. Ct., 723 P.2d 1034 (Or. App. 1986) 6.71n7

O'Neill v. Burns, 198 So. 2d 1 (Fla. 1967) 6.22n8

O'Neill v. Zoning Bd. of Adjustment 254 A.2d 12 (Pa. 1969) 6.42n4

Onslow County v. Moore, 499 S.E.2d 780 (N.C. App. 1998) 5.66n1

Open Door Alcoholism Program, Inc. v. Board of Adjustment, 491 A.2d 17 (N.J. App. Div. 1985) 5.08n11

Open Door Baptist Church v. Clark County, 995 P.2d 33 . . . . 6.57n13

Opp v. Portland, City of, 16 P.3d 520 . . . 6.71n6

Orange County v. Apopka, City of, 299 So. 2d 652 (Fla. App. 1974) 4.38n1

Orange County Publications v. Council of City of Newburgh, 401 N.Y.S.2d 84 (App. Div. 1978) 6.76n10

Orange Lake Assocs. v. Kirkpatrick, 21 F.3d 1214 (2d Cir. 1994) 7.03n5; 7.05n6; 8.35n4

Orangetown, Town of v. Magee, 665 N.E.2d 1061 (N.Y. 1996) 6.20n1

Orazio v. North Hempstead, Town of, 426 F. Supp. 1144 (E.D.N.Y. 1977) 11.23n5

Oregon City v. Hartke, 400 P.2d 255 (Or. 1965) . . 5.42n2; 11.05n1; 11.08n3

Oregon State Homebuilders Ass'n v. Tigard, City of, 604 P.2d 886 (Or. App. 1979) 9.22n1

Orinda Ass'n v. Board of Supervisors, 227 Cal. Rptr. 688 (Cal. App. 1986) 6.48n10

Orinda Homeowners Comm. v. Board of Supvrs., 90 Cal. Rptr. 88 (Cal. App. 1970) 9.26n3

Orion Corp. v. State (II), 747 P.2d 1062 (Wash. 1987) 2.37n4

Osborne v. Planning Bd., 536 N.Y.S.2d 244 (Sup. Ct. 1989) 5.20n4

Oshry v. Zoning Bd. of Appeals, 713 N.Y.S.2d 564 . . . . 6.76n16

Osius v. St. Clair Shores, City of, 75 N.W.2d 25 (Mich. 1956) 6.02n4; 6.03n4

Otto v. Steinhilber 6.44

Ottowa County Farms, Inc. v. Township of Polkton, 345 N.W.2d 672 (Mich. App. 1983) . . 5.37n2

Ouimette v. Somersworth, City of, 402 A.2d 159 (N. H.1979) 6.48n2

Our Saviour's Evangelical Lutheran Ch. v. Naperville, City of, 541 N.E.2d 1150 (Ill. App. 1989) 6.57n14

Ours Properties v. Ley, 96 S.E.2d 754 (Va. 1957) 6.03n3

Outdoor Graphics v. Burlington, City of, 103 F.3d 690 (8th Cir. 1996) 11.13n3

Outdoor Graphics, Inc. v. Burlington, City of, 103 F.2d 690 (8th Cir. 1996) 5.84n7

Outdoor Graphics, Inc. v. Burlington, City of, 103 F.3d 690 (8th Cir. 1996) 11.07n16

Outdoor Sys., Inc. v. Mesa, City of, 997 F.2d 604 (9th Cir. 1993) 6.57n4; 11.07n12; 11.11n9; 11.19n14

Outdoor Sys., Inc. v. Mesa, City of 997 F.2d 604 (9th Cir. 1993) 11.07n15

Outdoor Systems v. Mesa, City of, 819 P.2d 44 (Ariz. 1991) 11.06n2

Outdoor Systems, Inc. v. Lenaxa, City of, 67 F. Supp.2d 1231 (D. Kan. 1999) 11.23n5

Outdoor Systems, Inc. v. Lenexa, City of, 67 F. Supp.2d 1241 (D. Kan. 1999) 11.17n4

Outdoor Systems, Inc. v. Merriam, City of, 67 F. Supp.2d 1258 (D. Kan. 1999) . 6.57n2; 11.19n7

Outdoor Systems, Inc. v. Mesa, City of, 819 P.2d 44 (Ariz. 1991) 11.11n9

Outdoor Systems, Inc. v. Mesa, City of, 997 F.2d 604 (9th Cir. 1993) 5.84n8; 11.18n2; 11.19n7

Overhill Bldg. Co. v. Delany, 271 N.E.2d 537 (N.Y. 1971) 6.50n4

Overstreet v. Zoning Hearing Bd., 412 A.2d 169 (Pa. Commw. 1980) 6.52n8

Owen v. Independence, City of 8.37n1

Oxford House v. Township of Cherry Hill, 799 F. Supp. 450 (D.N.J. 1992) 5.14n1

Oxford House-C v. St. Louis, City of, 77 F.3d 249 (8th Cir. 1996) 5.14n4

Oxford-House Evergreen v. Plainfield, City of, 769 F. Supp. 1329 (D.N.J. 1991) . . . 8.42n10; 8.45n3

P

P Assocs. v. Raleigh, City of 258 S.E.2d 444 (N.C. 1979) 11.29n5; 11.32n5

Pace Resources, Inc. v. Shrewsbury Township, 808 F.2d 1023 (3d Cir.) 2.30n5

Pace Resources, Inc. v. Shrewsbury Township, 808 F.2d 1023 (3d Cir. 1987) 6.36n1

Pace Resources, Inc. v. Shrewsbury Twp., 808 F.2d 1023 (3d Cir. 1987) 2.30n9

Pace Resources, Inc. v. Shrewsbury Twp. Planning Comm'n, 492 A.2d 818 (Pa. Commw. 1985) . . 6.37n6, n12

Pacesetter Constr. Co.; State v., 571 P.2d 196 (Wash. 1977) 5.74n6

Pacesetter Constr. Co.; State v. 571 P.2d 196 (Wash. 1977) 2.37n4

Pacesetter Homes v. Olympia Fields, Village of, 244 N.E.2d 369 (Ill. App. 1968) 11.25n3

Pacific Blvd. Assocs. v. Long Beach, City of, 368 N.Y.S.2d 867 (Sup. Ct. 1975) 6.37n15

Padillo v. Lawrence, 685 P.2d 964 (N.M. App. 1984) 4.05n1

Paedae v. Escambia County, 709 So.2d 575 (Fla. App. 1998) 8.23n1

Painesville Bldg. Dep't, City of v. Dworken & Bernstein Co., 733 N.E.2d 1152 . . . . . . 11.23n6

Paladac v. Rockland, City of, 558 A.2d 372 (Me. 1989) 5.26n3

Palatine I v. Planning Bd., 628 A.2d 321 (N.J. 1993) 6.66n11

Palatine Nat'l Bank v. Barrington, Village of, 532 N.E.2d 955 (Ill. App. 1988) 3.15n9

Palatine, Village of v. LaSalle Nat'l Bank, 445 N.E.2d 1277 (Ill. App. 1983) 6.21n2

Palatine, Village of; United States v. , 37 F.3d 1230 (7th Cir. 1994) 5.13n3

Palazzola v. Gulfport, City of, 52 So. 2d 611 (Miss. 1951) 5.80n2, n11

Palazzolo v. Rhode Island, State of . . . 12.07n14

Palazzolo v. Rhode Island, State of, 533 U.S. 606 . . . 2.09n5; 2.16n11; 6.50n9; 12.07n14

Palazzolo v. Rhode Island, State of 533 U.S. 606 . . . . 2.28n3

Palazzolo State Dep't of Envtl. Protection v. Burgess, 772 So.2d 540 . . . . 2.16n12

Palermo Land Co. v. Planning Comm'n, 561 So. 2d 482 (La. 1990) 4.30n5

Palermo Land Co. v. Planning Comm'n of Calcasieu Parish, 561 So. 2d 482 (La. 1990) . . . 6.15n1; 6.31n5; 6.37n7

Palisades Props., Inc. v. Brunetti, 207 A.2d 523 (N.J. 1965) 6.29n9

Palm Beach County v. Wright 641 So. 2d 50 (Fla. 1994) 10.15n9

Palm Beach Isles Assocs. v. United States, 208 F.3d 1374 . . . . 2.19n4; 12.07n12

Palm Beach, Town of v. Gradison, 296 So. 2d 473 (Fla. App. 1974) 6.76n3

Palmer v. Board of Zoning Adjustment, 287 A.2d 535 (D.C. App. 1972) 6.48n8

Palmer v. Jackson, 617 F.2d 424 (5th Cir. 1980) . . 8.43n4

Palmer v. St. Louis County, 591 S.W.2d 39 (Mo. App. 1980) 8.02n7, n10; 8.04n6

Palmieri v. Zoning Bd. of Appeals, 349 A.2d 731 (Conn. Super. 1975) 8.08n1

Pan Pac. Props. v. Santa Cruz, County of, 146 Cal. Rptr. 428 (Cal. App. 1978) 8.10n1

Papalia v. Inspector of Bldgs., 217 N.E.2d 911 (Mass. 1966) 6.22n9

Par Developers v. Planning & Zoning Comm'n, 655 A.2d 1164 (Conn. App. 1995) 8.14n5

Par Mar v. Parkersburg, City of, 398 S.E.2d 532 (W.Va. 1990) 2.37n7

Paradise Valley, Town of v. Gulf Leisure Corp., 557 P.2d 532 (Ariz. App. 1976) . . 6.21n1; 8.11n18

Paradyne Corp. v. State Dep't of Transp., 528 So. 2d 291 (Fla. App. 1988) 9.13n4

Paragon Props. Co. v. Novi, City of, 550 N.W.2d 772 (Mich. 1996) 8.09n4, n6

Parishville, Town of v. Contore Co., 667 N.Y.S.2d 453 (App. Div. 1998) 4.30n11

Park Area Neighbors v. Fairfax, Town of, 35 Cal. Rptr. 2d 334 (Cal. App. 1994) 8.10n1

Park Ave. Tower Assocs. v. New York, City of, 746 F.2d 135 (2d Cir. 1984) 6.36n1

Park Constr. Corp. v. Board of County Comm'rs, 227 A.2d 15 (Md. 1967) 6.31n5

Park Home v. Williamsport, City of, 680 A.2d 835 (Pa. 1996) 11.35n5

Park Ridge, City of; People v. , 166 N.E.2d 635 (Ill. App. 1960) 9.06n2

Park View Heights Corp. v. Black Jack, City of, 467 F.2d 1208 (8th Cir. 1972) 7.04n4

Park View Heights Corp. v. Black Jack, City of, 605 F.2d 1033 (8th Cir. 1979) 7.06n1

Parker v. Beacon Hill Arch. Ass'n, 536 N.E.2d 1108 (Mass. 1989) 11.29n4

Parker v. Brown 317 U.S. 341 (1943) . . . 5.50n1

Parker v. Gardiner, Town of, 585 N.Y.S.2d 571 (App. Div. 1992) 6.74n12

Parkersburg Bldrs. Material Co. v. Barrack 191 S.E. 368, 192 S.E. 291 (W. Va. 1937) 4.09n1

Parking Ass'n of Ga. v. Atlanta, City of, 450 S.E.2d 200 (Ga. 1994) 5.36n4

Parking Ass'n of Georgia v. Atlanta, City of, 450 S.E.2d 200 (Ga. 1994) 5.77n2

Parkowners Ass'n v. Montclair, City of, 211 F.3d 1144 . . . . 8.42n3

Parkridge v. Seattle, City of 573 P.2d 359 (Wash. 1978) 6.31n7

Parkridge v. Seattle, City of 573 P.2d 359 (Wash. 1978) 6.38n1

Parks v. Board of Adjustment, 566 S.W.2d 365 (Tex. Civ. App. 1978) 5.20n4

Parks v. Board of County Comm'rs, 501 P.2d 85 (Or. App. 1972) 8.14n12

Parks v. Watson, 716 F.2d 646 (9th Cir. 1983) . . . 5.54n1

Parkview Assocs. v. New York, City of, 519 N.E.2d 1372 (N.Y. 1988) 6.17n1

Parkview Assocs. Partnership v. Lebanon, City of, 225 F.3d 321 . . . . 2.34n4

Parma, City of; United States v. , 494 F. Supp. 1049 (N.D. Ohio 1980), *aff'd,* 661 F.2d 562 (6th Cir. 1981), *cert. denied* *7.06n2*

Parma Heights, City of v. Jaros, 591 N.E.2d 726 (Ohio App. 1990) 6.05n13

Parranto Bros. v. New Brighton, City of, 425 N.W.2d 585 (Minn. App. 1988) 6.37n6, n15

Parranto Bros., Inc. v. New Brighton, City of, 425 N.W.2d 585 (Minn. App. 1988) . . . 2.16n8, n9

Parratt v. Taylor 8.33

Parratt in Logan v. Zimmerman Brush Co . . 8.33

Parratt in Zinermon v. Burch 494 U.S. 113 (1990) 8.33n6

Paruszewski v. Township of Elsinboro, 711 A.2d 273 (N.J. 1998) 6.74n11

Pasadena Airport Auth. v. Los Angeles, City of, 979 F.2d 1338 (9th Cir. 1992) 4.43n5

Pasco, City of v. Rhine, 753 P.2d 993 (Wash. App. 1988) 6.57n15

Pasco Cty. v. Tampa Farm Serv., 573 So. 2d 909 (Fla. App. 1990) 12.11n7

Passaic, City of v. Paterson Bill Posting, Adv. & Sign Painting Co 11.03

Pate v. City Council, 622 So.2d 405 (Ala. Civ. App. 1993) 5.54n5

Patenaude v. Meredith, Town of, 392 A.2d 582 (N.H. 1978) 9.19n4

Patsy v. Florida Bd. of Regents, 457 U.S. 496 (1982) 8.33n1

Patterson v. Alpine Village, 663 P.2d 95 (Utah 1983) 9.22n1

Patterson v. Tehama, County of, 235 Cal. Rptr. 867 (Cal. App. 1987) 6.83n8

Pattey v. Board of County Comm'rs, 317 A.2d 142 (Md. 1974) 6.31n7

Pattison v. Corby, 172 A.2d 490 (Md. 1961) 8.04n6

Patzau v. New Jersey Dep't of Transp., 638 A.2d 866 (N.J. App. Div. 1994) 5.39n6

PDR Dev. Corp. v. Santa Fe, City of, 900 P.2d 973 (N.M. App. 1995) 8.21n1

Peachtree Dev. Co. v. Paul, 423 N.E.2d 1087 (Ohio 1981) 6.03n4

Peachtree Dev. Co. v. Paul 423 N.E.2d 1087 (Ohio 1981) 9.27n4

Peacock v. Sacramento, County of, 77 Cal. Rptr. 391 (Cal. App. 1969) 2.23n4; 8.21n2

Pearce v. Edina, Village of, 118 N.W.2d 659 (Minn. 1962) 5.46n1

Pearl Inv. Co. v. City & County of San Francisco, 774 F.2d 1460 (9th Cir. 1985) . . . 8.43n6, n9, n11

Pearson v. Evans, 320 P.2d 300 (Wash. 1958) 5.19n2

Pearson v. Grand Blanc, City of, 961 F.2d 1211 (6th Cir. 1992) . . . 2.32n3; 2.39n5; 2.40n2; 6.25n13

Pearson Kent Corp. v. Bear 271 N.E.2d 218 (N.Y. 1971) 9.09n17

Pease Hill Community Group v. Spokane, County of, 816 P.2d 37 (Wash. App. 1991) 6.70n10

Pellegrino Food Prods. Co. v. Warren, City of, 136 F. Supp. 2d 391 . . . . 5.55n8

Pellegrino Food Prods. Co. v. Warren, City of, 136 F.Supp.2d 391 . . . . 8.46n11

Peltz v. South Euclid, City of, 228 N.E.2d 320 (Ohio 1967) 11.23n3

Pembaur v. Cincinnati, City of 475 U.S. 469 (1986) 8.31n4

Pemberton v. Montgomery County, 340 A.2d 240 (Md. 1975) 6.21n3

Pence v. State, 652 N.E.2d 486 (Ind. 1995) 8.02n4

Pendleton Constr. Co. v. Rockbridge County, 652 F. Supp. 312 (W.D. Va. 1987) . . . 5.54n3; 5.55n6

Pendoley v. Ferreira, 187 N.E.2d 142 (Mass. 1963) 4.12n6

Pengilly v. Multnomah County, 810 F. Supp. 1111 (D. Or. 1992) 9.15n4; 9.16n11

Peninsula Corp. v. Planning & Zoning Comm'n, 199 A.2d 1 (Conn. 1964) 9.05n7

Penn Advertising of Baltimore, Inc. v. Mayor & Council, 63 F.3d 1318 (4th Cir. 1995), *modified* *11.19n5*

Penn Cent. Transp. Co. v. New York City, 438 U.S. 104 (1978) 2.25n1

Penn Central Transp. Co. v. New York City 438 U.S. 104 (1978) 2.07n1

Pennhurst State School & Hosp. v. Halderman, 451 U.S. 1 (1981) 8.29n5

Pennsylvania Coal Co. v. Mahon 260 U.S. 393 (1922) 2.05n1

Pennsylvania Nw. Distribs., Inc. v. Zoning Hearing Bd., 584 A.2d 1372 (Pa. 1990) 5.85n5

Penobscot Area Hous. Dev. Corp. v. Brewer, City of, 434 A.2d 14 (Me. 1981) 5.08n3

Penobscot, Inc. v. Board of County Comm'rs, 642 P.2d 915 (Colo. 1982) 9.05n7

People v. (see name of defendant)

People ex (see name of defendant)

People ex rel. (see name of defendant)

People of Village of Cahokia v. Wright, 311 N.E.2d 153 . . . . 5.23n3

People Tags, Inc. v. Jackson County Legislature, 636 F. Supp. 1345 (W.D. 1986) 8.43n8

People Tags, Inc. v. Jackson County Legislature, 636 F. Supp. 1345 (W.D. Mo. 1986) 5.63n8; 8.43n9; 8.44n6

Pepper v. J.J. Welcome Constr. Co., 871 P.2d 601 (Wash. App. 1994) 8.23n17

Perez; People v. , 29 Cal. Rptr. 781 (Cal. App. 1963) 6.54n4

Perkins v. Madison County Livestock & Fair Ass'n, 613 N.W.2d 264 . . . . 4.05n1

Perlmart of Lacey, Inc. v. Lacey Township Planning Bd., 684 A.2d 1005 (N.J. App. Div. 1996) . . . 6.70n5

Perron v. Concord, City of, 150 A.2d 403 (N.H. 1959) 5.19n2

Perron v. New Brighton, Village of, 145 N.W.2d 425 (Minn. 1966) 2.46n5

Perry-Worth Concerned Citizens v. Board of Comm'rs, 723 N.E.2d 457 . . . . 6.74n5

Personnel Adm'r of Mass. v. Feeney, 442 U.S. 256 (1979) 7.03n2

Peru, City of v. Nienaber, 424 N.E.2d 85 (Ill. App. 1981) 5.19n7

Peru, City of v. Querciagrossa, 392 N.E.2d 778 (Ill. App. 1979) 6.17n2

Pestey v. Cushman, 788 A.2d 496 . . . . . 4.02n2

Petersburg Cellular Partnership v. Board of Supervisors, 29 F. Supp.2d 701 (E.D. Va. 1998) 4.42n10

Petersen v. Chicago Plan Comm'n, 707 N.E.2d 150 (Ill. App. 1998) 6.70n3

Petersen v. Clemson, City of, 439 S.E.2d 317 (S.C. App. 1993) 6.70n8; 9.28n2

Petersen v. Dane County, 402 N.W.2d 376 (Wis. App. 1987) 6.33n1; 12.13n6

Petersen v. Decorah, City of, 259 N.W.2d 553 (Iowa App. 1977) 5.17n6

Peterson v. Mayor & Council, 21 A.2d 777 (N.J. 1941) 5.47n5

Peterson Outdoor Advertising v. Myrtle Beach, City of, 489 S.E.2d 630 (S.C. 1997) 11.24n2

Petition of (see name of party)

Petrick v. Planning Bd., 671 A.2d 140 (N.J. App. Div. 1996) 6.74n9

Petrosky v. Zoning Hearing Bd., 402 A.2d 1385 (Pa. 1979) 6.12n1; 6.17n2

Petruzzi v. Zoning Board of Appeals, 176 Conn. 479, 408 A.2d 243 (1979) 5.78n2

Petterson v. Naperville, City of, 137 N.E.2d 371 (Ill. 1956) 9.03n11

Petty v. Barrentine, 594 S.W.2d 903 (Ky. App. 1980) 6.18n7

Pfile v. Zoning Bd. of Adjustment, 298 A.2d 598 (Pa. Commw. 1972) 8.19n8

Pharr, City of v. Tippitt, 616 S.W.2d 173 (Tex. 1981) 6.28n2

Pheasant Ridge Assocs. v. Burlington, Town of, 506 N.E.2d 1152 (Mass. 1987) 7.31n9

Pheasant Ridge Corp. v. Township of Warren, 777 A.2d 334 . . . . 2.22n9; 5.32n2

Philanz Oldsmobile, Inc. v. Keating, 381 N.Y.S.2d 916 (App. Div. 1976) 5.86n6

Phillipi v. Sublimity., City of 662 P.2d 325 (Or.1983) 3.17n2

Phillips v. Borough of Keyport, 107 F.3d 164 (3d Cir. 1997) 2.39n7

Phillips v. Brookhaven, Town of, 628 N.Y.S.2d 723 (App. Div. 1995) 5.54n5

Phillips v. Homewood, City of, 50 So. 2d 267 (Ala. 1951) 8.15n2

Philric Assocs. v. South Portland, 595 A.2d 1061 (Me. 1991) 2.22n3, n7

Phoenix City Council v. Canyon Ford, Inc., 473 P.2d 797 (Ariz. App. 1970) 6.21n1

Phoenix, City of v. Beall, 524 P.2d 1314 (Ariz. App. 1974) 2.36n2

Phoenix, City of v. Fehlner 5.38

Pica v. Sarno, 907 F. Supp. 795 (D.N.J. 1995) . . . 11.19n18

Picha v. McLeod, County of, 634 N.W.2d 739 . . . 6.56n8

Pickle v. Board of Cty. Comm'rs, 764 P.2d 262 (Wyo. 1988) 8.23n8

Pierson v. Henry County, 417 N.E.2d 234 (Ill. App. 1981) 12.13n6

Pierson v. Ray, 386 U.S. 547 (1967) 8.36n5

Pierson Trapp Co. v. Peak, 340 S.W.2d 456 (Ky. 1960) 5.36n10

Pigg v. State Dep't of Hwys., 746 P.2d 961 (Colo. 1987) 11.19n7

Piggott v. Borough of Hopewell, 91 A.2d 667 (N.J. 1952) 6.74n10

Pine Ridge Recycling, Inc. v. Butts County, 855 F. Supp. 1264 (M.D. Ga. 1994) 5.54n5

Pinecrest Lakes, Inc. v. Shidel, 705 So.2d 191 . . . 8.15n10

Pinecrest Lakes, Inc. v. Shidel, 795 So.2d 191 . . . 6.33n2

Pinehurst Enters. v. Southern Pines, Town of, 690 F. Supp. 444 (M.D.N.C. 1988) 5.54n3

Piney Mt. Neighborhood Ass'n v. Chapel Hill, Town of, 304 S.E.2d 251 (N.C. App. 1983) 6.56n11; 6.58n4

Pingitore v. Cave Creek, Town of, 981 P.2d 129 (Ariz. App 1999) 6.16n7; 6.18n3

Pioneer Trust Co. v. Pima Cty., 811 P.2d 22 (Ariz. 1991) 6.82n7

Pioneer Trust & Sav. Bank v. McHenry, County of, 241 N.E.2d 454 (Ill. 1968) 5.25n2

Pioneer Trust & Sav. Bank v. Mount Prospect, Village of 176 N.E.2d 799 (Ill. 1961) 9.19n1

Pirolo v. Clearwater, City of, 711 F.2d 1006 (11th Cir. 1983) 4.43n3

Piscitelli v. Township Comm., 248 A.2d 274 (N.J.L. Div. 1968) 11.25n2

Pisello v. Brookhaven, Town of, 933 F.Supp 202 (E.D. N.Y. 1996) 8.46n11

Pitcher v. Heidelberg Township Bd. of Supervisors, 637 A.2d 715 (Pa. Commw. 1994) . . . 9.16n11

Pitts v. Pilkerton, 714 F. Supp. 285 (M.D. Tenn. 1989) 2.53n3

Pitts, State ex rel. v. Board of Zoning Adjustments, 327 So. 2d 140 (La. App. 1976) 6.45n7

Pittsburgh, Historic Review Comm'n, City of v. Weinberg, 676 A.2d 207 (Pa. 1996) . . 11.35n5

Pittsfield Charter Township v. Washtenaw County, 633 N.W.2d 10 . . . . 4.38n3

Pizzo Mantin Group v. Township of Randolph, 645 A.2d 89 (N.J. 1994) 9.09n2

Plainfield, City of v. Borough of Middlesex, 173 A.2d 785 (N.J.L. Div. 1961) 2.23n4

Plan Comm'n of Harrison County v. Aulbach, 748 N.E..2d 926 (Ind. App. 2001) 9.09n1

Plandome Doughnuts v. Mammima, 692 N.Y.S2d 111 (App. Div. 1999) 6.59n4

Planning & Zoning Comm'n v. Synanon Found., Inc., 216 A.2d 442 (Conn. 1966) 5.08n11

Plano, City of v. Allen, City of, 395 S.W.2d 927 (Tex. App. 1965) 4.39n2

Platte, County of v. Chipman, 512 S.W.2d 199 (Mo. App. 1974) 8.10n3

Plattsburgh, City of v. Mannix, 432 N.Y.S.2d 910 (Sup. Ct. 1980) 8.07n1

Plaza Mobile & Modular Homes, Inc. v. Colchester, Town of, 639 F. Supp. 140 (D. Conn. 1986) . . 5.54n3

Pleas v. Seattle, City of, 774 P.2d 1158 (Wash. 1989) 8.23n6

Pleasant Valley Neighborhood Ass'n v. Planning & Zoning Comm'n, 543 A.2d 296 (Conn. App. 1988) 6.61n3

Pleasureland Museum, Inc. v. Beutter, 288 F.3d 988 . . . . 5.64n3; 5.65n2

Plymouth Charter Twp. v. Department of Soc. Servs., 501 N.W.2d 186 (Mich. App. 1993) . . 5.15n1

PNA AOA Media, L.L.C. v. Jackson County, 554 S.E.2d 657 . . . . 11.06n6

POA Co. v. Findlay Township Zoning Hearing Bd., 679 A.2d 1342 (Pa. Commw. 1996) . . . 6.50n8

Poe v. Baltimore, City of, 216 A.2d 707 (Md. 1966) 8.08n1; 8.11n6

Poirier v. Grand Blanc Township (II), 481 N.W.2d 762 (Mich. App. 1992) 8.21n6

Poirier v. Grand Blanc Tp., 423 N.W.2d 351 (Mich. App. 1988) 8.26n2

Poirier v. Grand Blanc Twp. (I), 423 N.W.2d 351 (Mich. App. 1988) 8.21n1

Pokoik v. Silsdorf, 358 N.E.2d 874 (N.Y. 1976) . . 6.16n1

Polk v. Lubec, Town of, 756 A.2d 510 . . 2.49n5

Pollard v. Palm Beach Cty., 560 So. 2d 1358 (Fla. App. 1990) 6.56n9

Pompano Beach, City of v. Yardarm Restaurant, 641 So. 2d 1377 (Fla. App. 1994) 2.21n1

Pompey, Town of v. Parker, 377 N.E.2d 741 (N.Y. 1978) 5.24n3

Pomponio v. Fauquier County Bd. of Supvrs., 21 F.3d 1319 (4th Cir. 1994) 8.44n9

Pond Brook Dev. Co. v. Twinsburg Township, 35 F. Supp. 2d 1025 (N.D. Ohio 1999) 2.30n6

Poole v. Berkeley County Planning Comm'n, 488 S.E.2d 349 (W. Va. 1997) 5.81n13

Pope v. Atlanta, City of, 249 S.E.2d 16 (Ga. 1978) 2.37n5

Pope v. Atlanta, City of, 418 F. Supp. 665 (Ga. 1977) 12.05n5

Pope v. Hinsdale, Town of, 624 A.2d 1360 (N.H. 1993) 5.26n2

Pope v. Little Bear's Head Dist., 764 A.2d 932 . . 2.49n5

Popisil v. Anderson, 527 N.Y.S.2d 819 (App. Div. 1988) 8.15n3

Poppell v. San Diego, City of, 149 F.3d 951 (9th Cir. 1998) 2.47n3; 2.49n3

Popular Refreshments, Inc. v. Fuller's Milk Bar, Inc., 205 A.2d 445 (N.J. App. Div. 1964) . . 9.06n5

Porpoise Point Pt'ship v. St. John's Cty., 532 So. 2d 727 (Fla. App. 1988) 9.27n6

Port Clinton Assocs. v. Board of Selectmen, 587 A.2d 126 (Conn. 1991) 8.09n3

Port of St. Helens v. Land Conservation & Dev. Comm'n, 996 P.2d 1014 . . . . 10.07n5

Port Orange, City of; State v., 650 So. 2d 1 (Fla. 1994) 9.21n2

Porter v. Southwestern Pub. Serv. Co., 489 S.W.2d 361 (Tex. 1972) 4.32n3

Portland, City of v. Carriage Inn, 676 P.2d 943 (Or. App. 1984) 1.13n2

Portland, City of v. Fisherman's Wharf Assocs. (II), 541 A.2d 160 (Me. 1988) 6.22n2

Portland Sand & Gravel v. Gray, Town of, 663 A.2d 41 (Me. 1995) 8.14n3

Portsmouth Advocates, Inc. v. Portsmouth, City of, 587 A.2d 600 (N.H. 1991) 11.28n3

Potomac Edison Co. v. Jefferson County Planning & Zoning Comm'n, 512 S.E.2d 576 (W.Va. 1998) 4.32n2

Potomac Greens Assocs. Pt'ship v. City Council of Alexandria, 761 F. Supp. 416 (E.D. Va. 1991) 6.05n23

Potomac Sand & Gravel Co. v. Governor of Md., 293 A.2d 241 (Md. 1972) 12.07n4

Potter v. Bryan Funeral Home, 817 S.W.2d 882 (Ark. 1991) 4.07n1

Potter v. Hartford Zoning Bd. of Adjustment, 407 A.2d 170 (Vt. 1979) 6.52n3

Pound Hill Corp. v. Perl 8.46

Powell v. Superior Portland Cement, 129 P.2d 536 (Wash. 1942) 4.04n2

Powell v. Taylor, 263 S.W.2d 906 (Ark. 1954) . . . 4.07n1

Powers v. Building Inspector, 296 N.E.2d 491 (Mass. 1973) 5.79n4

Powers v. Skagit County, 835 P.2d 230 (Wash. App. 1992) 12.09n10

Prah v. Moretti, 321 N.W.2d 182 (Wis. 1982) . . . 4.09n4

Prater v. Burnside, City of, 289 F.3d 417 . . . . . . 5.70n6

Pratt v. Building Inspector, 113 N.E.2d 816 (Mass. 1953) 5.19n3

PRB Enters. v. South Brunswick Planning Bd., 518 A.2d 1099 (N.J. 1987) 6.66n10

Precision Equities, Inc. v. Franklin Park Borough Zoning Hearing Bd., 646 A.2d 756 (Pa. Commw. 1994) 7.20n5

Preferred Sites, LLC v. Troup County, 296 F.3d 1210 . . . . 4.42n13

Prekeges v. King County, 990 P.2d 405 (Wash. App. 1999) 6.70n5

Presbyterian Church of Washington County, State ex rel. v. Washington, City of, 911 S.W.2d 697 (Mo. App. 1995) 6.56n8

Presbytery of Seattle v. King County, 787 P.2d 907 (Wash.1990) 8.11n16

Presnell v. Leslie, 144 N.E.2d 381 (N.Y. 1959) . . 5.19n2

Pressman v. Baltimore, City of, 160 A.2d 379 (Md. 1960) 6.63n6

Price v. Fayette County Bd. of County Comm'rs, 958 P.2d 583 (Idaho 1998) 6.34n1

Price v. Lakewood, City of, 818 P.2d 763 (Colo. 1991) 6.05n3

Price v. Smith, 207 A.2d 887 (Pa. 1965) 6.18n1; 6.21n2

Primerica v. Planning & Zoning Comm'n, 558 A.2d 646 (Conn. 1989) 5.38n3

Prince George's County v. Blumberg, 407 A.2d 1151 (Md. 1979) 6.21n3

Prince George's County v. Equitable Trust Co., 408 A.2d 737 (Md. 1970) 6.22n8

Prince George's County v. M & B Constr. Co . . . 9.26

Prince George's County v. Sunrise Dev. Ltd. Partnership, 623 A.2d 1296 (Md. 1993) 6.21n3

Pritchett v. Nathan Rodgers Constr. & Realty Corp., 379 So. 2d 545 (Ala. 1979) 6.11n2

Pro-Eco, Inc. v. Board of Comm'rs, 57 F.3d 305 (7th Cir. 1995) 2.42n2

Pro-Eco, Inc. v. Board of Comm'rs, 57 F.3d 505 . . 2.42n10

Professional Real Estate Investors, Inc. v. Columbia Pictures Indus., Inc., 508 U.S. 49 (1993) 5.55

Professional Real Estate Investors, Inc. v. Columbia Pictures Industries, Inc., 508 U.S. 49 (1993) . . . 5.55n7; 8.46n5

Project Home, Inc. v. Astatula, Town of, 373 So. 2d 710 (Fla. App. 1979) 6.16n6

Protect Hamden/North Haven From Excessive Traffic & Poll v. Planning & Zoning Comm'n, 600 A.2d 757 (Conn. 1991) 6.30n3

Protect Our Mountain Env't, Inc. (POME) v. District Ct., 677 P.2d 1361 (Colo. 1984) 8.46n7

Prudco Realty Corp. v. Palermo, 455 N.E.2d 483 (N.Y. 1983) 5.81n8

Prudential Ins. Co. v. Board of Appeals, 502 N.E.2d 137 (Mass. App. 1986) 6.66n10

Prudential Trust Co. v. Laramie, City of, 492 P.2d 971 (Wyo. 1972) 9.09n13

PruneYard Shopping Center v. Robins 447 U.S. 74 (1980) 2.18n3

Public Serv. Co. v. Hampton, Town of, 411 A.2d 164 (N.H. 1980) 4.32n5

PUDs. Lutz v. Longview, City of 520 P.2d 1374 (Wash. 1974) 9.27n3

Pulaski Hwy., Inc. v. Perryville, Town of, 519 A.2d 206 (Md. App. 1987) 6.57n4

Pullum v. Johnson, 647 So.2d 254 (Fla. App. 1994) 8.46n9

Pure Oil Div. v. Columbia, City of, 173 S.E.2d 140 (S.C. 1970) 6.16n2; 6.21n4

Puritan-Greenfield Imp. Ass'n v. Leo, 153 N.W.2d 162 (Mich. App. 1967) . . . 6.44n3; 6.45n4, n9; 6.46n4

Purze v. Winthrop Harbor, Village of, 236 F.3d 452 . . . . 2.49n4

Putnam County Envtl. Council, Inc. v. Board of County Comm'rs, 757 So.2d 590 . . . . 8.06n2

Pyramid Corp. v. DeSoto County Bd. of Supvrs., 366 F. Supp. 1299 (N.D. Miss. 1973) 8.15n4

Q

Q.C. Constr. Co. v. Gallo, 549 F. Supp. 1331 (D.R.I. 1986), aff'd mem. 836 F.2d 1340 (1st Cir. 1987) 6.11n2

Quackenbush v. Allstate Ins. Co., 517 U.S. 706 (1996) 8.41n4; 8.42n7; 8.44n2, n5

Quality Refrigerated Servs. v. Spencer, City of, 586 N.W.2d 202 (Iowa 1998) 6.70n5

Quarry Knoll II Corp. v. Planning & Zoning Comm'n, 780 A.2d 1 . . . . 7.31n6

Queen Creek Land & Cattle Corp. v. Yavapai County Bd. of Supvrs., 501 P.2d 391 (Ariz. 1972) 6.82n3

Quern v. Jordon, 440 U.S. 332 (1979) . . .   8.29n2

Quinlan v. Dover, City of, 614 A.2d 1057 (N.H. 1992)
. . . . 6.26n5

Quirk v. New Boston, Town of, 663 A.2d 1328 (N.H. 1995) 2.19n1; 5.71n2

R

R" Us v. Silva, 676 N.E.2d 862 (N.Y. 1996) . . . .
5.81n4

R & Y, Inc. v. Municipality of Anchorage, 34 P.3d 289 . . . . 2.37n1; 12.07n7

R.A. Vachon & Son v. Concord, City of, 289 A.2d 646 (N.H. 1972) 9.07n8

Raabe v. Walker, City of, 174 N.W.2d 789 (Mich. 1970) 3.15n7

Racetrac Petroleum, Inc. v. Prince George's County, 601 F. Supp. 892 (D. Md. 1985) 5.55n2

Racetrac Petroleum, Inc. v. Prince George's County 601 F. Supp. 892 (D. Md. 1985), aff'd . . . . . .
5.54n4

Racich v. Boone, County of, 625 N.E.2d 1095 (Ill. App. 1993) 12.13n6

Racine County v. Cape, 639 N.W.2d 782 . . . . . .
5.79n4

Raczkowski v. Zoning Comm'n, 733 A.2d 862 (Conn. App. 1999) 6.56n8

Radach v. Gunderson, 695 P.2d 128 (Wash. App. 1985) 8.15n7

Ragucci v. Metropolitan Dev. Comm'n, 702 N.E.2d 677 (Ind. 1998) 5.79n1, n2

Railroad Comm'n of Texas. v. Pullman Co . . . .
8.43

Railway Express Agency v. New York, City of, 336 U.S. 106 (1949) 11.07n2

Raleigh, City of v. Morand, 100 S.E.2d 870 (N.C. 1957) 4.23n1

Raleigh, City of, In re Application of , 421 S.E.2d 179 (N.C. App. 1992) 6.73n2

Ralph L. Wadsworth Constr., Inc. v. West Jordan City, 999 P.2d 1240 . . . . 6.56n9

Ramirez v. Santa Fe, City of, 852 P.2d 690 (N.M. App. 1993) 8.04n1

Ramona Convent of the Holy Name v. Alhambra, City of, 26 Cal. Rptr. 2d 140 (Cal. App. 1993) . . . .
2.19n1; 2.21n2

Ramsey, County of v. Stevens, 283 N.W.2d 918 (Minn. 1979) 12.08n5

Ranch House, Inc. v. Amerson, 238 F.3d 1273 . . .
5.63n2

Rancho Colorado, Inc. v. Bloomfield, City of, 586 P.2d 659 (Colo. 1978) 9.21n2

Rancho Palos Verdes Corp. v. Laguna Beach, City of, 547 F.2d 1092 (9th Cir. 1976) 8.44n7

Rancho Viejo, LLC v. Tres Amigos Viejos, LLC, 123 Cal. Rptr.2d 479 . . . . 12.11n2

Rancourt v. Barnstead, Town of, 523 A.2d 55 (N.H. 1986) 10.04n4

Rando v. North Attleboro, Town of, 692 N.E.2d 544 (Mass. App. 1998) 6.29n8; 6.64n1

Randolph v. Brookhaven, Town of, 337 N.E.2d 763 (N.Y. 1975) 6.29n8

Randy's Sanitation v. Wright County, 65 F. Supp. 2d 1017 (D.C. Minn. 1999) 8.46n7

Ranjel v. Lansing, City of, 417 F.2d 321 (6th Cir. 1969) 6.80n6

Ranken v. Lavine, 363 N.E.2d 343 (N.Y. 1977) . .
2.46n6

Rappa v. New Castle County, 18 F.3d 1043 (3d Cir. 1994) 8.36n9; 11.19n15

Rappa v. Newcastle County, 18 F.3d 1043 (3rd Cir. 1994) 11.13n3

Raritan Dev. Corp. v. Silva, 689 N.E.2d 1373 (N.Y. 1997) 5.75n1

Rasmussen v. Lake Forest, City of, 404 F. Supp. 148 (N.D. Ill. 1975) 8.43n8

Ratliff v. Phillips, 746 S.W.2d 405 (Ky. 1988) . . .
8.14n3

Raum v. Board of Supvrs., 342 A.2d 450 (Pa. Commw. 1975) 9.30n5

Raum v. Board of Supvrs., 370 A.2d 777 (Pa. Commw. 1977) 6.21n6

Raybestos-Manhattan, Inc. v. Planning & Zoning Comm'n, 442 A.2d 65 (Conn. 1982) . . 9.09n13

Raynes v. Leavenworth, 821 P.2d 1204 (Wash. 1992) 6.26n7

Raynes v. Leavenworth, City of, 821 P.2d 1204 (Wash. 1992) 6.72n5

Ray's Stateline Market v. Pelham, Town of, 605 A.2d 1068 (N.H. 1995) 5.79n5

Ray's Stateline Market, Inc. v. Pelham, Town of, 665 A.2d 1068 (N.H. 1995) 5.79n9

Reahard v. Lee County (II), 30 F.3d 1412 . . . . .
2.31n2

Real Estate Bd. of Metropolitan St. Louis v. Jennings, City of, 808 S.W.2d 7 (Mo. App. 1991) . . . . .
11.18n2

Reale Inv., Inc. v. Colorado Springs, City of, 856 P.2d 91 (Colo. 1993) 8.09n2

Rebholz v. Floyd, 327 So. 2d 806 (Fla. App. 1976) 8.14n11

Rebman v. Springfield, City of, 250 N.E.2d 282 (Ill. App. 1969) 11.32n5

Recreational Vehicle United Citizens Ass'n v. Sterling Heights, City of, 418 N.W.2d 702 (Mich. App. 1987) 5.19n12

Rector, Wardens & Vestry of St. Bartholomew's Ch. v. New York, City of, 914 F.2d 348 (2d Cir. 1990) 11.35n3; 11.37n3

Red Dog Saloon v. Sedgwick County Bd. of Comm'rs, 33 P.3d 869 . . . . 4.18n1

Red Maple Properties v. Zoning Comm'n, 610 A.2d 1238 (Conn. 1992) 6.69n2

Red Roof Inns, Inc. v. Ridgeland, City of, 797 So.2d 898 . . . . 5.84n8

Redfearn v. Creppel, 455 So. 2d 1356 (La. 1984) 5.19n1

Redfearn v. Creppel, 455 So.2d 1356 (La. 1984) . . 5.79n4

Redmond, City of v. Central Puget Sound Growth Mgt. Hearings Bd., 959 P.2d 1091 (Wash. 1998) 10.07n4

Redner v. Dean, 29 F.3d 1495 (11th Cir. 1994) . . 6.57n8

Reduce Urban Blight v. Zoning Bd. of Adjustment, 771 A.2d 874 . . . . 6.48n13

Reduce Urban Blight (SCRUB) v. Zoning Bd. of Adjustment, 729 A.2d 117 (Pa. Commw. 1999) 8.02n7

Reduce Urban Blight (SCRUB) v. Zoning Bd. of Adjustment, 787 A.2d 1123 . . . . 6.42n2

Redwood City Company of Jehovah's Witnesses, Inc. v. Menlo Park, City of, 335 P.2d 195 (Cal. App. 1959) 6.03n4

Reedy v. Wheaton, City of, 430 N.E.2d 273 (Ill. App. 1981) 5.36n9

Regents of Univ. of Cal. v. Santa Monica, City of, 143 Cal Rptr. 276 (Cal. App. 1978) 4.27n1

Region 10 Client Mgt., Inc. v. Hampstead, Town of, 424 A.2d 207 (N.H. 1980) 5.10n1

Regional Economic Community Action Program, Inc. v. Middletown, City of, 294 F.3d 35 . . 5.13n1

Reid v. Architectural Bd. of Review, 192 N.E.2d 74 (Ohio App. 1963) 11.25n6

Reid v. Brodsky, 156 A.2d 334 (Pa. 1959) 4.06n5

Reid v. Brodsky 156 A.2d 334 (Pa. 1959) 4.06n4

Reid Dev. Corp. v. Parsippany-Troy Hills Twp., 107 A.2d 20 (N.J. App. Div. 1954) 10.10n4

Reinking v. Metropolitan Bd. of Zoning Appeals, 671 N.E.2d 137 (Ind. App. 1996) 6.50n6

Reinman v. Little Rock, 237 U.S. 171 (1915) . . . 2.04n3

Reiter v. Beloit, City of, 947 P.2d 425 (Kan. 1997) 11.34n2

Remington v. Boonville, City of, 701 S.W.2d 804 (Mo. App. 1985) 6.76n8

Renard v. Dade County, 261 So. 2d 832 (Fla. 1972) 8.02n10; 8.03n2

Reno, City of v. Harris, 895 P.2d 663 (Nev. 1995) 6.56n18; 6.58n4

Renton, City of v. Playtime Theatres, Inc. 475 U.S. 41 (1986) 5.61n1

Resident Advisory Bd. v. Rizzo, 564 F.2d 126 (3d Cir. 1977) 7.05n4

Residents of Beverly Glen, Inc. v. Los Angeles, City of 109 Cal. Rptr. 724 (Cal. App. 1973) 8.06n5

Resolution Trust Corp. v. Highland Beach, Town of, 18 F.3d 1536 (11th Cir. 1994) 2.30n9; 2.39n7; 2.42n10

Resolution Trust Corp. v. Highland Beach, Town of, 18 F.3d 536 (11th Cir. 1994) 2.16n4

Resource Conservation Mgt., Inc. v. Board of Supvrs., 380 S.E.2d 879 (Va. 1989) 4.30n3, n6

Restigouche, Inc. v. Jupiter, Town of, 59 F.3d 1208 (11th Cir. 1995) 5.35n3

Restivo v. Lynch, 707 A.2d 663 (R.I. 1998) 6.70n8

Retail Property Trust v. Board of Zoning Appeals, 722 N.Y.S.2d 244 . . . . 6.56n8

Reuschenberg v. Huntington, Town of, 532 N.Y.S.2d 148 (App. Div. 1988) 2.36n6

Reynolds v. City Council, 680 P.2d 1350 (Colo. App. 1984) 9.09n2

Reynolds v. Dittmer, 312 N.W.2d 75 (Iowa App. 1981) 8.04n1

Reznik, The Distinction Between Legislative and Adjudicative v. Tigard, City of, 75 N.Y.U.L. Rev. 242

R.G. Moore Bldg. Co. v. Committee for the Repeal of Ordinance R(C)-88-13, 391 S.E.2d 587 (Va. 1990) 6.82n3

Rhodes v. Woodstock, Town of, 318 A.2d 170 (Vt. 1974) 8.13n2

Riccobono v. Whitpain Twp., 497 F. Supp. 1364 (E.D. Pa. 1980) 8.44n8

Richard Roesser Professional Bldr., Inc. v. Anne Arundel County, 793 A.2d 545 . . . . . . 6.50n6

Richardson v. City & County of Honolulu, 124 F.3d 1150 (9th Cir. 1997) 2.39n5

Richardson v. Little Rock Planning Comm'n, City of, 747 S.W.2d 115 (Ark. 1988) 9.09n2

Richmarr Holy Hills, Inc. v. American PCS, L.P., 701 A.2d 879 (Md. App. 1997) 6.58n4

Richmond, City of v. Board of Supvrs., 101 S.E.2d 641 (Va. 1958) 4.37n1

Richmond, City of v. Randall, 211 S.E.2d 56 (Va. 1975) 8.19n6

Richmond, City of v. Southern Ry., 123 S.E.2d 641 (Va. 1962) 4.32n3

Richmond Heights, City of v. Richmond Heights Presbyterian Church, 764 S.W.2d 647 (Mo. 1989) 5.68n5

Richmond, Town of v. Murdock, 235 N.W.2d 497 (Wis. 1975) 6.03n4

Ridenour v. Jessamini County Fiscal Court, 842 S.W.2d 532 (Ky. App. 1992) 6.76n5

Ridgefield Land Co. v. Detroit, City of, 217 N.W.2d 58 (Mich. 1926) 9.12n1

Riegert Apts. Corp. v. Planning Bd., 441 N.E.2d 1067 (N.Y. 1982) 6.66n8

Riggs v. Burson, 941 S.W.2d 44 (Tenn. 1997) . . . 4.43n5

Riggs v. Township of Long Beach, 514 A.2d 45 (N.J. App. Div. 1986) 6.37n11

Riggs v. Township of Long Beach, 538 A.2d 808 (N.J. 1988) 2.23n6

Right-Price Recreation, LLC v. Connells Prairie Community Council, 46 P.3d 789 . . . . . . 8.47n3

Riley v. Boxa, 542 N.W.2d 519 (Iowa 1996) 8.11n1

The Ripeness of Regulatory Takings Claims After Palazzolo v. Rhode Island,46 St. Louis U.L.J. 833

Rippley v. Lincoln, City of, 330 N.W.2d 505 (N.D. 1983) 8.21n2

Risner v. Wyoming, City of, 383 N.W.2d 226 (Mich. App. 1985) 11.20n1

Rispo Inv. Co. v. Seven Hills, City of, 629 N.E.2d 3 (Ohio App. 1993) 6.04n4

Rispo Realty & Dev. Co. v. Parma, City of, 564 N.E.2d 425 (Ohio 1990) 4.25n2

Riter v. Keokuk Electro-Metals Co., 82 N.W.2d 151 (Iowa 1957) 4.12n3

Rith Energy, Inc. v. United States, 271 F.3d 1347 . . . . 2.21n2

River Park, Inc. v. Highland Park, City of, 23 F.3d 164 (7th Cir. 1994) 2.32n4

River Park, Inc. v. Highland Park, City of, 667 N.E.2d 499 (Ill. App. 1996) 8.23n6

River Springs Ltd. Liability Co. v. Board of County Comm'rs, 899 P.2d 1329 (Wyo. 1995) 4.30n10

Riverside Bayview Homes, Inc.; United States v. , 474 U.S. 121 (1986) 12.06n3, n11

Riverside Groups, Inc. v. Smith, 497 So. 2d 988 (Fla. App. 1986) 6.70n8

Riverview Park, Inc. v. Hinsdale, Town of, 313 A.2d 733 (N.H. 1973) 5.21n1

Rives v. Clarksville, City of, 618 S.W.2d 502 (Tenn. App. 1981) 5.84n6

Riviera Beach, City of v. Shillingburg, 659 So.2d 1174 (Fla. App. 1995) 8.09n1

RK Dev. Corp. v. Norwalk, City of 242 A.2d 781 (Conn. 1968) 9.28n3

Roach v. Milton Zoning Bd. of Appeals, Town of, 530 N.Y.S.2d 321 (App. Div. 1988) 8.04n1

Roark v. Caldwell, City of, 394 P.2d 641 (Idaho 1964) 5.39n8

Robbins Auto Parts, Inc. v. Laconia, City of, 371 A.2d 1167 (N.H. 1977) 6.66n8

Robert E. Kurzius, Inc. v. Incorporated Village of Upper Bronxville,414 N.E.2d 680 (N.Y. 1980), cert. denied, 450 U.S. 1042 (1981) . . . 7.15n1

Robert L. Rieke Bldg. Co. v. Olathe, City of, 697 P.2d 72 (Kan. App. 1985) 6.21n5

Robert L. Rieke Bldg. Co. v. Overland Park, City of, 657 P.2d 1121 (Kan. 1983) . . 11.07n3; 11.10n5

Robert Lee Realty Co. v. Spring Valley, Village of, 462 N.E.2d 1193 (N.Y. 1984) 6.56n12

Robertson v. Salem, City of, 191 F. Supp. 604 (D. Or. 1961) 2.23n6

Robes v. Hartford, Town of, 636 A.2d 342 (Vt. 1993) 9.21n3, n10

Robie v. Lillie, 299 A.2d 155 (N.H. 1972) 4.09n2

Robie v. Lillis, 299 A.2d 155 (N.H. 1972) 4.09n3

Robinson v. Bloomfield Hills, City of 86 N.W.2d 166 (Mich. 1957) 2.36n3

Robinson v. Boulder, City of 547 P.2d 228 (Colo. 1976) 10.10n5

Robinson v. Indianola Mun. Separate School Dist., 467 So. 2d 911 (Miss. 1985) 4.28n3

Robinson v. Lintz, 420 P.2d 923 (Ariz. 1966) . . . 9.07n4

Robinson Twp. v. Knoll 302 N.W.2d 146 (Mich. 1981) 5.23n4

Rochester Bus. Inst. v. Rochester, City of, 267 N.Y.S.2d 274 (App. Div. 1966) 10.15n9

Rochester, City of v. Barcomb, 169 A.2d 281 (N.H. 1961) 6.20n2

Rochester, City of; State v. , 268 N.W.2d 885 (Minn. 1978) 6.26n5; 6.30n1

Rochester, City of v. Superior Plastics, Inc., 480 N.W.2d 620 (Mich. App. 1992) 5.41n1

Rochester Hills, City of v. Schultz, 592 N.W.2d 69 (Mich. 1999) 11.18n7

Rochester Hills, City of v. Six Star, Ltd., 423 N.W.2d 322 (Mich. App. 1988) 8.23n1

Rockenbach v. Apostle, 47 N.W.2d 636 (Mich. 1951) 4.10n1, n2

Rockford Blacktop Constr. Co. v. Boone, County of, 635 N.E.2d 1077 (Ill. App. 1994) 6.59n3

Rockhill v. Chesterfield Twp., 128 A.2d 473 (N.J. 1957) 6.61n4

Rockville Fuel & Feed Co. v. Gaithersburg, City of, 291 A.2d 672 (Md. 1972) 6.16n4

Rocky Mount, Town of v. Southside Investors, Inc., 487 S.E.2d 855 (Va. 1997) 6.16n8

Rocky Mount, Town of v. Wenco, Inc., 506 S.E.2d 17 (Va. 1998) 10.10n7

Rocky Point Plaza Corp., In re , 621 N.E.2d 566 (Ohio App. 1993) 6.70n14

Rodgers v. Tarrytown, Village of 96 N.E.2d 731 (N.Y. 1951) 6.61n2

Rodgers v. Zoning Bd. of Adjustment, 707 A.2d 1090 (N.J. App. Div. 1998) 5.81n14

Rodine v. Zoning Bd. of Adj., 434 N.W.2d 124 (Iowa App. 1988) 6.69n4

Rodo Land, Inc. v. Board of County Comm'rs, 517 P.2d 873 (Colo. App. 1974) . . 5.17n6; 5.31n2

Rodriguez v. Hawaii, County of, 823 F. Supp. 798 (D. Haw. 1993) 8.42n13

Rodriguez v. Larchmont, Village of, 608 F. Supp. 467 (S.D.N.Y. 1985) 8.36n2

Rodriguez v. Prince George's Cty., 558 A.2d 742 (Md. App. 1989) 6.63n1

Rodriguez v. Solis, 2 Cal. Rptr. 2d 50 (Cal. App. 1991) 11.19n4

Rodriguez v. Solis, 2 Cal. Rptr.2d 50 (Cal. App. 1991) 6.57n2

Rodrock Enters., L.P. v. Olathe, City of, 21 P.3d 598 . . . . 8.14n1

Roeder v. Borough Council, 266 A.2d 691 (Pa. 1970) 8.03n2

Rogers v. Cheyenne, City of, 747 P.2d 1137 (Wyo. 1987) 5.39n6

Rogers v. Norfolk, Town of, 734 N.E.2d 1143 . . . 8.16n6

Rogers v. Zoning Board of Adjustment, 707 A.2d 1090 (N.J. App. Div. 1998) 5.79n5

Rogers Machinery, Inc. v. Washington County, 45 P.3d 963 . . . . 9.22n9

Rogin v. Bensalem Township, 616 F.2d 680 (3d Cir. 1980) 6.36n1, n2

Rogin v. Bensalem Township 616 F.2d 580 (3d Cir. 1980) 2.42n2

Rogin v. Bensalem Twp., 616 F.2d 680 (3d Cir. 1980) 8.39, n7

Rogue Valley Ass'n of Realtors v. Ashland, City of, 970 P.2d 685 (Or. 1999) 6.03n2

Rogue Valley Ass'n of Realtors v. Ashland, City of, 970 P.2d 685 (Or. App. 1999) 7.30n4

Rohn v. Vasalia, City of, 263 Cal. Rptr. 319 (Cal. App. 1989) 9.13n3

Rolf v. San Antonio, City of, 77 F.3d 823 (5th Cir. 1996) 2.51n6

Rolling Pines Ltd. Partnership v. Little Rock, City of, 40 S.W.2d 828 . . . . 6.56n10

Rolling Pines Ltd. Partnership v. Little Rock, City of, 40 S.W.3d 828 . . . . 6.05n6

Roman Catholic Welfare Corporation of San Francisco v. Piedmont, City of, 289 P.2d 438 (Cal. 1955) 5.27n2

Romaz Props., Ltd. v. McGowan, 657 N.Y.S.2d 942 (App. Div. 1997) 10.14n1

Rome, City of v. Pilgrim, 271 S.E.2d 189 (Ga. 1980) 8.11n2

Ron Rose Group, Inc. v. Baum, 712 N.Y.S.2d 174 . . . . 6.48n17

Roney v. Board of Supvrs., 292 P.2d 529 (Cal. App. 1956) 5.43n2

Rooker v. Fidelity Trust Co., 263 U.S. 413 (1923) 2.34n1

Roosevelt v. Beau Monde Co., 384 P.2d 96 (Colo. 1963) 6.69n4

Root Outdoor Adv. v. Ft. Collins, City of, 788 P.2d 149 (Colo. 1990) 11.11n4

Rose v. Chaiken, 453 A.2d 1378 (N.J. Ch. Div. 1982) 4.05n1

Rose v. Plymouth Town, 173 P.2d 285 (Utah 1946) 10.10n2

Rosenaur v. Scherer, 105 Cal. Rptr. 2d 674 . . . . . 8.47n1

Rosenschein Assocs. v. Borough of Paradise Park, 701 A.2d 448 (N.J. App. Div. 1997) 7.13n1

Rothrock v. Zoning Hearing Bd. 319 A.2d 432 (1974) 5.80n7

Rotter v. Coconino Cty., 818 P.2d 704 (Ariz. 1991) 1.13n3

Rowell v. Board of Adj., 446 N.W.2d 917 (Minn. App. 1989) 6.48n15; 6.74n7

Roy v. Chevrolet Motor Car Co., 247 N.W. 774 (Mich. 1933) 4.12n4

Royal Foods Systems, Inc. v. Missouri Hwy. & Transp. Comm'n, 876 S.W.2d 38 (Mo. App. 1994) 5.80n6

R.R.I. Realty Corp. v. Southampton, Village of, 870 F.2d 911 (2d Cir. 1989) 2.40n6

R.T.G., Inc., State ex rel. v. Ohio, State of, 753 N.E.2d 869 . . . . 2.09n3

Rubinovitz v. Rogato, 60 F.3d 906 (1st Cir. 1995) 2.47n4

Ruckelshaus v. Monsanto Co., 467 U.S. 986 (1984) 2.16n1

Ruckelshaus v. Monsanto Co. 467 U.S. 986 (1984) 2.16n5

Ruf v. Buckinham Township, 765 A.2d 1166 . . . . . 9.10n4

Rumson Estates, Inc. v. Mayor & Council, 795 A.2d 290 . . . . 5.29n7

Runyon v. Fasi, 762 F. Supp. 280 (D. Haw. 1991) 11.23n4

Runyon v. Fasi, 762 F. Supp. 949 (D. Hawaii 1991) 11.23n3

Rusk, City of v. Cox, 665 S.W.2d 233 (Tex. App. 1984) 6.29n5; 8.18n2

Russell v. District of Columbia Bd. of Adjustment, 402 A.2d 1231 (D.C. App. 1979) . . . 6.48n16

Russell v. Kansas City (I), 690 F. Supp. 947 (D. Kan. 1988) 5.54n3

Russell v. Kansas City (II), 1988 U.S. Dist. Lexis 1217 (D. Kan. 1988) 5.56n5

Russell v. Penn Twp. Planning Comm'n, 348 A.2d 499 (Pa. Commw. 1975) 3.15n8

Rutgers v. Piluso 4.27; 4.38

Rutland Envtl. Protection Ass'n v. Kane County 9.26

Rymer v. Douglas County, 764 F.2d 796 (11th Cir. 1985) 8.33n4

Rzadkowolski v. Lake Orion, 845 F.2d 653 (6th Cir. 1988) 11.19n3

S

S. Kemble Fischer Realty Trust v. Board of Appeals, 402 N.E.2d 100 (Mass. App. 1980) . . 12.09n3

S & L Assocs. v. Township of Washington, 160 A.2d 635 (N.J. 1960) 6.74n5

Saah v. District of Columbia Bd. of Zoning Adjustment, 433 A.2d 1114 (D.C. App. 1981) 6.17n2

Saco, City of v. Tweedie, 314 A.2d 135 (Me. 1974) 5.23n3

Sacramento, County of v. Lewis, 523 U.S. 833 (1998) 2.39n8

Saddle River Country Day School v. Borough of Saddle River, 144 A.2d 425 (N.J. App. Div. 1958) 6.66n10

Saenz v. Roe, 526 U.S. 489 (1999) 10.08n5

Safe Grant v. Lone Oak Sportsmen's Club, Inc. 624 N.W.2d 796 . . . . 4.05n1

Safe Neighborhood v. Seattle, City of, 836 P.2d 235 (Wash. App. 1992) 5.08n6

Sage & Audubon Soc'y, Inc. v. Planning Comm'n, 668 P.2d 664 (Cal. 1983) 8.11n14

Sakolsky v. Coral Gables, City of, 151 So. 2d 433 (Fla. 1963) 6.18n5

Salamar Bldrs. Corp. v. Tuttle, 275 N.E.2d 585 (N.Y. 1971) 5.31n5

Salt Lake County v. Liquor Control Comm'n, 357 P.2d 488 (Utah 1960) 4.33n2

Salt Lake County Cottonwood Sanitary Dist. v. Sandy City, 879 P.2d 1379 (Utah App. 1994) 6.55n3

Samaad v. Dallas., City of 940 F.2d 925 (5th Cir. 1991) 2.24n5

Samaad v. Dallas, City of, 940 F.2d 925 (5th Cir. 1991) 2.31n1

Samaritan Center, Inc. v. Borough of Englishtown, 683 A.2d 611 (N.J.L. Div. 1996) 7.11n6; 7.13n6

Sameric Corp. v. Philadelphia, City of, 142 F.3d 582 (3d Cir. 1998) 2.32n2

Sammamish County Council v. Bellevue, City of, 29 P.3d 728 . . . . 10.05n6

Sampieri v. Inland Wetlands Agency, 628 A.2d 1286 (Conn. 1993) 12.05n2

Sams Land Co. v. Soap Lake, City of, 23 P.3d 477 . . . . 9.21n2

San Antonio River Auth. v. Garrett Bros., 528 S.W.2d 266 (Tex. Civ. App. 1977) 2.23n4

San Diego Bldg. Contractors Ass'n v. City Council, 529 P.2d 570 (Cal. 1974) 6.83n5

San Diego Gas & Elec. Co. v. San Diego, City of, 450 U.S. 621 (1981) 8.38n10

San Diego Gas & Elec. Co. v. San Diego, City of 450 U.S. 621 (1981) 2.25n3

San Diego Gas & Elec. Co. v. San Diego 450 U.S. 621 (1981) 8.25n2

San Miguel v. Windcrest, City of, 40 S.W.3d 104 . . . . 8.15n6

San Pedro N., Ltd. v. San Antonio, City of, 562 S.W.2d 260 (Tex. Civ. App. 1978) . . . 6.82n1

San Remo Hotel v. City & County of San Francisco, 145 F.3d 1095 (9th Cir. 1998) 2.31n5; 8.42n10, n13; 8.43n6

San Remo Hotel v. City & County of San Francisco, 41 P.3d 87 . . . . 5.18n8

San Remo Hotel, L.P. v. City & County of San Francisco, 41 P.3d 87 . . . . . 9.22n8, n10, n11; 9.23n3

San Telmo Assocs. v. Seattle, City of, 735 P.2d 673 (Wash. 1987) 7.28n1; 9.23n2

Sanchez v. Board of Zoning Adjustments, 488 So. 2d 1277 (La. App. 1986) 6.50n5

Sandbothe v. Olivette, City of, 647 S.W.2d 198 (Mo. App. 1983) 6.59n4

Sanders v. Board of Adjustment, 445 So. 2d 909 (Ala. App. 1983) 5.19n7

Sandgate, Town of v. Colehamer, 589 A.2d 1205 (Vt. 1990) 11.05n1

Sandy Beach Defense Fund v. City Council, 773 P.2d 250 (Hawaii 1989) 6.69n2, n4

Sanguinetti; State v. , 449 A.2d 922 (Vt. 1982) . . 11.10n6

Sanibel, City of v. Buntrock, 409 So. 2d 1072 (Fla. App. 1981) 6.07n2

Sanitary & Imp. Dist. No. 347 v. Omaha, City of, 589 N.W.2d 160 (Neb. App. 1999) 8.04n4

Sansoucy v. Planning Bd., 246 N.E.2d 811 (Mass. 1969) 9.09n15

Santa Barbara, City of v. Adamson 610 P.2d 436 (Cal. 1980) 5.05n4

Santa Fe, City of v. Gamble-Skogmo, Inc., 389 P.2d 13 (N.M. 1964) 11.28n1; 11.29n4, n6

Santa Fe Land Imp. Co. v. Chula Vista, City of, 596 F.2d 838 (9th Cir. 1979) 8.44n6

Santa Margarita Residents Together v. San Luis Obispo County 6.23n6

Santini v. Connecticut Hazardous Waste Mgt. Serv., 739 A.2d 680 (Conn. 1999) 3.21n2

Sapakoff v. Hague Zoning Bd. of Appeals, Town of, 621 N.Y.S.2d 215 (App. Div. 1995) . . 5.81n10

Sartoga v. Borough of West Paterson, 788 A.2d 841
. . . . 7.12n8

Sasso v. Osgood, 657 N.E.2d 254 (N.Y. 1995) . . .
6.48n12

Saunders v. Clark County Zoning Dep't, 421 N.E.2d
152 (Ohio 1981) 5.08n6

Saunders, County of v. Moore, 155 N.W.2d 317 (Neb.
1967) 6.21n4

Savago v. New Paltz, Village of, 214 F. Supp.2d 252
. . . . 11.21n1

Save El Toro Ass'n v. Days, 141 Cal. Rptr. 282 (Cal.
App. 1977) 3.22n6

Save Elkhart Lake, Inc. v. Elkhart Lake, Village of,
512 N.W.2d 202 (Wis. App. 1993) . . . 6.23n6

Save Historic Rhodes Tavern v. District of Columbia
Dep't of Hous. & Community Dev., 432 A.2d 710
(D.C. App. 1981) 11.34n6

Save Historic Rhodes Tavern v. District of Columbia
Dep't of Hous. & Urban Dev., 432 A.2d 710 (D.C.
App. 1981) 11.36n3

Save Lake Tahoe v. Crystal Enters., 490 F. Supp. 995
(D. Nev. 1980) 6.22n9

Save Our Forest Action Coalition Inc. v. Kingston,
City of, 675 N.Y.S.2d 451 (App. Div. 1998) . .
6.29n12

Save Our Rural Env't v. Snohomish County, 662 P.2d
816 (Wash. 1983) 6.30n4; 6.34n4

Save Our State Park v. Board of Clallam County
Comm'rs, 875 P.2d 673 (Wash. App. 1994) . . .
6.77n2

Save the Pine Bush, Inc. v. Albany, City of, 512
N.E.2d 526 (N.Y. 1987) 6.03n3

Save the Pine Bush, Inc., Matter of v. Albany, City of,
512 N.E.2d 526 (N.Y. 1987) 6.05n8

Saveland Park Holding Corp., State ex rel. v. Wieland
69 N.W.2d 217 (Wis.1955) 11.25n4

Sawyer Env't Recovery Facilities, Inc. v. Hampden,
Town of, 760 A.2d 257 . . . . 4.30n12

SCA Chem. Waste Serv., Inc. v. Konigsberg, 636
S.W.2d 430 (Tenn. 1982) 6.10n1

SCA Chem. Waste Serv., State ex rel. v. Konigsberg,
636 S.W.2d 430 (Tenn. 1982) 6.07n1

Scadron v. Des Plaines, City of, 606 N.E.2d 1154 (Ill.
1992) 4.25n2; 11.06n6

Scadron v. Des Plaines, City of, 734 F. Supp. 1437
(N.D. Ill. 1990), aff'd 11.19n16

Scenic Community v. Los Angeles, County of . . .
6.52

Scenic Community v. Los Angeles, County of, 263
Cal. Rptr. 214 (Cal. App. 1989) 9.03n8

Schad v. Borough of Mount Ephraim 452 U.S. 61
(1981) 5.60n1

Schad; State v. , 733 A.2d 1159 (N.J. 1999) . . . .
6.05n11; 11.18n5

Schaefer, State ex rel. v. Cleveland, 847 S.W.2d 867
(Mo. App. 1993) 9.09n7

Schafer v. New Orleans, City of, 743 F.2d 1086 (5th
Cir. 1984) 6.09n2

Schaffer v. Omaha, City of, 248 N.W.2d 764 (Neb.
1977) 11.10n4

Schalow v. Waupaca County, 407 N.W.2d 316 (Wis.
App. 1987) 6.50n6

Schalow v. Waupaca Cty., 407 N.W.2d 316 (Wis.
App. 1987) 6.68n3; 6.70n14

Schauer v. Miami Beach, City of, 112 So. 2d 838 (Fla.
1959) 6.72n2

Schaumburg, Village of v. Jeep Eagle Sales Corp., 676
N.E.2d 200 (Ill. App. 1996) 11.19n15

Scheer v. Township of Evesham, 445 A.2d 46 (N.J.
App. Div. 1982) 8.21n2

Schenkolewski; State v. , 693 A.2d 1173 (N.J. App.
Div. 1997) 6.74n1

Scheuer v. Rhodes, 416 U.S. 232 (1974) . . 8.36n5

Schillerstrom Homes, Inc. v. Naperville, City of, 762
N.E.2d 494 . . . . 4.25n9

Schindler; State v. , 604 So.2d 565 (Fla. App. 1992)
. . . . 12.07n9

Schlega v. Detroit Bd. of Zoning Appeals, 382
N.W.2d 737 (Mich. App. 1985) 8.12n1

Schlientz v. North Platte, City of, 110 N.W.2d 58
(Neb. 1961) 4.23n3

Schlotfelt v. Vinton Farmers' Supply Co . . 4.05;
4.12

Schlotfelt v. Vinton Farmers' Supply Co., 109 N.W.2d
695 (Iowa 1961) 4.04n1

Schmalenberg v. Tacoma News, 943 P.2d 350 (Wash.
App. 1997) 8.46n8

Schmalz v. Buckingham Twp. Zoning Bd. of Adjustment, 132 A.2d 233 (Pa. 1957) 5.71n3

Schmidt v. Kenosha, City of, 571 N.W.2d 892 (Wis.
App. 1997) 4.23n3

Schneider v. Ramsey, City of, 800 F. Supp. 815 (D.
Minn. 1992) 8.32n3

Schneiderman v. Shenkenberg, 281 N.Y.S.2d 459
(Sup. Ct. 1967) 5.46n1

Schnuck v. Santa Monica, City of, 935 F.2d 171 (9th
Cir. 1991) 2.31n4

Schoen v. Cherokee County, 530 S.E.2d 226 . . . .
6.76n15

Schofield v. Spokane County, 980 P.2d 277 (Wash.
App. 1999) 6.33n3

School Dist. of Philadelphia v. Zoning Bd. of Adjustment, 207 A.2d 864 (Pa. 1965) 4.25n6;
4.26n2; 4.28n3

Schoonover v. Klamath Cty., 806 P.2d 156 (Or. App.
1991) 9.13n2

Schrader v. Guilford Planning & Zoning Comm'n,
418 A.2d 93 (Conn. Super. 1980) 6.07n2;
8.14n2

Schrader, In re , 660 P.2d 135 (Okla. 1983) . . . .
. . . . 6.50n1

Schubert Organization, Inc. v. Landmarks Preservation Comm'n, 570 N.Y.S.2d 504 (App. Div. 1991)
. . . . 11.34n3

Schultz v. Board of Adjustment, 139 N.W.2d 448 (Iowa 1966) 6.03n4

Schultz v. Grants Pass, City of, 884 P.2d 569 (Or. App. 1994) 9.16n12, n15; 9.22n9

Schultz v. Pritts, 432 A.2d 1319 (Md. 1981) . . . .
. . . . 6.56n11

Schulz v. Milne, 849 F. Supp. 708 (N.D. Cal. 1994)
. . . . 6.04n3

Schwartz v. Flint, City of, 395 N.W.2d 678 (Mich. 1986) 8.19n2

Schwarz v. Glendale, City of, 950 P.2d 167 (Ariz. App. 1997) 6.04n2

Schweitzer v. Board of Zoning Appeals, 167 N.Y.S.2d 767 (Misc. 1957) 5.20n4

Schwing v. Baton Rouge, City of, 249 So. 2d 304 (La. App. 1971) 9.19n1

Schwing v. Baton Rouge, City of, 249 So. 2d 304 (La. App.1971) 9.16n10

Sciacca v. Caruso, 769 A.2d 578 . . 6.50n2; 6.52n6

SCIT, Inc. v. Planning Bd., 472 N.E.2d 269 (Mass. App. 1984) 6.54n5

Scituate, Town of v. O'Rourke, 239 A.2d 176 (R.I. 1968) 5.81n16

Sclavenitis v. Cherry Hills Bd. of Adj., 751 P.2d 661 (Colo. App. 1988) 6.68n3; 6.70n13

Scotch Plains Twp. v. Westfield, Town of, 199 A.2d 673 (N.J.L. Div. 1964) 4.34n1

Scott v. Greenville County, 716 F.2d 1409 (4th Cir. 1983) 2.40n8; 7.02n4; 8.35n6, n7

Scott v. Greenville County, 716 F.2d 1409 (4th Cir. 1985) 7.03n6

Scott v. Indian Wells, City of, 492 P.2d 1137 (Cal. 1972) 6.68n3; 6.69n4

Scott v. Indian Wells, City of 492 P.2d 1137 (Cal. 1972) 8.05n3

Scott Ventures v. Hayes Township, 537 N.W.2d 610 (Mich. App. 1995) 5.32n2

Scottsdale v. Scottsdale Assoc. Merchants, 583 P.2d 891 (Ariz. 1978) 5.82n2

Scottsdale, City of v. Arizona Sign Ass'n, Inc., 564 P.2d 922 (Ariz. App. 1977) 8.16n2

Scottsdale, City of v. Municipal Court of Tempe, 368 P.2d 637 (Ariz. 1962) 4.35n1

Scottsdale, City of v. Superior Court, 439 P.2d 290 (Ariz. 1968) 6.83n1

Scoville v. Ronalter, 291 A.2d 222 (Conn. 1971) . .
. . . . 4.05n2

Scranton, Town of v. Willoughby, 412 S.E.2d 424 (S.C. 1991) 5.23n3

Scrutton v. Sacramento, County of, 79 Cal. Rptr. 872 (Cal. App. 1969) 6.63n4; 6.64n3

Scudder v. Greendale, Town of, 704 F.2d 999 (7th Cir. 1983) 2.47n1; 8.33n1

Scurlock v. Lynn Haven, City of, 858 F.2d 1521 (11th Cir. 1988) 5.26n8

SDDS, Inc. v. State, 650 N.W.2d 1 . . . . . 8.26n9

SDJ, Inc. v. Houston, City of, 636 F. Supp. 1359 (S.D. Tex. 1986), aff'd, 837 F.2d 1268 (5th Cir. 1988)
. . . . 5.63n7

SDJ, Inc. v. Houston, City of, 837 F.2d 1268 (5th Cir. 1988) 5.64n3

Sea Cabins on the Ocean IV Homeowners Ass'n, Inc. v. N. Myrtle Beach, City of, 523 S.E.2d 193 (S.C. App. 1999) 2.19n3

Sea & Sage Audubon Soc'y, Inc. v. Planning Comm'n, 668 P.2d 664 (Cal. 1983) . . 8.11n16

Seabrook, Town of v. Vachon Mgt., Inc., 745 A.2d 1155 . . . . 5.79n3

Seabrook, Town of v. Yachon Mgt., Inc., 745 A.2d 1155 . . . . 6.15n1

Sealand Sisters, Inc. v. Planning Bd., 737 N.E.2d 503
. . . . 9.09n2

Seattle, City of v. Martin, 342 P.2d 602 (Wash. 1959)
. . . . 5.84n6

Seattle, City of; State v. , 615 P.2d 461 (Wash. 1980)
. . . . 4.37n3

Sechrist v. Municipal Court, 134 Cal. Rptr. 733 (Cal. App. 1976) 5.19n11

Security Mgt. Corp. v. Baltimore County, 655 A.2d 1326 . . . . 5.31n6

Security Mgt. Corp. v. Baltimore County, 655 A.2d 1326 (Md. App. 1995) 2.35n2; 12.03n1

Security Nat'l Bank v. Olathe, City of, 589 P.2d 589 (Kan. 1979) 6.33n7

Sedney v. Lloyd, 410 A.2d 616 (Md. 1980) . . . .
. . . . 8.18n5

Segal v. Zoning Hearing Bd., 771 A.2d 90 . . . . .
. . . . 6.42n1

Segalla v. Planning Bd., 611 N.Y.S.2d 287 (App. Div. 1994) 6.74n3

Segalla v. Planning Bd., 611 N.Y.S.2d 287 (App. Div. 1995) 6.74n3

Seguin v. Sterling Heights, City of, 968 F.2d 584 (6th Cir. 1992) 2.32n2

Seichner v. Islip, Town of, 439 N.E.2d 352 (N.Y. 1982) 12.15n2

Seiler v. Granite City, City of, 625 N.E.2d 1170 (Ill. App. 1993) 8.18n5

Selby Realty Co. v. San Buenaventura, City of 514 P.2d 111 (Cal. 1973) 3.21n3

Seldon v. Manitou Springs, City of, 745 P.2d 229 (Colo. 1987) 12.02n1

Selligman v. Von Allmen Bros., Inc., 179 S.W.2d 207 (Ky. 1944) 5.80n10

Sellon v. Manitou Springs, 745 P.2d 229 (Colo. 1987) 6.05n6

Senders v. Columbia Falls, Town of, 647 A.2d 93 (Me. 1994) 4.27n1

Senefsky v. Lawler, 12 N.W.2d 387 (Mich. 1943) 5.29n2

Senior v. Zoning Comm'n of New Canaan, 153 A.2d 415 (Conn. 1959) 5.31n2

Senior Estates, State ex rel. v. Clarke, 530 S.W.2d 30 (Mo. App. 1975) 2.23n4

Sequoyah Hills Homeowners Ass'n v. Oakland, City of, 29 Cal. Rptr. 2d 182 (Cal. App. 1994) 9.03n8

Serpa v. Washoe, County of, 901 P.2d 690 (Nev. 1995) 9.09n2

Service Oil Co. v. Rhodus, 500 P.2d 807 (Colo. 1972) 5.81n8; 5.82n5

Service Oil Co. v. Rhodus 500 P.2d 807 (Colo. 1972) 4.25n3

7-Eleven, Inc. v. McClain, 422 P.2d 455 (Okla. 1967) 4.33n2

751 Orange Ave, Inc. v. W. Haven, City of, 761 F.2d 105 (2d Cir. 1985) 5.64n1

S.E.W. Friel v. Triangle Oil Co., 543 A.2d 863 (Md. App. 1988) 6.11n6; 6.66n10

Seward Chapel, Inc. v. Seward, City of, 655 P.2d 1293 (Alaska 1982) 5.68n1

Seward County Bd. of Comm'rs v. Seward, City of, 242 N.W.2d 849 (Neb. 1976) 4.36n1

Seymour, City of v. Onyx Paving Co., 541 N.E.2d 951 (Ind. App. 1989) 8.23n5

Sgro v. Howarth, 203 N.E.2d 173 (Ill. App. 1964) 6.21n6

Shaari v. Harvard Student Agencies, Inc., 691 N.E.2d 925 (Mass. 1998) 8.47n1

Shannon v. Forsyth, City of, 666 P.2d 750 (Mont. 1982) 6.04n4

Shannon & Riordan v. Board of Zoning Appeals, 451 N.W.2d 479 (Wis. App. 1989) 5.10n5

Shapell Indus. v. Governing Bd., 1 Cal. Rptr. 2d 818 (Cal. App. 1991) 9.21n10

Shapiro v. Oyster Bay, Town of, 211 N.Y.S.2d 414 (Sup. Ct. 1961), aff'd, 249 N.Y.S.2d 663 (App. Div. 1964) 9.06n4

Shapiro v. Thompson 394 U.S. 618 (1969) 10.08n4

Sharp v. Zoning Hearing Bd., 628 A.2d 1223 (Pa. Commw. 1993) 6.29n11

Shaw v. Planning Comm'n, 500 A.2d 1338 (Conn. App. 1985) 6.68n2

Shell Oil Co. v. Board of Adjustment, 185 A.2d 201 (N.J. 1962) 4.26n3

Shellburne, Inc. v. Buck, 240 A.2d 757 (Del. 1968) 8.15n3

Shelton v. College Station, City of, 780 F.2d 475 (5th Cir. 1986) 2.39n5

Shemo, State ex rel. v. Maryland Heights, City of, 765 N.E.2d 345 . . . . 2.21n1

Shepard v. Woodland Twp. Comm. & Planning Bd., 364 A.2d 1005 (N.J. 1976) 7.10n1

Sherbert v. Verner, 374 U.S. 398 (1963) . . 5.69n5

Sheridan v. Planning Bd., 266 A.2d 396 (Conn. 1969) 6.61n1, n3

Sheridan Planning Comm'n v. Board of Sheridan County Comm'rs, 924 P.2d 988 (Wyo. 1996) . . 9.27n2, n4

Sherman v. Colorado Springs Planning Comm'n, City of, 680 P.2d 1302 (Colo. App. 1983), aff'd . . . 6.66n10

Sherman v. Colorado Springs Planning Comm'n, City of, 763 P.2d 292 (Colo. 1988) 8.13n8

Sherman v. Frazier, 446 N.Y.S.2d 372 (App. Div. 1982) 4.25n6

Sherrill House, Inc. v. Board of Appeal, 473 N.E.2d 716 (Mass. App. 1986) 8.04n1

Sherwood v. Grant County, 699 P.2d 243 (Wash. App. 1985) 6.46n4

Shire Inn v. Borough of Avon -By-The- . . 7.13n1

The Shopco Group v. Springdale, City of, 586 N.E.2d 145 (Ohio App.) 8.26n1

Shoptaugh v. Board of County Comm'rs, 543 P.2d 524 (Colo. App. 1976) 9.06n5; 9.09n15

Shors v. Johnson, 581 N.W.2d 648 (Iowa 1998) . . 8.11n1

Shoultes v. Laidlaw, 886 F.2d 114 (6th Cir. 1989) 8.35n4; 8.36n2

Sica v. Board of Adj., 603 A.2d 30 (N.J. 1992) . . 6.41n5

Siegert v. Gilley, 500 U.S. 226 (1991) . . 8.36n11

Sierra Club v. Morton, 405 U.S. 727 (1972) 8.06n3

Sierra Club v. Sigler, 695 F.2d 957 (5th Cir. 1983) 12.06n10

Sierra Screw Prods. v. Azusa Greens, Inc., 151 Cal. Rptr. 799 (Cal. App. 1979) 4.10n2, n6

Sign v. Rockford, City of 406 N.E.2d 943 (Ill. App. 1980) 11.10n7

Silva v. Township of Ada, 330 N.W.2d 663 (Mich. 1982) 2.04n4

Silver v. Franklin Township Board of Zoning Appeals, 966 F.2d 1031 (6th Cir. 1991) 2.31n2

Silverco, Inc. v. Zoning Bd. of Adjustment, 109 A.2d 147 (Pa. 1954) 6.41n10

Simko v. Ervin, 661 A.2d 1018 (Conn. 1995) . . . 8.11n9

Simms v. Sherman, City of, 181 S.W.2d 100 (Tex. Civ. App.), aff'd, 183 S.W.2d 415 (Tex. 1944) 5.68n3

Simon v. Needham 42 N.E.2d 516 (Mass. 1942) . .
    5.31n1

Simplex Technologies, Inc. v. Newington, Town of,
    766 A.2d 713 . . . . 6.44n7

Sinaloa Lake Owners Assoc. v. Simi Valley, 852 F.2d
    1398 (9th Cir. 1989) 2.32n4

Sinclair Oil Corp. v. Santa Barbara., County of 96
    F.3d 401 (9th Cir. 1996) 2.24n5

Sinclair Oil Corp. v. Santa Barbara, County of, 96
    F.3d 401 (9th Cir. 1996) 2.40n3

Sinclair Pipe Line Co. v. Richton Park, Village of, 167
    N.E.2d 406 (Ill. 1960) 6.43n4; 8.11n2

Sinclair Pipe Line Co. v. Richton Park, Village of 167
    N.E.2d 406 (Ill. 1960) 8.19n2

Sinn v. Board of Selectmen of Acton, 259 N.E.2d 557
    (Mass. 1970) 4.34n1

Sintra, Inc. v. Seattle, City of, 829 P.2d 765 (Wash.
    1992) 9.23n2

SK Finance SA v. La Plata County, Bd. of County
    Com'rs, 126 F.3d 1272 (10th Cir. 1997) . . . . .
    2.24n5

Skelly Oil Co., State ex rel. v. Common Council, 207
    N.W.2d 585 (Wis. 1973) 6.55n3

Skipper v. Hambleton Meadows Architectural Review
    Comm., 996 F. Supp. 478 (D. Md. 1998) . . . .
    8.45n3

Skokie Town House Bldrs., Inc., People ex rel. v.
    Morton Grove, Village of 157 N.E.2d 33 (Ill. 1959)
    . . . . 5.43n1

Skokie, Village of v. Walton on Dempster, Inc., 456
    N.E.2d 293 (Ill. App. 1983) . . 5.86n6; 11.10n2

Slavin v. Ingraham, 339 N.E.2d 157 (N.Y. 1975)
    . . . . 9.05n6

Slevin v. Long Island Jewish Medical Center, 319
    N.Y.S.2d 937 (Misc. 1971) 5.68n5

Slips v. State, 628 N.W.2d 781 . . . . . . 12.07n9

SLS Partnership v. Apple Valley, City of, 496 N.W.2d
    429 (Minn. App. 1993) 5.79n4

Smart SMR of N.Y., Inc. v. Borough of Fair Lawn Bd.
    of Adjustment, 704 A.2d 1271 (N.J. 1998) . . .
    6.47n3

Smart SMR of N.Y., Inc. v. Zoning Comm'n, 995 F.
    Supp. 52 (D. Conn. 1998) 4.42n13

SMD, L.L.P. v. Boswell, City of, 555 S.E.2d 813
    . . . . 8.39n1

Smeja v. Boone, County of, 339 N.E.2d 452 (Ill. App.
    1975) 12.13n6

Smeltzer v. Messer, 225 S.W.2d 96 (Ky. 1949) . .
    4.22n1

Smith v. Board of Adj., 460 N.W.2d 854 (Iowa 1990)
    . . . . 5.81n7

Smith v. Board of Adjustment, 460 N.W.2d 854 (Iowa
    1990) 5.81n10

Smith v. Clearwater, City of, 383 So. 2d 681 (Fla.
    App. 1980) 6.16n3; 6.18n4

Smith v. Fair Haven Zoning Bd. of Adjustment, 761
    A.2d 111 . . . . 6.71n7, n9

Smith v. Georgetown County Council, 355 S.E.2d 864
    (S.C. App. 1987) 9.28n2, n4

Smith v. Gill, 310 So. 2d 214 (Ala. 1975) . . . . .
    4.08n2

Smith v. Grant, 943 S.W.2d 319 (Mo. App. 1997)
    . . . . 8.07n1

Smith v. Los Angeles, County of, 29 Cal. Rptr. 2d 680
    (Cal. App. 1994) 6.57n2

Smith v. Lower Merion Twp., 1991 U.S. Dist. Lexis
    1110 (E.D. Pa. 1991) 10.08n8

Smith v. Mobile, City of 9.09

Smith v. Normal, Town of, 605 N.E.2d 727 (Ill. App.
    1992) 6.05n14

Smith v. Santa Barbara, County of, 9 Cal. Rptr. 2d 120
    (Cal. App. 1992) 6.17n1

Smith v. St. Johnsbury, Town of, 554 A.2d 233 (Vt.
    1988) 6.29n12; 6.33n5

Smith; State v. , 618 S.W.2d 474 (Tenn. 1981) . . .
    11.05n1

Smith v. Township Comm., 244 A.2d 145 (N.J. App.
    Div. 1968) 9.10n4

Smith v. Township of Livingston, 256 A.2d 85 (N.J.
    Ch.), aff'd, 257 A.2d 698 (N.J. 1969) . . 6.83n1

Smith v. Wade, 461 U.S. 30 (1983) 8.38n4

Smith v. Winhall Planning Comm'n, 436 A.2d 760
    . . . . 9.07n4

Smith v. Winhall Planning Comm'n, 436 A.2d 760
    (Vt. 1981) 6.16n1

Smith v. Wolfeboro, Town of, 615 A.2d 1252 (N.H.
    1992) 9.09n16

Smith v. Zoning Bd. of Appeals, 387 A.2d 542 (Conn.
    1978) 6.46n4

Smith v. Zoning Bd. of Appeals, 629 A.2d 1089
    (Conn. 1993) 9.09n3

Smith-Birch v. Baltimore County, 68 F. Supp.2d 602
    . . . . 2.42n9

Smith Inv. Co. v. Sandy City, 958 P.2d 245 (Utah
    App. 1998) 6.37n2, n13

Smith & Lee Assocs. v. Taylor (II), City of, 102 F.3d
    781 (6th Cir. 1996) 5.13n4

Smithfield v. Fanning, 602 A.2d 939 (R.I. 1992) . .
    4.38n3

Smithfield Concerned Citizens for Fair Zoning v.
    Smithfield, Town of, 907 F.2d 239 (1st Cir. 1990)
    . . . . 2.32n5; 6.36n2

Smoke v. Seattle, City of, 937 P.2d 186 (Wash. 1997)
    . . . . 8.11n1

Smoke Rise, Inc. v. Washington Sub. San. Comm'n,
    400 F. Supp. 1369 (1975) 6.11n5

Smoke Rise, Inc. v. Washington Sub. San. Comm'n,
    400 F. Supp. 1369 (D. Md. 1975) . . 6.10n4, n6

Smythe v. Butler Twp., 620 N.E.2d 901 (Ohio App.
    1993) 12.13n6

Snake River Brewing Co. v. Jackson, Town of, 39 P.3d 397 . . . . 5.81n5

Sneed v. Riverside, County of, 32 Cal. Rptr. 318 (Cal. App. 1962) 5.39n8

Snider v. Board of County Comm'rs, 932 P.2d 704 (Wash. App. 1997) 9.16n14

Snohomish County v. Anderson, 868 P.2d 116 (Wash. 1994) 6.77n2

Snohomish County v. State, 648 P.2d 430 (Wash. 1982) 4.27n2

Snowden v. Hughes, 321 U.S. 1 (1944) . . 2.49n2

Snyder v. Board of County Comm'rs 6.26

Snyder v. Board of County Comm'rs, 627 So. 2d 469 (Fla. 1993) 6.33n5

Snyder v. City Council, 531 P.2d 643 (Colo. App. 1975) 8.04n2

Snyder v. Lakewood, City of, 542 P.2d 371 (Colo. 1975) 8.13n9; 8.16n7; 8.22n1

Snyder v. Minneapolis, City of, 441 N.W.2d 781 (Minn. 1989) 8.23n5

Snyder v. Owensboro, 528 S.W.2d 663 (Ky. 1975) 9.09n2

Snyder v. Waukesha County Zoning Bd. of Adjustment, 247 N.W.2d 98 (Wis. 1976) . . . 6.48n2

Snyder v. Zoning Bd., 200 A.2d 222 (R.I. 1964) . . 9.06n4

Soaring Vista Props. v. Board of County Comm'rs, 741 A.2d 1110 (Md. 1999) 4.30n11

Soble Constr. Co. v. Zoning Hearing Bd. 329 A.2d 912 (Pa. Commw. 1974) 9.25n9

Society for Ethical Culture v. Spatt 415 N.E.2d 922 (N.Y. 1980) 11.37n2

Society of Jesus v. Boston Landmarks Comm'n, 564 N.E.2d 571 (Mass. 1990) . . . 5.69n4; 11.37n7

Soho Alliance v. New York City Bd. of Standards & Appeals, 741 N.E.2d 106 . . . . 6.45n2

Sokolinski v. Municipal Council, 469 A.2d 96 (N.J. App. Div. 1983) 6.74n9

Solar v. Zoning Bd. of Appeals, 600 N.E.2d 187 (Mass. App. 1992) 6.59n4

Solid Rock Ministries Int'l v. Board of Zoning Appeals, 740 N.E.2d 320 . . . . 5.68n5

Solid Waste Agency v. United States Army Corps of Eng'rs, 531 U.S. 159 . . . . 12.06n4

Sonn v. Planning Comm'n, 374 A.2d 159 (Conn. 1976) 9.09n7

Sorg v. North Hero Zoning Bd. of Adjustment, 378 A.2d 98 (Vt. 1977) 6.41n8

Sosna v. Iowa, 419 U.S. 393 (1975) . . . 10.08n5

South Brunswick Assocs. v. Township Council, 667 A.2d 1 (N.J.L. Div. 1995) 6.73n2

South County Sand & Gravel Co. v. South Kingstown, Town of, 160 F.3d 834 (1st Cir. 1998) 2.40n3

South County Sand & Gravel Co.. Inc. v. South Kingston, 160 F, Town of 2.08n8

South E. Prop. Owners & Residents Ass'n v. City Plan Comm'n, 244 A.2d 394 (Conn. 1968) . . 9.10n2

South Gwinnett Venture v. Pruitt, 491 F.2d 5 . . . 6.26n5

South Gwinnett Venture v. Pruitt, 491 F.2d 5 (5th Cir.1974) 6.25n13

South Hill Sewer Dist. v. Pierce County, 591 P.2d 877 (Wash. App. 1979) 4.36n1

South Maple St. Ass'n v. Board of Adjustment, 230 N.W.2d 471 (Neb. 1975) 6.52n4

South of Second Assocs. v. Georgetown, 580 P.2d 807 (Colo. 1978) 6.05n15; 11.30n2

South of Sunnyside Neighborhood League v. Board of Comm'rs, 569 P.2d 1063 (Or. 1977) . . 6.34n2

South-Suburban Housing Center v. Greater South Suburban Bd. of Realtors, 935 F.2d 868 (7th Cir. 1991) 11.18n2, n4; 11.22n1

Southeastern Displays, Inc. v. Ward, 414 S.W.2d 573 (Ky. 1967) 11.06n7

Southern Alameda Spanish Speaking Org. v. Union City, City of, 424 F.2d 291 (9th Cir. 1970) . . . 6.80n6

Southern Burlington County NAACP v. Township of Mt. Laurel, 456 A.2d 390 (N.J. 1983) . . 5.24n2

Southern Burlington County NAACP v. Township of Mt. Laurel (I), 336 A.2d 713 (N.J.) . . 10.08n1

Southern Equipment Co. v. Winstead, 342 S.E.2d 524 (N.C. App. 1986) 5.81n11

Southern Motor Carriers Rate Conference, Inc. v. United States, 471 U.S. 48 (1985) 5.53n6

Southern Nat'l Bank v. Austin, City of, 582 S.W.2d 229 (Tex. Civ. App. 1979) . . 8.16n2; 11.31n1

Southern Nevada Homebuilders Ass'n v. North Las Vegas, City of, 913 P.2d 1276 (Nev. 1996) . . . 9.21n5

Southern Pacific Transp. Co. v. Los Angeles, City of, 922 F.2d 4988 (9th Cir. 1990) 2.30n8

Southern Pines, Town of v. Mohr, 226 S.E.2d 865 (N.C. 1976) 5.10n1

Southlake Property Associates, Ltd. v. Morrow, City of, 112 F.3d 1114 (11th Cir. 1997) . . 11.19n10

Southland Corp. v. Mayor & City Council, 541 A.2d 653 (Md. App. 1988) 6.66n7

Southview Assoc., Ltd. v. Bongartz, 980 F.2d 84 (2d Cir. 1992) 2.30n5

Southview Assocs., Ltd. v. Bongartz, 980 F.2d 84 (2d Cir. 1992) 2.31n3; 2.32n4

Southwest Diversified, Inc. v. Brisbane, City of, 280 Cal. Rptr. 869 (Cal. App. 1991) 6.82n8

Southwestern Bell Mobile Systems v. Todd, 244 F.3d 51 . . . . 4.42n10

Southwestern Bell Mobile Systems, Inc. v. Todd, 244 F.3d 51 . . . . 4.42n12, n14

Southwick, Inc. v. Lacey, City of, 795 P.2d 712 (Wash. App. 1990) 6.66n2

Souza v. Lauppe, 69 Cal. Rptr.2d 494 (Cal. App. 1997) 12.11n3

Sovereign v. Dunn, 498 N.W.2d 62 (Minn. App. 1993) 6.76n9

Sowin Assocs. v. Planning & Zoning Comm'n, 580 A.2d 91 (Conn. App. 1990) 9.09n18

Spaid v. Board of County Comm'rs, 269 A.2d 797 (Md. 1970) 5.38n1

Sparks v. Bolton, 335 S.W.2d 780 (Tex. Civ. App. 1960) 8.11n7

Sparks v. Douglas County, 904 P.2d 738 (Wash. 1995) 9.16n14

Speedway Bd. of Zoning Appeals v. Popcheff, 385 N.E.2d 1179 (Ind. App. 1979) 6.68n3; 6.70n10, n11

Spence v. Board of Zoning Appeals, 496 S.E.2d 61 (Va. 1998) 6.50n6

Spence v. Zimmennan, 873 F.2d 256 . . . . 2.39n5

Spence v. Zimmerman, 873 F.2d 256 (11th Cir. 1989) 2.40n6

Spenger, Grubb & Assocs. v. Hailey, City of, 903 P.2d 741 (Idaho 1995) 6.33n2

Spero v. Zoning Bd. of Appeals, 586 A.2d 590 (Conn. 1991) 6.05n24

Sprenger, Grubb & Assocs. v. Hailey, City of, 986 P.2d 343 (Idaho 1999) 3.22n1

Sprenger, Grubb & Assocs., Inc. v. Hailey, City of, 903 P.2d 741 (Idaho 1995) . . . 5.48n2; 6.37n2, n11

Spriggs v. South Strabane Township Zoning Hearing Bd., 786 A.2d 333 . . . . 11.18n7

Springfield, City of v. Goff, 918 S.W.2d 786 (Mo. 1996) 4.25n9; 6.04n2

Sprint Spectrum, L.P. v. Borough of Upper Saddle River Zoning Bd. of Adjustment, 801 A.2d 336 . . . . 4.42n1

Sprint Spectrum L.P. v. Easton, Town of, 982 F. Supp. 47 (D. Mass. 1997) 4.42n13

Sprint Spectrum, L.P. v. Willoth, 176 F.3d 630 (2d Cir. 1999) 4.42n6, n8

Sproul Homes v. State Dep't of Highways, 611 P.2d 620 (Nev. 1980) 2.23n5

Spur Indus. v. Del E. Webb Dev. Co. 494 P.2d 700 (Ariz. 1972) 4.14n1

Spurgeon v. Board of Comm'rs, 317 P.2d 798 (Kan. 1957) 5.84n6

Srovnal, State ex rel. v. Linton, 346 N.E.2d 764 (Ohio 1976) 6.82n8

SRW Assocs. v. Bellport Beach Property Owners, 517 N.Y.S.2d 741 (App. Div. 1987) 8.46n9

St. Ann, City of v. Elam, 661 S.W.2d 632 (Mo. App. 1983) 8.11n19

St. Bartholomew's Church v. New York, City of, 65 St. John's L. Rev. 553 (1991)

St. Charles, City of v. DeVault Mgt. Co., 959 S.W.2d 815 (Mo. App. 1998) 6.34n2

St. Charles Gaming Co. v. Riverboat Gaming Comm'n, 648 So. 2d 1310 (La. 1995) . . 4.31n5

St. Clair v. Chico, City of, 880 F.2d 199 (9th Cir.1989) 2.24n2

St. Clair v. City 2.24n3

St. Corp. v. Von Gutfield, 603 N.E.2d 930 (N.Y. 1992) 8.46n9

St. John's County v. Northeast Florida Builders Ass'n, 583 So. 2d 635 (Fla. 1991) 9.22n3

St. Joseph, City of v. Preferred Family Healthcare, Inc., 859 S.W.2d 723 (Mo. App. 1993) 5.14n4

St. Louis, City of v. Bridgeton, City of, 705 S.W.2d 524 (Mo. App. 1985) 4.38n3

St. Louis, City of v. Brune, 515 S.W.2d 471 (Mo. 1974) 11.36n2

St. Louis, City of v. Golden Gate Corp., 421 S.W.2d 4 (Mo. 1967) 4.10n5

St. Louis, City of v. Praprotnik 485 U.S. 112 (1988) 8.31n6

St. Louis Gunning Adv. Co. v. St. Louis, City of, 137 S.W. 929 (Mo. 1911) 11.03n3

St. Louis Poster Adv. Co. v. St. Louis, City of, 249 U.S. 269 (1919) 11.10n1

St. Onge v. Donovan, 522 N.E.2d 1019 (N.Y. 1988) 6.51n4

St. Paul, City of v. Chicago, St. Paul, Minneapolis & Omaha Ry., 413 F.2d 762 (8th Cir. 1969) 5.74n6

St. Petersburg, City of v. Schweitzer, 297 So. 2d 74 (Fla. App. 1974) 6.03n2

Stafford, City of v. Gullo, 886 S.W.2d 524 (Tex. App. 1994) 9.16n1

Stahl v. Upper Southampton Twp. Zoning Hearing Bd., 606 A.2d 960 (Pa. Commw. 1992) 7.20n4

Staller v. Cranston Zoning Bd. of Review, 215 A.2d 418 (R.I. 1965) 6.43n4

Standard Oil Co. v. Warrensville Heights, City of, 355 N.E.2d 495 (Ohio App. 1976) 6.43n2

Stansberry v. Holmes, 613 F.2d 1285 (5th Cir. 1980) 5.65n4

Stanton, City of v. Cox, 255 Cal. Rptr. 682 (Cal. App. 1989) 5.63n8

Star Vector Corp. v. Windham, Town of, 776 A.2d 138 . . . . 6.66n11

State v. (see name of defendant)

State Bd. of Health v. Atnip Design & Supply Center, Inc., 385 So. 2d 1307 (Ala. 1980) . . . 8.14n10

State Dep't of Envtl. Protection v. Burgess, 772 So.2d 540 . . . . 2.21n3

State Dep't of Roads v. Popco, Inc., 528 N.W.2d 281 (Neb. 1995) 11.09n2

State ex (see name of state)

State ex rel. (see name of state)

State of (see name of state)

Staubes v. Folly Beach, City of, 500 S.E.2d 160 (S.C. App. 1998) 8.23n3; 8.26n1

Steadham v. Board of Zoning Adjustment, 629 So. 2d 647 (Ala. 1993) 8.04n1

Steakhouse, Inc. v. Raleigh, City of, 166 F.3d 634 (4th Cir. 1999) 6.57n4, n9

Steel Hill Dev., Inc. v. Sanbornton, Town of, 469 F.2d 956 (1st Cir. 1972) 5.31n2; 6.37n15

Steffens v. Keeler, 503 N.W.2d 675 (Mich. App. 1993) 12.11n2

Stegeman v. Ann Arbor, City of, 540 N.W.2d 724 (Mich. App. 1995) 5.05n3

Steinbergh v. Cambridge, City of, 604 N.E.2d 1269 (Mass. 1992) 8.26n2

Steinke; State v. , 96 N.W.2d 356 (Wis. 1959) . . . 5.80n11

Steinlage v. New Hampton, City of, 567 N.W.2d 438 (Iowa App. 1997) 8.14n4

Stephans v. Tahoe Regional Planning Agency, 697 F. Supp. 1149 (D. Nev. 1988) 2.30n7

Stephen Renedy Mem. Fund v. Old Saybrook, Town of, 492 A.2d 533 (Conn. App. 1985) . . 5.41n2

Stephens v. Cobb Cty., 684 F. Supp. 703 (N.D. Ga. 1988) 8.45n3

Stephens v. Vista, City of, 994 F.2d 650 (9th Cir. 1993) 6.23n6

Stephens City, Town of v. Russell, 399 S.E.2d 814 (Va. 1991) 6.15n1

Sterling Homes Corp. v. Anne Arundel County, 695 A.2d 1238 (Md. App. 1997) . . 6.15n4; 6.21n4

Stevens v. Cannon Beach, City of, 854 P.2d 449 (Or. 1993) 12.15n3

Stevens v. Huntington, Town of 229 N.E.2d 591 (N.Y. 1967) 2.36n8

Stewart v. Humpheries, 132 N.E.2d 758 (Ohio 1955) 5.20n4

Stice v. Gribben-Allen Motors, Inc., 534 P.2d 1267 (Kan. 1975) 6.43n2

Stickelman v. Harrison Township Bd. of Zoning Appeals, 772 N.E.2d 683 . . . . 6.48n14

Still v. Board of County Comm'rs, 600 P.2d 433 (Or. App.1979) 12.12n3

Stillwater Condominium Ass'n v. Salem, Town of, 668 P.2d 38 (N.H. 1995) 8.23n17

Stocks v. Irvine, City of 170 Cal. Rptr. 724 (Cal. App. 1981) 7.07n2

Stocksdale v. Barnard, 212 A.2d 282 (Md. 1965) 8.06n1

Stokes v. Mishawaka, City of, 441 N.E.2d 24 (Ind. App. 1982) 8.05n2

Stone v. Maitland, City of, 446 F.2d 83 (5th Cir. 1971) 5.47n6

Stone v. Wilton, City of, 331 N.W.2d 398 (Iowa 1983) 6.21n5; 6.37n17; 7.03n5

Stoner v. Township of Lower Merion, 587 A.2d 879 (Pa. Commw. 1991) 8.26n1

Stoner McCray Sys. v. Des Moines, City of, 78 N.W.2d 783 (Iowa 1956) 5.85n2

Stoner McCray Sys. v. Des Moines, City of, 78 N.W.2d 843 (Iowa 1956) 11.08n6

Stonewood, Town of v. Bell, 270 S.E.2d 787 (W. Va. 1980) 5.23n3

Stoney-Brook Dev. Corp. v. Fremont, Town of, 474 A.2d 561 (N.H. 1984) 10.04n4

Stop & Shop Supermarket Co. v. Board of Adjustment, 744 A.2d 1169 . . . . 6.41n6

Storegard v. Board of Election, 255 N.E.2d 880 (Ohio 1969) 6.83n2

Storey v. Central Hide & Rendering Co., 226 S.W.2d 615 (Tex. 1950) 4.12n1

Stowe v. Burke, 122 S.E.2d 374 (N.C. 1961) 6.18n2

Stoyanoff, State ex rel. v. Berkeley 458 S.W.2d 305 (Mo. 1970) 11.25n6

Straatmann Enters., Inc. v. Franklin, County of, 4 S.W.2d 641 (Mo. App. 1999) 11.06n4

Strandberg v. Kansas City, 415 S.W.2d 737 (Mo. 1967) 6.74n11

Strange v. Board of Zoning Appeals, 428 N.E.2d 1328 (Ind. App. 1981) 6.43n1

Stratford v. Crossman, 655 S.W.2d 500 (Ky. App. 1983) 8.14n11

Stratford Arms, Inc. v. Zoning Bd. of Adjustment, 239 A.2d 325 (Pa. 1968) 6.17n1

Stratos v. Ravenel, Town of, 376 S.E.2d 783 (S.C. App. 1989) 8.14n2

Strazzulla v. Building Inspector, 260 N.E.2d 163 (Mass. 1970) 11.06n2

Strickland v. Alderman, 74 F.3d 260 (11th Cir. 1996) 2.30n13, n14; 2.32n4; 2.47n3

Stringfellow's of New York v. New York, City of, 91 N.E.2d 382 (N.Y. 1998) 5.63n4, n7

Stroud v. Aspen, City of, 532 P.2d 720 (Colo. 1975) 5.77n2

Stroud & Trevarthen, Defensible Exactions After Nollan v. California Coastal Commission and Dolan

Strucker v. Summit County, 870 P.2d 283 (Utah App. 1994) 6.04n2

Stuart v. Board of County Comm'rs, 699 P.2d 978 (Colo. App. 1985) 6.26n8

Stuckman v. Kosciusko County Bd. of Zoning Appeals, 506 N.E.2d 1079 (Ind. 1987) . . . 5.79n8

Studen v. Beebe, 588 F.2d 560 (6th Cir. 1978) . . . 2.47n1

Sturdy Homes, Inc. v. Township of Redford, 186 N.W.2d 43 (Mich. App. 1971) 12.09n4

Sturgeon v. Retherford Publications, 987 P.2d 1218 (Okla. App. 1999) 8.46n8

Sturges v. Chilmark, Town of, 402 N.E.2d 1346 (Mass. 1980) 10.06n2

Stutsman, County of v. State Historical Soc'y, 371 N.W.2d 321 (N.D. 1985) 11.34n6

Subaru of N.E. v. Board of Appeals, 395 N.E.2d 880 (Mass. App. 1979) 12.09n4

Subdivision Servs. Bd. v. Zoning Hearing Bd., 784 A.2d 850 . . . . 11.06n3

Suburban Lodges of America, Inc. v. Columbus Graphics Comm'n, City of, 761 N.E.2d 1060 . . 11.18n6

Suburban Ready Mix Corp. v. Wheeling, Village of, 185 N.E.2d 665 (Ill. 1962) 5.37n6

Sucesion Suarez v. Gelabert, 541 F. Supp. 1253 (D.P.R. 1982) 2.04n4

Sucesion Suarez v. Gelabert, 541 F. Supp. 1253 (D.P.R. 1982), aff'd, 701 F.2d 231 (1st Cir. 1983) 2.16n6

Suddeth v. Forsyth Cty., 373 S.E.2d 746 (Ga. 1988) 6.03n3

Suess v. Vogelgesang, 281 N.E.2d 536 (Ind. App. 1972) 6.49n3

Suess Bldrs. Co. v. Beaverton, City of, 656 P.2d 306 (Or. 1982) 3.21n4

Suffolk Hous. Serv. v. Brookhaven, Town of, 397 N.Y.S.2d 302 (Sup. Ct. 1978), aff'd . . . 7.07n4

Suffolk Interreligious Coalition on Housing v. Brookhaven, Town of, 575 N.Y.S.2d 548 (App. Div. 1991) 7.05n6; 7.16n2

Suffolk Outdoor Adv. Co. v. Hulse, 373 N.E.2d 263 (N.Y. 1977) 11.08n3

Suffolk Outdoor Adv. Co. v. Southampton, Town of, 449 N.Y.S.2d 766 (App. Div. 1982), aff'd, 455 N.E.2d 1245 (N.Y. 1983) 5.86n4

Suffolk Outdoor Adv. Co. v. Southampton, Town of, 455 N.E.2d 1245 (N.Y. 1983) 11.11n8

Sugar Creek, City of v. Reese, 969 S.W.2d 888 (Mo. App. 1998) 5.79n1

Sugarloaf Citizens Ass'n v. Gudis, 573 A.2d 1325 (Md. 1990) 6.72n4

Sugarman v. Chester, Village of, 192 F. Supp.2d 282 . . . . 11.17n3; 11.23n8

Sugarman v. Lewis, 488 A.2d 709 (R.I. 1985) . . . 9.05n9

Suitum v. Tahoe Regional Planning Agency, 520 U.S. 725 . . . . 11.38n8

Suitum v. Tahoe Regional Planning Agency 520 U.S. 725 (1997) 2.28n1

Sullivan v. Acton, Town of, 645 N.E.2d 700 (Mass. App. 1995) 6.37n1

Sullivan v. Northwest Garage & Storage Company, 165 A.2d 881 (Md. 1960) 6.76n6

Sullivan v. Pittsburgh, City of, 811 F.2d 171 (3d Cir. 1987) 8.42n10, n12

Sullivan v. Pittsburgh, City of, 815 F.2d 171 (3rd Cir. 1987) 5.12n3

Sullivan v. Planning Bd., 645 N.E.2d 703 (Mass. App. 1995) 9.16n1

Sullivan v. Salem, Town of, 805 F.2d 81 (2d Cir. 1986) 8.31n5; 8.33n5; 8.36n4

Sullivan v. Zoning Bd. of Adjustment, 478 A.2d 912 (Pa. Commw. 1984) 5.84n6

Summey Outdoor Adv., Inc. v. Henderson, County of, 386 S.E.2d 439 (N.C. App. 1989) . . 11.07n13; 11.09n2

Sun-Brite Car Wash, Inc. v. Board of Zoning & Appeals, 508 N.E.2d 130 (N.Y. 1987) 5.46n3; 8.04n2

Sun Communities v. Leroy Township, 617 N.W.2d 42 . . . . 8.13n4

Sun Oil Co. v. Arlington, City of, 379 N.E.2d 266 (Ohio App. 1977) 11.10n2

Sun Oil Co. v. Madison Heights, City of, 199 N.W.2d 525 (Mich. App. 1972) 11.07n3

Sun Oil Co. v. Upper Arlington, City of, 379 N.E.2d 266 (Ohio App. 1977) 11.08n7

Sun Oil Co. v. Zoning Bd. of Adjustment, 169 A.2d 294 (Pa. 1961) 6.66n1

Sun Prairie, Town of v. Storms, 327 N.W.2d 642 (Wis. 1983) 9.06n3

Sun Ray Homes, Inc. v. Dade, County of, 166 So. 2d 827 (Fla. App. 1964) 8.13n11

Sun Ridge Dev., Inc. v. Cheyenne, City of, 787 P.2d 583 (Wyo. 1990) 6.10n1

Sun Suites Holdings, LLC v. Board of Aldermen, 535 S.E.2d 525 . . . . 6.56n8

Sundberg v. Evans, 897 P.2d 1285 (Wash. App. 1995) 8.23n7

Sunrise, City of v. D.C.A. Homes, Inc., 421 So. 2d 1084 (Fla. App. 1982) 11.18n4

Sunset View Cem. Ass'n v. Kraintz, 16 Cal. Rptr. 317 (Cal. App. 1961) 6.16n4

SuperAmerican Group, Inc. v. Little Canada, City of, 539 N.W.2d 264 (Minn. App. 1995) . . 6.58n4

Superior-FCR Landfill, Inc. v. Wright, County of, 59 F. Supp.2d 929 (D. Minn. 1999) 5.54n5

Superior Uptown, Inc. v. Cleveland, City of, 313 N.E.2d 820 (Ohio 1974) 6.37n9

Support Ministries for Persons With AIDS, Inc. v. Waterford, Village of, 808 F. Supp. 120 (N.D.N.Y. 1992) 5.14n1

Surfside Colony, Ltd. v. California Coastal Comm'n, 277 Cal. Rptr. 371 (Cal. App. 1991) . . 9.13n4

Surrick v. Zoning Hearing Bd 7.20

Surrick in BAC, Inc. v. Board of Supervisors of Millcreek Township 7.20

Suter v. Artist M., 503 U.S. 347 (1992) . . 8.29n5

Suttton v. United States Airlines, 527 U.S. 471 (1999) 5.12n3

Suzuki v. Los Angeles, City of, 51 Cal. Rptr.2d 880 (Cal. App. 1996) 5.78n2

Swain v. Board of Adjustment, 433 S.W.2d 727 (Tex. App. 1968) 6.43n2

Swain v. Winnebago, County of, 250 N.E.2d 439 (Ill. App. 1969) 5.46n3

Swain v. Winnebago, County of 250 N.E.2d 439 (Ill. App. 1969) 5.48n1

Swann v. Board of Adjustment, 459 So. 2d 896 (Ala. Civ. App. 1984) 6.43n2

Swansea, Village of v. St. Clair, County of, 359 N.E.2d 866 (Ill. App. 1977) 4.37n2

Swedenberg v. Phillips, 562 So. 2d 170 (Ala. 1990) 12.11n4

Sweetman v. Cumberland, Town of, 364 A.2d 1277 (R.I. 1977) 6.62n1

Swerdlick v. Koch, 721 A.2d 849 (R.I. 1998) . . 8.46n8

Swimming River Golf & Country Club v. Borough of New Shrewsbury, 152 A.2d 135 (N.J. 1959) . . 6.55n2

Sycamore Realty Co., Inc. v. People's Counsel, 684 A.2d 1331 (Md. 1996) 6.13n2

Sylvania Elec. Prods., Inc. v. Newton, City of, 183 N.E.2d 118 (Mass. 1962) 6.64n1

Sylvia Dev. Co. v. Calvert, 48 F.3d 819 (4th Cir. 1995) 2.47n1

Sylvia Dev. Co. v. Calvert County, 48 F.3d 810 (4th Cir. 1995) 2.40n6; 2.42n7; 2.47n1

Synod of Ohio, State ex rel. v. Joseph, 39 N.E.2d 515 (Ohio 1942) 5.68n3

Syracuse Aggregate Corp. v. Weise, 414 N.E.2d 651 (N.Y. 1980) 5.79n7

Szymanski; State v. , 189 A.2d 514 (Conn. Cir. Ct. App. Div. 1967) 5.79n4

T

T. Dev., L.L.C. v. Board of County Comm'rs, 32 P.3d 784 . . . . 9.09n2

Tabb Lakes v. United States, 10 F.3d 796 (D.C. Cir. 1993) 2.22n8

Tabb Lakes, Ltd. v. United States, 10 F.3d 796 (Fed. Cir. 1993) 2.19n3; 2.22n2; 12.07n12

Taber v. Benton Harbor, City of, 274 N.W. 324 (Mich. 1937) 4.35n1

Tahoe Keys Prop. Owners' Ass'n v. State Water Resources Bd., 28 Cal. Rptr. 2d 734 (Cal. App. 1994) 8.15n2; 9.22n3

Tahoe Reg'l Planning Agency v. King, 285 Cal. Rptr. 335 (Cal. App. 1991) 5.84n3; 11.05n1

Tahoe-Sierra Preservation Council v. Tahoe Regional Planning Agency, 638 F. Supp. 126 (D. Nev. 1986) 8.36n4

Tahoe-Sierra Preservation Council v. Tahoe Regional Planning Agency, 535 U.S. . . 5.39n3; 10.03n2

Tahoe-Sierra Preservation Council v. Tahoe Regional Planning Agency, 533 U.S. . . 2.07n3; 2.37n2

Tahoe-Sierra Preservation Council, Inc. v. Tahoe Regional Plan. Agency(II), 938 F.2d 153 (9th Cir. 1991) 2.30n8

Tahoe-Sierra Preservation Council, Inc. v. Tahoe Regional Planning Agency, 911 F.2d 1331 (9th Cir. 1990) 2.30n14

Tahoe-Sierra Preservation Council, Inc. v. Tahoe Regional Planning Agency, 535 U.S. 2.01n2; 2.02n2; 2.03n5; 2.07n6; 2.08n5; 2.09n6; 8.25n5; 8.32n2; 12.01n3; 12.07n15; 12.15n4

Tahoe-Sierra Regional Preservation Council, Inc. v. Tahoe Regional Planning Agency. . . . 2.20n2

Talbut v. Perryburg, City of, 594 N.E.2d 1046 (Ohio App. 1991) 8.13n10

Tall Trees Constr. Corp. v. Zoning Bd. of Appeals, 761 N.E.2d 565 . . . . 6.48n16

Tan v. Collier County, 56 F.3d 1533 (11th Cir. 1995) 2.31n5

Tandem Holding Corp. v. Board of Zoning Appeals, 373 N.E.2d 282 (N.Y. 1977) 6.56n11

Tangen v. State Ethics Comm'n, 550 P.2d 1275 (Haw. 1976) 6.74n7

Target Advertising, Inc.; People v. , 708 N.Y.S.2d 597 . . . . 11.18n1

Tata v. Babylon, Town of, 276 N.Y.S.2d 426 (Sup. Ct. 1967) 8.04n4

Tate v. Stephens, 265 S.E.2d 811 (Ga. 1980) 8.03n1

Taub v. Deer Park, City of, 882 S.W.2d 824 (Tex. 1994) 2.21n2

Tauber v. Longmeadow, Town of, 695 F. Supp. 1358 (D. Mass. 1988) 11.23n4

Taxpayers Ass'n of Weymouth Twp. v. Weymouth Twp 7.10

Taylor v. District of Columbia Bd. of Zoning Adjustment, 308 A.2d 230 (D.C. App. 1973) 6.42n5

Taylor v. North Palm Beach, Village of, 659 So. 2d 1167 (Fla. App. 1995) 3.21n6

Taylor v. Riviera Beach, City of, 801 So.2d 259 . . 8.09n6

Taylor v. Stevens County, 759 P.2d 447 (Wash. 1988) 8.23n14

Taylor v. Swanson, 187 Cal. Rptr. 111 (Cal. App. 1982) 8.16n7

Taylor v. Zoning Bd. of Appeals, 783 A.2d 526 . . 5.78n2, n7

Taylor Inv. v. Upper Darby Township, 983 F.2d 1285 . . . . 2.32n4

Taylor Inv., Ltd. v. Upper Darby Township, 983 F.2d 1285 (3d Cir. 1993) 2.24n3; 2.32n2

Taylor Props., Inc. v. Union County, 583 N.W.2d 638 (S.D. 1998) 6.80n7; 6.82n3

Tealin Co. v. Ladue, City of, 541 S.W.2d 544 (Mo. 1976) 5.35n2

Technical & Professional Serv. v. Board of Zoning Adjustment, 558 S.W.2d 798 (Mo. App. 1977) 5.47n1

Telluride, Town of v. Lot Thirty-Four Venture, L.L.C., 3 P.2d 30 . . . . 7.27n4

Temkin v. Karagheuzoff, 313 N.E.2d 770 (N.Y. 1974) 6.22n8

Tempe, City of v. Outdoor Systems, Inc., 32 P.3d 31 . . . . 5.80n1

Tempe, City of v. Rasor, 536 P.2d 239 (Ariz. App. 1975) 5.38n3

Temple Baptist Church, Inc. v. Albuquerque, City of, 646 P.2d 565 (N.M. 1982) . . 5.84n6; 11.08n7; 11.10n2

Temple Terrace, City of v. Hillsborough Ass'n for Retarded Citizens, 322 So. 2d 571 (Fla. App. 1975), aff'd, 332 So. 2d 610 (Fla. 1976) 5.10n1

Temple Terrace, City of v. Hillsborough Ass'n for Retarded Citizens 322 So. 2d 571 (Fla. App. 1975), aff'd, 332 So. 2d 610 (Fla. 1976) 4.38n4

Tenn v. 889 Assocs., 500 A.2d 366 (N.H. 1985) . . 4.09n4

Tenney v. Brandhove 341 U.S. 367 (1951) 8.35n1

Tennison v. Shomette, 379 A.2d 187 (Md. App. 1978) 6.29n11

Terino v. Hartford Zoning Bd. of Adj., Town of, 538 A.2d 160 (Vt. 1987) 5.41n1

Terminal Plaza Corp. v. City & County of San Francisco, 223 Cal. Rptr. 379 (Cal. App. 1986) . . . 9.23n2

Terminals Equip. Co. v. City & Cty. of San Francisco, 270 Cal. Rptr. 329 (Cal. App. 1990) . . 2.36n6

Tex-1, Inc. v. Dayton Bd. of Zoning Appeals, City of, 758 N.E.2d 768 . . . . 4.33n2

Texas Antiquities Comm. v. Dallas County Community College Dist., 554 S.W.2d 924 (Tex. 1977) 11.34n6

Texas Manufactured Housing Ass'n v. Nederland, City of, 101 F.3d 1095 (5th Cir. 1996) 2.48n3

Thames Enterprises v. St. Louis, City of, 851 F.2d 199 (8th Cir. 1988) 5.63n2

Theobald v. Board of County Comm'rs, 644 P.2d 942 (Colo. 1982) 3.13n1; 3.14n1

Thomas v. Chicago Park Dist., 534 U.S. 316 . . . . 6.57n5

Thomas v. Chicago Park District 534 U.S. 316 . . . 6.57n10

Thomas v. West Haven, City of, 734 A.2d 535 (Conn. 1999) 2.47n4

Thomas v. Zoning Bd. of Appeals, 381 A.2d 643 (Me. 1978) 6.21n5

Thomas Cusack Co. v. Chicago, City of, 242 U.S. 526 (1917) 6.04n3

Thompson v. Carrollton, City of, 211 S.W.2d 970 (Tex. App. 1948) 5.29n2

Thompson v. Cook County Zoning Bd. of Appeals, 421 N.E.2d 285 (Ill. 1981) 4.25n4

Thompson v. Hancock County, 531 N.W.2d 181 (Iowa 1995) 8.16n6

Thompson v. Newark, Village of, 768 N.E.2d 856 . . . . 9.21n1

Thomson v. State, Dep't of Envtl. Reg., 493 So. 2d 1032 (Fla. App. 1986) 6.68n3

Thornber v. N. Barrington, Village of, 747 N.E.2d 513 . . . . 6.65n3

Thornhill v. Alabama, 310 U.S. 88 (1940) 11.17n2

Thorp v. Lebanon, Town of, 612 N.W.2d 59 . . . . 2.47n4; 12.12n1

350 Lake Shore Assocs. v. Hill, 761 N.E.2d 760 . . 8.14n1

314 Quality Sand & Gravel, Inc. v. Planning & Zoning Comm'n, 738 A.2d 1157 (Conn. App. 1999) . . 6.56n4

360 Degree Communications Co. v. Board of Supervisors, 211 F.3d 79 . . . . 4.42n9

Tidewater Ass'n of Homeowners v. Virginia Beach, City of, 400 S.E.2d 523 (Va. 1991) . . . 9.21n3; 9.22n1

Tidewater Oil Co. v. Mayor and Council of Carteret, 209 A.2d 105 (N.J. 1965) 2.46n7

Tidewater Oil Co. v. Mayor & Council, 209 A.2d 105 (N.J. 1965) 1.17n1; 5.40n1

Tilles v. Huntington, Town of, 547 N.E.2d 90 (N.Y. 1989) 2.36n1

Tillo v. Sioux Falls, City of, 147 N.W.2d 128 (S.D. 1966) 2.36n2

Tim Thompson, Inc. v. Hinsdale, Village of, 617 N.E.2d 1227 (Ill. App. 1993) . . 2.21n2; 6.37n2

Timber Trails Corp. v. Planning & Zoning Comm'n, 610 A.2d 620 (Conn. 1992) 8.06n2

Tisei v. Ogunquit, Town of, 491 A.2d 564 (Me. 1985) 4.25n9; 6.10n1

Titman v. Zoning Hearing Bd., 408 A.2d 167 (Pa. Commw. 1979) 6.59n3

TJ's South, Inc. v. Lowell, Town of, 895 F. Supp. 1124 (N.D. Ind. 1995) 6.57n2

TK's Video, Inc. v. Denton County, 24 F.3d 705 (5th Cir. 1994) 6.57n12

TLC Dev. Co. v. Planning & Zoning Comm'n, 577 A.2d 288 (Conn. 1990) 6.66n4

TLC Dev., Inc. v. Branford, Town of, 855 F. Supp. 555 (D. Conn. 1994) 8.37n1

Todd-Mart, Inc. v. Town Bd. of Webster, 370 N.Y.S.2d 683 (App. Div. 1975) 9.27n4

Toigo v. Ross, Town of, 82 Cal. Rptr. 2d 649 (Cal. App. 1998) 8.09n6

Toigo v. Ross, Town of, 82 Cal.Rptr. 2d 649 (Cal. App. 1998) 8.09n3

Toll Bros., Inc. v. Township of West Windsdor 803 A.2d 53 . . . . 7.13n3

Toll Bros., Inc. v. West Windsor Township, 712 A.2d 266 (N.J. App. 1998) 6.07n4

Tollis v. San Bernardino County, 827 F.2d 1329 (9th Cir. 1987) 5.65n3

Tolman; People v. , 168 Cal. Rptr. 328 (Cal. App. 1980) 5.19n12

Topanga Press, Inc. v. Los Angeles, City of, 989 F.2d 1524 (9th Cir. 1993) 5.63n9

Topliss v. Planning Comm'n, 842 P.2d 648 (Hawaii App. 1993) 12.14n2

Torbett v. Anderson, 564 S.W.2d 676 (Tenn. App. 1978) 8.15n9

Torrance, City of v. Transitional Living Centers for Los Angeles, Inc., 638 P.2d 1304 (Cal. 1982) . . 5.10n4

Toso v. Santa Barbara, City of, 162 Cal. Rptr. 210 (Cal. App.1980) 2.23n5; 8.14n2

Tovar v. Billmeyer, 609 F.2d 1291 (9th Cir. 1990) 8.45n3

Towle v. Nashua, 212 A.2d 204 (N.H. 1965) 8.03n2

Town Close Assocs. v. Planning & Zoning Comm'n, 679 A.2d 378 (Conn. App. 1996) 7.31n3

Town Council of New Harmony v. Parker, 726 N.E.2d 1217 . . . . 8.11n16

Town Pump, Inc. v. Board of Adjustment, 971 P.2d 349 (Mont. 1998) 4.33n2

Township Bd. of Supvrs. v. Golla, 452 A.2d 1337 (Pa. 1982) 7.21n3

Township of Berlin v. Christiansen, 215 A.2d 593 (N.J.L. Div. 1965) 5.19n5

Township of Bernards v. State Dep't of Community Affairs, 558 A.2d 1 (N.J. App. Div. 1989) . . . 7.12n9

Township of Chartiers v. William H. Martin, Inc., 542 A.2d 985 (Pa. 1988) 5.79n11

Township of Dover v. Board of Adjustment, 386 A.2d 421 (N.J. App. Div. 1978) 8.07n1

Township of Dover v. Board of Adjustment 386 A.2d 421 (N.J. App. Div. 1978) 6.43n5

Township of Livingston v. Marchev, 205 A.2d 65 (N.J. App. Div. 1964) 5.19n12

Township of Middleton v. Abel, 297 A.2d 525 (Pa. Commw. 1972) 9.30n5

Township of Pittsfield v. Malcolm, 134 N.W.2d 166 (Mich. 1965) 6.21n2

Township of Randolph v. Lamprecht, 542 A.2d 36 (N.J. App. Div. 1988) 5.19n8

Township of Richmond v. Erbes, 489 N.W.2d 504 (Mich. App. 1992) 12.11n2

Township of Saddle Brook v. A.B. Family Center, Inc., 722 A.2d 530 (N.J. 1999) 5.66n1

Township of Sparta v. Spillane 312 A.2d 154 (N.J. App. 1973) 6.82n1

Township of Warren, In re , 622 A.2d 1257 (N.J. 1993) 7.03n5; 7.12n10

Township of West Orange v. Whitman, 8 F. Supp.2d 408 (D.N.J. 1998) 4.27n3

Township of Willistown v. Chesterdale Farms, Inc., 341 A.2d 466 (Pa. 1975) 7.20n2

Toys R Us v. Silva, 676 N.E.2d 862 (N.Y. 1996) 5.81n7

TPW, Inc. v. New Hope, City of, 388 N.W.2d 390 (Minn. App. 1986) 6.09n1

Trachtman; State v. , 947 P.2d 905 (Ariz. App. 1997) 6.05n13

Trademark Constr., Inc. v. Marion County Bd. of Comm'rs, 962 P.2d 772 (Or. 1998) . . . 6.58n5

Tran v. Gwinn, 554 S.E.2d 63 . . . . 6.57n13

Tranner v. Helmer, 878 P.2d 787 (Idaho 1994) . . . 8.14n1

Transamerica Title Ins. Co. v. Tucson, City of, 533 P.2d 693 (Ariz. App. 1975) 6.64n3

Transamerica Title Ins. Co. Trust v. Tucson, City of, 757 P.2d 1055 (Ariz. 1988) 6.83n1

Transylvania County v. Moody, 565 S.E.2d 720 . . 11.06n2; 11.07n1

Travis v. Moore, 377 So. 2d 609 (Miss. 1979) . . . 4.07n1

Travis v. Preston, 643 N.W.2d 235 . . . 12.11n11

Traweek v. City & Cty. of San Francisco, 920 F.2d 989 (9th Cir. 1990) 5.54n3

Treisman v. Bedford, Town of, 563 A.2d 786 (N.H. 1989) 3.22n5

Tremarco Corp. v. Garzio, 161 A.2d 241 (N.J. 1960) 6.20n3; 6.21n6

Treme v. St. Louis County, 609 S.W.2d 706 (Mo. App. 1980) 6.61n3

Trent v. Pittsburg, City of, 619 P.2d 1171 (Kan. 1980) 5.19n8

Trent Meredith, Inc. v. Oxnard, City of, 170 Cal. Rptr. 685 (Cal. App. 1981) 9.18n1

Tri County Indus., Inc. v. District of Columbia, 104 F.3d 455 (D.C. Cir. 1997) 2.40n2

Tri-State Generation & Transmission Co. v. Thornton, City of, 647 P.2d 670 (Colo. 1982) . . . 9.25n6

Trianon Park Condo. Ass'n v. Hialeah, City of, 468 So. 2d 912 (Fla. 1985) 8.23n5

Trible v. Bland, 458 S.E.2d 297 (Va. 1995) 5.10n2

Trice v. Pine Bluff, City of, 649 S.W.2d 179 (Ark. 1983) 6.05n3

Trimen Dev. Co. v. King County, 877 P.2d 187 (Wash. 1994) 9.21n10

Triomphe Investors v. Northwood, City of, 49 F.3d 198 (6th Cir. 1995) 2.40n6

Trisko v. Waite Park, City of, 566 N.W.2d 349 (Minn. App. 1997) 6.56n14

Trust Co. of Chicago v. Chicago, City of, 96 N.E.2d 499 (Ill. 1951) 6.37n6

Trust Co. of New Jersey v. Planning Bd., 582 A.2d 1295 (N.J. App. Div. 1990) 6.74n11

Trust Estate of (see name of party)

Trustees of Tufts College v. Medford, City of, 616 N.E.2d 433 (Mass. 1993) 5.27n5

Trustees of Union College v. Members of Schenectady City Council, 690 N.E.2d 862 (N.Y. 1998) . . . 5.27n2

Trustees of Union College v. Members of the Schenectady City Council, 690 N.E.2d 862 (N.Y. 1998) 11.28n6

Trustees Under Will of Pomeroy v. Westlake, Town of, 357 So. 2d 1299 (La. App. 1978) . . 8.19n4

Tsombandis v. West Haven, City of, 180 F. Supp.2d 262 . . . . 5.12n6

Tugwell v. Kititas County, 951 P.2d 272 (Wash. App. 1998) 6.31n2

Tullo v. Millburn Twp., 149 A.2d 620 (N.J. App. Div. 1959) 6.54n1

Tulsa, City of v. Swanson, 366 P.2d 629 (Okla. 1961) 5.38n1

Turf Valley Assocs. v. Zoning Bd., 278 A.2d 574 (Md. 1971) 6.73n3

Turner v. Del Norte, County of, 101 Cal. Rptr. 93 (Cal. App. 1972) 12.09n4

Turnpike Realty Co. v. Dedham, Town of, 284 N.E.2d 891 (Mass. 1972) 12.08n7

Turnpike Realty Co. v. Dedham, Town of 284 N.E.2d 891 (Mass. 1972) 12.09n2

Tuscaloosa, City of v. Bryan, 505 So. 2d 330 (Ala. 1987) 9.28n1

Tuscon, City of v. Whiteco Metrocom, Inc., 983 P.2d 759 (Ariz. App. 1999) 5.80n5

Tustin Heights Ass'n v. Board of Supvrs., 339 P.2d 914 (Cal. App. 1959) 8.14n11

Twain Harte Assocs. v. Tuolumne, County of, 265 Cal. Rptr. 737 (Cal. App. 1990) 2.19n1

Twain Harte Homeowners Ass'n v. Tuolumne, County of 188 Cal. Rptr. 233 (Cal. App. 1982) 3.22n9

TWC Realty Partnership v. Zoning Bd. of Adjustment, 717 A.2d 439 (N.J.L. Div. 1998), aff'd, 728 A.2d 338 (N.J. App. Div. 1999) 6.41n12

Twigg v. Kennebunk, Town of, 662 A.2d 914 (1995) 6.50n6

Twigg v. Kennebunk, Town of, 662 A.2d 914 (Me. 1995) 6.50n7

Twin Rocks Watseco Defense Comm. v. Sheets, 516 P.2d 472 (Or. App. 1973) 6.15n1

2BD Ltd. Partnership v. County Comm'rs, 896 F. Supp. 528 (D. Md. 1995) 8.35n5

216 Sutter Bay Assocs. v. Sutter County, 68 Cal. Rptr.2d 492 (Cal. App. 1997) 6.23n1

21st Century Dev. Co. v. Watts, 958 S.W.2d 25 (Ky. App. 1997) 6.33n3

2700 Irving Park Bldg. Corp. v. Chicago, City of, 69 N.E.2d 827 (Ill. 1946) 8.15n2

222 E. Chestnut St. Corp. v. Board of Appeals, 152 N.E.2d 465 (Ill. 1958) 8.04n4

U

U-Haul Co. v. St. Louis, City of, 855 S.W.2d 424 (Mo. App. 1993) 6.05n23

Udall v. Cresswell, 960 P.2d 818 (N.M. App. 1998) 9.05n5

Udell v. Haas, 235 N.E.2d 897 (N.Y. 1968) 3.14n1; 6.37n12

Udell v. Haas 235 N.E.2d 897 (N.Y. 1968) 3.14n5

Uncle v. New Jersey Pinelands Comm'n, 645 A.2d 788 (N.J. App. Div. 1994) 5.78n1

Understanding Lucas v. South Carolina Coastal Council, 45 Stan. L. Rev. 1433 (1993)

Ungar v. State, 492 A.2d 1336 (Md. 1985) 6.10n4; 6.11n5

Unification Theological Seminary v. Poughkeepsie, City of, 607 N.Y.S.2d 383 (App. Div. 1994) . . 5.08n8

Union City Bd. of Zoning Appeals v. Justice Outdoor Displays, 467 S.E.2d 875 (Ga. 1996) 11.19n10

Union City Bd. of Zoning Appeals v. Justice Outdoor Displays, Inc., 467 S.E.2d 875 (Ga. 1996) 11.23n5

Union Elec. Co. v. Crestwood, City of, 499 S.W.2d 480 (Mo. 1973) 4.32n1

Union Nat'l Bank v. Glenwood, Village of, 348 N.E.2d 226 (Ill. App. 1976) 6.23n5

Union Oil Co. v. Board of County Comm'rs, 724 P.2d 341 (Or. App. 1986) 6.21n6

Union Oil Co. of Cal. v. Worthington, City of, 405 N.E.2d 277 (Ohio 1980) 8.19n4

Union Quarries, Inc. v. Board of County Comm'rs, 478 P.2d 181 (Kan. 1970) 5.81n3

United Adv. Corp. v. Borough of Metuchen, 198 A.2d 447 (N.J. 1964) 11.08n3; 11.09n3

United Adv. Corp. v. Borough of Metuchen 198 A.2d 447 (N.J. 1964) 11.04n2

United Bank of Denver v. Reed, 635 P.2d 922 (Colo. App. 1981) 8.16n2

United Mine Workers v. Pennington, 381 U.S. 657 (1965) 5.55n1

United Property Owners Ass'n v. Borough of Belmar, 777 A.2d 950 . . . . 11.18n7

United States v. (see name of defendant)

United States Cellular Corp. v. Board of Adjustment, 589 N.W.2d 712 (Iowa 1999) 6.12n2

United States Trust Co. v. New Jersey 431 U.S. 1 (1977) 2.52n2

Unity Ventures v. Lake, County of, 631 F. Supp. 181 (N.D. Ill. 1986), *aff'd on other grounds*, 841 F.2d 770 . . . . 6.10n4

Unity Ventures v. Lake, County of, 841 F.2d 770 (7th Cir. 1988) 2.30n14; 2.32n2

Unity Ventures v. Lake, County of, 841 F.2d 770 (7th Cir.1988) 2.24n2

University City v. Dively Auto Body Co., 417 S.W.2d 107 (Mo. 1967) 5.84n6

University Place, City of v. McGuire, 30 P.3d 453 . . . . 5.79n7; 5.81n3

Unlimited v. Kitsap County, 750 P.2d 651 (Wash. App. 1988) 9.13n4

Uphold Rural El Dorado County v. Board of Supervisors, 74 Cal. Rptr. 2d 1 (Cal. App. 1998) 6.33n3; 9.03n4

Upper Salford Township v. Collins, 669 A.2d 335 (Pa. 1995) 7.21n3

Urban v. Planning Bd. of Manasquan, 592 A.2d 240 (N.J. 1991) 9.05n9

Urbanizadora Versalles, Inc. v. Rivera Rios, 701 F.2d 993 (1st Cir. 1983) . . 8.43n8; 8.44n6; 10.15n4

Urrutia v. Blaine County, 2 P.3d 738 . . . . 9.09n2

U.S. Outdoor Advertising v. Indiana Dep't of Transp., 714 N.E.2d 1244 (Ind. App. 1999) . . . 5.80n6

U.S. Outdoor Advertising Co., Inc. v. Indiana Dep't of Transp., 714 N.E.2d 1244 (Ind. App. 1999) 11.19n4

U.S. Partners Financial Corp. v. Kansas City, 707 F. Supp. 1090 (W.D. Mo. 1989) 5.63n5

Usdin v. State, 414 A.2d 280 (N.J.L. Div. 1980), *aff'd*, 430 A.2d 949 (N.J. App. Div. 1981) . . 12.09n6

Utah County v. Baxter, 635 P.2d 61 (Utah 1981) 8.15n6

V

Vagim v. Board of Supvrs., 40 Cal. Rptr. 760 (Cal. App. 1964) 4.28n1

Valatie, Village of v. Smith, 632 N.E.2d 1264 (N.Y. 1994) 5.78n5

Valkanet v. Chicago, City of, 148 N.E.2d 767 (Ill. 1958) 6.04n6

Valley Poultry Farms, Inc. v. Preece, 406 S.W.2d 413 (Ky. 1966) 4.10n2

Valley View Civic Ass'n v. Zoning Bd. of Adjustment, 462 A.2d 637 (Pa. 1983) 6.45n10

Valley View Indus. Park v. Richmond, City of, 733 P.2d 182 (Wash. 1987) 6.22n2

Valley View Village, Inc. v. Proffett, 221 F.2d 412 (6th Cir. 1955) 5.17n8

Valuable Env't v. Bothell, City of, 576 P.2d 401 (Wash. 1978) 6.74n8; 8.06n2

Valuable Env't (SAVE) v. Bothell, City of 6.35

Value Oil Co. v. Irvington, Town of, 377 A.2d 1225 (N.J.L. 1977) 6.56n13

Van v. Travel Information Council, 628 P.2d 1217 (Or. 1981) 11.23n5

Van Abbema v. Fornell, 807 F.2d 633 (7th Cir. 1986) 12.06n7

Van Duyne v. Crest Hill, City of, 483 N.E.2d 1307 (Ill. App. 1985) 8.22n1

Van Horn v. Castine, Town of, 167 F. Supp.2d 103 . . . . 11.29n1; 11.32n1

Van Landschoot v. Mendota Heights, City of, 336 N.W.2d 503 (Minn. 1983) 9.10n5

Van Laten v. Chicago, City of, 190 N.E.2d 717 (Ill. 1963) 8.11n16

Van Sicklen v. Browne 92 Cal. Rptr. 786 (Cal. App. 1971) 5.47n2

Vanderburgh County. v. Rittenhouse, 575 N.E.2d 663 (Ind. App. 1991) 12.13n6

Vari-Build, Inc. v. Reno, City of, 596 F. Supp. 673 (D. Nev. 1984) 8.33n5

Varnado v. Southern Univ. at New Orleans, 621 So. 2d 176 (La. App. 1993) 4.27n1

Vatalaro v. Department of Envtl. Regulation, 601 So. 2d 1223 (Fla. App. 1992) 12.07n6

Veling v. Borough of Ramsey, 228 A.2d 873 (N.J. App. Div. 1967) 8.23n5

Vella v. Camden, Town of, 677 A.2d 1051 (Me. 1996) 6.33n4

Venango, County of v. Borough of Sugarcreek Zoning Hearing Bd., 626 A.2d 489 (Pa. 1993) 4.37n1

Ventures in Prop. I v. Wichita, City of, 594 P.2d 671 (Kan. 1979) 8.21n2; 10.14n7

Venuto v. Owens-Corning Fiberglas Corp., 99 Cal. Rptr. 350 (Cal. App. 1971) 4.10n6

Verilli v. Concord, City of, 548 F.2d 262 (9th Cir. 1977) 11.23n1

Verland C.L.A., Inc. v. Zoning Hearing Bd., 556 A.2d 4 (Pa. Commw. 1989) 5.10n5

Vermont Div. of State Bldgs. v. Castleton Bd. of Adjustment, Town of, 415 A.2d 188 (Vt. 1980) 4.40n1

Vermont Elec. Power Co. v. Bandel, 375 A.2d 975 (Vt. 1977) 4.32n8

Vermont Nat'l Bank, In re , 597 A.2d 317 (Vt. 1991) 6.05n15

Vermont Railway, In re , 769 A.2d 648 . . 4.41n1

Verner v. Redman, 271 P.2d 468 (Ariz. 1954) . . . 6.21n3

Verona, Inc. v. Mayor & Council of West Caldwell, 229 A.2d 651 (N.J. 1967) 6.39n1; 6.56n8

Victor Rechhia Residential Constr., Inc. v. Zoning Bd. Of Adjustment, 768 A.2d 803 . . . . . . 3.18n1

Victoria Corp. v. Atlanta Merchandise Mart, Inc., 112 S.E.2d 793 (Ga. App. 1960) 8.04n6

Vidal v. Lisanti Foods, 679 A.2d 206 (N.J. App. 1996) 6.46n4

Video Int'l Prods., Inc. v. Warner-Amex Cable Communications, Inc., 858 F.2d 1075 (5th Cir. 1988) 8.31n2

Vigilant Invs. Corp. v. Hempstead, Town of, 312 N.Y.S.2d 1022 (App. Div. 1970) 8.19n4

Villa at Greely, Inc. v. Hopper, 917 P.2d 350 (Colo. App. 1996) 6.22n5

Village Bd. v. Jarrold, 423 N.E.2d 385 (N.Y. 1981) 6.45n3; 6.52n3

Village Bd. of Trustees v. Zoning Bd. of Appeals, 562 N.Y.S.2d 973 (App. Div. 1990) 5.23n1

Village Centers, Inc. v. DeKalb County, 281 S.E.2d 522 (Ga. 1981) 8.10n5

Village Creek Property Owners' Ass'n v. Edenton, Town of, 520 S.E.2d 793 (N.C. App. 1999) . . . 8.16n2

Village Lutheran Church v. Ladue, City of, 935 S.W.2d 720 (Mo. App. 1997) 5.68n3

Village Lutheran Church v. Ladue, Village of, 997 S.W.2d 506 (Mo. App. 1999) 5.69n2

Villager Pond, Inc. v. Darien, Town of, 56 F.3d 375 (2d Cir. 1995) 2.31n2

Villari v. Zoning Bd. of Adjustment, 649 A.2d 98 (N.J. App. Div. 1994) 5.81n3

Villas of Lake Jackson v. Leon County, 121 F.3d 610 (11th Cir. 1997) 2.40n3

Vim, Inc. v. Somerset Hotel Ass'n, 19 F. Supp. 2d 422 (W.D. Pa. 1998), aff'd 5.55n6

Vincent v. Broward County, 200 F.3d 1325 . . . . 5.63n10

Vinita Park, City of v. Girls Sheltercare, Inc., 664 S.W.2d 256 (Mo. App. 1984) . . 4.35n1; 5.08n8

Vintage Constr. Co. v. Bothell, City of, 922 P.2d 828 (Wash. App. 1996) 9.21n10

Vinyard v. St. Louis County, 399 S.W.2d 99 (Mo. 1966) 9.05n2

Virginia Beach Beautification Comm'n v. Board of Zoning Appeals, 344 S.E.2d 899 (Va. 1986) . . 8.06n1

Virginia Beach, City of v. Bell, 498 S.E.2d 414 (Va. 1998) 12.15n5

Virginia Beach, City of v. Virginia Land Inv. Ass'n No. 1, 389 S.E.2d 312 (Va. 1990) 6.38n1

Virginia State Bd. of Pharmacy v. Virginia Citizens Consumer Council, 425 U.S. 748 (1976) 2.50n1; 11.18n6

Virginia Vermiculite, Ltd. v. W.R. Grace & Co., 144 F.Supp.2d 558 . . . . 8.46n8

Visionquest Nat'l, Ltd. v. Board of Supvrs., 569 A.2d 915 (Pa. 1990) 6.56n10

Vislisel v. Board of Adjustment, 372 N.W.2d 316 (Iowa App. 1985) 5.20n5

Visser; State v. , 767 P.2d 858 (Mont. 1988) 9.05n7

Vito v. Garfield Heights, City of, 200 N.E.2d 501 (Ohio App. 1962) 4.25n4

Vittands v. Sudduth, 730 N.E.2d 325 . . . 8.46n11

Vlahos Realty Co. v. Little Boar's Head Dist., 146 A.2d 257 (N.H. 1958) 6.51n6

Vogelaar v. Polk County Zoning Bd. of Adjustment, 188 N.W.2d 860 (Iowa 1971) 6.39n1

Volkema v. Department of Natural Resources, 542 N.W.2d 282 (Mich. App. 1995) 2.19n3

Volpe's Appeal, In re , 121 A.2d 97 (Pa. 1956) . . 6.50n2

Volusia County v. Aberdeen at Ormond Beach, L.P., 760 So.2d 126 . . . . 9.22n11, n13

Vrabel v. Mayor & Council, 601 A.2d 229 (N.J. App. 1991) 9.16n10

Vulcan Materials Co. v. Guilford County, 444 S.E.2d 639 (N.C. App. 1994) 6.56n10

Vulcan Materials Co. v. Tehuacana, City of, 238 F.3d 382 . . . . 2.24n5

Vulcan Materials Co. v. Tehucacana, City of, 238 F.3d 382 . . . . 2.47n2

W

Waddill; State v. , 318 S.W.2d 281 (Mo. 1958) . . 6.03n2

Wade v. Fuller, 365 P.2d 802 (Utah 1961) 4.06n5

Wahlmann, State ex rel. v. Reim, 445 S.W.2d 336 (Mo. 1969) 6.82n6

Wait v. Scottsdale, City of, 618 P.2d 601 (Ariz. 1980) 6.26n5

the Wake of Lucas v. South Carolina Coastal Council
Wakefield v. Kraft, 96 A.2d 27 (Md. 1953) . . . . .
6.31n1
Walcek v. United States, 303 F.3d 1356 . . 8.26n6
Walcek v. United States, 49 Fed. Cl. 248 . . . . . .
12.07n9
Walcek v. United States (II), 49 Fed. Cl. 248 . . .
2.19n3
Wald Corp. v. Metropolitan Dade County, 338 So. 2d
863 (Fla. App. 1976) 9.16n8
Walker v. Kansas City, City of, 911 F.2d 80 (8th Cir.
1990) 2.42n7
Wallace v. Andersonville Docks, Inc., 489 S.W.2d
532 (Tenn. App. 1972) 4.03n1
Wallace v. Brown County Area Plan Comm'n, 689
N.E.2d 491 (Ind. App. 1998) 11.18n5
Walls v. Planning & Zoning Comm'n, 408 A.2d 252
(Conn. 1979) 8.04n4
Walnut Creek, City of v. Leadership Hous. Sys., Inc.,
140 Cal. Rptr. 690 (Cal. App. 1977) . . 2.23n5
Walnut Grove, City of v. Questco, Ltd., 564 S.E.2d
445 . . . . 11.06n1
Walnut Properties, Inc. v. Whittier (II), City of, 861
F.2d 1102 (9th Cir. 1988) . . . 5.63n8; 8.36n14
Walnut Props., Inc. v. Whittier, City of, 861 F.2d 1102
(9th Cir. 1988) 8.36n12
Walton Cty. v. Scenic Hills Estates, 401 S.E.2d 513
(Ga. 1991) 8.13n8
Walworth v. Elkhorn, City of, 133 N.W.2d 257 (Wis.
1965) 4.23n1
Walworth Co. v. Elkhorn, City of, 133 N.W.2d 257
(Wis. 1965) 6.09n1
Walworth Leasing Corp. v. Sterni, 316 N.Y.S.2d 851
(Sup. Ct. 1970) 5.25n2
Wampler v. Higgins, 752 N.E.2d 962 . . . 8.46n8
Wanamaker v. City Council, 19 Cal. Rptr. 554 (Cal.
App. 1962) 4.18n2
Wandyful Stadium v. Hempstead, Town of, 939 F.
Supp. 585 (E.D.N.Y. 1997) 8.42n2
Ward v. Bennett, 625 N.Y.S.2d 609 (App. Div. 1995)
. . . . 10.15n2
Ward v. Orange, County of, 217 F.3d 1350 . . . . .
5.63n2
Ward v. Rock Against Racism, 491 U.S. 781 (1989)
. . . . 2.50n6
Ward v. Scott, 93 A.2d 385 (N.J. 1952) . . 6.02n1;
6.03n4
Ward's Cove Packing Co. v. Atonio, 490 U.S. 642
(1989) 7.04n1
Warren v. Board of Appeals, 416 N.E.2d 1382 (Mass.
1981) 6.52n1
Warren v. Municipal Officers, 431 A.2d 624 (Me.
1981) 5.21n3; 5.26n4
Warren, Town of v. Frost, 301 A.2d 572 (R.I. 1973)
. . . . 6.51n2

Warren, Town of v. Hazardous Waste Facility Site
Safety Council, 466 N.E.2d 102 (Mass. 1984) . .
6.05n8
Warth v. Seldin
Warth v. Seldin and City of Eastlake
Warth v. Seldin. Arlington Heights 7.03
Warth v. Seldin 422 U.S. 490 (1974) 8.06n4
Warth v. Seldin 422 U.S. 490 (1975) 7.02n1
Washington v. Davis, 426 U.S. 229 (1976) . . . . .
6.80n4; 7.03n2
Washington v. Seattle School Dist. No. 1, 458 U.S.
457 (1982) 6.80n3
Washington, City of v. Warren County, 899 S.W.2d
863 (Mo. 1995) 4.36n1
Washington Cty. Cease, Inc. v. Persico, 473 N.Y.S.2d
610 (App. Div. 1984), aff'd, 477 N.E.2d 1084
(N.Y. 1985) 6.71n10
Washington ex rel. Seattle Title Trust Co. v. Roberge,
278 U.S. 116 (1928) 6.04n3
Washington Manufactured Housing Ass'n v. Public
Util. Dist. No. 3, 878 P.2d 1213 (Wash. 1994)
. . . . 5.26n6
Washington State Dep't of Corrections v. Kennewick,
City of, 937 P.2d 1119 (Wash. App. 1997) . . .
6.56n12; 6.75n3
Washington Sub. San. Comm'n v. TKU Assocs., 376
A.2d 505 (Md. 1977) 6.37n9
Waste Management v. Pollution Control Bd., 530
N.E.2d 682 (Ill. App. 1986) 6.71n5
Waste Management of Illinois, Inc. v. Pollution Con-
trol Bd., 530 N.E.2d 682 (Ill. App. 1988) . . . .
6.70n2
Water Dist. No. 1 v. City Council, 871 P.2d 1256
(Kan. 1994) 6.59n3
Water Dist. No. 1 of Johnson County v. City Council
of Kansas City, 871 P.2d 1256 (Kan. 1994) . . .
4.30n3
Waterfront Estates Dev., Inc. v. Palos Hills, City of,
597 N.E.2d 641 (Ill. App. 1992) 6.05n23;
11.25n3
Waterloo, City of v. Markham, 600 N.E.2d 1320 (Ill.
App. 1992) 11.23n6
Waterman v. Kaufman, 221 N.Y.S.2d 526 (Sup. Ct.
1961) 6.20n2
Waters Landing Ltd. Partnership v. Montgomery
County, 650 A.2d 712 (Md. 1994) . . . 9.21n3
Watson v. Town Council, 805 P.2d 641 (N.M. App.
1991) 6.29n12; 6.32n2; 6.33n2
Waukesha, City of v. Town Bd., 543 N.W.2d 515
(Wis. App. 1995) 9.27n4
Weaver v. Bishop, 52 P.2d 853 (Okla. 1935) . . . .
4.10n4
Webb v. Giltner, 468 N.W.2d 838 (Iowa App. 1991)
. . . . 6.32n2

Webster Assocs. v. Webster, Town of, 451 N.E.2d 189 (N.Y. 1983) 6.73n3

Weed v. King County, 677 P.2d 179 (Wash. App. 1984) 8.14n3

Weida v. Ferry, 493 A.2d 824 (R.I. 1985) 4.04n1

Weigel v. Planning & Zoning Comm'n, 278 A.2d 766 (Conn. 1971) 6.34n1

Weinberg v. Whatcom County, 241 F.3d 746 . . . . 2.42n7; 8.33n9

Weiner v. Board of Supvrs., 547 A.2d 833 (Pa. Commw. 1988) 7.20n4

Weiner v. Los Angeles, City of, 441 P.2d 293 (Cal. 1968) 6.05n16; 6.21n4

Weinman Assocs. General Partnership v. Huntersville, Town of, 555 S.E.2d 342 . . . . 6.22n4

Weinstein, The Myth of Ministry v. Mortar

Welch v. Paicos, 66 F.Supp.2d 138 (D. Mass. 1999) 2.51n1, n8

Welch v. Swasey 214 U.S. 91 (1909) . . . 5.74n1

Wells v. Libertyville, Village of, 505 N.E.2d 740 (Ill. App. 1987) 6.69n4

Wellspring Zendo, Inc. v. Trippe, 625 N.Y.S.2d 334 (App. Div. 1995) 5.68n4

Welsh v. Orono, City of 355 N.W.2d 117 (Minn. 1984) 4.30n9

Weltshe v. Graf, 82 N.E.2d 795 (Mass. 1948) . . . 4.10n1, n2

Wengert v. Zoning Hearing Bd., 414 A.2d 148 (Pa. Commw. 1980) 5.08n12

Wentworth Hotel v. New Castle, Town of, 287 A.2d 615 (N.H. 1972) 6.51n6

Wesley Chapel Bluemount Ass'n v. Baltimore County, 699 A.2d 434 (Md. 1997) . . . 6.76n7

Wesley Inv. Co. v. Alameda, County of, 198 Cal. Rptr. 872 (Cal. App. 1984) 6.66n10

West v. Mills, 380 S.E.2d 917 (Va. 1989) 9.28n1

West Bloomfield Charter Twp. v. Karchon, 530 N.W.2d 99 (Mich. App. 1995) 6.05n4

West Bluff Neighborhood Ass'n v. Albuquerque, City of 3.15n9

West Chester Township Zoning v. Fromm, 762 N.E.2d 400 . . . . 6.05n19

West Greenwich, Town of v. A. Cardi Realty Associates, 786 A.2d 354 . . . . 5.81n3

West Greenwich, Town of v. A. Cardi Realty Assocs., 786 A.2d 354 . . . . 5.79n7

West Hall Citizens for Controlled Dev. Density v. King County Council, 627 P.2d 1002 (Wash. App. 1981) 3.14n1

West Hartford Interfaith Coalition, Inc. v. Town Council, 636 A.2d 1342 (Conn. 1994) . . 7.31n2

West Hartford Methodist Church v. Zoning Bd. of Appeals, 121 A.2d 640 (Conn. 1956) . . 5.68n1; 6.57n15

West Hartford, Town of v. Rechel, 459 A.2d 1015 (Conn. 1983) 6.17n2

West Main Assocs. v. Bellevue, City of, 720 P.2d 782 (Wash. 1986) 6.22n7

West Monroe, City of v. Ouachita Ass'n for Retarded Children, Inc., 402 So. 2d 259 (La. App. 1981) 5.08n7

West Montgomery County Citizens Ass'n v. Maryland-Nat'l Capital Park & Planning Comm'n, 522 A.2d 1328 (Md. 1987) 12.16n8

West Old Town Neighborhood Ass'n v. Albuquerque, City of, 927 P.2d 529 (N.M. App. 1996) 6.26n2

West Palm Beach, City of v. State, 30 So. 2d 491 (Fla. 1947) 11.25n2

West Park Ave., Inc. v. Township of Ocean, 224 A.2d 1 (N.J. 1966) 9.18n2

West Ridge, Inc. v. McNamara, 160 A.2d 907 (Md. 1960) 6.31n7

West Slope Community Council v. Tacoma, City of, 569 P.2d 1183 (Wash. App. 1977) . . . 6.02n6; 6.74n12

Westborough Mall, Inc. v. Cape Girardeau, City of, 693 F.2d 733 (8th Cir.1983) 5.54n2

Westborough Mall, Inc. v. Cape Girardeau (I), City of 8.32n4

Westborough Mall, Inc. v. Cape Girardeau (IV), City of, 953 F.2d 345 (8th Cir. 1991) 8.32n4

Westborough, Town of v. Department of Pub. Utils., 267 N.E.2d 110 (Mass. 1971) 4.40n1

Westbrook v. Board of Adjustment, 262 S.E.2d 785 (Ga. 1980) 2.46n5

Western Air Lines, Inc. v. Port Auth., 817 F.2d 222 (2d Cir. 1987) 4.43n3

Western Land Equities, Inc. v. Logan, City of . . . 6.16

Western Land Equities, Inc. v. Logan, City of, 617 P.2d 388 (Utah 1980) 9.07n8

Western Presbyterian Church v. Board of Zoning Adjustment, 849 F. Supp. 77 (D.D.C. 1994) . . . 5.69n4

Westfield Motor Sales Co. v. Westfield, Town of 324 A.2d 113 (N.J.L. Div. 1974) 11.10n3

Westfield Partners Ltd. v. Hogan, 740 F. Supp. 523 (N.D. Ill. 1990) 8.46n3

Westfield Partners, Ltd. v. Hogan, 744 F. Supp. 189 (N.D. Ill. 1990) 8.46n4

Westford, Town of v. Kilburn, 300 A.2d 523 (Vt. 1973) 6.04n4

Westgate Families v. County Clerk, 667 P.2d 453 (N.M. 1983) 6.82n1

Westgate Shopping Village v. Toledo, City of, 639 N.E.2d 126 (Ohio App. 1994) 5.46n3

Westside Enters. v. Dexter, City of, 559 S.W.2d 638 (Mo. App. 1977) 8.10n2

Westside Hilltop Survival Comm. v. King County, 634 P.2d 862 (1981) 3.22n4

Westwood Forest Estates, Inc. v. South Nyack, Village of, 244 N.E.2d 700 (N.Y. 1969) . . 6.10n3

Westwood Forum, Inc. v. Springfield, City of, 634 N.E.2d 1154 (Ill. App. 1994) 8.06n1

Westwood Meat Mkt., Inc. v. McLucas, 361 P.2d 776 (Colo. 1961) 5.46n3

Wetlake v. Mascot Petroleum Co., 573 N.E.2d 1068 (Ohio 1991) 4.33n2

Whaley v. Dorchester County Zoning Bd. of Appeals, 524 S.E.2d 404 (S.C. 1999) 5.19n11

Whatcom County v. Brisane, 884 P.2d 1326 (Wash. 1994) 6.77n2

Wheeler v. Berkeley, City of, 485 S.W.2d 707 (Mo. App. 1972) 5.18n4

Wheeler v. Commissioner of Highways, 822 F.2d 586 (6th Cir. 1987) 11.19n4, n8, n13

Wheeler v. Commissioner of Hwys., 822 F.2d 586 (6th Cir. 1987) 11.19n14

Wheeler v. Gregg, 203 P.2d 37 (Cal. App. 1949) 6.02n4

Wheeler v. Pleasant Grove (II), City of, 833 F.2d 267 (11th Cir. 1987) 8.38n9, n11

Wheeler v. Pleasant Grove (III), City of 833 F.2d 267 (11th Cir. 1987) 8.26n4

Wheeler v. Pleasant Grove (IV), City of, 896 F.2d 1347 (11th Cir. 1990) 8.26n5

Whispering Woods v. Township of Middleton Planning Bd., 531 A.2d 770 (N.J. App. Div. 1987) 6.76n15

Whistler v. Burlington N.R.R., 741 P.2d 422 (Mont. 1987) 1.13n1

Whitcomb v. Woodward, City of, 616 P.2d 455 (Okla. App. 1980) 6.52n8

White v. Board of Comm'rs, 555 S.E.2d 45 . . . . 6.74n6

White v. Board of Zoning Appeals, 451 N.E.2d 756 (Ohio 1983) 5.08n6

White v. Brentwood, City of, 799 S.W.2d 890 (Mo. App. 1990) 2.16n9; 2.37n3

White v. Dallas, City of 517 S.W.2d 344 (Tex. Civ. App. 1974) 4.25n7

White v. Hollis, Town of, 589 A.2d 46 (Me. 1991) 6.68n3; 6.70n10

White v. Lee, 227 F.3d 1214 . . . . 5.55n8

White v. North, 675 A.2d 1023 (Md. App. 1996) 12.04n7

White Adv. Metro v. Zoning Hearing Bd., 453 A.2d 29 (Pa. Commw. 1982) 6.57n2

White Bear Docking & Storage, Inc. v. White Bear Lake, City of, 324 N.W.2d 174 (Minn. 1982) . . 6.56n10

White Plains, City of v. Ferraioli 313 N.E.2d 756 (N.Y. 1974) 5.08n10

Whiteco Indus. v. Bowers, 965 S.W.2d 203 . . . . 11.06n7

Whiteco Outdoor Advertising v. Tucson, City of, 972 P.2d 647 (Ariz. App. 1999) . 11.06n2; 11.11n8

Whitehead Oil Co. v. Lincoln, City of, 451 N.W.2d 702 (Neb. 1990) 6.20n3

Whitehead Oil Co. v. Lincoln (II), City of, 515 N.E.2d 390 (Neb. 1994) 6.16n4

Whitehead Oil Co. v. Lincoln (III), City of, 515 N.W.2d 401 (Neb. 1994) 8.09n6; 8.21n1; 8.26n1, n4

Whitesell v. Kosciusko Cty. Bd. of Zoning Appeals, 558 N.E.2d 889 (Ind. App. 1990) 9.28n1

Whitted v. Canyon County Board of Comm'rs, 44 P.3d 1173 . . . . 12.12n5

Whittingham v. Woodridge, Village of, 249 N.E.2d 332 (Ill. App. 1969) 8.05n2

Whitton v. Gladstone, City of, 54 F.3d 1400 (8th Cir. 1995) 11.23n5, n6

Whitton v. Gladstone, City of 54 F.3d 1499 (8th Cir. 1995) 11.23n7

Wiener v. San Diego, County of, 23 F.3d 263 (9th Cir. 1994) 8.42n11

Wiggers v. Skagit, County of, 596 P.2d 1345 (Wash. App. 1979) 9.25n8

Wilcox v. Superior Ct., 33 Cal. Rptr. 2d 446 (Cal. App. 1994) 8.47n1

Wilcox v. Zoning Bd. of Appeals, 217 N.E.2d 633 (N.Y. 1966) 6.42n3

Wildwood, Village of v. Olech 528 U.S. 562 . . . . 2.49n1

Wiley v. Hanover, County of, 163 S.E.2d 160 (Va. 1968) 6.05n21

Wilkinsburg-Penn Joint Water Auth. v. Borough of Churchill 207 A.2d 905 (Pa. 1965) . . . 4.37n1

Wilkinson v. Atkinson, 218 A.2d 503 (Md. 1966) 8.04n4

Wilkinson v. Board of County Comm'rs, 872 P.2d 1269 (Colo. App. 1994) 10.06n2

Wilkinson v. Pitkin County Bd. of County Comm'rs, 142 F.3d 1319 (11th Cir. 1998) 2.33n2

Willamette Univ. v. Land Conservation and Dev. Comm'n, 608 P.2d 1178 (Or. App. 1980) . . 10.07n4

Willey, In re , 140 A.2d 11 (Vt. 1958) . . . 5.22n2

William C. Haas & Co. v. City & County of San Francisco, 605 F.2d 1117 (9th Cir. 1979) 6.36n1

William C. Haas & Co. v. City & County of San Francisco 605 F.2d 1117 (9th Cir. 1979) 5.74n5

William S. Hart Union High Sch. Dist. v. Regional Planning Comm'n, 277 Cal. Rptr. 645 (Cal. App. 1991) 10.06n5

Williams v. Central, City of, 907 P.2d 701 (Colo. App. 1995) 6.09n3

Williams v. City & County of Denver, 622 P.2d 542 (Colo. 1981) 11.18n4

Williams v. Oeder, 659 N.E.2d 379 (Ohio App. 1995) 4.04n1

Williams v. Spencer, Town of, 500 S.E.2d 473 (N.C. App. 1998) . . . . : 5.80n2

Williams v. Whitten, 451 S.W.2d 535 (Tex. App. 1970) 6.04n4

Williams v. Wofford, 140 S.E.2d 190 (Ga. 1965) 6.22n8

Williamson County Regional Planning Comm'n v. Hamilton Bank 2.26

Willott v. Beachwood, Village of, 197 N.E.2d 201 (Ohio 1964) 6.30n6

Willow Creek Ranch, LLC v. Shelby, Town of, 611 N.W.2d 693 . . . . 4.31n7; 8.23n2, n5

Wilmette Park Dist. v. Wilmette, Village of, 490 N.E.2d 1282 (Ill. 1986) 4.37n1

Wilson v. Borough of Mountainside, 201 A.2d 540 (N.J. 1964) 2.46n6

Wilson v. Interlake Steel Co., 649 P.2d 922 (Cal. 1982) 4.05n1

Wilson v. Louisville, City of, 957 F. Supp. 948 (W.D. Ky. 1997) 11.07n16

Wilson v. Manning, 657 P.2d 251 (Utah 1982) . . . 6.82n7

Wilson v. Sherborn, Town of, 326 N.E.2d 922 (Mass. App. 1975) 7.31n9

Wiltshire v. Superior Court, 218 Cal. Rptr. 199 (Cal. App. 1985) 6.83n8

Win-Tasch Corp. v. Merrimack, Town of, 411 A.2d 144 (N.H. 1980) 8.23n5

Wincamp Partnership v. Anne Arundel County, 458 F. Supp. 1009 (D. Md. 1978) 6.10n4

Windward Marina, L.L.C. v. Destin, City of, 743 So.2d 635 (Fla. App. 1999) 6.33n3

Wine v. Council of City of Los Angeles, 2 Cal. Rptr. 94 (Cal. App. 1960) 8.03n1

Winget v. Winn-Dixie Stores, Inc., 130 S.E.2d 363 (S.C. 1963) 4.06n3; 4.10n3

Winnebago County; State v. , 540 N.W.2d 6 (Wis. App. 1995) 6.41n3; 6.45n7; 6.46n2

Winnebago, County of v. Hartman, 242 N.E.2d 916 (Ill. App. 1968) 5.26n1

Winters v. Commerce City, City of, 648 P.2d 175 (Colo. App. 1982) 8.23n7

Wisconsin Correctional Serv. v. Milwaukee, City of, 173 F. Supp.2d 842 . . . . 5.16n2

Wisconsin Lutheran High School Conference v. Sinar, 65 N.W.2d 43 (Wis. 1954) 5.27n2

Wisniowski v. Planning Comm'n, 655 A.2d 1146 (Conn. 1995) 7.31n3

Withrow v. Larkin, 421 U.S. 35 (1976) . . 2.42n9

Witt v. Borough of Maywood, 746 A.2d 73 (N.J.L. Div. 1998), aff'd, 746 A.2d 25 (N.J. App. Div. 1999) 6.33n1

W.J.F. Realty Corp. v. State, 672 N.Y.S.2d 1007 (Sup. Ct. 1998) 11.38n7; 12.16n6

W.L. Goodfellows & Co. v. Washington Township Planning Bd., 783 A.2d 750 . . . . . . 6.66n11

WMM Props., Inc. v. Cobb County, 339 S.E.2d 252 (Ga. 1986) 6.16n1

Wnuk v. Zoning Bd. of Appeals, 626 A.2d 698 (Conn. 1993) 6.44n5

Wolf v. District of Columbia Bd. of Zoning Adjustment, 397 A.2d 936 (D.C. App. 1979) 6.48n15; 6.52n5

Wolf v. Mt. Prospect, Village of, 40 N.E.2d 778 (Ill. App. 1942) 4.32n3

Wolff v. Dade County, 370 So. 2d 839 (Fla. App. 1979) 6.34n2

Wolff v. Mooresville Planning Comm'n, 754 N.E.2d 589 . . . . 6.05n16

Wolfman v. Board of Appeals, 444 N.E.2d 942 (Mass. App. 1983) 6.46n4

Wollen v. Borough of Fort Lee, 142 A.2d 881 (N.J. 1958) 6.73n3

Wood v. North Salt Lake, 390 P.2d 858 (Utah 1964) 9.07n8

Wood Bros. Homes v. Colorado Springs, City of, 568 P.2d 487 (Colo. 1977) 9.09n18

Wood Marine Serv., Inc. v. Harahan, City of, 858 F.2d 1061 (5th Cir. 1988) 5.35n2

Woodall v. El Paso, City of, 49 F.3d 1120 (5th Cir. 1995) 5.63n9

Woodall v. El Paso, City of, 959 F.2d 1305 (5th Cir. 1992) 5.63n9

Woodbury Place Partners, Inc. v. Woodbury, City of, 492 N.W.2d 258 (Minn. App. 1992) . . 6.09n3

Woodhouse v. Board of Comm'rs, 261 S.E.2d 882 (N.C. 1980) 9.28n1, n3

Woodinville Water Dist. v. King County, 21 P.3d 209 . . . . 6.59n4

Woodland Estates, Inc. v. Building Inspector of Methuen, 358 N.E.2d 468 (Mass. App. 1976) 6.29n8

Woodland Hills Conservation Ass'n v. Jackson, City of, 443 So. 2d 1173 (Miss. 1983) 6.26n2

Woodland Hills Residents Ass'n v. City Council, 609 P.2d 1029 (Cal. 1980) 6.72n2; 6.73n5

Woods v. Newton, City of, 208 N.E.2d 508 (Mass. 1965) 8.16n2

Woodwind Estates, Ltd. v. Gretkowski, 205 F.3d 118 . . . . 2.39n7; 2.40n6

Wooten v. South Carolina Coastal Comm'n, 510 S.E.2d 716 (S.C. 1999) 12.15n5

Work; State v. , 449 P.2d 806 (Wash. 1969) 5.22n2

World Diversified, Inc.; State v. , 576 N.W.2d 198 (Neb 1998) 5.80n7

World Famous Drinking Emporium, Inc. v. Tempe, City of, 820 F.2d 1079 (9th Cir. 1987) 8.42n11

World Wide Video, Inc. v. Tukwila, City of, 816 P.2d 18 (Wash. 1991) 5.63n2

Worldwide Video v. Tukwila, 816 P.2d 18 (Wash. 1991) 5.65n5

Wright v. Zoning Bd. of Appeals, 391 A.2d 146 (Conn. 1978) 6.51n4

Wright, County of v. Kennedy, 415 N.W.2d 728 (Minn. App. 1987) 11.25n1

Wrigley Props., Inc. v. Ladue, City of 369 S.W.2d 397 (Mo. 1963) 5.37n7

W.W. Dean & Assocs. v. South San Francisco, City of, 236 Cal. Rptr. 11 (Cal. App. 1987) 6.82n8

Wyatt v. United States, 271 F.3d 1090 . . . 2.22n5

Wyer v. Board of Envtl. Protection, 747 A.2d 192 . . . . 2.21n6

Wyzkowski v. Rizas, 626 A.2d 406 (N.J. 1993) . . 6.73n2

X

Xanthos v. Board of Adjustment, 685 P.2d 1032 (Utah 1984) 6.46n5

Y

Yale Auto Parts, Inc. v. Jackson, 758 F.2d 54 (2d Cir. 1985) 2.42n7

Yanow v. Seven Oaks Park, 94 A.2d 482 (N.J. 1953) 5.27n2

Yara Eng'r Corp. v. Newark, City of, 40 A.2d 559 (N.J. 1945) 5.39n8

Yarbrough v. Arkansas State Hwy. Comm'n, 539 S.W.2d 419 (Ark. 1976) 11.07n1, n9

Yaro v. Board of Appeals of Newburyport, 410 N.E.2d 725 (Mass. App. 1980) 6.76n14

Yates v. Mayor & Comm'rs, 244 So. 2d 724 (Miss. 1971) 5.77n2

Y.D. Dugout, Inc. v. Board of Appeals, 255 N.E.2d 732 (Mass. 1970) 6.66n2

Yeager v. Zoning Hearing Bd., 779 A.2d 595 . . . 6.48n13

Yee v. Escondido, City of 2.03

Yee v. Escondido, City of, 503 U.S. 519 (1992) . . 2.24n6

Yellow Lantern Kampground v. Cortlandville, Town of, 716 N.Y.S.2d 786 . . . . 6.29n12

Yeshiva Chofetz Chaim Radin, Inc. v. New Hempstead, Village of, 98 F. Supp. 2d 347 . . 8.47n1

Yocum v. Power, 157 A.2d 368 (Pa. 1960) 6.18n4

York v. Ogunquit, Town of, 769 A.2d 172 . . . . . 9.10n4

York v. Stallings, 341 P.2d 529 (Or. 1959) 4.12n3, n4

York, Town of v. Cragin, 541 A.2d 932 (Me. 1988) 9.05n4

Young v. American Mini Theatres, Inc . . . 5.59

Young v. Jewish Welfare Fed'n, 371 S.W.2d 767 (Tex. Civ. App. 1963) 8.23n5

Young v. Roseville, City of, 78 F. Supp.2d 970 (D. Minn. 1999) 11.21n1

Young v. Simi Valley, City of, 216 F.3d 807 . . . . 5.63n9, n12

Youngblood v. Board of Supvrs., 586 P.2d 556 (Cal. 1979) 9.07n7

Younger v. Harris 401 U.S. 31 (1971) . . . 8.42n1

Y.W.C.A. v. Board of Adjustment, 341 A.2d 356 (N.J. 1975) 5.08n9

Z

Zack; State v. , 674 P.2d 329 (Ariz. App. 1983) . . 5.41n2

Zagoreos v. Conklin, 491 N.Y.S.2d 358 (App. Div. 1985) 6.74n9

Zahra v. Southold, Town of, 48 F.3d 674 (2d Cir. 1995) 2.47n3; 8.36n14

Zalea & 35th, Inc. v. Snohomish County, 959 P.2d 1024 (Wash. 1998) 5.78n4

Zalea & 35th, Inc. v. Snohomish County, 959 P.2d 1024 (Wash. App. 1998) 5.78n2

Zanin v. Iacono, 487 A.2d 780 (N.J.L. Div. 1984) 9.25n6

Zarrinnia v. Zoning Hearing Bd., 639 A.2d 1276 (Pa. Commw. 1994) 5.17n3

Zaruta v. Zoning Hearing Bd., 543 A.2d 1282 (Pa. Commw. 1988) 6.46n5

Zealy v. Waukesha, City of, 548 N.W.2d 528 (Wis. 1996) 2.19n1; 2.35n2; 12.07n2

Zealy v. Waukesha, City of,153 F. Supp.2d 279 . . 2.34n3

Zebulon Enters. v. DuPage, County of, 496 N.E.2d 1256 (Ill. App. 1986) 6.57n2

Zell v. Borough of Roseland, 125 A.2d 890 (N.J. 1956) 6.74n10

Zeller v. Consolini, 758 A.2d 376 . 5.55n6; 8.46n3

Zeltig Land Dev. Corp. v. Bainbridge Township Bd. of Trustees, 599 N.E.2d 383 (Ohio App. 1991) 5.32n1

Zelvin v. Zoning Bd. of Appeals, 306 A.2d 151 (Conn. C.P. 1973) 5.18n6

Zerbetz v. Municipality of Anchorage, 856 P.2d 777 (Alaska 1993) 12.07n8

Zieky v. Town Plan & Zoning Comm., 196 A.2d 758 (Conn. 1963) 6.52n3

Zilber v. Moraga, 692 F. Supp. 1195 (N.D. Cal. 1988) 2.30n7

Zilber v. Moraga, Town of, 692 F. Supp. 1195 (N.D. Cal. 1988) 6.11n6

Zilinsky v. Zoning Bd. of Adjustment 521 A.2d 841 (N.J. 1987) 5.77n2

Zinermon v. Burch, Federal Rights, and State Remedies Thirty Years After

Zinn v. State, 334 N.W.2d 67 (Wis. 1983) 8.21n5

Z.J. Gifts D-2, L.L.C. v. Aurora, City of, 136 F.3d 683 (10th Cir. 1998) 5.63n4, n5

Zobel v. Williams, 457 U.S. 55 (1982) . . 10.08n5

Zoning Bd. of Appeals v. Ardemore Apartments, 767 N.E.2d 584 . . . . 7.31n9

Zoning Bd. of Appeals v. Planning & Zoning Comm'n, 605 A.2d 885 (Conn. App. 1992) . . . 6.43n2

Zoning Comm'n v. Lescynski, 453 A.2d 1144 (Conn. 1982) 6.15n4

Zoning Comm'n v. New Canaan Bldg. Co., 148 A.2d 330 (Conn. 1959) 6.31n2

Zoning Variance Application, In re , 449 A.2d 910 (Vt. 1982) 6.50n7

Zubli v. Community Mainstreaming Assocs., 423 N.Y.S.2d 982 (1979) 4.40n1

Zubli v. Community Mainstreaming Assocs., 423 N.Y.S.2d 982 (Sup. Ct. 1979) 5.10n4

Zukis v. Fitzwilliam, Town of, 604 A.2d 956 (N.H. 1992) 9.09n10

Zupancic, State ex rel. v. Schimenz 174 N.W.2d 533 (Wis. 1970) 6.63n5

Zygmont v. Planning & Zoning Comm'n, 210 A.2d 172 (Conn. 1965) 5.31n5

Zylka v. Crystal, City of, 167 N.W.2d 45 (Minn. 1969) 6.55n7

INDEX

[References are to sections.]

A

ABANDONMENT
Nonconforming uses, termination of . . . 5.81

ABSTENTION
Federal courts, of (See REMEDIES, subhead: Abstention)

ACCESSORY USES
Residential areas, in . . . 5.19

ADA (See AMERICANS WITH DISABILITIES ACT (ADA))

ADEQUATE PUBLIC FACILITIES REQUIRE-MENTS
Generally . . . 10.02; 10.05

ADULT BUSINESSES, ZONING FOR
Generally . . . 5.63
Alameda Books case . . . 5.62
Content-neutral time, place and manner regulations, upholding of . . . 5.61
Deconcentration zoning strategies, upholding of . . . 5.59
Defining adult uses . . . 5.65
Existing uses, applicability of ordinances to 5.64
Free speech considerations
  Generally . . . 5.58
  Alameda Books case . . . 5.62
  Content-neutral time, place and manner regula-tions, upholding of . . . 5.61
  Deconcentration zoning strategies, upholding of . . . 5.59
  Mini-Theatres case . . . 5.59
  Preclusion claims . . . 5.63
  Renton case . . . 5.61
  Schad case . . . 5.60
  Secondary effects of adult use businesses . . 5.62
Mini-Theatres case . . . 5.59
Preclusion claims . . . 5.63
Renton case . . . 5.61
Schad case . . . 5.60
Secondary effects of adult use businesses . . 5.62
State legislation . . . 5.66

AESTHETIC ZONING
Generally . . . 11.01
Architectural controls (See ARCHITECTURAL DE-SIGN REVIEW)

AESTHETIC ZONING—Cont.
Billboards, regulation of (See SIGNS AND BILL-BOARDS, REGULATION OF)
Due process considerations . . . 11.01
Free speech issues involving sign regulations . . . 11.01
Historical background . . . 11.03
Historic districts (See HISTORIC DISTRICTS)
Historic landmarks (See LANDMARK PRESERVA-TION)
Regulatory purpose, aesthetics as
  Generally . . . 11.03
  Historical background . . . 11.03
  Majority view holding aesthetics as regulatory purpose . . . 11.05
  Minority view holding aesthetics as factor in land use regulation . . . 11.04
  Property values, protection of . . . 11.04
Signs, regulation of (See SIGNS AND BILL-BOARDS, REGULATION OF)
Takings considerations . . . 11.01

AGRICULTURAL LAND, PRESERVATION OF
Generally . . . 12.01; 12.10
Agricultural district laws . . . 12.10
Agricultural zoning
  Generally . . . 12.12
  Takings considerations . . . 12.13
Exclusive agricultural zoning . . . 12.12
Farmland Policy Protection Act . . . 12.10
Federal programs . . . 12.10
Local programs . . . 12.10
Nonexclusive agricultural zoning . . . 12.12
Real property tax preference programs . . . 12.10
Right-to-farm (RTF) laws . . . 12.11
State programs . . . 12.10
Takings considerations . . . 12.13

AIRPORTS, ZONING FOR
Generally . . . 4.43; 5.39
Federal Aviation Act of 1958 . . . 4.43
Height and use restrictions . . . 5.39
Preemption of local zoning ordinances . . . 4.43
Takings considerations . . . 5.39

ALCOHOL (See LIQUOR AND LIQUOR STORES)

AMENDMENTS TO ORDINANCES (See RE-ZONING AND ZONING AMENDMENTS)

AMERICANS WITH DISABILITIES ACT (ADA)
Group homes, provisions regarding . . . 5.16

(5ᵗʰ Ed.—02/03)

[References are to sections.]

AMORTIZATION ORDINANCES
Nonconforming uses (See NONCONFORMING USES)

ANTITRUST LAWS, FEDERAL (See FEDERAL ANTITRUST LAWS)

APARTMENTS AND APARTMENT HOUSES
Generally . . . 5.18

APPEALS
Generally . . . 8.12; 8.13
Affordable housing denials or restrictions, of . . . 7.31
State court appellate structure . . . 1.17

ARCHITECTURAL DESIGN REVIEW
Generally . . . 1.07; 11.24
Appearance codes . . . 11.24
Constitutionality of . . . 11.25
Design review boards, creation and authority of . . . 11.24
Free speech considerations . . . 11.25

B

BIAS
Decision-making process, in . . . 6.72; 6.73

BILLBOARDS, REGULATION OF (See SIGNS AND BILLBOARDS, REGULATION OF)

BOARD OF ADJUSTMENT
Generally . . . 4.19

BUILDER EXACTIONS (See EXACTIONS)

BUILDING PERMITS
Estoppel and vested rights doctrines (See ESTOPPEL AND VESTED RIGHTS DOCTRINES)
Subdivision regulation, building permit denials as sanction for violations of . . . 9.08

C

CALIFORNIA
Exclusionary zoning . . . 7.24
Inclusionary zoning . . . 7.29

CELLULAR TOWERS, ZONING FOR
Generally . . . 4.42
Preemption of local zoning ordinances . . . 4.42
Telecommunications Act of 1996 . . . 4.42

CERTIORARI REVIEW
Generally . . . 8.12; 8.13

CHANGE–MISTAKE RULE
Downzoning, applicability to . . . 6.38

CHANGE–MISTAKE RULE—Cont.
Spot zoning, applicability to . . . 6.31

CIVIL RIGHTS ACTIONS, SECTION 1983 (See SECTION 1983 ACTIONS)

CLEAN WATER ACT
Wetlands areas, permit requirements for . . . 12.01; 12.06

COASTAL ZONE MANAGEMENT
Generally . . . 12.01; 12.14
National Coastal Zone Management Act . . . 12.01; 12.14
National programs . . . 12.14
State programs . . . 12.14
Takings considerations . . . 12.15

COMMERCIAL USES AND ZONING
Generally . . . 5.33
Airports (See AIRPORTS, ZONING FOR)
Antitrust laws (See FEDERAL ANTITRUST LAWS)
Business districts, use of zoning ordinances for protection of . . . 5.48
Classification of commercial districts . . . 5.36
Compatibility principle . . . 5.36
Competition, zoning for purpose of control of
    Generally . . . 5.44
    Antitrust laws (See FEDERAL ANTITRUST LAWS)
    Approval of; case law . . . 5.47
    Business districts, protection of . . . 5.48
    Disapproval of; case law . . . 5.46
    Federal antitrust law (See FEDERAL ANTITRUST LAWS)
Control of competition, zoning for purpose of (See subhead: Competition, zoning for purpose of control of)
Exclusion of . . . 5.37
Exclusive commercial zoning, problems with . . . 5.43
Federal antitrust law (See FEDERAL ANTITRUST LAWS)
Mapping considerations . . . 5.35
Noncumulative zoning . . . 5.43
Nuisance actions to enjoin commercial uses from residential neighborhoods . . . 4.06
Ribbon development . . . 5.38
Site development standards, imposition of . . . 5.36
Total commercial exclusion . . . 5.37
Use classifications . . . 5.36

COMPETITION
Zoning for purpose of control of (See COMMERCIAL USES AND ZONING)

[References are to sections.]

COMPREHENSIVE PLANS

Generally . . . 1.01; 3.01

Adoption of plan . . . 3.08

Consistency of zoning with comprehensive plan, requirements regarding

Generally . . . 3.13

Floating zones, applicability of consistency requirements to . . . 6.61

Majority judicial view . . . 3.14

Minority judicial view . . . 3.15

No plan required for exercise of zoning power . . . 3.14

Special exceptions and conditional uses, applicability of consistency requirements to 6.58

Spot zoning, applicability of consistency requirements to (See SPOT ZONING, subhead: Consistency with comprehensive plan, requirements regarding)

Standard Zoning Act . . . 3.13

Statutory consistency requirements

Generally . . . 3.16

Definitions of consistency . . . 3.16

Land use conflicts . . . 3.18

Upzoning to comply with plan . . 3.17

Variances, applicability of consistency requirements to . . . 6.49

Elements of plan

Generally . . . 3.01

Housing element . . . 3.11

Standard Planning Act . . . 3.07

State planning legislation . . . 3.10; 3.11

Floating zones, applicability of consistency requirements to . . . 6.61

Housing element . . . 3.11

"In accordance" requirement (See subhead: Consistency of zoning with comprehensive plan, requirements regarding)

Incremental planning as alternative to . . . 3.03

Judicial review . . . 3.22

Lower-income housing, planning policies for . . . 3.11

Planning commission . . . 3.06

Planning goals and policies, development of 3.02

Planning process

Generally . . . 3.02

Criticisms of . . . 3.03

Current planning practice . . . 3.04

Incremental planning as alternative . . . 3.03

Planning goals and policies, development of . . . 3.02

Revision of ordinances or comprehensive plans, interim development controls for purposes of providing time for . . . 6.09

COMPREHENSIVE PLANS—Cont.

Special exceptions and conditional uses, applicability of consistency requirements to . . . 6.58

Spot zoning, applicability of consistency requirements to (See SPOT ZONING, subhead: Consistency with comprehensive plan, requirements regarding)

Standard Planning Act

Generally . . . 3.05

Adoption of plan . . . 3.08

Elements of plan . . . 3.07

Planning commission . . . 3.06

Standard Zoning Act requirements regarding consistency of zoning with comprehensive plan 3.13

State planning legislation

Generally . . . 3.09

Elements of plan . . . 3.10; 3.11

Housing element . . . 3.11

Lower-income housing, planning policies for . . . 3.11

Mandatory planning, legislation requiring . . 3.12

Mandatory planning elements . . . 3.10

Optional planning elements . . . 3.10

Required planning elements . . . 3.10

Takings considerations

Defense to taking, plan as . . . 3.20

Taking, plan as . . . 3.21

Variances, applicability of consistency requirements to . . . 6.49

Zoning "in accordance with" plan (See subhead: Consistency of zoning with comprehensive plan, requirements regarding)

CONDITIONAL USES AND SPECIAL EXCEPTIONS (See SPECIAL EXCEPTIONS AND CONDITIONAL USES)

CONFLICTS OF INTERESTS

Decision-making process, in . . . 6.72; 6.74

CONSTITUTIONAL ISSUES

Architectural design review, involving . . . 11.25

Bivens actions . . . 8.39

Contract clause

Generally . . . 2.52; 2.53

Keystone Bituminous Coal case . . . 2.53

Due process (See DUE PROCESS)

Equal protection (See EQUAL PROTECTION)

Extraterritorial zoning, involving . . . 4.23

Federal and state constitutional law differences . . 1.02

First Amendment issues (See FREE SPEECH CLAUSE)

Free speech clause (See FREE SPEECH CLAUSE)

[References are to sections.]

CONSTITUTIONAL ISSUES—Cont.

Historic district designations, involving . . 11.29; 11.32

Implied constitutional cause of action . . . 8.39

Initiatives, involving . . . 6.78

Interim development controls, regarding (See INTERIM DEVELOPMENT CONTROLS)

Moratoria on development, regarding (See MORATORIA ON DEVELOPMENT)

Nonconforming uses, involving (See NONCONFORMING USES)

Referendum, involving . . . 6.78

Religious uses, involving . . . 5.69

Residential use, constitutionality of zoning for . . . 5.02

Special exceptions and conditional uses . . . 6.57

Spot zoning, involving . . . 6.29

State and federal constitutional law differences . . 1.02

Taking of property (See TAKING OF PROPERTY)

Transfer of development rights (TDRs) programs, involving

    Historic landmark preservation, TDRs for . . 11.38

    Natural resource area protections, TDRs for . . . 12.16

CONSTRUCTION OF ORDINANCES

Generally . . . 1.13

CONTRACT AND CONDITIONAL ZONING

Generally . . . 6.60; 6.62

Bilateral contract zoning

    Generally . . . 6.62

    Case law . . . 6.63

Proper purpose view . . . 6.65

Unilateral contract zoning

    Generally . . . 6.62

    Case law . . . 6.64

    Proper purpose view . . . 6.65

CONTRACT CLAUSE

Generally . . . 2.52; 2.53

Keystone Bituminous Coal case . . . 2.53

CORRIDOR PRESERVATION

Generally . . . 1.08; 10.12

Legislation for . . . 10.13

Official maps, use of . . . 10.13; 10.14

Takings considerations . . . 10.14

CRITICAL AREA CONTROLS

Generally . . . 12.04

D

DAMAGES

Section 1983 actions . . . 8.38

DECISION-MAKING PROCEDURES

Generally . . . 6.67; 6.70

Bias . . . 6.72; 6.73

Conflicts of interest . . . 6.72; 6.74

Entitlement interest, procedural due process protections for landowners with . . . 6.69

Expectancy interest, procedural due process protections for landowners with . . . 6.69

Impartial decision-maker, requirement for . . 6.71

Legislative and quasi-judicial decisions distinguished . . . 6.68

Neighborhood opposition, impact of . . . 6.75

Open meeting laws . . . 6.76

Procedural due process protections

    Generally . . . 6.67

    Bias . . . 6.72; 6.73

    Conflicts of interest . . . 6.72; 6.74

    Entitlement interests, for . . . 6.69

    Expectancy interests, for . . . 6.69

    Impartial decision-maker, requirement for . . 6.71

    Legislative vs. quasi-judicial decisions 6.68

    Neighborhood opposition, impact of . . 6.75

    Open meeting laws . . . 6.76

    Required procedures . . . 6.70

Quasi-judicial and legislative decisions distinguished . . . 6.68

DECLARATORY JUDGMENT

Generally . . . 8.12; 8.16

DELEGATION OF POWERS

Generally . . . 6.02

Compatibility standards . . . 6.03

Hearing examiner, use of . . . 6.02

Neighbors, delegation to . . . 6.04

Special permits, special exceptions and conditional uses (See SPECIAL EXCEPTIONS AND CONDITIONAL USES)

Standards for zoning . . . 6.03

Standard Zoning Act . . . 6.03

Statutory standards . . . 6.03

Vagueness claims . . . 6.05

Void for vagueness challenges . . . 6.05

DENSITY CONTROLS

Generally . . . 1.04

Bonuses . . . 5.76

Group homes . . . 5.15

Incentives . . . 5.76

[References are to sections.]

DENSITY CONTROLS—Cont.

Lot size requirements (See LOT SIZE REGULA-TIONS)

Site development requirements (See SITE DEVEL-OPMENT REQUIREMENTS)

DEVELOPMENT AGREEMENTS

Generally . . . 6.23

DISCRIMINATION

Civil rights actions under Section 1983 (See SEC-TION 1983 ACTIONS)

Exclusionary zoning (See EXCLUSIONARY ZONING)

Familial status discrimination, prohibition under Fair Housing Act of . . . 5.06

Group homes, discrimination against handicapped persons in (See GROUP HOMES)

Inclusionary zoning (See INCLUSIONARY PLAN-NING AND ZONING)

Section 1983 actions (See SECTION 1983 AC-TIONS)

DOWNZONING

Generally . . . 6.36

Change-mistake rule . . . 6.38

Compatibility with adjacent uses as factor in . . . 6.37

Reverse spot zoning . . . 6.37

Tests applied in review of . . . 6.37

DUE PROCESS

Generally . . . 1.01

Aesthetic zoning . . . 11.01

Federal and state constitutional law differences . . 1.02

Inclusionary zoning . . . 7.27

Procedural due process

    (See also DECISION-MAKING PROCEDURES)

    Generally . . . 2.41

    Federal courts, in . . . 2.42

    State courts, in . . . 2.43; 6.67 – 6.76

Ripeness doctrine, applicability of . . . 2.32

State and federal constitutional law differences . . 1.02

Substantive due process

    Generally . . . 2.39

    Aesthetic zoning . . . 11.01

    Arbitrary and irrational test . . . 2.39

    Entitlement rule . . . 2.40

    Federal courts, barriers to litigation in 2.40

    Rational relationship standard . . . 2.39

    "Shocks the conscience" test . . . 2.39

E

EDUCATIONAL USES (See SCHOOLS AND SCHOOL DISTRICTS)

ENVIRONMENTAL LAND USE CONTROLS

Generally . . . 1.06; 12.01

Agricultural land, preservation of (See AGRICUL-TURAL LAND, PRESERVATION OF)

Coastal zone management (See COASTAL ZONE MANAGEMENT)

Critical area controls . . . 12.04

Floodplain regulations (See FLOODPLAIN REGU-LATIONS)

Groundwater protection ordinances . . . 12.03

Slope protection ordinances . . . 12.02

State environmental programs, preemption of local zoning ordinances for . . . 4.30

Takings considerations (See TAKING OF PROP-ERTY)

View protection ordinances . . . 12.02

Wetlands regulations (See WETLANDS REGULA-TIONS)

EQUAL PROTECTION

Generally . . . 1.01; 2.44

Cleburne case . . . 2.48

Discriminatory intent requirement in racial discrimi-nation claims . . . 2.45

Exclusionary zoning . . . 1.01

Federal and state constitutional law differences . . 1.02

Middle-tier standard . . . 2.45

Olech case . . . 2.49

Rational relationship standard

    Generally . . . 2.45

    Cleburne case . . . 2.48

    Federal courts, application of standard in . . . 2.47

    Olech case . . . 2.49

    Selective enforcement, claims of

        Generally . . . 2.47

        Olech case . . . 2.49

    State courts, application of standard in 2.46

Relaxed rational relationship standard . . . 2.45

Ripeness doctrine, applicability of . . . 2.32

Selective enforcement, claims of

    Generally . . . 2.47

    Olech case . . . 2.49

Standards for judicial review

    Generally . . . 2.45

    Middle-tier standard . . . 2.45

    Rational relationship standard (See subhead: Rational relationship standard)

[References are to sections.]

EQUAL PROTECTION—Cont.
Standards for judicial review—Cont.
    Relaxed rational relationship standard . . . .
    2.45
    Strict scrutiny standard . . . 2.45
State and federal constitutional law differences . .
    1.02
Strict scrutiny standard . . . 2.45
Types of cases . . . 2.44

ESTOPPEL AND VESTED RIGHTS DOCTRINES
Generally . . . 6.12; 6.13
Building permit requirement, case law regarding
    Illegal building permits . . . 6.17
    No requirement for building permit . . . 6.16
    Requirement, building permit as . . . 6.15
Detrimental reliance
    Generally . . . 6.19
    Commitment to project, level of . . . 6.21
    Substantial reliance test . . . 6.20
Development agreements . . . 6.23
Good faith, requirement for . . . 6.18
Governmental act requirement
    Generally . . . 6.14
    Building permit requirement, case law regarding
    (See subhead: Building permit requirement,
    case law regarding)
Illegally issued building permits, effect of . . 6.17
Informal acts of municipality as basis for estoppel,
    reliance on . . . 6.16
Ordinance protections . . . 6.22
Reliance
    Detrimental reliance (See subhead: Detrimental
    reliance)
    Informal acts of municipality as basis for estop-
    pel, reliance on . . . 6.16
Rezoning and zoning amendments as basis for estop-
    pel . . . 6.16
Site plan and special exception approvals as basis for
    estoppel . . . 6.16
Statutory protections . . . 6.22
Subdivision plats or plans . . . 9.07

EXACTIONS
Generally . . . 1.09; 9.11
Authority for
    Generally . . . 9.11
    Impact fees . . . 9.21
    Park and school exactions . . . 9.18
Dedications and fees in lieu of dedication
    Generally . . . 9.11
    Parks and schools, dedications for . . . 9.18
Fees in lieu of
    Generally . . . 9.11
    Parks and schools, in-lieu fees for . . . 9.18
    Tax, challenges of in-lieu fees as unauthorized
    . . . 9.11; 9.18

EXACTIONS—Cont.
Impact fees (See IMPACT FEES)
Linkage programs . . . 9.23
Off-site streets and improvements . . . 9.11; 9.16
On-site streets and improvements . . . 9.11; 9.15
Park and school exactions
    Authority for . . . 9.18
    Dedications for . . . 9.18
    In-lieu fees for . . . 9.18
    Takings considerations . . . 9.19
School exactions (See subhead: Park and school
    exactions)
Takings considerations (See TAKING OF PROP-
    ERTY)

EXCLUSIONARY ZONING
Generally . . . 1.10; 7.01
Arlington Heights case; equal protection consider-
    ations . . . 7.03
California . . . 7.24
Commercial uses, total exclusion of . . . 5.37
Equal protection considerations . . . 7.03
Fair Housing Act, racial discrimination challenges
    under
    Generally . . . 7.04
    Disparate impact test, applicability of . . . .
    7.05
    Four-factor test for review of . . . 7.05
    Remedies . . . 7.06
    Standing to sue . . . 7.04
    Violations of act, determination of . . . 7.05
Federal courts, litigation in
    Generally . . . 7.02
    Equal protection considerations . . . 7.03
    Fair Housing Act (See subhead: Fair Housing
    Act, racial discrimination challenges under)
    Racial discrimination (See subhead: Racial
    discrimination)
    Standing to sue
    Generally . . . 7.02
    Fair Housing Act challenges . . . 7.04
Growth management programs . . . 10.08
Industrial uses, total exclusion of . . . 5.42
Low income housing . . . 1.10
Michigan . . . 7.23
Mobile homes, exclusion of
    Partial exclusion . . . 5.23
    Total exclusion . . . 5.24
New Hampshire . . . 7.25
New Jersey (See NEW JERSEY)
New York (See NEW YORK)
Pennsylvania (See PENNSYLVANIA)
Racial discrimination
    Generally . . . 7.02
    Arlington Heights case . . . 7.03

[References are to sections.]

EXCLUSIONARY ZONING—Cont.
Racial discrimination—Cont.
    Equal protection challenges . . . 7.03
    Fair Housing Act (See subhead: Fair Housing
      Act, racial discrimination challenges under)
    Standing to sue . . . 7.02
Standing to sue
    Fair Housing Act provisions . . . 7.04
    Federal courts, litigation in
      Generally . . . 7.02
      Fair Housing Act provisions . . . 7.04
    State courts, litigation in . . . 7.07
State courts, litigation in
    California . . . 7.24
    Michigan . . . 7.23
    New Hampshire . . . 7.25
    New Jersey (See NEW JERSEY)
    New York (See NEW YORK)
    Pennsylvania (See PENNSYLVANIA)
    Standing to sue . . . 7.07

EXTRATERRITORIAL ZONING
Generally . . . 4.22
Constitutional issues . . . 4.23
Right-to-vote problems . . . 4.23
Statutory authority . . . 4.22; 4.23

F

FAIR HOUSING ACT (FHA)
Exclusionary zoning (See EXCLUSIONARY
    ZONING)
Familial status discrimination, prohibition of . . . .
    5.06
Group homes for handicapped, provisions regarding
    (See GROUP HOMES)

FARMLAND POLICY PROTECTION ACT
Generally . . . 12.10

FEDERAL ANTITRUST LAWS
Generally . . . 5.49
Basis for liability . . . 5.56
Boulder case . . . 5.51
Conspiracy exception to state action immunity . .
    5.53
Damages, immunity of local governments from
    . . . 5.57
Home rule authority, immunity under . . . 5.51
Immunity
    Conspiracy exception to state action immunity
      . . . 5.53
    Damages, immunity of local governments from
      . . . 5.57
    Home rule authority, immunity under . . . .
      5.51

FEDERAL ANTITRUST LAWS—Cont.
Immunity—Cont.
    State action doctrine, immunity of municipalities
    under
      Generally . . . 5.50
      Conspiracy exception to state action immu-
        nity . . . 5.53
Local Government Antitrust Act . . . 5.57
Noerr-Pennington doctrine . . . 5.55
Omnie case . . . 5.53
Post-*Omnie* land use cases . . . 5.54
Sham exception to *Noerr-Pennington* doctrine . . .
    5.55
Standards for antitrust liability . . . 5.56
State action doctrine, immunity of municipalities
    under
      Generally . . . 5.50
      Conspiracy exception to state action immunity
        . . . 5.53
Town of Hallie case . . . 5.52

FEDERAL COURTS
Abstention (See REMEDIES, subhead: Abstention)
Due process
    Procedural due process . . . 2.42
    Substantive due process . . . 2.40
Exclusionary zoning (See EXCLUSIONARY
    ZONING)
Inverse condemnation (See INVERSE CONDEMNA-
    TION)
Judicial review
    Generally . . . 1.14
    Remedies (See REMEDIES)
Rational relationship standard . . . 2.47
Remedies (See REMEDIES)
Ripeness Doctrine; Futility rule . . . 2.30
Section 1983 actions removal to . . . 8.40

FHA (See FAIR HOUSING ACT (FHA))

FIRST AMENDMENT ISSUES (See FREE SPEECH
    CLAUSE)

FLEXIBLE ZONING TECHNIQUES
Generally . . . 6.60
Contract and conditional zoning (See CONTRACT
    AND CONDITIONAL ZONING)
Floating zones (See FLOATING ZONES)
Site plan reviews (See SITE PLAN REVIEWS)

FLOATING ZONES
Generally . . . 6.60; 6.61
Challenges to . . . 6.61
Consistency requirements . . . 6.61
Standards for approval of . . . 6.61

[References are to sections.]

FLOODPLAIN REGULATIONS
Generally . . . 12.01; 12.08
Local programs . . . 12.08
National Flood Insurance Act . . . 12.08
State programs . . . 12.08
Takings considerations . . . 12.09

FLOOR AREA RATIO REQUIREMENTS
Generally . . . 5.75

FREE SPEECH CLAUSE
Generally . . . 2.50
Adult businesses, zoning for (See ADULT BUSI-
NESSES, ZONING FOR)
Architectural design review ordinances . . . 11.25
Billboards, regulation of (See SIGNS AND BILL-
BOARDS, REGULATION OF)
Central Hudson tests . . . 2.50
Commercial speech, applicability to land use regula-
tions affecting . . . 2.50
Content-neutral regulations, tests applicable to . . .
2.50
Retaliatory governmental conduct, applicability to
. . . 2.51
Signs, regulation of (See SIGNS AND BILL-
BOARDS, REGULATION OF)
Special exceptions and conditional use permits . .
6.57
Time, place and manner regulations, tests applicable
to . . . 2.50
Viewpoint-neutral regulations, tests applicable to
. . . 2.50

FRONTAGE REQUIREMENTS
Generally . . . 5.72

FUNERAL PARLORS
Nuisance actions to enjoin funeral parlors from residential neighborhoods . . . 4.07

G

GENERAL PLANS (See COMPREHENSIVE
PLANS)

**GOVERNMENTAL IMMUNITY FROM ZON-
ING REGULATION**
Generally . . . 4.26
Airports and surrounding areas, regulation of . . .
4.43
Balancing test for local intergovernmental conflicts
. . . 4.38
Cellular towers, zoning for . . . 4.42
Eminent domain rule . . . 4.36
Environmental programs, preemption of local zoning
ordinances for . . . 4.30

**GOVERNMENTAL IMMUNITY FROM ZON-
ING REGULATION**—Cont.
Federal preemption
Generally . . . 4.41
Airports and surrounding areas . . . 4.43
Cellular towers . . . 4.42
Governmental-proprietary rule . . . 4.35
Home rule considerations . . . 4.39
Legislative interpretation rule . . . 4.26
Legislative solutions . . . 4.40
Liquor licensees, preemption from local zoning of
. . . 4.33
Local governments, immunity of
Generally . . . 4.34
Balancing test . . . 4.38
Eminent domain rule . . . 4.36
Governmental-proprietary rule . . . 4.35
State functions, immunity of local governments
exercising . . . 4.28
Superior power rule . . . 4.37
Private activities requiring state permits, preemption
of local zoning ordinances for . . . 4.31
Private utilities, immunity of . . . 4.32
School districts, exemption from local zoning of
. . . 4.28
Sovereign immunity rule . . . 4.26
State agencies, immunity of . . . 4.27
State-regulated and licensed facilities and businesses,
conflicts arising between local ordinances and
Generally . . . 4.29
Environmental programs . . . 4.30
Liquor licensees . . . 4.33
Private activities requiring state permits . . .
4.31
Private utilities . . . 4.32
Superior power rule . . . 4.37

**GOVERNMENT AND GOVERNMENT-
REGULATED LAND DEVELOPMENT, ZON-
ING FOR**
Immunity of government from zoning regulation (See
GOVERNMENTAL IMMUNITY FROM ZON-
ING REGULATION)

GROUNDWATER PROTECTION ORDINANCES
Generally . . . 12.03

GROUP HOMES
Americans with Disabilities Act (ADA) provisions
. . . 5.16
Conditional use, as . . . 5.09
Discrimination against handicapped persons, Fair
Housing Act provisions regarding (See subhead:
Fair Housing Act provisions regarding group homes
for handicapped persons)

[References are to sections.]

GROUP HOMES—Cont.

Fair Housing Act provisions regarding group homes for handicapped persons

     Generally . . . 5.12

     Discrimination defined . . . 5.12

     Handicapped defined . . . 5.12

     Occupancy restrictions . . . 5.14

     Quota requirements . . . 5.15

     Reasonable accommodation requirement . . . 5.12; 5.13

     Spacing requirements . . . 5.15

     Special use permits and variances . . . 5.13

"Family", group homes as permitted . . . 5.08

Functional equivalency rule . . . 5.08

Handicapped persons, group homes for

     Americans with Disabilities Act (ADA) provisions . . . 5.16

     Fair Housing Act provisions (See subhead: Fair Housing Act provisions regarding group homes for handicapped persons)

     Rehabilitation Act (RA) provisions . . . 5.16

Nuisance actions to prohibit group homes from residential neighborhoods . . . 4.08

Occupancy restrictions . . . 5.14

Quota requirements . . . 5.15

Reasonable accommodation requirement . . . 5.12; 5.13

Rehabilitation Act (RA) provisions . . . 5.16

Spacing requirements . . . 5.15

Special use permits and variances . . . 5.13

State legislative regulation . . . 5.10

GROWTH MANAGEMENT PROGRAMS

Generally . . . 1.08; 10.01; 10.02

Adequate public facilities (APF) requirements . . . 10.02; 10.05

Concurrency requirements . . . 10.05

Corridor preservation (See CORRIDOR PRESERVATION)

Exclusionary effects of . . . 10.08

Legal problems associated with . . . 10.03

Phasing programs (See subhead: Timing and phasing programs)

Public utilities and service as (See PUBLIC UTILITIES)

Quota controls

     Generally . . . 10.02

     Case law . . . 10.06

     Legal problems associated with . . . 10.03

     Petaluma case . . . 10.06

Right-to-travel objections to . . . 10.08

Timing and phasing programs

     Generally . . . 10.02

     Legal problems associated with . . . 10.03

     Ramapo case . . . 10.04

GROWTH MANAGEMENT PROGRAMS—Cont.

Urban growth boundaries and service areas 10.02; 10.07

H

HEIGHT LIMITATIONS

Generally . . . 5.74

Airports, zoning for . . . 5.39

HIGHWAY BEAUTIFICATION ACT

Amortization of outdoor advertising, prohibition of . . . 5.83; 11.11

Sign regulation . . . 11.06; 11.11

HIGHWAYS (See STREETS AND HIGHWAYS)

HISTORIC DISTRICTS

Generally . . . 1.05; 11.26

Constitutionality of . . . 11.29; 11.32

Delegation of power challenges . . . 11.30

Enabling legislation and ordinances . . . 11.28

Interim controls . . . 11.31

Takings considerations . . . 11.32

Transfer of development rights (TDRs), preservation by means of . . . 11.38

Vagueness challenges . . . 11.30

HISTORIC LANDMARKS (See LANDMARK PRESERVATION)

HISTORIC PRESERVATION

Generally . . . 11.26

Historic districts (See HISTORIC DISTRICTS)

Historic landmarks (See LANDMARK PRESERVATION)

Landmark preservation (See LANDMARK PRESERVATION)

National Historic Preservation Act . . . 11.26

Purpose of . . . 11.26

HOME OCCUPATIONS

Generally . . . 5.20

HOME RULE PROVISIONS

Generally . . . 4.24

Antitrust law, immunity from . . . 5.51

Constitutional home rule authority . . . 4.24

Land use powers . . . 4.25

Legislative home rule provisions . . . 4.24

Preemption of home rule zoning ordinances by legislature . . . 4.39

Traditional home rule provisions . . . 4.24

[References are to sections.]

I

IMMUNITY
Federal antitrust laws, from (See FEDERAL ANTI-
TRUST LAWS)
Governmental immunity from zoning regulation (See
GOVERNMENTAL IMMUNITY FROM ZON-
ING REGULATION)
Section 1983 actions (See SECTION 1983 AC-
TIONS)
Tort liability, from . . . 8.23

IMPACT FEES
Generally . . . 1.09; 9.11; 9.20
Authority for . . . 9.21
Takings considerations . . . 9.22

INCENTIVE ZONING
Generally . . . 7.27

INCLUSIONARY PLANNING AND ZONING
Generally . . . 7.26
Affordable housing appeals laws . . . 7.31
Appeals of affordable housing denials or restrictions
. . . 7.31
California legislation . . . 7.29
Due process challenges . . . 7.27
Incentive zoning . . . 7.27
Mandatory set asides . . . 7.27
Office-housing linkage programs . . . 7.28
Oregon legislation . . . 7.30
Set asides, mandatory . . . 7.27
Taking of property, as . . . 7.27

INDUSTRIAL USES AND ZONING
Generally . . . 5.33; 5.40
Exclusion of . . . 5.42
Exclusive industrial zoning, problems with . . 5.43
Noncumulative zoning . . . 5.43
Performance standards . . . 5.41
Total industrial exclusion . . . 5.42

INITIATIVE
Generally . . . 6.77
Actions subject to . . . 6.77
Availability in zoning process . . . 6.81
Constitutional issues . . . 6.78

INJUNCTIVE RELIEF
Judicial review of zoning determinations . . 8.12;
8.15
Nuisance actions (See NUISANCE ACTIONS)

INTERIM DEVELOPMENT CONTROLS
Generally . . . 6.06
Authority to enact regulations . . . 6.07

INTERIM DEVELOPMENT CONTROLS—Cont.
Constitutional considerations
Generally . . . 6.09
As applied challenges . . . 6.11
Lake Tahoe case . . . 6.09
Revision of ordinances or comprehensive plans,
interim development controls for purposes of
providing time for . . . 6.09

INVERSE CONDEMNATION
Generally . . . 8.20
Federal courts, in
Generally . . . 8.25
Compensation, availability and measurement of
. . . 8.26
First English case . . . 8.25
Highest and best use of property, compensation
based on . . . 8.26
Jury trial, availability of . . . 8.27
Land development cost approach for determin-
ing market value . . . 8.26
Market value test, use in permanent takings
cases of . . . 8.26
Rental value standard . . . 8.26
State courts, in
Generally . . . 8.20
Available remedy, case law upholding inverse
condemnation as . . . 8.21
Not available as remedy, case law holding in-
verse condemnation . . . 8.22

J

JUDICIAL REVIEW
Appeal and certiorari . . . 8.12; 8.13
Comprehensive plans, of . . . 3.22
Declaratory judgment . . . 8.12; 8.16
Federal courts
Generally . . . 1.14
Remedies (See REMEDIES)
Injunction . . . 8.12; 8.15
Judicial relief, availability of
Generally . . . 8.17
Alternative specific remedies . . . 8.19
Not available . . . 8.18
Specific relief available . . . 8.17; 8.19
Mandamus . . . 8.12; 8.14
Presumption of constitutionality for land use regula-
tion . . . 1.12
Remedies (See REMEDIES)
Special exceptions and conditional uses . . . 6.56
Standards of judicial review . . . 1.12
State courts
Generally . . . 1.15; 1.16; 8.12

[References are to sections.]

JUDICIAL REVIEW—Cont.
State courts—Cont.
    Appeal and certiorari . . . 8.12; 8.13
    Appellate court structure . . . 1.17
    Declaratory judgment . . . 8.12; 8.16
    Injunction . . . 8.12; 8.15
    Judicial relief (See subhead: Judicial relief, availability of)
    Mandamus . . . 8.12; 8.14
    Remedies (See REMEDIES)
    Variations among states . . . 1.16
Variances . . . 6.52

JURY TRIALS
Inverse condemnation cases, in . . . 8.27

L

LANDMARK PRESERVATION
Generally . . . 1.05; 11.26; 11.33
Enabling legislation and ordinances . . . 11.34
Maintenance and repair requirements . . . 11.36
Religious uses, takings problems in application of landmark ordinances to . . . 11.37
Takings considerations
    Generally . . . 11.35
    Maintenance and repair requirements 11.36
    Religious uses, in application of landmark ordinances to . . . 11.37
Transfer of development rights (TDRs), preservation by means of . . . 11.38

LAND USE CONTROLS (See ZONING (GENERALLY))

LAND USE LITIGATION (See JUDICIAL REVIEW; LITIGATION (GENERALLY))

LINKAGE
Exaction programs . . . 9.23
Inclusionary zoning . . . 7.28

LIQUOR AND LIQUOR STORES
State liquor licensees, preemption from local zoning of . . . 4.33

LITIGATION (GENERALLY)
Generally . . . 8.01
Judicial review (See JUDICIAL REVIEW)
Nuisance actions (See NUISANCE ACTIONS)
Remedies (See REMEDIES)
SLAPP suits (See SLAPP SUITS)
Standing to sue (See STANDING TO SUE)
Torts . . . 8.23

LOCAL GOVERNMENT ANTITRUST ACT
Generally . . . 5.57

LOT SIZE REGULATIONS
Generally . . . 5.28
Large-lot zoning
    Generally . . . 5.30
    Invalid, cases holding large-lot zoning as . . 5.32
    Valid, cases holding large-lot zoning as . . . 5.31
Maximum house size restrictions . . . 5.29
Minimum house size restrictions . . . 5.29

LOWER-INCOME HOUSING
Comprehensive plans, state legislative planning policies for lower-income housing in . . . 3.11
Exclusionary zoning . . . 1.10

M

MANDAMUS
Generally . . . 8.12; 8.14

MAPS (See OFFICIAL MAPS; ZONING MAPS)

MASTER PLANS (See COMPREHENSIVE PLANS)

MICHIGAN
Exclusionary zoning . . . 7.23

MOBILE HOMES, ZONING FOR
Generally . . . 5.21
Conditional use, as . . . 5.25
Dwelling, mobile home as . . . 5.22
Exclusionary zoning practices
    Partial exclusion . . . 5.23
    Total exclusion . . . 5.24
Federal regulations . . . 5.26
Preemption of local zoning for state or federally regulated mobile homes . . . 5.26
State regulations . . . 5.26

MORATORIA ON DEVELOPMENT
Generally . . . 6.06
Authority to enact regulations . . . 6.07
Constitutional considerations
    As applied challenges . . . 6.11
    Inadequate public facilities, moratoria on development for purposes of remedying . . 6.10
    Lake Tahoe case . . . 6.09
    Revision of ordinances or comprehensive plans, moratoria on development for purposes of providing time for . . . 6.09
    Takings considerations . . . 6.09
Limitations on . . . 6.07

[References are to sections.]

N

NATIONAL COASTAL ZONE MANAGEMENT ACT
Generally . . . 12.01; 12.14

NATIONAL HISTORIC PRESERVATION ACT
Generally . . . 11.26

NEW HAMPSHIRE
Exclusionary zoning . . . 7.25

NEW JERSEY
Exclusionary zoning
    Council on Affordable Housing (COAH), creation and functions of . . . 7.12
    Fair Housing Act, adoption of . . . 7.12
    Fair share doctrine . . . 7.09; 7.11; 7.12
    Mt. Laurel (I) case . . . 7.09
    Mt. Laurel (II) case . . . 7.11
    Post *Mt. Laurel (II)* cases . . . 7.13
    Weymouth case . . . 7.10

NEW YORK
Exclusionary zoning
    Asian Americans for Equality case . . . 7.17
    Berenson case . . . 7.15
    Brookhaven case . . . 7.16
    Regional housing need requirement . . . 7.15
    Remedies . . . 7.18

NONCONFORMING USES
Generally . . . 5.78
Abandonment of use, termination due to . . . 5.81
Amortization, termination of use via
    Generally . . . 5.78; 5.82
    Constitutionality of . . . 5.78; 5.84 – 5.86
    Highway Beautification Act, prohibition of amortization of outdoor advertising covered by . . . 5.83; 11.11
    Reasonableness of amortization period 5.86
Changes in nonconforming use . . . 5.79
Constitutional considerations
    Generally . . . 5.78
    Amortization, termination of use via . . 5.78; 5.84 – 5.86
Discontinuance of use as abandonment . . . 5.81
Expansion of nonconforming use . . . 5.79
Highway Beautification Act, prohibition of amortization of outdoor advertising covered by . . 5.83; 11.11
Reconstruction, permissibility of . . . 5.80
Repairs, permissibility of . . . 5.80
Restoration of structure, permissibility of . . 5.80
Retroactive elimination of . . . 5.78; 5.84
Signs and billboards . . . 5.83; 11.11

NONCUMULATIVE ZONING
Generally . . . 5.43

NUISANCE ACTIONS
Generally . . . 1.04
Aesthetic nuisances . . . 4.09
Anticipatory nuisances . . . 4.03
Commercial uses in residential areas, actions to prohibit . . . 4.06
Compensation to defendant as condition of injunctive relief . . . 4.14
Funeral parlors in residential neighborhoods, actions to prohibit . . . 4.07
Group homes in residential neighborhoods, actions to prohibit . . . 4.08
Half-way houses in residential neighborhoods, actions to prohibit . . . 4.08
Injunctions
    Anticipatory nuisances . . . 4.03
    Balancing of equities by courts . . . 4.12
    Cases not allowing injunction . . . 4.13
    Compensation to defendant as condition of injunctive relief . . . 4.14
Legalizing nuisances through zoning . . . 4.10
Nuisance per accidens . . . 4.02
Nuisance per se . . . 4.02
People as nuisances . . . 4.08
Priority of occupation rule . . . 4.04
Private actions . . . 4.02
Residential neighborhoods, nuisances in
    Generally . . . 4.05
    Aesthetic nuisances . . . 4.09
    Commercial uses . . . 4.06
    Funeral parlors . . . 4.07
    Group homes . . . 4.08
    Half-way houses . . . 4.08
    People as nuisances . . . 4.08

O

OFFICIAL MAPS
Corridor preservation, for . . . 10.13; 10.14
Takings considerations . . . 10.14

OFF-STREET PARKING REQUIREMENTS
Generally . . . 5.77

OPEN MEETING LAWS
Generally . . . 6.76

ORDINANCES
Generally . . . 1.04
Amendments (See REZONING AND ZONING AMENDMENTS)
Construction of ordinances . . . 1.13

[References are to sections.]

ORDINANCES—Cont.
Rezoning (See REZONING AND ZONING AMENDMENTS)

OREGON
Inclusionary zoning legislation . . . 7.30

OVERLAY ZONES (See FLOATING ZONES)

P

PARKING
Off-street parking requirements . . . 5.77

PARKS
Exactions for (See EXACTIONS, subhead: Park and school exactions)

PENNSYLVANIA
Exclusionary zoning
    Generally . . . 7.19
    Fernley case . . . 7.21
    Partial exclusion; *Surrick* case . . . 7.20
    Remedies . . . 7.22
    Surrick case . . . 7.20
    Total exclusion; *Fernley* case . . . 7.21

PERFORMANCE STANDARDS
Industrial zoning and uses . . . 5.41

PHASED GROWTH PROGRAMS (See GROWTH MANAGEMENT PROGRAMS, subhead: Timing and phasing programs)

PLANNED UNIT DEVELOPMENTS (PUDs)
Generally . . . 1.09; 9.01; 9.24
Amendments to plan . . . 9.29
Authority to approve PUDs
    Generally . . . 9.27
    Delegation of . . . 9.27
    Standard Zoning Act . . . 9.26
    State legislation . . . 9.30
Delegation of authority to review PUD applications
    . . . 9.27
Discretion to approve or reject . . . 9.28
Ordinance criteria . . . 9.25
Purpose clauses . . . 9.28
Review process
    Generally . . . 9.25
    Regulatory techniques . . . 9.27
Rezoning . . . 9.27
Standard Zoning Act provisions . . . 9.26
State legislation . . . 9.30

PLANS AND PLANNING
Comprehensive plans (See COMPREHENSIVE PLANS)

PLANS AND PLANNING—Cont.
Inclusionary planning and zoning (See INCLUSIONARY PLANNING AND ZONING)
Planned Unit Developments (PUDs) (See PLANNED UNIT DEVELOPMENTS (PUDs))
Planning commission, delegation of authority to . . . 6.55
Site plan reviews (See SITE PLAN REVIEWS)
Standard Planning Act (See STANDARD PLANNING ACT)
State land use planning
    Generally . . . 1.16
    Variations among states . . . 1.16
Subdivision plats or plans . . . 9.07

PREEMPTION OF LOCAL ZONING ORDINANCES (See GOVERNMENTAL IMMUNITY FROM ZONING REGULATION)

PROCEDURAL ISSUES (See DECISION-MAKING PROCEDURES)

PUBLIC UTILITIES
Growth management control, as
    Generally . . . 10.10
    Duty to serve . . . 10.10
    Refusals to extend service . . . 10.10
    Takings considerations . . . 10.11

PUDs (See PLANNED UNIT DEVELOPMENTS (PUDs))

Q

QUOTA CONTROLS (See GROWTH MANAGEMENT PROGRAMS)

R

RA (See REHABILITATION ACT (RA))

REFERENDUM
Generally . . . 6.77; 6.80
Actions subject to . . . 6.77
Availability in zoning process . . . 6.80
Constitutional issues . . . 6.78

REHABILITATION ACT (RA)
Group homes, provisions regarding . . . 5.16

RELIGIOUS FREEDOM RESTORATION ACT
Generally . . . 5.70

RELIGIOUS LAND USE AND INSTITUTIONALIZED PERSONS ACT
Generally . . . 5.70

[References are to sections.]

RELIGIOUS USES AND FACILITIES
Constitutional considerations . . . 5.69
Establishment clause of Constitution, violation of
. . . 5.69
Free exercise clause of Constitution, violation of
. . . 5.69
Landmark preservation ordinances . . . 11.37
Religious Freedom Restoration Act . . . 5.70
Religious Land Use and Institutionalized Persons Act
. . . 5.70
Schools . . . 5.27
Special exceptions and conditional use permits . .
6.57
State court decisions . . . 5.68
State religious freedom acts . . . 5.70

REMEDIES
Abstention
     Generally . . . 8.41
     Burford abstention . . . 8.44
     Colorado River abstention . . . 8.45
     Mirror image abstention . . . 8.43
     Pullman abstention . . . 8.43
     Younger abstention . . . 8.42
Bivens actions . . . 8.39
Civil rights actions under Section 1983 (See SEC-
TION 1983 ACTIONS)
Exhaustion of remedies
     Generally . . . 8.08
     Exceptions . . . 8.11
     Futility rule . . . 8.11
     Remedies which must be exhausted . . 8.10
     Ripeness distinguished . . . 8.08
     Section 1983 actions, applicability to . . 8.33
Federal courts, in
     Abstention (See subhead: Abstention)
     Bivens actions . . . 8.39
     Civil rights actions under Section 1983 (See
     SECTION 1983 ACTIONS)
     Implied constitutional cause of action . . . .
     8.39
     Inverse condemnation (See INVERSE CON-
     DEMNATION)
     Removal to Federal court . . . 8.40
     Section 1983 actions (See SECTION 1983
     ACTIONS)
Implied constitutional cause of action . . . 8.39
Inverse condemnation (See INVERSE CONDEMNA-
TION)
Judicial remedies (See JUDICIAL REVIEW)
Ripeness doctrine (See RIPENESS DOCTRINE)
Section 1983 actions (See SECTION 1983 AC-
TIONS)
State courts, in
     Exhaustion of remedies (See subhead: Exhaus-
     tion of remedies)

REMEDIES—Cont.
State courts, in—Cont.
     Inverse condemnation (See INVERSE CON-
     DEMNATION)
     Judicial remedies (See JUDICIAL REVIEW)
     Tort liability . . . 8.23
Tort liability . . . 8.23

RESIDENTIAL USES AND ZONING
Generally . . . 1.04; 5.01; 9.01
Accessory uses in residential areas . . . 5.19
Apartments . . . 5.18
Constitutionality of zoning for residential use . . .
5.02
Euclid; constitutionality of zoning for residential use
. . . 5.02
Group homes (See GROUP HOMES)
Home occupations, permissibility of . . . 5.20
Mobile homes, zoning for (See MOBILE HOMES,
ZONING FOR)
Nuisances in residential neighborhoods (See NUI-
SANCE ACTIONS)
Planned unit developments (PUDs) (See PLANNED
UNIT DEVELOPMENTS (PUDs))
Private schools in residential zones . . . 5.27
Religious schools in residential zones . . . 5.27
Single-family house districts (See SINGLE-FAMILY
HOUSE DISTRICTS)
Subdivision controls (See SUBDIVISION REGULA-
TION)

REZONING AND ZONING AMENDMENTS
Generally . . . 6.24
Authority to amend ordinances . . . 4.18; 6.24
Downzoning (See DOWNZONING)
Estoppel, as basis for . . . 6.16
Fasano rule . . . 6.26
Legislative act, rezoning as . . . 6.26
Planned unit developments . . . 9.27
Quasi-judicial, rezoning as . . . 6.26
Refusals to rezone . . . 6.25
Spot zoning challenges (See SPOT ZONING)
Standard Zoning Act . . . 4.18; 6.24

RIGHT-OF-WAY RESERVATIONS (See CORRI-
DOR PRESERVATION)

RIPENESS DOCTRINE
Generally . . . 1.02; 8.08
Exhaustion of remedies, distinguished . . . 8.08
Futility rule
     Federal courts, in . . . 2.30
     State courts, in . . . 8.09
State courts, in . . . 8.09
Takings claims, applicability to (See TAKING OF
PROPERTY)

[References are to sections.]

S

SCHOOLS AND SCHOOL DISTRICTS
Exactions for (See EXACTIONS, subhead: Park and school exactions)
Exemption from local zoning for . . . 4.28
Private schools . . . 5.27
Religious schools . . . 5.27

SECTION 1983 ACTIONS
Generally . . . 8.29
Adequacy of state remedies, requirements regarding . . . 8.33
Cases not actionable . . . 8.30
Causation, requirements regarding . . . 8.32
"Color of law" requirement . . . 8.31
"Custom and usage" requirement . . . 8.31
Damages . . . 8.38
Exhaustion of state remedies requirement, applicability of . . . 8.33
Fault, requirement for showing of . . . 8.32
Federal court, removal to . . . 8.40
Immunity
    Land use agencies and officials, of . . . 8.36
    Legislative bodies, of . . . 8.35
    Legislative versus administrative acts . . 8.35
    Local governments, of . . . 8.37
Land use agencies and officials, immunity of . . . 8.36
Legislative bodies, immunity of . . . 8.35
Local governments, immunity of . . . 8.37
Official policy requirement . . . 8.31
Policy defined . . . 8.31
Property rights as right protected by Section 1983 . . . 8.29
Punitive damages . . . 8.38
Scope of statute . . . 8.29

SET ASIDES
Generally . . . 7.27

SETBACK REQUIREMENTS
Generally . . . 5.71

SIGNS AND BILLBOARDS, REGULATION OF
Generally . . . 1.07; 11.06
Aesthetics as basis for sign regulation . . . 11.17
Authority to enact regulations . . . 11.06
Campaign signs, regulation of . . . 11.23
Classification of signs . . . 11.06; 11.19
Content-based sign definitions . . . 11.21
Content neutrality in regulations . . . 11.17
Controls on display of signs . . . 11.10
Display of signs, controls on . . . 11.10
Exclusion of billboards, regulations for . . . 11.08; 11.19

SIGNS AND BILLBOARDS, REGULATION OF—Cont.
Federal regulations . . . 11.06
For sale signs, regulation of . . . 11.22
Free speech issues
    Generally . . . 11.01; 11.12
    Aesthetics as basis for sign regulation 11.17
    Campaign signs, regulation of . . . 11.23
    Classification of off-or on-premises signs . . 11.19
    Content-based sign definitions . . . 11.21
    Content neutrality in regulations . . . 11.17
    Exemption of off-or on-premises signs 11.19
    For sale signs, regulation of . . . 11.22
    Ladue case . . . 11.15
    Location of signs, restrictions on 11.16
    Lorillard case . . . 11.16
    Metromedia case . . . 11.13; 11.17
    Off-premises signs, regulation of . . . 11.19
    On-premises signs, regulation of . . . 11.19
    Political signs, regulation of . . . 11.23
    Portable signs, regulation of . . . 11.20
    Prohibitions of off-or on-premises signs . . . 11.19
    Residential signs, regulation of . . . 11.15
    Standing to sue . . . 11.17
    Taxpayers for Vincent case . . . 11.14
    Temporary signs, regulation of . . . 11.23
    Time, place and manner restrictions . . 11.18
Highway Beautification Act . . . 11.06; 11.11
Ladue case . . . 11.15
Local regulations . . . 11.06
Location of signs, restrictions on . . . 11.16
Lorillard case . . . 11.16
Metromedia case . . . 11.13; 11.17
Nonconforming signs, regulation of . . 5.83; 11.11
Off-premises signs, regulation of . . . 11.19
On-premise signs, exemption for . . . 11.09; 11.19
Political signs, regulation of . . . 11.23
Portable signs, regulation of . . . 11.20
Prohibitions of signs . . . 11.08; 11.19
Residential signs, regulation of . . . 11.15
Standing to sue in free speech cases . . . 11.17
State regulations . . . 11.06
Takings issues associated with sign regulations on streets and highways . . . 11.07
Taxpayers for Vincent case . . . 11.14
Temporary signs, regulation of . . . 11.23
Time, place and manner restrictions . . . 11.18

SINGLE-FAMILY HOUSE DISTRICTS
Generally . . . 5.17
Constitutionality of . . . 5.02

SINGLE-FAMILY HOUSE DISTRICTS—Cont.

Discrimination against families with children under
    Fair Housing Act . . . 5.06
Euclid; constitutionality of single-family districts
    . . . 5.02
Fair Housing Act, prohibition of familial status dis-
    crimination under . . . 5.06
Family defined
    Generally . . . 5.03
    Belle Terre case . . . 5.04; 5.05
    Discrimination against families with children
        under Fair Housing Act . . . 5.06
    Fair Housing Act provisions . . . 5.06
    Group homes as permitted "family" use . . .
        5.08
    Moor case . . . 5.04
    State courts decisions . . . 5.05
Group homes in (See GROUP HOMES)

SITE AREA RATIO REQUIREMENTS

Generally . . . 5.73

SITE DEVELOPMENT REQUIREMENTS

Density bonuses and incentives . . . 5.76
Floor area ratio requirements . . . 5.75
Frontage requirements . . . 5.72
Height limitations . . . 5.74
Lot size regulations (See LOT SIZE REGULA-
    TIONS)
Off-street parking requirements . . . 5.77
Setback requirements . . . 5.71
Site area ratio requirements . . . 5.73
Yard requirements . . . 5.71

SITE PLAN REVIEWS

Generally . . . 6.66
Authority to enact regulations . . . 6.66
Estoppel, as basis for . . . 6.16

SLAPP SUITS

Generally . . . 8.46
Anti-SLAPP statutes . . . 8.47
Counterclaims to . . . 8.46
Limitations on . . . 8.47
SLAPPback suits . . . 8.46

SLOPE PROTECTION ORDINANCES

Generally . . . 12.02

**SPECIAL EXCEPTIONS AND CONDITIONAL
    USES**

Generally . . . 6.53; 6.54
Authority to regulate permits
    Generally . . . 6.39
    Delegation of authority (See subhead: Delega-
        tion of authority)
    Standard Zoning Act provisions 4.19;
        6.39; 6.53

**SPECIAL EXCEPTIONS AND CONDITIONAL
    USES—Cont.**

Classification of use as one requiring conditional use
    approval . . . 6.54
Conditions to permit . . . 6.59
Consistency with comprehensive plan, requirements
    regarding . . . 6.58
Constitutional considerations . . . 6.57
Delegation of authority
    Generally . . . 6.03; 6.55
    Legislature, delegation to . . . 6.55
    Planning commission, delegation to . . . 6.55
Estoppel, special exception approvals as basis for
    . . . 6.16
Free-speech protected uses . . . 6.57
Function of . . . 6.54
Group homes, for . . . 5.09
Judicial review . . . 6.56
Legislature, delegation of authority to . . . 6.55
Mobile homes, for . . . 5.25
Planning commission, delegation of authority to
    . . . 6.55
Religious uses . . . 6.57
Role of . . . 6.54
Standards for . . . 6.53
Standard Zoning Act provisions . . . 4.19; 6.39; 6.53
Variances distinguished . . . 6.39; 6.54

SPECIAL PERMITS (See SPECIAL EXCEPTIONS
    AND CONDITIONAL USES)

SPOT ZONING

Generally . . . 6.28
Adjacent communities, effect on . . . 6.35
Balancing test for review of . . . 6.29
Change-mistake rule . . . 6.31
Comprehensive plan, requirements regarding consis-
    tency with (See subhead: Consistency with compre-
    hensive plan, requirements regarding)
Consistency with comprehensive plan, requirements
    regarding
    Generally . . . 6.29; 6.32
    Spot planning, use of . . . 6.34
    Zoning decisions, applicability to . . . 6.33
Constitutional considerations . . . 6.29
Definitions . . . 6.28
"In accordance" requirement . . . 6.29
Public need test . . . 6.30
Public purpose test . . . 6.30
Spot planning, use of . . . 6.34

STANDARD CITY PLANNING ENABLING ACT
    (See STANDARD PLANNING ACT)

STANDARD PLANNING ACT

Generally . . . 1.01; 3.05

[References are to sections.]

STANDARD PLANNING ACT—Cont.

Comprehensive plans (See COMPREHENSIVE PLANS)

Optional plan-making as feature of . . . 3.05

Planning commission, membership on and role of . . . 3.06

Process-oriented requirements of . . . 3.05

Subdivision controls . . . 9.02; 9.03

STANDARD ZONING ACT

Generally . . . 1.01; 4.15; 6.01

Adoption of zoning ordinances . . . 4.18

Amendment of zoning ordinances . . . 4.18; 6.24

Board of Adjustment, powers of . . . 4.19

Comprehensive plan, requirement for consistency of zoning with . . . 3.13

Delegation of powers . . . 6.03

District concept . . . 4.17

Enforcement . . . 4.20

Planned unit developments (PUDs) . . . 9.26

Purposes . . . 4.16

Special exceptions (conditional uses) . . 4.19; 6.39; 6.53

Standing of third parties . . . 8.02

Third-party standing . . . 8.02

Variances, authorization of . . . 4.15; 6.39; 6.41

Zoning commission . . . 4.15

STANDARD ZONING ENABLING ACT (SZEA) (See STANDARD ZONING ACT)

STANDING TO SUE

Generally . . . 8.02

Associations, standing of . . . 8.06

Citizens, standing of . . . 8.03

Exclusionary zoning practices, challenges to (See EXCLUSIONARY ZONING)

Municipalities, standing of . . . 8.07

Neighborhood organizations and associations, standing of . . . 8.06

Nonresident landowners, standing of . . . 8.05

Organizations, standing of . . . 8.06

Resident landowners, standing of . . . 8.04

Signs and billboards, standing in free speech cases involving regulation of . . . 11.17

Special damages to interest or property right, requirement for . . . 8.02

Standard Zoning Act provisions . . . 8.02

Taxpayers, standing of . . . 8.03

Third-party standing in state courts

    Generally . . . 8.02

    Associations, standing of . . . 8.06

    Citizens, standing of . . . 8.03

    Municipalities, standing of . . . 8.07

    Neighborhood organizations and associations, standing of . . . 8.06

STANDING TO SUE—Cont.

Third-party standing in state courts—Cont.

    Nonresident landowners, standing of . . 8.05

    Organizations, standing of . . . 8.06

    "Prudential" standing limitation . . . 8.02

    Resident landowners, standing of . . . 8.04

    Special damages to interest or property right, requirement for . . . 8.02

    Standard Zoning Act provisions . . . 8.02

    Taxpayers, standing of . . . 8.03

STATE COURTS

Appellate court structure . . . 1.17

Due process in, procedural . . . 2.43; 6.67 – 6.76

Exclusionary zoning, litigation regarding (See EXCLUSIONARY ZONING)

Inverse condemnation (See INVERSE CONDEMNATION)

Judicial review (See JUDICIAL REVIEW)

Rational relationship standard . . . 2.46

Religious uses and facilities, decisions regarding . . . 5.68

Remedies (See REMEDIES)

Ripeness Doctrine . . . 8.09

Standing to sue; third-party standing in state courts (See STANDING TO SUE, subhead: Third-party standing in state courts)

Taking of property, regarding . . . 2.35

STATE LAND USE PLANNING

Generally . . . 1.16

Variations among states . . . 1.16

STREETS AND HIGHWAYS

Generally . . . 1.08

Billboards, regulation of (See SIGNS AND BILLBOARDS, REGULATION OF)

Corridor preservation (See CORRIDOR PRESERVATION)

Exactions in subdivision regulations for on-and off-site streets and improvements . . 9.11; 9.15; 9.16

Signs and billboards, regulation of (See SIGNS AND BILLBOARDS, REGULATION OF)

SUBDIVISION REGULATION

Generally . . . 1.09; 9.01

Approval requirements . . . 9.04

Builder exactions (See EXACTIONS)

Building permit denials as sanction . . . 9.08

Enabling legislation . . . 9.02; 9.03

Enforcement . . . 9.08

Exactions (See EXACTIONS)

Exemptions from . . . 9.05

Historical background . . . 9.02

Impact fees (See IMPACT FEES)

Plat requirements . . . 9.04

[References are to sections.]

SUBDIVISION REGULATION—Cont.
Procedures . . . 9.04
Purpose of . . . 9.02
Sanctions . . . 9.08
Scope of subdivision control authority 9.03; 9.09
Standard Planning Act . . . 9.02; 9.03
Subdivision defined . . . 9.05
Taking considerations . . . 9.09
Variances . . . 9.10
Vested rights . . . 9.07
Waivers of ordinance requirements . . . 9.10
Zoning, relationship to . . . 9.06

SUNSHINE LAWS (See OPEN MEETING LAWS)

SZEA (See STANDARD ZONING ACT)

T

TAKING OF PROPERTY
Generally . . . 1.01; 2.01; 2.02; 2.14
Acquisitory intent cases . . . 2.23
Aesthetic zoning . . . 11.01
Agins v. City of Tiburon case . . . 2.08; 2.25
Agricultural zoning . . . 12.13
Airport zoning regulations as . . . 5.39
"As-applied" zoning cases . . . 2.36
Average reciprocity of advantage maxim . . . 2.15
Balancing test . . . 2.37
Coastal setback legislation . . . 12.15
Compensation as remedy . . . 2.31
Comprehensive plans
    Defense to taking, plan as . . . 3.20
    Taking, plan as . . . 3.21
Conceptual segmentation . . . 2.17; 2.18
Condemnation powers, takings related to improper use of . . . 2.23
Corridor preservation . . . 10.14
Delay in decision making as . . . 2.22
Del Monte Dunes case . . . 2.13
Denominator issue (See subhead: Segmentation issue)
Diminution in value of land, "as-applied" cases claiming . . . 2.36
Dolan case . . . 2.12; 9.14
Due process claims . . . 2.32
Economically viable use of land, determinations regarding . . . 2.36
Environmental land use controls
    Generally . . . 12.01
    Agricultural zoning . . . 12.13
    Coastal setback legislation . . . 12.15
    Floodplain regulations . . . 12.09
    Slope protection ordinances . . . 12.02
    View protection ordinances . . . 12.02

TAKING OF PROPERTY—Cont.
Environmental land use controls—Cont.
    Wetlands regulations . . . 12.07
Equal protection claims . . . 2.32
Euclid case . . . 2.06
Exactions
    Generally . . . 2.10; 9.12
    Del Monte Dunes case . . . 2.13
    Dolan case . . . 2.12; 9.14
    Impact fees as taking . . . 9.22
    Nexus test . . . 2.11; 9.12; 9.13
    Nollan case . . . 2.11; 9.13
    Off-site streets and improvements . . . 9.16
    On-site streets and improvements . . . 9.15
    Parks and schools, land dedications or in-lieu fees for . . . 9.19
    Rough proportionality test . . 2.12; 2.13; 9.12; 9.14
"Facial" takings . . . 2.01
Final decision rule . . . 2.30
Floodplain regulations . . . 12.09
Futility exception to final decision rule . . . 2.30
Geographic segmentation . . . 2.19
Goldblatt case . . . 2.04
Hadacheck case . . . 2.04
Hamilton Bank case . . . 2.26
Historic district regulations as . . . 11.32
Impact analysis . . . 2.38
Inclusionary zoning as . . . 7.27
Inverse condemnation (See INVERSE CONDEMNATION)
Investment-backed expectations as takings factor . . . 2.16
Keystone Bituminous case . . . 2.05
Landmark regulation (See LANDMARK PRESERVATION)
"Line-drawing" cases . . . 2.36
Loretto case . . . 2.03
Loss of value of land, "as-applied" cases claiming . . . 2.36
Lucas case . . . 2.09; 2.21
Moratoria on development as . . . 6.09
Mugler case . . . 2.01
Multi-factor test . . . 2.37
Nectow v. City of Cambridge case . . . 2.06
Nexus test . . . 2.11; 9.12; 9.13
Nollan case . . . 2.11; 9.13
Noxious use cases . . . 2.04
Official map legislation . . . 10.14
Palazzolo case . . . 2.28
Penn Central case . . . 2.07
Pennsylvania Coal case . . . 2.05
Physical takings
    Generally . . . 2.02; 2.03

[References are to sections.]

TAKING OF PROPERTY—Cont.
Physical takings—Cont.
　　Loretto case . . . 2.03
　　Per se takings . . . 2.03
　　Yee case . . . 2.03
Public services, refusal of municipality to provide
　　. . . 10.11
Refusal of municipality to provide public services
　　. . . 10.11
Regulatory takings
　　Generally . . . 2.01
　　Per se regulatory takings . . . 2.02
Right to exclude, takings of . . . 2.17; 2.18
Ripeness doctrine
　　Generally . . . 2.24
　　Agins case . . . 2.25
　　Compensation requirement . . . 2.31
　　Due process claims, applicability to . . 2.32
　　Equal protection claims, applicability to . . .
　　　　2.32
　　Federal Court cases . . . 2.29 – 2.33
　　Final decision rule . . . 2.30
　　Futility exception to final decision rule . . . .
　　　　2.30
　　Hamilton Bank case . . . 2.26
　　Palazzolo case . . . 2.28
　　San Diego Gas & Elec. Co. case . . . 2.25
　　Suitum case . . . 2.28
　　Supreme Court cases . . . 2.25 – 2.28
　　Yolo County case . . . 2.27
Rooker-Feldman doctrine . . . 2.34
Rough proportionality test . . . 2.12; 2.13; 9.12;
　　9.14
San Diego Gas & Elec. Co. case . . . 2.25
Segmentation issue
　　Generally . . . 2.17
　　Conceptual segmentation . . . 2.17; 2.18
　　Geographic segmentation . . . 2.17; 2.19
　　Lucas case, applicability of . . . 2.21
　　Temporal segmentation . . . 2.17; 2.20
Sign regulations on streets and highways, takings
　　issues associated with . . . 11.07
Slope protection ordinances . . . 12.02
State court doctrines . . . 2.35
State statutes . . . 2.38
Subdivision controls . . . 9.09
Suitum case . . . 2.28
Temporal segmentation . . . 2.17; 2.20
Transfer of development rights (TDRs) programs
　　. . . 11.38
View protection ordinances . . . 12.02
Village of Euclid, Ohio v. Amber Realty Co. case
　　. . . 2.06
Wetlands regulations . . . 12.07

TAKING OF PROPERTY—Cont.
Whole parcel rule . . . 2.17
Yee case . . . 2.03
Yolo County case . . . 2.27

TDRs (See TRANSFER OF DEVELOPMENT
　　RIGHTS (TDRs))

TELECOMMUNICATIONS ACT OF 1996
Generally . . . 4.42

THIRD PARTIES
Standing to sue (See STANDING TO SUE)

TIMED GROWTH PROGRAMS (See GROWTH
　　MANAGEMENT PROGRAMS)

TORTS
Generally . . . 8.23
Immunity from tort liability . . . 8.23
Public duty rule . . . 8.23

**TRANSFER OF DEVELOPMENT RIGHTS
　　(TDRs)**
Generally . . . 11.38; 12.16
Constitutional considerations
　　Historic landmarks, TDRs for protection of
　　　　. . . 11.38
　　Natural resource areas, TDRs for protection of
　　　　. . . 12.16
Historic landmarks, for protection of . . . 11.38
Natural resource areas, for protection of . . 12.16
Statutory authority . . . 11.38
Takings considerations . . . 11.38

U

URBAN GROWTH BOUNDARIES
Generally . . . 10.02; 10.07

UTILITIES
Private utilities, immunity from local zoning ordi-
　　nances of . . . 4.32
Public utilities (See PUBLIC UTILITIES)

V

VARIANCES
Generally . . . 6.39
Area variances
　　Generally . . . 6.42
　　Availability of . . . 6.48
　　Practical difficulties test . . . 6.48
　　Unnecessary hardship test . . . 6.48
　　Use variances distinguished from . . . 6.42;
　　　　6.48
Authority to grant variances . . . 4.15; 6.39; 6.41

[References are to sections.]

VARIANCES—Cont.

Conditions to . . . 6.51

Consistency with comprehensive plan, requirements regarding . . . 6.49

Findings of fact in variance cases, requirements regarding . . . 6.52

Function of . . . 6.41

Hardship variance (See subhead: Unnecessary hardship test)

Judicial review . . . 6.52

Limitations on variance conditions . . . 6.51

Practical difficulties test . . . 6.48

Role of . . . 6.41

Self-created hardship . . . 6.50

Special exceptions and conditional uses distinguished . . . 6.39; 6.54

Standards for granting variances . . . 6.41 – 6.50

Standard Zoning Act provisions . . 4.15; 6.39; 6.41

Subdivision control ordinance requirements, from . . . 9.10

Unnecessary hardship test

    Generally . . . 6.44

    Area variances, for . . . 6.48

    Impact on the neighborhood as factor 6.47

    "No reasonable return" rule . . . 6.45

    Reasonable return test . . . 6.45

    Unique hardship requirement . . . 6.46

    Use variances, for . . . 6.48

Use variances

    Generally . . . 6.42

    Area variances distinguished from . . . 6.42; 6.48

    Prohibition of . . . 6.43

    Unnecessary hardship test . . . 6.48

VESTED RIGHTS (See ESTOPPEL AND VESTED RIGHTS DOCTRINES)

VIEW PROTECTION ORDINANCES

Generally . . . 12.02

W

WETLANDS REGULATIONS

Generally . . . 12.01; 12.05

Clean Water Act permit requirements . . . 12.01; 12.06

Local programs . . . 12.05

State programs . . . 12.05

Takings considerations . . . 12.07

Y

YARD REQUIREMENTS

Generally . . . 5.71

Z

ZONING (GENERALLY)

Generally . . . 1.01; 1.03; 1.04; 1.11; 4.01; 6.01

Aesthetic zoning (See AESTHETIC ZONING)

Amendments (See REZONING AND ZONING AMENDMENTS)

Architectural design review (See ARCHITECTURAL DESIGN REVIEW)

Billboards, regulation of (See SIGNS AND BILLBOARDS, REGULATION OF)

Commercial uses and zoning (See COMMERCIAL USES AND ZONING)

Comprehensive plans (See COMPREHENSIVE PLANS)

Constitutional issues (See CONSTITUTIONAL ISSUES)

Contract and conditional zoning (See CONTRACT AND CONDITIONAL ZONING)

Downzoning (See DOWNZONING)

Environmental land use controls (See ENVIRONMENTAL LAND USE CONTROLS)

Exclusionary zoning (See EXCLUSIONARY ZONING)

Extraterritorial zoning (See EXTRATERRITORIAL ZONING)

Floating zones (See FLOATING ZONES)

Historical background . . . 1.01

Historic districts (See HISTORIC DISTRICTS)

Historic landmarks (See LANDMARK PRESERVATION)

Home rule provisions (See HOME RULE PROVISIONS)

Immunity of government from zoning ordinances (See GOVERNMENTAL IMMUNITY FROM ZONING REGULATION)

Industrial uses and zoning (See INDUSTRIAL USES AND ZONING)

Landmark preservation (See LANDMARK PRESERVATION)

Maps (See ZONING MAPS)

Modern zoning legislation . . . 4.21

Nonconforming uses (See NONCONFORMING USES)

Nuisance actions, judicial zoning through (See NUISANCE ACTIONS)

Residential uses and zoning (See RESIDENTIAL USES AND ZONING)

[References are to sections.]

ZONING (GENERALLY)—Cont.

Rezoning (See REZONING AND ZONING AMENDMENTS)

Signs, regulation of (See SIGNS AND BILLBOARDS, REGULATION OF)

Spot zoning (See SPOT ZONING)

Stages of land use law . . . 1.18

Standard Zoning Act (See STANDARD ZONING ACT)

Statutory authority
    Extraterritorial zoning, for . . . 4.22; 4.23
    Modern zoning legislation . . . 4.21
    Standard Zoning Act (See STANDARD ZONING ACT)

Subdivision regulation, relationship to . . . 9.06

Taking of property, regulations as (See TAKING OF PROPERTY)

ZONING MAPS

Generally . . . 1.04; 3.01; 3.02

ZONING MAPS—Cont.

Amendments to (See REZONING AND ZONING AMENDMENTS)

Commercial uses and zoning . . . 5.35

ZONING POWERS

Generally . . . 1.01

Delegation of power (See DELEGATION OF POWERS)

Interim development controls, authority regarding . . . 6.07

Moratoria on development, authority regarding . . . 6.07

Police power as basis of zoning power . . . 1.01

Site plan reviews . . . 6.66

Special exceptions and conditional uses (See SPECIAL EXCEPTIONS AND CONDITIONAL USES, subhead: Authority to regulate permits)

Variances, authority to grant . . . 4.15; 6.39; 6.41

(5th Ed.—02/03)